eGrade Plus

www.wiley.com/college/black

Based on the Activities You Do Every Day

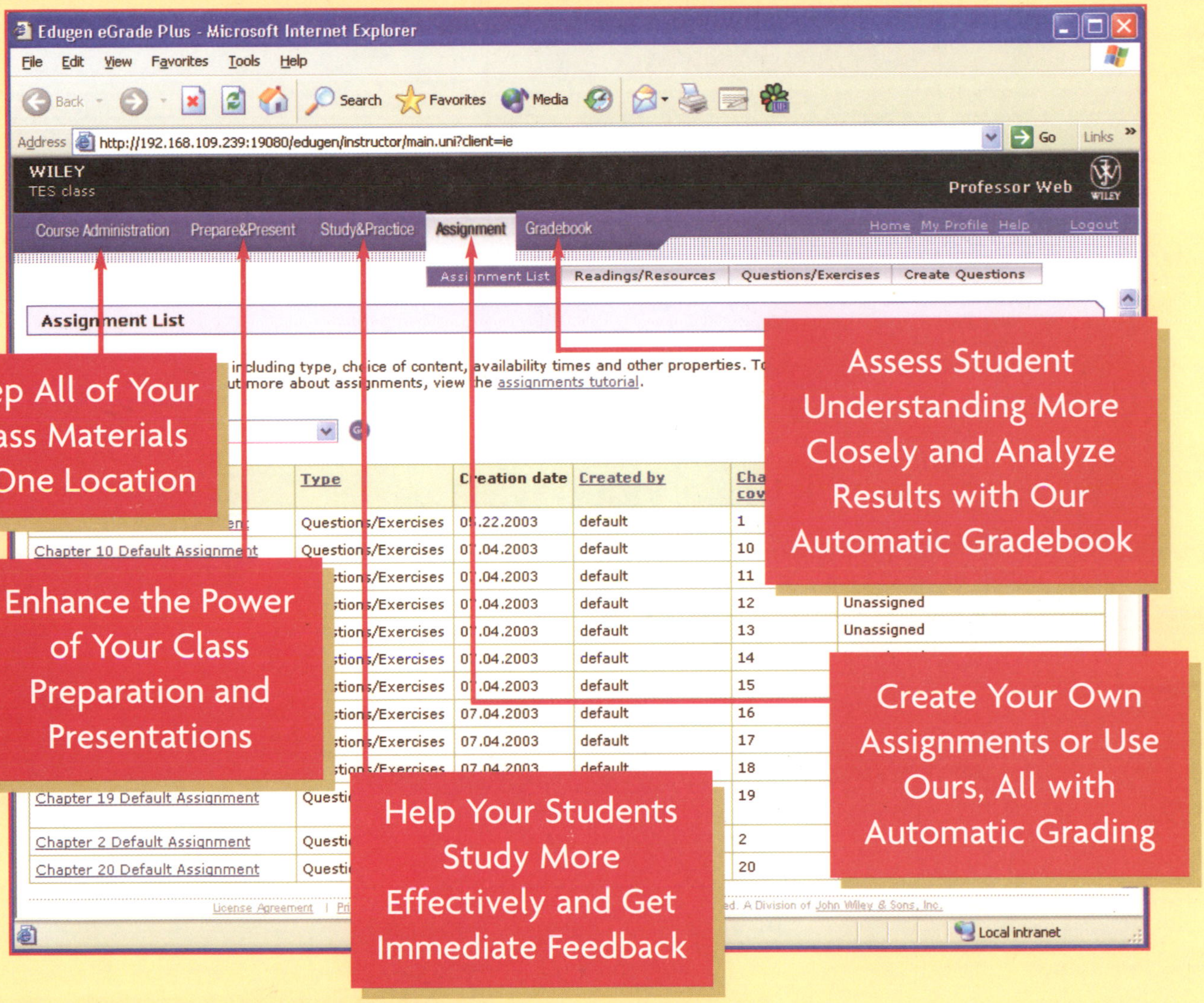

Keep All of Your Class Materials in One Location

Enhance the Power of Your Class Preparation and Presentations

Help Your Students Study More Effectively and Get Immediate Feedback

Assess Student Understanding More Closely and Analyze Results with Our Automatic Gradebook

Create Your Own Assignments or Use Ours, All with Automatic Grading

(Screenshot: Edugen eGrade Plus — Microsoft Internet Explorer)
Address: http://192.168.109.239:19080/edugen/instructor/main.uni?client=ie

WILEY — TES class — Professor Web

Course Administration | Prepare&Present | Study&Practice | Assignment | Gradebook — Home | My Profile | Help | Logout

Assignment List | Readings/Resources | Questions/Exercises | Create Questions

Assignment List

...including type, choice of content, availability times and other properties. To ...ut more about assignments, view the assignments tutorial.

	Type	Creation date	Created by	Chapters cov...
...ent	Questions/Exercises	05.22.2003	default	1
Chapter 10 Default Assignment	Questions/Exercises	07.04.2003	default	10
	...tions/Exercises	07.04.2003	default	11
	...tions/Exercises	07.04.2003	default	12	Unassigned
	...tions/Exercises	07.04.2003	default	13	Unassigned
	...tions/Exercises	07.04.2003	default	14	
	...tions/Exercises	07.04.2003	default	15	
	...tions/Exercises	07.04.2003	default	16	
	...tions/Exercises	07.04.2003	default	17	
	...tions/Exercises	07.04.2003	default	18	
Chapter 19 Default Assignment	Questi...			19
Chapter 2 Default Assignment	Questi...			2
Chapter 20 Default Assignment	Questi...			20

License Agreement | Pri... ...ed. A Division of John Wiley & Sons, Inc. — Local intranet

All the content and tools you need, all in one location, in an easy-to-use browser format. Choose the resources you need, or rely on the arrangement supplied by us.

Now, many of Wiley's textbooks are available with eGrade Plus, a powerful online tool that provides a completely integrated suite of teaching and learning resources in one easy-to-use Web site. eGrade Plus integrates Wiley's world-renowned content with media, including a multimedia version of the text, PowerPoint slides, and more. Upon adoption of eGrade Plus, you can begin to customize your course with the resources shown here.

See for yourself!

Go to www.wiley.com/college/egradeplus for an online demonstration of this powerful new software.

Students,
eGrade Plus Allows You to:

Study More Effectively

Get Immediate Feedback When You Practice on Your Own

eGrade Plus problems link directly to relevant sections of the **electronic book content,** so that you can review the text while you study and complete homework online. Additional resources include **page activities, student quizzes** and other problem-solving resources.

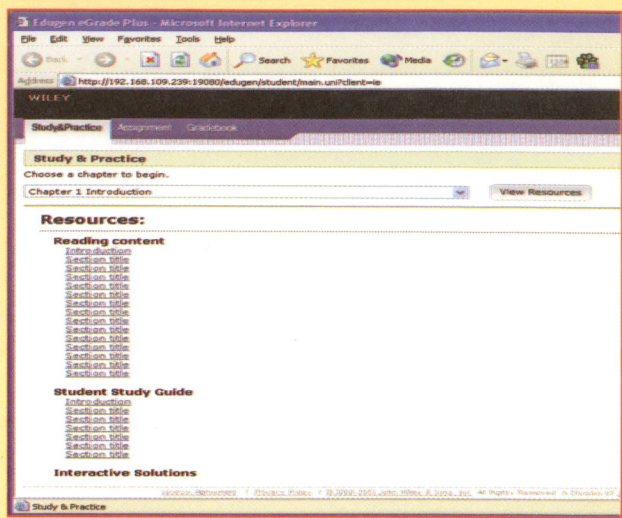

Complete Assignments/Get Help with Problem Solving

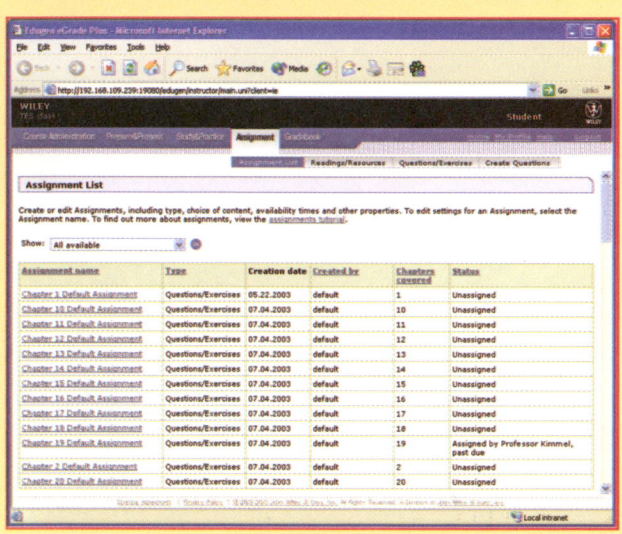

An **"Assignment"** area keeps all your assigned work in one location, making it easy for you to stay on task. In addition, many homework problems contain a **link** to the relevant section of the **electronic book,** providing you with a text explanation to help conquer problem-solving obstacles as they arise.

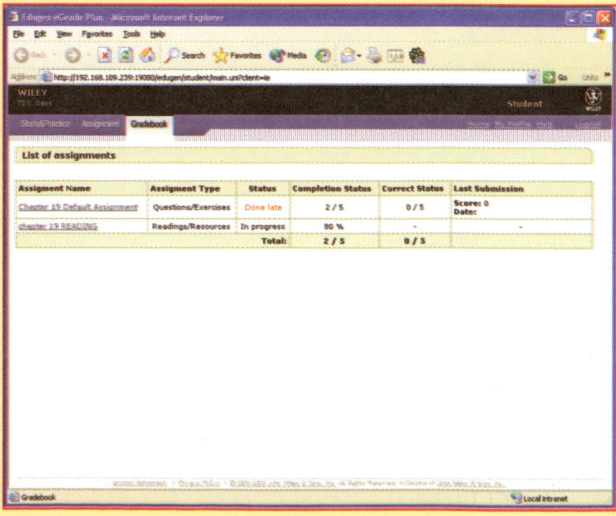

Keep Track of How You're Doing

A **Personal Gradebook** allows you to view your results from past assignments at any time.

BUSINESS STATISTICS

FOR CONTEMPORARY DECISION MAKING

4TH EDITION UPDATE

Ken Black

University of Houston–Clear Lake

www.wiley.com/college/black

Acquisitions Editor   *Beth Lang Golub*
Marketing Manager   *Jillian Rice*
Managing Editor   *Kevin Dodds*
Associate Editor   *Lorraina Raccuia*
Editorial Assistant   *Jen Snyder*
Developmental Editor   *Camille McMorrow*
Designer   *Jennifer Wasson*
Cover Design   *Kris Pauls/Benjamin Reece*
Cover Images   Front cover: circuitboard: Stockbyte; doughnuts: Courtesy of Krispy Kreme Doughnut Corporation; spices: PhotoDisc, Inc., Neil Beer. Back cover: single doughnut: Photodisc, Inc.

This book was set in Minion by Leyh Publishing LLC and printed and bound by Courier Kendallville.

This book is printed on acid free paper.∞

ISBN 0-471-70563-2

Printed in the United States of America

10 9 8 7 6 5 4

For Carolyn, Caycee, and Wendi

BRIEF CONTENTS

The following materials are available at: www.wiley.com/college/black

CONTENTS

4   Probability   96

9 Statistical Inference: Hypothesis Testing for Single Populations   288

10 Statistical Inferences about Two Populations   340

12 Analysis of Categorical Data   454

13 Simple Regression Analysis   480

14 Multiple Regression Analysis   522

The following materials are available at: www.wiley.com/college/black

PREFACE

The fourth edition Update of *Business Statistics: Contemporary Decision Making*, while continuing to retain the clear, crisp pedagogy of previous editions, adds new features and an even stronger emphasis on practical, applied statistics that will enhance the text's position as a leader in presenting business statistics in a decision-making setting. In addition, the Update edition contains the powerful new resource, *eGrade Plus,* which is an integrated suite of teaching and learning resources to give the instructor many more options in delivering an effective business statistics course.

This edition is written and designed for a two-semester introductory undergraduate business statistics course or an MBA-level introductory course. In addition, with 18 chapters, the fourth edition lends itself nicely to adaptation for a one-semester introductory business statistics course. The text is written with the assumption that the student has a college algebra mathematical background. No calculus is used in the presentation of material in the text.

An underlying philosophical approach to the text is that every statistical tool presented in the book has some business application. While the text contains statistical rigor, it is written so that the student can readily see that the proper application of statistics in the business world goes hand-in-hand with good decision making. In this edition, statistics are presented as a means for converting data into useful information that can be used to assist the business decision maker in making more thoughtful, information-based decisions. Thus, the text presents business statistics as "value added" tools in the process of converting data into useful information.

CHANGES FOR THE FOURTH EDITION UPDATE

Change in the Presentation of the Usage of *z* and *t* Statistics in Hypothesis Testing and Estimation

In the 4th edition Update, Chapters 8, 9, and 10 have been rewritten to reflect the more common and rigorous approach to the usage of the *z* and *t* statistics in making inferences about a population mean. In previous editions, the *z* statistic has been presented as the statistic of choice for hypothesis testing and confidence interval estimation about the population mean whenever sample size was large, $n \geq 30$, regardless of whether σ was known or unknown. The *t* statistic was reserved for usage when σ was unknown *and* sample size was small. In the Update edition, the position is that in making inferences about population means, the *t* statistic is *always* used whenever σ is unknown, *regardless of sample size.* The *z* statistic, on the other hand, is used only in situations in which σ is known. In this edition, the pedagogy, examples, problems, and other materials in chapters 8, 9, and 10 have been rewritten to consistently support this position. All ancillary materials have been updated to support this point of view.

Deletion of Probability Statements with Confidence Intervals

In previous editions, probability statements have been included in the presentation of confidence interval material in Chapters 8 and 10. In the 4th edition Update, all confidence interval probability statements and any related material have been deleted from the text.

While all other explanation and presentation of confidence intervals remains complete and thorough, the Update contains no probability statements about confidence intervals. Chapter 8 and 10 examples, Demonstration Problems, and problem solutions have been modified to reflect this change.

eGrade

Both Wiley and the author are very pleased to announce the addition of *eGrade Plus* to the 4th edition of *Business Statistics for Contemporary Decision Making* at the Update. *eGrade Plus* is an integrated suite of teaching and learning resources that are now available to aid the instructor in saving time preparing lectures, developing stronger problem-solving skills, and managing homework. *eGrade Plus* includes an online version of Black's *Business Statistics for Contemporary Decision Making, Fourth Edition Update* giving the instructor, and the institution many more ways to effectively and efficiently present the course. With this, there are a wealth of Wiley-provided resources for creating class presentations that will help you adapt, customize, and add to this content to meet the needs of your course. By using Wiley-provided question banks or by writing your own, you can automate the assigning and grading of homework or quizzes. Student results will be automatically graded and recorded in your gradebook. An instructor's gradebook allows you to analyze individual and overall class results to determine each student's progress and level of understanding. In addition, *eGrade Plus* can easily be integrated with another course management system, gradebook, or other resources used in the class. It can link homework problems to the relevant section of the online text, providing context-sensitive help. Please contact your Wiley sales representative for ordering information.

CHANGES FOR THE FOURTH EDITION

Decision Dilemma and In Response

The Decision Dilemma and In Response features that were so popular in the 2nd edition but were moved to the CD-ROM for the 3rd edition have been brought back into the text for the 4th edition. The Decision Dilemma is a real business vignette that opens each chapter. It sets the tone for the chapter by presenting a business or industry dilemma and asking a number of managerial or statistical questions, the solution of which will require the use of techniques presented in the chapter. It creates a setting for business statistics to be presented in the chapter. Located immediately at the end of each chapter, the In Response feature discusses and answers the managerial and statistical questions posed in the Decision Dilemma using techniques from the chapter, thus bringing closure to the chapter. In the 4th edition, seven new Decision Dilemmas and In Responses have been added since the feature last appeared in print in the 2nd edition, and virtually all others have been updated. The new Decision Dilemmas include: 1.) Laundry Statistics; 2.) Forecasting Air Pollution; 3.) How is the Doughnut Business? (featuring Krispy Kreme); 4.) State of Auto Manufacturing; 5.) Comparing International Labor Statistics; 6.) Predicting the Annual Sales Volume of Real-Estate Brokerage Firms by the Average Price of the Sale; and 7.) Are You Going to Hate Your Job?.

As an example, the Chapter 17 Decision Dilemma—How is the Doughnut Business?—presents Krispy Kreme as a rapidly growing international company specializing in doughnuts. The company, established in 1937 by Vernon Rudolph, began as a small manufacturer and supplier of doughnuts to local grocery stores in Winston-Salem, North Carolina, expanded rapidly to locations outside of the Southeast in the 1990s, and is growing internationally in the twenty-first century. With such rapid expansion, one concern might be consistency in doughnut size. The Decision Dilemma presents a situation in which quality management people at Krispy Kreme have conducted an experiment to compare the doughnut sizes of doughnuts produced by four different machines. Doughnuts produced by each machine are randomly selected and tested to determine if there is a significant difference in doughnut size by machine. Unfortunately, the assumptions underlying the use of a one-way ANOVA cannot be met. The dilemma is how to analyze the data under these conditions. Chapter 17 is about nonparametric statistics. The In Response feature at the end of the chapter shows the student how the dilemma can be solved by using a Kruskal-Wallis test. Two other dilemmas are presented in this Decision Dilemma and answered in the In Response feature using the Wilcoxon Matched-Pairs Signed Rank *t* test and Spearman's Rank Correlation. One deals with analyzing sales data before and after a sales campaign and the other deals with determining the strength of correlation between a store's sales and its size using ranked data.

Cases

Virtually all cases have been updated for this edition, and three new cases have been written for the 4th edition using contemporary companies: (1) Foot Locker in the Shoe Mix, Chapter 12 (Analysis of Categorical Data); (2) Starbucks Introduces Debit Card, Chapter 14 (Introduction to Multiple Regression); and (3) Schwinn, Chapter 17 (Nonparametric Statistics). The Starbucks' case presents one of business's contemporary success stories as the company has grown from one coffee house in 1971 to well over 5,000 today. In November of 2001, Starbucks attempted to implement a new concept by launching its prepaid (debit) Starbucks Card. The card was so popular when it was first released that many stores ran out. By mid-2002, Starbucks had activated over 5 million of these cards. It is believed that the card accounted for a large portion of the company's 7 percent same-store increase in sales in early 2002 and that it is responsible for attracting many of the new patrons to the store. In this case, students explore ways to predict the amount spent on the prepaid cards using regression methodology and demographic variables. In addition, multiple regression is used to develop models to predict a store's sales revenues. The second new case features Foot Locker, the world's number one retailer of athletic shoes and apparel, with approximately 3,600 retail stores located in 14 different companies across North America, Europe, and Australia. In this case, presented in the new categorical analysis (chi-square) chapter, distributions of sales across various pricing levels are compared from one year to the next in an effort to determine if shopping patterns are changing. Cross-tabulation analyses are undertaken to study the relationship between the gender of shoppers and geography and to examine market share by location. The third new case features Schwinn, an old-line bicycle company with a long history of innovation. Presently, the company is very successful in the mountain biking market as a premier producer of bicycles. In this case, housed in the nonparametrics chapter, students are asked to apply nonparametric statistical techniques to study quality control questions about the difference in suppliers and the randomness of paint flaws. In addition, the case includes a study of the differences in age of purchasers in two cities.

Statistics in Business Today

As with previous editions, the 4th edition includes a Statistics in Business Today feature in every chapter. This feature presents a real-life example of how the statistics presented in that chapter apply in the business world today. Five of the chapters in the 4th edition have new Statistics in Business Today features including: 1.) U.S. Wireless Usage Grows, Chapter 1—Introduction to Statistics; 2.) Telecommuting Statistics, Chapter 3—Descriptive Statistics; 3.) Predicting the Price of an SUV, Chapter 13—Simple Regression Analysis; 4.) Predicting Export Intensity of Chinese Manufacturing Firms Using Multiple Regression Analysis, Chapter 15—Building Multiple Regression Models; and 5.) Profiling Online Users, Chapter 17—Nonparametric Statistics.

As an example, from Telecommuting Statistics, a study by Telework America revealed that 28 million Americans are teleworking. It is estimated that by the end of 2004 there will be nearly 30 million regular teleworkers in the U.S. The typical telecommuter lives in the west or the northeast, is male, has a college education, is between 35 and 44 years of age, is married, and earns at least $40,000 per year. The mean income for teleworkers is $44,000. Most telecommuters work in IT, real estate, or enterprise management. Teleworkers typically drive 18 miles to work and save nearly 53 minutes of commuting time each workday. Teleworkers are relatively satisfied with their work. Seventy-five percent of home workers reported a quantifiable increase in productivity and work quality when they switched from tradition at work jobs to telecommuting. Two-thirds of teleworkers expressed increased job satisfaction. Teleworkers say that they work longer hours than non teleworkers but that their job interferes less with their personal lives.

Topical Changes

To provide greater emphasis and clarity on more important topics, the 4th edition contains two new chapters: (1) Chapter 15, Building Multiple Regression Models—a second chapter on multiple regression and (2) Chapter 12, Analysis of Categorical Data—a chapter on chi-square tests of categorical data. Separating the multiple regression presentation into two chapters allows the instructor the option of limiting the student's exposure to multiple regression using just an introduction (Chapter 14) or exploring more fully and in more detail multiple regression analysis through the use of modeling techniques such as stepwise regression and curvilinear models (Chapter 15). The chi-square tests have been extracted from the nonparametric statistics chapter (16) and given stand-alone status earlier in the 4th edition (Chapter 12) because of their more widespread usage in business areas such as marketing. In addition, to allow more time for instruction on key topics, one chapter of the 3rd edition, Index Numbers, has been reduced to a section in the 4th edition (Chapter 16, Times Series Forecasting and Index Numbers). Other changes that have been manifest in the 4th edition include moving Pareto Charts and Scatter Plots to Chapter 2 (Charts and Graphs), moving measures of association (correlation coefficient) to Chapter 3 (Descriptive Statistics), and introducing the HTAB system in Chapter 9 (Hypothesis Testing).

HTAB System and Hypothesis Testing

To advance the notion of business statistics in a setting of decision making, the 4th edition introduces, for the first time, the HTAB system. While most texts merely present the important hypothesis testing process as an 8-step method, the HTAB system reorganizes the hypothesis testing procedure into 4 major tasks, placing special emphasis on business decision making. The HTAB acronym stands for **H**ypothesize-**T**est-**A**ction-**B**usiness Implications. The HTAB tasks move the student through four distinct phases culminating in a business decision. The HTAB system places emphasis on determining what business implications, if any, result from the hypothesis test. To further underscore the emphasis on decision making, the 4th edition contains a presentation of *substantive* hypotheses within a context of *research* and *statistical* hypotheses. In examining substantive hypotheses, the student learns to differentiate between statistical *significance* and business *importance*.

New Problems

All third-edition problems were examined for timeliness, appropriateness, clarity, and logic before inclusion in the fourth edition Update. Those that fell short were replaced or rewritten. Several new problems were constructed in an effort to maximize student learning. Most problems with time-based values were updated. While the total number of problems in the text is still around 950, a concerted effort has been made to include only problems that make a significant contribution to the learning process.

All demonstration problems and example problems were thoroughly reviewed and edited for effectiveness. A demonstration problem is an extra example containing both an problem and its solution and is used as an additional pedagogical tool to supplement explanations and examples in the chapters. Virtually all example and demonstration problems in the fourth edition are business-oriented and contain the most current data available.

As with the previous edition, problems are located at the end of most sections in the chapters. A significant number of additional problems are provided at the end of each chapter in the Supplementary Problems. The Supplementary Problems are "scrambled"— problems using the various techniques in the chapter are mixed—so that students can test themselves on their ability to discriminate and differentiate ideas and concepts.

FEATURES AND BENEFITS

Each chapter of the fourth edition Update contains Learning Objectives, a Decision Dilemma, Demonstration Problems, Section Problems, Statistics in Business Today, an In Response, a Chapter Summary, Key Terms, Formulas, Ethical Considerations, Supplementary Problems, Analyzing the Databases, a Case, a Using the Computer, and Computer Output from both Excel 2000 and MINITAB Release 13.

- **Learning Objectives.** Each chapter begins with a statement of the chapter's main learning objectives. This statement gives the reader a list of key topics that will be discussed and the goals to be achieved from studying the chapter.

- **Decision Dilemma.** At the beginning of each chapter, a short case describes a real company or business situation in which managerial and statistical questions are raised. In most Decision Dilemmas, actual data are given and the student is asked to consider how the data can be analyzed to answer the questions.

- **Demonstration Problems.** Virtually every section of every chapter in the fourth edition contains demonstration problems. A demonstration problem contains both an example problem and its solution, and is used as an additional pedagogical tool to supplement explanations and examples.

- **Section Problems.** There are over 950 problems in the text. Problems for practice are found at the end of almost every section of the text. Most problems utilize real data gathered from a plethora of sources. Included here are a few brief excerpts from some of the real-life problems in the text: "The Wall Street Journal reported that 40% of all workers say they would change jobs for 'slightly higher pay.' In addition, 88% of companies say that there is a shortage of qualified job candidates." "In a study by Peter D. Hart Research Associates for the Nasdaq Stock Market, it was determined that 20% of all stock investors are retired people. In addition, 40% of all U.S. adults have invested in mutual funds." "A survey conducted for the Northwestern National Life Insurance Company revealed that 70% of American workers say job stress caused frequent health problems." "According to Padgett Business Services, 20% of all small-business owners say the most important advice for starting a business is to prepare for long hours and hard work. Twenty-five percent say the most important advice is to have good financing ready." "According to a study conducted for Gateway Computers, 59% of men and 70% of women say that weight is an extremely/very important factor in purchasing a laptop computer."

- **Statistics in Business Today.** Every chapter in the 4th edition contains a Statistics in Business Today feature. These focus boxes contain an interesting application of how techniques of that particular chapter are used in the business world today. They are usually based on real companies, surveys, or published research.

- **In Response.** Situated at the end of the chapter, the In Response feature addresses the managerial and statistical questions raised in the Decision Dilemma. Data given in the Decision Dilemma are analyzed computationally and by computer using techniques presented in the chapter. Answers to the managerial and statistical questions raised in the Decision Dilemma are arrived at by applying chapter concepts, thus bringing closure to the chapter.

- **Chapter Summary.** Each chapter concludes with a summary of the important concepts, ideas, and techniques of the chapter. This feature can serve as a preview of the chapter as well as a chapter review.

- **Key Terms.** Important terms are bolded and their definitions italicized throughout the text as they are discussed. At the end of the chapter, a list of the key terms from the chapter is presented. In addition, these terms appear with their definitions in an end-of-book Glossary.

- **Formulas.** Important formulas in the text are highlighted to make it easy for a reader to locate them. At the end of the chapter, most of the chapter's formulas are listed together as a handy reference.

- **Ethical Considerations.** Each chapter contains an Ethical Considerations feature that is very timely given the serious breach of ethics and lack of moral leadership of some business executives in recent months. With the abundance of statistical data and analysis, there is considerable potential for the misuse of statistics in business dealings. The important Ethical Considerations feature underscores this potential misuse by discussing such topics as lying with statistics, failing to meet statistical assumptions, failing to include pertinent information for decision makers, and other such matters of principle. Through this feature, instructors can begin to integrate the topic of ethics with applications of business statistics. Here are a few excerpts from Ethical Considerations features: "It is unprofessional and unethical to draw cause-and-effect conclusions just because two variables are correlated." "The business researcher needs to conduct the experiment in an environment such that as many concomitant variables are controlled as possible. To the extent that this is not done, the researcher has an ethical responsibility to report that fact in the findings." "The reader is warned that the value of lambda is assumed to be constant in a Poisson distribution experiment. Business researchers may produce spurious results if the value of lambda is used throughout a study; but because the study is conducted during different time periods, the value of lambda is actually changing." "In describing a body of data to an audience, it is best to use whatever statistical measures it takes to present a 'full' picture of the data. By limiting the descriptive measures used, the business researcher may give the audience only part of the picture and skew the way the receiver understands the data."

- **Supplementary Problems.** At the end of each chapter is an extensive set of additional problems. The Supplementary Problems are divided into three groups: Calculating the Statistics, which are strictly computational problems; Testing Your Understanding, which are problems for application and understanding; and Interpreting the Output, which are problems that require the interpretation and analysis of software output.

- **Analyzing the Databases.** There are seven major databases located on the student companion Web site that accompanies the fourth edition. The end-of-chapter Analyzing the Databases section contains several questions/problems that require the application of techniques from the chapter to data in the variables of the databases. It is assumed that most of these questions/problems will be solved using a computer.

- **Case.** Each end-of-chapter case is based on a real company. These cases give the student an opportunity to use statistical concepts and techniques presented in the chapter to solve a business dilemma. Some cases feature very large companies—such as Shell Oil, Coca-Cola, or Colgate-Palmolive. Others pertain to small businesses—such as Thermatrix, Robotron, or DeBourgh—that have overcome obstacles to survive and thrive. Most cases include raw data (also located on the CD-ROM) for analysis and questions that encourage the student to use several of the techniques presented in the chapter. In many cases, the student must analyze software output in order to reach conclusions or make decisions.

- **Using the Computer.** The Using the Computer section contains directions for producing the Excel 2000 and MINITAB Release 13 software output presented in the chapter. It is assumed that students have a general understanding of a Microsoft® Windows environment. Directions include specifics about menu bars, drop-down menus, and dialog boxes. Not every detail of every dialog box is discussed; the intent is to provide enough information for students to produce the same statistical output analyzed and discussed in the chapter.

■ **Presentation of Microsoft® Excel and MINITAB Software Output.** The fourth edition has a strong focus on both Excel and MINITAB software packages. More than 250 Excel 2000 or MINITAB Release 13 computer-generated outputs are displayed. Excel, because it is a part of Microsoft Office, has been installed on millions of computers around the world. Most students have access to Excel at home, school, or work. Because of the one-two punch of the Data Analysis tool and the Paste Function feature, Excel has considerable statistical capability. MINITAB is also featured because it has done an excellent job of keeping pace with the continual changes and demands of statistics in business. MINITAB Release 13, featured in this text, has techniques for analyzing proportions, greater data and file management capabilities including multiple worksheets, the capability of performing polynomial regression, and clarified and strengthened presentation of quality tools. In addition, the MINITAB spreadsheet is easier than ever to use.

■ **Databases.** The fourth edition Update contains seven databases (located on the student companion Web site), all of which are available in both Excel and MINITAB format ready for use. A manufacturing database, a financial database, a stock market database, an international employment database, an energy database, a healthcare database, and an agri-business database provide over 8350 observations and 56 variables. All data are real and from reliable sources that users will recognize: the U.S. Bureau of Labor Statistics, the New York Stock Exchange, the U.S. Department of Agriculture, Moody's Handbook of Common Stocks, the American Hospital Association, and the U.S. Bureau of the Census. Four of the seven databases have time-series data; one contains 168 months of time-series data ideal for demonstrating and analyzing forecasting decomposition techniques.

ANCILLARY TEACHING AND LEARNING MATERIALS

Students' Companion Site

The student companion Web site contains:

■ All databases in both Excel and MINITAB formats for easy access and use.

■ Excel and MINITAB files of data from all text problems and all cases. Instructors and students now have the option of analyzing any of the data sets using the computer.

■ Full, complete, and updated version of Chapter 19, Decision Analysis, in PDF format. This allows an instructor the option of covering the material in this chapter in the normal manner, while keeping the text manageable in size and length.

■ A section on Advanced Exponential Smoothing Techniques (from Chapter 16) which offers the instructor an opportunity to delve deeper into exponential smoothing if so desired. Derivation of the slope and intercept formulas from Chapter 13.

■ A tutorial on summation theory.

Instructor's Resource Kit

All instructor ancillaries are provided on a CD-ROM. Included in this convenient format are:

■ *Instructor's Manual:* Prepared by Ken Black, this manual contains the worked out solutions to virtually all problems in the text. In addition, this manual contains chapter objectives, chapter outlines, chapter teaching strategies, and solutions to the cases.

- *PowerPoint™ Presentation Slides:* The presentation slides contain graphics to help instructors create stimulating lectures. The PowerPoint 2000 slides may be adapted using PowerPoint software to facilitate classroom use.
- *Test Bank:* Prepared by Aaron Brown of Arkansas State University, the Test Bank includes multiple-choice questions for each chapter. The Test Bank is provided in Microsoft® Word format.

ACKNOWLEDGMENTS

John Wiley & Sons, Leyh Publishing, and I would like to thank the reviewers and advisors who cared enough and took the time to provide us with their excellent insights and advice, which was used to reshape and mold the text into the fourth edition. These colleagues include:

Thomas McCullough, University of California–Berkeley

Tade O. Okediji, University of Oklahoma

Michael Panik, University of Hartford

Randall K. Russell, Yavapai College

Daniel Shimshak, University of Massachusetts–Boston

Abbas A. Taheri, University of Wisconsin, Fox Valley

Michael Walcott, Faulkner University

Special thanks to Aaron Brown, Arkansas State University, who again prepared the Test Bank for the fourth edition. As always, I wish to recognize my colleagues at the University of Houston–Clear Lake for their continued interest and support of this project. In particular, I want to thank William Staples, President; Jim Hayes, Provost; and Ted Cummings, Dean of the School of Business and Public Administration, for their personal interest in the book and their administrative support. Three faculty members of the School of Business and Public Administration at UHCL who have especially given me much assistance and encouragement on this project are Mike Hanna, Vance Etnyre, and Lee Revere.

There are several people within the John Wiley & Sons publishing group whom I would like to thank for their invaluable assistance on this project. These include: Gitti Lindner, marketing manager; Beth Golub, executive editor; and Susan Elbe, publishing editor. I would like also to thank Rick Leyh, president of Leyh Publishing, who envisioned the potential for this project and who has provided constant support and motivation. Also from Leyh Publishing, I would like to thank Kevin Dodds and Lari Bishop for their efforts on behalf of the book, Benjamin Reece for his daily assistance on detailed matters and production work, as well as Michele Chancellor and Jennifer Wasson for their assistance.

I want to express a special appreciation to my wife of 34 years, Carolyn, who is the love of my life and continues to provide both professional and personal support in my writing. Thanks also to my daughters, Wendi and Caycee, for their patience, love, and support.

—Ken Black

ABOUT THE AUTHOR

Ken Black is currently Professor of Decision Sciences in the School of Business and Public Administration at the University of Houston–Clear Lake. Born in Cambridge, Massachusetts and raised in Missouri, he earned a Bachelor's degree in mathematics from Graceland College, a Master's degree in math education from the University of Texas at El Paso, a Ph.D. in business administration in management science, and a Ph.D. in educational research from the University of North Texas.

Since joining the faculty in 1979, Professor Black has taught all levels of statistics courses, forecasting, management science, market research, and production/operations management. He has published fifteen journal articles and over twenty professional papers, as well as two textbooks: Business Statistics: An Introductory Course and Business Statistics: Contemporary Decision Making. Black has consulted for many different companies, including Aetna, City of Houston, NYLCare, AT&T, Johnson Space Center, Southwest Information Resources, Connect Corporation, and Eagle Engineering.

Ken Black and his wife Carolyn have two daughters, Caycee and Wendi. His hobbies include playing the guitar, reading, traveling, and participating in Master's track and field as a long jumper.

Business Statistics

For Contemporary Decision Making

CHAPTER 1

Introduction to Statistics

LEARNING OBJECTIVES

The primary objective of Chapter 1 is to introduce you to the world of statistics, thereby enabling you to:

1. Define statistics.
2. Become aware of a wide range of applications of statistics in business.
3. Differentiate between descriptive and inferential statistics.
4. Classify numbers by level of data and understand why doing so is important.

Statistics Describe the State of Business in India's Countryside

India is the second largest country in the world, with more than a billion people. Three-quarters of the people live in rural areas, yet the rural market accounts for only about one-third of total national product sales. However, because of free-market reforms in the 1990s and a strong agricultural output, India's rural market has become more open for trade in consumer goods. Although India's urban market seems to be saturated, markets in rural India are relatively untapped, offering enormous potential. Because of these factors, many U.S. firms, such as Microsoft, General Electric, Kellogg's, and others, have entered the Indian market.

Presently, rural India can be described as poor and semi-illiterate. More than 65% of the people in rural India earn less than $574 annually, and 23% earn between $574 and $1,146. Sixty-six percent of the women are illiterate, as are 38% of the men. These rates are about double those for urban Indians. Seventy-seven percent of the households in rural India use wood as the cooking fuel, 39% have electricity, 18% have piped water, and 7% have flush toilets.

Nevertheless, conditions are changing and companies are moving into this relatively untapped market. For example, by the late 1990s, Colgate-Palmolive planned to increase its rural marketing budget to five times that of 1991. Colgate-Palmolive India's goal is that more than half its revenue by the year 2003 comes from rural India, which presently accounts for only about 30% of business.

Marketing to rural India is a challenging task and requires some nontraditional approaches because the illiteracy rates are high and only about one-third of the households have a television. One such technique is the use of video vans in which half-hour infomercials are carried through the countryside. A video van cruises into a small hamlet with speakers playing a popular movie melody. As shoppers congregate to the van, a marketer opens the door and plays a video on a screen with scenarios depicting the need for a particular product. After the video is completed, free samples are distributed. Hindustan Lever Ltd., India's leading consumer-products company, estimates that the cost per contact of such marketing is about four times the cost to city dwellers. However, the rural market for personal care products is growing about three times faster than city markets, which makes such marketing efforts more viable. Other companies use direct door-to-door campaigns to promote products to rural India. In addition, the advent of satellite television to rural homes and villages in India opens up some new avenues for advertising and marketing to this population segment.

Statistics available from the first half of the 1990s shed some light on the potential market of rural India. Toothpaste consumption in rural India doubled from 8,825 metric tons in 1990 to 17,023 in 1994. The annual per capita consumption for toothpaste is still only 30 grams per person in rural India compared to 160 grams in urban India and 400 grams in the United States. Thus, the potential for much growth is there. Sales of other products have been growing rapidly in this emerging market. The sales of laundry detergent increased from 272,540 metric tons in 1990 to 422,741 metric tons in 1994. Toilet soap went from 158,919 metric tons in 1990 to 231,084 metric tons in 1994. Shampoo increased in sales nearly fourfold from 497,000 liters in 1990 to 2,116,000 liters in 1994.

Rural India is a huge untapped market for businesses. Some evidence indicates that rural Indian consumers are buying products in increasing numbers. However, annual income statistics show a limited purchasing capacity. The dilemma facing companies is whether to enter this marketplace, and if so, to what extent and how.

Managerial and Statistical Questions

1. What kinds of statistics are presented in this report?
2. Are these data exact figures or estimates?
3. How would researchers go about gathering such data?
4. In measuring rural India as a marketplace, what other statistics could be gathered?
5. What levels of data measurement are represented in these data? If other statistics were gathered, what other levels of data measurement might be represented?
6. How could managers use these statistics to make better decisions about entering this marketplace?

Source: Adapted from Raja Ramachandran, "Understanding the Market Environment of India," *Business Horizons,* January 2000; Miriam Jordan, "In Rural India, Video Vans Sell Toothpaste and Shampoo," *Wall Street Journal,* 10 January 1996; Rinku Pegu, "Maya bazar," *The Week,* 30 May 1999, http://www.the-week.com/99may30/biz2.htm.

Every minute of the working day, decisions are made by businesses around the world that determine whether companies will be profitable and growing or whether they will stagnate and die. Most of these decisions are made with the assistance of information gathered about the marketplace, the economic and financial environment, the workforce, the competition, and other factors. Such information usually comes in the form of data or is accompanied by data. Business statistics provides the tool through which such data are collected, analyzed, summarized, and presented to facilitate the decision-making process. Thus, in the twenty-first century, business statistics plays an important role in the ongoing saga of decision making within the dynamic world of business.

1.1 STATISTICS IN BUSINESS

Virtually every area of business uses statistics in decision making. Here are examples of the use of statistics in several areas of business.

Best Way to Market

A survey conducted by Pitney Bowes of 302 directors and vice presidents of marketing and marketing communications at midsize and large U.S. companies revealed that almost 35% said that direct mail or catalogs were the most cost-effective way to reach customers. Eleven percent felt that the Internet was most cost-effective. The study also showed that more than 25% said that the best way to increase brand identity was through direct mail or catalogs. These and other statistics gathered and summarized in this study can help decision makers solve the dilemma of finding cost-effective vehicles for their products.

Stress on the Job

If decision makers are looking for ways to reduce healthcare expenses among their workforce, then they might do well to learn from a study of some 46,000 employees conducted by the Health Enhancement Research Organization. In it, the researchers discovered that depression and stress seem to have a greater impact on higher medical expenses than do high blood sugar, obesity, or smoking. The study showed that depressed workers had medical expenses 70% higher than nondepressed workers and that workers who said they were under constant stress had expenditures 46% higher than stress-free peers. On the other hand, the medical expenses for people who suffer from high blood pressure were just 11% higher than for those who do not. This information, along with other statistics reported in this study, can help decision makers to develop a strategy for reducing medical expenses among workers.

Financial Decisions

In a study reported by RHI Management Resources, chief financial officers were asked which *one* of the following initiatives they would most likely put on hold in an uncertain economy: (1) expansion, (2) merger or acquisition, (3) new product or service launch, (4) technology upgrade, (5) none, and (6) other. Thirty-two percent of the respondents indicated that they would put expansion plans on hold in an uncertain economy followed by merger or acquisition (23%), technology upgrade (18%), new product or service launch (10%), none (9%), and other (8%).

How Is the Economy Doing?

A *Wall Street Journal* report published to help investors and other decision makers track the state of the economy included such business statistics as the number of new home sales, an index of consumer confidence, the percentage increase in the gross domestic product, the number of initial jobless claims, and the unemployment rate. These statistics and others can serve as indicators of economic and financial states to come and can be used by forecasters as they attempt to predict future business climates. Figure 1.1 is an Excel-produced graph of the Consumer Price Index for all urban consumers every five years for the past 40 years. The data were published by the Federal Reserve Bank in St. Louis.

The Impact of Technology at Work

Greenfield Online conducted an Internet survey of 1,403 respondents for the Society of Financial Service Professionals to determine whether technology users appreciate the benefits of technology more in 2001 than in 1998. Eighty-seven percent of the respondents in 2001 said that technology expands job-related knowledge compared to 54% in 1998. Eighty percent in 2001 agreed that technology increases productivity during normal work hours compared to 66% in 1998. Eighty percent in 2001 responded that technology improves communication with clients and customers compared to only 42% in 1998. Fifty-four percent in 2001 said that technology relieves job stress as compared to only 26% in 1998.

In this text we will examine several types of graphs for depicting data as we study ways to arrange or structure data into forms that are both meaningful and useful to decision makers. We will learn about techniques for sampling from a population that allow studies of the business world to be conducted more inexpensively and in a more timely manner. We will explore various ways to forecast future values and examine techniques for predicting trends. This text also includes many statistical tools for testing hypotheses and for estimating population values. These and many other exciting statistics and statistical techniques await us on this journey through business statistics. Let us begin.

FIGURE 1.1

Consumer Price Index for All Urban Customers (1960-2000)

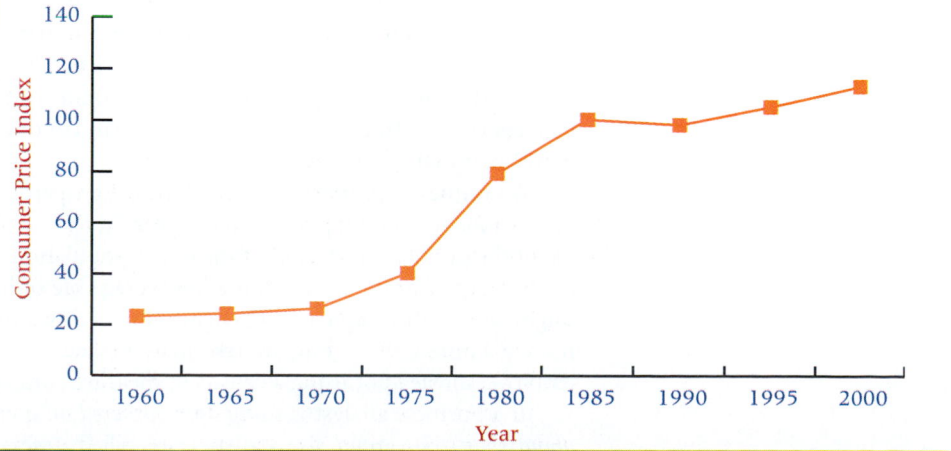

1.2 BASIC STATISTICAL CONCEPTS

Business statistics, like many areas of study, has its own language. It is important to begin our study with an introduction of some basic concepts in order to understand and communicate about the subject. We begin with a discussion of the word *statistics*. The word statistics has many different meanings in our culture. *Webster's Third New International Dictionary* gives a comprehensive definition of **statistics** as *a science dealing with the collection, analysis, interpretation, and presentation of numerical data.* Viewed from this perspective, statistics includes all the topics presented in this text. Statistics also is a branch of mathematics, and most of the science of statistics is based on mathematical thought and derivation. Many academic areas, including business, offer statistics courses within their own disciplines. However, statistics has become a course of study in its own right.

People often use the word *statistics* to refer to a group of data. They may say, for example, that they gathered statistics from their business operation. What they are referring to is measured facts and figures. The media and others also use the word *statistic* to refer to a death. Becoming a statistic in this sense of the word obviously is undesirable.

The word *statistics* is used in at least two other important ways. First, statistics can be descriptive measures computed from a sample and used to make determinations about a population. This usage is discussed later. Second, statistics can be the distributions used in the analysis of data. For example, a researcher using the *t* distribution to analyze data might refer to use of the *t* statistic in analyzing the data.

The following are some of the common uses of the word *statistics*.

1. Science of gathering, analyzing, interpreting, and presenting data
2. Branch of mathematics
3. Course of study
4. Facts and figures
5. A death
6. Measurement taken on a sample
7. Type of distribution used to analyze data

The study of statistics can be organized in a variety of ways. One of the main ways is to subdivide statistics into two branches: descriptive statistics and inferential statistics. To understand the difference between descriptive and inferential statistics, definitions of population and sample are helpful. *Webster's Third New International Dictionary* defines **population** as *a collection of persons, objects, or items of interest.* The population can be a widely defined category, such as "all automobiles," or it can be narrowly defined, such as "all Ford Mustang cars produced from 1998 to 2002." A population can be a group of people, such as "all workers presently employed by Microsoft," or it can be a set of objects, such as "all dishwashers produced on February 3, 2003, by the General Electric Company at the Louisville plant." The researcher defines the population to be whatever he or she is studying. When researchers *gather data from the whole population for a given measurement of interest*, they call it a **census.** Most people are familiar with the U.S. Census. Every 10 years, the government attempts to measure all persons living in this country. If a researcher is interested in ascertaining the Scholastic Aptitude Test (SAT) scores for all students at the University of Arizona, one way to do so is to conduct a census of all students currently enrolled at that university.

A **sample** is *a portion of the whole* and, if properly taken, is representative of the whole. For various reasons (explained in Chapter 7), researchers often prefer to work with a sample of the population instead of the entire population. For example, in conducting quality control experiments to determine the average life of lightbulbs, a lightbulb manufacturer might randomly sample only 75 lightbulbs during a production run. Because of time and money limitations, a human resources manager might take a random sample of 40 employees instead of using a census to measure company morale.

If a business analyst is *using data gathered on a group to describe or reach conclusions about that same group*, the statistics are called **descriptive statistics.** For example, if an instructor produces statistics to summarize a class's examination effort and uses those statistics to reach conclusions about that class only, the statistics are descriptive. The instructor can use these statistics to discuss class average, talk about the range of class scores, or present any other data measurements for the class based on the test.

Most athletic statistics, such as batting average, rebounds, and first downs, are descriptive statistics because they are used to describe an individual or team effort. Many of the statistical data generated by businesses are descriptive. They might include number of employees on vacation during June, average salary at the Denver office, corporate sales for 2002, average managerial satisfaction score on a company-wide census of employee attitudes, and average return on investment for the Lofton Company for the years 1988 through 2002.

Another type of statistics is called **inferential statistics.** If a researcher *gathers data from a sample and uses the statistics generated to reach conclusions about the population from which the sample was taken*, the statistics are inferential statistics. The data gathered are used to infer something about a larger group. Inferential statistics are sometimes referred to as *inductive statistics*. The use and importance of inferential statistics continue to grow.

One application of inferential statistics is in pharmaceutical research. Some new drugs are expensive to produce, and therefore tests must be limited to small samples of patients. Utilizing inferential statistics, researchers can design experiments with small randomly selected samples of patients and attempt to reach conclusions and make inferences about the population.

Market researchers use inferential statistics to study the impact of advertising on various market segments. Suppose a soft drink company creates an advertisement depicting a dispensing machine that talks to the buyer and market researchers want to measure the impact of the new advertisement on various age groups. The researcher could stratify the population into age categories ranging from young to old, randomly sample each stratum, and use inferential statistics to determine the effectiveness of the advertisement for the various age groups in the population. The advantage of using inferential statistics is that they enable the researcher to study effectively a wide range of phenomena without having to conduct a census. Most of the topics discussed in this text pertain to inferential statistics.

A *descriptive measure of the population* is called a **parameter.** Parameters are usually denoted by Greek letters. Examples of parameters are population mean (μ), population variance (σ^2), and population standard deviation (σ). A *descriptive measure of a sample* is called a **statistic.** Statistics are usually denoted by Roman letters. Examples of statistics are sample mean ($\bar{x}$), sample variance (s^2), and sample standard deviation (s).

Differentiation between the terms *parameter* and *statistic* is important only in the use of inferential statistics. A business researcher often wants to estimate the value of a parameter or conduct tests about the parameter. However, the calculation of parameters is usually either impossible or infeasible because of the amount of time and money required to take a census. In such cases, the business researcher can take a random sample of the population, calculate a statistic on the sample, and infer by estimation the value of the parameter. The basis for inferential statistics, then, is the ability to make decisions about parameters without having to complete a census of the population.

For example, a manufacturer of washing machines would probably want to determine the average number of loads that a new machine can wash before it needs repairs. The parameter is the population mean or average number of washes per machine before repair. A company statistician takes a sample of machines, computes the number of washes before repair for each machine, averages the numbers, and estimates the population value or parameter by using the statistic, which in this case is the sample average. Figure 1.2 demonstrates the inferential process.

Inferences about parameters are made under uncertainty. Unless parameters are computed directly from the population, the statistician never knows with certainty whether the estimates or inferences made from samples are true. In an effort to estimate the level of confidence in the result of the process, statisticians use probability statements. Therefore, part of this text is devoted to probability (Chapter 4).

FIGURE 1.2

Process of Inferential
Statistics to Estimate a
Population Mean (μ)

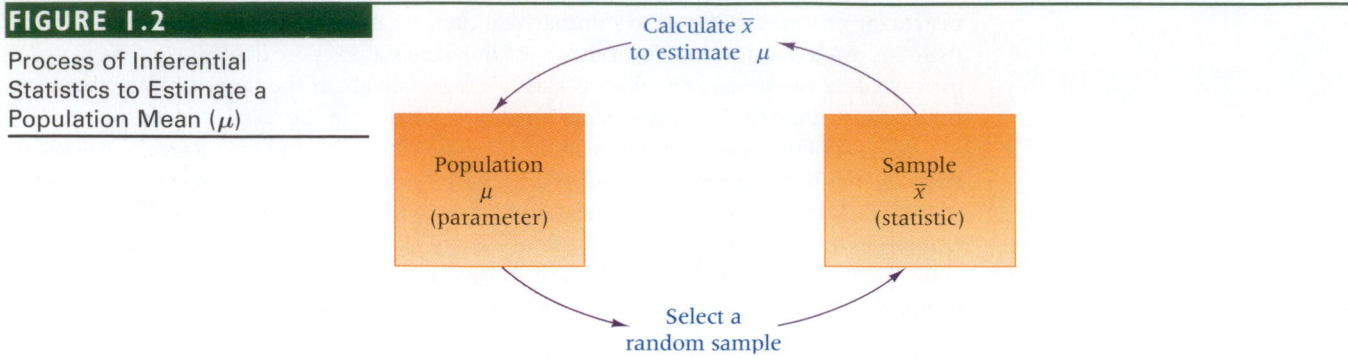

1.3 DATA MEASUREMENT

Millions of numerical data are gathered in businesses every day, representing myriad items. For example, numbers represent dollar costs of items produced, geographical locations of retail outlets, weights of shipments, and rankings of subordinates at yearly reviews. All such data should not be analyzed the same way statistically because the entities represented by the numbers are different. For this reason, the business researcher needs to know the *level of data measurement* represented by the numbers being analyzed.

The disparate use of numbers can be illustrated by the numbers 40 and 80, which could represent the weights of two objects being shipped, the ratings received on a consumer test by two different products, or the football jersey numbers of a fullback and a wide receiver. Although 80 pounds is twice as much as 40 pounds, the wide receiver is probably not twice as big as the fullback! Averaging the two weights seems reasonable but averaging the football jersey numbers makes no sense. The appropriateness of the data analysis depends on the level of measurement of the data gathered. The phenomenon represented by the numbers determines the level of data measurement. Four common levels of data measurement follow.

1. Nominal
2. Ordinal
3. Interval
4. Ratio

Nominal Level

The *lowest level of data measurement* is the **nominal level.** Numbers representing nominal-level data (the word *level* often is omitted) can be *used only to classify or categorize.* Employee identification numbers are an example of nominal data. The numbers are used only to differentiate employees and not to make a value statement about them. Many demographic questions in surveys result in data that are nominal because the questions are used for classification only. The following is an example of such a question that would result in nominal data:

Which of the following employment classifications best describes your area of work?

a. Educator
b. Construction worker
c. Manufacturing worker
d. Lawyer
e. Doctor
f. Other

Suppose that, for computing purposes, an educator is assigned a 1, a construction worker is assigned a 2, a manufacturing worker is assigned a 3, and so on. These numbers should be used only to classify respondents. The number 1 does not denote the top classification. It is used only to differentiate an educator (1) from a lawyer (4).

Some other types of variables that often produce nominal-level data are gender, religion, ethnicity, geographic location, and place of birth. Social security numbers, telephone numbers, employee ID numbers, and ZIP code numbers are further examples of nominal data. Statistical techniques that are appropriate for analyzing nominal data are limited. However, some of the more widely used statistics, such as the chi-square statistic, can be applied to nominal data, often producing useful information.

Ordinal Level

Ordinal-level data measurement is higher than the nominal level. In addition to the nominal-level capabilities, ordinal-level measurement can be used to rank or order objects. For example, using ordinal data, a supervisor can evaluate three employees by ranking their productivity with the numbers 1 through 3. The supervisor could identify one employee as the most productive, one as the least productive, and one as somewhere between by using ordinal data. However, the supervisor could not use ordinal data to establish that the intervals between the employees ranked 1 and 2 and between the employees ranked 2 and 3 are equal; that is, she could not say that the differences in the amount of productivity between workers ranked 1, 2, and 3 are necessarily the same. With ordinal data, the distances or spacing represented by consecutive numbers are not always equal.

Some questionnaire Likert-type scales are considered by many researchers to be ordinal in level. The following is an example of one such scale:

This computer tutorial is	___	___	___	___	___
	not helpful	somewhat helpful	moderately helpful	very helpful	extremely helpful
	1	2	3	4	5

When this survey question is coded for the computer, only the numbers 1 through 5 will remain, not the adjectives. Virtually everyone would agree that a 5 is higher than a 4 on this scale and that ranking responses is possible. However, most respondents would not consider the differences between not helpful, somewhat helpful, moderately helpful, very helpful, and extremely helpful to be equal.

Mutual funds as investments are sometimes rated in terms of risk by using measures of default risk, currency risk, and interest rate risk. These three measures are applied to investments by rating them as having high, medium, and low risk. Suppose high risk is assigned a 3, medium risk a 2, and low risk a 1. If a fund is awarded a 3 rather than a 2, it carries more risk, and so on. However, the differences in risk between categories 1, 2, and 3 are not necessarily equal. Thus, these measurements of risk are only ordinal-level measurements. Another example of the use of ordinal numbers in business is the ranking of the top 50 most admired companies in *Fortune* magazine. The numbers ranking the companies are only ordinal in measurement. Certain statistical techniques are specifically suited to ordinal data, but many other techniques are not appropriate for use on ordinal data.

Because nominal and ordinal data are often derived from imprecise measurements such as demographic questions, the categorization of people or objects, or the ranking of items, *nominal and ordinal data* are **nonmetric data** and are sometimes referred to as *qualitative data*.

Interval Level

Interval-level data measurement is the *next to the highest level of data in which the distances between consecutive numbers have meaning and the data are always numerical.* The distances represented by the differences between consecutive numbers are equal; that is, interval data have equal intervals. An example of interval measurement is Fahrenheit temperature. With Fahrenheit temperature numbers, the temperatures can be ranked, and the amounts of heat between consecutive readings, such as 20°, 21°, and 22°, are the same.

In addition, with interval-level data, the zero point is a matter of convention or convenience and not a natural or fixed zero point. Zero is just another point on the scale and does not mean the absence of the phenomenon. For example, zero degrees Fahrenheit is not the lowest possible temperature. Some other examples of interval level data are the percentage change in employment, the percentage return on a stock, and the dollar change in stock price.

With interval level data, converting the units from one measurement to another involves multiplying by some factor, a, and adding another factor, b, such that $y = b + ax$. As an example, converting from centigrade temperature to Fahrenheit temperature involves the relationship.

$$\text{Fahrenheit} = 32 + \frac{9}{5}\text{centigrade}$$

Ratio Level

Ratio-level data measurement is *the highest level of data measurement*. Ratio data *have the same properties as interval data*, but ratio data have an *absolute zero* and *the ratio of two numbers is meaningful*. The notion of absolute zero means that zero is fixed, and *the zero value in the data represents the absence of the characteristic being studied*. The value of zero cannot be arbitrarily assigned because it represents a fixed point. This definition enables the statistician to create *ratios* with the data.

Examples of ratio data are height, weight, time, volume, and Kelvin temperature. With ratio data, a researcher can state that 180 pounds of weight is twice as much as 90 pounds or, in other words, make a ratio of 180:90. Many of the data gathered by machines in industry are ratio data.

Other examples in the business world that are ratio level in measurement are production cycle time, work measurement time, passenger miles, number of trucks sold, complaints per 10,000 fliers, and number of employees. With ratio-level data, no b factor is required in converting units from one measurement to another, that is, $y = ax$. As an example, in converting height from yards to feet: feet = 3 · yards.

Because interval- and ratio-level data are usually gathered by precise instruments often used in production and engineering processes, in national standardized testing, or in standardized accounting procedures, they are called **metric data** and are sometimes referred to as *quantitative* data.

Comparison of the Four Levels of Data

Figure 1.3 shows the relationships of the usage potential among the four levels of data measurement. The concentric squares denote that each higher level of data can be analyzed by any of the techniques used on lower levels of data but, in addition, can be used in other statistical techniques. Therefore, ratio data can be analyzed by any statistical technique applicable to the other three levels of data plus some others.

Nominal data are the most limited data in terms of the types of statistical analysis that can be used with them. Ordinal data allow the researcher to perform any analysis that can be done with nominal data and some additional analyses. With ratio data, a statistician can make ratio comparisons and appropriately do any analysis that can be performed on nominal, ordinal, or interval data. Some statistical techniques require ratio data and cannot be used to analyze other levels of data.

Statistical techniques can be separated into two categories: parametric statistics and nonparametric statistics. **Parametric statistics** require that data be interval or ratio. If the data are nominal or ordinal, **nonparametric statistics** must be used. Nonparametric statistics can also be used to analyze interval or ratio data. This text focuses largely on parametric statistics, with the exception of Chapter 12 and Chapter 17, which contain nonparametric techniques. Thus much of the material in this text requires that data be interval or ratio data.

FIGURE 1.3

Usage Potential of Various Levels of Data

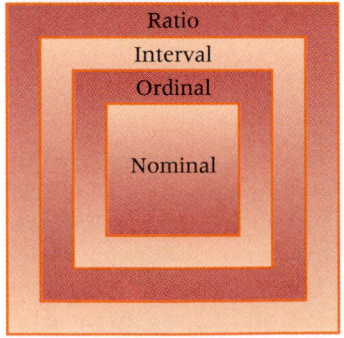

<table>
<tr><td>

DEMONSTRATION PROBLEM 1.1

</td><td>

Many changes continue to occur in the healthcare industry. Because of increased competition for patients among providers and the need to determine how providers can better serve their clientele, hospital administrators sometimes mail a quality satisfaction survey to their patients after the patient is released. The following types of questions are sometimes asked on such a survey. These questions will result in what level of data measurement?

</td></tr>
</table>

1. How long ago were you released from the hospital?
2. Which type of unit were you in for most of your stay?
   ___ Coronary care
   ___ Intensive care
   ___ Maternity care
   ___ Medical unit
   ___ Pediatric/children's unit
   ___ Surgical unit
3. In choosing a hospital, how important was the hospital's location?

   (circle one)

Very	Somewhat	Not Very	Not at All
Important	Important	Important	Important

4. How serious was your condition when you were first admitted to the hospital?
   ___Critical   ___Serious   ___Moderate   ___Minor
5. Rate the skill of your doctor:
   ___Excellent   ___Very Good   ___Good   ___Fair   ___Poor
6. On the following scale from one to seven, rate the nursing care:

   Poor   1   2   3   4   5   6   7   Excellent

Solution

Question 1 is a time measurement with an absolute zero and is therefore ratio-level measurement. A person who has been out of the hospital for two weeks has been out twice as long as someone who has been out of the hospital for one week.

Question 2 yields nominal data because the patient is asked only to categorize the type of unit he or she was in. This question does not require a hierarchy or ranking of the type of unit. Questions 3, 4, and 5 are likely to result in ordinal-level data. Suppose a number is assigned the descriptors in each of these three questions. For question 3, "very important" might be assigned a 4, "somewhat important" a 3, "not very important" a 2, and "not at all important" a 1. Certainly, the higher the number, the more important is the hospital's location. Thus, these responses can be ranked by selection. However, the increases in importance from 1 to 2 to 3 to 4 are not necessarily equal. This same logic applies to the numeric values assigned in questions 4 and 5.

Question 6 displays seven numeric choices with equal distances between the numbers shown on the scale and no adjective descriptors assigned to the numbers. Many researchers would declare this to be interval-level measurement because of the equal distance between numbers and the absence of a true zero on this scale. Some researchers might argue that because of the imprecision of the scale and the vagueness of selecting values between "poor" and "excellent" the measurement is only ordinal in level.

Statistical Analysis Using the Computer: Excel and MINITAB

The advent of the modern computer opened many new opportunities for statistical analysis. The computer allows for storage, retrieval, and transfer of large data sets. Furthermore, computer software has been developed to analyze data by means of sophisticated statistical techniques. Some widely used statistical techniques, such as multiple regression, are so tedious and cumbersome to compute manually that they were of little practical use to researchers before computers were developed.

Business statisticians use many popular statistical software packages, including MINITAB, SAS, and SPSS. Many computer spreadsheet software packages also have the capability of analyzing data statistically. In this text, the computer statistical output presented is from both the MINITAB and the Microsoft Excel software.

Statistics Describe the State of Business in India's Countryside

In the Decision Dilemma, many statistics were reported about rural India, its potential as a market, and its sales. Total sales figures are given for both 1990 and 1994 for four different products. The average annual consumption of toothpaste per person is reported. Percentages describing demographic characteristics of rural India are given including illiteracy rates and possession of household conveniences. The authors of the sources from which the Decision Dilemma is drawn never state whether the figures are actual figures drawn from a census of rural Indians or estimates taken from a sample of such people. If the figures come from a census, then the totals, averages, and percentages presented in the Decision Dilemma are parameters. Because governments sometimes conduct censuses, these data could be parameters. However, more often than not, data are gathered from samples of people or things. In many countries, researchers are capable of gathering relatively accurate, useful data by taking a well-planned sample that is representative of the population. The resulting data are analyzed producing statistics that, in turn, can be used to estimate population parameters. This process is an inferential process. A variety of reasons would make the use of an inferential process preferable to conducting a census. In Chapter 7, we will explore the use of sampling in greater detail.

In this particular situation, whether to market to rural India, researchers could be sent to representative areas of rural India and consumers could be surveyed about their economic state, their ownership of possessions, their personal and family characteristics, their consumer usage of products, and their willingness to expand their purchasing. A wide variety of statistics could be gathered representing several levels of data. For example, ratio-level measurements on such things as income, number of children, age of household

U.S. Wireless Usage Grows

According to a Cellular Telecommunications & Internet Association's semiannual wireless industry survey, more than 110 million customers in the United States used wireless in the year 2001. This figure represented a growth of almost 28% from the end of 1999. Not only were more people using wireless devices, they were using them more often. The average length of a call by 2001 was 3 minutes compared to 2 minutes and 38 seconds at the end of 1999. The average monthly bill for wireless usage, reflecting this increase in usage, went from $41.24 to $45.27 over the same one-year period.

Total revenues for U.S. wireless operators topped $50 billion for the year 2000. Roaming revenues were down reflecting continued network expansion. As carriers expand their covered territories, roaming revenues decrease because users are in the network more often.

What will happen to wireless usage in the future? As the market becomes more mature, will usage level off? Will factors such as public safety concerns, driving laws, personal safety, or etiquette debates curb the usage of wireless devices? These and other questions can be addressed through the gathering and analysis of business statistics.

Source: Adapted from "No Slump in U.S. Wireless Usage," *allNetDevices*, 27 April 2001, http://www.allnetdevices.com/wireless/news/2001/04/27/no_slump.html

ETHICAL CONSIDERATIONS

With the abundance and proliferation of statistical data, potential misuse of statistics in business dealings is a concern. It is, in effect, unethical business behavior to use statistics out of context. Unethical business people might use only selective data from studies to underscore their point, omitting statistics from the same studies that argue against their case. The results of statistical studies can be misstated or overstated to gain favor.

This chapter noted that if data are nominal or ordinal, then only nonparametric statistics are appropriate for analysis. The use of parametric statistics to analyze nominal and/or ordinal data is wrong and could be considered under some circumstances to be unethical.

In this text, each chapter contains a section on ethics that discusses how businesses can misuse the techniques presented in the chapter in an unethical manner. As both users and producers, business students need to be aware of the potential ethical pitfalls that can occur with statistics.

heads, number of livestock, value of house/land, and grams of toothpaste consumed per year might be obtained. In some instances, Likert scales (1-to-5 measurements) are used to gather responses about interests and likes, thus producing an ordinal-level of measurement. For privacy reasons, some question topics such as age or income are stated in class ranges also resulting in an ordinal level of measurement. In addition, rural Indians may be asked to rank a variety of products in terms of which they would be most likely to purchase, yielding ordinal data. Other variables such as geographic location, political party affiliation, occupation, and religion result in nominal data.

The decision to enter the rural India market is not just a marketing decision. It involves production capacity and schedule issues, transportation challenges, financial commitments, managerial growth or reassignment, accounting issues (accounting for rural India may differ from techniques used in traditional markets), information systems, and other related areas. With so much on the line, company decision makers need as much relevant information available as possible. In this Decision Dilemma, it is obvious to the decision maker that rural India is still quite poor and illiterate. Its capacity as a market is great. The statistics on the increasing sales of a few personal-care products look promising. What are the future forecasts for the earning power of people in rural India? Will major cultural issues block the adoption of the types of products that companies want to sell there? The answers to these and many other interesting and useful questions can be obtained by the appropriate use of statistics. The 750 million people living in rural India represent the second largest group of people in the world. It certainly is a market segment worth studying further.

SUMMARY

Statistics is an important decision-making tool in business and is used in virtually every area of business. The word *statistics* has many different connotations. Among the more common meanings of the word are (1) the science of gathering, analyzing, interpreting, and presenting data, (2) a branch of mathematics, (3) a course of study, (4) facts and figures, (5) a death, (6) sample measurement, and (7) type of distribution used to analyze data. Statistics are broadly used in business, including the disciplines of accounting, decision sciences, economics, finance, management, management information systems, marketing, and production.

The study of statistics can be subdivided into two main areas: *descriptive statistics* and *inferential statistics*.

Descriptive statistics result from gathering data from a body, group, or population and reaching conclusions only about that group. Inferential statistics are generated from the process of gathering sample data from a group, body, or population and reaching conclusions about the larger group from which the sample was drawn.

The appropriate type of statistical analysis depends on the level of data measurement, which can be (1) *nominal,* (2) *ordinal,* (3) *interval,* or (4) *ratio.* Nominal is the lowest level, representing classification of only such data as geographic location, gender, or social security number. The next level is ordinal, which provides rank ordering measurements in which the intervals between consecutive numbers do not necessarily represent equal distances. Interval is the next to highest level of data measurement in which the distances represented by consecutive numbers are equal. The highest level of data measurement is ratio, which has all the qualities of interval measurement, but ratio data contain an absolute zero and ratios between numbers are meaningful. Interval and ratio data sometimes are called *metric* or *quantitative* data. Nominal and ordinal data sometimes are called *nonmetric* or *qualitative* data.

The two major types of inferential statistics are (1) *parametric statistics* and (2) *nonparametric statistics*. Use of parametric statistics requires interval or ratio data and certain assumptions about the distribution of the data. The techniques presented in this text are largely parametric. If data are only nominal or ordinal in level, nonparametric statistics must be used.

KEY TERMS

census	metric data	ordinal-level data	ratio-level data
descriptive statistics	nominal-level data	parameter	sample
inferential statistics	nonmetric data	parametric statistics	statistic
interval-level data	nonparametric statistics	population	statistics

SUPPLEMENTARY PROBLEMS

1.1 Give a specific example of data that might be gathered from each of the following business disciplines: accounting, finance, human resources, marketing, information systems, production, and management. An example in the marketing area might be "number of sales per month by each salesperson."

1.2 State examples of data that can be gathered for decision-making purposes from each of the following industries: manufacturing, insurance, travel, retailing, communications, computing, agriculture, banking, and healthcare. An example in the travel industry might be the cost of business travel per day in various European cities.

1.3 Give an example of *descriptive* statistics in the recorded music industry. Give an example of how *inferential* statistics could be used in the recorded music industry. Compare the two examples. What makes them different?

1.4 Suppose you are an operations manager for a plant that manufactures batteries. Give an example of how you could use *descriptive* statistics to make better managerial decisions. Give an example of how you could use *inferential* statistics to make better managerial decisions.

1.5 Classify each of the following as nominal, ordinal, interval, or ratio data.

   a. The time required to produce each tire on an assembly line
   b. The number of quarts of milk a family drinks in a month
   c. The ranking of four machines in your plant after they have been designated as excellent, good, satisfactory, and poor
   d. The telephone area code of clients in the United States

   e. The age of each of your employees
   f. The dollar sales at the local pizza house each month
   g. An employee's ID number
   h. The response time of an emergency unit

1.6 Classify each of the following as nominal, ordinal, interval, or ratio data.

   a. The ranking of a company by *Fortune* 500
   b. The number of tickets sold at a movie theater on any given night
   c. The identification number on a questionnaire
   d. Per capita income
   e. The trade balance in dollars
   f. Socioeconomic class (low, middle, upper)
   g. Profit/loss in dollars
   h. A company's tax ID
   i. The Standard & Poor's bond ratings of cities based on the following scales.

Rating	Grade
Highest quality	AAA
High quality	AA
Upper medium quality	A
Medium quality	BBB
Somewhat speculative	BB
Low quality, speculative	B
Low grade, default possible	CCC
Low grade, partial recovery possible	CC
Default, recovery unlikely	C

1.7 The Rathburn Manufacturing Company makes electric wiring, which it sells to contractors in the construction industry. Approximately 900 electric contractors purchase wire from Rathburn annually. Rathburn's director of marketing wants to determine electric contractors' satisfaction with Rathburn's wire. He developed a questionnaire that yields a satisfaction score between 10 and 50 for participant responses. A random sample of 35 of the 900 contractors is asked to complete a satisfaction survey. The satisfaction scores for the 35 participants are averaged to produce a mean satisfaction score.

a. What is the population for this study?

b. What is the sample for this study?

c. What is the statistic for this study?

d. What would be a parameter for this study?

ANALYZING THE DATABASES

see www.wiley.com/college/black

Seven major databases constructed for this text can be used for applying the techniques presented in this course. These databases are found on the CD-ROM that accompanies this text, and each of these databases is available in either MINITAB or Excel format for your convenience. These seven databases represent a wide variety of business areas, such as the stock market, manufacturing, international labor, finance, energy, healthcare, and agribusiness. Altogether, these databases contain 56 variables and 8,350 observations. The data are gathered from such reliable sources as the U.S. government's Bureau of Labor, the New York Stock Exchange, the U.S. Department of Agriculture, *Moody's Handbook of Common Stocks,* the American Hospital Association, and the U.S. Census Bureau. Four of the seven databases contain time-series data that can be especially useful in forecasting and regression analysis. Here is a description of each database along with information that may help you to interpret outcomes.

Stock Market Database

The stock market database contains eight variables on the New York Stock Exchange. Three observations per month for nine years yields a total of 324 observations per variable. The variables include Composite Index, Industrial Index, Transportation Index, Utility Index, Stock Volume, Reported Trades, Dollar Value, and Warrants Volume. Dollar value is reported in units of millions of dollars. Recognizing that time of the month may make a difference in the value of an observation, each variable contains an observation from on or near to the tenth of the month denoted in the database as 1 under the variable Part of the Month, an observation from on or near to the twentieth of the month denoted as 2, and an observation from on or near to the thirtieth of the month denoted as 3. This database was constructed from data displayed on the Internet by the New York Stock Exchange. The original data can be accessed at the Data Library at http://www.nyse.com/marketinfo/marketinfo.html under the title "NYSE Statistics Archive."

Manufacturing Database

This database contains eight variables taken from 20 industries and 140 subindustries in the United States. The source of the database is the *1996 Annual Survey of Manufactures,* which is published by the Census Bureau of the U.S. Department of Commerce. Some of the industries are food products, textile mill products, furniture, chemicals, rubber products, primary metals, industrial machinery, and transportation equipment. The eight variables are Number of Employees, Number of Production Workers, Value Added by Manufacture, Cost of Materials, Value of Industry Shipments, New Capital Expenditures, End-of-Year Inventories, and Industry Group. Two variables, Number of Employees and Number of Production Workers, are in units of 1,000. Four variables, Value Added by Manufacture, Cost of Materials, New Capital Expenditures, and End-of-Year Inventories, are in million-dollar units. The Industry Group variable consists of numbers from 1 to 20 to denote the industry group to which the particular subindustry belongs. Value of Industry Shipments has been recoded to the following 1-to-4 scale.

1 = $0 to $4.9 billion

2 = $5 billion to $13.9 billion

3 = $14 billion to $28.9 billion

4 = $29 billion or more

International Labor Database

This time-series database contains the civilian unemployment rates in percent from seven countries presented yearly from 1959 through 1998. The data are published by the Bureau of Labor Statistics of the U.S. Department of Labor. The countries are the United States, Canada, Australia, Japan, France, Germany, and Italy.

Financial Database

The financial database contains observations on eight variables for 100 companies. The variables are Type of Industry, Total Revenues ($ millions), Total Assets ($ millions), Return on Equity (%), Earnings per Share ($), Average Yield (%), Dividends per Share ($), and Average Price per Earnings (P/E) ratio. The data were gathered from *Moody's Handbook of Common Stocks* (Summer 1998). The companies represent seven different types of industries. The variable "Type" displays a company's industry type as:

1 = apparel

2 = chemical

3 = electric power

4 = grocery

5 = healthcare products

6 = insurance

7 = petroleum

Energy Database

The energy database consists of data on seven energy variables over a period of 26 years. The database is adopted from *Monthly Energy Review*, February 1999 (Office of Energy Markets and End Use, Energy Information Administration, U.S. Department of Energy). The seven variables are World Crude Oil Production (million barrels per day), U.S. Energy Consumption (quadrillion BTUs per year), U.S. Nuclear Electricity Gross Generation (billion kilowatt-hours), U.S. Coal Production (million short tons), U.S. Total Dry Gas Production (million cubic feet), U.S. Fuel Rate for Automobiles (miles per gallon), and Cost of Unleaded (regular) Gasoline (U.S. city average).

Hospital Database

This database contains observations for 11 variables on U.S. hospitals. These variables include Geographic Region, Control, Service, Number of Beds, Number of Admissions, Census, Number of Outpatients, Number of Births, Total Expenditures, Payroll Expenditures, and Personnel. Information for these databases is taken from the *American Hospital Association Guide to the Health-Care Field*, 1998–99 edition, published in Chicago, Illinois.

The region variable is coded from 1 to 7, and the numbers represent the following regions.

1 = South

2 = Northeast

3 = Midwest

4 = Southwest

5 = Rocky Mountain

6 = California

7 = Northwest

Control is a type of ownership. Four categories of control are included in the database:

1 = government, nonfederal

2 = nongovernment, not-for-profit

3 = for-profit

4 = federal government

Service is the type of hospital. The two types of hospitals used in this database are:

1 = general medical

2 = psychiatric

The total expenditures and payroll variables are in units of $1,000.

Agribusiness Time-Series Database

The agribusiness time-series database contains the monthly weight (in 1,000 lbs.) of cold storage holdings for six different vegetables and for total frozen vegetables over a 14-year period. Each of the seven variables represents 168 months of data from 1984 to 1997. The six vegetables are green beans, broccoli, carrots, sweet corn, onions, and green peas. The data are published by the National Agricultural Statistics Service of the U.S. Department of Agriculture.

Use the databases to answer the following questions.

1. In the manufacturing database, what is the level of data for each of the following variables?

   a. Number of production workers

   b. Cost of materials

   c. Value of industry shipments

   d. Industry group

2. In the hospital database, what is the level of data for each of the following variables?

   a. Region

   b. Control

   c. Number of beds

   d. Personnel

3. In the financial database, what is the level of data for each of the following variables?

   a. Type of industry

   b. Total assets

   c. P/E ratio

CASE: DIGIORNO PIZZA: INTRODUCING A FROZEN PIZZA TO COMPETE WITH CARRY-OUT

In 1996, Kraft's DiGiorno Pizza hit the market. DiGiorno Pizza was a booming success with sales of $120 million the first year followed by $200 million the next year. It was neither luck nor coincidence that DiGiorno Pizza was an instant success. Kraft conducted extensive research about the product and the marketplace before introducing this product to the public. Many questions had to be answered before Kraft began production. For example, why do people eat pizza? When do they eat pizza? Do consumers believe that carry-out pizza is always more tasty?

SMI-Alcott conducted a research study for Kraft in which they sent out 1,000 surveys to pizza lovers. The results indicated that people ate pizza during fun social occasions or at home when no one wanted to cook. People used frozen pizza mostly for convenience but selected carry-out pizza for a variety of other reasons, including quality and the avoidance of cooking. The Loran Marketing Group conducted focus groups for Kraft with women ages 25 to 54. Their findings showed that consumers used frozen pizza for convenience but wanted carry-out pizza taste. To satisfy these seemingly divergent goals (convenience and taste), Kraft developed DiGiorno Pizza, which rises in the oven as it cooks. This impressed focus group members, and in a series of blind taste tests conducted by Product Dynamics, DiGiorno Pizza beat out all frozen pizzas and finished second overall behind one carry-out brand.

Through advertising Kraft was able to overcome two concerns that were raised by marketing research: people had trouble pronouncing "DiGiorno" and people needed to be convinced that the frozen pizza actually tasted good. Kraft had the name DiGiorno repeated several times in advertisements to make certain that consumers could pronounce the name. As a by-product, the ads also generated strong brand identification. In addition, the ads emphasized "fresh-baked taste" and the rising dough aspect of the product, which helped convince people of DiGiorno's higher quality of taste.

DiGiorno Pizza now has a 13% market share of the U.S. $2.3 billion frozen pizza category. It is the fastest Kraft product ever to break the $200 million barrier.

Discussion

Think about the market research that was conducted by Kraft and the fact that they used several companies. If you were in charge of conducting this research to help launch such a new product, what decisions would you make about whom to survey, where and when to survey, and what to measure?

1. What are some of the populations that Kraft might have been interested in measuring for these studies? Did Kraft actually attempt to contact entire populations? What samples were taken? In light of these two questions, how was the inferential process used by Kraft in their market research? Can you think of any descriptive statistics that might have been used by Kraft in their decision-making process?

2. In the various market research efforts made by Kraft for DiGiorno, some of the possible measurements appear in the following list. Categorize these by level of data. Think of some other measurements that Kraft researchers might have made to help them in this research effort and categorize them by level of data.

   a. Number of pizzas consumed per week per household
   b. Age of pizza purchaser
   c. Zip code of the survey respondent
   d. Dollars spent per month on pizza per person
   e. Time in between purchases of pizza
   f. Rating of taste of a given pizza brand on a scale from 1 to 10, where 1 is very poor tasting and 10 is excellent taste
   g. Ranking of the taste of four pizza brands on a taste test
   h. Number representing the geographic location of the survey respondent
   i. Quality rating of a pizza brand as excellent, good, average, below average, poor
   j. Number representing the pizza brand being evaluated.
   k. Gender of survey respondent

Source: Adapted from "Upper Crust," *American Demographics,* March 1999, p. 58; *Marketwatch—News That Matters* Web sites, "What's in a Name? Brand Extension Potential" and "DiGiorno Rising Crust Delivers $200 Million," formerly at http://www.foodexplorer.com/BUSINESS/Products/MarketAnalysis/PF02896b.htm, last accessed in 1999.

Charts and Graphs

LEARNING OBJECTIVES

The overall objective of Chapter 2 is for you to master several techniques for summarizing and depicting data, thereby enabling you to:

1. Recognize the difference between grouped and ungrouped data.
2. Construct a frequency distribution.
3. Construct a histogram, a frequency polygon, an ogive, a pie chart, a stem and leaf plot, a Pareto chart, and a scatter plot.

State of Auto Manufacturing

According to data released by the Automotive News Data Center, General Motors Corporation is number one in the world in total vehicle sales of cars and light trucks. Ford Motor Company is number two followed by Toyota Motor Corporation and Volkswagen, respectively. Between 1999 and 2000, while General Motors maintained its number one position, it sold nearly 200,000 fewer cars worldwide. During this same period, Ford Motor increased sales by more than 200,000. The greatest percentage growth from 1999 to 2000 was for PSA Peugeot-Citroen, which increased sales by 14.2%. The global sales figures for the top 10 auto manufacturers of cars and light trucks for both 1999 and 2000 follow.

Company	1999	2000	% Change
General Motors	8,786,000	8,591,327	-2.2
Ford Motor	7,148,000	7,350,495	2.8
Toyota Motor	5,359,000	5,703,446	6.4
Volkswagen	4,860,203	5,161,188	6.2
DaimlerChrysler	4,864,500	4,749,000	-2.4
PSA Peugeot-Citroen	2,519,600	2,877,900	14.2
Fiat	2,521,000	2,646,500	5.0
Hyundai Motor	2,600,862	2,634,530	1.3
Nissan Motor	2,567,878	2,629,044	2.4
Honda Motor	2,395,000	2,540,000	6.1

Managerial and Statistical Questions

Suppose you are a business analyst for one of these companies. Your manager asks you to prepare a brief report showing the state of car and light truck sales in the world. You are to compare your company's position with other firms.

1. What is the best way to convey the sales data in a report? Is the raw data enough? Can you effectively display the data graphically?

2. Suppose DaimlerChrysler randomly samples 40 dealerships and discovers that the following data tell how many car and light trucks were sold at these dealerships last month. How can you summarize these data in a report?

   34 58 40 49 49 57 44 57 69 45 64 31 47 30 44 44 51 65 60 65
   61 62 68 43 66 63 44 34 57 44 67 61 47 67 52 34 58 59 45 33

3. How might you graphically depict the 1999 data against the 2000 data?

Source: Adapted from Automotive News Data Center, "Top 10 Auto Manufacturers," *Ad Age Almanac*, 31 December 2001, p. 23.

TABLE 2.1

Unemployment Rates for France Over 40 Years (Ungrouped Data)

1.6	2.1	4.2	8.6	9.6
1.5	2.7	4.6	10.0	10.4
1.2	2.3	5.2	10.5	11.8
1.4	2.5	5.4	10.6	12.3
1.6	2.8	6.1	10.8	11.8
1.2	2.9	6.5	10.3	12.5
1.6	2.8	7.6	9.6	12.4
1.6	2.9	8.3	9.1	11.8

In Chapters 2 and 3 many techniques are presented for reformatting or reducing data so that the data are more manageable and can be used to assist decision makers more effectively. Two techniques for grouping data are the frequency distribution and the stem and leaf plot presented in this chapter. In addition, Chapter 2 discusses and displays several graphical tools for summarizing and presenting data, including histogram, frequency polygon, ogive, pie chart, and Pareto chart for one-variable data; and the scatter plot for two-variable numerical data. By using these and other techniques, decision makers can begin to "get a handle" on information contained in data and begin to use the data to enhance the decision-making process.

Raw data, or *data that have not been summarized in any way,* are sometimes referred to as **ungrouped data.** Table 2.1 contains raw data of the unemployment rates for France over 40 years. *Data that have been organized into a frequency distribution* are called **grouped data.** Table 2.2 presents a frequency distribution for the data displayed in Table 2.1. The distinction between ungrouped and grouped data is important because the calculation of statistics differs between the two types of data. This chapter focuses on organizing ungrouped data into grouped data and displaying them graphically.

2.1 FREQUENCY DISTRIBUTIONS

One particularly useful tool for grouping data is the **frequency distribution,** which is *a summary of data presented in the form of class intervals and frequencies.* How is a frequency distribution constructed from raw data? That is, how are frequency distributions like the one displayed in Table 2.2 constructed from raw data like those presented in Table 2.1? Frequency distributions are relatively easy to construct. Although some guidelines and rules of thumb help in their construction, frequency distributions vary in final shape and design, even when the original raw data are identical. In a sense, frequency distributions are constructed according to individual business researchers' taste.

When constructing a frequency distribution, the business researcher should first determine the range of the raw data. The **range** often is defined as *the difference between the largest and smallest numbers.* The range for the data in Table 2.1 is 11.3 (12.5 − 1.2).

The second step in constructing a frequency distribution is to determine how many classes it will contain. One rule of thumb is to select between *5 and 15 classes.* If the frequency distribution contains too few classes, the data summary may be too general to be useful. Too many classes may result in a frequency distribution that does not aggregate the data enough to be helpful. The final number of classes is arbitrary. The business researcher arrives at a number by examining the range and determining a number of classes that will span the range adequately and also be meaningful to the user. The data in Table 2.1 were grouped into six classes for Table 2.2.

After selecting the number of classes, the business researcher must determine the width of the class interval. An approximation of the class width can be calculated by dividing the range by the number of classes. For the data in Table 2.1, this approximation would be 11.3/6, or 1.9. Normally, the number is rounded up to the next whole number, which in this case is 2. The frequency distribution must start at a value equal to or lower than the lowest number of the ungrouped data and end at a value equal to or higher than the highest number. The lowest unemployment rate is 1.2 and the highest is 12.5, so the business researcher starts the frequency distribution at 1 and ends it at 13. Table 2.2 contains the completed frequency distribution for the data in Table 2.1. Class endpoints are selected so that no value of the data can fit into more than one class. The class interval expression, "under," in the distribution of Table 2.2 avoids such a problem.

TABLE 2.2

Frequency Distribution of the Unemployment Rates of France (Grouped Data)

Class Interval	Frequency
1–under 3	16
3–under 5	2
5–under 7	4
7–under 9	3
9–under 11	9
11–under 13	6

Class Midpoint

The *midpoint of each class interval* is called the **class midpoint** and is sometimes referred to as the **class mark.** It is *the value halfway across the class interval* and can be calculated as *the* *average of the two class endpoints*. For example, in the distribution of Table 2.2, the midpoint of the class interval 3–under 5 is 4, or (3+5)/2. A second way to obtain the class midpoint is to calculate one-half the distance across the class interval (half the class width) and add it to the class beginning point, as for the unemployment rates distribution:

$$\text{Class Beginning Point} = 3$$
$$\text{Class Width} = 2$$
$$\text{Class Midpoint} = 3 + \frac{1}{2}(2) = 4$$

The class midpoint is important, because it becomes the representative value for each class in most group statistics calculations. The third column in Table 2.3 contains the class midpoints for all classes of the data from Table 2.2.

Relative Frequency

Relative frequency is *the proportion of the total frequency that is in any given class interval in a frequency distribution*. Relative frequency is the individual class frequency divided by the total frequency. For example, from Table 2.3, the relative frequency for the class interval 5–under 7 is 4/40, or .10. Consideration of the relative frequency is preparatory to the study of probability in Chapter 4. Indeed, if values were selected randomly from the data in Table 2.1, the probability of drawing a number that is "5–under 7" would be .10, the relative frequency for that class interval. The fourth column of Table 2.3 lists the relative frequencies for the frequency distribution of Table 2.2.

Cumulative Frequency

The **cumulative frequency** is *a running total of frequencies through the classes of a frequency distribution*. The cumulative frequency for each class interval is the frequency for that class interval added to the preceding cumulative total. In Table 2.3 the cumulative frequency for the first class is the same as the class frequency: 16. The cumulative frequency for the second class interval is the frequency of that interval (2) plus the frequency of the first interval (16), which yields a new cumulative frequency of 18. This process continues through the last interval, at which point the cumulative total equals the sum of the frequencies (40). The concept of cumulative frequency is used in many areas, including sales cumulated over a fiscal year, sports scores during a contest (cumulated points), years of service, points earned in a course, and costs of doing business over a period of time. Table 2.3 gives cumulative frequencies for the data in Table 2.2.

TABLE 2.3					
Class Midpoints, Relative Frequencies, and Cumulative Frequencies for Unemployment Data	Interval	Frequency	Class Midpoint	Relative Frequency	Cumulative Frequency
	1–under 3	16	2	.400	16
	3–under 5	2	4	.050	18
	5–under 7	4	6	.100	22
	7–under 9	3	8	.075	25
	9–under 11	9	10	.225	34
	11–under 13	6	12	.150	40
	Totals	40		1.000	

<table>
<tr><td>DEMONSTRATION
PROBLEM 2.1</td><td colspan="5">The following data are the average weekly mortgage interest rates for a 60-week period.</td></tr>
</table>

7.29	7.03	7.14	6.77	6.35
6.69	7.02	7.40	7.16	6.96
6.98	7.56	6.75	6.87	7.11
7.39	7.28	6.97	6.90	6.57
7.11	6.95	7.23	7.31	7.00
7.30	7.17	6.96	6.78	7.30
7.16	6.78	6.79	7.07	7.03
6.87	6.80	7.10	7.13	6.95
7.08	7.24	7.34	7.47	7.31
6.96	6.70	6.57	6.88	6.84
7.02	7.40	7.12	7.16	7.16
6.99	6.94	7.29	7.05	6.84

Construct a frequency distribution for these data. Calculate and display the class midpoints, relative frequencies, and cumulative frequencies for this frequency distribution.

Solution

How many classes should this frequency distribution contain? The range of the data is 1.21 (7.56-6.35). If 13 classes are used, each class width is approximately:

$$\text{Class Width} = \frac{\text{Range}}{\text{Number of Classes}} = \frac{1.21}{13} = 0.093$$

If a class width of .10 is used, a frequency distribution can be constructed with endpoints that are more uniform looking and allow presentation of the information in categories more familiar to mortgage interest rate users.

The first class endpoint must be 6.35 or lower to include the smallest value; the last endpoint must be 7.56 or higher to include the largest value. In this case the frequency distribution begins at 6.30 and ends at 7.60. The resulting frequency distribution, class midpoints, relative frequencies, and cumulative frequencies are listed in the following table.

Class Interval	Frequency	Class Midpoint	Relative Frequency	Cumulative Frequency
6.30–under 6.40	1	6.35	.0167	1
6.40–under 6.50	0	6.45	.0000	1
6.50–under 6.60	2	6.55	.0333	3
6.60–under 6.70	1	6.65	.0167	4
6.70–under 6.80	6	6.75	.1000	10
6.80–under 6.90	6	6.85	.1000	16
6.90–under 7.00	10	6.95	.1667	26
7.00–under 7.10	8	7.05	.1333	34
7.10–under 7.20	11	7.15	.1833	45
7.20–under 7.30	5	7.25	.0833	50
7.30–under 7.40	6	7.35	.1000	56
7.40–under 7.50	3	7.45	.0500	59
7.50–under 7.60	1	7.55	.0167	60
Totals	60		1.0000	

The frequencies and relative frequencies of these data reveal the mortgage interest rate classes that are likely to occur during the period. Most of the mortgage interest rates (52 of the 60) are in the classes starting with (6.70–under 6.80) and going through (7.30–under 7.40). The rates with the greatest frequency, 11, are in the (7.10–under 7.20) class.

2.1 PROBLEMS

2.1   The following data represent the afternoon high temperatures for 50 construction days during a year in St. Louis.

42	70	64	47	66
55	85	10	24	45
16	40	81	15	35
38	79	35	36	23
31	38	52	16	81
69	73	38	48	25
31	62	47	63	84
17	40	36	44	17
64	75	53	31	60
12	61	43	30	33

a.   Construct a frequency distribution for the data using five class intervals.

b.   Construct a frequency distribution for the data using 10 class intervals.

c.   Examine the results of (a) and (b) and comment on the usefulness of the frequency distribution in terms of temperature summarization capability.

2.2   A packaging process is supposed to fill small boxes of raisins with approximately 50 raisins so that each box will weigh the same. However, the number of raisins in each box will vary. Suppose 100 boxes of raisins are randomly sampled, the raisins counted, and the following data are obtained.

57	51	53	52	50	60	51	51	52	52
44	53	45	57	39	53	58	47	51	48
49	49	44	54	46	52	55	54	47	53
49	52	49	54	57	52	52	53	49	47
51	48	55	53	55	47	53	43	48	46
54	46	51	48	53	56	48	47	49	57
55	53	50	47	57	49	43	58	52	44
46	59	57	47	61	60	49	53	41	48
59	53	45	45	56	40	46	49	50	57
47	52	48	50	45	56	47	47	48	46

Construct a frequency distribution for these data. What does the frequency distribution reveal about the box fills?

2.3   The owner of a fast-food restaurant ascertains the ages of a sample of customers. From these data, the owner constructs the frequency distribution shown. For each class interval of the frequency distribution, determine the class midpoint, the relative frequency, and the cumulative frequency.

Class Interval	Frequency
0–under 5	6
5–under 10	8
10–under 15	17
15–under 20	23
20–under 25	18
25–under 30	10
30–under 35	4

What does the relative frequency tell the fast-food restaurant owner about customer ages?

2.4   The human resources manager for a large company commissions a study in which the employment records of 500 company employees are examined for absenteeism during the past year. The business researcher conducting the study organizes the data into a frequency distribution to assist the human resources manager in analyzing the data. The frequency distribution is shown. For each class of the frequency distribution, determine the class midpoint, the relative frequency, and the cumulative frequency.

Class Interval	Frequency
0–under 2	218
2–under 4	207
4–under 6	56
6–under 8	11
8–under 10	8

2.5   List three specific uses of cumulative frequencies in business.

2.2 GRAPHICAL DEPICTION OF DATA

One of the most effective mechanisms for presenting data in a form meaningful to decision makers is graphical depiction. Through graphs and charts, the decision maker can often get an overall picture of the data and reach some useful conclusions merely by studying the chart or graph. Converting data to graphics can be creative and artful. Often the most difficult step in this process is to reduce important and sometimes expensive data to a graphic picture that is both clear and concise and yet consistent with the message of the original data. One of the most important uses of graphical depiction in statistics is to help the researcher determine the shape of a distribution. Six types of graphic depiction are presented here: (1) histogram, (2) frequency polygon, (3) ogive, (4) pie chart, (5) stem and leaf plot, and (6) Pareto chart.

Histograms

A **histogram** is *a type of vertical bar chart that is used to depict a frequency distribution.* Construction involves labeling the x axis (abscissa) with the class endpoints and the y axis (ordinate) with the frequencies, drawing a horizontal line segment from class endpoint to class endpoint at each frequency value, and connecting each line segment vertically from the frequency value to the x axis to form a series of rectangles. Figure 2.1 is a histogram of the frequency distribution in Table 2.2 produced by using the software package MINITAB.

A histogram is a useful tool for differentiating the frequencies of class intervals. A quick glance at a histogram reveals which class intervals produce the highest frequency totals. Figure 2.1 clearly shows that the class interval 1–under 3 yields by far the highest frequency count (16). Examination of the histogram reveals where large increases or decreases occur between classes, such as from the 1–under 3 class to the 3–under 5 class, a decrease of 14, and from the 7–under 9 class to the 9–under 11 class, an increase of 6.

Note that the scales used along the x and y axes for the histogram in Figure 2.1 are almost identical. However, because ranges of meaningful numbers for the two variables being graphed often differ considerably, the graph may have different scales on the two axes. Figure 2.2 shows what the histogram of unemployment rates would look like if the scale on the y axis were more compressed than that on the x axis. Notice that less difference in the length of the rectangles appears to represent the frequencies in Figure 2.2. It is important that the user of the graph clearly understands the scales used for the axes of a

FIGURE 2.1

MINITAB Histogram of French Unemployment Data

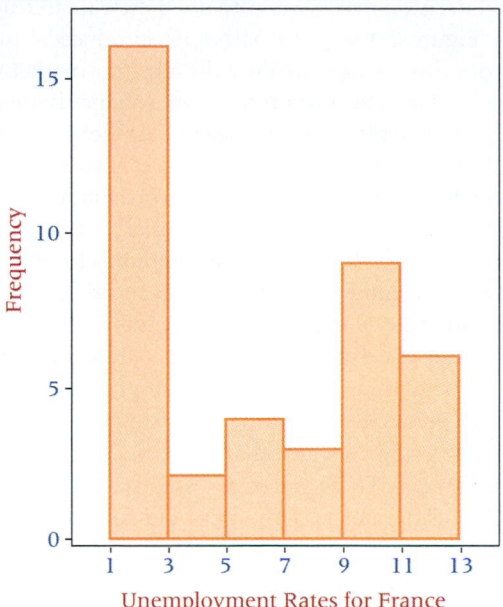

histogram. Otherwise, a graph's creator can "lie with statistics" by stretching or compressing a graph to make a point.*

Using Histograms to Get an Initial Overview of the Data

Because of the widespread availability of computers and statistical software packages to business researchers and decision makers, the histogram continues to become more important. Sometimes decision makers are presented with a large database of information and do not know where to begin in attempting to understand what the data mean. Histogram analysis of such data can yield initial information about the shape of the distribution of the data, the amount of variability of data, the central location of the data, and outlier data. Although most of these concepts are presented in Chapter 3, the notion of histogram as an initial tool to access these data characteristics is presented here.

For example, one of the variables in the Stock Market database (displayed on the CD-ROM) is Stock Volume. The database contains 324 stock volume observations. Suppose a

FIGURE 2.2

MINITAB Histogram of French Unemployment Data (*y* axis compressed)

* It should be pointed out that the software package Excel uses the term *histogram* to refer to a frequency distribution. However, by checking Chart Output in the Excel histogram dialog box, a graphical histogram is also created.

financial decision maker wants to use these data to reach some conclusions about the stock market. Figure 2.3 shows a MINITAB-produced histogram of these data. What can we learn from this histogram? Virtually all stock market volumes fall between zero and 1 billion shares. The distribution takes on a shape that is high on the left end and tapered to the right. In Chapter 3 we will learn that the shape of this distribution is skewed toward the right end. In statistics, it is often useful to determine whether data are approximately normally distributed (bell-shaped curve) as shown in Figure 2.4. We can see by examining the histogram in Figure 2.3 that the stock market volume data are not normally distributed. Although the center of the histogram is located near 500 million shares, a large portion of stock volume observations falls in the lower end of the data somewhere between 100 million and 400 million shares. In addition, the histogram shows some outliers in the upper end of the distribution. Outliers are data points that appear outside of the main body of observations and may represent phenomena that differ from those represented by other data points. By observing the histogram, we notice a few data observations near 1 billion. One could conclude that on a few stock market days an unusually large volume of shares are traded. These and other insights can be gleaned by examining the histogram and show that histograms play an important role in the initial analysis of data.

Frequency Polygons

A **frequency polygon** is *a graph in which line segments "connecting the dots" depict a frequency distribution.* Construction of a frequency polygon begins, as with a histogram, by scaling class endpoints along the *x* axis and the frequency values along the *y* axis. A dot is plotted for the frequency value at the midpoint of each class interval (class midpoint). Connecting these midpoint dots completes the graph. Figure 2.5 shows a frequency polygon of the distribution data from Table 2.2 produced by using the software package Excel. The information gleaned from frequency polygons and histograms is similar. As with the histogram, changing the scales of the axes can compress or stretch a frequency polygon, which affects the user's impression of what the graph represents.

Ogives

An **ogive** (o-jive) is *a cumulative frequency polygon.* Again, construction begins by labeling the *x* axis with the class endpoints and the *y* axis with the frequencies. However, the use of cumulative frequency values requires that the scale along the *y* axis be great enough to include the frequency total. A dot of zero frequency is plotted at the beginning of the first class and construction proceeds by marking a dot at the *end* of each class interval for the cumulative value. Connecting the dots then completes the ogive. Figure 2.6 presents an ogive produced by using Excel for the data in Table 2.2.

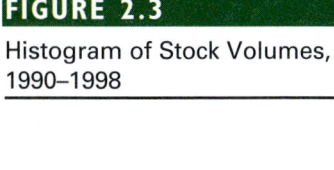

FIGURE 2.3

Histogram of Stock Volumes, 1990–1998

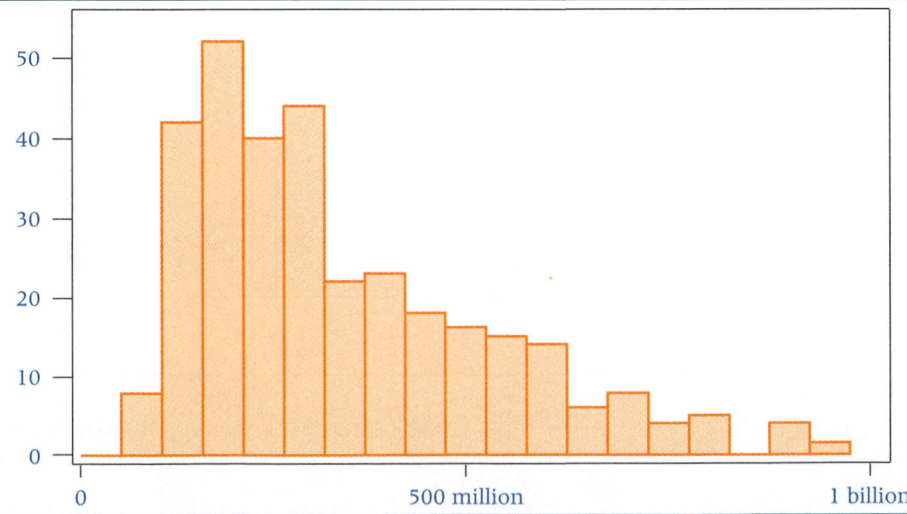

FIGURE 2.4

Normal Distribution

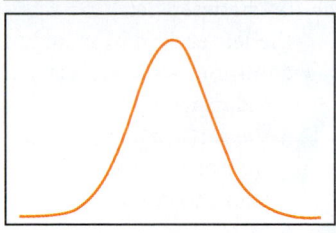

Ogives are most useful when the decision maker wants to see *running totals*. For example, if a comptroller is interested in controlling costs, an ogive could depict cumulative costs over a fiscal year.

Steep slopes in an ogive can be used to identify sharp increases in frequencies. In Figure 2.6 steep slopes occur in the 1–under 3 class and the 9–under 11 class, signifying large class frequency totals.

Pie Charts

A **pie chart** is *a circular depiction of data where the area of the whole pie represents 100% of the data being studied and slices represent a percentage breakdown of the sublevels*. Pie charts show the relative magnitudes of parts to a whole. They are widely used in business, particularly to depict such things as budget categories, market share, and time and resource allocations. However, the use of pie charts is minimized in the sciences and technology because pie charts can lead to less accurate judgments than are possible with other

FIGURE 2.5

Excel-Produced Frequency Polygon of the Unemployment Data

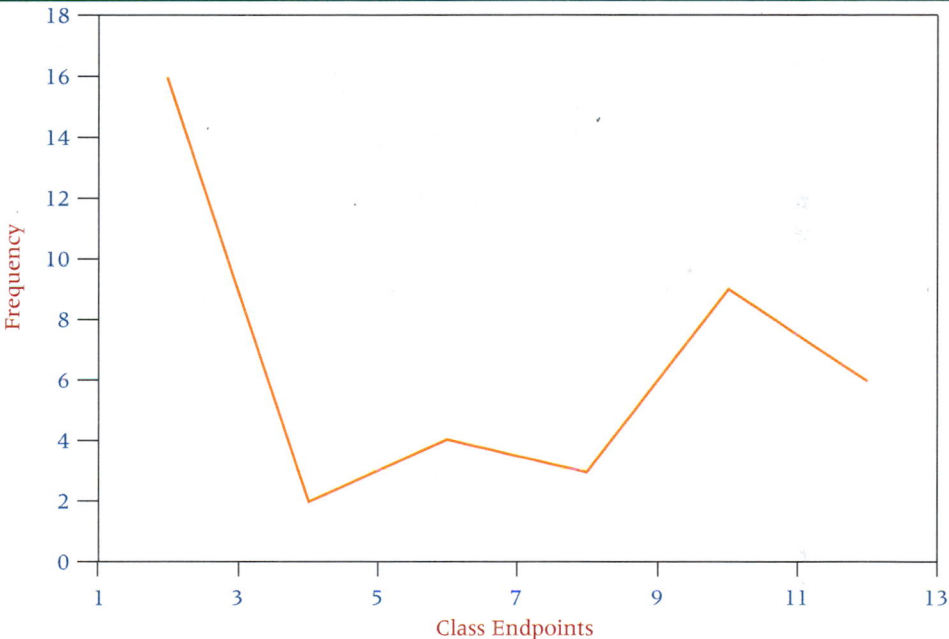

FIGURE 2.6

Excel Ogive of the Unemployment Data

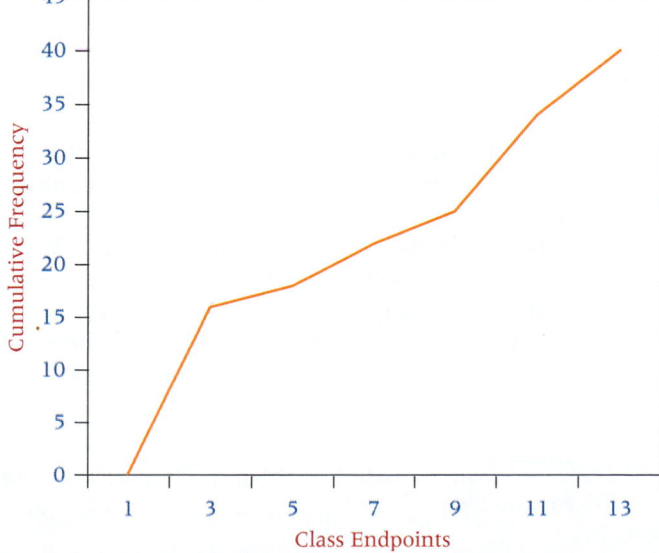

STATISTICS IN BUSINESS TODAY

Where Are Soft Drinks Sold?

The soft drink market is an extremely large and growing market in the United States and worldwide. In a recent year, 9.6 billion cases of soft drinks were sold in the United States alone. Where are soft drinks sold? The following data from Sanford C. Bernstein research indicate that the four leading places for soft drink sales are supermarkets, fountains, convenience/gas stores, and vending machines.

Place of Sales	Percentage
Supermarket	44
Fountain	24
Convenience/gas stations	16
Vending	11
Mass merchandisers	3
Drugstores	2

These data can be displayed graphically several ways. Displayed here is an Excel pie chart and a MINITAB bar chart of the data. Some statisticians prefer the histogram or the bar chart over the pie chart because they believe it is easier to compare categories that are similar in size with the histogram or the bar chart rather than the pie chart.

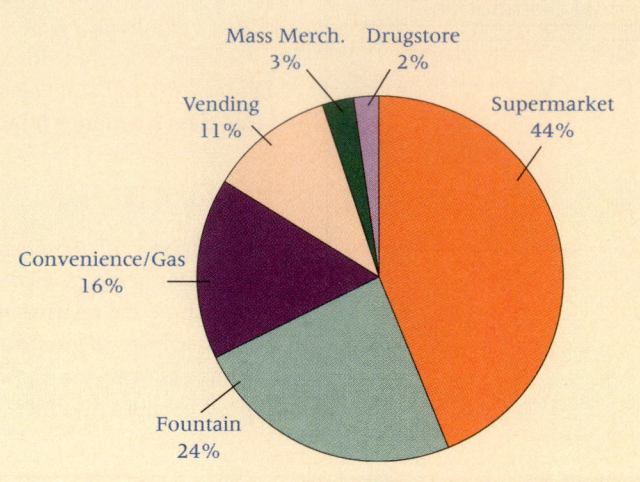

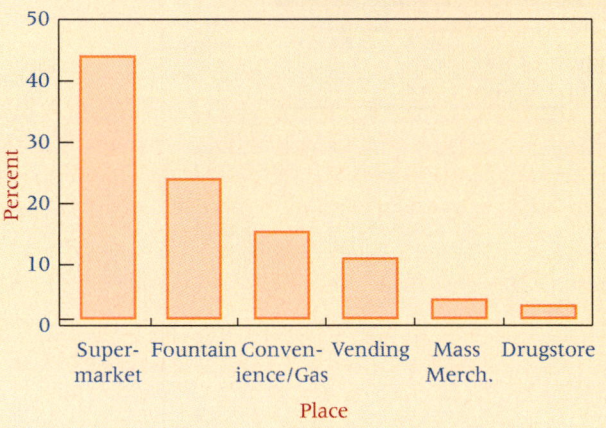

types of graphs.* Generally, it is more difficult for the viewer to interpret the relative size of angles in a pie chart than to judge the length of rectangles in a histogram or the relative distance of a frequency polygon dot from the x axis. In the feature, Statistics in Business Today, "Where Are Soft Drinks Sold?" graphical depictions of the percentage of sales by place were displayed by both a pie chart and a vertical bar chart.

Construction of the pie chart begins by determining the proportion of the subunit to the whole. Table 2.4 contains sales figures generated by Information Resources, Inc., for the top 10 toothpaste brands for a recent year. First, the whole-number sales figures are converted to proportions by dividing each sales figure by the total sales figure. This proportion is analogous to the relative frequency computed for frequency distributions. Because a circle contains 360°, each proportion is multiplied by 360 to obtain the correct number of degrees to represent each item. For example, Aquafresh sales of $177,989,000 represent a .1319 proportion of the total sales (177,989,000/1,349,326,000 = .1319). Multiplying this value by 360° results in 47.48°. Aquafresh sales will account for 47.48° of the pie. The pie chart is then completed by using a compass to lay out the slices. The pie chart in Figure 2.7, constructed by using MINITAB, depicts the data from Table 2.4.

---

*William S. Cleveland, *The Elements of Graphing Data* (Monterey, CA: Wadsworth Advanced Books and Software, 1985).

TABLE 2.4

Sales of Toothpaste for Top 10 Brands

Brand	Sales	Proportion	Degrees
Crest	$370,437,000	.2745	98.82
Colgate	321,084,000	.2380	85.68
Aquafresh	177,989,000	.1319	47.48
Mentadent	170,630,000	.1265	45.55
Arm & Hammer	109,512,000	.0812	29.23
Rembrandt	52,067,000	.0386	13.90
Sensodyn	50,133,000	.0372	13.39
Listerine	40,107,000	.0297	10.69
Closeup	32,009,000	.0237	8.53
Ultrabrite	25,358,000	.0187	6.73
Totals	$1,349,326,000	1.0000	360.00

FIGURE 2.7

MINITAB Pie Chart of Toothpaste Sales by Brand

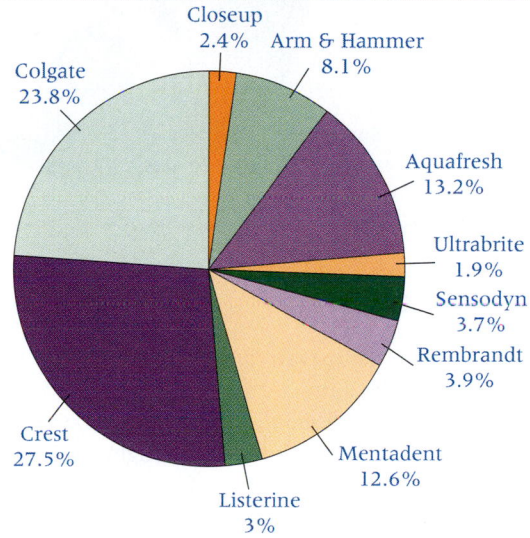

DEMONSTRATION PROBLEM 2.2

According to the National Retail Federation and Center for Retailing Education at the University of Florida, the four main sources of inventory shrinkage are employee theft, shoplifting, administrative error, and vendor fraud. The estimated annual dollar amount in shrinkage ($ millions) associated with each of these sources follows:

Employee theft	$17,918.6
Shoplifting	15,191.9
Administrative error	7,617.6
Vendor fraud	2,553.6
Total	$43,281.7

Construct a pie chart to depict these data.

Solution

Convert each raw dollar amount to a proportion by dividing each individual amount by the total.

Employee theft	17,918.6/43,281.7 = .414
Shoplifting	15,191.9/43,281.7 = .351
Administrative error	7,617.6/43,281.7 = .176
Vendor fraud	2,553.6/43,281.7 = .059
Total	1.000

Convert each proportion to degrees by multiplying each proportion by 360°.

Employee theft	$.414 \cdot 360°$	$=$	$149.0°$
Shoplifting	$.351 \cdot 360°$	$=$	$126.4°$
Administrative error	$.176 \cdot 360°$	$=$	$63.4°$
Vendor fraud	$.059 \cdot 360°$	$=$	$\underline{21.2°}$
Total			$360.0°$

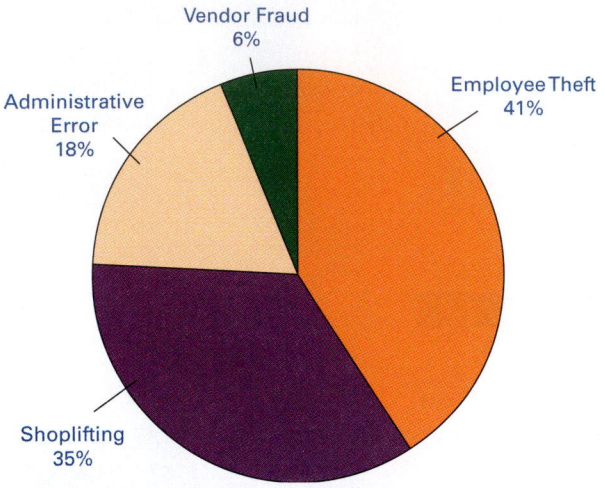

Stem and Leaf Plots

Another way to organize raw data into groups is by a **stem and leaf plot.** This technique is simple and provides a unique view of the data. A stem and leaf plot is *constructed by separating the digits for each number of the data into two groups, a stem and a leaf.* The leftmost digits are the stem and consist of the higher valued digits. The rightmost digits are the leaves and contain the lower values. If a set of data has only two digits, the stem is the value on the left and the leaf is the value on the right. For example, if 34 is one of the numbers, the stem is 3 and the leaf is 4. For numbers with more than two digits, division of stem and leaf is a matter of researcher preference.

Table 2.5 contains scores from an examination on plant safety policy and rules given to a group of 35 job trainees. A stem and leaf plot of these data is displayed in Table 2.6. One advantage of such a distribution is that the instructor can readily see whether the scores are in the upper or lower end of each bracket and also determine the spread of the scores. A second advantage of stem and leaf plots is that the values of the original raw data

TABLE 2.5

Safety Examination Scores for Plant Trainees

86	77	91	60	55
76	92	47	88	67
23	59	72	75	83
77	68	82	97	89
81	75	74	39	67
79	83	70	78	91
68	49	56	94	81

TABLE 2.6

Stem and Leaf Plot for Plant Safety Examination Data

Stem	Leaf									
2	3									
3	9									
4	7	9								
5	5	6	9							
6	0	7	7	8	8					
7	0	2	4	5	5	6	7	7	8	9
8	1	1	2	3	3	6	8	9		
9	1	1	2	4	7					

are retained (whereas most frequency distributions and graphic depictions use the class midpoint to represent the values in a class).

DEMONSTRATION PROBLEM 2.3	

The following data represent the costs (in dollars) of a sample of 30 postal mailings by a company.

3.67	2.75	5.47	4.65	3.32	2.09
1.83	10.94	1.93	3.89	7.20	2.78
3.34	7.80	3.20	3.21	3.55	3.53
3.64	4.95	5.42	8.64	4.84	4.10
9.15	3.45	5.11	1.97	2.84	4.15

Using dollars as a stem and cents as a leaf, construct a stem and leaf plot of the data.

Solution

Stem	Leaf								
1	83	93	97						
2	09	75	78	84					
3	20	21	32	34	45	53	55	64	67	89
4	10	15	65	84	95				
5	11	42	47						
6									
7	20	80							
8	64								
9	15								
10	94								

Pareto Charts

An important concept and movement in business is Total Quality Management (see Chapter 18). One of the important aspects of total quality management is the constant search for causes of problems in products and processes. A graphical technique for displaying problem causes is Pareto analysis. Pareto analysis is a quantitative tallying of the number and types of defects that occur with a product or service. Analysts use this tally to produce *a vertical bar chart that displays the most common types of defects, ranked in order of occurrence from left to right.* The bar chart is called a **Pareto chart.**

Pareto charts were named after an Italian economist, Vilfredo Pareto, who observed more than 100 years ago that most of Italy's wealth was controlled by a few families who were the major drivers behind the Italian economy. Quality expert J. M. Juran applied this notion to the quality field by observing that poor quality can often be addressed by attacking a few major causes that result in most of the problems. A Pareto chart enables quality control decision makers to separate the most important defects from trivial defects, which helps them to set priorities for needed quality improvement work.

Suppose the number of electric motors being rejected by inspectors for a company has been increasing. Company officials examine the records of several hundred of the motors in which at least one defect was found to determine which defects occurred more frequently. They find that 40% of the defects involved poor wiring, 30% involved a short in the coil, 25% involved a defective plug, and 5% involved cessation of bearings. Figure 2.8 is a Pareto chart constructed from this information. It shows that the main three problems with defective motors—poor wiring, a short in the coil, and a defective plug—account for 95% of the problems. From the Pareto chart, decision makers can formulate a logical plan for reducing the number of defects.

Company officials and workers would probably begin to improve quality by examining the segments of the production process that involve the wiring. Next, they would study the construction of the coil, then examine the plugs used and the plug-supplier process.

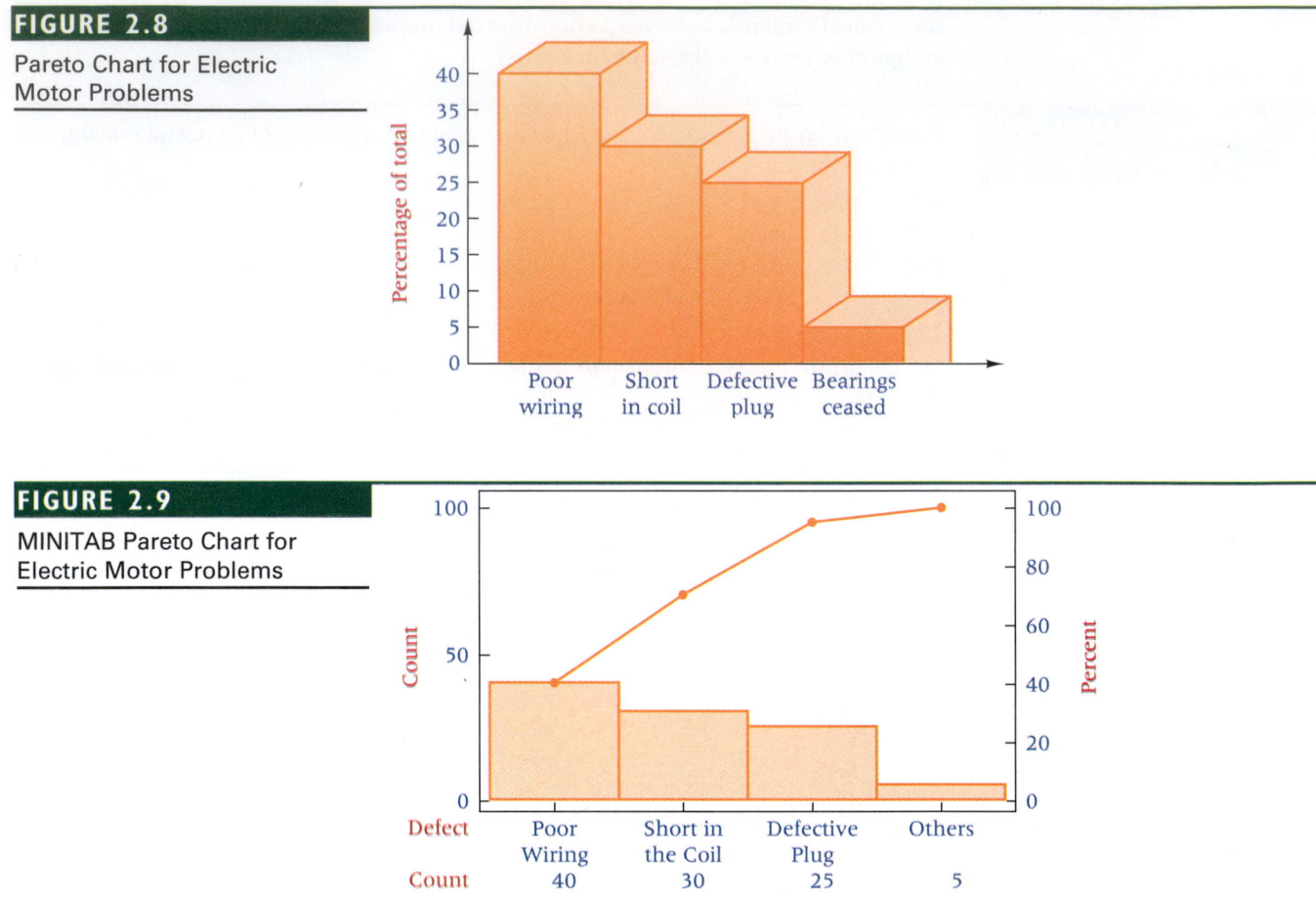

FIGURE 2.8

Pareto Chart for Electric Motor Problems

FIGURE 2.9

MINITAB Pareto Chart for Electric Motor Problems

Defect	Poor Wiring	Short in the Coil	Defective Plug	Others
Count	40	30	25	5
Percent	40.0	30.0	25.0	5.0
Cum %	40.0	70.0	95.0	100.0

Figure 2.9 is a MINITAB rendering of this Pareto chart. In addition to the bar chart analysis, the MINITAB Pareto analysis contains a cumulative percentage line graph. Observe the slopes on the line graph. The steepest slopes represent the more frequently occurring problems. As the slopes level off, the problems occur less frequently. The line graph gives the decision maker another tool for determining which problems to solve first.

2.2 PROBLEMS

2.6   Construct a histogram and a frequency polygon for the following data.

Class Interval	Frequency
30–under 32	5
32–under 34	7
34–under 36	15
36–under 38	21
38–under 40	34
40–under 42	24
42–under 44	17
44–under 46	8

2.7 Construct a histogram and a frequency polygon for the following data.

Class Interval	Frequency
10–under 20	9
20–under 30	7
30–under 40	10
40–under 50	6
50–under 60	13
60–under 70	18
70–under 80	15

2.8 Construct an ogive for the following data.

Class Interval	Frequency
3–under 6	2
6–under 9	5
9–under 12	10
12–under 15	11
15–under 18	17
18–under 21	5

2.9 Construct a stem and leaf plot using two digits for the stem.

212	239	240	218	222	249	265	224
257	271	266	234	239	219	255	260
243	261	249	230	246	263	235	229
218	238	254	249	250	263	229	221
253	227	270	257	261	238	240	239
273	220	226	239	258	259	230	262
255	226						

2.10 A list of the largest accounting firms in the United States along with their net revenue figures for 1997 ($ millions) according to the Public Accounting Report follows.

Firm	Revenue
Andersen Worldwide	$5,445
Ernst & Young	4,416
Deloitte & Touche	3,600
KPMG Peat Marwick	2,698
Coopers & Lybrand	2,504
PriceWaterhouse	2,344
Grant Thornton	289
McGladrey & Pullen	270
BDO Seidman	240

Construct a pie chart to represent these data. Label the slices with the appropriate percentages. Comment on the effectiveness of using a pie chart to display the revenue of these top accounting firms.

2.11 According to the Air Transport Association of America, Delta Airlines led all U.S. carriers in the number of passengers flown in a recent year. The top five airlines were Delta, United, American, US Airways, and Southwest. The number of passengers flown (in thousands) by each of these airlines follows:

TABLE 2.7

Value of New Construction Over a 35-Year Period

Residential	Nonresidential
169635	96497
155113	115372
149410	96407
175822	129275
162706	140569
134605	145054
195028	131289
231396	155261
234955	178925
266481	163740
267063	160363
263385	164191
252745	169173
228943	167896
197526	135389
232134	120921
249757	122222
274956	127593
251937	139711
281229	153866
280748	166754
297886	177639
315757	175048

Source: U.S. Census Bureau, *Current Construction Reports* (in millions of constant dollars).

Airline	Passengers
Delta	103,133
United	84,203
American	81,083
US Airways	58,659
Southwest	55,946

Construct a pie chart to depict this information.

2.12 Information Resources, Inc., reports that in a recent year, Huggies was the top-selling diaper brand in the United States with 41.3% of the market share. Other leading brands included Pampers with 25.6%, Luvs with 12.1%, Drypers with 3.3%, Fitti with 0.9%, and private labels with 15.8%. Use this information to construct a pie chart of the diaper market shares.

2.13 The following data represent the number of passengers per flight in a sample of 50 flights from Wichita, Kansas, to Kansas City, Missouri.

23	46	66	67	13	58	19	17	65	17
25	20	47	28	16	38	44	29	48	29
69	34	35	60	37	52	80	59	51	33
48	46	23	38	52	50	17	57	41	77
45	47	49	19	32	64	27	61	70	19

Construct a stem and leaf plot for these data. What does the stem and leaf plot tell you about the number of passengers per flight?

2.14 An airline company uses a central telephone bank and a semiautomated telephone process to take reservations. It has been receiving an unusually high number of customer complaints about its reservation system. The company conducted a survey of customers, asking them whether they had encountered any of the following problems in making reservations: busy signal, disconnection, poor connection, too long a wait to talk to someone, could not get through to an agent, connected with the wrong person. Suppose a survey of 744 complaining customers resulted in the following frequency tally.

Number of Complaints	Complaint
184	Too long a wait
10	Transferred to the wrong person
85	Could not get through to an agent
37	Got disconnected
420	Busy signal
8	Poor connection

Construct a Pareto diagram from this information to display the various problems encountered in making reservations.

2.3 GRAPHICAL DEPICTION OF TWO-VARIABLE NUMERICAL DATA: SCATTER PLOTS

Many times in business research it is important to explore the relationship between two numerical variables. More detailed statistical approaches are given in Chapters 3 and 13, but here we present a graphical mechanism for examining the relationship between two numerical variables, the scatter plot (or scatter diagram). A **scatter plot** is *a two-dimensional graph plot of pairs of points from two numerical variables.*

As an example of two numerical variables, consider the data in Table 2.7. Displayed are the values of new residential and new nonresidential buildings in the United States for

FIGURE 2.10

MINITAB Scatter Plot of New
Residential and New
Nonresidential Construction

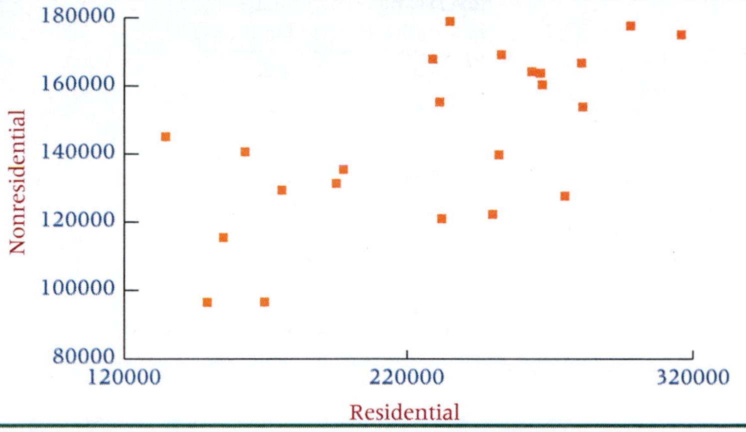

various years over a 35-year period. Do these two numerical variables exhibit any relationship? It might seem logical when new construction booms that it would boom in both residential building and in nonresidential building at the same time. However, the MINITAB scatter plot of these data displayed in Figure 2.10 shows somewhat mixed results. The apparent tendency is that more new residential building construction occurs when more new nonresidential building construction is also taking place and less new residential building construction when new nonresidential building construction is also at lower levels. The scatter plot also shows that in some years more new residential building and less new nonresidential building happened at the same time, and vice versa.

2.3 PROBLEMS

2.15 The U.S. National Oceanic and Atmospheric Administration, National Marine Fisheries Service, publishes data on the quantity and value of domestic fishing in the United States. The quantity (in millions of pounds) of fish caught and used for human food and for industrial products (oil, bait, animal food, etc.) over a decade follows. Is a relationship evident between the quantity used for human food and the quantity used for industrial products for a given year? Construct a scatter plot of the data. Examine the plot and discuss the strength of the relationship of the two variables.

Human Food	Industrial Product
3654	2828
3547	2430
3285	3082
3238	3201
3320	3118
3294	2964
3393	2638
3946	2950
4588	2604
6204	2259

2.16 Are the advertising dollars spent by a company related to total sales revenue? The following data represent the advertising dollars and the sales revenues for various companies in a given industry during a recent year. Construct a scatter plot of the data from the two variables and discuss the relationship between the two variables.

Advertising (in $millions)	Sales (in $millions)
4.2	155.7
1.6	87.3
6.3	135.6
2.7	99.0
10.4	168.2
7.1	136.9
5.5	101.4
8.3	158.2

IN RESPONSE

State of Auto Manufacturing

Because the raw data in the Decision Dilemma are in the millions, it is advantageous to represent the data graphically for the reader/listener. As examples of what can be done graphically, the 1999 market share data are shown in a MINITAB pie chart in Figure 2.11; the 2000 data are shown in an Excel histogram in Figure 2.12.

The dealership data can be summarized using either a frequency distribution or a stem and leaf plot. The following frequency distribution of the data shows the range of the data to be $69 - 30 = 39$. If the class widths are 5 and the frequency distribution begins at 30, 8 classes are needed.

30–under 35	6
35–under 40	0
40–under 45	7
45–under 50	6
50–under 55	2
55–under 60	6
60–under 65	6
65–under 70	7

ETHICAL CONSIDERATIONS

Ethical considerations for techniques learned in Chapter 2 begin with the data chosen for representation. With the abundance of available data in business, the person constructing the data summary must be selective in choosing the reported variables. The potential is great for the analyst to select variables or even data within variables that are favorable to his or her own situation or that are perceived to be well received by the listener.

Section 2.1 noted that the number of classes and the size of the intervals in frequency distributions are usually selected by the researcher. The researcher should be careful to select values and sizes that will give an honest, accurate reflection of the situation and not a biased over- or understated case.

Sections 2.2 and 2.3 discussed the construction of charts and graphs. It pointed out that in many instances, it makes sense to use unequal scales on the axes. However, doing so opens the possibility of "cheating with statistics" by stretching or compressing of the axes to underscore the researcher's or analyst's point. It is imperative that frequency distributions and charts and graphs be constructed in a manner that most reflects actual data and not merely the researcher's own agenda.

A stem and leaf plot of these data would appear as follows.

Stem	Leaf
3	0 1 3 4 4 4
4	0 3 4 4 4 4 4 5 5 7 7 9 9
5	1 2 7 7 7 8 8 9
6	0 1 1 2 3 4 5 5 6 7 7 8 9

A scatter plot can be used to examine the relationship between the 1999 and the 2000 data. An Excel plot of these two numerical variables is shown in Figure 2.13.

FIGURE 2.11

Pie Chart of Company

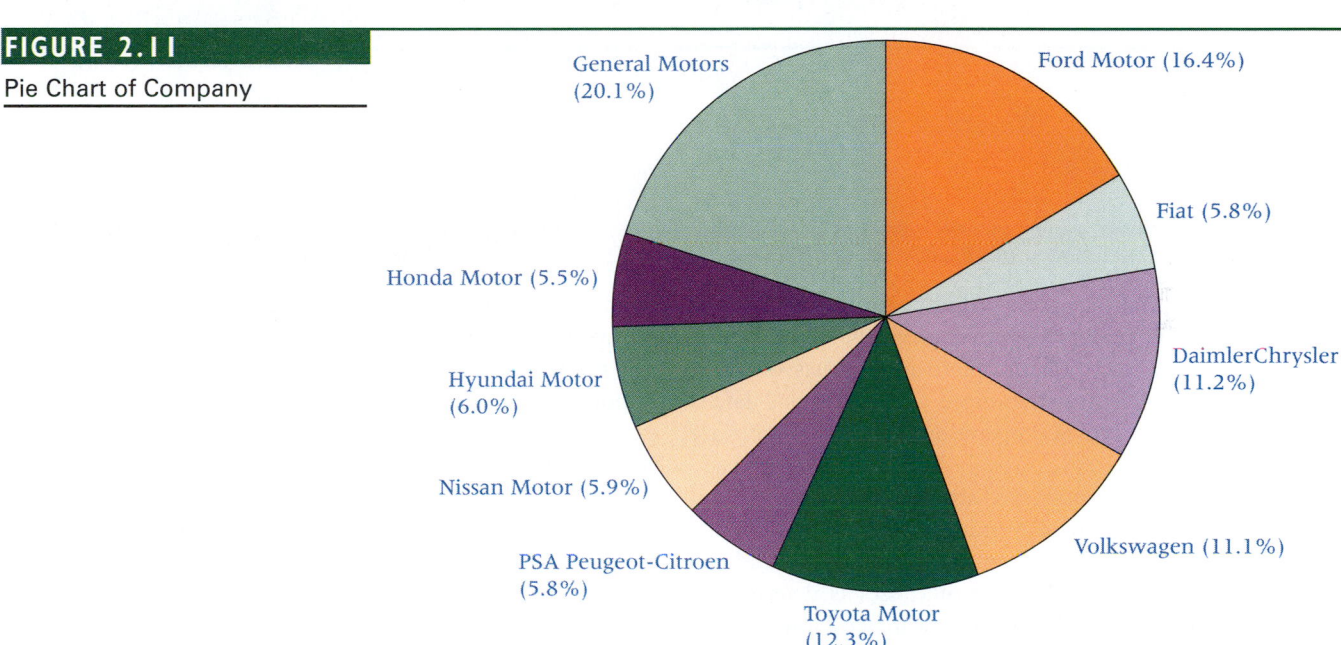

FIGURE 2.12

Histogram of Company Sales Data

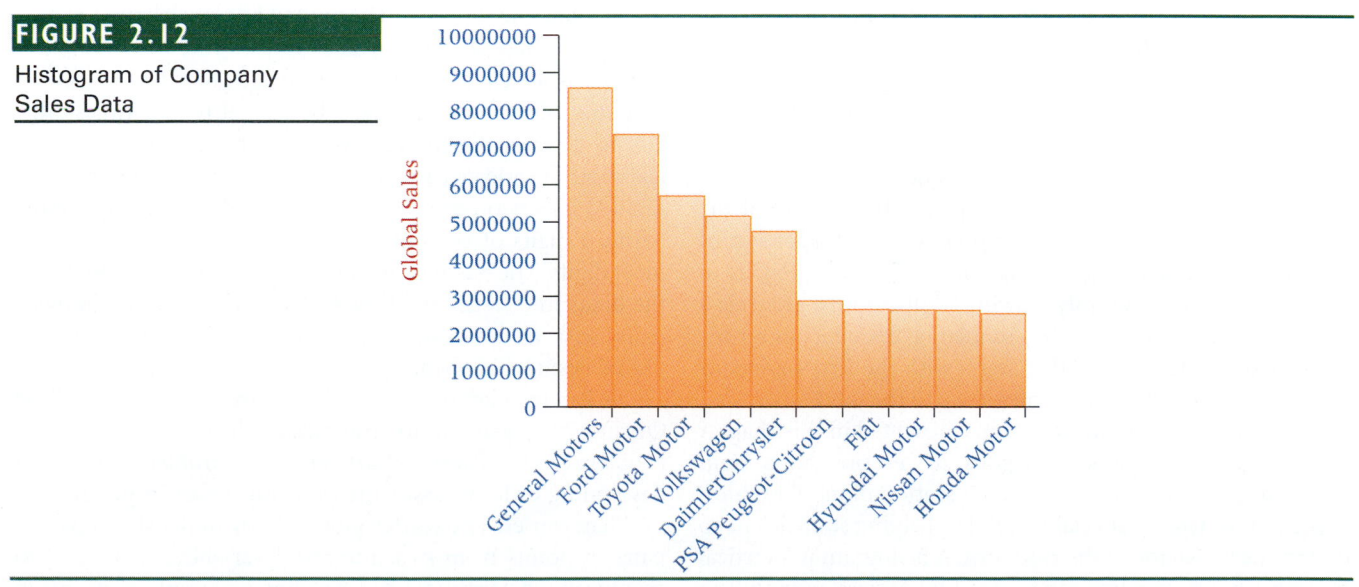

FIGURE 2.13

A Scatter Plot of Company Sales Data for 1999 and 2000

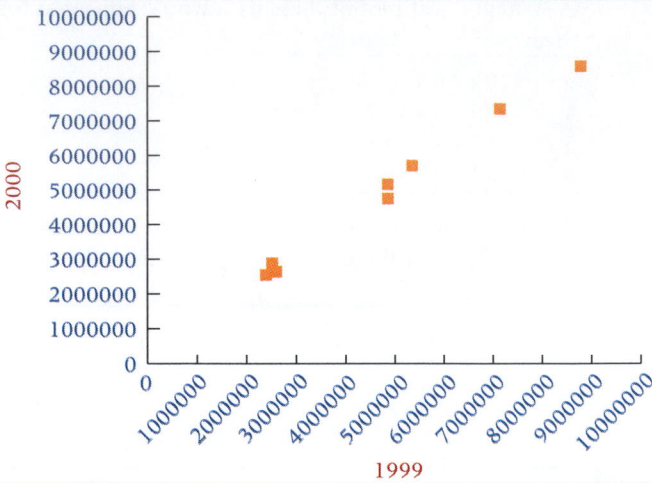

SUMMARY

The two types of data are grouped and ungrouped. Most statistical analysis is performed on ungrouped, or raw, data. Grouped data are data organized into a frequency distribution. Differentiating between grouped and ungrouped data is important, because statistical operations on the two types are computed differently.

Constructing a frequency distribution involves several steps. The first step is to determine the range of the data, which is the difference between the largest value and the smallest value. Next, the number of classes is determined, which is an arbitrary choice of the researcher. However, too few classes overaggregate the data into meaningless categories, and too many classes do not summarize the data enough to be useful. The third step in constructing the frequency distribution is to determine the width of the class interval. Dividing the range of values by the number of classes yields the approximate width of the class interval.

The class midpoint is the midpoint of a class interval. It is the average of the class endpoints and represents the halfway point of the class interval. Relative frequency is a value computed by dividing an individual frequency by the sum of the frequencies. Relative frequency represents the proportion of total values that is in a given class interval. It is analogous to the probability of randomly drawing a value from a given class interval out of all values. The cumulative frequency is a running total frequency tally that starts with the first frequency value and adds each ensuing frequency to the total.

The types of graphic depictions presented in this chapter are histograms, frequency polygons, ogives, pie charts, stem and leaf plots, Pareto charts, and scatter plots. Graphical depiction of data is especially useful in helping statisticians to determine the shape of distributions. A histogram is a vertical bar chart in which a line segment connects class endpoints at the value of the frequency. Two vertical lines connect this line segment down to the x axis, forming a rectangle. Histograms are taking on a growing importance as an initial analysis tool. The statistician can learn much about the shape of the distribution and other important characteristics of the data by examining a histogram of the data. A frequency polygon is constructed by plotting a dot at the midpoint of each class interval for the value of each frequency and then connecting the dots. Ogives are cumulative frequency polygons. Points on an ogive are plotted at the class endpoints. The ogive graph starts at the beginning of the first class interval with a value of zero and continues through the values of the cumulative frequencies to the class endpoints.

A pie chart is a circular depiction of data. The amount of each category is represented as a slice of the pie proportionate to the total. The slices are determined by multiplying the proportion of each category by 360° to compute the number of degrees of the circle allotted to each category. The researcher is cautioned in using pie charts because it is sometimes difficult to differentiate the relative sizes of the slices. Stem and leaf plots are another way to organize data. The numbers are divided into two parts, a stem and a leaf. The stems are the leftmost digits of the numbers and the leaves are the rightmost digits. The business researcher determines how to divide the digits into stems and leaves. The stems are listed individually, with all leaf values corresponding to each stem displayed beside that stem.

A Pareto chart is a vertical bar chart that is used in Total Quality Management to graphically display the causes of problems. The Pareto chart presents problem causes in descending order to assist the decision maker in prioritizing problem causes. The scatter plot is a two-dimensional plot of pairs of points from two numerical variables. It is used to graphically determine whether any apparent relationship exists between the two variables.

KEY TERMS

class mark	frequency polygon	Pareto chart	scatter plot
class midpoint	grouped data	pie chart	stem and leaf plot
cumulative frequency	histogram	range	ungrouped data
frequency distribution	ogive	relative frequency	

SUPPLEMENTARY PROBLEMS

CALCULATING THE STATISTICS

2.17 For the following data, construct a frequency distribution with six classes.

57	23	35	18	21
26	51	47	29	21
46	43	29	23	39
50	41	19	36	28
31	42	52	29	18
28	46	33	28	20

2.18 For each class interval of the frequency distribution given, determine the class midpoint, the relative frequency, and the cumulative frequency.

Class Interval	Frequency
20–under 25	17
25–under 30	20
30–under 35	16
35–under 40	15
40–under 45	8
45–under 50	6

2.19 Construct a histogram, a frequency polygon, and an ogive for the following frequency distribution.

Class Interval	Frequency
50–under 60	13
60–under 70	27
70–under 80	43
80–under 90	31
90–under 100	9

2.20 Construct a pie chart from the following data.

Label	Value
A	55
B	121
C	83
D	46

2.21 Construct a stem and leaf plot for the following data. Let the leaf contain one digit.

312	324	289	335	298
314	309	294	326	317
290	311	317	301	316
306	286	308	284	324

2.22 An examination of rejects shows at least 10 problems. A frequency tally of the problems follows. Construct a Pareto chart for these data.

Problem	Frequency
1	673
2	29
3	108
4	379
5	73
6	564
7	12
8	402
9	54
10	202

2.23 Construct a scatter plot for the following two numerical variables.

x	y
12	5
17	3
9	10
6	15
10	8
14	9
8	8

TESTING YOUR UNDERSTANDING

2.24 The Whitcomb Company manufactures a metal ring for industrial engines that usually weighs about 50 ounces. A random sample of 50 of these metal rings produced the following weights (in ounces).

51	53	56	50	44	47
53	53	42	57	46	55
41	44	52	56	50	57
44	46	41	52	69	53
57	51	54	63	42	47
47	52	53	46	36	58
51	38	49	50	62	39
44	55	43	52	43	42
57	49				

Construct a frequency distribution for these data using eight classes. What can you observe about the data from the frequency distribution?

2.25 A northwestern distribution company surveyed 53 of its midlevel managers. The survey obtained the ages of these managers, which later were organized into the frequency distribution shown. Determine the class midpoint, relative frequency, and cumulative frequency for these data.

Class Interval	Frequency
20–under 25	8
25–under 30	6
30–under 35	5
35–under 40	12
40–under 45	15
45–under 50	7

2.26 The following data are shaped roughly like a normal distribution (discussed in Chapter 6).

61.4	27.3	26.4	37.4	30.4	47.5
63.9	46.8	67.9	19.1	81.6	47.9
73.4	54.6	65.1	53.3	71.6	58.6
57.3	87.8	71.1	74.1	48.9	60.2
54.8	60.5	32.5	61.7	55.1	48.2
56.8	60.1	52.9	60.5	55.6	38.1
76.4	46.8	19.9	27.3	77.4	58.1
32.1	54.9	32.7	40.1	52.7	32.5
35.3	39.1				

Construct a frequency distribution starting with 10 as the lowest class beginning point and use a class width of 10. Construct a histogram and a frequency polygon for this frequency distribution and observe the shape of a normal distribution. On the basis of your results from these graphs, what does a normal distribution look like?

2.27 Use the data from Problem 2.25.

   a. Construct a histogram and a frequency polygon.
   b. Construct an ogive.

2.28 In a medium-sized southern city, 86 houses are for sale, each having about 2000 square feet of floor space. The asking prices vary. The frequency distribution shown contains the price categories for the 86 houses. Construct a histogram, a frequency polygon, and an ogive from these data.

Asking Price	Frequency
$ 60,000–under $ 70,000	21
70,000–under 80,000	27
80,000–under 90,000	18
90,000–under 100,000	11
100,000–under 110,000	6
110,000–under 120,000	3

2.29 Good, relatively inexpensive prenatal care often can prevent a lifetime of expense owing to complications resulting from a baby's low birth weight. A survey of a random sample of 57 new mothers asked them to estimate how much they spent on prenatal care. The researcher tallied the results and presented them in the frequency distribution shown. Use these data to construct a histogram, a frequency polygon, and an ogive.

Amount Spent on Prenatal Care	Frequency of New Mothers
$ 0–under $100	3
100–under 200	6
200–under 300	12
300–under 400	19
400–under 500	11
500–under 600	6

2.30 A consumer group surveyed food prices at 87 stores on the East Coast. Among the food prices being measured was that of sugar. From the data collected, the group constructed the frequency distribution of the prices of 5 pounds of Domino's sugar in the stores surveyed. Compute a histogram, a frequency polygon, and an ogive for the following data.

Price	Frequency
$1.75–under $1.90	9
1.90–under 2.05	14
2.05–under 2.20	17
2.20–under 2.35	16
2.35–under 2.50	18
2.50–under 2.65	8
2.65–under 2.80	5

2.31 The top music genres according to SoundScan for a recent year are R&B, Alternative (Rock) Music, Rap, and Country. These and other music genres along with the number of albums sold in each (in millions) are shown.

Genre	Albums Sold
R&B	146.4
Alternative	102.6
Rap	73.7
Country	64.5
Soundtrack	56.4
Metal	26.6
Classical	14.8
Latin	14.5

Construct a pie chart for these data displaying the percentage of the whole that each of these genres represents.

2.32 The following figures for U.S. imports of agricultural products and manufactured goods were taken from selected years between 1970 and 2000 (in $ billions). The source of the data is the U.S. International Trade Administration. Construct a scatter plot for these data and determine whether any relationship is apparent between the U.S. imports of agricultural products and the U.S. imports of manufactured goods during this time period.

Agricultural Products	Manufactured Goods
5.8	27.3
9.5	54.0
17.4	133.0
19.5	257.5
22.3	388.8
29.3	629.7

2.33 We show a list of the industries with the largest total release of toxic chemicals in 1998 according to the U.S. Environmental Protection Agency. Construct a pie chart to depict this information.

Industry	Total Release (pounds)
Chemicals	737,100,000
Primary metals	566,400,000
Paper	229,900,000
Plastics and rubber	109,700,000
Transportation equipment	102,500,000
Food	89,300,000
Fabricated metals	85,900,000
Petroleum	63,300,000
Electrical equipment	29,100,000

2.34 A manufacturing company produces plastic bottles for the dairy industry. Some of the bottles are rejected because of poor quality. Causes of poor-quality bottles include faulty plastic, incorrect labeling, discoloration, incorrect thickness, broken handle, and others. The following data for 500 plastic bottles that were rejected include the problems and the frequency of the problems. Use these data to construct a Pareto chart. Discuss the implications of the chart.

Problem	Number
Discoloration	32
Thickness	117
Broken handle	86
Fault in plastic	221
Labeling	44

2.35 A research organization selected 50 U.S. towns with Census 2000 populations between 4,000 and 6,000 as a sample to represent small towns for survey purposes. The populations of these towns follow.

4420	5221	4299	5831	5750
5049	5556	4361	5737	4654
4653	5338	4512	4388	5923
4730	4963	5090	4822	4304
4758	5366	5431	5291	5254
4866	5858	4346	4734	5919
4216	4328	4459	5832	5873
5257	5048	4232	4878	5166
5366	4212	5669	4224	4440
4299	5263	4339	4834	5478

Construct a stem and leaf plot for the data, letting each leaf contain two digits.

2.36 Listed here are 30 different weekly Dow Jones industrial stock averages.

2656	2301	2975	3002	2468
2742	2830	2405	2677	2990
2200	2764	2337	2961	3010
2976	2375	2602	2670	2922
2344	2760	2555	2524	2814
2996	2437	2268	2448	2460

Construct a stem and leaf plot for these 30 values. Let the stem contain two digits.

INTERPRETING THE OUTPUT

2.37 Suppose 150 shoppers at an upscale mall are interviewed and one of the questions asked is the household income. Study the MINITAB histogram of the following data and discuss what can be learned about the shoppers.

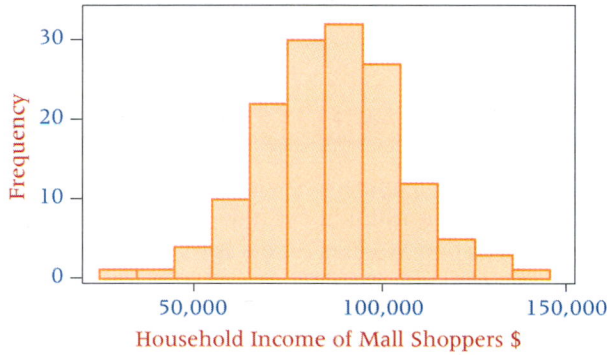

2.38 Shown here is an Excel-produced pie chart representing physician specialties. What does the chart tell you about the various specialties?

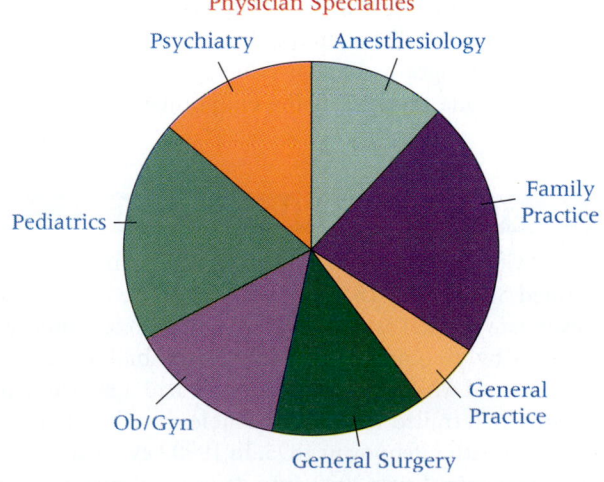

2.39 Suppose 100 CPA firms are surveyed to determine how many audits they perform over a certain time. The data are summarized using the MINITAB stem and leaf plot shown. What can you learn about the number of audits being performed by these firms from this plot?

Character Stem and Leaf Display

Stem and leaf of Number of Audits   N = 100
Leaf Unit = 1.0

9	1	222333333
16	1	4445555
26	1	6666667777
35	1	888899999
39	2	0001
44	2	22333
49	2	55555
(9)	2	677777777
42	2	8888899
35	3	000111
29	3	223333
23	3	44455555
15	3	67777
10	3	889
7	4	0011
3	4	222

2.40 The following Excel ogive shows toy sales by a company over a 12-month period. What conclusions can you reach about toy sales at this company?

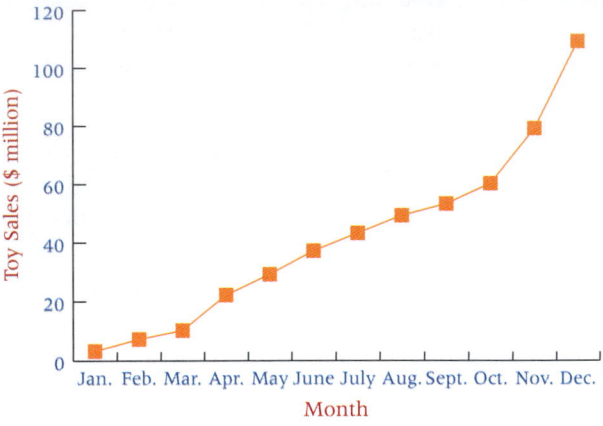

ANALYZING THE DATABASES

see www.wiley.com/college/black

1. Using the manufacturing database, construct a frequency distribution for the variable, Number of Production Workers Across All Industries. In Excel the frequency distribution is referred to a histogram. In MINITAB, produce a frequency distribution by constructing a histogram checking *Frequency* under *Options* and by checking *Show Data Labels* under *Annotation*, thereby revealing the class frequency counts. What does the frequency distribution reveal about the number of production workers?

2. Using the stock market database, construct a histogram for the variable, Reported Trades. How is the histogram shaped? Is it high in the middle or near one or both of the endpoints? Is it relatively constant in size across the classes (uniform) or does it appear to have no shape? Does it appear to be "normally" distributed?

3. Construct an ogive for the variable, Type, in the financial database. The 100 companies in this database are each categorized into one of seven types of companies. These types are listed at the end of Chapter 1. Construct a pie chart of these types and discuss the output. For example, which type is most prevalent in the database and which is the least?

4. Using the international unemployment database, construct a stem and leaf plot for Italy. What does the plot show about unemployment for Italy over the past 40 years? What does the plot fail to show?

CASE: SOAP COMPANIES DO BATTLE

Procter & Gamble has been the leading soap manufacturer in the United States since 1879, when it introduced Ivory soap. However, late in 1991 its major rival, Lever Bros. (Unilever), overtook it by grabbing 31.5% of the $1.6 billion personal soap market, of which Procter & Gamble had a 30.5% share. Lever Bros. had trailed Procter & Gamble since it entered the soap market with Lifebuoy in 1895. In 1990 Lever Bros. introduced a new soap, Lever 2000, into its product mix as a soap for the entire family. A niche for such a soap had been created because of the segmentation of the soap market into specialty soaps for children, women, and men. Lever Bros. felt that it could sell a soap for everyone in the family. Consumer response was strong; Lever 2000 rolled up $113 million in sales in 1991, putting Lever Bros. ahead of Procter & Gamble for the first time in the personal-soap revenue contest. Procter & Gamble still sells more soap, but Lever's brands cost more, thereby resulting in greater overall sales.

Needless to say, Procter & Gamble was quick to search for a response to the success of Lever 2000. Procter & Gamble looked at several possible strategies, including repositioning Safeguard, which has been seen as a male soap. Ultimately, Procter & Gamble responded to the challenge by introducing its Oil of Olay Moisturizing Bath Bar. In its first year of national distribution, this product was backed by a $24 million media effort. The new bath bar was quite successful and helped Procter & Gamble regain market share.

The following represent the latest figures on the leading personal soaps in the United States with their respective sales figures. Each of these soaps is produced by one of four soap manufacturers: Unilever, Procter & Gamble, Dial, and Colgate-Palmolive.

Soap	Manufacturer	Sales ($ millions)
Dove	Unilever	271
Dial	Dial	193
Lever 2000	Unilever	138
Irish Spring	Colgate-Palmolive	121
Zest	Procter & Gamble	115
Ivory	Procter & Gamble	94
Caress	Unilever	93
Olay	Procter & Gamble	69
Safeguard	Procter & Gamble	48
Coast	Dial	44

In 1983 the market shares for soap were Procter & Gamble with 37.1%, Lever Bros. (Unilever) with 24%, Dial with 15%, Colgate-Palmolive with 6.5%, and all others with 17.4%. By 1991 the market shares for soap were Lever Bros. (Unilever) with 31.5%, Procter & Gamble with 30.5%, Dial with 19%, Colgate-Palmolive with 8%, and all others with 11%.

DISCUSSION

1. Suppose you are making a report for Procter & Gamble displaying their share of the market along with the share of other companies for the years 1983, 1991, and the latest figures. Using either Excel or MINITAB, produce graphs for the market shares of personal soap for each of these years. For the latest figures data, assume that the "all others" total is about $119 million. What do you observe about the market shares of the various companies by studying the graphs? In particular, how is Procter & Gamble doing relative to previous years?

2. Suppose Procter & Gamble sells about 20 million bars of soap per week, but the demand is not constant and production management would like to get a better handle on how sales are distributed over the year. Let the following sales figures given in units of million bars represent the sales of bars per week over one year.

Construct a histogram to represent these data. What do you see in the graph that might be helpful to the production (and sales) people?

17.1	19.6	15.4	17.4	15.0	18.5	20.6	18.4
20.0	20.9	19.3	18.2	14.7	17.1	12.2	19.9
18.7	20.4	20.3	15.5	16.8	19.1	20.4	15.4
20.3	17.5	17.0	18.3	13.6	39.8	20.7	21.3
22.5	21.4	23.4	23.1	22.8	21.4	24.0	25.2
26.3	23.9	30.6	25.2	26.2	26.9	32.8	26.3
26.6	24.3	26.2	23.8				

Construct a stem and leaf plot using the whole numbers as the stems. What advantages does the stem and leaf plot of these sales figures offer over the histogram? What are some disadvantages? Which would you use in discussions with production people and why?

3. A random sample of finished soap bars in their packaging is tested for quality. All defective bars are examined for problem causes. Among the problems found were improper packaging, poor labeling, bad seal, shape of bar wrong, bar surface marred, wrong color in bar, wrong bar fragrance, wrong soap consistency, and others. Some of the leading problem causes and the number of each are given here. Use a Pareto chart to analyze these problem causes. Based on your findings, what would you recommend to the company?

Problem Cause	Frequency
Bar surface	89
Color	17
Fragrance	2
Label	32
Shape	8
Seal	47
Labeling	5
Soap consistency	3

Source: Adapted from Valerie Reitman, "Buoyant Sales of Lever 2000 Soap Bring Sinking Sensation to Procter & Gamble," *Wall Street Journal*, 19 March 1992, p. B1. Reprinted by permission of The Wall Street Journal © 1992, Dow Jones & Company, Inc. All rights reserved worldwide; Pam Weisz, "$40 M Extends Lever 2000 Family," *Brandweek*, vol. 36, no. 32 (21 August 1995), p. 6; Laurie Freeman, "P&G Pushes Back against Unilever in Soap," *Advertising Age*, vol. 65, no. 41 (28 September 1994), p. 21; Jeanne Whalen and Pat Sloan, "Intros Help Boost Soap Coupons," *Advertising Age*, vol. 65, no. 19 (2 May 1994), p. 30; and "P&G Places Coast Soap Up for Sale," *The Post*, World Wide Web Edition of *The Cincinnati Post*, 2 February 1999, http://www.cincypost.com.business /pg022599.html.

USING THE COMPUTER

EXCEL

With **Chart Wizard,** Excel offers the capability of producing many of the charts and graphs presented in this chapter. In addition, Excel can generate frequency distributions and histograms using **Data Analysis.**

Many of the techniques in this course can be done on Excel using a tool called **Data Analysis.** To access the **Data** Analysis feature, select **Tools** on the menu bar. **Data Analysis** is located at the bottom of the **Tools** pull-down menu. If **Data Analysis** does not appear on this menu, it must be added in. This add-in need only be done once. To add in **Data Analysis,** select **Add-ins** on the **Tools** menu. On the **Add-ins** dialog box that appears, check **Analysis ToolPak** (not **Analysis ToolPak—VBA**). Click OK and **Analysis ToolPak** will be added to the **Tools** capability.

Excel refers to frequency distributions as histograms. In Excel the classes are called bins. If you do not specify bins, Excel will automatically determine the number of bins. If you want to specify the bins, load the class endpoints into a column. To compute the frequency distribution, select **Tools** on the Excel menu bar. Select **Data Analysis** from the **Tools** pull-down menu and select **Histogram** from the **Data Analysis** dialog box. Place the location of the raw values of data into **Input Range.** If you want to specify class endpoints, place the location of the endpoints into **Bin Range.** If you want Excel to automatically determine the bins, leave this blank. If you have labels, then check **Labels.** If you want a histogram graph, check **Chart Output** at the bottom of the dialog box. If you want an ogive, select **Cumulative Percentage** along with **Chart Output,** and Excel will yield a histogram graph with an ogive overlaid on it. Select one of the output options. After clicking OK you will get a frequency distribution as output with bins and frequencies along with a histogram graph.

After constructing a frequency distribution, you can construct histograms, frequency polygons, and ogives with the **Chart Wizard** feature. To access the **Chart Wizard** select **Insert** on the menu bar. From the pull-down menu select **Chart.** A variety of charts and graphs are available here. The first is called **Column.** With it a histogram-type chart can be constructed. These Column charts are actually vertical bar charts with spaces between the classes. Select **Column,** and then move through the four dialog boxes that follow, filling in the appropriate information. In the data range box place the location of the bins and the frequencies from the frequency distribution. In the **Chart Wizard** it is possible to modify the titles, axes, legend, and location of the output as desired. To convert a vertical bar graph into a histogram by eliminating the gap between bars, right click on one of the bars of the graph. From the menu that appears, select **Format Data Series.** From the dialog box that appears, select **Options.** In the space beside **Gap width,** place a zero or reduce the number to zero. Click OK. The gap will disappear.

A frequency polygon can be constructed by selecting **Line** on the **Chart Wizard.** The steps are virtually the same for the Line chart as for the Column chart.

To construct an ogive, the data must be cumulated first when the frequency distribution is being constructed by checking **Cumulative Percentage** in the Histogram dialog box. The **Chart Wizard** can then be used to construct the ogive by selecting **Line** chart. The four-step dialog boxes are virtually the same as those used to construct vertical bar charts and frequency polygons except that at step 2 you must select the **Series** tab. Under **Series,** highlight **Frequency** and select **Remove,** which leaves you with just the cumulative percentages or an ogive.

To construct a pie chart in Excel, load the labels (company, person, etc.) into one column and the values (frequency, dollar value, percentage, etc.) into another column. Select **Insert** from the menu bar, then select **Chart** from the pull-down menu. Select **Pie** from this menu and follow the directions through the four steps. You have the option of including a legend, determining what data labels to use if any, and determining the final location of the pie chart.

To construct a scatter plot in Excel, load the data for each variable in a separate column. Select **Insert** from the menu bar, then select **Chart** from the pull-down menu. Select **XY (Scatter)** from this menu and follow the directions through the four steps. You have the option of including a legend, determining what data labels to use if any, and determining the final location of the scatter plot.

MINITAB

MINITAB has the capability of constructing histograms, frequency polygons, ogives, pie charts, stem and leaf charts, Pareto charts, and scatter plots along with the essentials needed to construct a frequency distribution. With the exception of Pareto charts, which are accessed through **Stat,** all of these charts and graphs are accessed by selecting **Graph** on the menu bar.

Histograms, frequency polygons, and ogives are constructed in MINITAB using the **Histogram** option on the **Graph** pull-down menu. To begin, insert the column location of the raw data into the first line under **Graph variables** in the **Histogram** dialog box. Multiple graphs can be made by inserting locations in several lines under **Graph variables.** Under **Data display,** select the type of graph desired. Use **Bar** for a histogram and **Connect** for a frequency polygon or an ogive. Several options are available in this dialog box for setting the number of classes, giving the graph a title, modifying the axes, and so on. The **Options** dialog box is especially important in modifying the number of classes, determining the type of intervals used, and constructing an ogive. To construct an ogive, select **Cumulative Frequency** in the **Options** dialog box. To construct a frequency polygon, a histogram, or to determine frequencies for a frequency distribution, select **Frequency.** Most of the essentials of a frequency distribution can be obtained by constructing a histogram, selecting **Annotation** from the Histogram dialog box, and then selecting **Data Labels.** In the **Data Labels** dialog box, check **Show data labels.** This option will add frequencies to the graph. From these frequencies and the class endpoints displayed on the graph, a frequency distribution can be constructed.

Pie charts are constructed by selecting **Pie Chart** on the **Graph** pull-down menu. In the **Pie Chart** dialog box, the two main options are **Chart data in** and **Chart table.** Use the **Chart data in** option if the values to be used in constructing the pie chart are in a single column. Use the **Chart table** option if the categories are in one column and the frequencies (values) are in another column. Other options are available, such as how to order the pie slices, exploding slices, colors, or labels.

Stem and leaf plots are constructed by selecting **Stem-and-leaf…** from the **Graph** pull-down menu. In the **Stem-and-leaf…** dialog box, enter the location of the data and click OK. The output contains stems and leaves but in addition gives a cumulative frequency count above and below the median value (displayed on the left of the output).

To construct a Pareto chart, begin by selecting **S̲tat** from the menu bar. From the pull-down menu that appears, select **Quality Tools.** From the **Quality Tools** pull-down menu select **P̲areto Chart.** From the **P̲areto Chart** dialog box select **C̲hart defects table** if you have a summary of the defects with the reasons (**L̲abels**) in one column and the frequency of occurrence (**F̲requencies**) in another column. Enter the location of the reasons in **L̲abels** and the location of the frequencies in **F̲requencies.** If you have unsummarized data, you can select **C̲hart defects data in.** In the space provided, give the location of the column with all the defects that occurred. It is possible to have the defects either by name or with some code. If you want to have the labels in one column and the defects in another, then select **B̲Y variable in** and place the location of the labels there.

To construct a scatter plot, select **G̲raph,** then select **P̲lot.** In the **P̲lot** dialog box under **G̲raph variables,** place the location of the y variable in the first space under **Y** and the location of the x variable in the second space under **X.** Multiple scatter plots can be created by filling in the spaces beside **Graph 2, Graph 3,** and so on. To get a scatter plot (instead of a line plot, etc.), select **Symbol** under **Display** in the **Data display** portion of the dialog box.

Descriptive Statistics

LEARNING OBJECTIVES

The focus of Chapter 3 is the use of statistical techniques to describe data, thereby enabling you to:

1. Distinguish between measures of central tendency, measures of variability, measures of shape, and measures of association.
2. Understand the meanings of mean, median, mode, quartile, percentile, and range.
3. Compute mean, median, mode, percentile, quartile, range, variance, standard deviation, and mean absolute deviation on ungrouped data.
4. Differentiate between sample and population variance and standard deviation.
5. Understand the meaning of standard deviation as it is applied by using the empirical rule and Chebyshev's theorem.
6. Compute the mean, mode, standard deviation, and variance on grouped data.
7. Understand skewness, kurtosis, and box and whisker plots.
8. Compute a coefficient of correlation and interpret it.

Laundry Statistics

According to Procter & Gamble, 35 billion loads of laundry are run in the United States each year. Every second, 1,100 loads are started. Statistics show that one person in the United States generates a quarter of a ton of dirty clothing each year. Americans appear to be spending more time doing laundry than they did 40 years ago. Today, the average American woman spends seven to nine hours a week on laundry. However, industry research shows that the result is dirtier laundry than in other developed countries. Various companies market new and improved versions of washers and detergents. Yet, Americans seem to be resistant to manufacturers' innovations in this area. In the United States, the average washing machine uses about 16 gallons of water. In Europe, the figure is about 4 gallons. The average wash cycle of an American wash is about 35 minutes compared to 90 minutes in Europe. Americans prefer top loading machines because they do not have to bend over, and the top loading machines are larger. Europeans use the smaller front-loading machines because of smaller living spaces.

Managerial and Statistical Questions

Virtually all of the statistics cited here are gleaned from studies or surveys.

1. Suppose a study of laundry usage is done in 50 U.S. households that contain washers and dryers. Water measurements are taken for the number of gallons of water used by each washing machine in completing a cycle. The following data are the number of gallons used by each washing machine during the washing cycle. Summarize the data so that study findings can be reported.

15	17	16	15	16	17	18	15	14	15
16	16	17	16	15	15	17	14	15	16
16	17	14	15	12	15	16	14	14	16
15	13	16	17	17	15	16	16	16	14
17	16	17	14	16	13	16	15	16	15

2. The average wash cycle for an American wash is 35 minutes. Suppose the standard deviation of a wash cycle for an American wash is 5 minutes. Within what range of time do most American wash cycles fall?

3. Is the amount of laundry done by a household each year related in some way to the household income? Suppose eight households of two adults and two children are randomly chosen for a study. Over a year period, a record is kept of the weight of clothing washed by each household, and their annual household income is ascertained. From the following study data, determine whether a relationship exists between a household's income and the amount of laundry done (in weight).

Amount of Laundry (weight in lbs.)	Household Income ($1,000s)
1,210	42
875	31
1,890	60
1,450	68
2,040	110
1,330	45
660	56
1,490	72
1,950	93

Source: Adapted from Emily Nelson, "In Doing Laundry, Americans Cling to Outmoded Ways," *Wall Street Journal,* 16 May 2002, pp. A1 & A10.

Chapter 2 described graphical techniques for organizing and presenting data. For example, we attempted to summarize 40 years of unemployment rates for France with a frequency distribution, a histogram, a frequency polygon, and an ogive. Even though these graphs allow the researcher to make some general observations about the shape and spread of the data, a more complete understanding of the data can be attained by summarizing the data using statistics. This chapter presents such statistical measures, including measures of central tendency, measures of variability, and measures of shape. The computation of these measures is different for ungrouped and grouped data. Hence we present some measures for both ungrouped and grouped data. In addition, one of the statistics presented can be used to compute the correlation or relatedness of two numerical variables.

3.1 MEASURES OF CENTRAL TENDENCY: UNGROUPED DATA

One type of measure that is used to describe a set of data is the **measure of central tendency.** Measures of central tendency *yield information about the center, or middle part, of a group of numbers.* Table 3.1 displays offer price for the 20 largest U.S. initial public offerings in a recent year according to Securities Data. For these data, measures of central tendency can yield such information as the average offer price, the middle offer price, and the most frequently occurring offer price. Measures of central tendency do not focus on the span of the data set or how far values are from the middle numbers. The measures of central tendency presented here for ungrouped data are the mode, the median, the mean, percentiles, and quartiles.

Mode

The **mode** is *the most frequently occurring value in a set of data.* For the data in Table 3.1 the mode is $19.00 because the offer price that recurred the most times (4) was $19.00. Organizing the data into an ordered array (an ordering of the numbers from smallest to largest) helps to locate the mode. The following is an ordered array of the values from Table 3.1.

7.00	11.00	14.25	15.00	15.00	15.50	19.00	19.00	19.00	19.00
21.00	22.00	23.00	24.00	25.00	27.00	27.00	28.00	34.22	43.25

This grouping makes it easier to see that 19.00 is the most frequently occurring number.

In the case of a tie for the most frequently occurring value, two modes are listed. Then the data are said to be **bimodal.** If a set of data is not exactly bimodal but contains two values that are more dominant than others, some researchers take the liberty of referring to the data set as bimodal even without an exact tie for the mode. Data sets with more than two modes are referred to as **multimodal.**

In the world of business, the concept of mode is often used in determining sizes. For example, shoe manufacturers might produce inexpensive shoes in three widths only: small, medium, and large. Each width size represents a modal width of feet. By reducing the number of sizes to a few modal sizes, companies can reduce total product costs by limiting machine setup costs. Similarly, the garment industry produces shirts, dresses, suits, and many other clothing products in modal sizes. For example, all size M shirts in a given lot are produced in the same size. This size is some modal size for medium-sized men.

The mode is an appropriate measure of central tendency for nominal-level data. The mode can be used to determine which category occurs most frequently.

Median

The **median** is *the middle value in an ordered array of numbers.* For an array with an odd number of terms, the median is the middle number. For an array with an even number of terms, the median is the average of the two middle numbers. The following steps are used to determine the median.

TABLE 3.1

Offer Prices for the 20 Largest U.S. Initial Public Offerings in a Recent Year

$14.25	$19.00	$11.00	$28.00
24.00	23.00	43.25	19.00
27.00	25.00	15.00	7.00
34.22	15.50	15.00	22.00
19.00	19.00	27.00	21.00

STEP 1. Arrange the observations in an ordered data array.
STEP 2. For an odd number of terms, find the middle term of the ordered array. It is the median.
STEP 3. For an even number of terms, find the average of the middle two terms. This average is the median.

Suppose a business researcher wants to determine the median for the following numbers.

15   11   14   3   21   17   22   16   19   16   5   7   19   8   9   20   4

The researcher arranges the numbers in an ordered array.

3   4   5   7   8   9   11   14   15   16   16   17   19   19   20   21   22

Because the array contains 17 terms (an odd number of terms), the median is the middle number, or 15.

If the number 22 is eliminated from the list, the array would contain only 16 terms.

3   4   5   7   8   9   11   14   15   16   16   17   19   19   20   21

Now, for an even number of terms, the statistician determines the median by averaging the two middle values, 14 and 15. The resulting median value is 14.5.

Another way to locate the median is by finding the $(n + 1)/2$ term in an ordered array. For example, if a data set contains 77 terms, the median is the 39th term. That is,

$$\frac{n+1}{2} = \frac{77+1}{2} = \frac{78}{2} = 39\text{th term}$$

This formula is helpful when a large number of terms must be manipulated.

Consider the offer price data in Table 3.1. Because this data set contains 20 values, or $n = 20$, the median for these data is located at the $(20+ 1)/2$ term, or the 10.5th term. This equation indicates that the median is located halfway between the 10th and 11th terms or the average of 19.00 and 21.00. Thus, the median offer price for the largest 20 U.S. initial public offerings is $20.00.

The median is unaffected by the magnitude of extreme values. This characteristic is an advantage, because large and small values do not inordinately influence the median. For this reason, the median is often the best measure of location to use in the analysis of variables such as house costs, income, and age. Suppose, for example, that a real estate broker wants to determine the median selling price of 10 houses listed at the following prices.

$67,000	$105,000	$148,000	$5,250,000
91,000	116,000	167,000	
95,000	122,000	189,000	

The median is the average of the two middle terms, $116,000 and $122,000, or $119,000. This price is a reasonable representation of the prices of the 10 houses. Note that the house priced at $5,250,000 did not enter into the analysis other than to count as one of the 10 houses. If the price of the tenth house were $200,000, the results would be the same. However, if all the house prices were averaged, the resulting average price of the original 10 houses would be $635,000, higher than nine of the 10 individual prices.

A disadvantage of the median is that not all the information from the numbers is used. For example, information about the specific asking price of the most expensive house does not really enter into the computation of the median. The level of data measurement must be at least ordinal for a median to be meaningful.

Mean

The **arithmetic mean** is *the average of a group of numbers* and is computed by summing all numbers and dividing by the number of numbers. Because the arithmetic mean is so widely used, most statisticians refer to it simply as the *mean*.

The population mean is represented by the Greek letter mu (μ). The sample mean is represented by $\bar{x}$. The formulas for computing the population mean and the sample mean are given in the boxes that follow.

POPULATION MEAN	$$\mu = \frac{\Sigma x}{N} = \frac{x_1 + x_2 + x_3 + \cdots + x_N}{N}$$
SAMPLE MEAN	$$\bar{x} = \frac{\Sigma x}{n} = \frac{x_1 + x_2 + x_3 \cdots + x_n}{n}$$

The capital Greek letter sigma (Σ) is commonly used in mathematics to represent a summation of all the numbers in a grouping.* Also, N is the number of terms in the population, and n is the number of terms in the sample. The algorithm for computing a mean is to sum all the numbers in the population or sample and divide by the number of terms.

A more formal definition of the mean is

$$\mu = \frac{\sum_{i=1}^{N} x_i}{N}$$

However, for the purposes of this text,

$$\Sigma x \text{ denotes } \sum_{i=1}^{N} x_i$$

It is inappropriate to use the mean to analyze data that are not at least interval level in measurement.

Suppose a company has five departments with 24, 13, 19, 26, and 11 workers each. The *population mean* number of workers in each department is 18.6 workers. The computations follow.

$$
\begin{array}{r}
24 \\
13 \\
19 \\
26 \\
\underline{11} \\
\Sigma x = \quad 93
\end{array}
$$

and

$$\mu = \frac{\Sigma x}{n} = \frac{93}{5} = 18.6$$

The calculation of a sample mean uses the same algorithm as for a population mean and will produce the same answer if computed on the same data. However, it is inappropriate to compute a sample mean for a population or a population mean for a sample. Because both populations and samples are important in statistics, a separate symbol is necessary for the population mean and for the sample mean.

DEMONSTRATION PROBLEM 3.1	The number of U.S. cars in service by top car rental companies in a recent year according to *Auto Rental News* follows.

Company	Number of Cars in Service
Enterprise	460,000
Hertz	350,000
ANC Rental Group	322,000
Avis	220,000
Budget	146,000
Dollar	78,000
Thrifty	51,000
U-Save	15,000
Toyota	12,000
Rent-a-Wreck	12,000
Advantage	12,000
Payless	8,000
ACE	8,000

* The mathematics of summations is not discussed here. A more detailed explanation is given on the CD-ROM.

Compute the mode, the median, and the mean.

Solution

Mode: 12,000

Median: With 13 different companies in this group, $n = 13$. The median is located at the $(13 + 1)/2 = 7$th position. Because the data are already ordered, the 7th term is 51,000, which is the median.

Mean: The total number of cars in service is $1,694,000 = \Sigma x$

$$\mu = \frac{\Sigma x}{n} = \frac{1,694,000}{13} = 130,307.7$$

The mean is affected by each and every value, which is an advantage. The mean uses all the data and each data item influences the mean. It is also a disadvantage, because extremely large or small values can cause the mean to be pulled toward the extreme value. Recall the preceding discussion of the 10 house prices. If the mean is computed for the 10 houses, the mean price is higher than the prices of nine of the houses because the $5,250,000 house is included in the calculation. The total price of the 10 houses is $6,350,000, and the mean price is $635,000.

The mean is the most commonly used measure of central tendency because it uses each data item in its computation, it is a familiar measure, and it has mathematical properties that make it attractive to use in inferential statistics analysis.

Percentiles

Percentiles are *measures of central tendency that divide a group of data into 100 parts*. There are 99 percentiles, because it takes 99 dividers to separate a group of data into 100 parts. The nth percentile is the value such that at least n percent of the data are below that value and at most $(100 - n)$ percent are above that value. Specifically, the 87th percentile is a value such that at least 87% of the data are below the value and no more than 13% are above the value. Percentiles are "stair-step" values, as shown in Figure 3.1, because the 87th percentile and the 88th percentile have no percentile between. If a plant operator takes a safety examination and 87.6% of the safety exam scores are below that person's score, he or she still scores at only the 87th percentile, even though more than 87% of the scores are lower.

Percentiles are widely used in reporting test results. Almost all college or university students have taken the SAT, ACT, GRE, or GMAT examination. In most cases, the results for these examinations are reported in percentile form and also as raw scores. Shown next is a summary of the steps used in determining the location of a percentile.

Steps in Determining the Location of a Percentile

1. Organize the numbers into an ascending-order array.
2. Calculate the percentile location (i) by:

$$i = \frac{P}{100}(n)$$

where

P = the percentile of interest
i = percentile location
n = number in the data set

FIGURE 3.1

Stair-Step Percentiles

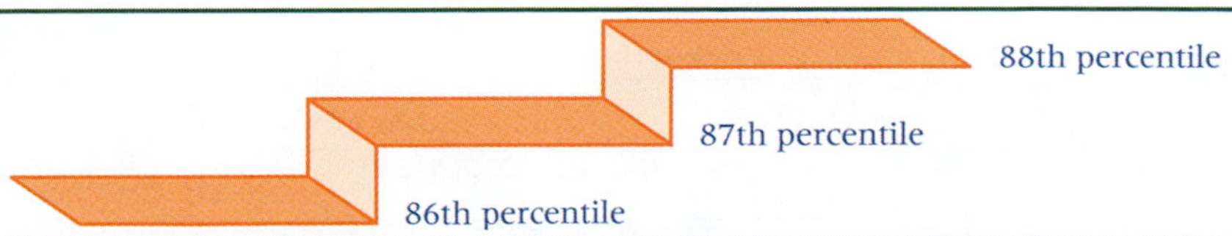

88th percentile

87th percentile

86th percentile

3. Determine the location by either (a) or (b).

    a. If i is a whole number, the Pth percentile is the average of the value at the ith location and the value at the $(i + 1)^{\text{st}}$ location.

    b. If i is not a whole number, the Pth percentile value is located at the whole number part of $i + 1$.

For example, suppose you want to determine the 80th percentile of 1240 numbers. P is 80 and n is 1240. First, order the numbers from lowest to highest. Next, calculate the location of the 80th percentile.

$$i = \frac{80}{100}(1240) = 992$$

Because $i = 992$ is a whole number, follow the directions in step 3(a). The 80th percentile is the average of the 992nd number and the 993rd number.

$$P_{80} = \frac{(992\text{nd number} + 993\text{rd number})}{2}$$

DEMONSTRATION PROBLEM 3.2

Determine the 30th percentile of the following eight numbers: 14, 12, 19, 23, 5, 13, 28, 17.

Solution

For these eight numbers, we want to find the value of the 30th percentile, so $n = 8$ and $P = 30$.

First, organize the data into an ascending-order array.

    5   12   13   14   17   19   23   28

Next, compute the value of i.

$$i = \frac{30}{100}(8) = 2.4$$

Because i is not a whole number, step 3(b) is used. The value of $i + 1$ is 2.4 + 1, or 3.4. The whole-number part of 3.4 is 3. The 30th percentile is located at the third value. The third value is 13, so 13 is the 30th percentile. Note that a percentile may or may not be one of the data values.

Quartiles

Quartiles are *measures of central tendency that divide a group of data into four subgroups or parts.* The three quartiles are denoted as Q_1, Q_2, and Q_3. The first quartile, Q_1, separates the first, or lowest, one-fourth of the data from the upper three-fourths and is equal to the 25th percentile. The second quartile, Q_2, separates the second quarter of the data from the third quarter. Q_2 is located at the 50th percentile and equals the median of the data. The third quartile, Q_3, divides the first three-quarters of the data from the last quarter and is equal to the value of the 75th percentile. These three quartiles are shown in Figure 3.2.

Suppose we want to determine the values of Q_1, Q_2, and Q_3 for the following numbers.

    106   109   114   116   121   122   125   129

FIGURE 3.2

Quartiles

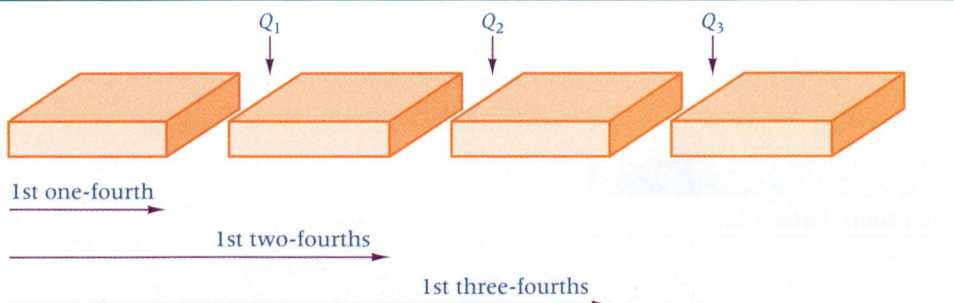

1st one-fourth

1st two-fourths

1st three-fourths

The value of Q_1 is found at the 25th percentile, P_{25}, by:

$$\text{For } n = 8, \ i = \frac{25}{100}(8) = 2$$

Because i is a whole number, P_{25} is found as the average of the second and third numbers.

$$P_{25} = \frac{(109 + 114)}{2} = 111.5$$

The value of Q_1 is $P_{25} = 111.5$. Notice that one-fourth, or two, of the values (106 and 109) are less than 111.5.

The value of Q_2 is equal to the median. Because the array contains an even number of terms, the median is the average of the two middle terms.

$$Q_2 = \text{median} = \frac{(116 + 121)}{2} = 118.5$$

Notice that exactly half of the terms are less than Q_2 and half are greater than Q_2.

The value of Q_3 is determined by P_{75} as follows.

$$i = \frac{75}{100}(8) = 6$$

Because i is a whole number, P_{75} is the average of the sixth and the seventh numbers.

$$P_{75} = \frac{(122 + 125)}{2} = 123.5$$

The value of Q_3 is $P_{75} = 123.5$. Notice that three-fourths, or six, of the values are less than 123.5 and two of the values are greater than 123.5.

<table>
<tr><td>

**DEMONSTRATION
PROBLEM 3.3**

</td><td>

The following shows revenues for the world's top advertising organizations according to *Advertising Age*. Determine the first, the second, and the third quartiles for these data.

</td></tr>
</table>

Ad Organization	Headquarters	Worldwide Gross Income ($ millions)
WPP Group	London	8165
Interpublic Group of Cos.	New York	7981
Omnicom Group	New York	7404
Publicis Communication	Paris	4770
Dentsu	Tokyo	2796
Havas Advertising	Paris	2733
Grey Advertising	New York	1864
Cordiant Communications Group	London	1175
Hakuhodo	Tokyo	874
Asatsu	Tokyo	396
TMP Worldwide	New York	359
Carlson Marketing Group	Minneapolis	356
Incepta Group	London	248
DigitasA	Boston	236
Tokyu Agency	Tokyo	204
Daiko Advertising	Tokyo	203

Solution

For 16 advertising organizations, $n = 16$. $Q_1 = P_{25}$ is found by

$$i = \frac{25}{100}(16) = 4$$

Because i is a whole number, Q_1 is found to be the average of the fourth and fifth values from the bottom.

$$Q_1 = \frac{248 + 356}{2} = 302$$

$Q_2 = P_{50}$ = median; with 16 terms, the median is the average of the eighth and ninth terms.

$$Q_2 = \frac{874 + 1175}{2} = 1024.5$$

$Q_3 = P_{75}$ is solved by

$$i = \frac{75}{100}(16) = 12$$

Q_3 is found by averaging the twelfth and thirteenth terms.

$$Q_3 = \frac{2796 + 4770}{2} = 3783$$

3.1 PROBLEMS

3.1   Determine the mode for the following numbers.

2   4   8   4   6   2   7   8   4   3   8   9   4   3   5

3.2   Determine the median for the numbers in Problem 3.1.

3.3   Determine the median for the following numbers.

213   345   609   073   167   243   444   524   199   682

3.4   Compute the mean for the following numbers.

17.3   44.5   31.6   40.0   52.8   38.8   30.1   78.5

3.5   Compute the mean for the following numbers.

7   −2   5   9   0   −3   −6   −7   −4   −5   2   −8

3.6   Compute the 35th percentile, the 55th percentile, Q_1, Q_2, and Q_3 for the following data.

16   28   29   13   17   20   11   34   32   27   25   30   19   18   33

3.7   Compute P_{20}, P_{47}, P_{83}, Q_1, Q_2, and Q_3 for the following data.

120	138	97	118	172	144
138	107	94	119	139	145
162	127	112	150	143	80
105	116	142	128	116	171

3.8   The following data show the number of cars and light trucks for a recent year for the largest automakers in the world, as reported by *AutoFacts*, a unit of Coopers & Lybrand Consulting. Compute the mean and median. Which of these two measures do you think is most appropriate for summarizing these data and why? What is the value of Q_2? Determine the 63rd percentile for the data. Determine the 29th percentile for the data.

Automaker	Production (1,000s)
General Motors	7880
Ford Motors	6359
Toyota	4580
Volkswagen	4161
Chrysler	2968
Nissan	2646
Honda	2436
Fiat	2264
Peugeot	1767
Renault	1567
Mitsubishi	1535
Hyundai	1434
BMW	1341
Daimler-Benz	1227
Daewoo	898

3.9 The following lists the biggest banks in the world ranked by assets according to *American Banker*. Compute the median, Q_3, P_{20}, P_{60}, P_{80}, and P_{93}.

Bank	Assets ($ billions)
Citigroup (New York)	902
Deutsche Bank (Frankfurt)	873
Bank of Tokyo-Mitsubishi	721
J.P.Morgan Chase (New York)	715
UBS (Zurich)	674
HSBC Holdings (London)	673
BHV AG (Munich)	654
BNP-SG-Paribas (Paris)	652
BankAmerica (Charlotte)	642
ING NV (Amsterdam)	613

3.10 The following lists the number of fatal accidents by scheduled commercial airline over a 17-year period according to the Air Transport Association of America. Using these data, compute the mean, median, and mode. What is the value of the third quartile? Determine P_{11}, P_{35}, P_{58}, and P_{67}.

4   4   4   1   4   2   4   3   8   6   4   4   1   4   2   3   3

3.2 MEASURES OF VARIABILITY: UNGROUPED DATA

Measures of central tendency yield information about particular points of a data set. However, business researchers can use another group of analytic tools to describe a set of data. These tools are **measures of variability,** which *describe the spread or the dispersion of a set of data.* Using measures of variability in conjunction with measures of central tendency makes possible a more complete numerical description of the data.

For example, a company has 25 salespeople in the field, and the median annual sales figure for these people is $1.2 million. Are the salespeople being successful as a group or not? The median provides information about the sales of the person in the middle, but what about the other salespeople? Are all of them selling $1.2 million annually, or do the sales figures vary widely, with one person selling $5 million annually and another selling only $150,000 annually? Measures of variability provide the additional information necessary to answer that question.

Figure 3.3 shows three distributions in which the mean of each distribution is the same ($\mu = 50$) but the variabilities differ. Observation of these distributions shows that a measure of variability is necessary to complement the mean value in describing the data. Methods of computing measures of variability differ for ungrouped data and grouped data. This section focuses on seven measures of variability for ungrouped data: range, interquartile range, mean absolute deviation, variance, standard deviation, Z scores, and coefficient of variation.

Range

The **range** is *the difference between the largest value of a data set and the smallest value.* Although it is usually a single numeric value, some business researchers define the range as the ordered pair of smallest and largest numbers (smallest, largest). It is a crude measure of variability, describing the distance to the outer bounds of the data set. It reflects those extreme values because it is constructed from them. An advantage of the range is its ease of computation. One important use of the range is in quality assurance, where the range is used to construct control charts. A disadvantage of the range is that, because it is computed with the values that are on the extremes of the data, it is affected by extreme values. Therefore its application as a measure of variability is limited.

The data in Table 3.1 represent the offer prices for the 20 largest U.S. initial public offerings in a recent year. The lowest offer price was $7.00 and the highest price was $43.25. The range of the offer prices can be computed as the difference of the highest and lowest values:

$$\text{Range} = \text{Highest} - \text{Lowest} = \$43.25 - \$7.00 = \$36.25$$

Interquartile Range

Another measure of variability is the **interquartile range**. The interquartile range is *the range of values between the first and third quartile.* Essentially, it is the range of the middle 50% of the data and is determined by computing the value of $Q_3 - Q_1$. The interquartile range is especially useful in situations where data users are more interested in values toward the middle and less interested in extremes. In describing a real estate housing market, realtors might use the interquartile range as a measure of housing prices when describing the middle half of the market for buyers who are interested in houses in the midrange. In addition, the interquartile range is used in the construction of box and whisker plots.

INTERQUARTILE RANGE	$Q_3 - Q_1$

The following data indicate the top 15 trading partners of the United States by U.S. exports to the country in a recent year according to the U.S. Census Bureau.

Country	Exports ($ billions)
Canada	$151.8
Mexico	71.4
Japan	65.5
United Kingdom	36.4
South Korea	25.0
Germany	24.5
Taiwan	20.4
Netherlands	19.8
Singapore	17.7
France	16.0
Brazil	15.9
Hong Kong	15.1
Belgium	13.4
China	12.9
Australia	12.1

FIGURE 3.3

Three Distributions with the Same Mean but Different Dispersions

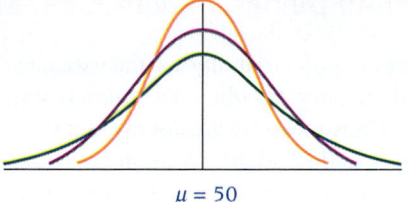

$\mu = 50$

What is the interquartile range for these data? The process begins by computing the first and third quartiles as follows.

Solving for $Q_1 = P_{25}$ when $n = 15$:

$$i = \frac{25}{100}(15) = 3.75$$

Because i is not a whole number, P_{25} is found as the fourth term from the bottom.

$$Q_1 = P_{25} = 15.1$$

Solving for $Q_3 = P_{75}$:

$$i = \frac{75}{100}(15) = 11.25$$

Because i is not a whole number, P_{75} is found as the 12th term from the bottom.

$$Q_3 = P_{75} = 36.4$$

The interquartile range is:

$$Q_3 - Q_1 = 36.4 - 15.1 = 21.3$$

The middle 50% of the exports for the top 15 U.S. trading partners spans a range of 21.3 ($ billions).

STATISTICS IN BUSINESS TODAY

Telecommuting Statistics

A study by Telework America sponsored by AT&T in 2001 revealed that 28 million Americans are teleworking. Of these, 24.1% work on the road, 21.7% work out of their home, 7.5% work in telework centers, and 4.2% work at satellite offices. More than 40% of these people work in more than one location. An estimated 30 million regular teleworkers will be working in the United States by the end of 2004.

The typical telecommuter lives in the West or the Northeast, is male, has a college education, is between 35 and 44 years of age, is married, and earns at least $ 40,000 per year. The mean income for teleworkers is $ 44,000. Most of telecommuters work in IT, real estate, or enterprise management. Teleworkers typically drive 18 miles to work and save nearly 53 minutes of commuting time each workday they telecommute. On average, teleworkers work one to two days per week away from home.

Teleworkers are relatively satisfied with their work. Seventy-five percent of home workers reported a quantifiable increase in productivity and work quality when they switched from traditional at-work jobs to telecommuting. Two-thirds of teleworkers expressed increased job satisfaction. Teleworkers say that they work longer hours than nonteleworkers but that their job interferes less with their personal lives.

Teleworking can result in cost savings for companies due to lack of absenteeism, reduced real estate costs, and job retention. It is estimated that employees who telework can save their employers an average of $10,000 each in reduced absenteeism and job retention. Real estate costs can be reduced from 25% to 90%. AT&T saves $3,000 per teleworker annually and has saved $25 million a year in real estate costs through employees who are full-time teleworkers.

Source: Adapted from YouCanWorkFromAnywhere.com at http://www.ycwfa.com/infocenter/facts.htm; Toni Kistner, "Annual Survey Helps Debunk Telework Myths," *Net.Worker*, 29 October 2001, at http://www.nwfusion.com/net.worker/columnists/2001/1029kistner.html.

Mean Absolute Deviation, Variance, and Standard Deviation

Three other measures of variability are the variance, the standard deviation, and the mean absolute deviation. They are obtained through similar processes and are, therefore, presented together. These measures are not meaningful unless the data are at least interval-level data. The variance and standard deviation are widely used in statistics. Although the standard deviation has some stand-alone potential, the importance of variance and standard deviation lies mainly in their role as tools used in conjunction with other statistical devices.

Suppose a small company started a production line to build computers. During the first five weeks of production, the output is 5, 9, 16, 17, and 18 computers, respectively. Which descriptive statistics could the owner use to measure the early progress of production? In an attempt to summarize these figures, the owner could compute a mean.

$$x$$

$$5$$

$$9$$

$$16$$

$$17$$

$$18$$

$$\Sigma x = 65 \qquad \mu = \frac{\Sigma x}{N} = \frac{65}{5} = 13$$

What is the variability in these five weeks of data? One way for the owner to begin to look at the spread of the data is to subtract the mean from each data value. *Subtracting the mean from each value of data* yields the **deviation from the mean** $(x - \mu)$. Table 3.2 shows these deviations for the computer company production. Note that some deviations from the mean are positive and some are negative. Figure 3.4 shows that geometrically the negative deviations represent values that are below (to the left of) the mean and positive deviations represent values that are above (to the right of) the mean.

An examination of deviations from the mean can reveal information about the variability of data. However, the deviations are used mostly as a tool to compute other measures of variability. Note that in both Table 3.2 and Figure 3.4 these deviations total zero. This phenomenon applies to all cases. For a given set of data, the sum of all deviations from the arithmetic mean is always zero.

TABLE 3.2

Deviations from the Mean for Computer Production

Number (x)	Deviations from the Mean $(x - \mu)$
5	$5 - 13 = -8$
9	$9 - 13 = -4$
16	$16 - 13 = +3$
17	$17 - 13 = +4$
18	$18 - 13 = \underline{+5}$
$\Sigma x = 65$	$\Sigma(x - \mu) = 0$

FIGURE 3.4

Geometric Distances from the Mean (from Table 3.2)

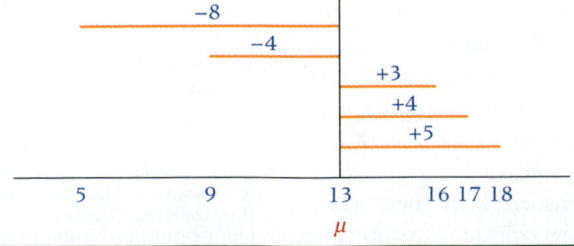

SUM OF DEVIATIONS FROM THE ARITHMETIC MEAN IS ALWAYS ZERO	$\Sigma(x - \mu) = 0$

This property requires considering alternative ways to obtain measures of variability.

One obvious way to force the sum of deviations to have a nonzero total is to take the absolute value of each deviation around the mean. Utilizing the absolute value of the deviations about the mean makes solving for the mean absolute deviation possible.

Mean Absolute Deviation

The **mean absolute deviation** (MAD) is *the average of the absolute values of the deviations around the mean for a set of numbers.*

MEAN ABSOLUTE DEVIATION	$MAD = \dfrac{\Sigma|x - \mu|}{N}$

Using the data from Table 3.2, the computer company owner can compute a mean absolute deviation by taking the absolute values of the deviations and averaging them, as shown in Table 3.3. The mean absolute deviation for the computer production data is 4.8.

Because it is computed by using absolute values, the mean absolute deviation is less useful in statistics than other measures of dispersion. However, in the field of forecasting, it is used occasionally as a measure of error.

Variance

Because absolute values are not conducive to easy manipulation, mathematicians developed an alternative mechanism for overcoming the zero-sum property of deviations from the mean. This approach utilizes the square of the deviations from the mean. The result is the variance, an important measure of variability.

The **variance** is *the average of the squared deviations about the arithmetic mean for a set of numbers.* The population variance is denoted by σ^2.

POPULATION VARIANCE	$\sigma^2 = \dfrac{\Sigma(x - \mu)^2}{N}$

Table 3.4 shows the original production numbers for the computer company, the deviations from the mean, and the squared deviations from the mean.

The sum of the squared deviations about the mean of a set of values—called the **sum of squares of x** and sometimes abbreviated as SS_x—is used throughout statistics. For the computer company, this value is 130. Dividing it by the number of data values (5 weeks) yields the variance for computer production.

$$\sigma^2 = \frac{130}{5} = 26.0$$

TABLE 3.3

MAD for Computer Production Data

x	$x - \mu$	$|x - \mu|$
5	−8	+8
9	−4	+4
16	+3	+3
17	+4	+4
18	+5	+5
$\Sigma x = 65$	$\Sigma(x - \mu) = 0$	$\Sigma|x - \mu| = 24$

$$MAD = \frac{\Sigma|x - \mu|}{n} = \frac{24}{5} = 4.8$$

Because the variance is computed from squared deviations, the final result is expressed in terms of squared units of measurement. Statistics measured in squared units are problematic to interpret. Consider, for example, Mattel Toys attempting to interpret production costs in terms of squared dollars or Troy-Bilt measuring production output variation in terms of squared lawn mowers. Therefore, when used as a descriptive measure, variance can be considered as an intermediate calculation in the process of obtaining the sample standard deviation.

Standard Deviation

The standard deviation is a popular measure of variability. It is used both as a separate entity and as a part of other analyses, such as computing confidence intervals and in hypothesis testing (see Chapters 8, 9, and 10).

POPULATION STANDARD DEVIATION	$\sigma = \sqrt{\dfrac{\Sigma(x-\mu)^2}{N}}$

The **standard deviation** is *the square root of the variance*. The population standard deviation is denoted by σ.

Like the variance, the standard deviation utilizes the sum of the squared deviations about the mean (SS_x). It is computed by averaging these squared deviations (SS_x/N) and taking the square root of that average. One feature of the standard deviation that distinguishes it from a variance is that the standard deviation is expressed in the same units as the raw data, whereas the variance is expressed in those units squared. Table 3.4 shows the standard deviation for the computer production company: $\sqrt{26}$, or 5.1.

What does a standard deviation of 5.1 mean? The meaning of standard deviation is more readily understood from its use, which is explored in the next section. Although the standard deviation and the variance are closely related and can be computed from each other, differentiating between them is important, because both are widely used in statistics.

Meaning of Standard Deviation

What is a standard deviation? What does it do, and what does it mean? The most precise way to define standard deviation is by reciting the formula used to compute it. However, insight into the concept of standard deviation can be gleaned by viewing the manner in which it is applied. Two ways of applying the standard deviation are the empirical rule and Chebyshev's theorem.

TABLE 3.4

Computing a Variance and a Standard Deviation from the Computer Production Data

x	$x - \mu$	$(x - \mu)^2$
5	−8	64
9	−4	16
16	+3	9
17	+4	16
18	+5	25
$\Sigma x = 65$	$\Sigma(x - \mu) = 0$	$\Sigma(x - \mu)^2 = 130$

$SS_x = \Sigma(x - \mu)^2 = 130$

$$\text{Variance} = \sigma^2 = \frac{SS_x}{N} = \frac{\Sigma(x-\mu)^2}{N} = \frac{130}{5} = 26.0$$

$$\text{Standard Deviation} = \sigma = \sqrt{\frac{\Sigma(x-\mu)^2}{N}} = \sqrt{\frac{130}{5}} = 5.1$$

FIGURE 3.5

Empirical Rule for One and Two
Standard Deviations of
Gasoline Prices

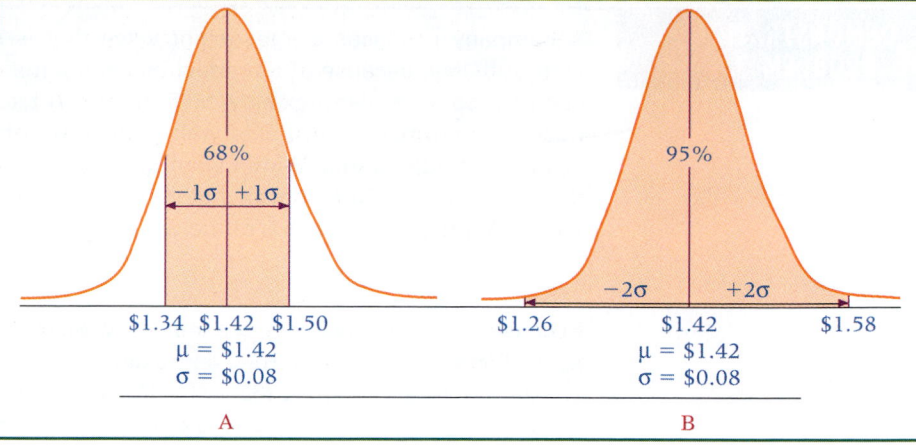

If a set of data is normally distributed, or bell shaped, approximately 68% of the data values are within one standard deviation of the mean, 95% are within two standard deviations, and almost 100% are within three standard deviations.

Empirical Rule

The **empirical rule** is an important rule of thumb that *is used to state the approximate percentage of values that lie within a given number of standard deviations from the mean of a set of data if the data are normally distributed.*

The empirical rule is used only for three numbers of standard deviations: 1σ, 2σ, and 3σ. More detailed analysis of other numbers of σ values is presented in Chapter 6. Also discussed in further detail in Chapter 6 is the normal distribution, a unimodal, symmetrical distribution that is bell (or mound) shaped. The requirement that the data be normally distributed contains some tolerance, and the empirical rule generally applies as long as the data are approximately mound shaped.

EMPIRICAL RULE*

Distance from the Mean	Values within Distance
$\mu \pm 1\sigma$	68%
$\mu \pm 2\sigma$	95%
$\mu \pm 3\sigma$	99.7%

*Based on the assumption that the data are approximately normally distributed.

If a set of data is normally distributed, or bell shaped, approximately 68% of the data values are within one standard deviation of the mean, 95% are within two standard deviations, and almost 100% are within three standard deviations.

Suppose a recent report states that for California, the average statewide price of a gallon of regular gasoline was $1.42. Suppose regular gasoline prices varied across the state with a standard deviation of $0.08 and were normally distributed. According to the empirical rule, approximately 68% of the prices should fall within $\mu \pm 1\sigma$, or $1.42 ± 1 ($0.08). Approximately 68% of the prices would be between $1.34 and $1.50, as shown in Figure 3.5A. Approximately 95% should fall within $\mu \pm 2\sigma$ or $1.42 ± 2($0.08) = $1.42 ± $0.16, or between $1.26 and $1.58, as shown in Figure 3.5B. Nearly all regular gasoline prices (99.7%) should fall between $1.16 and $1.66 ($\mu \pm 3\sigma$).

Note that with 68% of the gasoline prices falling within one standard deviation of the mean, approximately 32% are outside this range. Because the normal distribution is symmetrical, the 32% can be split in half such that 16% lie in each tail of the distribution. Thus, approximately 16% of the gasoline prices should be less than $1.34 and approximately 16% of the prices should be greater than $1.50.

Many phenomena are distributed approximately in a bell shape, including most human characteristics such as height and weight; therefore the empirical rule applies in many situations and is widely used.

DEMONSTRATION PROBLEM 3.4	A company produces a lightweight valve that is specified to weigh 1365 grams. Unfortunately, because of imperfections in the manufacturing process not all of the valves produced weigh exactly 1365 grams. In fact, the weights of the valves produced are normally distributed with a mean weight of 1365 grams and a standard deviation of 294 grams. Within what range of weights would approximately 95% of the valve weights fall? Approximately 16% of the weights would be more than what value? Approximately 0.15% of the weights would be less than what value?

Solution

Because the valve weights are normally distributed, the empirical rule applies. According to the empirical rule, approximately 95% of the weights should fall within $\mu \pm 2\sigma = 1365 \pm 2(294) = 1365 \pm 588$. Thus, approximately 95% should fall between 777 and 1953. Approximately 68% of the weights should fall within $\mu \pm 1\sigma$ and 32% should fall outside this interval. Because the normal distribution is symmetrical, approximately 16% should lie above $\mu + 1\sigma = 1365 + 294 = 1659$. Approximately 99.7% of the weights should fall within $\mu \pm 3\sigma$ and .3% should fall outside this interval. Half of these or .15% should lie below $\mu - 3\sigma = 1365 - 3(294) = 1365 - 882 = 483$.

Chebyshev's Theorem

The empirical rule applies only when data are known to be approximately normally distributed. What do researchers use when data are not normally distributed or when the shape of the distribution is unknown? Chebyshev's theorem applies to all distributions regardless of their shape and thus can be used whenever the data distribution shape is unknown or is nonnormal. Even though Chebyshev's theorem can in theory be applied to data that are normally distributed, the empirical rule is more widely known and is preferred whenever appropriate. Chebyshev's theorem is not a rule of thumb, as is the empirical rule, but rather it is presented in formula format and therefore can be more widely applied. **Chebyshev's theorem** states that *at least $1 - 1/k^2$ values will fall within $\pm k$ standard deviations of the mean regardless of the shape of the distribution.*

CHEBYSHEV'S THEOREM	Within k standard deviations of the mean, $\mu \pm k\sigma$, lie at least $$1 - \frac{1}{k^2}$$ proportion of the values. Assumption: $k > 1$

Specifically, Chebyshev's theorem says that at least 75% of all values are within $\pm 2\sigma$ of the mean regardless of the shape of a distribution because if $k = 2$, then $1 - 1/k^2 = 1 - 1/2^2 = 3/4 = .75$. Figure 3.6 provides a graphic illustration. In contrast, the empirical rule states that if the data are normally distributed 95% of all values are within $\mu \pm 2\sigma$. According to Chebyshev's theorem, the percentage of values within three standard deviations of the mean is at least 89%, in contrast to 99.7% for the empirical rule. Because a formula is used to compute proportions with Chebyshev's theorem, any value of k greater than 1 ($k > 1$) can be used. For example, if $k = 2.5$, at least .84 of all values are within $\mu \pm 2.5\sigma$, because $1 - 1/k^2 = 1 - 1/(2.5)^2 = .84$.

FIGURE 3.6

Application of Chebyshev's Theorem for Two Standard Deviations

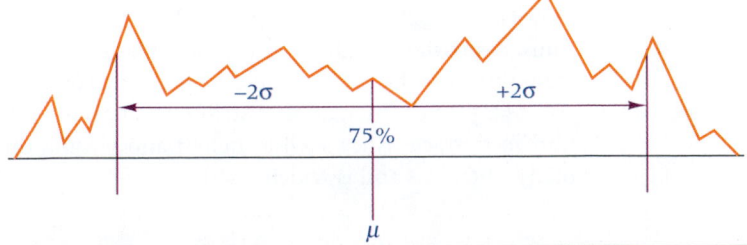

DEMONSTRATION PROBLEM 3.5

In the computing industry the average age of professional employees tends to be younger than in many other business professions. Suppose the average age of a professional employed by a particular computer firm is 28 with a standard deviation of 5 years. A histogram of professional employee ages with this firm reveals that the data are not normally distributed but rather are amassed in the twenties and that few workers are over 40. Apply Chebyshev's theorem to determine within what range of ages would at least 85% of the workers' ages fall.

Solution

Because the ages are not normally distributed, it is not appropriate to apply the empirical rule; and therefore, Chebyshev's theorem must be applied to answer the question.

Chebyshev's theorem states that at least $1 - 1/k^2$ proportion of the values are within $\mu \pm k\sigma$. Because 85% of the values are within this range, let

$$1 - \frac{1}{k^2} = .85$$

Solving for k yields

$$.15 = \frac{1}{k^2}$$
$$k^2 = 6.667$$
$$k = 2.58$$

Chebyshev's theorem says that at least .85 of the values are within $\pm 2.58\sigma$ of the mean. For $\mu = 28$ and $\sigma = 5$, at least .85, or 85%, of the values are within $28 \pm 2.58(5) = 28 \pm 12.9$ years of age or between 15.1 and 40.9 years old.

Population versus Sample Variance and Standard Deviation

The sample variance is denoted by s^2 and the sample standard deviation by s. The main use for sample variances and standard deviations is as estimators of population variances and standard deviations. Because of this, computation of the sample variance and standard deviation differs slightly from computation of the population variance and standard deviation. Both the sample variance and sample standard deviation use $n - 1$ in the denominator instead of n because using n in the denominator of a sample variance results in a statistic that tends to underestimate the population variance. While discussion of the properties of *good estimators* is beyond the scope of this text, one of the properties of a good estimator is being *unbiased*. Whereas, using n in the denominator of the sample variance makes it a *biased* estimator, using $n - 1$ allows it to be an *unbiased* estimator, which is a desirable property in inferential statistics.

SAMPLE VARIANCE	
	$s^2 = \dfrac{\Sigma(x - \bar{x})^2}{n - 1}$

SAMPLE STANDARD DEVIATION	
	$s = \sqrt{\dfrac{\Sigma(x - \bar{x})^2}{n - 1}}$

Shown here is a sample of six of the largest accounting firms in the United States and the number of partners associated with each firm as reported by the *Public Accounting Report*.

Firm	Number of Partners
PriceWaterhouse	1062
McGladrey & Pullen	381
Deloitte & Touche	1719
Andersen Worldwide	1673
Coopers & Lybrand	1277
BDO Seidman	217

The sample variance and sample standard deviation can be computed by:

x	$(x-\bar{x})^2$
1062	51.41
381	454,046.87
1719	441,121.79
1673	382,134.15
1277	49,359.51
217	701,959.11
$\Sigma x = 6329$	$\Sigma(x-\bar{x})^2 = 2,028,672.84$

$$\bar{x} = \frac{6329}{6} = 1054.83$$

$$s^2 = \frac{\Sigma(x-\bar{x})^2}{n-1} = \frac{2,028,672.84}{5} = 405,734.57$$

$$s = \sqrt{s^2} = \sqrt{405,734.57} = 636.97$$

The sample variance is 405,734.57 and the sample standard deviation is 636.97.

Computational Formulas for Variance and Standard Deviation

An alternative method of computing variance and standard deviation, sometimes referred to as the computational method or shortcut method, is available. Algebraically,

$$\Sigma(x-\mu)^2 = \Sigma x^2 - \frac{(\Sigma x)^2}{N}$$

and

$$\Sigma(x-\bar{x})^2 = \Sigma x^2 - \frac{(\Sigma x)^2}{n}$$

Substituting these equivalent expressions into the original formulas for variance and standard deviation yields the following computational formulas.

COMPUTATIONAL FORMULA FOR POPULATION VARIANCE AND STANDARD DEVIATION	$\sigma^2 = \dfrac{\Sigma x^2 - \dfrac{(\Sigma x)^2}{N}}{N}$ $\sigma = \sqrt{\sigma^2}$

COMPUTATIONAL FORMULA FOR SAMPLE VARIANCE AND STANDARD DEVIATION	$s^2 = \dfrac{\Sigma x^2 - \dfrac{(\Sigma x)^2}{n}}{n-1}$ $s = \sqrt{s^2}$

These computational formulas utilize the sum of the x values and the sum of the x^2 values instead of the difference between the mean and each value and computed deviations. In the precalculator/computer era, this method usually was faster and easier than using the original formulas.

For situations in which the mean is already computed or is given, alternative forms of these formulas are

$$\sigma^2 = \frac{\Sigma x^2 - N\mu^2}{N}$$

$$s^2 = \frac{\Sigma x^2 - n(\bar{x})^2}{n-1}$$

TABLE 3.5

Computational Formula Calculations of Variance and Standard Deviation for Computer Production Data

x	x^2
5	25
9	81
16	256
17	289
18	324
$\Sigma x = 65$	$\Sigma x^2 = 975$

$$\sigma^2 = \frac{975 - \dfrac{(65)^2}{5}}{5} = \frac{975 - 845}{5} = \frac{130}{5} = 26$$

$$\sigma = \sqrt{26} = 5.1$$

Using the computational method, the owner of the start-up computer production company can compute a population variance and standard deviation for the production data, as shown in Table 3.5. (Compare these results with those in Table 3.4.)

DEMONSTRATION PROBLEM 3.6

The effectiveness of district attorneys can be measured by several variables, including the number of convictions per month, the number of cases handled per month, and the total number of years of conviction per month. A researcher uses a sample of five district attorneys in a city and determines the total number of years of conviction that each attorney won against defendants during the past month, as reported in the first column in the following tabulations. Compute the mean absolute deviation, the variance, and the standard deviation for these figures.

Solution

The researcher computes the mean absolute deviation, the variance, and the standard deviation for these data in the following manner.

x	$\lvert x - \bar{x} \rvert$	$(x - \bar{x})^2$
55	41	1,681
100	4	16
125	29	841
140	44	1,936
60	36	1,296
$\Sigma x = 480$	$\Sigma \lvert x - \bar{x} \rvert = 154$	$\Sigma(x - \bar{x})^2 = 5,770$

$$\bar{x} = \frac{\Sigma x}{n} = \frac{480}{5} = 96$$

$$MAD = \frac{154}{5} = 30.8$$

$$s^2 = \frac{5,770}{4} = 1,442.5 \text{ and } s = \sqrt{s^2} = 37.98$$

She then uses computational formulas to solve for s^2 and s and compares the results.

x	x^2
55	3,025
100	10,000
125	15,625
140	19,600
60	3,600
$\Sigma x = 480$	$\Sigma x^2 = 51,850$

$$s^2 = \frac{51,850 - \dfrac{(480)^2}{5}}{4} = \frac{51,850 - 46,080}{4} = \frac{5,770}{4} = 1,442.5$$

$$s = \sqrt{1,442.5} = 37.98$$

The results are the same. The sample standard deviation obtained by both methods is 37.98, or 38, years.

z Scores

A **z score** represents the number of standard deviations a value (x) is above or below the mean of a set of numbers when the data are normally distributed. Using z scores allows translation of a value's raw distance from the mean into units of standard deviations.

z SCORE	$$z = \frac{x - \mu}{\sigma}$$

For samples,

$$z = \frac{x - \bar{x}}{s}$$

If a z score is negative, the raw value (x) is below the mean. If the z score is positive, the raw value (x) is above the mean.

For example, for a data set that is normally distributed with a mean of 50 and a standard deviation of 10, suppose a statistician wants to determine the z score for a value of 70. This value ($x = 70$) is 20 units above the mean, so the z value is

$$z = \frac{70 - 50}{10} = +2.00$$

This z score signifies that the raw score of 70 is two standard deviations above the mean. How is this z score interpreted? The empirical rule states that 95% of all values are within two standard deviations of the mean if the data are approximately normally distributed. Figure 3.7 shows that because the value of 70 is two standard deviations above the mean ($z = +2.00$) 95% of the values are between 70 and the value ($x = 30$), that is two standard deviations below the mean, or $z = (30 - 50)/10 = -2.00$. Because 5% of the values are outside the range of two standard deviations from the mean and the normal distribution is symmetrical, 2½% (½ of the 5%) are below the value of 30. Thus 97½% of the values are below the value of 70. Because a z score is the number of standard deviations an individual data value is from the mean, the empirical rule can be restated in terms of z scores.

Between $z = -1.00$ and $z = +1.00$ are approximately 68% of the values.
Between $z = -2.00$ and $z = +2.00$ are approximately 95% of the values.
Between $z = -3.00$ and $z = +3.00$ are approximately 99.7% of the values.

The topic of z scores is discussed more extensively in Chapter 6.

Coefficient of Variation

The **coefficient of variation** is a statistic that is *the ratio of the standard deviation to the mean expressed in percentage* and is denoted CV.

COEFFICIENT OF VARIATION	$$CV = \frac{\sigma}{\mu}(100)$$

The coefficient of variation essentially is a relative comparison of a standard deviation to its mean. The coefficient of variation can be useful in comparing standard deviations that have been computed from data with different means.

Suppose five weeks of average prices for stock A are 57, 68, 64, 71, and 62. To compute a coefficient of variation for these prices, first determine the mean and standard deviation: $\mu = 64.40$ and $\sigma = 4.84$. The coefficient of variation is:

$$CV_A = \frac{\sigma_A}{\mu_A}(100) = \frac{4.84}{64.40}(100) = .075 = 7.5\%$$

FIGURE 3.7

Percentage Breakdown of
Scores Two Standard
Deviations from the Mean

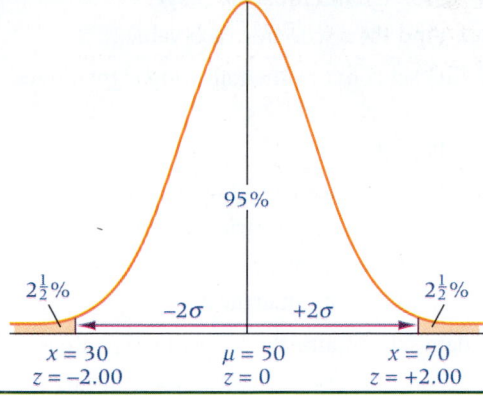

The standard deviation is 7.5% of the mean.

Sometimes financial investors use the coefficient of variation or the standard deviation or both as measures of risk. Imagine a stock with a price that never changes. An investor bears no risk of losing money from the price going down because no variability occurs in the price. Suppose, in contrast, that the price of the stock fluctuates wildly. An investor who buys at a low price and sells for a high price can make a nice profit. However, if the price drops below what the investor buys it for, the stock owner is subject to a potential loss. The greater the variability is, the more the potential for loss. Hence, investors use measures of variability such as standard deviation or coefficient of variation to determine the risk of a stock. What does the coefficient of variation tell us about the risk of a stock that the standard deviation does not?

Suppose the average prices for a second stock, B, over these same five weeks are 12, 17, 8, 15, and 13. The mean for stock B is 13.00 with a standard deviation of 3.03. The coefficient of variation can be computed for stock B as:

$$CV_B = \frac{\sigma_B}{\mu_B}(100) = \frac{3.03}{13}(100) = .233 = 23.3\%$$

The standard deviation for stock B is 23.3% of the mean.

With the standard deviation as the measure of risk, stock A is more risky over this period of time because it has a larger standard deviation. However, the average price of stock A is almost five times as much as that of stock B. Relative to the amount invested in stock A, the standard deviation of $4.84 may not represent as much risk as the standard deviation of $3.03 for stock B, which has an average price of only $13.00. The coefficient of variation reveals the risk of a stock in terms of the size of standard deviation relative to the size of the mean (in percentage). Stock B has a coefficient of variation that is nearly three times as much as the coefficient of variation for stock A. Using coefficient of variation as a measure of risk indicates that stock B is riskier.

The choice of whether to use a coefficient of variation or raw standard deviations to compare multiple standard deviations is a matter of preference. The coefficient of variation also provides an optional method of interpreting the value of a standard deviation.

3.2 PROBLEMS

3.11 A data set contains the following seven values.

6   2   4   9   1   3   5

a. Find the range.

b. Find the mean absolute deviation.

c. Find the population variance.

d. Find the population standard deviation.

    e. Find the interquartile range.

    f. Find the z score for each value.

3.12 A data set contains the following eight values.

4	3	0	5	2	9	4	5

    a. Find the range.

    b. Find the mean absolute deviation.

    c. Find the sample variance.

    d. Find the sample standard deviation.

    e. Find the interquartile range.

3.13 A data set contains the following six values.

12	23	19	26	24	23

    a. Find the population standard deviation using the formula containing the mean (the original formula).

    b. Find the population standard deviation using the computational formula.

    c. Compare the results. Which formula was faster to use? Which formula do you prefer? Why do you think the computational formula is sometimes referred to as the "shortcut" formula?

3.14 Use your calculator or computer to find the sample variance and sample standard deviation for the following data.

57	88	68	43	93
63	51	37	77	83
66	60	38	52	28
34	52	60	57	29
92	37	38	17	67

3.15 Use your calculator or computer to find the population variance and population standard deviation for the following data.

123	090	546	378
392	280	179	601
572	953	749	075
303	468	531	646

3.16 Determine the interquartile range on the following data.

44	18	39	40	59
46	59	37	15	73
23	19	90	58	35
82	14	38	27	24
71	25	39	84	70

3.17 According to Chebyshev's theorem, at least what proportion of the data will be within $\mu \pm k\sigma$ for each value of k?

    a. $k = 2$

    b. $k = 2.5$

    c. $k = 1.6$

    d. $k = 3.2$

3.18 Compare the variability of the following two sets of data by using both the standard deviation and the coefficient of variation.

Data Set 1	Data Set 2
49	159
82	121
77	138
54	152

3.19 A sample of 12 small accounting firms reveals the following numbers of professionals per office.

7	10	9	14	11	8
5	12	8	3	13	6

a. Determine the mean absolute deviation.

b. Determine the variance.

c. Determine the standard deviation.

d. Determine the interquartile range.

e. What is the z score for the firm that has six professionals?

f. What is the coefficient of variation for this sample?

3.20 The following, supplied by Marketing Intelligence Service, is a list of the companies with the most new products in a recent year.

Company	Number of New Products
Avon Products	768
L'Oreal	429
Unilever U.S.	323
Revlon	306
Garden Botanika	286
Philip Morris	262
Procter & Gamble	215
Nestlé	172
Paradiso	162
Tsumura International	148
Grand Metropolitan	145

a. Find the range.

b. Find the mean absolute deviation.

c. Find the population variance.

d. Find the population standard deviation.

e. Find the interquartile range.

f. Find the z score for Nestlé.

g. Find the coefficient of variation.

3.21 A distribution of numbers is approximately bell shaped. If the mean of the numbers is 125 and the standard deviation is 12, between what two numbers would approximately 68% of the values fall? Between what two numbers would 95% of the values fall? Between what two values would 99.7% of the values fall?

3.22 Some numbers are not normally distributed. If the mean of the numbers is 38 and the standard deviation is 6, what proportion of values would fall between 26 and 50? What proportion of values would fall between 14 and 62? Between what two values would 89% of the values fall?

3.23 According to Chebyshev's theorem, how many standard deviations from the mean would include at least 80% of the values?

3.24 The time needed to assemble a particular piece of furniture with experience is normally distributed with a mean time of 43 minutes. If 68% of the assembly times are between 40 and 46 minutes, what is the value of the standard deviation? Suppose 99.7% of the assembly times are between 35 and 51 minutes and the mean is still 43 minutes. What would the value of the standard deviation be now? Suppose the time needed to assemble another piece of furniture is not normally distributed and that the mean assembly time is 28 minutes. What is the value of the standard deviation if at least 77% of the assembly times are between 24 and 32 minutes?

3.25 Environmentalists are concerned about emissions of sulfur dioxide into the air. The average number of days per year in which sulfur dioxide levels exceed 150 milligrams per cubic meter in Milan, Italy, is 29. The number of days per year in which emission limits are exceeded is normally distributed with a standard deviation of 4.0 days. What percentage of the years would average between 21 and 37 days of excess emissions of sulfur dioxide? What percentage of the years would exceed 37 days? What percentage of the years would exceed 41 days? In what percentage of the years would there be fewer than 25 days with excess sulfur dioxide emissions?

3.26 The *Runzheimer Guide* publishes a list of the most inexpensive cities in the world for the business traveler. Listed are the 10 most inexpensive cities with their respective per diem costs. Use this list to calculate the *z* scores for Bordeaux, Montreal, Edmonton, and Hamilton. Treat this list as a sample.

City	Per Diem ($)
Hamilton, Ontario	97
London, Ontario	109
Edmonton, Alberta	111
Jakarta, Indonesia	118
Ottawa	120
Montreal	130
Halifax, Nova Scotia	132
Winnipeg, Manitoba	133
Bordeaux, France	137
Bangkok, Thailand	137

3.3 MEASURES OF CENTRAL TENDENCY AND VARIABILITY: GROUPED DATA

Grouped data do not provide information about individual values. Hence, measures of central tendency and variability for grouped data must be computed differently from those for ungrouped or raw data.

Measures of Central Tendency

Two measures of central tendency are presented here for grouped data: the mean and the mode.

Mean

For ungrouped data, the mean is computed by summing the data values and dividing by the number of values. With grouped data, the specific values are unknown. What can be used to represent the data values? The midpoint of each class interval is used to represent all the values in a class interval. This midpoint is weighted by the frequency of values in that class interval. The mean for grouped data is then computed by summing the products of the class midpoint and the class frequency for each class and dividing that sum by the total number of frequencies. The formula for the mean of grouped data follows.

MEAN OF GROUPED DATA

$$\mu_{grouped} = \frac{\sum fM}{N} = \frac{\sum fM}{\sum f} = \frac{f_1 M_1 + f_2 M_2 + \cdots + f_i M_i}{f_1 + f_2 + \cdots + f_i}$$

where

i = the number of classes
f = class frequency
N = total frequencies

TABLE 3.6
Frequency Distribution of the Unemployment Rates of France

Class Interval	Frequency
1–under 3	16
3–under 5	2
5–under 7	4
7–under 9	3
9–under 11	9
11–under 13	6

Table 3.6 gives the frequency distribution of the unemployment rates of France from Table 2.2. To find the mean of these data, we need Σf and ΣfM. The value of Σf can be determined by summing the values in the frequency column. To calculate ΣfM, we must first determine the values of M, or the class midpoints. Next we multiply each of these class midpoints by the frequency in that class interval, f, resulting in fM. Summing these values of fM yields the value of ΣfM.

Table 3.7 contains the calculations needed to determine the group mean. The group mean for the unemployment data is 6.25. Remember that because each class interval was represented by its class midpoint rather than by actual values, the group mean is only approximate.

Mode

The *mode* for grouped data is *the class midpoint of the modal class. The modal class is the class interval with the greatest frequency.* Using the data from Table 3.7, the 1–under 3 class interval contains the greatest frequency, 16. Thus, the modal class is 1–under 3. The class midpoint of this modal class is 2. Therefore, the mode for the frequency distribution shown in Table 3.7 is 2. The modal unemployment rate is 2%.

Measures of Variability

Two measures of variability for grouped data are presented here: the variance and the standard deviation. Again, the standard deviation is the square root of the variance. Both measures have original and computational formulas.

FORMULAS FOR POPULATION VARIANCE AND STANDARD DEVIATION OF GROUPED DATA

Original Formula	Computational Version
$\sigma^2 = \dfrac{\sum f(M - \mu)^2}{N}$	$\sigma^2 = \dfrac{\sum fM^2 - \dfrac{(\sum fM)^2}{N}}{N}$
$\sigma = \sqrt{\sigma^2}$	

where:

f = frequency
M = class midpoint
N = Σf, or total frequencies of the population
μ = grouped mean for the population

TABLE 3.7
Calculation of Grouped Mean

Class Interval	Frequency (f)	Class Midpoint (M)	fM
1–under 3	16	2	32
3–under 5	2	4	8
5–under 7	4	6	24
7–under 9	3	8	24
9–under 11	9	10	90
11–under 13	6	12	72
	$\Sigma f = N = 40$		$\Sigma fM = 250$

$$\mu = \frac{\sum fM}{\sum f} = \frac{250}{40} = 6.25$$

TABLE 3.8

Calculating Grouped Variance
and Standard Deviation with
the Original Formula

Class Interval	f	M	fM	$M-\mu$	$(M-\mu)^2$	$f(M-\mu)^2$
1–under 3	16	2	32	−4.25	18.063	289.008
3–under 5	2	4	8	−2.25	5.063	10.126
5–under 7	4	6	24	−0.25	0.063	0.252
7–under 9	3	8	24	1.75	3.063	9.189
9–under 11	9	10	90	3.75	14.063	126.567
11–under 13	6	12	72	5.75	33.063	198.378
	$\Sigma f = N = 40$		$\Sigma fM = 250$			$\Sigma f(M-\mu)^2 = 633.520$

$$\mu = \frac{\Sigma fM}{\Sigma f} = \frac{250}{40} = 6.25$$

$$\sigma^2 = \frac{\Sigma f(M-\mu)^2}{N} = \frac{633.520}{40} = 15.838$$

$$\sigma = \sqrt{15.838} = 3.980$$

TABLE 3.9

Calculating Grouped Variance
and Standard Deviation with
the Computational Formula

Class Interval	f	M	fM	fM^2
1–under 3	16	2	32	64
3–under 5	2	4	8	32
5–under 7	4	6	24	144
7–under 9	3	8	24	192
9–under 11	9	10	90	900
11–under 13	6	12	72	864
	$f = N = 40$		$fM = 250$	$fM^2 = 2196$

$$\sigma^2 = \frac{\Sigma fM^2 - \dfrac{(\Sigma fM)^2}{n}}{n} = \frac{2196 - \dfrac{(250)^2}{40}}{40} = \frac{2196 - 1562.5}{40} = \frac{633.5}{40} = 15.838$$

$$\sigma = \sqrt{15.838} = 3.980$$

FORMULAS FOR SAMPLE VARIANCE AND STANDARD DEVIATION OF GROUPED DATA

Original Formula

$$s^2 = \frac{\Sigma f(M-\bar{x})^2}{n-1}$$

$$s = \sqrt{s^2}$$

Computational Version

$$s^2 = \frac{\Sigma fM^2 - \dfrac{(\Sigma fM)^2}{n}}{n-1}$$

where:

f = frequency
M = class midpoint
N = Σf, or total of the frequencies of the population
μ = grouped mean for the sample

For example, let us calculate the variance and standard deviation of the French unemployment data grouped as a frequency distribution in Table 3.6. If the data are treated as a population, the computations are as follows.

For the original formula, the computations are given in Table 3.8. The method of determining σ^2 and σ by using the computational formula is shown in Table 3.9. In either case, the variance of the unemployment data is 15.838 (squared percent) and the standard deviation is 3.98%. As with the computation of the grouped mean, the class midpoint is used to represent all values in a class interval. This approach may or may not be appropriate, depending on whether the average value in a class is at the midpoint. If this situation does not occur, then the variance and the standard deviation are only approximations. Because grouped statistics are usually computed without knowledge of the actual data, the statistics computed potentially may be only approximations.

DEMONSTRATION PROBLEM 3.7

Compute the mean, mode, variance, and standard deviation on the following sample data.

Class Interval	Frequency
10–under 15	6
15–under 20	22
20–under 25	35
25–under 30	29
30–under 35	16
35–under 40	8
40–under 45	4
45–under 50	2

Solution

The mean is computed as follows.

Class	f	M	fM
10–under 15	6	12.5	75.0
15–under 20	22	17.5	385.0
20–under 25	35	22.5	787.5
25–under 30	29	27.5	797.5
30–under 35	16	32.5	520.0
35–under 40	8	37.5	300.0
40–under 45	4	42.5	170.0
45–under 50	2	47.5	95.0
	$\Sigma f = n = 122$		$\Sigma fM = 3130.0$

$$\bar{x} = \frac{\Sigma fM}{\Sigma f} = \frac{3130}{122} = 25.66$$

The grouped mean is 25.66.

The grouped mode can be determined by finding the class midpoint of the class interval with the greatest frequency. The class with the greatest frequency is 20–under 25 with a frequency of 35. The midpoint of this class is 22.5, which is the grouped mode.

The variance and standard deviation can be found as shown next. First, use the original formula.

Class	f	M	$M - \bar{x}$	$(M - \bar{x})^2$	$f(M - \bar{x})^2$
10–under 15	6	12.5	−13.16	173.19	1039.14
15–under 20	22	17.5	−8.16	66.59	1464.98
20–under 25	35	22.5	−3.16	9.99	349.65
25–under 30	29	27.5	1.84	3.39	98.31
30–under 35	16	32.5	6.84	46.79	748.64
35–under 40	8	37.5	11.84	140.19	1121.52
40–under 45	4	42.5	16.84	283.59	1134.36
45–under 50	2	47.5	21.84	476.99	953.98
	$\Sigma f = n = 122$				$\Sigma f(M - \bar{x})^2 = 6910.58$

$$s^2 = \frac{\Sigma f(M - \bar{x})^2}{n-1} = \frac{6910.58}{121} = 57.11$$

$$s = \sqrt{57.11} = 7.56$$

Next, use the computational formula.

Class	f	M	fM	fM²
10–under 15	6	12.5	75.0	937.50
15–under 20	22	17.5	385.0	6,737.50
20–under 25	35	22.5	787.5	17,718.75
25–under 30	29	27.5	797.5	21,931.25
30–under 35	16	32.5	520.0	16,900.00
35–under 40	8	37.5	300.0	11,250.00
40–under 45	4	42.5	170.0	7,225.00
45–under 50	2	47.5	95.0	4,512.50
	$\Sigma f = n = 122$		$\Sigma fM = 3{,}130.0$	$\Sigma fM^2 = 87{,}212.50$

$$s^2 = \frac{\Sigma fM^2 - \dfrac{\left(\Sigma fM\right)^2}{n}}{n-1} = \frac{87{,}212.5 - \dfrac{(3{,}130)^2}{122}}{121} = \frac{6{,}910.04}{121} = 57.11$$

$$s = \sqrt{57.11} = 7.56$$

The sample variance is 57.11 and the standard deviation is 7.56.

3.3 PROBLEMS

3.27 Compute the mean and the mode for the following data.

Class	f
0–under 2	39
2–under 4	27
4–under 6	16
6–under 8	15
8–under 10	10
10–under 12	8
12–under 14	6

3.28 Compute the mean and the mode for the following data.

Class	f
1.2–under 1.6	220
1.6–under 2.0	150
2.0–under 2.4	90
2.4–under 2.8	110
2.8–under 3.2	280

3.29 Determine the population variance and standard deviation for the following data by using the original formula.

Class	f
20–under 30	7
30–under 40	11
40–under 50	18
50–under 60	13
60–under 70	6
70–under 80	4

3.30 Determine the sample variance and standard deviation for the following data by using the computational formula.

Class	f
5–under 9	20
9–under 13	18
13–under 17	8
17–under 21	6
21–under 25	2

3.31 A random sample of voters in Nashville, Tennessee, is classified by age group, as shown by the following data.

Age Group	Frequency
18–under 24	17
24–under 30	22
30–under 36	26
36–under 42	35
42–under 48	33
48–under 54	30
54–under 60	32
60–under 66	21
66–under 72	15

a. Calculate the mean of the data.

b. Calculate the mode.

c. Calculate the variance.

d. Calculate the standard deviation.

3.32 The following data represent the number of appointments made per 15-minute interval by telephone solicitation for a lawn-care company.

Number of Appointments	Frequency of Occurrence
0–under 1	31
1–under 2	57
2–under 3	26
3–under 4	14
4–under 5	6
5–under 6	3

a. Calculate the mean of the data.

b. Calculate the mode.

c. Calculate the variance.

d. Calculate the standard deviation.

3.33 The Air Transport Association of America publishes figures on the busiest airports in the United States. The following frequency distribution has been constructed from these figures for a recent year.

Number of Passengers Arriving and Departing (millions)	Number of Airports
20–under 30	8
30–under 40	7
40–under 50	1
50–under 60	0
60–under 70	3
70–under 80	1

    a. Calculate the mean of these data.

    b. Calculate the mode.

    c. Calculate the variance.

    d. Calculate the standard deviation.

3.34 The frequency distribution shown represents the number of farms per state for 49 of the 50 states, based on information from the U.S. Department of Agriculture. Determine the average number of farms per state from these data. The mean computed from the original ungrouped data was 37,816 and the standard deviation was 29,341. How do your answers for these grouped data compare? Why might they differ?

Number of Farms per State	f
0–under 20,000	16
20,000–under 40,000	11
40,000–under 60,000	10
60,000–under 80,000	6
80,000–under 100,000	5
100,000–under 120,000	1

3.4 MEASURES OF SHAPE

Measures of shape are *tools that can be used to describe the shape of a distribution of data.* In this section, we examine two measures of shape, skewness and kurtosis. We also look at box and whisker plots.

Skewness

A distribution of data in which the right half is a mirror image of the left half is said to be *symmetrical*. One example of a symmetrical distribution is the normal distribution, or bell curve, which is presented in more detail in Chapter 6.

    Skewness is when *a distribution is asymmetrical or lacks symmetry.* The distribution in Figure 3.8 has no skewness because it is symmetric. Figure 3.9 shows a distribution that is skewed left, or negatively skewed, and Figure 3.10 shows a distribution that is skewed right, or positively skewed.

    The skewed portion is the long, thin part of the curve. Many researchers use skewed distribution to denote that the data are sparse at one end of the distribution and piled up at the other end. Instructors sometimes refer to a grade distribution as skewed, meaning that few students scored at one end of the grading scale, and many students scored at the other end.

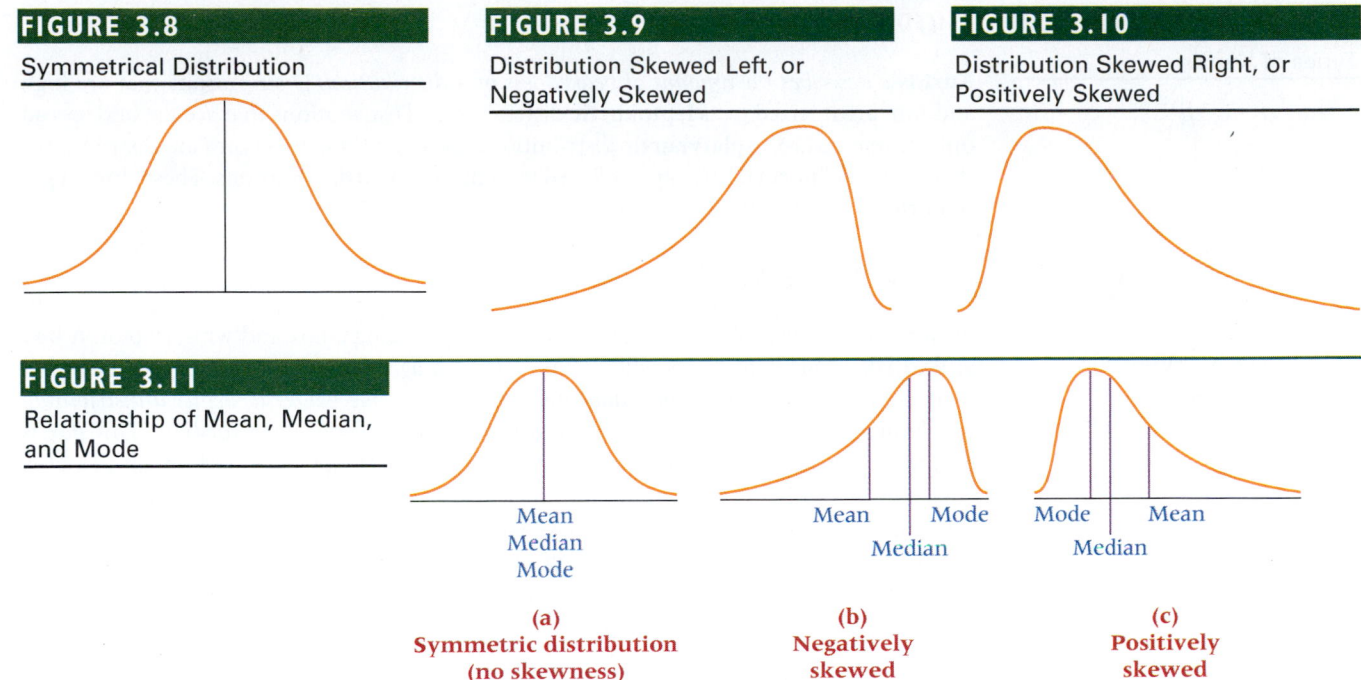

FIGURE 3.8

Symmetrical Distribution

FIGURE 3.9

Distribution Skewed Left, or Negatively Skewed

FIGURE 3.10

Distribution Skewed Right, or Positively Skewed

FIGURE 3.11

Relationship of Mean, Median, and Mode

| (a) | (b) | (c) |
| Symmetric distribution (no skewness) | Negatively skewed | Positively skewed |

Skewness and the Relationship of the Mean, Median, and Mode

The concept of skewness helps to understand the relationship of the mean, median, and mode. In a unimodal distribution (distribution with a single peak or mode) that is skewed, the mode is the apex (high point) of the curve and the median is the middle value. The mean tends to be located toward the tail of the distribution, because the mean is affected by all values, including the extreme ones. A bell-shaped or normal distribution with the mean, median, and mode all at the center of the distribution has no skewness. Figure 3.11 displays the relationship of the mean, median, and mode for different types of skewness.

Coefficient of Skewness

Statistician Karl Pearson is credited with developing at least two coefficients of skewness that can be used to determine the degree of skewness in a distribution. We present one of these coefficients here, referred to as a Pearsonian **coefficient of skewness.** This coefficient *compares the mean and median in light of the magnitude of the standard deviation.* Note that if the distribution is symmetrical, the mean and median are the same value and hence the coefficient of skewness is equal to zero.

COEFFICIENT OF SKEWNESS	$$S_k = \frac{3(\mu - M_d)}{\sigma}$$

where

S_k = coefficient of skewness
M_d = median

Suppose, for example, that a distribution has a mean of 29, a median of 26, and a standard deviation of 12.3. The coefficient of skewness is computed as

$$S_k = \frac{3(29 - 26)}{12.3} = +0.73$$

Because the value of S_k is positive, the distribution is positively skewed. If the value of S_k is negative, the distribution is negatively skewed. The greater the magnitude of S_k, the more skewed is the distribution.

FIGURE 3.12

Types of Kurtosis

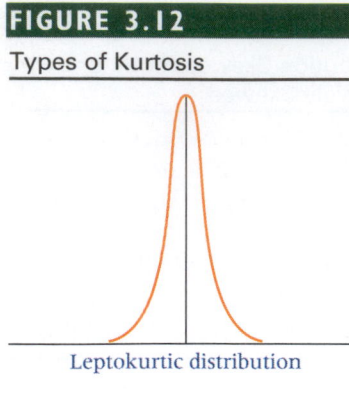

Leptokurtic distribution

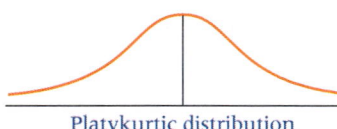

Platykurtic distribution

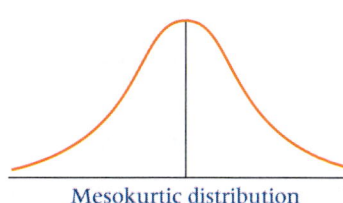

Mesokurtic distribution

Kurtosis

Kurtosis *describes the amount of peakedness of a distribution.* Distributions that are high and thin are referred to as **leptokurtic** distributions. Distributions that are flat and spread out are referred to as **platykurtic** distributions. Between these two types are distributions that are more "normal" in shape, referred to as **mesokurtic** distributions. These three types of kurtosis are illustrated in Figure 3.12.

Box and Whisker Plots

Another way to describe a distribution of data is by using a box and whisker plot. A **box and whisker plot**, sometimes called a *box plot*, is *a diagram that utilizes the upper and lower quartiles along with the median and the two most extreme values to depict a distribution graphically.* The plot is constructed by using a box to enclose the median. This *box* is extended outward from the median along a continuum to the lower and upper quartiles, enclosing not only the median but also the middle 50% of the data. From the lower and upper quartiles, lines referred to as *whiskers* are extended out from the box toward the outermost data values. The box and whisker plot is determined from five specific numbers.

1. The median (Q_2).
2. The lower quartile (Q_1).
3. The upper quartile (Q_3).
4. The smallest value in the distribution.
5. The largest value in the distribution.

The box of the plot is determined by locating the median and the lower and upper quartiles on a continuum. A box is drawn around the median with the lower and upper quartiles (Q_1 and Q_3) as the box endpoints. These box endpoints (Q_1 and Q_3) are referred to as the *hinges* of the box.

Next the value of the interquartile range (IQR) is computed by $Q_3 - Q_1$. The interquartile range includes the middle 50% of the data and should equal the length of the box. However, here the interquartile range is used outside of the box also. At a distance of $1.5 \cdot$ IQR outward from the lower and upper quartiles are what are referred to as *inner fences.* A *whisker*, a line segment, is drawn from the lower hinge of the box outward to the smallest data value. A second whisker is drawn from the upper hinge of the box outward to the largest data value. The inner fences are established as follows.

$$Q_1 - 1.5 \cdot \text{IQR}$$
$$Q_3 + 1.5 \cdot \text{IQR}$$

If data fall beyond the inner fences, then *outer* fences can be constructed:

$$Q_1 - 3.0 \cdot \text{IQR}$$
$$Q_3 + 3.0 \cdot \text{IQR}$$

Figure 3.13 shows the features of a box and whisker plot.

Data values outside the mainstream of values in a distribution are viewed as *outliers.* Outliers can be merely the more extreme values of a data set. However, sometimes outliers occur due to measurement or recording errors. Other times they are values so unlike the other values that they should not be considered in the same analysis as the rest of the distribution. Values in the data distribution that are outside the inner fences but within the outer fences are referred to as *mild outliers.* Values that are outside the outer fences are called

FIGURE 3.13

Box and Whisker Plot

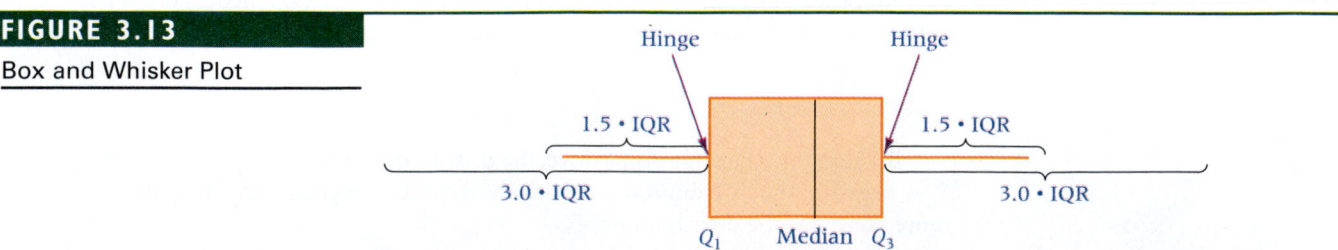

extreme outliers. Thus, one of the main uses of a box and whisker plot is to identify outliers. In some computer-produced box and whisker plots, the whiskers are drawn to the largest and smallest data values within the inner fences. An asterisk is then printed for each data value located between the inner and outer fences to indicate a mild outlier. Values outside the outer fences are indicated by a zero on the graph. These values are extreme outliers.

Another use of box and whisker plots is to determine whether a distribution is skewed. The location of the median in the box can relate information about the skewness of the middle 50% of the data. If the median is located on the right side of the box, then the middle 50% are skewed to the left. If the median is located on the left side of the box, then the middle 50% are skewed to the right. By examining the length of the whiskers on each side of the box, a business researcher can make a judgment about the skewness of the outer values. If the longest whisker is to the right of the box, then the outer data are skewed to the right and vice versa. We shall use the data given in Table 3.10 to construct a box and whisker plot.

After organizing the data into an ordered array, as shown in Table 3.11, it is relatively easy to determine the values of the lower quartile (Q_1), the median, and the upper quartile (Q_3). From these, the value of the interquartile range can be computed.

The hinges of the box are located at the lower and upper quartiles, 69 and 80.5. The median is located within the box at distances of 4 from the lower quartile and 6.5 from the upper quartile. The distribution of the middle 50% of the data is skewed right, because the median is nearer to the lower or left hinge. The inner fence is constructed by

$$Q_1 - 1.5 \cdot IQR = 69 - 1.5(11.5) = 69 - 17.25 = 51.75$$

and

$$Q_3 + 1.5 \cdot IQR = 80.5 + 1.5(11.5) = 80.5 + 17.25 = 97.75$$

The whiskers are constructed by drawing a line segment from the lower hinge outward to the smallest data value and a line segment from the upper hinge outward to the largest data value. An examination of the data reveals that no data values in this set of numbers are outside the inner fence. The whiskers are constructed outward to the lowest value, which is 62, and to the highest value, which is 87.

To construct an outer fence, we calculate $Q_1 - 3 \cdot IQR$ and $Q_3 + 3 \cdot IQR$, as follows.

$$Q_1 - 3 \cdot IQR = 69 - 3(11.5) = 69 - 34.5 = 34.5$$
$$Q_3 + 3 \cdot IQR = 80.5 + 3(11.5) = 80.5 + 34.5 = 115.0$$

Figure 3.14 is the MINITAB computer printout for this box and whisker plot.

TABLE 3.10

Data for Box and Whisker Plot

71	87	82	64	72	75	81	69
76	79	65	68	80	73	85	71
70	79	63	62	81	84	77	73
82	74	74	73	84	72	81	65
74	62	64	68	73	82	69	71

TABLE 3.11

Data in Ordered Array with Quartiles and Median

87	85	84	84	82	82	82	81	81	81
80	79	79	77	76	75	74	74	74	73
73	73	73	72	72	71	71	71	70	69
69	68	68	65	65	64	64	63	62	62

$$Q_1 = 69$$
$$Q_2 = \text{median} = 73$$
$$Q_3 = 80.5$$
$$IQR = Q_3 - Q_1 = 80.5 - 69 = 11.5$$

FIGURE 3.14

MINITAB Box and Whisker Plot

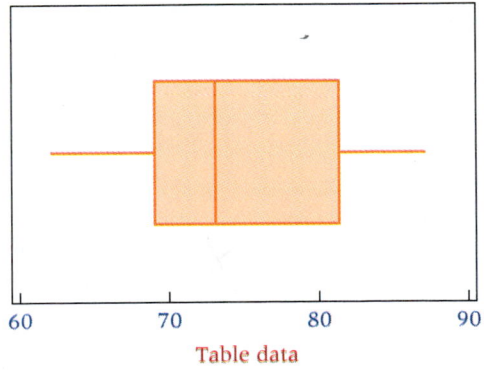

Table data

3.4 PROBLEMS

3.35   On a certain day the average closing price of a group of stocks on the New York Stock Exchange is $35 (to the nearest dollar). If the median value is $33 and the mode is $21, is the distribution of these stock prices skewed? If so, how?

3.36   A local hotel offers ballroom dancing on Friday nights. A researcher observes the customers and estimates their ages. Discuss the skewness of the distribution of ages if the mean age is 51, the median age is 54, and the modal age is 59.

3.37   The sales volumes for the top real estate brokerage firms in the United States for a recent year were analyzed using descriptive statistics. The mean annual dollar volume for these firms was $5.51 billion, the median was $3.19 billion, and the standard deviation was $9.59 billion. Compute the value of the Pearsonian coefficient of skewness and discuss the meaning of it. Is the distribution skewed? If so, to what extent?

3.38   Suppose the following data are the ages of Internet users obtained from a sample. Use these data to compute a Pearsonian coefficient of skewness. What is the meaning of the coefficient?

41	15	31	25	24
23	21	22	22	18
30	20	19	19	16
23	27	38	34	24
19	20	29	17	23

3.39   Construct a box and whisker plot on the following data. Do the data contain any outliers? Is the distribution of data skewed?

540	690	503	558	490	609
379	601	559	495	562	580
510	623	477	574	588	497
527	570	495	590	602	541

3.40   Suppose a consumer group asked 18 consumers to keep a yearly log of their shopping practices and that the following data represent the number of coupons used by each consumer over the yearly period. Use the data to construct a box and whisker plot. List the median, Q_1, Q_3, the endpoints for the inner fences, and the endpoints for the outer fences. Discuss the skewness of the distribution of these data and point out any outliers.

81	68	70	100	94	47	66	70	82
110	105	60	21	70	66	90	78	85

3.5 MEASURES OF ASSOCIATION

Measures of association are statistics that yield information about the relatedness of numerical variables. In this chapter, we discuss only one measure of association, correlation, and do so only for two numerical variables.

Correlation

Correlation is *a measure of the degree of relatedness of variables.* It can help a business researcher determine, for example, whether the stocks of two airlines rise and fall in any related manner. Logically, the prices of two stocks in the same industry should be related. For a sample of pairs of data, correlation analysis can yield a numerical value that represents the degree of relatedness of the two stock prices over time. In the transportation industry, is a correlation evident between the price of transportation and the weight of the

TABLE 3.12

Data for the
Economics Example

Day	Interest Rate	Futures Index
1	7.43	221
2	7.48	222
3	8.00	226
4	7.75	225
5	7.60	224
6	7.63	223
7	7.68	223
8	7.67	226
9	7.59	226
10	8.07	235
11	8.03	233
12	8.00	241

object being shipped? Do price and distance show any correlation? How strong are the correlations? Pricing decisions can be based in part on shipment costs that are correlated with other variables. In economics and finance, how strong is the correlation between the producer price index and the unemployment rate? In retail sales, what variables are related to a particular store's sales? Are sales related to population density, number of competitors, size of the store, amount of advertising, or other variables?

Several measures of correlation are available, the selection of which depends mostly on the level of data being analyzed. Ideally, researchers would like to solve for ρ, the population coefficient of correlation. However, because researchers virtually always deal with sample data, this section introduces a widely used sample **coefficient of correlation,** r. This measure is applicable only if both variables being analyzed have at least an interval level of data. Chapter 17 presents a correlation measure that can be used when the data are ordinal.

The statistic r is the **Pearson product-moment correlation coefficient,** named after Karl Pearson (1857–1936), an English statistician who developed several coefficients of correlation along with other significant statistical concepts. The term r is a *measure of the linear correlation of two variables.* It is a number that ranges from −1 to 0 to +1, representing the strength of the relationship between the variables. An r value of +1 denotes a perfect positive relationship between two sets of numbers. An r value of −1 denotes a perfect negative correlation, which indicates an inverse relationship between two variables: as one variable gets larger, the other gets smaller. An r value of 0 means no linear relationship is present between the two variables.

PEARSON PRODUCT-MOMENT CORRELATION COEFFICIENT

$$r = \frac{\sum(x-\bar{x})(y-\bar{y})}{\sqrt{\sum(x-\bar{x})^2 \sum(y-\bar{y})^2}} = \frac{\sum xy - \frac{(\sum x \sum y)}{n}}{\sqrt{\left[\sum x^2 - \frac{(\sum x)^2}{n}\right]\left[\sum y^2 - \frac{(\sum y)^2}{n}\right]}}$$

Figure 3.15 depicts five different degrees of correlation: (a) represents strong negative correlation, (b) represents moderate negative correlation, (c) represents moderate positive correlation, (d) represents strong positive correlation, and (e) contains no correlation.

TABLE 3.13

Computation of r for the
Economics Example

Day	Interest x	Futures Index y	x^2	y^2	xy
1	7.43	221	55.205	48,841	1,642.03
2	7.48	222	55.950	49,284	1,660.56
3	8.00	226	64.000	51,076	1,808.00
4	7.75	225	60.063	50,625	1,743.75
5	7.60	224	57.760	50,176	1,702.40
6	7.63	223	58.217	49,729	1,701.49
7	7.68	223	58.982	49,729	1,712.64
8	7.67	226	58.829	51,076	1,733.42
9	7.59	226	57.608	51,076	1,715.34
10	8.07	235	65.125	55,225	1,896.45
11	8.03	233	64.481	54,289	1,870.99
12	8.00	241	64.000	58,081	1,928.00
	$\sum x = 92.93$	$\sum y = 2{,}725$	$\sum x^2 = 720.220$	$\sum y^2 = 619{,}207$	$\sum xy = 21{,}115.07$

$$r = \frac{(21{,}115.07) - \frac{(92.93)(2725)}{12}}{\sqrt{\left[(720.22) - \frac{(92.93)^2}{12}\right]\left[(619{,}207) - \frac{(2725)^2}{12}\right]}} = .815$$

FIGURE 3.15 Five Correlations

(a) Strong Negative Correlation (r = −.933)

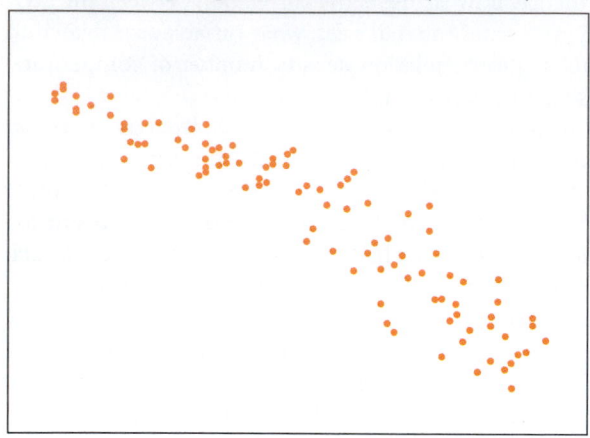

(b) Moderate Negative Correlation (r = −.674)

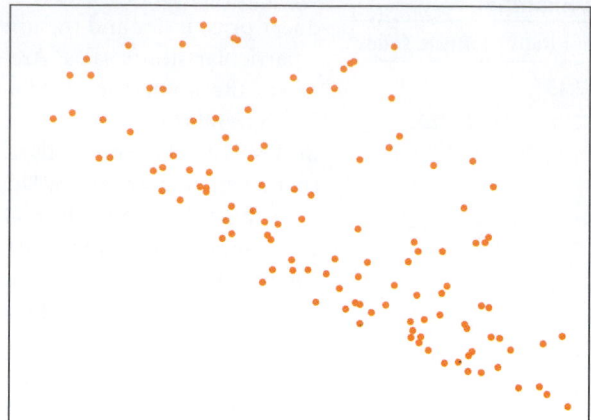

(c) Moderate Positive Correlation (r = .518)

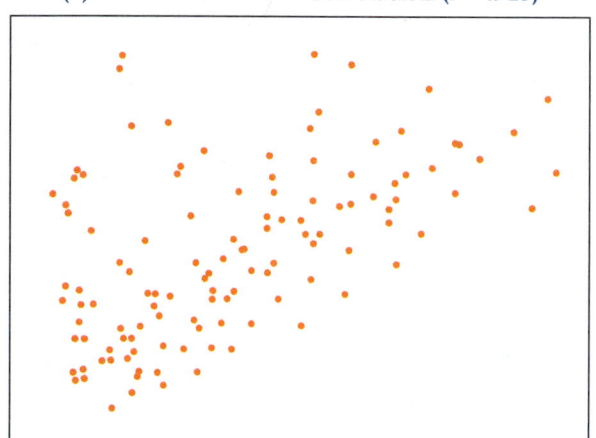

(d) Strong Positive Correlation (r = .909)

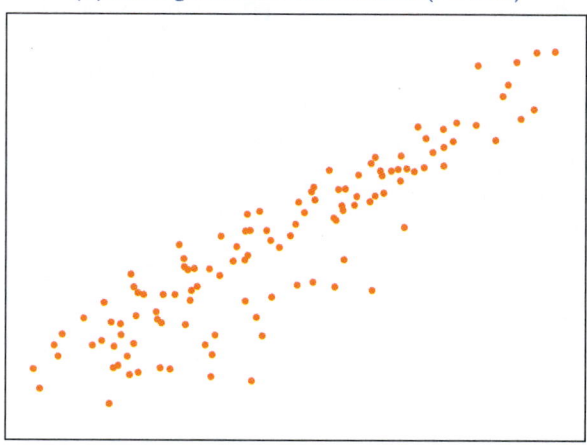

(e) Virtually No Correlation (r = −.004)

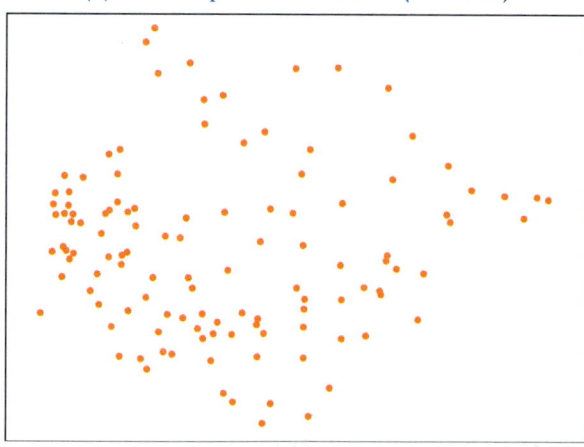

FIGURE 3.16

Excel and MINITAB Output for the Economics Example

Excel Output

	A	B	C
1		Interest Rate	Futures Index
2	Interest Rate	1	
3	Futures Index	0.815	1

MINITAB Output

Correlations: INTEREST RATE, FUTURES INDEX

Pearson correlation of INTEREST RATE and FUTURES INDEX = 0.815

What is the measure of correlation between the interest rate of federal funds and the commodities futures index? With data such as those shown in Table 3.12, which represent the values for interest rates of federal funds and commodities futures indexes for a sample of 12 days, a correlation coefficient, r, can be computed.

Examination of the formula for computing a Pearson product-moment correlation coefficient reveals that the following values must be obtained to compute r: Σx, Σx^2, Σy, Σy^2, Σxy, and n. In correlation analysis, it does not matter which variable is designated x and which is designated y. For this example, the correlation coefficient is computed as shown in Table 3.13. The r value obtained ($r = .815$) represents a relatively strong positive relationship between interest rates and commodities futures index over this 12-day period.

Figure 3.16 shows both Excel and MINITAB output for this problem.

3.5 PROBLEMS

3.41 Determine the value of the coefficient of correlation, r, for the following data.

X	4	6	7	11	14	17	21
Y	18	12	13	8	7	7	4

3.42 Determine the value of r for the following data.

X	158	296	87	110	436
Y	349	510	301	322	550

3.43 In an effort to determine whether any correlation exists between the price of stocks of airlines, an analyst sampled six days of activity of the stock market. Using the following prices of Delta stock and Southwest stock, compute the coefficient of correlation. Stock prices have been rounded off to the nearest tenth for ease of computation.

Delta	Southwest
47.6	15.1
46.3	15.4
50.6	15.9
52.6	15.6
52.4	16.4
52.7	18.1

3.44 The following data are the claims (in $ millions) for BlueCross BlueShield benefits for nine states, along with the surplus (in $ millions) that the company had in assets in those states.

State	Claims	Surplus
Alabama	$1425	$277
Colorado	273	100
Florida	915	120
Illinois	1687	259
Maine	234	40
Montana	142	25
North Dakota	259	57
Oklahoma	258	31
Texas	894	141

Use the data to compute a correlation coefficient, r, to determine the correlation between claims and surplus.

3.45 The National Safety Council released the following data on the incidence rates for fatal or lost-worktime injuries per 100 employees for several industries in three recent years.

Industry	Year 1	Year 2	Year 3
Textile	.46	.48	.69
Chemical	.52	.62	.63
Communication	.90	.72	.81
Machinery	1.50	1.74	2.10
Services	2.89	2.03	2.46
Nonferrous metals	1.80	1.92	2.00
Food	3.29	3.18	3.17
Government	5.73	4.43	4.00

Compute r for each pair of years and determine which years are most highly correlated.

3.6 DESCRIPTIVE STATISTICS ON THE COMPUTER

Both MINITAB and Excel yield extensive descriptive statistics. Even though each computer package can compute individual statistics such as a mean or a standard deviation, they can also produce multiple descriptive statistics at one time. Figure 3.17 displays a MINITAB output for the descriptive statistics associated with the computer production data presented earlier in this section. The MINITAB output contains, among other things, the mean, the median, the sample standard deviation, the minimum and maximum (which can then be used to compute the range), and Q_1 and Q_3 (from which the interquartile range can be computed). Excel's descriptive statistics output for the same computer production data is displayed in Figure 3.18. The Excel output contains the mean, the median, the mode, the sample standard deviation, the sample variance, and the range. The descriptive statistics feature on either of these computer packages yields a lot of useful information about a data set. MINITAB and Excel also have the capability of computing the correlation coefficient, r.

FIGURE 3.17
MINITAB Output for the Computer Production Problem

DESCRIPTIVE STATISTICS

Variable	N	Mean	Median	TrMean	StDev	SE Mean
Computer	5	13.00	16.00	13.00	5.70	2.55

Variable	Minimum	Maximum	Q_1	Q_3
Computer	5.00	18.00	7.00	17.50

FIGURE 3.18
Excel Output for the Computer Production Problem

COMPUTER PRODUCTION DATA

	A	B
1	Mean	13
2	Standard error	2.5495
3	Median	16
4	Mode	N/A
5	Standard deviation	5.7009
6	Sample variance	32.5
7	Kurtosis	−1.7112
8	Skewness	−0.8096
9	Range	13
10	Minimum	5
11	Maximum	18
12	Sum	65
13	Count	5

Laundry Statistics

The descriptive statistics presented in this chapter are excellent for summarizing and presenting data sets in more concise formats. For example, question 1 of the managerial and statistical questions in the Decision Dilemma reports water measurements for 50 U.S. households. Using Excel and/or MINITAB, many of the descriptive statistics presented in this chapter can be applied to these data. The results are shown in Figures 3.19 and 3.20.

These computer outputs show that the average water usage is 15.48 gallons with a standard deviation of about 1.233 gallons. The median is 16 gallons with a range of 6 gallons (12 to 18). The first quartile is 15 gallons and the third quartile is 16 gallons. The mode is also 16 gallons. The MINITAB graph and the skewness measures show that the data are slightly skewed to the left. Applying Chebyshev's Theorem to the mean and standard deviation shows that at least 88.9% of the measurements should fall between 11.78 gallons and 19.18 gallons. An examination of the data and the minimum and maximum reveals that 100% of the data actually fall within these limits.

According to the Decision Dilemma, the mean wash cycle time is 35 minutes with a standard deviation of 5 minutes. If the wash cycle times are approximately normally distributed, we can apply the empirical rule. According to the empirical rule, 68% of the times would fall within 30 and 40 minutes, 95% of the times would fall within 25 and 45 minutes, and 99.7% of the wash times would fall within 20 and 50 minutes. If the data are not normally distributed, Chebyshev's theorem reveals that at least 75% of the times should fall between 25 and 45 minutes and 88.9% should fall between 20 and 50 minutes.

Is amount of laundry correlated to household income? If a correlation coefficient is computed on the data from the Decision Dilemma, an r of .723 is found. This result indicates that some correlation is likely between the two sets of data. However, it is not a perfect correlation nor is it a very strong correlation. The tendency appears to be that households with higher incomes do larger amounts of laundry. However, in some cases households with lower incomes still do relatively large amounts of laundry and households with higher incomes sometimes do less laundry.

FIGURE 3.19

Excel Descriptive Statistics

WATER USAGE

	A	B
1	Mean	15.48
2	Standard error	0.174
3	Median	16
4	Mode	16
5	Standard deviation	1.233
6	Sample variance	1.52
7	Kurtosis	0.264
8	Skewness	−0.531
9	Range	6
10	Minimum	12
11	Maximum	18
12	Sum	774
13	Count	50

FIGURE 3.20

MINITAB Descriptive Statistics

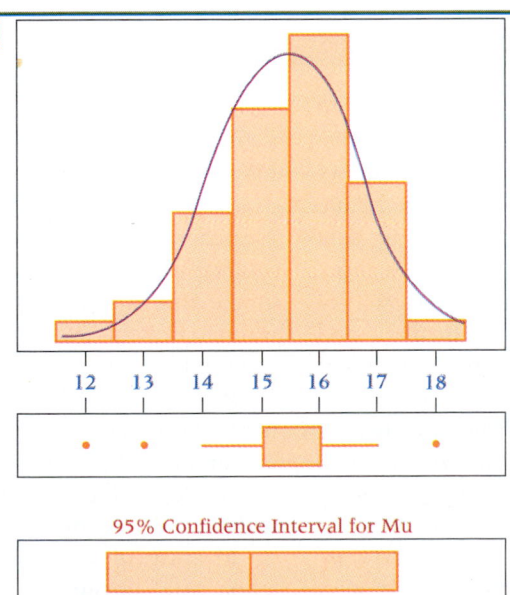

Variable: Water Usage

Anderson-Darling Normality Test

A-Squared	1.598
P-Value	0.000
Mean	15.4800
St Dev	1.2329
Variance	1.52
Skewness	−5.3E−01
Kurtosis	0.263785
N	50
Minimum	12.0000
1st Quartile	15.0000
Median	16.0000
3rd Quartile	16.0000
Maximum	18.0000

95% Confidence Interval for Mu
15.1296	15.8304

95% Confidence Interval for Sigma
1.0299	1.5363

95% Confidence Interval for Median
15.0000	16.0000

95% Confidence Interval for Mu

95% Confidence Interval for Median

ETHICAL CONSIDERATIONS

In describing a body of data to an audience, it is best to use whatever measures it takes to present a "full" picture of the data. By limiting the descriptive measures used, the business researcher may give the audience only part of the picture and can skew the way the receiver understands the data. For example, if a researcher presents only the mean, the audience will have no insight into the variability of the data; in addition, the mean might be inordinately large or small because of extreme values. Likewise, the choice of the median precludes a picture that includes the extreme values. Using the mode can cause the receiver of the information to focus only on values that occur often.

At least one measure of variability is usually needed with at least one measure of central tendency for the audience to begin to understand what the data look like. Unethical researchers might be tempted to present only the descriptive measure that will convey the picture of the data that they wants the audience to see. Ethical researchers will instead use any and all methods that will present the fullest, most informative picture possible from the data.

A strong correlation does not necessarily indicate cause and effect. It is unprofessional and unethical to draw cause-and-effect conclusions just because two variables are related. For example, suppose the number of moving vans leased is shown to increase with temperature. Some decision makers might believe that the hotter the day, the more people tend to move. The reality might be that people tend to move after school is out for the year in order to be less disruptive of their children's schooling. School is usually out during the summer in most of the country when the temperatures are hotter. Hence, it may be the school schedule that actually drives the moves, not the temperature. A hot spell in January therefore does not necessarily generate a lot of moves.

Former governor of Colorado Richard Lamm has been quoted as having said that "Demographers are academics who can statistically prove that the average person in Miami is born Cuban and dies Jewish…."* People are more likely to reach this type of conclusion if incomplete or misleading descriptive statistics are provided by researchers.

*Alan L. Otten. "People Patterns/Odds and Ends," *The Wall Street Journal*, 29 June 1992, p. B1. Reprinted by permission of *The Wall Street Journal* © 1992, Dow Jones & Company, Inc. All Rights Reserved Worldwide.

SUMMARY

Statistical descriptive measures include measures of central tendency, measures of variability, and measures of shape. Measures of central tendency and measures of variability are computed differently for ungrouped and grouped data. Measures of central tendency are useful in describing data because they communicate information about the more central portions of the data. The most common measures of central tendency are the three Ms: mode, median, and mean. In addition, percentiles and quartiles are measures of central tendency.

The mode is the most frequently occurring value in a set of data. If two values tie for the mode, the data are bimodal. Data sets can be multimodal. Among other things, the mode is used in business for determining sizes.

The median is the middle term in an ordered array of numbers containing an odd number of terms. For an array with an even number of terms, the median is the average of the two middle terms. The formula $(n + 1)/2$ specifies the location of the median. A median is unaffected by the magnitude of extreme values. This characteristic makes the median a most useful and appropriate measure of location in reporting such things as income, age, and prices of houses.

The arithmetic mean is widely used and is usually what researchers are referring to when they use the word *mean*. The arithmetic mean is the average. The population mean and the sample mean are computed in the same way but are denoted by different symbols. The arithmetic mean is affected by every value and can be inordinately influenced by extreme values.

Percentiles divide a set of data into 100 groups, which means 99 percentiles are needed. Quartiles divide data into four groups. The three quartiles are Q_1, which is the lower quartile; Q_2, which is the middle quartile and equals the median; and Q_3, which is the upper quartile.

Measures of variability are statistical tools used in combination with measures of central tendency to describe data. Measures of variability provide a description of data that measures of central tendency cannot give: information about the spread of the data values. These measures include the range, mean absolute deviation, variance, standard deviation, interquartile range, and coefficient of variation for ungrouped data.

One of the most elementary measures of variability is the range. It is the difference between the largest and smallest values. Although the range is easy to compute, it has limited usefulness. The interquartile range is the difference between the third and first quartile. It equals the range of the middle 50% of the data.

The mean absolute deviation (MAD) is computed by averaging the absolute values of the deviations from the mean. The mean absolute deviation provides the magnitude of the average deviation but without specifying its direction. The mean absolute deviation has limited usage in statistics, but interest is growing for the use of MAD in the field of forecasting.

Variance is widely used as a tool in statistics but is used little as a stand-alone measure of variability. The variance is the average of the squared deviations about the mean.

The square root of the variance is the standard deviation. It also is a widely used tool in statistics. It is used more often than the variance as a stand-alone measure. The standard deviation is best understood by examining its applications in determining where data are in relation to the mean. The empirical rule and Chebyshev's theorem are statements about the proportions of data values that are within various numbers of standard deviations from the mean.

The empirical rule reveals the percentage of values that are within one, two, or three standard deviations of the mean for a set of data. The empirical rule applies only if the data are in a bell-shaped distribution. According to the empirical rule, approximately 68% of all values of a normal distribution are within plus or minus one standard deviation of the mean. Ninety-five percent of all values are within two standard deviations either side of the mean, and virtually all values are within three standard deviations of the mean.

Chebyshev's theorem also delineates the proportion of values that are within a given number of standard deviations from the mean. However, it applies to any distribution. According to Chebyshev's theorem, at least $1 - 1/k^2$ values are within k standard deviations of the mean. The z score represents the number of standard deviations a value is from the mean for normally distributed data.

The coefficient of variation is a ratio of a standard deviation to its mean, given as a percentage. It is especially useful in comparing standard deviations or variances that represent data with different means.

Some measures of central tendency and some measures of variability are presented for grouped data. These measures include mean, mode, variance, and standard deviation. Generally, these measures are only approximate for grouped data because the values of the actual raw data are unknown.

Two measures of shape are skewness and kurtosis. Skewness is the lack of symmetry in a distribution. If a distribution is skewed, it is stretched in one direction or the other. The skewed part of a graph is its long, thin portion. One measure of skewness is the Pearsonian coefficient of skewness.

Kurtosis is the degree of peakedness of a distribution. A tall, thin distribution is referred to as leptokurtic. A flat distribution is platykurtic, and a distribution with a more normal peakedness is said to be mesokurtic.

A box and whisker plot is a graphical depiction of a distribution. The plot is constructed by using the median, the lower quartile, and the upper quartile. It can yield information about skewness and outliers.

Bivariate correlation can be accomplished with several different measures. In this chapter, only one coefficient of correlation is presented: the Pearson product-moment coefficient of correlation, r. This value ranges from −1 to 0 to +1. An r value of +1 is perfect positive correlation, and an r value of −1 is a perfect negative correlation. Negative correlation means that as one variable increases in value, the other variable tends to decrease. For r values near zero, little or no correlation is present.

KEY TERMS

arithmetic mean	deviation from the mean	measures of shape	quartiles
bimodal	empirical rule	measures of variability	range
box and whisker plot	interquartile range	median	skewness
Chebyshev's theorem	kurtosis	mesokurtic	standard deviation
coefficient of correlation (r)	leptokurtic	mode	sum of squares of x
coefficient of skewness	mean absolute deviation	multimodal	variance
coefficient of variation (CV)	(MAD)	percentiles	z score
correlation	measures of central tendency	platykurtic	

FORMULAS

Population mean (ungrouped)

$$\mu = \frac{\Sigma x}{N}$$

Sample mean (ungrouped)

$$\bar{x} = \frac{\Sigma x}{n}$$

Mean absolute deviation

$$MAD = \frac{\Sigma |x - \mu|}{N}$$

Population variance (ungrouped)

$$\sigma^2 = \frac{\Sigma (x - \mu)^2}{N}$$

$$\sigma^2 = \frac{\Sigma x^2 - \frac{(\Sigma x)^2}{N}}{N}$$

$$\sigma^2 = \frac{\Sigma x^2 - N\mu^2}{N}$$

Population standard deviation (ungrouped)

$$\sigma = \sqrt{\sigma^2}$$

$$\sigma = \sqrt{\frac{\Sigma (x - \mu)^2}{N}}$$

$$\sigma = \sqrt{\frac{\Sigma x^2 - \frac{(\Sigma x)^2}{N}}{N}}$$

$$\sigma = \sqrt{\frac{\Sigma x^2 - N\mu^2}{N}}$$

Grouped mean

$$\mu_{grouped} = \frac{\Sigma fM}{N}$$

Population variance (grouped)

$$\sigma^2 = \frac{\Sigma f(M - \mu)^2}{N} = \frac{\Sigma fM^2 - \frac{(\Sigma fM)^2}{N}}{N}$$

Population standard deviation (grouped)

$$\sigma = \sqrt{\frac{\Sigma f(M - \mu)^2}{N}} = \sqrt{\frac{\Sigma fM^2 - \frac{(\Sigma fM)^2}{N}}{N}}$$

Sample variance

$$s^2 = \frac{\Sigma (x - \bar{x})^2}{n - 1}$$

$$s^2 = \frac{\Sigma x^2 - \frac{(\Sigma x)^2}{n}}{n - 1}$$

$$s^2 = \frac{\Sigma x^2 - n(\bar{x})^2}{n - 1}$$

Sample standard deviation

$$s = \sqrt{s^2}$$

$$s = \sqrt{\frac{\Sigma (x - \bar{x})^2}{n - 1}}$$

$$s = \sqrt{\frac{\Sigma x^2 - \frac{(\Sigma x)^2}{n}}{n - 1}}$$

$$s = \sqrt{\frac{\Sigma x^2 - n(\bar{x})^2}{n - 1}}$$

Chebyshev's theorem

$$1 - \frac{1}{k^2}$$

z score

$$z = \frac{x - \mu}{\sigma}$$

Coefficient of variation

$$CV = \frac{\sigma}{\mu}(100)$$

Interquartile range

$$IQR = Q_3 - Q_1$$

Sample variance (grouped)

$$s^2 = \frac{\Sigma f(M - \bar{x})^2}{n - 1} = \frac{\Sigma fM^2 - \frac{(\Sigma fM)^2}{n}}{n - 1}$$

Sample standard deviation (grouped)

$$s = \sqrt{\frac{\Sigma f(M - \bar{x})^2}{n - 1}} = \sqrt{\frac{\Sigma fM^2 - \frac{(\Sigma fM)^2}{n}}{n - 1}}$$

Pearsonian coefficient of skewness

$$S_k = \frac{3(\mu - M_d)}{\sigma}$$

Pearson's product-moment correlation coefficient

$$r = \frac{\Sigma (x - \bar{x})(y - \bar{y})}{\sqrt{\Sigma (x - \bar{x})^2 \Sigma (y - \bar{y})^2}} = \frac{\Sigma xy - \frac{(\Sigma x \Sigma y)}{n}}{\sqrt{\left[\Sigma x^2 - \frac{(\Sigma x)^2}{n}\right]\left[\Sigma y^2 - \frac{(\Sigma y)^2}{n}\right]}}$$

SUPPLEMENTARY PROBLEMS

CALCULATING THE STATISTICS

3.46 The 2000 U.S. Census asked every household to report information on each person living there. Suppose for a sample of 30 households selected, the number of persons living in each was reported as follows.

2 3 1 2 6 4 2 1 5 3 2 3 1 2 2

1 3 1 2 2 4 2 1 2 8 3 2 1 1 3

Compute the mean, median, mode, range, lower and upper quartiles, and interquartile range for these data.

3.47 The 2000 U.S. Census also asked for each person's age. Suppose that a sample of 40 households taken from the census data showed the age of the first person recorded on the census form to be as follows.

42 29 31 38 55 27 28

33 49 70 25 21 38 47

63 22 38 52 50 41 19

22 29 81 52 26 35 38

29 31 48 26 33 42 58

40 32 24 34 25

Compute P_{10}, P_{80}, Q_1, Q_3, the interquartile range, and the range for these data.

3.48 According to the National Association of Investment Clubs, PepsiCo is the most popular stock with investment clubs with 11,388 clubs holding PepsiCo stock. Intel is a close second, followed by Motorola. For the following list of the most popular stocks with investment clubs, compute the mean, median, P_{30}, P_{60}, P_{90}, Q_1, Q_3, range, and interquartile range.

Company	Number of Clubs Holding Stock
PepsiCo	11,388
Intel	11,019
Motorola	9,863
Tricon Global Restaurants	9,168
Merck & Co.	8,687
AFLAC	6,796
Diebold	6,552
McDonald's	6,498
Coca-Cola	6,101
Lucent Technologies	5,563
Home Depot	5,414
Clayton Homes	5,390
RPM	5,033
Cisco Systems	4,541
General Electric	4,507
Johnson & Johnson	4,464
Microsoft	4,152
Wendy's International	4,150
Walt Disney	3,999
AT&T	3,619

3.49 *Editor & Publisher International Yearbook* published a listing of the top 10 daily newspapers in the United States, as shown here. Use these population data to compute a mean and a standard deviation. The figures are given in average daily circulation from Monday through Friday. Because the numbers are large, it may save you some effort to recode the data. One way to recode these data is to move the decimal point six places to the left (e.g., 1,774,880 becomes 1.77488). If you recode the data this way, the resulting mean and standard deviation will be correct for the recoded data. To rewrite the answers so that they are correct for the original data, move the decimal point back to the right six places in the answers.

Newspaper	Average Daily Circulation
Wall Street Journal	1,762,751
USA Today	1,692,666
New York Times	1,097,180
Los Angeles Times	1,033,399
Washington Post	762,009
(New York) Daily News	704,463
Chicago Tribune	661,699
Long Island Newsday	576,345
Houston Chronicle	546,799
Dallas Morning News	495,597

3.50 We show the companies with the largest oil refining capacity in the world according to the *Petroleum Intelligence Weekly*. Use these population data and answer the questions.

Company	Capacity (barrels per day in 1,000s)
ExxonMobil	6,300
Royal Dutch/Shell	3,791
China Petrochemical	2,867
Petroleos de Venezuela	2,437
Saudi Arabian Oil	1,970
BP Amoco	1,965
Chevron	1,661
Petrobras	1,540
Texaco	1,532
Petroleos Mexicanos (Pemex)	1,520
National Iranian Oil	1,092

a. What are the values of the mean and the median? Compare the answers and state which you prefer as a measure of location for these data and why.

b. What are the values of the range and interquartile range? How do they differ?

c. What are the values of variance and standard deviation for these data?

d. What is the z score for Texaco? What is the z score for ExxonMobil? Interpret these z scores.

e. Calculate the Pearsonian coefficient of skewness and comment on the skewness of this distribution.

3.51 The U.S. Department of the Interior releases figures on mineral production. Following are the 10 leading states in nonfuel mineral production in the United States.

State	Value ($ millions)
California	3,350
Nevada	2,800
Arizona	2,550
Texas	2,050
Florida	1,920
Michigan	1,670
Georgia	1,660
Minnesota	1,570
Utah	1,420
Missouri	1,320

a. Calculate the mean, median, and mode.
b. Calculate the range, interquartile range, mean absolute deviation, sample variance, and sample standard deviation.
c. Compute the Pearsonian coefficient of skewness for these data.
d. Sketch a box and whisker plot.

3.52 The radio music listener market is diverse. Listener formats might include adult contemporary, album rock, top 40, oldies, rap, country and western, classical, and jazz. In targeting audiences, market researchers need to be concerned about the ages of the listeners attracted to particular formats. Suppose a market researcher surveyed a sample of 170 listeners of oldies stations and obtained the following age distribution.

Age	Frequency
15–under 20	9
20–under 25	16
25–under 30	27
30–under 35	44
35–under 40	42
40–under 45	23
45–under 50	7
50–under 55	2

a. What are the mean and modal ages of oldies listeners?
b. What are the variance and standard deviation of the ages of oldies listeners?

3.53 A research agency administers a demographic survey to 90 telemarketing companies to determine the size of their operations. When asked to report how many employees now work in their telemarketing operation, the companies gave responses ranging from 1 to 100. The agency's analyst organizes the figures into a frequency distribution.

Number of Employees Working in Telemarketing	Number of Companies
0–under 20	32
20–under 40	16
40–under 60	13
60–under 80	10
80–under 100	19

a. Compute the mean and mode for this distribution.
b. Compute the standard deviation for these data.

3.54 Determine the Pearson product-moment correlation coefficient for the following data.

X	1	10	9	6	5	3	2
Y	8	4	4	5	7	7	9

TESTING YOUR UNDERSTANDING

3.55 Financial analysts like to use the standard deviation as a measure of risk for a stock. The greater the deviation in a stock price over time, the more risky it is to invest in the stock. However, the average prices of some stocks are considerably higher than the average price of others, allowing for the potential of a greater standard deviation of price. For example, a standard deviation of $5.00 on a $10.00 stock is considerably different from a $5.00 standard deviation on a $40.00 stock. In this situation, a coefficient of variation might provide insight into risk. Suppose stock X costs an average of $32.00 per share and showed a standard deviation of $3.45 for the past 60 days. Suppose stock Y costs an average of $84.00 per share and showed a standard deviation of $5.40 for the past 60 days. Use the coefficient of variation to determine the variability for each stock.

3.56 The Polk Company reported that the average age of a car on U.S. roads in a recent year was 7.5 years. Suppose the distribution of ages of cars on U.S. roads is approximately bell-shaped. If 99.7% of the ages are between 1 year and 14 years, what is the standard deviation of car age? Suppose the standard deviation is 1.7 years and the mean is 7.5 years. Between what two values would 95% of the car ages fall?

3.57 According to a *Human Resources* report, a worker in the industrial countries spends on average 419 minutes a day on the job. Suppose the standard deviation of time spent on the job is 27 minutes.

a. If the distribution of time spent on the job is approximately bell shaped, between what two times would 68% of the figures be? 95%? 99.7%?
b. If the shape of the distribution of times is unknown, approximately what percentage of the times would be between 359 and 479 minutes?
c. Suppose a worker spent 400 minutes on the job. What would that worker's Z score be and what would it tell the researcher?

3.58 During the 1990s, businesses were expected to show a lot of interest in Central and Eastern European countries. As new markets began to open, American business people needed a better understanding of the market potential there. The following are the per capita GDP figures for eight of these European countries published by the *World Almanac*.

Country	Per Capita GDP (U.S. $)
Albania	1,650
Bulgaria	4,300
Croatia	5,100
Germany	22,700
Hungary	7,800
Poland	7,200
Romania	3,900
Bosnia/Herzegovina	1,770

a. Compute the mean and standard deviation for Albania, Bulgaria, Croatia, and Germany.
b. Compute the mean and standard deviation for Hungary, Poland, Romania, and Bosnia/Herzegovina.
c. Use a coefficient of variation to compare the two standard deviations. Treat the data as population data.

3.59 According to the Bureau of Labor Statistics, the average annual salary of a worker in Detroit, Michigan, is $35,748. Suppose the median annual salary for a worker in this group is $31,369 and the mode is $29,500. Is the distribution of salaries for this group skewed? If so, how and why? Which of these measures of central tendency would you use to describe these data? Why?

3.60 How strong is the correlation between the inflation rate and 30-year treasury yields? The following data published by Fuji Securities are given as pairs of inflation rates and treasury yields for selected years over a 35-year period.

Inflation Rate	30-Year Treasury Yield
1.57%	3.05%
2.23	3.93
2.17	4.68
4.53	6.57
7.25	8.27
9.25	12.01
5.00	10.27
4.62	8.45

Compute the Pearson product-moment correlation coefficient to determine the strength of the correlation between these two variables. Comment on the strength and direction of the correlation.

3.61 According to the U.S. Army Corps of Engineers, the top 20 U.S. ports, ranked by total tonnage (in million tons), were as follows.

Port	Total Tonnage
South Louisiana, LA	214.2
Houston, TX	158.8
New York, NY and NJ	133.7
New Orleans, LA	87.5
Corpus Christi, TX	78.0
Beaumont, TX	69.4
Baton Rouge, LA	63.7
Port of Plaguemines, LA	62.5
Long Beach, CA	60.9
Valdez, AK	53.4
Pittsburgh, PA	52.9
Tampa, FL	51.5
Lake Charles, LA	50.7
Texas City, TX	49.5
Mobile, AL	45.4
Duluth-Superior, MN and WI	42.3
Los Angeles, CA	42.3
Norfolk Harbor, VA	40.8
Philadelphia, PA	39.3
Baltimore, MD	37.3

a. Construct a box and whisker plot for these data.
b. Discuss the shape of the distribution from the plot.
c. Are there outliers?
d. What are they and why do you think they are outliers?

3.62 *Runzheimer International* publishes data on overseas business travel costs. They report that the average per diem total for a business traveler in Paris, France, is $349. Suppose the shape of the distribution of the per diem costs of a business traveler to Paris is unknown, but that 53% of the per diem figures are between $317 and $381. What is the value of the standard deviation? The average per diem total for a business traveler in Moscow is $415. If the shape of the distribution of per diem costs of a business traveler in Moscow is unknown and if 83% of the per diem costs in Moscow lie between $371 and $459, what is the standard deviation?

INTERPRETING THE OUTPUT

3.63 *American Banker* compiled a list of the top 100 banking companies in the world according to total assets. Leading the list is the Bank of Tokyo–Mitsubishi, followed by the Deutsche Bank. The following Excel descriptive statistics output lists the variable total assets ($ millions) for these 100 banks. Study the output and describe in your own words what you can learn about the assets of these top 100 world banks.

	A	B
1	**Top World Banks**	
2	Mean	213496.77
3	Standard error	12972.00
4	Median	164573
5	Mode	N/A
6	Standard deviation	129720
7	Sample variance	16827278273
8	Kurtosis	1.05
9	Skewness	1.18
10	Range	615029
11	Minimum	76891
12	Maximum	691920
13	Sum	21349677
14	Count	100

3.64 *Hispanic Business, Inc.*, compiled a list of the top advertisers cultivating the Hispanic market. These data ($ millions) were entered into a MINITAB spreadsheet and analyzed using the graphical descriptive statistics feature. Study the output and describe the expenditures of these top Hispanic market advertisers.

Variable: Media Expenditures

Mean	7.8560
Standard deviation	5.8860
Variance	34.6455
Skewness	3.6214
Kurtosis	17.7851
N	50
Minimum	3.25
1st Quartile	4.50
Median	5.75
3rd Quartile	8.625
Maximum	40.00
95% Confidence Interval for Mu	
6.1832	9.5288

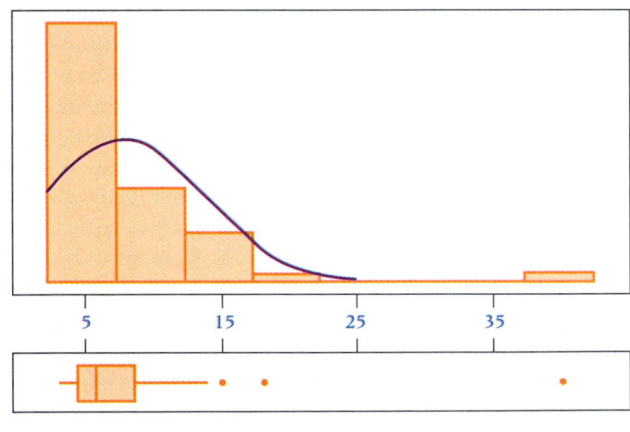

95% Confidence Interval for Mu

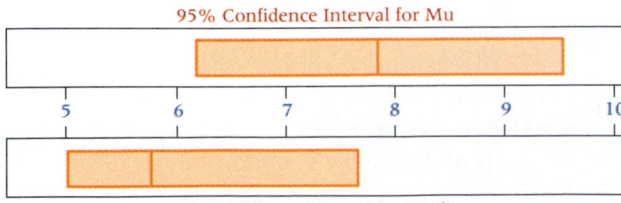

95% Confidence Interval for Median

3.65 Many large companies are located around the world. The number of employees for 46 of the largest employers with headquarters outside the United States were analyzed with Excel's descriptive statistics feature. The data follow. Summarize what you have learned about the number of employees for these companies by studying this output.

	A	B
1	**Large Employers Outside of the United States**	
2	Mean	183327.1304
3	Standard error	9480.8850
4	Median	157670
5	Mode	135000
6	Standard deviation	64302.4905
7	Sample variance	4134810279
8	Kurtosis	0.8266
9	Skewness	1.2996
10	Range	256106
11	Minimum	125894
12	Maximum	382000
13	Sum	8433048
14	Count	46

3.66 The Competitive Media Reporting and Publishers Information Bureau compiled a list of the top 25 advertisers in the United States for a recent year. The total advertising expenditures for each company ($1,000s) were analyzed using MINITAB's numerical descriptive statistics feature and its box plot feature, both of which are displayed. Study this output and summarize the expenditures of the top 25 advertisers in your own words.

Descriptive Statistics

Variable	N	Mean	Median	TrMean	StDev	SE Mean
Top 25 A	25	772702	613823	723681	436067	87213

Variable	Minimum	Maximum	Q_1	Q_3
Top 25 A	445958	2226934	484600	788256

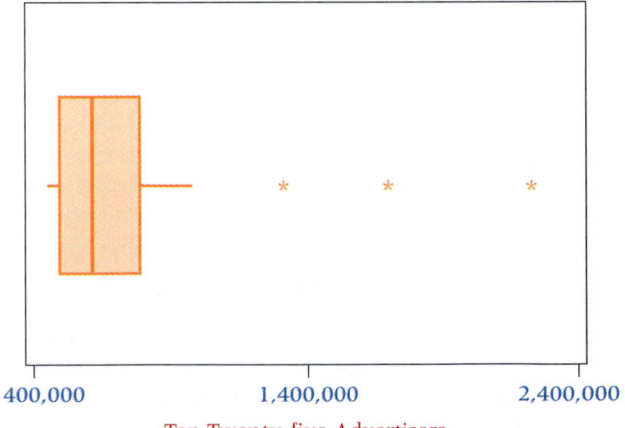

Top Twenty-five Advertisers

ANALYZING THE DATABASES

see www.wiley.com/college/black

1. Use the manufacturing database. What is the mean amount of New Capital Expenditures? What is the median amount of New Capital Expenditures? What does the comparison of the mean and the median tell you about the data?

2. For the stock market database "describe" the Dollar Value variable. Include measures of central tendency, variability, and skewness. What did you find?

3. Using the financial database study Earnings per Share for Type 2 and Type 7 (chemical companies and petrochemical companies). Compute a coefficient of variation for Type 2 and for Type 7. Compare the two coefficients and comment. Use the hospital database. Construct a box and whisker plot for Births. Thinking about hospitals and birthing facilities, comment on why the box and whiskers plot may look the way it does.

4. Produce a correlation matrix for the variables Beds, Admissions, Census, Outpatient Visits, Births, Total Expenditures, Payroll Expenditures, and Personnel for the hospital database. Which variables are most highly correlated? Which variables are least correlated?

CASE: COCA-COLA GOES SMALL IN RUSSIA

The Coca-Cola Company is the number-one seller of soft drinks in the world. Every day an average of more than 1 billion servings of Coca-Cola, Diet Coke, Sprite, Fanta, and other products of Coca-Cola are enjoyed around the world. The company has the world's largest production and distribution system for soft drinks and sells more than twice as many soft drinks as its nearest competitor. Coca-Cola products are sold in more than 200 countries around the globe.

For several reasons, the company believes it will continue to grow internationally. One reason is that disposable income is rising. Another is that outside the United States and Europe, the world is getting younger. In addition, reaching world markets is becoming easier as political barriers fall and transportation difficulties are overcome. Still another reason is that the sharing of ideas, cultures, and news around the world creates market opportunities. Part of the company mission is for Coca-Cola to maintain the world's most powerful trademark and effectively utilize the world's most effective and pervasive distribution system.

In June 1999 Coca-Cola Russia introduced a 200-milliliter (about 6.8 oz.) Coke bottle in Volgograd, Russia, in a campaign to market Coke to its poorest customers. This strategy was successful for Coca-Cola in other countries, such as India. The bottle sells for 12 cents, making it affordable to almost everyone. In 2001, Coca-Cola enjoyed a 25% volume growth in Russia including an 18% increase in unit case sales of Coca-Cola.

Discussion

1. Because of the variability of bottling machinery, it is likely that every 200-milliliter bottle of Coca-Cola does not contain exactly 200 milliliters of fluid. Some bottles may contain more fluid and others less. Because 200-milliliter bottle fills are somewhat unusual, a production engineer wants to test some of the bottles from the first production runs to determine how close they are to the 200-milliliter specification. Suppose the following data are the fill measurements from a random sample of 50 bottles. Use the techniques presented in this chapter to describe the sample. Consider measures of central tendency, variability, and skewness. Based on this analysis, how is the bottling process working?

200.1	199.9	200.2	200.2	200.0
200.1	200.9	200.1	200.3	200.5
199.7	200.4	200.3	199.8	199.3
200.1	199.4	199.6	199.2	200.2
200.4	199.8	199.9	200.2	199.6
199.6	200.4	200.4	200.6	200.6
200.1	200.8	199.9	200.0	199.9
200.3	200.5	199.9	201.1	199.7
200.2	200.5	200.2	199.7	200.9
200.2	199.5	200.6	200.3	199.8

2. Suppose that at another plant Coca-Cola is filling bottles with the more traditional 20 ounces of fluid. A lab randomly samples 150 bottles and tests the bottles for fill volume. The descriptive statistics are given in both MINITAB and Excel computer output. Write a brief report to supervisors summarizing what this output is saying about the process.

Descriptive Statistics: Bottle Fills

Variable	N	Mean	Median	TrMean	StDev	SE Mean
Bottle F	150	20.003	20.005	20.003	0.027	0.002

Variable	Minimum	Maximum	Q_1	Q_3
Bottle F	19.920	20.090	19.985	20.021

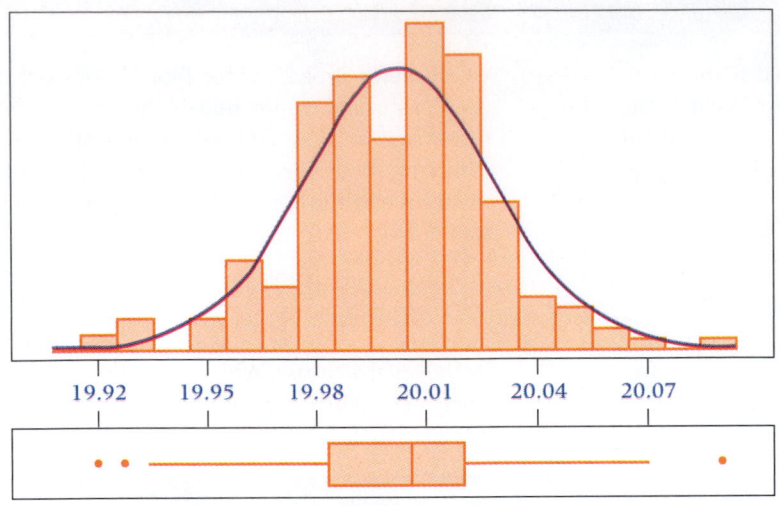

Variable: Bottle Fills

Anderson-Darling Normality Test

A-Squared	0.588
P-Value	0.123
Mean	20.0028
St Dev	0.0266
Variance	7.09E−04
Skewness	−8.6E−02
Kurtosis	1.01598
N	150
Minimum	19.9200
1st Quartile	19.9851
Median	20.0046
3rd Quartile	20.0208
Maximum	20.0896

95% Confidence Interval for Mu

19.9985	20.0071

95% Confidence Interval for Sigma

0.0239	0.0300

95% Confidence Interval for Median

19.9977	20.0091

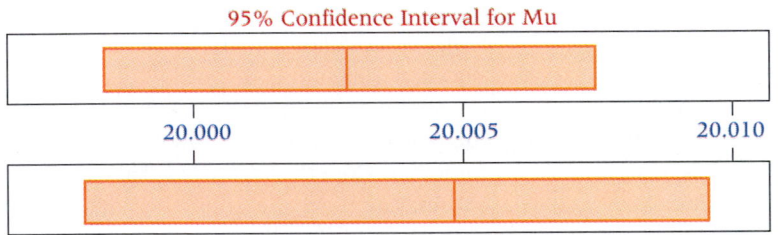

95% Confidence Interval for Median

Excel Output

	A	B
1	**Bottle Fills**	
2	Mean	20.003
3	Standard error	0.002
4	Median	20.005
5	Mode	20.004
6	Standard deviation	0.027
7	Sample variance	0.001
8	Kurtosis	1.015
9	Skewness	−0.085
10	Range	0.170
11	Minimum	19.92
12	Maximum	20.090
13	Sum	3000.416
14	Count	150

Source: Adapted from "Coke, Avis Adjust in Russia," *Advertising Age*, 5 July 1999, p. 25; Coca-Cola Web site at http://www.coca-cola.com/home.html. The Coca-Cola company's 2001 annual report found at: http://www2.coca-cola.com/investors/annualreport/2001/index.html.

USING THE COMPUTER

EXCEL

Excel can analyze data by using several of the techniques presented in this chapter. It has one particularly powerful command that generates many descriptive statistics.

Descriptive Statistics

Several of the descriptive statistics presented in this chapter can be accessed by Excel through the use of the Descriptive Statistics command. Begin by selecting **Tools** on the Excel menu bar. On the pull-down menu select **Data Analysis**. In the data analysis dialog box, select the option **Descriptive Statistics**. Input the range of the data to be described. Check whether the data are grouped by column or row. Check for labels in the first row. Of particular importance is to check the box at the bottom left entitled **Summary statistics**. Checking this box tells Excel to include a wide range of descriptive measures.

The output includes mean, median, mode, standard deviation, sample variance, a measure of kurtosis, a measure of skewness, range, minimum, maximum, sum, and count.

Rank and Percentile

Excel has a command called Rank and Percentile that orders the data, assigns ranks to the data, and outputs the percentiles of the data. To access this command, select **Tools** from the menu bar of Excel. On the pull-down menu that appears, select **Data Analysis**. The data analysis dialog box will appear. Select **Rank and Percentile**. A rank and percentile dialog box will appear. Input the range of data. Check whether the data are in columns or rows and for labels in the first row.

MINITAB

MINITAB Windows is capable of performing many of the tasks presented in this chapter, including descriptive statistics and box plots.

Descriptive Statistics

Through the use of the Descriptive Statistics command, MINITAB yields a considerable number of the statistical techniques mentioned in this chapter. The process begins with the selection of **Stat** on the menu bar.

From the pull-down menu, select **Basic Statistics**. From the basic statistics pull-down menu, select **Display Descriptive Statistics** and a dialog box appears. Input the column(s) to be analyzed. If you click on **OK**, then your output will include the sample size, mean, median, standard deviation, minimum, maximum, the first quartile, and the third quartile. However, if you select the option, **Graph…**, you will have several other output options that are relatively self-explanatory. The options include **Histogram of data**, **Histogram of data with normal curve, Dotplot of data, Boxplot of data,** and **Graphical summary**. If you select **Graphical summary**, you will get output like that shown in the Case as "Bottle Fills." This output includes the features mentioned under tabular output plus a histogram of the data overlaid with a normal curve, a box plot, and other output that will be explained later in the text.

Column Statistics

Column statistics can be obtained by selecting the command **Calc** on the MINITAB Windows menu bar. From the pull-down menu, select the **Column Statistics** command. The column statistics dialog box will appear. Check off the statistics you would like to calculate. Input the column with the data. The output will include the items you asked for.

A **Row Statistics** item can also be found on the **Calc** pull-down menu. Use it if your data are located in a row. You will get a row statistics dialog box that is virtually identical to the column statistics dialog box. Follow the same steps as those used with column statistics to get output on row data.

Box and Whisker Plot

A box and whisker plot can be produced by selecting **Graph** on the menu bar. On the graph pull-down menu that appears, select **Boxplot** from the menu and a box plot dialog box will appear. Enter the variable location in **Y**. Select **IQRange Box** under Display. Several graphical options such as adding a title are given at the bottom of the dialog box. One particularly useful option is transposing the graph so that the whiskers parallel the X axis. To do this, select **Options** at the bottom of the dialog box. You will then have the opportunity to check a box denoting that you want to transpose X and Y. The resulting output is a box and whisker plot with an asterisk representing outliers.

CHAPTER 4

Probability

LEARNING OBJECTIVES

The main objective of Chapter 4 is to help you understand the basic principles of probability, thereby enabling you to:

1. Comprehend the different ways of assigning probability.
2. Understand and apply marginal, union, joint, and conditional probabilities.
3. Select the appropriate law of probability to use in solving problems.
4. Solve problems by using the laws of probability, including the law of addition, the law of multiplication, and the law of conditional probability.
5. Revise probabilities by using Bayes' rule.

Gender Equity in the Workplace

The Civil Rights Act was signed into law in the United States in 1964 by President Lyndon Johnson. This law, which was amended in 1972, resulted in several "titles" that addressed discrimination in American society at various levels. One is Title VII, which pertains specifically to employment discrimination. It applies to all employers with more than 15 employees, along with other institutions. One of the provisions of Title VII makes it illegal to refuse to hire a person on the basis of the person's gender.

Today, company hiring procedures must be within the preview and framework of the Equal Employment Opportunity Commission (EEOC) guidelines and Title VII. How does a company defend its hiring practices or know when they are within acceptable bounds? How can individuals or groups who feel they have been the victims of illegal hiring practices "prove" their case? How can a group demonstrate that they have been "adversely impacted" by a company's discriminatory hiring practices?

Statistics are widely used in employment discrimination actions and by companies in attempting to meet EEOC guidelines. Substantial quantities of human resources data are logged and analyzed on a daily basis. A small portion of the human resource data was gathered on a client company.

CLIENT COMPANY HUMAN RESOURCE DATA BY GENDER

Type of Position	Gender		Total
	Male	Female	
Managerial	8	3	11
Professional	31	13	44
Technical	52	17	69
Clerical	9	22	31
Total	100	55	155

Managerial and Statistical Questions

1. Suppose some legal concern has been expressed that a disproportionate number of managerial people at the client company are men. If a worker is randomly selected from the client company, what is the probability that the worker is a woman? If a managerial person is randomly selected, what is the probability that the person is a woman? What factors might enter into the apparent discrepancy between probabilities?

2. Suppose a special bonus is being given to one person in the technical area this year. If the bonus is randomly awarded, what is the probability that it will go to a woman given that worker is in the technical area? Is this discrimination against male technical workers? What factors might enter into the awarding of the bonus other than random selection?

3. Suppose that at the annual holiday party the name of an employee of the client company will be drawn randomly to win a trip to Hawaii. What is the probability that a professional person will be the winner?

4. What is the probability that the winner will be either a man or a clerical worker? What is the probability that the winner will be a woman and in management? Suppose the winner is a man. What is the probability that he is from the technical group?

Source: EEOC information adapted from Richard D. Arvey and Robert H. Faley, Fairness in Selecting Employees, 2nd ed. (Reading, MA: Addison-Wesley Publishing Company, 1992.

In business, most decision making involves uncertainty. For example, an operations manager does not know definitely whether a valve in the plant is going to malfunction or continue to function—or, if it continues, for how long. When should it be replaced? What is the chance that the valve will malfunction within the next week? In the banking industry, what are the new vice president's prospects for successfully turning a department around? The answers to these questions are uncertain.

In the case of a high-rise building, what are the chances that a fire-extinguishing system will work when needed if redundancies are built in? Businesspeople must address these and thousands of similar questions daily. Because most such questions do not have definite answers, the decision making is based on uncertainty. In many of these situations, a probability can be assigned to the likelihood of an outcome. This chapter is about learning how to determine or assign probabilities.

4.1 INTRODUCTION TO PROBABILITY

Chapter 1 discussed the difference between descriptive and inferential statistics. Much statistical analysis is inferential, and probability is the basis for inferential statistics. Recall that inferential statistics involves taking a sample from a population, computing a statistic on the sample, and inferring from the statistic the value of the corresponding parameter of the population. The reason for doing so is that the value of the parameter is unknown. Because it is unknown, the analyst conducts the inferential process under uncertainty. However, by applying rules and laws, the analyst can often assign a probability of obtaining the results. Figure 4.1 depicts this process.

Suppose a quality control inspector selects a random sample of 40 lightbulbs from a population of brand X bulbs and computes the average number of hours of luminance for the sample bulbs. By using techniques discussed later in this text, the specialist estimates the average number of hours of luminance for the *population* of brand X lightbulbs from this sample information. Because the lightbulbs being analyzed are only a sample of the population, the average number of hours of luminance for the 40 bulbs may or may not accurately estimate the average for all bulbs in the population. The results are uncertain. By applying the laws presented in this chapter, the inspector can assign a value of probability to this estimate.

In addition, probabilities are used directly in certain industries and industry applications. For example, the insurance industry uses probabilities in actuarial tables to determine the likelihood of certain outcomes in order to set specific rates and coverages. The gaming industry uses probability values to establish charges and payoffs. One way to determine whether a company's hiring practices meet the government's EEOC guidelines mentioned in the Decision Dilemma is to compare various proportional breakdowns of their employees (by ethnicity, gender, age, etc.) to the proportions in the general population from which the employees are hired. In comparing the company figures with those of the general population, the courts could study the probabilities of a company randomly hiring a certain profile of employees from a given population. In other industries, such as

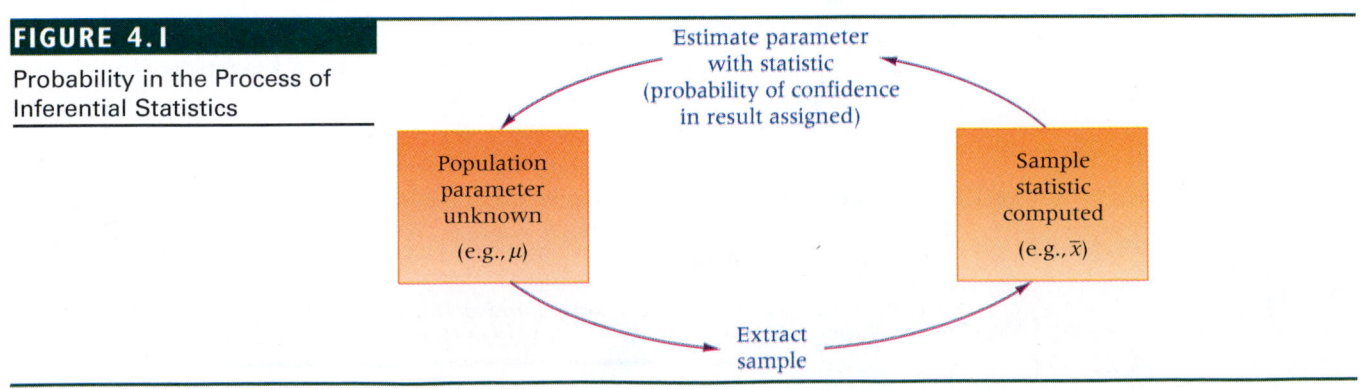

FIGURE 4.1

Probability in the Process of Inferential Statistics

manufacturing and aerospace, it is important to know the life of a mechanized part and the probability that it will malfunction at any given length of time in order to protect the firm from major breakdowns.

4.2 METHODS OF ASSIGNING PROBABILITIES

The three general methods of assigning probabilities are (1) the classical method, (2) the relative frequency of occurrence method, and (3) subjective probabilities.

Classical Method of Assigning Probabilities

When probabilities are assigned based on laws and rules, the method is referred to as the **classical method of assigning probabilities**. This method involves an experiment, which is *a process that produces outcomes, and an event, which is an outcome of an experiment.*

When we assign probabilities using the classical method, the probability of an individual event occurring is determined as the ratio of the number of items in a population containing the event (n_e) to the total number of items in the population (N). That is, $P(E) = n_e/N$. For example, if a company has 200 workers and 70 are female, the probability of randomly selecting a female from this company is 70/200 = .35.

CLASSICAL METHOD OF ASSIGNING PROBABILITIES	$$P(E) = \frac{n_e}{N}$$

where
N = total possible number of outcomes of an experiment
n_e = the number of outcomes in which the event occurs out of N outcomes

For example, in a particular plant, three machines make a given product. Machine A always produces 40% of the total number of this product. Ten percent of the items produced by machine A are defective. If the finished products are well mixed with regard to which machine produced them and if one of these products is randomly selected, the classical method of assigning probabilities tells us that the probability that the part was produced by machine A and is defective is .04. This probability can be determined even before the part is sampled because with the classical method, the probabilities can be determined **a priori;** that is, *they can be determined prior to the experiment.*

Because n_e can never be greater than N (no more than N outcomes in the population could possibly have attribute e), the highest value of any probability is 1. If the probability of an outcome occurring is 1, the event is certain to occur. The smallest possible probability is 0. If none of the outcomes of the N possibilities has the desired characteristic, e, the probability is $0/N = 0$, and the event is certain not to occur.

RANGE OF POSSIBLE PROBABILITIES	$$0 \leq P(E) \leq 1$$

Thus, probabilities are nonnegative proper fractions or nonnegative decimal values less than or equal to 1.

Probability values can be converted to percentages by multiplying by 100. Meteorologists often report weather probabilities in percentage form. For example, when they forecast a 60% chance of rain for tomorrow, they are saying that the probability of rain tomorrow is .60.

Relative Frequency of Occurrence

The **relative frequency of occurrence method** of assigning probabilities is based on cumulated historical data. With this method, *the probability of an event occurring is equal to the number of times the event has occurred in the past divided by the total number of opportunities for the event to have occurred.*

PROBABILITY BY RELATIVE FREQUENCY OF OCCURRENCE	Number of Times an Event Occurred
	Total Number of Opportunities for the Event to Occur

Relative frequency of occurrence is not based on rules or laws but on what has occurred in the past. For example, a company wants to determine the probability that its inspectors are going to reject the next batch of raw materials from a supplier. Data gathered from company record books show that the supplier sent the company 90 batches in the past, and inspectors rejected 10 of them. By the method of relative frequency of occurrence, the probability of the inspectors rejecting the next batch is 10/90 or .11. If the next batch is rejected, the relative frequency of occurrence probability for the subsequent shipment would change to 11/91= .12.

Subjective Probability

The **subjective method** of *assigning probability is based on the feelings or insights of the person determining the probability*. Subjective probability comes from the person's intuition or reasoning. Although not a scientific approach to probability, the subjective method often is based on the accumulation of knowledge, understanding, and experience stored and processed in the human mind. At times it is merely a guess. At other times, subjective probability can potentially yield accurate probabilities. Subjective probability can be used to capitalize on the background of experienced workers and managers in decision making.

Suppose a director of transportation for an oil company is asked the probability of getting a shipment of oil out of Saudi Arabia to the United States within three weeks. A director who has scheduled many such shipments, has a knowledge of Saudi politics, and has an awareness of current climatological and economic conditions may be able to give an accurate probability that the shipment can be made on time.

Subjective probability also can be a potentially useful way of tapping a person's experience, knowledge, and insight and using them to forecast the occurrence of some event. An experienced airline mechanic can usually assign a meaningful probability that a particular plane will have a certain type of mechanical difficulty. Physicians sometimes assign subjective probabilities to the life expectancy of people who have cancer.

4.3 STRUCTURE OF PROBABILITY

In the study of probability, developing a language of terms and symbols is helpful. The structure of probability provides a common framework within which the topics of probability can be explored.

Experiment

As previously stated, an **experiment** is *a process that produces outcomes*. Examples of business-oriented experiments with outcomes that can be statistically analyzed might include the following.

- Interviewing 20 randomly selected consumers and asking them which brand of appliance they prefer
- Sampling every 200th bottle of ketchup from an assembly line and weighing the contents
- Testing new pharmaceutical drugs on samples of cancer patients and measuring the patients' improvement
- Auditing every 10th account to detect any errors
- Recording the Dow Jones Industrial Average on the first Monday of every month for 10 years

Event

Because an **event** is *an outcome of an experiment*, the experiment defines the possibilities of the event. If the experiment is to sample five bottles coming off a production line, an event could be to get one defective and four good bottles. In an experiment to roll a die, one event could be to roll an even number and another event could be to roll a number greater than two. Events are denoted by uppercase letters; italic capital letters (e.g., A and E_1, E_2, …) represent the general or abstract case, and Roman capital letters (e.g., H and T for heads and tails) denote specific things and people.

Elementary Events

Events that cannot be decomposed or broken down into other events are called **elementary events**. Elementary events are denoted by lowercase letters (e.g., e_1, e_2, e_3, …). Suppose the experiment is to roll a die. The elementary events for this experiment are to roll a 1 or roll a 2 or roll a 3, and so on. Rolling an even number is an event, but it is not an elementary event because the even number can be broken down further into events 2, 4, and 6.

In the experiment of rolling a die, there are six elementary events {1, 2, 3, 4, 5, 6}. Rolling a pair of dice results in 36 possible elementary events (outcomes). For each of the six elementary events possible on the roll of one die, there are six possible elementary events on the roll of the second die, as depicted in the tree diagram in Figure 4.2. Table 4.1 contains a list of these 36 outcomes.

In the experiment of rolling a pair of dice, other events could include outcomes such as two even numbers, a sum of 10, a sum greater than five, and others. However, none of these events is an elementary event because each can be broken down into several of the elementary events displayed in Table 4.1.

Sample Space

A **sample space** is *a complete roster or listing of all elementary events for an experiment*. Table 4.1 is the sample space for the roll of a pair of dice. The sample space for the roll of a single die is {1, 2, 3, 4, 5, 6}.

FIGURE 4.2

Possible Outcomes for the Roll of a Pair of Dice

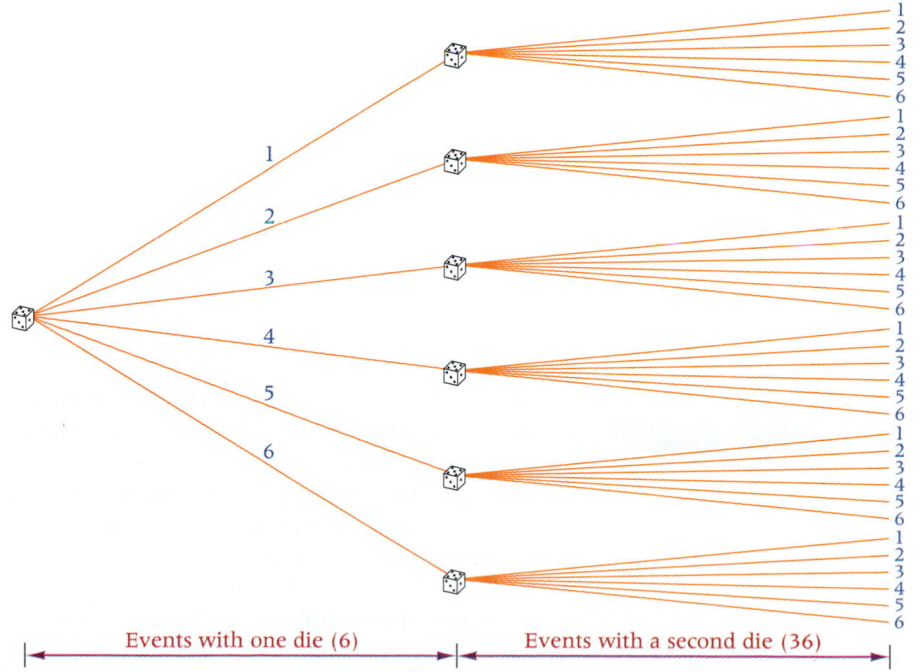

Events with one die (6)   Events with a second die (36)

TABLE 4.1					
(1,1)	(2,1)	(3,1)	(4,1)	(5,1)	(6,1)
(1,2)	(2,2)	(3,2)	(4,2)	(5,2)	(6,2)
(1,3)	(2,3)	(3,3)	(4,3)	(5,3)	(6,3)
(1,4)	(2,4)	(3,4)	(4,4)	(5,4)	(6,4)
(1,5)	(2,5)	(3,5)	(4,5)	(5,5)	(6,5)
(1,6)	(2,6)	(3,6)	(4,6)	(5,6)	(6,6)

All Possible Elementary Events in the Roll of a Pair of Dice (Sample Space)

Sample space can aid in finding probabilities. Suppose an experiment is to roll a pair of dice. What is the probability that the dice will sum to 7? An examination of the sample space shown in Table 4.1 reveals that there are six outcomes in which the dice sum to 7—{(1,6), (2,5), (3,4), (4,3), (5,2), (6,1)}—in the total possible 36 elementary events in the sample space. Using this information, we can conclude that the probability of rolling a pair of dice that sum to 7 is 6/36, or .1667. However, using the sample space to determine probabilities is unwieldy and cumbersome when the sample space is large. Hence statisticians usually use other more effective methods of determining probability.

Unions and Intersections

Set notation, the use of braces to group numbers, is used as *a symbolic tool for unions and intersections* in this chapter. The **union** of X, Y is *formed by combining elements from both sets* and is denoted $X \cup Y$. An element qualifies for the union of X, Y if it is in either X or Y or in both X and Y. The union expression $X \cup Y$ can be translated to "X or Y." For example, if

$$X = \{1,4,7,9\} \text{ and } Y = \{2,3,4,5,6\}$$
$$X \cup Y = \{1,2,3,4,5,6,7,9\}$$

Note that all the values of X and all the values of Y qualify for the union. However, none of the values is listed more than once in the union. In Figure 4.3, the shaded region of the Venn diagram denotes the union.

An intersection is denoted $X \cap Y$. To qualify for intersection, an element must be in both X and Y. The **intersection** *contains the elements common to both sets.* Thus the intersection symbol, $\cap$, is often read as *and*. The intersection of X, Y is referred to as X and Y. For example, if

$$X = \{1,4,7,9\} \text{ and } Y = \{2,3,4,5,6\}$$
$$X \cap Y = \{4\}$$

Note that only the value 4 is common to both sets X and Y. The intersection is more exclusive than and hence equal to or (usually) smaller than the union. Elements must be characteristic of both X and Y to qualify. In Figure 4.4, the shaded region denotes the intersection.

Mutually Exclusive Events

Two or more events are **mutually exclusive events** if *the occurrence of one event precludes the occurrence of the other event(s)*. This characteristic means that mutually exclusive events cannot occur simultaneously and therefore can have no intersection.

The variable "gender" presents two mutually exclusive outcomes, male and female: An employee randomly selected to be part of a study is either male or female but cannot be both. A manufactured part is either defective or okay: The part cannot be both okay and defective at the same time because "okay" and "defective" are mutually exclusive categories. In a sample of the manufactured products, the event of selecting a defective part is mutually exclusive with the event of selecting a nondefective part. Suppose an office building is for sale and two different potential buyers have placed bids on the building. It is not possible for both buyers to purchase the building, therefore, the event of buyer A purchasing

FIGURE 4.3

A Union

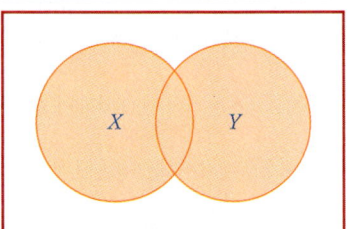

FIGURE 4.4

An Intersection

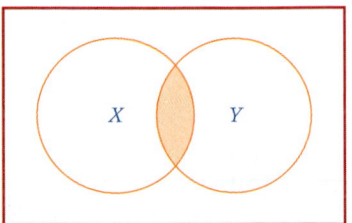

the building is mutually exclusive with the event of buyer B purchasing the building. In the toss of a single coin, heads and tails are mutually exclusive events. The person tossing the coin gets either a head or a tail but never both. On a toss of a pair of dice, the event $(6, 6)$, "boxcars," is mutually exclusive with the event $(1, 1)$, "snake eyes." Getting both boxcars and snake eyes on the same roll of the dice is impossible.

The probability of two mutually exclusive events occurring at the same time is zero.

MUTUALLY EXCLUSIVE EVENTS X AND Y	$P(X \cap Y) = 0$

Independent Events

Two or more events are **independent events** if *the occurrence or nonoccurrence of one of the events does not affect the occurrence or nonoccurrence of the other event(s)*. Certain experiments, such as rolling dice, yield independent events; each die is independent of the other. Whether a 6 is rolled on the first die has no influence on whether a 6 is rolled on the second die. Coin tosses always are independent of each other. The event of getting a head on the first toss of a coin is independent of getting a head on the second toss. It is generally believed that certain human characteristics are independent of other events. For example, left-handedness is probably independent of the possession of a credit card. Whether a person wears glasses or not is probably independent of the brand of milk preferred.

Many experiments using random selection can produce either independent or nonindependent events. In these experiments, the outcomes are independent if sampling is done with replacement; that is, after each item is selected and the outcome is determined, the item is restored to the population and the population is shuffled. This way, each draw becomes independent of the previous draw. Suppose an inspector is randomly selecting bolts from a bin that contains 5% defects. If the inspector samples a defective bolt and returns it to the bin, on the second draw there are still 5% defects in the bin regardless of the fact that the first outcome was a defect. If the inspector does not replace the first draw, the second draw is not independent of the first; in this case, fewer than 5% defects remain in the population. Thus the probability of the second outcome is dependent on the first outcome.

If X and Y are independent, the following symbolic notation is used.

INDEPENDENT EVENTS X AND Y	$P(X\|Y) = P(X)$ and $P(Y\|X) = P(Y)$

$P(X|Y)$ denotes the probability of X occurring given that Y has occurred. If X and Y are independent, then the probability of X occurring given that Y has occurred is just the probability of X occurring. Knowledge that Y has occurred does not impact the probability of X occurring because X and Y are independent. For example, $P(\text{prefers Pepsi}|\text{person is right-handed}) = P(\text{prefers Pepsi})$ because a person's handedness is independent of brand preference.

Collectively Exhaustive Events

A list of **collectively exhaustive events** contains *all possible elementary events for an experiment*. Thus, all sample spaces are collectively exhaustive lists. The list of possible outcomes for the tossing of a pair of dice contained in Table 4.1 is a collectively exhaustive list. The sample space for an experiment can be described as a list of events that are mutually exclusive and collectively exhaustive. Sample space events do not overlap or intersect, and the list is complete.

Complementary Events

The **complement** of event A is denoted A', pronounced "not A." All *the elementary events of an experiment not in A comprise its complement*. For example, if in rolling one die, event

A is getting an even number, the complement of *A* is getting an odd number. If event *A* is getting a 5 on the roll of a die, the complement of *A* is getting a 1, 2, 3, 4, or 6. The complement of event *A* contains whatever portion of the sample space that event *A* does not contain, as the Venn diagram in Figure 4.5 shows.

Using the complement of an event sometimes can be helpful in solving for probabilities because of the following rule.

PROBABILITY OF THE COMPLEMENT OF *A*	$$P(A') = 1 - P(A)$$

Suppose 32% of the employees of a company have a college degree. If an employee is randomly selected from the company, the probability that the person does not have a college degree is $1 - .32 = .68$. Suppose 42% of all parts produced in a plant are molded by machine A and 31% are molded by machine B. If a part is randomly selected, the probability that it was molded by neither machine A nor machine B is $1 - .73 = .27$. (Assume that a part is only molded on one machine.)

Counting the Possibilities

In statistics, a collection of techniques and rules for counting the number of outcomes that can occur for a particular experiment can be used. Some of these rules and techniques can delineate the size of the sample space. Presented here are three of these counting methods.

The *mn* Counting Rule

Suppose a customer decides to buy a certain brand of new car. Options for the car include two different engines, five different paint colors, and three interior packages. If each of these options is available with each of the others, how many different cars could the customer choose from? To determine this number, we can use the **mn counting rule.**

THE *mn* COUNTING RULE	For an operation that can be done *m* ways and a second operation that can be done *n* ways, the two operations then can occur, in order, in *mn* ways. This rule can be extended to cases with three or more operations.

Using the *mn* counting rule, we can determine that the automobile customer has $(2)(5)(3) = 30$ different car combinations of engines, paint colors, and interiors available.

Suppose a scientist wants to set up a research design to study the effects of gender (M, F), marital status (single never married, divorced, married), and economic class (lower, middle, and upper) on the frequency of airline ticket purchases per year. The researcher would set up a design in which 18 different samples are taken to represent all possible groups generated from these customer characteristics.

$$\text{Number of Groups} = (\text{Gender})(\text{Marital Status})(\text{Economic Class})$$
$$= (2)(3)(3) = 18 \text{ Groups}$$

Sampling from a Population with Replacement

In the second counting method, sampling *n* items from a population of size *N with replacement* would provide

$$(N)^n \text{ possibilities}$$

where
  N = population size
  n = sample size

For example, each time a die, which has six sides, is rolled, the outcomes are independent (with replacement) of the previous roll. If a die is rolled three times in succession, how

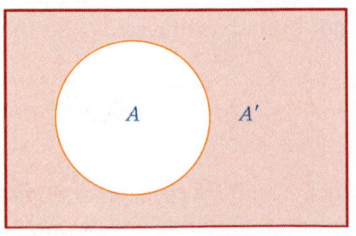

FIGURE 4.5

The Complement of Event *A*

many different outcomes can occur? That is, what is the size of the sample space for this experiment? The size of the population, N, is 6, the six sides of the die. We are sampling three dice rolls, $n = 3$. The sample space is

$$(N)^n = (6)^3 = 216$$

Suppose in a lottery six numbers are drawn from the digits 0 through 9, with replacement (digits can be reused). How many different groupings of six numbers can be drawn? N is the population of 10 numbers (0 through 9) and n is the sample size, six numbers.

$$(N)^n = (10)^6 = 1,000,000$$

That is, a million six-digit numbers are available!

Combinations: Sampling from a Population without Replacement

The third counting method uses **combinations,** sampling n items from a population of size N without replacement provides

$$_NC_n = \binom{N}{n} = \frac{N!}{n!(N-n)!}$$

possibilities.

For example, suppose a small law firm has 16 employees and three are to be selected randomly to represent the company at the annual meeting of the American Bar Association. How many different combinations of lawyers could be sent to the meeting? This situation does not allow sampling with replacement because three different lawyers will be selected to go. This problem is solved by using combinations. $N = 16$ and $n = 3$, so

$$_NC_n = {}_{16}C_3 = \frac{16!}{3!13!} = 560$$

A total of 560 combinations of three lawyers could be chosen to represent the firm.

4.3 PROBLEMS

4.1   A supplier shipped a lot of six parts to a company. The lot contained three defective parts. Suppose the customer decided to randomly select two parts and test them for defects. How large a sample space is the customer potentially working with? List the sample space. Using the sample space list, determine the probability that the customer will select a sample with exactly one defect.

4.2   Given $X = \{1, 3, 5, 7, 8, 9\}$, $Y = \{2, 4, 7, 9\}$, and $Z = \{1, 2, 3, 4, 7\}$, solve the following.

    a. $X \cup Z = $ ___
            b. $X \cap Y = $ ___

    c. $X \cap Z = $ ___
            d. $X \cup Y \cup Z = $ ___

    e. $X \cap Y \cap Z = $ ___
       f. $(X \cup Y) \cap Z = $ ___

    g. $(Y \cap Z) \cup (X \cap Y) = $ ___
   h.   X or Y = ___

    i.   Y and X = ___

4.3   If a population consists of the positive even numbers through 30 and if $A = \{2, 6, 12, 24\}$, what is A'?

4.4   A company's customer service 800 telephone system is set up so that the caller has six options. Each of these six options leads to a menu with four options. For each of these four options, three more options are available. For each of these three options, another three options are presented. If a person calls the 800 number for assistance, how many total options are possible?

4.5   A bin contains six parts. Two of the parts are defective and four are acceptable. If three of the six parts are selected from the bin, how large is the sample space?

Which counting rule did you use and why? For this sample space, what is the probability that exactly one of the three sampled parts is defective?

4.6   A company places a seven-digit serial number on each part that is made. Each digit of the serial number can be any number from 0 through 9. Digits can be repeated in the serial number. How many different serial numbers are possible?

4.7   A small company has 20 employees. Six of these employees will be selected randomly to be interviewed as part of an employee satisfaction program. How many different groups of six can be selected?

4.4 MARGINAL, UNION, JOINT, AND CONDITIONAL PROBABILITIES

Four particular types of probability are presented in this chapter. The first type is **marginal probability**. Marginal probability is denoted $P(E)$, where E is some event. A marginal probability is usually *computed by dividing some subtotal by the whole*. An example of marginal probability is the probability that a person owns a Ford car. This probability is computed by dividing the number of Ford owners by the total number of car owners. The probability of a person wearing glasses is also a marginal probability. This probability is computed by dividing the number of people wearing glasses by the total number of people.

A second type of probability is the union of two events. Union probability is denoted $P(E_1 \cup E_2)$, where E_1 and E_2 are two events. $P(E_1 \cup E_2)$ is the probability that E_1 will occur or that E_2 will occur or that both E_1 and E_2 will occur. An example of union probability is the probability that a person owns a Ford or a Chevrolet. To qualify for the union, the person only has to have at least one of these cars. Another example is the probability of a person wearing glasses or having red hair. All people wearing glasses are included in the union, along with all redheads and all redheads who wear glasses. In a company, the probability that a person is male or a clerical worker is a union probability. A person qualifies for the union by being male or by being a clerical worker or by being both (a male clerical worker).

A third type of probability is the intersection of two events, or joint probability. The joint probability of events E_1 and E_2 occurring is denoted $P(E_1 \cap E_2)$. Sometimes $P(E_1 \cap E_2)$ is read as the probability of E_1 and E_2. To qualify for the intersection, both events must occur. An example of joint probability is the probability of a person owning both a Ford and a Chevrolet. Owning one type of car is not sufficient. A second example of joint probability is the probability that a person is a redhead and wears glasses.

The fourth type is conditional probability. Conditional probability is denoted $P(E_1|E_2)$. This expression is read: the probability that E_1 will occur given that E_2 is known to have occurred. Conditional probabilities involve knowledge of some prior information. The information that is known or given is written to the right of the vertical line in the probability statement. An example of conditional probability is the probability that a person owns a Chevrolet given that she owns a Ford. This conditional probability is only a measure of the proportion of Ford owners who have a Chevrolet—not the proportion of total car owners who own a Chevrolet. Conditional probabilities are computed by determining the number of items that have an outcome out of some subtotal of the population. In the car owner example, the possibilities are reduced to Ford owners, and then the number of Chevrolet owners out of those Ford owners is determined. Another example of a conditional probability is the probability that a worker in a company is a professional given that he is male. Of the four probability types, only conditional probability does not have the population total as its denominator. Conditional probabilities have a population subtotal in the denominator. Figure 4.6 summarizes these four types of probability.

4.5 ADDITION LAWS

Several tools are available for use in solving probability problems. These tools include sample space, tree diagrams, the laws of probability, probability matrices, and insight. Because

FIGURE 4.6

Marginal, Union, Joint, and
Conditional Probabilities

Marginal	Union	Joint	Conditional
$P(X)$	$P(X \cup Y)$	$P(X \cap Y)$	$P(X \mid Y)$
The probability of X occurring	The probability of X or Y occurring	The probability of X and Y occurring	The probability of X occurring given that Y has occurred
Uses total possible outcomes in denominator	Uses total possible outcomes in denominator	Uses total possible outcomes in denominator	Uses subtotal of the possible outcomes in denominator

of the individuality and variety of probability problems, some techniques apply more readily in certain situations than in others. No best method is available for solving all probability problems. In some instances, the probability matrix lays out a problem in a readily solvable manner. In other cases, setting up the probability matrix is more difficult than solving the problem in another way. The probability laws almost always can be used to solve probability problems. However, for some problems the solution can be determined without formally applying the laws.

One of the tools already presented is sample space; others include the laws of probability. Four laws of probability are presented in this chapter: The addition laws, conditional probability, the multiplication laws, and Bayes' rule. The addition laws and the multiplication laws each have a general law and a special law. The general law of addition is used to find the probability of the union of two events, $P(X \cup Y)$. The expression $P(X \cup Y)$ denotes the probability of X occurring or Y occurring or both X and Y occurring.

GENERAL LAW OF ADDITION
$$P(X \cup Y) = P(X) + P(Y) - P(X \cap Y)$$
where X, Y are events and $(X \cap Y)$ is the intersection of X and Y.

Yankelovich Partners conducted a survey for the American Society of Interior Designers in which workers were asked which changes in office design would increase productivity. Respondents were allowed to answer more than one type of design change. The number one change that 70% of the workers said would increase productivity was reducing noise. In second place was more storage/filing space, selected by 67%. If one of the survey respondents was randomly selected and asked what office design changes would increase worker productivity, what is the probability that this person would select reducing noise *or* more storage/filing space?

Let N represent the event "reducing noise." Let S represent the event "more storage/filing space." The probability of a person responding with N *or* S can be symbolized statistically as a union probability by using the law of addition.

$$P(N \cup S)$$

To successfully satisfy the search for a person who responds with reducing noise *or* more storage/filing space, we need only find someone who wants *at least one* of those two events. Because 70% of the surveyed people responded that reducing noise would create more productivity, $P(N) = .70$. In addition, because 67% responded that increased storage space would improve productivity, $P(S) = .67$. Either of these would satisfy the requirement of the union. Thus, the solution to the problem seems to be

$$P(N \cup S) = P(N) + P(S) = .70 + .67 = 1.37$$

FIGURE 4.7

Solving for the Union in the Office Productivity Problem

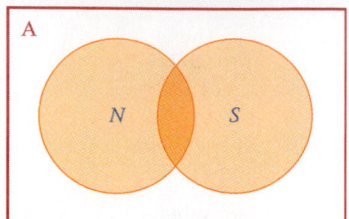

A

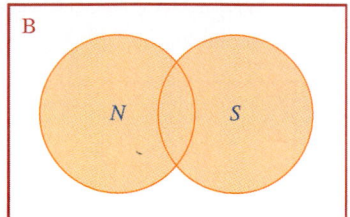

B

However, we already established that probabilities cannot be more than 1.00. What is the problem here? Notice that all people who responded that *both* reducing noise *and* increasing storage space would improve productivity are included in *each* of the marginal probabilities $P(N)$ and $P(S)$. Certainly a respondent who recommends both of these improvements should be included as favoring at least one. However, because they are included in the $P(N)$ *and* the $P(S)$, the people who recommended both improvements are *double counted*. For that reason, the general law of addition subtracts the intersection probability, $P(N \cap S)$.

In Figure 4.7, Venn diagrams illustrate this discussion. Notice that the intersection area of N and S is double shaded in diagram A, indicating that it has been counted twice. In diagram B, the shading is consistent throughout N and S because the intersection area has been subtracted out. Thus diagram B illustrates the proper application of the general law of addition.

So what is the answer to Yankelovich Partners' union probability question? Suppose 56% of all respondents to the survey had said that *both* noise reduction *and* increased storage/filing space would improve productivity: $P(N \cap S) = .56$. Then we could use the general law of addition to solve for the probability that a person responds that *either* noise reduction *or* increased storage space would improve productivity.

$$P(N \cup S) = P(N) + P(S) - P(N \cap S) = .70 + .67 - .56 = .81$$

Hence, 81% of the workers surveyed responded that *either* noise reduction *or* increased storage space would improve productivity.

Probability Matrices

In addition to the formulas, another useful tool in solving probability problems is a probability matrix. A **probability matrix** *displays the marginal probabilities and the intersection probabilities of a given problem.* Union probabilities and conditional probabilities must be computed from the matrix. Generally, a probability matrix is constructed as a two-dimensional table with one variable on each side of the table. For example, in the office design problem, noise reduction would be on one side of the table and increased storage space on the other. In this problem, a Yes row and a No row would be created for one variable and a Yes column and a No column would be created for the other variable, as shown in Table 4.2.

Once the matrix is created, we can enter the marginal probabilities. $P(N) = .70$ is the marginal probability that a person responds yes to noise reduction. This value is placed in the "margin" in the row of Yes to noise reduction, as shown in Table 4.3. If $P(N) = .70$, then 30% of the people surveyed did not think that noise reduction would increase productivity. Thus, $P(\text{not } N) = 1 - .70 = .30$. This value, also a marginal probability, goes in the row indicated by No under noise reduction. In the column under Yes for increased storage space, the marginal probability $P(S) = .67$ is recorded. Finally, the marginal probability of No for increased storage space, $P(\text{not } S) = 1 - .67 = .33$, is placed in the No column.

TABLE 4.2

Probability Matrix for the Office Design Problem

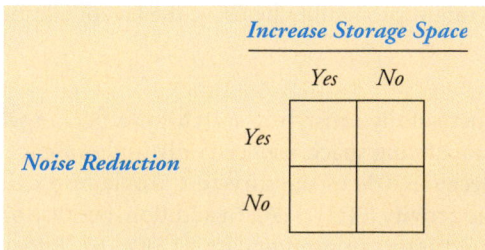

	Increase Storage Space	
	Yes	*No*
Noise Reduction — *Yes*		
No		

TABLE 4.3

Probability Matrix for the Office Design Problem

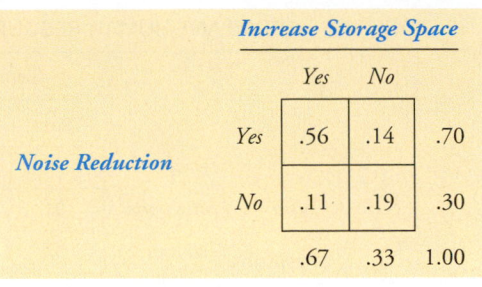

TABLE 4.4

Yes Row and Column for Probability Matrix of the Office Design Problem

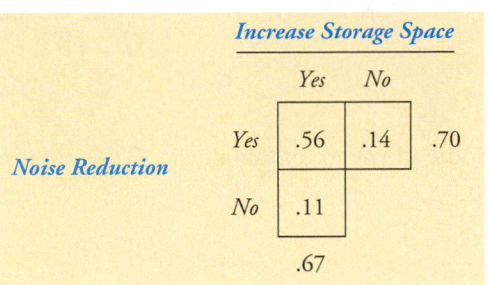

In this probability matrix, all four marginal probabilities are given or can be computed simply by using the probability of a complement rule, $P(\text{not } S) = 1 - P(S)$. The intersection of noise reduction and increased storage space is given as $P(N \cap S) = .56$. This value is entered into the probability matrix in the cell under Yes Yes, as shown in Table 4.3. The rest of the matrix can be determined by subtracting the cell values from the marginal probabilities. For example, subtracting .56 from .70 and getting .14 yields the value for the cell under Yes for noise reduction and No for increased storage space. In other words, 14% of all respondents said that noise reduction would improve productivity but increased storage space would not. Filling out the rest of the matrix results in the probabilities shown in Table 4.3.

Now we can solve the union probability, $P(N \cup S)$, in at least two different ways using the probability matrix. The focus is on the Yes row for noise reduction and the Yes column for increase storage space, as displayed in Table 4.4. The probability of a person suggesting noise reduction *or* increased storage space as a solution for improving productivity, $P(N \cup S)$, can be determined from the probability matrix by adding the marginal probabilities of Yes for noise reduction and Yes for increased storage space and then subtracting the Yes Yes cell, following the pattern of the general law of probabilities.

$$P(N \cup S) = .70 \text{ (from Yes row)} + .67 \text{ (from Yes column)}$$
$$- .56 \text{ (From Yes Yes cell)} = .81$$

Another way to solve for the union probability from the information displayed in the probability matrix is to sum all cells in any of the Yes rows or columns. Observe the following from Table 4.4.

$$P(N \cup S) = .56 \text{ (from Yes Yes cell)}$$
$$+ .14 \text{ (from Yes on noise reduction and No on increase storage space)}$$
$$+ .11 \text{ (from No on noise reduction and Yes on increase storage space)}$$
$$= .81$$

DEMONSTRATION PROBLEM 4.1

The client company data from the Decision Dilemma reveal that 155 employees worked one of four types of positions. Shown here again is the raw values matrix (also called a contingency table) with the frequency counts for each category and for subtotals and totals containing a breakdown of these employees by type of position and by gender. If an employee of the company is selected randomly, what is the probability that the employee is female or a professional worker?

COMPANY HUMAN RESOURCE DATA

		Gender		
		Male	Female	
Type of Position	Managerial	8	3	11
	Professional	31	13	44
	Technical	52	17	69
	Clerical	9	22	31
		100	55	155

Solution

Let F denote the event of female and P denote the event of professional worker. The question is

$$P(F \cup P) = ?$$

By the general law of addition,

$$P(F \cup P) = P(F) + P(P) - P(F \cap P)$$

Of the 155 employees, 55 are women. Therefore, $P(F) = 55/155 = .355$. The 155 employees include 44 professionals. Therefore, $P(P) = 44/155 = .284$. Because 13 employees are both female and professional, $P(F \cap P) = 13/155 = .084$. The union probability is solved as

$$P(F \cup P) = .355 + .284 - .084 = .555.$$

To solve this probability using a matrix, you can either use the raw values matrix shown previously or convert the raw values matrix to a probability matrix by dividing every value in the matrix by the value of N, 155. The raw value matrix is used in a manner similar to that of the probability matrix. To compute the union probability of selecting a person who is either female or a professional worker from the raw value matrix, add the number of people in the Female column (55) to the number of people in the Professional row (44), then subtract the number of people in the intersection cell of Female and Professional (13). This step yields the value $55 + 44 - 13 = 86$. Dividing this value (86) by the value of N (155) produces the union probability.

$$P(F \cup P) = 86/155 = .555$$

A second way to produce the answer from the raw value matrix is to add all the cells one time that are in either the Female column or the Professional row

$$3 + 13 + 17 + 22 + 31 = 86$$

and then divide by the total number of employees, $N = 155$, which gives

$$P(F \cup P) = 86/155 = .555$$

DEMONSTRATION PROBLEM 4.2

Shown here are the raw values matrix and corresponding probability matrix for the results of a national survey of 200 executives who were asked to identify the geographic locale of their company and their company's industry type. The executives were only allowed to select one locale and one industry type.

RAW VALUES MATRIX

		Geographic Location				
		Northeast D	Southeast E	Midwest F	West G	
Industry Type	Finance A	24	10	8	14	56
	Manufacturing B	30	6	22	12	70
	Communications C	28	18	12	16	74
		82	34	42	42	200

PROBABILITY MATRIX

		Geographic Location				
		Northeast D	Southeast E	Midwest F	West G	
Industry Type	Finance A	.12	.05	.04	.07	.28
	Manufacturing B	.15	.03	.11	.06	.35
	Communications C	.14	.09	.06	.08	.37
		.41	.17	.21	.21	1.00

Suppose a respondent is selected randomly from these data.

a. What is the probability that the respondent is from the Midwest (F)?

b. What is the probability that the respondent is from the communications industry (C) or from the Northeast (D)?

c. What is the probability that the respondent is from the Southeast (E) or from the finance industry (A)?

Solution

a. $P(\text{Midwest}) = P(F) = .21$

b. $P(C \cup D) = P(C) + P(D) - P(C \cap D) = .37 + .41 - .14 = .64$

c. $P(E \cup A) = P(E) + P(A) - P(E \cap A) = .17 + .28 - .05 = .40$

In computing the union by using the general law of addition, the intersection probability is subtracted because it is already included in both marginal probabilities. This adjusted probability leaves a union probability that properly includes both marginal values and the intersection value. If the intersection probability is subtracted out a second time, the intersection is removed, leaving the probability of *X or Y* but not *both*.

$P(X \text{ or } Y \text{ but not both}) = P(X) + P(Y) - P(X \cap Y) - P(X \cap Y) = P(X \cup Y) - P(X \cap Y)$

Figure 4.8 is the Venn diagram for this probability.

Complement of a Union

The probability of the union of two events X and Y represents the probability that the outcome is *either X or* it is *Y or* it is *both X and Y*. The union includes everything except the possibility that it is neither (*X or Y*). Another way to state it is as *neither X nor Y*, which can

FIGURE 4.8

The *X* or *Y* but Not Both Case

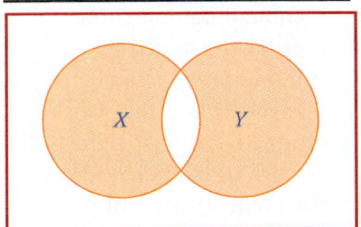

FIGURE 4.9

The Complement of a Union: The Neither/Nor Region

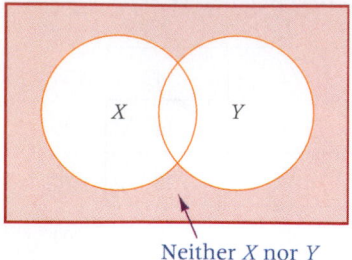

Neither *X* nor *Y*

symbolically be represented as $P(\text{not } X \cap \text{not } Y)$. Because it is the only possible case other than the union of X or Y, it is the **complement of a union.** Stated more formally,

$$P(\text{neither } X \text{ nor } Y) = P(\text{not } X \cap \text{not } Y) = 1 - P(X \cup Y).$$

Examine the Venn diagram in Figure 4.9. Note that the complement of the union of X, Y is the shaded area outside the circles. This area represents the neither X nor Y region.

In the survey about increasing worker productivity by changing the office design discussed earlier, the probability that a randomly selected worker would respond with noise reduction *or* increased storage space was determined to be

$$P(N \cup S) = P(N) + P(S) - P(N \cap S) = .70 + .67 - .56 = .81$$

The probability that a worker would respond with *neither* noise reduction *nor* increased storage space is calculated as the complement of this union.

$$P(\text{neither } N \text{ nor } S) = P(\text{not } N \cap \text{not } S) = 1 - P(N \cup S) = 1 - .81 = .19$$

Thus 19% of the workers selected neither noise reduction nor increased storage space as solutions to increasing productivity. In Table 4.3, this *neither/nor* probability is found in the No No cell of the matrix, .19.

Special Law of Addition

If two events are mutually exclusive, the probability of the union of the two events is the probability of the first event plus the probability of the second event. Because mutually exclusive events do not intersect, nothing has to be subtracted.

SPECIAL LAW OF ADDITION	If X, Y are mutually exclusive, $P(X \cup Y) = P(X) + P(Y)$.

The special law of addition is a special case of the general law of addition. In a sense, the general law fits all cases. However, when the events are mutually exclusive, a zero is inserted into the general law formula for the intersection, resulting in the special law formula.

In the survey about improving productivity by changing office design, the respondents were allowed to choose more than one possible office design change. Therefore, it is most likely that virtually none of the change choices were mutually exclusive, and the special law of addition would not apply to that example.

In another survey, however, respondents were allowed to select only one option for their answer, which made the possible options mutually exclusive. In this survey, conducted by Yankelovich Partners for William M. Mercer, Inc., workers were asked what most hinders their productivity and were given only the following selections from which to choose only one answer.

- Lack of direction
- Lack of support
- Too much work
- Inefficient process
- Not enough equipment/supplies
- Low pay/chance to advance

Lack of direction was cited by the most workers (20%), followed by lack of support (18%), too much work (18%), inefficient process (8%), not enough equipment/supplies (7%), low pay/chance to advance (7%), and a variety of other factors added by respondents. If a worker who responded to this survey is selected (or if the survey actually reflects the views of the working public and a worker in general is selected) and that worker is asked which of the given selections most hinders his or her productivity, what is the probability that the worker will respond that it is either too much work or inefficient process?

Let M denote the event "too much work" and I denote the event "inefficient process." The question is:

$$P(M \cup I) = ?$$

Because 18% of the survey respondents said "too much work,"

$$P(M) = .18$$

Because 8% of the survey respondents said "inefficient process,"

$$P(I) = .08$$

Because it was not possible to select more than one answer,

$$P(M \cap I) = .0000$$

Implementing the special law of addition gives

$$P(M \cup I) = P(M) + P(I) = .18 + .08 = .26$$

DEMONSTRATION PROBLEM 4.3

If a worker is randomly selected from the company described in Demonstration Problem 4.1, what is the probability that the worker is either technical or clerical? What is the probability that the worker is either a professional or a clerical?

Solution

Examine the raw value matrix of the company's human resources data shown in Demonstration Problem 4.1. In many raw value and probability matrices like this one, the rows are nonoverlapping or mutually exclusive, as are the columns. In this matrix, a worker can be classified as being in only one type of position and as either male or female but not both. Thus, the categories of type of position are mutually exclusive, as are the categories of gender, and the special law of addition can be applied to the human resource data to determine the union probabilities.

Let T denote technical, C denote clerical, and P denote professional. The probability that a worker is either technical or clerical is

$$P(T \cup C) = P(T) + P(C) = \frac{69}{155} + \frac{31}{155} = \frac{100}{155} = .645$$

The probability that a worker is either professional or clerical is

$$P(P \cup C) = P(P) + P(C) = \frac{44}{155} + \frac{31}{155} = \frac{75}{155} = .484$$

DEMONSTRATION PROBLEM 4.4

Use the data from the matrices in Demonstration Problem 4.2. What is the probability that a randomly selected respondent is from the Southeast or the West?

$$P(E \cup G) = ?$$

Solution

Because geographic location is mutually exclusive (the work location is either in the Southeast or in the West but not in both),

$$P(E \cup G) = P(E) + P(G) = .17 + .21 = .38$$

4.5 PROBLEMS

4.8 Given $P(A) = .10$, $P(B) = .12$, $P(C) = .21$, $P(A \cap C) = .05$, and $P(B \cap C) = .03$, solve the following.

a. $P(A \cup C) = $ ____

b. $P(B \cup C) = $ ____

c. If A and B are mutually exclusive, $P(A \cup B) = $ ____

4.9 Use the values in the matrix to solve the equations given.

	D	E	F
A	5	8	12
B	10	6	4
C	8	2	5

a. $P(A \cup D) = $ ____

b. $P(E \cup B) = $ ____

c. $P(D \cup E) = $ ____

d. $P(C \cup F) = $ ____

4.10 Use the values in the matrix to solve the equations given.

	E	F
A	.10	.03
B	.04	.12
C	.27	.06
D	.31	.07

a. $P(A \cup F) = $ ____

b. $P(E \cup B) = $ ____

c. $P(B \cup C) = $ ____

d. $P(E \cup F) = $ ____

4.11 Suppose that 47% of all Americans have flown in an airplane at least once and that 28% of all Americans have ridden on a train at least once. What is the probability that a randomly selected American has either ridden on a train or flown in an airplane? Can this problem be solved? Under what conditions can it be solved? If the problem cannot be solved, what information is needed to make it solvable?

4.12 According to the U.S. Bureau of Labor Statistics, 75% of the women 25 through 49 years of age participate in the labor force. Suppose 78% of the women in that age group are married. Suppose also that 61% of all women 25 through 49 years of age are married and are participating in the labor force.

a. What is the probability that a randomly selected woman in that age group is married or is participating in the labor force?

b. What is the probability that a randomly selected woman in that age group is married or is participating in the labor force but not both?

c. What is the probability that a randomly selected woman in that age group is neither married nor participating in the labor force?

4.13 According to Nielsen Media Research, approximately 67% of all U.S. households with television have cable TV. Seventy-four percent of all U.S. households with television have two or more TV sets. Suppose 55% of all U.S. households with television have cable TV and two or more TV sets. A U.S. household with television is randomly selected.

a. What is the probability that the household has cable TV or two or more TV sets?

b. What is the probability that the household has cable TV or two or more TV sets but not both?

    c. What is the probability that the household has neither cable TV nor two or more TV sets?

    d. Why does the special law of addition not apply to this problem?

4.14 A survey conducted by the Northwestern University Lindquist-Endicott Report asked 320 companies about the procedures they use in hiring. Only 54% of the responding companies review the applicant's college transcript as part of the hiring process, and only 44% consider faculty references. Assume that these percentages are true for the population of companies in the United States and that 35% of all companies use both the applicant's college transcript and faculty references.

    a. What is the probability that a randomly selected company uses either faculty references or college transcript as part of the hiring process?

    b. What is the probability that a randomly selected company uses either faculty references or college transcript but not both as part of the hiring process?

    c. What is the probability that a randomly selected company uses neither faculty references nor college transcript as part of the hiring process?

    d. Construct a probability matrix for this problem and indicate the locations of your answers for parts (a), (b), and (c) on the matrix.

4.6 MULTIPLICATION LAWS

General Law of Multiplication

As stated in Section 4.4, the probability of the intersection of two events $(X \cap Y)$ is called the joint probability. The general law of multiplication is used to find the joint probability.

GENERAL LAW OF MULTIPLICATION	$P(X \cap Y) = P(X) \cdot P(Y|X) = P(Y) \cdot P(X|Y)$

The notation $X \cap Y$ means that both X *and* Y must *happen*. The general law of multiplication gives the probability that *both* event X and event Y will occur at the same time.

According to the U.S. Bureau of Labor Statistics, 46% of the U.S. labor force is female. In addition, 25% of the women in the labor force work part time. What is the probability that a randomly selected member of the U.S. labor force is a woman *and* works part time? This question is one of joint probability, and the general law of multiplication can be applied to answer it.

Let W denote the event that the member of the labor force is a woman. Let T denote the event that the member is a part-time worker. The question is:

$$P(W \cap T) = ?$$

FIGURE 4.10

Joint Probability that a Woman is in the Labor Force and is a Part-Time Worker

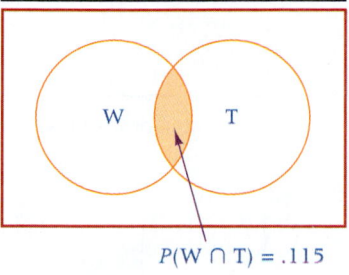

$P(W \cap T) = .115$

According to the general law of multiplication, this problem can be solved by

$$P(W \cap T) = P(W) \cdot P(T|W)$$

Since 46% of the labor force is women, $P(W) = .46$. $P(T|W)$ is a conditional probability that can be stated as the probability that a worker is a part-time worker given that the worker is a woman. This condition is what was given in the statement that 25% *of the women in the labor force* work part time. Hence, $P(T|W) = .25$. From there it follows that

$$P(W \cap T) = P(W) \cdot P(T|W) = (.46)(.25) = .115$$

It can be stated that 11.5% of the U.S. labor force are women *and* work part time. The Venn diagram in Figure 4.10 shows these relationships and the joint probability.

TABLE 4.5

Probability Matrix of Company Human Resource Data

		Gender		
		Male	Female	
Type of Position	Managerial	.052	.019	.071
	Professional	.200	.084	.284
	Technical	.335	.110	.445
	Clerical	.058	.142	.200
		.645	.355	1.000

Determining joint probabilities from raw value or probability matrices is easy because every cell of these matrices is a joint probability. In fact, some statisticians refer to a probability matrix as a *joint probability table*.

For example, suppose the raw value matrix of the client company data from Demonstration Problem 4.1 and the Decision Dilemma is converted to a probability matrix by dividing by the total number of employees ($N = 155$), resulting in Table 4.5. Each value in the cell of Table 4.5 is an intersection, and the table contains all possible intersections (joint probabilities) for the events of gender and type of position. For example, the probability that a randomly selected worker is male *and* a technical worker, $P(M \cap T)$, is .335. The probability that a randomly selected worker is female *and* a professional worker, $P(F \cap P)$, is .084. Once a probability matrix is constructed for a problem, usually the easiest way to solve for the joint probability is to find the appropriate cell in the matrix and select the answer. However, sometimes because of what is given in a problem, using the formula is easier than constructing the matrix.

DEMONSTRATION PROBLEM 4.5

A company has 140 employees, of which 30 are supervisors. Eighty of the employees are married, and 20% of the married employees are supervisors. If a company employee is randomly selected, what is the probability that the employee is married and is a supervisor?

Solution

Let M denote married and S denote supervisor. The question is:

$$P(M \cap S) = ?$$

First, calculate the marginal probability.

$$P(M) = \frac{80}{140} = .5714$$

Then, note that 20% of the married employees are supervisors, which is the conditional probability, $P(S|M) = .20$. Finally, applying the general law of multiplication gives

$$P(M \cap S) = P(M) \cdot P(S|M) = (.5714)(.20) = .1143$$

Hence, 11.43% of the 140 employees are married and are supervisors.

DEMONSTRATION PROBLEM 4.6

From the data obtained from the interviews of 200 executives in Demonstration Problem 4.2, find:

a. $P(B \cap E)$

b. $P(G \cap A)$

c. $P(B \cap C)$

RAW VALUES MATRIX

		Northeast D	Southeast E	Midwest F	West G	
	Finance A	24	10	8	14	56
Industry Type	Manufacturing B	30	6	22	12	70
	Communications C	28	18	12	16	74
		82	34	42	42	200

Geographic Location spans Northeast D, Southeast E, Midwest F, West G.

PROBABILITY MATRIX

		Northeast D	Southeast E	Midwest F	West G	
	Finance A	.12	.05	.04	.07	.28
Industry Type	Manufacturing B	.15	.03	.11	.06	.35
	Communications C	.14	.09	.06	.08	.37
		.41	.17	.21	.21	1.00

Geographic Location spans Northeast D, Southeast E, Midwest F, West G.

Solution

a. From the cell of the probability matrix, $P(B \cap E) = 6/200 = .03$. To solve by the formula, $P(B \cap E) = P(B) \cdot P(E|B)$, first find $P(B)$:

$$P(B) = \frac{70}{200} = .35$$

The probability of E occurring given that B has occurred, $P(E|B)$, can be determined from the probability matrix as $P(E|B) = .03/.35$. Therefore,

$$P(B \cap E) = P(B) \cdot P(E|B) = (.35)\left(\frac{.03}{.35}\right) = .03$$

Although the formula works, finding the joint probability in the cell of the probability matrix is faster than using the formula.

An alternative formula is $P(B \cap E) = P(E) \cdot P(B|E)$, but $P(E) = .17$. Then $P(B|E)$ means the probability of B if E is given. There are .17 Es in the probability matrix and .03 Bs in these Es. Hence,

$$P(B|E) = \frac{.03}{.17} \text{ and } P(B \cap E) = P(E) \cdot P(B|E) = (.17)\left(\frac{.03}{.17}\right) = .03$$

b. To obtain $P(G \cap A)$, find the intersecting cell of G and A in the probability matrix, .07, or use one of the following formulas:

$$P(G \cap A) = P(G) \cdot P(A|G) = (.21)\left(\frac{.07}{.21}\right) = .07$$

or

$$P(G \cap A) = P(A) \cdot P(G|A) = (.28)\left(\frac{.07}{.28}\right) = .07$$

TABLE 4.6

Contingency Table of Data from Independent Events

	D	E	
A	8	12	20
B	20	30	50
C	6	9	15
	34	51	85

c. The probability $P(B \cap C)$ means that one respondent would have to work both in the manufacturing industry and the communications industry. The survey used to gather data from the 200 executives, however, requested that each respondent specify only one industry type for his or her company. The matrix shows no intersection for these two events. Thus B and C are mutually exclusive. None of the respondents is in both manufacturing and communications. Hence,

$$P(B \cap C) = .0$$

Special Law of Multiplication

If events X and Y are independent, a special law of multiplication can be used to find the intersection of X and Y. This special law utilizes the fact that when two events X, Y are independent, $P(X|Y) = P(X)$ and $P(Y|X) = P(Y)$. Thus, the general law of multiplication,

$P(X \cap Y) = P(X) \cdot P(Y|X)$, becomes $P(X \cap Y) = P(X) \cdot P(Y)$ when X and Y are independent.

SPECIAL LAW OF MULTIPLICATION	If X, Y are independent, $P(X \cap Y) = P(X) \cdot P(Y)$

A study released by Bruskin-Goldring Research for SEIKO found that 28% of U.S. adults believe that the automated teller has had a most significant impact on everyday life. Another study by David Michaelson & Associates for Dale Carnegie & Associates examined employee views on team spirit in the workplace and discovered that 72% of all employees believe that working as a part of a team lowers stress. Are people's views on automated tellers independent of their views on team spirit in the workplace? If they are independent, then the probability of a person being randomly selected who believes that the automated teller has had a most significant impact on everyday life *and* that working as part of a team lowers stress is found as follows. Let A denote automated teller and S denote teamwork lowers stress.

$$P(A) = .28$$
$$P(S) = .72$$
$$P(A \cap S) = P(A) \cdot P(S) = (.28)(.72) = .2016$$

Therefore, 20.16% of the population believes that the automated teller has had a most significant impact on everyday life *and* that working as part of a team lowers stress.

DEMONSTRATION PROBLEM 4.7

A manufacturing firm produces pads of bound paper. Three percent of all paper pads produced are improperly bound. An inspector randomly samples two pads of paper, one at a time. Because a large number of pads are being produced during the inspection, the sampling being done, in essence, is with replacement. What is the probability that the two pads selected are both improperly bound?

Solution

Let I denote improperly bound. The problem is to determine

$$P(I_1 \cap I_2) = ?$$

The probability of I = .03, or 3% are improperly bound. Because the sampling is done with replacement, the two events are independent. Hence,

$$P(I_1 \cap I_2) = P(I_1) \cdot P(I_2) = (.03)(.03) = .0009$$

Most probability matrices contain variables that are not independent. If a probability matrix contains independent events, the special law of multiplication can be applied. If not, the special law cannot be used. In Section 4.7 we explore a technique for determining whether events are independent. Table 4.6 contains data from independent events.

DEMONSTRATION PROBLEM 4.8

Use the data from Table 4.6 and the special law of multiplication to find $P(B \cap D)$.

Solution

$$P(B \cap D) = P(B) \cdot P(D) = \frac{50}{85} \cdot \frac{34}{85} = .2353$$

This approach works *only* for contingency tables and probability matrices in which the variable along one side of the matrix is *independent* of the variable along the other side of the matrix. Note that the answer obtained by using the formula is the same as the answer obtained by using the cell information from Table 4.6.

$$P(B \cap D) = \frac{20}{85} = .2353$$

4.6 PROBLEMS

4.15 Use the values in the contingency table to solve the equations given.

	C	D	E	F
A	5	11	16	8
B	2	3	5	7

   a. $P(A \cap E) =$ ____
   b. $P(D \cap B) =$ ____
   c. $P(D \cap E) =$ ____
   d. $P(A \cap B) =$ ____ .

4.16 Use the values in the probability matrix to solve the equations given.

	D	E	F
A	.12	.13	.08
B	.18	.09	.04
C	.06	.24	.06

   a. $P(E \cap B) =$ ____
   b. $P(C \cap F) =$ ____
   c. $P(E \cap D) =$ ____

4.17 a. A batch of 50 parts contains six defects. If two parts are drawn randomly one at a time without replacement, what is the probability that both parts are defective?
   b. If this experiment is repeated, with replacement, what is the probability that both parts are defective?

4.18 According to the nonprofit group Zero Population Growth, 78% of the U.S. population now lives in urban areas. Scientists at Princeton University and the University of Wisconsin report that about 15% of all U.S. adults care for ill relatives. Suppose that 11% of adults living in urban areas care for ill relatives.

    a. Use the general law of multiplication to determine the probability of randomly selecting an adult from the U.S. population who lives in an urban area and is caring for an ill relative.

    b. What is the probability of randomly selecting an adult from the U.S. population who lives in an urban area and does not care for an ill relative?

    c. Construct a probability matrix and show where the answer to this problem lies in the matrix.

    d. From the probability matrix, determine the probability that an adult lives in a nonurban area and cares for an ill relative.

4.19 A study by Peter D. Hart Research Associates for the Nasdaq Stock Market revealed that 43% of all U.S. adults are stockholders. In addition, the study determined that 75% of all U.S. adult stockholders have some college education. Suppose 37% of all U.S. adults have some college education. A U.S. adult is randomly selected.

    a. What is the probability that the adult does not own stock?

    b. What is the probability that the adult owns stock and has some college education?

    c. What is the probability that the adult owns stock or has some college education?

    d. What is the probability that the adult has neither some college education nor owns stock?

    e. What is the probability that the adult does not own stock or has no college education?

    f. What is the probability that the adult has some college education and owns no stock?

4.20 According to the Consumer Electronics Manufacturers Association, 10% of all U.S. households have a fax machine and 52% have a personal computer. Suppose 91% of all U.S. households having a fax machine have a personal computer. A U.S. household is randomly selected.

    a. What is the probability that the household has a fax machine and a personal computer?

    b. What is the probability that the household has a fax machine or a personal computer?

    c. What is the probability that the household has a fax machine and does not have a personal computer?

    d. What is the probability that the household has neither a fax machine nor a personal computer?

    e. What is the probability that the household does not have a fax machine and does have a personal computer?

4.21 A study by Becker Associates, a San Diego travel consultant, found that 30% of the traveling public said that their flight selections are influenced by perceptions of airline safety. Thirty-nine percent of the traveling public wants to know the age of the aircraft. Suppose 87% of the traveling public who say that their flight selections are influenced by perceptions of airline safety wants to know the age of the aircraft.

    a. What is the probability of randomly selecting a member of the traveling public and finding out that she says that flight selection is influenced by perceptions of airline safety and she does not want to know the age of the aircraft?

    b. What is the probability of randomly selecting a member of the traveling public and finding out that she says that flight selection is neither influenced by perceptions of airline safety nor does she want to know the age of the aircraft?

    c. What is the probability of randomly selecting a member of the traveling public and finding out that he says that flight selection is not influenced by perceptions of airline safety and he wants to know the age of the aircraft?

4.22 The U.S. Energy Department states that 60% of all U.S. households have ceiling fans. In addition, 29% of all U.S. households have an outdoor grill. Suppose 13% of all U.S. households have both a ceiling fan and an outdoor grill. A U.S. household is randomly selected.

a. What is the probability that the household has a ceiling fan or an outdoor grill?

b. What is the probability that the household has neither a ceiling fan nor an outdoor grill?

c. What is the probability that the household does not have a ceiling fan and does have an outdoor grill?

d. What is the probability that the household does have a ceiling fan and does not have an outdoor grill?

4.7 CONDITIONAL PROBABILITY

Conditional probabilities are computed based on the prior knowledge that a statistician has on one of the two events being studied. If X, Y are two events, the conditional probability of X occurring given that Y is known or has occurred is expressed as $P(X|Y)$ and is given in the *law of conditional probability*.

LAW OF CONDITIONAL PROBABILITY	$$P(X|Y) = \frac{P(X \cap Y)}{P(Y)} = \frac{P(X) \cdot P(Y|X)}{P(Y)}$$

The conditional probability of $(X|Y)$ is the probability that X will occur given Y. The formula for conditional probability is derived by dividing both sides of the general law of multiplication by $P(Y)$.

In the study by Yankelovich Partners to determine what changes in office design would improve productivity, 70% of the respondents believed noise reduction would improve productivity and 67% said increased storage space would improve productivity. In addition, suppose 56% of the respondents believed both noise reduction and increased storage space would improve productivity. A worker is selected randomly and asked about changes in office design. This worker believes that noise reduction would improve productivity. What is the probability that this worker believes increased storage space would improve productivity? That is, what is the probability that a randomly selected person believes storage space would improve productivity *given that* he or she believes noise reduction improves productivity? In symbols, the question is

$$P(S|N) = ?$$

Note that the given part of the information is listed to the right of the vertical line in the conditional probability. The formula solution is

$$P(S|N) = \frac{P(S \cap N)}{P(N)}$$

$$P(N) = .70 \text{ and } P(S \cap N) = .56$$

$$P(S|N) = \frac{P(S \cap N)}{P(N)} = \frac{.56}{.70} = .80$$

Eighty percent of workers who believe noise reduction would improve productivity believe increased storage space would improve productivity.

Note in Figure 4.11 that the area for N in the Venn diagram is completely shaded because it is given that the worker believes noise reduction will improve productivity. Also notice that the intersection of N and S is more heavily shaded. This portion of noise reduction includes increased storage space. It is the only part of increased storage space that is

FIGURE 4.11.

Conditional Probability of Increased Storage Space Given Noise Reduction

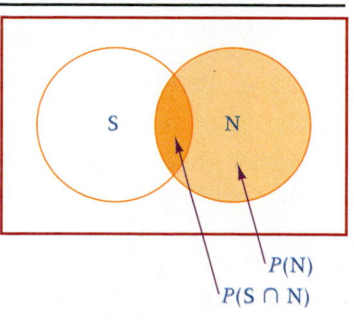

$P(N)$
$P(S \cap N)$

in noise reduction, and because the person is known to favor noise reduction, it is the only area of interest that includes increased storage space.

Examine the probability matrix in Table 4.7 for the office design problem. None of the probabilities given in the matrix are conditional probabilities. To reiterate what has been previously stated, a probability matrix contains only two types of probabilities, marginal and joint. The cell values are all joint probabilities and the subtotals in the margins are marginal probabilities. How are conditional probabilities determined from a probability matrix? The law of conditional probabilities shows that a conditional probability is computed by dividing the joint probability by the marginal probability. Thus, the probability matrix has all the necessary information to solve for a conditional probability.

What is the probability that a randomly selected worker believes noise reduction would not improve productivity given that the worker does believe increased storage space would improve productivity? That is,

$$P(\text{not N}|\text{S}) = ?$$

The law of conditional probability states that

$$P(\text{not N}|\text{S}) = \frac{P(\text{not N} \cap \text{S})}{P(\text{S})}$$

Notice that because S is given, we are interested only in the column that is shaded in Table 4.7, which is the Yes column for increased storage space. The marginal probability, $P(\text{S})$, is the total of this column and is found in the margin at the bottom of the table as .67. $P(\text{not N} \cap \text{S})$ is found as the intersection of No for noise and Yes for storage. This value is .11. Hence, $P(\text{not N} \cap \text{S})$ is .11. Therefore,

$$P(\text{not N}|\text{S}) = \frac{P(\text{not N} \cap \text{S})}{P(\text{S})} = \frac{.11}{.67} = .164$$

The second version of the conditional probability law formula is

$$P(X|Y) = \frac{P(X) \cdot P(Y|X)}{P(Y)}$$

This version is more complex than the first version, $P(X \cap Y)/P(Y)$. However, sometimes the second version must be used because of the information given in the problem—for example, when solving for $P(X|Y)$ but $P(Y|X)$ is given. The second version of the formula is obtained from the first version by substituting the formula for $P(X \cap Y) = P(X) \cdot P(Y|X)$ into the first version.

As an example, in Section 4.6, data relating to women in the U.S. labor force were presented. Included in this information was the fact that 46% of the U.S. labor force is female and that 25% of the females in the U.S. labor force work part time. In addition, 17.4% of all U.S. laborers are known to be part-time workers. What is the probability that

TABLE 4.7

Office Design Problem
Probability Matrix

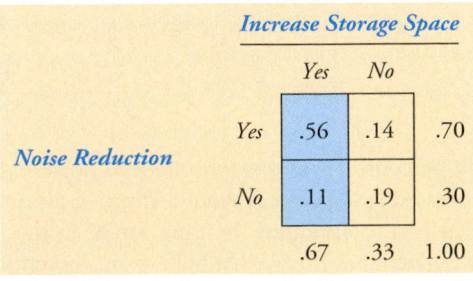

		Increase Storage Space		
		Yes	*No*	
Noise Reduction	*Yes*	.56	.14	.70
	No	.11	.19	.30
		.67	.33	1.00

a randomly selected U.S. worker is a woman if that person is known to be a part-time worker? Let W denote the event of selecting a woman and T denote the event of selecting a part-time worker. In symbols, the question to be answered is

$$P(W|T) = ?$$

The first form of the law of conditional probabilities is

$$P(W|T) = \frac{P(W \cap T)}{P(T)}$$

Note that this version of the law of conditional probabilities requires knowledge of the joint probability, $P(W \cap T)$, which is not given here. We therefore try the second version of the law of conditional probabilities, which is

$$P(W|T) = \frac{P(W) \cdot P(T|W)}{P(T)}$$

For this version of the formula, everything is given in the problem.

$$P(W) = .46$$
$$P(T) = .174$$
$$P(T|W) = .25$$

The probability of a laborer being a woman given that the person works part time can now be computed.

$$P(W|T) = \frac{P(W) \cdot P(T|W)}{P(T)} = \frac{(.46)(.25)}{(.174)} = .661$$

Hence, 66.1% of the part-time workers are women.

In general, this second version of the law of conditional probabilities is likely to be used when $P(X \cap Y)$ is unknown but $P(Y|X)$ is known.

DEMONSTRATION PROBLEM 4.9

The data from the executive interviews given in Demonstration Problem 4.2 are repeated here. Use these data to find:

a. $P(B|F)$

b. $P(G|C)$

c. $P(D|F)$

RAW VALUES MATRIX

		Geographic Location				
		Northeast D	Southeast E	Midwest F	West G	
	Finance A	24	10	8	14	56
Industry Type	Manufacturing B	30	6	22	12	70
	Communications C	28	18	12	16	74
		82	34	42	42	200

PROBABILITY MATRIX

		Geographic Location				
		Northeast D	Southeast E	Midwest F	West G	
Industry Type	Finance A	.12	.05	.04	.07	.28
	Manufacturing B	.15	.03	.11	.06	.35
	Communications C	.14	.09	.06	.08	.37
		.41	.17	.21	.21	1.00

Solution

a.
$$P(B|F) = \frac{P(B \cap F)}{P(F)} = \frac{.11}{.21} = .524$$

Determining conditional probabilities from a probability matrix by using the formula is a relatively painless process. In this case, the joint probability, $P(B \cap F)$, appears in a cell of the matrix (.11); the marginal probability, $P(F)$, appears in a margin (.21). Bringing these two probabilities together by formula produces the answer, .11/.21 = .524. This answer means that 52.4% of the Midwest executives (the F values) are in manufacturing (the B values).

b.
$$P(G|C) = \frac{P(G \cap C)}{P(C)} = \frac{.08}{.37} = .216$$

This result means that 21.6% of the responding communications industry executives, (C) are from the West (G).

c.
$$P(D|F) = \frac{P(D \cap F)}{P(F)} = \frac{.00}{.21} = .00$$

Because D and F are mutually exclusive, $P(D \cap F)$ is zero and so is $P(D|F)$. The rationale behind $P(D|F) = 0$ is that, if F is given (the respondent is known to be located in the Midwest), the respondent could not be located in D (the Northeast).

Independent Events

INDEPENDENT EVENTS X, Y To determine whether X and Y are independent events, the following definition can be used.

$$P(X|Y) = P(X) \quad \text{and} \quad P(Y|X) = P(Y)$$

In each equation, it does not matter that X or Y is given because X and Y are *independent*. When X and Y are independent, the conditional probability is solved as a marginal probability.

Sometimes, it is important to test a contingency table of raw data to determine whether events are independent. If *any* combination of two events from the different sides of the matrix fail the test, $P(X|Y) = P(X)$, the matrix does not contain independent events.

DEMONSTRATION PROBLEM 4.10

Test the matrix for the 200 executive responses to determine whether industry type is independent of geographic location.

STATISTICS IN BUSINESS TODAY

HMOs: The Probabilities of Regulating and Reforming

The movement toward HMOs from traditional healthcare providers occurred quite rapidly in the past decade. Although some people are satisfied with HMOs, others believe that they need to be reformed. An article published in *The Wall Street Journal* on June 25, 1998, presents many statistics with regard to Americans and their healthcare. The article states that 51% of consumers believe that passing new regulations on HMOs is a good idea, but 32% of consumers believe it is a bad idea. These two figures can be seen as marginal probabilities:

$$P(\text{good idea}) = .51 \text{ and } P(\text{bad idea}) = .32$$

The support for passing such regulation varies by political party affiliation, age, and type of insurance held. For example, 57% of democrats believe that passing new regulations on HMOs is a good idea, but only 43% of republicans think so. Fifty-five percent of consumers ages 18 to 29 believe that new regulations are a good idea, but the figure drops to 46% for consumers 65 and over. Forty-nine percent of consumers who have Medicare/Medicaid support new regulations, and 60% of consumers who have no insurance support new regulations. These figures can be stated as conditional probabilities.

$$P(\text{good idea}|\text{democrat}) = .57$$
$$P(\text{good idea}|\text{republican}) = .43$$
$$P(\text{good idea}|\text{18 to 29}) = .55$$
$$P(\text{good idea}|\text{65 and over}) = .46$$

$$P(\text{good idea}|\text{Medicare/Medicaid}) = .49$$
$$P(\text{good idea}|\text{no insurance}) = .60$$

In addition, the U.S. Census Bureau reports that 12.6% of the population is at least 65 years of age and 16.1% of the U.S. population has no insurance:

$$P(\geq 65) = .126 \text{ and } P(\text{no insurance}) = .161$$

Some of these probabilities can be combined to produce intersection probabilities such as:

$$P(\geq 65 \cap \text{good idea}) = P(\geq 65) \cdot P(\text{good idea}|\geq 65)$$
$$= (.126)(.46) = .058$$

$$P(\text{no insurance} \cap \text{good idea}) =$$

$$P(\text{no insurance}) \cdot P(\text{good idea}|\text{no insurance})$$
$$= (.161)(.60) = .097$$

According to these figures, 5.8% of consumers are at least 65 years of age *and* think that new regulations for HMOs are a good idea; whereas 9.7% of consumers have no insurance and think that new regulations for HMOs are a good idea.

Using the addition law, we can also compute union probabilities such as the probability that a randomly selected consumer has no insurance or thinks that new regulations for HMOs are a good idea:

$$P(\text{no insurance} \cup \text{good idea}) =$$

$$P(\text{no insurance}) + P(\text{good idea})$$
$$- P(\text{no insurance} \cap \text{good idea})$$
$$= .161 + .51 - .097 = .574$$

RAW VALUES MATRIX

		Geographic Location				
		Northeast D	Southeast E	Midwest F	West G	
Industry Type	Finance A	24	10	8	14	56
	Manufacturing B	30	6	22	12	70
	Communications C	28	18	12	16	74
		82	34	42	42	200

Solution

Select one industry and one geographic location (say, A—Finance and G—West). Does $P(A|G) = P(A)$?

$$P(A|G) = \frac{14}{42} \text{ and } P(A) = \frac{56}{200}$$

Does 14/42 = 56/200? No, .33 ≠ .28. Industry and geographic location are not independent because at least one exception to the test is present.

DEMONSTRATION PROBLEM 4.11

Determine whether the contingency table shown as Table 4.6 and repeated here contains independent events.

	D	E	
A	8	12	20
B	20	30	50
C	6	9	15
	34	51	85

Solution

Check the first cell in the matrix to find whether $P(A|D) = P(A)$.

$$P(A|D) = \frac{8}{34} = .2353$$

$$P(A) = \frac{20}{85} = .2353$$

The checking process must continue until all the events are determined to be independent. In this matrix, all the possibilities check out. Thus, Table 4.6 contains independent events.

4.7 PROBLEMS

4.23   Use the values in the contingency table to solve the equations given.

	E	F	G
A	15	12	8
B	11	17	19
C	21	32	27
D	18	13	12

   a. $P(G|A) =$ ___
   b. $P(B|F) =$ ___
   c. $P(C|E) =$ ___
   d. $P(E|G) =$ ___

4.24   Use the values in the probability matrix to solve the equations given.

	C	D
A	.36	.44
B	.11	.09

   a. $P(C|A) =$ ___
   b. $P(B|D) =$ ___
   c. $P(A|B) =$ ___

4.25 The results of a survey asking, "Do you have a calculator and/or a computer in your home?" follow.

		Calculator		
		Yes	No	
Computer	Yes	46	3	49
	No	11	15	26
		57	18	75

Is the variable "calculator" independent of the variable "computer"? Why or why not?

4.26 In 1997, business failures in the United States numbered 83,384, according to Dun & Bradstreet. The construction industry accounted for 10,867 of these business failures. The South Atlantic states accounted for 8,010 of the business failures. Suppose that 1,258 of all business failures were construction businesses located in the South Atlantic states. A failed business from 1997 is randomly sampled.

a. What is the probability that the business is located in the South Atlantic states?

b. What is the probability that the business is in the construction industry or located in the South Atlantic states?

c. What is the probability that the business is in the construction industry if it is known that the business is located in the South Atlantic states?

d. What is the probability that the business is located in the South Atlantic states if it is known that the business is a construction business?

e. What is the probability that the business is not located in the South Atlantic states if it is known that the business is not a construction business?

f. Given that the business is a construction business, what is the probability that the business is not located in the South Atlantic states?

4.27 Arthur Andersen Enterprise Group/National Small Business United, Washington, conducted a national survey of small-business owners to determine the challenges for growth for their businesses. The top challenge, selected by 46% of the small-business owners, was the economy. A close second was finding qualified workers (37%). Suppose 15% of the small-business owners selected both the economy and finding qualified workers as challenges for growth. A small-business owner is randomly selected.

a. What is the probability that the owner believes the economy is a challenge for growth if the owner believes that finding qualified workers is a challenge for growth?

b. What is the probability that the owner believes that finding qualified workers is a challenge for growth if the owner believes that the economy is a challenge for growth?

c. Given that the owner does not select the economy as a challenge for growth, what is the probability that the owner believes that finding qualified workers is a challenge for growth?

d. What is the probability that the owner believes neither that the economy is a challenge for growth nor that finding qualified workers is a challenge for growth?

4.28 Late in 1998, a study of online users was conducted by Jupiter Communications to determine for which type of purchase a consumer prefers live customer service. Forty-seven percent of the users replied that when purchasing airline tickets, they prefer live customer service. Suppose that of those who prefer live customer service for purchasing airline tickets, 81% prefer live customer service for transacting loans. If an online user is randomly selected, determine the following probabilities:

   a. The online user prefers live customer service for both purchasing airline tickets and for transacting loans.

   b. The online user does not prefer live customer service for transacting loans given that she does prefer live customer service for purchasing airline tickets.

   c. The online user does not prefer live customer service for transacting loans and does prefer live customer service for purchasing airline tickets.

4.29 *Accounting Today* reported that 37% of accountants purchase their computer hardware by mail order direct and that 54% purchase their computer software by mail order direct. Suppose that 97% of the accountants who purchase their computer hardware by mail order direct purchase their computer software by mail order direct. If an accountant is randomly selected, determine the following probabilities:

   a. The accountant does not purchase his computer software by mail order direct given that he does purchase his computer hardware by mail order direct.

   b. The accountant does purchase his computer software by mail order direct given that he does not purchase his computer hardware by mail order direct.

   c. The accountant does not purchase his computer hardware by mail order direct if it is known that he does purchase his computer software by mail order direct.

   d. The accountant does not purchase his computer hardware by mail order direct if it is known that he does not purchase his computer software by mail order direct.

4.8 REVISION OF PROBABILITIES: BAYES' RULE

An extension to the conditional law of probabilities is Bayes' rule, which was developed by and named for Thomas Bayes (1702–1761). **Bayes' rule** is *a formula that extends the use of the law of conditional probabilities to allow revision of original probabilities with new information.*

BAYES' RULE	$$P(X_i|Y) = \frac{P(X_i) \cdot P(Y|X_i)}{P(X_1) \cdot P(Y|X_1) + P(X_2) \cdot P(Y|X_2) + \cdots + P(X_n) \cdot P(Y|X_n)}$$

Recall that the law of conditional probability for

$$P(X_i|Y)$$

is

$$P(X_i|Y) = \frac{P(X_i) \cdot P(Y|X_i)}{P(Y)}$$

    Compare Bayes' rule to this law of conditional probability. The numerators of Bayes' rule and the law of conditional probability are the same, the intersection of X_i and Y shown in the form of the general rule of multiplication. The new feature that Bayes' rule uses is found in the denominator of the rule:

$$P(X_1) \cdot P(Y|X_1) + P(X_2) \cdot P(Y|X_2) + \cdots + P(X_n) \cdot P(Y|X_n)$$

    The denominator of Bayes' rule includes a product expression (intersection) for every partition in the sample space, Y, including the event (X_i) itself. The denominator is thus a collective exhaustive listing of mutually exclusive outcomes of Y. This denominator is sometimes referred to as the "total probability formula." It represents a weighted average of the conditional probabilities, with the weights being the prior probabilities of the corresponding event.

By expressing the law of conditional probabilities in this new way, Bayes' rule enables the statistician to make new and different applications using conditional probabilities. In particular, statisticians use Bayes' rule to "revise" probabilities in light of new information.

A particular type of printer ribbon is produced by only two companies, Alamo Ribbon Company and South Jersey Products. Suppose Alamo produces 65% of the ribbons and that South Jersey produces 35%. Eight percent of the ribbons produced by Alamo are defective and 12% of the South Jersey ribbons are defective. A customer purchases a new ribbon. What is the probability that Alamo produced the ribbon? What is the probability that South Jersey produced the ribbon? The ribbon is tested, and it is defective. Now what is the probability that Alamo produced the ribbon? That South Jersey produced the ribbon?

The probability was .65 that the ribbon came from Alamo and .35 that it came from South Jersey. These are called prior probabilities because they are based on the original information.

The new information that the ribbon is defective changes the probabilities because one company produces a higher percentage of defective ribbons than the other company does. How can this information be used to update or revise the original probabilities? Bayes' rule allows such updating. One way to lay out a revision of probabilities problem is to use a table. Table 4.8 shows the analysis for the ribbon problem.

The process begins with the prior probabilities: .65 Alamo and .35 South Jersey. These prior probabilities appear in the second column of Table 4.8. Because the product is found to be defective, the conditional probabilities, $P(\text{defective}|\text{Alamo})$ and $P(\text{defective}|\text{South Jersey})$ should be used. Eight percent of Alamo's ribbons are defective: $P(\text{defective}|\text{Alamo})$ = .08. Twelve percent of South Jersey's ribbons are defective: $P(\text{defective}|\text{South Jersey})$ = .12. These two conditional probabilities appear in the third column. Eight percent of Alamo's 65% of the ribbons are defective: (.08)(.65) = .052, or 5.2% of the total. This figure appears in the fourth column of Table 4.8; it is the joint probability of getting a ribbon that was made by Alamo and is defective. Because the purchased ribbon is defective, these are the only Alamo ribbons of interest. Twelve percent of South Jersey's 35% of the ribbons are defective. Multiplying these two percentages yields the joint probability of getting a South Jersey ribbon that is defective. This figure also appears in the fourth column of Table 4.8: (.12)(.35) = .042; that is, 4.2% of all ribbons are made by South Jersey and are defective. This percentage includes the only South Jersey ribbons of interest because the ribbon purchased is defective.

Column 4 is totaled to get .094, indicating that 9.4% of all ribbons are defective (Alamo and defective = .052 + South Jersey and defective = .042). The other 90.6% of the ribbons, which are acceptable, are not of interest because the ribbon purchased is defective. To compute the fifth column, the posterior or revised probabilities, involves dividing each value in column 4 by the total of column 4. For Alamo, .052 of the total ribbons are Alamo and defective out of the total of .094 that are defective. Dividing .052 by .094 yields .553 as a revised probability that the purchased ribbon was made by Alamo. This probability is lower than the prior or original probability of .65 because fewer of Alamo's ribbons (as a percentage) are defective than those produced by South Jersey. The defective ribbon is now less likely to have come from Alamo than before the knowledge of the defective ribbon. South Jersey's probability is revised by dividing the .042 joint probability of the ribbon being made by South Jersey and defective by the total probability of the ribbon being defective (.094).

TABLE 4.8	**Event**	**Prior Probability** $P(E_i)$	**Conditional Probability** $P(d\|E_i)$	**Joint Probability** $P(E_i \cap d)$	**Posterior or Revised Probability**
Bayesian Table for Revision of Ribbon Problem Probabilities	Alamo	.65	.08	.052	$\dfrac{.052}{.094} = .553$
	South Jersey	.35	.12	.042	$\dfrac{.042}{.094} = .447$
				$P(\text{defective}) = .094$	

FIGURE 4.12

Tree Diagram for Ribbon
Problem Probabilities

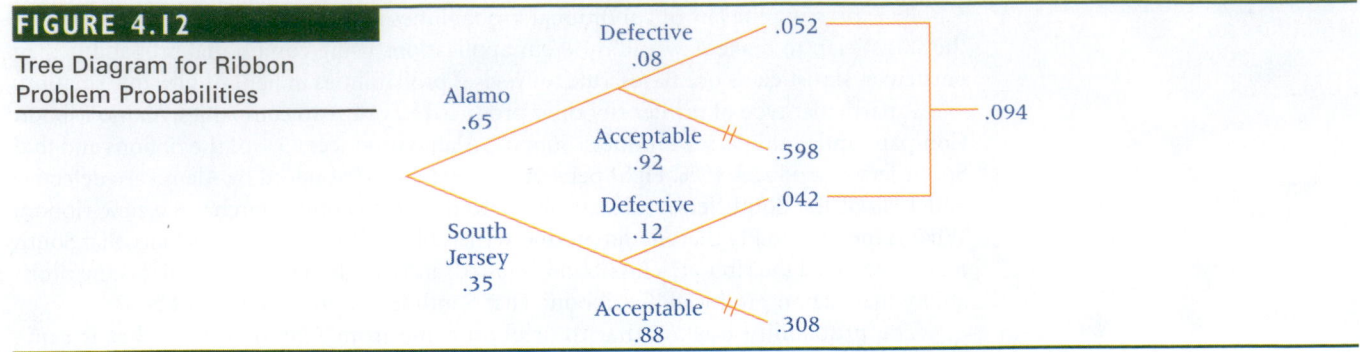

The result is .042/.094 = .447. The probability that the defective ribbon is from South Jersey increased because a higher percentage of South Jersey ribbons are defective.

Tree diagrams are another common way to solve Bayes' rule problems. Figure 4.12 shows the solution for the ribbon problem. Note that the tree diagram contains all possibilities, including both defective and acceptable ribbons. When new information is given, only the pertinent branches are selected and used. The joint probability values at the end of the appropriate branches are used to revise and compute the posterior possibilities. Using the total number of defective ribbons, .052 + .042 = .094, the calculation is as follows.

$$\text{Revised Probability: Alamo} = \frac{.052}{.094} = .553$$

$$\text{Revised Probability: South Jersey} = \frac{.042}{.094} = .447$$

DEMONSTRATION PROBLEM 4.12

Machines A, B, and C all produce the same two parts, X and Y. Of all the parts produced, machine A produces 60%, machine B produces 30%, and machine C produces 10%. In addition,

40% of the parts made by machine A are part X.

50% of the parts made by machine B are part X.

70% of the parts made by machine C are part X.

A part produced by this company is randomly sampled and is determined to be an X part. With the knowledge that it is an X part, revise the probabilities that the part came from machine A, B, or C.

Solution

The prior probability of the part coming from machine A is .60, because machine A produces 60% of all parts. The prior probability is .30 that the part came from B and .10 that it came from C. These prior probabilities are more pertinent if nothing is known about the part. However, the part is known to be an X part. The conditional probabilities show that different machines produce different proportions of X parts. For example, .40 of the parts made by machine A are X parts, but .50 of the parts made by machine B and .70 of the parts made by machine C are X parts. It makes sense that the probability of the part coming from machine C would increase and that the probability that the part was made on machine A would decrease because the part is an X part.

The following table shows how the prior probabilities, conditional probabilities, joint probabilities, and marginal probability, $P(X)$, can be used to revise the prior probabilities to obtain posterior probabilities.

Event	Prior $P(E_i)$	Conditional $P(X\|E_i)$	Joint $P(X \cap E_i)$	Posterior
A	.60	.40	$(.60)(.40) = .24$	$\dfrac{.24}{.46} = .52$
B	.30	.50	.15	$\dfrac{.15}{.46} = .33$
C	.10	.70	.07	$\dfrac{.07}{.46} = .15$
			$P(X) = .46$	

After the probabilities are revised, it is apparent that the probability of the part being made at machine A decreased and that the probabilities that the part was made at machines B and C increased. A tree diagram presents another view of this problem.

Revised Probabilities: Machine A: $\dfrac{.24}{.46} = .52$

Machine B: $\dfrac{.15}{.46} = .33$

Machine C: $\dfrac{.07}{.46} = .15$

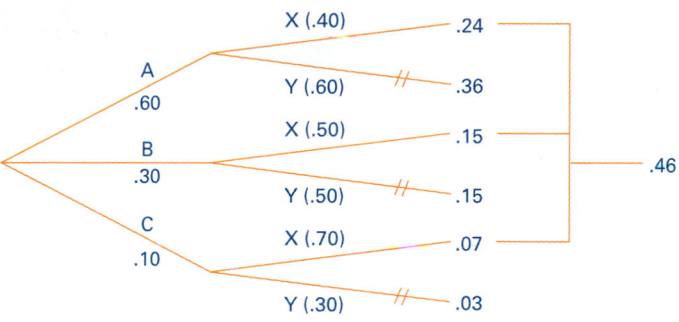

4.8 PROBLEMS

4.30 In a manufacturing plant, machine A produces 10% of a certain product, machine B produces 40% of this product, and machine C produces 50% of this product. Five percent of machine A products are defective, 12% of machine B products are defective, and 8% of machine C products are defective. The company inspector has just sampled a product from this plant and has found it to be defective. Determine the revised probabilities that the sampled product was produced by machine A, machine B, or machine C.

4.31 Alex, Alicia, and Juan fill orders in a fast-food restaurant. Alex incorrectly fills 20% of the orders he takes. Alicia incorrectly fills 12% of the orders she takes. Juan incorrectly fills 5% of the orders he takes. Alex fills 30% of all orders, Alicia fills 45% of all orders, and Juan fills 25% of all orders. An order has just been filled.

a. What is the probability that Alicia filled the order?

b. If the order was filled by Juan, what is the probability that it was filled correctly?

c. Who filled the order is unknown, but the order was filled incorrectly. What are the revised probabilities that Alex, Alicia, or Juan filled the order?

d. Who filled the order is unknown, but the order was filled correctly. What are the revised probabilities that Alex, Alicia, or Juan filled the order?

4.32   In a small town, two lawn companies fertilize lawns during the summer. Tri-State Lawn Service has 72% of the market. Thirty percent of the lawns fertilized by Tri-State could be rated as very healthy one month after service. Greenchem has the other 28% of the market. Twenty percent of the lawns fertilized by Greenchem could be rated as very healthy one month after service. A lawn that has been treated with fertilizer by one of these companies within the last month is selected randomly. If the lawn is rated as very healthy, what are the revised probabilities that Tri-State or Greenchem treated the lawn?

4.33   Companies provide training to employees for many different reasons. Among them are employee loyalty, employee retention, and quality of employee work. Suppose 65% of all companies give some training to their employees but that this figure varies by company size. Suppose further that 18% of all companies using training are small companies and that 75% of all companies that do not use training are small companies. A company is randomly sampled without regard to size. What is the probability that the company uses training? Suppose it is determined that the selected company is not a small company. What is the revised probability that the company uses training? What proportion of all companies is not small?

Gender Equity in the Workplace

The client company data given in the Decision Dilemma are displayed in a raw values matrix form. Using the techniques presented in this chapter, it is possible to statistically answer the managerial questions. If a worker is randomly selected from the 155 employees, the probability that the worker is a woman, $P(W)$, is 55/155 or .355. This marginal probability indicates that roughly 35.5% of all employees of the client company are women. Given that the employee has a managerial position, the probability that the employee is a woman, $P(W|M)$ is 3/11 or .273. The proportion of managers at the company who are women is lower than the proportion of all workers at the company who are women. Several factors might be related to this discrepancy, some of which may be defensible by the company—including experience, education, and prior history of success—and some may not.

Suppose a technical employee is randomly selected for a bonus. What is the probability that a female would be selected given that the worker is a technical employee? That is, $P(F|T) = ?$ Applying the law of conditional probabilities to the raw values matrix given in the Decision Dilemma, $P(F|T) = 17/69 = .246$. Using the concept of complementary events, the probability that a man is selected given that the employee is a technical person is $1 - .246 = .754$. It is more than three times as likely that a randomly selected technical person is a male. If a woman were the one chosen for the bonus, a man could argue discrimination based on the mere probabilities. However, the company decision makers could then present documentation of the choice criteria based on productivity, technical suggestions, quality measures, and others.

Suppose a client company employee is randomly chosen to win a trip to Hawaii. The marginal probability that the winner is a professional is $P(P) = 44/155 = .284$. The probability that the winner is either a male or is a clerical worker is a union probability is:

$$P(M \cup C) = P(M) + P(C) - P(M \cap C) = \frac{100}{155} + \frac{31}{155} - \frac{9}{155} = \frac{122}{155} = .787$$

The probability of a male or clerical employee at the client company winning the trip is .787. The probability that the winner is a woman *and* a manager is a joint probability is

$$P(F \cap M) = 3/155 = .019$$

There is less than a 2% chance that a female manager will be selected randomly as the trip winner.

What is the probability that the winner is from the technical group if it is known that the employee is a male? This conditional probability is as follows:

$$P(T|M) = 52/100 = .52.$$

Many other questions can be answered about the client company's human resource situation using probabilities.

The probability approach to a human resource pool is a factual, numerical approach to people selection taken without regard to individual talents, skills, and worth to the company. Of course, in most instances, many other considerations go into the hiring, promoting, and rewarding of workers besides the random draw of their name. However, company management should be aware that attacks on hiring, promotion, and reward practices are sometimes made using statistical analyses such as those presented here. It is not being argued here that management should base decisions merely on the probabilities within particular categories. Nevertheless, being aware of the probabilities, management can proceed to undergird their decisions with documented evidence of worker productivity and worth to the organization.

ETHICAL CONSIDERATIONS

One of the potential misuses of probability occurs when subjective probabilities are used. Most subjective probabilities are based on a person's feelings, intuition, or experience. Almost everyone has an opinion on something and is willing to share it. As professional people, it is important that we do not give our "best-guess" probability of an occurrence if we are not relatively confident of what will happen. Optimistic people will tend to give higher probabilities of the likelihood of a company or client attaining some goal. Pessimistic people may tend to dampen the probability of such a goal being attained. Although such probabilities are not strictly unethical to report, they can be misleading and disastrous to other decision makers. We should be cautious in offering our subjective probabilities in decision-making situations where our opinion is highly valued. In addition, subjective probabilities leave the door open for unscrupulous people to overemphasize their point of view by manipulating the probability.

Relative frequency of occurrence probabilities are basically computed on historical figures. It is important that such historical information be accurate and valid. "Padding" the figures from the past can lead to incorrect and misleading probabilities.

The decision maker should remember that the laws and rules of probability are for the "long run." If a coin is tossed, even though the probability of getting a head is .5, the result will be either a head or a tail. It isn't possible to get a half head. The probability of getting a head (.5) will probably work out in the long run, but in the short run an experiment might produce 10 tails in a row. Suppose the probability of striking oil on a geological formation like the one on which a company is drilling is .10. This probability means that, in the long run, if the company drills enough holes on this type of formation, it should strike oil in about 10% of the holes. However, if the company has only enough money to drill one hole, it will either strike oil or have a dry hole. The probability figure of .10 may mean something different to the company that can afford to drill only one hole than to the company that can drill many hundreds. Classical probabilities could be used unethically to lure a company or client into a potential short-run investment with the expectation of getting at least something in return, when in actuality the investor will either win or lose. The oil company that drills only one hole will not get 10% back from the hole. It will either win or lose on the hole. Thus, classical probabilities open the door for unsubstantiated expectations, particularly in the short run.

SUMMARY

The study of probability addresses ways of assigning probabilities, types of probabilities, and laws of probabilities. Probabilities support the notion of inferential statistics. Using sample data to estimate and test hypotheses about population parameters is done with uncertainty. If samples are taken at random, probabilities can be assigned to outcomes of the inferential process.

Three methods of assigning probabilities are (1) the classical method, (2) the relative frequency of occurrence method, and (3) subjective probabilities. The classical method can assign probabilities a priori, or before the experiment takes place. It relies on the laws and rules of probability. The relative frequency of occurrence method assigns probabilities based on historical data or empirically derived data. Subjective probabilities are based on the feelings, knowledge, and experience of the person determining the probability.

Certain special types of events necessitate amendments to some of the laws of probability: mutually exclusive events and independent events. Mutually exclusive events are events that cannot occur at the same time, so the probability of their intersection is zero. In determining the union of two mutually exclusive events, the law of addition is amended by the deletion of the intersection. With independent events, the occurrence of one has no impact or influence on the occurrence of the other. Certain experiments, such as those involving coins or dice, naturally produce independent events. Other experiments produce independent events when the experiment is conducted with replacement. If events are independent, the joint probability is computed by multiplying the individual probabilities, which is a special case of the law of multiplication.

Three techniques for counting the possibilities in an experiment are the mn counting rule, the N^n possibilities, and combinations. The mn counting rule is used to determine how many total possible ways an experiment can occur in a series of sequential operations. The N^n formula is applied when sampling is being done with replacement or events are independent. Combinations are used to determine the possibilities when sampling is being done without replacement.

Four types of probability are marginal probability, conditional probability, joint probability, and union probability. The general law of addition is used to compute the probability of a union. The general law of multiplication is used to compute joint probabilities. The conditional law is used to compute conditional probabilities.

Bayes' rule is a method that can be used to revise probabilities when new information becomes available; it is a variation of the conditional law. Bayes' rule takes prior probabilities of events occurring and adjusts or revises those probabilities on the basis of information about what subsequently occurs.

KEY TERMS

a priori	complement	joint probability	sample space
Bayes' rule	conditional probability	marginal probability	set notation
classical method of assigning probabilities	elementary events	*mn* counting rule	subjective probability
	event	mutually exclusive events	union
collectively exhaustive events	experiment	probability matrix	union probability
combinations	independent events	relative frequency of occurrence	
complement of a union	intersection		

FORMULAS

Counting rule

$$mn$$

Sampling with replacement

$$N^n$$

Sampling without replacement

$$_NC_n$$

Combination formula

$$_NC_n = \binom{N}{n} = \frac{N!}{n!(N-n)!}$$

General law of addition

$$P(X \cup Y) = P(X) + P(Y) - P(X \cap Y)$$

Special law of addition

$$P(X \cup Y) = P(X) + P(Y)$$

General law of multiplication

$$P(X \cap Y) = P(X) \cdot P(Y|X) = P(Y) \cdot P(X|Y)$$

Special law of multiplication

$$P(X \cap Y) = P(X) \cdot P(Y)$$

Law of conditional probability

$$P(X|Y) = \frac{P(X \cap Y)}{P(Y)} = \frac{P(X) \cdot P(Y|X)}{P(Y)}$$

Bayes' rule

$$P(X_i|Y) = \frac{P(X_i) \cdot P(Y|X_i)}{P(X_1) \cdot P(Y|X_1) + P(X_2) \cdot P(Y|X_2) + \cdots + P(X_n) \cdot P(Y|X_n)}$$

SUPPLEMENTARY PROBLEMS

CALCULATING THE STATISTICS

4.34 Use the values in the contingency table to solve the equations given.

		D	E
	A	10	20
Variable 2	B	15	5
	C	30	15

  a. $P(E) =$ ___
  b. $P(B \cup D) =$ ___
  c. $P(A \cap E) =$ ___
  d. $P(B|E) =$ ___
  e. $P(A \cup B) =$ ___
  f. $P(B \cap C) =$ ___
  g. $P(D|C) =$ ___
  h. $P(A|B) =$ ___
  i. Are variables 1 and 2 independent? Why or why not?

4.35 Use the values in the contingency table to solve the equations given.

	D	E	F	G
A	3	9	7	12
B	8	4	6	4
C	10	5	3	7

  a. $P(F \cap A) =$ ___
  b. $P(A|B) =$ ___
  c. $P(B) =$ ___
  d. $P(E \cap F) =$ ___
  e. $P(D|B) =$ ___
  f. $P(B|D) =$ ___
  g. $P(D \cup C) =$ ___
  h. $P(F) =$ ___

4.36 The following probability matrix contains a breakdown on the age and gender of U.S. physicians in a recent year, as reported by the American Medical Association.

U.S. PHYSICIANS IN A RECENT YEAR

		<35	35–44	45–54	55–64	>65	
	Male	.11	.20	.19	.12	.16	.78
Gender	Female	.07	.08	.04	.02	.01	.22
		.18	.28	.23	.14	.17	1.00

(Age (years))

  a. What is the probability that one randomly selected physician is 35–44 years old?
  b. What is the probability that one randomly selected physician is both a woman and 45–54 years old?
  c. What is the probability that one randomly selected physician is a man or is 35–44 years old?
  d. What is the probability that one randomly selected physician is less than 35 years old or 55–64 years old?
  e. What is the probability that one randomly selected physician is a woman if she is 45–54 years old?
  f. What is the probability that a randomly selected physician is neither a woman nor 55–64 years old?

TESTING YOUR UNDERSTANDING

4.37 Purchasing Survey asked purchasing professionals what sales traits impressed them most in a sales representative. Seventy-eight percent selected "thoroughness." Forty percent responded "knowledge of your own product." The purchasing professionals were allowed to list more than one trait. Suppose 27% of the purchasing professionals listed both "thoroughness" and "knowledge of your own product" as sales traits that impressed them most. A purchasing professional is randomly sampled.

  a. What is the probability that the professional selected "thoroughness" or "knowledge of your own product"?
  b. What is the probability that the professional selected neither "thoroughness" nor "knowledge of your own product"?
  c. If it is known that the professional selected "thoroughness," what is the probability that the professional selected "knowledge of your own product"?
  d. What is the probability that the professional did not select "thoroughness" and did select "knowledge of your own product"?

4.38 The U.S. Bureau of Labor Statistics publishes data on the benefits offered by small companies to their employees. Only 42% offer retirement plans while 61% offer life insurance. Suppose 33% offer both retirement plans and life insurance as benefits. If a small company is randomly selected, determine the following probabilties:

  a. The company offers a retirement plan given that they offer life insurance.
  b. The company offers life insurance given that they offer a retirement plan.
  c. The company offers life insurance or a retirement plan.
  d. The company offers a retirement plan and does not offer life insurance.
  e. The company does not offer life insurance if it is known that they offer a retirement plan.

4.39 According to Link Resources, 16% of the U.S. population is technology-driven. However, these figures vary by region. For example, in the West the figure is 20% and in the Northeast the figure is 17%. Twenty-one percent of the U.S. population in general is in the West and 20% of the U.S. population is in the Northeast. Suppose an American is chosen randomly.

  a. What is the probability that the person lives in the West and is a technology-driven person?
  b. What is the probability that the person lives in the Northeast and is a technology-driven person?
  c. Suppose the chosen person is known to be technology-driven. What is the probability that the person lives in the West?
  d. Suppose the chosen person is known not to be technology-driven. What is the probability that the person lives in the Northeast?
  e. Suppose the chosen person is known to be technology-driven. What is the probability that the person lives in neither the West nor the Northeast?

4.40 In a certain city, 30% of the families have a MasterCard, 20% have an American Express card, and 25% have a Visa card. Eight percent of the families have both a MasterCard and an American Express card. Twelve percent have both a Visa card and a MasterCard. Six percent have both an American Express card and a Visa card.

  a. What is the probability of selecting a family that has either a Visa card or an American Express card?
  b. If a family has a MasterCard, what is the probability that it has a Visa card?
  c. If a family has a Visa card, what is the probability that it has a MasterCard?
  d. Is possession of a Visa card independent of possession of a MasterCard? Why or why not?
  e. Is possession of an American Express card mutually exclusive of possession of a Visa card?

4.41 A few years ago, a survey commissioned by *The World Almanac* and *Maturity News* Service reported that 51% of the respondents did not believe the Social Security system will be secure in 20 years. Of the respondents who were age 45 or older, 70% believed the system will be secure in 20 years. Of the people surveyed, 57% were under age 45. One respondent is selected randomly.

  a. What is the probability that the person is age 45 or older?
  b. What is the probability that the person is younger than age 45 and believes that the Social Security system will be secure in 20 years?
  c. If the person selected believes the Social Security system will be secure in 20 years, what is the probability that the person is 45 years old or older?
  d. What is the probability that the person is younger than age 45 or believes the Social Security system will not be secure in 20 years?

4.42 A telephone survey conducted by the Maritz Marketing Research company found that 43% of Americans expect to save more money next year than they saved last year. Forty-five percent of those surveyed plan to reduce debt next year. Of those who expect to save more money next year, 81% plan to reduce debt next year. An American is selected randomly.

  a. What is the probability that this person expects to save more money next year and plans to reduce debt next year?
  b. What is the probability that this person expects to save more money next year or plans to reduce debt next year?
  c. What is the probability that this person neither expects to save more money next year nor plans to reduce debt next year?
  d. What is the probability that this person expects to save more money next year and does not plan to reduce debt next year?

4.43 The Steelcase Workplace Index studied the types of work-related activities that Americans did while on vacation in the summer. Among other things, 40% read work-related material. Thirty-four percent checked in with the boss. Respondents to the study were allowed to select more than one activity. Suppose that of those who read work-related material, 78% checked in with the boss. One of these survey respondents is selected randomly.

  a. What is the probability that while on vacation this respondent checked in with the boss and read work-related material?
  b. What is the probability that while on vacation this respondent neither read work-related material nor checked in with the boss?
  c. What is the probability that while on vacation this respondent read work-related material given that the respondent checked in with the boss?
  d. What is the probability that while on vacation this respondent did not check in with the boss given that the respondent read work-related material?

e. What is the probability that while on vacation this respondent did not check in with the boss given that the respondent did not read work-related material?

f. Construct a probability matrix for this problem.

4.44 Health Rights Hotline published the results of a survey of 2,400 people in Northern California in which consumers were asked to share their complaints about managed care. The number one complaint was denial of care, with 17% of the participating consumers selecting it. Several other complaints were noted including inappropriate care (14%), customer service (14%), payment disputes (11%), specialty care (10%), delays in getting care (8%), and prescription drugs (7%). These complaint categories are mutually exclusive. Assume that the results of this survey can be inferred to all managed care consumers. If a managed care consumer is randomly selected, determine the following probabilities:

a. The consumer complains about payment disputes or specialty care.

b. The consumer complains about prescription drugs and customer service.

c. The consumer complains about inappropriate care given that the consumer complains about specialty care.

d. The consumer does not complain about delays in getting care nor does the consumer complain about payment disputes.

4.45 Companies use employee training for various reasons including employee loyalty, certification, quality, and process improvement. In a national survey of companies, BI Learning Systems reported that 56% percent of the responding companies named employee retention as a top reason for training. Suppose 36% of the companies replied that they use training for process improvement and for employee retention. In addition, suppose that of the companies that use training for process improvement, 90% use training for employee retention. A company that uses training is randomly selected.

a. What is the probability that the company uses training for employee retention and not for process improvement?

b. If it is known that the company uses training for employee retention, what is the probability that it uses training for process improvement?

c. What is the probability that the company uses training for process improvement?

d. What is the probability that the company uses training for employee retention or process improvement?

e. What is the probability that the company neither uses training for employee retention nor uses training for process improvement?

f. Suppose it is known that the company does not use training for process improvement. What is the probability that the company does use training for employee retention?

4.46 Pitney Bowes surveyed 302 directors and vice presidents of marketing at large and midsized U.S. companies to determine what they believe is the best vehicle for educating decision makers on complex issues in selling products and services. The highest percentage of companies chose direct mail/catalogs, followed by direct sales/sales rep. Direct mail/catalogs was selected by 38% of the companies. None of the companies selected both direct mail/catalogs and direct sales/sales rep. Suppose also that 41% selected neither direct mail/catalogs nor direct sales/sales rep. If one of these companies is selected randomly and their top marketing person interviewed about this matter, determine the following probabilities:

a. The marketing person selected direct mail/catalogs and did not select direct sales/sales rep.

b. The marketing person selected direct sales/sales rep.

c. The marketing person selected direct sales/sales rep given that the person selected direct mail/catalogs.

d. The marketing person did not select direct mail/catalogs given that the person did not select direct sales/sales rep.

4.47 A small independent physicians' practice has three doctors. Dr. Sarabia sees 41% of the patients, Dr. Tran sees 32%, and Dr. Jackson sees the rest. Dr. Sarabia requests blood tests on 5% of her patients, Dr. Tran requests blood tests on 8% of his patients, and Dr. Jackson requests blood tests on 6% of her patients. An auditor randomly selects a patient from the past week and discovers that the patient had a blood test as a result of the physician visit. Knowing this information, what is the probability that the patient saw Dr. Sarabia? For what percentage of all patients at this practice are blood tests requested?

4.48 A survey by the Arthur Andersen Enterprise Group/National Small Business United attempted to determine what the leading challenges are for the growth and survival of small businesses. Although the economy and finding qualified workers were the leading challenges, several others were listed in the results of the study, including regulations, listed by 30% of the companies, and the tax burden, listed by 35%. Suppose that 71% of the companies listing regulations as a challenge listed the tax burden as a challenge. Assume these percentages hold for all small businesses. If a small business is randomly selected, determine the following probabilities:

a. The small business lists both the tax burden and regulations as a challenge.

b. The small business lists either the tax burden or regulations as a challenge.

c. The small business lists either the tax burden or regulations but not both as a challenge.

d. The small business lists regulations as a challenge given that it lists the tax burden as a challenge.

e. The small business does not list regulations as a challenge given that it lists the tax burden as a challenge.

f. The small business does not list regulations as a challenge given that it does not list the tax burden as a challenge.

4.49 According to the Public Voice for Food and Health Policy, approximately 27% of all soup products in a recent year did not carry nutritional labeling. Approximately 83% of breakfast meats and about 59% of hot dog products did not have nutritional labeling. Assume that if these three groups of foods were combined, 60% would be soup products, 35% would be breakfast meats, and 5% would be hot dogs. A researcher is blindly given a food product from one of these three groups and is told that the product does have nutritional labeling. Revise the probabilities that the product is a soup product, a breakfast meat, and a hot dog product.

4.50 A survey conducted for Lifetime's daily half-hour series "The Great American TV Poll" asked Americans what they consider to be the most important thing in their lives. Twenty-nine percent said "good health," 21% responded "a happy marriage," and 40% replied "faith in God." Because they were asked which of these things is the most important thing, a respondent could not select more than one answer.

a. What is the probability that a person replied "a happy marriage" or "faith in God"?

b. What is the probability that a person replied "a happy marriage" or "faith in God" or "good health"?

c. What is the probability that a person replied "faith in God" and "good health"?

d. What is the probability that a person replied neither "faith in God" nor "good health" nor "a happy marriage"?

ANALYZING THE DATABASES

see www.wiley.com/college/black

1. In the manufacturing database, what is the probability that a randomly selected SIC Code industry is in industry group 13? What is the probability that a randomly selected SIC Code industry has a value of industry shipments of 4? What is the probability that a randomly selected SIC Code industry is in industry group 13 and has a value of industry shipments of 2? What is the probability that a randomly selected SIC Code industry is in industry group 13 or has a value of industry shipments of 2? What is the probability that a randomly selected SIC code industry neither is in industry group 13 nor has a value of industry shipments of 2?

2. Use the hospital database. Construct a raw values matrix for region and for type of control. You should have a 7 × 4 matrix. Using this matrix, answer the following questions. (Refer to Chapter 1 for category members.) What is the probability that a randomly selected hospital is in the Midwest if the hospital is known to be for-profit? If the hospital is known to be in the South, what is the probability that it is a government, nonfederal hospital? What is the probability that a hospital is in the Rocky Mountain region or a not-for-profit, nongovernment hospital? What is the probability that a hospital is a for-profit hospital located in California?

CASE: COLGATE-PALMOLIVE MAKES A "TOTAL" EFFORT

In the mid-1990s, Colgate-Palmolive developed a new toothpaste for the U.S. market, Colgate Total, with an antibacterial ingredient that was already being successfully sold overseas. However, the word *antibacterial* was not allowed for such products by the Food and Drug Administration rules. So Colgate-Palmolive had to come up with another way of marketing this and other features of their new toothpaste to U.S. consumers. Market researchers told Colgate-Palmolive that consumers were weary of trying to discern among the different advantages of various toothpaste brands and wanted simplification in their shopping lives. In response, the name "Total" was given to the product in the United States: The one word would convey that the toothpaste is the "total" package of various benefits.

Young & Rubicam developed several commercials illustrating Total's benefits and tested the commercials with focus groups. One commercial touting Total's long-lasting benefits was particularly successful. Meanwhile, in 1997, Colgate-Palmolive received FDA approval for Total, five years after the company had applied for it. The product was launched in the United States in January of 1998 using commercials that were designed from the more successful ideas of the focus group tests. A print campaign followed.

Within three months, Colgate-Palmolive grabbed the number one market share for toothpaste. Ten months later, 21% of all U.S. households had purchased Total for the first time. During this same time period, 43% of those who initially tried Total purchased it again. Colgate Total had been successfully introduced into the U.S. market.

Discussion

1. What probabilities are given in this case? Use these probabilities and the probability laws to determine what percentage of U.S. households purchased Total at least twice in the first 10 months of its release.

2. Is age category independent of willingness to try new products? According to the U.S. Census

Bureau, approximately 20% of all Americans are in the 45–64 age category. Suppose 24% of the consumers who purchased Total for the first time during the initial 10-month period were in the 45–64 age category. Use this information to determine whether age is independent of the initial purchase of Total during the introductory time period. Explain your answer.

3. Using the probabilities given in Question 2, calculate the probability that a randomly selected U.S. consumer is either in the 45–64 age category or purchased Total during the initial 10-month period. What is the probability that a randomly selected person purchased Total in the first 10 months given that the person is in the 45–64 age category?

4. Suppose 32% of all toothpaste consumers in the United States saw the Total commercials. Of those who saw the commercials, 40% purchased Total at least once in the first 10 months of its introduction. Of those who did not see the commercials, 12.06% purchased Total at least once in the first 10 months of its introduction. Suppose a toothpaste consumer is randomly selected and it is learned that they purchased Total during the first 10 months of its introduction. Revise the probability that this person saw the Total commercials and the probability that the person did not see the Total commercials.

CHAPTER 5

Discrete Distributions

LEARNING OBJECTIVES

The overall learning objective of Chapter 5 is to help you understand a category of probability distributions that produces only discrete outcomes, thereby enabling you to:

1. Distinguish between discrete random variables and continuous random variables.
2. Know how to determine the mean and variance of a discrete distribution.
3. Identify the type of statistical experiments that can be described by the binomial distribution and know how to work such problems.
4. Decide when to use the Poisson distribution in analyzing statistical experiments and know how to work such problems.
5. Decide when binomial distribution problems can be approximated by the Poisson distribution and know how to work such problems.
6. Decide when to use the hypergeometric distribution and know how to work such problems.

The Good and the Bad of the Banking Industry's Public Image

In recent years, the banking industry has been faced with many new challenges and opportunities. A series of bank failures due to competition within the industry, alternative banking options, and poor management, along with financial losses due to risky real estate and other loans in the late 1980s and early 1990s resulted in an apparent slide in consumer faith in banks. Today some business leaders believe that banks are out of touch and have lost their usefulness. Others believe that consumers' perception of the banking industry has improved in recent years particularly after the industry experienced three straight years of record profits. How does the consumer actually view the banking industry?

A recent study by the Gallup Organization commissioned by the American Bankers Association surveyed 1,002 consumers who currently do business with a bank. Results of the survey were mixed and varied. The good news for banks is that 80% of bank users considered a bank to be their primary financial institution and that 65% were "very satisfied" with their primary institution. Seventy-nine percent said that banks were "very important" to the health of the economy, and 64% believed that banks are more competitive today than five years ago. Eighty-seven percent of those surveyed felt safe using an ATM (automatic teller machine). On the negative side, 41% of those who had applied for a loan at a bank said that the process was somewhat or very difficult. Fifty-two percent of consumers believed that it was not appropriate for banks to charge fees for their services and only 33% strongly agreed that bank services represented good value for the money. Even though 87% believed that bankers should care about their communities, only 31% strongly agreed that they do. Only 29% strongly agreed that banks are flexible in meeting consumers' financial needs.

Some other findings of the study included the following: 39% of all consumers said that convenience is the most important reason to maintain a relationship in their primary financial institution followed by friendly/good service (19%), long-standing relationship (14%), checking held there (11%), and good loan interest rates (11%). Poor customer service led the list of reasons why people changed or considered changing primary financial institutions (19%) followed by moved (18%), fees/service changes (18%), interest rates (16%), and location/convenience (13%).

Managerial and Statistical Questions

1. This study was conducted nationwide by the Gallup Organization. Are these results reflective of your geographic region in the United States or for financial consumers in other countries?

2. The study suggests that 80% of all financial consumers consider their bank to be their primary financial institution. Suppose you randomly select 25 financial consumers in your community, what is the probability that 18 or more of these consumers consider their bank to be their primary financial institution if the 80% figure holds in your community?

3. According to the survey, 65% of all financial consumers are very satisfied with their primary institution. Suppose 15 financial consumers are randomly selected, based on the survey figures what is the expected number of these 15 who are very satisfied with their primary institution?

4. Suppose we conduct a local survey of 32 bank consumers and find out that 26 feel safe in using ATMs. If we randomly select 7 of these 32 to do some additional interviews, what is the probability that exactly 4 of the 7 feel safe in using ATMs?

5. A bank conducts a customer traffic study to determine arrival patterns from 10 A.M. to 11 A.M. on weekdays. The results show that, on average, 3.8 customers arrive at the bank every two minutes. Based on this information, suppose a two-minute time period is randomly selected, what is the probability that no customers would arrive during this time? What is the probability that more than five customers would arrive in this two-minute time period? What is the probability that fewer than three customers would arrive in a randomly selected four-minute interval?

Source: Adapted from "Do Banks Have an Image Problem? You Decide," Supplement to *ABA Banking Journal,* October 1995, pp. S2–S20.

In statistical experiments involving chance, outcomes occur randomly. Suppose as an example of such an experiment, a battery manufacturer randomly selects three batteries from a large batch of batteries to be tested for quality. Each selected battery is to be rated as good or defective. The batteries are numbered from 1 to 3, a defective battery is designated with a D, and a good battery is designated with a G. All possible outcomes are shown in Table 5.1. The expression, $D_1 G_2 D_3$, denotes one particular outcome in which the first and third batteries are defective and the second battery is good. In this chapter, we examine the probabilities of various outcomes that can occur with particular types of experiments.

5.1 DISCRETE VERSUS CONTINUOUS DISTRIBUTIONS

A **random variable** is *a variable that contains the outcomes of a chance experiment.* For example, suppose an experiment is to measure the arrivals of automobiles at a turnpike tollbooth during a 30-second period. The possible outcomes are: 0 cars, 1 car, 2 cars, …, *n* cars. These numbers (0, 1, 2, …, *n*) are the values of a random variable. Suppose another experiment is to measure the time between the completion of two tasks in a production line. The values will range from 0 seconds to *n* seconds. These time measurements are the values of another random variable. The two categories of random variables are (1) discrete random variables and (2) continuous random variables.

A random variable is a **discrete random variable** *if the set of all possible values is at most a finite or a countably infinite number of possible values.* In most statistical situations, discrete random variables produce values that are nonnegative whole numbers. For example, if six people are randomly selected from a population and how many of the six are left-handed is to be determined, the random variable produced is discrete. The only possible numbers of left-handed people in the sample of six are 0, 1, 2, 3, 4, 5, and 6. There cannot be 2.75 left-handed people in a group of six people; obtaining nonwhole number values is impossible. Other examples of experiments that yield discrete random variables include the following:

1. Randomly selecting 25 people who consume soft drinks and determining how many people prefer diet soft drinks
2. Determining the number of defects in a batch of 50 items
3. Counting the number of people who arrive at a store during a five-minute period
4. Sampling 100 registered voters and determining how many voted for the president in the last election

The battery experiment described at the beginning of the chapter produces a distribution that has discrete outcomes. Any one trial of the experiment will contain 0, 1, 2, or 3 defective batteries. It is not possible to get 1.58 defective batteries. It could be said that discrete random variables are usually generated from experiments in which things are "counted" not "measured."

Continuous random variables *take on values at every point over a given interval.* Thus continuous random variables have no gaps or unassumed values. It could be said that

TABLE 5.1
All Possible Outcomes for the Battery Experiment
$G_1\ G_2\ G_3$
$D_1\ G_2\ G_3$
$G_1\ D_2\ G_3$
$G_1\ G_2\ D_3$
$D_1\ D_2\ G_3$
$D_1\ G_2\ D_3$
$G_1\ D_2\ D_3$
$D_1\ D_2\ D_3$

continuous random variables are generated from experiments in which things are "measured" not "counted." For example, if a person is assembling a product component, the time it takes to accomplish that feat could be any value within a reasonable range such as 3 minutes 36.4218 seconds or 5 minutes 17.5169 seconds. A list of measures for which continuous random variables might be generated would include time, height, weight, and volume. Other examples of experiments that yield continuous random variables include the following:

1. Sampling the volume of liquid nitrogen in a storage tank
2. Measuring the time between customer arrivals at a retail outlet
3. Measuring the lengths of newly designed automobiles
4. Measuring the weight of grain in a grain elevator at different points of time

Once continuous data are measured and recorded, they become discrete data because the data are rounded off to a discrete number. Thus in actual practice, virtually all business data are discrete. However, for practical reasons, data analysis is facilitated greatly by using continuous distributions on data that were continuous originally.

The outcomes for random variables and their associated probabilities can be organized into distributions. The two types of distributions are **discrete distributions,** *constructed from discrete random variables,* and **continuous distributions,** *based on continuous random variables.* Discrete distributions include the binomial distribution, Poisson distribution, and hypergeometric distribution. Continuous distributions include the normal distribution, uniform distribution, exponential distribution, *t* distribution, chi-square distribution, and *F* distribution. In this chapter, we will explore discrete distributions. Chapter 6 addresses continuous distributions.

5.2 DESCRIBING A DISCRETE DISTRIBUTION

How can we describe a discrete distribution? One way is to construct a graph of the distribution and study the graph. Chapter 2 discussed some types of graphs that might suffice for this task, including the histogram and the frequency polygon. The histogram, or vertical bar chart, is probably the most common graphical way to depict a discrete distribution. However, some distributions contain outcomes for only certain data points and leave a void between values. Therefore, the histogram used often involves thin lines or sticks rather than bars or rectangles.

Observe the discrete distribution in Table 5.2. An executive is considering out-of-town business travel for a given Friday. She recognizes that at least one crisis could occur on the day that she is gone and she is concerned about that possibility. Table 5.2 shows a discrete distribution that contains the number of crises that could occur during the day that she is gone and the probability that each number will occur. For example, there is a .37 probability that no crisis will occur, a .31 probability of one crisis, and so on. The histogram in Figure 5.1 depicts the distribution given in Table 5.2. Notice that the *x* axis of the histogram contains the possible outcomes of the experiment (number of crises that might occur) and that the *y* axis contains the probabilities of these occurring.

It is readily apparent from studying the graph of Figure 5.1 that the most likely number of crises is 0 or 1. In addition, we can see that the distribution is discrete in that no probabilities are shown for values in between the whole-number crises.

Mean, Variance, and Standard Deviation of Discrete Distributions

What additional mechanisms can be used to describe discrete distributions besides depicting them graphically? The measures of central tendency and measures of variability discussed in Chapter 3 for grouped data can be applied to discrete distributions to compute a mean, a variance, and a standard deviation. Each of those three descriptive measures (mean, variance, and standard deviation) is computed on grouped data by using the class midpoint as the value to represent the data in the class interval. With discrete distributions, using the class midpoint is not necessary because the discrete value of an outcome (0, 1, 2, 3, ...) is used to represent itself. Thus, instead of using the value of the class midpoint (*M*)

TABLE 5.2

Discrete Distribution of Occurrence of Daily Crises

Number of Crises	Probability
0	.37
1	.31
2	.18
3	.09
4	.04
5	.01

FIGURE 5.1

MINITAB Histogram of Discrete Distribution of Crises Data

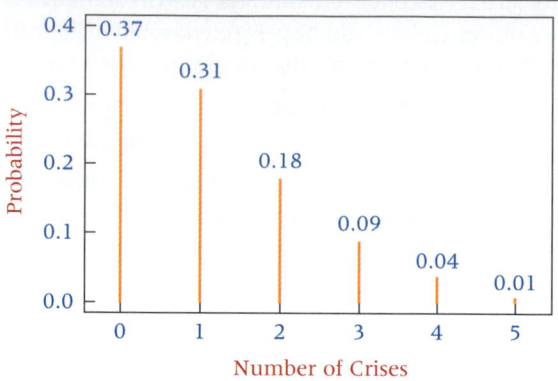

TABLE 5.3

Computing the Mean of the Crises Data

x	$P(x)$	$x \cdot P(x)$
0	.37	.00
1	.31	.31
2	.18	.36
3	.09	.27
4	.04	.16
5	.01	.05

$$\sum[x \cdot P(x)] = 1.15$$

$$\mu = 1.15 \text{ crises}$$

in computing these descriptive measures for grouped data, the discrete experiment's outcomes (x) are used. In computing these descriptive measures on grouped data, the frequency of each class interval is used to weight the class midpoint. With discrete distribution analysis, the probability of each occurrence is used as the weight.

Mean or Expected Value

The **mean** or **expected value** of a discrete distribution is *the long-run average of occurrences.* We must realize that any one trial using a discrete random variable yields only one outcome. However, if the process is repeated long enough (the game is played long enough), the average of the outcomes are most likely to approach a long-run average, expected value, or mean value. This mean, or expected, value is computed as follows.

MEAN OR EXPECTED VALUE OF A DISCRETE DISTRIBUTION where	$$\mu = E(x) = \Sigma[x \cdot P(x)]$$

$E(x)$ = long-run average
x = an outcome
$P(x)$ = probability of that outcome

As an example, let's compute the mean or expected value of the distribution given in Table 5.2. See Table 5.3 for the resulting values. In the long run, the mean or expected number of crises on a given Friday for this executive is 1.15 crises. Of course, the executive will never have 1.15 crises.

Variance and Standard Deviation of a Discrete Distribution

The variance and standard deviation of a discrete distribution are solved for by using the outcomes (x) and probabilities of outcomes [$P(x)$] in a manner similar to that of computing a mean. In addition, the computations for variance and standard deviations use the mean of the discrete distribution. The formula for computing the variance follows.

VARIANCE OF A DISCRETE DISTRIBUTION where	$$\sigma^2 = \Sigma[(x - \mu)^2 \cdot P(x)]$$

x = an outcome
$P(x)$ = probability of a given outcome
μ = mean

TABLE 5.4

Calculation of Variance and Standard Deviation on Crises Data

x	$P(x)$	$(x-\mu)^2$	$(x-\mu)^2 \cdot P(x)$
0	.37	$(0-1.15)^2 = 1.32$	$(1.32)(.37) = .49$
1	.31	$(1-1.15)^2 = .02$	$(0.02)(.31) = .01$
2	.18	$(2-1.15)^2 = .72$	$(0.72)(.18) = .13$
3	.09	$(3-1.15)^2 = 3.42$	$(3.42)(.09) = .31$
4	.04	$(4-1.15)^2 = 8.12$	$(8.12)(.04) = .32$
5	.01	$(5-1.15)^2 = 14.82$	$(14.82)(.01) = .15$
			$\Sigma[(x-\mu)^2 \cdot P(x)] = 1.41$

The variance of $\sigma^2 = \Sigma[(x-\mu)^2 \cdot P(x)] = 1.41$

The standard deviation is $\sigma = \sqrt{1.41} = 1.19$ crises.

The standard deviation is then computed by taking the square root of the variance.

STANDARD DEVIATION OF A DISCRETE DISTRIBUTION

$$\sigma = \sqrt{\Sigma[(x-\mu)^2 \cdot P(x)]}$$

The variance and standard deviation of the crisis data in Table 5.2 are calculated and shown in Table 5.4. The mean of the crisis data is 1.15 crises. The standard deviation is 1.19 crises, and the variance is 1.41.

DEMONSTRATION PROBLEM 5.1

During one holiday season, the Texas lottery played a game called the Stocking Stuffer. With this game, total instant winnings of $34.8 million were available in 70 million $1 tickets, with ticket prizes ranging from $1 to $1,000. Shown here are the various prizes and the probability of winning each prize. Use these data to compute the expected value of the game, the variance of the game, and the standard deviation of the game.

Prize (x)	Probability P(x)
$1,000	.00002
100	.00063
20	.00400
10	.00601
4	.02403
2	.08877
1	.10479
0	.77176

Solution

The mean is computed as follows.

Prize (x)	Probability P(x)	x · P(x)
$1,000	.00002	.02000
100	.00063	.06300
20	.00400	.08000
10	.00601	.06010
4	.02403	.09612
2	.08877	.17754
1	.10479	.10479
0	.77176	.00000
		$\Sigma[x \cdot P(x)] = .60155$

$\mu = E(x) = \Sigma[x \cdot P(x)] = .60155$

The expected payoff for a $1 ticket in this game is 60.2 cents. If a person plays the game for a long time, he or she could expect to average about 60 cents in winnings.

In the long run, the participant will lose about $1.00 − .602 = .398, or about 40 cents a game. Of course, an individual will never win 60 cents in any one game.

Using this mean, $\mu = .60155$, the variance and standard deviation can be computed as follows.

x	P(x)	$(x - \mu)^2$	$(x - \mu)^2 \cdot P(x)$
$1,000	.00002	998797.26190	19.97595
100	.00063	9880.05186	−6.22443
20	.00400	376.29986	−1.50520
10	.00601	88.33086	−0.53087
4	.02403	11.54946	−0.27753
2	.08877	1.95566	−0.17360
1	.10479	0.15876	−0.01664
0	.77176	0.36186	−0.27927

$$\Sigma[(x - \mu)^2 \cdot P(x)] = 28.98349$$

$$\sigma^2 = \Sigma[(x - \mu)^2 \cdot P(x)] = 28.98349$$

$$\sigma = \sqrt{\sigma^2} = \sqrt{\Sigma[(x - \mu)^2 \cdot P(x)]} = \sqrt{28.98349} = 5.38363$$

The variance is 28.98351 (dollars)^2 and the standard deviation is $5.38.

5.2 PROBLEMS

5.1   Determine the mean, the variance, and the standard deviation of the following discrete distribution.

x	P(x)
1	.238
2	.290
3	.177
4	.158
5	.137

5.2   Determine the mean, the variance, and the standard deviation of the following discrete distribution.

x	P(x)
0	.103
1	.118
2	.246
3	.229
4	.138
5	.094
6	.071
7	.001

5.3   The following data are the result of a historical study of the number of flaws found in a porcelain cup produced by a manufacturing firm. Use these data and the associated probabilities to compute the expected number of flaws and the standard deviation of flaws.

Flaws	Probability
0	.461
1	.285
2	.129
3	.087
4	.038

5.4   Suppose 20% of the people in a city prefer Pepsi-Cola as their soft drink of choice. If a random sample of six people is chosen, the number of Pepsi drinkers could range from zero to six. Shown here are the possible numbers of Pepsi drinkers in a sample of six people and the probability of that number of Pepsi drinkers occurring in the sample. Use the data to determine the mean number of Pepsi drinkers in a sample of six people in the city and compute the standard deviation.

Number of Pepsi Drinkers	Probability
0	.262
1	.393
2	.246
3	.082
4	.015
5	.002
6	.000

5.3 BINOMIAL DISTRIBUTION

Perhaps the most widely known of all discrete distributions is the **binomial distribution.** The binomial distribution has been used for hundreds of years. Several assumptions underlie the use of the binomial distribution:

ASSUMPTIONS OF THE BINOMIAL DISTRIBUTION	■ The experiment involves n identical trials. ■ Each trial has only two possible outcomes denoted as success or as failure. ■ Each trial is independent of the previous trials. ■ The terms p and q remain constant throughout the experiment, where the term p is the probability of getting a success on any one trial and the term $q = (1 - p)$ is the probability of getting a failure on any one trial.

As the word *binomial* indicates, any single trial of a binomial experiment contains only two possible outcomes. These two outcomes are labeled *success* or *failure*. Usually the outcome of interest to the researcher is labeled a success. For example, if a quality control analyst is looking for defective products, he would consider finding a defective product a success even though the company would not consider a defective product a success. If researchers are studying left-handedness, the outcome of getting a left-handed person in a trial of an experiment is a success. The other possible outcome of a trial in a binomial experiment is called a failure. The word *failure* is used only in opposition to success. In the preceding experiments, a failure could be to get an acceptable part (as opposed to a defective part) or to get a right-handed person (as opposed to a left-handed person). In a binomial distribution experiment, any one trial can have only two possible, mutually exclusive outcomes (right-handed/left-handed, defective/good, male/female, etc.).

The binomial distribution is a discrete distribution. In n trials, only x successes are possible, where x is a whole number between 0 and n. For example, if five parts are randomly selected from a batch of parts, only 0, 1, 2, 3, 4, or 5 defective parts are possible in that sample. In a sample of five parts, getting 2.714 defective parts is not possible, nor is getting eight defective parts possible.

In a binomial experiment, the trials must be independent. This constraint means that either the experiment is by nature one that produces independent trials (such as tossing coins or rolling dice) or the experiment is conducted with replacement. The effect of the independent trial requirement is that p, the probability of getting a success on one trial, remains constant from trial to trial. For example, suppose 5% of all parts in a bin are defective. The probability of drawing a defective part on the first draw is $p = .05$. If the first part drawn is not replaced, the second draw is not independent of the first, and the p value will change for the next draw. The binomial distribution does not allow for p to change from trial to trial within an experiment. However, if the population is large in comparison with the sample size, the effect of sampling without replacement is minimal, and the independence assumption essentially is met, that is, p remains relatively constant.

Generally, if the sample size, n, is less than 5% of the population, the independence assumption is not of great concern. Therefore the acceptable sample size for using the binomial distribution with samples taken *without* replacement is

$$n < 5\% \, N$$

where

n = sample size
N = population size

For example, suppose 10% of the population of the world is left-handed and that a sample of 20 people is selected randomly from the world's population. If the first person selected is left-handed—and the sampling is conducted without replacement—the value of $p = .10$ is virtually unaffected because the population of the world is so large. In addition, with many experiments the population is continually being replenished even as the sampling is being done. This condition often is the case with quality control sampling of products from large production runs. Some examples of binomial distribution problems follow.

1. Suppose a machine producing computer chips has a 6% defective rate. If a company purchases 30 of these chips, what is the probability that none is defective?

2. One ethics study suggested that 84% of U.S. companies have an ethics code. From a random sample of 15 companies, what is the probability that at least 10 have an ethics code?

3. Suppose brand X car battery has a 35% market share. If 70 cars are selected at random, what is the probability that at least 30 cars have a brand X battery?

4. A survey found that nearly 67% of company buyers stated that their company had programs for preferred buyers. If a random sample of 50 company buyers is taken, what is the probability that 40 or more have companies with programs for preferred buyers?

Solving a Binomial Problem

A survey of relocation administrators by Runzheimer International revealed several reasons why workers reject relocation offers. Included in the list were family considerations, financial reasons, and others. Four percent of the respondents said they rejected relocation offers because they received too little relocation help. Suppose five workers who just rejected relocation offers are randomly selected and interviewed. Assuming the 4% figure holds for all workers being offered relocation, what is the probability that the first worker interviewed rejected the offer because of too little relocation help and the next four workers rejected the offer for other reasons?

Let T represent too little relocation help and R represent other reasons. The sequence of interviews for this problem is as follows:

$$T_1, R_2, R_3, R_4, R_5$$

The probability of getting this sequence of workers is calculated by using the special rule of multiplication for independent events (assuming the workers are independently selected from a large population of workers). If 4% of the workers rejecting relocation offers do so for too little relocation help, the probability of one person being randomly selected from workers rejecting relocation offers who does so for that reason is .04, which is the value of p. The other 96% of the workers who reject relocation offers do so for other reasons. Thus the probability of randomly selecting a worker from those who reject relocation offers who does so for other reasons is $1 - .04 = .96$, which is the value for q. The probability of obtaining this sequence of five workers who have rejected relocation offers is

$$P(T_1 \cap R_2 \cap R_3 \cap R_4 \cap R_5) = (.04)(.96)(.96)(.96)(.96) = .03397$$

Obviously, in the random selection of workers who rejected relocation offers, the worker who did so because of too little relocation help could have been the second worker or the third or the fourth or the fifth. All the possible sequences of getting one worker who rejected relocation because of too little help and four workers who did so for other reasons follow.

$$T_1, R_2, R_3, R_4, R_5$$
$$R_1, T_2, R_3, R_4, R_5$$
$$R_1, R_2, T_3, R_4, R_5$$
$$R_1, R_2, R_3, T_4, R_5$$
$$R_1, R_2, R_3, R_4, T_5$$

The probability of each of these sequences occurring is calculated as follows:

$$(.04)(.96)(.96)(.96) = .03397$$
$$(.96)(.04)(.96)(.96) = .03397$$
$$(.96)(.96)(.04)(.96) = .03397$$
$$(.96)(.96)(.96)(.04) = .03397$$
$$(.96)(.96)(.96)(.96)(.04) = .03397$$

Note that in each case the final probability is the same. Each of the five sequences contains the product of .04 and four .96s. The commutative property of multiplication allows for the reordering of the five individual probabilities in any one sequence. The probabilities in each of the five sequences may be reordered and summarized as $(.04)^1 (.96)^4$. Each sequence contains the same five probabilities, which makes recomputing the probability of each sequence unnecessary. What *is* important is to determine how many different ways the sequences can be formed and multiply that figure by the probability of one sequence occurring. For the five sequences of this problem, the total probability of getting exactly one worker who rejected relocation because of too little relocation help in a random sample of five workers who rejected relocation offers is

$$5(.04)^1(.96)^4 = .16985$$

An easier way to determine the number of sequences than by listing all possibilities is to use *combinations* to calculate them. (The concept of combinations was introduced in Chapter 4.) Five workers are being sampled, so $n = 5$, and the problem is to get one worker who rejected a relocation offer because of too little relocation help, $x = 1$. Hence $_nC_x$ will yield the number of possible ways to get x successes in n trials. For this problem, $_5C_1$ tells the number of sequences of possibilities.

$$_5C_1 = \frac{5!}{1!(5-1)!} = 5$$

Weighting the probability of one sequence with the combination yields

$$_5C_1(.04)^1(.96)^4 = .16985.$$

Using combinations simplifies the determination of how many sequences are possible for a given value of x in a binomial distribution.

Now suppose 70% of all Americans believe cleaning up the environment is an important issue. What is the probability of randomly sampling four Americans and having exactly two of them say that they believe cleaning up the environment is an important issue? Let E represent the success of getting a person who believes cleaning up the environment is an important issue. For this example, $p = .70$. Let N represent the failure of not getting a person who believes cleaning up is an important issue (N denotes not important). The probability of getting one of these persons is $q = .30$.

The various sequences of getting two Es in a sample of four follow.

$$E_1, E_2, N_3, N_4$$
$$E_1, N_2, E_3, N_4$$
$$E_1, N_2, N_3, E_4$$
$$N_1, E_2, E_3, N_4$$
$$N_1, E_2, N_3, E_4$$
$$N_1, N_2, E_3, E_4$$

Two successes in a sample of four can occur six ways. Using combinations, the number of sequences is

$$_4C_2 = 6 \text{ ways}$$

The probability of selecting any individual sequence is

$$(.70)^2(.30)^2 = .0441$$

Thus the overall probability of getting exactly two people who believe cleaning up the environment is important out of four randomly selected people, when 70% of Americans believe cleaning up the environment is important, is

$$_4C_2(.70)^2(.30)^2 = .2646$$

Generalizing from these two examples yields the binomial formula, which can be used to solve binomial problems.

BINOMIAL FORMULA

$$P(x) = {_nC_x} \cdot p^x \cdot q^{n-x} = \frac{n!}{x!(n-x)!} \cdot p^x \cdot q^{n-x}$$

where

n = the number of trials (or the number being sampled)
x = the number of successes desired
p = the probability of getting a success in one trial
q = $1 - p$ = the probability of getting a failure in one trial

---

The binomial formula summarizes the steps presented so far to solve binomial problems. The formula allows the solution of these problems quickly and efficiently.

DEMONSTRATION PROBLEM 5.2

The Gallup survey discussed in the Decision Dilemma found that 65% of all financial consumers were very satisfied with their primary financial institution. If this figure still holds true today, suppose 40 financial consumers are sampled randomly. What is the probability that exactly 23 of the 40 are very satisfied with their primary financial institution?

Solution

The value of p is .65 (very satisfied), the value of $q = 1 - p = 1 - .65 = .35$ (not very satisfied), $n = 40$, and $x = 23$. The binomial formula yields the final answer.

$$_{40}C_{23}(.65)^{23}(.35)^{17} = (88732378800)(.000049775)(.000000018) = .0784$$

If 65% of the financial consumers are very satisfied, about 7.84% of the time the researcher would get exactly 23 out of 40 financial consumers who are very satisfied with their financial institution. The odds are against getting 23 out of 40 financial consumers by chance who are very satisfied with their financial institution. How many very satisfied financial consumers would one expect to get in 40 randomly selected financial consumers? If 65% of the financial consumers are very satisfied with their primary financial institution, one would expect to get about 65% of 40 or $(.65)(40) = 26$ very satisfied financial consumers. In any individual sample of 40 financial consumers, the number who are very satisfied is likely to differ from 26. On average, the expected number is 26. A researcher who gets 23 very satisfied financial consumers out of 40 can view this number in light of the 26 that would be expected.

DEMONSTRATION PROBLEM 5.3

According to the U.S. Census Bureau, approximately 6% of all workers in Jackson, Mississippi, are unemployed. In conducting a random telephone survey in Jackson, what is the probability of getting two or fewer unemployed workers in a sample of 20?

Solution

This problem must be worked as the union of three problems: (1) zero unemployed, $x = 0$; (2) one unemployed, $x = 1$; and (3) two unemployed, $x = 2$. In each problem, $p = .06$, $q = .94$, and $n = 20$. The binomial formula gives the following result.

$x = 0$		$x = 1$		$x = 2$	
$_{20}C_0(.06)^0(.94)^{20}$	$+$	$_{20}C_1(.06)^1(.94)^{19}$	$+$	$_{20}C_2(.06)^2(.94)^{18}$	$=$
.2901	$+$	.3703	$+$	.2246	$= .8850$

If 6% of the workers in Jackson, Mississippi, are unemployed, the telephone surveyor would get zero, one, or two unemployed workers 88.5% of the time in a random sample of 20 workers. The requirement of getting two or fewer is satisfied by getting zero, one, or two unemployed workers. Thus this problem is the union of three probabilities. Whenever the binomial formula is used to solve for cumulative success (not an exact number), the probability of each x value must be solved and the probabilities summed. If an actual survey produced such a result, it would serve to validate the census figures.

Using the Binomial Table

Anyone who works enough binomial problems will begin to recognize that the probability of getting $x = 5$ successes from a sample size of $n = 30$ when $p = .10$ is the same no matter whether the five successes are left-handed people, defective parts, brand X purchasers, or any other variable. Whether the sample involves people, parts, or products does not matter in terms of the final probabilities. The essence of the problem is the same: $n = 30$, $x = 5$, and $p = .10$. Recognizing this fact, mathematicians constructed a set of binomial tables containing presolved probabilities.

Two parameters, n and p, describe or characterize a binomial distribution. Binomial distributions actually are a family of distributions. Every different value of n and/or every different value of p gives a different binomial distribution, and tables are available for various combinations of n and p values. Because of space limitations, the binomial tables presented in this text are limited. Table A.2 in Appendix A contains binomial tables. Each table is headed by a value of n. Nine values of p are presented in each table of size n. In the column below each value of p is the binomial distribution for that combination of n and p. Table 5.5 contains a segment of Table A.2 with the binomial probabilities for $n = 20$.

DEMONSTRATION PROBLEM 5.4	Solve the binomial probability for $n = 20$, $p = .40$, and $x = 10$ by using Table A.2, Appendix A.

Solution

To use Table A.2, first locate the value of n. Because $n = 20$ for this problem, the portion of the binomial tables containing values for $n = 20$ presented in Table 5.5 can be used. After locating the value of n, search horizontally across the top of the table for the appropriate value of p. In this problem, $p = .40$. The column under .40 contains the probabilities for the binomial distribution of $n = 20$ and $p = .40$. To get the probability of $x = 10$, find the value of x in the leftmost column and locate the probability in the table at the intersection of $p = .40$ and $x = 10$. The answer is .117. Working this problem by the binomial formula yields the same result.

$$_{20}C_{10}(.40)^{10}(.60)^{10} = .1171$$

DEMONSTRATION PROBLEM 5.5	According to Information Resources, which publishes data on market share for various products, Oreos control about 10% of the market for cookie brands. Suppose 20

purchasers of cookies are selected randomly from the population. What is the probability that fewer than four purchasers choose Oreos?

Solution

For this problem, $n = 20$, $p = .10$, and $x < 4$. Because $n = 20$, the portion of the binomial tables presented in Table 5.5 can be used to work this problem. Search along the row of p values for .10. Determining the probability of getting $x < 4$ involves summing the probabilities for $x = 0$, 1, 2, and 3. The values appear in the x column at the intersection of each x value and $p = .10$.

x Value	Probability
0	.122
1	.270
2	.285
3	.190
	$(x < 4) = .867$

If 10% of all cookie purchasers prefer Oreos and 20 cookie purchasers are randomly selected, about 86.7% of the time fewer than four of the 20 will select Oreos.

Using the Computer to Produce a Binomial Distribution

Both Excel and MINITAB can be used to produce the probabilities for virtually any binomial distribution. Such computer programs offer yet another option for solving binomial problems besides using the binomial formula or the binomial tables. Actually, the computer packages in effect print out what would be a column of the binomial table. The advantages of using statistical software packages for this purpose are convenience (if the binomial tables are not readily available and a computer is) and the potential for generating tables for many more values than those printed in the binomial tables.

TABLE 5.5

Excerpt from Table A.2, Appendix A

$n = 20$				Probability					
X	.1	.2	.3	.4	.5	.6	.7	.8	.9
0	.122	.012	.001	.000	.000	.000	.000	.000	.000
1	.270	.058	.007	.000	.000	.000	.000	.000	.000
2	.285	.137	.028	.003	.000	.000	.000	.000	.000
3	.190	.205	.072	.012	.001	.000	.000	.000	.000
4	.090	.218	.130	.035	.005	.000	.000	.000	.000
5	.032	.175	.179	.075	.015	.001	.000	.000	.000
6	.009	.109	.192	.124	.037	.005	.000	.000	.000
7	.002	.055	.164	.166	.074	.015	.001	.000	.000
8	.000	.022	.114	.180	.120	.035	.004	.000	.000
9	.000	.007	.065	.160	.160	.071	.012	.000	.000
10	.000	.002	.031	.117	.176	.117	.031	.002	.000
11	.000	.000	.012	.071	.160	.160	.065	.007	.000
12	.000	.000	.004	.035	.120	.180	.114	.022	.000
13	.000	.000	.001	.015	.074	.166	.164	.055	.002
14	.000	.000	.000	.005	.037	.124	.192	.109	.009
15	.000	.000	.000	.001	.015	.075	.179	.175	.032
16	.000	.000	.000	.000	.005	.035	.130	.218	.090
17	.000	.000	.000	.000	.001	.012	.072	.205	.190
18	.000	.000	.000	.000	.000	.003	.028	.137	.285
19	.000	.000	.000	.000	.000	.000	.007	.058	.270
20	.000	.000	.000	.000	.000	.000	.001	.012	.122

For example, the study of bank customers presented in the Decision Dilemma stated that 64% of all financial consumers believe banks are more competitive today than they were five years ago. Suppose 23 financial consumers are selected randomly and we wanted to determine the probabilities of various x values occurring. Table A.2 in Appendix A could not be used because only nine different p values are included and $p = .64$ is not one of those values. In addition, $n = 23$ is not included in the table. Without the computer, we are left with the binomial formula as the only option for solving binomial problems for $n = 23$ and $p = .64$. Particularly if the cumulative probability questions are asked (for example, $x \leq 10$), the binomial formula can be a tedious way to solve the problem.

Shown in Table 5.6 is the MINITAB output for the binomial distribution of $n = 23$ and $p = .64$. With this computer output, a researcher could obtain or calculate the probability of any occurrence within the binomial distribution of $n = 23$ and $p = .64$. Table 5.7 contains MINITAB output for the particular binomial problem, $P(x \leq 10)$ when $n = 23$ and $p = .64$, solved by using MINITAB's cumulative probability capability.

Shown in Table 5.8 is Excel output for all values of x that have probabilities greater than .000001 for the binomial distribution discussed in Demonstration Problem 5.3 ($n = 20$, $p = .06$) and the solution to the question posed in Demonstration Problem 5.3.

Mean and Standard Deviation of a Binomial Distribution

A binomial distribution has an expected value or a long-run average, which is denoted by μ. The value of μ is determined by $n \cdot p$. For example, if $n = 10$ and $p = .4$, then $\mu = n \cdot p = (10)(.4) = 4$. The long-run average or expected value means that, if n items are sampled over and over for a long time and if p is the probability of getting a success on one trial, the average number of successes per sample is expected to be $n \cdot p$. If 40% of all graduate business students at a large university are women and if random samples of 10 graduate business students are selected many times, the expectation is that, on average, four of the 10 students would be women.

TABLE 5.6

MINITAB Output for the Binomial Distribution of $n = 23$, $p = .64$

```
   PROBABILITY DENSITY
         FUNCTION

Binomial with n = 23 and
p = 0.640000
   x   P( X = x )
 0.00    0.0000
 1.00    0.0000
 2.00    0.0000
 3.00    0.0000
 4.00    0.0000
 5.00    0.0000
 6.00    0.0002
 7.00    0.0009
 8.00    0.0031
 9.00    0.0090
10.00    0.0225
11.00    0.0473
12.00    0.0840
13.00    0.1264
14.00    0.1605
15.00    0.1712
16.00    0.1522
17.00    0.1114
18.00    0.0660
19.00    0.0309
20.00    0.0110
21.00    0.0028
22.00    0.0005
23.00    0.0000
```

TABLE 5.7

MINITAB Output for the Binomial Problem, $P(x) \leq 10 \mid n = 23$ and $p = .64$

```
 CUMULATIVE DISTRIBUTION FUNCTION

Binomial with n = 23 and p = 0.640000
   x   P( X <= x )
10.00      0.0357
```

TABLE 5.8

Excel Output for Demonstration Problem 5.3 and the Binomial Distribution of $n = 20$, $p = .06$

	A	B	C	D	E	F
1	x	Prob(x)				
2	0	0.2901				
3	1	0.3703				
4	2	0.2246				
5	3	0.0860				
6	4	0.0233				
7	5	0.0048				
8	6	0.0008				
9	7	0.0001				
10	8	0.0000				
11	9	0.0000				
12	The probability $x \leq 2$ when $n = 20$ and $p = .06$ is: **0.8850**					

MEAN AND STANDARD DEVIATION OF A BINOMIAL DISTRIBUTION	$\mu = n \cdot p$ $\sigma = \sqrt{n \cdot p \cdot q}$

Examining the mean of a binomial distribution gives an intuitive feeling about the likelihood of a given outcome. For example, suppose researchers generally agree that 10% of all people are left-handed. However, suppose a researcher believes, as some have theorized, that this figure is higher for children who are born to women over the age of 35. In an attempt to gather evidence, she randomly selects 100 children who were born to women over the age of 35 and 20 turn out to be left-handed. Is it likely that she would have gotten 20 left-handed people in a sample of 100? How many would she have expected to get in a sample of 100? The mean or expected value for $n = 100$ and $p = .10$ is $(100)(.10) = 10$ left-handed people. Did the 20 left-handed children in a sample of 100 happen by chance or is the researcher drawing from a different population than the general population that produces 10% left-handed people? She can investigate this outcome further by examining the binomial probabilities for this problem. However, the mean of the distribution gives her an expected value from which to work.

According to one study, 64% of all financial consumers believe banks are more competitive today than they were five years ago. If 23 financial consumers are selected randomly, what is the expected number who believe banks are more competitive today than they were five years ago? This problem can be described by the binomial distribution of $n = 23$ and $p = .64$ given in Table 5.6. The mean of this binomial distribution yields the expected value for this problem.

$$\mu = n \cdot p = 23(.64) = 14.72$$

In the long run, if 23 financial consumers are selected randomly over and over and if indeed 64% of all financial consumers believe banks are more competitive today, then the experiment should average 14.72 financial consumers out of 23 who believe banks are more competitive today. Realize that because the binomial distribution is a discrete distribution you will never actually get 14.72 people out of 23 who believe banks are more competitive today. The mean of the distribution does reveal the relative likelihood of any individual occurrence. Examine Table 5.6. Notice that the highest probabilities are those near $x = 14.72$: $P(x = 15) = .1712$, $P(x = 14) = .1605$, and $P(x = 16) = .1522$. All other probabilities for this distribution are less than these probabilities.

The standard deviation of a binomial distribution is denoted σ and is equal to $\sqrt{n \cdot p \cdot q}$. For the left-handedness example, $\sigma = \sqrt{100(.10)(.90)} = 3$. The standard deviation for the financial consumer problem described by the binomial distribution in Table 5.6 is

$$\sigma = \sqrt{n \cdot p \cdot q} = \sqrt{(23)(.64)(.36)} = 2.30$$

Chapter 6 shows that some binomial distributions are nearly bell-shaped and can be approximated by using the normal curve. The mean and standard deviation of a binomial distribution are the tools used to convert these binomial problems to normal curve problems.

Graphing Binomial Distributions

The graph of a binomial distribution can be constructed by using all the possible x values of a distribution and their associated probabilities. The x values usually are graphed along the x axis and the probabilities are graphed along the y axis.

Table 5.9 lists the probabilities for three different binomial distributions: $n = 8$ and $p = .20$, $n = 8$ and $p = .50$, and $n = 8$ and $p = .80$. Figure 5.2 displays Excel graphs for each of these three binomial distributions. Observe how the shape of the distribution changes as the value of p increases. For $p = .50$, the distribution is symmetrical. For $p = .20$ the distribution is skewed right and for $p = .80$ the distribution is skewed left. This pattern makes sense because the mean of the binomial distribution $n = 8$ and $p = .50$ is 4, which is in the middle of the distribution. The mean of the distribution $n = 8$ and $p = .20$ is 1.6, which results in the highest probabilities being near $x = 2$ and $x = 1$. This graph peaks early and

TABLE 5.9

Probabilities for Three Binomial Distributions with $n = 8$

	Probabilities for		
x	$p = .20$	$p = .50$	$p = .80$
0	.1678	.0039	.0000
1	.3355	.0312	.0001
2	.2936	.1094	.0011
3	.1468	.2187	.0092
4	.0459	.2734	.0459
5	.0092	.2187	.1468
6	.0011	.1094	.2936
7	.0001	.0312	.3355
8	.0000	.0039	.1678

FIGURE 5.2

Excel Graphs of Three Binomial Distributions with $n = 8$

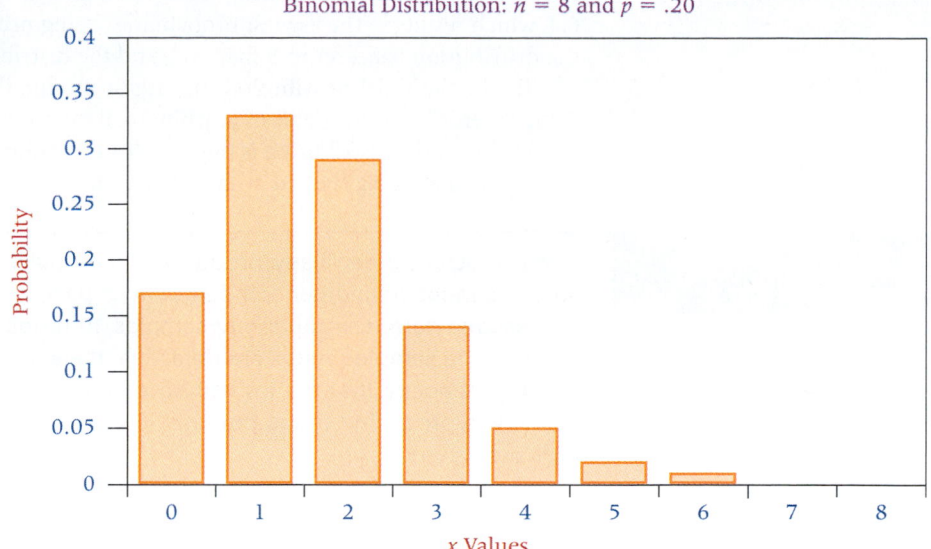

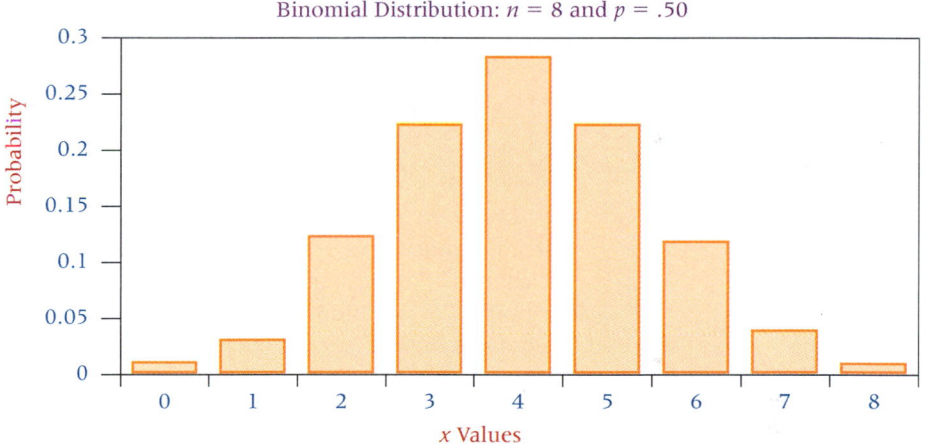

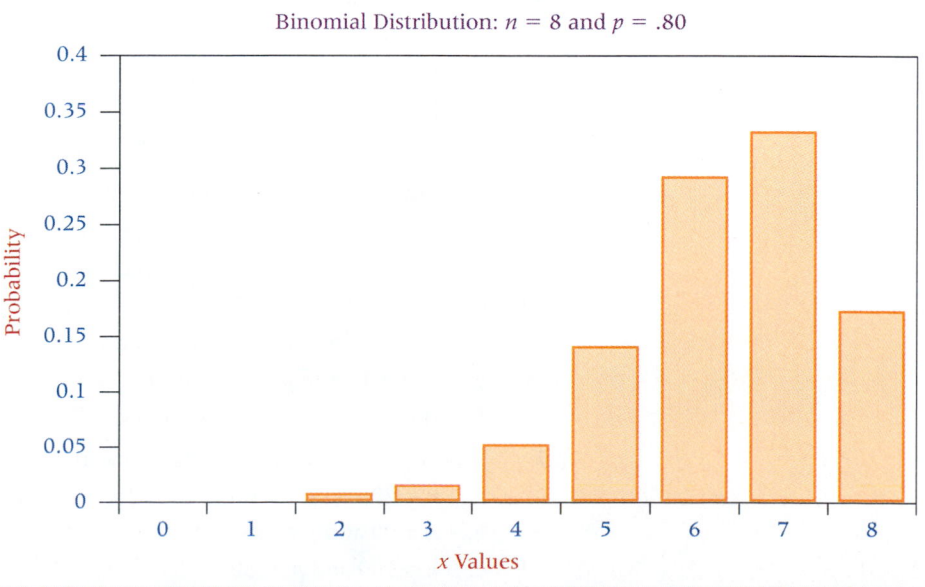

stretches toward the higher values of x. The mean of the distribution $n = 8$ and $p = .80$ is 6.4, which results in the highest probabilities being near $x = 6$ and $x = 7$. Thus the peak of the distribution is nearer to 8 than to 0 and the distribution stretches back toward $x = 0$.

In any binomial distribution the largest x value that can occur is n and the smallest value is zero. Thus the graph of any binomial distribution is constrained by zero and n. If the p value of the distribution is not .50, this constraint will result in the graph "piling up" at one end and being skewed at the other end.

DEMONSTRATION PROBLEM 5.6	A manufacturing company produces 10,000 plastic mugs per week. This company supplies mugs to another company, which packages the mugs as part of picnic sets. The second company randomly samples 10 mugs sent from the supplier. If two or fewer of the sampled mugs are defective, the second company accepts the lot. What is the probability that the lot will be accepted if the mug manufacturing company actually is producing mugs that are 10% defective? 20% defective? 30% defective? 40% defective?

Solution

In this series of binomial problems, $n = 10$, $x \leq 2$, and p ranges from .10 to .40. From Table A.2—and cumulating the values—we have the following probability of $x \leq 2$ for each p value and the expected value ($\mu = n \cdot p$).

p	Lot Accepted $P(x \leq 2)$	Expected Number of Defects (μ)
.10	.930	1.0
.20	.677	2.0
.30	.382	3.0
.40	.167	4.0

These values indicate that if the manufacturing company is producing 10% defective mugs, the probability is relatively high (.930) that the lot will be accepted by chance. For higher values of p, the probability of lot acceptance by chance decreases. In addition, as p increases, the expected value moves away from the acceptable values, $x \leq 2$. This move reduces the chances of lot acceptance.

5.3 PROBLEMS

5.5 Solve the following problems by using the binomial formula.
  a. If $n = 4$ and $p = .10$, find $P(x = 3)$.
  b. If $n = 7$ and $p = .80$, find $P(x = 4)$.
  c. If $n = 10$ and $p = .60$, find $P(x \geq 7)$.
  d. If $n = 12$ and $p = .45$, find $P(5 \leq x \leq 7)$.

5.6 Solve the following problems by using the binomial tables (Table A.2).
  a. If $n = 20$ and $p = .50$, find $P(x = 12)$.
  b. If $n = 20$ and $p = .30$, find $P(x > 8)$.
  c. If $n = 20$ and $p = .70$, find $P(x < 12)$.
  d. If $n = 20$ and $p = .90$, find $P(x \leq 16)$.
  e. If $n = 15$ and $p = .40$, find $P(4 \leq x \leq 9)$.
  f. If $n = 10$ and $p = .60$, find $P(x \geq 7)$.

5.7 Solve for the mean and standard deviation of the following binomial distributions.
  a. $n = 20$ and $p = .70$
  b. $n = 70$ and $p = .35$
  c. $n = 100$ and $p = .50$

5.8 Use the probability tables in Table A.2 and sketch the graph of each of the following binomial distributions. Note on the graph where the mean of the distribution falls.

 a. $n = 6$ and $p = .70$

 b. $n = 20$ and $p = .50$

 c. $n = 8$ and $p = .80$

5.9 *Purchasing* magazine reported the results of a survey in which buyers were asked a series of questions with regard to Internet usage. One question asked was how they would use the Internet if security and other issues could be resolved. Seventy-eight percent said they would use it for pricing information, 75% said they would use it to send purchase orders, and 70% said they would use it for purchase order acknowledgments. Assume that these percentages hold true for all buyers. A researcher randomly samples 20 buyers and asks them how they would use the Internet if security and other issues could be resolved.

 a. What is the probability that exactly 14 of these buyers would use the Internet for pricing information?

 b. What is the probability that all of the buyers would use the Internet to send purchase orders?

 c. What is the probability that fewer than 12 would use the Internet for purchase order acknowledgments?

5.10 *The Wall Street Journal* reported some interesting statistics on the job market. One statistic is that 40% of all workers say they would change jobs for "slightly higher pay." In addition, 88% of companies say that there is a shortage of qualified job candidates. Suppose 16 workers are randomly selected and asked if they would change jobs for "slightly higher pay." What is the probability that nine or more say yes? What is the probability that three, four, five, or six say yes? If 13 companies are contacted, what is the probability that exactly 10 say there is a shortage of qualified job candidates? What is the probability that all of the companies say there is a shortage of qualified job candidates? What is the expected number of companies that would say there is a shortage of qualified job candidates?

5.11 An increasing number of consumers believe they have to look out for themselves in the marketplace. According to a survey conducted by the Yankelovich Partners for *USA WEEKEND* magazine, 60% of all consumers have called an 800 or 900 telephone number for information about some product. Suppose a random sample of 25 consumers is contacted and interviewed about their buying habits.

 a. What is the probability that 15 or more of these consumers have called an 800 or 900 telephone number for information about some product?

 b. What is the probability that more than 20 of these consumers have called an 800 or 900 telephone number for information about some product?

 c. What is the probability that fewer than 10 of these consumers have called an 800 or 900 telephone number for information about some product?

5.12 Graph the distribution for Problem 5.11. For which values of x are the probabilities highest? Determine the expected value of this distribution. How does the expected value compare with the values of x that have the highest probabilities? Compute the standard deviation. Determine the interval $\mu \pm 2\sigma$ for this distribution. Between what two values of x does this interval lie? What is the percentage of values within this interval? How does this answer compare with what Chebyshev's theorem or the empirical rule presented in Chapter 3 would yield?

5.13 In the past few years outsourcing overseas has become more frequently used than ever before by U.S. companies. However, outsourcing is not without problems. A recent survey by *Purchasing* indicates that 20% of the companies that outsource overseas use a consultant. Suppose 15 companies that outsource overseas are randomly selected.

a. What is the probability that exactly five companies that outsource overseas use a consultant?

b. What is the probability that more than nine companies that outsource overseas use a consultant?

c. What is the probability that none of the companies that outsource overseas use a consultant?

d. What is the probability that between four and seven (inclusive) companies that outsource overseas use a consultant?

e. Construct a graph for this binomial distribution. In light of the graph and the expected value, explain why the probability results from parts (a) through (d) were obtained.

5.14   According to Cerulli Associates of Boston, 30% of all CPA financial advisors have an average client size between $500,000 and $1 million. Thirty-four percent have an average client size between $1 million and $5 million. Suppose a complete list of all CPA financial advisors is available and 18 are randomly selected from that list.

a. What is the expected number of CPA financial advisors that have an average client size between $500,000 and $1 million? What is the expected number with an average client size between $1 million and $5 million?

b. What is the probability that at least eight CPA financial advisors have an average client size between $500,000 and $1 million?

c. What is the probability that two, three, or four CPA financial advisors have an average client size between $1 million and $5 million?

d. What is the probability that none of the CPA financial advisors have an average client size between $500,000 and $1 million? What is the probability that none have an average client size between $1 million and $5 million? Which probability is higher and why?

5.4 POISSON DISTRIBUTION

The Poisson distribution is another discrete distribution. It is named after Simeon-Denis Poisson (1781–1840), a French mathematician, who published its essentials in a paper in 1837. The Poisson distribution and the binomial distribution have some similarities, but also several differences. The binomial distribution describes a distribution of two possible outcomes designated as successes and failures from a given number of trials. The **Poisson distribution** *focuses only on the number of discrete occurrences over some interval or continuum.* A Poisson experiment does not have a given number of trials (n) as a binomial experiment does. For example, whereas a binomial experiment might be used to determine how many U.S.-made cars are in a random sample of 20 cars, a Poisson experiment might focus on the number of cars randomly arriving at an automobile repair facility during a 10-minute interval.

The Poisson distribution describes the occurrence of *rare events*. In fact, the Poisson formula has been referred to as the *law of improbable events*. For example, serious accidents at a chemical plant are rare, and the number per month might be described by the Poisson distribution. The Poisson distribution often is used to describe the number of random arrivals per some time interval. If the number of arrivals per interval is too frequent, the time interval can be reduced enough so that a rare number of occurrences is expected. Another example of a Poisson distribution is the number of random customer arrivals per five-minute interval at a small boutique on weekday mornings.

The Poisson distribution also has an application in the field of management science. The models used in queuing theory (theory of waiting lines) usually are based on the assumption that the Poisson distribution is the proper distribution to describe random arrival rates over a period of time.

The Poisson distribution has the following characteristics:

- It is a discrete distribution.
- It describes rare events.

- Each occurrence is independent of the other occurrences.
- It describes discrete occurrences over a continuum or interval.
- The occurrences in each interval can range from zero to infinity.
- The expected number of occurrences must hold constant throughout the experiment.

Examples of Poisson-type situations include the following:

1. Number of telephone calls per minute at a small business
2. Number of cases of a rare blood disease per 100,000 people
3. Number of hazardous waste sites per county in the United States
4. Number of major oil spills in the New England region per month
5. Number of arrivals at a turnpike toll booth per minute between 3 a.m. and 4 a.m. in January on the Kansas Turnpike
6. Number of times a one-year-old personal computer printer breaks down per quarter (3 months)
7. Number of sewing flaws per pair of jeans during production
8. Number of times a tire blows on a commercial airplane per week
9. Number of paint spots per new automobile
10. Number of flaws per bolt of cloth

Each of these examples represents a rare occurrence of events for some interval. Note that, although time is a more common interval for the Poisson distribution, intervals can range from a county in the United States to a pair of jeans. Some of the intervals in these examples might have zero occurrences. Moreover, the average occurrence per interval for many of these examples is probably in the single digits (1–9).

If a Poisson-distributed phenomenon is studied over a long period of time, a *long-run average* can be determined. This average is denoted **lambda (λ).** Each Poisson problem contains a lambda value from which the probabilities of particular occurrences are determined. Although n and p are required to describe a binomial distribution, a Poisson distribution can be described by λ alone. The Poisson formula is used to compute the probability of occurrences over an interval for a given lambda value.

POISSON FORMULA

$$P(x) = \frac{\lambda^x e^{-\lambda}}{x!}$$

where

x = 0, 1, 2, 3, …
λ = long-run average
e = 2.718282

Here, x is the number of occurrences per interval for which the probability is being computed, λ is the long-run average, and $e = 2.718282$ is the base of natural logarithms.

A word of caution about using the Poisson distribution to study various phenomena is necessary. The λ value must hold constant throughout a Poisson experiment. The researcher must be careful not to apply a given lambda to intervals for which lambda changes. For example, the average number of customers arriving at a Sears store during a one-minute interval will vary from hour to hour, day to day, and month to month. Different times of the day or week might produce different lambdas. The number of flaws per pair of jeans might vary from Monday to Friday. The researcher should be specific in describing the interval for which λ is being used.

Working Poisson Problems by Formula

Suppose bank customers arrive randomly on weekday afternoons at an average of 3.2 customers every 4 minutes. What is the probability of exactly five customers arriving in a 4-minute interval on a weekday afternoon? The lambda for this problem is 3.2 customers per 4 minutes. The value of x is five customers per 4 minutes. The probability of five customers randomly arriving during a 4-minute interval when the long-run average has been 3.2 customers per 4-minute interval is

$$\frac{(3.2^5)(e^{-3.2})}{5!} = \frac{(335.54)(.0408)}{120} = .1141$$

If a bank averages 3.2 customers every 4 minutes, the probability of five customers arriving during any one 4-minute interval is .1141.

DEMONSTRATION PROBLEM 5.7	Bank customers arrive randomly on weekday afternoons at an average of 3.2 customers every 4 minutes. What is the probability of having more than seven customers in a 4-minute interval on a weekday afternoon?

Solution

$$\lambda = 3.2 \text{ customers/4 minutes}$$
$$x > 7 \text{ customers/4 minutes}$$

In theory, the solution requires obtaining the values of $x = 8, 9, 10, 11, 12, 13, 14,$ ... ∞. In actuality, each x value is determined until the values are so far away from $\lambda = 3.2$ that the probabilities approach zero. The exact probabilities are then summed to find $x > 7$.

$$P(x = 8|\lambda = 3.2) = \frac{(3.2^8)(e^{-3.2})}{8!} = .0111$$
$$P(x = 9|\lambda = 3.2) = \frac{(3.2^9)(e^{-3.2})}{9!} = .0040$$
$$P(x = 10|\lambda = 3.2) = \frac{(3.2^{10})(e^{-3.2})}{10!} = .0013$$
$$P(x = 11|\lambda = 3.2) = \frac{(3.2^{11})(e^{-3.2})}{11!} = .0004$$
$$P(x = 12|\lambda = 3.2) = \frac{(3.2^{12})(e^{-3.2})}{12!} = .0001$$
$$P(x = 13|\lambda = 3.2) = \frac{(3.2^{13})(e^{-3.2})}{13!} = .0000$$
$$P(x > 7) = P(x \geq 8) = .0169$$

If the bank has been averaging 3.2 customers every 4 minutes on weekday afternoons, it is unlikely that more than seven people would randomly arrive in any one 4-minute period. This answer indicates that more than seven people would randomly arrive in a 4-minute period only 1.69% of the time. Bank officers could use these results to help them make staffing decisions.

DEMONSTRATION PROBLEM 5.8	A bank has an average random arrival rate of 3.2 customers every 4 minutes. What is the probability of getting exactly 10 customers during an 8-minute interval?

Solution

$$\lambda = 3.2 \text{ customers/4 minutes}$$
$$x = 10 \text{ customers/8 minutes}$$

This example is different from the first two Poisson examples in that the intervals for lambda and the sample are different. The intervals must be the same in order to use λ and x together in the probability formula. The right way to approach this dilemma is to adjust the interval for lambda so that it and x have the same interval. The interval for x is 8 minutes, so lambda should be adjusted to an 8-minute interval. Logically, if the bank averages 3.2 customers every 4 minutes, it should average twice as many, or 6.4 customers every 8 minutes. If x were for a 2-minute interval, the value of lambda would be halved from 3.2 to 1.6 customers per 2-minute interval. The wrong approach to this dilemma is to equalize the intervals by changing the x value. Never adjust or change x in a problem. Just because 10 customers arrive in one 8-minute interval does not mean that there would necessarily have been five customers in a 4-minute interval. There is no guarantee how the 10 customers are spread over the 8-minute interval. Always adjust the lambda value. After lambda has been adjusted for an 8-minute interval, the solution is

$$\lambda = 6.4 \text{ customers/8 minutes}$$
$$x = 10 \text{ customers/8 minutes}$$
$$\frac{(6.4)^{10} e^{-6.4}}{10!} = .0528$$

Using the Poisson Tables

Every value of lambda determines a different Poisson distribution. Regardless of the nature of the interval associated with a lambda, the Poisson distribution for a particular lambda is the same. Table A.3, Appendix A, contains the Poisson distributions for selected values of lambda. Probabilities are displayed in the table for each x value associated with a given lambda if the probability has a nonzero value to four decimal places. Table 5.10 presents a portion of Table A.3 that contains the probabilities of $x \leq 9$ if lambda is 1.6.

<table><tr><td>**DEMONSTRATION PROBLEM 5.9**</td><td>If a real estate office sells 1.6 houses on an average weekday and sales of houses on weekdays are Poisson distributed, what is the probability of selling exactly four houses in one day? What is the probability of selling no houses in one day? What is the probability of selling more than five houses in a day? What is the probability of selling 10 or more houses in a day? What is the probability of selling exactly four houses in two days?</td></tr></table>

Solution

$$\lambda = 1.6 \text{ houses/day}$$
$$P(x = 4| \lambda = 1.6) = ?$$

Table 5.10 gives the probabilities for $\lambda = 1.6$. The left column contains the x values. The line $x = 4$ yields the probability .0551. If a real estate firm has been averaging 1.6 houses sold per day, only 5.51% of the days would it sell exactly four houses and still maintain the lambda value. Line 1 of Table 5.10 shows the probability of selling no houses in a day (.2019). That is, on 20.19% of the days, the firm would sell no houses if sales are Poisson distributed with $\lambda = 1.6$ houses per day. Table 5.10 is not cumulative. To determine $P(x > 5)$, more than five houses, find the probabilities of $x = 6$, $x = 7$, $x = 8$, $x = 9$, ... $x = ?$. However, at $x = 9$, the probability to four decimal places is zero, and Table 5.10 stops when an x value zeros out at four decimal places. The answer for $x > 5$ follows.

x	Probability
6	.0047
7	.0011
8	.0002
9	.0000
$x > 5 =$	.0060

TABLE 5.10

Poisson Table for $\lambda = 1.6$

x	Probability
0	.2019
1	.3230
2	.2584
3	.1378
4	.0551
5	.0176
6	.0047
7	.0011
8	.0002
9	.0000

What is the probability of selling 10 or more houses in one day? As the table zeros out at $x = 9$, the probability of $x \geq 10$ is essentially .0000—that is, if the real estate office has been averaging only 1.6 houses sold per day, it is virtually impossible to sell 10 or more houses in a day. What is the probability of selling exactly four houses in two days? In this case, the interval has been changed from one day to two days. Lambda is for one day, so an adjustment must be made: A lambda of 1.6 for one day converts to a lambda of 3.2 for two days. Table 5.10 no longer applies, so Table A.3 must be used to solve this problem. The answer is found by looking up $\lambda = 3.2$ and $x = 4$ in Table A.3: the probability is .1781.

Mean and Standard Deviation of a Poisson Distribution

The mean or expected value of a Poisson distribution is λ. It is the long-run average of occurrences for an interval if many random samples are taken. Lambda usually is not a whole number, so most of the time actually observing lambda occurrences in an interval is impossible.

For example, suppose $\lambda = 6.5$/interval for some Poisson-distributed phenomenon. The resulting numbers of x occurrences in 20 different random samples from a Poisson distribution with $\lambda = 6.5$ might be as follows.

6   9   7   4   8   7   6   6   10   6   5   5   8   4   5   8   5   4   9   10

Computing the mean number of occurrences from this group of 20 intervals gives 6.6. In theory, for infinite sampling the long-run average is 6.5. Note from the samples that, when λ is 6.5, several 5s and 6s occur. Rarely would sample occurrences of 1, 2, 3, 11, 12, 13, ... occur when $\lambda = 6.5$. Understanding the mean of a Poisson distribution gives a feel for the actual occurrences that are likely to happen.

The variance of a Poisson distribution also is λ. The standard deviation is $\sqrt{\lambda}$. Combining the standard deviation with Chebyshev's theorem indicates the spread or dispersion of a Poisson distribution. For example, if $\lambda = 6.5$, the variance also is 6.5, and the standard deviation is 2.55. Chebyshev's theorem states that at least $1 - 1/k^2$ values are within k standard deviations of the mean. The interval $\mu \pm 2\sigma$ contains at least $1 - (1^2/2) = .75$ of the values. For $\mu = \lambda = 6.5$ and $\sigma = 2.55$, 75% of the values should be within the $6.5 \pm 2(2.55) = 6.5 \pm 5.1$ range. That is, the range from 1.4 to 11.6 should include at least 75% of all the values. An examination of the 20 values randomly generated for a Poisson distribution with $\lambda = 6.5$ shows that actually 100% of the values are within this range.

Graphing Poisson Distributions

The values in Table A.3, Appendix A, can be used to graph a Poisson distribution. The x values are on the x axis and the probabilities are on the y axis. Figure 5.3 is a MINITAB graph for the distribution of values for $\lambda = 1.6$.

The graph reveals a Poisson distribution skewed to the right. With a mean of 1.6 and a possible range of x from zero to infinity, the values obviously will "pile up" at 0 and 1. Consider, however, the MINITAB graph of the Poisson distribution for $\lambda = 6.5$ in Figure 5.4. Note that with $\lambda = 6.5$, the probabilities are greatest for the values of 5, 6, 7, and 8. The graph has less skewness, because the probability of occurrence of values near zero is small, as are the probabilities of large values of x.

Using the Computer to Generate Poisson Distributions

Using the Poisson formula to compute probabilities can be tedious when one is working problems with cumulative probabilities. The Poisson tables in Table A.3, Appendix A, are faster to use than the Poisson formula. However, Poisson tables are limited by the amount of space available, and Table A.3 only includes probability values for Poisson distributions with lambda values to the tenths place in most cases. For researchers who want to use lambda values with more precision or who feel that the computer is more convenient than textbook tables, some statistical computer software packages are an attractive option.

STATISTICS IN BUSINESS TODAY

Air Passengers' Complaints

In recent months, airline passengers have expressed much more dissatisfaction with airline service than ever before. It is not clear whether passengers are actually more dissatisfied with their flying experiences or they are just more vocal. Complaints include flight delays, lost baggage, long runway delays with little or no onboard service, overbooked flights, cramped space due to fuller flights, canceled flights, and grumpy airline employees. A majority of dissatisfied fliers merely grin and bear it. However, an increasing number of passengers log complaints with the U.S. Department of Transportation. In the mid 1990s, the average number of complaints per 100,000 passengers boarded was .66. In ensuing years, the average rose to .74, .86, and 1.08.

In a recent year, according to the Department of Transportation, Southwest Airlines had the fewest average number of complaints per 100,000 with .25, followed by Alaska Airlines with .54, Delta Air Lines with .79, US Airways with .84, and Continental with 1.02. Within the top 10 largest U.S. airlines, Northwest had the highest average number of complaints logged against it—2.21 complaints per 100,000 passengers.

Because these average numbers are relatively small, it appears that the actual number of complaints per 100,000 is rare and may follow a Poisson distribution. In this case, λ represents the average number of complaints and the interval is 100,000 passengers. For example, using $\lambda = 1.08$ complaints (average for all airlines), if 100,000 boarded passengers were contacted, the probability that exactly three of them logged a complaint to the Department of Transportation could be computed as

$$\frac{(1.08)^3 e^{-1.08}}{3!} = .0713$$

That is, if 100,000 boarded passengers were contacted over and over, 7.13% of the time exactly three would have logged complaints with the Department of Transportation.

MINITAB will produce a Poisson distribution for virtually any value of lambda. For example, one study by the National Center for Health Statistics claims that, on average, an American has 1.9 acute illnesses or injuries per year. If these cases are Poisson distributed, lambda is 1.9 per year. What does the Poisson probability distribution for this lambda look like? Table 5.11 contains the MINITAB computer output for this distribution.

Excel can also generate probabilities of different values of X for any Poisson distribution. Table 5.12 displays the probabilities produced by Excel for the real estate problem from Demonstration Problem 5.9 using a lambda of 1.6.

Approximating Binomial Problems by the Poisson Distribution

Certain types of binomial distribution problems can be approximated by using the Poisson distribution. Binomial problems with large sample sizes and small values of p, which then generate rare events, are potential candidates for use of the Poisson distribution. As a rule of thumb, if $n > 20$ and $n \cdot p \leq 7$, the approximation is close enough to use the Poisson distribution for binomial problems.

FIGURE 5.3

MINITAB Graph of the Poisson Distribution for $\lambda = 1.6$

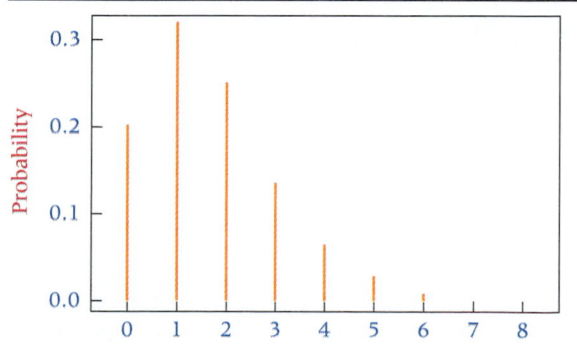

FIGURE 5.4

MINITAB Graph of the Poisson Distribution for $\lambda = 6.5$

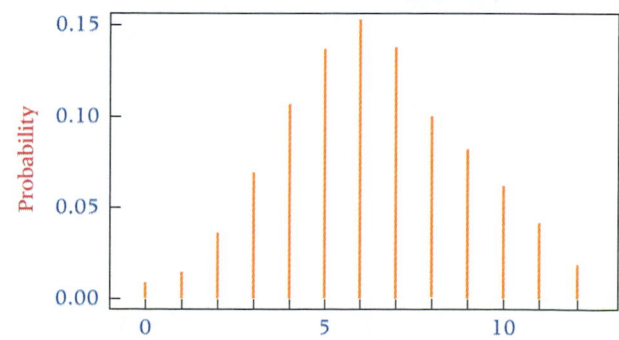

TABLE 5.11
MINITAB Output for the Poisson Distribution λ=1.9

PROBABILITY DENSITY FUNCTION

Poisson with mu = 1.90000

x	P(X = x)
0.00	0.1496
1.00	0.2842
2.00	0.2700
3.00	0.1710
4.00	0.0812
5.00	0.0309
6.00	0.0098
7.00	0.0027
8.00	0.0006
9.00	0.0001
10.00	0.0000

TABLE 5.12
Excel Output for the Poisson Distribution λ=1.6

	A	B
1	x	Probability
2	0	0.2019
3	1	0.3230
4	2	0.2584
5	3	0.1378
6	4	0.0551
7	5	0.0176
8	6	0.0047
9	7	0.0011
10	8	0.0002
11	9	0.0000

If these conditions are met and the binomial problem is a candidate for this process, the procedure begins with computation of the mean of the binomial distribution, $\mu = n \cdot p$. Because μ is the expected value of the binomial, it translates to the expected value, λ, of the Poisson distribution. Using μ as the λ value and using the x value of the binomial problem allows approximation of the probability from a Poisson table or by the Poisson formula.

Large values of n and small values of p usually are not included in binomial distribution tables thereby precluding the use of binomial computational techniques. Using the Poisson distribution as an approximation to such a binomial problem in such cases is an attractive alternative; and indeed, when a computer is not available, it can be the only alternative.

As an example, the following binomial distribution problem can be worked by using the Poisson distribution: $n = 50$ and $p = .03$. What is the probability that $x = 4$? That is, $P(x = 4 | n = 50 \text{ and } p = .03) = ?$

To solve this equation, first determine lambda:

$$\lambda = \mu = n \cdot p = (50)(.03) = 1.5$$

As $n > 20$ and $n \cdot p \leq 7$, this problem is a candidate for the Poisson approximation. For $x = 4$, Table A.3 yields a probability of .0471 for the Poisson approximation. For comparison, working the problem by using the binomial formula yields the following results:

$$_{50}C_4(.03)^4(.97)^{46} = .0459$$

The Poisson approximation is .0012 different from the result obtained by using the binomial formula to work the problem.

A MINITAB graph of this binomial distribution follows.

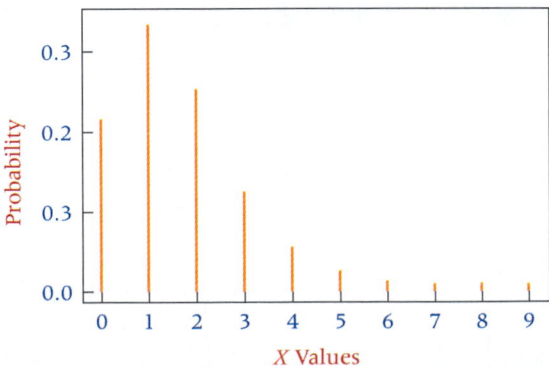

With $\lambda = 1.5$, the Poisson distribution can be generated. A MINITAB graph of this Poisson distribution follows.

In comparing the two graphs, it is difficult to tell the difference between the binomial distribution and the Poisson distribution because the approximation of the binomial distribution by the Poisson distribution is close.

DEMONSTRATION PROBLEM 5.10	Suppose the probability of a bank making a mistake in processing a deposit is .0003. If 10,000 deposits (n) are audited, what is the probability that more than six mistakes were made in processing deposits?

Solution

$$\lambda = \mu = n \cdot p = (10,000)(.0003) = 3.0$$

Because $n > 20$ and $n \cdot p \le 7$, the Poisson approximation is close enough to analyze $x > 6$. Table A.3 yields the following probabilities.

$\lambda = 3.0$

x	Probability
7	.0216
8	.0081
9	.0027
10	.0008
11	.0002
12	.0001
	$x > 6 = .0335$

To work this problem by using the binomial formula requires starting with $x = 7$.

$$_{10,000}C_7(.0003)^7(.9997)^{9993}$$

This process would continue for x values of 8, 9, 10, 11, ..., until the probabilities approach zero. Obviously, this process is impractical, making the Poisson approximation an attractive alternative.

5.4 PROBLEMS

5.15 Find the following values by using the Poisson formula.
  a. $P(x = 5|\lambda = 2.3)$
  b. $P(x = 2|\lambda = 3.9)$
  c. $P(x \le 3|\lambda = 4.1)$
  d. $P(x = 0|\lambda = 2.7)$
  e. $P(x = 1|\lambda = 5.4)$
  f. $P(4 < x < 8|\lambda = 4.4)$

5.16 Find the following values by using the Poisson tables in Appendix A.
  a. $P(x = 6|\lambda = 3.8)$
  b. $P(x > 7|\lambda = 2.9)$
  c. $P(3 \le x \le 9|\lambda = 4.2)$
  d. $P(x = 0|\lambda = 1.9)$

e. $P(x \leq 6 | \lambda = 2.9)$

f. $P(5 < x \leq 8 | \lambda = 5.7)$

5.17   Sketch the graphs of the following Poisson distributions. Compute the mean and standard deviation for each distribution. Locate the mean on the graph. Note how the probabilities are graphed around the mean.

a. $\lambda = 6.3$

b. $\lambda = 1.3$

c. $\lambda = 8.9$

d. $\lambda = 0.6$

5.18   On Monday mornings, the First National Bank only has one teller window open for deposits and withdrawals. Experience has shown that the average number of arriving customers in a 4-minute interval on Monday mornings is 2.8, and each teller can serve more than that number efficiently. These random arrivals at this bank on Monday mornings are Poisson distributed.

a.   What is the probability that on a Monday morning exactly six customers will arrive in a 4-minute interval?

b.   What is the probability that no one will arrive at the bank to make a deposit or withdrawal during a 4-minute interval?

c.   Suppose the teller can serve no more than four customers in any 4-minute interval at this window on a Monday morning. What is the probability that, during any given 4-minute interval, the teller will be unable to meet the demand? What is the probability that the teller will be able to meet the demand? When demand cannot be met during any given interval, a second window is opened. What percentage of the time will a second window have to be opened?

d.   What is the probability that exactly three people will arrive at the bank during a 2-minute period on Monday mornings to make a deposit or a withdrawal? What is the probability that five or more customers will arrive during an 8-minute period?

5.19   A restaurant manager is interested in taking a more statistical approach to predicting customer load. She begins the process by gathering data. One of the restaurant hosts or hostesses is assigned to count customers every 5 minutes from 7 P.M. until 8 P.M. every Saturday night for three weeks. The data are shown here. After the data are gathered, the manager computes lambda using the data from all three weeks as one data set as a basis for probability analysis. What value of lambda did she find? Assume that these customers randomly arrive and that the arrivals are Poisson distributed. Use the value of lambda computed by the manager and help the manager calculate the probabilities in parts (a) through (e) for any given 5-minute interval between 7 P.M. and 8 P.M. on Saturday night.

Number of Arrivals

Week 1	Week 2	Week 3
3	1	5
6	2	3
4	4	5
6	0	3
2	2	5
3	6	4
1	5	7
5	4	3
1	2	4
0	5	8
3	3	1
3	4	3

a. What is the probability that no customers arrive during any given 5-minute interval?

b. What is the probability that six or more customers arrive during any given 5-minute interval?

c. What is the probability that during a 10-minute interval fewer than four customers arrive?

d. What is the probability that between three and six (inclusive) customers arrive in any 10-minute interval?

e. What is the probability that exactly eight customers arrive in any 15-minute interval?

5.20 According to the United National Environmental Program and World Health Organization, in Bombay, India, air pollution standards for particulate matter are exceeded an average of 5.6 days in every three-week period. Assume that the distribution of number of days exceeding the standards per three-week period is Poisson distributed.

a. What is the probability that the standard is not exceeded on any day during a three-week period?

b. What is the probability that the standard is exceeded exactly 6 days of a three-week period?

c. What is the probability that the standard is exceeded 15 or more days during a three-week period? If this outcome actually occurred, what might you conclude?

5.21 The average number of annual trips per family to amusement parks in the United States is Poisson distributed, with a mean of 0.6 trips per year. What is the probability of randomly selecting an American family and finding the following:

a. The family did not make a trip to an amusement park last year?

b. The family took exactly one trip to an amusement park last year?

c. The family took two or more trips to amusement parks last year?

d. The family took three or fewer trips to amusement parks over a three-year period?

e. The family took exactly four trips to amusement parks during a six-year period?

5.22 Ship collisions in the Houston Ship Channel are rare. Suppose the number of collisions are Poisson distributed, with a mean of 1.2 collisions every four months.

a. What is the probability of having no collisions occur over a four-month period?

b. What is the probability of having exactly two collisions in a two-month period?

c. What is the probability of having one or fewer collisions in a six-month period? If this outcome occurred, what might you conclude about ship channel conditions during this period? What might you conclude about ship channel safety awareness during this period? What might you conclude about weather conditions during this period? What might you conclude about lambda?

5.23 A pen company averages 1.2 defective pens per carton produced (200 pens). The number of defects per carton is Poisson distributed.

a. What is the probability of selecting a carton and finding no defective pens?

b. What is the probability of finding eight or more defective pens in a carton?

c. Suppose a purchaser of these pens will quit buying from the company if a carton contains more than three defective pens. What is the probability that a carton contains more than three defective pens?

5.24 A medical researcher estimates that .00004 of the population has a rare blood disorder. If the researcher randomly selects 100,000 people from the population, what is the probability that seven or more people will have the rare blood disorder? What is the probability that more than 10 people will have the rare blood disorder? Suppose the researcher gets more than 10 people who have the rare blood disorder in the sample of 100,000 but that the sample was taken from a particular geographic region. What might the researcher conclude from the results?

5.25 A data firm records a large amount of data. Historically, .9% of the pages of data recorded by the firm contain errors. If 200 pages of data are randomly selected,

    a. What is the probability that six or more pages contain errors?

    b. What is the probability that more than 10 pages contain errors?

    c. What is the probability that none of the pages contain errors?

    d. What is the probability that fewer than five pages contain errors?

5.26 A high percentage of people who fracture or dislocate a bone see a doctor for that condition. Suppose the percentage is 99%. Consider a sample in which 300 people are randomly selected who have fractured or dislocated a bone.

    a. What is the probability that exactly five of them did not see a doctor?

    b. What is the probability that fewer than four of them did not see a doctor?

    c. What is the expected number of people who would not see a doctor?

5.5 HYPERGEOMETRIC DISTRIBUTION

Another discrete statistical distribution is the hypergeometric distribution. Statisticians often use the **hypergeometric distribution** to complement the types of analyses that can be made by using the binomial distribution. Recall that the binomial distribution applies, in theory, only to experiments in which the trials are done with replacement (independent events). The hypergeometric distribution applies only to experiments in which the trials are done without replacement.

The hypergeometric distribution, like the binomial distribution, consists of two possible outcomes: success and failure. However, the user must know the size of the population and the proportion of successes and failures in the population to apply the hypergeometric distribution. In other words, because the hypergeometric distribution is used when sampling is done without replacement, information about population makeup must be known in order to redetermine the probability of a success in each successive trial as the probability changes.

The hypergeometric distribution has the following characteristics:

- It is discrete distribution.
- Each outcome consists of either a success or a failure.
- Sampling is done without replacement.
- The population, N, is finite and known.
- The number of successes in the population, A, is known.

HYPERGEOMETRIC FORMULA

$$P(x) = \frac{{}_A C_x \cdot {}_{N-A} C_{n-x}}{{}_N C_n}$$

where

    N = size of the population
    n = sample size
    A = number of successes in the population
    x = number of successes in the sample; sampling is done *without* replacement

---

A hypergeometric distribution is characterized or described by three parameters: N, A, and n. Because of the multitude of possible combinations of these three parameters, creating tables for the hypergeometric distribution is practically impossible. Hence, the researcher who selects the hypergeometric distribution for analyzing data must use the hypergeometric formula to calculate each probability. Because this task can be tedious and time-consuming, most researchers use the hypergeometric distribution as a fall-back position when working binomial problems without replacement. Even though the binomial distribution theoretically applies only when sampling is done with replacement and p stays constant, recall that, if the population is large enough in comparison with the sample size, the impact of sampling without replacement on p is minimal. Thus the binomial distribution can be used in some situations when sampling is done without replacement. Because of the tables available, using the binomial distribution instead of the hypergeometric distribution whenever possible is preferable. As a rule of thumb, if the sample size is less than 5% of the population, use of the binomial distribution rather than the hypergeometric distribution is acceptable when sampling is done without replacement. The hypergeometric distribution yields the exact probability, and the binomial distribution yields a good approximation of the probability in these situations.

In summary, the hypergeometric distribution should be used instead of the binomial distribution when the following conditions are present:

1. Sampling is being done without replacement.
2. $n \geq 5\% \ N$.

Hypergeometric probabilities are calculated under the assumption of equally likely sampling of the remaining elements of the sample space.

As an application of the hypergeometric distribution, consider the following problem. Twenty-four people, of whom eight are women, apply for a job. If five of the applicants are sampled randomly, what is the probability that exactly three of those sampled are women?

This problem contains a small, finite population of 24, or $N = 24$. A sample of five applicants is taken, or $n = 5$. The sampling is being done without replacement, because the five applicants selected for the sample are five different people. The sample size is 21% of the population, which is greater than 5% of the population ($n/N = 5/24 = .21$). The hypergeometric distribution is the appropriate distribution to use. The population breakdown is $A = 8$ women (successes) and $N - A = 24 - 8 = 16$ men. The probability of getting $x = 3$ women in the sample of $n = 5$ is

$$\frac{_8C_3 \cdot _{16}C_2}{_{24}C_5} = \frac{(56)(120)}{42{,}504} = .1581$$

Conceptually, the combination in the denominator of the hypergeometric formula yields all the possible ways of getting n samples from a population, N, including the ones with the desired outcome. In this problem, there are 42,504 ways of selecting five people from 24 people. The numerator of the hypergeometric formula computes all the possible ways of getting x successes from the A successes available and $n - x$ failures from the $N - A$ available failures in the population. There are 56 ways of getting three women from a pool of eight and there are 120 ways of getting two men from a pool of 16. The combinations of each are multiplied in the numerator because the joint probability of getting x successes *and* $n - x$ failures is being computed.

DEMONSTRATION PROBLEM 5.11	Suppose 18 major computer companies operate in the United States and that 12 are located in California's Silicon Valley. If three computer companies are selected randomly from the entire list, what is the probability that one or more of the selected companies are located in the Silicon Valley?

Solution

$$N = 18, \ n = 3, \ A = 12, \ \text{and} \ x \geq 1$$

This problem is actually three problems in one: $x = 1$, $x = 2$, and $x = 3$. Sampling is being done without replacement, and the sample size is 16.6% of the population. Hence this problem is a candidate for the hypergeometric distribution. The solution follows.

$$
\begin{array}{ccc}
x = 1 & x = 2 & x = 3 \\
\dfrac{_{12}C_1 \cdot _6C_2}{_{18}C_3} + & \dfrac{_{12}C_2 \cdot _6C_1}{_{18}C_3} + & \dfrac{_{12}C_3 \cdot _6C_0}{_{18}C_3} = \\
.2206 \ + & .4853 \ + & .2696 \quad = .9755
\end{array}
$$

An alternative solution method using the law of complements would be one minus the probability that none of the companies is located in Silicon Valley, or

$$1 - P(x = 0 | N = 18, n = 3, A = 12)$$

Thus,

$$1 - \frac{{}_{12}C_0 \cdot {}_6C_3}{{}_{18}C_3} = 1 - .0245 = .9755$$

Using the Computer to Solve for Hypergeometric Distribution Probabilities

Using MINITAB or Excel, it is possible to solve for hypergeometric distribution probabilities on the computer. Both software packages require the input of N, A, n, and x. In either package, the resulting output is the exact probability for that particular value of x. The MINITAB output for the example presented in this section, where $N = 24$ people of whom $A = 8$ are women, $n = 5$ are randomly selected, and $x = 3$ are women, is displayed in Table 5.13. The Excel output for this same problem is presented in Table 5.14.

5.5 PROBLEMS

5.27 Compute the following probabilities by using the hypergeometric formula.
   a. The probability of $x = 3$ if $N = 11$, $A = 8$, and $n = 4$
   b. The probability of $x < 2$ if $N = 15$, $A = 5$, and $n = 6$
   c. The probability of $x = 0$ if $N = 9$, $A = 2$, and $n = 3$
   d. The probability of $x > 4$ if $N = 20$, $A = 5$, and $n = 7$

5.28 Shown here are the top 19 companies in the world in terms of oil refining capacity. Some of the companies are privately owned and others are state owned. Suppose six companies are randomly selected.
   a. What is the probability that exactly one company is privately owned?
   b. What is the probability that exactly four companies are privately owned?
   c. What is the probability that all six companies are privately owned?
   d. What is the probability that none of the companies are privately owned?

Company	Ownership Status
ExxonMobil	Private
Royal Dutch/Shell	Private
BP Amoco	Private
Totalfinaelf	Private
Petroleos de Venezuela	State
Sinopec	Private
Saudi Aramco	State
China Petrochemical	State
Petroleo Brasileiro	State
Petroleo Mexicanos	State
National Iraniam Oil	State
Texaco	Private
Chevron	Private
Repsol-YPF	Private
Kuwait Petroleum	State
Agip Petroli	Private
Nippon Mitsubishi Oil	Private
Marathon Ashland Petro	Private
Pertamina	State

5.29   *Catalog Age* lists the top 17 U.S. firms in annual catalog sales. Dell Computer is number one followed by Gateway and J.C. Penney. Of the 17 firms on the list, eight are in some type of computer-related business. Suppose four firms are randomly selected.

    a.   What is the probability that none of the firms are in some type of computer-related business?

    b.   What is the probability that all four firms are in some type of computer-related business?

    c.   What is the probability that exactly two are in non-computer-related business?

5.30   W. Edwards Deming in his red bead experiment had a box of 4,000 beads, of which 800 were red and 3,200 were white.* Suppose a researcher were to conduct a modified version of the red bead experiment. In her experiment, she has a bag of 20 beads, of which four are red and 16 are white. This experiment requires a participant to reach into the bag and randomly select five beads without replacement.

    a.   What is the probability that the participant will select exactly four white beads?

    b.   What is the probability that the participant will select exactly four red beads?

    c.   What is the probability that the participant will select all red beads?

5.31   Shown here are the top 10 U.S. cities ranked by number of hotel rooms as compiled by Smith Travel Research.

Rank	City	Number of Rooms
1	Las Vegas, NV	106,100
2	Orlando, FL	92,200
3	Los Angeles–Long Beach, CA	80,000
4	Atlanta, GA	73,100
5	Chicago, IL	71,000
6	Washington, DC	68,700
7	New York, NY	66,600
8	Dallas, TX	48,500
9	San Diego, CA	47,200
10	Anaheim–Santa Ana, CA	44,600

Suppose four of these cities are selected randomly.

    a.   What is the probability that exactly two cities are in California?

    b.   What is the probability that none of the cities are east of the Mississippi River?

    c.   What is the probability that exactly three of the cities are ones with more than 70,000 rooms?

5.32   A company produces and ships 16 personal computers knowing that four of them have defective wiring. The company that purchased the computers is going to thoroughly test three of the computers. The purchasing company can detect the defective wiring. What is the probability that the purchasing company will find the following?

    a.   No defective computers

    b.   Exactly three defective computers

    c.   Two or more defective computers

    d.   One or fewer defective computer

5.33   A western city has 18 police officers eligible for promotion. Eleven of the 18 are Hispanic. Suppose only five of the police officers are chosen for promotion and that one is Hispanic. If the officers chosen for promotion had been selected by chance alone, what is the probability that one or fewer of the five promoted officers would have been Hispanic? What might this result indicate?

---

*Mary Walton, "Deming's Parable of Red Beads," *Across the Board* (February 1987): 43–48.

TABLE 5.13

MINITAB Output for
Hypergeometric Problem

Probability Density Function
Hypergeometric with $N = 24$, $X = 8$, and $n = 5$

x	P(X = x)
3.00	0.1581

TABLE 5.14

Excel Output for a Hypergeometric Problem

	A	B	C
1	The probability of x=3 when N=24, n=5, and A=8 is: **0.1581**		

IN RESPONSE

The Good and the Bad of the Banking Industry's Public Image

If the results of the national banking survey can be accepted as population figures, the many percentages presented can be used as p values and applied to sample analysis using the binomial distribution. For example, 80% of all financial consumers consider their bank to be their primary financial institution. If 25 financial consumers are randomly selected, the expected number of these who consider the bank to be their primary financial institution can be determined along with the probability of any particular number from 0 to 25. The value of n is 25 and p is .80. The expected number is $\mu = n \cdot p = (25)(.80) = 20$. One would expect that 20 of the 25 selected people consider the bank to be their primary financial institution. The probability of 18 or more considering their bank to be their primary institution can be obtained by summing values of x from 18 to 25 in table A.2 resulting in .997. Almost all the time in a random sample of 25 financial consumers, 18 or more will say that their bank is their primary financial institution if indeed 80% of all financial consumers feel that way.

Similarly, if 65% of all financial consumers are very satisfied with their primary institution and 15 financial consumers are randomly selected, the binomial distribution ($n = 15$, $p = .65$) can be applied. The expected number is $\mu = n \cdot p = 15(.65) = 9.75$. We realize that with this discrete distribution, we will never obtain 9.75 financial consumers out of 15 who are very satisfied. However, the probabilities for the x values around this figure should be the highest for this distribution.

Suppose a local survey of 32 bank consumers reveals that 26 feel safe in using ATMs. If a random sample of 7 of these 32 is taken, what is the probability that exactly 4 of the 7 feel safe using ATMs? In this hypergeometric problem, $N = 32$, $n = 7$, $A = 26$, and $x = 4$. Applying the hypergeometric formula yields a probability of .0888. In this population, 26 out of 32 or about 81% feel safe in using ATMs. Yet, in the sample of 7, only 4 or about 51% feel safe in using ATMs. The probability, .0888, means that only about 8.88% of the time would this result (4 out of 7) occur by chance from this population.

Random arrival problems are often described by the Poisson distribution. If, on average, a bank has 3.8 customers arriving every 2 minutes, then probability questions about specific customer arrival questions can likely be answered by using the Poisson distribution with lambda equal to 3.8 and the interval being 2 minutes. The probability of no arrivals in a 2-minute period ($x = 0$) is .0224 obtained by using Table A.3 in the Appendix. The probability of more than five customers arriving in a 2-minute period is .1844. If a 4-minute interval is used, lambda is adjusted by doubling lambda to meet the doubled interval resulting in a lambda of 7.6 for 4 minutes. The probability of getting fewer than three customers in a 4-minute interval is .0188.

SUMMARY

Probability experiments produce random outcomes. A variable that contains the outcomes of a random experiment is called a random variable. Random variables such that the set of all possible values is at most a finite or countably infinite number of possible values are called discrete random variables. Random variables that take on values at all points over a given interval are called continuous random variables. Discrete distributions are constructed from discrete random variables. Continuous distributions are constructed from continuous random variables. Three discrete distributions are the binomial distribution, Poisson distribution, and hypergeometric distribution.

The binomial distribution fits experiments when only two mutually exclusive outcomes are possible. In theory, each trial in a binomial experiment must be independent of the other trials. However, if the population size is large enough in relation to the sample size ($n < 5\%N$), the binomial distribution can be used where applicable in cases where the trials are not independent. The probability of getting a desired outcome on any one trial is denoted as p, which is the probability of getting a success. The binomial distribution can be used to analyze discrete studies involving such things as heads/tails, defective/good, and male/female. The binomial formula is used to determine the probability of obtaining x outcomes in n trials. Binomial distribution problems can be solved more rapidly with the use of binomial tables than by formula. A binomial table can be constructed for every different pair of n and p values. Table A.2 of Appendix A contains binomial tables for selected values of n and p. The mean, or long-run average, of a binomial distribution is $\mu = n \cdot p$. The standard deviation of a binomial distribution is $\sqrt{n \cdot p \cdot q}$.

The Poisson distribution usually is used to analyze phenomena that produce rare occurrences. The only information required to generate a Poisson distribution is the long-run average, which is denoted by lambda (λ). The Poisson distribution pertains to occurrences over some interval. The assumptions are that each occurrence is independent of other occurrences and that the value of lambda remains constant throughout the experiment. Some examples of Poisson-type experiments are number of flaws per page of paper, number of crashes per 1,000 commercial airline flights, and number of calls per minute to a switchboard. Poisson probabilities can be determined by either the Poisson formula or the Poisson tables in Table A.3 of Appendix A. Lambda is both the mean and the variance of a Poisson distribution. The Poisson distribution can be used to approximate binomial distribution problems when n is large ($n > 20$), p is small, and $n \cdot p \leq 7$.

The hypergeometric distribution is a discrete distribution that is usually used for binomial-type experiments when the population is small and finite and sampling is done without replacement. Because using the hypergeometric distribution is a tedious process, using the binomial distribution whenever possible is generally more advantageous.

KEY TERMS

binomial distribution	discrete distributions	lambda (λ)	random variable
continuous distributions	discrete random variables	mean or expected value	
continuous random variables	hypergeometric distribution	Poisson distribution	

FORMULAS

Mean (expected) value of a discrete distribution
$$\mu = E(x) = \Sigma[x \cdot P(x)]$$

Variance of a discrete distribution
$$\sigma^2 = \Sigma[(x - \mu)^2 \cdot P(x)]$$

Standard deviation of a discrete distribution
$$\sigma = \sqrt{\Sigma[(x - \mu)^2 \cdot P(x)]}$$

Binomial formula
$$_nC_x \cdot p^x \cdot q^{n-x} = \frac{n!}{x!(n-x)!} \cdot p^x \cdot q^{n-x}$$

Mean of a binomial distribution
$$\mu = n \cdot p$$

Standard deviation of a binomial distribution
$$\sigma = \sqrt{n \cdot p \cdot q}$$

Poisson formula
$$P(x) = \frac{\lambda^x e^{-\lambda}}{x!}$$

Hypergeometric formula
$$P(x) = \frac{_AC_x \cdot {}_{N-A}C_{n-x}}{_NC_n}$$

ETHICAL CONSIDERATIONS

Several points must be emphasized about the use of discrete distributions to analyze data. The independence and/or size assumptions must be met in using the binomial distribution in situations where sampling is done without replacement. Size and λ assumptions must be satisfied in using the Poisson distribution to approximate binomial problems. In either case, failure to meet such assumptions can result in spurious conclusions.

As n increases, the use of binomial distributions to study exact x-value probabilities becomes questionable in decision making. Although the probabilities are mathematically correct, as n becomes larger, the probability of any particular x value becomes lower because there are more values among which to split the probabilities. For example, if $n = 100$ and $p = .50$, the probability of $x = 50$ is .0796. This probability of occurrence appears quite low, even though $x = 50$ is the expected value of this distribution and is also the value most likely to occur. It is more useful to decision makers and, in a sense, probably more ethical to present cumulative values for larger sizes of n. In this example, it is probably more useful to examine $P(x > 50)$ than $P(x = 50)$.

The reader is warned in the chapter that the value of λ is assumed to be constant in a Poisson distribution experiment. Researchers may produce spurious results because the λ value changes during a study. For example, suppose the value of λ is obtained for the number of customer arrivals at a toy store between 7 P.M. and 9 P.M. in the month of December. Because December is an active month in terms of traffic volume through a toy store, the use of such a λ to analyze arrivals at the same store between noon and 2 P.M. in February would be inappropriate and, in a sense, unethical.

Errors in judgment such as these are probably more a case of misuse than lack of ethics. However, it is important that statisticians and researchers adhere to assumptions and appropriate applications of these techniques. The inability or unwillingness to do so opens the way for unethical decision making.

SUPPLEMENTARY PROBLEMS

CALCULATING THE STATISTICS

5.34 Solve for the probabilities of the following binomial distribution problems by using the binomial formula.

  a. If $n = 11$ and $p = .23$, what is the probability that $x = 4$?
  b. If $n = 6$ and $p = .50$, what is the probability that $x \geq 1$?
  c. If $n = 9$ and $p = .85$, what is the probability that $x > 7$?
  d. If $n = 14$ and $p = .70$, what is the probability that $x \leq 3$?

5.35 Use Table A.2, Appendix A, to find the values of the following binomial distribution problems.

  a. $P(x = 14 | n = 20$ and $p = .60)$
  b. $P(x < 5 | n = 10$ and $p = .30)$
  c. $P(x \geq 12 | n = 15$ and $p = .60)$
  d. $P(x > 20 | n = 25$ and $p = .40)$

5.36 Use the Poisson formula to solve for the probabilities of the following Poisson distribution problems.

  a. If $\lambda = 1.25$, what is the probability that $x = 4$?
  b. If $\lambda = 6.37$, what is the probability that $x \leq 1$?
  c. If $\lambda = 2.4$, what is the probability that $x > 5$?

5.37 Use Table A.3, Appendix A, to find the following Poisson distribution values.

  a. $P(x = 3 | \lambda = 1.8)$
  b. $P(x < 5 | \lambda = 3.3)$
  c. $P(x \geq 3 | \lambda = 2.1)$
  d. $P(2 < x \leq 5 | \lambda = 4.2)$

5.38 Solve the following problems by using the hypergeometric formula.

  a. If $N = 6$, $n = 4$, and $A = 5$, what is the probability that $x = 3$?
  b. If $N = 10$, $n = 3$, and $A = 5$, what is the probability that $x \leq 1$?
  c. If $N = 13$, $n = 5$, and $A = 3$, what is the probability that $x \geq 2$?

TESTING YOUR UNDERSTANDING

5.39 In a study by Peter D. Hart Research Associates for the Nasdaq Stock Market, it was determined that 20% of all stock investors are retired people. In addition, 40% of all U.S. adults invest in mutual funds. Suppose a random sample of 25 stock investors is taken. What is the probability that exactly seven are retired people? What is the probability that 10 or more are retired people? How many retired people would you expect to find in a random sample of 25 stock investors? Suppose a random sample of 20 U.S. adults is taken. What is the probability that exactly eight adults invested in mutual funds? What is the probability that fewer than six adults invested in mutual funds? What is the probability that none of the adults invested in mutual funds? What is the probability that 12 or more adults invested in mutual funds? For which exact number of adults is the probability the highest? How does this figure compare to the expected number?

5.40 A service station has a pump that distributes diesel fuel to automobiles. The station owner estimates that only about 3.2 cars use the diesel pump every 2 hours. Assume the arrivals of diesel pump users are Poisson distributed.

a. What is the probability that three cars will arrive to use the diesel pump during a 1-hour period?

b. Suppose the owner needs to shut down the diesel pump for half an hour to make repairs. However, the owner hates to lose any business. What is the probability that no cars will arrive to use the diesel pump during a half-hour period?

c. Suppose five cars arrive during a 1-hour period to use the diesel pump. What is the probability of five or more cars arriving during a 1-hour period to use the diesel pump? If this outcome actually occurred, what might you conclude?

5.41 In a particular manufacturing plant, two machines (A and B) produce a particular part. One machine (B) is newer and faster. In one 5-minute period, a lot consisting of 32 parts is produced. Twenty-two are produced by machine B and the rest by machine A. Suppose an inspector randomly samples a dozen of the parts from this lot.

a. What is the probability that exactly three parts were produced by machine A?

b. What is the probability that half of the parts were produced by each machine?

c. What is the probability that all of the parts were produced by machine B?

d. What is the probability that seven, eight, or nine parts were produced by machine B?

5.42 Suppose that, for every lot of 100 computer chips a company produces, an average of 1.4 are defective. Another company buys many lots of these chips at a time, from which one lot is selected randomly and tested for defects. If the tested lot contains more than three defects, the buyer will reject all the lots sent in that batch. What is the probability that the buyer will accept the lots? Assume that the defects per lot are Poisson distributed.

5.43 The National Center for Health Statistics reports that 25% of all Americans between the ages of 65 and 74 have a chronic heart condition. Suppose you live in a state where the environment is conducive to good health and low stress and you believe the conditions in your state promote healthy hearts. To investigate this theory, you conduct a random telephone survey of 20 persons 65 to 74 years of age in your state.

a. On the basis of the figure from the National Center for Health Statistics, what is the expected number of persons 65 to 74 years of age in your survey who have a chronic heart condition?

b. Suppose only one person in your survey has a chronic heart condition. What is the probability of getting one or fewer people with a chronic heart condition in a sample of 20 if 25% of the population in this age bracket has this health problem? What do you conclude about your state from the sample data?

5.44 A survey conducted for the Northwestern National Life Insurance Company revealed that 70% of American workers say job stress caused frequent health problems. One in three said they expected to burn out in the job in the near future. Thirty-four percent said they thought seriously about quitting their job last year because of workplace stress. Fifty-three percent said they were required to work more than 40 hours a week very often or somewhat often.

a. Suppose a random sample of 10 American workers is selected. What is the probability that more than seven of them say job stress caused frequent health problems? What is the expected number of workers who say job stress caused frequent health problems?

b. Suppose a random sample of 15 American workers is selected. What is the expected number of these sampled workers who say they will burn out in the near future? What is the probability that none of the workers say they will burn out in the near future?

c. Suppose a sample of seven workers is selected randomly. What is the probability that all seven say they are asked very often or somewhat often to work more than 40 hours a week? If this outcome actually happened, what might you conclude?

5.45 According to Padgett Business Services, 20% of all small-business owners say the most important advice for starting a business is to prepare for long hours and hard work. Twenty-five percent say the most important advice is to have good financing ready. Nineteen percent say having a good plan is the most important advice; 18% say studying the industry is the most important advice; and 18% list other advice. Suppose 12 small-business owners are contacted, and assume that the percentages hold for all small-business owners.

a. What is the probability that none of the owners would say preparing for long hours and hard work is the most important advice?

b. What is the probability that six or more owners would say preparing for long hours and hard work is the most important advice?

c. What is the probability that exactly five owners would say having good financing ready is the most important advice?

d. What is the expected number of owners who would say having a good plan is the most important advice?

5.46 According to a recent survey, the probability that a passenger files a complaint with the Department of Transportation about a particular U.S. airline is .000014. Suppose 100,000 passengers who flew with this particular airline are randomly contacted.

a. What is the probability that exactly five passengers filed complaints?

b. What is the probability that none of the passengers filed complaints?

c. What is the probability that more than six passengers filed complaints?

5.47 A hair stylist has been in business one year. Sixty percent of his customers are walk-in business. If he randomly samples eight of the people from last week's list of customers, what is the probability that three or fewer were walk-ins? If this outcome actually occurred, what would be some of the explanations for it?

5.48 According to the U.S. Census Bureau, about 20% of Idaho residents live in metropolitan areas. This percentage is the lowest of all 50 states. A catalog sales company in Georgia just purchased a list of Idaho consumers. Its market analyst randomly selects 25 people from this list.

  a. What is the probability that exactly eight people live in metropolitan areas?
  b. What is the probability that the analyst would get more than 10 people in this sample who live in metropolitan areas?
  c. Suppose the analyst got more than 10 people who live in metropolitan areas from the group of 25. What might she conclude about the company's list of Idaho consumers? What might she conclude about the census figure?

5.49 Suppose that, for every family vacation trip by car of more than 2,000 miles, an average of .60 flat tires occurs. Suppose also that the distribution of the number of flat tires per trip of more than 2,000 miles is Poisson. What is the probability that a family will take a trip of more than 2,000 miles and have no flat tires? What is the probability that the family will have three or more flat tires on such a trip? Suppose trips are independent and the value of lambda holds for all trips of more than 2,000 miles. If a family takes two trips of more than 2,000 miles during a summer, what is the probability that the family will have no flat tires on either trip?

5.50 *Editor and Publisher Yearbook* releases figures on the top newspapers in the United States. Shown here are the top 25 daily city newspapers in the United States ranked according to circulation.

Rank	Newspaper
1	New York Times (NY)
2	Los Angeles Times (CA)
3	Washington Post (DC)
4	New York Daily News (NY)
5	Chicago Tribune (IL)
6	Long Island Newsday (NY)
7	Houston Chronicle (TX)
8	Dallas Morning News (TX)
9	Chicago Sun-Times (IL)
10	Boston Globe (MA)
11	San Francisco Chronicle (CA)
12	Phoenix Arizona Republic (AZ)
13	New York Post (NY)
14	Denver Rocky Mountain News (CO)
15	Denver Post (CO)
16	Newark Star-Ledger (NJ)
17	Philadelphia Inquirer (PA)
18	San Diego Union-Tribune (CA)
19	Detroit Free Press (MI)
20	Cleveland Plain Dealer (OH)
21	Orange County Register (CA)
22	Portland Oregonian (OR)
23	Miami Herald (FL)
24	Minneapolis Star Tribune (MN)
25	St. Petersburg Times (FL)

Suppose a researcher wants to sample a portion of these newspapers and compare the sizes of the business sections of the Sunday papers. She randomly samples eight of these newspapers.

  a. What is the probability that the sample contains exactly one newspaper located in New York state?
  b. What is the probability that half of the newspapers are ranked in the top 10 by circulation?
  c. What is the probability that none of the newspapers are located in California?
  d. What is the probability that exactly three of the newspapers are located in states that begin with the letter M?

5.51 An office in Albuquerque has 24 workers including management. Eight of the workers commute to work from the west side of the Rio Grande River. Suppose six of the office workers are randomly selected.

  a. What is the probability that all six workers commute from the west side of the Rio Grande?
  b. What is the probability that none of the workers commute from the west side of the Rio Grande?
  c. Which probability from parts (a) and (b) was greatest? Why do think this is?
  d. What is the probability that half of the workers do not commute from the west side of the Rio Grande?

5.52 According to the U.S. Census Bureau, 20% of the workers in Atlanta use public transportation. If 25 Atlanta workers are randomly selected, what is the expected number to use public transportation? Graph the binomial distribution for this sample. What are the mean and the standard deviation for this distribution? What is the probability that more than 12 of the selected workers use public transportation? Explain conceptually and from the graph why you would get this probability. Suppose you randomly sample 25 Atlanta workers and actually get 14 who use public transportation. Is this outcome likely? How might you explain this result?

5.53 One of the earliest applications of the Poisson distribution was in analyzing incoming calls to a telephone switchboard. Analysts generally believe that random phone calls are Poisson distributed. Suppose phone calls to a switchboard arrive at an average rate of 2.4 calls per minute.

a. If an operator wants to take a 1-minute break, what is the probability that there will be no calls during a 1-minute interval?

b. If an operator can handle at most five calls per minute, what is the probability that the operator will be unable to handle the calls in any 1-minute period?

c. What is the probability that exactly three calls will arrive in a 2-minute interval?

d. What is the probability that one or fewer calls will arrive in a 15-second interval?

5.54 Only 1% of all American households do not have a color television set. A television marketing analyst randomly selects 160 American households.

a. How many households would he expect to not have a color television set?

b. What is the probability that eight or more households do not have a color television set?

c. What is the probability that between two and six households (inclusive) do not have a color television set?

5.55 Suppose that in the bookkeeping operation of a large corporation the probability of a recording error on any one billing is .005. Suppose the probability of a recording error from one billing to the next is constant, and 1,000 billings are randomly sampled by an auditor.

a. What is the probability that fewer than four billings contain a recording error?

b. What is the probability that more than 10 billings contain a billing error?

c. What is the probability that all 1,000 billings contain no recording errors?

5.56 According to the American Medical Association, about 36% of all U.S. physicians under the age of 35 are women. Your company has just hired eight physicians under the age of 35 and none is a woman. If a group of women physicians under the age of 35 want to sue your company for discriminatory hiring practices, would they have a strong case based on these numbers? Use the binomial distribution to determine the probability of

the company's hiring result occurring randomly and comment on the potential justification for a lawsuit.

5.57 The following table lists the 32 largest U.S. universities according to enrollment figures from the *World Almanac*.

University	Enrollment
University of Phoenix (AZ)	66,534
University of Texas at Austin (TX)	49,996
Ohio State University–Columbus (OH)	47,952
University of Minnesota (MN)	45,481
University of Florida (FL)	45,114
Arizona State University (AZ)	44,126
Texas A&M University–College Station (TX)	44,026
Michigan State University (MI)	43,366
University of Wisconsin–Madison (WI)	41,219
Pennsylvania State–University Park (PA)	40,571
University of Illinois–Champaign (IL)	37,965
Purdue University–West Lafayette (IN)	37,871
University of Michigan (MI)	37,595
New York University (NY)	37,150
Indiana University–Bloomington (IN)	37,076
University of California at Los Angeles (CA)	36,890
University of Washington (WA)	36,134
University of South Florida (FL)	36,015
Rutgers University (NJ)	35,237
University of Arizona (AZ)	34,560
Florida State University (FL)	33,951
University of Central Florida (FL)	33,713
University of Maryland–College Park (MD)	33,189
Brigham Young University (UT)	32,554
University of Houston (TX)	32,123
Florida International University (FL)	31,945
San Diego State University (CA)	31,609
University of California at Berkeley (CA)	31,347
University of Georgia (GA)	31,288
California State University Long Beach (CA)	30,918
Louisiana State University (LA)	30,861
Wayne State University (MI)	30,408

a. If five different universities are selected randomly from the list, what is the probability that three of them have enrollments of 40,000 or more?

b. If eight different universities are selected randomly from the list, what is the probability that two or fewer are universities in Michigan or Arizona?

c. Suppose universities are being selected randomly from this list with replacement. If five universities are sampled, what is the probability that the sample will contain exactly two universities in Texas?

5.58 In one midwestern city, the government has 14 repossessed houses, which are evaluated to be worth about the same. Ten of the houses are on the north side of town and the rest are on the west side. A local contractor submitted a bid to purchase four of the houses. Which houses the contractor will get is subject to a random draw.

a. What is the probability that all four houses selected for the contractor will be on the north side of town?

b. What is the probability that all four houses selected for the contractor will be on the west side of town?

c. What is the probability that half of the houses selected for the contractor will be on the west side and half on the north side of town?

5.59 The Public Citizen's Health Research Group studied the serious disciplinary actions that were taken during a recent year on nonfederal medical doctors in the United States. The national average was 3.84 serious actions per 1,000 doctors. The state with the lowest number was Minnesota, with 1.6 serious actions per 1,000 doctors. Assume that the numbers of serious actions per 1,000 doctors in both the United States and in Minnesota are Poisson distributed.

a. What is the probability of randomly selecting 1,000 U.S. doctors and finding no serious actions taken?

b. What is the probability of randomly selecting 2,000 U.S. doctors and finding six serious actions taken?

c. What is the probability of randomly selecting 3,000 Minnesota doctors and finding fewer than seven serious actions taken?

INTERPRETING THE OUTPUT

5.60 Study the MINITAB output. Discuss the type of distribution, the mean, standard deviation, and why the probabilities fall as they do.

```
Probability Density Function
────────────────────────────────────────
Binomial with n = 15 and p = 0.360000
   x      P(X = x)
 0.00     0.0012
 1.00     0.0104
 2.00     0.0411
 3.00     0.1002
 4.00     0.1692
 5.00     0.2093
 6.00     0.1963
 7.00     0.1419
 8.00     0.0798
 9.00     0.0349
10.00     0.0118
11.00     0.0030
12.00     0.0006
13.00     0.0001
14.00     0.0000
15.00     0.0000
────────────────────────────────────────
```

5.61 Study the Excel output. Explain the distribution in terms of shape and mean. Are these probabilities what you would expect? Why or why not?

	A	B
1	x Values	
2	0	0.0620
3	1	0.1725
4	2	0.2397
5	3	0.2221
6	4	0.1544
7	5	0.0858
8	6	0.0398
9	7	0.0158
10	8	0.0055
11	9	0.0017
12	10	0.0005
13	11	0.0001

5.62 Study the graphical output from Excel. Describe the distribution and explain why the graph takes the shape it does.

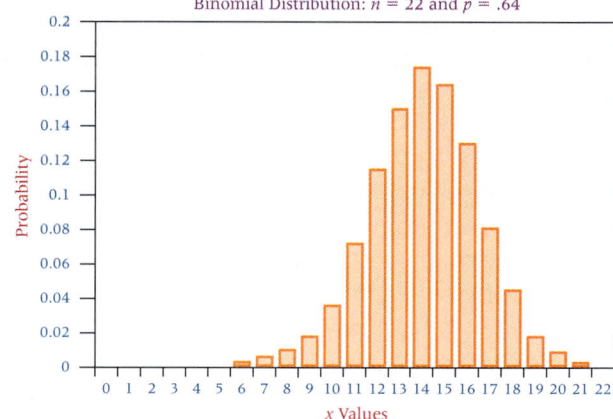

Binomial Distribution: $n = 22$ and $p = .64$

5.63 Study the MINITAB graph. Discuss the distribution including type, shape, and probability outcomes.

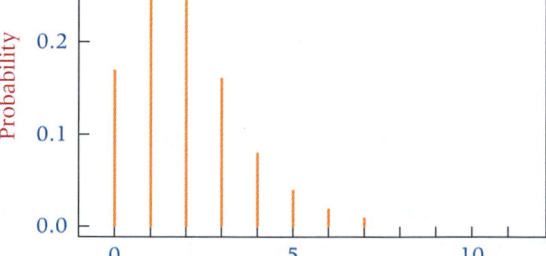

Poisson Distribution: Lambda = 1.784

ANALYZING THE DATABASES

see www.wiley.com/college/black

1. Use the manufacturing database. What is the probability that a randomly selected SIC code industry has a value of industry shipments equal to 2? Use this as the p value for a binomial experiment. If you were to randomly select 12 SIC code industries, what is the probability that fewer than three would have a value of industry shipments equal to 2? If you were to randomly select 25 SIC code industries, what is the probability that exactly eight would have a value of industry shipments equal to 2?

2. Use the hospital database. In this population of 200, what is the breakdown between hospitals that are general medical hospitals and psychiatric hospitals? Using those figures as a breakdown of the population and the hypergeometric distribution, what is the probability of randomly selecting 16 hospitals from this database and getting exactly nine that are psychiatric hospitals? Using the number of hospitals in this database that are for-profit, compute p = probability that a hospital is for-profit. Now use the binomial formula to determine the probability of randomly selecting 30 hospitals and getting exactly 10 that are for-profit.

3. Use the financial database of chemical companies. If five of these companies are selected randomly, what is the probability that exactly three have a return on equity of 15% or more? *Hint:* Use the hypergeometric distribution and a breakdown of this population of 19 companies to compute this probability. What is the probability of randomly selecting eight insurance companies and getting exactly four of them with average yields of less than 1%?

CASE: FUJI FILM INTRODUCES APS

In the early 1990s, Fuji Photo Film, USA, joined forces with four of its rivals to create the Advanced Photo System (APS), which is hailed as the first major development in the film industry since 35-millimeter technology was introduced. In February 1996, the new 24-millimeter system, promising clearer and sharper pictures, was launched. By the end of the year, the lack of communications and a limited supply of products made retailers angry and consumers baffled. Advertising was almost nonexistent. Because the product was developed by five industry rivals, the companies had enacted a secrecy agreement in which no one outside of company management, including the company's sales force, would know details about the product until each company introduced its APS products on the same day. When the product was actually introduced, it came with little communication to retailers about the product, virtually no training of sales representatives on the product (so that they could demonstrate and explain the features), and a great underestimation of demand for the product. Fortunately, Fuji pressed on by taking an "honesty is the best policy" stance and explaining to retailers and other customers what had happened and asking for patience. In addition, Fuji increased its research to better ascertain market positioning and size. By 1997, Fuji had geared up production to meet the demand and was increasing customer promotion. APS products were on the road to success. By 1998, APS cameras owned 20% of the point-and-shoot camera market.

Discussion

Suppose you are a part of a Fuji team whose task it is to examine issues about market share, customer acceptance, complaints, and the reasons why new products are successful.

1. As stated, by 1998 APS cameras owned 20% of the point-and-shoot camera market. Now it is the year 2003 and the market share might be nearer to 40%. Suppose 30 customers from the point-and-shoot camera market are randomly selected. If the market share is really .40, what is the expected number of point-and-shoot camera customers who purchase an APS camera? What is the probability that six or fewer purchase an APS camera? Suppose you actually got six or fewer APS customers in the sample of 30. Based on the probability just calculated, is this enough evidence to convince you that the market share is not 40%? Why or why not?

2. Suppose customer complaints on the 24-millimeter film are Poisson distributed at an average rate of 2.4 complaints/100,000 rolls sold. Suppose further that Fuji is having trouble with shipments being late and one batch of 100,000 rolls yields seven complaints from customers. Assuming that it is unacceptable to management for the average rate of complaints to increase, is this enough evidence to convince management that the average rate of complaints has increased, or can it be written off as a random occurrence that happens quite frequently? Produce the Poisson distribution for this question and discuss its implication for this problem.

3. One study of 52 product launches found that those undertaken with revenue growth as the main objective are more likely to fail than those undertaken to increase customer satisfaction or to create a new market such as the APS system. Suppose of the 52 products launched, 34 were launched with revenue growth as the main objective and the rest were launched to increase customer satisfaction or to create a new market. Now suppose only 10 of these products were successful (the rest failed) and seven were products that were launched to increase customer satisfaction or to create a new market. What is the probability of this result occurring by chance? What does this probability tell you about the basic premise regarding the importance of the main objective?

USING THE COMPUTER

EXCEL

Excel can be used to compute exact or cumulative probabilities for problems using the binomial, hypergeometric, or Poisson distributions. For each of these computations, the process begins by selecting the Paste Function key, f_x, on the tool bar, which will cause the Paste Function dialog box to appear.

Binomial Distribution

To work a binomial distribution problem by using Excel, select the function name, **BINOMDIST**, from the Paste Function dialog box. The BINOMDIST dialog box will appear. Four lines of information must be completed to use this function. The first line requires the number of successes, x. The second line is for the sample size, n. Place the value of p, the probability of a single success, in the third line. The fourth line, cumulative, is a logical value that determines whether the answer is given as an exact probability or a cumulative probability. If you enter FALSE on the line, the answer will be the exact probability of getting x successes in n trials. If you enter TRUE, the answer will be cumulative probability of getting from zero to x successes. The outcome is the probability value.

Poisson Distribution

Poisson distribution problems can be solved by using the **POISSON** option selected from the Paste Function dialog box. In the POISSON dialog box that appears, three lines must be completed to obtain an answer. The first line requires the number of successes, x. The second line is for the value of λ. The third line is a logical value that determines whether the answer is given as an exact probability or a cumulative probability. If you respond with FALSE on the line, the answer will be given as an exact probability. If a TRUE is placed on the line, the answer will be given as the cumulative probability of values between zero and x.

Hypergeometric Distribution

When you select the **HYPGEOMDIST** option from the Paste Function dialog box, another dialog box will appear. Four lines must be completed to use this function. The first line requires the number of successes in the sample, x. The second line asks for the sample size, n. The third line is the number of successes in the population, A, and the fourth line is for the size of the population, N. The output will be an exact probability value.

MINITAB

MINITAB Windows allows you to produce a binomial distribution, a Poisson distribution, or a hypergeometric distribution. The process begins by selecting the option **Calc** on the menu bar. This selection will cause a pull-down menu to appear.

Select the option **Probability Distributions**. Another pull-down menu will appear.

Binomial Distribution

To obtain a binomial distribution, select the option **Binomial**. A dialog box will appear. From the box, choose how the probabilities are calculated by selecting either **Probability**, **Cumulative Probability**, or **Inverse Probability**. Probability yields the exact probabilities for each x value. Cumulative Probability yields the cumulative probability for each and every number of possible successes from zero to x. Inverse Probability yields the inverse of the cumulative probabilities. **Number of trials** is the sample size, n, and **Probability of a success** is the value of p. If you want to have probabilities computed for several values of x, place them in a column, select the input column option, and list the column location of the x values. If you only want to compute the probability for a particular value of x, check **Input constant** and input the number of successes you want to evaluate, x. The output will be the exact probability, the cumulative probability, or the inverse cumulative probability.

Poisson Distribution

To obtain a Poisson distribution, select the option **Poisson** from the pull-down menu. A dialog box will appear. Choose how the probabilities are calculated by selecting either **Probability**, **Cumulative Probability**, or **Inverse Probability**. Probability yields the exact probabilities for each x value. Cumulative Probability yields the cumulative probability for each and every number of possible successes from zero to x. Inverse Probability yields the inverse of the cumulative probabilities. On the line, **Mean**, enter the value of λ. If you want to have probabilities computed for several values of x, place them in a column, select the input column option, and list the column location of the x values. If you only want to compute the probability for a particular value of x, check **Input constant** and input the number of successes you want to evaluate, x. The output will be the exact probability, the cumulative probability, or the inverse cumulative probability.

Hypergeometric Distribution

To obtain a Hypergeometric distribution, select the option **Hypergeometric** from the pull-down menu. A dialog box will appear. Choose how the probabilities are calculated by selecting either **Probability**, **Cumulative Probability**, or **Inverse Probability**. Probability yields the exact probabilities for each x value. Cumulative Probability yields the cumulative probability for each and every number of possible successes from zero to x. Inverse Probability yields the inverse of the cumulative probabilities. On the fourth line enter the population size, N. In the next line, enter the number of successes in the population, A. In the following line, enter the sample size, n. If you want to have probabilities computed for several values of x, place them in a column, select the input column option, and list the column location of the x values. If you only want to compute the probability for a particular value of x, check **Input constant** and input the number of successes you want to evaluate, x. The output will be the exact probability, the cumulative probability, or the inverse cumulative probability.

CHAPTER 6

Continuous Distributions

LEARNING OBJECTIVES

The primary learning objective of Chapter 6 is to help you understand continuous distributions, thereby enabling you to:

1. Understand concepts of the uniform distribution.
2. Appreciate the importance of the normal distribution.
3. Recognize normal distribution problems and know how to solve such problems.
4. Decide when to use the normal distribution to approximate binomial distribution problems and know how to work such problems.
5. Decide when to use the exponential distribution to solve problems in business and know how to work such problems.

The Changing Faces of the Insurance Industry

The insurance industry faced many challenges in the 1990s. Traditional markets eroded and new opportunities arose. In past decades, traditional one-income families relied heavily on life insurance coverage against the premature death of the breadwinner. In this decade, couples marry later, have fewer children, and often have two breadwinners. These trends along with others result in less dependence on life insurance. In fact, a study by the Life Insurance Marketing and Research Association showed that only 59% of Americans now believe that life insurance is the best way to protect a family financially against the premature death of the breadwinner. This figure is down from 72% in the early 1980s. Financially, industry analysts say this drop cost insurance companies $700 billion in coverage and $4.7 billion in premium revenue. Insurance marketers now are looking more closely at previously underutilized markets for new sales, such as those traditionally considered more risky, including families with single parents or low incomes.

Health insurance, homeowner insurance, automobile insurance, and other types of insurance providers face similar challenges, except in those areas where insurance coverage is mandatory. The average U.S. household spends $2,100 on all types of insurance according to the Bureau of Labor Statistics' Consumer Expenditure Survey. This figure does not include health and life insurance paid for in full or in part by employers. A breakdown by type of insurance is 39% for health coverage, 33 percent for vehicles, 19% for life and other personal nonhealth insurance, and 9% for homeowners and related insurance.

Geographic location is a strong influence on the insurance rates paid by consumers. On average, a U.S. consumer spends $691 a year on automobile insurance. The highest rates are in New Jersey ($1,100 per year), New York ($960 per year), and Hawaii ($959 per year). The lowest rates are in North Dakota where the average rate per year is $402. The average U.S. figure for homeowner's insurance was $420, with Alaska and Hawaii excluded. Texas recorded the highest annual homeowner's insurance cost at $592 per household with Massachusetts second at $548. The lowest average annual per household cost was in Wisconsin where the figure was only $274.

Insurance costs also vary with the value of vehicles and the size and location of the home. Households with middle-aged adults and children are more likely to spend more on insurance. Health insurance spending increases with age.

Managerial and Statistical Questions

1. The average yearly cost in the United States for automobile insurance is $691. Since this figure varies by states, locales, and individuals, what probability distribution best describes the yearly costs for automobile insurance in the United States? Are the data uniformly distributed or normally distributed? If the data are uniformly distributed, between what two values would the middle 50% lie? If the data are normally distributed with a mean of $691 and a standard deviation of $109, what percentage of consumers pay more than $874?

2. According to the Bureau of Labor Statistics' survey, the average homeowner insurance cost in the United States is $420 per year. If homeowner insurance costs across the United States are uniformly distributed, what is the probability that an individual homeowner is paying less than $400? Suppose homeowner insurance costs are normally distributed in the state of Texas with a mean cost of $592 and a standard deviation of $78. What is the probability that a randomly selected Texas household is paying between $500 and $650 for homeowner insurance?

3. The survey reported by the Life Insurance Marketing and Research Association showed that 20% of all insurance consumers prefer purchasing insurance over the phone or by mail. Suppose a survey of 80 randomly selected Americans is taken. What is the probability that 21 or more of those selected believe that life insurance is the best way to protect a family financially against the premature death of the breadwinner?

4. Suppose insurance annuity tables show that, on average, 1.8 houses are destroyed by fire every hour in the United States. What is the probability that an hour and a half goes by without a house being destroyed by fire?

Source: Adapted from Jan Larson, "Insurance at Risk," *American Demographics*, October 1995, pp. 53–57; National Association of Insurance Commissioners, *The Wall Street Journal Almanac 1999*, Ronald J. Alsop, ed. (New York: Ballantine Books, 1999), p. 659.

Whereas Chapter 5 focused on the characteristics and applications of discrete distributions, Chapter 6 concentrates on information about continuous distributions. Continuous distributions are constructed from continuous random variables in which values are taken on for every point over a given interval and are usually generated from experiments in which things are "measured" as opposed to "counted." With continuous distributions, probabilities of outcomes occurring between particular points are determined by calculating the area under the curve between those points. In addition, the entire area under the whole curve is equal to 1. The many continuous distributions in statistics include the uniform distribution, the normal distribution, the exponential distribution, the *t* distribution, the chi-square distribution, and the *F* distribution. This chapter presents the uniform distribution, the normal distribution, and the exponential distribution.

6.1 THE UNIFORM DISTRIBUTION

The **uniform distribution,** sometimes referred to as the **rectangular distribution,** is *a relatively simple continuous distribution in which the same height, or f(x), is obtained over a range of values.* The following probability density function defines a uniform distribution.

PROBABILITY DENSITY FUNCTION OF A UNIFORM DISTRIBUTION	$$f(x) = \begin{cases} \dfrac{1}{b-a} & \text{for } a \leq x \leq b \\ 0 & \text{for all other values} \end{cases}$$

Figure 6.1 is an example of a uniform distribution. In a uniform, or rectangular, distribution, the total area under the curve is equal to the product of the length and the width of the rectangle and equals 1. Because the distribution lies, by definition, between the *x* values of *a* and *b*, the length of the rectangle is $(b-a)$. Combining this area calculation with the fact that the area equals 1, the height of the rectangle can be solved as follows.

FIGURE 6.1

Uniform Distribution

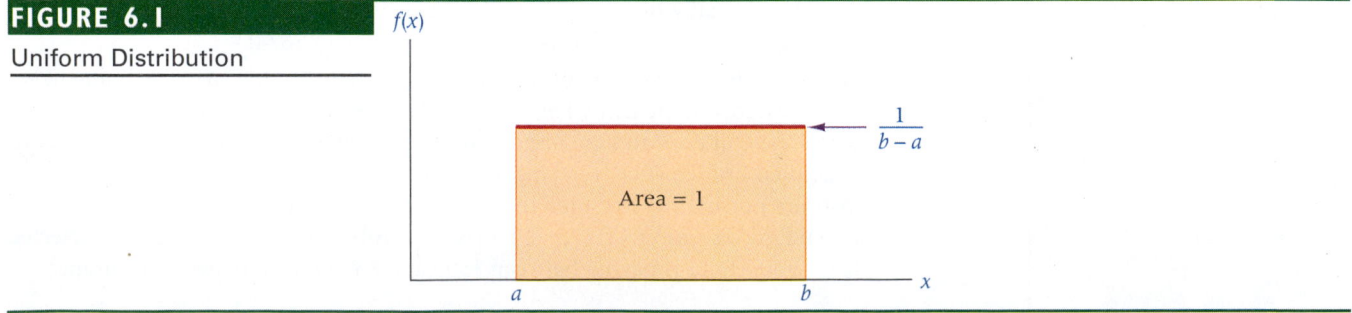

$$\text{Area of Rectangle} = (\text{Length})(\text{Height}) = 1$$

But

$$\text{Length} = (b-a)$$

Therefore,

$$(b-a)(\text{Height}) = 1$$

and

$$\text{Height} = \frac{1}{(b-a)}$$

These calculations show why, between the x values of a and b, the distribution has a constant height of $1/(b-a)$.

The mean and standard deviation of a uniform distribution are given as follows.

MEAN AND STANDARD DEVIATION OF A UNIFORM DISTRIBUTION	$\mu = \dfrac{a+b}{2}$ $\sigma = \dfrac{b-a}{\sqrt{12}}$

Many possible situations arise in which data might be uniformly distributed. As an example, suppose a production line is set up to manufacture machine braces in lots of five per minute during a shift. When the lots are weighed, variation among the weights is detected, with lot weights ranging from 41 to 47 grams in a uniform distribution. The height of this distribution is

$$f(x) = \text{Height} = \frac{1}{(b-a)} = \frac{1}{(47-41)} = \frac{1}{6}$$

The mean and standard deviation of this distribution are

$$\text{Mean} = \frac{a+b}{2} = \frac{41+47}{2} = \frac{88}{2} = 44$$

$$\text{Standard Deviation} = \frac{b-a}{\sqrt{12}} = \frac{47-41}{\sqrt{12}} = \frac{6}{3.464} = 1.732$$

Figure 6.2 provides the uniform distribution for this example, with its mean, standard deviation, and the height of the distribution.

Determining Probabilities in a Uniform Distribution

With discrete distributions, the probability function yields the value of the probability. For continuous distributions, probabilities are calculated by determining the area over an interval of the function. With continuous distributions, any single value is possible but it has a probability of zero. There is no area under the curve for a single point. The following equation is used to determine the probabilities of x for a uniform distribution between a and b.

FIGURE 6.2
Distribution of Lot Weights

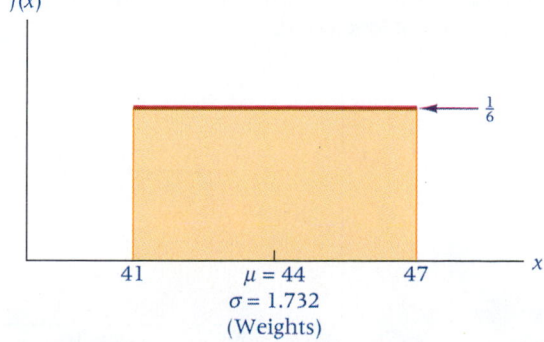

FIGURE 6.3

Solved Probability in a
Uniform Distribution

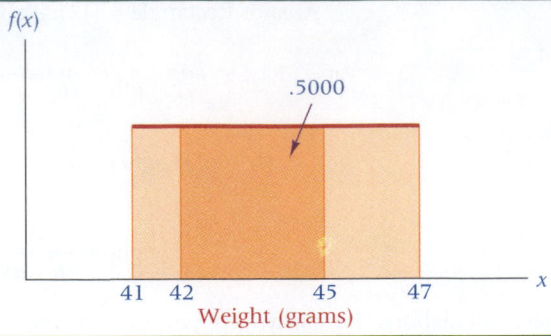

PROBABILITIES IN A UNIFORM DISTRIBUTION	$$P(x) = \frac{x_2 - x_1}{b - a}$$

where:

$$a \leq x_1 \leq x_2 \leq b$$

Remember that the area between a and b is equal to 1. The probability for any interval that includes a and b is 1. The probability of $x \geq b$ or of $x \leq a$ is zero because there is no area above b or below a.

Suppose that on the machine braces problem we want to determine the probability that a lot weighs between 42 and 45 grams. This probability is computed as follows:

$$P(x) = \frac{x_2 - x_1}{b - a} = \frac{45 - 42}{47 - 41} = \frac{3}{6} = .5000$$

Figure 6.3 displays this solution.

The probability that a lot weighs more than 48 grams is zero, because $x = 48$ is greater than the upper value, $x = 47$, of the uniform distribution. A similar argument gives the probability of a lot weighing less than 40 grams. Because 40 is less than the lowest value of the uniform distribution range, 41, the probability is zero.

DEMONSTRATION PROBLEM 6.1

Suppose the amount of time it takes to assemble a plastic module ranges from 27 to 39 seconds and that assembly times are uniformly distributed. Describe the distribution. What is the probability that a given assembly will take between 30 and 35 seconds? Fewer than 30 seconds?

Solution

$$f(x) = \frac{1}{39 - 27} = \frac{1}{12}$$

$$\mu = \frac{a + b}{2} = \frac{39 + 27}{2} = 33$$

$$\sigma = \frac{b - a}{\sqrt{12}} = \frac{39 - 27}{\sqrt{12}} = \frac{12}{\sqrt{12}} = 3.464$$

The height of the distribution is 1/12. The mean time is 33 seconds with a standard deviation of 3.464 seconds.

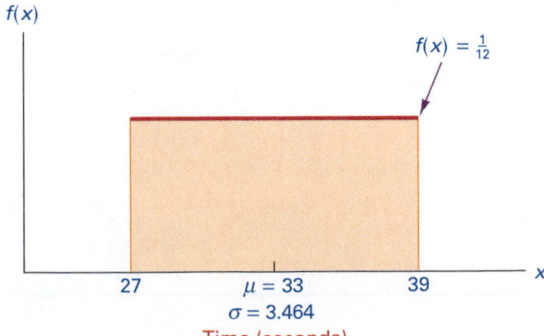

$$P(30 \leq x \leq 35) = \frac{35-30}{39-27} = \frac{5}{12} = .4167$$

There is a .4167 probability that it will take between 30 and 35 seconds to assemble the module.

$$P(x < 30) = \frac{30-27}{39-27} = \frac{3}{12} = .2500$$

There is a .2500 probability that it will take less than 30 seconds to assemble the module. Because there is no area less than 27 seconds, $P(x < 30)$ is determined by using only the interval $27 \leq x < 30$. In a continuous distribution, there is no area at any one point (only over an interval). Thus the probability $x < 30$ is the same as the probability of $x \leq 30$.

DEMONSTRATION PROBLEM 6.2

According to the National Association of Insurance Commissioners, the average annual cost for automobile insurance in the United States is $691. Suppose automobile insurance costs are uniformly distributed in the United States with a range of from $200 to $1,182. What is the standard deviation of this uniform distribution? What is the height of the distribution? What is the probability that a person's annual cost for automobile insurance in the United States is between $410 and $825?

Solution

The mean is given as $691. The value of a is $200 and b is $1,182.

$$\sigma = \frac{b-a}{\sqrt{12}} = \frac{1,182-200}{\sqrt{12}} = 283.5$$

The height of the distribution is $\dfrac{1}{1,182-200} = \dfrac{1}{982} = .001$. $x_1 = 410$ and $x_2 = 825$

$$P(410 \leq x \leq 825) = \frac{825-410}{1,182-200} = \frac{415}{982} = .4226$$

The probability that a randomly selected person pays between $410 and $825 annually for automobile insurance in the United States is .4226. That is, about 42.26% of all people in the United States pay in that range.

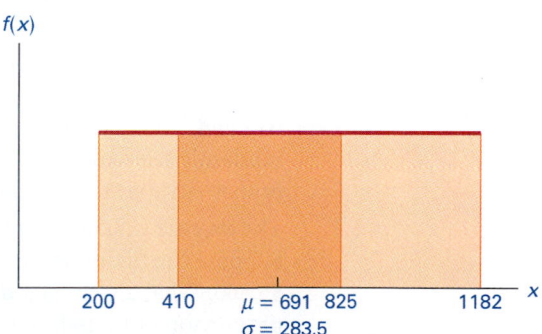

Using the Computer to Solve for Uniform Distribution Probabilities

Using the values of a, b, and x, MINITAB has the capability of computing probabilities for the uniform distribution. The resulting computation is a cumulative probability from the left end of the distribution to each x value. As an example, the probability question, $P(410 \leq x \leq 825)$, from Demonstration Problem 6.2 can be worked using MINITAB.

TABLE 6.1	CUMULATIVE DISTRIBUTION FUNCTION
MINITAB Output for Uniform Distribution	Continuous uniform on 200.000 to 1182.00
	x P(X <= x)
	825.0000 0.6365
	410.0000 0.2138

MINITAB computes the probability of $x \leq 825$ and the probability of $x \leq 410$, and these results are shown in Table 6.1. The final answer to the probability question from Demonstration Problem 6.2 is obtained by subtracting these two probabilities:

$$P(410 \leq x \leq 825) = .6365 - .2138 = .4227$$

Excel does not have the capability of directly computing probabilities for the uniform distribution.

6.1 PROBLEMS

6.1   Values are uniformly distributed between 200 and 240.
   a.   What is the value of $f(x)$ for this distribution?
   b.   Determine the mean and standard deviation of this distribution.
   c.   Probability of $(x > 230) = ?$
   d.   Probability of $(205 \leq x \leq 220) = ?$
   e.   Probability of $(x \leq 225) = ?$

6.2 x is uniformly distributed over a range of values from 8 to 21.
   a.   What is the value of $f(x)$ for this distribution?
   b.   Determine the mean and standard deviation of this distribution.
   c.   Probability of $(10 \leq x < 17) = ?$
   d.   Probability of $(x < 22) = ?$
   e.   Probability of $(x \geq 7) = ?$

6.3   The retail price of a medium-sized box of a well-known brand of cornflakes ranges from $2.80 to $3.14. Assume these prices are uniformly distributed. What are the average price and standard deviation of prices in this distribution? If a price is randomly selected from this list, what is the probability that it will be between $3.00 and $3.10?

6.4   The average fill volume of a regular can of soft drink is 12 ounces. Suppose the fill volume of these cans ranges from 11.97 to 12.03 ounces and is uniformly distributed. What is the height of this distribution? What is the probability that a randomly selected can contains more than 12.01 ounces of fluid? What is the probability that the fill volume is between 11.98 and 12.01 ounces?

6.5   The average U.S. household spends $2,100 a year on all types of insurance. Suppose the figures are uniformly distributed between the values of $400 and $3,800. What are the standard deviation and the height of this distribution? What proportion of households spends more than $3,000 a year on insurance? More than $4,000? Between $700 and $1,500?

6.2 NORMAL DISTRIBUTION

Probably the most widely known and used of all distributions is the **normal distribution.** It fits many human characteristics, such as height, weight, length, speed, IQ, scholastic achievement, and years of life expectancy, among others. Like their human counterparts,

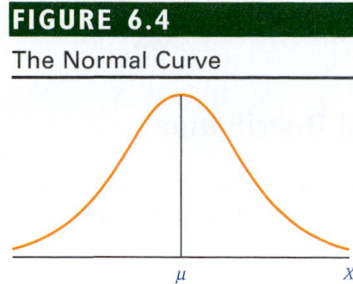

FIGURE 6.4

The Normal Curve

living things in nature, such as trees, animals, insects, and others, have many characteristics that are normally distributed.

Many variables in business and industry also are normally distributed. Some examples of variables that could produce normally distributed measurements include the annual cost of household insurance, the cost per square foot of renting warehouse space, and managers' satisfaction with support from ownership on a five-point scale. In addition, most items produced or filled by machines are normally distributed.

Because of its many applications, the normal distribution is an extremely important distribution. Besides the many variables mentioned that are normally distributed, the normal distribution and its associated probabilities are an integral part of statistical process control (see Chapter 18). When large enough sample sizes are taken, many statistics are normally distributed regardless of the shape of the underlying distribution from which they are drawn (as discussed in Chapter 7). Figure 6.4 is the graphic representation of the normal distribution: the normal curve.

History of the Normal Distribution

Discovery of the normal curve of errors is generally credited to mathematician and astronomer Karl Gauss (1777–1855), who recognized that the errors of repeated measurement of objects are often normally distributed.[*] Thus the normal distribution is sometimes referred to as the *Gaussian distribution* or the *normal curve of error*. A modern-day analogy of Gauss's work might be the distribution of measurements of machine-produced parts, which often yield a normal curve of error around a mean specification.

To a lesser extent, some credit has been given to Pierre-Simon de Laplace (1749–1827) for discovering the normal distribution. However, many people now believe that Abraham de Moivre (1667–1754), a French mathematician, first understood the normal distribution. De Moivre determined that the binomial distribution approached the normal distribution as a limit. De Moivre worked with remarkable accuracy. His published table values for the normal curve are only a few ten-thousandths off the values of currently published tables.[†]

The normal distribution exhibits the following characteristics.

- It is a continuous distribution.
- It is a symmetrical distribution about its mean.
- It is asymptotic to the horizontal axis.
- It is unimodal.
- It is a family of curves.
- Area under the curve is 1.

The normal distribution is symmetrical. Each half of the distribution is a mirror image of the other half. Many normal distribution tables contain probability values for only one side of the distribution because probability values for the other side of the distribution are identical because of symmetry.

In theory, the normal distribution is asymptotic to the horizontal axis. That is, it does not touch the *x* axis, and it goes forever in each direction. The reality is that most applications of the normal curve are experiments that have finite limits of potential outcomes. For example, even though SAT scores are analyzed by the normal distribution, the range of scores on each part of the SAT is only from 200 to 800.

The normal curve sometimes is referred to as the *bell-shaped curve*. It is unimodal in that values *mound up* in only one portion of the graph—the center of the curve. The normal distribution actually is a family of curves. Every unique value of the mean and every unique value of the standard deviation result in a different normal curve. In addition, *the total area under any normal distribution is 1.* The area under the curve yields the probabilities, so the

---

[*] John A. Ingram and Joseph G. Monks, *Statistics for Business and Economics* (San Diego: Harcourt Brace Jovanovich, Publishers, 1989).

[†] Roger E. Kirk, *Statistical Issues: A Reader for the Behavioral Sciences* (Monterey, CA: Brooks/Cole Publishing Co., 1972).

total of all probabilities for a normal distribution is 1. Because the distribution is symmetric, the area of the distribution on each side of the mean is 0.5.

Probability Density Function of the Normal Distribution

The normal distribution is described or characterized by two parameters: the mean, μ, and the standard deviation, σ. The values of μ and σ produce a normal distribution. The density function of the normal distribution is

$$f(x) = \frac{1}{\sigma\sqrt{2\pi}} e^{-(1/2)[(x-\mu)/\sigma)]^2}$$

where

μ = mean of x
σ = standard deviation of x
π = 3.14159..., and
e = 2.71828....

Because the formula is so complex, using it to determine areas under the curve is cumbersome and time-consuming. Virtually all researchers use table values to analyze normal distribution problems rather than this formula.

Standardized Normal Distribution

Every unique pair of μ and σ values defines a different normal distribution. Figure 6.5 shows the MINITAB graphs of normal distributions for the following three pairs of parameters.

1. $\mu = 50$ and $\sigma = 5$
2. $\mu = 80$ and $\sigma = 5$
3. $\mu = 50$ and $\sigma = 10$

Note that every change in a parameter (μ or σ) determines a different normal distribution. This characteristic of the normal curve (a family of curves) could make analysis by the normal distribution tedious because volumes of normal curve tables—one for each different combination of μ and σ—would be required. Fortunately, a mechanism was developed by which all normal distributions can be converted into a single distribution: the z distribution. This process yields the **standardized normal distribution** (or curve). The conversion formula for any x value of a given normal distribution follows.

z FORMULA	$z = \dfrac{x - \mu}{\sigma}, \quad \sigma \neq 0$

A **z score** is *the number of standard deviations that a value, x, is above or below the mean.* If the value of x is less than the mean, the z score is negative; if the value of x is more than the mean, the z score is positive; and if the value of x equals the mean, the associated

---

FIGURE 6.5

Normal Curves for Three Different Combinations of Means and Standard Deviations

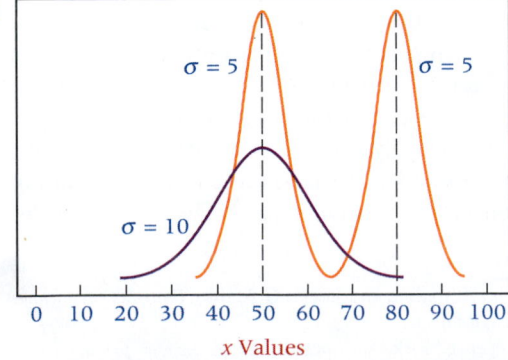

z score is zero. This formula allows conversion of the distance of any x value from its mean into standard deviation units. A standard z score table can be used to find probabilities for any normal curve problem that has been converted to z scores. The **z distribution** is *a normal distribution with a mean of 0 and a standard deviation of 1.* Any value of x at the mean of a normal curve is zero standard deviations from the mean. Any value of x that is one standard deviation above the mean has a z value of 1. The empirical rule, introduced in Chapter 3, is based on the normal distribution in which about 68% of all values are within one standard deviation of the mean regardless of the values of μ and σ. In a z distribution, about 68% of the z values are between $z = -1$ and $z = +1$.

The z distribution probability values are given in Table A.5. Because it is so frequently used, the z distribution is also printed inside the cover of this text. For discussion purposes, a list of z distribution values is presented in Table 6.2.

Table A.5 gives the total area under the z curve between 0 and any point on the positive z-axis. Since the curve is symmetric, the area under the curve between z and 0 is the same whether z is positive or negative (the sign on the z value designates whether the z score is above or below the mean). The table areas or probabilities are always positive.

Solving Normal Curve Problems

The mean and standard deviation of a normal distribution and the z formula and table enable a researcher to determine the probabilities for intervals of any particular values of a normal curve. One example is the many possible probability values of GMAT scores examined next.

The Graduate Management Aptitude Test (GMAT), produced by the Educational Testing Service in Princeton, New Jersey, is widely used by graduate schools of business in the United States as an entrance requirement. Assuming that the scores are normally distributed, probabilities of achieving scores over various ranges of the GMAT can be determined. In a recent year, the mean GMAT score was 494 and the standard deviation was about 100. What is the probability that a randomly selected score from this administration of the GMAT is between 600 and the mean? That is,

$$P(494 \leq x \leq 600 | \mu = 494 \text{ and } \sigma = 100) = ?$$

FIGURE 6.6

Graphical Depiction of the Area Between a Score of 600 and a Mean on a GMAT

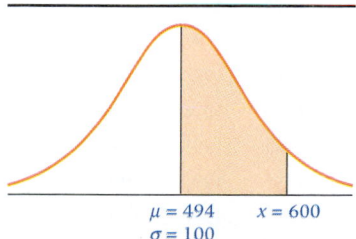

$\mu = 494$ $x = 600$
$\sigma = 100$

Figure 6.6 is a graphical representation of this problem.

The z formula yields the number of standard deviations that the x value, 600, is away from the mean.

$$z = \frac{x - \mu}{\sigma} = \frac{600 - 494}{100} = \frac{106}{100} = 1.06$$

The z value of 1.06 reveals that the GMAT score of 600 is 1.06 standard deviations more than the mean. The z distribution values in Table 6.2 give the probability of a value being between this value of x and the mean. The whole-number and tenths-place portion of the z score appear in the first column of Table 6.2 (the 1.0 portion of this z score). Across the top of the table are the values of the hundredths-place portion of the z score. For this z score, the hundredths-place value is 6. The probability value in Table

FIGURE 6.7

Graphical Solutions to the GMAT Problem

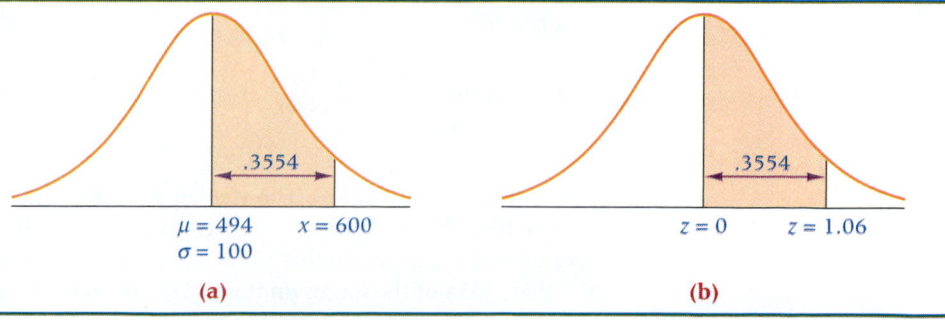

(a)   (b)

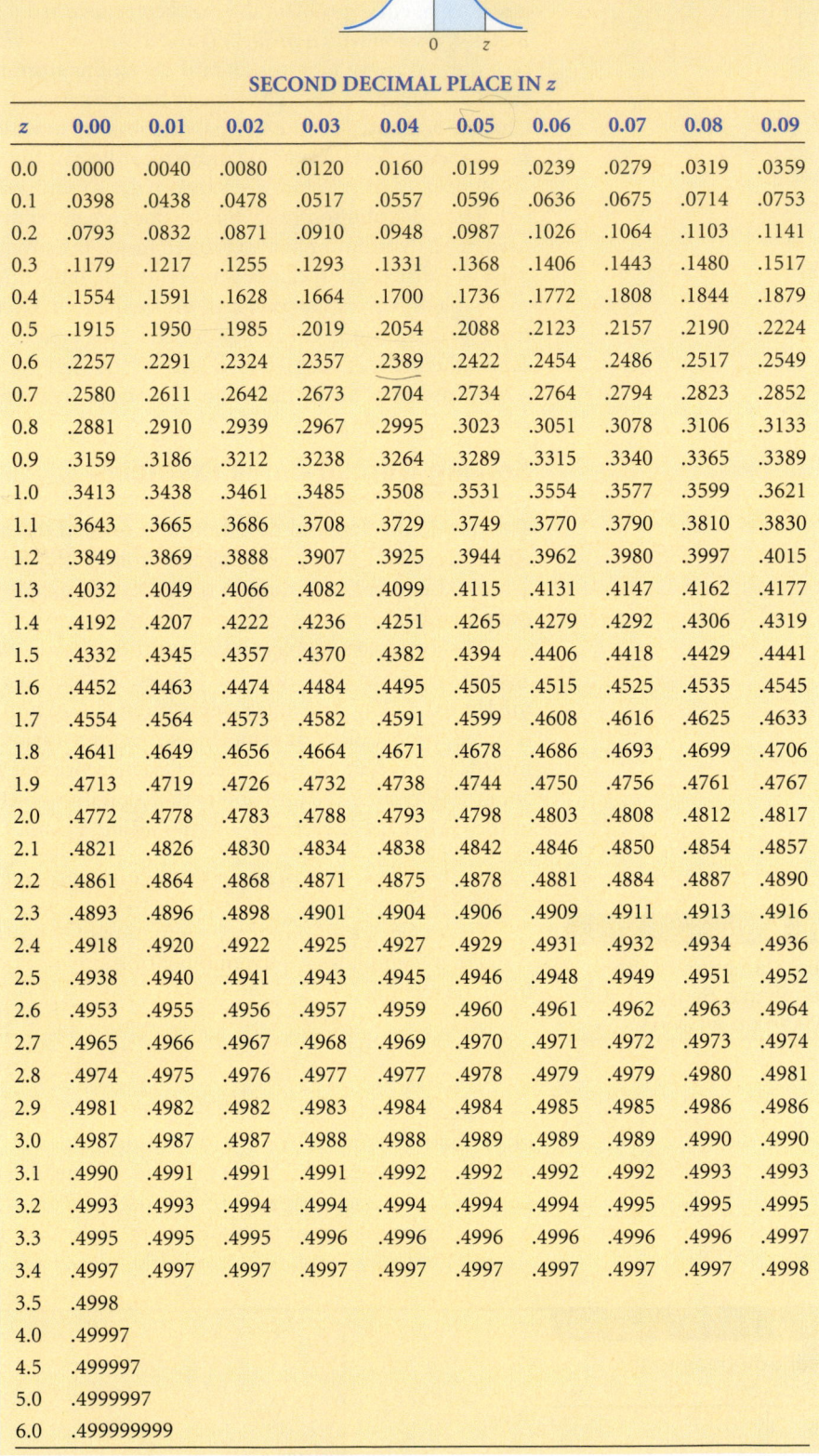

				SECOND DECIMAL PLACE IN *z*					
z	0.00	0.01	0.02	0.03	0.04	0.05	0.06	0.07	0.08	0.09
0.0	.0000	.0040	.0080	.0120	.0160	.0199	.0239	.0279	.0319	.0359
0.1	.0398	.0438	.0478	.0517	.0557	.0596	.0636	.0675	.0714	.0753
0.2	.0793	.0832	.0871	.0910	.0948	.0987	.1026	.1064	.1103	.1141
0.3	.1179	.1217	.1255	.1293	.1331	.1368	.1406	.1443	.1480	.1517
0.4	.1554	.1591	.1628	.1664	.1700	.1736	.1772	.1808	.1844	.1879
0.5	.1915	.1950	.1985	.2019	.2054	.2088	.2123	.2157	.2190	.2224
0.6	.2257	.2291	.2324	.2357	.2389	.2422	.2454	.2486	.2517	.2549
0.7	.2580	.2611	.2642	.2673	.2704	.2734	.2764	.2794	.2823	.2852
0.8	.2881	.2910	.2939	.2967	.2995	.3023	.3051	.3078	.3106	.3133
0.9	.3159	.3186	.3212	.3238	.3264	.3289	.3315	.3340	.3365	.3389
1.0	.3413	.3438	.3461	.3485	.3508	.3531	.3554	.3577	.3599	.3621
1.1	.3643	.3665	.3686	.3708	.3729	.3749	.3770	.3790	.3810	.3830
1.2	.3849	.3869	.3888	.3907	.3925	.3944	.3962	.3980	.3997	.4015
1.3	.4032	.4049	.4066	.4082	.4099	.4115	.4131	.4147	.4162	.4177
1.4	.4192	.4207	.4222	.4236	.4251	.4265	.4279	.4292	.4306	.4319
1.5	.4332	.4345	.4357	.4370	.4382	.4394	.4406	.4418	.4429	.4441
1.6	.4452	.4463	.4474	.4484	.4495	.4505	.4515	.4525	.4535	.4545
1.7	.4554	.4564	.4573	.4582	.4591	.4599	.4608	.4616	.4625	.4633
1.8	.4641	.4649	.4656	.4664	.4671	.4678	.4686	.4693	.4699	.4706
1.9	.4713	.4719	.4726	.4732	.4738	.4744	.4750	.4756	.4761	.4767
2.0	.4772	.4778	.4783	.4788	.4793	.4798	.4803	.4808	.4812	.4817
2.1	.4821	.4826	.4830	.4834	.4838	.4842	.4846	.4850	.4854	.4857
2.2	.4861	.4864	.4868	.4871	.4875	.4878	.4881	.4884	.4887	.4890
2.3	.4893	.4896	.4898	.4901	.4904	.4906	.4909	.4911	.4913	.4916
2.4	.4918	.4920	.4922	.4925	.4927	.4929	.4931	.4932	.4934	.4936
2.5	.4938	.4940	.4941	.4943	.4945	.4946	.4948	.4949	.4951	.4952
2.6	.4953	.4955	.4956	.4957	.4959	.4960	.4961	.4962	.4963	.4964
2.7	.4965	.4966	.4967	.4968	.4969	.4970	.4971	.4972	.4973	.4974
2.8	.4974	.4975	.4976	.4977	.4977	.4978	.4979	.4979	.4980	.4981
2.9	.4981	.4982	.4982	.4983	.4984	.4984	.4985	.4985	.4986	.4986
3.0	.4987	.4987	.4987	.4988	.4988	.4989	.4989	.4989	.4990	.4990
3.1	.4990	.4991	.4991	.4991	.4992	.4992	.4992	.4992	.4993	.4993
3.2	.4993	.4993	.4994	.4994	.4994	.4994	.4994	.4995	.4995	.4995
3.3	.4995	.4995	.4995	.4996	.4996	.4996	.4996	.4996	.4996	.4997
3.4	.4997	.4997	.4997	.4997	.4997	.4997	.4997	.4997	.4997	.4998
3.5	.4998									
4.0	.49997									
4.5	.499997									
5.0	.4999997									
6.0	.499999999									

6.2 for *z* = 1.06 is .3554. The shaded portion of the curve at the top of the table indicates that the probability value given *always* is the probability or area between an *x* value and the mean. In this particular example, that is the desired area. Thus the answer is that .3554 of the scores on the GMAT are between a score of 600 and the mean of 494. Figure 6.7(a) depicts graphically the solution in terms of *x* values. Figure 6.7(b) shows the solution in terms of *z* values.

DEMONSTRATION PROBLEM 6.3	What is the probability of obtaining a score greater than 700 on a GMAT test that has a mean of 494 and a standard deviation of 100? Assume GMAT scores are normally distributed.

$$P(x > 700 | \mu = 494 \text{ and } \sigma = 100) = ?$$

Solution

Examine the following diagram.

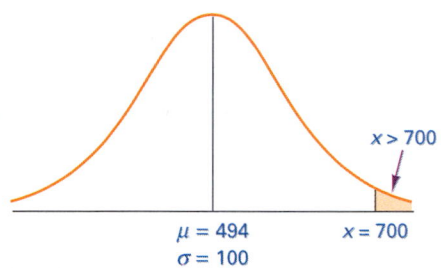

This problem calls for determining the area of the upper tail of the distribution. The z score for this problem is

$$z = \frac{x - \mu}{\sigma} = \frac{700 - 494}{100} = \frac{206}{100} = 2.06$$

Table 6.2 gives a probability of .4803 for this z score. This value is the probability of randomly drawing a GMAT with a score between the mean and 700. Finding the probability of getting a score greater than 700, which is the tail of the distribution, requires subtracting the probability value of .4803 from .5000, because each half of the distribution contains .5000 of the area. The result is .0197. Note that an attempt to determine the area of $x \geq 700$ instead of $x > 700$ would have made no difference because, in continuous distributions, the area under an exact number such as $x = 700$ is zero. A line segment has no width and hence no area.

.5000 (probability of x greater than the mean)
− .4803 (probability of x between 700 and the mean)
.0197 (probability of x greater than 700)

The solution is depicted graphically in (a) for x values and in (b) for z values.

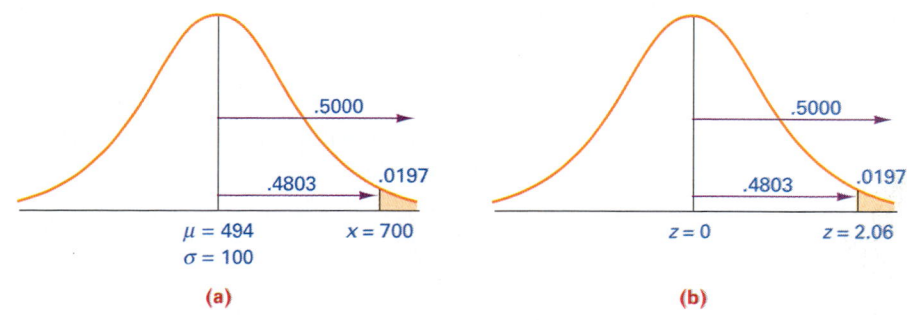

DEMONSTRATION PROBLEM 6.4	For the same GMAT examination, what is the probability of randomly drawing a score that is 550 or less?

$$P(x \leq 550 | \mu = 494 \text{ and } \sigma = 100) = ?$$

Solution

A sketch of this problem is shown here. Determine the area under the curve for all values less than or equal to 550.

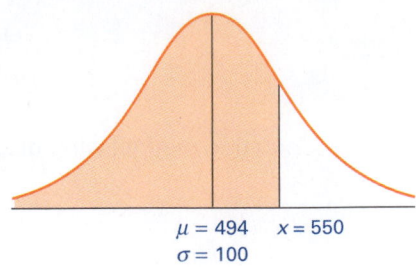

$$\mu = 494 \qquad x = 550$$
$$\sigma = 100$$

The *z* formula yields the area between 550 and the mean.

$$z = \frac{x - \mu}{\sigma} = \frac{550 - 494}{100} = \frac{56}{100} = 0.56$$

The area under the curve for $z = 0.56$ is .2123, which is the probability of getting a score between 550 and the mean. However, obtaining the probability for all values less than or equal to 550 also requires including the values less than the mean. Because one-half or .5000 of the values are less than the mean, the probability of $x \leq 550$ is found as follows.

$\quad$ .5000 (probability of values less than the mean)
$\underline{+.2123}$ (probability of values between 550 and the mean)
$\quad$ .7123 (probability of values $\leq$ 550)

This solution is depicted graphically in (a) for *x* values and in (b) for *z* values.

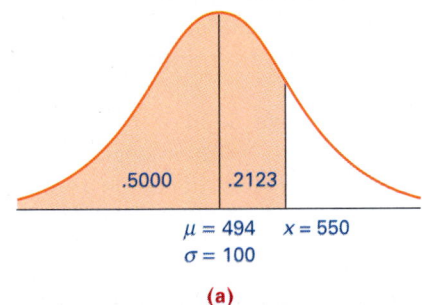

$$\mu = 494 \qquad x = 550$$
$$\sigma = 100$$

(a)

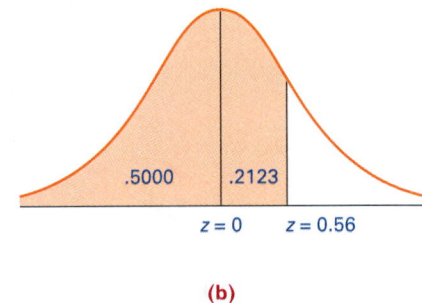

$$z = 0 \qquad z = 0.56$$

(b)

DEMONSTRATION PROBLEM 6.5

What is the probability of getting a score of less than 400 on the same GMAT test?

$$P(x < 400 | \mu = 494 \text{ and } \sigma = 100) = ?$$

Solution

The following sketch reveals that the problem is to determine the area of the lower tail of the distribution.

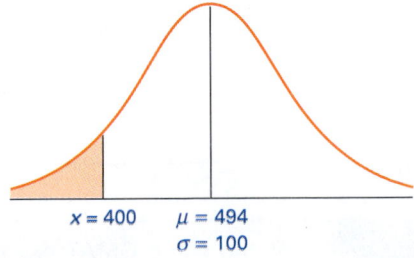

$$x = 400 \qquad \mu = 494$$
$$\sigma = 100$$

The *z* score for this problem is

$$z = \frac{x - \mu}{\sigma} = \frac{400 - 494}{100} = \frac{-94}{100} = -0.94$$

Note that this z value is negative. A negative z value indicates that the x value is below the mean and the z value is on the left side of the distribution. None of the z values in Table 6.2 is negative. However, because the normal distribution is symmetric, probabilities for z values on the left side of the distribution are the same as the values on the right side of the distribution. The negative sign in the z value merely indicates that the area is on the left side of the distribution. The probability is always positive. Table 6.2 yields a probability of .3264 for a z value of 0.94. The problem is to find the area in the lower tail of the distribution, so the probability, .3264, must be subtracted from .5000 to obtain the answer.

.5000 (probability of value less than the mean)
−.3264 (probability of value between 400 and the mean)
.1736 (probability of value less than 400)

Graphically, the solution is shown in (a) for x values and in (b) for z values.

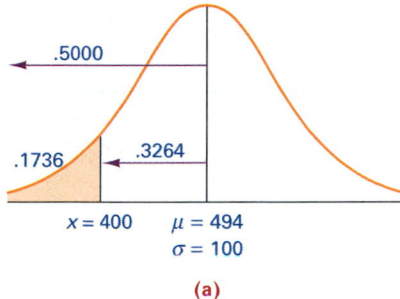

(a)

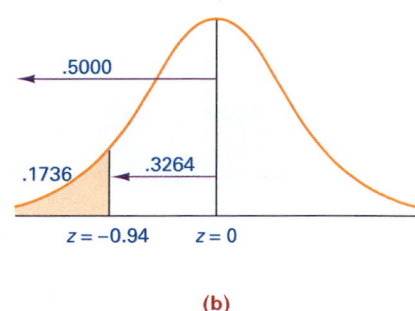

(b)

DEMONSTRATION PROBLEM 6.6

What is the probability of randomly obtaining a score between 300 and 600 on the GMAT exam?

$$P(300 < x < 600 | \mu = 494 \text{ and } \sigma = 100) = ?$$

Solution

The following sketch depicts the problem graphically: determine the area between x = 300 and x = 600, which spans the mean value. Because areas in the z distribution are given in relation to the mean, this problem must be worked as two separate problems and the results combined.

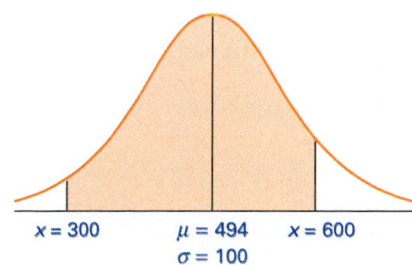

A z score is determined for each x value.

$$z = \frac{x - \mu}{\sigma} = \frac{600 - 494}{100} = \frac{106}{100} = 1.06$$

and

$$z = \frac{x - \mu}{\sigma} = \frac{300 - 494}{100} = \frac{-194}{100} = -1.94$$

The probability for $z = 1.06$ is .3554; the probability for $z = -1.94$ is .4738. The solution of $P(300 < x < 600)$ is obtained by summing the probabilities.

.3554 (probability of a value between the mean and 600)
+.4738 (probability of a value between the mean and 300)
.8292 (probability of a value between 300 and 600)

Graphically, the solution is shown in (a) for x values and in (b) for z values.

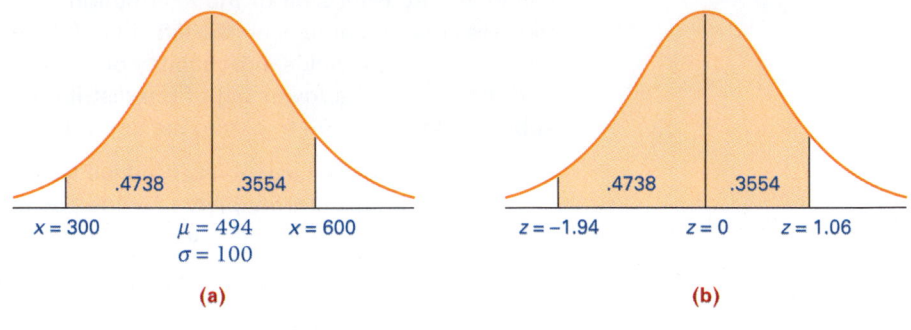

(a)   (b)

DEMONSTRATION PROBLEM 6.7	What is the probability of getting a score between 350 and 450 on the same GMAT exam?

$$P(350 < x < 450 \mid \mu = 494 \text{ and } \sigma = 100) = ?$$

Solution

The following sketch reveals that the solution to the problem involves determining the area of the shaded slice in the lower half of the curve.

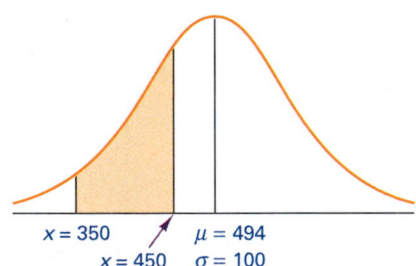

In this problem, the two x values are on the same side of the mean. The areas or probabilities of each x value must be determined and the final probability found by determining the difference between the two areas.

$$z = \frac{x - \mu}{\sigma} = \frac{350 - 494}{100} = \frac{-144}{100} = -1.44$$

and

$$z = \frac{x - \mu}{\sigma} = \frac{450 - 494}{100} = \frac{-44}{100} = -0.44$$

The probability associated with $z = -1.44$ is .4251.
The probability associated with $z = -0.44$ is .1700.

Subtracting gives the solution.

.4251 (probability of a value between 350 and the mean)
−.1700 (probability of a value between 450 and the mean)
.2551 (probability of a value between 350 and 450)

Graphically, the solution is shown in (a) for *x* values and in (b) for *z* values.

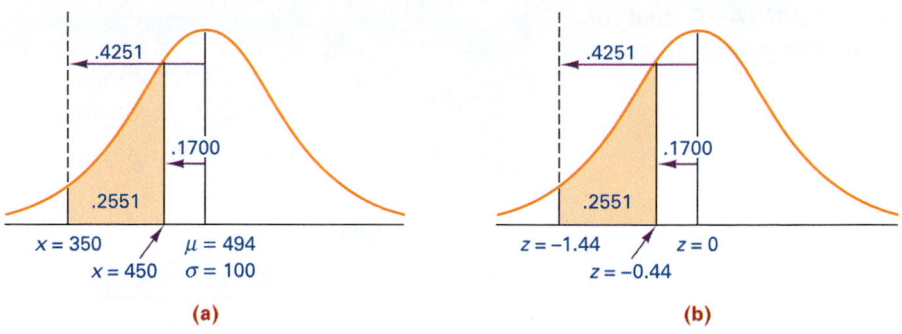

(a)   (b)

DEMONSTRATION
PROBLEM 6.8

Runzheimer International publishes business travel costs for various cities throughout the world. In particular, they publish per diem totals, which represent the average costs for the typical business traveler including three meals a day in business-class restaurants and single-rate lodging in business-class hotels and motels. If 86.65% of the per diem costs in Buenos Aires, Argentina, are less than $449 and if the standard deviation of per diem costs is $36, what is the average per diem cost in Buenos Aires? Assume that per diem costs are normally distributed.

Solution

In this problem, the standard deviation and an *x* value are given; the object is to determine the value of the mean. Examination of the *z* score formula reveals four variables: *x*, μ, σ, and *z*. In this problem, only two of the four variables are given. Because solving one equation with two unknowns is impossible, one of the other unknowns must be determined. The value of *z* can be determined from the normal distribution table (Table 6.2).

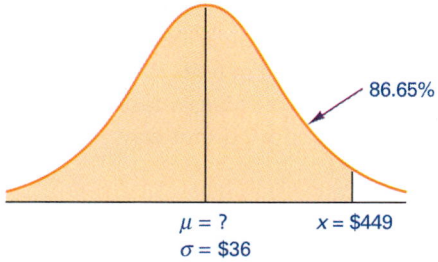

Because 86.65% of the values are less than *x* = $449, 36.65% of the per diem costs are between $449 and the mean. The other 50% of the per diem costs are in the lower half of the distribution. Converting the percentage to a proportion yields .3665 of the values between the *x* value and the mean. What *z* value is associated with this area? This area, or probability, of .3665 in Table 6.2 is associated with the *z* value of 1.11. This *z* value is positive, because it is in the upper half of the distribution. Using the *z* value of 1.11, the *x* value of $449, and the σ value of $36 allows solving for the mean algebraically.

$$z = \frac{x - \mu}{\sigma}$$

$$1.11 = \frac{\$449 - \mu}{\$36}$$

and

$$\mu = \$449 - (\$36)(1.11) = \$449 - \$39.96 = \$409.04$$

The mean per diem cost for business travel in Buenos Aires is $409.04.

TABLE 6.3

Excel and MINITAB Output for
Normal Distribution

Excel Output

	A	B
1	x Value	
2	450	0.3300
3	350	0.0749
4		
5		**0.2551**

MINITAB Output

CUMULATIVE DISTRIBUTION FUNCTION

Normal with mean = 494.000 and
standard deviation = 100.000

x	P(X <= x)
450.0000	0.3300
350.0000	0.0749

Prob (350 < x < 450) = 0.2551

**DEMONSTRATION
PROBLEM 6.9**

The U.S. Environmental Protection Agency publishes figures on solid waste generation in the United States. One year, the average number of waste generated per person per day was 3.58 pounds. Suppose the daily amount of waste generated per
person is normally distributed, with a standard deviation of 1.04 pounds. Of the daily
amounts of waste generated per person, 67.72% would be greater than what amount?

Solution

The mean and standard deviation are given, but x and z are unknown. The problem is
to solve for a specific x value when .6772 of the x values are greater than that value.

If .6772 of the values are greater than x, then .1772 are between x and the mean
(.6772 − .5000). Table 6.2 shows that the probability of .1772 is associated with a z
value of 0.46. Because x is less than the mean, the z value actually is −0.46. Whenever
an x value is less than the mean, its associated z value is negative and should be
reported that way.

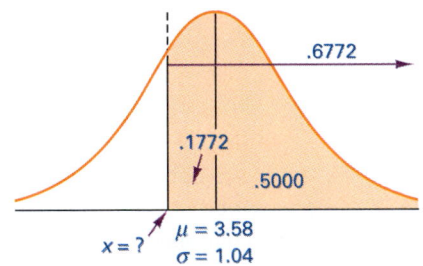

Solving the z equation yields

$$z = \frac{x - \mu}{\sigma}$$

$$-0.46 = \frac{x - 3.58}{1.04}$$

and

$$x = 3.58 + (-0.46)(1.04) = 3.10$$

Thus 67.72% of the daily average amount of solid waste per person weighs more
than 3.10 pounds.

Warehousing

Tompkins Associates conducted a national study of warehousing in the United States. The study revealed many interesting facts. Warehousing is a labor-intensive industry that presents considerable opportunity for improvement in productivity. What does the "average" warehouse look like? The construction of new warehouses is restricted by prohibitive expense. Perhaps for that reason, the average age of a warehouse is 19 years. Warehouses vary in size, but the average size is about 50,000 square feet. To visualize such an "average" warehouse, picture one that is square with

about 224 feet on each side or a rectangle that is 500 feet by 100 feet. The average clear height of a warehouse in the United States is 22 feet.

Suppose the ages of warehouses, the sizes of warehouses, and the clear heights of warehouses are normally distributed. Using the mean values already given and the standard deviations, techniques presented in this section could be used to determine, for example, the probability that a randomly selected warehouse is less than 15 years old, is larger than 60,000 square feet, or has a clear height between 20 and 25 feet.

Using the Computer to Solve for Normal Distribution Probabilities

Both Excel and MINITAB can be used to solve for normal distribution probabilities. In each case, the computer package uses μ, σ, and the value of x to compute a cumulative probability from the left. Shown in Table 6.3 are Excel and MINITAB output for the probability question addressed in Demonstration Problem 6.7: $P(350 < x < 450 \mid \mu = 494$ and $\sigma = 100)$. Since both computer packages yield probabilities cumulated from the left, this problem is solved manually with the computer output by finding the difference in $P(x < 450)$ and $P(x < 350)$.

6.2 PROBLEMS

6.6 Determine the probability or area for the portions of the normal distribution described.

   a. $z \geq 1.96$

   b. $z < 0.73$

   c. $-1.46 < z \leq 2.84$

   d. $-2.67 \leq z \leq 1.08$

   e. $-2.05 < z \leq -0.87$

6.7 Determine the probabilities for the following normal distribution problems.

   a. $\mu = 604, \sigma = 56.8, x \leq 635$

   b. $\mu = 48, \sigma = 12, x < 20$

   c. $\mu = 111, \sigma = 33.8, 100 \leq x < 150$

   d. $\mu = 264, \sigma = 10.9, 250 < x < 255$

   e. $\mu = 37, \sigma = 4.35, x > 35$

   f. $\mu = 156, \sigma = 11.4, x \geq 170$

6.8 Tompkins Associates reports that the mean clear height for a Class A warehouse in the United States is 22 feet. Suppose clear heights are normally distributed and that the standard deviation is 4 feet. A Class A warehouse in the United States is randomly selected.

   a. What is the probability that the clear height is greater than 17 feet?

   b. What is the probability that the clear height is less than 13 feet?

   c. What is the probability that the clear height is between 25 and 31 feet?

6.9 According to the Cellular Telecommunications Industry Association, the average local monthly cell phone bill is $42.78. Suppose local monthly cell phone bills are normally distributed, with a standard deviation of $11.35.

a. What is the probability that a randomly selected cell phone bill is more than $67.75?

b. What is the probability that a randomly selected cell phone bill is between $30 and $50?

c. What is the probability that a randomly selected cell phone bill is no more than $25?

d. What is the probability that a randomly selected cell phone bill is between $45 and $55?

6.10 According to the Internal Revenue Service, income tax returns one year averaged $1,332 in refunds for taxpayers. One explanation of this figure is that taxpayers would rather have the government keep back too much money during the year than to owe it money at the end of the year. Suppose the average amount of tax at the end of a year is a refund of $1,332, with a standard deviation of $725. Assume that amounts owed or due on tax returns are normally distributed.

a. What proportion of tax returns show a refund greater than $2,000?

b. What proportion of the tax returns show that the taxpayer owes money to the government?

c. What proportion of the tax returns show a refund between $100 and $700?

6.11 Toolworkers are subject to work-related injuries. One disorder, caused by strains to the hands and wrists, is called carpal tunnel syndrome. It strikes as many as 23,000 workers per year. The U.S. Labor Department estimates that the average cost of this disorder to employers and insurers is approximately $30,000 per injured worker. Suppose these costs are normally distributed, with a standard deviation of $9,000.

a. What proportion of the costs are between $15,000 and $45,000?

b. What proportion of the costs are greater than $50,000?

c. What proportion of the costs are between $5,000 and $20,000?

d. Suppose the standard deviation is unknown, but 90.82% of the costs are more than $7,000. What would be the value of the standard deviation?

e. Suppose the mean value is unknown, but the standard deviation is still $9,000. How much would the average cost be if 79.95% of the costs were less than $33,000?

6.12 Suppose you are working with a data set that is normally distributed, with a mean of 200 and a standard deviation of 47. Determine the value of x from the following information.

a. 60% of the values are greater than x.

b. x is less than 17% of the values.

c. 22% of the values are less than x.

d. x is greater than 55% of the values.

6.13 Work the following problems, assuming that the data are normally distributed.

a. The standard deviation of the distribution is 12.56, and 71.97% of the values are greater than 56. What is the value of μ?

b. The mean of the distribution is 352, and only 13.35% of the values are less than 300. What is the value of σ?

6.14 Suppose the standard deviation for Problem 6.8 is unknown but the mean is still 22 feet. If 72.4% of all U.S. Class A warehouses have a clear height greater than 18.5 feet, what is the standard deviation?

6.15 Suppose the mean clear height of all U.S. Class A warehouses is unknown but the standard deviation is known to be 4 feet. What is the value of the mean clear height if 29% of U.S. Class A warehouses have a clear height less than 20 feet?

6.16 Data accumulated by the National Climatic Data Center shows that the average wind speed in miles per hour for St. Louis, Missouri, is 9.7. Suppose wind speed measurements are normally distributed for a given geographic location. If

22.45% of the time the wind speed measurements are more than 11.6 miles per hour, what is the standard deviation of wind speed in St. Louis?

6.3 USING THE NORMAL CURVE TO APPROXIMATE BINOMIAL DISTRIBUTION PROBLEMS

For certain types of binomial distribution problems, the normal distribution can be used to approximate the probabilities. As sample sizes become large, binomial distributions approach the normal distribution in shape regardless of the value of p. This phenomenon occurs faster (for smaller values of n) when p is near .50. Figures 6.8 through 6.10 show three binomial distributions. Note in Figure 6.8 that even though the sample size, n, is only 10, the binomial graph bears a strong resemblance to a normal curve.

The graph in Figure 6.9 ($n = 10$ and $p = .20$) is skewed to the right because of the low p value and the small size. For this distribution, the expected value is only 2 and the probabilities pile up at $x = 0$ and 1. However, when n becomes large enough, as in the binomial distribution ($n = 100$ and $p = .20$) presented in Figure 6.10, the graph is relatively symmetric around the mean ($\mu = n \cdot p = 20$) because enough possible outcome values to the left of $x = 20$ allow the curve to fall back to the x axis.

For large n values, the binomial distribution is cumbersome to analyze without a computer. Table A.2 goes only to $n = 25$. Because of the size of the factorials involved, using calculators to work binomial problems when n is large is difficult or impossible. Fortunately,

FIGURE 6.8

The Binomial Distribution for $n = 10$ and $p = .50$

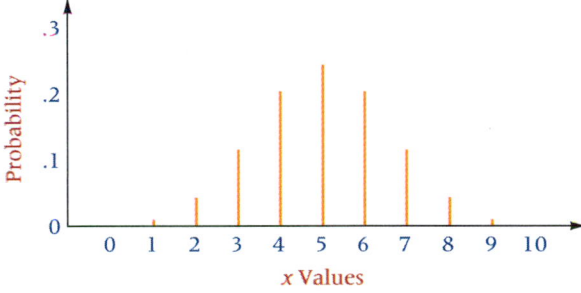

FIGURE 6.9

The Binomial Distribution for $n = 10$ and $p = .20$

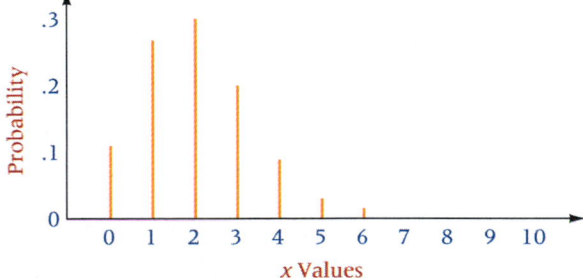

FIGURE 6.10

The Binomial Distribution for $n = 100$ and $p = .20$

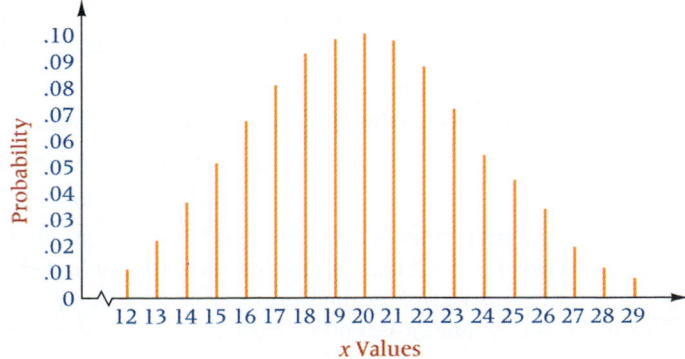

FIGURE 6.11

Graph of the Binomial Problem: $n = 60$ and $p = .30$

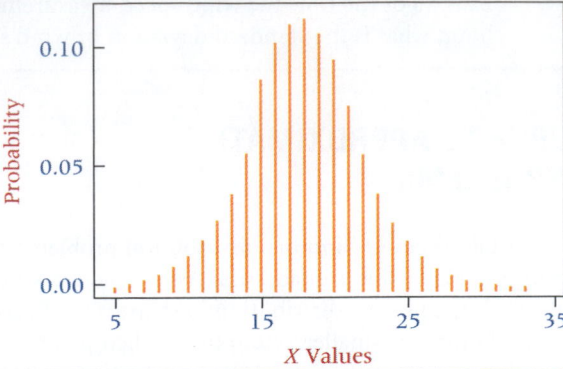

FIGURE 6.12

Graph of Apparent Solution of Binomial Problem Worked by the Normal Curve

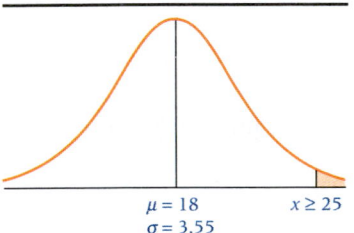

$\mu = 18$ $x \geq 25$
$\sigma = 3.55$

TABLE 6.4

Rules of Thumb for the Correction for Continuity

Values Being Determined	Corrections
$x >$	$+.50$
$x \geq$	$-.50$
$x <$	$-.50$
$x \leq$	$+.50$
$\leq x \leq$	$-.50$ and $+.50$
$< x <$	$+.50$ and $-.50$
$x =$	$-.50$ and $+.50$

the normal distribution is a good approximation for binomial distribution problems for large values of n.

To work a binomial problem by the normal curve requires a translation process. The first part of this process is to convert the two parameters of a binomial distribution, n and p, to the two parameters of the normal distribution, μ and σ. This process utilizes formulas from Chapter 5:

$$\mu = n \cdot p \text{ and } \sigma = \sqrt{n \cdot p \cdot q}$$

After completion of this, a test must be made to determine whether the normal distribution is a good enough approximation of the binomial distribution:

Does the interval $\mu \pm 3\sigma$ lie between 0 and n?

Recall that the empirical rule states that approximately 99.7%, or almost all, of the values of a normal curve are within three standard deviations of the mean. For a normal curve approximation of a binomial distribution problem to be acceptable, all possible x values should be between 0 and n, which are the lower and upper limits, respectively, of a binomial distribution. If $\mu \pm 3\sigma$ is not between 0 and n, do *not* use the normal distribution to work a binomial problem because the approximation is not good enough. Upon demonstration that the normal curve is a good approximation for a binomial problem, the procedure continues. Another rule of thumb for determining when to use the normal curve to approximate a binomial problem is that the approximation is good enough if both $n \cdot p > 5$ and $n \cdot q > 5$.

The process can be illustrated in the solution of the binomial distribution problem.

$$P(x \geq 25 | n = 60 \text{ and } p = .30) = ?$$

Note that this binomial problem contains a relatively large sample size and that none of the binomial tables in Appendix A.2 can be used to solve the problem. This problem is a good candidate for use of the normal distribution.

Translating from a binomial problem to a normal curve problem gives

$$\mu = n \cdot p = (60)(.30) = 18 \text{ and } \sigma = \sqrt{n \cdot p \cdot q} = 3.55$$

The binomial problem becomes a normal curve problem.

$$P(x \geq 25 | \mu = 18 \text{ and } \sigma = 3.55) = ?$$

Next, the test is made to determine whether the normal curve sufficiently fits this binomial distribution to justify the use of the normal curve.

$$\mu \pm 3\sigma = 18 \pm 3(3.55) = 18 \pm 10.65$$
$$7.35 \leq \mu \pm 3\sigma \leq 28.65$$

This interval is between 0 and 60, so the approximation is sufficient to allow use of the normal curve. Figure 6.11 is a MINITAB graph of this binomial distribution. Notice how closely it resembles the normal curve. Figure 6.12 is the apparent graph of the normal curve version of this problem.

FIGURE 6.13

Graph of a Portion of the Binomial Problem: $n = 60$ and $p = .30$

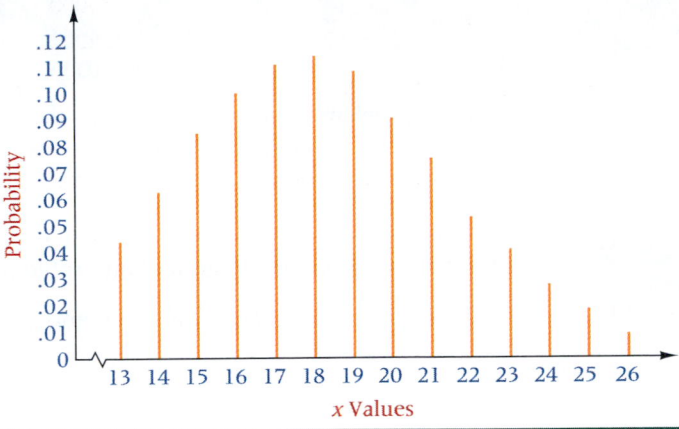

FIGURE 6.14

Graph of the Solution to the Binomial Problem Worked by the Normal Curve

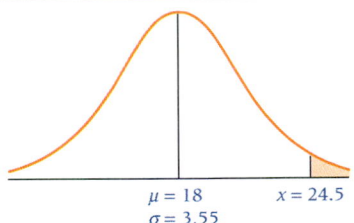

TABLE 6.5

Probability Values for the Binomial Problem: $n = 60$, $p = .30$, and $x \geq 25$

x Value	Probability
25	.0167
26	.0096
27	.0052
28	.0026
29	.0012
30	.0005
31	.0002
32	.0001
33	.0000
$x \geq 25$	.0361

Correcting for Continuity

The translation of a discrete distribution to a continuous distribution is not completely straightforward. A correction of $+.50$ or $-.50$ or $\pm.50$, depending on the problem, is required. This correction ensures that most of the binomial problem's information is correctly transferred to the normal curve analysis. This correction is called the **correction for continuity**, which is *made during conversion of a discrete distribution into a continuous distribution.*

Figure 6.13 is a portion of the graph of the binomial distribution, $n = 60$ and $p = .30$. Note that with a binomial distribution, all the probabilities are concentrated on the whole numbers. Thus, the answers for $x \geq 25$ are found by summing the probabilities for $x = 25$, 26, 27, ..., 60. There are no values between 24 and 25, 25 and 26, ..., 59, and 60. Yet, the normal distribution is continuous, and values are present all along the x axis. A correction must be made for this discrepancy for the approximation to be as accurate as possible.

As an analogy, visualize the process of melting iron rods in a furnace. The iron rods are like the probability values on each whole number of a binomial distribution. Note that the binomial graph in Figure 6.13 looks like a series of iron rods in a line. When the rods are placed in a furnace, they melt down and spread out. Each rod melts and moves to fill the area between it and the adjacent rods. The result is a continuous sheet of solid iron (continuous iron) that looks like the normal curve. The melting of the rods is analogous to spreading the binomial distribution to approximate the normal distribution.

How far does each rod spread toward the others? A good estimate is that each rod goes about halfway toward the adjacent rods. In other words, a rod that was concentrated at $x = 25$ spreads to cover the area from 24.5 to 25.5; $x = 26$ becomes continuous from 25.5 to 26.5; and so on. For the problem $P(x \geq 25 | n = 60$ and $p = .30)$, conversion to a continuous normal curve problem yields $P(x \geq 24.5 | \mu = 18$ and $\sigma = 3.55)$. The correction for continuity was $-.50$ because the problem called for the inclusion of the value of 25 along with all greater values; the binomial value of $x = 25$ translates to the normal curve value of 24.5 to 25.5. Had the binomial problem been to analyze $P(x > 25)$, the correction would have been $+.50$, resulting in a normal curve problem of $P(x \geq 25.5)$. The latter case would begin at more than 25 because the value of 25 would not be included.

The decision as to how to correct for continuity depends on the equality sign and the direction of the desired outcomes of the binomial distribution. Table 6.4 lists some rules of thumb that can help in the application of the correction for continuity.

For the binomial problem $P(x \geq 25 | n = 60$ and $p = .30)$, the normal curve becomes $P(x \geq 24.5 | \mu = 18$ and $\sigma = 3.55)$, as shown in Figure 6.14, and

$$z = \frac{x - \mu}{\sigma} = \frac{24.5 - 18}{3.55} = 1.83$$

The probability (Table 6.2) of this z value is .4664. The answer to this problem lies in the tail of the distribution, so the final answer is obtained by subtracting.

$$.5000$$
$$-.4664$$
$$.0336$$

Had this problem been worked by using the binomial formula, the solution would have been as shown in Table 6.5. The difference between the normal distribution approximation and the actual binomial values is only .0025 (.0361 − .0336).

DEMONSTRATION PROBLEM 6.10

Work the following binomial distribution problem by using the normal distribution.

$$P(x = 12 | n = 25 \text{ and } p = .40) = ?$$

Solution

Find μ and σ.

$$\mu = n \cdot p = (25)(.40) = 10.0$$
$$\sigma = \sqrt{n \cdot p \cdot q} = \sqrt{(25)(.40)(.60)} = 2.45$$

Test: $\mu \pm 3\sigma = 10.0 \pm 3(2.45) = 2.65 \text{ to } 17.35$

This range is between 0 and 25, so the approximation is close enough. Correct for continuity next. Because the problem is to determine the probability of x being exactly 12, the correction entails both −.50 and +.50. That is, a binomial probability at $x = 12$ translates to a continuous normal curve area that lies between 11.5 and 12.5. The graph of the problem follows:

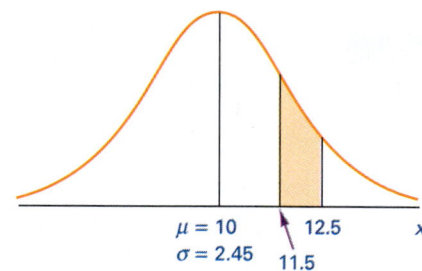

Then,

$$z = \frac{x - \mu}{\sigma} = \frac{12.5 - 10}{2.45} = 1.02$$

and

$$z = \frac{x - \mu}{\sigma} = \frac{11.5 - 10}{2.45} = 0.61$$

$z = 1.02$ produces a probability of .3461.
$z = 0.61$ produces a probability of .2291.

The difference in areas yields the following answer:

$$.3461 - .2291 = .1170$$

Had this problem been worked by using the binomial tables, the resulting answer would have been .114. The difference between the normal curve approximation and the value obtained by using binomial tables is only .003.

DEMONSTRATION PROBLEM 6.11

Solve the following binomial distribution problem by using the normal distribution.

$$P(x < 27 | n = 100 \text{ and } p = .37) = ?$$

Solution

Because neither the sample size nor the p value is contained in Table A.2, working this problem by using binomial distribution techniques is impractical. It is a good candidate for the normal curve. Calculating μ and σ yields

$$\mu = n \cdot p = (100)(.37) = 37.0$$

$$\sigma = \sqrt{n \cdot p \cdot q} = \sqrt{(100)(.37)(.63)} = 4.83$$

Testing to determine the closeness of the approximation gives

$$\mu \pm 3\sigma = 37 \pm 3(4.83) = 37 \pm 14.49$$

The range 22.51 to 51.49 is between 0 and 100. This problem satisfies the conditions of the test. Next, correct for continuity: $x < 27$ as a binomial problem translates to $x \leq 26.5$ as a normal distribution problem. The graph of the problem follows.

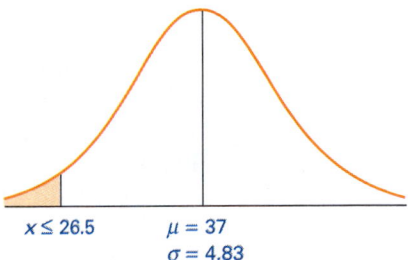

$x \leq 26.5$ $\mu = 37$
$\sigma = 4.83$

Then,

$$z = \frac{x - \mu}{\sigma} = \frac{26.5 - 37}{4.83} = -2.17$$

Table 6.2 shows a probability of .4850. Solving for the tail of the distribution gives

$$.5000 - .4850 = .0150$$

which is the answer.

Had this problem been solved by using the binomial formula, the probabilities would have been the following.

x Value	Probability
26	.0059
25	.0035
24	.0019
23	.0010
22	.0005
21	.0002
20	.0001
x < 27	.0131

The answer obtained by using the normal curve approximation (.0150) compares favorably to this exact binomial answer. The difference is only .0019.

6.3 PROBLEMS

6.17 Convert the following binomial distribution problems to normal distribution problems. Use the correction for continuity.

a. $P(x \leq 16 | n = 30 \text{ and } p = .70)$

b. $P(10 < x \leq 20) | n = 25 \text{ and } p = .50)$

c. $P(x = 22 | n = 40 \text{ and } p = .60)$

d. $P(x > 14 | n = 16 \text{ and } p = .45)$

6.18   Use the test $\mu \pm 3\sigma$ to determine whether the following binomial distributions can be approximated by using the normal distribution.
   a. $n = 8$ and $p = .50$
   b. $n = 18$ and $p = .80$
   c. $n = 12$ and $p = .30$
   d. $n = 30$ and $p = .75$
   e. $n = 14$ and $p = .50$

6.19   Where appropriate, work the following binomial distribution problems by using the normal curve. Also, use Table A.2 to find the answers by using the binomial distribution and compare the answers obtained by the two methods.
   a. $P(x = 8 | n = 25$ and $p = .40) = ?$
   b. $P(x \geq 13 | n = 20$ and $p = .60) = ?$
   c. $P(x = 7 | n = 15$ and $p = .50) = ?$
   d. $P(x < 3 | n = 10$ and $p = .70) = ?$

6.20   The Zimmerman Agency conducted a study for Residence Inn by Marriott of business travelers who take trips of five nights or more. According to this study, 37% of these travelers enjoy sightseeing more than any other activity that they do not get to do as much at home. Suppose 120 randomly selected business travelers who take trips of five nights or more are contacted. What is the probability that fewer than 40 enjoy sightseeing more than any other activity that they do not get to do as much at home?

6.21   One study on managers' satisfaction with management tools reveals that 59% of all managers use self-directed work teams as a management tool. Suppose 70 managers selected randomly in the United States are interviewed. What is the probability that fewer than 35 use self-directed work teams as a management tool?

6.22   According to The Yankee Group, 53% of all cable households rate cable companies as good or excellent in quality transmission. Sixty percent of all cable households rate cable companies as good or excellent in having professional personnel. Suppose 300 cable households are randomly contacted.
   a.   What is the probability that more than 175 cable households rate cable companies as good or excellent in quality transmission?
   b.   What is the probability that between 165 and 170 (inclusive) cable households rate cable companies as good or excellent in quality transmission?
   c.   What is the probability that between 155 and 170 (inclusive) cable households rate cable companies as good or excellent in having professional personnel?
   d.   What is the probability that fewer than 200 cable households rate cable companies as good or excellent in having professional personnel?

6.23   The International Data Corporation reports that Compaq is number one in PC market share in the United States with 16% of the market. Suppose a researcher randomly selects 130 recent purchasers of PCs.
   a.   What is the probability that more than 25 PC purchasers bought a Compaq?
   b.   What is the probability that between 15 and 23 (inclusive) PC purchasers bought a Compaq?
   c.   What is the probability that fewer than 12 PC purchasers bought a Compaq?
   d.   What is the probability that exactly 22 PC purchasers bought a Compaq?

6.24   A study about strategies for competing in the global marketplace states that 52% of the respondents agreed that companies need to make direct investments in foreign countries. It also states that about 70% of those responding agree that it is attractive to have a joint venture to increase global competitiveness. Suppose CEOs of 95 manufacturing companies are randomly contacted about global strategies.
   a.   What is the probability that between 44 and 52 (inclusive) CEOs agree that companies should make direct investments in foreign countries?

    b. What is the probability that more than 56 CEOs agree with that assertion?

    c. What is the probability that fewer than 60 CEOs agree that it is attractive to have a joint venture to increase global competitiveness?

    d. What is the probability that between 55 and 62 (inclusive) CEOs agree with that assertion?

6.4 EXPONENTIAL DISTRIBUTION

Another useful continuous distribution is the exponential distribution. It is closely related to the Poisson distribution. Whereas the Poisson distribution is discrete and describes random occurrences over some interval, the **exponential distribution** is *continuous and describes a probability distribution of the times between random occurrences.* The following are the characteristics of the exponential distribution.

- It is a continuous distribution.
- It is a family of distributions.
- It is skewed to the right.
- The x values range from zero to infinity.
- Its apex is always at $x = 0$.
- The curve steadily decreases as x gets larger.

The exponential probability distribution is determined by the following.

EXPONENTIAL PROBABILITY DENSITY FUNCTION	$$f(x) = \lambda e^{-\lambda x}$$ where $x \geq 0$ $\lambda > 0$ and $e = 2.71828 \ldots$

An exponential distribution can be characterized by the one parameter, λ. Each unique value of λ determines a different exponential distribution, resulting in a family of exponential distributions. Figure 6.15 shows graphs of exponential distributions for four values of λ. The points on the graph are determined by using λ and various values of x in the probability density formula. The mean of an exponential distribution is $\mu = 1/\lambda$, and the standard deviation of an exponential distribution is $\sigma = 1/\lambda$.

Probabilities of the Exponential Distribution

Probabilities are computed for the exponential distribution by determining the area under the curve between two points. Applying calculus to the exponential probability density function produces a formula that can be used to calculate the probabilities of an exponential distribution.

PROBABILITIES OF THE RIGHT TAIL OF THE EXPONENTIAL DISTRIBUTION	$$P(x \geq x_0) = e^{-\lambda x_0}$$ where: $x_0 \geq 0$

To use this formula requires finding values of e^{-x}. These values can be computed on most calculators or obtained from Table A.4, which contains the values of e^{-x} for selected values of x. x_0 is the fraction of the interval or the number of intervals between arrivals in the probability question and λ is the average arrival rate.

For example, arrivals at a bank are Poisson distributed with a λ of 1.2 customers every minute. What is the average time between arrivals and what is the probability that at least 2 minutes will elapse between one arrival and the next arrival? Since the interval for

FIGURE 6.15

Graphs of Some Exponential Distributions

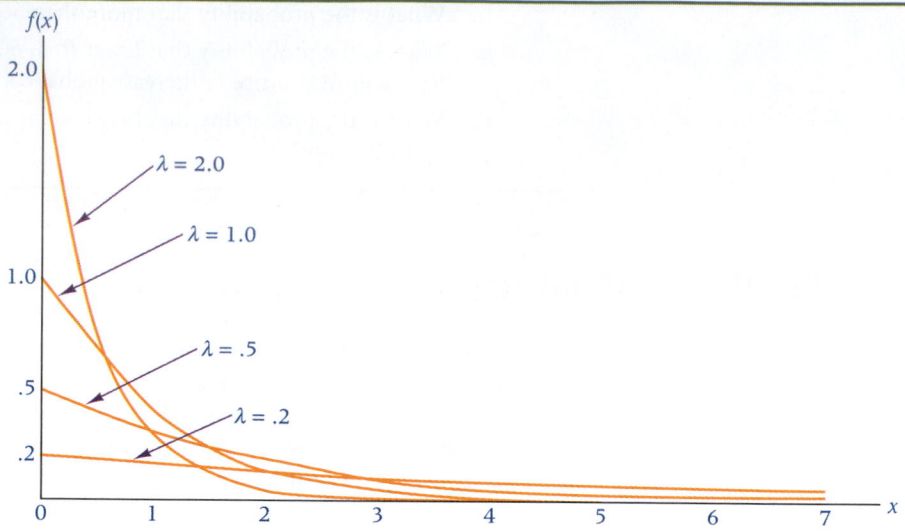

FIGURE 6.16

Exponential Distribution for $\lambda = 1.2$ and Solution for $x \geq 2$

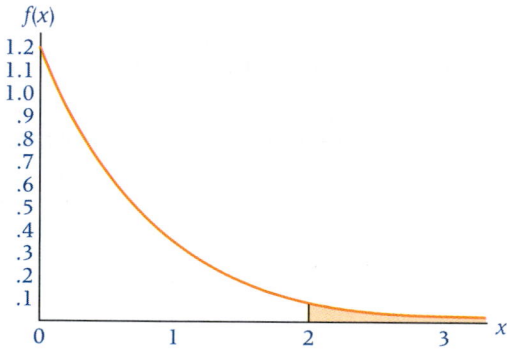

TABLE 6.6

Excel and MINITAB Output for Exponential Distribution

Excel Output

	A	B
1	x Value	Probability < x Value
2		
3	0.75	0.6448

MINITAB Output

Cumulative Distribution Function

Exponential with mean = 0.724600

    x   P(X <= x)

0.7500 0.6448

lambda is 1 minute and we want to know the probability that at least 2 minutes transpire between arrivals (twice the lambda interval), x_0 is 2.

Interarrival times of random arrivals are exponentially distributed. The mean of this exponential distribution is $\mu = 1/\lambda = 1/1.2 = .833$ minute (50 seconds). On average, .833 minute, or 50 seconds, will elapse between arrivals at the bank. The probability of an interval of 2 minutes or more between arrivals can be calculated by

$$P(x \geq 2 | \lambda = 1.2) = e^{-1.2(2)} = .0907.$$

About 9.07% of the time when the rate of random arrivals is 1.2 per minute, 2 minutes or more will elapse between arrivals, as shown in Figure 6.16.

This problem underscores the potential of using the exponential distribution in conjunction with the Poisson distribution to solve problems. In operations research and management science, these two distributions are used together to solve queuing problems (theory of waiting lines). The Poisson distribution can be used to analyze the arrivals to the queue, and the exponential distribution can be used to analyze the interarrival time.

DEMONSTRATION PROBLEM 6.12	A manufacturing firm has been involved in statistical quality control for several years. As part of the production process, parts are randomly selected and tested. From the records of these tests, it has been established that a defective part occurs in a pattern that is Poisson distributed on the average of 1.38 defects every 20 minutes during production runs. Use this information to determine the probability that less than 15 minutes will elapse between any two defects.

Solution

The value of λ is 1.38 defects per 20-minute interval. The value of μ can be determined by

$$\mu = \frac{1}{\lambda} = \frac{1}{1.38} = .7246$$

On the average, it is .7246 of the interval, or (.7246)(20 minutes) = 14.49 minutes, between defects. The value of x_0 represents the desired number of intervals between arrivals or occurrences for the probability question. In this problem, the probability question involves 15 minutes and the interval is 20 minutes. Thus x_0 is 15/20, or .75 of an interval. The question here is to determine the probability of there being less than 15 minutes between defects. The probability formula always yields the right tail of the distribution—in this case, the probability of there being 15 minutes or more between arrivals. By using the value of x_0 and the value of λ, the probability of there being 15 minutes or more between defects can be determined.

$$P(x \geq x_0) = P(x \geq .75) = e^{-\lambda x_0} = e^{(-1.38)(.75)} = e^{-1.035} = .3552$$

The probability of .3552 is the probability that at least 15 minutes will elapse between defects. To determine the probability of there being less than 15 minutes between defects, compute $1 - P(x)$. In this case, $1 - .3552 = .6448$. There is a probability of .6448 that less than 15 minutes will elapse between two defects when there is an average of 1.38 defects per 20-minute interval or an average of 14.49 minutes between defects.

Using the Computer to Determine Exponential Distribution Probabilities

Both Excel and MINITAB can be used to solve for exponential distribution probabilities. Excel uses the value of λ and x_0, but MINITAB requires μ (equals $1/\lambda$) and x_0. In each case, the computer yields the cumulative probability from the left (the complement of what the probability formula shown in this section yields). Table 6.6 provides Excel and MINITAB output for the probability question addressed in Demonstration Problem 6.12.

6.4 PROBLEMS

6.25   Use the probability density formula to sketch the graphs of the following exponential distributions.

    a. $\lambda = 0.1$

    b. $\lambda = 0.3$

    c. $\lambda = 0.8$

    d. $\lambda = 3.0$

6.26 Determine the mean and standard deviation of the following exponential distributions.

    a. $\lambda = 3.25$

    b. $\lambda = 0.7$

    c. $\lambda = 1.1$

    d. $\lambda = 6.0$

6.27 Determine the following exponential probabilities.

    a. $P(x \geq 5 | \lambda = 1.35)$

    b. $P(x < 3 | \lambda = 0.68)$

    c. $P(x > 4 | \lambda = 1.7)$

    d. $P(x < 6 | \lambda = 0.80)$

6.28 The average length of time between arrivals at a turnpike tollbooth is 23 seconds. Assume that the time between arrivals at the tollbooth is exponentially distributed.

    a. What is the probability that a minute or more will elapse between arrivals?

    b. If a car has just passed through the tollbooth, what is the probability that no car will show up for at least 3 minutes?

6.29 A busy restaurant determined that between 6:30 P.M. and 9:00 P.M. on Friday nights, the arrivals of customers are Poisson distributed with an average arrival rate of 2.44 per minute.

    a. What is the probability that at least 10 minutes will elapse between arrivals?

    b. What is the probability that at least 5 minutes will elapse between arrivals?

    c. What is the probability that at least 1 minute will elapse between arrivals?

    d. What is the expected amount of time between arrivals?

6.30 During the summer at a small private airport in western Nebraska, the unscheduled arrival of airplanes is Poisson distributed with an average arrival rate of 1.12 planes per hour.

    a. What is the average interarrival time between planes?

    b. What is the probability that at least 2 hours will elapse between plane arrivals?

    c. What is the probability of two planes arriving less than 10 minutes apart?

6.31 The exponential distribution can be used to solve Poisson-type problems in which the intervals are not time. The Air Travel Consumer Report published by the U.S. Department of Transportation reported that in a recent year, America West led the nation in fewest occurrences of mishandled baggage, with a mean rate of 3.39 per 1,000 passengers. Assume mishandled baggage occurrences are Poisson distributed. Using the exponential distribution to analyze this problem, determine the average number of passengers between occurrences. Suppose baggage has just been mishandled. What is the probability that at least 500 passengers will have their baggage handled properly before the next mishandling occurs? What is the probability that the number will be fewer than 200 passengers?

6.32 The Foundation Corporation specializes in constructing the concrete foundations for new houses in the South. The company knows that because of soil types, moisture conditions, variable construction, and other factors, eventually most foundations will need major repair. On the basis of its records, the company's president believes that a new house foundation on average will not need major repair for 20 years. If she wants to guarantee the company's work against major repair but wants to have to honor no more than 10% of its guarantees, for how many years should the company guarantee its work? Assume that occurrences of major foundation repairs are Poisson distributed.

6.33 During the dry month of August, one U.S. city has measurable rain on average only 2 days per month. If the arrival of rainy days is Poisson distributed in this city during the month of August, what is the average number of days that will pass between measurable rain? What is the standard deviation? What is the probability during this month that there will be a period of less than 2 days between rain?

The Changing Faces of the Insurance Industry

The study reports the average insurance expenditures for automobile insurance, homeowner insurance, and all insurance. Other mean values are given for some of the more extreme states. Probability questions can be answered regarding these data if it is known how the population data are distributed. Techniques for testing the fit of various distributions to the data are presented in a later chapter. However, if the data are uniformly distributed and the minimum and maximum values are known (a and b), probability questions regarding particular intervals can be answered. For example, suppose nationally annual automobile insurance rates range from \$274 to \$1,108 ($a = 274$, $b = 1,108$). Between what two values would the middle 50% of the data lie? The difference between a and b is 834. In order for the uniform distribution probability to equal .50, $x_2 - x_1$ would have to be 417. The mean, \$691, is halfway between a and b and is also halfway between $x_2 - x_1$ in solving for the middle 50%. The middle 50% lies between \$691 $\pm$ ½(\$417) = \$691 $\pm$ \$208.50 = \$482.50 and \$899.50. Suppose the range of annual payments for homeowner insurance in the United States is from \$100 to \$740 with a mean of \$420. The probability of a randomly selected person paying less than \$400 can be computed from section 6.1 techniques with

$$a = \$100, b = \$740, x_2 = \$400, \text{ and } x_1 = \$100 \text{ as } .4688$$

Suppose annual automobile insurance rates are normally distributed with a mean of \$691 and a standard deviation of \$109. Using techniques presented in section 6.2, it can be determined that the z value for $x = \$874$ is 1.68 with an associated probability from standard normal distribution table as .4535. The probability that a randomly selected person is paying more than \$874 annually for automobile insurance is .5000 − .4535, or about .0465. Suppose that annual homeowner insurance costs are normally distributed. The mean cost in Texas is \$592. Suppose the standard deviation is \$78. Using techniques presented in section 6.2, it can be determined that the probability that a randomly selected Texan pays between \$500 and \$650 annually for homeowner insurance is .6514.

Chapter 6 presented techniques for working binomial problems with the normal distribution. Twenty percent of Americans prefer purchasing life insurance over the phone or by mail. Suppose 80 Americans are randomly selected, what is the probability that 21 or more believe this way? In this binomial distribution problem, $n = 80$, $p = .20$, and $x = 21$. The data pass the test to indicate that the normal distribution would be a good enough approximation of this problem to use as a tool. The data are converted to normal distribution parameters resulting in $\mu = 16$ and $\sigma = 3.58$. The value of x is corrected to 20.5 yielding a z value of 1.26 and a probability of .1038 (.5000 - .3962).

Suppose that life insurance experts state that, on average, 1.8 houses are destroyed by fire in the United States every hour. If it can be assumed that occurrence of fire is Poisson distributed, then $\lambda = 1.8$ houses per hour. Using information presented in section 6.4, the average time between houses being destroyed by fire is .555 of an hour or every 33.3 minutes. What is the probability that it would be at least one and one-half hours between house destroying fires? Using the exponential distribution, $x_0 = 1.5$ and the probability is .0672. Life insurance experts can use these types of probabilities to assist them in setting rates.

ETHICAL CONSIDERATIONS

Several points must be considered in working with continuous distributions. Is the population being studied the same population from which the parameters (mean, standard deviation, λ) were determined? If not, the results may not be valid for the analysis being done. Invalid or spurious results can be obtained by using the parameters from one population to analyze another population. For example, a market study in New England may result in the conclusion that the amount of fish eaten per month by adults is normally distributed with the average of 2.3 pounds of fish per month. A market researcher in the Southwest should not assume that these figures apply to her population. People in the Southwest probably have quite different fish-eating habits than people in New England, and the application of New England population parameters to the Southwest probably will result in questionable conclusions.

As was true with the Poisson distribution in Chapter 5, the use of λ in the exponential distribution should be judicious because a λ for one interval in a given time period or situation may not be the same as the λ for the same interval in a different time period or situation. For example, the number of arrivals per 5-minute time period at a restaurant on Friday night is not likely to be the same as the number of arrivals in a 5-minute time period at that same restaurant from 2 P.M. to 4 P.M. on weekdays. In using established parameters such as μ and λ, a researcher should be certain that the population from which the parameter was determined is, indeed, the same population being studied.

Sometimes a normal distribution is used to analyze data when, in fact, the data are not normal. Such an analysis can contain bias and produce false results. Certain techniques for testing a distribution of data can determine whether they are distributed a certain way. Some of the techniques are presented in Chapter 17. In general, Chapter 6 techniques can be misused if the wrong type of distribution is applied to the data or if the distribution used for analysis is the right one but the parameters (μ, σ, λ) do not fit the data of the population being analyzed.

SUMMARY

This chapter discussed three different continuous distributions: the uniform distribution, the normal distribution, and the exponential distribution. With continuous distributions, the value of the probability density function does not yield the probability, but instead gives the height of the curve at any given point. In fact, with continuous distributions, the probability at any discrete point is .0000. Probabilities are determined over an interval. In each case, the probability is the area under the curve for the interval being considered. In each distribution, the probability or total area under the curve is 1.

Probably the simplest of these distributions is the uniform distribution, sometimes referred to as the rectangular distribution. The uniform distribution is determined from a probability density function that contains equal values along some interval between the points a and b. Basically, the height of the curve is the same everywhere between these two points. Probabilities are determined by calculating the portion of the rectangle between the two points a and b that is being considered.

The most widely used of all distributions is the normal distribution. Many phenomena are normally distributed, including characteristics of most machine-produced parts, many measurements of the biological and natural environment, and many human characteristics such as height, weight, IQ, and achievement test scores. The normal curve is continuous, symmetrical, unimodal, and asymptotic to the axis; actually, it is a family of curves.

The parameters necessary to describe a normal distribution are the mean and the standard deviation. For convenience, data that are being analyzed by the normal curve should be standardized by using the mean and the standard deviation to compute z scores. A z score is the distance that an x value is from the mean, μ, in units of standard deviations. With the z score of an x value, the probability of that value occurring by chance from a given normal distribution can be determined by using a table of z scores and their associated probabilities.

The normal distribution can be used to work certain types of binomial distribution problems. Doing so requires converting the n and p values of the binomial distribution to μ and σ of the normal distribution. When worked by using the normal distribution, the binomial distribution solution is only an approximation. If the values of $\mu \pm 3\sigma$ are within a range from 0 to n, the approximation is reasonably accurate. Adjusting for the fact that a discrete distribution problem is being worked by using a continuous distribution requires a correction for continuity. The correction for continuity involves adding or subtracting .50 to the x value being analyzed. This correction usually improves the normal curve approximation.

Another continuous distribution is the exponential distribution. It complements the discrete Poisson distribution. The exponential distribution is used to compute the probabilities of times between random occurrences. The exponential distribution is a family of distributions described by one parameter, σ. The distribution is skewed to the right and always has its highest value at $x = 0$.

KEY TERMS

correction for continuity	rectangular distribution	z distribution
exponential distribution	standardized normal distribution	z score
normal distribution	uniform distribution	

FORMULAS

Probability density function of a uniform distribution

$$f(x) = \begin{cases} \dfrac{1}{b-a} & \text{for } a \le x \le b \\ 0 & \text{for all other values} \end{cases}$$

Mean and standard deviation of a uniform distribution

$$\mu = \frac{a+b}{2}$$

$$\sigma = \frac{b-a}{\sqrt{12}}$$

Probability density function of the normal distribution

$$f(x) = \frac{1}{\sigma\sqrt{2\pi}} e^{-(1/2)[(x-\mu)/\sigma)]^2}$$

z formula

$$z = \frac{x-\mu}{\sigma}$$

Conversion of a binomial problem to the normal curve

$$\mu = n \cdot p \text{ and } \sigma = \sqrt{n \cdot p \cdot q}$$

Exponential probability density function

$$f(x) = \lambda e^{-\lambda x}$$

Probabilities of the right tail of the exponential distribution

$$P(x \ge x_0) = e^{-\lambda x_0}$$

SUPPLEMENTARY PROBLEMS

CALCULATING THE STATISTICS

6.34 Data are uniformly distributed between the values of 6 and 14. Determine the value of $f(x)$. What are the mean and standard deviation of this distribution? What is the probability of randomly selecting a value greater than 11? What is the probability of randomly selecting a value between 7 and 12?

6.35 Assume a normal distribution and find the following probabilities.

  a. $P(x < 21 | \mu = 25 \text{ and } \sigma = 4)$
  b. $P(x \ge 77 | \mu = 50 \text{ and } \sigma = 9)$
  c. $P(x > 47 | \mu = 50 \text{ and } \sigma = 6)$
  d. $P(13 < x < 29 | \mu = 23 \text{ and } \sigma = 4)$
  e. $P(x \ge 105 | \mu = 90 \text{ and } \sigma = 2.86)$

6.36 Work the following binomial distribution problems by using the normal distribution. Check your answers by using Table A.2 to solve for the probabilities.

  a. $P(x = 12 | n = 25 \text{ and } p = .60)$

  b. $P(x > 5 | n = 15 \text{ and } p = .50)$
  c. $P(x \le 3 | n = 10 \text{ and } p = .50)$
  d. $P(x \ge 8 | n = 15 \text{ and } p = .40)$

6.37 Find the probabilities for the following exponential distribution problems.

  a. $P(x \ge 3 | \lambda = 1.3)$
  b. $P(x < 2 | \lambda = 2.0)$
  c. $P(1 \le x \le 3 | \lambda = 1.65)$
  d. $P(x > 2 | \lambda = .405)$

TESTING YOUR UNDERSTANDING

6.38 The U.S. Bureau of Labor Statistics reports that of persons who usually work full time, the average number of hours worked per week is 43.4. Assume that the number of hours worked per week for those who usually work full time is normally distributed. Suppose 12% of these workers work more 48 hours. Based on this percentage, what is the standard deviation of number of hours worked per week for these workers?

6.39 A U.S. Bureau of Labor Statistics survey showed that one in five people 16 years of age or older volunteers some of his or her time. If this figure holds for the entire population and if a random sample of 150 people 16 years of age or older is taken, what is the probability that more than 50 of those sampled do volunteer work?

6.40 An entrepreneur opened a small hardware store in a strip mall. During the first few weeks, business was slow, with the store averaging only one customer every 20 minutes in the morning. Assume that the random arrival of customers is Poisson distributed.

  a. What is the probability that at least 1 hour would elapse between customers?

  b. What is the probability that 10 to 30 minutes would elapse between customers?

  c. What is the probability that less than 5 minutes would elapse between customers?

6.41 In a recent year, the average price of a Microsoft Windows Upgrade was $90.28 according to *PC Data*. Assume that prices of the Microsoft Windows Upgrade that year were normally distributed, with a standard deviation of $8.53. If a retailer of computer software was randomly selected that year, what is the probability that the price of a Microsoft Windows Upgrade was below $80? What is the probability that the price was above $95? What is the probability that the price was between $83 and $87?

6.42 According to the U.S. Department of Agriculture, Alabama egg farmers produce millions of eggs every year. Suppose egg production per year in Alabama is normally distributed, with a standard deviation of 83 million eggs. If during only 3% of the years Alabama egg farmers produce more than 2,655 million eggs, what is the mean egg production by Alabama farmers?

6.43 The U.S. Bureau of Labor Statistics releases figures on the number of full-time wage and salary workers with flexible schedules. The numbers of full-time wage and salary workers in each age category are almost uniformly distributed by age, with ages ranging from 18 to 65 years. If a worker with a flexible schedule is randomly drawn from the U.S. workforce, what is the probability that he or she will be between 25 and 50 years of age? What is the mean value for this distribution? What is the height of the distribution?

6.44 A business convention holds its registration on Wednesday morning from 9:00 A.M. until 12:00 noon. Past history has shown that registrant arrivals follow a Poisson distribution at an average rate of 1.8 every 15 seconds. Fortunately, several facilities are available to register convention members.

  a. What is the average number of seconds between arrivals to the registration area for this conference based on past results?

  b. What is the probability that 25 seconds or more would pass between registration arrivals?

  c. What is the probability that less than 5 seconds will elapse between arrivals?

  d. Suppose the registration computers went down for a 1-minute period. Would this condition pose a problem? What is the probability that at least 1 minute will elapse between arrivals?

6.45 *M/PF Research, Inc.* lists the average monthly apartment rent in some of the most expensive apartment rental locations in the United States. According to their report, the average cost of renting an apartment in Minneapolis is $951. Suppose that the standard deviation of the cost of renting an apartment in Minneapolis is $96 and that apartment rents in Minneapolis are normally distributed. If a Minneapolis apartment is randomly selected, what is the probability that the price is:

  a. $1,000 or more?

  b. Between $900 and $1,100?

  c. Between $825 and $925?

  d. Less than $700?

6.46 According to *The Wirthlin Report*, 24% of all workers say that their job is very stressful. If 60 workers are randomly selected, what is the probability that 17 or more say that their job is very stressful? What is the probability that more than 22 say that their job is very stressful? What is the probability that between 8 and 12 (inclusive) say that their job is very stressful?

6.47 The U.S. Bureau of Labor Statistics reports that the average annual salary in the metropolitan Boston area is $45,121. Suppose annual salaries in the metropolitan Boston area are normally distributed, with a standard deviation of $4,246. A Boston area worker is randomly selected.

  a. What is the probability that the worker's annual salary is more than $50,000?

  b. What is the probability that the worker's annual salary is less than $40,000?

  c. What is the probability that the worker's annual salary is more than $35,000?

  d. What is the probability that the worker's annual salary is between $39,000 and $47,000?

6.48 Suppose interarrival times at a hospital emergency room during a weekday are exponentially distributed, with an average interarrival time of 9 minutes. If the arrivals are Poisson distributed, what would the average number of arrivals per hour be? What is the probability that less than 5 minutes will elapse between any two arrivals?

6.49 Suppose the average speeds of passenger trains traveling from Newark, New Jersey, to Philadelphia, Pennsylvania, are normally distributed, with a mean average speed of 88 miles per hour and a standard deviation of 6.4 miles per hour.

a. What is the probability that a train will average less than 70 miles per hour?

b. What is the probability that a train will average more than 80 miles per hour?

c. What is the probability that a train will average between 90 and 100 miles per hour?

6.50 The Conference Board published information on why companies expect to increase the number of part-time jobs and reduce full-time positions. Eighty-one percent of the companies said the reason was to get a flexible workforce. Suppose 200 companies that expect to increase the number of part-time jobs and reduce full-time positions are identified and contacted. What is the expected number of these companies that would agree that the reason is to get a flexible workforce? What is the probability that between 150 and 155 (not including the 150 or the 155) would give that reason? What is the probability that more than 158 would give that reason? What is the probability that fewer than 144 would give that reason?

6.51 According to the U.S. Bureau of the Census, about 75% of commuters in the United States drive to work alone. Suppose 150 U.S. commuters are randomly sampled.

a. What is the probability that fewer than 105 commuters drive to work alone?

b. What is the probability that between 110 and 120 (inclusive) commuters drive to work alone?

c. What is the probability that more than 95 commuters drive to work alone?

6.52 According to figures released by the National Agricultural Statistics Service of the U.S. Department of Agriculture, the U.S. production of wheat over the past 20 years has been approximately uniformly distributed. Suppose the mean production over this period was 2.165 billion bushels. If the height of this distribution is .862 billion bushels, what are the values of a and b for this distribution?

6.53 The Federal Reserve System publishes data on family income based on its Survey of Consumer Finances. When the head of the household has a college degree, the mean before-tax family income is $85,200. Suppose that 60% of the before-tax family incomes when the head of the household has a college degree are between $75,600 and $94,800 and that these incomes are normally distributed. What is the standard deviation of before-tax family incomes when the head of the household has a college degree?

6.54 According to The Polk Company, a survey of households using the Internet in buying or leasing cars reported that 81% were seeking information about prices. In addition, 44% were seeking information

about products offered. Suppose 75 randomly selected households who are using the Internet in buying or leasing cars are contacted.

a. What is the expected number of households who are seeking price information?

b. What is the expected number of households who are seeking information about products offered?

c. What is the probability that 67 or more households are seeking information about prices?

d. What is the probability that fewer than 23 households are seeking information about products offered?

6.55 Coastal businesses along the Gulf of Mexico from Texas to Florida worry about the threat of hurricanes during the season from June through October. Businesses become especially nervous when hurricanes enter the Gulf of Mexico. Suppose the arrival of hurricanes during this season is Poisson distributed, with an average of three hurricanes entering the Gulf of Mexico during the 5-month season. If a hurricane has just entered the Gulf of Mexico, what is the probability that at least 1 month will pass before the next hurricane enters the Gulf? What is the probability that another hurricane will enter the Gulf of Mexico in 2 weeks or less? What is the average amount of time between hurricanes entering the Gulf of Mexico?

6.56 With the growing emphasis on technology and the changing business environment, many workers are discovering that training such as reeducation, skill development, and personal growth are of great assistance in the job marketplace. A recent Gallup survey found that 80% of Generation Xers considered the availability of company-sponsored training as a factor to weigh in taking a job. If 50 Generation Xers are randomly sampled, what is the probability that fewer than 35 consider the availability of company-sponsored training as a factor to weigh in taking a job? What is the expected number? What is the probability that between 42 and 47 (inclusive) consider the availability of company-sponsored training as a factor to weigh in taking a job?

6.57 According to the Air Transport Association of America, the average operating cost of an MD-80 jet airliner is $2,087 per hour. Suppose the operating costs of an MD-80 jet airliner are normally distributed with a standard deviation of $175 per hour. At what operating cost would only 20% of the operating costs be less? At what operating cost would 65% of the operating costs be more? What operating cost would be more than 85% of operating costs?

6.58 Supermarkets usually become busy at about 5 P.M. on weekdays, because many workers stop by on the way home to shop. Suppose at that time arrivals at a supermarket's express checkout station are Poisson distributed, with an average of .8 person/minute. If the clerk has just checked out the last person in line, what is the probability that at least 1 minute will elapse before the next customer arrives? Suppose the clerk wants to go to the manager's office to ask a quick question and needs 2.5 minutes to do so. What is the probability that the clerk will get back before the next customer arrives?

6.59 According to *Editor and Publisher Yearbook*, the average daily circulation of *The Wall Street Journal* based on 2000 figures is 1,762,751. Suppose the standard deviation is 50,940. Assume the paper's daily circulation is normally distributed. On what percentage of days would it surpass a circulation of 1,850,000? Suppose the paper cannot support the fixed expenses of a full-production setup if the circulation drops below 1,620,000. If the probability of this event occurring is low, the production manager might try to keep the full crew in place and not disrupt operations. How often will this event happen, based on the historical information?

6.60 Incoming phone calls generally are thought to be Poisson distributed. If an operator averages 2.2 phone calls every 30 seconds, what is the expected (average) amount of time between calls? What is the probability that a minute or more would elapse between incoming calls? Two minutes?

INTERPRETING THE OUTPUT

6.61 Shown here is a MINITAB output. Suppose the data represent the number of sales associates who are working in a department store in any given retail day. Describe the distribution including the mean and standard deviation. Interpret the shape of the distribution and the mean in light of the data being studied. What do the probability statements mean?

CUMULATIVE DISTRIBUTION FUNCTION

Continuous uniform on 11.0000
to 32.0000
         x   P(X <= x)
   28.0000   0.8095
   34.0000   1.0000
   16.0000   0.2381
   21.0000   0.4762

6.62 A manufacturing company produces a metal rod. Use the Excel output shown here to describe the weight of the rod. Interpret the probability values in terms of the manufacturing process.

	A	B	C	D
1	**Normal Distribution**			
2	Mean = 227 mg.			
3	Standard Deviation = 2.3 mg.			
4				
5	x Value	Probability < x Value		
6	220	0.0012		
7	225	0.1923		
8	227	0.5000		
9	231	0.9590		
10	238	1.0000		

6.63 Suppose the MINITAB output shown here represents the analysis of the length of home-use cell phone calls in terms of minutes. Describe the distribution of cell phone call lengths and interpret the meaning of the probability statements.

CUMULATIVE DISTRIBUTION FUNCTION

Normal with mean = 2.35000 and
standard deviation = 0.110000
       x   P(X <= x)
   2.6000   0.9885
   2.4500   0.8183
   2.3000   0.3247
   2.0000   0.0007

6.64 A restaurant averages 4.51 customers per 10 minutes during the summer in the late afternoon. Shown here are Excel and MINITAB output for this restaurant. Discuss the type of distribution used to analyze the data and the meaning of the probabilities.

	A	B
1		
2	x Values	
3	0.1	0.3630
4	0.2	0.5942
5	0.5	0.8951
6	1.0	0.9890
7	2.4	1.0000

CUMULATIVE DISTRIBUTION FUNCTION

Exponential with mean = 0.221729
       x   P(X <= x)
   0.1000   0.3630
   0.2000   0.5942
   0.5000   0.8951
   1.0000   0.9890
   2.4000   1.0000

ANALYZING THE DATABASES

see **www.wiley.com/college/black**

1. Select the agribusiness time-series database. Create a histogram graph for onions and for broccoli. Each of these variables is approximately normally distributed. Compute the mean and the standard deviation for each distribution. The data in this database represent the monthly weight (in thousands of pounds) of each vegetable. In terms of monthly weight, describe each vegetable (onions and broccoli). If a month were randomly selected from the onion distribution, what is the probability that the weight would be more than 50,000? What is the probability that the weight would be between 25,000 and 35,000? If a month were randomly selected from the broccoli distribution, what is the probability that the weight would be more than 100,000? What is the probability that the weight would be between 135,000 and 170,000?

2. Use the manufacturing database. The industry group variable is nearly uniformly distributed in this database, with values from $a = 1$ to $b = 20$. What is the height of this distribution? What is the probability of randomly selecting an industry group from 7 to 13 (inclusive) from this population if the distribution is uniform? (Use the uniform distribution theory to work this problem, not the actual numbers from the database).

3. Construct histogram graphs of all variables in the manufacturing database. Find at least one graph that appears to take on the shape of an exponential distribution. Compute descriptive statistics for that variable. Study the statistics and discuss what information relayed by the statistics would indicate that the shape of the distribution might be exponential.

CASE: MERCEDES GOES AFTER YOUNGER BUYERS

Mercedes and BMW have been competing head-to-head for market share in the luxury-car market for more than three decades. Back in 1959, BMW (Bayerische Motoren Werke) almost went bankrupt and nearly sold out to Daimler-Benz, the maker of Mercedes-Benz cars. BMW was able to recover to the point that in 1992 it passed Mercedes in worldwide sales. Among the reasons for BMW's success was its ability to sell models that were more luxurious than previous models but still focused on consumer quality and environmental responsibility. In particular, BMW targeted its sales pitch to the younger market, whereas Mercedes retained a more mature customer base.

In response to BMW's success, Mercedes has been trying to change their image by launching several products in an effort to attract younger buyers who are interested in sporty, performance-oriented cars. BMW, influenced by Mercedes, is pushing for more refinement and comfort. In fact, one automotive expert says that Mercedes wants to become BMW, and vice versa. However, according to one recent automotive expert, the focus is still on luxury and comfort for Mercedes while BMW focuses on performance and driving dynamics. Even though each company produces many different models, two relatively comparable coupe automobiles are the BMW 330ci and the Mercedes CLK 320. As of 2002, the average price for a 330ci was $34,990 as compared to $43,215 for a CLK 320. Gas mileage for the 330ci is 30 miles per gallon on the highway and 21 miles per gallon in town as compared to 29 miles per gallon on the highway and 21 miles per gallon in town for the CLK 320.

Discussion

1. Suppose Mercedes is concerned that dealer prices of the CLK 320 are not consistent and that even though the average price is $43,215, the prices are actually normally distributed with a standard deviation of $2,981. Suppose also that Mercedes believes that at $42,000, the CLK 320 is priced out of the BMW 330ci market. What percentage of the dealer prices for the Mercedes CLK 320 is more than $42,000 and hence priced out of the BMW 330ci market? The average price for a BMW 330ci is $34,990. Suppose these prices are also normally distributed with a standard deviation of $2,367. What percentage of BMW dealers are pricing the 330ci at more than the average price for a CLK 320? What percentage of Mercedes dealers are pricing the CLK 320 at less than the average price for a 330ci? Suppose a BMW dealer is selling a 330ci for $37,059. What percentage of Mercedes dealers prices the CLK 320 less than this price? In terms of the CLK 320 competing with the 330ci pricewise, what do these data tell you?

2. Suppose that gas mileage rates for various CLK cars (including the fact that some drivers are less efficient than others) are uniformly distributed over a range from 24 miles per gallon to 34 miles per gallon on the road. What proportion of cars fall into the 26 to 30 miles per gallon range? Suppose that gas mileage rates for various 330ci cars are uniformly distributed over a range from 25 miles per gallon to 35 miles per gallon on the road. What proportion of 330ci cars fall into the 26 to 30 miles per gallon range? How does this percentage compare to the figure for the CLK? What does this comparison mean? Suppose these figures were true and Mercedes wanted to appeal to environmentally conscious shoppers on the basis of fuel economy. Compute the proportion of each of the two car models that gets 30 or more miles per gallon according to these figures, and compare the results.

3. Suppose that in one dealership an average of 1.37 CLKs is sold every 3 hours (during a 12-hour showroom day) and that sales are Poisson distributed. The following Excel-produced probabilities indicate the occurrence of different intersales times based on this information. Study the output and interpret it for the salespeople. For example, what is the probability that less than an hour will elapse between sales? What is the probability that more than a day (12-hour day) will pass before the next sale after a car has been sold? What can the dealership managers do with such information? How can it help in staffing? How can such information be used as a tracking device for the impact of advertising? Is there a

chance that these probabilities would change during the year? If so, why?

Portion of 3-Hour Time Frame	Cumulative Exponential Probabilities from Left
0.167	0.2045
0.333	0.3663
0.667	0.5990
1	0.7459
2	0.9354
3	0.9836
4	0.9958
5	0.9989

USING THE COMPUTER

EXCEL

Excel can be used to compute cumulative probabilities for particular values of x from either an exponential distribution or a normal distribution. In either case, begin by selecting the function key, f_x, on the tool bar. It will produce the **Paste Function.** Next select the function, **Statistical,** on the left side of the Paste Function window. A new list of options will appear on the right side.

Normal Distribution

Normal curve probabilities can be obtained by selecting the **NORMDIST** function from the right side of the **Statistical** function. A dialog box will appear. The dialog box has four lines to which you must respond. Enter the value of x on the first line, the mean on the second line, and the standard deviation in the third line. The fourth line requires a logical response of either TRUE or FALSE. If you enter TRUE, you will get the cumulative probabilities for all values up to x. If you enter FALSE, you will get the value of the probability density function for that combination of x, μ, and σ. In this chapter, we are interested in solving for and using probabilities and will therefore almost always use the logical response TRUE.

Exponential Distribution

Probabilities from an exponential distribution can be obtained by selecting the **EXPONDIST** function from the right side list of the **Statistical** function. An EXPONDIST dialog box will appear. This dialog box contains three lines to which you must respond. Place the value of x_0 on the first line and the value of λ on the second line. The third line requires a logical response of either TRUE or FALSE. If you enter TRUE, you will get the cumulative probabilities from zero to the value of x_0. If you enter FALSE, you will get the value of the probability density formula. For problems worked in this text, we are mostly interested in the cumulative probabilities and will place a TRUE response in this box.

MINITAB

MINITAB offers the capability of producing probabilities for exponential distributions, normal distributions, or uniform distributions. Begin the process by selecting the option **Calc** on the menu bar, which results in a pull-down menu. On this menu, select **Probability Distributions.** When you select this option, another pull-down menu will appear.

Uniform Distribution

To use MINITAB Windows to compute probabilities from a uniform distribution, select **Uniform** from the **Probability Distributions** pull-down menu. This selection will result in a dialog box. Choose how the probabilities are calculated by selecting **Probability Density, Cumulative Probability,** or **Inverse Probability.** Probability Density yields the value of the probability density for a particular combination of a, b, and x. Cumulative Probability produces the cumulative probabilities for values less than or equal to x. Inverse Probability yields the inverse of the cumulative probabilities. Here we are mostly interested in cumulative probability. On the line, **Lower endpoint,** enter the value of a. On the line, **Upper endpoint,** enter the value of b. If you want to have probabilities computed for several values of x, place them in a column, select the input column option, and list the column location of the x values. If you only want to compute the probability for a particular value of x, check input constant and input x.

Normal Distribution

To use MINITAB to compute probabilities from a normal distribution, select **Normal** from the **Probability Distributions** pull-down menu. This selection will result in a dialog box. Choose how the probabilities are calculated by selecting **Probability Density, Cumulative Probability,** or **Inverse Probability.** Probability Density yields the value of the probability density for a particular combination of x, μ, and σ. Cumulative Probability produces the cumulative probabilities for values less than or equal to *x*. Inverse Probability yields the inverse of the cumulative probabilities. Here we are mostly interested in cumulative probability. On the line, **Mean,** enter the value of μ, and on the line, **Standard deviation,** enter the value of σ. If you want to have probabilities computed for several values of *x*, place them in a column, select the input column option, and list the column location of the *x* values. If you only want to compute the probability for a particular value of *x*, check input constant and input *x*.

Exponential Distribution

To use MINITAB to compute probabilities from an exponential distribution, select **Exponential** from the **Probability Distributions** pull-down menu. This selection will result in a

dialog box. Choose how the probabilities are calculated by selecting **Probability Density, Cumulative Probability,** or **Inverse Probability.** Probability Density yields the value of the probability density for a particular combination of x_0 and μ. Cumulative Probability produces the cumulative probabilities for values less than or equal to x_0. Inverse Probability yields the inverse of the cumulative probabilities. Here we are mostly interested in cumulative probability. On the line, **Mean,** enter the value of μ. If you want to have probabilities computed for several values of x_0, place them in a column, select the input column option, and list the column location of the x_0 values. If you only want to compute the probability for a particular value of x_0, check input constant and input x_0. *Note:* MINITAB uses the mean, $\mu = 1/\lambda$, not the value of λ.

Sampling and Sampling Distributions

LEARNING OBJECTIVES

The two main objectives for Chapter 7 are to give you an appreciation for the proper application of sampling techniques and an understanding of the sampling distributions of two statistics, thereby enabling you to:

1. Determine when to use sampling instead of a census.

2. Distinguish between random and nonrandom sampling.

3. Decide when and how to use various sampling techniques.

4. Be aware of the different types of errors that can occur in a study.

5. Understand the impact of the central limit theorem on statistical analysis.

6. Use the sampling distributions of $\bar{x}$ and $\hat{p}$.

Early in the 1960s, the government of Mexico established the maquiladora program. This program allowed U.S.-owned corporations to build manufacturing facilities inside the Mexican border where they could import supplies and materials from the United States free of duty, to assemble or produce products, and then export the finished items back to the United States. The idea was to entice U.S. firms to build in Mexico because of the cheap labor pool available there, and thus create jobs for Mexicans.

The program has been successful, with more than 3,500 registered companies taking part. By 2000, more than 1.1 million maquiladora workers were employed. An estimated $50 billion (U.S.) was spent by maquiladoras with suppliers in 1999, with maquiladora industry exports at about $65 billion (U.S.). Nearly 85% of maquiladora manufacturing is in Mexico's northern states, those bordering the United States. These firms are concentrated in Ciudad Juarez, Tijuana, Mexicali, Nuevo Laredo, and Matamoras. The maquiladora program now encompasses companies from all over the world including Japan, Korea, China, Canada, and many European countries.

What are the Mexican maquiladora workers like? What are their attitudes toward their jobs and their companies? Are there cultural gaps between company and worker that must be bridged in order to utilize the human resources more effectively? What culture-based attitudes and expectations do the maquiladora laborers bring to the work situation? How does a business researcher go about surveying workers?

Managerial and Statistical Questions

Suppose researchers decide to survey maquiladora workers to ascertain the workers' attitudes toward and expectations of the work environment and the company.

1. Should the researchers take a census of all maquiladora workers or just a sample? What are reasons for each?
2. If a sample is used, what type of sampling technique would gain the most valid information? How can the researchers be certain that the sample of workers is representative of the population?
3. What types of questions should be asked and how should they be stated?
4. Can the questions be analyzed quantitatively? If so, which statistical techniques are most appropriate?
5. In what format can the researchers most effectively convey the results of the study to management?
6. How can management fully utilize the study results to effect a more productive work environment?

Source: Adapted from Cheryl L. Noll, "Mexican Maquiladora Workers: An Attitude Toward Working," *Southwest Journal of Business and Economics*, vol. IX, no. 1 (Spring 1992), pp. 1–8; *Maquila Magazine,* http://www.mexico-maquila.com/mi.htm, accessed 2000; Steven B. Zisser, "Maquiladora 2001 Understanding and Preparing," available at http://www.maqguide.com/zisser1.htm.

This chapter explores the process of sampling and the sampling distributions of some statistics. How do we obtain the data used in statistical analysis? Why do researchers often take a sample rather than conduct a census? What are the differences between random and nonrandom sampling? This chapter addresses these and other questions about sampling.

Also presented are the distributions of two statistics: the sample mean and the sample proportion. It has been determined that statistics such as these are approximately normally distributed under certain conditions. Knowledge of the uses of the sample mean and sample proportion is important in the study of statistics and is basic to much of statistical analysis.

7.1 SAMPLING

Sampling is widely used in business as a means of gathering useful information about a population. Data are gathered from samples and conclusions are drawn about the population as a part of the inferential statistics process. In the Decision Dilemma on maquiladora workers, a random sample of workers could be taken from a wide selection of companies in several industries in many of the key border cities. A carefully constructed questionnaire that is culturally sensitive to Mexicans could be administered to the selected workers to determine work attitudes, expectations, and cultural differences between workers and companies. The researchers could compile and analyze the data gleaned from the responses. Summaries and observations could be made about worker outlook and culture in the maquiladora program. Management and decision makers could then attempt to use the results of the study to improve worker performance and motivation. Often, a sample provides a reasonable means for gathering such useful decision-making information that might be otherwise unattainable and unaffordable.

Reasons for Sampling

Taking a sample instead of conducting a census offers several advantages.

1. The sample can save money.
2. The sample can save time.
3. For given resources, the sample can broaden the scope of the study.
4. Because the research process is sometimes destructive, the sample can save product.
5. If accessing the population is impossible, the sample is the only option.

A sample can be cheaper to obtain than a census for a given magnitude of questions. For example, if an 8-minute telephone interview is being undertaken, conducting the interviews with a sample of 100 customers rather than with a population of 100,000 customers obviously is less expensive. In addition to the cost savings, the significantly smaller number of interviews usually requires less total time. Thus, if obtaining the results is a matter of urgency, sampling can provide them more quickly. With the volatility of some markets and the constant barrage of new competition and new ideas, sampling has a strong advantage over a census in terms of research turnaround time.

If the resources allocated to a research project are fixed, more detailed information can be gathered by taking a sample than by conducting a census. With resources concentrated on fewer individuals or items, the study can be broadened in scope to allow for more specialized questions. One organization budgeted $100,000 for a study and opted to take a census instead of a sample by using a mail survey. The researchers mass-mailed thousands of copies of a computer card that looked like a major league baseball all-star ballot. The card contained 20 questions to which the respondent could answer Yes or No by punching out a perforated hole. The information retrieved amounted to the percentages of respondents who answered Yes and No on the 20 questions. For the same amount of money, the company could have taken a random sample from the population, held interactive one-on-one sessions with highly trained interviewers, and gathered detailed information about the process being studied. By using the money for a sample, the researchers could have spent significantly more time with each respondent and thus increased the potential for gathering useful information.

Some research processes are destructive to the product or item being studied. For example, if light bulbs are being tested to determine how long they burn or if candy bars are being taste tested to determine whether the taste is acceptable, the product is destroyed. If a census were conducted for this type of research, no product would be left to sell. Hence, taking a sample is the only realistic option for testing such products.

Sometimes a population is virtually impossible to access for research. For example, some people refuse to answer sensitive questions, and some telephone numbers are unlisted. Some items of interest (like a 1957 Chevrolet) are so scattered that locating all of them would be extremely difficult. When the population is inaccessible for these or other reasons, sampling is the only option.

Reasons for Taking a Census

Sometimes taking a census makes more sense than using a sample. One reason to take a census is to eliminate the possibility that by chance a randomly selected sample might not be representative of the population. Even when all the proper sampling techniques are implemented, a sample that is nonrepresentative of the population can be selected by chance. For example, if the population of interest is all truck owners in the state of Colorado, a random sample of owners could yield mostly ranchers, when in fact many of the truck owners in Colorado are urban dwellers.

A second reason to take a census is that the client (person authorizing and/or underwriting the study) does not have an appreciation for random sampling and feels more comfortable with conducting a census. Both of these reasons for taking a census are based on the assumption that enough time and money are available to conduct such a census.

Frame

Every research study has a target population that consists of the individuals, institutions, or entities that are the object of investigation. The sample is taken from a population *list, map, directory, or other source used to represent the population.* This list, map, or directory is called the **frame,** which can be school lists, trade association lists, or even lists sold by list brokers. Ideally, a one-to-one correspondence exists between the frame units and the population units. In reality, the frame and the target population are often different. For example, suppose the target population is all families living in Detroit. A feasible frame would be the residential pages of the Detroit telephone books. How would the frame differ from the target population? Some families have no telephone. Other families have unlisted numbers. Still other families might have moved and/or changed numbers since the directory was printed. Some families even have multiple listings under different names.

Frames that have *overregistration* contain all the target population units plus some additional units. Frames that have *underregistration* contain fewer units than does the target population. Sampling is done from the frame, not the target population. In theory, the target population and the frame are the same. In reality, a researcher's goal is to minimize the differences between the frame and the target population.

Random versus Nonrandom Sampling

The two main types of sampling are random and nonrandom. In **random sampling** *every unit of the population has the same probability of being selected into the sample.* Random sampling implies that chance enters into the process of selection. For example, most Americans would like to believe that winners of nationwide magazine sweepstakes are selected by some random draw of numbers. Late in the 1960s when the military draft lottery was being used, most people eligible for the draft trusted that a given birthdate was selected by chance as the first date used to draft people. In both of these situations, members of the population believed that selections were made by chance.

In **nonrandom sampling** *not every unit of the population has the same probability of being selected into the sample.* Members of nonrandom samples are not selected by chance. For example, they might be selected because they are at the right place at the right time or because they know the people conducting the research.

Sometimes random sampling is called *probability sampling* and nonrandom sampling is called *nonprobability sampling.* Because every unit of the population is not equally likely to be selected, assigning a probability of occurrence in nonrandom sampling is impossible. The statistical methods presented and discussed in this text are based on the assumption that the data come from random samples. *Nonrandom sampling methods are not appropriate techniques for gathering data to be analyzed by most of the statistical methods presented in this text.* However, several nonrandom sampling techniques are described in this section, primarily to alert you to their characteristics and limitations.

Random Sampling Techniques

The four basic random sampling techniques are simple random sampling, stratified random sampling, systematic random sampling, and cluster (or area) random sampling. Each technique offers advantages and disadvantages. Some techniques are simpler to use, some are less costly, and others show greater potential for reducing sampling error.

Simple Random Sampling

The most elementary random sampling technique is **simple random sampling.** Simple random sampling can be viewed as the basis for the other random sampling techniques. With simple random sampling, each unit of the frame is numbered from 1 to N (where N is the size of the population). Next, a table of random numbers or a random number generator is used to select n items into the sample. A random number generator is usually a computer program that allows computer-calculated output to yield random numbers. Table 7.1 contains a brief table of random numbers. Table A.1 in Appendix A contains a full table of random numbers. These numbers are random in all directions. The spaces in the table are there only for ease of reading the values. For each number, any of the 10 digits (0–9) is equally likely, so getting the same digit twice or more in a row is possible.

As an example, from the population frame of companies listed in Table 7.2, we will use simple random sampling to select a sample of six companies. First, we number every member of the population. We select as many digits for each unit sampled as there are in the largest number in the population. For example, if a population has 2,000 members, we select four-digit numbers. Because the population in Table 7.2 contains 30 members, only two digits need be selected for each number. The population is numbered from 01 to 30, as shown in Table 7.3.

The object is to sample six companies, so six different two-digit numbers must be selected from the table of random numbers. Because this population contains only 30 companies, all numbers greater than 30 (31–99) must be ignored. If, for example, the number 67 is selected, the process is continued until a value between 1 and 30 is obtained. If the same number occurs more than once, we proceed to another number. For ease of understanding, we start with the first pair of digits in Table 7.1 and proceed across the first row until $n = 6$ different values between 01 and 30 are selected. If additional numbers are needed, we proceed

TABLE 7.1							
A Brief Table of Random Numbers							

91567	42595	27958	30134	04024	86385	29880	99730
46503	18584	18845	49618	02304	51038	20655	58727
34914	63976	88720	82765	34476	17032	87589	40836
57491	16703	23167	49323	45021	33132	12544	41035
30405	83946	23792	14422	15059	45799	22716	19792
09983	74353	68668	30429	70735	25499	16631	35006
85900	07119	97336	71048	08178	77233	13916	47564

TABLE 7.2

A Population Frame of
30 Companies

Alaska Airlines	DuPont	Lucent
Alcoa	Exxon Mobil	Mattel
Ashland	General Dynamics	Mead
Bank of America	General Electric	Microsoft
BellSouth	General Mills	Occidental Petroleum
Chevron	Halliburton	JCPenney
Citigroup	IBM	Procter & Gamble
Clorox	Kellogg	Ryder
Delta Air Lines	Kmart	Sears
Disney	Lowe's	Time Warner

TABLE 7.3

Numbered Population of
30 Companies

01 Alaska Airlines	11 DuPont	21 Lucent
02 Alcoa	12 Exxon Mobil	22 Mattel
03 Ashland	13 General Dynamics	23 Mead
04 Bank of America	14 General Electric	24 Microsoft
05 BellSouth	15 General Mills	25 Occidental Petroleum
06 Chevron	16 Halliburton	26 JCPenney
07 Citigroup	17 IBM	27 Procter & Gamble
08 Clorox	18 Kellogg	28 Ryder
09 Delta Air Lines	19 Kmart	29 Sears
10 Disney	20 Lowe's	30 Time Warner

across the second row, and so on. Often a researcher will start at some randomly selected location in the table and proceed in a predetermined direction to select numbers.

In the first row of digits in Table 7.1, the first number is 91. This number is out of range so it is cast out. The next two digits are 56. Next is 74, followed by 25, which is the first usable number. From Table 7.3, we see that 25 is the number associated with Occidental Petroleum, so Occidental Petroleum is the first company selected into the sample. The next number is 95, unusable, followed by 27, which is usable. Twenty-seven is the number for Procter & Gamble, so this company is selected. Continuing the process, we pass over the numbers 95 and 83. The next usable number is 01, which is the value for Alaska Airlines. Thirty-four is next, followed by 04 and 02, both of which are usable. These numbers are associated with Bank of America and Alcoa, respectively. Continuing along the first row, the next usable number is 29, which is associated with Sears. Because this selection is the sixth, the sample is complete. The following companies constitute the final sample.

> Alaska Airlines
> Alcoa
> Bank of America
> Occidental Petroleum
> Procter & Gamble
> Sears

Simple random sampling is easier to perform on small than on large populations. The process of numbering all the members of the population and selecting items is cumbersome for large populations.

Stratified Random Sampling

A second type of random sampling is **stratified random sampling,** in which the population is divided into nonoverlapping subpopulations called strata. The researcher then extracts a simple random sample from each of the subpopulations. The main reason for using stratified random sampling is that it has the potential for reducing sampling error.

Sampling error occurs when, by chance, the sample does not represent the population. With stratified random sampling, the potential to match the sample closely to the population is greater than it is with simple random sampling because portions of the total sample are taken from different population subgroups. However, stratified random sampling is generally more costly than simple random sampling because each unit of the population must be assigned to a stratum before the random selection process begins.

Strata selection is usually based on available information. Such information may have been gleaned from previous censuses or surveys. Stratification benefits increase as the strata differ more. Internally, a stratum should be relatively homogeneous; externally, strata should contrast with each other. Stratification is often done by using demographic variables, such as gender, socioeconomic class, geographic region, religion, and ethnicity. For example, if a U.S. presidential election poll is to be conducted by a market research firm, what important variables should be stratified? The gender of the respondent might make a difference because a gender gap in voter preference has been noted in past elections; that is, men and women tended to vote differently in national elections. Geographic region also provides an important variable in national elections because voters are influenced by local cultural values that differ from region to region. Voters in the South voted almost exclusively for Democrats in the past, but recently they tended to vote for Republican candidates in national elections. Voters in the Rocky Mountain states supported Republican presidential candidates; in the industrial Northeast, voters were more inclined toward Democratic candidates.

In FM radio markets, age of listener is an important determinant of the type of programming used by a station. Figure 7.1 contains a stratification by age with three strata, based on the assumption that age makes a difference in preference of programming. This stratification implies that listeners 20 to 30 years of age tend to prefer the same type of programming, which is different from that preferred by listeners 30 to 40 and 40 to 50 years of age. Within each age subgroup (stratum), *homogeneity* or alikeness is present; between each pair of subgroups a difference, or *heterogeneity,* is present.

Stratified random sampling can be either proportionate or disproportionate. **Proportionate stratified random sampling** occurs *when the percentage of the sample taken from each stratum is proportionate to the percentage that each stratum is within the whole population.* For example, suppose voters are being surveyed in Boston and the sample is being stratified by religion as Catholic, Protestant, Jewish, and others. If Boston's population is 90% Catholic and if a sample of 1,000 voters is taken, the sample would require inclusion of 900 Catholics to achieve proportionate stratification. Any other number of Catholics would be disproportionate stratification. The sample proportion of other religions would also have to follow population percentages. Or consider the city of El Paso, Texas, where the population is approximately 77% Hispanic. If a researcher is conducting a citywide poll in El Paso and if stratification is by ethnicity, a proportionate stratified random sample should contain 77% Hispanics. Hence, an ethnically proportionate stratified

FIGURE 7.1

Stratified Random Sampling of FM Radio Listeners

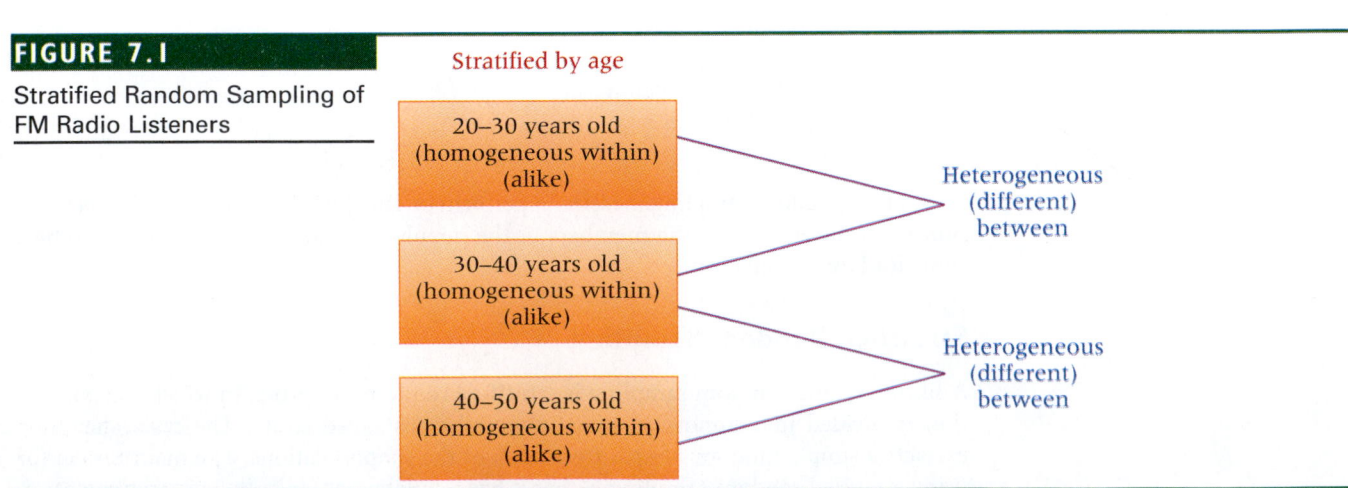

sample of 160 residents from El Paso's 600,000 residents should contain approximately 123 Hispanics. *Whenever the proportions of the strata in the sample are different from the proportions of the strata in the population,* **disproportionate stratified random sampling** occurs.

Systematic Sampling

Systematic sampling is a third random sampling technique. Unlike stratified random sampling, systematic sampling is not done in an attempt to reduce sampling error. Rather, systematic sampling is used because of its convenience and relative ease of administration. With **systematic sampling,** *every kth item is selected to produce a sample of size n from a population of size N.* The value of k, sometimes called the sampling cycle, can be determined by the following formula. If k is not an integer value, the whole-number value should be used.

DETERMINING THE VALUE OF k	$$k = \frac{N}{n}$$

where

n = sample size
N = population size
k = size of interval for selection

As an example of systematic sampling, a management information systems researcher wanted to sample the manufacturers in Texas. He had enough financial support to sample 1,000 companies (n). The *Directory of Texas Manufacturers* listed approximately 17,000 total manufacturers in Texas (N) in alphabetical order. The value of k was 17 (17,000/1,000) and the researcher selected every 17th company in the directory for his sample.

Did the researcher begin with the first company listed or the 17th or one somewhere between? In selecting every kth value, a simple random number table should be used to select a value between 1 and k inclusive as a starting point. The second element for the sample is the starting point plus k. In the example, $k = 17$, so the researcher would have gone to a table of random numbers to determine a starting point between 1 and 17. Suppose he selected the number 5. He would have started with the 5th company, then selected the 22nd (5 + 17), and then the 39th, and so on.

Besides convenience, systematic sampling has other advantages. Because systematic sampling is evenly distributed across the frame, a knowledgeable person can easily determine whether a sampling plan has been followed in a study. However, a problem with systematic sampling can occur if the data are subject to any periodicity, and the sampling interval is in syncopation with it. In such a case, the sampling would be nonrandom. For example, if a list of 150 college students is actually a merged list of five classes with 30 students in each class and if each of the lists of the five classes has been ordered with the names of top students first and bottom students last, then systematic sampling of every 30th student could cause selection of all top students, all bottom students, or all mediocre students; that is, the original list is subject to a cyclical or periodic organization. Systematic sampling methodology is based on the assumption that the source of population elements is random.

Cluster (or Area) Sampling

Cluster (or area) sampling is a fourth type of random sampling. **Cluster (or area) sampling** involves dividing the population into nonoverlapping areas or clusters. However, in contrast to stratified random sampling where strata are homogeneous, cluster sampling identifies clusters that tend to be internally heterogeneous. In theory, each cluster contains a wide variety of elements, and the cluster is a miniature, or microcosm, of the population. Examples of clusters are towns, companies, homes, colleges, areas of a city, and geographic regions. Often clusters are naturally occurring groups of the population and are already identified, such as states or Standard Metropolitan Statistical Areas. Although area sampling usually refers to clusters that are areas of the population, such as geographic regions and cities, the terms *cluster sampling* and *area sampling* are used interchangeably in this text.

After choosing the clusters, the researcher randomly selects individual elements into the sample from the clusters. One example of business research that makes use of clustering is test marketing of new products. Often in test marketing, the United States is divided into clusters of test market cities, and individual consumers within the test market cities are surveyed. Figure 7.2 shows some U.S. test market cities that are used as clusters to test products. The Statistics in Business Today feature on test market cities discusses some of the more frequently researched U.S. cities.

Sometimes the clusters are too large, and a second set of clusters is taken from each original cluster. This technique is called **two-stage sampling.** For example, a researcher could divide the United States into clusters of cities. She could then divide the cities into clusters of blocks and randomly select individual houses from the block clusters. The first stage is selecting the test cities and the second stage is selecting the blocks.

Cluster or area sampling offers several advantages. Two of the foremost advantages are convenience and cost. Clusters are usually convenient to obtain, and the cost of sampling from the entire population is reduced because the scope of the study is reduced to the clusters. The cost per element is usually lower in cluster or area sampling than in stratified sampling because of lower element listing or locating costs. The time and cost of contacting elements of the population can be reduced, especially if travel is involved, because clustering reduces the distance to the sampled elements. In addition, administration of the sample survey can be simplified. Sometimes cluster or area sampling is the only feasible approach because the sampling frames of the individual elements of the population are unavailable and therefore other random sampling techniques cannot be used.

Cluster or area sampling also has several disadvantages. If the elements of a cluster are similar, cluster sampling may be statistically less efficient than simple random sampling. In an extreme case—when the elements of a cluster are the same—sampling from the cluster may be no better than sampling a single unit from the cluster. Moreover, the costs and problems of statistical analysis are greater with cluster or area sampling than with simple random sampling.

Nonrandom Sampling

Sampling techniques used to select elements from the population by any mechanism that does not involve a random selection process are called **nonrandom sampling techniques.** Because chance is not used to select items from the samples, these techniques are nonprobability techniques and are not desirable for use in gathering data to be analyzed by the methods of

FIGURE 7.2

Some Test Market Cities

Test Market Cities

Particular cities are chosen as test markets for a variety of reasons, including demographics, psychographics, familiarity, convenience, and others. The most surveyed metropolitan area in the United States is Odessa–Midland, Texas, where residents receive more calls per capita than those in any other area. Odessa–Midland is followed by Portland, Maine, and Boulder–Longmont, Colorado, respectively. The table shows the 10 most surveyed metropolitan areas according to Survey Sampling of Fairfield, Connecticut.

The most surveyed cities are not necessarily the most representative of the United States. Tulsa is not one of the most surveyed cities but is believed to be the city that comes closest to the national demographic profile in terms of population, age, ethnicity, and housing values. The runner-up is Charleston, West Virginia.

Market researchers have different criteria for selecting test market cities. Some of the rationale is proprietary. A test market is sometimes chosen because the company has used that city in a previous test and the product went on to be successful. Other markets are convenient or comfortable to the researcher.

Certain products are targeted toward particular demographic or psychographic segments of the population. The selection of a test market city might be based on which city has the highest number or proportion of people in those targeted segments. Still other factors can enter into the selection of a test market city. Spill-in occurs when two or more markets are so close together that people from other areas come "in" to shop. Spill-over occurs when a test market is influenced by media from other areas. Both are problems that are taken into consideration in selecting a test market city. For example, even though Baltimore is the number one city psychographically, it is affected by spill-in from Washington, D.C., so the Baltimore market is difficult to isolate and study without taking Washington, D.C., into consideration. For this reason and others, *Marketing News* rated Boise, Idaho, as one of the best places to market consumer goods in the United States. It is a microcosm of the nation, yet is an isolated media island that allows for research design control.

MOST SURVEYED METROPOLITAN AREAS

Rank	Metropolitan Area
1	Odessa–Midland, TX
2	Portland, ME
3	Boulder–Longmont, CO
4	Grand Forks, ND–MN
5	Phoenix–Mesa, AZ
6	Denver, CO
7	Fargo–Moorhead, ND–MN
8	Boise, ID
9	Tucson, AZ
10	Pittsfield, MA

inferential statistics presented in this text. Sampling error cannot be determined objectively for these sampling techniques. Four nonrandom sampling techniques are presented here: convenience sampling, judgment sampling, quota sampling, and snowball sampling.

Convenience Sampling

In **convenience sampling,** *elements for the sample are selected for the convenience of the researcher.* The researcher typically chooses elements that are readily available, nearby, or willing to participate. The sample tends to be less variable than the population because in many environments the extreme elements of the population are not readily available. The researcher will select more elements from the middle of the population. For example, a convenience sample of homes for door-to-door interviews might include houses where people are at home, houses with no dogs, houses near the street, first-floor apartments, and houses with friendly people. In contrast, a random sample would require the researcher to gather data only from houses and apartments that have been selected randomly, no matter how inconvenient or unfriendly the location. If a research firm is located in a mall, a convenience sample might be selected by interviewing only shoppers who pass the shop and look friendly.

Judgment Sampling

Judgment sampling occurs when *elements selected for the sample are chosen by the judgment of the researcher.* Researchers often believe they can obtain a representative sample by using sound judgment, which will result in saving time and money. Sometimes ethical, professional researchers might believe they can select a more representative sample than the random process will provide. They might be right! However, some studies show that random sampling methods outperform judgment sampling in estimating the population mean even when the researcher who is administering the judgment sampling is trying to put together a representative sample. When sampling is done by judgment, calculating the probability that an element is going to be selected into the sample is not possible. The sampling error cannot be determined objectively because probabilities are based on *nonrandom* selection.

Other problems are associated with judgment sampling. The researcher tends to make errors of judgment in one direction. These systematic errors lead to what are called *biases*. The researcher also is unlikely to include extreme elements. Judgment sampling provides no objective method for determining whether one person's judgment is better than another's.

Quota Sampling

A third nonrandom sampling technique is **quota sampling,** which appears to be similar to stratified random sampling. Certain population subclasses, such as age group, gender, or geographic region, are used as strata. However, instead of randomly sampling from each stratum, the researcher uses a nonrandom sampling method to gather data from one stratum until the desired quota of samples is filled. Quotas are described by quota controls, which set the sizes of the samples to be obtained from the subgroups. Generally, a quota is based on the proportions of the subclasses in the population. In this case, the quota concept is similar to that of proportional stratified sampling.

Quotas often are filled by using available, recent, or applicable elements. For example, instead of randomly interviewing people to obtain a quota of Italian Americans, the researcher would go to the Italian area of the city and interview there until enough responses are obtained to fill the quota. In quota sampling, an interviewer would begin by asking a few filter questions; if the respondent represents a subclass whose quota has been filled, the interviewer would terminate the interview.

Quota sampling can be useful if no frame is available for the population. For example, suppose a researcher wants to stratify the population into owners of different types of cars but fails to find any lists of Toyota van owners. Through quota sampling, the researcher would proceed by interviewing all car owners and casting out non–Toyota van owners until the quota of Toyota van owners is filled.

Quota sampling is less expensive than most random sampling techniques because it essentially is a technique of convenience. However, cost may not be meaningful because the quality of nonrandom and random sampling techniques cannot be compared. Another advantage of quota sampling is the speed of data gathering. The researcher does not have to call back or send out a second questionnaire if he does not receive a response; he just moves on to the next element. Also, preparatory work for quota sampling is minimal.

The main problem with quota sampling is that, when all is said and done, it still is only a *nonrandom* sampling technique. Some researchers believe that if the quota is filled by *randomly* selecting elements and discarding those not from a stratum, quota sampling is essentially a version of stratified random sampling. However, most quota sampling is carried out by the researcher going where the quota can be filled quickly. The object is to gain the benefits of stratification without the high field costs of stratification. Ultimately, it remains a nonprobability sampling method.

Snowball Sampling

Another nonrandom sampling technique is **snowball sampling,** in which *survey subjects are selected based on referral from other survey respondents.* The researcher identifies a person who fits the profile of subjects wanted for the study. The researcher then asks this person for the names and locations of others who would also fit the profile of subjects wanted for the study. Through these referrals, survey subjects can be identified cheaply and efficiently, which is particularly useful when survey subjects are difficult to locate. It is the main advantage of snowball sampling; its main disadvantage is that it is nonrandom.

Sampling Error

Sampling error occurs *when the sample is not representative of the population.* When random sampling techniques are used to select elements for the sample, sampling error occurs by chance. Many times the statistic computed on the sample is not an accurate estimate of the population parameter because the sample was not representative of the population. This result is caused by sampling error. With random samples, sampling error can be computed and analyzed.

Nonsampling Errors

All errors other than sampling errors are **nonsampling errors.** The many possible nonsampling errors include missing data, recording errors, input processing errors, and analysis errors. Other nonsampling errors result from the measurement instrument, such as errors of unclear definitions, defective questionnaires, and poorly conceived concepts. Improper definition of the frame is a nonsampling error. In many cases, finding a frame that perfectly fits the population is impossible. Insofar as it does not fit, a nonsampling error has been committed.

Response errors are also nonsampling errors. They occur when people do not know, will not say, or overstate. Virtually no statistical method is available to measure or control for nonsampling errors. The statistical techniques presented in this text are based on the assumption that none of these nonsampling errors were committed. The researcher must eliminate these errors through carefully planning and executing the research study.

7.1 PROBLEMS

7.1 Develop a frame for the population of each of the following research projects.
  a. Measuring the job satisfaction of all union employees in a company
  b. Conducting a telephone survey in Utica, New York, to determine the level of interest in opening a new hunting and fishing specialty store in the mall
  c. Interviewing passengers of a major airline about its food service
  d. Studying the quality control programs of boat manufacturers
  e. Attempting to measure the corporate culture of cable television companies

7.2 Make a list of 20 people you know. Include men and women, various ages, various educational levels, and so on. Number the list and then use the random number list in Table 7.1 to select six people randomly from your list. How representative of the population is the sample? Find the proportion of men in your population and in your sample. How do the proportions compare? Find the proportion of 20-year-olds in your sample and the proportion in the population. How do they compare?

7.3 Use the random numbers in Table A.1 of Appendix A to select 10 of the companies from the 30 companies listed in Table 7.2. Compare the types of companies in your sample with the types in the population. How representative of the population is your sample?

7.4 For each of the following research projects, list three variables for stratification of the sample.
  a. A nationwide study of motels and hotels is being conducted. An attempt will be made to determine the extent of the availability of online links for customers. A sample of motels and hotels will be taken.
  b. A consumer panel is to be formed by sampling people in Michigan. Members of the panel will be interviewed periodically in an effort to understand current consumer attitudes and behaviors.
  c. A large soft drink company wants to study the characteristics of the U.S. bottlers of its products, but the company does not want to conduct a census.

d. The business research bureau of a large university is conducting a project in which the bureau will sample paper-manufacturing companies.

7.5 In each of the following cases, the variable represents one way that a sample can be stratified in a study. For each variable, list some strata into which the variable can be divided.

a. Age of respondent (person)
b. Size of company (sales volume)
c. Size of retail outlet (square feet)
d. Geographic location
e. Occupation of respondent (person)
f. Type of business (company)

7.6 A city's telephone book lists 100,000 people. If the telephone book is the frame for a study, how large would the sample size be if systematic sampling were done on every 200th person?

7.7 If every 11th item is systematically sampled to produce a sample size of 75 items, approximately how large is the population?

7.8 If a company employs 3,500 people and if a random sample of 175 of these employees has been taken by systematic sampling, what is the value of k? The researcher would start the sample selection between what two values? Where could the researcher obtain a frame for this study?

7.9 For each of the following research projects, list at least one area or cluster that could be used in obtaining the sample.

a. A study of road conditions in the state of Missouri
b. A study of U.S. offshore oil wells
c. A study of the environmental effects of petrochemical plants west of the Mississippi River

7.10 Give an example of how judgment sampling could be used in a study to determine how district attorneys feel about attorneys advertising on television.

7.11 Give an example of how convenience sampling could be used in a study of *Fortune* 500 executives to measure corporate attitude toward paternity leave for employees.

7.12 Give an example of how quota sampling could be used to conduct sampling by a company test marketing a new personal computer.

7.2 SAMPLING DISTRIBUTION OF $\bar{x}$

In the inferential statistics process, a researcher selects a random sample from the population, computes a statistic on the sample, and reaches conclusions about the population parameter from the statistic. In attempting to analyze the sample statistic, it is essential to know the distribution of the statistic. So far we studied several distributions, including the binomial distribution, the Poisson distribution, the hypergeometric distribution, the uniform distribution, the normal distribution, and the exponential distribution.

In this section we explore the sample mean, $\bar{x}$, as the statistic. The sample mean is one of the more common statistics used in the inferential process. To compute and assign the probability of occurrence of a particular value of a sample mean, the researcher must know the distribution of the sample means. One way to examine the distribution possibilities is to take a population with a particular distribution, randomly select samples of a given size, compute the sample means, and attempt to determine how the means are distributed.

Suppose a small finite population consists of only $N = 8$ numbers:

54   55   59   63   64   68   69   70

Using an Excel-produced histogram, we can see the shape of the distribution of this population of data.

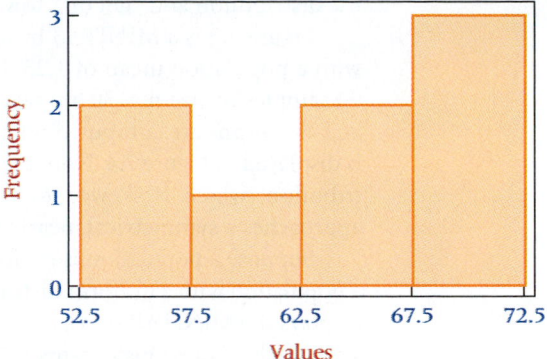

Suppose we take all possible samples of size $n = 2$ from this population with replacement. The result is the following pairs of data.

(54,54)	(55,54)	(59,54)	(63,54)
(54,55)	(55,55)	(59,55)	(63,55)
(54,59)	(55,59)	(59,59)	(63,59)
(54,63)	(55,63)	(59,63)	(63,63)
(54,64)	(55,64)	(59,64)	(63,64)
(54,68)	(55,68)	(59,68)	(63,68)
(54,69)	(55,69)	(59,69)	(63,69)
(54,70)	(55,70)	(59,70)	(63,70)
(64,54)	(68,54)	(69,54)	(70,54)
(64,55)	(68,55)	(69,55)	(70,55)
(64,59)	(68,59)	(69,59)	(70,59)
(64,63)	(68,63)	(69,63)	(70,63)
(64,64)	(68,64)	(69,64)	(70,64)
(64,68)	(68,68)	(69,68)	(70,68)
(64,69)	(68,69)	(69,69)	(70,69)
(64,70)	(68,70)	(69,70)	(70,70)

The means of each of these samples follow.

54	54.5	56.5	58.5	59	61	61.5	62
54.5	55	57	59	59.5	61.5	62	62.5
56.5	57	59	61	61.5	63.5	64	64.5
58.5	59	61	63	63.5	65.5	66	66.5
59	59.5	61.5	63.5	64	66	66.5	67
60	61.5	63.5	65.5	66	68	68.5	69
61.5	62	64	66	66.5	68.5	69	69.5
62	62.5	64.5	66.5	67	69	69.5	70

Again using an Excel-produced histogram, we can see the shape of the distribution of these sample means.

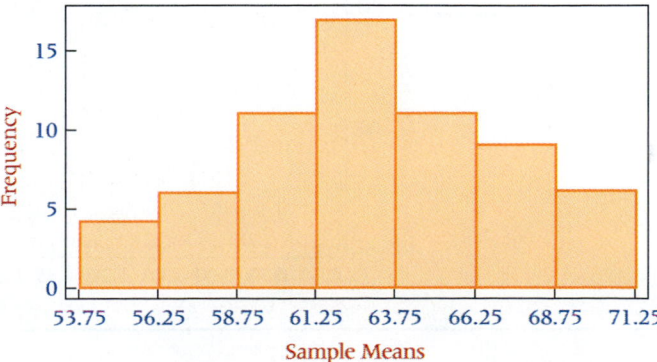

Notice that the shape of the histogram for sample means is quite unlike the shape of the histogram for the population. The sample means appear to "pile up" toward the middle of the distribution and "tail off" toward the extremes.

Figure 7.3 is a MINITAB histogram of the data from a Poisson distribution of values with a population mean of 1.25. Note that the histogram is skewed to the right. Suppose 90 samples of size $n = 30$ are taken randomly from a Poisson distribution with $\lambda = 1.25$ and the means are computed on each sample. The resulting distribution of sample means is displayed in Figure 7.4. Notice that although the samples were drawn from a Poisson distribution, which is skewed to the right, the sample means form a distribution that approaches a symmetrical, nearly normal-curve-type distribution.

Suppose a population is uniformly distributed. If samples are selected randomly from a population with a uniform distribution, how are the sample means distributed? Figure 7.5 displays the MINITAB histogram distributions of sample means from five different sample sizes. Each of these histograms represents the distribution of sample means from 90 samples generated randomly from a uniform distribution in which $a = 10$ and $b = 30$. Observe the shape of the distributions. Notice that even for small sample sizes, the distributions of sample means for samples taken from the uniformly distributed population begin to "pile up" in the middle. As sample sizes become much larger, the sample mean distributions begin to approach a normal distribution and the variation among the means decreases.

So far, we examined three populations with different distributions. However, the sample means for samples taken from these populations appear to be approximately normally distributed, especially as the sample sizes become larger. What would happen to the distribution of sample means if we studied populations with differently shaped distributions? The answer to that question is given in the **central limit theorem.**

FIGURE 7.3

MINITAB Histogram of a Poisson Distributed Population, $\lambda = 1.25$

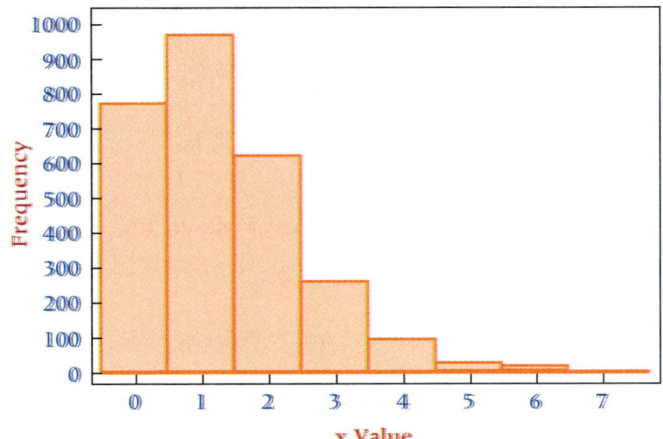

FIGURE 7.4

MINITAB Histogram of Sample Means

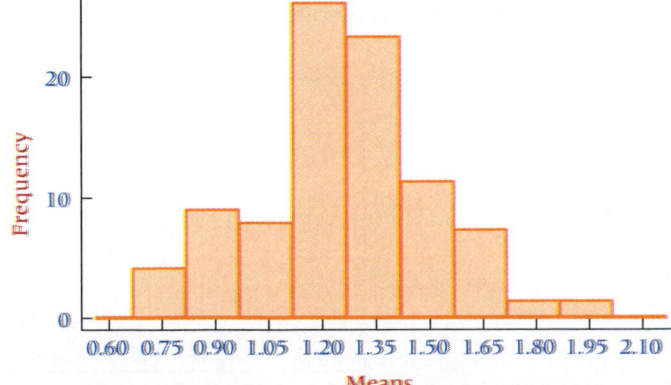

FIGURE 7.5   MINITAB Outputs for Sample Means from 90 Samples Ranging in Size from $n = 2$ to $n = 30$ from a Uniformly Distributed Population with $a = 10$ and $b = 30$

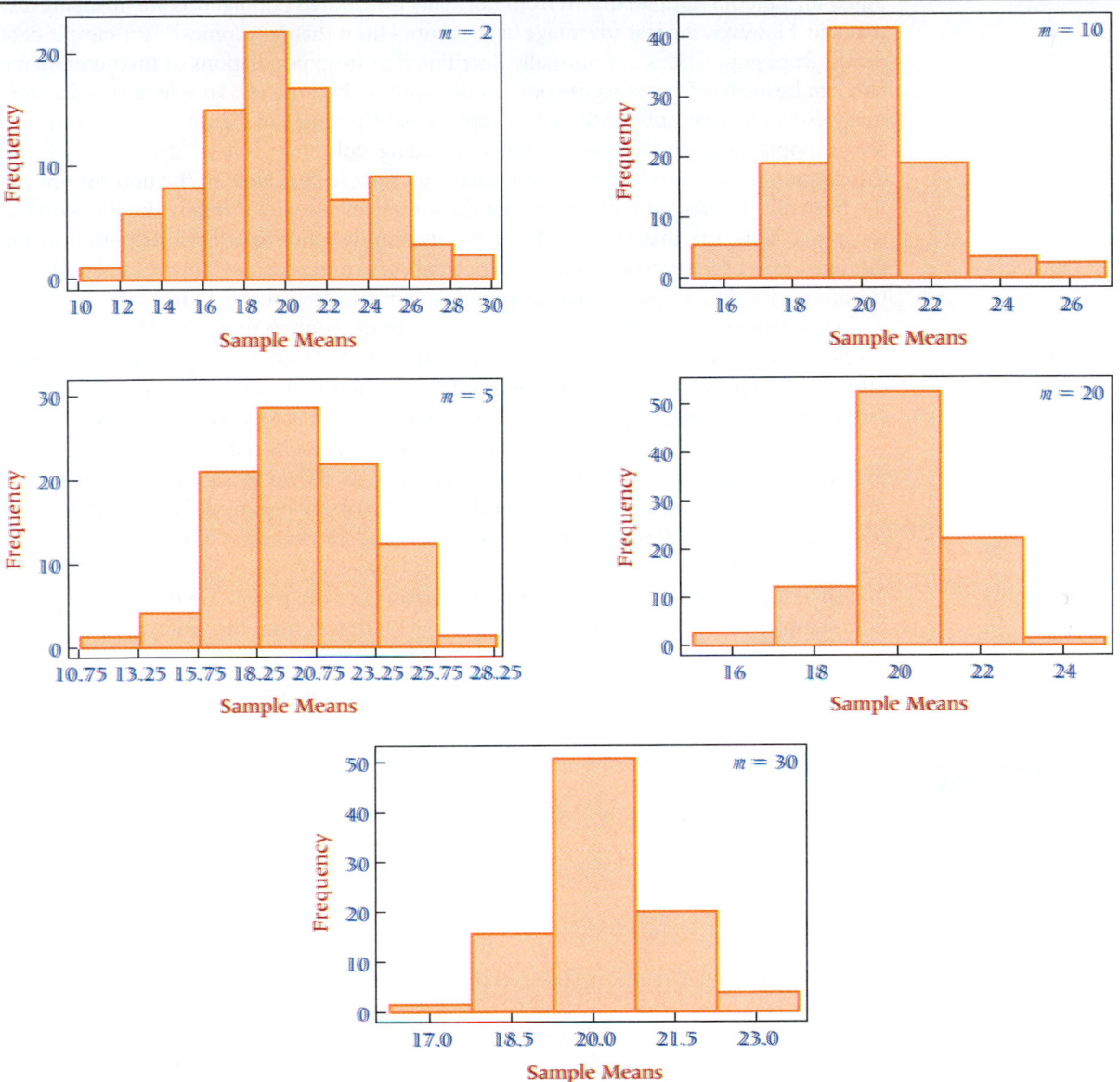

CENTRAL LIMIT THEOREM	If samples of size n are drawn randomly from a population that has a mean of μ and a standard deviation of σ, the sample means, $\bar{x}$, are approximately normally distributed for sufficiently large sample sizes ($n \geq 30$) regardless of the shape of the population distribution. If the population is normally distributed, the sample means are normally distributed for any size sample.

From mathematical expectation,* it can be shown that the mean of the sample means is the population mean.

$$\mu_{\bar{x}} = \mu$$

and the standard deviation of the sample means (called the standard error of the mean) is the standard deviation of the population divided by the square root of the sample size.

$$\sigma_{\bar{x}} = \frac{\sigma}{\sqrt{n}}$$

*The derivations are beyond the scope of this text and are not shown.

The central limit theorem creates the potential for applying the normal distribution to many problems when sample size is sufficiently large. Sample means that have been computed for random samples drawn from normally distributed populations are normally distributed. However, the real advantage of the central limit theorem comes when sample data drawn from populations not normally distributed or from populations of unknown shape also can be analyzed by using the normal distribution because the sample means are normally distributed for sufficiently large sample sizes.* Column 1 of Figure 7.6 shows four different population distributions. Each succeeding column displays the shape of the distribution of the sample means for a particular sample size. Note in the bottom row for the normally distributed population that the sample means are normally distributed even for $n = 2$. Note also that with the other population distributions, the distribution of the sample means begins to approximate the normal curve as n becomes larger. For all four distributions, the distribution of sample means is approximately normal for $n = 30$.

How large must a sample be for the central limit theorem to apply? The sample size necessary varies according to the shape of the population. However, in this text (as in many others), a sample of *size 30 or larger* will suffice. Recall that if the population is normally distributed, the sample means are normally distributed for sample sizes as small as $n = 1$.

The shapes displayed in Figure 7.6 coincide with the results obtained empirically from the random sampling shown in Figures 7.4 and 7.5. As shown in Figure 7.6, and as indicated in Figure 7.5, as sample size increases, the distribution narrows, or becomes more leptokurtic. This trend makes sense because the standard deviation of the mean is $\sigma/\sqrt{n}$. This value will become smaller as the size of n increases.

In Table 7.4, the means and standard deviations of the means are displayed for random samples of various sizes ($n = 2$ through $n = 30$) drawn from the uniform distribution

---

* The actual form of the central limit theorem is a limit function of calculus. As the sample size increases to infinity, the distribution of sample means literally becomes normal in shape.

FIGURE 7.6

Shapes of the Distributions of Sample Means for Three Sample Sizes Drawn from Four Different Population Distributions

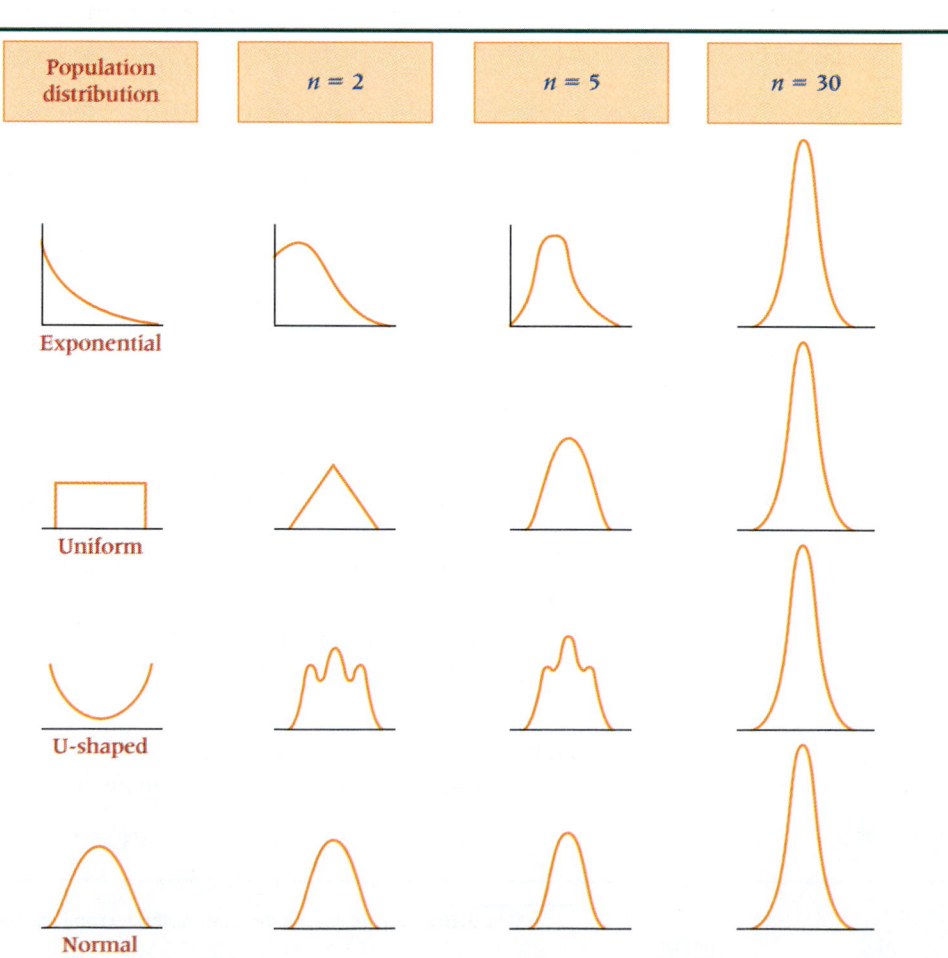

TABLE 7.4	Sample Size	Mean of Sample Means	Standard Deviation of Sample Means	μ	$\dfrac{\sigma}{\sqrt{n}}$
$\mu_{\bar{x}}$ and $\sigma_{\bar{x}}$ of 90 Random Samples for Five Different Sizes*	$n = 2$	19.92	3.87	20	4.08
	$n = 5$	20.17	2.65	20	2.58
	$n = 10$	20.04	1.96	20	1.83
	$n = 20$	20.20	1.37	20	1.29
	$n = 30$	20.25	0.99	20	1.05

*Randomly generated by using MINITAB from a uniform distribution with $a = 10$, $b = 30$.

of $a = 10$ and $b = 30$ shown in Figure 7.5. The population mean is 20, and the standard deviation of the population is 5.774. Note that the mean of the sample means for each sample size is approximately 20 and that the standard deviation of the sample means for each set of 90 samples is approximately equal to $\sigma/\sqrt{n}$. A small discrepancy occurs between the standard deviation of the sample means and $\sigma/\sqrt{n}$, because not all possible samples of a given size were taken from the population (only 90). In theory, if all possible samples for a given sample size are taken exactly once, the mean of the sample means will equal the population mean and the standard deviation of the sample means will equal the population standard deviation divided by the square root of n.

The central limit theorem states that sample means are normally distributed regardless of the shape of the population for large samples and for any sample size with normally distributed populations. Thus, sample means can be analyzed by using z scores. Recall from Chapters 3 and 6 the formula to determine z scores for individual values from a normal distribution:

$$z = \frac{x - \mu}{\sigma}$$

If sample means are normally distributed, the z score formula applied to sample means would be

$$z = \frac{\bar{x} - \mu_{\bar{x}}}{\sigma_{\bar{x}}}$$

This result follows the general pattern of z scores: the difference between the statistic and its mean divided by the statistic's standard deviation. In this formula, the mean of the statistic of interest is $\mu_{\bar{x}}$, and *the standard deviation of the statistic of interest is $\sigma_{\bar{x}}$*, sometimes referred to as **the standard error of the mean.** To determine $\mu_{\bar{x}}$, the researcher would randomly draw out all possible samples of the given size from the population, compute the sample means, and average them. This task is virtually impossible to accomplish in any realistic period of time. Fortunately, $\mu_{\bar{x}}$ equals the population mean, μ, which is easier to access. Likewise, to determine directly the value of $\sigma_{\bar{x}}$, the researcher would take all possible samples of a given

FIGURE 7.7

Graphical Solution to the Tire Store Example

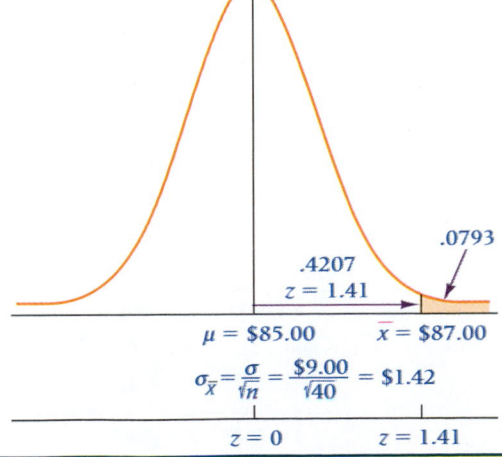

.0793

.4207
$z = 1.41$

$\mu = \$85.00$ $\bar{x} = \$87.00$

$\sigma_{\bar{x}} = \dfrac{\sigma}{\sqrt{n}} = \dfrac{\$9.00}{\sqrt{40}} = \$1.42$

$z = 0$ $z = 1.41$

size from a population, compute the sample means, and determine the standard deviation of sample means. This task also is practically impossible. Fortunately, $\sigma_{\bar{x}}$ can be computed by using the population standard deviation divided by the square root of the sample size.

As sample size increases, the standard deviation of the sample means becomes smaller and smaller because the population standard deviation is being divided by larger and larger values of the square root of n. The ultimate benefit of the central limit theorem is a practical, useful version of the z formula for sample means.

z **FORMULA FOR SAMPLE MEANS**	$$z = \dfrac{\bar{x} - \mu}{\dfrac{\sigma}{\sqrt{n}}}$$

When the population is normally distributed and the sample size is 1, this formula for sample means becomes the z formula for individual values that we used in Chapter 6. The reason is that the mean of one value is that value, and when $n = 1$ the value of $\sigma/\sqrt{n} = \sigma$.

Suppose, for example, that the mean expenditure per customer at a tire store is $85.00, with a standard deviation of $9.00. If a random sample of 40 customers is taken, what is the probability that the sample average expenditure per customer for this sample will be $87.00 or more? Because the sample size is greater than 30, the central limit theorem can be used, and the sample means are normally distributed. With $\mu = \$85.00$, $\sigma = \$9.00$, and the z formula for sample means, z is computed as

$$z = \frac{\bar{x} - \mu}{\dfrac{\sigma}{\sqrt{n}}} = \frac{\$87.00 - \$85.00}{\dfrac{\$9.00}{\sqrt{40}}} = \frac{\$2.00}{\$1.42} = 1.41$$

From the z distribution (Table A.5), $z = 1.41$ produces a probability of .4207. This number is the probability of getting a sample mean between $87.00 and $85.00 (the population mean). Solving for the tail of the distribution yields

$$.5000 - .4207 = .0793$$

which is the probability of $\bar{x} \geq \$87.00$. That is, 7.93% of the time, a random sample of 40 customers from this population will yield a sample mean expenditure of $87.00 or more. Figure 7.7 shows the problem and its solution.

DEMONSTRATION PROBLEM 7.1

Suppose that during any hour in a large department store, the average number of shoppers is 448, with a standard deviation of 21 shoppers. What is the probability that a random sample of 49 different shopping hours will yield a sample mean between 441 and 446 shoppers?

Solution

For this problem, $\mu = 448$, $\sigma = 21$, and $n = 49$. The problem is to determine $P(441 \leq \bar{x} \leq 446)$. The following diagram depicts the problem.

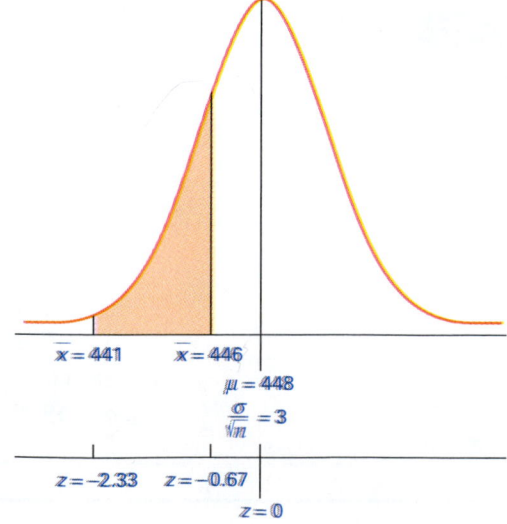

Solve this problem by calculating the *z* scores and using Table A.5 to determine the probabilities.

$$z = \frac{441 - 448}{\frac{21}{\sqrt{49}}} = \frac{-7}{3} = -2.33$$

and

$$z = \frac{446 - 448}{\frac{21}{\sqrt{49}}} = \frac{-2}{3} = -0.67$$

z Value	Probability
−2.33	.4901
−0.67	−.2486
	.2415

The probability of a value being between $z = -2.33$ and −0.67 is .2415; that is, there is a 24.15% chance of randomly selecting 49 hourly periods for which the sample mean is between 441 and 446 shoppers.

Sampling from a Finite Population

The example shown in this section and Demonstration Problem 7.1 was based on the assumption that the population was infinitely or extremely large. In cases of a finite population, *a statistical adjustment can be made to the z formula for sample means.* The adjustment is called the **finite correction factor:** $\sqrt{(N-n)/(N-1)}$. It operates on the standard deviation of sample means, $\sigma_{\bar{x}}$. Following is the *z* formula for sample means when samples are drawn from finite populations.

Z FORMULA FOR SAMPLE MEANS OF A FINITE POPULATION	$z = \dfrac{\bar{x} - \mu}{\dfrac{\sigma}{\sqrt{n}}\sqrt{\dfrac{N-n}{N-1}}}$

If a random sample of size 35 were taken from a finite population of only 500, the sample mean would be less likely to deviate from the population mean than would be the case if a sample of size 35 were taken from an infinite population. For a sample of size 35 taken from a finite population of size 500, the finite correction factor is

$$\sqrt{\frac{500 - 35}{500 - 1}} = \sqrt{\frac{465}{499}} = .965$$

TABLE 7.5			
Finite Correction Factor for Some Sample Sizes	**Population Size**	**Sample Size**	**Value of Correction Factor**
	2000	30 (<5%N)	.993
	2000	500	.866
	500	30	.971
	500	200	.775
	200	30	.924
	200	75	.793

Thus the standard deviation of the mean—sometimes referred to as the standard error of the mean—is adjusted downward by using .965. As the size of the finite population becomes larger in relation to sample size, the finite correction factor approaches 1. In theory, whenever researchers are working with a finite population, they can use the finite correction factor. A rough rule of thumb for many researchers is that, if the sample size is less than 5% of the finite population size or $n/N < 0.05$, the finite correction factor does not significantly modify the solution. Table 7.5 contains some illustrative finite correction factors.

DEMONSTRATION PROBLEM 7.2	A production company's 350 hourly employees average 37.6 years of age, with a standard deviation of 8.3 years. If a random sample of 45 hourly employees is taken, what is the probability that the sample will have an average age of less than 40 years?

Solution

The population mean is 37.6, with a population standard deviation of 8.3; that is, $\mu = 37.6$ and $\sigma = 8.3$. The sample size is 45, but it is being drawn from a finite population of 350; that is, $n = 45$ and $N = 350$. The sample mean under consideration is 40, or $\bar{x} = 40$. The following diagram depicts the problem on a normal curve.

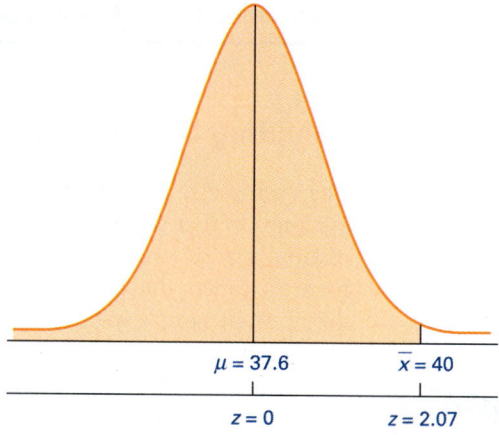

$$\mu = 37.6 \qquad \bar{x} = 40$$
$$z = 0 \qquad z = 2.07$$

Using the *z* formula with the finite correction factor gives

$$z = \frac{40 - 37.6}{\dfrac{8.3}{\sqrt{45}}\sqrt{\dfrac{350 - 45}{350 - 1}}} = \frac{2.4}{1.157} = 2.07$$

This *z* value yields a probability (Table A.5) of .4808. Therefore, the probability of getting a sample average age of less than 40 years is .4808 + .5000 = .9808. Had the finite correction factor not been used, the z value would have been 1.94, and the final answer would have been .9738.

7.2 PROBLEMS

7.13   A population has a mean of 50 and a standard deviation of 10. If a random sample of 64 is taken, what is the probability that the sample mean is each of the following?

   a.   Greater than 52

   b.   Less than 51

   c.   Less than 47

   d.   Between 48.5 and 52.4

   e.   Between 50.6 and 51.3

7.14   A population is normally distributed, with a mean of 23.45 and a standard deviation of 3.8. What is the probability of each of the following?

a.   Taking a sample of size 10 and obtaining a sample mean of 22 or more

b.   Taking a sample of size 4 and getting a sample mean of more than 26

7.15   Suppose a random sample of size 36 is drawn from a population with a mean of 278. If 86% of the time the sample mean is less than 280, what is the population standard deviation?

7.16   A random sample of size 81 is drawn from a population with a standard deviation of 12. If only 18% of the time a sample mean greater than 300 is obtained, what is the mean of the population?

7.17   Find the probability in each case.

a. $N = 1000$, $n = 60$, $\mu = 75$, and $\sigma = 6$; $P(\bar{x} < 76.5) = ?$

b. $N = 90$, $n = 36$, $\mu = 108$, and $\sigma = 3.46$; $P(107 < \bar{x} < 107.7) = ?$

c. $N = 250$, $n = 100$, $\mu = 35.6$, and $\sigma = 4.89$; $P(\bar{x} \geq 36) = ?$

d. $N = 5000$, $n = 60$, $\mu = 125$, and $\sigma = 13.4$; $P(\bar{x} \leq 125) = ?$

7.18   The Statistical Abstract of the United States published by the U.S. Census Bureau reports that the average annual consumption of fresh fruit per person is 99.9 pounds. The standard deviation of fresh fruit consumption is about 30 pounds. Suppose a researcher took a random sample of 38 people and had them keep a record of the fresh fruit they ate for one year.

a.   What is the probability that the sample average would be less than 90 pounds?

b.   What is the probability that the sample average would be between 98 and 105 pounds?

c.   What is the probability that the sample average would be less than 112 pounds?

d.   What is the probability that the sample average would be between 93 and 96 pounds?

7.19   Suppose a subdivision on the southwest side of Denver, Colorado, contains 1,500 houses. The subdivision was built in 1983. A sample of 100 houses is selected randomly and evaluated by an appraiser. If the mean appraised value of a house in this subdivision for all houses is $177,000, with a standard deviation of $8,500, what is the probability that the sample average is greater than $185,000?

7.20   Suppose the average checkout tab at a large supermarket is $65.12, with a standard deviation of $21.45. Twenty-three percent of the time when a random sample of 45 customer tabs is examined, the sample average should exceed what value?

7.21   According to Nielsen Media Research, the average number of hours of TV viewing per household per week in the United States is 50.4 hours. Suppose the standard deviation is 11.8 hours and a random sample of 42 U.S. households is taken.

a.   What is the probability that the sample average is more than 52 hours?

b.   What is the probability that the sample average is less than 47.5 hours?

c.   What is the probability that the sample average is less than 40 hours? If the sample average actually is less than 40 hours, what would it mean in terms of the Nielsen Media Research figures?

d.   Suppose the population standard deviation is unknown. If 71% of all sample means are greater than 49 hours and the population mean is still 50.4 hours, what is the value of the population standard deviation?

7.3 SAMPLING DISTRIBUTION OF $\hat{p}$

Sometimes in analyzing a sample, a researcher will choose to use the sample proportion, denoted $\hat{p}$. If research produces *measurable* data such as weight, distance, time, and income, the sample mean is often the statistic of choice. However, if research results in

FIGURE 7.8

Graphical Solution to the
Electrical Contractor Example

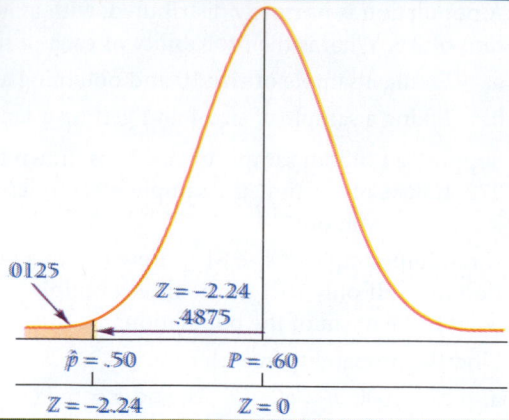

countable items such as how many people in a sample choose Dr. Pepper as their soft drink
or how many people in a sample have a flexible work schedule, the sample proportion is
often the statistic of choice. Whereas the mean is computed by averaging a set of values,
the **sample proportion** is *computed by dividing the frequency with which a given characteristic occurs in a sample by the number of items in the sample.*

SAMPLE PROPORTION

$$\hat{p} = \frac{x}{n}$$

where

x = number of items in a sample that have the characteristic
n = number of items in the sample

For example, in a sample of 100 factory workers, 30 workers might belong to a union.
The value of $\hat{p}$ for this characteristic, union membership, is $30/100 = .30$. In a sample of
500 businesses in suburban malls, if 10 are shoe stores, then the sample proportion of shoe
stores is $10/500 = .02$. The sample proportion is a widely used statistic and is usually computed on questions involving Yes or No answers. For example, do you have at least a high
school education? Are you predominantly right-handed? Are you female? Do you belong
to the student accounting association?

How does a researcher use the sample proportion in analysis? The central limit theorem applies to sample proportions in that the normal distribution approximates the shape
of the distribution of sample proportions if $n \cdot p > 5$ and $n \cdot q > 5$ (p is the population proportion and $q = 1 - p$). The mean of sample proportions for all samples of size n randomly
drawn from a population is p (the population proportion) and the standard deviation of
sample proportions is $\sqrt{(p \cdot q)/n}$, sometimes referred to as the **standard error of the proportion.** Sample proportions also have a z formula.

**z FORMULA FOR SAMPLE
PROPORTIONS FOR $n \cdot P > 5$
AND $n \cdot Q > 5$**

$$z = \frac{\hat{p} - p}{\sqrt{\dfrac{p \cdot q}{n}}}$$

where

$\hat{p}$ = sample proportion
n = sample size
p = population proportion
q = $1 - p$

Suppose 60% of the electrical contractors in a region use a particular brand of wire.
What is the probability of taking a random sample of size 120 from these electrical contractors and finding that .50 or less use that brand of wire? For this problem,

$$p = .60 \quad \hat{p} = .50 \quad n = 120$$

The z formula yields

$$z = \frac{.50 - .60}{\sqrt{\dfrac{(.60)(.40)}{120}}} = \frac{-.10}{.0447} = -2.24$$

From Table A.5, the probability corresponding to $z = -2.24$ is .4875. For $z < -2.24$ (the tail of the distribution), the answer is $.5000 - .4875 = .0125$. Figure 7.8 shows the problem and solution graphically.

This answer indicates that a researcher would have difficulty (probability of .0125) finding that 50% or less of a sample of 120 contractors use a given brand of wire if indeed the population market share for that wire is .60. If this sample result actually occurs, either it is a rare chance result, the .60 proportion does not hold for this population, or the sampling method may not have been random.

DEMONSTRATION PROBLEM 7.3	If 10% of a population of parts is defective, what is the probability of randomly selecting 80 parts and finding that 12 or more parts are defective?

Solution

Here, $p = .10$, $\hat{p} = 12/80 = .15$, and $n = 80$. Entering these values in the z formula yields

$$z = \frac{.15 - .10}{\sqrt{\dfrac{(.10)(.90)}{80}}} = \frac{.05}{.0335} = 1.49$$

Table A.5 gives a probability of .4319 for a z value of 1.49, which is the area between the sample proportion, .15, and the population proportion, .10. The answer to the question is

$$P(\hat{p} \geq .15) = .5000 - .4319 = .0681.$$

Thus, about 6.81% of the time, 12 or more defective parts would appear in a random sample of 80 parts when the population proportion is .10. If this result actually occurred, the 10% proportion for population defects would be open to question. The diagram shows the problem graphically.

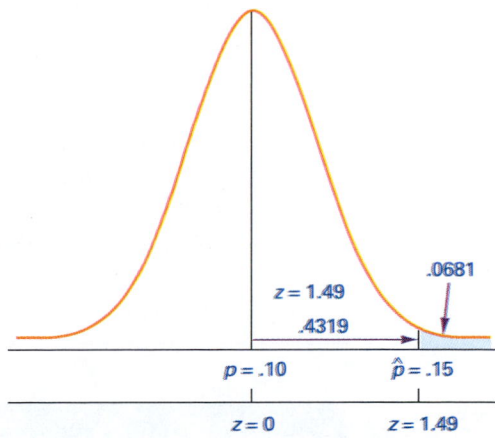

7.3 PROBLEMS

7.22 A given population proportion is .25. For the given value of n, what is the probability of getting each of the following sample proportions?

  a. $n = 110$ and $\hat{p} \leq .21$
  b. $n = 33$ and $\hat{p} > .24$

    c. $n = 59$ and $.24 \leq \hat{p} < .27$

    d. $n = 80$ and $\hat{p} > .30$

    e. $n = 800$ and $\hat{p} > .30$

7.23 A population proportion is .58. Suppose a random sample of 660 items is sampled randomly from this population.

    a. What is the probability that the sample proportion is greater than .60?

    b. What is the probability that the sample proportion is between .55 and .65?

    c. What is the probability that the sample proportion is greater than .57?

    d. What is the probability that the sample proportion is between .53 and .56?

    e. What is the probability that the sample proportion is less than .48?

7.24 Suppose a population proportion is .40, and 80% of the time when you draw a random sample from this population you get a sample proportion of .35 or more. How large a sample were you taking?

7.25 If a population proportion is .28 and if the sample size is 140, 30% of the time the sample proportion will be less than what value if you are taking random samples?

7.26 According to a study by Decision Analyst, 21% of the people who have credit cards are very close to the total limit on the card(s). Suppose a random sample of 600 credit card users is taken. What is the probability that more than 150 credit card users are very close to the total limit on their card(s)?

7.27 According to a survey by Accountemps, 48% of executives believe that employees are most productive on Tuesdays. Suppose 200 executives are randomly surveyed.

    a. What is the probability that fewer than 90 of the executives believe employees are most productive on Tuesdays.

    b. What is the probability that more than 100 of the executives believe employees are most productive on Tuesdays.

    c. What is the probability that more than 80 of the executives believe employees are most productive on Tuesdays

7.28 The Travel Weekly International Air Transport Association survey asked business travelers about the purpose for their most recent business trip. Nineteen percent responded that it was for an internal company visit. Suppose 950 business travelers are randomly selected.

    a. What is the probability that more than 25% of the business travelers say that the reason for their most recent business trip was an internal company visit?

    b. What is the probability that between 15% and 20% of the business travelers say that the reason for their most recent business trip was an internal company visit?

    c. What is the probability that between 133 and 171 of the business travelers say that the reason for their most recent business trip was an internal company visit?

Surveying Maquiladora Workers

Because of limited resources, limited time, and a large population of workers, most work attitude and cultural studies of maquiladora workers probably would be accomplished through the use of random sampling. To ensure the inclusion of certain groups and in an effort to reduce sampling error, a proportionate stratified sampling technique might be selected. Such a sampling plan could include as strata such things as geographic location of the border city (Texas, New Mexico, Arizona, California), size of the city, type of industry, size of the plant, number of maquiladora workers at that facility, age of the worker, gender of the worker, level of responsibility of the worker, and other seemingly important variables.

Each company is likely to have a complete list of all workers. These lists could serve as a frame for the study. If granted permission to use the lists, the researcher could then identify strata within the lists and randomly sample workers from those lists.

Attitude and culture questions are not easy to formulate in a way that produces valid data. Experts on the measurement of such things should be consulted. However, if questions were asked in a way that produced numerical responses that could be averaged, sample means could be computed. If sample sizes were large enough, the central limit theorem could be invoked, enabling the researcher to analyze mean sample responses as though they came from normally distributed populations.

Suppose a stratified random sample of 50 maquiladora workers produces a mean age of 26.9 years. If the population mean age of these workers is 28.1 years with a standard deviation of 8.4 years, what is the probability that a researcher would get a sample mean of 26.9 years or less? The techniques of this chapter can be applied to obtain the following probability:

$$z = \frac{\bar{x} - \mu}{\frac{\sigma}{\sqrt{n}}} = \frac{26.9 - 28.1}{\frac{8.4}{\sqrt{50}}} = 1.01$$

This z value yields a probability of .3438 between the sample mean and the population mean. There is a probability of .5000 − .3438 = .1562 of obtaining a sample mean less than 26.9 if the population mean is 28.1.

Some of the questions asked might require only a Yes or No response. For example, "Are working conditions in a U.S.-company-owned maquiladora plant considerably different from those in a plant owned by an equivalent Mexican company?" requires only a Yes or No response. Such questions can be summarized by using sample proportions. If the sample sizes are large enough, the researcher can assume from the central limit theorem that sample proportions come from a normal distribution, which can provide the basis for analysts.

Suppose a stratified random sample of 350 workers is asked whether working conditions in a U.S. company-owned maquiladora plant are considerably different from those in a plant owned by an equivalent Mexican company. What is the probability that more than .44 of the sample would agree with the statement if .40 of the population actually agreed that it is true? That is, what is the probability of getting a sample proportion of more than .44 if the population proportion is actually .40? The probability can be obtained by using techniques from this chapter.

$$z = \frac{\hat{p} - p}{\sqrt{\frac{p \cdot q}{n}}} = \frac{.44 - .40}{\sqrt{\frac{(.40)(.60)}{350}}} = 1.53$$

This z value yields a probability of .4370. There is a .5000 − .4370 = .0630 probability of obtaining a sample proportion of more than .44 if the population proportion is .40 and 350 people are sampled. The beauty of the central limit theorem in such a study is that if sample sizes are large enough, the analysis of sample means and sample proportions can be done with the assumption that the normal distribution fits the statistics without the researcher having to study the shape of the population on each question.

ETHICAL CONSIDERATIONS

The art and science of sampling has potential for breeding unethical behavior. Considerable research is reported under the guise of random sampling when, in fact, nonrandom sampling is used. Remember, if nonrandom sampling is used, probability statements about sampling error are not appropriate. Some researchers purport to be using stratified random sampling when they are actually using quota sampling. Others claim to be using systematic random sampling when they are actually using convenience or judgment sampling.

In the process of inferential statistics, researchers use sample results to make conclusions about a population. These conclusions are disseminated to the interested public. The public often assumes that sample results truly reflect the state of the population. If the sample does not reflect the population because questionable sampling practices were used, it could be argued that unethical research behavior occurred. Valid, representative sampling is not an easy task. Researchers and statisticians should exercise extreme caution in taking samples to be sure the results obtained reflect the conditions in the population as nearly as possible.

The central limit theorem is based on large samples unless the population is normally distributed. In analyzing small-sample data, it is an unethical practice to assume a sample mean is from a normal distribution unless the population can be shown with some confidence to be normally distributed. Using the normal distribution to analyze sample proportions is also unethical if sample sizes are smaller than those recommended by the experts.

SUMMARY

For much business research, successfully conducting a census is virtually impossible and the sample is a feasible alternative. Other reasons for sampling include cost reduction, potential for broadening the scope of the study, and loss reduction when the testing process destroys the product.

To take a sample, a population must be identified. Often the researcher cannot obtain an exact roster or list of the population and so must find some way to identify the population as closely as possible. The final list or directory used to represent the population and from which the sample is drawn is called the frame.

The two main types of sampling are random and nonrandom. Random sampling occurs when each unit of the population has the same probability of being selected for the sample. Nonrandom sampling is any sampling that is not random. The four main types of random sampling discussed are simple random sampling, stratified sampling, systematic sampling, and cluster or area sampling.

In simple random sampling, every unit of the population is numbered. A table of random numbers or a random number generator is used to select n units from the population for the sample.

Stratified random sampling uses the researcher's prior knowledge of the population to stratify the population into subgroups. Each subgroup is internally homogeneous but different from the others. Stratified random sampling is an attempt to reduce sampling error and ensure that at least some of each of the subgroups appears in the sample. After the strata are identified, units can be sampled randomly from each stratum. If the proportions of units selected from each subgroup for the sample are the same as the proportions of the subgroups in the population, the process is called proportionate stratified sampling. If not, it is called disproportionate stratified sampling.

With systematic sampling, every kth item of the population is sampled until n units have been selected. Systematic sampling is used because of its convenience and ease of administration.

Cluster or area sampling involves subdividing the population into nonoverlapping clusters or areas. Each cluster or area is a microcosm of the population and is usually heterogeneous within. Individual units are then selected randomly from the clusters or areas to get the final sample. Cluster or area sampling is usually done to reduce costs. If a set of second clusters or areas is selected from the first set, the method is called two-stage sampling.

Four types of nonrandom sampling were discussed: convenience, judgment, quota, and snowball. In convenience sampling, the researcher selects units from the population to be in the sample for convenience. In judgment sampling, units are selected according to the judgment of the researcher. Quota sampling is similar to stratified sampling, with the researcher identifying subclasses or strata. However, the researcher selects units from each stratum by some nonrandom technique until a specified quota from each stratum is filled. With snowball sampling, the researcher obtains additional sample members by asking current sample members for referral information.

Sampling error occurs when the sample does not represent the population. With random sampling, sampling error occurs by chance. Nonsampling errors are all other research and analysis errors that occur in a study. They include recording errors, input errors, missing data, and incorrect definition of the frame.

According to the central limit theorem, if a population is normally distributed, the sample means for samples taken from that population also are normally distributed regardless of sample size. The central limit theorem also says that if the sample sizes are large ($n \geq 30$), the sample mean is approximately normally distributed regardless of the distribution shape of the population. This theorem is extremely useful because it enables researchers to analyze sample data by using the normal distribution for virtually any type of study in which means are an appropriate statistic, as long as the sample size is large enough. The central limit theorem states that sample proportions are normally distributed for large sample sizes.

KEY TERMS

central limit theorem
cluster (or area) sampling
convenience sampling
disproportionate stratified
    random sampling
finite correction factor
frame

judgment sampling
nonrandom sampling
nonrandom sampling
    techniques
nonsampling errors
proportionate stratified
    random sampling

quota sampling
random sampling
sample proportion
sampling error
simple random sampling
snowball sampling
standard error of the mean

standard error of the
    proportion
stratified random sampling
systematic sampling
two-stage sampling

FORMULAS

Determining the value of k

$$k = \frac{N}{n}$$

z formula for sample means

$$z = \frac{\bar{x} - \mu}{\frac{\sigma}{\sqrt{n}}}$$

z formula for sample means when there is a finite population

$$z = \frac{\bar{x} - \mu}{\frac{\sigma}{\sqrt{n}}\sqrt{\frac{N-n}{N-1}}}$$

Sample proportion

$$\hat{p} = \frac{x}{n}$$

z formula for sample proportions

$$z = \frac{\hat{p} - p}{\sqrt{\frac{p \cdot q}{n}}}$$

SUPPLEMENTARY PROBLEMS

CALCULATING THE STATISTICS

7.29 The mean of a population is 76 and the standard deviation is 14. The shape of the population is unknown. Determine the probability of each of the following occurring from this population.

  a. A random sample of size 35 yielding a sample mean of 79 or more
  b. A random sample of size 140 yielding a sample mean of between 74 and 77
  c. A random sample of size 219 yielding a sample mean of less than 76.5

7.30 Forty-six percent of a population possesses a particular characteristic. Random samples are taken from this population. Determine the probability of each of the following occurrences.

  a. The sample size is 60 and the sample proportion is between .41 and .53.
  b. The sample size is 458 and the sample proportion is less than .40.
  c. The sample size is 1350 and the sample proportion is greater than .49.

TESTING YOUR UNDERSTANDING

7.31 Suppose the age distribution in a city is as follows.

Under 18	22%
18–25	18%
26–50	36%
51–65	10%
Over 65	14%

A researcher is conducting proportionate stratified random sampling with a sample size of 250. Approximately how many people should he sample from each stratum?

7.32 Candidate Jones believes she will receive .55 of the total votes cast in her county. However, in an attempt to validate this figure, her pollster contacts a random sample of 600 registered voters in the county. The poll results show that 298 of the voters say they are committed to voting for her. If she actually has .55 of the total vote, what is the probability of getting a sample proportion this small or smaller? Do you think she actually has 55% of the vote? Why or why not?

7.33 Determine a possible frame for conducting random sampling in each of the following studies.

   a. The average amount of overtime per week for production workers in a plastics company in Pennsylvania
   b. The average number of employees in all Alpha/Beta supermarkets in California
   c. A survey of commercial lobster catchers in Maine

7.34 A particular automobile costs an average of $17,755 in the Pacific Northwest. The standard deviation of prices is $650. Suppose a random sample of 30 dealerships in Washington and Oregon is taken, and their managers are asked what they charge for this automobile. What is the probability of getting a sample average cost of less than $17,500? Assume that only 120 dealerships in the entire Pacific Northwest sell this automobile.

7.35 A company has 1,250 employees, and you want to take a simple random sample of $n = 60$ employees. Explain how you would go about selecting this sample by using the table of random numbers. Are there numbers that you cannot use? Explain.

7.36 Suppose the average client charge per hour for out-of-court work by lawyers in the state of Iowa is $125. Suppose further that a random telephone sample of 32 lawyers in Iowa is taken and that the sample average charge per hour for out-of-court work is $110. If the population variance is $525, what is the probability of getting a sample mean of $110 or larger? What is the probability of getting a sample mean larger than $135 per hour? What is the probability of getting a sample mean of between $120 and $130 per hour?

7.37 A survey of 2,645 consumers by DDB Needham Worldwide of Chicago for public relations agency Porter/Novelli showed that how a company handles a crisis when at fault is one of the top influences in consumer buying decisions, with 73% claiming it is an influence. Quality of product was the number one influence, with 96% of consumers stating that quality

influences their buying decisions. How a company handles complaints was number two, with 85% of consumers reporting it as an influence in their buying decisions. Suppose a random sample of 1,100 consumers is taken and each is asked which of these three factors influence their buying decisions.

   a. What is the probability that more than 810 consumers claim that how a company handles a crisis when at fault is an influence in their buying decisions?
   b. What is the probability that fewer than 1,030 consumers claim that quality of product is an influence in their buying decisions?
   c. What is the probability that between 82% and 84% of consumers claim that how a company handles complaints is an influence in their buying decisions?

7.38 Suppose you are sending out questionnaires to a randomly selected sample of 100 managers. The frame for this study is the membership list of the American Managers Association. The questionnaire contains demographic questions about the company and its top manager. In addition, it asks questions about the manager's leadership style. Research assistants are to score and enter the responses into the computer as soon as they are received. You are to conduct a statistical analysis of the data. Name and describe four nonsampling errors that could occur in this study.

7.39 A researcher is conducting a study of a *Fortune* 500 company that has factories, distribution centers, and retail outlets across the country. How can she use cluster or area sampling to take a random sample of employees of this firm?

7.40 A directory of personal computer retail outlets in the United States contains 12,080 alphabetized entries. Explain how systematic sampling could be used to select a sample of 300 outlets.

7.41 In an effort to cut costs and improve profits, many U.S. companies have been turning to outsourcing. In fact, according to *Purchasing* magazine, 54% of companies surveyed outsourced some part of their manufacturing process in the past two to three years. Suppose 565 of these companies are contacted.

   a. What is the probability that 339 or more companies outsourced some part of their manufacturing process in the past two to three years?
   b. What is the probability that 288 or more companies outsourced some part of their manufacturing process in the past two to three years?
   c. What is the probability that 50% or less of these companies outsourced some part of their manufacturing process in the past two to three years?

7.42 The average cost of a one-bedroom apartment in a town is $550 per month. What is the probability of randomly selecting a sample of 50 one-bedroom apartments in this town and getting a sample mean of less than $530 if the population standard deviation is $100?

7.43 The Aluminum Association reports that the average American uses 56.8 pounds of aluminum in a year. A random sample of 51 households is monitored for one year to determine aluminum usage. If the population standard deviation of annual usage is 12.3 pounds, what is the probability that the sample mean will be each of the following?

  a. More than 60 pounds
  b. More than 58 pounds
  c. Between 56 and 57 pounds
  d. Less than 55 pounds
  e. Less than 50 pounds

7.44 Use Table A.1 to select 20 three-digit random numbers. Did any of the numbers occur more than once? How is it possible for a number to occur more than once? Make a stem and leaf plot of the numbers with the stem being the left digit. Do the numbers seem to be equally distributed, or are they bunched together?

7.45 Direct marketing companies are turning to the Internet for new opportunities. A recent study by Gruppo, Levey, & Co. showed that 73% of all direct marketers conduct transactions on the Internet. Suppose a random sample of 300 direct marketing companies is taken.

  a. What is the probability that between 210 and 234 (inclusive) direct marketing companies are turning to the Internet for new opportunities?
  b. What is the probability that 78% or more of direct marketing companies are turning to the Internet for new opportunities?
  c. Suppose a random sample of 800 direct marketing companies is taken. Now what is the probability that 78% or more are turning to the Internet for new opportunities? How does this answer differ from the answer in part (b)? Why do the answers differ?

7.46 According to the U.S. Bureau of Labor Statistics, 20% of all people 16 years of age or older do volunteer work. Women volunteer slightly more than men, with 22% of women volunteering and 19% of men volunteering. What is the probability of randomly sampling 140 women 16 years of age or older and getting 35 or more who do volunteer work? What is the probability of getting 21 or fewer from this group? Suppose a sample of 300 men and women 16 years of age or older is selected randomly from the U.S. population. What is

the probability that the sample proportion of those who do volunteer work is between 18% and 25%?

7.47 Suppose you work for a large firm that has 20,000 employees. The CEO calls you in and asks you to determine employee attitudes toward the company. She is willing to commit $100,000 to this project. What are the advantages of taking a sample versus conducting a census? What are the trade-offs?

7.48 In a particular area of the Northeast, an estimated 75% of the homes use heating oil as the principal heating fuel during the winter. A random telephone survey of 150 homes is taken in an attempt to determine whether this figure is correct. Suppose 120 of the 150 homes surveyed use heating oil as the principal heating fuel. What is the probability of getting a sample proportion this large or larger if the population estimate is true?

7.49 The U.S. Bureau of Labor Statistics released hourly wage figures for western countries for workers in the manufacturing sector. The hourly wage was $21.24 in Switzerland, $22.00 in Japan, and $19.86 in the United States. Suppose 40 manufacturing workers are selected randomly from across Switzerland and asked what their hourly wage is. What is the probability that the sample average will be between $21 and $22? Suppose 35 manufacturing workers are selected randomly from across Japan. What is the probability that the sample average will exceed $23? Suppose 50 manufacturing workers are selected randomly from across the United States. What is the probability that the sample average will be less than $18.90? Assume that in all three countries, the standard deviation of hourly labor rates is $3.

7.50 Give a variable that could be used to stratify the population for each of the following studies. List at least four subcategories for each variable.

  a. A political party wants to conduct a poll prior to an election for the office of U.S. senator in Minnesota.
  b. A soft drink company wants to take a sample of soft drink purchases in an effort to estimate market share.
  c. A retail outlet wants to interview customers over a one-week period.
  d. An eyeglasses manufacturer and retailer wants to determine the demand for prescription eyeglasses in its marketing region.

7.51 According to Runzheimer International, a typical business traveler spends an average of $281 per day in Chicago. This cost includes hotel, meals, car rental, and incidentals. A survey of 65 randomly selected business travelers who have been to Chicago on business recently is taken. For the population mean of $281 per day, what is the probability of getting a sample average of more than $273 per day if the population standard deviation is $47?

1. Let the manufacturing database be the frame for a population of manufacturers that are to be studied. This database has 140 different SIC Codes. How would you proceed to take a simple random sample of size 6 from these industries? Explain how you would take a systematic sample of size 10 from this frame. Examine the variables in the database. Name two variables that could be used to stratify the population. Explain how these variables could be used in stratification and why they might be important strata.

2. Assume the manufacturing database is the population of interest. Compute the mean and standard deviation for cost of materials on this population. Take a random sample of 32 of the SIC Code categories and compute the sample mean cost of materials on this sample. Using techniques presented in this chapter, determine the probability of getting a mean this large or larger from the population. Note that the population contains only 140 items. Work this problem with and without the finite correction factor. Compare the results and discuss the differences in answers.

3. Use the hospital database to calculate the mean and standard deviation of personnel. Assume that these figures are true for the population of hospitals in the United States. Suppose a random sample of 36 hospitals is taken from hospitals in the United States. What is the probability that the sample mean of personnel is less than 650? What is the probability that the sample mean of personnel is between 700 and 1,100? What is the probability that the sample mean is between 900 and 950?

Determine the proportion of the hospital database that is under the control of nongovernment not-for-profit organizations (category 2). Assume that this proportion represents the entire population of hospitals. If you randomly selected 500 hospitals from across the United States, what is the probability that 45% or more are under the control of nongovernment not-for-profit organizations? If you randomly selected 100 hospitals, what is the probability that less than 40% are under the control of nongovernment not-for-profit organizations?

CASE: SHELL ATTEMPTS TO RETURN TO PREMIERE STATUS

The Shell Oil Company, which began about 1912, had been for decades a household name as a quality oil company in the United States. However, by the late 1970s much of its prestige as a premiere company had disappeared. How could Shell regain its high status?

In the 1990s, Shell undertook an extensive research effort to find out what it needed to do to improve its image. As a first step, Shell hired Responsive Research and the Opinion Research Corporation to conduct a series of focus groups and personal interviews among various segments of the population. Included in these were youths, minorities, residents in neighborhoods near Shell plants, legislators, academics, and present and past employees of Shell. The researchers learned that people believe that top companies are integral parts of the communities in which the companies are located rather than separate entities. These studies and others led to the development of materials that Shell used to explain their core values to the general public.

Next, PERT Survey Research ran a large quantitative study to determine which values were best received by the target audience. Social issues emerged as the theme with the most support. During the next few months, the advertising agency of Ogilvy & Mather, hired by Shell, developed several campaigns with social themes. Two market research companies were hired to evaluate the receptiveness of the various campaigns. The result was the "Count on Shell" campaign, which featured safety messages with useful information about what to do in various dangerous situations.

A public "Count on Shell" campaign was launched in February 1998 and met with considerable success: the ability to recall Shell advertising jumped from 20% to 32% among opinion influencers; more than 1 million copies of Shell's free safety brochures were distributed; and activity on Shell's Internet "Count on Shell" site remains extremely strong. By promoting itself as a reliable company that cares, Shell seems to be regaining its premiere status.

Today, Shell continues its efforts to be "community friendly." United Way of America announced Shell Oil Company as one of its three Spirit of America Summit Award winners for 2002 and commended the company for its outstanding volunteer and corporate contributions programs. Several Shell employees were recognized by the Houston Minority Business Council for their continued efforts to provide windows of opportunity for minority business owners and strengthen Shell's commitment to supplier diversity. Recently, the Shell Oil Company Foundation donated $120,000 to the National Action Council for Minorities in Engineering in support of the organization's mission to increase the representation of successful African-American, American-Indian and Latino women and men in engineering and technology-, math-, and science-based careers.

Discussion

1. Suppose you were asked to develop a sampling plan to determine what a "premiere company" is to the general public. What sampling plan would you use?

What is the target population? What would you use for a frame? Which of the four types of random sampling discussed in this chapter would you use? Could you use a combination of two or more of the types (two-stage sampling)? If so, how?

2. It appears that at least one of the research companies hired by Shell used some stratification in their sampling. What are some of the variables on which they are stratified? If you were truly interested in ascertaining opinions from a variety of segments of the population with regard to opinions on "premiere" companies or about Shell, what strata might make sense? Name at least five and justify why you would include them.

3. Suppose that in 1979 only 12% of the general adult U.S. public believed that Shell was a "premiere" company. Suppose further that you randomly selected 350 people from the general adult U.S. public this year and 25% said that Shell was a "premiere" company. If only 12% of the general adult U.S. public still believes that Shell is a "premiere" company, how likely is it that the 25% figure is a chance result in sampling 350 people? *Hint:* Use the techniques in this chapter to determine the probability of the 25% figure occurring by chance.

4. PERT Survey Research conducted quantitative surveys in an effort to measure the effectiveness of various campaigns. Suppose they used a 1-to-5 scale where 1 denotes that the campaign is not effective at all, 5 denotes that the campaign is extremely effective, and 2, 3, and 4 fall in between on an interval scale. Suppose also that a particular campaign received an average of 1.8 on the scale with a standard deviation of .7 early in the tests. Later, after the campaign had been critiqued and improved, a survey of 35 people was taken and a sample mean of 2.0 was recorded. What is the probability of this sample mean or greater occurring if the actual population mean is still just 1.8? Based on this probability, do you think that a sample mean of 2.0 is just a chance fluctuation on the 1.8 population mean, or do you think that perhaps it indicates the population mean is now greater than 1.8? Support your conclusion. Suppose a sample mean of 2.5 is attained. What is the likelihood of this result occurring by chance when the population mean is 1.8? Suppose this increase actually happens after the campaign has been improved. What does it mean?

Source: Adapted from "Count on It," *American Demographics*, March 1999, p. 60; "Shell in the U.S.," 2002, available at http://www.shellus.com/.

USING THE COMPUTER

EXCEL

Random numbers can be generated from Excel for several different distributions. The procedure begins with the selection of **Tools** on the menu bar. From the pull-down menu, choose **Data Analysis.** From the menu provided in the **Data Analysis** dialog box, select **Random Number Generation**. In the third line of the Random Number Generation dialog box are the choices of distributions. Select the distribution from which you want to generate random numbers. The options and required responses in the Random Number Generation dialog box will change with the chosen distribution. In each case, the number of variables goes on the first line and the number of random numbers to be generated goes into the second line.

For random number generation from a binomial distribution, place the value of p on the **p Value** = line and n in the **Number of Trials** = line. For random number generation from a normal distribution, place the value of μ on the **Mean** = line and the value of σ on the **Standard Deviation** = line. For random number generation from a Poisson distribution, place the value of λ in the **Lambda** = line. For random number generation from the uniform distribution, place the value of a in the first space after **Between** and the value of b in the second space.

MINITAB

MINITAB Windows has the capability of generating random numbers from many different distributions. We will focus here on the normal distribution, the uniform distribution, the binomial distribution, the Poisson distribution, and the exponential distribution. Begin by selecting **Calc** on the menu bar. On the pull-down menu that appears, select **Random Data.** When the pull-down menu appears, select the distribution from which you want to generate random numbers. A dialog box for the distribution selected will open, which asks you to signify how many rows of data you want to generate. Basically, it wants to know how many random numbers you want to generate for each column. Next, you are asked to signify the columns in which you want the data loaded. For example, if you want to generate 100 random numbers in column 1, you would place 100 (rows of data) on line 1 and C1 on line 2. Each distribution also requires specific parameters. The binomial distribution dialog box asks for **Number of trials:** (place the value of n there) and **Probability of success:** (place the value of p). The exponential distribution dialog box asks for the **Mean:**. Place the value of μ on this line. The normal distribution dialog box asks for the **Mean** (place μ on this line) and the **Standard deviation:** (place σ on this line). The Poisson distribution dialog box asks for the **Mean:**. Place the value of λ on this line. The uniform distribution dialog box asks for the **Lower endpoint:** (place the value of a) and the **Upper endpoint:** (place the value of b).

CHAPTER 8

Statistical Inference: Estimation for Single Populations

LEARNING OBJECTIVES

The overall learning objective of Chapter 8 is to help you understand estimating parameters of single populations, thereby enabling you to:

1. Know the difference between point and interval estimation.
2. Estimate a population mean from a sample mean when σ is known.
3. Estimate a population mean from a sample mean when σ is unknown.
4. Estimate a population proportion from a sample proportion.
5. Estimate the population variance from a sample variance.
6. Estimate the minimum sample size necessary to achieve given statistical goals.

A Report of Surveys on Productivity, Compensation, and Benefits

A number of surveys and studies set out to determine the state of compensation and benefits in the United States. One survey of 1,200 employees found that 25% of U.S. workers believed that they could accomplish at least 50% more on the job each day. Some of the barriers to productivity according to workers and the associated% of the survey respondents who cited them include the following: companies not supervising their work closely enough (37%), companies not involving them enough in decision making (34%), companies not rewarding them for a good job performance (29%), and companies not giving them advancement or promotion opportunities (29%). Twenty-eight% of the workers said that their companies do not train employees to a great extent, and 26% said that companies do not hire the right people.

A survey of 231 human resource specialists conducted by *Compensation & Benefits Review* reported that 12.12% cited managing performance as the dominant issue facing compensation and benefits managers. In addition, 10.39% named team-based pay and 9.96% named competency-based pay as the most pressing issues.

ECS/Watson Wyatt Data Services studied 1,500 companies and found that more than 75% of companies use variable pay for middle managers. The favorite variable pay approach, according to the survey, was annual bonuses. Two-thirds of those companies reporting variable pay plans for middle managers use bonuses. Another survey by Watson Wyatt showed that 26% of supervisors were given cash awards, usually some sort of bonus.

Edward Perlin Associates surveyed sixty-three companies with data-processing professionals to ascertain the prevalence of computer security-related jobs in light of the increase of computer viruses and the compensation for such employees. The average annual compensation including base salary and bonuses for security managers is $79,900. Security heads earn an average total yearly compensation of $94,800. The average figure for security specialists is $42,900.

A survey of 4,800 members of the Institute of Management Accountants showed that the average annual salary in the 30- to 39-year age bracket is $57,937 for certified management accountants compared to $47,332 for uncertified management accountants. In the 19- to 29-year-old age bracket, for certified management accountants the average annual salary is $40,185 and $31,008 for uncertified management accountants.

A survey of 1,935 Internet workers by the Association of Internet Professions revealed that the average annual salary for an online services manager was $59,781, for a software development person was $64,024, and for a media production person was $42,455.

Managerial and Statistical Questions

1. How can the national average salary for computer security positions be estimated using sample data? How much error is involved in such an estimation? How much confidence do we have in this estimation?

2. This Decision Dilemma reports average annual salaries for certified and uncertified management accountants and of Internet workers. However, these figures are based on sample information. How does a business researcher use sample information to estimate population parameters like the mean national average annual salary for accountants? For Internet workers? What is the error in such a process? Are we certain of the results?

3. One survey reported that 37% of the workers felt that companies are not supervising their work enough. This figure came from a survey of 1,200 employees and is only a sample statistic. Can we say from this survey that 37% of all employees in the United States feel this way? Why or why not? Can we use the 37% as an estimate for the population parameter? If we do, how much error is there; and how much confidence do we have in the final results?

4. A survey of 231 human resource specialists found that 12.12% cited that managing performance is the dominant issue facing compensation and benefits managers. Can this figure be used to represent all compensation and benefits managers? If so, how much potential error is there in doing so? Since this sample size is 231 and the sample size for the employee survey on productivity uses a sample size of 1,200, does the accuracy of the results of the two surveys differ? Does the size of the sample enter in to the predictability of a survey's results?

5. Why did these research companies choose to sample 1,200, 231, 1,500, 63, and 4,800 firms or people, respectively? What is the rationale for determining how many to sample other than to sample as few as possible to save time or money? Is a minimum sample size necessary to accomplish estimations?

Source: Adapted from William Lissy and Marlene L. Morgenstern, "Currents in Compensation and Benefits," *Compensation & Benefits Review* (November–December 1995), pp. 15–25; "Compensation by Job Category," *Internet World* (1 February 2000), p. 1.

The central limit theorem presented in Chapter 7 states that certain statistics of interest, such as the sample mean and the sample proportion, are approximately normally distributed for large sample sizes regardless of the shape of the population distribution. The z formulas for each statistic that were developed and discussed can be used in parametric estimation, hypothesis testing, and determination of sample size. This chapter describes how these z formulas can be manipulated algebraically into a format for estimating population parameters and determining the size of samples necessary to conduct research. In addition, mechanisms are introduced for the estimation of population means when the population standard deviation is unknown and for the estimation of population variance.

8.1 ESTIMATING THE POPULATION MEAN USING THE z STATISTIC (σ KNOWN)

On many occasions estimating the population mean is useful in business research. For example, the manager of human resources in a company might want to estimate the average number of days of work an employee misses per year because of illness. If the firm has thousands of employees, direct calculation of a population mean such as this may be practically impossible. Instead, a random sample of employees can be taken, and the sample mean number of sick days can be used to estimate the population mean. Suppose another company developed a new process for prolonging the shelf life of a loaf of bread. The company wants to be able to date each loaf for freshness, but company officials do not know exactly how long the bread will stay fresh. By taking a random sample and determining the sample mean shelf life, they can estimate the average shelf life for the population of bread.

As the cellular telephone industry matures, a cellular telephone company is rethinking its pricing structure. Users appear to be spending more time on the phone and are shopping around for the best deals. To do better planning, the cellular company wants to ascertain the average number of minutes of time used per month by each of its residential users but does not have the resources available to examine all monthly bills and extract the information. The company decides to take a sample of customer bills and estimate the population mean from sample data. A researcher for the company takes a random sample of 85 bills for a recent month and from these bills computes a sample mean of 153 minutes. This sample mean, which is a statistic, is used to estimate the population mean, which is a parameter. If the company uses the sample mean of 153 minutes as an estimate for the population mean, then the sample mean is used as a *point estimate*.

A **point estimate** is *a statistic taken from a sample that is used to estimate a population parameter*. A point estimate is only as good as the representativeness of its sample. If other random samples are taken from the population, the point estimates derived from those samples are likely to vary. Because of variation in sample statistics, estimating a population parameter with an interval estimate is often preferable to using a point estimate. An **interval estimate** (confidence interval) is *a range of values within which the analyst can declare, with some confidence, the population parameter lies.* Confidence intervals can be two-sided or one-sided. This text presents only two-sided confidence intervals. How are confidence intervals constructed?

As a result of the central limit theorem, the following z formula for sample means can be used when sample sizes are large, regardless of the shape of the population distribution, or for smaller sizes if the population is normally distributed.

$$z = \frac{\bar{x} - \mu}{\frac{\sigma}{\sqrt{n}}}$$

Rearranging this formula algebraically to solve for μ gives

$$\mu = \bar{x} - z \frac{\sigma}{\sqrt{n}}$$

Because a sample mean can be greater than or less than the population mean, z can be positive or negative. Thus the preceding expression takes the following form.

$$\bar{x} \pm z \frac{\sigma}{\sqrt{n}}$$

Rewriting this expression yields the confidence interval formula for estimating μ with large sample sizes.

100(1 − α)% CONFIDENCE INTERVAL TO ESTIMATE μ (8.1)

$$\bar{x} \pm z_{\alpha/2} \frac{\sigma}{\sqrt{n}}$$

or

$$\bar{x} - z_{\alpha/2} \frac{\sigma}{\sqrt{n}} \leq \mu \leq \bar{x} + z_{\alpha/2} \frac{\sigma}{\sqrt{n}}$$

where
α = the area under the normal curve outside the confidence interval area
$\alpha/2$ = the area in one end (tail) of the distribution outside the confidence interval

---

Alpha (α) is the area under the normal curve in the tails of the distribution outside the area defined by the confidence interval. We will focus more on α in Chapter 9. Here we use α to locate the z value in constructing the confidence interval as shown in Figure 8.1. Because the standard normal table is based on areas between a z of 0 and $z_{\alpha/2}$, the table z value is found by locating the area of .5000 − $\alpha/2$, which is the part of the normal curve between the middle of the curve and one of the tails. Another way to locate this z value is to change the confidence level from percentage to proportion, divide it in half, and go to the table with this value. The results are the same.

The confidence interval formula (8.1) yields a range (interval) within which we feel with some confidence the population mean is located. It is not certain that the population mean is in the interval unless we have a 100% confidence interval that is infinitely

---

FIGURE 8.1

z Scores for Confidence Intervals in Relation to α

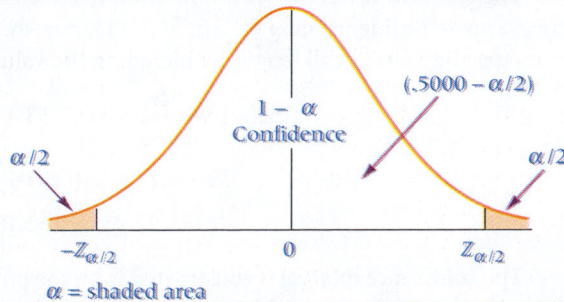

α = shaded area

FIGURE 8.2

Distribution of Sample Means for 95% Confidence

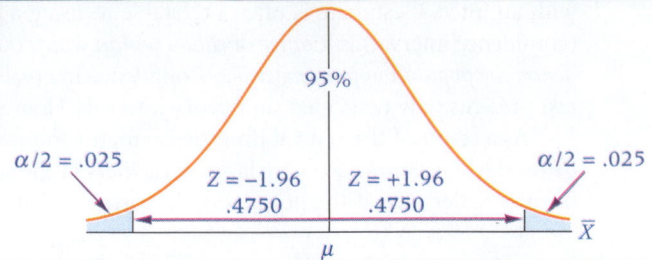

FIGURE 8.3

Twenty 95% Confidence Intervals of μ

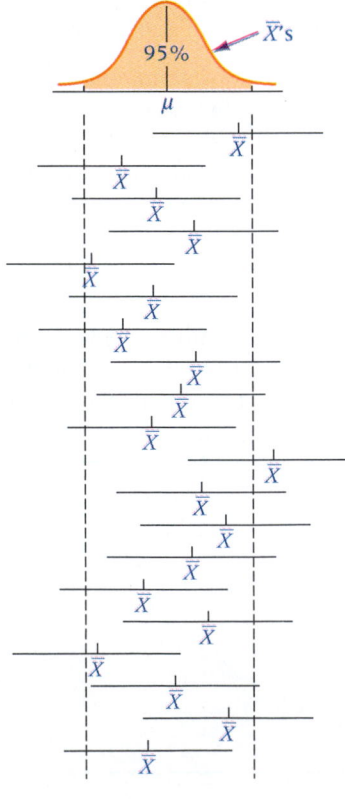

wide. If we want to construct a 95% confidence interval, the level of confidence is 95% or .95. If 100 such intervals are constructed by taking random samples from the population, it is likely that 95 of the intervals would include the population mean and five would not.

As an example, in the cellular telephone company problem of estimating the population mean number of minutes called per residential user per month, from the sample of 85 bills it was determined that the sample mean is 153 minutes. Using this sample mean, a confidence interval can be calculated within which the researcher is relatively confident the actual population mean is located. To make this calculation using formula 8.1, the value of the population standard deviation and the value of z (in addition to the sample mean, 153, and the sample size, 85) must be known. Suppose past history and similar studies indicate that the population standard deviation is 46 minutes.

The value of z is driven by the level of confidence. An interval with 100% confidence is so wide that it is meaningless. Some of the more common levels of confidence used by business researchers are 90%, 95%, 98%, and 99%. Why would a business researcher not just select the highest confidence and always use that level? The reason is that trade-offs between sample size, interval width, and level of confidence must be considered. For example, as the level of confidence is increased, the interval gets wider, provided the sample size and standard deviation remain constant.

For the cellular telephone problem, suppose the business researcher decided on a 95% confidence interval for the results. Figure 8.2 shows a normal distribution of sample means about the population mean. When using a 95% level of confidence, the researcher selects an interval centered on μ within which 95% of all sample mean values will fall and then uses the width of that interval to create an interval around the *sample mean* within which he has some confidence the population mean will fall.

For 95% confidence, $\alpha = .05$ and $\alpha/2 = .025$. The value of $z_{\alpha/2}$ or $z_{.025}$ is found by looking in the standard normal table under $.5000 - .0250 = .4750$. This area in the table is associated with a z value of 1.96. Another way can be used to locate the table z value. Because the distribution is symmetric and the intervals are equal on each side of the population mean, ½(95%), or .4750, of the area is on each side of the mean. Table A.5 yields a z value of 1.96 for this portion of the normal curve. Thus the z value for a 95% confidence interval is always 1.96. In other words, of all the possible $\bar{x}$ values along the horizontal axis of the diagram, 95% of them should be within a z score of 1.96 from the population mean.

The business researcher can now complete the cellular telephone problem. To determine a 95% confidence interval for $\bar{x} = 153$, $\sigma = 46$, $n = 85$, and $z = 1.96$, the researcher estimates the average call length by including the value of z in formula 8.1.

$$153 - 1.96 \frac{46}{\sqrt{85}} \leq \mu \leq 153 + 1.96 \frac{46}{\sqrt{85}}$$

$$153 - 9.78 \leq \mu \leq 153 + 9.78$$

$$143.22 \leq \mu \leq 162.78$$

The confidence interval is constructed from the point estimate, which in this problem is 153 minutes, and the error of this estimate, which is ±9.78 minutes. The resulting confidence interval is $143.22 \leq \mu \leq 162.78$. The cellular telephone company researcher is 95% confident that the average length of a call for the population is between 143.22 and 162.78 minutes.

What does being 95% confident that the population mean is in an interval actually indicate? It indicates that, if the company researcher were to randomly select 100 samples of 85 calls and use the results of each sample to construct a 95% confidence interval, approximately 95 of the 100 intervals would contain the population mean. It also indicates that 5% of the intervals would not contain the population mean. The company researcher is likely to take only a single sample and compute the confidence interval from that sample information. That interval either contains the population mean or it does not. Figure 8.3 depicts the meaning of a 95% confidence interval for the mean. Note that if 20 random samples are taken from the population, 19 of the 20 are likely to contain the population mean if a 95% confidence interval is used (19/20 = 95%). If a 90% confidence interval is constructed, only 18 of the 20 intervals are likely to contain the population mean.

DEMONSTRATION PROBLEM 8.1

A survey was taken of U.S. companies that do business with firms in India. One of the questions on the survey was: Approximately how many years has your company been trading with firms in India? A random sample of 44 responses to this question yielded a mean of 10.455 years. Suppose the population standard deviation for this question is 7.7 years. Using this information, construct a 90% confidence interval for the mean number of years that a company has been trading in India for the population of U.S. companies trading with firms in India.

Solution

Here, $n = 44$, $\bar{x} = 10.455$, and $\sigma = 7.7$. To determine the value of $z_{\alpha/2}$, divide the 90% confidence in half, or take $.5000 - \alpha/2 = .5000 - .0500$. The z distribution of $\bar{x}$ around μ contains .4500 of the area on each side of μ, or ½(90%). Table A.5 yields a z value of 1.645 for the area of .4500 (interpolating between .4495 and .4505). The confidence interval is

$$\bar{x} - z\frac{\sigma}{\sqrt{n}} \leq \mu \leq \bar{x} + z\frac{\sigma}{\sqrt{n}}$$

$$10.455 - 1.645\frac{7.7}{\sqrt{44}} \leq \mu \leq 10.455 + 1.645\frac{7.7}{\sqrt{44}}$$

$$10.455 - 1.91 \leq \mu \leq 10.455 + 1.91$$

$$8.545 \leq \mu \leq 12.365$$

The analyst is 90% confident that if a census of all U.S. companies trading with firms in India were taken at the time of this survey, the actual population mean number of years a company would have been trading with firms in India would be between 8.545 and 12.365. The point estimate is 10.455 years.

TABLE 8.1

Values of *z* for Common Levels of Confidence

Confidence Level	z Value
90%	1.645
95%	1.96
98%	2.33
99%	2.575

For convenience, Table 8.1 contains some of the more common levels of confidence and their associated *z* values.

Finite Correction Factor

Recall from Chapter 7 that if the sample is taken from a finite population, a finite correction factor may be used to increase the accuracy of the solution. In the case of interval estimation, the finite correction factor is used to reduce the width of the interval. As stated in Chapter 7, if the sample size is less than 5% of the population, the finite correction factor does not significantly alter the solution. If formula 8.1 is modified to include the finite correction factor, the result is formula 8.2.

CONFIDENCE INTERVAL TO ESTIMATE μ USING THE FINITE CORRECTION FACTOR (8.2)	$$\bar{x} - z_{\alpha/2}\frac{\sigma}{\sqrt{n}}\sqrt{\frac{N-n}{N-1}} \leq \mu \leq \bar{x} + z_{\alpha/2}\frac{\sigma}{\sqrt{n}}\sqrt{\frac{N-n}{N-1}}$$

Demonstration Problem 8.2 shows how the finite correction factor can be used.

A study is conducted in a company that employs 800 engineers. A random sample of 50 engineers reveals that the average sample age is 34.3 years. Historically, the population standard deviation of the age of the company's engineers is approximately 8 years. Construct a 98% confidence interval to estimate the average age of all the engineers in this company.

Solution

This problem has a finite population. The sample size, 50, is greater than 5% of the population, so the finite correction factor may be helpful. In this case $N = 800$, $n = 50$, $\bar{x} = 34.3$, and $\sigma = 8$. The z value for a 98% confidence interval is 2.33 (.98 divided into two equal parts yields .4900; the z value is obtained from Table A.5 by using .4900). Substituting into formula 8.2 and solving for the confidence interval gives

$$34.3 - 2.33 \frac{8}{\sqrt{50}} \sqrt{\frac{750}{799}} \leq \mu \leq 34.3 + 2.33 \frac{8}{\sqrt{50}} \sqrt{\frac{750}{799}}$$

$$34.3 - 2.55 \leq \mu \leq 34.3 + 2.55$$

$$31.75 \leq \mu \leq 36.85$$

Without the finite correction factor, the result would have been

$$34.3 - 2.64 \leq \mu \leq 34.3 + 2.64$$

$$31.66 \leq \mu \leq 36.94$$

The finite correction factor takes into account the fact that the population is only 800 instead of being infinitely large. The sample, $n = 50$, is a greater proportion of the 800 than it would be of a larger population, and thus the width of the confidence interval is reduced.

Estimating the Population Mean Using the z Statistic when the Sample Size is Small

In the formulas and problems presented so far in this section, sample size was large ($n \geq 30$). However, quite often in the business world, sample sizes are small. While the Central Limit Theorem applies only when sample size is large, the distribution of sample means is approximately normal even for small sizes **if** the *population* is normally distributed. This is visually displayed in the bottom row of Figure 7.6 in Chapter 7. Thus, if it is known that the population from which the sample is being drawn is normally distributed and if σ is known, the z formulas presented in this section can still be used to estimate a population mean even if the sample size is small ($n < 30$).

As an example, suppose a U.S. car rental firm wants to estimate the average number of miles traveled per day by each of its cars rented in California. A random sample of 20 cars rented in California reveals that the sample mean travel distance per day is 85.5 miles, with a population standard deviation of 19.3 miles. Compute a 99% confidence interval to estimate μ.

Here, $n = 20$, $\bar{x} = 85.5$, and $\sigma = 19.3$. For a 99% level of confidence, a z value of 2.575 is obtained. Assume that number of miles traveled per day is normally distributed in the population. The confidence interval is

$$\bar{x} - z_{\alpha/2} \frac{\sigma}{\sqrt{n}} \leq \mu \leq \bar{x} + z_{\alpha/2} \frac{\sigma}{\sqrt{n}}$$

$$85.5 - 2.575 \frac{19.3}{\sqrt{20}} \leq \mu \leq 85.5 + 2.575 \frac{19.3}{\sqrt{20}}$$

$$85.5 - 11.1 \leq \mu \leq 85.5 + 11.1$$

$$74.4 \leq \mu \leq 96.6$$

FIGURE 8.4

Excel and MINITAB Output for the Cellular Telephone Example

Excel Output

	A	B
1	The sample mean is:	153
2	The error of the interval is:	9.779
3	The confidence interval is:	153 ± 9.779
4	The confidence interval is:	$143.221 \leq Mu \leq 162.779$

MINITAB Output

One-Sample z: Minutes

The assumed sigma = 46.0

Variable	n	Mean	StDev	95.0% CI
Minutes	85	153.00	46	(143.22, 162.78)

The point estimate indicates that the average number of miles traveled per day by a rental car in California is 85.5. With 99% confidence, we estimate that the population mean is somewhere between 74.4 and 96.6 miles per day.

Using the Computer to Construct z Confidence Intervals for the Mean

It is possible to construct a z confidence interval for the mean with either Excel or MINITAB. Excel yields the $\pm$ error portion of the confidence interval that must be placed with the sample mean to construct the complete confidence interval. MINITAB constructs the complete confidence interval. Figure 8.4 shows both the Excel output and the MINITAB output for the cellular telephone example.

8.1 PROBLEMS

8.1 Use the following information to construct the confidence intervals specified to estimate μ.

  a. 95% confidence for $\bar{x} = 25$, $\sigma = 3.5$, and $n = 60$

  b. 98% confidence for $\bar{x} = 119.6$, $\sigma = 23.89$, and $n = 75$

  c. 90% confidence for $\bar{x} = 3.419$, $\sigma = 0.974$, and $n = 32$

  d. 80% confidence for $\bar{x} = 56.7$, $\sigma = 12.1$, $N = 500$, and $n = 47$

8.2 For a random sample of 36 items and a sample mean of 211, compute a 95% confidence interval for μ if the population standard deviation is 23.

8.3 A random sample of 81 items is taken, producing a sample mean of 47. The population standard deviation is 5.89. Construct a 90% confidence interval to estimate the population mean.

8.4 A random sample of size 70 is taken from a population that has a variance of 49. The sample mean is 90.4 What is the point estimate of μ? Construct a 94% confidence interval for μ.

8.5 A random sample of size 39 is taken from a population of 200 members. The sample mean is 66 and the population standard deviation is 11. Construct a 96% confidence interval to estimate the population mean. What is the point estimate of the population mean?

8.6 A candy company fills a 20-ounce package of Halloween candy with individually wrapped pieces of candy. The number of pieces of candy per package varies because the package is sold by weight. The company wants to estimate the number of pieces per package. Inspectors randomly sample 120 packages of this candy and count the number of pieces in each package. They find that the sample mean number of pieces is 18.72. Assuming a population standard deviation of .8735, what is the point estimate of the number of pieces per package? Construct a 99% confidence interval to estimate the mean number of pieces per package for the population.

8.7   A small lawnmower company produced 1,500 lawnmowers in 1995. In an effort to determine how maintenance-free these units were, the company decided to conduct a multiyear study of the 1995 lawnmowers. A sample of 200 owners of these lawnmowers was drawn randomly from company records and contacted. The owners were given an 800 number and asked to call the company when the first major repair was required for the lawnmowers. Owners who no longer used the lawnmower to cut their grass were disqualified. After many years, 187 of the owners had reported. The other 13 disqualified themselves. The average number of years until the first major repair was 5.3 for the 187 owners reporting. It is believed that the population standard deviation was 1.28 years. If the company wants to advertise an average number of years of repair-free lawn mowing for this lawnmower, what is the point estimate? Construct a 95% confidence interval for the average number of years until the first major repair.

8.8   The average total dollar purchase at a convenience store is less than that at a supermarket. Despite smaller-ticket purchases, convenience stores can still be profitable because of the size of operation, volume of business, and the markup. A researcher is interested in estimating the average purchase amount for convenience stores in suburban Long Island. To do so, she randomly sampled 24 purchases from several convenience stores in suburban Long Island and tabulated the amounts to the nearest dollar. Use the following data to construct a 90% confidence interval for the population average amount of purchases. Assume that the population standard deviation is 3.23 and the population is normally distributed.

$2	$11	$8	$7	$9	$3
5	4	2	1	10	8
14	7	6	3	7	2
4	1	3	6	8	4

8.9   A community health association is interested in estimating the average number of maternity days women stay in the local hospital. A random sample is taken of 36 women who had babies in the hospital during the past year. The following numbers of maternity days each woman was in the hospital are rounded to the nearest day.

3	3	4	3	2	5	3	1	4	3
4	2	3	5	3	2	4	3	2	4
1	6	3	4	3	3	5	2	3	2
3	5	4	3	5	4				

Use these data and a population standard deviation of 1.17 to construct a 98% confidence interval to estimate the average maternity stay in the hospital for all women who have babies in this hospital.

8.10   A meat-processing company in the Midwest produces and markets a package of eight small sausage sandwiches. The product is nationally distributed, and the company is interested in knowing the average retail price charged for this item in stores across the country. The company cannot justify a national census to generate this information. Based on the company information system's list of all retailers who carry the product, a researcher for the company contacts 36 of these retailers and ascertains the selling prices for the product. Use the following price data and a population standard deviation of 0.113 to determine a point estimate for the national retail price of the product. Construct a 90% confidence interval to estimate this price.

$2.23	$2.11	$2.12	$2.20	$2.17	$2.10
2.16	2.31	1.98	2.17	2.14	1.82
2.12	2.07	2.17	2.30	2.29	2.19
2.01	2.24	2.18	2.18	2.32	2.02
1.99	1.87	2.09	2.22	2.15	2.19
2.23	2.10	2.08	2.05	2.16	2.26

8.11 According to the U.S. Census Bureau, the average travel time to work in Philadelphia is 27.4 minutes. Suppose a business researcher wants to estimate the average travel time to work in Cleveland using a 95% level of confidence. A random sample of 45 Cleveland commuters is taken and the travel time to work is obtained from each. The data follow. Assuming a population standard deviation of 5.124, compute a 95% confidence interval on the data. What is the point estimate and what is the error of the interval? Explain what these results means in terms of Philadelphia commuters.

27	25	19	21	24	27	29	34	18	29	16	28
20	32	27	28	22	20	14	15	29	28	29	33
16	29	28	28	27	23	27	20	27	25	21	18
26	14	23	27	27	21	25	28	30			

8.12 In a recent year, turkey prices increased because of a high rate of turkey deaths caused by a heat wave and a fatal illness that spread across North Carolina, the top turkey-producing state. Suppose a random sample of turkey prices is taken from across the nation in an effort to estimate the average turkey price per pound in the United States. Shown here is the MINITAB output for such a sample. Examine the output. What is the point estimate? What is the value of the assumed population standard deviation? How large is the sample? What level of confidence is being used? What table value is associated with this level of confidence? What is the confidence interval? Often the portion of the confidence interval that is added and subtracted from the mean is referred to as the error of the estimate. How much is the error of the estimate in this problem?

```
                 Z CONFIDENCE INTERVALS
_____
The assumed sigma = 0.140
Variable    n    Mean    StDev    SE Mean      95.0 % CI
Price per   41   0.5765  0.1394   0.0219    (0.5336, 0.6193)
```

8.2 ESTIMATING THE POPULATION MEAN USING THE *t* STATISTIC (σ UNKNOWN)

In Section 8.1, we learned how to estimate a population mean by using the sample mean when the population standard deviation is known. In most instances, if a business researcher desires to estimate a population mean, the population standard deviation will be unknown and thus, techniques presented in section 8.1 will not be applicable. When the population standard deviation is unknown, the sample standard deviation must be used in the estimation process. In this section, a statistical technique is presented to estimate a population mean using the sample mean when the population standard deviation is unknown.

Suppose a business researcher is interested in estimating the average flying time of a DC-10 jet from New York to Los Angeles. Since the business researcher does not know the population mean or average time, it is likely that she also does not know the population standard deviation. By taking a random sample of flights, the researcher can compute a sample mean and a sample standard deviation from which the estimate can be constructed. Another business researcher is studying the impact of movie video advertisements on consumers using a random sample of people. The researcher wants to estimate the mean response for the population, but has no idea what is the population standard deviation. He will have the sample mean and sample standard deviation available to perform this analysis.

The z formulas presented in Section 8.1 are inappropriate for use when the population standard deviation is unknown (and is replaced by the sample standard deviation). Instead, another mechanism to handle such cases was developed by a British statistician, William S. Gosset.

Gosset was born in 1876 in Canterbury, England. He studied chemistry and mathematics, and in 1899 went to work for the Guinness Brewery in Dublin, Ireland. Gosset was involved in quality control at the brewery, studying variables such as raw materials and temperature. Because of the circumstances of his experiments, Gosset conducted many studies where the population standard deviation was unavailable. He discovered that using the standard z test with a sample standard deviation produced inexact and incorrect distributions. This finding led to his development of the distribution of the sample standard deviation and the t test.

Gosset was a student and close personal friend of Karl Pearson. When Gosset's first work on the t test was published, he used the pen name "Student." As a result, the t test is sometimes referred to as the Student's t test. Gosset's contribution was significant because it led to more exact statistical tests, which some scholars say marked the beginning of the modern era in mathematical statistics.*

The *t* Distribution

Gosset developed the ***t* distribution,** which is used instead of the z distribution for doing inferential statistics on the population mean when the population standard deviation is unknown and the population is normally distributed. The formula for the ***t* value** is

$$t = \frac{\bar{x} - \mu}{\frac{s}{\sqrt{n}}}$$

This formula is essentially the same as the z formula, but the distribution table values are different. The t distribution values are contained in Table A.6 and, for convenience, inside the back cover of the text.

The t distribution actually is a series of distributions because every sample size has a different distribution, thereby creating the potential for many t tables. To make these t values more manageable, only select key values are presented; each line in the table contains values from a different t distribution. An assumption underlying the use of the t statistic is that the population is normally distributed. If the population distribution is not normal or is unknown, nonparametric techniques (presented in Chapter 17) should be used.

Robustness

Most statistical techniques have one or more underlying assumptions. If a statistical technique is relatively insensitive to minor violations in one or more of its underlying assumptions, the technique is said to be **robust** to that assumption. The t statistic for estimating a population mean is relatively robust to the assumption that the population is normally distributed.

Some statistical techniques are not robust, and a statistician should exercise extreme caution to be certain that the assumptions underlying a technique are being met before using

---

* Adapted from Arthur L. Dudycha and Linda W. Dudycha, "Behavioral Statistics: An Historical Perspective," in *Statistical Issues: A Reader for the Behavioral Sciences,* Roger Kirk, ed. (Monterey, CA: Brooks/Cole, 1972).

it or interpreting statistical output resulting from its use. A business analyst should always beware of statistical assumptions and the robustness of techniques being used in an analysis.

Characteristics of the *t* Distribution

Figure 8.5 displays two *t* distributions superimposed on the standard normal distribution. Like the standard normal curve, *t* distributions are symmetric, unimodal, and a family of curves. The *t* distributions are flatter in the middle and have more area in their tails than the standard normal distribution.

An examination of *t* distribution values reveals that the *t* distribution approaches the standard normal curve as *n* becomes large. The *t* distribution is the appropriate distribution to use any time the population variance or standard deviation is unknown, regardless of sample size.

Reading the *t* Distribution Table

To find a value in the *t* distribution table requires knowing the degrees of freedom; each different value of degrees of freedom is associated with a different *t* distribution. The *t* distribution table used here is a compilation of many *t* distributions, with each line of the table having different degrees of freedom and containing *t* values for different *t* distributions. The **degrees of freedom** for the *t* statistic presented in this section are computed by $n - 1$. The term **degrees of freedom** refers to *the number of independent observations for a source of variation minus the number of independent parameters estimated in computing the variation.*[*] In this case, one independent parameter, the population mean, μ, is being estimated by $\bar{x}$ in computing *s*. Thus, the degrees of freedom formula is *n* independent observations minus one independent parameter being estimated $(n - 1)$.

Because the degrees of freedom are computed differently for various *t* formulas, a degrees of freedom formula is given along with each *t* formula in the text.

In Table A.6, the degrees of freedom are located in the left column. The *t* distribution table in this text does not use the area between the statistic and the mean as does the *z* distribution (standard normal distribution). Instead, the *t* table uses the area in the tail of the distribution. The emphasis in the *t* table is on α, and each tail of the distribution contains $\alpha/2$ of the area under the curve when confidence intervals are constructed. For confidence intervals, the table *t* value is found in the column under the value of $\alpha/2$ and in the row of the degrees of freedom (df) value.

For example, if a 90% confidence interval is being computed, the total area in the two tails is 10%. Thus, α is .10 and $\alpha/2$ is .05, as indicated in Figure 8.6. The *t* distribution table shown in Table 8.2 contains only six values of $\alpha/2$ (.10, .05, .025, .01, .005, .001). The *t* value is located at the intersection of the df value and the selected $\alpha/2$ value. So if the degrees of freedom for a given *t* statistic are 24 and the desired $\alpha/2$ value is .05, the *t* value is 1.711.

FIGURE 8.5

Comparison of Two *t* Distributions to the Standard Normal Curve

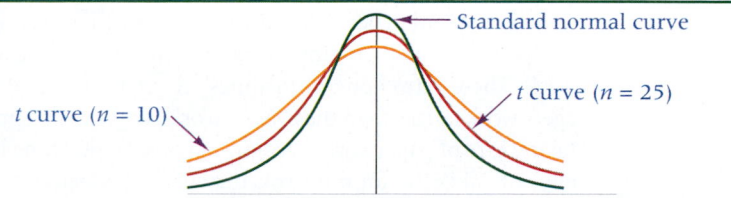

Standard normal curve

t curve (*n* = 25)

t curve (*n* = 10)

---

* Roger E. Kirk. *Experimental Design: Procedures for the Behavioral Sciences.* Belmont, California: Brooks/Cole Publishing Company, 1968.

FIGURE 8.6

Distribution with Alpha
for 90% Confidence

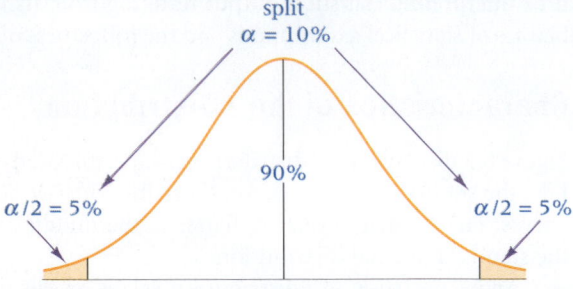

TABLE 8.2

t Distribution

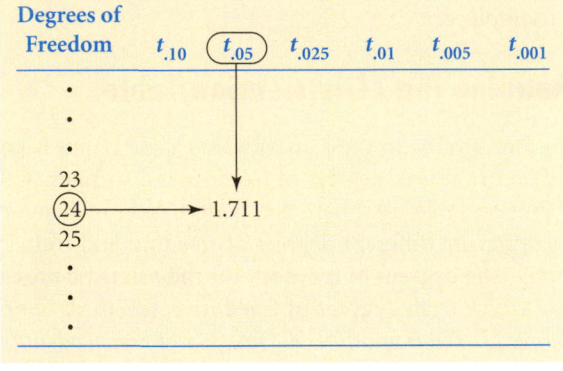

Confidence Intervals to Estimate the Population Mean Using the *t* Statistic

The *t* formula

$$t = \frac{\bar{x} - \mu}{\frac{s}{\sqrt{n}}}$$

can be manipulated algebraically to produce a formula for estimating the population mean when σ is unknown and the population is normally distributed. The results are the formulas given next.

CONFIDENCE INTERVAL TO ESTIMATE μ: POPULATION STANDARD DEVIATION UNKNOWN AND THE POPULATION NORMALLY DISTRIBUTED (8.3)	$$\bar{x} \pm t_{\alpha/2,n-1} \frac{s}{\sqrt{n}}$$ $$\bar{x} - t_{\alpha/2,n-1} \frac{s}{\sqrt{n}} \leq \mu \leq \bar{x} + t_{\alpha/2,n-1} \frac{s}{\sqrt{n}}$$ $$\text{df} = n - 1$$

Formula 8.3 can be used in a manner similar to methods presented in Section 8.1 for constructing a confidence interval to estimate μ. For example, in the aerospace industry some companies allow their employees to accumulate extra working hours beyond their 40-hour week. These extra hours sometimes are referred to as *green* time, or *comp* time. Many managers work longer than the 8-hour workday preparing proposals, overseeing crucial tasks, and taking care of paperwork. Recognition of such overtime is important. Most managers are usually not paid extra for this work, but a record is kept of this time and occasionally the manager is allowed to use some of this comp time as extra leave or vacation time. Suppose a researcher wants to estimate the average amount of comp time accumulated per week for managers in the aerospace industry. He randomly samples 18 managers and measures the amount of extra time they work during a specific week and obtains the results shown (in hours).

6	21	17	20	7	0	8	16	29
3	8	12	11	9	21	25	15	16

He constructs a 90% confidence interval to estimate the average amount of extra time per week worked by a manager in the aerospace industry. He assumes that comp time is normally distributed in the population. The sample size is 18, so df = 17. A 90% level of confidence results in $\alpha/2 = .05$ area in each tail. The table *t* value is

$$t_{.05,17} = 1.740$$

The subscripts in the *t* value denote to other researchers the area in the right tail of the *t* distribution (for confidence intervals $\alpha/2$) and the number of degrees of freedom. The sample mean is 13.56 hours, and the sample standard deviation is 7.8 hours. The confidence interval is computed from this information as

$$\bar{x} \pm t_{\alpha/2,n-1} \frac{s}{\sqrt{n}}$$

$$13.56 \pm 1.740 \frac{7.8}{\sqrt{18}} = 13.56 \pm 3.20$$

$$10.36 \leq \mu \leq 16.76$$

The point estimate for this problem is 13.56 hours, with an error of ±3.20 hours. The researcher is 90% confident that the average amount of comp time accumulated by a manager per week in this industry is between 10.36 and 16.76 hours.

From these figures, aerospace managers could attempt to build a reward system for such extra work or evaluate the regular 40-hour week to determine how to use the normal work hours more effectively and thus reduce comp time.

DEMONSTRATION PROBLEM 8.3

The owner of a large equipment rental company wants to make a rather quick estimate of the average number of days a piece of ditchdigging equipment is rented out per person per time. The company has records of all rentals, but the amount of time required to conduct an audit of *all* accounts would be prohibitive. The owner decides to take a random sample of rental invoices. Fourteen different rentals of ditchdiggers are selected randomly from the files, yielding the following data. She uses these data to construct a 99% confidence interval to estimate the average number of days that a ditchdigger is rented and assumes that the number of days per rental is normally distributed in the population.

$$3 \quad 1 \quad 3 \quad 2 \quad 5 \quad 1 \quad 2 \quad 1 \quad 4 \quad 2 \quad 1 \quad 3 \quad 1 \quad 1$$

Solution

As $n = 14$, the df = 13. The 99% level of confidence results in $\alpha/2 = .005$ area in each tail of the distribution. The table *t* value is

$$t_{.005,13} = 3.012$$

The sample mean is 2.14 and the sample standard deviation is 1.29. The confidence interval is

$$\bar{x} \pm t \frac{s}{\sqrt{n}}$$

$$2.14 \pm 3.012 \frac{1.29}{\sqrt{14}} = 2.14 \pm 1.04$$

$$1.10 \leq \mu \leq 3.18$$

The point estimate of the average length of time per rental is 2.14 days, with an error of ±1.04. With a 99% level of confidence, the company's owner can estimate that the average length of time per rental is between 1.10 and 3.18 days. Combining this figure with variables such as frequency of rentals per year can help the owner estimate potential profit or loss per year for such a piece of equipment.

FIGURE 8.7

Excel and MINITAB Output for
the Comp Time Example

Excel Output

	A	B
1	Comp Time	
2	Mean	13.56
3	Standard Error	1.8386
4	Standard Deviation	7.8006
5	Confidence Level (90.0%)	3.20

MINITAB Output

```
      One-Sample T: Comp Time

Variable     n    Mean   StDev   SE Mean      90.0% CI
Comp Time   18   13.56    7.80      1.84    (10.36, 16.75)
```

Using the Computer to Construct
t Confidence Intervals for the Mean

Both Excel and MINITAB can be used to construct confidence intervals for μ using the
t distribution. Figure 8.7 displays Excel output and MINITAB output for the aerospace
comp time problem. The Excel output includes the mean, the standard error, the sample
standard deviation, and the error of the confidence interval, referred to by Excel as the
"confidence level." The standard error of the mean is computed by dividing the standard
deviation (7.8006) by square root of n (4.243). When using the Excel output, the confidence interval must be computed from the sample mean and the confidence level (error
of the interval).

The MINITAB output yields the confidence interval endpoints (10.36, 16.75). The
"SE Mean" is the standard error of the mean. The error of the confidence interval is computed by multiplying the standard error of the mean by the table value of t. Adding and
subtracting this error from the mean yields the confidence interval endpoints produced
by MINITAB.

8.2 PROBLEMS

8.13 Suppose the following data are selected randomly from a population of normally
distributed values.

40   51   43   48   44   57   54
39   42   48   45   39   43

Construct a 95% confidence interval to estimate the population mean.

8.14 Assuming x is normally distributed, use the following information to compute a
90% confidence interval to estimate μ.

313   320   319   340   325   310
321   329   317   311   307   318

8.15 If a random sample of 41 items produces $\bar{x} = 128.4$ and $s = 20.6$, what is the 98%
confidence interval for μ? Assume x is normally distributed for the population.
What is the point estimate?

8.16 A random sample of 15 items is taken, producing a sample mean of 2.364 with a
sample variance of .81. Assume x is normally distributed and construct a 90%
confidence interval for the population mean.

8.17 Use the following data to construct a 99% confidence interval for μ.

16.4	17.1	17.0	15.6	16.2
14.8	16.0	15.6	17.3	17.4
15.6	15.7	17.2	16.6	16.0
15.3	15.4	16.0	15.8	17.2
14.6	15.5	14.9	16.7	16.3

Assume x is normally distributed. What is the point estimate for μ?

8.18 According to Runzheimer International, the average cost of a domestic trip for business travelers in the financial industry is $1,250. Suppose another travel industry research company takes a random sample of 22 business travelers in the financial industry and determines that the sample average cost of a domestic trip is $1,192, with a sample standard deviation of $279. Construct a 98% confidence interval for the population mean from these sample data. Assume that the data are normally distributed in the population. Now go back and examine the $1,250 figure published by Runzheimer International. Does it fall into the confidence interval computed from the sample data? What does it tell you?

8.19 A valve manufacturer produces a butterfly valve composed of two semicircular plates on a common spindle that is used to permit flow in one direction only. The semicircular plates are supplied by a vendor with specifications that the plates be 2.37 millimeters thick and have a tensile strength of 5 pounds per millimeter. A random sample of 20 such plates is taken. Electronic calipers are used to measure the thickness of each plate; the measurements are given here. Assuming that the thicknesses of such plates are normally distributed, use the data to construct a 95% level of confidence for the population mean thickness of these plates. What is the point estimate? How much is the error of the interval?

2.4066	2.4579	2.6724	2.1228	2.3238
2.1328	2.0665	2.2738	2.2055	2.5267
2.5937	2.1994	2.5392	2.4359	2.2146
2.1933	2.4575	2.7956	2.3353	2.2699

8.20 Some fast-food chains offer a lower-priced combination meal in an effort to attract budget-conscious customers. One chain test-marketed a burger, fries, and a drink combination for $1.71. The weekly sales volume for these meals was impressive. Suppose the chain wants to estimate the average amount its customers spent on a meal at their restaurant while this combination offer was in effect. An analyst gathers data from 28 randomly selected customers. The following data represent the sample meal totals.

$3.21	5.40	3.50	4.39	5.60	8.65	5.02	4.20	1.25	7.64
3.28	5.57	3.26	3.80	5.46	9.87	4.67	5.86	3.73	4.08
5.47	4.49	5.19	5.82	7.62	4.83	8.42	9.10		

Use these data to construct a 90% confidence interval to estimate the population mean value. Assume the amounts spent are normally distributed.

8.21 The marketing director of a large department store wants to estimate the average number of customers who enter the store every 5 minutes. She randomly selects 5-minute intervals and counts the number of arrivals at the store. She obtains the figures 58, 32, 41, 47, 56, 80, 45, 29, 32, and 78. The analyst assumes the number of arrivals is normally distributed. Using these data, the analyst computes a 95% confidence interval to estimate the mean value for all 5-minute intervals. What interval values does she get?

8.22 Runzheimer International publishes results of studies on overseas business travel costs. Suppose as a part of one of these studies the following per diem travel accounts (in dollars) are obtained for 14 business travelers staying in Johannesburg, South Africa. Use these data to construct a 98% confidence interval to estimate the average per diem expense for businesspeople traveling to

Johannesburg. What is the point estimate? Assume per diem rates for any locale are approximately normally distributed.

142.59	148.48	159.63	171.93	146.90	168.87	141.94
159.09	156.32	142.49	129.28	151.56	132.87	178.34

8.3 ESTIMATING THE POPULATION PROPORTION

Business decision makers and researchers often need to be able to estimate a population proportion. For most businesses, estimating market share (their proportion of the market) is important because many company decisions evolve from market share information. Companies spend thousands of dollars estimating the proportion of produced goods that are defective. Market segmentation opportunities come from a knowledge of the proportion of various demographic characteristics among potential customers or clients.

Methods similar to those in Section 8.1 can be used to estimate the population proportion. The central limit theorem for sample proportions led to the following formula in Chapter 7.

$$z = \frac{\hat{p} - p}{\sqrt{\dfrac{p \cdot q}{n}}}$$

where $q = 1 - p$. Recall that this formula can be applied only when $n \cdot p$ and $n \cdot q$ are greater than 5.

Algebraically manipulating this formula to estimate p involves solving for p. However, p is in both the numerator and the denominator, which complicates the resulting formula. For this reason—for confidence interval purposes only and for large sample sizes—$\hat{p}$ is substituted for p in the denominator, yielding

$$z = \frac{\hat{p} - p}{\sqrt{\dfrac{\hat{p} \cdot \hat{q}}{n}}}$$

where $\hat{q} = 1 - \hat{p}$. Solving for p results in the confidence interval in formula (8.4).*

CONFIDENCE INTERVAL TO ESTIMATE p (8.4)

$$\hat{p} - z_{\alpha/2}\sqrt{\frac{\hat{p} \cdot \hat{q}}{n}} \leq p \leq \hat{p} + z_{\alpha/2}\sqrt{\frac{\hat{p} \cdot \hat{q}}{n}}$$

where
$\hat{p}$ = sample proportion
$\hat{q} = 1 - \hat{p}$
p = population proportion
n = sample size

In this formula, $\hat{p}$ is the point estimate and $\pm z_{\alpha/2}\sqrt{\dfrac{\hat{p} \cdot \hat{q}}{n}}$ is the error of the estimation.

---

*Because we are not using the true standard deviation of $\hat{p}$, the correct divisor of the standard error of $\hat{p}$ is $n - 1$. However, for large sample sizes, the effect is negligible. Although technically the minimal sample size for the techniques presented in this section is $n \cdot p$ and $n \cdot q$ greater than 5, in actual practice sample sizes of several hundred are more commonly used. As an example, for $\hat{p}$ and $\hat{q}$ of .50 and $n = 300$, the standard error of $\hat{p}$ is .02887 using n and .02892 using $n - 1$, a difference of only .00005.

Coffee Consumption in the United States

In 1969, more people drank coffee than soft drinks in the United States. In fact, according to Jack Maxwell of *Beverage Digest*, U.S. consumption of coffee in 1969 was close to 40 gallons per capita compared to about 20 gallons of soft drinks. However, by 1998, coffee consumption was down to about 20 gallons per capita annually compared to more than 50 gallons for soft drink consumption. Although coffee lost out to soft drinks as a beverage leader in the past three decades, it made a comeback recently with the increase in the popularity of coffee shops in the United States.

What is the state of coffee consumption in the United States now? A survey conducted by the National Coffee Association revealed that 80 percent of Americans now drink coffee at least occasionally. Out-of-home consumption has grown to 39%. Daily consumption among 18- to 24-year-olds rose to 25% compared to 74% of the over-60-year-olds. The average consumption per drinker rose to 3.3 cups per day. However, the 18- to 24-year-olds who drink coffee average 4.6 cups per day, whereas the over-60-year-olds average only 2.8 cups. Coffee consumption also varies by geographic region. Fifty-three percent of Northeasterners surveyed had drunk coffee the previous day compared to 47% of Westerners. Only 16% of Northeasterners drink their coffee black compared to 33% of Westerners and 42% of people in the North Central region.

How does U.S. consumption of coffee compare to other countries? The U.S. per capita consumption of coffee is 4 kilograms, compared to 5.56 kilograms in Europe in general and 11 kilograms in Finland.

Because much of the information presented here was gleaned from some survey, virtually all of the percentages and means are sample statistics and not population parameters. Thus, what are presented as coffee population statistics are actually point estimates. Using the sample size (3,300) and a level of confidence, confidence intervals can be constructed for the proportions. Confidence intervals for means can be constructed from these point estimates if the value of the standard deviation can be determined.

Source: Adapted from Nikhil Deogun, "Joe Wakes Up, Smells the Soda," The Wall Street Journal (8 June 1999), p. B1; "Better Latte than Never," Prepared Foods (March 2001), p. 1; "Coffee Consumption on the Rise," Nation's Restaurant News (2 July 2001), p. 1. Other sources include the National Coffee Association, Jack Maxwell, the International Coffee Organization, and Datamonitor.

As an example, a study of 87 randomly selected companies with a telemarketing operation revealed that 39% of the sampled companies used telemarketing to assist them in order processing. Using this information, how could a researcher estimate the *population* proportion of telemarketing companies that use their telemarketing operation to assist them in order processing?

The sample proportion, $\hat{p} = .39$, is the *point estimate* of the population proportion, p. For $n = 87$ and $\hat{p} = .39$, a 95% confidence interval can be computed to determine the interval estimation of p. The z value for 95% confidence is 1.96. The value of $\hat{q} = 1 - \hat{p} = 1 - .39 = .61$. The confidence interval estimate is

$$.39 - 1.96\sqrt{\frac{(.39)(.61)}{87}} \le p \le .39 + 1.96\sqrt{\frac{(.39)(.61)}{87}}$$

$$.39 - .10 \le p \le .39 + .10$$

$$.29 \le p \le .49$$

This interval suggests that the population proportion of telemarketing firms that use their operation to assist order processing is somewhere between .29 and .49, based on the point estimate of .39 with an error of ±.10. This result has a 95% level of confidence.

DEMONSTRATION PROBLEM 8.4

Coopers & Lybrand surveyed 210 chief executives of fast-growing small companies. Only 51% of these executives had a management succession plan in place. A spokesperson for Cooper & Lybrand said that many companies do not worry about management succession unless it is an immediate problem. However, the unexpected exit of a corporate leader can disrupt and unfocus a company for long enough to cause it to lose its momentum.

Use the data given to compute a 92% confidence interval to estimate the proportion of *all* fast-growing small companies that have a management succession plan.

Solution

The point estimate is the sample proportion given to be .51. It is estimated that .51, or 51% of all fast-growing small companies have a management succession plan. Realizing that the point estimate might change with another sample selection, we calculate a confidence interval.

The value of n is 210; $\hat{p}$ is .51, and $\hat{q} = 1 - \hat{p} = .49$. Because the level of confidence is 92%, the value of $z_{.04} = 1.75$. The confidence interval is computed as

$$.51 - 1.75\sqrt{\frac{(.51)(.49)}{210}} \leq p \leq .51 + 1.75\sqrt{\frac{(.51)(.49)}{210}}$$

$$.51 - .06 \leq p \leq .51 + .06$$

$$.45 \leq p \leq .57$$

It is estimated with 92% confidence that the proportion of the population of fast-growing small companies that have a management succession plan is between .45 and .57.

DEMONSTRATION PROBLEM 8.5

A clothing company produces men's jeans. The jeans are made and sold with either a regular cut or a boot cut. In an effort to estimate the proportion of their men's jeans market in Oklahoma City that prefers boot-cut jeans, the analyst takes a random sample of 212 jeans sales from the company's two Oklahoma City retail outlets. Only 34 of the sales were for boot-cut jeans. Construct a 90% confidence interval to estimate the proportion of the population in Oklahoma City who prefer boot-cut jeans.

Solution

The sample size is 212, and the number preferring boot-cut jeans is 34. The sample proportion is $\hat{p} = 34/212 = .16$. A point estimate for boot-cut jeans in the population is .16, or 16%. The z value for a 90% level of confidence is 1.645, and the value of $\hat{q} = 1 - \hat{p} = 1 - .16 = .84$. The confidence interval estimate is

$$.16 - 1.645\sqrt{\frac{(.16)(.84)}{212}} \leq p \leq .16 + 1.645\sqrt{\frac{(.16)(.84)}{212}}$$

$$.16 - .04 \leq p \leq .16 + .04$$

$$.12 \leq p \leq .20$$

The analyst estimates that the population proportion of boot-cut jeans purchases is between .12 and .20. The level of confidence in this result is 90%.

Using the Computer to Construct Confidence Intervals of the Population Proportion

MINITAB has the capability of producing confidence intervals for proportions. Figure 8.8 contains MINITAB output for Demonstration Problem 8.5. The output contains the sample size (labeled as N), the number in the sample containing the characteristic of interest (X), the sample proportion, the level of confidence, and the endpoints of the confidence interval. Note that the endpoints of the confidence interval are essentially the same as those computed in Demonstration Problem 8.5.

FIGURE 8.8

MINITAB Output for Demonstration Problem 8.5

```
              TEST AND CI FOR ONE PROPORTION

Test of p = 0.5 vs p not = 0.5
Sample   X    N    Sample p         90.0% CI          P-Value
1        34   212  0.160377  (0.120328, 0.207718)     0.000
```

8.3 PROBLEMS

8.23 Use the information about each of the following samples to compute the confidence interval to estimate p.

    a. $n = 44$ and $\hat{p} = .51$; compute a 99% confidence interval.

    b. $n = 300$ and $\hat{p} = .82$; compute a 95% confidence interval.

    c. $n = 1,150$ and $\hat{p} = .48$; compute a 90% confidence interval.

    d. $n = 95$ and $\hat{p} = .32$; compute an 88% confidence interval.

8.24 Use the following sample information to calculate the confidence interval to estimate the population proportion. Let x be the number of items in the sample having the characteristic of interest.

    a. $n = 116$ and $x = 57$, with 99% confidence

    b. $n = 800$ and $x = 479$, with 97% confidence

    c. $n = 240$ and $x = 106$, with 85% confidence

    d. $n = 60$ and $x = 21$, with 90% confidence

8.25 Suppose a random sample of 85 items has been taken from a population and 40 of the items contain the characteristic of interest. Use this information to calculate a 90% confidence interval to estimate the proportion of the population that has the characteristic of interest. Calculate a 95% confidence interval. Calculate a 99% confidence interval. As the level of confidence changes and the other sample information stays constant, what happens to the confidence interval?

8.26 A study released by Scoop Marketing showed that Universal/PolyGram held a 24.5% share of the music CD market. Suppose this figure is actually a point estimate obtained by interviewing 1,003 people who purchased a music CD. Use this information to compute a 99% confidence interval for the proportion of the market that is held by Universal/PolyGram. Suppose the figure was obtained from a survey of 10,000 people. Recompute the confidence interval and compare your results with the first confidence interval. How did they differ? What might you conclude about sample size and confidence intervals?

8.27 According to the Stern Marketing Group, 9 out of 10 professional women say that financial planning is more important today than it was five years ago. Where do these women go for help in financial planning? Forty-seven percent use a financial advisor (broker, tax consultant, financial planner). Twenty-eight percent use written sources such as magazines, books, and newspapers. Suppose these figures were obtained by taking a sample of 560 professional women who said that financial planning is more important today than it was five years ago. Construct a 95% confidence interval for the proportion of professional women who use a financial advisor. Use the percentage given in this problem as the point estimate. Construct a 90% confidence interval for the proportion of professional women who use written sources. Use the percentage given in this problem as the point estimate.

8.28 What proportion of pizza restaurants that are primarily for walk-in business have a salad bar? Suppose that, in an effort to determine this figure, a random sample of 1,250 of these restaurants across the United States based on the *Yellow Pages* is called. If 997 of the restaurants sampled have a salad bar, what is the 98% confidence interval for the population proportion?

8.29 The highway department wants to estimate the proportion of vehicles on Interstate 25 between the hours of midnight and 5:00 A.M. that are 18-wheel tractor trailers. The estimate will be used to determine highway repair and construction considerations and in highway patrol planning. Suppose researchers for the highway department counted vehicles at different locations on the interstate for several nights during this time period. Of the 3,481 vehicles counted, 927 were 18-wheelers.

    a. Determine the point estimate for the proportion of vehicles traveling Interstate 25 during this time period that are 18-wheelers.

    b. Construct a 99% confidence interval for the proportion of vehicles on Interstate 25 during this time period that are 18-wheelers.

8.30 What proportion of commercial airline pilots are more than 40 years of age? Suppose a researcher has access to a list of all pilots who are members of the Commercial Airline Pilots Association. If this list is used as a frame for the study, she can randomly select a sample of pilots, contact them, and ascertain their ages. From 89 of these pilots so selected, she learns that 48 are more than 40 years of age. Construct an 85% confidence interval to estimate the population proportion of commercial airline pilots who are more than 40 years of age.

8.31 According to Runzheimer International, in a survey of relocation administrators 63% of all workers who rejected relocation offers did so for family considerations. Suppose this figure was obtained by using a random sample of the files of 672 workers who had rejected relocation offers. Use this information to construct a 95% confidence interval to estimate the population proportion of workers who reject relocation offers for family considerations.

8.4 ESTIMATING THE POPULATION VARIANCE

At times in statistical analysis, the researcher is more interested in the population variance than in the population mean or population proportion. For example, in the total quality movement, suppliers who want to earn world-class supplier status or even those who want to maintain customer contracts are often asked to show continual reduction of variation on supplied parts. Tests are conducted with samples in efforts to determine lot variation and to determine whether variability goals are being met.

Estimating the variance is important in many other instances in business. For example, variations between airplane altimeter readings need to be minimal. It is not enough just to know that, on the average, a particular brand of altimeter produces the correct altitude. It is also important that the variation between instruments be small. Thus measuring the variation of altimeters is critical. Parts being used in engines must fit tightly on a consistent basis. A wide variability among parts can result in a part that is too large to fit into its slots or so small that it results in too much tolerance, which causes vibrations. How can variance be estimated?

You may recall from Chapter 3 that sample variance is computed by using the formula

$$s^2 = \frac{\sum(x - \bar{x})^2}{n - 1}$$

Because sample variances are typically used as estimators or estimations of the population variance, as they are here, a mathematical adjustment is made in the denominator by using $n - 1$ to make the sample variance an unbiased estimator of the population variance.

Suppose a researcher wants to estimate the population variance from the sample variance in a manner that is similar to the estimation of the population mean from a sample mean. The relationship of the sample variance to the population variance is captured by the **chi-square distribution** (x^2). The ratio of the sample variance (s^2) multiplied by $n - 1$ to the population variance (σ^2) is approximately chi-square distributed, as shown in formula 8.5, if the population from which the values are drawn is normally distributed.

Caution: *Use of the chi-square statistic to estimate the population variance is extremely sensitive to violations of the assumption that the population is normally distributed. For that reason, some researchers do not include this technique among their statistical repertoire. Although the technique is still rather widely presented as a mechanism for constructing confidence intervals to estimate a population variance, you should proceed with extreme caution and apply the technique only in cases where the population is known to be normally distributed. We can say that this technique lacks robustness.*

Like the t distribution, the chi-square distribution varies by sample size and contains a degrees-of-freedom value. The number of degrees of freedom for the chi-square formula (8.5) is $n - 1$.

χ^2 FORMULA FOR SINGLE VARIANCE (8.5)	$$\chi^2 = \frac{(n-1)s^2}{\sigma^2}$$ $$\text{df} = n - 1$$

The chi-square distribution is not symmetrical, and its shape will vary according to the degrees of freedom. Figure 8.9 shows the shape of chi-square distributions for three different degrees of freedom.

Formula 8.5 can be rearranged algebraically to produce a formula that can be used to construct confidence intervals for population variances. This new formula is shown as formula 8.6.

CONFIDENCE INTERVAL TO ESTIMATE THE POPULATION VARIANCE (8.6)	$$\frac{(n-1)s^2}{\chi^2_{\alpha/2}} \leq \sigma^2 \leq \frac{(n-1)s^2}{\chi^2_{1-\alpha/2}}$$ $$\text{df} = n - 1$$

The value of alpha (α) is equal to 1 – (level of confidence expressed as a proportion). Thus, if we are constructing a 90% confidence interval, alpha is 10% of the area and is expressed in proportion form: $\alpha = .10$.

How can this formula be used to estimate the population variance from a sample variance? Suppose eight purportedly 7-centimeter aluminum cylinders in a sample are measured in diameter, resulting in the following values:

| 6.91 cm | 6.93 cm | 7.01 cm | 7.02 cm |
| 7.05 cm | 7.00 cm | 6.98 cm | 7.01 cm |

In estimating a population variance from these values, the sample variance must be computed. This value is $s^2 = .0022125$. If a point estimate is all that is required, the point estimate is the sample variance, .0022125. However, realizing that the point estimate will probably change from sample to sample, we want to construct an interval estimate. To do this, we must know the degrees of freedom and the table values of the chi-squares. Because $n = 8$, the degrees of freedom are $\text{df} = n - 1 = 7$. What are the chi-square values necessary to complete the information needed in formula 8.6? Assume the population of cylinder diameters is normally distributed.

Suppose we are constructing a 90% confidence interval. The value of α is $1 - .90 = .10$. It is the portion of the area under the chi-square curve that is outside the confidence interval. This outside area is needed because the chi-square table values given in Table A.8 are listed according the area in the right tail of the distribution. In a 90% confidence interval, $\alpha/2$ or .05 of the area is in the right tail of the distribution and .05 is in the left tail of the distribution. The chi-square value for the .05 area on the right tail of the distribution can be obtained directly from the table by using the degrees of freedom, which in this case are 7. Thus the right-side chi-square, $\chi^2_{.05,7}$, is 14.0671. Because Table A.8 lists chi-square values for areas in the right tail, the chi-square value for the left tail must be obtained by determining how much area lies to the right of the left tail. If .05 is to the left of the confidence interval, then $1 - .05 = .95$ of the area is to the right of the left tail. This calculation is consistent with the $1 - \alpha/2$

FIGURE 8.9

Three Chi-Square Distributions

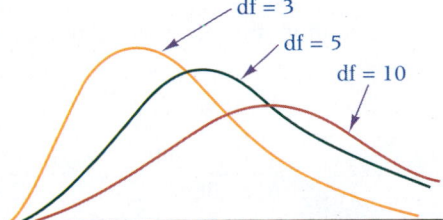

FIGURE 8.10

Two Table Values of Chi-Square

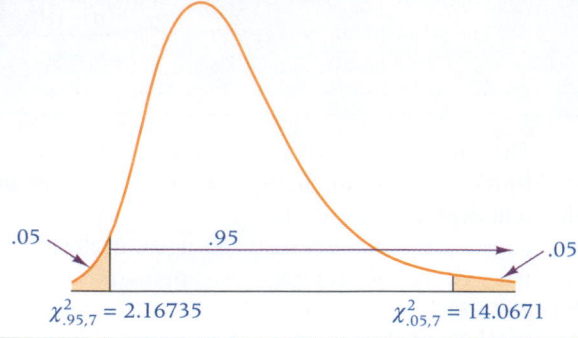

$$\chi^2_{.95,7} = 2.16735 \qquad \chi^2_{.05,7} = 14.0671$$

expression used in formula (8.6). Thus the chi-square for the left tail is $\chi^2_{.95,7} = 2.16735$. Figure 8.10 shows the two table values of χ^2 on a chi-square distribution.

Incorporating these values into the formula, we can construct the 90% confidence interval to estimate the population variance of the 7-centimeter aluminum cylinders.

$$\frac{(n-1)s^2}{\chi^2_{\alpha/2}} \leq \sigma^2 \leq \frac{(n-1)s^2}{\chi^2_{1-\alpha/2}}$$

$$\frac{(7)(.0022125)}{14.0671} \leq \sigma^2 \leq \frac{(7)(.0022125)}{2.16735}$$

$$.001101 \leq \sigma^2 \leq .007146$$

The confidence interval says that with 90% confidence, the population variance is somewhere between .001101 and .007146.

<table>
<tr><td>

DEMONSTRATION PROBLEM 8.6

</td><td>

The U.S. Bureau of Labor Statistics publishes data on the hourly compensation costs for production workers in manufacturing for various countries. The latest figures published for Greece show that the average hourly wage for a production worker in manufacturing is $9.63. Suppose the business council of Greece wants to know how consistent this figure is. They randomly select 25 production workers in manufacturing from across the country and determine that the standard deviation of hourly wages for such workers is $1.12. Use this information to develop a 95% confidence interval to estimate the population variance for the hourly wages of production workers in manufacturing in Greece. Assume that the hourly wages for production workers across the country in manufacturing are normally distributed.

</td></tr>
</table>

Solution

By squaring the standard deviation, $s = 1.12$, we can obtain the sample variance, $s^2 = 1.2544$. This figure provides the point estimate of the population variance. Because the sample size, n, is 25, the degrees of freedom, $n - 1$, are 24. A 95% confidence means that alpha is $1 - .95 = .05$. This value is split to determine the area in each tail of the chi-square distribution: $\alpha/2 = .025$. The values of the chi-squares obtained from Table A.8 are

$$\chi^2_{.025,24} = 39.3641 \text{ and } \chi^2_{.975,24} = 12.4011$$

From this information, the confidence interval can be determined.

$$\frac{(n-1)s^2}{\chi^2_{\alpha/2}} \leq \sigma^2 \leq \frac{(n-1)s^2}{\chi^2_{1-\alpha/2}}$$

$$\frac{(24)(1.2544)}{39.3641} \leq \sigma^2 \leq \frac{(24)(1.2544)}{12.4011}$$

$$0.7648 \leq \sigma^2 \leq 2.4277$$

The business council can estimate with 95% confidence that the population variance of the hourly wages of production workers in manufacturing in Greece is between 0.7648 and 2.4277.

8.4 PROBLEMS

8.32 For each of the following sample results, construct the requested confidence interval. Assume the data come from normally distributed populations.
   a. $n = 12$, $\bar{x} = 28.4$, $s^2 = 44.9$; 99% confidence for σ^2
   b. $n = 7$, $\bar{x} = 4.37$, $s = 1.24$; 95% confidence for σ^2
   c. $n = 20$, $\bar{x} = 105$, $s = 32$; 90% confidence for σ^2
   d. $n = 17$, $s^2 = 18.56$; 80% confidence for σ^2

8.33 Use the following sample data to estimate the population variance. Produce a point estimate and a 98% confidence interval. Assume the data come from a normally distributed population.

27	40	32	41	45	29	33	39
30	28	36	32	42	40	38	46

8.34 The Interstate Conference of Employment Security Agencies says the average workweek in the United States is down to only 35 hours, largely because of a rise in part-time workers. Suppose this figure was obtained from a random sample of 20 workers and that the standard deviation of the sample was 4.3 hours. Assume hours worked per week are normally distributed in the population. Use this sample information to develop a 98% confidence interval for the population variance of the number of hours worked per week for a worker. What is the point estimate?

8.35 A manufacturing plant produces steel rods. During one production run of 20,000 such rods, the specifications called for rods that were 46 centimeters in length and 3.8 centimeters in width. Fifteen of these rods comprising a random sample were measured for length; the resulting measurements are shown here. Use these data to estimate the population variance of length for the rods. Assume rod length is normally distributed in the population. Construct a 99% confidence interval. Discuss the ramifications of the results.

44 cm	47 cm	43 cm	46 cm	46 cm
45 cm	43 cm	44 cm	47 cm	46 cm
48 cm	48 cm	43 cm	44 cm	45 cm

8.36 Suppose a random sample of 14 people 30–39 years of age produced the household incomes shown here. Use these data to determine a point estimate for the population variance of household incomes for people 30–39 years of age and construct a 95% confidence interval. Assume household income is normally distributed.

$37,500	44,800
33,500	36,900
42,300	32,400
28,000	41,200
46,600	38,500
40,200	32,000
35,500	36,800

8.5 ESTIMATING SAMPLE SIZE

In most business research that uses sample statistics to infer about the population, being able to *estimate the size of sample necessary to accomplish the purposes of the study* is important. The need for this **sample-size estimation** is the same for the large corporation investing tens of thousands of dollars in a massive study of consumer preference and for students undertaking a small case study and wanting to send questionnaires to local businesspeople. In either case, such things as level of confidence, sampling error, and width of estimation interval are closely tied to sample size. If the large corporation is undertaking a market study, should it sample 40 people or 4,000 people? The question is an important one. In most cases, because of cost considerations, business researchers do not want to sample any more units or individuals than necessary.

Sample Size When Estimating μ

In research studies when μ is being estimated, the size of sample can be determined by using the z formula for sample means to solve for n. Consider,

$$z = \frac{\bar{x} - \mu}{\frac{\sigma}{\sqrt{n}}}$$

The difference between $\bar{x}$ and μ is the **error of estimation** resulting from the sampling process. Let $E = (\bar{x} - \mu) =$ the error of estimation. Substituting E into the preceding formula yields

$$z = \frac{E}{\frac{\sigma}{\sqrt{n}}}$$

Solving for n yields a formula that can be used to determine sample size.

SAMPLE SIZE WHEN ESTIMATING μ (8.7)	$n = \dfrac{z_{\alpha/2}^2 \sigma^2}{E^2} = \left(\dfrac{z_{\alpha/2}\sigma}{E}\right)^2$

Sometimes in estimating sample size the population variance is known or can be determined from past studies. Other times, the population variance is unknown and must be estimated to determine the sample size. In such cases, it is acceptable to use the following estimate to represent σ.

$$\sigma \approx \frac{1}{4}(range)$$

Using formula (8.7), the business researcher can estimate the sample size needed to achieve the goals of the study before gathering data. For example, suppose a researcher wants to estimate the average monthly expenditure on bread by a family in Chicago. She wants to be 90% confident of her results. How much error is she willing to tolerate in the results? Suppose she wants the estimate to be within $1.00 of the actual figure and the standard deviation of average monthly bread purchases is $4.00. What is the sample size estimation for this problem? The value of z for a 90% level of confidence is 1.645. Using formula (8.7) with $E = \$1.00$, $\sigma = \$4.00$, and $z = 1.645$ gives

$$n = \frac{z_{\alpha/2}^2 \sigma^2}{E^2} = \frac{(1.645)^2 (4)^2}{1^2} = 43.30$$

That is, at least $n = 43.3$ must be sampled randomly to attain a 90% level of confidence and produce an error within $1.00 for a standard deviation of $4.00. Sampling 43.3 units is impossible, so this result should be rounded up to $n = 44$ units.

In this approach to estimating sample size, we view the error of the estimation as the amount of difference between the statistic (in this case, $\bar{x}$) and the parameter (in this case, μ). The error could be in either direction; that is, the statistic could be over or under the parameter. Thus, the error, E, is actually $\pm E$ as we view it. So when a problem states that the researcher wants to be within \$1.00 of the actual monthly family expenditure for bread, it means that the researcher is willing to allow a tolerance within $\pm$\$1.00 of the actual figure. Another name for this error is the **bounds** of the interval.

DEMONSTRATION PROBLEM 8.7

Suppose you want to estimate the average age of all Boeing 727 airplanes now in active domestic U.S. service. You want to be 95% confident, and you want your estimate to be within two years of the actual figure. The 727 was first placed in service about 30 years ago, but you believe that no active 727s in the U.S. domestic fleet are more than 25 years old. How large a sample should you take?

Solution

Here, $E = 2$ years, the z value for 95% is 1.96, and σ is unknown, so it must be estimated by using $\sigma \approx (1/4) \cdot$ (range). As the range of ages is 0 to 25 years, $\sigma = (1/4)(25) = 6.25$. Use formula (8.7).

$$n = \frac{z^2 \sigma^2}{E^2} = \frac{(1.96)^2 (6.25)^2}{2^2} = 37.52$$

Because you cannot sample 37.52 units, the required sample size is 38. If you randomly sample 38 units, you have an opportunity to estimate the average age of active 727s within 2 years and be 95% confident of the results. If you want to be within 1 year for the estimate ($E = 1$), the sample-size estimate changes to

$$n = \frac{z^2 \sigma^2}{E^2} = \frac{(1.96)^2 (6.25)^2}{1^2} = 150.1$$

Note that cutting the error by a factor of ½ increases the required sample size by a factor of 4. The reason is the squaring factor in formula (8.7). If you want to reduce the error to one-half of what you used before, you must be willing to incur the cost of a sample that is four times larger, for the same level of confidence.

Note: *Sample-size estimates for the population mean where σ is unknown using the t distribution are not shown here. Because a sample size must be known to determine the table value of t, which in turn is used to estimate the sample size, this procedure usually involves an iterative process.*

Determining Sample Size When Estimating *p*

Determining the sample size required to estimate the population proportion, p, also is possible. The process begins with the z formula for sample proportions.

$$z = \frac{\hat{p} - p}{\sqrt{\dfrac{p \cdot q}{n}}}$$

where $q = 1 - p$.

As various samples are taken from the population, $\hat{p}$ will rarely equal the population proportion, p, resulting in an error of estimation. The difference between $\hat{p}$ and p is the error of estimation, so $E = \hat{p} - p$.

$$z = \frac{E}{\sqrt{\dfrac{p \cdot q}{n}}}$$

Solving for n yields the formula for determining sample size.

SAMPLE SIZE WHEN ESTIMATING p (8.8)	$n = \dfrac{z^2 pq}{E^2}$

where

p = population proportion
$q = 1 - p$
E = error of estimation
n = sample size

How can the value of n be determined prior to a study if the formula requires the value of p and the study is being done to estimate p? Although the actual value of p is not known prior to the study, similar studies might have generated a good approximation for p. If no previous value is available for use in estimating p, some possible p values, as shown in Table 8.3, might be considered.

Note that, as p · q is in the numerator of the sample size formula, $p = .5$ will result in the largest sample sizes. Often *if p is unknown, researchers use .5 as an estimate of p* in formula 8.8. This selection results in the largest sample size that could be determined from formula 8.8 for a given z value and a given error value.

DEMONSTRATION PROBLEM 8.8

Hewitt Associates conducted a national survey to determine the extent to which employers are promoting health and fitness among their employees. One of the questions asked was, Does your company offer on-site exercise classes? Suppose it was estimated before the study that no more than 40% of the companies would answer Yes. How large a sample would Hewitt Associates have to take in estimating the population proportion to ensure a 98% confidence in the results and to be within .03 of the true population proportion?

TABLE 8.3

p · q for Various Selected Values of p

p	$p \cdot q$
.5	.25
.4	.24
.3	.21
.2	.16
.1	.09

Solution

The value of E for this problem is .03. Because it is estimated that no more than 40% of the companies would say Yes, $p = .40$ can be used. A 98% confidence interval results in a z value of 2.33. Inserting these values into formula (8.8) yields

$$n = \frac{(2.33)^2(.40)(.60)}{(.03)^2} = 1447.7$$

Hewitt Associates would have to sample 1,448 companies to be 98% confident in the results and maintain an error of .03.

8.5 PROBLEMS

8.37 Determine the sample size necessary to estimate μ for the following information.
  a. $\sigma = 36$ and $E = 5$ at 95% confidence
  b. $\sigma = 4.13$ and $E = 1$ at 99% confidence
  c. Values range from 80 to 500, error is to be within 10, and the confidence level is 90%
  d. Values range from 50 to 108, error is to be within 3, and the confidence level is 88%

8.38 Determine the sample size necessary to estimate p for the following information.
  a. $E = .02$, p is approximately .40, and confidence level is 96%
  b. E is to be within .04, p is unknown, and confidence level is 95%
  c. E is to be within 5%, p is approximately 55%, and confidence level is 90%
  d. E is to be no more than .01, p is unknown, and confidence level is 99%

8.39 A bank officer wants to determine the amount of the average total monthly deposits per customer at the bank. He believes an estimate of this average amount using a confidence interval is sufficient. How large a sample should he take to be within $200 of the actual average with 99% confidence? He assumes the standard deviation of total monthly deposits for all customers is about $1,000.

8.40 Suppose you have been following a particular airline stock for many years. You are interested in determining the average daily price of this stock in a 10-year period and you have access to the stock reports for these years. However, you do not want to average all the daily prices over 10 years because of the more than 2,500 data points, so you decide to take a random sample of the daily prices and estimate the average. You want to be 90% confident of your results, you want the estimate to be within $2.00 of the true average, and you believe the standard deviation of the price of this stock is about $12.50 over this period of time. How large a sample should you take?

8.41 A group of investors wants to develop a chain of fast-food restaurants. In determining potential costs for each facility, they must consider, among other expenses, the average monthly electric bill. They decide to sample some fast-food restaurants currently operating to estimate the monthly cost of electricity. They want to be 90% confident of their results and want the error of the interval estimate to be no more than $100. They estimate that such bills range from $600 to $2,500. How large a sample should they take?

8.42 Suppose a production facility purchases a particular component part in large lots from a supplier. The production manager wants to estimate the proportion of defective parts received from this supplier. She believes the proportion defective is no more than .20 and wants to be within .02 of the true proportion of defective parts with a 90% level of confidence. How large a sample should she take?

8.43 What proportion of secretaries of *Fortune* 500 companies has a personal computer at his or her workstation? You want to answer this question by conducting a random survey. How large a sample should you take if you want to be 95% confident of the results and you want the error of the confidence interval to be no more than .05? Assume no one has any idea of what the proportion actually is.

8.44 What proportion of shoppers at a large appliance store actually makes a large-ticket purchase? To estimate this proportion within 10% and be 95% confident of the results, how large a sample should you take? Assume you have no idea what proportion of all shoppers actually make a large-ticket purchase.

A Report of Surveys on Productivity, Compensation, and Benefits

National average annual salary figures in most industries are likely to be based on random samples of data. Techniques presented in this chapter in Sections 8.1 and 8.2 are applicable to estimate a mean for the population. In most cases, the population variance or standard deviation is unavailable; and the sample variance or standard deviation is used. If the population standard deviation is unknown, the *t* distribution should be used. Remember, there is an assumption that the population data are normally distributed when using the *t* distribution. The error of the estimation is a function of the level of confidence, the standard deviation of the population, and the sample size. Most researchers use confidence levels that are at least 90%. As the level of confidence increases (all other things staying constant), the wider the confidence interval will be; and hence, the greater the error will be. As sample size increases, the error becomes smaller.

According to the Decision Dilemma, 63 companies were randomly surveyed and the resulting sample mean annual salary for security managers was $79,900. This figure is actually only a point estimate of the population mean. If another 63 companies were randomly sampled, the point estimate ($79,900) is likely to change. Suppose the population standard deviation of these salaries is $5,500. The resulting 95% confidence interval would be:

$$79,900 \pm 1.96 \frac{5,500}{\sqrt{63}} = 79,900 \pm 1,358$$

Thus, the point estimate reported by Edward Perlin Associates would have an error of ±$1,358.

One survey of 1,200 employees found that .37 of the workers felt that companies are not supervising employees enough. Because this 37% comes from a sample, it is only a point estimate of the population proportion. If we compute a 95% confidence interval using this information, then we get

$$.37 \pm 1.96 \sqrt{\frac{(.37)(.63)}{1200}} = .37 \pm .027$$

When used as a part of a 95% confidence interval, the .37 is a point estimate with an error of .027 or 2.7%.

A survey of 231 human resource specialists found that 12.12% of them believed that managing performance is the dominant issue facing compensation and benefits managers. This .1212 is actually a point estimate. Using this information, we can compute a 90% confidence interval to estimate the population proportion of human resource specialists who feel this way:

$$.1212 \pm 1.645 \sqrt{\frac{(.1212)(.8788)}{231}} = .1212 \pm .035$$

The confidence interval includes an error of .035 or 3.5%. Thus, the 12.12% figure presented by the researcher might have an error of as much as ±3.5% under a 90% level of confidence. Had a sample size of 1,200 been used in these computations, the error would reduce to .015. Increasing the sample size by more than five times reduces the error by a factor of about 2.3 (due to the fact that the sample size is under the square root sign).

In determining how large of a sample to take, a company must consider such variables as size of acceptable error and level of confidence. The trade-offs with these variables affect the cost of the study. The smaller the acceptable error, the greater is the required sample size (all other things being the same). Increased sample size results in increased cost to the company. If cost is a factor, the decision makers should go with the largest error that they feel they can tolerate and still get useful information. If the confidence level is increased (all other things being the same), then the required sample size will also increase resulting in increased cost.

ETHICAL CONSIDERATIONS

Using sample statistics to estimate population parameters poses a couple of ethical concerns. Many survey reports and advertisers use point estimates as the values of the population parameter. No error value is stated, as would be the case if a confidence interval had been computed. These point estimates are subject to change if another sample is taken. It is probably unethical to state as a conclusion that a point estimate is the population parameter without some sort of disclaimer or explanation about what a point estimate is.

The misapplication of t formulas when data are not normally distributed in the population is also of concern. Although some studies have shown that the t formula analyses are robust, a researcher should be careful not to violate the assumptions underlying the use of the t formulas. An even greater potential for misuse lies in using the chi-square for the estimation of a population variance because this technique is highly sensitive to violations of the assumption that the data are normally distributed.

SUMMARY

Techniques for estimating population parameters from sample statistics are important tools for business research. These tools include techniques for estimating population means, techniques for estimating the population proportion and the population variance, and methodology for determining how large a sample to take.

At times in business research, a product is new or untested or information about the population is unknown. In such cases, gathering data from a sample and making estimates about the population is useful and can be done with a point estimate or an interval estimate. A point estimate is the use of a statistic from the sample as an estimate for a parameter of the population. Because point estimates vary with each sample, it is usually best to construct an interval estimate. An interval estimate is a range of values computed from the sample within which the researcher believes with some confidence that the population parameter lies. Certain levels of confidence seem to be used more than others: 90%, 95%, 98%, and 99%.

If the population standard deviation is known, the z statistic is used to estimate the population mean. If the population standard deviation is unknown, the t distribution should be used instead of the z distribution. It is assumed when using the t distribution that the population from which the samples are drawn is normally distributed. However, the technique for estimating a population mean by using the t test is robust, which means it is relatively insensitive to minor violations to the assumption. The population variance can be estimated by using sample variance and the chi-square distribution. The chi-square technique for estimating the population variance is not robust; it is sensitive to violations of the assumption that the population is normally distributed. Therefore, extreme caution must be exercised in using this technique.

The formulas in Chapter 7 resulting from the central limit theorem can be manipulated to produce formulas for estimating sample size for large samples. Determining the sample size necessary to estimate a population mean, if the population standard deviation is unavailable, can be based on one-fourth the range as an approximation of the population standard deviation. Determining sample size when estimating a population proportion requires the value of the population proportion. If the population proportion is unknown, the population proportion from a similar study can be used. If none is available, using a value of .50 will result in the largest sample size estimation for the problem if other variables are held constant. Sample size determination is used mostly to provide a ballpark figure to give researchers some guidance. Larger sample sizes usually result in greater costs.

KEY TERMS

bounds	interval estimate	t distribution
chi-square distribution	point estimate	t value
degrees of freedom (df)	robust	
error of estimation	sample-size estimation	

FORMULAS

(8.1) $100(1-\alpha)\%$ confidence interval to estimate μ

$$\bar{x} - z_{\alpha/2}\frac{\sigma}{\sqrt{n}} \le \mu \le \bar{x} + z_{\alpha/2}\frac{\sigma}{\sqrt{n}}$$

(8.2) Confidence interval to estimate μ using the finite correction factor

$$\bar{x} - z_{\alpha/2}\frac{\sigma}{\sqrt{n}}\sqrt{\frac{N-n}{N-1}} \le \mu \le \bar{x} + z_{\alpha/2}\frac{\sigma}{\sqrt{n}}\sqrt{\frac{N-n}{N-1}}$$

(8.3) Confidence interval to estimate μ: population standard deviation unknown

$$\bar{x} - t_{\alpha/2,n-1}\frac{s}{\sqrt{n}} \le \mu \le \bar{x} + t_{\alpha/2,n-1}\frac{s}{\sqrt{n}}$$

$$df = n - 1$$

(8.4) Confidence interval to estimate p

$$\hat{p} - z_{\alpha/2}\sqrt{\frac{\hat{p}\cdot\hat{q}}{n}} \le p \le \hat{p} + z_{\alpha/2}\sqrt{\frac{\hat{p}\cdot\hat{q}}{n}}$$

(8.5) χ^2 formula for single variance

$$\chi^2 = \frac{(n-1)s^2}{\sigma^2}$$

$$df = n - 1$$

(8.6) Confidence interval to estimate the population variance

$$\frac{(n-1)s^2}{\chi^2_{\alpha/2}} \le \sigma^2 \le \frac{(n-1)s^2}{\chi^2_{1-\alpha/2}}$$

$$df = n - 1$$

(8.7) Sample size when estimating μ

$$n = \frac{z^2_{\alpha/2}\sigma^2}{E^2} = \left(\frac{z_{\alpha/2}\sigma}{E}\right)^2$$

(8.8) Sample size when estimating p

$$n = \frac{z^2 pq}{E^2}$$

SUPPLEMENTARY PROBLEMS

CALCULATING THE STATISTICS

8.45 Use the following data to construct 80%, 94%, and 98% confidence intervals to estimate μ. Assume that σ is 7.75. State the point estimate.

44	37	49	30	56	48	53	42	51
38	39	45	47	52	59	50	46	34
39	46	27	35	52	51	46	45	58
51	37	45	52	51	54	39	48	

8.46 Construct 90%, 95%, and 99% confidence intervals to estimate μ from the following data. State the point estimate. Assume the data come from a normally distributed population.

12.3	11.6	11.9	12.8	12.5	11.4	12.0
11.7	11.8	12.3				

8.47 Use the following information to compute the confidence interval for the population proportion.

   a. $n = 715$ and $x = 329$, with 95% confidence
   b. $n = 284$ and $\hat{p} = .71$, with 90% confidence
   c. $n = 1250$ and $\hat{p} = .48$, with 95% confidence
   d. $n = 457$ and $x = 270$, with 98% confidence

8.48 Use the following data to construct 90% and 95% confidence intervals to estimate the population variance. Assume the data come from a normally distributed population.

212	229	217	216	223	219	208
214	232	219				

8.49 Determine the sample size necessary under the following conditions.

   a. To estimate μ with $\sigma = 44$, $E = 3$, and 95% confidence
   b. To estimate μ with a range of values from 20 to 88 with $E = 2$ and 90% confidence
   c. To estimate p with p unknown, $E = .04$, and 98% confidence
   d. To estimate p with $E = .03$, 95% confidence, and p thought to be approximately .70

TESTING YOUR UNDERSTANDING

8.50 In planning both market opportunity and production levels, being able to estimate the size of a market can be important. Suppose a diaper manufacturer wants to know how many diapers a 1-month-old baby uses during a 24-hour period. To determine this usage, the manufacturer's analyst randomly selects 17 parents of 1-month-olds and asks them to keep track of diaper usage for 24 hours. The results are shown. Construct a 99% confidence interval to estimate the average daily diaper usage of a 1-month-old baby. Assume diaper usage is normally distributed.

12	8	11	9	13	14	10
10	9	13	11	8	11	15
10	7	12				

8.51 Suppose you want to estimate the proportion of cars that are sport utility vehicles (SUVs) being driven in Kansas City, Missouri, at rush hour by standing on the corner of I-70 and I-470 and counting SUVs. You believe the figure is no higher than .40. If you want the error of the confidence interval to be no greater than .03, how many cars should you randomly sample? Use a 90% level of confidence.

8.52 Use the data in Problem 8.50 to construct a 99% confidence interval to estimate the population variance for the number of diapers used during a 24-hour period for 1-month-olds. How could information about the population variance be used by a manufacturer or marketer in planning?

8.53 What is the average length of a company's policy book? Suppose policy books are sampled from 45 medium-sized companies. The average number of pages in the sample books is 213 and the population standard deviation of 48. Use this information to construct a 98% confidence interval to estimate the mean number of pages for the population of medium-sized company policy books.

8.54 A random sample of small-business managers was given a leadership style questionnaire. The results were scaled so that each manager received a score for initiative. Suppose the following data are a random sample of these scores.

37	42	40	39	38	31	40
37	35	45	30	33	35	44
36	37	39	33	39	40	41
33	35	36	41	33	37	38
40	42	44	35	36	33	38
32	30	37	42			

   Assuming σ is 3.891, use these data to construct a 90% confidence interval to estimate the average score on initiative for all small-business managers.

8.55 A national beauty salon chain wants to estimate the number of times per year a woman has her hair done at a beauty salon if she uses one at least once a year. The chain's researcher estimates that, of those women who use a beauty salon at least once a year, the standard deviation of number of times of usage is approximately 6. The national chain wants the estimate to be within one time of the actual mean value. How large a sample should the researcher take to obtain a 98% confidence level?

8.56 Is the environment a major issue with Americans? To answer that question, a researcher conducts a survey of 1,255 randomly selected Americans. Suppose 714 of the sampled people replied that the environment is a major issue with them. Construct a 95% confidence interval to estimate the proportion of Americans who feel that the environment is a major issue with them. What is the point estimate of this proportion?

8.57 According to a survey by Topaz Enterprises, a travel auditing company, the average error by travel agents is $128. Suppose this figure was obtained from a random sample of 41 travel agents and the sample standard deviation is $21. What is the point estimate of the national average error for all travel agents? Compute a 98% confidence interval for the national average error based on these sample results. Assume the travel agent errors are normally distributed in the population. How wide is the interval? Interpret the interval.

8.58 A national survey on telemarketing was undertaken. One of the questions asked was: How long has your organization had a telemarketing operation? Suppose the following data represent some of the answers received to this question. Suppose further that only 300 telemarketing firms comprised the population when this survey was taken. Use the following data to compute a 98% confidence interval to estimate the average number of years a telemarketing organization has had a telemarketing operation. The population standard deviation is 3.06.

5	5	6	3	6	7	5
5	6	8	4	9	6	4
10	5	10	11	5	14	7
5	9	6	7	3	4	3
7	5	9	3	6	8	16
12	11	5	4	3	6	5
8	3	5	9	7	13	4
6	5	8	3	5	8	7
11	5	14	4			

8.59 An entrepreneur wants to open an appliance service repair shop. She would like to know about what the average home repair bill is, including the charge for the service call for appliance repair in the area. She wants the estimate to be within $20 of the actual figure. She believes the range of such bills is between $30 and $600. How large a sample should the entrepreneur take if she wants to be 95% confident of the results?

8.60 A national survey of insurance offices was taken, resulting in a random sample of 245 companies. Of these 245 companies, 189 responded that they were going to purchase new software for their offices in the next year. Construct a 90% confidence interval to estimate the population proportion of insurance offices that intend to purchase new software during the next year.

8.61 A national survey of companies included a question that asked whether the company had at least one bilingual telephone operator. The sample results of 90 companies follow (Y denotes that the company does have at least one bilingual operator; N denotes that it does not).

N	N	N	N	Y	N	Y	N	N
Y	N	N	N	Y	Y	N	N	N
N	N	Y	N	Y	N	Y	N	Y
Y	Y	N	Y	N	N	N	Y	N
N	Y	N	N	N	N	N	N	N
Y	N	Y	Y	N	N	Y	N	Y
N	N	Y	Y	N	N	N	N	N
Y	N	N	N	N	Y	N	N	N
Y	Y	Y	N	N	Y	N	N	N
N	N	N	Y	Y	N	N	Y	N

Use this information to estimate with 95% confidence the proportion of the population that does have at least one bilingual operator.

8.62 A movie theater has had a poor accounting system. The manager has no idea how many large containers of popcorn are sold per movie showing. She knows that the amounts vary by day of the week and hour of the day. However, she wants to estimate the overall average per movie showing. To do so, she randomly selects 12 movie performances and counts the number of large containers of popcorn sold between 30 minutes before the movie showing and 15 minutes after the movie showing. The sample average was 43.7 containers, with a variance of 228. Construct a 95% confidence interval to estimate the mean number of large containers of popcorn sold during a movie showing. Assume the number of large containers of popcorn sold per movie is normally distributed in the population. Use this information to construct a 98% confidence interval to estimate the population variance.

8.63 According to a survey by Runzheimer International, the average cost of a fast-food meal (quarter-pound cheeseburger, large fries, medium soft drink, excluding taxes) in Seattle is $4.82. Suppose this figure was based on a sample of 27 different establishments and the standard deviation was $0.37. Construct a 95% confidence interval for the population mean cost for all fast-food meals in Seattle. Assume the costs of a fast-food meal in Seattle are normally distributed. Using the interval as a guide, is it likely that the population mean is really $4.50? Why or why not?

8.64 A survey of 77 commercial airline flights of under 2 hours resulted in a sample average late time for a flight of 2.48 minutes. The population standard deviation was 12 minutes. Construct a 95% confidence interval for the average time that a commercial flight of under 2 hours is late. What is the point estimate? What does the interval tell about whether the average flight is late?

8.65 A regional survey of 560 companies asked the vice president of operations how satisfied he or she was with the software support received from the computer staff of the company. Suppose 33% of the 560 vice presidents said they were satisfied. Construct a 99% confidence interval for the proportion of the population of vice presidents who would have said they were satisfied with the software support if a census had been taken.

8.66 A research firm has been asked to determine the proportion of all restaurants in the state of Ohio that serve alcoholic beverages. The firm wants to be 98%

confident of its results but has no idea of what the actual proportion is. The firm would like to report an error of no more than .05. How large a sample should it take?

8.67 A national magazine marketing firm attempts to win subscribers with a mail campaign that involves a contest using magazine stickers. Often when people subscribe to magazines in this manner they sign up for multiple magazine subscriptions. Suppose the marketing firm wants to estimate the average number of subscriptions per customer of those who purchase at least one subscription. To do so, the marketing firm's researcher randomly selects 65 returned contest entries. Twenty-seven contain subscription requests. Of the 27, the average number of subscriptions is 2.10, with a standard deviation of .86. The researcher uses this information to compute a 98% confidence interval to estimate μ and assumes that x is normally distributed. What does the researcher find?

8.68 A national survey showed that Hillshire Farm Deli Select cold cuts were priced, on the average, at $5.20 per pound. Suppose a national survey of 23 retail outlets was taken and the price per pound of Hillshire Farm Deli Select cold cuts was ascertained. If the following data represent these prices, what is a 90% confidence interval for the population variance of these prices? Assume prices are normally distributed in the population.

5.18	5.22	5.25	5.19	5.30
5.17	5.15	5.28	5.20	5.14
5.05	5.19	5.26	5.23	5.19
5.22	5.08	5.21	5.24	5.33
5.22	5.19	5.19		

8.69 The price of a head of iceberg lettuce varies greatly with the season and the geographic location of a store. During February a researcher contacts a random sample of 39 grocery stores across the United States and asks the produce manager of each to state the current price charged for a head of iceberg lettuce. Using the researcher's results that follow, construct a 99% confidence interval to estimate the mean price of a head of iceberg lettuce in February in the United States. Assume that σ is 0.205.

1.59	1.25	1.65	1.40	0.89
1.19	1.50	1.49	1.30	1.39
1.29	1.60	0.99	1.29	1.19
1.20	1.50	1.49	1.29	1.35
1.10	0.89	1.10	1.39	1.39
1.50	1.50	1.55	1.20	1.15
0.99	1.00	1.30	1.25	1.10
1.00	1.55	1.29	1.39	

INTERPRETING THE OUTPUT

8.70 A soft drink company produces a cola in a 12-ounce can. Even though their machines are set to fill the cans with 12 ounces, variation due to calibration, operator error, and other things sometimes precludes the cans having the correct fill. To monitor the can fills, a quality team randomly selects some filled 12-ounce cola cans and measures their fills in the lab. A confidence interval for the population mean is constructed from the data. Shown here is the MINITAB output from this effort. Discuss the output.

```
                 One-Sample Z: Can Fills

The assumed sigma = 0.0536

Variable    N     Mean    StDev   SE Mean       99.0% CI
Can Fills  58  11.9788   0.0556   0.0070  (11.9607, 11.9970)
```

8.71 A company has developed a new light bulb that seems to burn longer than most residential bulbs. To determine how long these bulbs burn, the company randomly selects a sample of these bulbs and burns them in the laboratory. The Excel output shown here is a portion of the analysis from this effort. Discuss the output.

	A	B
1	Bulb Burn	
2	Mean	2198.217
3	Standard Deviation	152.9907
4	Count	84
5	Confidence Level (90.0%)	27.76691

8.72 Suppose a researcher wants to estimate the average age of a person who is a first-time home buyer. A random sample of first-time home buyers is taken and their ages are ascertained. The MINITAB output shown here is an analysis of that data. Study the output and explain its implication.

```
                One-Sample T: Ages

Variable    N    Mean   StDev   SE Mean      98.0% CI
Ages       21   27.63    6.54      1.43   (24.02, 31.24)
```

8.73 What proportion of all American workers drive their cars to work? Suppose a poll of American workers is taken in an effort to answer that question, and the MINITAB output shown here is an analysis of the data from the poll. Explain the meaning of the output in light of the question.

```
           Test and CI for One Proportion

Test of p = 0.5 vs p not = 0.5

Sample   X    N   Sample p         95.0% CI         P-Value
1      506  781  0.647887  (0.613240, 0.681413)    0.000
```

ANALYZING THE DATABASES

see www.wiley.com/college/black

1. Construct a 95% confidence interval for the population mean number of production workers using the manufacturing database as a sample. What is the point estimate? How much is the error of the estimation? Comment on the results.

2. Construct a 90% confidence interval to estimate the average census for hospitals using the hospital database. State the point estimate and the error of the estimation. Change the level of confidence to 99%. What happened to the interval? Did the point estimate change?

3. The financial database contains financial data on 100 companies. Use this database as a sample and estimate the earnings per share for all corporations from these data. Select several levels of confidence and compare the results.

4. Using the tally or frequency feature of the computer software, determine the sample proportion of the hospital database under the variable "service" that are "general medical" (category 1). From this statistic, construct a 95% confidence interval to estimate the population proportion of hospitals that are "general medical." What is the point estimate? How much error is there in the interval?

CASE: THERMATRIX

In 1985, a company called In-Process Technology was set up to produce and sell a thermal oxidation process that could be used to reduce industrial pollution. The initial investors acquired the rights to technology developed at a federal government laboratory. However, for years the company performed dismally and by 1991 was still only earning $264,000 annually.

In 1992, current CEO John Schofield was hired to turn things around. Under his tutelage, the company was reorganized and renamed Thermatrix. Schofield realized the potential of the technology in the environmental marketplace. He was able to raise more than $20 million in private equity offerings over several years to produce, market, and distribute the product. In June of 1996, there was a successful public offering of Thermatrix in the financial markets.

Thermatrix's philosophy was to give customers more than competitors gave without charging more. The company targeted large corporations as customers, hoping to use its client list as a selling tool. In addition, realizing that they were a small, thinly capitalized company, Thermatrix partnered with many of its clients in developing solutions to the clients' specific environment problems.

Eventually, Schofield located the Thermatrix operations group in Knoxville, Tennessee, because of the low cost of living and the large pool of highly trained professional workers. Thermatrix was able to attract good employees using stock options and other competitive compensation. Sixty employees presently work for the company, and annual sales have risen to about $15 million.

Thermatrix also has become a player in the international marketplace. In 1997, 35% of company revenue came from overseas business. By 1998, it was expected that more than 60% of its revenues would be derived from overseas customers. A main key to the company's success has been its customer satisfaction. In 2001, Thermatrix sold its Wahlco Environment Systems assets and refocused its efforts on its core business, the application of its flameless thermal oxidation technology.

Discussion

1. Thermatrix has grown and flourished because of its good customer relationships, which include partnering, delivering a quality product on time, and listening to the customer's needs. Suppose company management wants to formally measure customer satisfaction at least once a year and develops a brief survey that includes the following four questions. Suppose 115 customers participated in this survey with the results shown. Use techniques presented in this chapter to analyze the data to estimate population responses to these questions.

Question	Yes	No
1. In general, were deliveries on time?	63	52
2. Were the contact people at Thermatrix helpful and courteous?	86	29
3. Was the pricing structure fair to your company?	101	14
4. Would you recommend Thermatrix to other companies?	105	10

2. Now suppose Thermatrix officers want to ascertain employee satisfaction with the company. They randomly sample nine employees and ask them to complete a satisfaction survey under the supervision of an independent testing organization. As part of this survey, employees are asked to respond to questions on a 5-point scale where 1 is low satisfaction and 5 is high satisfaction. Assume the data are at least interval and that the overall responses on questions are normally distributed.

The questions and the results of the survey are shown here. Analyze the results by using techniques from this chapter.

Question	Mean	Standard Deviation
1. Are you treated fairly as an employee?	3.79	.86
2. Has the company given you the training you need to do the job adequately?	2.74	1.27
3. Does management seriously consider your input in making decisions about production?	4.18	.63
4. Is your physical work environment acceptable?	3.34	.81
5. Is the compensation for your work adequate and fair?	3.95	.21

Source: Adapted from "Thermatrix: Selling Products, Not Technology," *Insights and Inspiration: How Businesses Succeed,* published by Nation's Business on behalf of MassMutual and the U.S. Chamber of Commerce in association with The Blue Chip Enterprise Initiative, 1997; and Thermatrix, Inc., available at http://www.thermatrix.com/text_version/background/backgrnd.html (Company Background) and http://www.thermatrix.com/overview.html (Background Information).

USING THE COMPUTER

EXCEL

Confidence intervals for a population mean can be constructed with Excel in two different ways. One way is to select **Tools** on the menu bar. From the pull-down menu, select **Data Analysis.** In the Data Analysis dialog box, select **Descriptive Statistics.** In the dialog box for Descriptive Statistics, place the **Input Range** of the data at the top of the box. Insert the level of confidence in the box with the percent sign and check if you want a separate line of output for the answer. Check and fill other boxes to obtain any desired descriptive statistics. The output is a single number that is the ± error portion of the confidence interval. Use this and the mean (point estimate) to construct a confidence interval to estimate the population mean. Excel computes the confidence interval error by multiplying the table value for the confidence interval (based on sample size and level of confidence) by the standard error of the mean (standard deviation). This method assumes that the population standard deviation is unknown (uses the sample standard deviation) and uses the *t* distribution.

The second way to construct confidence intervals for the mean with Excel is by using the Paste Function. Begin by clicking the Paste Function, f_x, on the standard tool bar. The Paste Function dialog box will appear. From the **Function category** on the left, select **Statistical.** A menu of statistical techniques will appear on the right. Select **CONFIDENCE** from this list. A dialog box will appear. This box requires the value of **Alpha** (1 − confidence level), the value of the population **Standard_deviation,** and the sample **Size.** The output is the same as that obtained by using the **Descriptive Statistics** command—the ± error of the confidence interval. The Paste Function uses *z* values and assumes that the population standard deviation is known. It will use the mean of the column as the point estimate.

MINITAB

MINITAB Windows has the capability of constructing confidence intervals for a population mean when the population standard deviation is known or when it is unknown. In either case, begin by selecting **Stat** on the menu bar. A pull-down menu will appear. Select **Basic Statistics** from the pull-down menu; a second pull-down menu will appear. To estimate the population mean when the population standard deviation is known, select **1–sample Z.** A dialog box will appear. Enter the column location of the data under **Variables.** Enter the value for the population standard deviation in the box labeled **Sigma.** You must enter a value for the population standard deviation. The default confidence level is 95%. To change this, select **Options…** and a dialog box will appear. In the line beside **Confidence level,** enter the level of confidence. The output consists of the known value of sigma, the sample size, the sample mean, the sample standard deviation, the standard error of the mean, and the endpoints of the confidence interval.

If the population standard deviation is unknown, select **1–sample t…** from the **Basic Statistics** pull-down menu. A dialog box will appear. Enter the column location of the data in the **Variables** box. The default confidence level is 95%. To change this, select **Options…** and a dialog box will appear. In the line beside **Confidence level,** enter the level of confidence. The output is the same as for **1 – sample Z** except that no known value of sigma is available to report.

CHAPTER 9

Statistical Inference: Hypothesis Testing for Single Populations

LEARNING OBJECTIVES

The main objective of Chapter 9 is to help you to learn how to test hypotheses on single populations, thereby enabling you to:

1. Understand the logic of hypothesis testing and know how to establish null and alternative hypotheses.
2. Understand Type I and Type II errors and know how to solve for Type II errors.
3. Know how to implement the HTAB system to test hypotheses.
4. Test hypotheses about a single population mean when σ is known.
5. Test hypotheses about a single population mean when σ is unknown.
6. Test hypotheses about a single population proportion.
7. Test hypotheses about a single population variance.

Business Referrals

Word-of-mouth information about products and services is exchanged on a daily basis by millions of consumers. Many of us seek out such advice because we want to obtain product information from a third party to assist us in the market decision-making process. What we receive is often subjective opinion that is flavored by other consumer's experiences or information they gathered from other sources. An underlying factor in the reliance on such word-of-mouth information is a trust in the source. It is important for businesses to understand the impact of such "business referrals."

The White House Office of Consumer Affairs determined in a study that at least 90% of unhappy customers will not do business with the offending company again. In addition, each unhappy customer will share his/her displeasure with at least nine other people. According to a study by Mediamark Research of New York City, about 50% of all Americans often seek the advice of others before buying services or products. In addition, almost 40% say that others seek out their advice before purchasing. Maritz Marketing Research of Fenton, Missouri, studied adults in an effort to determine for which products or services they seek advice. Forty-six percent seek advice when selecting a physician, 44% for a mechanic, and 42% for legal advice. In looking for a restaurant in which to celebrate a special occasion, 38% of all consumers seek out advice and information from others.

Some advice givers are referred to as *influentials*. Influentials are "trendsetting opinion leaders whose activism and expertise make them the natural source for word-of-mouth referrals." This group represents about 10% of all adult Americans. A report issued by Roper Starch Worldwide and cosponsored by *The Atlantic Monthly* stated that influentials tend to be among the first to try new products. They are looking for new restaurants and vacation spots to try, are activists on the job and in their community, and are self-indulgent. Businesses would do well to seek out such influentials and win them over to the company's products, thereby tapping into the word-of-mouth pipeline. On average, an influential recommends restaurants to 5.0 people a year. The following chart shows the average number of recommendations made by influentials per year on other items. These data were compiled and released by Roper Starch Worldwide.

Product or Service	Average Number of Recommendations
Office equipment	5.8
Vacation destination	5.1
TV show	4.9
Retail store	4.7
Clothing	4.5
Consumer electronics	4.5
Car	4.1
Stocks, mutual funds, CDs, etc.	3.4

Managerial and Statistical Questions

1. Each of the figures enumerated in this Decision Dilemma were derived by studies conducted on samples and published as fact. If we want to challenge these figures by conducting surveys of our own, then how would we go about testing these results? Are these studies dated now? Do they apply to all market segments (geographically, economically, etc.)? How could we test to determine whether these results apply to our market segment today?

2. The Roper Starch Worldwide study listed the mean number of recommendations made by influentials per year for different products or services. If these figures become accepted by industry users, how can we conduct our own tests to determine whether they are actually true? If we randomly sampled some influentials and our mean figures did not match these figures, then could we automatically conclude that their figures are not true? How much difference would we have to obtain to reject their claims? Is there a possibility that we could make an error in conducting such research?

3. The studies by the White House Office of Consumer Affairs, Mediamark Research, and Maritz Marketing Research produced a variety of proportions about word-of-mouth advertising and advice seeking. Are these figures necessarily true? Since these figures are based on sample information and are probably point estimates, could there be error in the estimations? How can we test to determine whether these figures that become accepted in the media as population parameters are actually true? Could there be differences in various population subgroups?

4. Suppose you have theories regarding word-of-mouth advertising, business referrals, or influentials. How would you test the theories to determine whether they are true?

Source: Adapted from Chip Walker, "Word of Mouth," *American Demographics* (July 1995), pp. 38–45.

A foremost statistical mechanism for decision making is the hypothesis test. The concept of hypothesis testing lies at the heart of inferential statistics, and the use of statistics to "prove" or "disprove" claims hinges on it. With **hypothesis testing,** business researchers are able *to structure problems in such a way that they can use statistical evidence to test various theories about business phenomena.* Business applications of statistical hypothesis testing run the gamut from determining whether a production line process is out of control to providing conclusive evidence that a new management leadership approach is significantly more effective than an old one.

9.1 INTRODUCTION TO HYPOTHESIS TESTING

In the field of business, decision makers are continually attempting to find answers to questions such as the following:

- What container shape is most economical and reliable for shipping a product?
- Which management approach best motivates employees in the retail industry?
- How can the company's retirement investment financial portfolio be diversified for optimum performance?
- What is the best way to link client databases for fast retrieval of useful information?
- Which indicator best predicts the general state of the economy in the next six months?
- What is the most effective means of advertising in a business-to-business setting?

Business researchers are often called upon to provide insights and information to decision makers to assist them in answering such questions. In searching for answers to questions and in attempting to find explanations for business phenomena, business researchers often develop "hypotheses" that can be studied and explored. **Hypotheses** are *tentative explanations of a principle operating in nature.** In this text, we will explore various types of hypotheses, how to test them, and how to interpret the results of such tests so that useful information can be brought to bear on the business decision-making process.

---

* Paraphrasing of definition published in *Merriam Webster's Collegiate Dictionary*, 10th ed. (Springfield, MA: Merriam Webster, Inc., 1993).

Types of Hypotheses

Three types of hypotheses that will be explored here:

1. *Research* hypotheses
2. *Statistical* hypotheses
3. *Substantive* hypotheses

Although much of the focus will be on testing statistical hypotheses, it is also important for business decision makers to have an understanding of both research and substantive hypotheses.

Research Hypotheses

Research hypotheses are most nearly like hypotheses defined earlier. A **research hypothesis** is *a statement of what the researcher believes will be the outcome of an experiment or a study*. Before studies are undertaken, business researchers often have some idea or theory based on experience or previous work as to how the study will turn out. These ideas, theories, or notions established before an experiment or study is conducted are research hypotheses. Some examples of research hypotheses in business might include:

- Older workers are more loyal to a company.
- Companies with more than $1 billion in assets spend a higher percentage of their annual budget on advertising than do companies with less than $1 billion in assets.
- The implementation of a Six Sigma quality approach in manufacturing will result in greater productivity.
- The price of scrap metal is a good indicator of the industrial production index six months later.
- Airline company stock prices are positively correlated with the volume of OPEC oil production.

Virtually all inquisitive, thinking businesspeople have similar research hypotheses concerning relationships, approaches, and techniques in business. Such hypotheses can lead decision makers to new and better ways to accomplish business goals. However, to formally test research hypotheses, it is generally best to state them as statistical hypotheses.

Statistical Hypotheses

In order to scientifically test research hypotheses, a more formal hypothesis structure needs to be set up using **statistical hypotheses.** Suppose business researchers want to "prove" the research hypothesis that older workers are more loyal to a company. A "loyalty" survey instrument is either developed or obtained. If this instrument is administered to both older and younger workers, how much higher do older workers have to score on the "loyalty" instrument (assuming higher scores indicate more loyal) than younger workers to prove the research hypothesis? What is the "proof threshold"? Instead of attempting to prove or disprove research hypotheses directly in this manner, business researchers convert their research hypotheses to statistical hypotheses and then test the statistical hypotheses using standard procedures.

All statistical hypotheses consist of two parts, a null hypothesis and an alternative hypothesis. These two parts are constructed to contain all possible outcomes of the experiment or study. Generally, the **null hypothesis** *states that the "null" condition exists; that is, there is nothing new happening, the old theory is still true, the old standard is correct, and the system is in control.* The **alternative hypothesis,** on the other hand, *states that the new theory is true, there are new standards, the system is out-of-control, and/or something is happening.* As an example, suppose flour packaged by a manufacturer is sold by weight; and a particular size of package is supposed to average 40 ounces. Suppose the manufacturer wants to test to determine whether their packaging process is out-of-control as determined by the weight of the flour packages. The null hypothesis for this experiment is that the average weight of the flour packages is 40 ounces (no problem). The alternative hypothesis is that the average is not 40 ounces (process is out-of-control).

It is common symbolism to represent the null hypothesis as H_0 and the alternative hypothesis as H_a. The null and alternative hypotheses for the flour example can be restated using these symbols and μ for the population mean as:

$$H_0: \mu = 40 \text{ oz.}$$

$$H_a: \mu \neq 40 \text{ oz.}$$

As another example, suppose a company has held an 18% share of the market. However, because of an increased marketing effort, company officials believe the company's market share is now greater than 18%, and the officials would like to prove it. The null hypothesis is that the market share is still 18% or perhaps it has even dropped below 18%. Converting the 18% to a proportion and using p to represent the population proportion, results in the following null hypothesis:

$$H_0: p \leq .18$$

The alternative hypothesis is that the population proportion is now greater than .18:

$$H_a: p > .18$$

Note that the "new idea" or "new theory" that company officials want to "prove" is stated in the alternative hypothesis. The null hypothesis states that the old market share of 18% is still true.

Generally speaking, new hypotheses that business researchers want to "prove" are stated in the alternative hypothesis. Because many business researchers only undertake an experiment to determine whether their new hypothesis is correct, they are hoping that the alternative hypothesis will be "proven" true. However, if a manufacturer is testing to determine whether his process is out-of-control as shown in the flour-packaging example, then he is most likely hoping that the alternative hypothesis is not "proven" true thereby demonstrating that the process is still in control.

Note in the market share example that the null hypothesis also contains the less than case ($<$) because between the two hypotheses (null and alternative), all possible outcomes must be included ($<$, $>$, and $=$). One could say that the null and alternative hypotheses are mutually exclusive (no overlap) and collectively exhaustive (all cases included). Thus, whenever a decision is made about which hypothesis is true, logically either one is true or the other but not both. Even though the company officials are not interested in "proving" that their market share is less than 18%, logically, it should be included as a possibility. On the other hand, many researchers and statisticians leave out the "less than" ($<$) portion of the null hypothesis on the market share problem because company officials are only interested in "proving" that the market share has increased and the inclusion of the "less than" sign in the null hypothesis is confusing. This approach can be justified in the way that statistical hypotheses are tested. If the equal part of the null hypothesis is rejected because the market share is seemingly greater, then certainly the "less than" portion of the null hypothesis is also rejected because it is further away from "greater than" than is "equal." Using this logic, the null hypothesis for the market share problem can be written as

$$H_0: p = .18$$

rather than

$$H_0: p \leq .18$$

Thus, in this form, the statistical hypotheses for the market share problem can be written as

$$H_0: p = .18$$
$$H_a: p > .18$$

Even though the "less than" sign, $<$, is not included in the null hypothesis, it is implied that it is there. We will adopt such an approach in this book; and thus, all *null* hypotheses presented in this book will be written with an equal sign only ($=$) rather than with a directional sign ($\leq$) or ($\geq$).

Statistical hypotheses are written so that they will produce either a one-tailed or a two-tailed test. The hypotheses shown already for the flour package manufacturing problem are two-tailed:

$$H_0\colon \mu = 40 \text{ oz.}$$

$$H_a\colon \mu \neq 40 \text{ oz.}$$

Two-tailed tests always use = and $\neq$ in the statistical hypotheses and are directionless in that the alternative hypothesis allows for either the greater than (>) or less than (<) possibility. In this particular example, if the process is "out-of-control," plant officials might not know whether machines are overfilling or underfilling packages and are interested in testing for either possibility.

The hypotheses shown for the market share problem are one-tailed:

$$H_0\colon p = .18$$

$$H_a\colon p > .18$$

One-tailed tests are always directional, and the alternative hypothesis uses either the greater than (>) or the less than (<) sign. A one-tailed test should only be used when the researcher knows for certain that the outcome of an experiment is going to occur only in one direction or the researcher is only interested in one direction of the experiment as in the case of the market share problem. In one-tailed problems, the researcher is trying to "prove" that something is older, younger, higher, lower, more, less, greater, and so on. These words are considered "directional" words in that they indicate the direction of the focus of the research. Without these words, the alternative hypothesis of a one-tailed test cannot be established.

In business research, the conservative approach is to conduct a two-tailed test because sometimes study results can be obtained that are in opposition to the direction that researchers thought would occur. For example, in the market share problem, it might turn out that the company had actually lost market share; and even though company officials were not interested in "proving" such a case, they may need to know that it is true. It is recommended that, if in doubt, business researchers should use a two-tailed test.

Substantive Hypotheses

In testing a statistical hypothesis, a business researcher reaches a conclusion based on the data obtained in the study. If the null hypothesis is rejected and therefore the alternative hypothesis is accepted, it is common to say that a statistically significant result has been obtained. For example, in the market share problem, if the null hypothesis is rejected, the result is that the market share is "significantly greater" than 18%. The word, *significant,* to statisticians and business researchers merely means that the result of the experiment is unlikely due to chance and a decision has been made to reject the null hypothesis. However, in everyday business life, the word, *significant,* is more likely to connote "important" or "a large amount." One problem that can arise in testing statistical hypotheses is that particular characteristics of the data can result in a statistically significant outcome that is not a significant business outcome.

As an example, consider the market share study. Suppose a large sample of potential customers is taken, and a sample market share of 18.2% is obtained. Suppose further that a statistical analysis of these data results in statistical significance. We would conclude statistically that the market share is significantly higher than 18%. This finding actually means that it is unlikely that the difference between the sample proportion and the population proportion of .18 is due just to chance. However, to the business decision maker, a market share of 18.2% might not be significantly higher than 18%. Because of the way the word *significant* is used to denote rejection of the null hypothesis rather than an important business difference, business decision makers need to exercise caution in interpreting the outcomes of statistical tests.

In addition to understanding a statistically significant result, business decision makers need to determine what, to them, is a *substantive* result. A **substantive result** is *when the outcome of a statistical study produces results that are important to the decision maker.* The importance to the researcher will vary from study to study. As an example, in a recent year, one healthcare administrator was excited because patient satisfaction had significantly increased (statistically) from one year to the next. However, an examination of the data revealed that on a five-point scale, their satisfaction ratings had gone up from 3.61 to only 3.63. Is going from a 3.61 rating to a 3.63 rating in one year really a substantive increase? On the other hand, increasing the average purchase at a large, high-volume store from $55.45 to $55.50 might be substantive as well as significant if volume is large enough to drive profits higher. Both business researchers and decision makers should be aware that statistically significant results are not always substantive results.

Using the HTAB System to Test Hypotheses

In conducting business research, the process of testing hypotheses involves four major tasks:

- Task 1. Establishing the hypotheses
- Task 2. Conducting the test
- Task 3. Taking statistical action
- Task 4. Determining the business implications

This process, depicted in Figure 9.1, is referred to here as the HTAB system where HTAB is an acronym for **H**ypothesize, **T**est, **A**ction, **B**usiness.

Task 1, establishing the hypotheses, encompasses all activities that lead up to the establishment of the statistical hypotheses being tested. These activities might include investigating a business opportunity or problem, developing theories about possible solutions, and establishing research hypotheses. Task 2, conducting the test, involves the selection of the proper statistical test, setting the value of alpha, establishing a decision rule, gathering sample data, and computing the statistical analysis. Task 3, taking statistical action, is making a statistical decision about whether or not to reject the null hypothesis based on the outcome of the statistical test. Task 4, determining the business implications, is deciding what the statistical action means in business terms, that is, interpreting the statistical outcome in terms of business decision making.

Typically, statisticians and researchers present the hypothesis testing process in terms of an eight-step approach. These eight steps are as follows:

- Step 1. Establish a null and alternative hypothesis.
- Step 2. Determine the appropriate statistical test.
- Step 3. Set the value of alpha, the Type I error rate.
- Step 4. Establish the decision rule.
- Step 5. Gather sample data.
- Step 6. Analyze the data.
- Step 7. Reach a statistical conclusion.
- Step 8. Make a business decision.

These eight steps fit nicely into the four HTAB tasks as a part of the HTAB paradigm. Figure 9.2 presents the HTAB paradigm incorporating the eight steps into the four HTAB tasks.

Task 1 of the HTAB system, hypothesizing, includes step 1, which is establishing a null and alternative hypothesis. In establishing the null and alternative hypotheses, it is important that the business researcher clearly identify what is being tested and whether the hypotheses are one-tailed or two-tailed. In hypothesis testing process, it is *always assumed that the null hypothesis is true* at the beginning of the study. In other words, it is assumed that the process is in control (no problem), that the market share has not increased, that older workers are not more loyal to a company than younger workers, and so on. This process is analogous to the U.S. trial system in which the accused is presumed innocent at the beginning of the trial.

Task 2 of the HTAB system, testing, includes steps 2 through 6. Step 2 is to select the most appropriate statistical test to use for the analysis. In selecting such a test, the business researcher needs to consider the type, number, and level of data being used in the study along with the statistic used in the analysis (mean, proportion, variance, etc.). In addition,

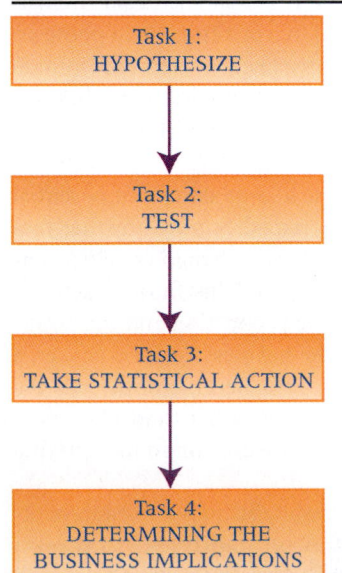

FIGURE 9.1

HTAB System of Testing Hypotheses

Task 1: HYPOTHESIZE

Task 2: TEST

Task 3: TAKE STATISTICAL ACTION

Task 4: DETERMINING THE BUSINESS IMPLICATIONS

FIGURE 9.2

HTAB Paradigm Incorporating the Eight Steps

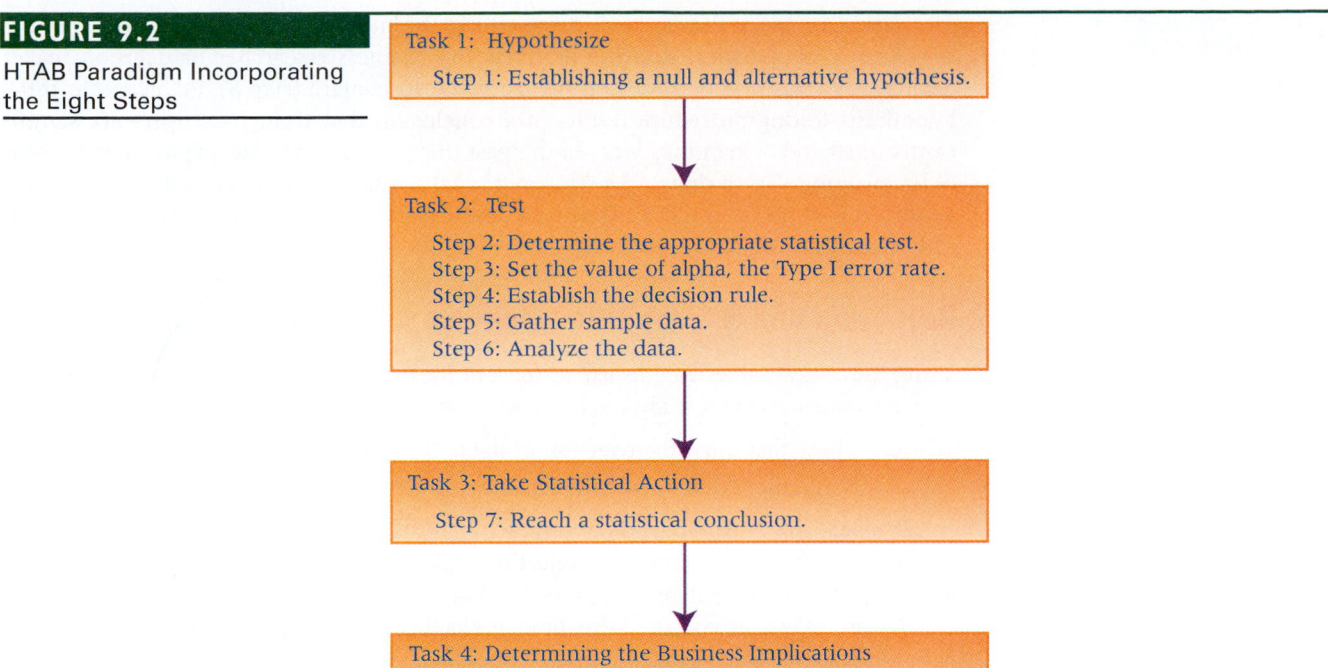

Task 1: Hypothesize

    Step 1: Establishing a null and alternative hypothesis.

Task 2: Test

    Step 2: Determine the appropriate statistical test.
    Step 3: Set the value of alpha, the Type I error rate.
    Step 4: Establish the decision rule.
    Step 5: Gather sample data.
    Step 6: Analyze the data.

Task 3: Take Statistical Action

    Step 7: Reach a statistical conclusion.

Task 4: Determining the Business Implications

    Step 8: Make a business decision.

business researchers should consider the assumptions underlying certain statistical tests and determine whether they can be met in the study before using such tests.

At step 3, the value of alpha is set. Alpha is the probability of committing a Type I error and will be discussed later. Common values of alpha include .05, .01, .10, and .001.

A decision rule should be established before the study is undertaken (step 4). Using alpha and the test statistic, critical values can be determined. These **critical values** are *used at the decision step to determine whether the null hypothesis is rejected* or not. If the *p*-value method (discussed later) is used, the value of alpha is used as a critical probability value. The process begins by assuming that the null hypothesis is true. Data are gathered and statistics computed. If the evidence is away from the null hypothesis, the business researcher begins to doubt that the null hypothesis is really true. If the evidence is far enough away from the null hypothesis that the critical value is surpassed, the business researcher will reject the null hypothesis and declare that a statistically significant result has been attained. Here again, it is analogous to the U.S. court of law system. Initially, a defendant is assumed to be innocent. Prosecuting attorneys present evidence against the defendant (analogous to data gathered and analyzed in a study). At some point, if enough evidence is presented against the defendant such that the jury no longer believes the defendant is innocent, a critical level of evidence has been reached and the jury finds the defendant guilty. The first four steps in testing hypotheses should *always* be completed *before* the study is undertaken. It is not sound research to gather data first and then try to determine what to do with the data.

Step 5 is to gather sample data. This step might include the construction and implementation of a survey, conducting focus groups, randomly sampling items from an assembly line, or even sampling from secondary data sources (e.g., financial databases). In gathering data, the business researcher is cautioned to recall the proper techniques of random sampling (presented in Chapter 7). Care should be taken in establishing a frame, determining the sampling technique, and constructing the measurement device. A strong effort should be made to avoid all nonsampling errors. After the data are sampled, the test statistic can be calculated (step 6).

Task 3 of the HTAB system, take statistical action, includes step 7. Using the previously established decision rule (in step 4) and the value of the test statistic, the business researcher can draw a statistical conclusion. In *all* hypothesis tests, the business researcher needs to conclude whether the null hypothesis is rejected or is not rejected (step 7).

Task 4 of the HTAB system, determining the business implications, incorporates step 8. After a statistical decision is made, the business researcher or decision maker decides what business implications the study results contain (step 8). For example, if the hypothesis-testing procedure results in a conclusion that train passengers are significantly older today than they were in the past, the manager may decide to cater to these older customers or to draw up a strategy to make ridership more appealing to younger people. It is at this step that the business decision maker must decide whether a statistically significant result is really a substantive result.

Rejection and Nonrejection Regions

Using the critical values established at step 4 of the hypothesis testing process, the possible statistical outcomes of a study can be divided into two groups:

1. Those that cause the rejection of the null hypothesis
2. Those that do not cause the rejection of the null hypothesis.

Conceptually and graphically, statistical outcomes that result in the rejection of the null hypothesis lie in what is termed the **rejection region.** Statistical outcomes that fail to result in the rejection of the null hypothesis lie in what is termed the **nonrejection region.**

As an example, consider the flour-packaging manufacturing example. The null hypothesis is that the average fill for the population of packages is 40 ounces. Suppose a sample of 100 such packages is randomly selected, and a sample mean of 40.01 ounces is obtained. Because this mean is not 40 ounces, should the business researcher decide to reject the null hypothesis? In the hypothesis test process we are using sample statistics (in this case, the sample mean of 40.1 ounces) to make decisions about population parameters (in this case, the population mean of 40 ounces). It makes sense that in taking random samples from a population with a mean of 40 ounces not all sample means will equal 40 ounces. In fact, the central limit theorem (see Chapter 7) states that for large sample sizes, sample means are normally distributed around the population mean. Thus, even when the population mean is 40 ounces, a sample mean might still be 40.1, 38.6, or even 44.2. However, suppose a sample mean of 50 ounces is obtained for 100 packages. This sample mean may be so far from what is reasonable to expect for a population with a mean of 40 ounces that the decision is made to reject the null hypothesis. This begs the question: when is the sample mean so far away from the population mean that the null hypothesis is rejected? The critical values established at step 4 of the hypothesis testing process are used to divide the means that lead to the rejection of the null hypothesis from those that do not. Figure 9.3 displays a normal distribution of sample means around a population mean of 40 ounces. Note the critical values in each end (tail) of the distribution. In each direction beyond the critical values lie the rejection regions. Any sample mean that falls in that region will lead the business researcher to reject the null hypothesis. Sample means that fall between the two critical values are close enough to the population mean that the business researcher will decide not to reject the null hypothesis. These means are in the nonrejection region.

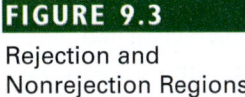

FIGURE 9.3

Rejection and
Nonrejection Regions

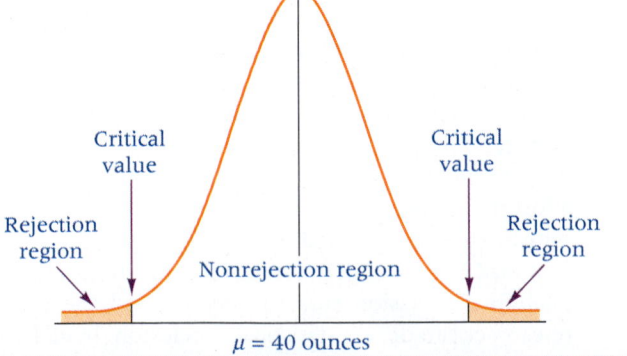

Type I and Type II Errors

Because the hypothesis testing process uses sample statistics calculated from random data to reach conclusions about population parameters, it is possible to make an incorrect decision about the null hypothesis. In particular, two types of errors can be made in testing hypotheses: Type I error and Type II error.

A **Type I error** is committed by *rejecting a true null hypothesis*. With a Type I error, the null hypothesis is true, but the business researcher decides that it is not. As an example, suppose the flour-packaging process actually is "in control" and is averaging 40 ounces of flour per package. Suppose also that a business researcher randomly selects 100 packages, weighs the contents of each, and computes a sample mean. It is possible, by chance, to randomly select 100 of the more extreme packages (mostly heavy weighted or mostly light weighted) resulting in a mean that falls in the rejection region. The decision is to reject the null hypothesis even though the population mean is actually 40 ounces. In this case, the business researcher has committed a Type I error.

The notion of a Type I error can be used outside the realm of statistical hypothesis testing in the business world. For example, if a manager fires an employee because some evidence indicates that she is stealing from the company and if she really is not stealing from the company, then the manager has committed a Type I error. As another example, suppose a worker on the assembly line of a large manufacturer hears an unusual sound and decides to shut the line down (reject the null hypothesis). If the sound turns out not to be related to the assembly line and no problems are occurring with the assembly line, then the worker has committed a Type I error. In U.S. industries in the 1950s, 1960s, and 1970s when U.S. products were in great demand, workers were strongly discouraged from making such Type I errors because the production downtime was so expensive. An analogous courtroom example of a Type I error is when an innocent person is sent to jail.

In Figure 9.3, the rejection regions represent the possibility of committing a Type I error. Means that fall beyond the critical values will be considered so extreme that the business researcher chooses to reject the null hypothesis. However, if the null hypothesis is true, any mean that falls in a rejection region will result in a decision that produces a Type I error. The *probability of committing a Type I error* is called **alpha (α)** or **level of significance.** Alpha equals the area under the curve that is in the rejection region beyond the critical value(s). The value of alpha is always set before the experiment or study is undertaken. As mentioned previously, common values of alpha are .05, .01, .10, and .001.

A **Type II error** is committed when a business researcher *fails to reject a false null hypothesis.* In this case, the null hypothesis is false, but a decision is made to not reject it. Suppose in the case of the flour problem that the packaging process is actually producing a population mean of 41 ounces even though the null hypothesis is 40 ounces. A sample of 100 packages yields a sample mean of 40.2 ounces, which falls in the nonrejection region. The business decision maker decides not to reject the null hypothesis. A Type II error has been committed. The packaging procedure is out-of-control and the hypothesis testing process does not identify it.

Suppose in the business world an employee is stealing from the company. A manager sees some evidence that the stealing is occurring but lacks enough evidence to conclude that the employee is stealing from the company. The manager decides not to fire the employee based on theft. The manager has committed a Type II error. Consider the manufacturing line with the noise. Suppose the worker decides not enough noise is heard to shut the line down, but in actuality, one of the cords on the line is unraveling, creating a dangerous situation. The worker is committing a Type II error. Beginning in the 1980s, U.S. manufacturers started protecting more against Type II errors. They found that in many cases, it was more costly to produce bad product (e.g., scrap/rework costs and loss of market share due to poor quality) than it was to make it right the first time. They encouraged workers to "shut down" the line if the quality of work was seemingly not what it should be (risking a Type I error) rather than allowing poor quality product to be shipped. In a court-of-law, a Type II error is committed when a guilty person is declared innocent.

The probability of committing a Type II error is **beta (β).** Unlike alpha, beta is not usually stated at the beginning of the hypothesis testing procedure. Actually, because beta occurs only when the null hypothesis is not true, the computation of beta varies with the many possible alternative parameters that might occur. For example, in the flour-packaging problem, if the population mean is not 40 ounces, then what is it? It could be 41, 38, or 42 ounces. A value of beta is associated with each of these alternative means.

How are alpha and beta related? First of all, because alpha can only be committed when the null hypothesis is rejected and beta can only be committed when the null hypothesis is not rejected, a business researcher cannot commit both a Type I error and a Type II error at the same time on the same hypothesis test. Generally, alpha and beta are inversely related. If alpha is reduced, then beta is increased, and vice versa. If the rejection regions displayed in Figure 9.3 are reduced, making it harder to reject the 40-ounce weight, it will be easier to not discern when the packaging process is out-of-control. In terms of the manufacturing assembly line, if management makes it harder for workers to shut down the assembly line (reduce Type I error), then there is a greater chance that bad product will be made or that a serious problem with the line will arise (increase Type II error). Legally, if the courts make it harder to send innocent people to jail, then they have made it easier let guilty people go free. One way to reduce both errors is to increase the sample size. If a larger sample is taken, it is more likely that the sample is representative of the population; which translates into a better chance that a business researcher will make the correct choice. Figure 9.4 shows the relationship between the two types of error. The "state of nature" is how things actually are and the "action" is the decision that the business researcher actually makes. Note that each action alternative contains only one of the errors along with the possibility that a correct decision has been made. **Power,** which is equal to $1 - \beta$, is *the probability of a test rejecting the null hypothesis when the null hypothesis is false.* Figure 9.4 shows the relationship between α, β, and power.

9.2 TESTING HYPOTHESES ABOUT A POPULATION MEAN USING THE z STATISTIC (σ KNOWN)

One of the most basic hypothesis tests is a test about a population mean. A business researcher might be interested in testing to determine whether an established or accepted mean value for an industry is still true or in testing a hypothesized mean value for a new theory or product. As an example, a computer products company sets up a telephone service to assist customers by providing technical support. The average wait time during weekday hours is 37 minutes. However, a recent hiring effort added technical consultants to the system, and management believes that the average wait time decreased, and they want to prove it. Other business scenarios resulting in hypothesis tests of a single mean might include the following:

- A financial investment firm wants to test to determine whether the average hourly change in the Dow Jones Average over a 10-year period is +0.25.

- A manufacturing company wants to test to determine whether the average thickness of a plastic bottle is 2.4 millimeters.

FIGURE 9.4			State of nature	
Alpha, Beta, and Power			Null true	Null false
		Fail to reject null	Correct decision	Type II error (β)
	Action			
		Reject null	Type I error (α)	Correct decision (power)

■   A retail store wants to test to determine whether the average age of its customers is less than 40 years.

Formula (9.1) can be used to test hypotheses about a single population mean if the sample size is large ($n \geq 30$) for any population and for small samples ($n < 30$) if x is known to be normally distributed.

z TEST FOR A SINGLE MEAN (9.1)	$$z = \frac{\bar{x} - \mu}{\dfrac{\sigma}{\sqrt{n}}}$$

A survey of CPAs across the United States found that the average net income for sole proprietor CPAs is \$74,914.* Because this survey is now more than ten years old, an accounting researcher wants to test this figure by taking a random sample of 112 sole proprietor accountants in the United States to determine whether the net income figure changed. The researcher could use the eight steps of hypothesis testing to do so. Assume the population standard deviation of net incomes for sole proprietor CPAs is \$14,530.

HYPOTHESIZE:

At step 1, the hypotheses must be established. Because the researcher is testing to determine whether the figure has changed, the alternative hypothesis is that the mean net income is not \$74,914. The null hypothesis is that the mean still equals \$74,914. These hypotheses follow.

$$H_0\text{: } \mu = \$74{,}914$$

$$H_a\text{: } \mu \neq \$74{,}914$$

TEST:

Step 2 is to determine the appropriate statistical test and sampling distribution. Because sample size is large ($n = 112$) and the researcher is using the sample mean as the statistic, the z test in formula (9.1) is the appropriate test statistic.

$$z = \frac{\bar{x} - \mu}{\dfrac{\sigma}{\sqrt{n}}}$$

Step 3 is to specify the Type I error rate, or alpha, which is .05 in this problem. Step 4 is to state the decision rule. Because the test is two-tailed and alpha is .05, there is $\alpha/2$ or .025 area in each of the tails of the distribution. Thus, the rejection region is in the two ends of the distribution with 2.5% of the area in each. There is a .4750 area between the mean and each of the critical values that separate the tails of the distribution (the rejection region) from the nonrejection region. By using this .4750 area and Table A.5, the critical z value can be obtained.

$$z_{\alpha/2} = \pm 1.96$$

Figure 9.5 displays the problem with the rejection regions and the critical values of z. The decision rule is that if the data gathered produce a z value greater than 1.96 or less than −1.96, the test statistic is in one of the rejection regions and the decision is to reject the null hypothesis. If the z value calculated from the data is between −1.96 and +1.96, the decision is to not reject the null hypothesis because the calculated z value is in the nonrejection region.

Step 5 is to gather the data. Suppose the 112 CPAs who respond produce a sample mean of \$78,695. At step 6, the value of the test statistic is calculated by using $\bar{x} = \$78{,}695$, $n = 112$, $\sigma = \$14{,}530$, and a hypothesized $\mu = \$74{,}914$:

$$z = \frac{78{,}695 - 74{,}914}{\dfrac{14{,}530}{\sqrt{112}}} = 2.75$$

---

*Adapted from Daniel J. Flaherty, Raymond A. Zimmerman, and Mary Ann Murray, "Benchmarking Against the Best," *Journal of Accountancy* (July 1995), pp. 85–88.

FIGURE 9.5

CPA Net Income Example

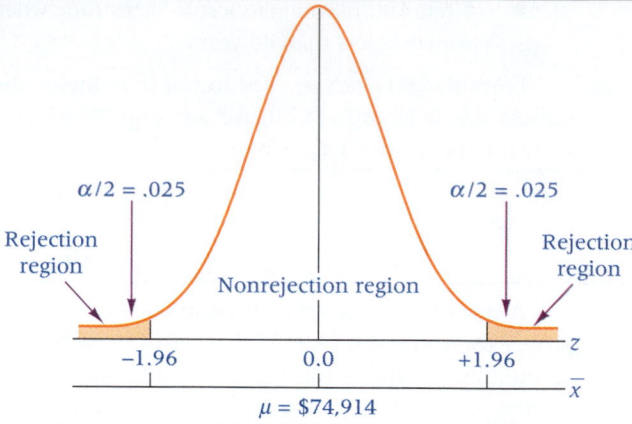

ACTION:

Because this test statistic, $z = 2.75$, is greater than the critical value of z in the upper tail of the distribution, $z = +1.96$, the statistical conclusion reached at step 7 of the hypothesis-testing process is to reject the null hypothesis. *The calculated test statistic* is often referred to as the **observed value.** Thus, the observed value of z for this problem is 2.75 and the critical value of z for this problem is 1.96.

BUSINESS IMPLICATION:

Step 8 is to make a managerial decision. What does this result mean? Statistically, the researcher has enough evidence to reject the figure of $74,914 as the true national average net income for sole proprietor CPAs. Although the researcher conducted a two-tailed test, the evidence gathered indicates that the national average may have increased. The sample mean of $78,695 is $3,781 higher than the national mean being tested. The researcher can conclude that the national average is more than before, but because the $78,695 is only a sample mean, it offers no guarantee that the national average for all sole proprietor CPAs is $3,781 more. If a confidence interval were constructed with the sample data, $78,695 would be the point estimate. Other samples might produce different sample means. Managerially, this statistical finding may mean that CPAs will be more expensive to hire either as full-time employees or as consultants. It may mean that consulting services have gone up in price. For new accountants, it may mean the potential for greater earning power. If the sample mean of $78,695 is the actual new population average for the year 2005, it would represent an increase of $3,781 over a ten-year period. This increase may or may not be substantive depending on one's point of view.

Testing the Mean with a Finite Population

If the hypothesis test for the population mean is being conducted with a known finite population, the population information can be incorporated into the hypothesis-testing formula. Doing so can increase the potential for rejecting the null hypothesis. However, remember from Chapter 7 that if the sample size is less than 5% of the population, the finite correction factor does not significantly alter the solution. Formula (9.1) can be amended to include the population information.

FORMULA TO TEST HYPOTHESES ABOUT μ WITH A FINITE POPULATION (9.2)	$z = \dfrac{\bar{x} - \mu}{\dfrac{\sigma}{\sqrt{n}} \sqrt{\dfrac{N-n}{N-1}}}$

In the CPA net income example, suppose only 600 sole proprietor CPAs practice in the United States. A sample of 112 CPAs taken from a population of only 600 CPAs is

18.67% of the population and therefore is much more likely to be representative of the population than a sample of 112 CPAs taken from a population of 20,000 CPAs (.56% of the population). The finite correction factor takes this difference into consideration and allows for an increase in the observed value of z. The observed z value would change to

$$ z = \frac{\overline{x} - \mu}{\dfrac{\sigma}{\sqrt{n}} \sqrt{\dfrac{N-n}{N-1}}} = \frac{78{,}695 - 74{,}914}{\dfrac{14{,}530}{\sqrt{112}} \sqrt{\dfrac{600-112}{600-1}}} = \frac{3{,}781}{1{,}239.2} = 3.05 $$

Use of the finite correction factor increased the observed z value from 2.75 to 3.05. The decision to reject the null hypothesis does not change with this new information. However, on occasion, the finite correction factor can make the difference between rejecting and failing to reject the null hypothesis.

Using the *p*-Value to Test Hypotheses

Another way to reach a statistical conclusion in hypothesis testing problems is by using the **p-value,** sometimes referred to as **observed significance level.** The *p*-value is growing in importance with the increasing use of statistical computer packages to test hypotheses. No preset value of α is given in the *p*-value method. Instead, the probability of getting a test statistic at least as extreme as the observed test statistic (computed from the data) is computed under the assumption that the null hypothesis is true. Virtually every statistical computer program yields this probability (*p*-value). The *p*-value defines the smallest value of alpha for which the null hypothesis can be rejected. For example, if the *p*-value of a test is .038, the null hypothesis cannot be rejected at $\alpha = .01$ because .038 is the smallest value of alpha for which the null hypothesis can be rejected. However, the null hypothesis can be rejected for $\alpha = .05$.

Suppose a researcher is conducting a one-tailed test with a rejection region in the upper tail and obtains an observed test statistic of $z = 2.04$ from the sample data. Using the standard normal table, Table A.5, we find that the probability of randomly obtaining a z value this great or greater by chance is $.5000 - .4793 = .0207$. The p value is .0207. Using this information, the researcher would reject the null hypothesis for $\alpha = .05$ or .10 or any value more than .0207. The researcher would not reject the null hypothesis for any alpha value less than or equal to .0207 (in particular, $\alpha = .01$, .001, etc.).

For a two-tailed test, recall that we split alpha to determine the critical value of the test statistic. With the *p*-value, the probability of getting a test statistic at least as extreme as the observed value is computed. This *p*-value is then compared to $\alpha/2$ for two-tailed tests to determine statistical significance. The business researcher should be cautioned that some statistical computer packages are programmed to double the observed probability and report that value as the *p*-value when the user signifies that a two-tailed test is being requested. The researcher then compares this *p*-value to alpha values to decide whether to reject the null hypothesis. In other words, rather than the researcher splitting alpha, the probability of the observed test statistic is doubled. The researcher must be sure she understands what the computer software package does to the *p*-value for a two-tailed test before she reaches a statistical conclusion.

As an example of using *p*-values with a two-tailed test, consider the CPA net income problem. The observed test statistic for this problem is $z = 2.75$. Using Table A.5, we know that the probability of obtaining a test statistic at least this extreme if the null hypothesis is true is $.5000 - .4970 = .0030$. Observe that in the MINITAB output in Figure 9.6 the *p*-value is .0060. MINITAB doubles the *p*-value on a two-tailed test so that the researcher can compare the *p*-value to α to reach a statistical conclusion. On the other hand, when Excel yields a *p*-value in its output, it always gives the one-tailed value, which in this case is .003 (see output in Figure 9.6). To reach a statistical conclusion from an Excel produced *p*-value when doing a two-tailed test, the researcher must either compare the *p*-value to $\alpha/2$ or double it and compare it to α.

FIGURE 9.6

MINITAB and Excel Output
with *p* Values

MINITAB Output

```
                              Z-TEST

Test of mu=74914 vs mu not=74914
The assumed sigma=14530

Variable      N     Mean    StDev   SE Mean     Z        p
Net Income   112    78695   14543     1373    2.75    0.0060
```

Excel Output

	A	B
1	Sample Mean	78695
2	Standard Error	1374
3	Standard Deviation	14543
4	Count (n)	112
5	Hypothesized Value of Mu	74914
6	P-value	0.003

Using the Critical Value Method to Test Hypotheses

Another method of testing hypotheses is the critical value method. In the CPA income example, the null hypothesis was rejected because the computed value of *z* was in the rejection zone. What mean income would it take to cause the observed *z* value to be in the rejection zone? The **critical value method** *determines the critical mean value required for z to be in the rejection region and uses it to test the hypotheses.*

This method also uses formula (9.1). However, instead of an observed *z*, a critical $\bar{x}$ value, $\bar{x}_C$, is determined. The critical table value of z_c is inserted into the formula, along with μ and σ. Thus,

$$z_c = \frac{\bar{x}_c - \mu}{\dfrac{\sigma}{\sqrt{n}}}$$

Substituting values from the CPA income example gives

$$\pm 1.96 = \frac{\bar{x}_c - 74{,}914}{\dfrac{14{,}530}{\sqrt{112}}}$$

or

$$\bar{x}_c = 74{,}914 \pm 1.96\frac{14{,}530}{\sqrt{112}} = 74{,}914 \pm 2{,}691$$

lower $\bar{x}_c = 72{,}223$ and upper $\bar{x}_c = 77{,}605$.

Figure 9.7 depicts graphically the rejection and nonrejection regions in terms of means instead of *z* scores.

With the critical value method, most of the computational work is done ahead of time. In this problem, before the sample means are computed, the analyst knows that a sample mean value of greater than $77,605 or less than $72,223 must be attained to reject the hypothesized population mean. Because the sample mean for this problem was $78,695, which is greater than $77,605, the analyst rejects the null hypothesis. This method is particularly attractive in industrial settings where standards can be set ahead of time and then quality control technicians can gather data and compare actual measurements of products to specifications.

FIGURE 9.7

Rejection and Nonrejection
Regions for Critical
Value Method

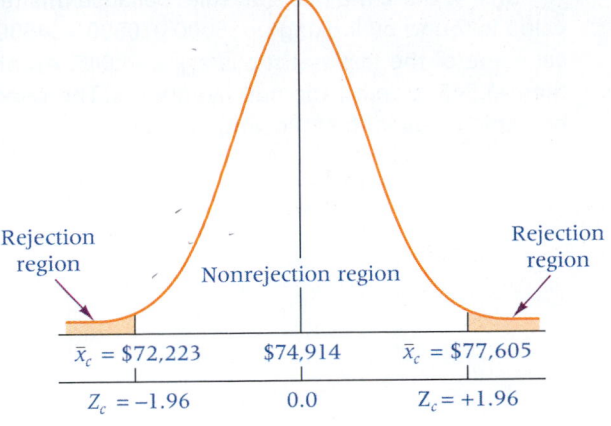

Rejection region

Nonrejection region

Rejection region

$\bar{x}_c = \$72{,}223$	$\$74{,}914$	$\bar{x}_c = \$77{,}605$
$Z_c = -1.96$	0.0	$Z_c = +1.96$

DEMONSTRATION PROBLEM 9.1

In an attempt to determine why customer service is important to managers in the United Kingdom, researchers surveyed managing directors of manufacturing plants in Scotland.* One of the reasons proposed was that customer service is a means of retaining customers. On a scale from 1 to 5, with 1 being low and 5 being high, the survey respondents rated this reason more highly than any of the others, with a mean response of 4.30. Suppose U.S. researchers believe American manufacturing managers would not rate this reason as highly and conduct a hypothesis test to prove their theory. Alpha is set at .05. Data are gathered and the following results are obtained. Use these data and the eight steps of hypothesis testing to determine whether U.S. managers rate this reason significantly lower than the 4.30 mean ascertained in the United Kingdom. Assume from previous studies that the population standard deviation is 0.574.

3	4	5	5	4	5	5	4	4	4	4
4	4	4	4	5	4	4	4	3	4	4
4	3	5	4	4	5	4	4	4	5	

Solution

HYPOTHESIZE:

STEP 1. Establish hypotheses. Because the U.S. researchers are interested only in "proving" that the mean figure is lower in the United States, the test is one-tailed. The alternative hypothesis is that the population mean is lower than 4.30. The null hypothesis states the equality case.

$$H_0: \mu = 4.30$$
$$H_a: \mu < 4.30$$

TEST:

STEP 2. Determine the appropriate statistical test. The test statistic is

$$z = \frac{\bar{x} - \mu}{\dfrac{\sigma}{\sqrt{n}}}$$

STEP 3. Specify the Type I error rate.

$$\alpha = .05$$

* William G. Donaldson, "Manufacturers Need to Show Greater Commitment to Customer Service," *Industrial Marketing Management*, vol. 24 (October 1995), pp. 421–430. The 1-to-5 scale has been reversed here for clarity of presentation.

STEP 4. State the decision rule. Because this test is a one-tailed test, the critical z value is found by looking up $.5000 - .0500 = .4500$ as the area in Table A.5. The critical value of the test statistic is $z_{.05} = -1.645$. An observed test statistic must be less than -1.645 to reject the null hypothesis. The rejection region and critical value can be depicted as in the following diagram.

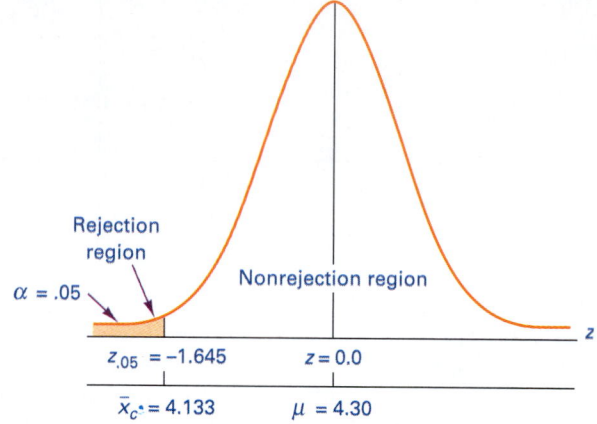

STEP 5. Gather the sample data. The data are shown.
STEP 6. Calculate the value of the test statistic.

$$\bar{x} = 4.156 \qquad \sigma = .574$$

$$z = \frac{4.156 - 4.30}{\dfrac{.574}{\sqrt{32}}} = -1.42$$

ACTION:

STEP 7. State the statistical conclusion. Because the observed test statistic is not less than the critical value and is not in the rejection region, the statistical conclusion is that the null hypothesis cannot be rejected.

BUSINESS IMPLICATION:

STEP 8. Make a managerial decision. The test does not result in enough evidence to conclude that U.S. managers think it is less important to use customer service as a means of retaining customers than do U.K. managers. Customer service is an important tool for retaining customers in both countries according to managers.

Using the p-value: The observed test statistic is $z = -1.42$. From Table A.5, the probability of getting a z value at least this extreme when the null hypothesis is true is $.5000 - .4222 = .0778$. Hence, the null hypothesis cannot be rejected at $\alpha = .05$ because the smallest value of alpha for which the null hypothesis can be rejected is $.0778$.

Using the critical value method: For what sample mean (or more extreme) value would the null hypothesis be rejected? This critical sample mean can be determined by using the critical z value associated with alpha, $z_{.05} = -1.645$.

$$z_c = \frac{\bar{x}_c - \mu}{\dfrac{\sigma}{\sqrt{n}}}$$

$$-1.645 = \frac{\bar{x}_c - 4.30}{\dfrac{.574}{\sqrt{32}}}$$

$$\bar{x}_c = 4.133$$

The decision rule is that a sample mean less than 4.133 would be necessary to reject the null hypothesis. Because the mean obtained from the sample data is 4.156, the researchers fail to reject the null hypothesis. The preceding diagram includes a scale with the critical sample mean and the rejection region for the critical value method.

FIGURE 9.8

MINITAB and Excel Output for Demonstration Problem 9.1

MINITAB Output

One-Sample Z: Ratings

```
Test of mu = 4.3 vs mu < 4.3
The assumed sigma = 0.574
```

Variable	N	Mean	StDev	SE Mean
Ratings	32	4.156	0.574	0.101

Variable	95.0% Upper Bound	Z	P
Ratings	4.323	-1.42	0.078

Excel Output

	A
1	
2	The p-value for the ratings problem is **0.078339**
3	

Using the Computer to Test Hypotheses About a Population Mean Using the z Statistic

Both MINITAB and Excel can be used to test hypotheses about a single population mean using the z statistic. Figure 9.8 contains output from both MINITAB and Excel for Demonstration Problem 9.1. For z tests, MINITAB requires knowledge of the population standard deviation. Note that the standard MINITAB output includes a statement of the one-tailed hypothesis, the observed z value, and the p-value. Because this test is a one-tailed test, the p-value was not doubled. The Excel output contains only the right-tailed p-value of the z statistic. With a negative observed z for Demonstration Problem 9.1, the p-value was calculated by taking $1 -$ (Excel's answer).

9.2 PROBLEMS

9.1 **a.** Use the data given to test the following hypotheses.

$$H_0: \mu = 25 \qquad H_a: \mu \neq 25$$
$$\bar{x} = 28.1, n = 57, \sigma = 8.46, \alpha = .01$$

  b. Use the p-value to reach a statistical conclusion

  c. Using the critical value method, what are the critical sample mean values?

9.2 Use the data given to test the following hypotheses. Assume the data are normally distributed in the population.

$$H_0: \mu = 7.48 \qquad H_a: \mu < 7.48$$
$$\bar{x} = 6.91, n = 24, \sigma = 1.21, \alpha = .01$$

9.3 **a.** Use the data given to test the following hypotheses.

$$H_0: \mu = 1200 \qquad H_a: \mu \geq 1200$$
$$\bar{x} = 1215, n = 113, \sigma = 100, \alpha = .10$$

  b. Use the p-value to obtain the results.

  c. Solve for the critical value required to reject the mean.

9.4 The Environmental Protection Agency releases figures on urban air soot in selected cities in the United States. For the city of St. Louis, the EPA claims that the average number of micrograms of suspended particles per cubic meter of air is 82. Suppose St. Louis officials have been working with businesses, commuters, and industries to reduce this figure. These city officials hire an environmental company to take random measures of air soot over a period of several weeks. The resulting data follow. Assume that the population standard deviation is 9.184. Use these data to determine whether the urban air soot in St. Louis is significantly lower than it was when the EPA conducted its measurements. Let $\alpha = .01$. If the null hypothesis is rejected, discuss the substantive hypothesis.

81.6	66.6	70.9	82.5	58.3	71.6	72.4
96.6	78.6	76.1	80.0	73.2	85.5	73.2
68.6	74.0	68.7	83.0	86.9	94.9	75.6
77.3	86.6	71.7	88.5	87.0	72.5	83.0
85.8	74.9	61.7	92.2			

9.5 According to the U.S. Bureau of Labor Statistics, the average weekly earnings of a production worker in 1997 were $424.20. Suppose a labor researcher wants to test to determine whether this figure is still accurate today. The researcher randomly selects 54 production workers from across the United States and obtains a representative earnings statement for one week from each. The resulting sample average is $432.69. Assuming a population standard deviation of $33.90, and a 5% level of significance, determine whether the mean weekly earnings of a production worker have changed.

9.6 According to a study several years ago by the Personal Communications Industry Association, the average wireless phone user earns $62,600 per year. Suppose a researcher believes that the average annual earnings of a wireless phone user are lower now, and he sets up a study in an attempt to prove his theory. He randomly samples 18 wireless phone users and finds out that the average annual salary for this sample is $58,974, with a population standard deviation of $7,810. Use $\alpha = .01$ to test the researcher's theory. Assume wages in this industry are normally distributed.

9.7 A manufacturing company produces valves in various sizes and shapes. One particular valve plate is supposed to have a tensile strength of 5 pounds per millimeter (lbs/mm). The company tests a random sample of 42 such valve plates from a lot of 650 valve plates. The sample mean is a tensile strength of 5.0611 lbs/mm, and the population standard deviation is .2803 lbs/mm. Use $\alpha = .10$ and test to determine whether the lot of valve plates has an average tensile strength of 5 lbs/mm.

9.8 A manufacturing firm has been averaging 18.2 orders per week for several years. However, during a recession, orders appeared to slow. Suppose the firm's production manager randomly samples 32 weeks and finds a sample mean of 15.6 orders. The population standard deviation is 2.3 orders. Test to determine whether the average number of orders is down by using $\alpha = .10$.

9.9 A study conducted by Runzheimer International showed that Paris is the most expensive place to live of the 12 European Union cities. Paris ranks second in housing expense, with a rental unit of six to nine rooms costing an average of $4,292 a month. Suppose a company's CEO believes this figure is too high and decides to conduct her own survey. Her assistant contacts the owners of 55 randomly selected rental units of six to nine rooms and finds that the sample average cost is $4,008. Assume that the population standard deviation is $386. Using the sample results and $\alpha = .01$, test to determine whether the figure published by Runzheimer International is too high. If the null hypothesis is rejected, discuss whether the results are substantive.

9.10 The American Water Works Association estimates that the average person in the United States uses 123 gallons of water per day. Suppose some researchers believe that more water is being used now and want to test to determine whether it is so. They randomly select a sample of Americans and carefully keep track of the water used by each sample member for a day, then analyze the results by using a statistical computer software package. The output is given here. Assume $\alpha = .05$.

How many people were sampled? What was the sample mean? Was this a one- or two-tailed test? What was the result of the study? What decision could be stated about the null hypothesis from these results?

```
           One-Sample Z: Wateruse

Test of mu = 123 vs mu > 123
The assumed sigma = 27.68

Variable   N    Mean    StDev   SE Mean
Wateruse   40   132.36  27.68   4.38

Variable   95.0% Lower Bound    Z     P
Wateruse         125.16         2.14  0.016
```

9.3 TESTING HYPOTHESES ABOUT A POPULATION MEAN USING THE t STATISTIC (σ UNKNOWN)

Very often when a business researcher is gathering data to test hypotheses about a single population mean, the value of the population standard deviation is unknown and the researcher must use the sample standard deviation as an estimate of it. In such cases, the z test cannot be used.

Chapter 8 presented the t distribution, which can be used to analyze hypotheses about a single population mean when σ is unknown if the population is normally distributed for the measurement being studied. In this section, we will examine the t test for a single population mean. In general, this t test is applicable whenever the researcher is drawing a single random sample to test the value of a population mean (μ), the population standard deviation is unknown, and the population is normally distributed for the measurement of interest. Recall from Chapter 8 that the assumption that the data be normally distributed in the population is rather robust.

The formula for testing such hypotheses follows.

t TEST FOR μ (9.3)	$$t = \frac{\bar{x} - \mu}{\frac{s}{\sqrt{n}}}$$ $$\mathrm{df} = n - 1$$

The U.S. Farmers' Production Company builds large harvesters. For a harvester to be properly balanced when operating, a 25-pound plate is installed on its side. The machine that produces these plates is set to yield plates that average 25 pounds. The distribution of plates produced from the machine is normal. However, the shop supervisor is worried that the machine is out of adjustment and is producing plates that do not average 25 pounds. To test this concern, he randomly selects 20 of the plates produced the day before and weighs them. Table 9.1 shows the weights obtained, along with the computed sample mean and sample standard deviation.

The test is to determine whether the machine is out of control, and the shop supervisor has not specified whether he believes the machine is producing plates that are too heavy or too light. Thus a two-tailed test is appropriate. The following hypotheses are tested.

$$H_0: \mu = 25 \text{ pounds}$$
$$H_a: \mu \neq 25 \text{ pounds}$$

An α of .05 is used. Figure 9.9 shows the rejection regions.

Because $n = 20$, the degrees of freedom for this test are 19 ($20 - 1$). The t distribution table is a one-tailed table but the test for this problem is two-tailed, so alpha must be split, which yields $\alpha/2 = .025$, the value in each tail. (To obtain the table t value when conducting

TABLE 9.1

Weights in Pounds of a Sample of 20 Plates

22.6	22.2	23.2	27.4	24.5
27.0	26.6	28.1	26.9	24.9
26.2	25.3	23.1	24.2	26.1
25.8	30.4	28.6	23.5	23.6

$\bar{x} = 25.51, s = 2.1933, n = 20$

FIGURE 9.9

Rejection Regions for the
Machine Plate Example

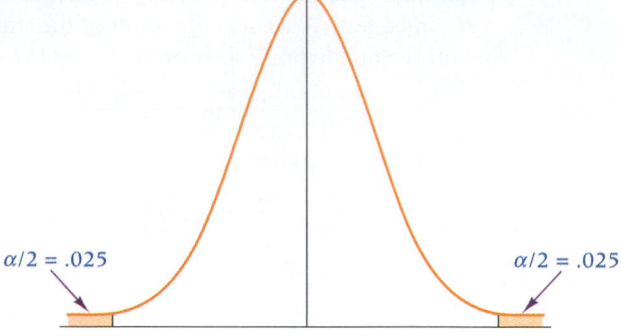

$\alpha/2 = .025$ $\alpha/2 = .025$

FIGURE 9.10

Graph of Observed and Critical
t Values for the Machine Plate
Example

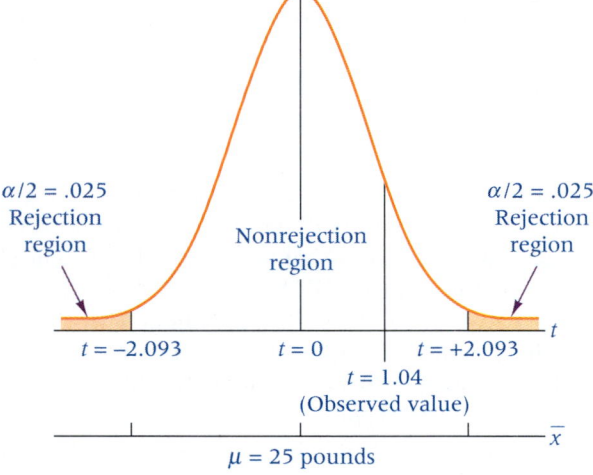

$\alpha/2 = .025$
Rejection
region

Nonrejection
region

$\alpha/2 = .025$
Rejection
region

$t = -2.093$ $t = 0$ $t = +2.093$

$t = 1.04$
(Observed value)

$\mu = 25$ pounds

FIGURE 9.11

MINITAB and Excel Output for
the Machine Plate Example

MINITAB Output

One-Sample T: Weight

Test of mu = 25 vs mu not = 25

Variable	N	Mean	StDev	SE Mean
Weight	20	25.510	2.193	0.490

Variable	95.0% CI	T	P
Weight	(24.484, 26.536)	1.04	0.311

Excel Output

	A	B
1	Mean	25.51
2	Variance	4.810
3	df	19
4	t Stat	1.04
5	P (T<=t) one-tail	0.1557
6	t Critical one-tail	1.73
7	P (T<=t) two-tail	0.3114
8	t Critical two-tail	2.09

---

a two-tailed test, always split alpha and use $\alpha/2$.) The table *t* value for this example is 2.093.
Table values such as this one are often written in the following form:

$$t_{.025,19} = 2.093$$

Figure 9.10 depicts the *t* distribution for this example, along with the critical values,
the observed *t* value, and the rejection regions. In this case, the decision rule is to reject the

null hypothesis if the observed value of t is less than -2.093 or greater than $+2.093$ (in the tails of the distribution). Computation of the test statistic yields

$$t = \frac{\bar{x} - \mu}{\frac{s}{\sqrt{n}}} = \frac{25.51 - 25.00}{\frac{2.1933}{\sqrt{20}}} = 1.04 \text{ (observed } t \text{ value)}$$

Because the observed t value is $+1.04$, the null hypothesis is not rejected. Not enough evidence is found in this sample to reject the hypothesis that the population mean is 25 pounds.

Figure 9.11 shows MINITAB and Excel output for this example. Note that the MINITAB output includes the observed t value (1.04) and the p-value (.311). Since this test is a two-tailed test, MINITAB has doubled the one-tailed p-value for $t = 1.04$. Thus the p-value of .311 can be compared directly to $\alpha = .05$ to reach the conclusion to fail to reject the null hypothesis.

The Excel output contains the observed t value (1.04) plus the p-value and the critical table t value for both a one-tailed and a two-tailed test. Since this test is a two-tailed test, the p-value of .3114 is used to compare to $\alpha = .05$. Excel also gives the table value of $t = 2.09$ for a two-tailed test, which allows one to verify that the statistical conclusion is to fail to reject the null hypothesis because the observed t value is only 1.04, which is less than 2.09.

DEMONSTRATION PROBLEM 9.2	Figures released by the U.S. Department of Agriculture show that the average size of farms has increased since 1940. In 1940, the mean size of a farm was 174 acres; by 1997, the average size was 471 acres. Between those years, the number of farms decreased but the amount of tillable land remained relatively constant, so now farms are bigger. This trend might be explained, in part, by the inability of small farms to compete with the prices and costs of large-scale operations and to produce a level of income necessary to support the farmers' desired standard of living. Suppose an agribusiness researcher believes the average size of farms increased from the 1997 mean figure of 471 acres. To test this notion, she randomly sampled 23 farms across the United States and ascertained the size of each farm from county records. The data she gathered follow. Use a 5% level of significance to test her hypothesis. Assume that number of acres per farm is normally distributed in the population.

445	489	474	505	553	477	454	463	466
557	502	449	438	500	466	477	557	433
545	511	590	561	560

Solution

HYPOTHESIZE:

STEP 1. The researcher's hypothesis is that the average size of a U.S. farm is more than 471 acres. Because this theory is unproven, it is the alternate hypothesis. The null hypothesis is that the mean is still 471 acres.

$$H_0: \mu = 471$$
$$H_a: \mu > 471$$

TEST:

STEP 2. The statistical test to be used is

$$t = \frac{\bar{x} - \mu}{\frac{s}{\sqrt{n}}}$$

STEP 3. The value of alpha is .05.

STEP 4. With 23 data points, df $= n - 1 = 23 - 1 = 22$. This test is one-tailed, and the critical table t value is

$$t_{.05,22} = 1.717$$

The decision rule is to reject the null hypothesis if the observed test statistic is greater than 1.717.

STEP 5. The gathered data are shown.

STEP 6. The sample mean is 498.78 and the sample standard deviation is 46.94. The observed t value is

$$t = \frac{\bar{x} - \mu}{\frac{s}{\sqrt{n}}} = \frac{498.78 - 471}{\frac{46.94}{\sqrt{23}}} = 2.84$$

ACTION:

STEP 7. The observed t value of 2.84 is greater than the table t value of 1.717, so the business researcher rejects the null hypothesis. She accepts the alternative hypothesis and concludes that the average size of a U.S. farm is now more than 471 acres. The following graph represents this analysis pictorially.

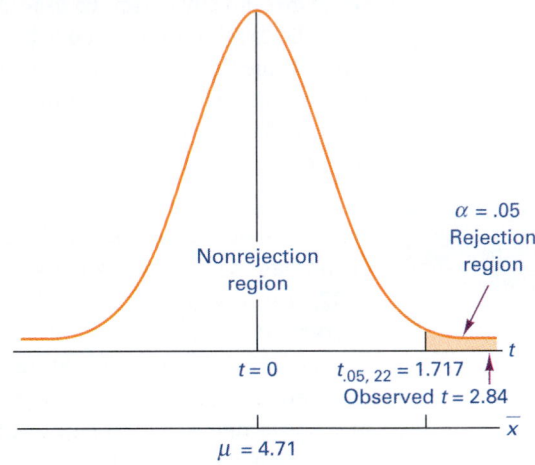

BUSINESS IMPLICATIONS:

STEP 8. Agribusiness researchers can speculate about what it means to have larger farms. If the average size of a farm has increased from 471 acres to almost 500 acres, it may represent a substantive increase.

It could mean that small farms are not financially viable. It might mean that corporations are buying out small farms and that large company farms are on the increase. Such a trend might spark legislative movements to protect the small farm. Larger farm sizes might also affect commodity trading.

FIGURE 9.12
MINITAB and Excel Output for Demonstration Problem 9.2

MINITAB Output

```
One-Sample T: Acres
```

```
Test of mu = 471 vs mu > 471
Variable    N    Mean    StDev   SE Mean
Acres       23   498.78  46.94    9.79

Variable    95.0% Lower Bound    T      P
Acres              481.97        2.84  0.005
```

Excel Output

	A	B
1	Mean	498.78
2	Variance	2203.63
3	Observations	23
4	df	22
5	t Stat	2.84
6	P (T<=t) one-tail	0.0048
7	t Critical one-tail	1.72
8	P (T<=t) two-tail	0.0096
9	t Critical two-tail	2.07

Using the Computer to Test Hypotheses About a Population Mean Using the *t* Test

MINITAB has the capability of computing a one-sample *t* test for means. Figure 9.12 contains MINITAB output for Demonstration Problem 9.2. The output contains the hypotheses being tested, the sample statistics, the observed *t* value (2.84), and the *p*-value (.005). Because the *p*-value is less than $\alpha = .05$, the decision is to reject the null hypothesis.

Excel does not have a one-sample *t* test function. However, by using the two-sample *t* test for means with unequal variances, the results for a one-sample test can be obtained. This is accomplished by inputting the sample data for the first sample and the value of the parameter being tested (in this case, $\mu = 471$) for the second sample. The output includes the observed *t* value (2.84) and both the table *t* values and *p*-values for one- and two-tailed tests. Because Demonstration Problem 9.2 was a one-tailed test, the *p*-value of .0048, which is the same value obtained using MINITAB, is used.

9.3 PROBLEMS

9.11 A random sample of size 20 is taken, resulting in a sample mean of 16.45 and a sample standard deviation of 3.59. Assume *x* is normally distributed and use this information and $\alpha = .05$ to test the following hypotheses.

$$H_0: \mu = 16 \qquad H_a: \mu \neq 16$$

9.12 A random sample of 51 items is taken, with $\bar{x} = 58.42$ and $s^2 = 25.68$. Use these data to test the following hypotheses, assuming you want to take only a 1% risk of committing a Type I error and that *x* is normally distributed.

$$H_0: \mu = 60 \qquad H_a: \mu < 60$$

9.13 The following data were gathered from a random sample of 11 items.

1200	1175	1080	1275	1201	1387
1090	1280	1400	1287	1225	

Use these data and a 5% level of significance to test the following hypotheses, assuming that the data come from a normally distributed population.

$$H_0: \mu = 1160 \qquad H_a: \mu > 1160$$

9.14 The following data (in pounds), which were selected randomly from a normally distributed population of values, represent measurements of a machine part that is supposed to weigh, on average, 8.3 pounds.

8.1	8.4	8.3	8.2	8.5	8.6	8.4	8.3	8.4	8.2
8.8	8.2	8.2	8.3	8.1	8.3	8.4	8.5	8.5	8.7

Use these data and $\alpha = .01$ to test the hypothesis that the parts average 8.3 pounds.

9.15 A hole-punch machine is set to punch a hole 1.84 centimeters in diameter in a strip of sheet metal in a manufacturing process. The strip of metal is then creased and sent on to the next phase of production, where a metal rod is slipped through the hole. It is important that the hole be punched to the specified diameter of 1.84 cm. To test punching accuracy, technicians have randomly sampled 12 punched holes and measured the diameters. The data (in centimeters) follow. Use an alpha of .10 to determine whether the holes are being punched an average of 1.84 centimeters. Assume the punched holes are normally distributed in the population.

1.81	1.89	1.86	1.83
1.85	1.82	1.87	1.85
1.84	1.86	1.88	1.85

9.16 Suppose a study reports that the average price for a gallon of self-serve regular unleaded gasoline is $1.16. You believe that the figure is higher in your area of the country. You decide to test this claim for your part of the United States by randomly calling gasoline stations. Your random survey of 25 stations produces the following prices.

$1.27	$1.29	$1.16	$1.20	$1.37
1.20	1.23	1.19	1.20	1.24
1.16	1.07	1.27	1.09	1.35
1.15	1.23	1.14	1.05	1.35
1.21	1.14	1.14	1.07	1.10

Assume gasoline prices for a region are normally distributed. Do the data you obtained provide enough evidence to reject the claim? Use a 1% level of significance.

9.17 Suppose that in past years the average price per square foot for warehouses in the United States has been $32.28. A national real estate investor wants to determine whether that figure has changed now. The investor hires a researcher who randomly samples 19 warehouses that are for sale across the United States and finds that the mean price per square foot is $31.67, with a standard deviation of $1.29. Assume that prices of warehouse footage are normally distributed in the population. If the researcher uses a 5% level of significance, what statistical conclusion can be reached? What are the hypotheses?

9.18 According to a National Public Transportation survey, the average commuting time for people who commute to a city with a population of 1 to 3 million is 19.0 minutes. Suppose a researcher lives in a city with a population of 2.4 million and wants to test this claim in her city. Assume that commuter times are normally distributed in the population. She takes a random sample of commuters and gathers data. The data are analyzed using both MINITAB and Excel, and the output is shown here. What are the results of the study? What are the hypotheses?

MINITAB Output:

One-Sample T: Commute Time

Test of mu = 19 vs mu not = 19

Variable	N	Mean	StDev	SE Mean
Commute Time	26	19.534	4.100	0.804

Variable	95.0% CI	T	P
Commute Time	(17.878, 21.190)	0.66	0.513

Excel Output:

	A	B
1	Mean	19.534
2	Variance	16.813
3	Observations	26
4	df	25
5	t Stat	0.66
6	P (T<=t) one-tail	0.256
7	t Critical one-tail	1.71
8	P (T<=t) two-tail	0.513
9	t Critical two-tail	2.06

9.4 TESTING HYPOTHESES ABOUT A PROPORTION

Data analysis used in business decision making often contains proportions to describe such aspects as market share, consumer makeup, quality defects, on-time deliver rate, profitable stocks, and others. Business surveys often produce information expressed in proportion form such as .45 of all businesses offer flexible hours to employees or .88 of all businesses have Web sites. Business researchers conduct hypothesis tests about such proportions to determine whether they have changed in some way. As an example, suppose a company held a 26% or .26 share of the market for several years. Due to a massive marketing effort and improved product quality, company officials believe that the market share increased; and they want to prove it. Other examples of hypothesis testing about a single population proportion might include:

- A market researcher wants to test to determine whether the proportion of new car purchasers who are female has increased.
- A financial researcher wants to test to determine whether the proportion of companies that were profitable last year in the average investment officer's portfolio is .60.
- A quality manager for a large manufacturing firm wants to test to determine whether the proportion of defective items in a batch is less than .04.

Formula (9.4) for inferential analysis of a proportion was introduced in section 7.3 of Chapter 7. Based on the central limit theorem, this formula makes possible the testing of hypotheses about the population proportion in a manner similar to that of the formula used to test sample means. Recall that $\hat{p}$ denotes a sample proportion and p denotes the population proportion. To validly use this test, the sample size must be large enough such that $n \cdot p \geq 5$ and $n \cdot q \geq 5$.

---

z TEST OF A POPULATION PROPORTION (9.4)

$$z = \frac{\hat{p} - p}{\sqrt{\dfrac{p \cdot q}{n}}}$$

where

$\hat{p}$ = sample proportion
p = population proportion
q = $1 - p$

A manufacturer believes exactly 8% of its products contain at least one minor flaw. Suppose a company researcher wants to test this belief. The null and alternative hypotheses are

$$H_0: p = .08$$

$$H_a: p \neq .08$$

This test is two-tailed because the hypothesis being tested is whether the proportion of products with at least one minor flaw is .08. Alpha is selected to be .10. Figure 9.13 shows the distribution, with the rejection regions and $z_{.05}$. Because α is divided for a two-tailed test, the table value for an area of $(1/2)(.10) = .05$ is $z_{.05} = \pm 1.645$.

FIGURE 9.13

Distribution with Rejection Regions for Flawed-Product Example

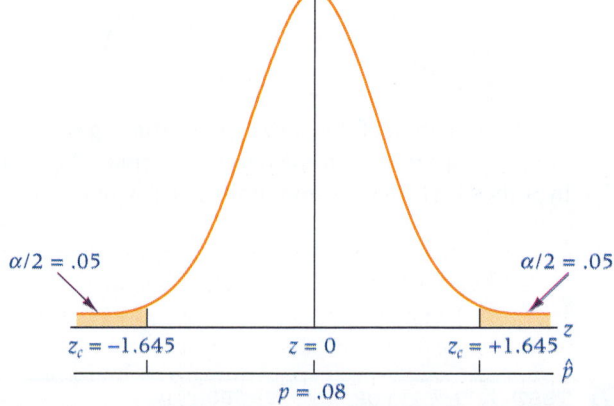

For the business researcher to reject the null hypothesis, the observed z value must be greater than 1.645 or less than −1.645. The business researcher randomly selects a sample of 200 products, inspects each item for flaws, and determines that 33 items have at least one minor flaw. Calculating the sample proportion gives

$$\hat{p} = \frac{33}{200} = .165$$

The observed z value is calculated as:

$$z = \frac{\hat{p} - p}{\sqrt{\dfrac{p \cdot q}{n}}} = \frac{.165 - .080}{\sqrt{\dfrac{(.08)(.92)}{200}}} = \frac{.085}{.019} = 4.43$$

Note that the denominator of the z formula contains the population proportion. Although the business researcher does not actually know the population proportion, he is testing a population proportion value. Hence he uses the hypothesized population value in the denominator of the formula as well as in the numerator. This method contrasts with the confidence interval formula, where the sample proportion is used in the denominator.

The observed value of z is in the rejection region (observed $z = 4.43 >$ table $z_{.05} = +1.645$), so the business researcher rejects the null hypothesis. He concludes that the proportion of items with at least one minor flaw in the population from which the sample of 200 was drawn is not .08. With $\alpha = .10$, the risk of committing a Type I error in this example is .10.

The observed value of $z = 4.43$ is outside the range of most values in virtually all z tables. Thus if the researcher were using the p-value to arrive at a decision about the null hypothesis, the probability would be .0000, and he would reject the null hypothesis.

The MINITAB output shown in Figure 9.14 displays a p-value of .000 for this problem, underscoring the decision to reject the null hypothesis.

Suppose the researcher wanted to use the critical value method. He would enter the table value of $z_{.05} = 1.645$ in the Z formula for single sample proportions, along with the hypothesized population proportion and n, and solve for the critical value of denoted as $\hat{p}_C$. The result is

$$z_{\alpha/2} = \frac{\hat{p}_c - p}{\sqrt{\dfrac{p \cdot q}{n}}}$$

$$\pm 1.645 = \frac{\hat{p}_c - .08}{\sqrt{\dfrac{(.08)(.92)}{200}}}$$

$$\hat{p}_c = .08 \pm 1.645 \sqrt{\frac{(.08)(.92)}{200}} = .08 \pm .032$$

$$= .048 \text{ and } .112$$

Examination of the sample proportion, $\hat{p} = .165$, and Figure 9.15 clearly show that the sample proportion is in the rejection region. The statistical conclusion is to reject the null hypothesis. The proportion of products with at least one flaw is not .08.

FIGURE 9.14

MINITAB Output for the
Flawed-Product Example

```
TEST AND CI FOR ONE PROPORTION

Test of p = 0.08 vs p not = 0.08

Sample   X    N    Sample p         90.0% CI           P-Value
1        33   200  0.165000  (0.123279, 0.214351)     0.000
```

STATISTICS IN BUSINESS TODAY

Testing Hypotheses about Commuting

How do Americans commute to work? A National Public Transportation survey taken a few years ago indicated that almost 80% of U.S. commuters drive alone to work, more than 11% carpool, and approximately 5% use public transportation. Using hypothesis testing methodology presented in this chapter, researchers can test whether these proportions still hold true today as well as how these figures vary by region. For example, in New York City it is almost certain that the proportion of commuters using public transportation is much higher than 5%. In rural parts of the country where public transportation is unavailable, the proportion of commuters using public transportation would be zero.

What is the average travel time of a commute to work in the United States? According to the National Public Transportation Survey, travel time varies according to the type of transportation used. For example, the average travel time of a commute using a private vehicle is 20 minutes as compared to 42 minutes using public transportation. In part, this difference can be accounted for by the travel speed in miles per hour: private vehicles average 35 miles per hour over a commute compared to 19 miles per hour averaged by public transportation vehicles. It is possible to test any of these means using hypothesis testing techniques presented in this chapter to either validate the figures or to determine whether the figures are no longer true.

FIGURE 9.15

Distribution Using Critical Value Method for the Flawed-Product Example

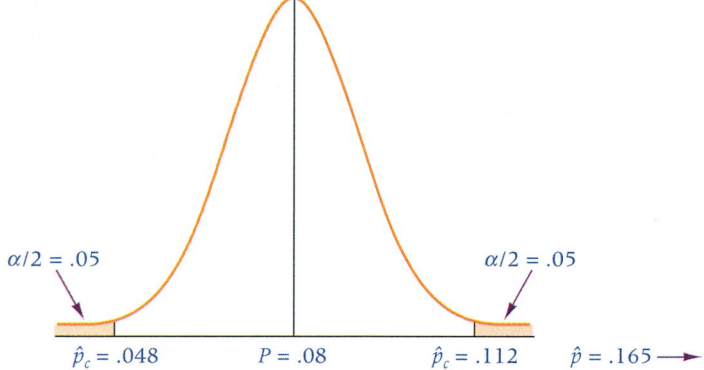

$\alpha/2 = .05$ $\alpha/2 = .05$

$\hat{p}_c = .048$ $P = .08$ $\hat{p}_c = .112$ $\hat{p} = .165 \longrightarrow$

DEMONSTRATION PROBLEM 9.3

A survey of the morning beverage market shows that the primary breakfast beverage for 17% of Americans is milk. A milk producer in Wisconsin, where milk is plentiful, believes the figure is higher for Wisconsin. To test this idea, she contacts a random sample of 550 Wisconsin residents and asks which primary beverage they consumed for breakfast that day. Suppose 115 replied that milk was the primary beverage. Using a level of significance of .05, test the idea that the milk figure is higher for Wisconsin.

Solution

HYPOTHESIZE:

STEP 1. The milk producer's theory is that the proportion of Wisconsin residents who drink milk for breakfast is higher than the national proportion, which is the alternative hypothesis. The null hypothesis is that the proportion in Wisconsin does not differ from the national average. The hypotheses for this problem are

$$H_0: p = .17$$
$$H_a: p > .17$$

TEST:

STEP 2. The test statistic is

$$z = \frac{\hat{p} - p}{\sqrt{\dfrac{p \cdot q}{n}}}$$

STEP 3. The Type I error rate is .05.

STEP 4. This test is a one-tailed test, and the table value is $z_{.05} = +1.645$. The sample results must yield an observed z value greater than 1.645 for the milk producer to reject the null hypothesis. The following diagram shows $z_{.05}$ and the rejection region for this problem.

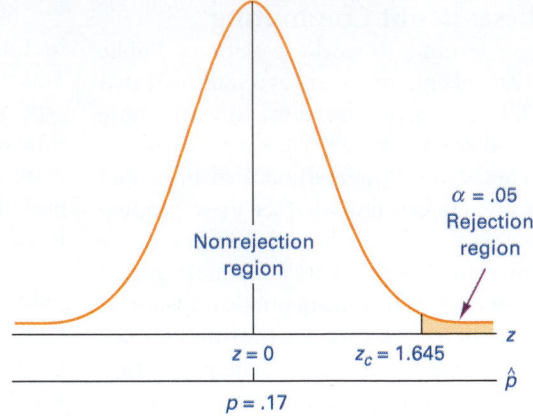

STEP 5. $n = 550$ and $x = 115$

$$\hat{p} = \frac{115}{550} = .209$$

STEP 6. $$z = \frac{\hat{p} - p}{\sqrt{\dfrac{p \cdot q}{n}}} = \frac{.209 - .17}{\sqrt{\dfrac{(.17)(.83)}{550}}} = \frac{.039}{.016} = 2.44$$

ACTION:

STEP 7. Because $z = 2.44$ is beyond $z_{.05} = 1.645$ in the rejection region, the milk producer rejects the null hypothesis. On the basis of the random sample, the producer is ready to conclude that the proportion of Wisconsin residents who drink milk as the primary beverage for breakfast is higher than the national proportion.

BUSINESS IMPLICATIONS:

STEP 8. If the proportion of residents who drink milk for breakfast is higher in Wisconsin than in other parts of the United States, milk producers might have a market opportunity in Wisconsin that is not available in other parts of the country. Perhaps Wisconsin residents are being loyal to home-state products, in which case marketers of other Wisconsin products might be successful in appealing to residents to support their products. The fact that more milk is sold in Wisconsin might mean that if Wisconsin milk producers appealed to markets outside Wisconsin in the same way they do inside the state, they might increase their market share of the breakfast beverage market in other states. Is a proportion of almost .21 really a substantive increase over .17? Certainly in a market of any size at all, an increase of almost 4% of the market share could be worth millions of dollars and in such a case, would be substantive.

The probability of obtaining a $z \geq 2.44$ by chance is .0073. Because this probability is less than $\alpha = .05$, the null hypothesis is also rejected with the p-value.

A critical proportion can be solved for by

$$z_{.05} = \frac{\hat{p}_c - p}{\sqrt{\dfrac{p \cdot q}{n}}}$$

$$1.645 = \frac{\hat{p}_c - .17}{\sqrt{\dfrac{(.17)(.83)}{550}}}$$

$$\hat{p}_c = .17 + 1.645 \sqrt{\frac{(.17)(.83)}{550}} = .17 + .026 = .196$$

With the critical value method, a sample proportion greater than .196 must be obtained to reject the null hypothesis. The sample proportion for this problem is .209, so the null hypothesis is also rejected with the critical value method.

FIGURE 9.16

MINITAB Output for
Demonstration Problem 9.3

Test and CI for One Proportion

```
Test of p = 0.17 vs p > 0.17
                                     Exact
Sample X     N      Sample p    90.0% Lower Bound   P-Value
1     115    550    0.209091    0.186770      0.010
```

Using the Computer to Test Hypotheses About a Population Proportion

MINITAB has the capability of testing hypotheses about a population proportion. Figure 9.16 shows the MINITAB output for Demonstration Problem 9.3. Notice that the output includes a restatement of the hypotheses, the sample proportion, and the p-value. From this information, a decision regarding the null hypothesis can be made by comparing the p-value (.010) to α (.050). Because the p-value is less than α, the decision is to reject the null hypothesis.

9.4 PROBLEMS

9.19 Suppose you are testing H_0: $p = .45$ versus H_a: $p > .45$. A random sample of 310 people produces a value of $\hat{p} = .465$. Use $\alpha = .05$ to test this hypothesis.

9.20 Suppose you are testing H_0: $p = .63$ versus H_a: $p < .63$. For a random sample of 100 people, $x = 55$, where x denotes the number in the sample that have the characteristic of interest. Use a .01 level of significance to test this hypothesis.

9.21 Suppose you are testing H_0: $p = .29$ versus H_a: $p \neq .29$. A random sample of 740 items shows that 207 have this characteristic. With a .05 probability of committing a Type I error, test the hypothesis. For the p-value method, what is the probability of the calculated z value for this problem? If you had used the critical value method, what would the two critical values be? How do the sample results compare with the critical values?

9.22 The Independent Insurance Agents of America conducted a survey of insurance consumers and discovered that 48% of them always reread their insurance policies, 29% sometimes do, 16% rarely do, and 7% never do. Suppose a large insurance company invests considerable time and money in rewriting policies so that they will be more attractive and easy to read and understand. After using the new policies for a year, company managers want to determine whether rewriting the policies significantly changed the proportion of policyholders who always reread their insurance policy. They contact 380 of the company's insurance consumers who purchased a policy in the past year and ask them whether they always reread their insurance policies. One hundred and sixty-four respond that they do. Use a 1% level of significance to test the hypothesis.

9.23 A study by Hewitt Associates showed that 79% of companies offer employees flexible scheduling. Suppose a researcher believes that in accounting firms this figure is lower. The researcher randomly selects 415 accounting firms and through interviews determines that 303 of these firms have flexible scheduling. With a 1% level of significance, does the test show enough evidence to conclude that a significantly lower proportion of accounting firms offer employees flexible scheduling?

9.24 A survey was undertaken by Bruskin/Goldring Research for Quicken to determine how people plan to meet their financial goals in the next year. Respondents were allowed to select more than one way to meet their goals. Thirty-one percent said that they were using a financial planner to help them meet their goals. Twenty-four percent were using family/friends to help them meet their financial goals followed by broker/accountant (19%), computer software (17%), and books (14%). Suppose another researcher takes a similar survey of 600 people to test these results. If 200 people respond that they are going to use a financial planner to help them meet their goals, is this proportion enough evidence to reject the 31% figure generated in the Bruskin/Goldring survey using $\alpha = .10$? If 130 respond that they are going to use family/friends to help them meet their financial goals, is this result enough evidence to declare that the proportion is significantly lower than Bruskin/Goldring's figure of .24 if $\alpha = .05$?

9.25 Eighteen percent of U.S.-based multinational companies provide an allowance for personal long-distance calls for executives living overseas, according to the Institute for International Human Resources and the National Foreign Trade Council. Suppose a researcher thinks that U.S.-based multinational companies are having a more difficult time recruiting executives to live overseas and that an increasing number of these companies are providing an allowance for personal long-distance calls to these executives to ease the burden of living away from home. To test this hypothesis, a new study is conducted by contacting 376 multinational companies. Twenty-two percent of these surveyed companies are providing an allowance for personal long-distance calls to executives living overseas. Does the test show enough evidence to declare that a significantly higher proportion of multinational companies provide a long-distance call allowance? Let $\alpha = .01$.

9.26 A large manufacturing company investigated the service it received from suppliers and discovered that, in the past, 32% of all materials shipments were received late. However, the company recently installed a just-in-time system in which suppliers are linked more closely to the manufacturing process. A random sample of 118 deliveries since the just-in-time system was installed reveals that 22 deliveries were late. Use this sample information to test whether the proportion of late deliveries was reduced significantly. Let $\alpha = .05$.

9.27 Where do CFOs get their money news? According to Robert Half International, 47% get their money news from newspapers, 15% get it from communication/colleagues, 12% get it from television, 11% from the Internet, 9% from magazines, 5% from radio, and 1% don't know. Suppose a researcher wants to test these results. She randomly samples 67 CFOs and finds that 40 of them get their money news from newspapers. Does the test show enough evidence to reject the findings of Robert Half International? Use $\alpha = .05$.

9.5 TESTING HYPOTHESES ABOUT A VARIANCE

At times a researcher needs to test hypotheses about a population variance. For example, in the area of statistical quality control, manufacturers try to produce equipment and parts that are consistent in measurement. Suppose a company produces industrial wire that is specified to be a particular thickness. Because of the production process, the thickness of the wire will vary slightly from one end to the other and from lot to lot and batch to batch. Even if the average thickness of the wire as measured from lot to lot is on specification, the variance of the measurements might be too great to be acceptable. In other words, on the average the wire is the correct thickness, but some portions of the wire might be too thin and others unacceptably thick. By conducting hypothesis tests for the variance of the thickness measurements, the quality control people can monitor for variations in the process that are too great.

The procedure for testing hypotheses about a population variance is similar to the techniques presented in Chapter 8 for estimating a population variance from the sample variance. Formula (9.5) used to conduct these tests assumes a normally distributed population.

FORMULA FOR TESTING HYPOTHESES ABOUT A POPULATION VARIANCE (9.5)	$$\chi^2 = \frac{(n-1)s^2}{\sigma^2}$$ $$df = n-1$$

Note: *As was mentioned in Chapter 8, the chi-square test of a population variance is extremely sensitive to violations of the assumption that the population is normally distributed.*

As an example, a manufacturing firm has been working diligently to implement a just-in-time inventory system for its production line. The final product requires the installation of a pneumatic tube at a particular station on the assembly line. With the just-in-time inventory system, the company's goal is to minimize the number of pneumatic tubes that are piled up at the station waiting to be installed. Ideally, the tubes would arrive just as the operator needs them. However, because of the supplier and the variables involved in getting the tubes to the line, most of the time there will be some buildup of tube inventory. The company expects that, on the average, about 20 pneumatic tubes will be at the station. However, the production superintendent does not want the variance of this inventory to be greater than 4. On a given day, the number of pneumatic tubes piled up at the workstation is determined eight different times and the following numbers of tubes are recorded.

$$23 \quad 17 \quad 20 \quad 29 \quad 21 \quad 14 \quad 19 \quad 24$$

Using these sample data, we can test to determine whether the variance is greater than 4. The hypothesis test is one-tailed. Assume the number of tubes is normally distributed. The null hypothesis is that the variance is acceptable with no problems—the variance is equal to 4. The alternative hypothesis is that the variance is greater than 4.

$$H_0: \sigma^2 = 4$$

$$H_a: \sigma^2 > 4$$

Suppose alpha is .05. Because the sample size is eight, the degrees of freedom for the critical table chi-square value are $8 - 1 = 7$. Using Table A.8, we find the critical chi-square value.

$$\chi^2_{.05, 7} = 14.0671$$

Because the alternative hypothesis is greater than 4, the rejection region is in the upper tail of the chi-square distribution. The sample variance is calculated from the sample data to be

$$s^2 = 20.9821$$

The observed chi-square value is calculated as

$$\chi^2 = \frac{(8-1)(20.9821)}{4} = 36.72$$

Because this observed chi-square value, $\chi^2 = 36.72$, is greater than the critical chi-square table value, $\chi^2_{.05, 7} = 14.0671$, the decision is to reject the null hypothesis. On the basis of this sample of eight data measurements, the population variance of inventory at this workstation is greater than 4. Company production personnel and managers might want to investigate further to determine whether they can find a cause for this unacceptable variance. Figure 9.17 shows a chi-square distribution with the critical value, the rejection region, the nonrejection region, the value of α, and the observed chi-square value.

Using Excel, the p-value of the observed chi-square, 36.72, is determined to be .0000053. Because this value is less than $\alpha = .05$, the conclusion is to reject the null hypothesis using the p-value. In fact, using this p-value, the null hypothesis could be rejected for

$$\alpha = .00001$$

FIGURE 9.17

Hypothesis Test Distribution for Pneumatic Tube Example

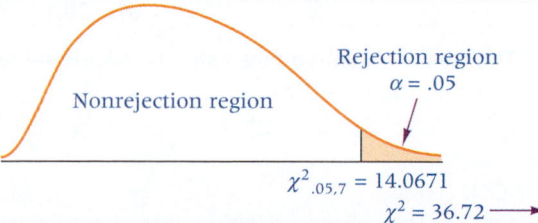

This null hypothesis can also be tested by the critical value method. Instead of solving for an observed value of chi-square, the critical chi-square value for alpha is inserted into formula (9.5) along with the hypothesized value of σ^2 and the degrees of freedom $(n-1)$. Solving for s^2 yields a critical sample variance value, s_c^2.

$$\chi_c^2 = \frac{(n-1)s_c^2}{\sigma^2}$$

$$s_c^2 = \frac{\chi_c^2 \cdot \sigma^2}{(n-1)} = \frac{(14.0671)(4)}{7} = 8.038$$

The critical value of the sample variance is $s_C^2 = 8.038$. Because the observed sample variance actually was 20.9821, which is larger than the critical variance, the null hypothesis is rejected.

DEMONSTRATION PROBLEM 9.4

A small business has 37 employees. Because of the uncertain demand for its product, the company usually pays overtime on any given week. The company assumed that about 50 total hours of overtime per week is required and that the variance on this figure is about 25. Company officials want to know whether the variance of overtime hours has changed. Given here is a sample of 16 weeks of overtime data (in hours per week). Assume hours of overtime are normally distributed. Use these data to test the null hypothesis that the variance of overtime data is 25. Let $\alpha = .10$.

57	56	52	44
46	53	44	44
48	51	55	48
63	53	51	50

Solution

HYPOTHESIZE:

STEP 1. This test is a two-tailed test. The null and alternative hypotheses are

$$H_0: \sigma^2 = 25$$
$$H_a: \sigma^2 \neq 25$$

TEST:

STEP 2. The test statistic is

$$\chi^2 = \frac{(n-1)s^2}{\sigma^2}$$

STEP 3. Because this test is two-tailed, $\alpha = .10$ must be split: $\alpha/2 = .05$.

STEP 4. The degrees of freedom are $16 - 1 = 15$. The two critical chi-square values are

$$\chi^2_{(1-.05),15} = \chi^2_{.95,15} = 7.26094$$

$$\chi^2_{.05,15} = 24.9958$$

The decision rule is to reject the null hypothesis if the observed value of the test statistic is less than 7.26094 or greater than 24.9958.

STEP 5. The data are as listed previously.

STEP 6. The sample variance is

$$s^2 = 28.1$$

The observed chi-square value is calculated as

$$\chi^2 = \frac{(n-1)s^2}{\sigma^2} = \frac{(15)(28.1)}{25} = 16.86$$

ACTION:

STEP 7. This observed chi-square value is in the nonrejection region because $\chi^2_{.95,15} = 7.26094 < \chi^2_{observed} = 16.86 < \chi^2_{.05,15} = 24.9958$. The company fails to reject the null hypothesis. The population variance of overtime hours per week is 25.

BUSINESS IMPLICATIONS:

STEP 8. This result indicates to the company managers that the variance of weekly overtime hours is about what they expected.

9.5 PROBLEMS

9.28 Test each of the following hypotheses by using the given information. Assume the populations are normally distributed.

    a. H_0: $\sigma^2 = 20$
           H_a: $\sigma^2 > 20$
           $\alpha = .05$, $n = 15$, $s^2 = 32$

    b. H_0: $\sigma^2 = 8.5$
           H_a: $\sigma^2 \neq 8.5$
           $\alpha = .10$, $n = 22$, $s^2 = 17$

    c. H_0: $\sigma^2 = 45$
           H_a: $\sigma^2 < 45$
           $\alpha = .01$, $n = 8$, $s = 4.12$

    d. H_0: $\sigma^2 = 5$
           H_a: $\sigma^2 \neq 5$
           $\alpha = .05$, $n = 11$, $s^2 = 1.2$

9.29 Previous experience shows the variance of a given process to be 14. Researchers are testing to determine whether this value has changed. They gather the following dozen measurements of the process. Use these data and $\alpha = .05$ to test the null hypothesis about the variance. Assume the measurements are normally distributed.

52	44	51	58	48	49
38	49	50	42	55	51

9.30 A manufacturing company produces bearings. One line of bearings is specified to be 1.64 centimeters (cm) in diameter. A major customer requires that the variance of the bearings be no more than .001 cm^2. The producer is required to test the bearings before they are shipped, and so the diameters of 16 bearings are measured with a precise instrument, resulting in the following values. Assume bearing diameters are normally distributed. Use the data and $\alpha = .01$ to test the data to determine whether the population of these bearings is to be rejected because of too high a variance.

1.69	1.62	1.63	1.70
1.66	1.63	1.65	1.71
1.64	1.69	1.57	1.64
1.59	1.66	1.63	1.65

9.31 A savings and loan averages about $100,000 in deposits per week. However, because of the way pay periods fall, seasonality, and erratic fluctuations in the local economy, deposits are subject to a wide variability. In the past, the variance for weekly deposits has been about $199,996,164. In terms that make more sense to managers, the standard deviation of weekly deposits has been $14,142. Shown here are data from a random sample of 13 weekly deposits for a recent period. Assume weekly deposits are normally distributed. Use these data and $\alpha = .10$ to test to determine whether the variance for weekly deposits has changed.

$93,000	$135,000	$112,000
68,000	46,000	104,000
128,000	143,000	131,000
104,000	96,000	71,000
87,000		

9.32 A company produces industrial wiring. One batch of wiring is specified to be 2.16 centimeters (cm) thick. A company inspects the wiring in seven locations and determines that, on the average, the wiring is about 2.16 cm thick. However, the measurements vary. It is unacceptable for the variance of the wiring to be more than .04 cm². The standard deviation of the seven measurements on this batch of wiring is .34 cm. Use $\alpha = .01$ to determine whether the variance on the sample wiring is too great to meet specifications. Assume wiring thickness is normally distributed.

9.6 SOLVING FOR TYPE II ERRORS

If a researcher reaches the statistical conclusion not to reject the null hypothesis, he makes either a correct decision or a Type II error. If the null hypothesis is true, the researcher makes a correct decision. If the null hypothesis is false, a Type II error results.

In business, failure to reject the null hypothesis may mean staying with the status quo, not implementing a new process, or not making adjustments. If a new process, product, theory, or adjustment is not significantly better than what is currently accepted practice, the decision maker makes a correct decision. However, if the new process, product, theory, or adjustment would significantly improve sales, the business climate, costs, or morale, the decision maker makes an error in judgment (Type II). In business, Type II errors can translate to lost opportunities, poor product quality (as a result of failure to discern a problem in the process), or failure to react to the marketplace. Sometimes the ability to react to changes, new developments, or new opportunities is what keeps a business moving and growing. The Type II error plays an important role in business statistical decision making.

Determining the probability of committing a Type II error is more complex than finding the probability of committing a Type I error. The probability of committing a Type I error either is given in a problem or is stated by the researcher before proceeding with the study. A Type II error, β, varies with possible values of the alternative parameter. For example, suppose a researcher is conducting a statistical test on the following hypotheses.

$$H_0: \mu = 12 \text{ ounces}$$

$$H_a: \mu < 12 \text{ ounces}$$

A Type II error can be committed only when the researcher fails to reject the null hypothesis and the null hypothesis is false. In these hypotheses, if the null hypothesis, $\mu = 12$ ounces, is false, what is the true value for the population mean? Is the mean really 11.99 or 11.90 or 11.5 or 10 ounces? For each of these possible values of the population mean, the researcher can compute the probability of committing a Type II error. Often, when the null hypothesis is false, the value of the alternative mean is unknown, so the researcher will compute the probability of committing Type II errors for several possible values. How can the probability of committing a Type II error be computed for a specific alternative value of the mean?

Suppose that, in testing the preceding hypotheses, a sample of 60 cans of beverage yields a sample mean of 11.985 ounces. Assume that the population standard deviation is 0.10 ounces. From $\alpha = .05$ and a one-tailed test, the table $z_{.05}$ value is -1.645. The observed z value from sample data is

$$z = \frac{11.985 - 12.00}{\frac{.10}{\sqrt{60}}} = -1.16$$

From this observed value of z, the researcher determines not to reject the null hypothesis. By not rejecting the null hypothesis, the researcher either makes a correct decision or commits a Type II error. What is the probability of committing a Type II error in this problem if the population mean actually is 11.99?

The first step in determining the probability of a Type II error is to calculate a critical value for the sample mean, $\bar{x}_c$. In testing the null hypothesis by the critical value method, this value is used as the cutoff for the nonrejection region. For any sample mean obtained that is less than $\bar{x}_c$ (or greater for an upper-tail rejection region), the null hypothesis is rejected. Any sample mean greater than $\bar{x}_c$ (or less for an upper-tail rejection region) causes the researcher to fail to reject the null hypothesis. Solving for the critical value of the mean gives

$$z_c = \frac{\bar{x}_c - \mu}{\frac{\sigma}{\sqrt{n}}}$$

$$-1.645 = \frac{\bar{x}_c - 12}{\frac{.10}{\sqrt{60}}}$$

$$\bar{x}_c = 11.979$$

Figure 9.18(a) shows the distribution of values when the null hypothesis is true. It contains a critical value of the mean, $\bar{x}_c = 11.979$ ounces, below which the null hypothesis will be rejected. Figure 9.18(b) shows the distribution when the alternative mean, $\mu_1 = 11.99$ ounces, is true. How often will the business researcher fail to reject the top distribution as true when, in reality, the bottom distribution is true? If the null hypothesis is false, the researcher will fail to reject the null hypotheses whenever $\bar{x}$ is in the nonrejection region, $\bar{x}_c \geq 11.979$ ounces. If μ actually equals 11.99 ounces, what is the probability of failing to reject $\mu = 12$ ounces when 11.979 ounces is the critical value? The business researcher calculates this probability by extending the critical value ($\bar{x}_c = 11.979$ ounces) from distribution (a) to distribution (b) and solving for the area to the right of $\bar{x}_c = 11.979$.

$$z_1 = \frac{\bar{x}_c - \mu_1}{\frac{\sigma}{\sqrt{n}}} = \frac{11.979 - 11.99}{\frac{.10}{\sqrt{60}}} = -0.85$$

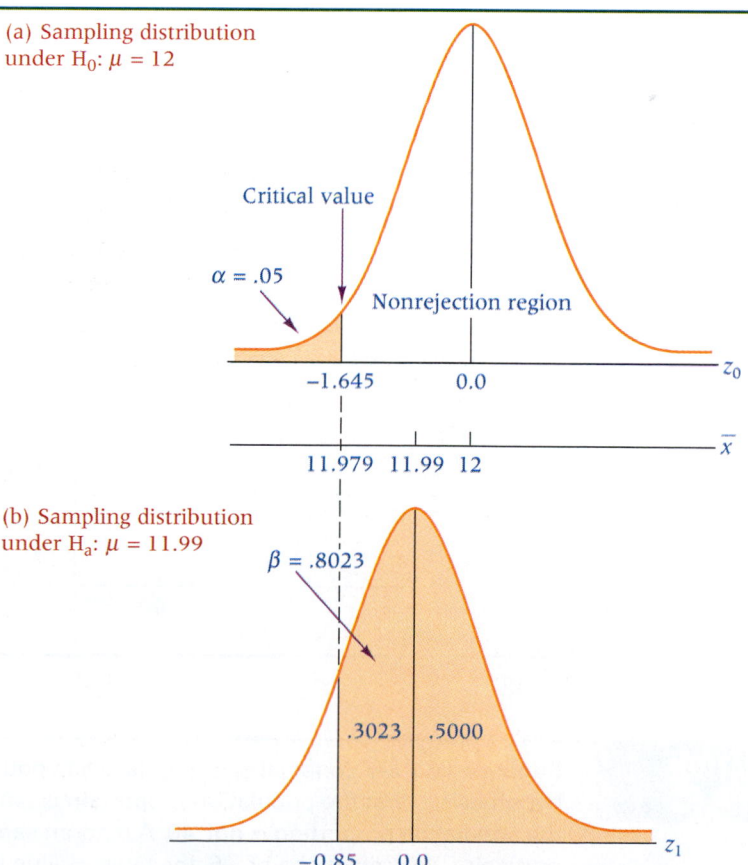

FIGURE 9.18

Type II Error for Soft Drink Example with Alternative Mean = 11.99 Ounces

(a) Sampling distribution under H_0: $\mu = 12$

Critical value

$\alpha = .05$

Nonrejection region

-1.645 0.0 z_0

11.979 11.99 12 $\bar{x}$

(b) Sampling distribution under H_a: $\mu = 11.99$

$\beta = .8023$

.3023 .5000

-0.85 0.0 z_1

This value of z yields an area of .3023. The probability of committing a Type II error is all the area to the right of $\bar{x}_c = 11.979$ in distribution (b), or $.3023 + .5000 = .8023$. Hence there is an 80.23% chance of committing a Type II error if the alternative mean is 11.99 ounces.

| DEMONSTRATION PROBLEM 9.5 | Recompute the probability of committing a Type II error for the soft drink example if the alternative mean is 11.96 ounces. |

Solution

Everything in distribution (a) of Figure 9.18 stays the same. The null hypothesized mean is still 12 ounces, the critical value is still 11.979 ounces, and $n = 60$. However, distribution (b) of Figure 9.18 changes with $\mu_1 = 11.96$ ounces, as the following diagram shows.

The z formula used to solve for the area of distribution (b), $\mu_1 = 11.96$, to the right of 11.979 is

$$z_1 = \frac{\bar{x}_c - \mu_1}{\frac{\sigma}{\sqrt{n}}} = \frac{11.979 - 11.96}{\frac{.10}{\sqrt{60}}} = 1.47$$

From Table A.5, only .0708 of the area is to the right of the critical value. Thus the probability of committing a Type II error is only .0708, as illustrated in the following diagram.

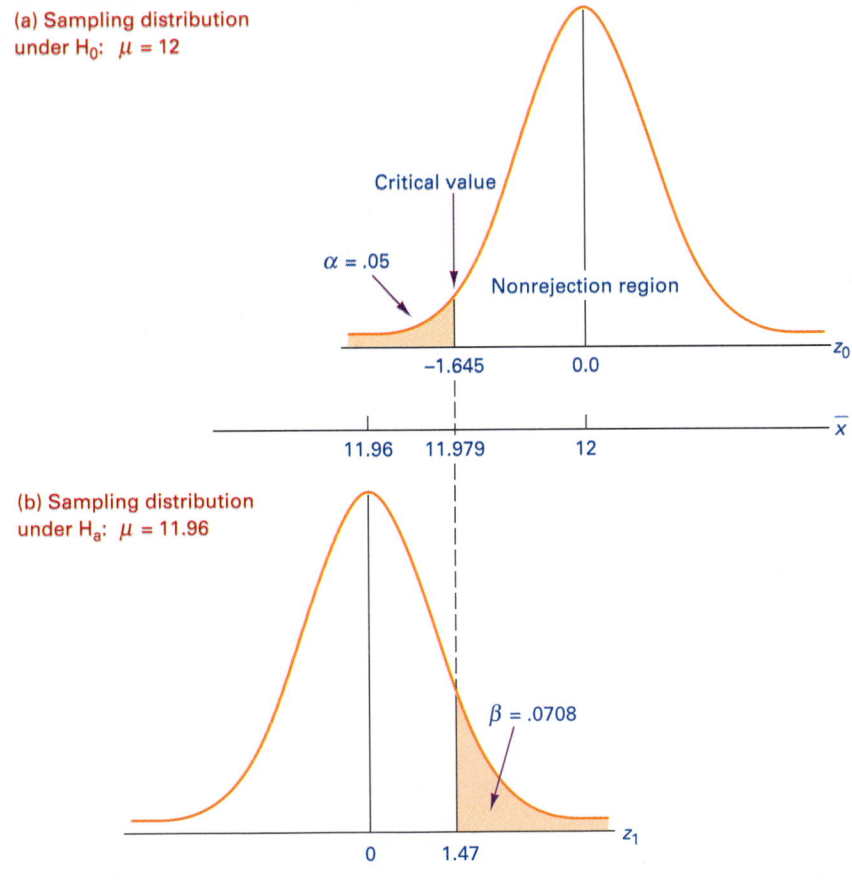

(a) Sampling distribution under H_0: $\mu = 12$

(b) Sampling distribution under H_a: $\mu = 11.96$

| DEMONSTRATION PROBLEM 9.6 | Suppose you are conducting a two-tailed hypothesis test of proportions. The null hypothesis is that the population proportion is .40. The alternative hypothesis is that the population proportion is not .40. A random sample of 250 produces a sample proportion of .44. With alpha of .05, the table z value for $\alpha/2$ is 1.96. The observed z from the sample information is |

$$z = \frac{\hat{p} - p}{\sqrt{\frac{p \cdot q}{n}}} = \frac{.44 - .40}{.031} = 1.29$$

Thus the null hypothesis is not rejected. Either a correct decision is made or a Type II error is committed. Suppose the alternative population proportion really is .36. What is the probability of committing a Type II error?

Solution

Solve for the critical value of the proportion.

$$z_c = \frac{\hat{p}_c - p}{\sqrt{\frac{p \cdot q}{n}}}$$

$$\pm 1.96 = \frac{\hat{p}_c - .40}{\sqrt{\frac{(.40)(.60)}{250}}}$$

$$\hat{p}_c = .40 \pm .06$$

The critical values are .34 on the lower end and .46 on the upper end. The alternative population proportion is .36. The following diagram illustrates these results and the remainder of the solution to this problem.

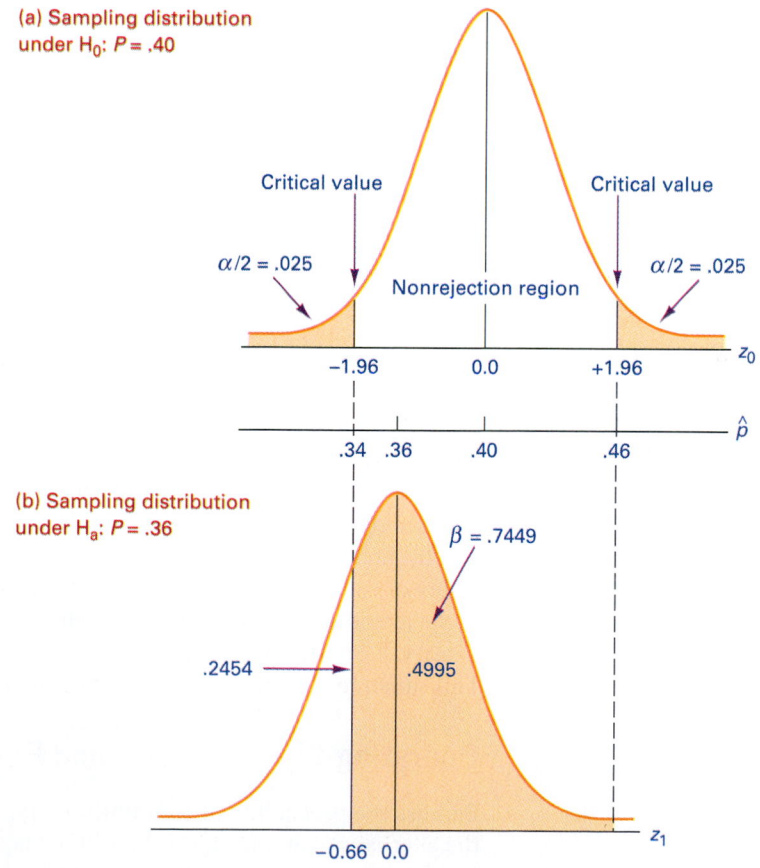

(a) Sampling distribution under H_0: $P = .40$

Critical value

Critical value

$\alpha/2 = .025$

Nonrejection region

$\alpha/2 = .025$

−1.96   0.0   +1.96 z_0

.34 .36   .40   .46 $\hat{p}$

(b) Sampling distribution under H_a: $P = .36$

$\beta = .7449$

.2454   .4995

−0.66 0.0 z_1

Solving for the area between $\hat{p}_c = .34$ and $p_1 = .36$ yields

$$z_1 = \frac{.34 - .36}{\sqrt{\frac{(.36)(.64)}{250}}} = -0.66$$

The area associated with $z_1 = -0.66$ is .2454.

The area between .36 and .46 of the sampling distribution under H_a: $p = .36$ (graph (b)) can be solved for by using the following z value.

$$z = \frac{.46 - .36}{\sqrt{\dfrac{(.36)(.64)}{250}}} = 3.29$$

The area from Table A.5 associated with $z = 3.29$ is .4995. Combining this value with the .2454 obtained from the left side of the distribution in graph (b) yields the total probability of committing a Type II error:

$$.2454 + .4995 = .7449$$

With two-tailed tests, both tails of the distribution contain rejection regions. The area between the two tails is the nonrejection region and the region where Type II errors can occur. If the alternative hypothesis is true, the area of the sampling distribution under H_a between the locations where the critical values from H_0 are located is β. In theory, both tails of the sampling distribution under H_a would be non-β area. However, in this problem, the right critical value is so far away from the alternative proportion ($p_1 = .36$) that the area between the right critical value and the alternative proportion is near .5000 (.4995) and virtually no area falls in the upper right tail of the distribution (.0005).

Some Observations About Type II Errors

Type II errors are committed only when the researcher fails to reject the null hypothesis but the alternative hypothesis is true. If the alternative mean or proportion is close to the hypothesized value, the probability of committing a Type II error is high. If the alternative value is relatively far away from the hypothesized value, as in the problem with $\mu = 12$ ounces and $\mu_a = 11.96$ ounces, the probability of committing a Type II error is small. The implication is that when a value is being tested as a null hypothesis against a true alternative value that is relatively far away, the sample statistic obtained is likely to show clearly which hypothesis is true. For example, suppose a researcher is testing to determine whether a company really is filling 2-liter bottles of cola with an average of 2 liters. If the company decides to underfill the bottles by filling them with only 1 liter, a sample of 50 bottles is likely to average a quantity near the 1-liter fill rather than near the 2-liter fill. Committing a Type II error is highly unlikely. Even a customer probably could see by looking at the bottles on the shelf that they are underfilled. However, if the company fills 2-liter bottles with 1.99 liters, the bottles are close in fill volume to those filled with 2.00 liters. In this case, the probability of committing a Type II error is much greater. A customer probably could not catch the underfill just by looking.

In general, if the alternative value is relatively far from the hypothesized value, the probability of committing a Type II error is smaller than it is when the alternative value is close to the hypothesized value. The probability of committing a Type II error decreases as alternative values of the hypothesized parameter move farther away from the hypothesized value. This situation is shown graphically in operating characteristic curves and power curves.

Operating Characteristic and Power Curves

Because the probability of committing a Type II error changes for each different value of the alternative parameter, it is best in managerial decision making to examine a series of possible alternative values. For example, Table 9.2 shows the probabilities of committing a Type II error (β) for several different possible alternative means for the soft drink example discussed in Demonstration Problem 9.5, in which the null hypothesis was H_0: $\mu = 12$ ounces and $\alpha = .05$.

As previously mentioned, power is the probability of rejecting the null hypothesis when it is false and represents the correct decision of selecting the alternative hypothesis when it is true. Power is equal to $1 - \beta$. Note that Table 9.2 also contains the power values for the alternative means and that the β and power probabilities sum to 1 in each case.

These values can be displayed graphically as shown in Figures 9.19 and 9.20. Figure 9.19 is a MINITAB-generated **operating characteristic (OC) curve** *constructed by plotting the β values against the various values of the alternative hypothesis.* Notice that when the alternative means are near the value of the null hypothesis, $\mu = 12$, the probability of committing a Type II error is high because it is difficult to discriminate between a distribution with a mean of 12 and a distribution with a mean of 11.999. However, as the values of the alternative means move away from the hypothesized value, $\mu = 12$, the values of β drop. This visual representation underscores the notion that it is easier to discriminate between a distribution with $\mu = 12$ and a distribution with $\mu = 11.95$ than between distributions with $\mu = 12$ and $\mu = 11.999$.

Figure 9.20 is an Excel **power curve** constructed by *plotting the power values $(1 - \beta)$ against the various values of the alternative hypotheses.* Note that the power increases as the alternative mean moves away from the value of μ in the null hypotheses. This relationship makes sense. As the alternative mean moves farther and farther away from the null hypothesized mean, a correct decision to reject the null hypothesis becomes more likely.

TABLE 9.2

β Values and Power Values for the Soft Drink Example

Alternative Mean	Probability of Committing A Type II Error, β	Power
$\mu_a = 11.999$	.94	.06
$\mu_a = 11.995$	.89	.11
$\mu_a = 11.99$	.80	.20
$\mu_a = 11.98$	.53	.47
$\mu_a = 11.97$	.24	.76
$\mu_a = 11.96$	.07	.93
$\mu_a = 11.95$	.01	.99

FIGURE 9.19

MINITAB Operating-Characteristic Curve for the Soft Drink Example

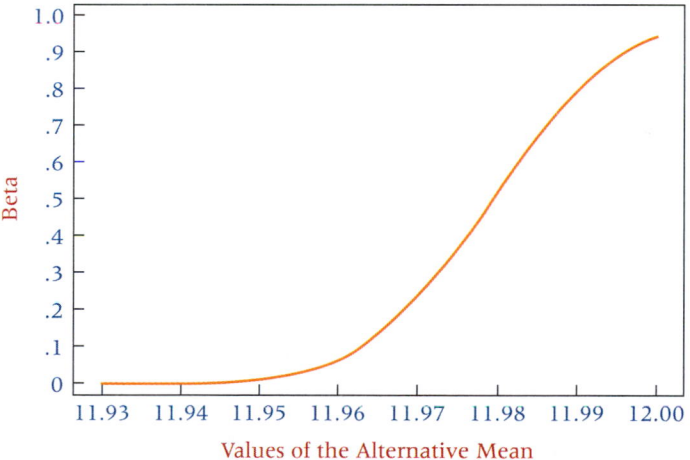

FIGURE 9.20

Excel Power Curve for the Soft Drink Example

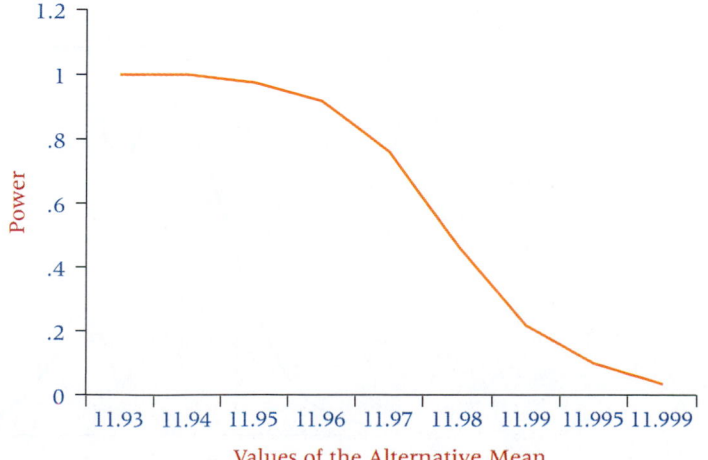

Effect of Increasing Sample Size on the Rejection Limits

The size of the sample affects the location of the rejection limits. Consider the soft drink example in which we were testing the following hypotheses.

$$H_0: \mu = 12.00 \text{ ounces}$$

$$H_a: \mu < 12.00 \text{ ounces}$$

Sample size was 60 ($n = 60$) and the standard deviation was .10 ($\sigma = .10$). With $\alpha = .05$, the critical value of the test statistic was $z_{.05} = -1.645$. From this information, a critical raw score value was computed:

$$z_C = \frac{\bar{x}_C - \mu}{\frac{\sigma}{\sqrt{n}}}$$

$$-1.645 = \frac{\bar{x}_C - 12}{\frac{.10}{\sqrt{60}}}$$

$$\bar{x}_C = 11.979$$

Any sample mean obtained in the hypothesis-testing process that is less than 11.979 will result in a decision to reject the null hypothesis.

Suppose the sample size is increased to 100. The critical raw score value is

$$-1.645 = \frac{\bar{x}_C - 12}{\frac{.10}{\sqrt{100}}}$$

$$\bar{x}_C = 11.984$$

FIGURE 9.21

Type II Error for Soft Drink Example with n Increased to 100

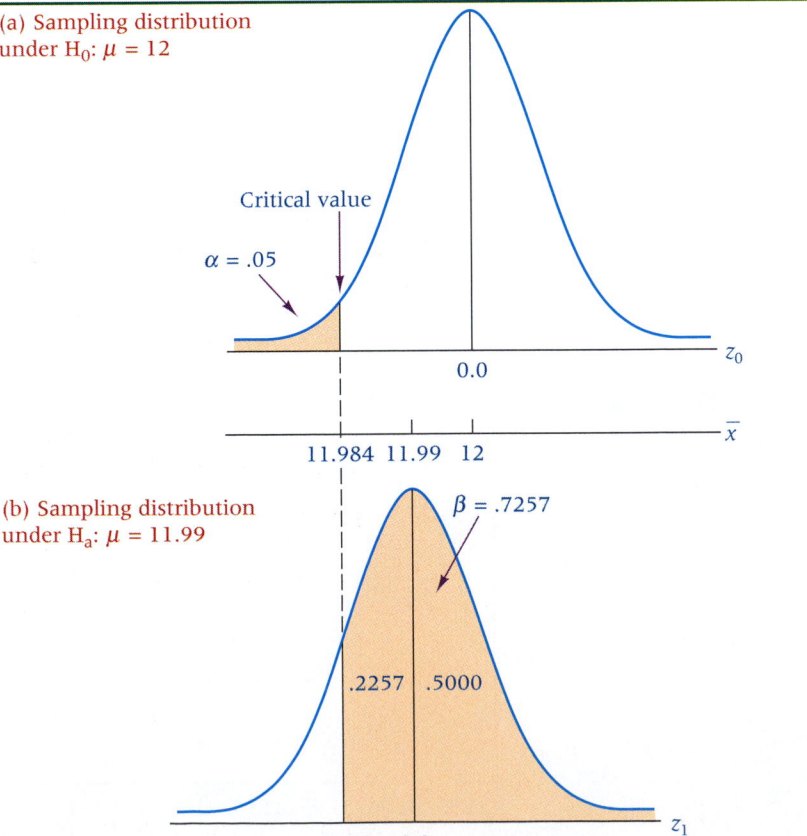

(a) Sampling distribution under H_0: $\mu = 12$

Critical value

$\alpha = .05$

0.0 z_0

11.984 11.99 12 $\bar{x}$

(b) Sampling distribution under H_a: $\mu = 11.99$

$\beta = .7257$

.2257 .5000

-0.60 0.0 z_1

Notice that the critical raw score value is nearer to the hypothesized value ($\mu = 12$) for the larger sample size than it was for a sample size of 60. Because n is in the denominator of the standard error of the mean ($\sigma/\sqrt{n}$), an increase in n results in a decrease in the standard error of the mean, which when multiplied by the critical value of the test statistic ($z_{\alpha/2}$) results in a critical raw score that is closer to the hypothesized value. For $n = 500$, the critical raw score value for this problem is 11.993.

Increased sample size not only affects the distance of the critical raw score value from the hypothesized value of the distribution, but also can result in reducing β for a given value of α. Examine Figure 9.18. Note that the critical raw score value is 11.979 with alpha equal to .05 for $n = 60$. The value of β for an alternative mean of 11.99 is .8023. Suppose the sample size is 100. The critical raw score value (already solved) is 11.984. The value of β is now .7257. The computation is

$$z = \frac{11.984 - 11.99}{\dfrac{.10}{\sqrt{100}}} = -0.60$$

The area under the standard normal curve for $z = -0.60$ is .2257. Adding .2257 + .5000 (from the right half of the H_a sampling distribution) results in a β of .7257. Figure 9.21 shows the sampling distributions with α and β for this problem. In addition, by increasing sample size a business researcher could reduce alpha without necessarily increasing beta. It is possible to reduce the probabilities of committing Type I and Type II errors simultaneously by increasing sample size.

9.6 PROBLEMS

9.33 Suppose a null hypothesis is that the population mean is greater than or equal to 100. Suppose further that a random sample of 48 items is taken and the population standard deviation is 14. For each of the following α values, compute the probability of committing a Type II error if the population mean actually is 99.

   a. $\alpha = .10$

   b. $\alpha = .05$

   c. $\alpha = .01$

   d.   Based on the answers to parts (a), (b), and (c), what happens to the value of β as α gets smaller?

9.34 For Problem 9.33, use $\alpha = .05$ and solve for the probability of committing a Type II error for the following possible true alternative means.

   a. $\mu_a = 98.5$

   b. $\mu_a = 98$

   c. $\mu_a = 97$

   d. $\mu_a = 96$

   e.   What happens to the probability of committing a Type II error as the alternative value of the mean gets farther from the null hypothesized value of 100?

9.35 Suppose a hypothesis states that the mean is exactly 50. If a random sample of 35 items is taken to test this hypothesis, what is the value of β if the population standard deviation is 7 and the alternative mean is 53? Use $\alpha = .01$.

9.36 An alternative hypothesis is that $p < .65$. To test this hypothesis, a random sample of size 360 is taken. What is the probability of committing a Type II error if $\alpha = .05$ and the alternative proportion is as follows?

   a. $p_a = .60$

   b. $p_a = .55$

   c. $p_a = .50$

9.37 The New York Stock Exchange recently reported that the average age of a female shareholder is 44 years. A broker in Chicago wants to know whether this figure is accurate for the female shareholders in Chicago. The broker secures a master list of shareholders in Chicago and takes a random sample of 58 women. Suppose the average age for shareholders in the sample is 45.1 years, with a population standard deviation of 8.7 years. Test to determine whether the broker's sample data differ significantly enough from the 44-years figure released by the New York Stock Exchange to declare that Chicago female shareholders are different in age from female shareholders in general. Use $\alpha = .05$. If no significant difference is noted, what is the broker's probability of committing a Type II error if the average age of a female Chicago shareholder is actually 45 years? 46 years? 47 years? 48 years? Construct an OC curve for these data. Construct a power curve for these data.

9.38 A Harris poll was taken to determine which of 13 major industries are doing a good job of serving their customers. Among the industries rated most highly by Americans for serving their customers were computer hardware and software companies, car manufacturers, and airlines. The industries rated lowest on serving their customers were tobacco companies, managed care providers, and health insurance companies. Seventy-one percent of those polled responded that airlines are doing a good job serving their customers. Suppose due to rising ticket prices, a researcher feels that this figure is now too high. He takes a poll of 463 Americans, and 324 say that the airlines are doing a good job of serving their customers. Does the survey show enough evidence to declare that the proportion of Americans saying that the airlines are doing a good job of serving their customers is significantly lower than stated in the Harris poll? Let alpha equal 10. If the researcher fails to reject the null hypothesis and if the figure is actually 69% now, what is the probability of committing a Type II error? What is the probability of committing a Type II error if the figure is really 66%? 60%?

Business Referrals

In the Decision Dilemma, many data facts are reported from numerous surveys about consumers seeking advice from others before purchasing items or services. Most of the statistics are stated as though they are facts about the population. For example, one study reports that 46% of all consumers seek advice when selecting a physician. Suppose a business researcher believes that this figure is not true, has changed over time, is not true for a particular region of the country, or is different for a particular type of medicine. Using hypothesis techniques presented in Section 9.4 of this chapter, this figure (46%) can be tested as a population proportion. Because the figures presented in the Decision Dilemma have been published and widely disseminated, the researcher who wants to test them would likely place these figures in the null hypothesis (e.g., H_0: $p = .46$), gather a random sample from whichever population is to be studied, and conduct a hypothesis test.

It was reported by Roper Starch Worldwide that influentials make recommendations about office equipment an average of 5.8 times per year. These and any of the other means reported in this study could be tested. The researcher would need to scientifically identify influentials in the population and randomly select a sample. A research mechanism could be set up whereby the number of referrals by each influential could be recorded for a year and averaged thereby producing a sample mean and a sample standard deviation. Using a selected value of alpha, the sample mean could be statistically tested against the population mean (in this case, $H_0: \mu = 5.8$). The probability of falsely rejecting a true null would be alpha. If the null was actually false ($\mu \neq 5.8$), the probability (β) of failing to reject the false null hypothesis would depend upon what the true number of mean referrals per year was for influentials on office equipment.

If a researcher has theories on influentials and these research theories can be stated as statistical hypotheses, the theory should be formulated as an alternate hypothesis; and the null hypothesis should be that the theory is not true. Samples are randomly selected. If the statistic of choice is a mean, then a z test or t test for a population mean should be used in the analysis dependent on whether or not the population standard deviation is known or unknown. In many studies, the sample standard deviation is used in the analysis instead of the unknown population standard deviation. In these cases, a t test should be used when the assumption that the population data are normally distributed can be made. If the statistic is a proportion, then the z test for a population proportion is appropriate. Techniques presented in Chapter 8, Section 8.5, can be used to assist the researcher in determining how large a sample to take. Using alpha, a critical table z value can be determined and inserted into the sample size determination formulas to determine sample size.

ETHICAL CONSIDERATIONS

The process of hypothesis testing encompasses several areas that could potentially lead to unethical activity, beginning with the null and alternative hypotheses. In the hypothesis-testing approach, the preliminary assumption is that the null hypothesis is true. If a researcher has a new theory or idea that he or she is attempting to prove, it is somewhat unethical to express that theory or idea as the null hypothesis. In doing so, the researcher is assuming that what he or she is trying to prove is true and the burden of proof is on the data to reject this idea or theory. Statistical hypothesis testing is set up so that the new idea or theory is not assumed to be true; the burden of proof is on the researcher to demonstrate through the data and the rejection of the null hypothesis that the new idea or theory is true. The researcher must take great care not to assume that what he or she is attempting to prove is true.

The value of alpha should be established before the experiment is undertaken. Too many researchers "data snoop"—that is, they look at the data and the results of the data analysis and then decide what alpha could be used in order to reject the null hypothesis.

Hypothesis testing through random sampling opens up many possible unethical situations that can occur in sampling, such as identifying a frame that is favorable to the outcome the researcher is seeking or using nonrandom sampling techniques to test hypotheses. In addition, the researcher should be careful to use the proper test statistic for tests of a population mean, particularly when σ is unknown. If t tests are used, or in testing a population variance, the researcher should be careful to apply the techniques only when it can be shown with some confidence that the population is normally distributed. The chi-square test of a population variance has been shown to be extremely sensitive to the assumption that the population is normally distributed. Unethical usage of this technique occurs when the statistician does not carefully check the population distribution shape for compliance with this assumption. Failure to do so can easily result in the reporting of spurious conclusions.

It can be unethical from a business decision-making point of view to knowingly use the notion of statistical significance to claim business significance when the results are not substantive. Therefore, it is unethical to intentionally attempt to mislead the business user by inappropriately using the word *significance*.

SUMMARY

Three types of hypotheses were presented in this chapter: research hypotheses, statistical hypotheses, and substantive hypotheses. Research hypotheses are statements of what the researcher believes will be the outcome of an experiment or study. In order to test hypotheses, business researchers formulate their research hypotheses into statistical hypotheses. All statistical hypotheses consist of two parts, a null hypothesis and an alternative hypothesis. The null and alternative hypotheses are structured so that either one or the other is true but not both. In testing hypotheses, the researcher assumes that the null hypothesis is true. By examining the sampled data, the researcher either rejects or does not reject the null hypothesis. If the sample data are significantly in opposition to the null hypothesis, the researcher rejects the null hypothesis and accepts the alternative hypothesis by default.

Hypothesis tests can be one-tailed or two-tailed. Two-tailed tests always utilize = and ≠ in the null and alternative hypotheses. These tests are nondirectional in that significant deviations from the hypothesized value that are either greater than or less than the value are in rejection regions. The one-tailed test is directional, and the alternative hypothesis contains < or > signs. In these tests, only one end or tail of the distribution contains a rejection region. In a one-tailed test, the researcher is interested only in deviations from the hypothesized value that are either greater than or less than the value but not both.

Not all statistically significant outcomes of studies are important business outcomes. A substantive result is when the outcome of a statistical study produces results that are important to the decision maker.

When a business researcher reaches a decision about the null hypothesis, the researcher either makes a correct decision or an error. If the null hypothesis is true, the researcher can make a Type I error by rejecting the null hypothesis. The probability of making a Type I error is alpha (α). Alpha is usually set by the researcher when establishing the hypotheses. Another expression sometimes used for the value of α is level of significance.

If the null hypothesis is false and the researcher fails to reject it, a Type II error is committed. Beta (β) is the probability of committing a Type II error. Type II errors must be computed from the hypothesized value of the parameter, α, and a specific alternative value of the parameter being examined. As many possible Type II errors in a problem exist as there are possible alternative statistical values.

If a null hypothesis is true and the researcher fails to reject it, no error is committed, and the researcher makes a correct decision. Similarly, if a null hypothesis is false and it is rejected, no error is committed. Power ($1 - \beta$) is the probability of a statistical test rejecting the null hypothesis when the null hypothesis is false.

An operating characteristic (OC) curve is a graphical depiction of values of β that can occur as various values of the alternative hypothesis are explored. This graph can be studied to determine what happens to β as one moves away from the value of the null hypothesis. A power curve is used in conjunction with an operating characteristic curve. The power curve is a graphical depiction of the values of power as various values of the alternative hypothesis are examined. The researcher can view the increase in power as values of the alternative hypothesis diverge from the value of the null hypothesis.

Included in this chapter were hypothesis tests for a single mean when σ is known and when σ is unknown, a test of a single population proportion, and a test for a population variance. Three different analytic approaches were presented: (1) standard method, (2) p-value, and (3) critical value method.

KEY TERMS

alpha (α)
alternative hypothesis
beta (β)
critical value
critical value method
hypothesis
hypothesis testing

level of significance
nonrejection region
null hypothesis
observed significance level
observed value
one-tailed test

operating characteristic
  (OC) curve
p-value
power
power curve
rejection region
research hypothesis

statistical hypothesis
substantive result
two-tailed test
Type I error
Type II error

FORMULAS

z test for a single mean (9.1)

$$z = \frac{\bar{x} - \mu}{\frac{\sigma}{\sqrt{n}}}$$

Formula to test hypotheses about μ with a finite population (9.2)

$$z = \frac{\bar{x} - \mu}{\frac{\sigma}{\sqrt{n}} \sqrt{\frac{N-n}{N-1}}}$$

t test for a single mean (9.3)

$$t = \frac{\bar{x} - \mu}{\frac{s}{\sqrt{n}}}$$

$$df = n - 1$$

z test of a population proportion (9.4)

$$z = \frac{\hat{p} - p}{\sqrt{\frac{p \cdot q}{n}}}$$

Formula for testing hypotheses about a population variance (9.5)

$$\chi^2 = \frac{(n-1)s^2}{\sigma^2}$$

$$df = n - 1$$

SUPPLEMENTARY PROBLEMS

CALCULATING THE STATISTICS

9.39 Use the information given and the HTAB system to test the hypotheses. Let $\alpha = .01$.

$H_0: \mu = 36$ $H_a: \mu \neq 36$ $n = 63$ $\bar{x} = 38.4$ $\sigma = 5.93$

9.40 Use the information given and the HTAB system to test the hypotheses. Let $\alpha = .05$. Assume the population is normally distributed.

$H_0: \mu = 7.82$ $H_a: \mu < 7.82$ $n = 17$ $\bar{x} = 17.1$ $s = 1.69$

9.41 For each of the following problems, test the hypotheses. Incorporate the HTAB system with its eight-step process.

a. $H_0: p = .28$ $H_a: p > .28$ $n = 783$ $x = 230$ $\alpha = .10$
b. $H_0: p = .61$ $H_a: p \neq .61$ $n = 401$ $\hat{p} = .56$ $\alpha = .05$

9.42 Test the following hypotheses by using the information given and the HTAB system. Let alpha be .01. Assume the population is normally distributed.

$H_0: \sigma^2 = 15.4$ $H_a: \sigma^2 > 15.4$ $n = 18$ $s^2 = 29.6$

9.43 Solve for the value of beta in each of the following problems.

a. $H_0: \mu = 130$ $H_a: \mu > 130$ $n = 75$ $\sigma = 12$ $\alpha = .01$.
The alternative mean is actually 135.
b. $H_0: p = .44$ $H_a: p < .44$ $n = 1095$ $\alpha = .05$.
The alternative proportion is actually .42.

TESTING YOUR UNDERSTANDING

9.44 According to a survey by ICR for Vienna Systems, a majority of American households have tried to cut long-distance phone bills. Of those who have tried to cut the bills, 32% have done so by switching long-distance companies. Suppose business researchers believe that this figure may be higher today. To test this theory, a researcher conducts another survey by randomly contacting 80 American households who have tried to cut long-distance phone bills. If 39% of the contacted households say they have tried to cut their long-distance phone bills by switching long-distance companies, is this result enough evidence to state that a significantly higher proportion of American households are trying to cut long-distance phone bills by switching companies? Let $\alpha = .01$.

9.45 According to Zero Population Growth, the average urban U.S. resident consumes 3.3 pounds of food per day. Is this figure accurate for rural U.S. residents? Suppose 64 rural U.S. residents are identified by a random procedure and their average consumption per day is 3.45 pounds of food. Assume a population variance of 1.31 pounds of food per day. Use a 5% level of significance to determine whether the Zero Population Growth figure for urban U.S. residents also is true for rural U.S. residents on the basis of the sample data.

9.46 Brokers generally agree that bonds are a better investment during times of low interest rates than during times of high interest rates. A survey of executives during a time of low interest rates showed that 57% of them had some retirement funds invested in bonds. Assume this percentage is constant for bond market investment by executives with retirement funds. Suppose interest rates have risen lately and the proportion of executives with retirement investment money in the bond market may have dropped. To test this idea, a researcher randomly samples 210 executives who have retirement funds. Of these, 93 now have retirement funds invested in bonds. For $\alpha = .10$, does the test show enough evidence to declare that the proportion of executives with retirement fund investments in the bond market is significantly lower than .57?

9.47 Highway engineers in Ohio are painting white stripes on a highway. The stripes are supposed to be approximately 10 feet long. However, because of the machine, the operator, and the motion of the vehicle carrying the equipment, considerable variation occurs among the stripe lengths. Engineers claim that the variance of stripes is not more than 16 inches. Use the sample lengths given here from 12 measured stripes to test the variance claim. Assume stripe length is normally distributed. Let $\alpha = .05$.

Stripe Lengths in Feet

10.3	9.4	9.8	10.1
9.2	10.4	10.7	9.9
9.3	9.8	10.5	10.4

9.48 A computer manufacturer estimates that its line of minicomputers has, on average, 8.4 days of downtime per year. To test this claim, a researcher contacts seven companies that own one of these computers and is allowed to access company computer records. It is determined that, for the sample, the average number of downtime days is 5.6, with a sample standard deviation of 1.3 days. Assuming that number of downtime days is normally distributed, test to determine whether these minicomputers actually average 8.4 days of downtime in the entire population. Let $\alpha = .01$.

9.49 A life insurance salesperson claims the average worker in the city of Cincinnati has no more than $25,000 of personal life insurance. To test this claim, you randomly sample 100 workers in Cincinnati. You find that this sample of workers averages $26,650 of personal life insurance. The population standard deviation is $12,000.

a. Determine whether the test shows enough evidence to reject the null hypothesis posed by the salesperson. Assume the probability of committing a Type I error is .05.

b. If the actual average for this population is $30,000, what is the probability of committing a Type II error?

9.50 A financial analyst has been watching a particular stock for several months. The price of this stock remained fairly stable during this time. In fact, the financial analyst claims that the variance of the price of this stock did not exceed $4 for the entire period. Recently, the market heated up, and the price of this stock appears more volatile. To determine whether it is more volatile, a sample of closing prices of this stock for 8 days is taken randomly. The sample mean price is $36.25, with a sample standard deviation of $7.80. Using a level of significance of .10, test to determine whether the financial analyst's previous variance figure is now too low. Assume stock prices are normally distributed.

9.51 A study of MBA graduates by Universum for The American Graduate Survey 1999 revealed that MBA graduates have several expectations of prospective employers beyond their base pay. In particular, according to the study 46% expect a performance-related bonus, 46% expect stock options, 42% expect a signing bonus, 28% expect profit sharing, 27% expect extra vacation/personal days, 25% expect tuition reimbursement, 24% expect health benefits, and 19% expect guaranteed annual bonuses. Suppose a study is conducted in an ensuing year to see whether these expectations have changed. If 125 MBA graduates are randomly selected and if 66 expect stock options, does this result provide enough evidence to declare that a significantly higher proportion of MBAs expect stock options? Let $\alpha = .05$. If the proportion really is .50, what is the probability of committing a Type II error?

9.52 Suppose the number of beds filled per day in a medium-sized hospital is normally distributed. A hospital administrator tells the board of directors that, on the average, at least 185 beds are filled on any given day. One of the board members believes this figure is inflated, and she manages to secure a random sample of figures for 16 days. The data are shown here. Use $\alpha = .05$ and the sample data to test whether the hospital administrator's statement is false. Assume the number of filled beds per day is normally distributed in the population.

Number of Beds Occupied per Day

173	149	166	180
189	170	152	194
177	169	188	160
199	175	172	187

9.53 According to the International Data Corporation, Compaq Computers holds a 16% share of the personal computer market in the United States and a 12.7% share of the worldwide market. Suppose a market researcher believes that Compaq holds a higher share of the market in the southwestern region of the United States. To verify this theory, he randomly selects 428 people who purchased a personal computer in the last month in the southwestern region of the United States. Eighty-four of these purchases were Compaq Computers. Using a 1% level of significance, test the market researcher's theory. What is the probability of making a Type I error? If the market share is really .21 in the southwestern region of the United States, what is the probability of making a Type II error?

9.54 A national publication reported that a college student living away from home spends, on average, no more than $15 per month on laundry. You believe this figure is too low and want to disprove this claim. To conduct the test, you randomly select 35 college students and ask them to keep track of the amount of money they spend during a given month for laundry. The sample produces an average expenditure on laundry of $19.34, with a population standard deviation of $4.52. Use these sample data to conduct the hypothesis test. Assume you are willing to take a 10% risk of making a Type I error.

9.55 A local company installs natural-gas grills. As part of the installation, a ditch is dug to lay a small natural-gas line from the grill to the main line. On the average, the depth of these lines seems to run about 1 foot. The company claims that the depth does not vary by more than 16 inches (the variance). To test this claim, a researcher randomly took 22 depth measurements at different locations. The sample average depth was 13.4 inches with a standard deviation of 6 inches. Is this enough evidence to reject the company's claim about the variance? Assume line depths are normally distributed. Let $\alpha = .05$.

9.56 A study of pollutants showed that certain industrial emissions should not exceed 2.5 parts per million. You believe a particular company may be exceeding this average. To test this supposition, you randomly take a sample of nine air tests. The sample average is 3.4 parts per million, with a sample standard deviation of .6. Does this result provide enough evidence for you to conclude that the company is exceeding the safe limit? Use $\alpha = .01$. Assume emissions are normally distributed.

9.57 The average cost per square foot for office rental space in the central business district of Philadelphia is $23.58, according to Cushman & Wakefield. A large real estate company wants to confirm this figure. The firm conducts a telephone survey of 95 offices in the central business district of Philadelphia and asks the office managers how much they pay in rent per square foot. Suppose the sample average is $22.83 per square foot. The population standard deviation is $5.11.

   a. Conduct a hypothesis test using $\alpha = .05$ to determine whether the cost per square foot reported by Cushman & Wakefield should be rejected.

   b. If the decision in part (a) is to fail to reject and if the actual average cost per square foot is $22.30, what is the probability of committing a Type II error?

9.58 The American Water Works Association reports that, on average, men use between 10 and 15 gallons of water daily to shave when they leave the water running. Suppose the following data are the numbers of gallons of water used in a day to shave by 12 randomly selected men and the data come from a normal distribution of data. Use these data and a 5% level of significance to test to determine whether the population variance for such water usage is 2.5 gallons.

10	8	13	17	13	15
12	13	15	16	9	7

INTERPRETING THE OUTPUT

9.59 According to the U.S. Census Bureau, the average American generates 4.4 pounds of garbage per day. Suppose we believe that because of recycling and a greater emphasis on the environment, the figure is now lower. To test this notion, we take a random sample of Americans and have them keep a log of their garbage for a day. We record and analyze the results by using a statistical computer package. The output follows. Describe the sample. What statistical decisions can be made on the basis of this analysis? Let alpha be .05. Assume that pounds of garbage per day are normally distributed in the population. Discuss any substantive results.

```
One-Sample T: Garbage

Test of mu = 4.4 vs mu < 4.4

Variable    N     Mean    StDev    SE Mean
Garbage     22    3.969   0.866    0.185

Variable    95.0% Upper Bound      T        P
Garbage          4.286           -2.34    0.015
```

9.60 One survey conducted by RHI Management Resources determined that the Lexus is the favorite luxury car for 25% of CFOs. Suppose a financial management association conducts its own survey of CFOs in an effort to determine whether this figure is correct. They use an alpha of .05. Following is the MINITAB output with the results of the survey. Discuss the findings, including the hypotheses, one- or two-tailed tests, sample statistics, and the conclusion. Explain from the data why you reached the conclusion you did. Are these results substantive?

```
Test and CI for One Proportion

Test of p = 0.25 vs p not = 0.25

Sample  X    N    Sample p        95.0% CI          P-Value
1       79   384  0.205729  (0.166399, 0.249663)    0.045
```

9.61 In a recent year, published statistics by the National Cattlemen's Beef Association claimed that the average retail beef price for USDA All Fresh beef was $2.51. Suppose a survey of retailers is conducted this year to determine whether the price of USDA All Fresh beef has increased. The Excel output of the results of the survey are shown here. Analyze the output and explain what it means in this study. An alpha of .05 was used in this analysis. Assume that beef prices are normally distributed in the population. Comment on any substantive results.

	A	B
1	Mean	2.55
2	Variance	0.0218
3	Observations	26
4	df	26
5	t Stat	1.51
6	P (T<=t) one-tail	0.072
7	t Critical one-tail	1.71
8	P (T<=t) two-tail	0.144
9	t Critical two-tail	2.06

9.62 The American Express Retail Index states that the average U.S. household will spend $2,747 on home improvement projects this year. Suppose a large national home improvement company wants to test that figure in the West, theorizing that the average might be lower in the West. The research firm hired to conduct the study arrives at the results shown here. Analyze the data and explain the results. Comment on any substantive findings.

```
One-Sample Z: Home Improv

Test of mu = 2747 vs mu < 2747
The assumed sigma = 1557

  Variable     N    Mean  StDev  SE Mean
Home Improv   67    2349   1818     190

  Variable    95.0%  Upper Bound     Z      P
Home Improv            2662        2.09  0.018
```

ANALYZING THE DATABASES   see www.wiley.com/college/black

1. Suppose the average number of employees per industry group in the manufacturing database is believed to be less than 150 (1,000s). Test this belief as the alternative hypothesis by using the 140 SIC Code industries given in the database as the sample. Let $\alpha = .01$. Assume that the number of employees per industry group are normally distributed in the population. What did you decide and why?

2. Examine the hospital database. Suppose you want to "prove" that the average hospital in the United States averages more than 700 births per year. Use the hospital database as your sample and test this hypothesis. Let alpha be .01. On average, do hospitals in the United States employ fewer than 900 personnel? Use the hospital database as your sample and an alpha of .10 to test this figure as the alternative hypothesis. Assume that the number of births and number of employees in hospitals are normally distributed in the population.

3. Consider the financial database. Are the average earnings per share for companies in the stock market less than $2.50? Use the sample of companies represented by this database to test that hypothesis. Let $\alpha = .05$. Test to determine whether the average return on equity for all companies is equal to 21. Use this database as the sample and $\alpha = .10$. Assume that the earnings per share and return on equity are normally distributed in the population.

4. Fifteen years ago, the average production in the United States for green beans was 166,770 pounds per month. Use the 12 months in 1997 (the last 12 months in the database) in the agriculture database as a sample to test to determine whether the mean monthly production figure for green beans in the United States is now different from the old figure. Let $\alpha = .01$. Assume that the monthly production of beans is normally distributed in the population.

CASE: FRITO-LAY TARGETS THE HISPANIC MARKET

Frito Company was founded in 1932 in San Antonio, Texas, by Elmer Doolin. H. W. Lay & Company was founded in Atlanta, Georgia, by Herman W. Lay in 1938. In 1961, the two companies merged to form Frito-Lay, Inc., with headquarters in Texas. Frito-Lay produced, distributed, and marketed snack foods with particular emphasis on various types of chips. In 1965, the company merged with Pepsi-Cola to form PepsiCo, Inc. Three decades later, Pepsi-Cola combined its domestic and international snack food operations into one business unit called Frito-Lay Company. According to data released by Information Resources, Frito-Lay brands account for more than 60% of the share of the snack chip market.

Despite its overall popularity, Frito-Lay faces a general lack of appeal in the Hispanic market, which is a growing segment of the U.S. population. In an effort to better penetrate that market, Frito-Lay hired various market researchers to determine why Hispanics do not purchase their products as often as company officials had hoped and what could be done about the problem.

Driving giant RVs through Hispanic neighborhoods and targeting Hispanic women (who tend to buy most of the groceries for their families), the researchers tested various brands and discovered several things. Hispanics thought Frito-Lay products were too bland, not spicy enough. Hispanics also were relatively unaware of Frito-Lay advertising. In addition, they tended to purchase snacks in small bags rather than in large family-style bags and at small local grocery stores rather than at large supermarkets.

After the "road test," focus groups composed of male teens and male young adults—a group that tends to consume a lot of chips—were formed. The researchers determined that even though many of the teens spoke English at school, they spoke Spanish at home with their family. From this discovery, it was concluded that Spanish advertisements would be needed to reach Hispanics. In addition, the use of Spanish rock music, a growing movement in the Hispanic youth culture, could be effective in some ads.

Researchers also found that using a "Happy Face" logo, which is an icon of Frito-Lay's sister company in Mexico, was effective. Because it reminded the 63% of all Hispanics in the

United States who are Mexican-American of snack foods from home, the logo increased product familiarity.

As a result of this research, Frito-Lay launched its first Hispanic products in San Antonio in 1997. Since that time, sales of the Doritos brand improved 32% in Hispanic areas and Doritos Salsa Verde sales have grown to represent 15% of all sales. Frito-Lay later expanded its line of products into other areas of the United States with large Hispanic populations.

Discussion

In the research process for Frito-Lay Company, many different numerical questions were raised regarding Frito-Lay products, advertising techniques, and purchase patterns among Hispanics. In each of these areas, statistics—in particular, hypothesis testing—plays a central role. Using the case information and the concepts of statistical hypothesis testing, discuss the following:

1. Many proportions were generated in the focus groups and market research that were conducted for this project, including the proportion of the market that is Hispanic, the proportion of Hispanic grocery shoppers that are women, the proportion of chip purchasers that are teens, and so on. Use techniques presented in this chapter to analyze each of the following and discuss how the results might affect marketing decision makers regarding the Hispanic market.

   a. The case information stated that 63% of all U.S. Hispanics are Mexican-American. How might we test that figure? Suppose 850 U.S. Hispanics are randomly selected using U.S. Census Bureau information. Suppose 575 state that they are Mexican-Americans. Test the 63% percentage using an alpha of .05.

   b. Suppose that in the past 94% of all Hispanic grocery shoppers were women. Perhaps due to changing cultural values, we believe that more Hispanic men are now grocery shopping. We randomly sample 689 Hispanic grocery shoppers from around the United States and 606 are women. Does this result provide enough evidence to conclude that a lower proportion of Hispanic grocery shoppers now are women?

   c. What proportion of Hispanics listen primarily to advertisements in Spanish? Suppose one source says that in the past the proportion has been about .83. We want to test to determine whether this figure is true. A random sample of 438 Hispanics is selected, and the MINITAB results of testing this hypothesis are shown here. Discuss and explain this output and the implications of this study using $\alpha = .05$.

```
Test and CI for One Proportion

Test of p = 0.83 vs p not = 0.83
Sample   X    N    Sample p        95.0% CI          P-Value
1       347  438   0.792237   (0.751184, 0.829290)   0.042
```

2. The statistical mean can be used to measure various aspects of the Hispanic culture and the Hispanic market, including size of purchase, frequency of purchase, age of consumer, size of store, and so on. Use techniques presented in this chapter to analyze each of the following and discuss how the results might affect marketing decisions.

   a. What is the average age of a purchaser of Doritos Salsa Verde? Suppose initial tests indicate that the mean age is 31. Is this figure really correct? To test whether it is, a researcher randomly contacts 24 purchasers of Doritos Salsa Verde with results shown in the following Excel output. Discuss the output in terms of a hypothesis test to determine whether the mean age is actually 31. Let α be .01. Assume that ages of purchasers are normally distributed in the population.

	A	B
1	Mean	28.81
2	Variance	50.2651
3	Observations	24
4	df	23
5	t Stat	−1.52
6	P (T<=t) one-tail	0.0716
7	t Critical one-tail	1.71
8	P (T<=t) two-tail	0.1431
9	t Critical two-tail	2.07

   b. What is the average expenditure of a Hispanic customer on chips per year? Suppose it is hypothesized that the figure is $45 per year. A researcher who knows the Hispanic market believes that this figure is too high and wants to prove her case. She randomly selects 18 Hispanics, has them keep a log of grocery purchases for one year, and obtains the following figures. Analyze the data using techniques from this chapter and an alpha of .05. Assume that expenditures per customer are normally distributed in the population.

$55	37	59	57	27	28
16	46	34	62	9	34
4	25	38	58	3	50

Source: Adapted from "From Bland to Brand," *American Demographics* (March 1999), p. 57; Frito-Lay, available at http://www.fritolay.com; and Ronald J. Alsop, ed., *The Wall Street Journal Almanac 1999* (New York: Ballantine Books, 1998), p. 202.

USING THE COMPUTER

EXCEL

Excel has somewhat limited capability for doing hypothesis testing with single samples. It can compute z tests for single population means by using the Paste Function. Begin by clicking on the Paste Function f_x on the standard tool bar. The Paste Function dialog box will appear. From the **Function category** on the left, select **Statistical**. A menu of statistical techniques will appear on the right. Select **ZTEST** from this list. A dialog box will appear. This box requires the location of the data array in the first space beside **Array**. Place the hypothesized value of the mean in the second space beside **X**. Record the population standard deviation in the third line beside **Sigma**. The output is the right-tailed p-value for the test statistic. If the z value is negative, subtract $1 - $ (Excel output) to obtain the p-value for the left tail.

A single-sample t test can be computed in Excel by "fooling" the Excel dialog box for **t-Test: Two-Sample Assuming Unequal Variances**. First load the single-sample data in a column. Next, place the value of the hypothesized mean in another column in as many cells as there are data in the single-sample data column. Next, select **Tools** from the menu bar. Select **Data Analysis** from the pull-down menu. From the Data Analysis dialog box, select **t-Test: Two-Sample Assuming Unequal Variances**. In the dialog box that appears, place the location of the cells containing the single-sample data in **Variable 1 Range**. Place the location of the cells containing the repeated value of the hypothesized mean in **Variable 2 Range**. Place 0 in **Hypothesized Mean Difference**. Finally, fill in the labels and alpha information. The result will be the output for a single-sample t test.

MINITAB

MINITAB Windows conducts hypothesis tests by using the same commands, pull-down menus, and dialog boxes as those used to construct confidence intervals (discussed in Chapter 8). Begin by selecting **Stat** from the menu bar. From the pull-down menu that appears, select **Basic Statistics**. A second pull-down menu will appear. To conduct hypothesis tests in which the population standard deviation is known, select **1–sample Z**. To conduct hypothesis tests in which the population standard deviation is unknown, select **1–sample t**.

In the dialog boxes of each, enter the column location of the data being tested in the first space, **Variables**. (If a z test is being conducted, enter the value of the known population standard deviation in the space labeled **Sigma**.) In the **Test Mean** space enter the hypothesized value of μ. Select **Options**. From the Options dialog box enter the level of confidence if different from 95% and select whether the alternative hypothesis is **less than**, **greater than**, or **not equal**. The output includes a statement of the hypotheses, the sample size, the sample mean and standard deviation, the standard error of the mean, the t statistics, and the p-value of the statistic.

MINITAB is able to test hypotheses about single proportions using the same process presented in Chapter 8. Begin the process by selecting **Stat** from the menu bar. From the pull-down menu, select **Basic Statistics**. From that pull-down menu, select **1 Proportion**. In the dialog box that appears, select either **Samples in columns** or **Summarized data**. If the data are in columns and if only one of two possible values is in each cell, then select **Samples in columns**. If you want to enter the summary data, select **Summarized data**. Using this option, place the size of the sample in the **Number of trials** space, and the number of items containing characteristic of interest, x, in the **Number of successes** space. To test a hypothesis, select **Options**. This command allows you to place the hypothesized proportion in **Test proportion**. Beside **Alternative** select the appropriate alternative hypothesis being tested. The resulting output includes a sample proportion, a confidence interval, and a p-value.

Statistical Inferences about Two Populations

LEARNING OBJECTIVES

The general focus of Chapter 10 is on testing hypotheses and constructing confidence intervals about parameters from two populations, thereby enabling you to:

1. Test hypotheses and construct confidence intervals about the difference in two population means using the z statistic.
2. Test hypotheses and construct confidence intervals about the difference in two population means using the t statistic.
3. Test hypotheses and construct confidence intervals about the mean difference in two related populations.
4. Test hypotheses and construct confidence intervals about the difference in two population proportions.
5. Test hypotheses and construct confidence intervals about the difference in two population variances.

Comparing International Labor Statistics

Labor statistics are used to compare various countries in such areas as productivity, cost, and job satisfaction. In particular, statistics can be used to determine whether a difference is evident between two countries on some labor measure or between periods of time in one country. For example, in 1992 the hourly compensation cost for production workers in manufacturing for Japan was $16.38. By the year 2000, this figure had risen to $22.00. In the United States, the hourly cost rose from $16.09 to $19.96 over this same period. Was Japanese labor more expensive than in the United States in 1992 if the hourly labor cost for Japan was $16.38 compared to $16.09 in the United States? What about in the year 2000? The hourly compensation cost for production workers in 1995 was $25.32 for Austria and $24.07 for Denmark. By the year 2000, the rates were $19.46 for Austria and $20.44 for Denmark.

A study conducted by the International Labor Organization (ILO) showed that the average workweek in the United States has declined from 40 hours in 1967 to 39.2 hours in 1998. The ILO also reported that in 1970, 43.3% of all women in the United States participated in the workforce and that by 1998, 59.8% of all women in the United States were participating in the workforce.

The Center for Survey Research and Analysis at the University of Connecticut revealed that 57% of Americans stated that they would work the same number of hours per week if given a choice, and 60% were very satisfied with their flexibility in hours or days worked.

Managerial and Statistical Questions

1. Suppose the labor data used to compute the hourly labor costs for Japan and the United States were actually sample data. Is the 1992 hourly labor cost in Japan ($16.38) significantly higher than the 1992 figure for the United States ($16.09), or is the difference merely due to chance? The hourly labor cost for Japan appears to have increased from 1992 to 2000. Is this due to chance in the random sampling or has there really been a significant increase in hourly labor costs for Japan?

2. The two labor cost statistics for Austria and Denmark are relatively close for both years that are reported. Because it is unlikely that all workers in Austria and Denmark were involved in the study and these statistics may have been gathered using samples, is the 98 cent difference between these two countries in 2000 really significant or just the chance result of sampling?

3. Has the average workweek in the United States actually declined from 40 hours to 39.2 hours over the 31-year period from 1967 until 1998 or is this just the chance difference of two samples of workers taken in these two years?

4. The studies showed that 57% of Americans stated that they would work the same number of hours per week if given a choice. Suppose 700 Americans took part in this study. Suppose further that a study of 850 Koreans was taken and 55% of Korean workers stated that they would work the same number of hours per week if given a choice. Based on these two samples, could we state that a significant lower percentage of Korean workers than U.S. workers would work the same number of hours per week if given a choice?

5. Sixty percent of American workers were very satisfied with their flexibility in hours or days worked. Suppose this figure is based on a sample of 375 workers taken in 1997. If a sample of 290 workers in the year 2000 is taken resulting in 64% stating that they are very satisfied with their flexibility in hours or days worked, could we state that a higher percentage of American workers are very satisfied with their flexibility in hours or days in the year 2000 than in 1997?

Source: Adapted from Foreign Labor Statistics of the Bureau of Labor Statistics, http://stats.bls.gov/news.release/ichcc.nws.htm, and http://www.bls.gov/fls/home.htm; Employment Policy Foundation, http://www.epf.org/ff/ff991014.htm.

To this point, all discussion of confidence intervals and hypothesis testing centered on samples drawn from a single population. We learned how to test hypotheses about a single population mean, a single population proportion, and a single population variance. Often, it is of equal interest to make inferences about two populations. A business analyst might want to compare the expenditures on shoes made in 1995 with those from 2005 in an effort to determine whether any change occurred over time. A researcher might want to estimate or test to determine the difference in the market proportions of two companies or the proportion of market share of one company in two different regions.

In this chapter, we will consider several different techniques for analyzing data that come from two samples. One technique is used with proportions, one is used with variances, and the others are used with means. The techniques for analyzing means are separated into those using the *z* statistic and those using the *t* statistic. In four of the five techniques presented in this chapter, the two samples are assumed to be **independent samples.** The samples are independent because *the items or people sampled in each group are in no way related to those in the other group.* Any similarity between items or people in the two samples is coincidental and due to chance. One of the techniques presented in the chapter is for analyzing data from dependent, or related, samples in which items or persons in one sample are matched in some way with items or persons in the other sample. For four of the five techniques, we will examine both hypothesis tests and confidence intervals. We begin with techniques for analyzing the difference in two means using the *z* statistic.

10.1 HYPOTHESIS TESTING AND CONFIDENCE INTERVALS ABOUT THE DIFFERENCE IN TWO MEANS USING THE *z* STATISTIC (POPULATION VARIANCES KNOWN)

In some research designs, the sampling plan calls for selecting two independent samples, calculating the sample means, and using the difference in the two sample means to estimate or test the difference in the two population means. The object might be to determine whether the two samples come from the same population or, if they come from different populations, to determine the amount of difference in the populations. This type of analysis can be used to determine, for example, whether the effectiveness of two brands of toothpaste differs or whether two brands of tires wear differently. Business research might be conducted to study the difference in the productivity of men and women on an assembly line under certain conditions. An engineer might want to determine differences in the strength of aluminum produced under two different temperatures. Does the average cost of a two-bedroom, one-story house differ between Boston and Seattle? If so, how much is the difference? These and many other interesting questions can be researched by comparing the difference in two sample means.

How does a researcher analyze the difference in two samples by using sample means? The central limit theorem states that the difference in two sample means, $\bar{x}_1 - \bar{x}_2$, is normally distributed for large sample sizes (both n_1 and $n_2 \geq 30$) regardless of the shape of the populations. It can also be shown that

$$\mu_{\bar{x}_1-\bar{x}_2} = \mu_1 - \mu_2$$

$$\sigma_{\bar{x}_1-\bar{x}_2} = \sqrt{\frac{\sigma_1^2}{n_1} + \frac{\sigma_2^2}{n_2}}$$

These expressions lead to a *z* formula for the difference in two sample means.

z FORMULA FOR THE DIFFERENCE IN TWO SAMPLE MEANS (INDEPENDENT SAMPLES AND POPULATION VARIANCES KNOWN) (10.1)	$$z = \frac{(\bar{x}_1 - \bar{x}_2) - (\mu_1 - \mu_2)}{\sqrt{\dfrac{\sigma_1^2}{n_1} + \dfrac{\sigma_2^2}{n_2}}}$$

where

μ_1 = the mean of population 1
μ_2 = the mean of population 2
n_1 = size of sample 1
n_2 = size of sample 2

This formula is the basis for statistical inferences about the difference in two means using two random independent samples.

Note: *If the populations are normally distributed on the measurement being studied and if the population variances are known, formula (10.1) can be used for small sample sizes.*

Hypothesis Testing

In many instances, a business researcher wants to test the differences in the mean values of two populations. One example might be to test the difference between the mean values of men and women for achievement, intelligence, or other characteristics. A consumer organization might want to test two brands of light bulbs to determine whether one burns longer than the other. A company wanting to relocate might want to determine whether a significant difference separates the average price of a home in Newark, New Jersey, from house prices in Cleveland, Ohio. Formula (10.1) can be used to test the difference between two population means.

As a specific example, suppose we want to conduct a hypothesis test to determine whether the average annual wage for an advertising manager is different from the average

TABLE 10.1

Wages for Advertising Managers and Auditing Managers ($1,000)

Advertising Managers		Auditing Managers	
74.256	64.276	69.962	67.160
96.234	74.194	55.052	37.386
89.807	65.360	57.828	59.505
93.261	73.904	63.362	72.790
103.030	54.270	37.194	71.351
74.195	59.045	99.198	58.653
75.932	68.508	61.254	63.508
80.742	71.115	73.065	43.649
39.672	67.574	48.036	63.369
45.652	59.621	60.053	59.676
93.083	62.483	66.359	54.449
63.384	69.319	61.261	46.394
57.791	35.394	77.136	71.804
65.145	86.741	66.035	72.401
96.767	57.351	54.335	56.470
77.242		42.494	67.814
67.056		83.849	71.492

$n_1 = 32$ $n_2 = 34$
$\bar{x}_1 = 70.700$ $\bar{x}_2 = 62.187$
$\sigma_1 = 16.253$ $\sigma_2 = 12.900$
$\sigma_1^2 = 264.164$ $\sigma_2^2 = 166.411$

annual wage of an auditing manager. Because we are testing to determine whether the means are different, it might seem logical that the null and alternative hypotheses would be

$$H_0: \mu_1 = \mu_2$$

$$H_a: \mu_1 \neq \mu_2$$

where advertising managers are population 1 and auditing managers are population 2. However, statisticians generally construct these hypotheses as

$$H_0: \mu_1 - \mu_2 = \delta$$

$$H_a: \mu_1 - \mu_2 \neq \delta$$

This format allows the business analyst not only to test if the population means are equal, but also affords her the opportunity to hypothesize about a particular difference in the means (δ). Generally speaking, most business analysts are only interested in testing whether the difference in the means is different. Thus, δ is set equal to zero resulting in the following hypotheses, which we will use for this problem and others.

$$H_0: \mu_1 - \mu_2 = 0$$

$$H_a: \mu_1 - \mu_2 \neq 0$$

A random sample of 32 advertising managers from across the United States is taken. The advertising managers are contacted by telephone and asked what is their annual salary. A similar random sample is taken of 34 auditing managers. The resulting salary data are listed in Table 10.1, along with the sample means, the population standard deviations, and the population variances.

In this problem, the business analyst is testing whether there is a difference in the average wage of an advertising manager and an auditing manager; therefore the test is

FIGURE 10.1

Critical Values and Rejection Regions for the Wage Example

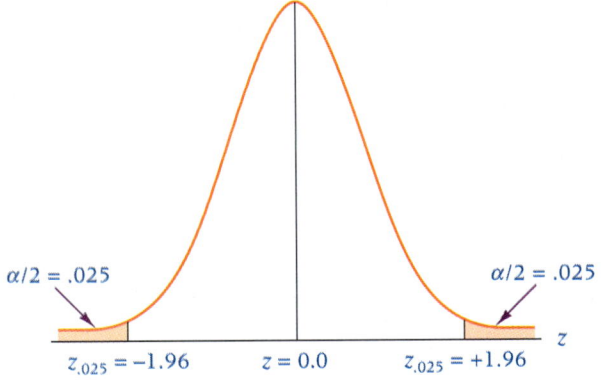

FIGURE 10.2

Location of Observed z Value for the Wage Example

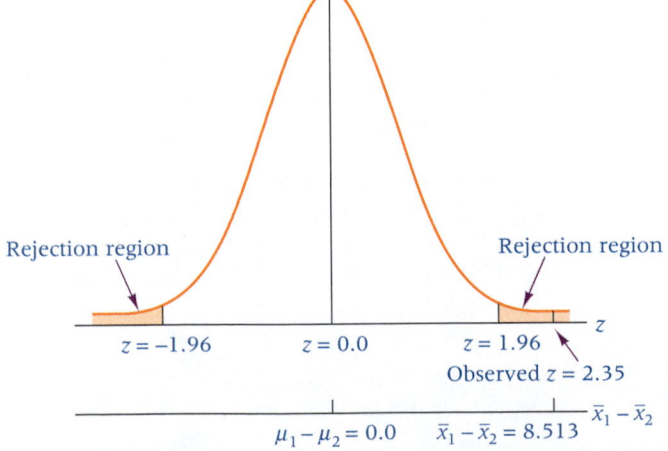

two-tailed. If the business analyst had hypothesized that one was paid more than the other, the test would have been one-tailed.

Suppose $\alpha = .05$. Because this test is a two-tailed test, each of the two rejection regions has an area of .025, leaving .475 of the area in the distribution between each critical value and the mean of the distribution. The associated critical table $z_{\alpha/2}$ value for this area is $z_{.025} = \pm 1.96$. Figure 10.1 shows the critical table z value along with the rejection regions.

Formula (10.1) and the data in Table 10.1 yield a z value to complete the hypothesis test

$$z = \frac{(70.700 - 62.187) - (0)}{\sqrt{\dfrac{264.164}{32} + \dfrac{166.411}{34}}} = 2.35$$

The observed value of 2.35 is greater than the critical value obtained from the z table, 1.96. The business researcher rejects the null hypothesis and can say that there is a significant difference between the average annual wage of an advertising manager and the average annual wage of an auditing manager. The business researcher then examines the sample means (70.700 for advertising managers and 62.187 for auditing managers) and uses common sense to conclude that advertising managers earn more, on the average, than do auditing managers. Figure 10.2 shows the relationship between the observed z and $z_{\alpha/2}$.

This conclusion could have been reached by using the p-value. Looking up the probability of $z \geq 2.35$ in the z distribution table in Appendix A.5 yields an area of $.5000 - .4906 = .0094$. This p-value (.0094) is less than $\alpha/2 = .025$. The decision is to reject the null hypothesis.

DEMONSTRATION PROBLEM 10.1	A sample of 87 professional working women showed that the average amount paid annually into a private pension fund per person was $3,352. The population standard deviation is $1,100. A sample of 76 professional working men showed that the average amount paid annually into a private pension fund per person was $5,727, with a population standard deviation of $1,700. A women's activist group wants to "prove" that women do not pay as much per year as men into private pension funds. If they use $\alpha = .001$ and these sample data, will they be able to reject a null hypothesis that women annually pay the same as or more than men into private pension funds? Use the eight-step hypothesis-testing process.

Solution

HYPOTHESIZE:

STEP 1. This test is one-tailed. Because the women's activist group wants to prove that women pay less than men into private pension funds annually, the alternative hypothesis should be $\mu_w - \mu_m < 0$, and the null hypothesis is that women pay the same as or more than men, $\mu_w - \mu_m = 0$.

TEST:

STEP 2. The test statistic is

$$z = \frac{(\bar{x}_1 - \bar{x}_2) - (\mu_1 - \mu_2)}{\sqrt{\dfrac{\sigma_1^2}{n_1} + \dfrac{\sigma_2^2}{n_2}}}$$

STEP 3. Alpha has been specified as .001.

STEP 4. By using this value of alpha, a critical $z_{.001} = -3.08$ can be determined. The decision rule is to reject the null hypothesis if the observed value of the test statistic, z, is less than -3.08.

STEP 5. The sample data follow.

Women	Men
$\bar{x}_1 = \$3352$	$\bar{x}_2 = \$5727$
$\sigma_1 = \$1100$	$\sigma_2 = \$1700$
$n_1 = 87$	$n_2 = 76$

STEP 6. Solving for z gives

$$z = \frac{(3352 - 5727) - (0)}{\sqrt{\frac{1100^2}{87} + \frac{1700^2}{76}}} = \frac{-2375}{227.9} = -10.42$$

ACTION:

STEP 7 The observed z value of -10.42 is deep in the rejection region, well past the table value of $z_c = -3.08$. Even with the small $\alpha = .001$, the null hypothesis is rejected.

BUSINESS IMPLICATIONS:

STEP 8. The evidence is substantial that women, on average, pay less than men into private pension funds annually. The following diagram displays these results.

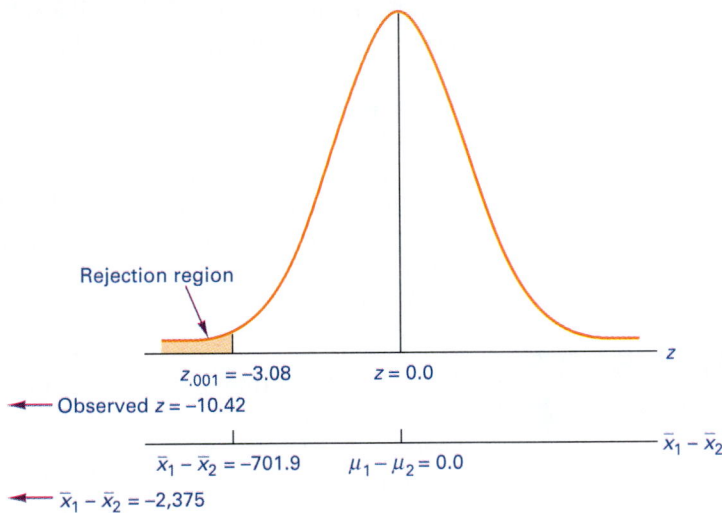

The probability of obtaining an observed z value of -10.42 by chance is virtually zero, because the value is beyond the limits of the z table. By the p-value, the null hypothesis is rejected because the probability is .0000, or less than $\alpha = .001$.

If this problem were worked by the critical value method, what critical value of the difference in the two means would have to be surpassed to reject the null hypothesis for a table z value of -3.08? The answer is

$$(\bar{x}_1 - \bar{x}_2)_C = (\mu_1 - \mu_2) - z\sqrt{\frac{\sigma_1^2}{n_1} + \frac{\sigma_2^2}{n_2}}$$

$$= 0 - 3.08(227.9) = -701.9$$

The difference in sample means would need to be at least 701.9 to reject the null hypothesis. The actual sample difference in this problem was -2375 ($3352 - 5727$), which is considerably larger than the critical value of difference. Thus, with the critical value method also, the null hypothesis is rejected.

Confidence Intervals

Sometimes being able to estimate the difference in the means of two populations is valuable. By how much do two populations differ in size or weight or age? By how much do two products differ in effectiveness? Do two different methods produce different mean results? The answers to these questions are often difficult to obtain through census techniques. The alternative is to take a random sample from each of the two populations and study the difference in the sample means.

Algebraically, formula (10.1) can be manipulated to produce a formula for constructing confidence intervals for the difference in two population means.

CONFIDENCE INTERVAL TO ESTIMATE $\mu_1 - \mu_2$ (10.2)	$(\bar{x}_1 - \bar{x}_2) - z\sqrt{\dfrac{\sigma_1^2}{n_1} + \dfrac{\sigma_2^2}{n_2}} \leq \mu_1 - \mu_2 \leq (\bar{x}_1 - \bar{x}_2) + z\sqrt{\dfrac{\sigma_1^2}{n_1} + \dfrac{\sigma_2^2}{n_2}}$

Suppose a study is conducted to estimate the difference between middle-income shoppers and low-income shoppers in terms of the average amount saved on grocery bills per week by using coupons. Random samples of 60 middle-income shoppers and 80 low-income shoppers are taken, and their purchases are monitored for one week. The average amounts saved with coupons, as well as sample sizes and population standard deviations, follow.

Middle-Income Shoppers	Low-Income Shoppers
$n_1 = 60$	$n_2 = 80$
$\bar{x}_1 = \$5.84$	$\bar{x}_2 = \$2.67$
$\sigma_1 = \$1.41$	$\sigma_2 = \$0.54$

This information can be used to construct a 98% confidence interval to estimate the difference between the mean amount saved with coupons by middle-income shoppers and the mean amount saved with coupons by low-income shoppers.

The z_c value associated with a 98% level of confidence is 2.33. This value, the data shown, and formula (10.2) can be used to determine the confidence interval.

$$(5.84 - 2.67) - 2.33\sqrt{\frac{1.41^2}{60} + \frac{0.54^2}{80}} \leq \mu_1 - \mu_2 \leq (5.84 - 2.67) + 2.33\sqrt{\frac{1.41^2}{60} + \frac{0.54^2}{80}}$$

$$3.17 - 0.45 \leq \mu_1 - \mu_2 \leq 3.17 + 0.45$$

$$2.72 \leq \mu_1 - \mu_2 \leq 3.62$$

There is a 98% level of confidence that the actual difference in the population mean coupon savings per week between middle-income and low-income shoppers is between $2.72 and $3.62. That is, the difference could be as little as $2.72 or as great as $3.62. The point estimate for the difference in mean savings is $3.17. Note that a zero difference in the population means of these two groups is unlikely, because zero is not in the 98% range.

DEMONSTRATION PROBLEM 10.2

A consumer test group wants to determine the difference in gasoline mileage of cars using regular unleaded gas and cars using premium unleaded gas. Researchers for the group divided a fleet of 100 cars of the same make in half and tested each car on one tank of gas. Fifty of the cars were filled with regular unleaded gas and 50 were filled with premium unleaded gas. The sample average for the regular gasoline group was 21.45 miles per gallon (mpg), and the sample average for the premium gasoline group was 24.6 mpg. Assume that the population standard deviation of the regular unleaded gas population is 3.46 mpg, and that the population standard deviation of the premium unleaded gas population is 2.99 mpg. Construct a 95% confidence interval to estimate the difference in the mean gas mileage between the cars using regular gasoline and the cars using premium gasoline.

Solution

The z value for a 95% confidence interval is 1.96. The other sample information follows.

Regular	Premium
$n_r = 50$	$n_p = 50$
$\bar{x}_r = 21.45$	$\bar{x}_p = 24.6$
$\sigma_r = 3.46$	$\sigma_p = 2.99$

Based on this information, the confidence interval is

$$(21.45 - 24.6) - 1.96\sqrt{\frac{3.46^2}{50} + \frac{2.99^2}{50}} \leq \mu_1 - \mu_2 \leq (21.45 - 24.6) + 1.96\sqrt{\frac{3.46^2}{50} + \frac{2.99^2}{50}}$$

$$-3.15 - 1.27 \leq \mu_1 - \mu_2 \leq -3.15 + 1.27$$

$$-4.42 \leq \mu_1 - \mu_2 \leq -1.88$$

We are 95% confident that the actual difference in mean gasoline mileage between the two types of gasoline is between –1.88 mpg and –4.42 mpg. The point estimate is –3.15 mpg.

Designating one group as group 1 and another group as group 2 is an arbitrary decision. If the two groups in Demonstration Problem 10.2 were reversed, the confidence interval would be the same, but the signs would be reversed and the inequalities would be switched. Thus the researcher must interpret the confidence interval in light of the sample information. For the confidence interval in Demonstration Problem 10.2, the population difference in mean mileage between regular and premium could be as much as –4.42 mpg. This result means that the premium gasoline could average 4.42 mpg more than regular gasoline. The other side of the interval shows that, on the basis of the sample information, the difference in favor of premium gasoline could be as little as 1.88 mpg.

If the confidence interval were being used to test the hypothesis that there is a difference in the average number of miles per gallon between regular and premium gasoline, the interval would tell us to reject the null hypothesis because the interval does *not* contain zero. When both ends of a confidence interval have the same sign, zero is not in the interval. In Demonstration Problem 10.2, the interval signs are both negative. We are 95% confident that the true difference in population means is negative. Hence, we are 95% confident that there is nonzero difference in means. For such a test, $\alpha = 1 - .95 = .05$. If the signs of the confidence interval for the difference of the sample means are different, the interval includes zero, and finding no significant difference in population means is possible.

Using the Computer to Test Hypotheses About the Difference in Two Population Means Using the *z* Test

Excel has the capability of testing hypotheses about two population means using a *z* test, but MINITAB does not. Figure 10.3 shows Excel output for the advertising manager and auditing manager wage problem. For *z* tests, Excel requires knowledge of the population variances. The standard output includes the sample means and **population** variances, the sample sizes, the hypothesized mean difference (which here, as in most cases, is zero), the observed *z* value, and the *p*-values and critical table *z* values for both a one-tailed and a two-tailed test. Note that the *p*-value for this two-tailed test is .0189, which is less than $\alpha = .05$ and thus indicates that the decision should be to reject the null hypothesis.

FIGURE 10.3

Excel Output for the Advertising Managers and Auditing Managers Wage Problem

		A	B	C
1		z-Test: Two Sample for Means		
2			Ad Mgr	Auditing Mgr
3		Mean	70.700	62.187
4		Known Variance	264.164	166.411
5		Observations	32	34
6		Hypothesized Mean Difference	0	
7		z	2.35	
8		P(Z<=z) one-tail	0.0094	
9		z Critical one-tail	1.64	
10		P(Z<=z) two-tail	0.0189	
11		z Critical two-tail	1.96	

10.1 PROBLEMS

10.1 **a.** Test the following hypotheses of the difference in population means by using the following data ($\alpha = .10$) and the eight-step process.

$$H_0: \mu_1 - \mu_2 = 0 \qquad H_a: \mu_1 - \mu_2 < 0$$

Sample 1	Sample 2
$\bar{x}_1 = 51.3$	$\bar{x}_2 = 53.2$
$\sigma_1^2 = 52$	$\sigma_2^2 = 60$
$n_1 = 31$	$n_2 = 32$

b. Use the critical value method to find the critical difference in the mean values required to reject the null hypothesis.

c. What is the p-value for this problem?

10.2 Use the following sample information to construct a 90% confidence interval for the difference in the two population means.

Sample 1	Sample 2
$n_1 = 32$	$n_2 = 31$
$\bar{x}_1 = 70.4$	$\bar{x}_2 = 68.7$
$\sigma_1 = 5.76$	$\sigma_2 = 6.1$

10.3 Examine the following data. Assume the variances for the two populations are 22.74 and 26.65 respectively.

a. Use the data to test the following hypotheses ($\alpha = .02$).

$$H_0: \mu_1 - \mu_2 = 0 \qquad H_a: \mu_1 - \mu_2 \neq 0$$

Sample 1			Sample 2		
90	88	80	78	85	82
88	87	91	90	80	76
81	84	84	77	75	79
88	90	91	82	83	88
89	95	97	80	90	74
88	83	94	81	75	76
81	83	88	83	88	77
87	87	93	86	90	75
88	84	83	80	80	74
95	93	97	89	84	79

b. Construct a 98% confidence interval to estimate the difference in population means using these data. How does your result validate the decision you reached in part (a)?

10.4 The Trade Show Bureau conducted a survey to determine why people go to trade shows. The respondents were asked to rate a series of reasons on a scale from 1 to 5, with 1 representing little importance and 5 representing great importance. One of the reasons suggested was general curiosity. The following responses for 50 people from the computers/electronics industry and 50 people from the food/beverage industry were recorded. Use these data and $\alpha = .01$ to determine whether there is a significant difference between people in these two industries on this question. Assume the variance for the computer/electronics population is 1.0188 and the variance for the food/beverager population is 0.9180.

Computers/Electronics					Food/Beverage				
1	2	1	3	2	3	3	2	4	3
0	3	3	2	1	4	5	2	4	3
3	3	1	2	2	3	2	3	2	3
3	2	2	2	2	4	3	3	3	3
1	2	3	2	1	2	4	2	3	3
1	1	3	3	2	2	4	4	4	4
2	1	4	1	4	3	5	3	3	2
2	3	0	1	0	2	0	2	2	5
3	3	2	2	3	4	3	3	2	3
2	1	0	2	3	4	3	3	3	2

10.5 Suppose you own a plumbing repair business and employ 15 plumbers. You are interested in estimating the difference in the average number of calls completed per day between two of the plumbers. A random sample of 40 days of plumber A's work results in a sample average of 5.3 calls, with a population variance of 1.99. A random sample of 37 days of plumber B's work results in a sample mean of 6.5 calls, with a population variance of 2.36. Use this information and a 95% level of confidence to estimate the difference in population mean daily efforts between plumber A and plumber B. Interpret the results. Is it possible that, for these populations of days, the average number of calls completed between plumber A and plumber B do not differ?

10.6 The Bureau of Labor Statistics shows that the average insurance cost to a company per employee per hour is $1.84 for managers and $1.99 for professional specialty workers. Suppose these figures were obtained from 35 managers and 41 professional specialty workers and that their respective population standard deviations are $.38 and $.51. Calculate a 98% confidence interval to estimate the difference in the mean hourly company expenditures for insurance for these two groups. What is the value of the point estimate? Test to determine whether there is a significant difference in the hourly rates employers pay for insurance between managers and professional specialty workers. Use a 2% level of significance.

10.7 A company's auditor believes the per diem cost in Nashville, Tennessee, rose significantly between 1994 and 2001. To test this belief, the auditor samples 51 business trips from the company's records for 1994; the sample average was $190 per day, with a population standard deviation of $18.50. The auditor selects a second random sample of 47 business trips from the company's records for 2001; the sample average was $198 per day, with a population standard deviation of $15.60. If he uses a risk of committing a Type I error of .01, does the auditor find that the per diem average expense in Nashville has gone up significantly?

10.8 Suppose a market analyst wants to determine the difference in the average price of a gallon of whole milk in Seattle and Atlanta. To do so, he takes a telephone survey of 31 randomly selected consumers in Seattle. He first asks whether they have purchased a gallon of milk during the past 2 weeks. If they say no, he continues to select consumers until he selects $n = 31$ people who say yes. If they say yes, he asks them how much they paid for the milk. The analyst undertakes a similar survey in Atlanta with 31 respondents. Using the resulting sample information that follows, compute a 99% confidence interval to estimate the difference in the mean price of a gallon of milk between the two cities. Assume the population variance for Seattle is 0.03, and the population variance for Atlanta is 0.015.

Seattle			Atlanta		
$2.55	$2.36	$2.43	$2.25	$2.40	$2.39
2.67	2.54	2.43	2.30	2.33	2.40
2.50	2.54	2.38	2.19	2.29	2.23
2.61	2.80	2.49	2.41	2.18	2.29

3.10	2.61	2.57	2.39	2.59	2.53
2.86	2.56	2.71	2.26	2.38	2.19
2.50	2.64	2.97	2.19	2.25	2.45
2.47	2.72	2.65	2.42	2.61	2.33
2.76	2.73	2.80	2.60	2.25	2.51
2.65	2.83	2.69	2.38	2.29	2.36
		2.71			2.44

10.9 Employee suggestions can provide useful and insightful ideas for management. Some companies solicit and receive employee suggestions more than others, and company culture influences the use of employee suggestions. Suppose a study is conducted to determine whether there is a significant difference in mean number of suggestions a month per employee between the Canon Corporation and the Pioneer Electronic Corporation. The study shows that the average number of suggestions per month is 5.8 at Canon and 5.0 at Pioneer. Suppose these figures were obtained from random samples of 36 and 45 employees, respectively. If the population standard deviations of suggestions per employee are 1.7 and 1.4 for Canon and Pioneer, respectively, is there a significant difference in the population means? Use $\alpha = .05$.

10.10 Two processes in a manufacturing line are performed manually: operation A and operation B. A random sample of 50 different assemblies using operation A shows that the sample average time per assembly is 8.05 minutes, with a population standard deviation of 1.36 minutes. A random sample of 38 different assemblies using operation B shows that the sample average time per assembly is 7.26 minutes, with a population standard deviation of 1.06 minutes. For $\alpha = .10$, is there enough evidence in these samples to declare that operation A takes significantly longer to perform than operation B?

10.2 HYPOTHESIS TESTING AND CONFIDENCE INTERVALS ABOUT THE DIFFERENCE IN TWO MEANS: INDEPENDENT SAMPLES AND POPULATION VARIANCES UNKNOWN

The techniques presented in Section 10.1 are for use whenever the population variances are known. On many occasions, statisticians test hypotheses or construct confidence intervals about the difference in two population means and the population variances are not known. If the population variances are not known, the z methodology is not appropriate. This section presents methodology for handling the situation when the population variances are unknown.

Hypothesis Testing

The hypothesis test presented in this section is a test that compares the means of two samples to determine whether there is a difference in the two population means from which the samples come. This technique is used whenever the population variances are unknown (and hence the sample variances must be used), and the samples are independent (not related in any way). *An assumption underlying this technique is that the measurement or characteristic being studied is normally distributed for both populations.* In Section 10.1, the difference in large sample means was analyzed by formula (10.1):

$$z = \frac{(\bar{x}_1 - \bar{x}_2) - (\mu_1 - \mu_2)}{\sqrt{\dfrac{\sigma_1^2}{n_1} + \dfrac{\sigma_2^2}{n_2}}}$$

If $\sigma_1^2 = \sigma_2^2$, formula (10.1) algebraically reduces to

$$z = \frac{(\bar{x}_1 - \bar{x}_2) - (\mu_1 - \mu_2)}{\sigma\sqrt{\dfrac{1}{n_1} + \dfrac{1}{n_2}}}$$

If σ is unknown, it can be estimated by *pooling* the two sample variances and computing a pooled sample standard deviation.

$$\sigma \approx s_p = \sqrt{\frac{s_1^2(n_1 - 1) + s_2^2(n_2 - 1)}{n_1 + n_2 - 2}}$$

s_p^2 is the weighted average of the two sample variances, s_1^2 and s_2^2. Substituting this expression for σ and changing z to t produces a formula to test the difference in means.

---

t FORMULA TO TEST THE
DIFFERENCE IN MEANS
ASSUMING σ_1^2, σ_2^2 (10.3)

$$t = \frac{(\bar{x}_1 - \bar{x}_2) - (\mu_1 - \mu_2)}{\sqrt{\dfrac{s_1^2(n_1 - 1) + s_2^2(n_2 - 1)}{n_1 + n_2 - 2}}\sqrt{\dfrac{1}{n_1} + \dfrac{1}{n_2}}}$$

$$df = n_1 + n_2 - 2$$

Formula (10.3) is constructed by assuming that the two population variances, σ_1^2 and σ_2^2, are equal. Thus, when using formula (10.3) to test hypotheses about the difference in two means for independent samples when the population variances are unknown, we must assume that the two samples come from populations in which the variances are essentially equal. If that is not possible, the following formula should be used.

---

t FORMULA TO TEST THE
DIFFERENCE IN MEANS (10.4)

$$t = \frac{(\bar{x}_1 - \bar{x}_2) - (\mu_1 - \mu_2)}{\sqrt{\dfrac{s_1^2}{n_1} + \dfrac{s_2^2}{n_2}}}$$

$$df = \frac{\left[\dfrac{s_1^2}{n_1} + \dfrac{s_2^2}{n_2}\right]^2}{\dfrac{\left(\dfrac{s_1^2}{n_1}\right)^2}{n_1 - 1} + \dfrac{\left(\dfrac{s_2^2}{n_2}\right)^2}{n_2 - 1}}$$

In formula (10.4), the population variances are not assumed to be equal. Because this formula requires a more complex degrees-of-freedom component, it may be unattractive to some users. Many statistical computer software packages offer the user a choice of the "pooled" formula or the "unpooled" formula. The "pooled" formula in the computer packages is formula (10.3), in which equal population variances are assumed. The "unpooled" formula is formula (10.4) and is used when population variances cannot be assumed to be equal. Again, in each of these formulas, the populations from which the two samples are drawn are assumed to be normally distributed for the phenomenon being measured.

At the Hernandez Manufacturing Company, an application of the test of the difference in small sample means arises. New employees are expected to attend a three-day seminar to learn about the company. At the end of the seminar, they are tested to measure their knowledge about the company. The traditional training method has been lecture and a question-and-answer session. Management decided to experiment with a different training procedure, which processes new employees in two days by using videocassettes and having no question-and-answer session. If this procedure works, it could save the company thousands of dollars over a period of several years. However, there is some concern about the effectiveness of the two-day method, and company managers would like to know whether there is any difference in the effectiveness of the two training methods.

To test the difference in the two methods, the managers randomly select one group of 15 newly hired employees to take the three-day seminar (method A) and a second group of 12 new employees for the two-day videocassette method (method B). Table 10.2 shows the test scores of the two groups. Using $\alpha = .05$, the managers want to determine whether there is a significant difference in the mean scores of the two groups. They assume that the scores for this test are normally distributed and that the population variances are approximately equal.

HYPOTHESIZE:

STEP 1. The hypotheses for this test follow.

$$H_0: \mu_1 - \mu_2 = 0$$

$$H_a: \mu_1 - \mu_2 \neq 0$$

TEST:

STEP 2. The statistical test to be used is formula (10.3).

STEP 3. The value of alpha is .05.

STEP 4. Because the hypotheses are = and $\neq$, this test is two-tailed. The degrees of freedom are 25 ($15 + 12 - 2 = 25$) and alpha is .05. The t table requires an alpha value for one tail only, and, because it is a two-tailed test, alpha is split from .05 to .025 to obtain the table t value: $t_{.025,25} = \pm 2.060$.

The null hypothesis will be rejected if the observed t value is less than -2.060 or greater than +2.060.

STEP 5. The sample data are given in Table 10.2. From these data, we can calculate the sample statistics. The sample means and variances follow.

Method A	Method B
$\bar{x}_1 = 47.73$	$\bar{x}_2 = 56.5$
$s_1^2 = 19.495$	$s_2^2 = 18.273$
$n_1 = 15$	$n_2 = 12$

STEP 6. The observed value of t is

$$t = \frac{(47.73 - 56.50) - (0)}{\sqrt{\dfrac{(19.495)(14) + (18.273)(11)}{(15 + 12 - 2)}} \sqrt{\dfrac{1}{15} + \dfrac{1}{12}}} = -5.20$$

ACTION:

STEP 7. Because the observed value, $t = -5.20$, is less than the lower critical table value, $t = -2.06$, the observed value of t is in the rejection region. The null hypothesis is rejected. There is a significant difference in the mean scores of the two tests.

BUSINESS IMPLICATIONS:

STEP 8. Figure 10.4 shows the critical areas, the observed t value, and the decision for this test. Note that the computed t value is -5.20, which is enough to cause the managers of the Hernandez Manufacturing Company to reject the null hypothesis. Their conclusion is that there is a significant difference in the effectiveness of the training methods. Upon examining the sample means, they realize that method B (the two-day videocassette method) actually produced an average score that was more than eight points higher than that for the group trained with method A.

In a test of this sort, which group is group 1 and which is group 2 is an arbitrary decision. If the two samples had been designated in reverse, the observed t value would have been $t = +5.20$ (same magnitude but different sign), and the decision would have been the same.

TABLE 10.2	**Training Method A**					**Training Method B**			
Test Scores for New Employees after Training	56	50	52	44	52	59	54	55	65
	47	47	53	45	48	52	57	64	53
	42	51	42	43	44	53	56	53	57

FIGURE 10.4

t Values for the Training
Methods Example

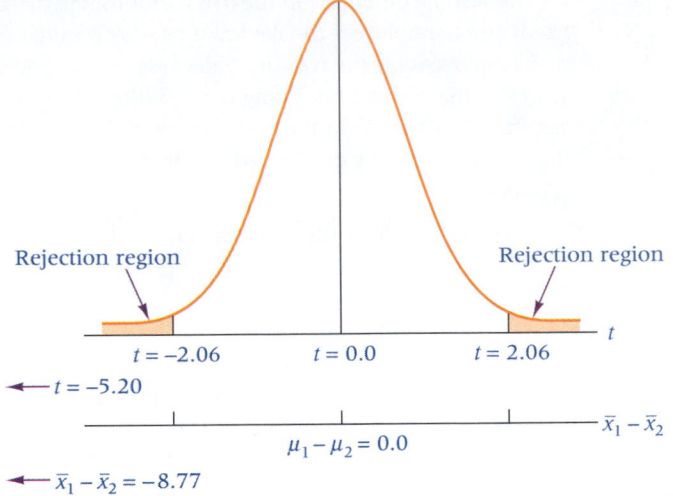

FIGURE 10.5

Excel and MINITAB Output for
the Training Methods Example

Excel Output

	A	B	C
1	z-Test: Two Sample Assuming Equal Variances		
2		Method A	Method B
3	Mean	47.73	56.50
4	Variance	19.495	18.273
5	Observations	15	12
6	Pooled Variance	18.957	
7	Hypothesized Mean Difference	0	
8	df	25	
9	t Stat	-5.20	
10	P(T<=t) one-tail	0.0000112	
11	t Critical one-tail	1.71	
12	P(T<=t) two-tail	0.0000223	
13	t Critical two-tail	2.06	

MINITAB Output

```
Two-sample T for Method A vs Method B

           N    Mean   StDev  SE Mean
Method A  15   47.73    4.42      1.1
Method B  12   56.50    4.27      1.2

Difference = mu Method A - mu Method B
Estimate for difference: -8.77
95% CI for difference: (-12.24, -5.29)
T-Test of difference = 0 (vs not =): t-Value = -5.20  p-Value =
0.000  DF = 25
Both use Pooled StDev = 4.35
```

Using the Computer to Test Hypotheses and Construct Confidence Intervals About the Difference in Two Population Means Using the *t* Test

Both Excel and MINITAB have the capability of analyzing *t* tests for the difference in two means. The two computer packages yield similar output. Figure 10.5 contains Excel and MINITAB output for the Hernandez Manufacturing Company training methods example. Notice that both outputs contain the same sample means, the degrees of freedom (df = 25), the observed *t* value −5.20 and the *p*-value (.0000223 on

Excel as two-tailed p and .0000 on MINITAB). This p-value can be compared directly with $\alpha = .05$ for decision-making purposes (reject the null hypothesis).

Each package offers other information. Excel displays the sample variances whereas MINITAB displays sample standard deviations. Excel displays the pooled variance whereas MINITAB displays the pooled standard deviation. Excel prints out p-values for both a one-tailed test and a two-tailed test, and the user must select the appropriate value for his or her test. Excel also prints out the critical t values for both one- and two-tailed tests. Notice that the critical t value for a two-tailed test (2.06) is the same as the critical t value obtained by using the t table (± 2.060). MINITAB yields the standard errors of the mean for each sample and the 95% confidence interval. MINITAB uses the same command for hypothesis testing and confidence interval estimation for the two-sample case. For this reason, MINITAB output for this type of problem always contains both the hypothesis-testing and confidence interval results.

DEMONSTRATION PROBLEM 10.3	Is there a difference in the way Chinese cultural values affect the purchasing strategies of industrial buyers in Taiwan and mainland China? A study by researchers at the National Chiao-Tung University in Taiwan attempted to determine whether there is a significant difference in the purchasing strategies of industrial buyers in the two countries based on the cultural dimension labeled "integration." Integration is being in harmony with one's self, family, and associates. For the study, 46 Taiwanese buyers and 26 mainland Chinese buyers were contacted and interviewed. Buyers were asked to respond to 35 items using a 9-point scale with possible answers ranging from no importance (1) to extreme importance (9). The resulting statistics for the two groups are shown in step 5. Using $\alpha = .01$, test to determine whether there is a significant difference between buyers of the two countries on integration. Assume that integration scores are normally distributed in the population.

Solution

HYPOTHESIZE:

STEP 1. If a two-tailed test is undertaken, the hypotheses and the table t value are as follows.

$$H_0: \mu_1 - \mu_2 = 0$$
$$H_a: \mu_1 - \mu_2 \neq 0$$

TEST:

STEP 2. The appropriate statistical test is formula (10.3).

STEP 3. The value of alpha is .01.

STEP 4. The sample sizes are 46 and 26. Thus, there are 70 degrees of freedom. With this figure and $\alpha/2 = .005$, critical table t values can be determined.

$$t_{.005,70} = 2.660$$

STEP 5. The sample data follow.

Integration

Taiwanese Buyers	Mainland Chinese Buyers
$n_1 = 46$	$n_2 = 26$
$\bar{x}_1 = 5.42$	$\bar{x}_2 = 5.04$
$s_1^2 = (.58)^2 = .3364$	$s_2^2 = (.49)^2 = .2401$
$df = n_1 + n_2 - 2 = 46 + 26 - 2 = 70$	

STEP 6. The observed t value is

$$t = \frac{(5.42 - 5.04) - (0)}{\sqrt{\dfrac{(.3364)(45) + (.2401)(25)}{46 + 26 - 2}}\sqrt{\dfrac{1}{46} + \dfrac{1}{26}}} = 2.82$$

ACTION:

STEP 7. Because the observed value of $t = 2.82$ is greater than the critical table value of $t = 2.66$, the decision is to reject the null hypothesis.

BUSINESS IMPLICATIONS

STEP 8. The Taiwan industrial buyers scored significantly higher than the mainland China industrial buyers on integration. Managers should keep in mind in dealing with Taiwanese buyers that they may be more likely to place worth on personal virtue and social hierarchy than do the mainland Chinese buyers.

The following graph shows the critical t values, the rejection regions, the observed t value, and the difference in the raw means.

TABLE 10.3

Conscientiousness Data on Phone Survey Respondents and Average Americans

Phone Survey Respondents	Average Americans
35.38	35.03
37.06	33.90
37.74	34.56
36.97	36.24
37.84	34.59
37.50	34.95
40.75	33.30
35.31	34.73
35.30	34.79
	37.83
$n_1 = 9$	$n_2 = 10$
$\bar{x}_1 = 37.09$	$\bar{x}_2 = 34.99$
$s_1 = 1.727$	$s_2 = 1.253$
df $= 9 + 10 - 2 = 17$	

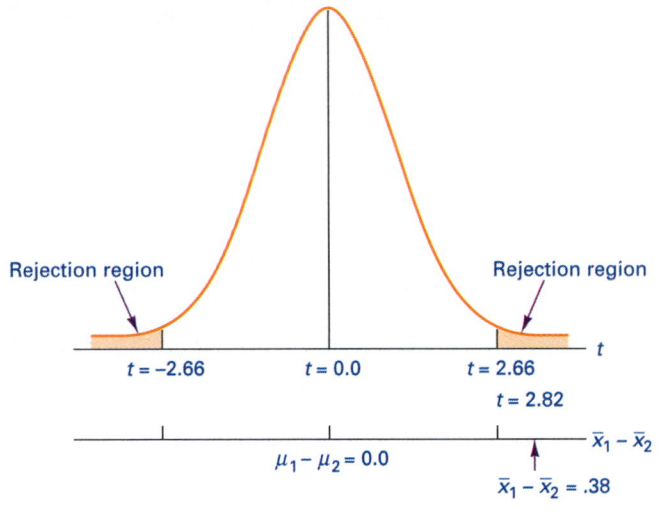

Confidence Intervals

Confidence interval formulas can be derived to estimate the difference in the population means for independent samples when the population variances are unknown. The focus in this section is only on confidence intervals when approximately equal population variances and normally distributed populations can be assumed.

CONFIDENCE INTERVAL TO ESTIMATE $\mu_1 - \mu_2$ ASSUMING THE POPULATION VARIANCES ARE UNKNOWN AND EQUAL (10.5)	$(\bar{x}_1 - \bar{x}_2) - t\sqrt{\dfrac{s_1^2(n_1-1) + s_2^2(n_2-1)}{n_1 + n_2 - 2}}\sqrt{\dfrac{1}{n_1} + \dfrac{1}{n_2}} \leq \mu_1 - \mu_2 \leq$ $(\bar{x}_1 - \bar{x}_2) + t\sqrt{\dfrac{s_1^2(n_1-1) + s_2^2(n_2-1)}{n_1 + n_2 - 2}}\sqrt{\dfrac{1}{n_1} + \dfrac{1}{n_2}}$ $\mathrm{df} = n_1 + n_2 - 2$

One group of researchers set out to determine whether there is a difference between "average Americans" and those who are "phone survey respondents."* Their study was based on a well-known personality survey that attempted to assess the personality profile of both average Americans and phone survey respondents. Suppose they sampled nine phone survey respondents and 10 average Americans in this survey and obtained the results on one personality factor, conscientiousness, which are displayed in Table 10.3. Assume that conscientiousness scores are normally distributed in the population.

---

*Source: Data adapted from David Whitlark and Michael Geurts, "Phone Surveys: How Well Do Respondents Represent Average Americans?" *Marketing Research* (Fall 1998), pp. 13–17. Note that the results on this portion of the actual study are about the same as those shown here except that in the actual study the sample sizes were in the 500–600 range.

FIGURE 10.6	**TWO-SAMPLE T FOR PHONE SURVEY RESPONDENTS VS AVERAGE AMERICANS**		

MINITAB Output for the Phone Survey Respondent and Average American Example

```
                N    Mean   StDev   SE Mean
Phone Su    9    37.09   1.73    0.58
Average    10    34.99   1.25    0.40
Difference = mu Phone Survey Respondents - mu Average Americans
Estimate for difference: 2.102
99% CI for difference: (0.112, 4.093)
T-Test of difference = 0 (vs not =): T-Value = 3.06
P-Value = 0.007   DF = 17
Both use Pooled StDev = 1.49
```

The table t value for a 99% level of confidence and 17 degrees of freedom is $t_{.005,17} = 2.898$. The confidence interval is

$$(37.09 - 34.99) \pm 2.898\sqrt{\frac{(1.727)^2(8) + (1.253)^2(9)}{9 + 10 - 2}}\sqrt{\frac{1}{9} + \frac{1}{10}}$$

$$2.10 \pm 1.99$$
$$0.11 \leq \mu_1 - \mu_2 \leq 4.09$$

The researchers are 99% confident that the true difference in population mean personality scores for conscientiousness between phone survey respondents and average Americans is between .11 and 4.09. Zero is not in this interval, so they can conclude that there is a significant difference in the average scores of the two groups. Higher scores indicate more conscientiousness. Therefore, it is possible to conclude from Table 10.3 and this confidence interval that phone survey respondents are significantly more conscientious than average Americans. These results indicate that researchers should be careful in using phone survey results to reach conclusions about average Americans.

Figure 10.6 contains MINITAB output for this problem. Note that the MINITAB output includes both the confidence interval (.112 to 4.093) and the observed t value (3.06) for hypothesis testing. Because the p-value is .007, which is less than .01, the MINITAB hypothesis-testing information validates the conclusion reached that there is a significant difference in the scores of the two groups.

DEMONSTRATION PROBLEM 10.4

A coffee manufacturer is interested in estimating the difference in the average daily coffee consumption of regular-coffee drinkers and decaffeinated-coffee drinkers. Its researcher randomly selects 13 regular-coffee drinkers and asks how many cups of coffee per day they drink. He randomly locates 15 decaffeinated-coffee drinkers and asks how many cups of coffee per day they drink. The average for the regular-coffee drinkers is 4.35 cups, with a standard deviation of 1.20 cups. The average for the decaffeinated-coffee drinkers is 6.84 cups, with a standard deviation of 1.42 cups. The researcher assumes, for each population, that the daily consumption is normally distributed, and he constructs a 95% confidence interval to estimate the difference in the averages of the two populations.

Solution

The table t value for this problem is $t_{.025,26} = 2.056$. The confidence interval estimate is

$$(4.35 - 6.84) \pm 2.056\sqrt{\frac{(1.20)^2(12) + (1.42)^2(14)}{13 + 15 - 2}}\sqrt{\frac{1}{13} + \frac{1}{15}}$$

$$-2.49 \pm 1.03$$
$$-3.52 \leq \mu_1 - \mu_2 \leq -1.46$$

The researcher is 95% confident that the difference in population average daily consumption of cups of coffee between regular- and decaffeinated-coffee drinkers is between 1.46 cups and 3.52 cups. The point estimate for the difference in population means is 2.49 cups, with an error of 1.03 cups.

Ethical Differences Between Men and Women

Is there a difference between men and women in making ethical managerial decisions? One study attempted to answer this question by studying 164 managers of a large financial conglomerate. A questionnaire was constructed using vignettes (brief, focused cases) to depict four ethical questions under two different scenarios. Vignettes dealt with (1) sale of an unsafe product, (2) bribery, (3) product misrepresentation, and (4) industrial espionage. These vignettes were to be considered under the scenarios of (a) enhancing the firm's profit position and (b) the individual's own economic gain. The questionnaire was structured to produce a score for each respondent on each ethical question without regard to scenario and a score for each respondent on each ethical question with regard to each scenario. The null hypothesis that there is no significant difference in the mean ethical scores of men and women was tested for each question using a t test for independent samples.

The results were mixed. In considering the responses to the four vignettes without regard to either of the two scenarios, there was a significant difference between men and women on the sale of an unsafe product at ($\alpha = .01$). On this question, women scored significantly higher (more ethical) than men, indicating that women are less likely to sell an unsafe product. On the questions of product misrepresentation and industrial espionage, women scored significantly higher on both ($\alpha = .10$). There was no significant difference between men and women on the question of bribery.

The results were somewhat different when the two scenarios were considered (firm profit position and personal economic gain). On the question of selling an unsafe product, women were significantly more ethical ($\alpha = .01$) when considered in light of enhancing the firm's profit position and significantly more ethical ($\alpha = .05$) when considering one's personal economic gain. On the question of bribery, there was no significant difference in the ethics scores of men and women in light of enhancing the firm's profit position but women were significantly more ethical ($\alpha = .10$) when considering one's personal economic gain. On the question of product misrepresentation, there was no significant difference between men and women when considering one's personal economic gain but women were significantly more ethical than men in light of enhancing the firm's profit position ($\alpha = .10$). On the question of industrial espionage, women were significantly more ethical than men ($\alpha = .10$) in light of enhancing the firm's profit position, and women were also significantly more ethical than men ($\alpha = .01$) when considering one's personal gain.

This study used two-sample hypothesis testing in an effort to determine whether there is a difference between men and women on ethical management issues. The results here can assist decision makers in assigning managers to various tasks that involve any of these four ethical questions. Interesting questions can be studied about why women might be more ethical than men in some managerial situations and what might be done to foster stronger ethics among men.

Source: Adapted from James J. Hoffman, "Are Women Really More Ethical Than Men? Maybe It Depends on the Situation," *Journal of Managerial Issues,* Vol. X, no. 1 (Spring 1998), pp. 60–73.

10.2 PROBLEMS

10.11 Use the data given and the eight-step process to test the following hypotheses.

$$H_0: \mu_1 - \mu_2 = 0 \qquad H_a: \mu_1 - \mu_2 < 0$$

Sample 1	Sample 2
$n_1 = 8$	$n_2 = 11$
$\bar{x}_1 = 24.56$	$\bar{x}_2 = 26.42$
$s_1^2 = 12.4$	$s_2^2 = 15.8$

Use a 1% level of significance, and assume that x is normally distributed.

10.12 a. Use the following data and $\alpha = .10$ to test the stated hypotheses. Assume x is normally distributed in the populations and the variances of the populations are approximately equal.

$$H_0: \mu_1 - \mu_2 = 0 \qquad H_a: \mu_1 - \mu_2 \neq 0$$

Sample 1	Sample 2
$n_1 = 20$	$n_2 = 20$
$\bar{x}_1 = 118$	$\bar{x}_2 = 113$
$s_1 = 23.9$	$s_2 = 21.6$

b. Use these data to construct a 90% confidence interval to estimate $\mu_1 - \mu_2$.

10.13 Suppose that for years the mean of population 1 has been accepted to be the same as the mean of population 2, but that now population 1 is believed to have a greater mean than population 2. Letting $\alpha = .05$ and assuming the populations have equal variances and x is approximately normally distributed, use the following data to test this belief.

Sample 1		Sample 2	
43.6	45.7	40.1	36.4
44.0	49.1	42.2	42.3
45.2	45.6	43.1	38.8
40.8	46.5	37.5	43.3
48.3	45.0	41.0	40.2

10.14 a. Suppose you want to determine whether the average values for populations 1 and 2 are different, and you randomly gather the following data.

Sample 1						Sample 2					
2	10	7	8	2	5	10	12	8	7	9	11
9	1	8	0	2	8	9	8	9	10	11	10
11	2	4	5	3	9	11	10	7	8	10	10

Test your conjecture, using a probability of committing a Type I error of .01. Assume the population variances are the same and x is normally distributed in the populations.

b. Use these data to construct a 98% confidence interval for the difference in the two population means.

10.15 Suppose a realtor is interested in comparing the asking prices of midrange homes in Peoria, Illinois, and Evansville, Indiana. The realtor conducts a small telephone survey in the two cities, asking the prices of midrange homes. A random sample of 21 listings in Peoria resulted in a sample average price of $86,900, with a standard deviation of $2,300. A random sample of 26 listings in Evansville resulted in a sample average price of $84,000, with a standard deviation of $1,750. The realtor assumes prices of midrange homes are normally distributed and the variance in prices in the two cities is about the same. What would he obtain for a 90% confidence interval for the difference in mean prices of midrange homes between Peoria and Evansville?

10.16 Test whether there is any difference in the mean prices of midrange homes of the two cities in Problem 10.15 for $\alpha = .05$.

10.17 Based on an indication that mean daily car rental rates may be higher for Boston than for Dallas, a survey of eight car rental companies in Boston is taken and the sample mean car rental rate is $47, with a standard deviation of $3. Further, suppose a survey of nine car rental companies in Dallas results in a sample mean of $44 and a standard deviation of $3. Use $\alpha = .01$ to test to determine whether the average daily car rental rates in Boston are significantly higher than those in Dallas. Assume car rental rates are normally distributed and the population variances are equal.

10.18 What is the difference in average daily hotel room rates between Minneapolis and New Orleans? Suppose we want to estimate this difference by taking hotel rate samples from each city and using a 98% confidence level. The data for such a study follow. Use these data to produce a point estimate for the mean difference in the hotel rates for the two cities. Assume the population variances are approximately equal and hotel rates in any given city are normally distributed.

Minneapolis	New Orleans
$n_M = 22$	$n_{NO} = 20$
$\bar{x}_M = \$112$	$\bar{x}_{NO} = \$122$
$s_M = \$11$	$s_{NO} = \$12$

10.19 A study was made to compare the costs of supporting a family of four Americans for a year in different foreign cities. The lifestyle of living in the United States on an annual income of $75,000 was the standard against which living in foreign cities was compared. A comparable living standard in Toronto and Mexico City was attained for about $64,000. Suppose an executive wants to determine whether there is any difference in the average annual cost of supporting her family of four in the manner to which they are accustomed between Toronto and Mexico City. She uses the following data, randomly gathered from 11 families in each city, and an alpha of .01 to test this difference. She assumes the annual cost is normally distributed and the population variances are equal. What does the executive find?

Toronto	Mexico City
$69,000	$65,000
64,500	64,000
67,500	66,000
64,500	64,900
66,700	62,000
68,000	60,500
65,000	62,500
69,000	63,000
71,000	64,500
68,500	63,500
67,500	62,400

10.20 Use the data in Problem 10.19 to construct a 95% confidence interval to estimate the difference in average annual costs between the two cities.

10.3 STATISTICAL INFERENCES FOR TWO RELATED POPULATIONS

In the preceding section, hypotheses were tested and confidence intervals constructed about the difference in two population means when the samples are independent. In this section, a method is presented to analyze **dependent samples** or related samples. Some researchers refer to this test as the **matched-pairs** test. Others call it the *t test for related measures* or the *correlated t test.*

What are some types of situations in which the two samples being studied are related or dependent? Let's begin with the before-and-after study. Sometimes as an experimental control mechanism, the same person or object is measured both before and after a treatment. Certainly, the after measurement is *not* independent of the before measurement because the measurements are taken on the same person or object in both cases. Table 10.4 gives data from a hypothetical study in which people were asked to rate a company before and after one week of viewing a 4-minute videocassette of the company twice a day. The before scores are one sample and the after scores are a second sample, but each pair of scores is related because the two measurements apply to the same person. The before scores and the after scores are not likely to vary from each other as much as scores gathered from independent samples because individuals bring their biases about businesses and the company to the study. These individual biases affect both the before scores and the after scores in the same way because each pair of scores is measured on the same person.

Other examples of related measures samples include studies in which twins, siblings, or spouses are matched and placed in two different groups. For example, a fashion merchandiser might be interested in comparing men's and women's perceptions of women's clothing. If the men and women selected for the study are spouses or siblings, a built-in relatedness to the measurements of the two groups in the study is likely. Their scores are more apt to be alike or related than those of randomly chosen independent groups of men and women because of similar backgrounds or tastes.

TABLE 10.4

Rating of a Company (on a Scale from 0 to 50)

Individual	Before	After
1	32	39
2	11	15
3	21	35
4	17	13
5	30	41
6	38	39
7	14	22

Hypothesis Testing

To ensure the use of the proper hypothesis-testing techniques, the researcher must determine whether the two samples being studied are dependent or independent. The approach to analyzing two *related* samples is different from the techniques used to analyze independent samples. Use of the techniques in Section 10.2 to analyze related group data can result in a loss of power and an increase in Type II errors.

The matched-pairs test for related samples requires that the two samples be the same size and that the individual related scores be matched. Formula (10.6) is used to test hypotheses about dependent populations.

t FORMULA TO TEST THE **DIFFERENCE IN TWO DEPENDENT POPULATIONS** **(10.6)**	$$t = \frac{\bar{d} - D}{\frac{s_d}{\sqrt{n}}}$$ $$\text{df} = n - 1$$ where n = number of pairs d = sample difference in pairs D = mean population difference s_d = standard deviation of sample difference $\bar{d}$ = mean sample difference

This *t* test for dependent measures uses the sample difference, d, between individual matched sample values as the basic measurement of analysis instead of individual sample values. Analysis of the d values effectively converts the problem from a two-sample problem to a single sample of differences, which is an adaptation of the single-sample means formula. This test utilizes the sample mean of differences,, and the standard deviation of differences, s_d, which can be computed by using formulas (10.7) and (10.8).

FORMULAS FOR $\bar{d}$ **AND** s_d **(10.7 AND 10.8)**	$$\bar{d} = \frac{\Sigma d}{n}$$ $$s_d = \sqrt{\frac{\Sigma(d - \bar{d})^2}{n-1}} = \sqrt{\frac{\Sigma d^2 - \frac{(\Sigma d)^2}{n}}{n-1}}$$

An assumption for this test is that the differences of the two populations are normally distributed.

Analyzing data by this method involves calculating a *t* value with formula (10.6) and comparing it with a critical *t* value obtained from the table. The critical *t* value is obtained from the *t* distribution table in the usual way, with the exception that, in the degrees of freedom $(n - 1)$, n is the number of matched pairs of scores.

Suppose a stock market investor is interested in determining whether there is a significant difference in the P/E (price to earnings) ratio for companies from one year to the next. In an effort to study this question, the investor randomly samples nine companies from the *Handbook of Common Stocks* and records the P/E ratios for each of these companies at the end of 2003 and at the end of 2004. The data are shown in Table 10.5.

These data are related data because each P/E value for 2003 has a corresponding 2004 measurement on the same company. Because no prior information indicates whether P/E ratios have gone up or down, the hypothesis tested is two-tailed. Assume $\alpha = .01$. Assume that differences in P/E ratios are normally distributed in the population. **HYPOTHESIZE:**

STEP 1.

$$H_0: \ D = 0$$
$$H_a: \ D \neq 0$$

TEST:

STEP 2. The appropriate statistical test is

$$t = \frac{\bar{d} - D}{\frac{s_d}{\sqrt{n}}}$$

STEP 3. $\alpha = .01$

STEP 4. Because $\alpha = .01$ and this test is two-tailed, $\alpha/2 = .005$ is used to obtain the table t value. With nine pairs of data, $n = 9$, df $= n - 1 = 8$. The table t value is $t_{.005,8} = \pm 3.355$. If the observed test statistic is greater than 3.355 or less than -3.355, the null hypothesis will be rejected.

STEP 5. The sample data are given in Table 10.5.

STEP 6. Table 10.6 shows the calculations to obtain the observed value of the test statistic, which is $t = -0.70$.

ACTION:

STEP 7. Because the observed t value is greater than the critical table t value in the lower tail ($t = -0.70 > t = -3.355$), it is in the nonrejection region.

BUSINESS IMPLICATIONS:

STEP 8. There is not enough evidence from the data to declare a significant difference in the average P/E ratio between 2003 and 2004. The graph in Figure 10.7 depicts the rejection regions, the critical values of t, and the observed value of t for this example.

TABLE 10.5	Company	2003 P/E Ratio	2004 P/E Ratio
P/E Ratios for Nine Randomly Selected Companies	1	8.9	12.7
	2	38.1	45.4
	3	43.0	10.0
	4	34.0	27.2
	5	34.5	22.8
	6	15.2	24.1
	7	20.3	32.3
	8	19.9	40.1
	9	61.9	106.5

TABLE 10.6	Company	2003 P/E	2004 P/E	d
Analysis of P/E Ratio Data	1	8.9	12.7	–3.8
	2	38.1	45.4	–7.3
	3	43.0	10.0	33.0
	4	34.0	27.2	6.8
	5	34.5	22.8	11.7
	6	15.2	24.1	–8.9
	7	20.3	32.3	–12.0
	8	19.9	40.1	–20.2
	9	61.9	106.5	–44.6

$$\bar{d} = -5.033, \quad s_d = 21.599, \quad n = 9$$

$$\text{Observed } t = \frac{-5.033 - 0}{\frac{21.599}{\sqrt{9}}} = -0.70$$

Using the Computer to Make Statistical Inferences About Two Related Populations

Both MINITAB and Excel can be used to make statistical inferences about two related populations. Figure 10.8 shows MINITAB and Excel output for the P/E Ratio problem. The MINITAB output contains summary data for each sample and the difference of the two samples along with a confidence interval of the difference, a restating of the tested hypotheses, the observed t value, and the p-value. Because the p-value (0.504) is greater than the value of alpha (.01), the decision is to fail to reject the null hypothesis.

FIGURE 10.7

Graphical Depiction of P/E Ratio Analysis

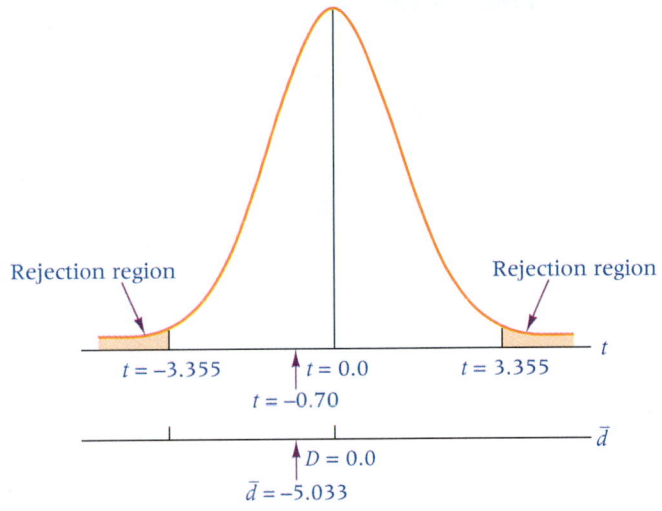

FIGURE 10.8

MINITAB and Excel Output for the P/E Ratio Example

MINITAB Output

PAIRED T FOR 2001 P/E - 2002 P/E

	N	Mean	StDev	SE Mean
2001 P/E	9	30.64	16.37	5.46
2002 P/E	9	35.68	28.94	9.65
Difference	9	-5.03	21.60	7.20

99% CI for mean difference: (-29.19, 19.13)

T-Test of mean difference = 0 (vs not = 0):
T-Value = -0.70 P-Value = 0.504

Excel Output

	A	B	C
1	t-Test: Paired Two Sample for Means		
2		2001 P/E	2002 P/E
3	Mean	30.64	35.68
4	Variance	268.135	837.544
5	Observations	9	9
6	Pearson Correlation	0.674357	
7	Hypothesized Mean Difference	0	
8	df	8	
9	t Stat	-0.70	
10	P(T<=t) one-tail	0.252	
11	t Critical one-tail	2.90	
12	P(T<=t) two-tail	0.504	
13	t Critical two-tail	3.36	

The Excel output contains the hypothesized mean difference, the observed t value (-0.70), and the critical t values and their associated p-values for both a one-tailed and a two-tailed test. The p-value for a two-tailed test is the same as that produced by MINITAB, indicating that the decision is to fail to reject the null hypothesis.

DEMONSTRATION PROBLEM 10.5

Let us revisit the hypothetical study discussed earlier in the section in which consumers are asked to rate a company both before and after viewing a video on the company twice a day for a week. The data from Table 10.4 are displayed again here. Use an alpha of .05 to test to determine whether there is a significant increase in the ratings of the company after the one-week video treatment. Assume that differences in ratings are normally distributed in the population.

Individual	Before	After
1	32	39
2	11	15
3	21	35
4	17	13
5	30	41
6	38	39
7	14	22

Solution

Because the same individuals are being used in a before-and-after study, it is a related measures study. The desired effect is to increase ratings, which means the hypothesis test is one-tailed.

HYPOTHESIZE:

STEP 1.

$$H_0: D = 0$$
$$H_a: D < 0$$

Because the researchers want to "prove" that the ratings increase from Before to After and because the difference is computed by subtracting After ratings from the Before ratings, the desired alternative hypothesis is $D < 0$.

TEST:

STEP 2. The appropriate test statistic is formula (10.6).

STEP 3. The Type I error rate is .05.

STEP 4. The degrees of freedom are $n - 1 = 7 - 1 = 6$. For $\alpha = .05$, the table t value is $t_{.05,6} = -1.943$. The decision rule is to reject the null hypothesis if the observed value is less than -1.943.

STEP 5. The sample data and some calculations follow.

Individual	Before	After	d
1	32	39	-7
2	11	15	-4
3	21	35	-14
4	17	13	4
5	30	41	-11
6	38	39	-1
7	14	22	-8

$\bar{d} = -5.857 \quad s_d = 6.0945$

STEP 6. The observed t value is:

$$t = \frac{-5.857 - 0}{\frac{6.0945}{\sqrt{7}}} = -2.54$$

ACTION:

STEP 7. Because the observed value of –2.54 is less than the critical, table value of –1.943, the decision is to reject the null hypothesis.

BUSINESS IMPLICATIONS:

STEP 8. There is enough evidence to conclude that, on average, the ratings have increased significantly. This result might be used by managers to support a decision to continue using the videos or to expand the use of such videos in an effort to increase public support for their company.

The following graph depicts the observed value, the rejection region, and the critical t value for the problem.

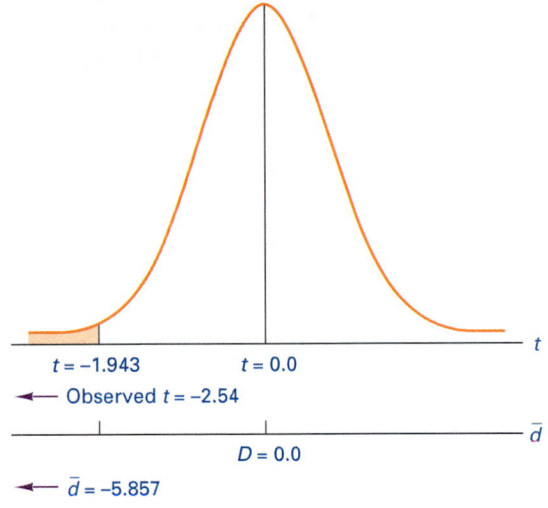

Confidence Intervals

Sometimes a researcher is interested in estimating the mean difference in two populations for related samples. A confidence interval for D, the mean population difference of two related samples, can be constructed by algebraically rearranging formula (10.6), which was used to test hypotheses about D. Again the assumption is that for small sample sizes the population differences are normally distributed.

CONFIDENCE INTERVAL FORMULA TO ESTIMATE THE DIFFERENCE IN RELATED POPULATIONS, D (10.9)	$$\bar{d} - t\frac{s_d}{\sqrt{n}} \leq D \leq \bar{d} + t\frac{s_d}{\sqrt{n}}$$ $$df = n - 1$$

The following housing industry example demonstrates the application of formula (10.9). The sale of new houses apparently fluctuates seasonally. Superimposed on the seasonality are economic and business cycles that also influence the sale of new houses. In certain parts of the country, new-house sales increase in the spring and early summer and drop off in the fall. Suppose a national real estate association wants to estimate the average difference in the number of new-house sales per company in Indianapolis between 2003 and 2004. To do so, the association randomly selects 18 real estate firms in the Indianapolis area and obtains their new-house sales figures for May 2003 and May 2004. The numbers of sales per company are shown in Table 10.7. Using these data, the association's analyst estimates the average difference in the number of sales per real estate company in Indianapolis for May 2003 and May 2004 and constructs a 99% confidence interval. The analyst assumes that differences in sales are normally distributed in the population.

TABLE 10.7		
Number of New House Sales in Indianapolis		
Realtor	**May 2003**	**May 2004**
1	8	11
2	19	30
3	5	6
4	9	13
5	3	5
6	0	4
7	13	15
8	11	17
9	9	12
10	5	12
11	8	6
12	2	5
13	11	10
14	14	22
15	7	8
16	12	15
17	6	12
18	10	10

TABLE 10.8			
Differences in Number of New House Sales, 2003–2004			
Realtor	**May 2003**	**May 2004**	**d**
1	8	11	-3
2	19	30	-11
3	5	6	-1
4	9	13	-4
5	3	5	-2
6	0	4	-4
7	13	15	-2
8	11	17	-6
9	9	12	-3
10	5	12	-7
11	8	6	+2
12	2	5	-3
13	11	10	+1
14	14	22	-8
15	7	8	-1
16	12	15	-3
17	6	12	-6
18	10	10	0
	$\bar{d} = -3.39$	and	$s_d = 3.27$

The number of pairs, n, is 18, and the degrees of freedom are 17. For a 99% level of confidence and these degrees of freedom, the table t value is $t_{.005,17} = 2.898$. The values for $\bar{d}$, and s_d are shown in Table 10.8.

The point estimate of the difference is $\bar{d}$ = -3.39. The 99% confidence interval is

$$\bar{d} - t\frac{s_d}{\sqrt{n}} \leq D \leq \bar{d} + t\frac{s_d}{\sqrt{n}}$$

$$-3.39 - 2.898\frac{3.27}{\sqrt{18}} \leq D \leq -3.39 + 2.898\frac{3.27}{\sqrt{18}}$$

$$-3.39 - 2.23 \leq D \leq -3.39 + 2.23$$

$$-5.62 = D = -1.16$$

The analyst estimates with a 99% level of confidence that the average difference in new-house sales for a real estate company in Indianapolis between 2003 and 2004 in May is somewhere between −5.62 and −1.16 houses. Because 2004 sales were subtracted from 2003 sales, the minus signs indicate more sales in 2004 than in 2003. Note that both ends of the confidence interval contain negatives. This result means that the analyst can be 99% confident that zero difference is not the average difference. If the analyst were using this confidence interval to test the hypothesis that there is no significant mean difference in average new-house sales per company in Indianapolis between May 2003 and May 2004, the null hypothesis would be rejected for $\alpha = .01$. The point estimate for this example is −3.39 houses, with an error of 2.23 houses. Figure 10.9 is the MINITAB computer output for the confidence interval.

FIGURE 10.9

MINITAB Output for the New House Sales Example

```
Paired T for May 2003 - May 2004

              N    Mean    StDev   SE Mean
May 2001     18    8.44    4.64    1.09
May 2002     18   11.83    6.54    1.54
Difference   18  -3.389    3.274   0.772
99% CI for mean difference: (-5.626, -1.152)
T-Test of mean difference = 0 (vs not = 0):
T-Value = -4.39 P-Value = 0.000
```

10.3 PROBLEMS

10.21 Use the data given and a 1% level of significance to test the following hypotheses. Assume the differences are normally distributed in the population.

$$H_0: D = 0 \qquad H_a: D > 0$$

Pair	Sample 1	Sample 2
1	38	22
2	27	28
3	30	21
4	41	38
5	36	38
6	38	26
7	33	19
8	35	31
9	44	35

10.22 Use the data given to test the following hypotheses ($\alpha = .05$). Assume the differences are normally distributed in the population.

$$H_0: D = 0 \qquad H_a: D \neq 0$$

Individual	Before	After
1	107	102
2	99	98
3	110	100
4	113	108
5	96	89
6	98	101
7	100	99
8	102	102
9	107	105
10	109	110
11	104	102
12	99	96
13	101	100

10.23 Construct a 98% confidence interval to estimate D from the following sample information. Assume the differences are normally distributed in the population.

$$\bar{d} = 40.56, \ s_d = 26.58, \ n = 22$$

10.24 Construct a 90% confidence interval to estimate D from the following sample information. Assume the differences are normally distributed in the population.

Client	Before	After
1	32	40
2	28	25
3	35	36
4	32	32
5	26	29
6	25	31
7	37	39
8	16	30
9	35	31

10.25 Because of uncertainty in real estate markets, many homeowners are considering remodeling and constructing additions rather than selling. Probably the most expensive room in the house to remodel is the kitchen, with an average cost of about $23,400. In terms of resale value, is remodeling the kitchen worth the cost? The following cost and resale figures are published by *Remodeling* magazine for 11 cities. Use these data to construct a 99% confidence interval for the difference between cost and added resale value of kitchen remodeling. Assume the differences are normally distributed in the population.

City	Cost	Resale
Atlanta	$20,427	$25,163
Boston	27,255	24,625
Des Moines	22,115	12,600
Kansas City, MO	23,256	24,588
Louisville	21,887	19,267
Portland, OR	24,255	20,150
Raleigh-Durham	19,852	22,500
Reno	23,624	16,667
Ridgewood, NJ	25,885	26,875
San Francisco	28,999	35,333
Tulsa	20,836	16,292

10.26 The vice president of marketing brought to the attention of sales managers that most of the company's manufacturer representatives contacted clients and maintained client relationships in a disorganized, haphazard way. The sales managers brought the reps in for a three-day seminar and training session on how to use an organizer to schedule visits and recall pertinent information about each client more effectively. Sales reps were taught how to schedule visits most efficiently to maximize their efforts. Sales managers were given data on the number of site visits by sales reps on a randomly selected day both before and after the seminar. Use the following data to test whether significantly more site visits were made after the seminar ($\alpha = .05$). Assume the differences in the number of site visits are normally distributed.

Rep	Before	After
1	2	4
2	4	5
3	1	3
4	3	3
5	4	3
6	2	5
7	2	6
8	3	4
9	1	5

10.27 Eleven employees were put under the care of the company nurse because of high cholesterol readings. The nurse lectured them on the dangers of this condition and put them on a new diet. Shown are the cholesterol readings of the 11 employees both before the new diet and one month after use of the diet began. Construct a 98% confidence interval to estimate the population mean difference of cholesterol readings for people who are involved in this program. Assume differences in cholesterol readings are normally distributed in the population.

Employee	Before	After
1	255	197
2	230	225
3	290	215
4	242	215
5	300	240
6	250	235
7	215	190
8	230	240
9	225	200
10	219	203
11	236	223

10.28 Lawrence and Glover published the results of a study in the *Journal of Managerial Issues* in which they examined the effects of accounting firm mergers on auditing delay. Auditing delay is the time between a company's fiscal year-end and the date of the auditor's report. The hypothesis is that with the efficiencies gained through mergers the length of the audit delay would decrease. Suppose to test their hypothesis, they examined the audit delays on 27 clients of Big Six firms from both before and after the Big Six firm merger (a span of 5 years). Suppose further that the mean difference in audit delay for these clients from before merger to after merger was a decrease in 3.71 days and the standard deviation of difference was 5 days. Use these data and $\alpha = .01$ to test whether the audit delays after the merger were significantly lower than before the merger. Assume that the differences in auditing delay are normally distributed in the population.

10.29 A nationally known supermarket decided to promote its own brand of soft drinks on TV for two weeks. Before the ad campaign, the company randomly selected 21 of its stores across the United States to be part of a study to measure the campaign's effectiveness. During a specified half-hour period on a certain Monday morning, all the stores in the sample counted the number of cans of its own brand of soft drink sold. After the campaign, a similar count was made. The average difference was an increase of 75 cans, with a standard deviation of difference of 30 cans. Using this information, construct a 90% confidence interval to estimate the population average difference in soft drink sales for this company's brand before and after the ad campaign. Assume the differences in soft drink sales for the company's brand are normally distributed in the population.

10.30 Is there a significant difference in the gasoline mileage of a car for regular unleaded and premium unleaded? To test this question, a researcher randomly selected 15 drivers for a study. They were to drive their cars for one month on regular unleaded and for one month on premium unleaded gasoline. The participants drove their own cars for this experiment. The average sample difference was 2.85 miles per gallon in favor of the premium unleaded, and the sample standard deviation of difference was 1.9 miles per gallon. For $\alpha = .01$, does the test show enough evidence for the researcher to conclude that there is a significant difference in mileage between regular unleaded and premium unleaded gasoline? Assume the differences in gasoline mileage figures are normally distributed in the population.

10.4 STATISTICAL INFERENCES ABOUT TWO POPULATION PROPORTIONS, $p_1 - p_2$

Sometimes a researcher wishes to make inferences about the difference in two population proportions. This type of analysis has many applications in business, such as comparing the market share of a product for two different markets, studying the difference in the proportion of female customers in two different geographic regions, or comparing the proportion of defective products from one period to another. In making inferences about the difference in two population proportions, the statistic normally used is the difference in the sample proportions: $\hat{p}_1 - \hat{p}_2$. This statistic is computed by taking random samples and determining $\hat{p}$ for each sample for a given characteristic, then calculating the difference in these sample proportions.

The central limit theorem states that for large samples (each of $n_1 \cdot \hat{p}_1$, $n_1 \cdot \hat{q}_1$, $n_2 \cdot \hat{p}_2$, and $n_2 \cdot \hat{q}_2 > 5$, where $\hat{q} = 1 - \hat{p}$), the difference in sample proportions is normally distributed with a mean difference of

$$\mu_{\hat{p}_1 - \hat{p}_2} = p_1 - p_2$$

and a standard deviation of the difference of sample proportions of

$$\sigma_{\hat{p}_1 - \hat{p}_2} = \sqrt{\frac{p_1 \cdot q_1}{n_1} + \frac{p_2 \cdot q_2}{n_2}}$$

From this information, a z formula for the difference in sample proportions can be developed.

z FORMULA FOR THE DIFFERENCE IN TWO POPULATION PROPORTIONS (10.10)	$$z = \frac{(\hat{p}_1 - \hat{p}_2) - (p_1 - p_2)}{\sqrt{\dfrac{p_1 \cdot q_1}{n_1} + \dfrac{p_2 \cdot q_2}{n_2}}}$$

where
$\hat{p}_1$ = proportion from sample 1
$\hat{p}_2$ = proportion from sample 2
n_1 = size of sample 1
n_2 = size of sample 2
p_1 = proportion from population 1
p_2 = proportion from population 2
$q_1 = 1 - p_1$
$q_2 = 1 - p_2$

Hypothesis Testing

Formula (10.10) is the formula that can be used to determine the probability of getting a particular difference in two sample proportions when given the values of the population proportions. In testing hypotheses about the difference in two population proportions, particular values of the population proportions are not usually known or assumed. Rather, the hypotheses are about the difference in the two population proportions ($p_1 - p_2$). Note that formula (10.10) requires knowledge of the values of p_1 and p_2. Hence, a modified version of formula (10.10) is used when testing hypotheses about $p_1 - p_2$. This formula utilizes a pooled value obtained from the sample proportions to replace the population proportions in the denominator of formula (10.10).

The denominator of formula (10.10) is the standard deviation of the difference in two sample proportions and uses the population proportions in its calculations. However, the population proportions are unknown, so an estimate of the standard deviation of the difference in two sample proportions is made by using sample proportions as point estimates of the population proportions. The sample proportions are combined by using a weighted average to produce $\bar{p}$, which, in conjunction with $\bar{q}$ and the sample sizes, produces a point estimate of the standard deviation of the difference in sample proportions. The result is formula (10.11), which we shall use to test hypotheses about the difference in two population proportions.

---

z FORMULA TO TEST THE DIFFERENCE IN POPULATION PROPORTIONS (10.11)

$$z = \frac{(\hat{p}_1 - \hat{p}_2) - (p_1 - p_2)}{\sqrt{(\bar{p} \cdot \bar{q})\left(\dfrac{1}{n_1} + \dfrac{1}{n_2}\right)}}$$

where $\bar{p} = \dfrac{x_1 + x_2}{n_1 + n_2} = \dfrac{n_1 \hat{p}_1 + n_2 \hat{p}_2}{n_1 + n_2}$ and $\bar{q} = 1 - \bar{p}$

Testing the difference in two population proportions is useful whenever the researcher is interested in comparing the proportion of one population that has a certain characteristic with the proportion of a second population that has the same characteristic. For example, a researcher might be interested in determining whether the proportion of people driving new cars (less than 1 year old) in Houston is different from the proportion in Denver. A study could be conducted with a random sample of Houston drivers and a random sample of Denver drivers to test this idea. The results could be used to compare the new-car potential of the two markets and the propensity of drivers in these areas to buy new cars.

Do consumers and CEOs have different perceptions of ethics in business? A group of researchers attempted to determine whether there was a difference in the proportion of consumers and the proportion of CEOs who believe that fear of getting caught or losing one's job is a strong influence of ethical behavior. In their study, they found that 57% of consumers said that fear of getting caught or losing one's job was a strong influence on ethical behavior but only 50% of CEOs felt the same way.

Suppose these data were determined from a sample of 755 consumers and 616 CEOs. Does this result provide enough evidence to declare that a significantly higher proportion of consumers than of CEOs believe fear of getting caught or losing one's job is a strong influence on ethical behavior?

HYPOTHESIZE:

STEP 1. Suppose sample 1 is the consumer sample and sample 2 is the CEO sample. Because we are trying to prove that a higher proportion of consumers than of CEOs believe fear of getting caught or losing one's job is a strong influence on ethical behavior, the alternative hypothesis should be $p_1 - p_2 > 0$. The following hypotheses are being tested.

$$H_0: p_1 - p_2 = 0$$
$$H_a: p_1 - p_2 > 0$$

where p_1 is the proportion of consumers who select the factor
            p_2 is the proportion of CEOs who select the factor

TEST:

STEP 2. The appropriate statistical test is formula (10.11).

STEP 3. Let $\alpha = .10$.

STEP 4. Because this test is a one-tailed test, the critical table z value is $z_c = 1.28$. If an observed value of z of more than 1.28 is obtained, the null hypothesis will be rejected. Figure 10.10 shows the rejection region and the critical value for this problem.

STEP 5. The sample information follows.

Consumers	CEOs
$n_1 = 755$	$n_2 = 616$
$\hat{p}_1 = .57$	$\hat{p}_2 = .50$

STEP 6.

$$\bar{p} = \frac{n_1 \hat{p}_1 + n_2 \hat{p}_2}{n_1 + n_2} = \frac{(755)(.57) + (616)(.50)}{755 + 616} = .539$$

FIGURE 10.10

Rejection Region for the
Ethics Example

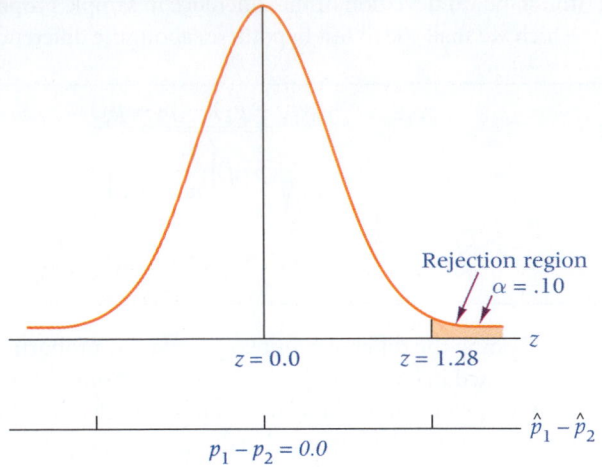

If the statistics had been given as raw data instead of sample proportions, we would have used the following formula.

$$\overline{p} = \frac{x_1 + x_2}{n_1 + n_2}$$

The observed z value is

$$z = \frac{(.57 - .50) - (0)}{\sqrt{(.539)(.461)\left(\dfrac{1}{755} + \dfrac{1}{616}\right)}} = 2.59$$

ACTION:
> STEP 7. Because $z = 2.59$ is greater than the critical table z value of 1.28 and is in the rejection region, the null hypothesis is rejected.

BUSINESS IMPLICATIONS:
> STEP 8. A significantly higher proportion of consumers than of CEOs believe fear of getting caught or losing one's job is a strong influence on ethical behavior. CEOs might want to take another look at ways to influence ethical behavior. If employees are more like consumers than CEOs, CEOs might be able to use fear of getting caught or losing one's job as a means of ensuring ethical behavior on the job. By transferring the idea of ethical behavior to the consumer, retailers might use fear of being caught and prosecuted to retard shoplifting in the retail trade.

DEMONSTRATION PROBLEM 10.6

A study of female entrepreneurs was conducted to determine their definition of success. The women were offered optional choices such as happiness/self-fulfillment, sales/profit, and achievement/challenge. The women were divided into groups according to the gross sales of their businesses. A significantly higher proportion of female entrepreneurs in the $100,000 to $500,000 category than in the less than $100,000 category seemed to rate sales/profit as a definition of success.

Suppose you decide to test this result by taking a survey of your own and identify female entrepreneurs by gross sales. You interview 100 female entrepreneurs with gross sales of less than $100,000, and 24 of them define sales/profit as success. You then interview 95 female entrepreneurs with gross sales of $100,000 to $500,000, and 39 cite sales/profit as a definition of success. Use this information to test to determine whether there is a significant difference in the proportions of the two groups that define success as sales/profit. Use $\alpha = .01$.

Solution

HYPOTHESIZE:

STEP 1. You are testing to determine whether there is a difference between two groups of entrepreneurs, so a two-tailed test is required. The hypotheses follow.

$$H_0: p_1 - p_2 = 0$$
$$H_a: p_1 - p_2 \neq 0$$

TEST:

STEP 2. The appropriate statistical test is formula (10.11).

STEP 3. Alpha has been specified as .01.

STEP 4. With $\alpha = .01$, you obtain a critical z value from Table A.5 for $\alpha/2 = .005$, $z_{.005} = \pm 2.575$. If the observed z value is more than 2.575 or less than −2.575, the null hypothesis is rejected.

STEP 5. The sample information follows.

Less Than $100,000	$100,000 to $500,000
$n_1 = 100$	$n_2 = 95$
$x_1 = 24$	$x_2 = 39$
$\hat{p}_1 = \dfrac{24}{100} = .24$	$\hat{p}_2 = \dfrac{39}{95} = .41$

where

$$\bar{p} = \frac{x_1 + x_2}{n_1 + n_2} = \frac{24 + 39}{100 + 95} = \frac{63}{195} = .323$$

x = the number of entrepreneurs who define sales/profits as success

STEP 6. The observed z value is

$$z = \frac{(\hat{p}_1 - \hat{p}_2) - (p_1 - p_2)}{\sqrt{(\bar{p} \cdot \bar{q})\left(\dfrac{1}{n_1} + \dfrac{1}{n_2}\right)}} = \frac{(.24 - .41) - (0)}{\sqrt{(.323)(.677)\left(\dfrac{1}{100} + \dfrac{1}{95}\right)}} = \frac{-.17}{.067} = -2.54$$

ACTION:

STEP 7. Although this observed value is near the rejection region, it is in the nonrejection region. The null hypothesis is not rejected. The test did not show enough evidence here to reject the null hypothesis and declare that the responses to the question by the two groups are different statistically. Note that alpha was small and that a two-tailed test was conducted. If a one-tailed test had been used, z_c would have been $z_{.01} = 2.33$, and the null hypothesis would have been rejected. If alpha had been .05, z_c would have been $z_{.025} = \pm 1.96$, and the null hypothesis would have been rejected. This result underscores the crucial importance of selecting alpha and determining whether to use a one-tailed or two-tailed test in hypothesis testing.

The following diagram shows the critical values, the rejection regions, and the observed value for this problem.

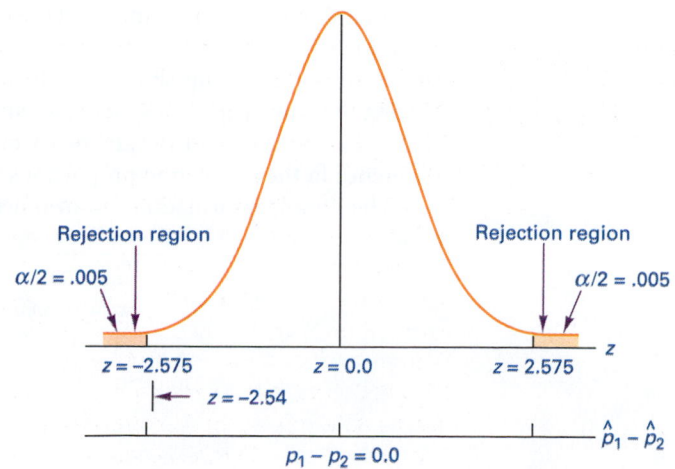

BUSINESS IMPLICATIONS:

STEP 8. We cannot statistically conclude that a greater proportion of female entrepreneurs in the higher gross sales category define success as sales/profit. One of the payoffs of such a determination is to find out what motivates the people with whom we do business. If sales/profits motivate people, offers or promises of greater sales and profits can be a means of attracting their services, their interest, or their business. If sales/profits do not motivate people, such offers would not generate the kind of response wanted and we would need to look for other ways to motivate them.

Confidence Intervals

Sometimes in business research the investigator wants to estimate the difference in two population proportions. For example, what is the difference, if any, in the population proportions of workers in the Midwest who favor union membership and workers in the South who favor union membership? In studying two different suppliers of the same part, a large manufacturing company might want to estimate the difference between suppliers in the proportion of parts that meet specifications. These and other situations requiring the estimation of the difference in two population proportions can be solved by using confidence intervals.

The formula for constructing confidence intervals to estimate the difference in two population proportions is a modified version of formula (10.10). Formula (10.10) for two proportions requires knowledge of each of the population proportions. Because we are attempting to estimate the difference in these two proportions, we obviously do not know their value. To overcome this lack of knowledge in constructing a confidence interval formula, we substitute the sample proportions in place of the population proportions and use these sample proportions in the estimate, as follows.

$$z = \frac{(\hat{p}_1 - \hat{p}_2) - (p_1 - p_2)}{\sqrt{\dfrac{\hat{p}_1 \cdot \hat{q}_1}{n_1} + \dfrac{\hat{p}_2 \cdot \hat{q}_2}{n_2}}}$$

Solving this equation for $p_1 - p_2$ produces the formula for constructing confidence intervals for $p_1 - p_2$.

CONFIDENCE INTERVAL TO ESTIMATE $p_1 - p_2$ (10.12)	$(\hat{p}_1 - \hat{p}_2) - z\sqrt{\dfrac{\hat{p}_1 \cdot \hat{q}_1}{n_1} + \dfrac{\hat{p}_2 \cdot \hat{q}_2}{n_2}} \leq p_1 - p_2 \leq (\hat{p}_1 - \hat{p}_2) + z\sqrt{\dfrac{\hat{p}_1 \cdot \hat{q}_1}{n_1} + \dfrac{\hat{p}_2 \cdot \hat{q}_2}{n_2}}$

To see how this formula is used, suppose that in an attempt to target its clientele, managers of a supermarket chain want to determine the difference between the proportion of morning shoppers who are men and the proportion of after–5 P.M. shoppers who are men. Over a period of two weeks, the chain's researchers conduct a systematic random sample survey of 400 morning shoppers, which reveals that 352 are women and 48 are men. During this same period, a systematic random sample of 480 after–5 P.M. shoppers reveals that 293 are women and 187 are men. Construct a 98% confidence interval to estimate the difference in the population proportions of men.

The sample information is shown here.

Morning Shoppers	After–5 P.M. Shoppers
$n_1 = 400$	$n_2 = 480$
$x_1 = 48$ men	$x_2 = 187$ men
$\hat{p}_1 = .12$	$\hat{p}_2 = .39$
$\hat{q}_1 = .88$	$\hat{q}_2 = .61$

FIGURE 10.11

MINITAB Output for the
Shopping Example

```
        TEST AND CI FOR TWO PROPORTIONS

Sample    X     N     Sample p
1        48    400    0.120000
2       187    480    0.389583

Estimate for p(1) − p(2):   −0.269583
98% CI for p(1) − p(2):   (−0.333692, −0.205474)
Test for p(1) − p(2) = 0 (vs not = 0):
Z = −9.78   P-Value = 0.000
```

For a 98% level of confidence, $z = 2.33$. Using formula (10.12) yields

$$(.12 - .39) - 2.33\sqrt{\frac{(.12)(.88)}{400} + \frac{(.39)(.61)}{480}} \le p_1 - p_2$$

$$\le (.12 - .39) + 2.33\sqrt{\frac{(.12)(.88)}{400} + \frac{(.39)(.61)}{480}}$$

$$-.27 - .064 \ge p_1 - p_2 \ge -.27 + .064$$

$$-.334 \ge p_1 - p_2 \ge -.206$$

There is a 98% level of confidence that the difference in population proportions is between −.334 and −.206. Because the after–5 p.m. shopper proportion was subtracted from the morning shoppers, the negative signs in the interval indicate a higher proportion of men in the after–5 p.m. shoppers than in the morning shoppers. Thus the confidence level is 98% that the difference in proportions is at least .206 and may be as much as .334.

Using the Computer to Analyze the Difference in Two Proportions

MINITAB has the capability of testing hypotheses or constructing confidence intervals about the difference in two proportions. Figure 10.11 shows MINITAB output for the shopping example. Notice that the output contains a summary of sample information along with the difference in sample proportions, the confidence interval, the computer z value for a hypothesis test, and the p-value. The confidence interval shown here is the same as the one we just computed except for rounding differences.

10.4 PROBLEMS

10.31 Using the given sample information, test the following hypotheses.

a. $H_0: p_1 - p_2 = 0$ $H_a: p_1 - p_2 \ne 0$

Sample 1	Sample 2	
$n_1 = 368$	$n_2 = 405$	
$x_1 = 175$	$x_2 = 182$	Let $\alpha = .05$.

Note that x is the number in the sample having the characteristic of interest.

b. $H_0: p_1 - p_2 = 0$ $H_a: p_1 - p_2 > 0$

Sample 1	Sample 2	
$n_1 = 649$	$n_2 = 558$	
$\hat{p}_1 = .38$	$\hat{p}_2 = .25$	Let $\alpha = .10$.

10.32 In each of the following cases, calculate a confidence interval to estimate $p_1 - p_2$.

    a. $n_1 = 85$, $n_2 = 90$, $\hat{p}_1 = .75$, $\hat{p}_2 = .67$; level of confidence = 90%

    b. $n_1 = 1100$, $n_2 = 1300$, $\hat{p}_1 = .19$, $\hat{p}_2 = .17$; level of confidence = 95%

    c. $n_1 = 430$, $n_2 = 399$, $x_1 = 275$, $x_2 = 275$; level of confidence = 85%

    d. $n_1 = 1500$, $n_2 = 1500$, $x_1 = 1050$, $x_2 = 1100$; level of confidence = 80%

10.33 According to a study conducted for Gateway Computers, 59% of men and 70% of women say that weight is an extremely/very important factor in purchasing a laptop computer. Suppose this survey was conducted using 374 men and 481 women. Do these data show enough evidence to declare that a significantly higher proportion of women than men believe that weight is an extremely/very important factor in purchasing a laptop computer? Use a 5% level of significance.

10.34 Does age make a difference in the amount of savings a worker feels is needed to be secure at retirement? A study by CommSciences for Transamerica Asset Management found that .24 of workers in the 25–33 age category feel that $250,000 to $500,000 is enough to be secure at retirement. However, .35 of the workers in the 34–52 age category feel that this amount is enough. Suppose 210 workers in the 25–33 age category and 176 workers in the 34–52 age category were involved in this study. Use these data to construct a 90% confidence interval to estimate the difference in population proportions on this question.

10.35 Companies that recently developed new products were asked to rate which activities are most difficult to accomplish with new products. Options included such activities as assessing market potential, market testing, finalizing the design, developing a business plan, and the like. A researcher wants to conduct a similar study to compare the results between two industries: the computer hardware industry and the banking industry. He takes a random sample of 56 computer firms and 89 banks. The researcher asks whether market testing is the most difficult activity to accomplish in developing a new product. Some 48% of the sampled computer companies and 56% of the sampled banks respond that it is the most difficult activity. Use a level of significance of .20 to test whether there is a significant difference in the responses to the question from these two industries.

10.36 A large production facility uses two machines to produce a key part for its main product. Inspectors have expressed concern about the quality of the finished product. Quality control investigation has revealed that the key part made by the two machines is defective at times. The inspectors randomly sampled 35 units of the key part from each machine. Of those produced by machine A, five were defective. Seven of the 35 sampled parts from machine B were defective. The production manager is interested in estimating the difference in proportions of the populations of parts that are defective between machine A and machine B. From the sample information, compute a 98% confidence interval for this difference.

10.37 According to a CCH Unscheduled Absence survey, 9% of small businesses use telecommuting of workers in an effort to reduce unscheduled absenteeism. This proportion compares to 6% for all businesses. Is there really a significant difference between small businesses and all businesses on this issue? Use these data and an alpha of .10 to test this question. Assume that there were 780 small businesses and 915 other businesses in this survey.

10.38 Many Americans spend time worrying about paying their bills. A survey by Fleishman-Hilliard Research for MassMutual discovered that 60% of Americans with kids say that paying bills is a major concern. This proportion compares to 52% of Americans without kids. Suppose 850 Americans with kids and 910 without kids were contacted for this study. Use these data to construct a 95% confidence interval to estimate the difference in population proportions between Americans with kids and Americans without kids on this issue.

10.5 TESTING HYPOTHESES ABOUT TWO POPULATION VARIANCES

Sometimes we are interested in studying the variance of a population rather than a mean or proportion. Section 9.5 discussed how to test hypotheses about a single population variance, but on some occasions business researchers are interested in testing hypotheses about the difference in two population variances. In this section, we examine how to conduct such tests. When would a business researcher be interested in the variances from two populations?

In quality control, analysts often examine both a measure of central tendency (mean or proportion) and a measure of variability. Suppose a manufacturing plant made two batches of an item, produced items on two different machines, or produced items on two different shifts. It might be of interest to management to compare the variances from two batches or two machines to determine whether there is more variability in one than another.

Variance is sometimes used as a measure of the risk of a stock in the stock market. The greater the variance, the greater is the risk. By using techniques discussed here, a financial researcher could determine whether the variances (or risk) of two stocks are the same.

In testing hypotheses about two population variances, the sample variances are used. It makes sense that if two samples come from the same population (or populations with equal variances), the ratio of the sample variances, s_1^2 / s_2^2 should be about 1. However, because of sampling error, sample variances even from the same population (or from two populations with equal variances) will vary. This *ratio of two sample variances* formulates what is called an **F value.**

$$F = \frac{s_1^2}{s_2^2}$$

These ratios, if computed repeatedly for pairs of sample variances taken from a population, are distributed as an **F distribution.** The F distribution will vary by the sizes of the samples, which are converted to degrees of freedom.

With the F distribution, there are degrees of freedom associated with the numerator (of the ratio) and the denominator. An assumption underlying the F distribution is that the populations from which the samples are drawn are normally distributed for x. The F test of two population variances is extremely sensitive to violations of the assumption that the populations are normally distributed. The statistician should carefully investigate the shape of the distributions of the populations from which the samples are drawn to be certain the populations are normally distributed. The formula used to test hypotheses comparing two population variances follows.

F TEST FOR TWO POPULATION VARIANCES (10.13)	$$F = \frac{s_1^2}{s_2^2}$$

$$\text{df}_{\text{numerator}} = v_1 = n_1 - 1$$
$$\text{df}_{\text{denominator}} = v_2 = n_2 - 1$$

Table A.7 contains F distribution table values for $\alpha = .10, .05, .025, .01,$ and $.005$. Figure 10.12 shows an F distribution for $v_1 = 6$ and $v_2 = 30$. Notice that the distribution is nonsymmetric, which can be a problem when we are conducting a two-tailed test and want to determine the critical value for the lower tail. Table A.7 contains only F values for the upper tail. However, the F distribution is not symmetric nor does it have a mean of zero as do the z and t distributions; therefore, we cannot merely place a minus sign on the upper-tail critical value and obtain the lower-tail critical value (in addition, the F ratio is always positive—it is the ratio of two variances). This dilemma can be solved by using formula (10.14), which essentially states that the critical F value for the lower tail $(1 - \alpha)$ can be solved for by taking the inverse of the F value for the upper tail (α). The degrees of freedom numerator for the upper-tail critical value is the degrees of freedom denominator for the lower-tail critical value, and the degrees of freedom denominator for the upper-tail critical value is the degrees of freedom numerator for the lower-tail critical value.

FIGURE 10.12

An F Distribution for $v_1 = 6$, $v_2 = 30$

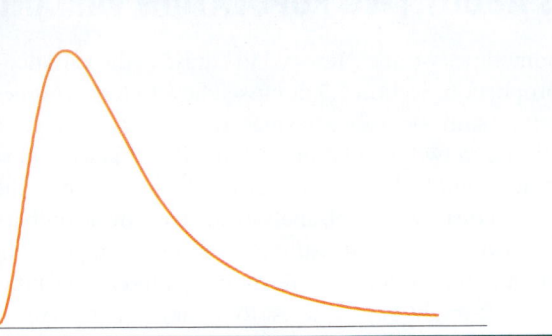

FORMULA FOR DETERMINING THE CRITICAL VALUE FOR THE LOWER-TAIL F (10.14)

$$F_{1-\alpha,v_2,v_1} = \frac{1}{F_{\alpha,v_1,v_2}}$$

A hypothesis test can be conducted using two sample variances and formula (10.13). The following example illustrates this process.

Suppose a machine produces metal sheets that are specified to be 22 millimeters thick. Because of the machine, the operator, the raw material, the manufacturing environment, and other factors, there is variability in the thickness. Two machines produce these sheets. Operators are concerned about the consistency of the two machines. To test consistency, they randomly sample 10 sheets produced by machine 1 and 12 sheets produced by machine 2. The thickness measurements of sheets from each machine are given in the accompanying table. Assume sheet thickness is normally distributed in the population. How can we test to determine whether the variance from each sample comes from the same population variance (population variances are equal) or from different population variances (population variances are not equal)?

HYPOTHESIZE:

STEP 1. Determine the null and alternative hypotheses. In this case, we are conducting a two-tailed test (variances are the same or not), and the following hypotheses are used.

$$H_0: \sigma_1^2 = \sigma_2^2$$
$$H_a: \sigma_1^2 \neq \sigma_2^2$$

TEST:

STEP 2. The appropriate statistical test is

$$F = \frac{s_1^2}{s_2^2}$$

STEP 3. Let $\alpha = .05$.

STEP 4. Because we are conducting a two-tailed test, $\alpha/2 = .025$. Because $n_1 = 10$ and $n_2 = 12$, the degrees of freedom numerator for the upper-tail critical value is $v_1 = n_1 - 1 = 10 - 1 = 9$ and the degrees of freedom denominator for the upper-tail critical value is $v_2 = n_2 - 1 = 12 - 1 = 11$. The critical F value for the upper tail obtained from Table A.7 is

$$F_{.025,9,11} = 3.59$$

Table 10.9 is a copy of the F distribution for a one-tailed $\alpha = .025$ (which yields equivalent values for two-tailed $\alpha = .05$ where the upper tail contains .025 of the area). Locate $F_{.025,9,11} = 3.59$ in the table. The lower-tail critical value can be calculated from the upper-tail value by using formula (10.14).

$$F_{.975,11,9} = \frac{1}{F_{.025,9,11}} = \frac{1}{3.59} = .28$$

The decision rule is to reject the null hypothesis if the observed F value is greater than 3.59 or less than .28.

STEP 5. Next we computed the sample variances. The data are shown here.

Machine 1		Machine 2	
22.3	21.9	22.0	21.7
21.8	22.4	22.1	21.9
22.3	22.5	21.8	22.0
21.6	22.2	21.9	22.1
21.8	21.6	22.2	21.9
		22.0	22.1

$$s_1^2 = .1138 \qquad s_2^2 = .0202$$
$$n_1 = 10 \qquad n_2 = 12$$

STEP 6.

$$F = \frac{s_1^2}{s_2^2} = \frac{.1138}{.0202} = 5.63$$

The ratio of sample variances is 5.63.

ACTION:

STEP 7. The observed F value is 5.63, which is greater than the upper-tail critical value of 3.59. As Figure 10.13 shows, this F value is in the rejection region. Thus, the decision is to reject the null hypotheses. The population variances are not equal.

BUSINESS IMPLICATIONS:

STEP 8. An examination of the sample variances reveals that the variance from machine 1 measurements is greater than that from machine 2 measurements. The operators and process managers might want to examine machine 1 further; an adjustment may be needed or some other reason may be causing the seemingly greater variations on that machine.

Using the Computer to Test Hypotheses About Two Population Variances

Excel has the capability of directly testing hypotheses about two population variances. Figure 10.14 shows Excel output for the sheet metal example. The output contains the two sample means, the two sample variances, the observed F value, the p-value for a one-tailed

---

FIGURE 10.13

MINITAB Graph of F Values and Rejection Region for the Sheet Metal Example

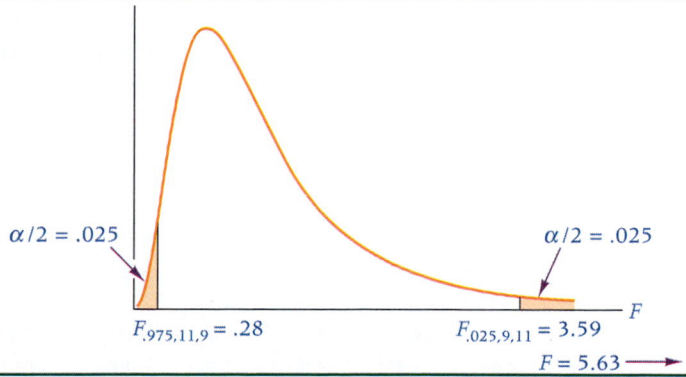

$\alpha/2 = .025$ $\alpha/2 = .025$

$F_{.975,11,9} = .28$ $F_{.025,9,11} = 3.59$

$F = 5.63$

FIGURE 10.14

Excel Output for the Sheet Metal Example

	A	B	C
1	F-Test Two-Sample for Variances		
2		Machine 1	Machine 2
3	Mean	22.04	21.975
4	Variance	0.113778	0.020227
5	Observations	10	12
6	df	9	11
7	F	5.62	
8	F F < = f) one-tail	0.0047	
9	F Critical one-tail	3.59	

TABLE 10.9   A Portion of the *F* Distribution Table

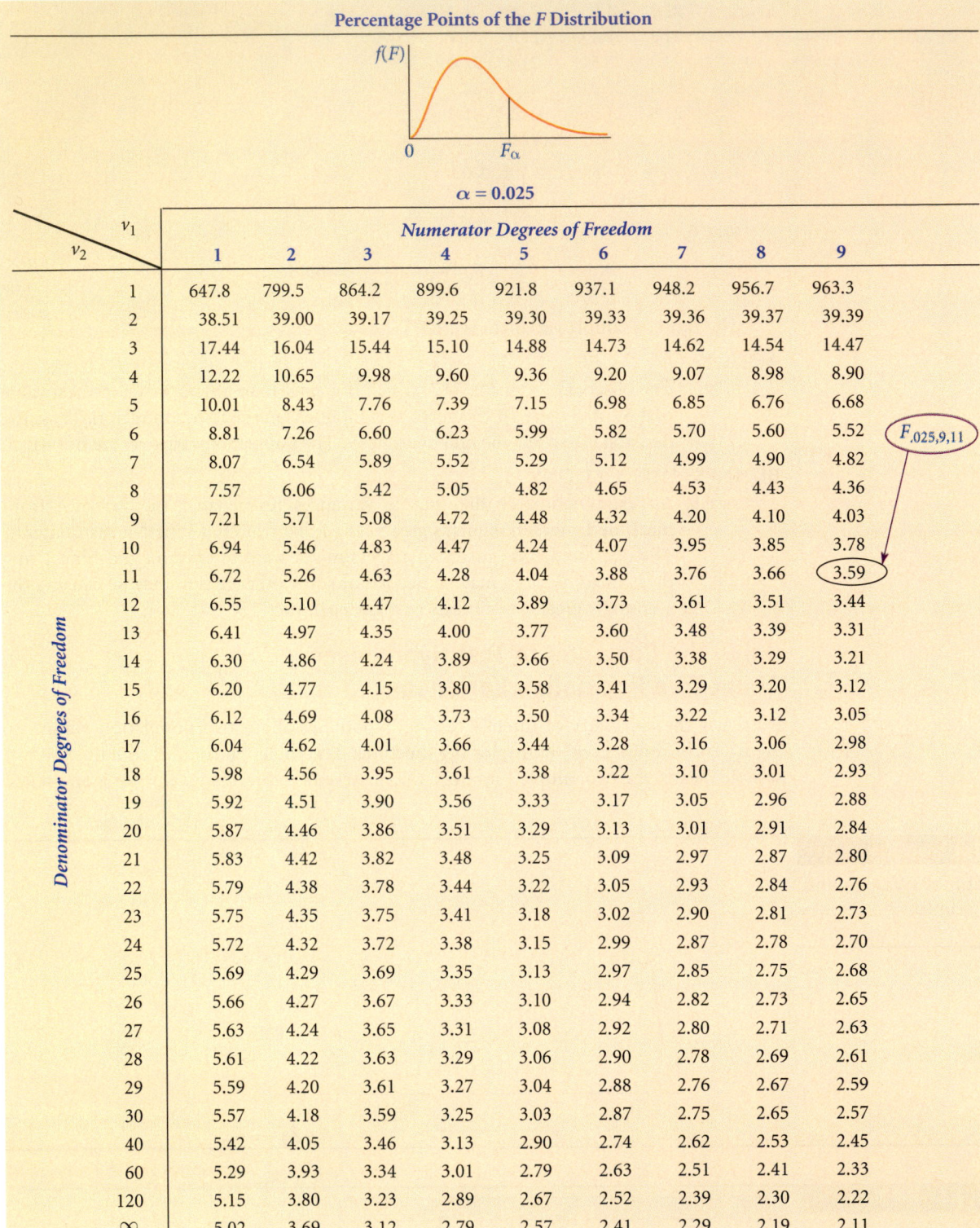

Percentage Points of the *F* Distribution

$f(F)$

0   F_α

$\alpha = 0.025$

v_2 \ v_1	1	2	3	4	5	6	7	8	9	
1	647.8	799.5	864.2	899.6	921.8	937.1	948.2	956.7	963.3	
2	38.51	39.00	39.17	39.25	39.30	39.33	39.36	39.37	39.39	
3	17.44	16.04	15.44	15.10	14.88	14.73	14.62	14.54	14.47	
4	12.22	10.65	9.98	9.60	9.36	9.20	9.07	8.98	8.90	
5	10.01	8.43	7.76	7.39	7.15	6.98	6.85	6.76	6.68	
6	8.81	7.26	6.60	6.23	5.99	5.82	5.70	5.60	5.52	$F_{.025,9,11}$
7	8.07	6.54	5.89	5.52	5.29	5.12	4.99	4.90	4.82	
8	7.57	6.06	5.42	5.05	4.82	4.65	4.53	4.43	4.36	
9	7.21	5.71	5.08	4.72	4.48	4.32	4.20	4.10	4.03	
10	6.94	5.46	4.83	4.47	4.24	4.07	3.95	3.85	3.78	
11	6.72	5.26	4.63	4.28	4.04	3.88	3.76	3.66	3.59	
12	6.55	5.10	4.47	4.12	3.89	3.73	3.61	3.51	3.44	
13	6.41	4.97	4.35	4.00	3.77	3.60	3.48	3.39	3.31	
14	6.30	4.86	4.24	3.89	3.66	3.50	3.38	3.29	3.21	
15	6.20	4.77	4.15	3.80	3.58	3.41	3.29	3.20	3.12	
16	6.12	4.69	4.08	3.73	3.50	3.34	3.22	3.12	3.05	
17	6.04	4.62	4.01	3.66	3.44	3.28	3.16	3.06	2.98	
18	5.98	4.56	3.95	3.61	3.38	3.22	3.10	3.01	2.93	
19	5.92	4.51	3.90	3.56	3.33	3.17	3.05	2.96	2.88	
20	5.87	4.46	3.86	3.51	3.29	3.13	3.01	2.91	2.84	
21	5.83	4.42	3.82	3.48	3.25	3.09	2.97	2.87	2.80	
22	5.79	4.38	3.78	3.44	3.22	3.05	2.93	2.84	2.76	
23	5.75	4.35	3.75	3.41	3.18	3.02	2.90	2.81	2.73	
24	5.72	4.32	3.72	3.38	3.15	2.99	2.87	2.78	2.70	
25	5.69	4.29	3.69	3.35	3.13	2.97	2.85	2.75	2.68	
26	5.66	4.27	3.67	3.33	3.10	2.94	2.82	2.73	2.65	
27	5.63	4.24	3.65	3.31	3.08	2.92	2.80	2.71	2.63	
28	5.61	4.22	3.63	3.29	3.06	2.90	2.78	2.69	2.61	
29	5.59	4.20	3.61	3.27	3.04	2.88	2.76	2.67	2.59	
30	5.57	4.18	3.59	3.25	3.03	2.87	2.75	2.65	2.57	
40	5.42	4.05	3.46	3.13	2.90	2.74	2.62	2.53	2.45	
60	5.29	3.93	3.34	3.01	2.79	2.63	2.51	2.41	2.33	
120	5.15	3.80	3.23	2.89	2.67	2.52	2.39	2.30	2.22	
∞	5.02	3.69	3.12	2.79	2.57	2.41	2.29	2.19	2.11	

Numerator Degrees of Freedom

Denominator Degrees of Freedom

test, and the critical F value for a one-tailed test. Because the sheet metal example is a two-tailed test, the p-value must be doubled to .0094 in order to reach a decision or just compare the p-value of .0047 to $\alpha/2 = .025$. Because this value is less than $\alpha = .05$, the decision is to reject the null hypothesis.

DEMONSTRATION PROBLEM 10.7	According to Runzheimer International, a family of four in Manhattan with $60,000 annual income spends more than $22,000 a year on basic goods and services. In contrast, a family of four in San Antonio with the same annual income spends only $15,460 on the same items. Suppose we want to test to determine whether the variance of money spent per year on the basics by families across the United States is greater than the variance of money spent on the basics by families in Manhattan—that is, whether the amounts spent by families of four in Manhattan are more homogeneous than the amounts spent by such families nationally. Suppose a random sample of eight Manhattan families produces the accompanying figures, which are given along with those reported from a random sample of seven families across the United States. Complete a hypothesis-testing procedure to determine whether the variance of values taken from across the United States can be shown to be greater than the variance of values obtained from families in Manhattan. Let $\alpha = .01$. Assume the amount spent on the basics is normally distributed in the population.

**Amount Spent on Basics By Family of Four
with $60,000 Annual Income**

Across United States	Manhattan
$18,500	$23,000
19,250	21,900
16,400	22,500
20,750	21,200
17,600	21,000
21,800	22,800
14,750	23,100
	21,300

Solution

HYPOTHESIZE:

STEP 1. This is a one-tailed test with the following hypotheses.

$$H_0: \sigma_1^2 = \sigma_2^2$$

$$H_a: \sigma_1^2 > \sigma_2^2$$

Note that what we are trying to prove—that the variance for the U.S. population is greater than the variance for families in Manhattan—is in the alternative hypothesis.

TEST:

STEP 2. The appropriate statistical test is

$$F = \frac{s_1^2}{s_2^2}$$

STEP 3. The Type I error rate is .01.

STEP 4. This test is a one-tailed test, so we will use the F distribution table in Appendix A.7 with $\alpha = .01$. The degrees of freedom for $n_1 = 7$ and $n_2 = 8$ are $v_1 = 6$ and $v_2 = 7$. The critical F value for the upper tail of the distribution is

$$F_{.01,6,7} = 7.19.$$

The decision rule is to reject the null hypothesis if the observed value of F is greater than 7.19.

STEP 5. The following sample variances are computed from the data.

$$s_1^2 = 5,961,428.6$$
$$n_1 = 7$$
$$s_2^2 = 737,142.9$$
$$n_2 = 8$$

STEP 6. The observed F value can be determined by

$$F = \frac{s_1^2}{s_2^2} = \frac{5,961,428.6}{737,142.9} = 8.09$$

ACTION:

STEP 7. Because the observed value of $F = 8.09$ is greater than the table critical F value of 7.19, the decision is to reject the null hypothesis.

BUSINESS IMPLICATIONS:

STEP 8. The variance for families in the United States is greater than the variance of families in Manhattan. Families in Manhattan are more homogeneous in amount spent on basics than families across the United States. Marketing managers need to understand this homogeneity as they attempt to find niches in the Manhattan population. Manhattan may not contain as many subgroups as can be found across the United States. The task of locating market niches may be easier in Manhattan than in the rest of the country because fewer possibilities are likely. The following MINITAB graph shows the rejection region as well as the critical and calculated values of F.

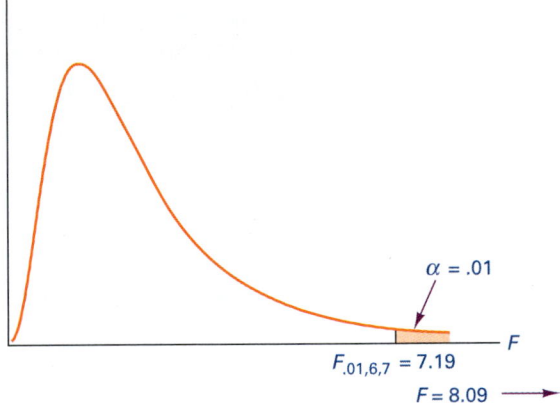

$\alpha = .01$

$F_{.01,6,7} = 7.19$

$F = 8.09$

Note: *Some authors recommend the use of this F test to determine whether the data being analyzed by a t test for two population means are meeting the assumption of equal population variances. However, some statistical researchers suggest that for equal sample sizes, the t test is insensitive to the equal variance assumption, and therefore the F test is not needed in that situation. For unequal sample sizes, the F test of variances is "not generally capable of detecting assumption violations that lead to poor performance" with the t test.* This text does not present the application of the F test to determine whether variance assumptions for the t test have been met.*

10.5 PROBLEMS

10.39 Test the following hypotheses by using the given sample information and $\alpha = .01$. Assume the populations are normally distributed.

$$H_0: \sigma_1^2 = \sigma_2^2 \quad H_a: \sigma_1^2 < \sigma_2^2$$

$$n_1 = 10, n_2 = 12, s_1^2 = 562, s_2^2 = 1013$$

*Carol A. Markowski and Edward P. Markowski, "Conditions for the Effectiveness of a Preliminary Test of Variance," *The American Statistician*, vol. 44 (November 1990), pp. 322–326.

10.40 Test the following hypotheses by using the given sample information and $\alpha = .05$. Assume the populations are normally distributed.

$$H_0: \sigma_1^2 = \sigma_2^2 \qquad H_a: \sigma_1^2 \neq \sigma_2^2$$
$$n_1 = 5, n_2 = 19, s_1 = 4.68, s_2 = 2.78$$

10.41 Suppose the data shown here are the results of a survey to investigate gasoline prices. Ten service stations were selected randomly in each of two cities and the figures represent the prices of a gallon of unleaded regular gasoline on a given day. Use the F test to determine whether there is a significant difference in the variances of the prices of unleaded regular gasoline between these two cities. Let $\alpha = .10$. Assume gasoline prices are normally distributed.

City 1			City 2		
1.18	1.07	1.13	1.08	1.05	1.19
1.15	1.14	1.13	1.17	1.21	1.12
1.14	1.13	1.03	1.14	1.14	1.13
	1.09			1.11	

10.42 How long are resale houses on the market? One survey by the Houston Association of Realtors reported that in Houston, resale houses are on the market an average of 112 days. Of course, the length of time varies by market. Suppose random samples of 13 houses in Houston and 11 houses in Chicago that are for resale are traced. The data shown here represent the number of days each house was on the market before being sold. Use the given data and a 1% level of significance to determine whether the population variances for the number of days until resale are different in Houston than in Chicago. Assume the numbers of days resale houses are on the market are normally distributed.

Houston		Chicago	
132	126	118	56
138	94	85	69
131	161	113	67
127	133	81	54
99	119	94	137
126	88	93	
134			

10.43 One recent study showed that the average annual amount spent by an East Coast household on frankfurters was $23.84 compared with an average of $19.83 for West Coast households. Suppose a random sample of 12 East Coast households showed that the standard deviation of these purchases (frankfurters) was $7.52, whereas a random sample of 15 West Coast households resulted in a standard deviation of $6.08. Do these samples provide enough evidence to conclude that the variance of annual frankfurter purchases for East Coast households is greater than the variance of annual frankfurter purchases for West Coast households? Let alpha be .05. Assume amounts spent per year on frankfurters are normally distributed. Suppose the data did show that the variance among East Coast households is greater than that among West Coast households. What might this variance mean to decision makers in the frankfurter industry?

10.44 According to the General Accounting Office of the U.S. government, the average age of a male federal worker is 43.6 years and that of a male worker in the nonfederal sector is 37.3 years. Is there any difference in the variation of ages of men in the federal sector and men in the nonfederal sector? Suppose a random sample of 15 male federal workers is taken and the variance of their ages is 91.5. Suppose also a random sample of 15 male nonfederal workers is taken and the variance of their ages is 67.3. Use these data and $\alpha = .01$ to answer the question. Assume ages are normally distributed.

Comparing International Labor Statistics

Various techniques in Chapter 10 can be used to analyze the international labor data presented in the Decision Dilemma if the data are actually only sample statistics. It is highly likely that the samples gathered in the United States and in Japan in 1992 and in 2000 are independent. It is almost certain that large sample sizes were used given the importance of the studies and the fact that the government agencies or contractors had the resources to conduct large-scale studies. Therefore, techniques from Section 10.1 would be appropriate to use for comparing Japanese figures to U.S. figures for each year (1992 and 2000). As an example, suppose the following data were gathered from samples in Japan and in the United States in order to compare hourly labor costs between the two countries.

	Year 1992		Year 2000	
	Japan	United States	Japan	United States
Sample size	73	67	88	94
Sample mean	16.38	16.09	22.00	19.96
Population standard deviation	2.17	2.13	2.34	2.42

The computations result in

For 1992:

$$z = \frac{(\bar{x}_1 - \bar{x}_2) - (\mu_1 - \mu_2)}{\sqrt{\dfrac{\sigma_1^2}{n_1} + \dfrac{\sigma_2^2}{n_2}}} = \frac{(16.38 - 16.09) - (0)}{\sqrt{\dfrac{(2.17)^2}{73} + \dfrac{(2.13)^2}{67}}} = 0.80$$

For 2000:

$$z = \frac{(\bar{x}_1 - \bar{x}_2) - (\mu_1 - \mu_2)}{\sqrt{\dfrac{\sigma_1^2}{n_1} + \dfrac{\sigma_2^2}{n_2}}} = \frac{(22.00 - 19.96) - (0)}{\sqrt{\dfrac{(2.34)^2}{88} + \dfrac{(2.42)^2}{94}}} = 5.78$$

Using a two-tailed test, an alpha of .05, and a critical z value of ± 1.96, we would fail to reject the null hypothesis for 1992 but reject the null hypothesis for 2000. Thus, the samples do not provide enough evidence to declare that labor costs are cheaper in the United States than in Japan in 1992 but that labor costs in the United States were significantly cheaper than labor costs in Japan in the year 2000. Similar analyses could be undertaken to compare the statistics of Austria to those of Denmark. In addition, statistics on the average length of workweek in the United States from 1967 to 1998 can be compared using the difference of means from two independent samples techniques presented in Sections 10.1 and 10.2.

The percentage figures for two populations can be compared and tested using the difference in two population proportions analysis presented in section 10.4. As an example, consider the data on the percentage of workers who would work the same number of hours per week if given the choice for the United States and for Korea shown here:

	United States	Korea
Sample size	700	850
Sample proportion	.57	.55

The computations result in

$$\bar{p} = \frac{(n_1 \hat{p}_1 + n_2 \hat{p}_2)}{n_1 + n_2} = \frac{700(.57) + 850(.55)}{1550} = .559$$

$$z = \frac{(\hat{p}_1 - \hat{p}_2) - (p_1 - p_2)}{\sqrt{\bar{p} \cdot \bar{q} \left(\frac{1}{n_1} + \frac{1}{n_2} \right)}} = \frac{(.57 - .55) - (0)}{\sqrt{(.559)(.441) \left(\frac{1}{700} + \frac{1}{850} \right)}} = 0.79$$

The results of this analysis do not show enough evidence to declare that a significantly lower proportion of Korean workers would work the same number of hours per week if given the choice even with alpha equal to .10. The difference is probably due to chance. Other differences in population proportions can be tested using Section 10.4 techniques on sample data such as the question on the difference in American workers' satisfaction with work time flexibility between 1997 and the year 2000. Work this problem out as a student exercise using $\alpha = .05$ and a two-tailed test.

ETHICAL CONSIDERATIONS

The statistical techniques presented in this chapter share some of the pitfalls of confidence interval methodology and hypothesis-testing techniques mentioned in preceding chapters. Included among these pitfalls are assumption violations. Remember, if small sample sizes are used in analyzing means, the z tests are valid only when the population is normally distributed and the population variances are known. If the population variances are unknown, a t test can be used if the population is normally distributed and if the population variances can be assumed to be equal. The z tests and confidence intervals for two population proportions also have a minimum sample-size requirement that should be met. In addition, it is assumed that both populations are normally distributed when the F test is used for two population variances.

Use of the t test for two independent populations is not unethical when the populations are related, but it is likely to result in a loss of power. As with any hypothesis-testing procedure, in determining the null and alternative hypotheses, make certain you are not assuming true what you are trying to prove.

SUMMARY

Business research often requires the analysis of two populations. Three types of parameters can be compared: means, proportions, and variances. Except for the F test for population variances, all techniques presented contain both confidence intervals and hypothesis tests. In each case, the two populations are studied through the use of sample data randomly drawn from each population.

The population means are analyzed by comparing two sample means. When sample sizes are large ($n \geq 30$) and population variances are known, a z test is used. When sample sizes are small, the population variances are known, and the populations are normally distributed, the z test is used to analyze the population means. If the population variances are unknown, and the populations are normally distributed, the t test of means for independent samples is used. For populations that are related on some measure, such as twins or before-and-after, a t test for dependent measures (matched pairs) is used. The difference in two population proportions can be tested or estimated using a z test.

The population variances are analyzed by an F test when the assumption that the populations are normally distributed is met. The F value is a ratio of the two variances. The F distribution is a distribution of possible ratios of two sample variances taken from one population or from two populations containing the same variance.

KEY TERMS

dependent samples	F value	matched-pairs test
F distribution	independent samples	related measures

FORMULAS

(10.1) z test for the difference in two independent sample means

$$z = \frac{(\bar{x}_1 - \bar{x}_2) - (\mu_1 - \mu_2)}{\sqrt{\dfrac{\sigma_1^2}{n_1} + \dfrac{\sigma_2^2}{n_2}}}$$

(10.2) Confidence interval for estimating the difference in two independent population means

$$(\bar{x}_1 - \bar{x}_2) - z\sqrt{\frac{\sigma_1^2}{n_1} + \frac{\sigma_2^2}{n_2}} \leq \mu_1 - \mu_2 \leq (\bar{x}_1 - \bar{x}_2) + z\sqrt{\frac{\sigma_1^2}{n_1} + \frac{\sigma_2^2}{n_2}}$$

(10.3) t test for two independent sample means, small samples, population variances unknown but assumed to be equal (assume also that the two populations are normally distributed)

$$t = \frac{(\bar{x}_1 - \bar{x}_2) - (\mu_1 - \mu_2)}{\sqrt{\dfrac{s_1^2(n_1 - 1) + s_2^2(n_2 - 1)}{n_1 + n_2 - 2}}\sqrt{\dfrac{1}{n_1} + \dfrac{1}{n_2}}}$$

$$df = n_1 + n_2 - 2$$

(10.4) t test for two independent sample means, small samples, population variances unknown and not assumed to be equal (assume also that the two populations are normally distributed)

$$t = \frac{(\bar{x}_1 - \bar{x}_2) - (\mu_1 - \mu_2)}{\sqrt{\dfrac{s_1^2}{n_1} + \dfrac{s_2^2}{n_2}}}$$

$$df = \frac{\left[\dfrac{s_1^2}{n_1} + \dfrac{s_2^2}{n_2}\right]^2}{\dfrac{\left(\dfrac{s_1^2}{n_1}\right)^2}{n_1 - 1} + \dfrac{\left(\dfrac{s_2^2}{n_2}\right)^2}{n_2 - 1}}$$

(10.5) Confidence interval for estimating the difference in two independent means, small samples, population

variances unknown but assumed to be equal (assume also that the two populations are normally distributed)

$$(\bar{x}_1 - \bar{x}_2) \pm t\sqrt{\frac{s_1^2(n_1 - 1) + s_2^2(n_2 - 1)}{n_1 + n_2 - 2}}\sqrt{\frac{1}{n_1} + \frac{1}{n_2}}$$

$$df = n_1 + n_2 - 2$$

(10.6) t test for the difference in two related samples (the differences are normally distributed in the population)

$$t = \frac{\bar{d} - D}{\dfrac{s_d}{\sqrt{n}}}$$

$$df = n - 1$$

(10.7 and 10.8) Formulas for $\bar{d}$ and s_d

$$\bar{d} = \frac{\Sigma d}{n}$$

$$s_d = \sqrt{\frac{\Sigma(d - \bar{d})^2}{n - 1}} = \sqrt{\frac{\Sigma d^2 - \dfrac{(\Sigma d)^2}{n}}{n - 1}}$$

(10.9) Confidence interval formula for estimating the difference in related samples (the differences are normally distributed in the population)

$$\bar{d} - t\frac{s_d}{\sqrt{n}} \leq D \leq \bar{d} + t\frac{s_d}{\sqrt{n}}$$

$$df = n - 1$$

(10.11) z formula for testing the difference in population proportions

$$z = \frac{(\hat{p}_1 - \hat{p}_2) - (p_1 - p_2)}{\sqrt{(\bar{p} \cdot \bar{q})\left(\dfrac{1}{n_1} + \dfrac{1}{n_2}\right)}}$$

where $\bar{p} = \dfrac{x_1 + x_2}{n_1 + n_2} = \dfrac{n_1\hat{p}_1 + n_2\hat{p}_2}{n_1 + n_2}$ and $\bar{q} = 1 - \bar{p}$

(10.12) Confidence interval to estimate $p_1 - p_2$

$$(\hat{p}_1 - \hat{p}_2) - z\sqrt{\frac{\hat{p}_1 \cdot \hat{q}_1}{n_1} + \frac{\hat{p}_2 \cdot \hat{q}_2}{n_2}} \leq p_1 - p_2$$

$$\leq (\hat{p}_1 - \hat{p}_2) + z\sqrt{\frac{\hat{p}_1 \cdot \hat{q}_1}{n_1} + \frac{\hat{p}_2 \cdot \hat{q}_2}{n_2}}$$

(10.13) F test for two population variances (assume the two populations are normally distributed)

$$F = \frac{s_1^2}{s_2^2}$$

$$df_{numerator} = v_1 = n_1 - 1$$
$$df_{denominator} = v_2 = n_2 - 1$$

(10.14) Formula for determining the critical value for the lower-tail F

$$F_{1-\alpha,v_2,v_1} = \frac{1}{F_{\alpha,v_1,v_2}}$$

SUPPLEMENTARY PROBLEMS

CALCULATING THE STATISTICS

10.45 Test the following hypotheses with the data given. Let $\alpha = .10$.

$$H_0: \mu_1 - \mu_2 = 0 \qquad H_a: \mu_1 - \mu_2 \neq 0$$

Sample 1	Sample 2
$\bar{x}_1 = 138.4$	$\bar{x}_2 = 142.5$
$\sigma_1 = 6.71$	$\sigma_2 = 8.92$
$n_1 = 48$	$n_2 = 39$

10.46 Use the following data to construct a 98% confidence interval to estimate the difference between μ_1 and μ_2.

Sample 1	Sample 2
$\bar{x}_1 = 34.9$	$\bar{x}_2 = 27.6$
$\sigma_1^2 = 2.97$	$\sigma_2^2 = 3.50$
$n_1 = 34$	$n_2 = 31$

10.47 The following data come from independent samples drawn from normally distributed populations. Use these data to test the following hypotheses. Let the Type I error rate be .05.

$$H_0: \mu_1 - \mu_2 = 0$$
$$H_a: \mu_1 - \mu_2 > 0$$

Sample 1	Sample 2
$\bar{x}_1 = 2.06$	$\bar{x}_2 = 1.93$
$s_1^2 = .176$	$s_2^2 = .143$
$n_1 = 12$	$n_2 = 15$

10.48 Construct a 95% confidence interval to estimate $\mu_1 - \mu_2$ by using the following data. Assume the populations are normally distributed.

Sample 1	Sample 2
$\bar{x}_1 = 74.6$	$\bar{x}_2 = 70.9$
$s_1^2 = 10.5$	$s_2^2 = 11.4$
$n_1 = 18$	$n_2 = 19$

10.49 The following data have been gathered from two related samples. The differences are assumed to be normally distributed in the population. Use these data and alpha of .01 to test the following hypotheses.

$$H_0: D = 0$$
$$H_a: D < 0$$

$$n = 21, \ \bar{d} = -1.16, s_d = 1.01$$

10.50 Use the following data to construct a 99% confidence interval to estimate D. Assume the differences are normally distributed in the population.

Respondent	Before	After
1	47	63
2	33	35
3	38	36
4	50	56
5	39	44
6	27	29
7	35	32
8	46	54
9	41	47

10.51 Test the following hypotheses by using the given data and alpha equal to .05.

$$H_0: p_1 - p_2 = 0$$
$$H_a: p_1 - p_2 \neq 0$$

Sample 1	Sample 2
$n_1 = 783$	$n_2 = 896$
$x_1 = 345$	$x_2 = 421$

10.52 Use the following data to construct a 99% confidence interval to estimate $p_1 - p_2$.

Sample 1	Sample 2
$n_1 = 409$	$n_2 = 378$
$\hat{p}_1 = .71$	$\hat{p}_2 = .67$

10.53 Test the following hypotheses by using the given data. Let alpha = .05.

$$H_0: \sigma_1^2 = \sigma_2^2$$

$$Ha: \sigma_1^2 \neq \sigma_2^2$$

$$n_1 = 8, n_2 = 10, s_1^2 = 46, s_2^2 = 37$$

TESTING YOUR UNDERSTANDING

10.54 Suppose a large insurance company wants to estimate the difference between the average amount of term life insurance purchased per family and the average amount of whole life insurance purchased per family. To obtain an estimate, one of the company's actuaries randomly selects 27 families who have term life insurance only and 29 families who have whole life policies only. Each sample is taken from families in which the leading provider is younger than 45 years of age. Use the data obtained to construct a 95% confidence interval to estimate the difference in means for these two groups. Assume the amount of insurance is normally distributed.

Term	Whole Life
$\overline{x}_T$ = $75,000	$\overline{x}_W$ = $45,000
s_T = $22,000	s_W = $15,500
n_T = 27	n_W = 29

10.55 A study is conducted to estimate the average difference in bus ridership for a large city during the morning and afternoon rush hours. The transit authority's researcher randomly selects nine buses because of the variety of routes they represent. On a given day the number of riders on each bus is counted at 7:45 A.M. and at 4:45 P.M., with the following results.

Bus	Morning	Afternoon
1	43	41
2	51	49
3	37	44
4	24	32
5	47	46
6	44	42
7	50	47
8	55	51
9	46	49

Use the data to compute a 90% confidence interval to estimate the population average difference. Assume that difference in ridership is normally distributed.

10.56 According to CardWeb Inc.'s CardData, Visa's share of the U.S. credit card market went from 44.7% in 1990 to 48.7% in 1997. How were these figures obtained? Possibly they were determined by examining the total dollar amounts of transactions for the population of credit card usage and determining Visa's portion. If so, certainly we could declare that Visa's market share increased. Suppose, however, that the 1990 figure was obtained by randomly selecting 1,300 credit card transactions and tallying the proportion done with a Visa card. Suppose also that the 1997 figure was obtained by randomly selecting 1,450 credit card transactions and doing the same thing. At a 5% level of significance, do the data present enough evidence to declare that Visa's market share increased significantly between 1990 and 1997?

10.57 A study was conducted to compare the salaries of accounting clerks and data entry operators. One of the hypotheses to be tested is that the variability of salaries among accounting clerks is the same as the variability of salaries of data entry operators. To test this hypothesis, a random sample of 16 accounting clerks was taken, resulting in a sample mean salary of $26,400 and a sample standard deviation of $1,200. A random sample of 14 data entry operators was taken as well, resulting in a sample mean of $25,800 and a sample standard deviation of $1,050. Use these data and α = .05 to test to determine whether the population variance of salaries is the same for accounting clerks as it is for data entry operators. Assume that salaries of data entry operators and accounting clerks are normally distributed in the population.

10.58 Is there more variation in the output of one shift in a manufacturing plant than in another shift? In an effort to study this question, plant managers gathered productivity reports from the 8 A.M. to 4 P.M. shift for 8 days. The reports indicated that the following numbers of units were produced on each day for this shift.

5528	4779	5112	5380
4918	4763	5055	5106

Productivity information was also gathered from 7 days for the 4 P.M. to midnight shift, resulting in the following data.

4325	4016	4872	4559
3982	4754	4116	

Use these data and α = .01 to test to determine whether the variances of productivity for the two shifts are the same. Assume productivity is normally distributed in the population.

10.59 A study was conducted to develop a scale to measure stress in the workplace. Respondents were asked to rate 26 distinct work events. Each event was to be compared with the stress of the first week on the job, which was awarded an arbitrary score of 500. Sixty professional men and 41 professional women participated in the study. One of the stress events was "lack of support from the boss." The men's sample average rating of this event was 631 and the women's sample average rating was 848. Suppose the population standard deviations for men and for women both were about 100. Construct a 95% confidence interval to estimate the difference in the population mean scores on this event for men and women.

10.60 A national grocery store chain wants to estimate the difference in the average weight of turkeys sold in Detroit and the average weight of turkeys sold in Charlotte. According to the chain's researcher, a random sample of 20 turkeys sold at the chain's stores in Detroit yielded a sample mean of 17.53 pounds, with a standard deviation of 3.2 pounds. Her random sample of 24 turkeys sold at the chain's stores in Charlotte yielded a sample mean of 14.89 pounds, with a standard deviation of 2.7 pounds. Use a 1% level of significance to determine whether there is a difference in the mean weight of turkeys sold in these two cities. Assume the population variances are approximately the same and that the weights of turkeys sold in the stores are normally distributed.

10.61 A tree nursery has been experimenting with fertilizer to increase the growth of seedlings. A sample of 35 two-year-old pine trees are grown for three more years with a cake of fertilizer buried in the soil near the trees' roots. A second sample of 35 two-year-old pine trees are grown for three more years under identical conditions (soil, temperature, water) as the first group, but not fertilized. Tree growth is measured over the three-year period with the following results.

Trees with Fertilizer	Trees without Fertilizer
$n_1 = 35$	$n_2 = 35$
$\bar{x}_1 = 38.4$ inches	$\bar{x}_1 = 23.1$ inches
$\sigma_1 = 9.8$ inches	$\sigma_2 = 7.4$ inches

Do the data support the theory that the population of trees with the fertilizer grew significantly larger during the period in which they were fertilized than the nonfertilized trees? Use $\alpha = .01$.

10.62 One of the most important aspects of a store's image is the perceived quality of its merchandise. Other factors include merchandise pricing, assortment of products, convenience of location, and service. Suppose image perceptions of shoppers of specialty stores and shoppers of discount stores are being compared. A random sample of shoppers is taken at each type of store, and the shoppers are asked whether the quality of merchandise is a determining factor in their perception of the store's image. Some 75% of the 350 shoppers at the specialty stores say Yes, but only 52% of the 500 shoppers at the discount store say Yes. Construct a 90% confidence interval for the difference in population proportions.

10.63 Use the data from Problem 10.54 to determine whether the variances of term and whole life insurance amounts are the same. Let $\alpha = .05$.

10.64 What is the average difference between the price of name-brand soup and the price of store-brand soup? To obtain an estimate, an analyst randomly samples eight stores. Each store sells its own brand and a national name brand. The prices of a can of name-brand tomato soup and a can of the store-brand tomato soup follow.

Store	Name Brand	Store Brand
1	54¢	49¢
2	55	50
3	59	52
4	53	51
5	54	50
6	61	56
7	51	47
8	53	49

Construct a 90% confidence interval to estimate the average difference. Assume that the differences in prices of tomato soup are normally distributed in the population.

10.65 As the prices of heating oil and natural gas increase, consumers become more careful about heating their homes. Researchers want to know how warm homeowners keep their houses in January and how the results from Wisconsin and Tennessee compare. The researchers randomly call 23 Wisconsin households between 7 P.M. and 9 P.M. on January 15 and ask the respondent how warm the house is according to the thermostat. The researchers then call 19 households in Tennessee the same night and ask the same question. The results follow.

Wisconsin				Tennessee			
71	71	65	68	73	75	74	71
70	61	67	69	74	73	74	70
75	68	71	73	72	71	69	72
74	68	67	69	74	73	70	72
69	72	67	72	69	70	67	
70	73	72					

For $\alpha = .01$, is the average temperature of a house in Tennessee significantly higher than that of a house in Wisconsin on the evening of January 15? Assume the population variances are equal and the house temperatures are normally distributed in each population.

10.66 In manufacturing, does worker productivity drop on Friday? In an effort to determine whether it does, a company's personnel analyst randomly selects from a manufacturing plant five workers who make the same part. He measures their output on Wednesday and again on Friday and obtains the following results.

Worker	Wednesday Output	Friday Output
1	71	53
2	56	47
3	75	52
4	68	55
5	74	58

The analyst uses $\alpha = .05$ and assumes the difference in productivity is normally distributed. Do the samples provide enough evidence to show that productivity drops on Friday?

10.67 A manufacturer uses two machines to drill holes in pieces of sheet metal used in engine construction. The workers who attach the sheet metal to the engine become inspectors in that they reject sheets so poorly drilled that they cannot be attached. The production manager is interested in knowing whether one machine produces more defective drillings than the other machine. As an experiment, employees mark the sheets so that the manager can determine which machine was used to drill the holes. A random sample of 191 sheets of metal drilled by machine 1 is taken, and 38 of the sheets are defective. A random sample of 202 sheets of metal drilled by machine 2 is taken, and 21 of the sheets are defective. Use $\alpha = .05$ to determine whether there is a significant difference in the proportion of sheets drilled with defective holes between machine 1 and machine 2.

10.68 Is there a difference in the proportion of construction workers who are under 35 years of age and the proportion of telephone repair people who are under 35 years of age? Suppose a study is conducted in Calgary, Alberta, using random samples of 338 construction workers and 281 telephone repair people. The sample of construction workers includes 297 people under 35 years of age and the sample of telephone repair people includes 192 people under that age. Use these data to construct a 90% confidence interval to estimate the difference in proportions of people under 35 years of age among construction workers and telephone repair people.

10.69 Executives often spend so many hours in meetings that they have relatively little time to manage their individual areas of operation. What is the difference in mean time spent in meetings by executives of the aerospace industry and executives of the automobile industry? Suppose random samples of 33 aerospace executives and 35 automobile executives are monitored for a week to determine how much time they spend in meetings. The results follow.

Aerospace	Automobile
$n_1 = 33$	$n_2 = 35$
$\bar{x}_1 = 12.4$ hours	$\bar{x}_2 = 4.6$ hours
$\sigma_1 = 2.9$ hours	$\sigma_2 = 1.8$ hours

Use the data to estimate the difference in the mean time per week executives in these two industries spend in meetings. Use a 99% level of confidence.

10.70 Various types of retail outlets sell toys during the holiday season. Among them are specialty toy stores, large discount toy stores, and other retailers that carry toys as only one part of their stock of goods. Is there any difference in the dollar amount of a customer purchase between a large discount toy store and a specialty toy store if they carry relatively comparable types of toys? Suppose in December a random sample of 60 sales slips is selected from a large discount toy outlet and a random sample of 40 sales slips is selected from a specialty toy store. The data gathered from these samples follow.

Large Discount Toy Store	Specialty Toy Store
$\bar{x}_D = \$47.20$	$\bar{x}_S = \$27.40$
$\sigma_D = \$12.45$	$\sigma_S = \$9.82$

Use $\alpha = .01$ and the data to determine whether there is a significant difference in the average size of purchases at these stores.

10.71 One of the new thrusts of quality control management is to examine the process by which a product is produced. This approach also applies to paperwork. In industries where large long-term projects are undertaken, days and even weeks may elapse as a change order makes its way through a maze of approvals before receiving final approval. This process can result in long delays and stretch schedules to the breaking point. Suppose a quality control consulting group claims that it can significantly reduce the number of days required for such paperwork to receive approval. In an attempt to "prove" its case, the group selects five jobs for which it revises the paperwork system. The following data show the number of days required for a change order to be approved before the group intervened and the number of days required for a change order to be approved after the group instituted a new paperwork system.

Before	After
12	8
7	3
10	8
16	9
8	5

Use $\alpha = .01$ to determine whether there was a significant drop in the number of days required to process paperwork to approve change orders. Assume that the differences in days are normally distributed.

10.72 For the two large newspapers in your city, you are interested in knowing whether there is a significant difference in the average number of pages in each dedicated solely to advertising. You randomly select 10 editions of newspaper A and six editions of newspaper B (excluding weekend editions). The data follow. Use $\alpha = .01$ to test whether there is a significant difference in averages. Assume the number of pages of advertising per edition is normally distributed and the population variances are approximately equal.

A		B	
17	17	8	14
21	15	11	10
11	19	9	6
19	22		
26	16		

INTERPRETING THE OUTPUT

10.73 A study by Colliers International presented the highest and the lowest global rental rates per year per square foot of office space. Among the cities with the lowest rates were Perth, Australia; Edmonton, Alberta, Canada; and Calgary, Alberta, Canada with rates of $8.81, $9.55, and $9.69, respectively. At the high end were Hong Kong; Bombay, India; and Tokyo, Japan with rates over $100. Suppose a researcher conducted her own survey of businesses renting office space to determine whether one city is significantly more expensive than another. The data are tallied and analyzed by using MINITAB. The results follow. Discuss the output. Assume that rental rates are normally distributed in the population. What cities were studied? How large were the samples? What were the sample statistics? What was the value of alpha? What were the hypotheses, and what was the conclusion?

```
Two-sample T for Hong Kong vs Bombay

            N    Mean   StDev   SE Mean
Hong Kong  19   130.4   12.9     3.0
Bombay     23   128.4   13.9     2.9

Difference = mu Hong Kong - mu Bombay
Estimate for difference:  2.00
98% CI for difference: (-8.11, 12.11)
T-Test of difference = 0 (vs not =):
T-Value = 0.48   P-Value = 0.634
DF = 40
Both use Pooled StDev = 13.5
```

10.74 Why do employees "blow the whistle" on other employees for unethical or illegal behavior? One study conducted by the AICPA reported the likelihood that employees would blow the whistle on another employee for such things as unsafe working conditions, unsafe products, and poorly managed operations. On a scale from 1 to 7, with 1 denoting highly improbable and 7 denoting highly probable, unnecessary purchases received a 5.72 in the study. Suppose this study was administered at a company and then all employees were subjected to a one-month series of seminars on reasons to blow the whistle on fellow employees. One month later the study was administered again to the same employees at the company in an effort to determine whether the treatment had any effect. The following Excel output shows the results of the study. What were the sample sizes? What might the hypotheses have been? If $\alpha = .05$, what conclusions could be made? Which of the statistical tests presented in this chapter is likely to have been used? Assume that differences in scores are normally distributed.

	A	B	C
1	t-Test: Paired Two Sample for Means		
2		Variable 1	Variable 2
3	Mean	4.357	5.214
4	Variance	1.170	0.951
5	Observations	14	14
6	Pearson Correlation	0.51	
7	Hypothesized Mean Difference	0	
8	df	13	
9	t Stat	-3.12	
10	P(T<=t) one-tail	0.0040	
11	t Critical one-tail	1.77	
12	P(T<=t) two-tail	0.0081	
13	t Critical two-tail	2.16	

10.75 A large manufacturing company produces computer printers that are distributed and sold all over the United States. Due to lack of industry information, the company has a difficult time ascertaining its market share in different parts of the country. They hire a market research firm to estimate their market share in a northern city and a southern city. They would also like to know whether there is a difference in their market shares in these two cities; if so, they want to estimate how much. The market research firm randomly selects printer customers from different locales across both cities and determines what brand of computer printer they purchased. The following MINITAB output shows the results from this study. Discuss the results including sample sizes, estimation of the difference in proportions, and any significant differences determined. What were the hypotheses tested?

```
Test and CI for Two Proportions

Sample   X    N    Sample p
  1     147  473   0.310782
  2     104  385   0.270130

Estimate for p(1) - p(2): 0.0406524
99% CI for p(1) - p(2): (-0.0393623, 0.120667)
Test for p(1) - p(2) = 0 (vs not = 0):
Z = 1.31   P-Value = 0.191
```

10.76 A manufacturing company produces plastic pipes that are specified to be 10 inches long and 1/8 inch thick with an opening of 3/4 inch. These pipes are molded on two different machines. To maintain consistency, the company periodically randomly selects pipes for testing. In one specific test, pipes were randomly sampled from each machine and the lengths were measured. A statistical test was computed using Excel in an effort to determine whether there was a significant difference in the variances of the lengths of the pipes produced by the two machines. The results are shown here. Discuss the outcome of this test along with some of the other information given in the output.

	A	B	C
1	F-Test Two-Sample for Variances		
2		Machine 1	Machine 2
3	Mean	9.9124	9.9250
4	Variance	0.019110	0.010664
5	Observations	26	26
6	df	25	25
7	F	1.79	
8	P(F<=f) one-tail	0.0758	
9	F Critical one-tail	1.96	

ANALYZING THE DATABASES

see www.wiley.com/college/black

1. Test to determine whether there is a significant difference between mean "Value added by the Manufacturer" and the mean "Cost of Materials" in manufacturing. Use the manufacturing database as the sample data and let alpha be .01.

2. Use the manufacturing database to test to determine whether there is a significantly greater variance among the values of "End-of-Year Inventories" than among "Cost of Materials." Let $\alpha = .05$.

3. Is there a difference between the average "Number of admissions" at a general medical hospital and a psychiatric hospital? Use the hospital database to test

this hypothesis with $\alpha = .10$. The variable "Service" in the hospital database differentiates general medical hospitals (coded 1) and psychiatric hospitals (coded 2). Now test to determine whether there is a difference between these two types of hospitals on the variables "Beds" and "Total Expenses."

4. Use the financial database to test whether there is a significant difference in the proportion of companies whose "Earnings per Share" are more than $2.00 and the proportion of companies whose "Dividends per Share" are more than $1.00. Let $\alpha = .05$.

CASE: SEITZ CORPORATION: PRODUCING QUALITY GEAR-DRIVEN AND LINEAR-MOTION PRODUCTS

The Seitz Corporation is a QS 9000 and ISO 9001 certified company that designs and manufactures thermoplastic mechanical drives, such as gears and pulleys, and pin-feed tractors for printers. They specialize in complete gear train design and converting drive systems from metals to plastics for cost reductions and higher performance. Founded in 1949 by the late Karl F. Seitz, this family-owned company based in Torrington, Connecticut, operates plants in Connecticut and Illinois and is in the process of opening a plant in Loveland, Colorado. Currently, Seitz's plants employ about 300 people; the new Loveland facility is expected to add another 200 employees to that number in the next two years.

Seitz began as a small toolmaking business and grew slowly. In the late 1960s, the company expanded its services to include custom injection molding. As their customer base grew to include leading printer manufacturers, Seitz developed and patented a proprietary line of perforated-form-handling tractors. Utilizing its injection-molding technology, the company engineered an all-plastic tractor called Data Motion, which replaced the costly metal version. By the late 1970s, business was booming, and Data Motion had become the worldwide industry leader.

In the 1980s, foreign competition entered the business equipment market, and many of Seitz's customers relocated or closed shop. The ripple effect hit Seitz as sales declined and profits eroded. Employment at the company dropped from a

high of 313 in 1985 to only 125 in 1987. Drastic changes had to be made at Seitz.

To meet the challenge in 1987, Seitz made a crucial decision to change the way it did business. The company implemented a formal five-year plan with measurable goals called "World-Class Excellence Through Total Quality." Senior managers devoted many hours to improving employee training and involvement. New concepts were explored and integrated into the business plan. Teams and programs were put into place to immediately correct deficiencies in Seitz's systems that were revealed in customer satisfaction surveys. All employees from machine operators to accountants were taught that quality means understanding customers' needs and fulfilling them correctly the first time.

Once the program started, thousands of dollars in cost savings and two new products generating almost $1 million in sales resulted. Annual sales grew from $10.8 million in 1987 to $19 million in 1990. Seitz's customer base expanded from 312 in 1987 to 550 at the end of 1990.

In the decade of the 1990s, Seitz continued its steady growth. By 1999, Seitz was shipping products to 28 countries, and customers included Xerox, Hewlett Packard, Canon, U.S. Tsubaki, and many more worldwide. By 1998, sales topped the $30 million mark. In the year 2000, Seitz introduced a new line of actuators to accommodate different levels of system intelligence in transportation HVAC applications. CEO and president Alan F. Seitz stated that the "Seitz Corporation is dedicated to providing products and services that consistently meet or exceed our customers' requirements."

Discussion

1. Seitz's list of several hundred business-to-business customers continues to grow. Managers would like to know whether the average dollar amount of sales per transaction per customer has changed from last year to this year. Suppose company accountants sampled 20 customers randomly from last year's records and determined that the mean sales per customer was $2,300, with a standard deviation of $500. They sampled 25 customers randomly from this year's files and determined that the mean sales per customer for this sample was $2,450, with a standard deviation of $540. Analyze these data and summarize your findings for managers. Explain how this information can be used by decision makers. Assume that sales per customer are normally distributed.

2. One common approach to measuring a company's quality is through the use of customer satisfaction surveys. Suppose in a random sample Seitz's customers are asked whether the plastic tractor produced by Seitz has outstanding quality (Yes or No). Assume Seitz produces these tractors at two different plant locations and that the tractor customers can be divided according to where their tractors were manufactured. Suppose a random sample of 45 customers who bought tractors made at plant 1 results in 18 saying the tractors have excellent quality and a random sample of 51 customers who bought tractors made at plant 2 results in 12 saying the tractors have excellent quality. Use a confidence interval to express the estimated difference in population proportions of excellent ratings between the two groups of customers. Does it seem to matter which plant produces the tractors in terms of the quality rating received from customers? What would you report from these data?

3. Suppose the customer satisfaction survey included a question on the overall quality of Seitz measured on a 5-point scale, with 1 indicating low quality and 5 indicating high quality. Company managers monitor the figures from year to year to help determine whether Seitz is improving customers' perception of its quality. Suppose random samples of the responses from 2001 customers and 2002 customers are taken and analyzed on this question, and the following MINITAB analysis of the data results. Help managers interpret this analysis so that comparisons can be made between 2001 and 2002. Discuss the samples, the statistics, and the conclusions.

Two-Sample t Test and Confidence Interval

```
Two sample T for 2001 vs 2002
        N    Mean   StDev   SE Mean
2001   75   3.268   0.195    0.023
2002   93   3.322   0.182    0.019

95% C.I. For mu 2001 - mu 2002:
(20.112, 0.004)

T-Test mu 2001 = mu 2002 (vs not =):
T = -1.83 P = 0.070 DF = 153
```

4. Suppose Seitz produces pulleys that are specified to be 50 millimeters (mm) in diameter. A large batch of pulleys is made in week 1 and another is made in week 5. Quality control people want to determine whether there is a difference in the variance of the diameters of the two batches. Assume that a sample of six pulleys from the week 1 batch results in the following diameter measurements (in mm): 51, 50, 48, 50, 49, 51. Assume that a sample of seven pulleys from the week 5 batch results in the following diameter measurements (in mm): 50, 48, 48, 51, 52, 50, 52. Conduct a test to determine whether the variance in diameters differs between these two populations. Why would the quality control people be interested in such a test? What results of this test would you relate to them? What about the means of these two batches? Analyze these data in terms of the means and report on the results. Assume that pulley diameters are normally distributed in the population.

Source: Adapted from "Seitz Corporation," *Strengthening America's Competitiveness: Resource Management Insights for Small Business Success,* published by Warner Books on behalf of Connecticut Mutual Life Insurance Company and the U.S. Chamber of Commerce in association with the Blue Chip Enterprise Initiative (1991). Case update based on Seitz Corporation, http://www.seitzcorp.com.

USING THE COMPUTER

EXCEL

With the exception of the difference in two proportions, the techniques presented in this chapter can be analyzed by using Excel. Many of the analyses are done by using the **Data Analysis** dialog box options. Begin by selecting **Tools** on the menu bar. From this menu select **Data Analysis**. Several possible options in the Data Analysis dialog box can be used to analyze two-sample data. To test the difference in two population variances, select the command **F-test Two-Sample for Variances**. A dialog box will appear. Enter the locations of the two samples in the two spaces appearing first. Select **Alpha**. The output consists of the mean, variance, and sample size for each sample along with the degrees of freedom, the F statistic, the p-value, and the critical F value.

To test the difference in two related populations, select **t Test: Paired Two-Sample for Means** from the **Data Analysis** dialog box. A dialog box will appear. Enter the locations of the two variables in the first two spaces. Enter the hypothesized mean difference in the third space and enter **Alpha**. The output will consist of the means, the variances, the sample sizes, the degrees of freedom, the hypothesized mean difference, the t statistic for a one-tailed test with its associated p-value, and the t statistic for a two-tailed test with its associated p-value.

Two t tests are available from the **Data Analysis** dialog box to test the difference in the means of two independent populations, one assuming equal variances and one assuming unequal variances. The command for the t test assuming equal variances is **t-Test: Two-Sample Assuming Equal Variances** and the command for the t test assuming unequal variances is **t-Test: Two-Sample Assuming Unequal Variances**. The required input is the same for both. Enter the location of the two samples of data in the first two spaces. In the third space, record the hypothesized value of the mean difference. Insert alpha in the **Alpha** space. The output is identical for each of these tests, but the test assuming equal variances will yield the value of the pooled variance in addition to the other output. The common output for the two tests consists of the means, the variances, the sample sizes, the hypothesized mean difference, the degrees of freedom, the t statistic, the p-value, and the critical t value for both one-tailed and two-tailed tests.

If the population variances are known, a z test for the difference in two means can be used to analyze the data. Select **z-Test: Two-Sample for Means** from the **Data Analysis** dialog box. A dialog box will appear. Enter the location of the two samples in the first two spaces. Enter the hypothesized mean difference in the third space. Enter the known variances in the next two boxes. Select **Alpha**. The output consists of the means, the variances, the sample sizes, the hypothesized mean differences, z, the p-value, and critical z for both one-tailed and two-tailed tests.

The Paste Function can be used to do some of the analysis from this chapter. Begin by clicking the Paste Function, f_x, on the standard tool bar. From the **Function category** on the left, select **Statistical**. From the menu on the right, select **FTEST** to test the difference in two variances and select **TTEST** to test the difference in two means. The dialog boxes for these selections will appear. Each of these dialog boxes requires the location of the data in the first two spaces. The **TTEST** dialog box requires that you place a 1 in the **Tails** space if you are requesting a one-tailed test and a 2 if you are requesting a two-tailed test. Insert a 1, a 2, or a 3 in the **Type** space. A 1 in the **Type** space signifies that you want to conduct a paired difference test. A 2 signifies a two-sample test of the means assuming equal variances, and a 3 signifies a two-sample test of the means assuming unequal variances. The output for each of these tests is the p-value.

MINITAB

MINITAB Windows has the capability of directly computing a two-sample t test. The output will contain both the t test and the confidence interval. Begin by selecting **Stat** on the menu bar and a pull-down menu will appear. Select **Basic Statistics** from the pull-down menu and a second pull-down menu will appear. From this menu, select **2-Sample t**. A dialog box will appear. If the data are located in two different columns, check **Samples in different columns**, and place the column locations of the data in the next two boxes. If the data are stacked, check the first circle, **Samples in one column**, and place the location of the stacked data in the next space and the location of the group identifiers in the space labeled **Subscripts**. Check to indicate whether you are assuming equal variances. In order enter the direction of the hypothesis and number of tails to be tested, select **Options**. The **Options** dialog box that appears asks three questions. In the first line, enter the level of confidence, in the second line enter the mean difference being tested, and in the third line select which of the three alternative hypotheses are being tested. The output consists of the sample means, the sample sizes, the sample standard deviations, the standard error of the mean, the confidence interval, the t statistic, the p-value, and the degrees of freedom.

MINITAB can compute inferences about the difference in two dependent populations. Select **Stat** from the menu bar. From the pull-down menu that appears, select **Basic Statistics**. From the next pull-down menu that appears, select **Paired t**. In that dialog box, enter the column with one set of data in the **First sample** line and the column with the other set of data in the **Second sample** line. Select **Options** to enter the confidence level, the test mean, and the alternative hypothesis. The output contains the sample means, the sample standard deviations, the standard errors of the means, the confidence interval of the population difference, a statement of the tested hypotheses, the observed t value, and the associated p-value.

MINITAB also has the capability of analyzing the difference in two population proportions. Begin by selecting **Stat** from the menu bar. From the pull-down menu that appears, select **Basic Statistics.** From the next pull-down menu that appears, select **2 Proportions.** That dialog box offers three major options. If the dichotomous data are in one column with subscripts in a second column, choose the first option, **Samples in one column.** If the dichotomous data are in two separate columns (one for each group that is being compared), use the second option, **Samples in different columns.** If you merely want to enter the two sample sizes and how many of each possess the characteristic of interest (n and x), use the third option, **Summarized data.** By selecting **Options,** you have the opportunity to enter the confidence level, the tested difference, and the alternative hypothesis. The output contains a breakdown of each sample including n, x, and the sample proportion. In addition, the output contains the difference in sample proportions between the groups, the confidence interval for the difference, a statement of the tested hypotheses, the observed z value, and the associated p-value.

CHAPTER 11

Analysis of Variance and Design of Experiments

LEARNING OBJECTIVES

The focus of this chapter is the design of experiments and the analysis of variance, thereby enabling you to:

1. Understand the differences between various experimental designs and when to use them.
2. Compute and interpret the results of a one-way ANOVA.
3. Compute and interpret the results of a random block design.
4. Compute and interpret the results of a two-way ANOVA.
5. Understand and interpret interaction.
6. Know when and how to use multiple comparison techniques.

Analyzing the Differences in Profitability of Companies in Three Countries

In a true global marketplace, little difference should separate the profitability of firms from various countries in like industries. The reasoning is that in a true global economy, companies in similar industries face the same obstacles, market economies, and opportunities. In addition, firms in the same line of business tend to develop similar organizational structures and strategies. Logically, it follows that if they are viable businesses and competitive players, these firms should earn similar rates of return.

Not all firms in like industries around the world achieve the same profits. Does it mean that a true global economy does not exist? Some people argue that the business scenario around the world is more multidomestic than global. Through trade agreements, some countries minimize barriers to trade. The result is that firms in various countries within the trade agreement area develop similar business profiles. However, barriers and obstacles to a completely open global economy remain.

Michael Blaine (Ohio State University) set out to determine whether statistically significant differences characterize the profitability of large German, Japanese, and U.S. companies. He randomly selected 100 companies from Disclosure/Worldscope's Industrial Company Profiles for each of the three countries. Data collected from these companies were used to calculate an annual national average indicator of profitability of large companies in each of the three countries over a six-year period. Three different measurements of profitability were used: (1) the average annual return on assets, (2) return on equity, and (3) operating margin. Some of the data gathered in the study follow.

Return on Assets

Year	Germany	Japan	United States
1	3.65	4.06	7.89
2	3.68	4.35	6.40
3	3.62	3.29	5.63
4	4.13	3.22	7.69
5	3.81	3.69	4.10
6	4.29	3.89	6.34

Return on Equity

Year	Germany	Japan	United States
1	8.86	8.48	15.24
2	10.56	10.40	12.05
3	10.58	6.73	6.89
4	9.77	6.12	15.20
5	10.33	7.90	6.02
6	13.02	9.65	9.17

Operating Margin

Year	Germany	Japan	United States
1	5.99	7.05	8.99
2	5.90	6.74	8.76
3	5.52	5.32	6.37
4	1.80	5.20	7.08
5	0.83	6.03	4.75
6	0.44	6.70	6.40

Managerial and Statistical Questions

1. In general, is an overall difference identified in the return on assets between large companies in Germany, Japan, and the United States? What about for return on equity and operating margin?

2. Statistically, could we test the preceding questions by using a series of *t* tests between each pair of countries? Suppose the researcher included seven countries in the study. To test the difference in each pair of countries would take 21 *t* tests for the means of independent samples (Chapter 10). Is there a better way? What about error rate?

3. Could other factors besides country be studied? Only large companies were included in the study. How could small and medium-sized companies be included in the analysis? Does the year make a difference? Is it possible to test to determine whether a statistically significant difference exists in return on assets, return on equity, or operating margin between years?

4. If we designed a study to include small, medium, and large companies in each of these three countries, is it possible to test to determine whether an interaction between company size and country is present? In other words, suppose large companies do better in Germany, but small companies do better in Japan. What statistical techniques might be used to analyze that interaction of company and country? How do the results affect the other parts of the study?

Source: Adapted from Michael Blaine, "Comparing the Profitability of Firms in Germany, Japan, and the United States," *Management International Review*, vol. 34, no. 2 (1994), pp. 125–148.

Sometimes business research entails more complicated hypothesis-testing scenarios than those presented to this point in the text. Instead of comparing the wear of tire tread for two brands of tires to determine whether there is a significant difference between the brands, as we could have done by using Chapter 10 techniques, a tire researcher may choose to compare three, four, or even more brands of tires at the same time. In addition, the researcher may want to include different levels of quality of tires in the experiment, such as low-quality, medium-quality, and high-quality tires. Tests may be conducted under varying conditions of temperature, precipitation, or road surface.

How does a researcher set up designs for such experiments? How can the data be analyzed? These questions can be answered, in part, through the use of analysis of variance and the design of experiments.

11.1 INTRODUCTION TO DESIGN OF EXPERIMENTS

An **experimental design** is *a plan and a structure to test hypotheses in which the researcher either controls or manipulates one or more variables.* It contains independent and dependent variables. In an experimental design, an **independent variable** may be either a treatment variable or a classification variable. A **treatment variable** is *a variable the experimenter controls or modifies in the experiment.* A **classification variable** is *some characteristic of the experimental subjects that was present prior to the experiment and is not a result of the experimenter's manipulations or control.* Independent variables are sometimes also referred to as **factors.** Wal-Mart executives might sanction an in-house study to compare daily sales volumes for a given size store in four different demographic settings: (1) inner-city stores (large city), (2) suburban stores (large city), (3) stores in a medium-sized city, and (4) stores in a small town. Managers might also decide to compare sales on the five different weekdays (Monday through Friday).

In this study, the independent variables are store demographics and day of the week. A finance researcher might conduct a study to determine whether there is a significant difference in application fees for home loans in five geographic regions of the United

States and might include three different types of lending organizations. In this study, the independent variables are geographic region and types of lending organizations. Or suppose a manufacturing organization produces a valve that is specified to have an opening of 6.37 centimeters. Quality controllers within the company might decide to test to determine how the openings for produced valves vary among four different machines on three different shifts. This experiment includes the independent variables of type of machine and work shift.

Whether an independent variable can be manipulated by the researcher depends on the concept being studied. Independent variables such as work shift, gender of employee, geographic region, type of machine, and quality of tire are classification variables with conditions that existed prior to the study. The business researcher cannot change the characteristic of the variable, so he or she studies the phenomenon being explored under several conditions of the various aspects of the variable. As an example, the valve experiment is conducted under the conditions of all three work shifts.

However, some independent variables can be manipulated by the researcher. For example, in the well-known Hawthorne studies of the Western Electric Company in the 1920s in Illinois, the amount of light in production areas was varied to determine the effect of light on productivity. In theory, this independent variable could be manipulated by the researcher to allow any level of lighting. Other examples of independent variables that can be manipulated include the amount of bonuses offered workers, level of humidity, and temperature.

Each independent variable has two or more levels, or classifications. **Levels,** or **classifications,** of independent variables are *the subcategories of the independent variable used by the researcher in the experimental design.* For example, the different demographic settings listed for the Wal-Mart study are four levels, or classifications, of the independent variable store demographics: (1) inner-city store, (2) suburban store, (3) store in a medium-sized city, and (4) store in small town. In the valve experiment, four levels or classifications of machines within the independent variable machine type are used: machine 1, machine 2, machine 3, and machine 4.

The other type of variable in an experimental design is a **dependent variable.** A dependent variable is *the response to the different levels of the independent variables.* It is the measurement taken under the conditions of the experimental design that reflect the effects of the independent variable(s). In the Wal-Mart study, the dependent variable is probably the dollar amount of daily total sales. For the study on loan application fees, the fee charged for a loan application is probably the dependent variable. In the valve experiment, the dependent variable is the size of the opening of the valve.

Experimental designs in this chapter are analyzed statistically by a group of techniques referred to as **analysis of variance,** or **ANOVA.** The analysis of variance concept begins with the notion that individual items being studied, such as employees, machine-produced products, district offices, hospitals, and so on, are not all the same. Note the measurements for the openings of 24 valves randomly selected from an assembly line that are given in Table 11.1. The mean opening is 6.34 centimeters (cm). Only one of the 24 valve openings is actually the mean. Why do the valve openings vary? Notice that the total sum of squares of deviation of these valve openings around the mean is .3915 cm^2. Why is this value not zero? Using various types of experimental designs, we can explore some possible reasons for this variance with analysis of variance techniques. As we explore each of the experimental designs and their associated analysis, note that the statistical technique is attempting to "break down" the total variance among the objects being studied

TABLE 11.1

Valve Opening Measurements (in cm) for 24 Valves Produced on an Assembly Line

6.26	6.19	6.33	6.26	6.50
6.19	6.44	6.22	6.54	6.23
6.29	6.40	6.23	6.29	6.58
6.27	6.38	6.58	6.31	6.34
6.21	6.19	6.36	6.56	

$\bar{x} = 6.34$ Total Sum of Squares Deviation = SST = $\Sigma(x_i - \bar{x})^2 = .3915$

into possible causes. In the case of the valve openings, this variance of measurements might be due to such variables as machine, operator, shift, supplier, and production conditions, among others.

Many different types of experimental designs are available to researchers. In this chapter, we will present and discuss three specific types of experimental designs: completely randomized design, randomized block design, and factorial experiments.

11.1 PROBLEMS

11.1 Some New York Stock Exchange analysts believe that 24-hour trading on the stock exchange is the wave of the future. As an initial test of this idea, the New York Stock Exchange opened two after-hour "crossing sections" in the early 1990s and studied the results of these extra-hour sessions for one year.

   a. State an independent variable that could have been used for this study.

   b. List at least two levels, or classifications, for this variable.

   c. Give a dependent variable for this study.

11.2 Southwest Airlines is able to keep fares low, in part because of relatively low maintenance costs on its airplanes. One of the main reasons for the low maintenance costs is that Southwest flies only one type of aircraft, the Boeing 737. However, Southwest flies three different versions of the 737. Suppose Southwest decides to conduct a study to determine whether there is a significant difference in the average annual maintenance costs for the three types of 737s used.

   a. State an independent variable for such a study.

   b. What are some of the levels or classifications that might be studied under this variable?

   c. Give a dependent variable for this study.

11.3 A large multinational banking company wants to determine whether there is a significant difference in the average dollar amounts purchased by users of different types of credit cards. Among the credit cards being studied are MasterCard, Visa, Discover, and American Express.

   a. If an experimental design were set up for such a study, what are some possible independent variables?

   b. List at least three levels, or classifications, for each independent variable.

   c. What are some possible dependent variables for this experiment?

11.4 Is there a difference in the family demographics of people who stay at motels? Suppose a study is conducted in which three categories of motels are used: economy motels, modestly priced chain motels, and exclusive motels. One of the dependent variables studied might be the number of children in the family of the person staying in the motel. Name three other dependent variables that might be used in this study.

11.2 THE COMPLETELY RANDOMIZED DESIGN (ONE-WAY ANOVA)

One of the simplest experimental designs is the completely randomized design. In the **completely randomized design,** *subjects are assigned randomly to treatments.* The completely randomized design contains only one independent variable, with two or more treatment levels, or classifications. If only two treatment levels, or classifications, of the independent variable are present, the design is the same one used to test the difference in means of two independent populations presented in Chapter 10, which used the *t* test to analyze the data.

In this section, we will focus on completely randomized designs with three or more classification levels. Analysis of variance, or ANOVA, will be used to analyze the data that result from the treatments.

A completely randomized design could be structured for a tire-quality study in which tire quality is the independent variable and the treatment levels are low, medium, and high quality. The dependent variable might be the number of miles driven before the tread fails state inspection. A study of daily sales volumes for Wal-Mart stores could be undertaken by using a completely randomized design with demographic setting as the independent variable. The treatment levels, or classifications, would be inner-city stores, suburban stores, stores in medium-sized cities, and stores in small towns. The dependent variable would be sales dollars.

As an example of a completely randomized design, suppose a researcher decides to analyze the effects of the machine operator on the valve opening measurements of valves produced in a manufacturing plant, like those shown in Table 11.1. The independent variable in this design is machine operator. Suppose further that four different operators operate the machines. These four machine operators are the levels of treatment, or classification, of the independent variable. The dependent variable is the opening measurement of the valve. Figure 11.1 shows the structure of this completely randomized design. Is there a significant difference in the mean valve openings of 24 valves produced by the four operators? Table 11.2 contains the valve opening measurements for valves produced under each operator.

One-Way Analysis of Variance

In the machine operator example, is it possible to analyze the four samples by using a t test for the difference in two sample means? These four samples would require $_4C_2 = 6$ individual t tests to accomplish the analysis of two groups at a time. Recall that if $\alpha = .05$ for a particular test, there is a 5% chance of rejecting a null hypothesis that is true (i.e., committing a Type I error). If enough tests are done, eventually one or more null hypotheses will be falsely rejected by chance. Hence, $\alpha = .05$ is valid only for one t test. In this problem, with six t tests, the error rate compounds, so when the analyst is finished with the problem there is a much greater than .05 chance of committing a Type I error. Fortunately, a technique has been developed that analyzes all the sample means at one time and thus precludes the buildup of error rate: analysis of variance (ANOVA). A completely randomized design is analyzed by a **one-way analysis of variance.**

In general, if k samples are being analyzed, the following hypotheses are being tested in a one-way ANOVA.

$$H_0: \mu_1 = \mu_2 = \mu_3 = \dots = \mu_k$$
$$H_a: \text{At least one of the means is different from the others.}$$

The null hypothesis states that the population means for all treatment levels are equal. Because of the way the alternative hypothesis is stated, if even one of the population means is different from the others, the null hypothesis is rejected.

TABLE 11.2
Valve Openings by Operator

1	2	3	4
6.33	6.26	6.44	6.29
6.26	6.36	6.38	6.23
6.31	6.23	6.58	6.19
6.29	6.27	6.54	6.21
6.40	6.19	6.56	
	6.50	6.34	
	6.19	6.58	
	6.22		

FIGURE 11.1
Completely Randomized Design

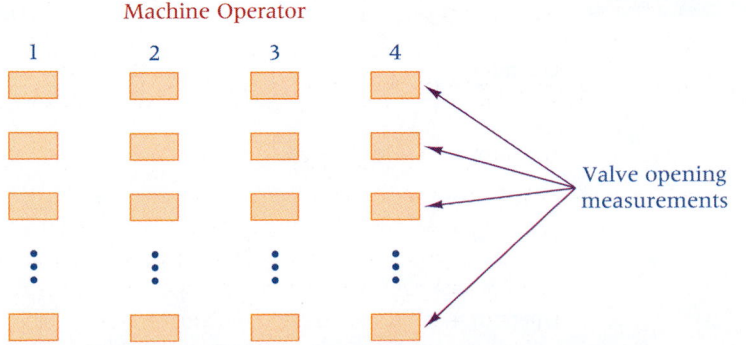

Testing these hypotheses by using one-way ANOVA is accomplished by partitioning the total variance of the data into the following two variances.

1. The variance resulting from the treatment (columns)
2. The error variance, or that portion of the total variance unexplained by the treatment

As part of this process, the total sum of squares of deviation of values around the mean can be divided into two additive and independent parts.

$$SST \qquad\qquad = \qquad\qquad SSC \qquad + \qquad\qquad SSE$$

$$\sum_{i=1}^{n_j}\sum_{j=1}^{C}(x_{ij}-\bar{x})^2 = \sum_{j=1}^{C}n_j(\bar{x}_j-\bar{x})^2 + \sum_{i=1}^{n_j}\sum_{j=1}^{C}(x_{ij}-\bar{x}_j)^2$$

where

i = particular member of a treatment level
j = a treatment level
C = number of treatment levels
n_j = number of observations in a given treatment level
$\bar{x}$ = grand mean
$\bar{x}_j$ = mean of a treatment group or level
x_{ij} = individual value

This relationship is shown in Figure 11.2. Observe that the total sum of squares of variation is partitioned into the sum of squares of treatment (columns) and the sum of squares of error.

The formulas used to accomplish one-way analysis of variance are developed from this relationship. The double summation sign indicates that the values are summed within a treatment level and across treatment levels. Basically, ANOVA compares the relative sizes of the *treatment* variation and the *error* variation (within-group variation). The error variation is unaccounted-for variation and can be viewed at this point as variation due to individual differences within treatment groups. If a significant difference in treatments is present, the treatment variation should be large relative to the error variation.

Figure 11.3 displays the data from the machine operator example in terms of treatment level. Note the variation of values (*x*) *within* each treatment level. Now examine the variation between levels 1 through 4 (the difference in the machine operators). In particular,

---

FIGURE 11.2

Partitioning Total Sum of Squares of Variation

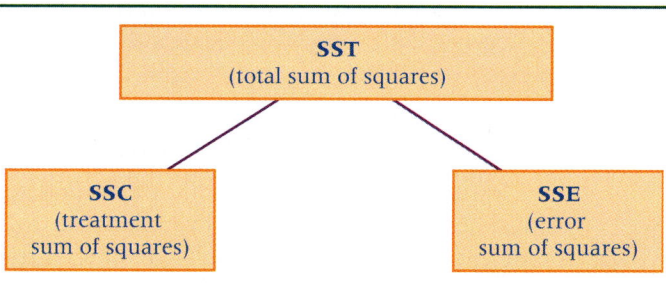

FIGURE 11.3

Location of Mean Value Openings by Operator

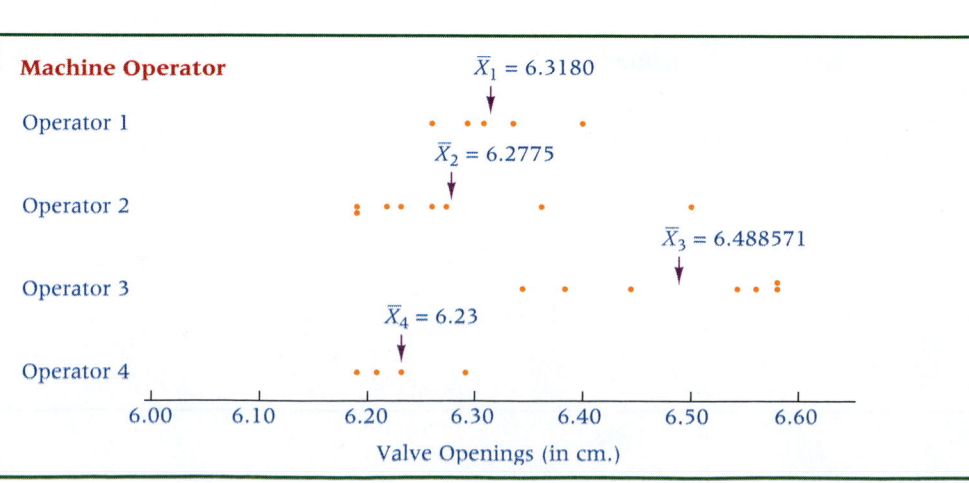

note that values for treatment level 3 seem to be located differently from those of levels 2 and 4. This difference also is underscored by the mean values for each treatment level:

$$\bar{x}_1 = 6.3180 \quad \bar{x}_2 = 6.2775 \quad \bar{x}_3 = 6.488571 \quad \bar{x}_4 = 6.23$$

Analysis of variance is used to determine statistically whether the variance between the treatment level means is greater than the variances within levels (error variance). Several important assumptions underlie analysis of variance:

1. Observations are drawn from normally distributed populations.
2. Observations represent random samples from the populations.
3. Variances of the populations are equal.

These assumptions are similar to those for using the *t* test for small independent samples in Chapter 10. It is assumed that the populations are normally distributed and that the population variances are equal. These techniques should be used only with random samples.

An ANOVA is computed with the three sums of squares: total, treatment (columns), and error. Shown here are the formulas to compute a one-way analysis of variance. The term SS represents sum of squares, and the term MS represents mean square. SSC is the sum of squares columns, which yields the sum of squares between treatments. It measures the variation between columns or between treatments since the independent variable treatment levels are presented as columns. SSE is the sum of squares of error, which yields the variation within treatments (or columns). Some say that it is a measure of the individual differences unaccounted for by the treatments. SST is the total sum of squares and is a measure of all variation in the dependent variable. As shown previously, SST contains both SSC and SSE and can be partitioned into SSC and SSE. MSC, MSE, and MST are the mean squares of column, error, and total, respectively. Mean square is an average and is computed by dividing the sum of squares by the degrees of freedom. Finally, the *F* value is determined by dividing the treatment variance (MSC) by the error variance (MSE). As discussed in Chapter 10, the *F* is a ratio of two variances. In the ANOVA situation, the **F value** is *a ratio of the treatment variance to the error variance.*

FORMULAS FOR COMPUTING A ONE-WAY ANOVA

$$\text{SSC} = \sum_{j=1}^{C} n_j (\bar{x}_j - \bar{x})^2$$

$$\text{SSE} = \sum_{i=1}^{n_j} \sum_{j=1}^{C} (x_{ij} - \bar{x}_j)^2$$

$$\text{SST} = \sum_{i=1}^{n_j} \sum_{j=1}^{C} (x_{ij} - \bar{x})^2$$

$$\text{df}_C = C - 1$$
$$\text{df}_E = N - C$$
$$\text{df}_T = N - 1$$

$$\text{MSC} = \frac{\text{SSC}}{\text{df}_C}$$

$$\text{MSE} = \frac{\text{SSE}}{\text{df}_E}$$

$$F = \frac{\text{MSC}}{\text{MSE}}$$

where

i = a particular member of a treatment level
j = a treatment level
C = number of treatment levels
n_j = number of observations in a given treatment level
$\bar{x}$ = grand mean
$\bar{x}_j$ = column mean
x_{ij} = individual value

Performing these calculations for the machine operator example yields the following.

Machine Operator

1	2	3	4
6.33	6.26	6.44	6.29
6.26	6.36	6.38	6.23
6.31	6.23	6.58	6.19
6.29	6.27	6.54	6.21
6.40	6.19	6.56	
	6.50	6.34	
	6.19	6.58	
	6.22		

T_j:　$T_1 = 31.59$　　$T_2 = 50.22$　　$T_3 = 45.42$　　$T_4 = 24.92$　　$T = 152.15$

n_j:　$n_1 = 5$　　　$n_2 = 8$　　　$n_3 = 7$　　　$n_4 = 4$　　　$N = 24$

$\bar{x}_j$:　$\bar{x}_1 = 6.318$　$\bar{x}_2 = 6.2775$　$\bar{x}_3 = 6.488571$　$\bar{x}_4 = 6.230$　$\bar{x} = 6.339583$

$$SSC = \sum_{j=1}^{C} n_j(\bar{x}_j - \bar{x})^2$$

$= [5(6.318 - 6.339583)^2 + 8(6.2775 - 6.339583)^2 + 7(6.488571$
$\quad - 6.339583)^2 + 4(6.230 - 6.339583)^2]$
$= 0.00233 + 0.03083 + 0.15538 + 0.04803$
$= 0.23658$

$$SSE = \sum_{i=1}^{n_j} \sum_{j=1}^{C} (x_{ij} - \bar{x}_j)^2$$

$= [(6.33 - 6.318)^2 + (6.26 - 6.318)^2 + (6.31 - 6.318)^2 +$
$\quad (6.29 - 6.318)^2 + (6.40 - 6.318)^2 + (6.26 - 6.2775)^2 +$
$\quad (6.36 - 6.2775)^2 + \ldots + (6.19 - 6.230)^2 + (6.21 - 6.230)^2$
$= 0.15492$

$$SST = \sum_{i=1}^{n_j} \sum_{j=1}^{C} (x_{ij} - \bar{x})^2$$

$= [(6.33 - 6.339583)^2 + (6.26 - 6.339583)^2 +$
$\quad (6.31 - 6.339583)^2 + \ldots + (6.19 - 6.339583)^2 +$
$\quad (6.21 - 6.339583)^2$
$= 0.39150$

$$df_C = C - 1 = 4 - 1 = 3$$
$$df_E = N - C = 24 - 4 = 20$$
$$df_T = N - 1 = 24 - 1 = 23$$

$$MSC = \frac{SSC}{df_C} = \frac{.23658}{3} = .078860$$

$$MSE = \frac{SSE}{df_E} = \frac{.15492}{20} = .007746$$

$$F = \frac{.078860}{.007746} = 10.18$$

From these computations, an analysis of variance chart can be constructed, as shown in Table 11.3. The observed F value is 10.18. It is compared to a critical value from the F table to determine whether there is a significant difference in treatment or classification.

Reading the *F* Distribution Table

The ***F* distribution** table is in Table A.7. Associated with every F value in the table are two unique df values: degrees of freedom in the numerator (df_C) and degrees of freedom in the

TABLE 11.3
Analysis of Variance for the Machine Operator Example

Source of Variance	df	SS	MS	F
Between	3	0.23658	0.078860	10.18
Error	20	0.15492	0.007746	
Total	23	0.39150		

denominator (df_E). To look up a value in the F distribution table, the researcher must know both degrees of freedom. Because each F distribution is determined by a unique pair of degrees of freedom, many F distributions are possible. Space constraints limit Table A.7 to F values for only $\alpha = .005, .01, .025, .05,$ and $.10$. However, statistical computer software packages for computing ANOVAs usually give a probability for the F value, which allows a hypothesis-testing decision for any alpha based on the p-value method.

In the one-way ANOVA, the df_C values are the treatment (column) degrees of freedom, $C - 1$. The df_E values are the error degrees of freedom, $N - C$. Table 11.4 contains an abbreviated F distribution table for $\alpha = .05$. For the machine operator example, $df_C = 3$ and $df_E = 20$. $F_{.05,3,20}$ from Table 11.4 is 3.10. This value is the critical value of the F test. Analysis of variance tests are always one-tailed tests with the rejection region in the upper tail. The decision rule is to reject the null hypothesis if the observed F value is greater than the critical F value ($F_{.05,3,20} = 3.10$). For the machine operator problem, the observed F value of 10.18 is larger than the table F value of 3.10. The null hypothesis is rejected. Not all means are equal, so there is a significant difference in the mean valve openings by machine operator. Figure 11.4 is a MINITAB graph of an F distribution showing the critical F value for this example and the rejection region. Note that the F distribution begins at zero and contains no negative values because the F value is the ratio of two variances, and variances are always positive.

Using the Computer for One-Way ANOVA

Many researchers use the computer to analyze data with a one-way ANOVA. Figure 11.5 shows the MINITAB and Excel output of the ANOVA computed for the machine operator example. The output includes the analysis of variance table presented in Table 11.3. Both MINITAB and Excel ANOVA tables display the observed F value, mean squares, sum of squares, degrees of freedom, and a value of p. The value of p is the probability of an F value of 10.18 occurring by chance in an ANOVA with this structure (same degrees of freedom) even if there is no difference between means of the treatment levels. Using the p-value method of testing hypotheses presented in Chapter 9, we can easily see that because this p-value is only .000279, the null hypothesis would be rejected using $\alpha = .05$. Most computer output yields the value of p, so there is no need to look up a table value

---

TABLE 11.4

An Abbreviated F Table for $\alpha = .05$

	NUMERATOR DEGREES OF FREEDOM								
Denominator Degrees of Freedom	1	2	3	4	5	6	7	8	9
.									
.									
.									
19	4.38	3.52	3.13	2.90	2.74	2.63	2.54	2.48	2.42
20	4.35	3.49	3.10	2.87	2.71	2.60	2.51	2.45	2.39
21	4.32	3.47	3.07	2.84	2.68	2.57	2.49	2.42	2.37

FIGURE 11.4

MINITAB Graph of F Values for the Machine Operator Example

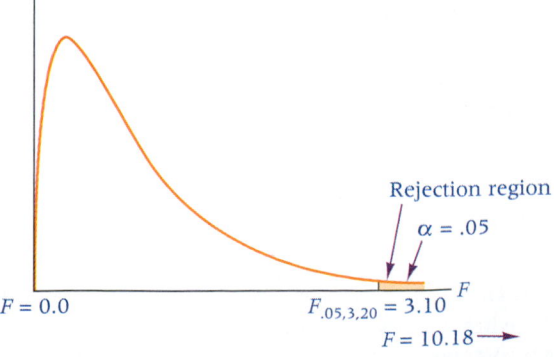

Rejection region
$\alpha = .05$

$F = 0.0$

$F_{.05,3,20} = 3.10$

$F = 10.18$

FIGURE 11.5

MINITAB and Excel Analysis of the Machine Operator Problem

MINITAB Output:

One-way ANOVA: Operator 1, Operator 2, Operator 3, Operator 4

```
Analysis of Variance
Source   DF        SS        MS        F        P
Factor    3    0.23658   0.07886   10.18    0.000
Error    20    0.15492   0.00775
Total    23    0.39150
                                Individual 95% CIs For Mean
                                Based on Pooled StDev
Level        N     Mean    StDev ---------+---------+---------+---------
Operator 1   5   6.3180   0.0526              (-----*-----)
Operator 2   8   6.2775   0.1053         (----*-----)
Operator 3   7   6.4886   0.1006                          (--- * ---)
Operator 4   4   6.2300   0.0432   (------*-------)
                                   ---------+---------+---------+---------
Pooled StDev = 0.0880                  6.24      6.36      6.48
```

Excel Output:

	A	B	C	D	E	F	G
1	Anova: Single Factor						
2							
3	SUMMARY						
4	Groups	Count	Sum	Average	Variance		
5	Operator 1	5	31.59	6.318000	0.002770		
6	Operator 2	8	50.22	6.277500	0.011079		
7	Operator 3	7	45.42	6.488571	0.010114		
8	Operator 4	4	24.92	6.230000	0.001867		
9							
10							
11	ANOVA						
12	Source of Variation	SS	df	MS	F	P-value	F crit
13	Between Groups	0.236580	3	0.078860	10.18	0.000279	3.10
14	Within Groups	0.154916	20	0.007746			
15							
16	Total	0.391496	23				

of F against which to compare the observed F value. The Excel output also includes the critical table F value for this problem, $F_{.05,3,20} = 3.10$.

The second part of the MINITAB output in Figure 11.5 contains the size of samples and sample means for each of the treatment levels. Displayed graphically are the 95% confidence levels for the population means of each treatment level group. These levels are computed by using a pooled standard deviation from all the treatment level groups. The researcher can visually observe the confidence intervals and make a subjective determination about the relative difference in the population means. More rigorous statistical techniques for testing the differences in pairs of groups are given in Section 11.3.

Comparison of *F* and *t* Values

Analysis of variance can be used to test hypotheses about the difference in two means. Analysis of data from two samples by both a t test and an ANOVA shows that the observed F value equals the observed t value squared.

$$F = t^2 \qquad \text{for } df_C = 1$$

The t test of independent samples actually is a special case of one-way ANOVA when there are only two treatment levels ($df_C = 1$). The t test is computationally simpler than ANOVA for two groups. However, some statistical computer software packages do not contain a t test. In these cases, the researcher can perform a one-way ANOVA and then either take the square root of the F value to obtain the value of t or use the generated probability with the p-value method to reach conclusions.

DEMONSTRATION PROBLEM 11.1

A company has three manufacturing plants, and company officials want to determine whether there is a difference in the average age of workers at the three locations. The following data are the ages of five randomly selected workers at each plant. Perform a one-way ANOVA to determine whether there is a significant difference in the mean ages of the workers at the three plants. Use $\alpha = .01$ and note that the sample sizes are equal.

Solution

HYPOTHESIZE:

STEP 1. The hypotheses follow.

$$H_0: \mu_1 = \mu_2 = \mu_3$$
$$H_a: \text{At least one of the means is different from the others.}$$

TEST:

STEP 2. The appropriate test statistic is the F test calculated from ANOVA.

STEP 3. The value of α is .01.

STEP 4. The degrees of freedom for this problem are $3 - 1 = 2$ for the numerator (treatments – columns) and $15 - 3 = 12$ for the denominator (error). The critical F value is $F_{.01,2,12} = 6.93$.

Because ANOVAs are always one-tailed with the rejection region in the upper tail, the decision rule is to reject the null hypothesis if the observed value of F is greater than 6.93.

STEP 5.

Plant (Employee Ages)

1	2	3
29	32	25
27	33	24
30	31	24
27	34	25
28	30	26

STEP 6.

$$T_j: \quad T_1 = 141 \quad T_2 = 160 \quad T_3 = 124 \quad T = 425$$
$$n_j: \quad n_1 = 5 \quad n_2 = 5 \quad n_3 = 5 \quad N = 15$$
$$\bar{x}_j: \quad \bar{x}_1 = 28.2 \quad \bar{x}_2 = 32.0 \quad \bar{x}_3 = 24.8 \quad \bar{x} = 28.33$$

$$SSC = 5(28.2 - 28.33)^2 + 5(32.0 - 28.33)^2 + 5(24.8 - 28.33)^2 = 129.73$$
$$SSE = (29 - 28.2)^2 + (27 - 28.2)^2 + \ldots + (25 - 24.8)^2 + (26 - 24.8)^2 = 19.60$$
$$SST = (29 - 28.33)^2 + (27 - 28.33)^2 + \ldots + (25 - 28.33)^2 +$$
$$(26 - 28.33)^2 = 149.33$$
$$df_C = 3 - 1 = 2$$
$$df_E = 15 - 3 = 12$$
$$df_T = 15 - 1 = 14$$

Source of Variance	SS	df	MS	F
Between	129.73	2	64.87	39.80
Error	19.60	12	1.63	
Total	149.33	14		

ACTION:

STEP 7. The decision is to reject the null hypothesis because the observed F value of 39.80 is greater than the critical table F value of 6.93.

BUSINESS IMPLICATIONS:

STEP 8. There is a significant difference in the mean ages of workers at the three plants. This difference can have hiring implications. Company leaders should understand that because motivation, discipline, and experience may differ with age, the differences in ages may call for different managerial approaches in each plant.

The following chart displays the dispersion of the ages of workers from the three samples, along with the mean age for each plant sample. Note the difference in group means. The significant F value says that the difference between the mean ages is relatively greater than the differences of ages within each group.

Following are the MINITAB and Excel output for this problem.

MINITAB Output:

One-way ANOVA: Plant 1, Plant 2, Plant 3

Analysis of Variance

Source	DF	SS	MS	F	P
Factor	2	129.73	64.87	39.71	0.000
Error	12	19.60	1.63		
Total	14	149.33			

Individual 95% CIs For Mean
Based on Pooled StDev

Level	N	Mean	StDev	--+---------+---------+---------+----
Plant 1	5	28.200	1.304	(---*---)
Plant 2	5	32.000	1.581	(---*---)
Plant 3	5	24.800	0.837	(---*---)

Pooled StDev =1.278   24.0   27.0   30.0   33.0

Excel Output

	A	B	C	D	E	F	G
1	Anova: Single Factor						
2							
3	SUMMARY						
4	Groups	Count	Sum	Average	Variance		
5	Plant 1	5	141	28.2	1.7		
6	Plant 2	5	160	32	2.5		
7	Plant 3	5	124	24.8	0.7		
8							
9							
10	ANOVA						
11	Source of Variation	SS	df	MS	F	P-value	F crit
12	Between Groups	129.7333	2	64.8667	39.71	0.0000051	3.89
13	Within Groups	19.6	12	1.6333			
14							
15	Total	149.3333	14				

11.2 PROBLEMS

11.5 Compute a one-way ANOVA on the following data.

1	2	3
2	5	3
1	3	4
3	6	5
3	4	5
2	5	3
1		5

Determine the observed F value. Compare the observed F value with the critical table F value and decide whether to reject the null hypothesis. Use $\alpha = .05$.

11.6   Compute a one-way ANOVA on the following data.

1	2	3	4	5
14	10	11	16	14
13	9	12	17	12
10	12	13	14	13
	9	12	16	13
	10		17	12
				14

Determine the observed F value. Compare the observed F value with the critical table F value and decide whether to reject the null hypothesis. Use $\alpha = .01$.

11.7   Develop a one-way ANOVA on the following data.

1	2	3	4
113	120	132	122
121	127	130	118
117	125	129	125
110	129	135	125

Determine the observed F value. Compare it to the critical F value and decide whether to reject the null hypothesis. Use a 1% level of significance.

11.8   Compute a one-way ANOVA on the following data.

1	2
27	22
31	27
31	25
29	23
30	26
27	27
28	23

Determine the observed F value. Compare it to the critical table F value and decide whether to reject the null hypothesis. Perform a t test for independent measures on the data. Compare the t and F values. Are the results different? Use $\alpha = .05$.

11.9   Suppose you are using a completely randomized design to study some phenomenon. There are five treatment levels and a total of 55 people in the study. Each treatment level has the same sample size. Complete the following ANOVA.

Source of Variation	SS	df	MS	F
Treatment	583.39			
Error	972.18			
Total	1555.57			

11.10   Suppose you are using a completely randomized design to study some phenomenon. There are three treatment levels and a total of 17 people in the study. Complete the following ANOVA table. Use $\alpha = .05$ to find the table F value and use the data to test the null hypothesis.

Source of Variation	SS	df	MS	F
Treatment	29.64			
Error	68.42			
Total				

11.11 A milk company has four machines that fill gallon jugs with milk. The quality control manager is interested in determining whether the average fill for these machines is the same. The following data represent random samples of fill measures (in quarts) for 19 jugs of milk filled by the different machines. Use $\alpha = .01$ to test the hypotheses. Discuss the business implications of your findings.

Machine 1	Machine 2	Machine 3	Machine 4
4.05	3.99	3.97	4.00
4.01	4.02	3.98	4.02
4.02	4.01	3.97	3.99
4.04	3.99	3.95	4.01
	4.00	4.00	
	4.00		

11.12 That the starting salaries of new accounting graduates would differ according to geographic regions of the United States seems logical. A random selection of accounting firms is taken from three geographic regions, and each is asked to state the starting salary for a new accounting graduate who is going to work in auditing. The data obtained follow. Use a one-way ANOVA to analyze these data. Note that the data can be restated to make the computations more reasonable (example: $32,500 = 3.25$). Use a 1% level of significance. Discuss the business implications of your findings.

South	Northeast	West
$30,500	$41,000	$35,500
31,500	39,500	33,500
30,000	39,000	35,000
31,000	38,000	36,500
31,500	39,500	36,000

11.13 A management consulting company presents a three-day seminar on project management to various clients. The seminar is basically the same each time it is given. However, sometimes it is presented to high-level managers, sometimes to midlevel managers, and sometimes to low-level managers. The seminar facilitators believe evaluations of the seminar may vary with the audience. Suppose the following data are some randomly selected evaluation scores from different levels of managers who attended the seminar. The ratings are on a scale from 1 to 10, with 10 being the highest. Use a one-way ANOVA to determine whether there is a significant difference in the evaluations according to manager level. Assume $\alpha = .05$. Discuss the business implications of your findings.

High Level	Midlevel	Low Level
7	8	5
7	9	6
8	8	5
7	10	7
9	9	4
	10	8
	8	

11.14 Family transportation costs are usually higher than most people believe because those costs include car payments, insurance, fuel costs, repairs, parking, and public transportation. Twenty randomly selected families in four major cities are asked to use their records to estimate a monthly figure for transportation cost. Use the data obtained and ANOVA to test whether there is a significant difference in monthly transportation costs for families living in these cities. Assume that $\alpha = .05$. Discuss the business implications of your findings.

Atlanta	New York	Los Angeles	Chicago
$650	$250	$850	$540
480	525	700	450
550	300	950	675
600	175	780	550
675	500	600	600

11.15 Shown here is the MINITAB output for a one-way ANOVA. Analyze the results. Include the number of treatment levels, the sample sizes, the F value, the overall statistical significance of the test, and the values of the means.

One-Way Analysis of Variance

Analysis of Variance

Source	df	SS	MS	F	p
Factor	3	1701	567	2.95	0.040
Error	61	11728	192		
Total	64	13429			

Individual 95% CIs For Mean Based on Pooled StDev

Level	N	Mean	StDev
C1	18	226.73	13.59
C2	15	238.79	9.41
C3	21	232.58	12.16
C4	11	239.82	20.96

Pooled StDev = 13.87   224.0   232.0   240.0   248.0

11.16 Business is very good for a chemical company. In fact, it is so good that workers are averaging more than 40 hours per week at each of the chemical company's five plants. However, management is not certain whether there is a difference between the five plants in the average number of hours worked per week per worker. Random samples of data are taken at each of the five plants. The data are analyzed using Excel. The results follow. Explain the design of the study and determine whether there is an overall significant difference between the means at $\alpha = .05$? Why or why not? What are the values of the means? What are the business implications of this study to the chemical company?

	A	B	C	D	E	F	G
1	Anova: Single Factor						
2							
3	SUMMARY						
4	Groups	Count	Sum	Average	Variance		
5	Plant 1	11	636.5577	57.87	63.5949		
6	Plant 2	12	601.7648	50.15	62.4813		
7	Plant 3	8	491.7352	61.47	47.4772		
	Plant 4	5	246.0172	49.20	65.6072		
	Plant 5	7	398.6368	56.95	140.3540		
8							
9							
10	ANOVA						
11	Source of Variation	SS	df	MS	F	P-value	F crit
12	Between Groups	900.0863	4	225.0216	3.10	0.026595	2.62
13	Within Groups	2760.136	38	72.63516			
14							
15	Total	3660.223	42				

11.3 MULTIPLE COMPARISON TESTS

Analysis of variance techniques are particularly useful in testing hypotheses about the differences of means in multiple groups because ANOVA utilizes only one single overall test. The advantage of this approach is that the probability of committing a Type I error, α, is controlled. As noted in Section 11.2, if four groups are tested two at a time, it takes six t tests ($_4C_2$) to analyze hypotheses between all possible pairs. In general, if k groups are tested two at a time, $_kC_2 = k(k-1)/2$ paired comparisons are possible.

Suppose alpha for an experiment is .05. If two different pairs of comparisons are made in the experiment using alpha of .05 in each, there is a .95 probability of not making a Type I error in each comparison. This approach results in a .9025 probability of not making a Type I error in either comparison (.95 × .95), and a .0975 probability of committing a Type I error in at least one comparison (1 − .9025). Thus, the probability of committing a Type I error for this experiment is not .05 but .0975. In an experiment where the means of four groups are being tested two at a time, six different tests are conducted. If each is analyzed using $\alpha = .05$, the probability that no Type I error will be committed in any of the six tests is .95 × .95 × .95 × .95 × .95 × .95 = .735 and the probability of committing at least one Type I error in the six tests is 1 − .735 = .265. If an ANOVA is computed on all groups simultaneously using $\alpha = .05$, the value of alpha is maintained in the experiment.

Sometimes the researcher is satisfied with conducting an overall test of differences in groups such as the one ANOVA provides. However, when it is determined that there is an overall difference in population means, it is often desirable to go back to the groups and determine from the data which pairs of means are significantly different. Such pairwise analyses can lead to the buildup of the Type I experimental error rate, as mentioned. Fortunately, several techniques, referred to as **multiple comparisons,** have been developed to handle this problem.

Multiple comparisons are to be used only when an overall significant difference between groups has been obtained by using the F value of the analysis of variance. Some of these techniques protect more for Type I errors and others protect more for Type II errors. Some multiple comparison techniques require equal sample sizes. There seems to be some difference of opinion in the literature about which techniques are most appropriate. Here we will consider only a posteriori or post hoc pairwise comparisons.

A **posteriori** or **post hoc** pairwise comparisons are made *after the experiment when the researcher decides to test for any significant differences in the samples based on a significant overall F value.* In contrast, **a priori** comparisons are made when the researcher *determines before the experiment which comparisons are to be made.* The error rates for these two types of comparisons are different, as are the recommended techniques. In this text, we only consider pairwise (two-at-a-time) multiple comparisons. Other types of comparisons are possible but belong in a more advanced presentation. The two multiple comparison tests discussed here are Tukey's HSD test for designs with equal sample sizes and the Tukey-Kramer procedure for situations in which sample sizes are unequal. MINITAB yields computer output for each of these tests.

Tukey's Honestly Significant Difference (HSD) Test: The Case of Equal Sample Sizes

Tukey's honestly significant difference (HSD) test, sometimes known as Tukey's T method, is a popular test for pairwise a posteriori multiple comparisons. This test, developed by John W. Tukey and presented in 1953, is somewhat limited by the fact that it requires equal sample sizes.

Tukey's HSD test takes into consideration the number of treatment levels, the value of mean square error, and the sample size. Using these values and a table value, q, the HSD determines the critical difference necessary between the means of any two treatment levels for the means to be significantly different. Once the HSD is computed, the researcher can examine the absolute value of any or all differences between pairs of means from treatment levels to determine whether there is a significant difference. The formula to compute a Tukey's HSD test follows.

TUKEY'S HSD TEST

$$\text{HSD} = q_{\alpha, C, N-C} \sqrt{\frac{\text{MSE}}{n}}$$

where:

MSE	= mean square error
n	= sample size
$q_{\alpha, C, N-C}$	= critical value of the studentized range distribution from Table A.10

In Demonstration Problem 11.1, an ANOVA test was used to determine that there was an overall significant difference in the mean ages of workers at the three different plants, as evidenced by the F value of 39.8. The sample data for this problem follow.

	PLANT		
	1	**2**	**3**
	29	32	25
	27	33	24
	30	31	24
	27	34	25
	28	30	26
Group Means	28.2	32.0	24.8
n_j	5	5	5

Because the sample sizes are equal in this problem, Tukey's HSD test can be used to compute multiple comparison tests between groups 1 and 2, 2 and 3, and 1 and 3. To compute the HSD, the values of MSE, n, and q must be determined. From the solution presented in Demonstration Problem 11.1, the value of MSE is 1.63. The sample size, n_j, is 5. The value of q is obtained from Table A.10 by using

$$\text{Number of Populations = Number of Treatment Means} = C$$

along with $\text{df}_E = N - C$

In this problem, the values used to look up q are

$$C = 3$$
$$\text{df}_E = N - C = 12.$$

Table A.10 has a q table for $\alpha = .05$ and one for $\alpha = .01$. In this problem, $\alpha = .01$. Shown in Table 11.5 is a portion of Table A.10 for $\alpha = .01$.

For this problem, $q_{.01,3,12} = 5.04$. HSD is computed as

$$\text{HSD} = q\sqrt{\frac{\text{MSE}}{n}} = 5.04\sqrt{\frac{1.63}{5}} = 2.88$$

Using this value of HSD, the business researcher can examine the differences between the means from any two groups of plants. Any of the pairs of means that differ by more than 2.88 are significantly different at $\alpha = .01$. Here are the differences for all three possible pairwise comparisons.

$$|\bar{x}_1 - \bar{x}_2| = |28.2 - 32.0| = 3.8$$
$$|\bar{x}_1 - \bar{x}_3| = |28.2 - 24.8| = 3.4$$
$$|\bar{x}_2 - \bar{x}_3| = |32.0 - 24.8| = 7.2$$

TABLE 11.5

q Values for $\alpha = .01$

Degrees of Freedom	**Number of Populations**				
	2	**3**	**4**	**5**	**...**
1	90	135	164	186	
2	14	19	22.3	24.7	
3	8.26	10.6	12.2	13.3	
4	6.51	8.12	9.17	9.96	
.					
.					
.					
11	4.39	5.14	5.62	5.97	
12	4.32	5.04	5.50	5.84	

TABLE 11.6

MINITAB Output for
Tukey's HSD

```
Tukey's pairwise
   comparisons
Family error rate = 0.0100
Individual error rate = 0.00385
Critical value = 5.05
Intervals for (column level mean) - (row level mean)
          1        2
2   -6.686
    -0.914
3    0.514    4.314
     6.286   10.086
```

All three comparisons are greater than the value of HSD, which is 2.88. Thus, the mean ages between any and all pairs of plants are significantly different.

Using the Computer to Do Multiple Comparisons

Table 11.6 shows the MINITAB output for computing a Tukey's HSD test. The computer output contains the confidence intervals for the differences in pairwise means for pairs of treatment levels. If the confidence interval includes zero, there is no significant difference in the pair of means. (If the interval contains zero, there is a possibility of no difference in the means.) Note in Table 11.6 that all three pairs of confidence intervals contain the same sign throughout the interval. For example, the confidence interval for estimating the difference in means from 1 and 2 is $-6.686 \leq \mu_1 - \mu_2 \leq -0.914$. This interval does not contain zero, so we are confident that there is more than a zero difference in the two means. The same holds true for levels 1 and 3 and levels 2 and 3. The computer output displays the family error rate ($\alpha = .01$).

DEMONSTRATION PROBLEM 11.2

A metal-manufacturing firm wants to test the tensile strength of a given metal under varying conditions of temperature. Suppose that in the design phase, the metal is processed under five different temperature conditions and that random samples of size five are taken under each temperature condition. The data follow.

Tensile Strength of Metal Produced Under Five Different Temperature Settings

1	2	3	4	5
2.46	2.38	2.51	2.49	2.56
2.41	2.34	2.48	2.47	2.57
2.43	2.31	2.46	2.48	2.53
2.47	2.40	2.49	2.46	2.55
2.46	2.32	2.50	2.44	2.55

A one-way ANOVA is performed on these data by using MINITAB, with the resulting analysis shown here.

One-Way ANOVA: Strength versus Temp

```
Analysis of Variance on Tensile
Source   df      SS          MS        F       p
Temp      4   0.108024   0.027006   43.70   0.000
Error    20   0.012360   0.000618
Total    24   0.120384

Individual 95% CIs For Mean
Based on Pooled StDev
                              --------+-------+-------+------
Level   N    Mean    StDev
  1     5   2.4460   0.0251                    (--*---)
  2     5   2.3500   0.0387   (---*--)
  3     5   2.4880   0.0192                         (--*---)
  4     5   2.4680   0.0192                      (---*--)
  5     5   2.5520   0.0148                                 (---*--)
                              --------+-------+-------+------
Pooled StDev = 0.0249                  2.380   2.450   2.520
```

Note from the ANOVA table that the F value of 43.70 is statistically significant at $\alpha = .01$. There is an overall difference in the population means of metal produced under the five temperature settings. Use the data to compute a Tukey's HSD to determine which of the five groups are significantly different from the others.

Solution

From the ANOVA table, the value of MSE is .000618. The sample size, n_j, is 5. The number of treatment means, C, is 5 and the df_E are 20. With these values and $\alpha = .01$, the value of q can be obtained from Table A.10.

$$q_{.01,5,20} = 5.29$$

HSD can be computed as

$$HSD = q\sqrt{\frac{MSE}{n}} = 5.29\sqrt{\frac{.000618}{5}} = .0588$$

The treatment group means for this problem follow.

Group 1 = 2.446
Group 2 = 2.350
Group 3 = 2.488
Group 4 = 2.468
Group 5 = 2.552

Computing all pairwise differences between these means (in absolute values) produces the following data.

	1	2	3	4	5
			Group		
1	—	.096	.042	.022	.106
2	.096	—	.138	.118	.202
3	.042	.138	—	.020	.064
4	.022	.118	.020	—	.084
5	.106	.202	.064	.084	—

Comparing these differences to the value of HSD = .0588, we can determine that the differences between groups 1 and 2 (.096), 1 and 5 (.106), 2 and 3 (.138), 2 and 4 (.118), 2 and 5 (.202), 3 and 5 (.064), and 4 and 5 (.084) are significant at $\alpha = .01$.

Not only is there an overall significant difference in the treatment levels as shown by the ANOVA results, but there is a significant difference in the tensile strength of metal between seven pairs of levels. By studying the magnitudes of the individual treatment levels' means, the steel-manufacturing firm can determine which temperatures result in the greatest tensile strength. The MINITAB output for this Tukey's HSD is shown here. Note that the family error rate was held at .01 and that the computer analysis shows significant differences between pairs 1 and 2, 1 and 5, 2 and 3, 2 and 4, 2 and 5, 3 and 5, and 4 and 5. These results are consistent with the manual calculations.

```
Tukey's pairwise comparisons

Family error rate = 0.0100
Individual error rate = 0.00128

Critical value = 5.29

Intervals for (column level mean) - (row level mean)

          1          2          3          4
2     0.03719
      0.15481
3    -0.10081   -0.19681
      0.01681   -0.07919
4    -0.08081   -0.17681   -0.03881
      0.03681   -0.05919    0.07881
5    -0.16481   -0.26081   -0.12281   -0.14281
     -0.04719   -0.14319   -0.00519   -0.02519
```

Tukey-Kramer Procedure: The Case of Unequal Sample Sizes

Tukey's HSD was modified by C. Y. Kramer in the mid-1950s to handle situations in which the sample sizes are unequal. The modified version of HSD is sometimes referred to as the **Tukey-Kramer procedure.** The formula for computing the significant differences with this procedure is similar to that for the equal sample sizes, with the exception that the mean square error is divided in half and weighted by the sum of the inverses of the sample sizes under the root sign.

TUKEY-KRAMER FORMULA

$$q_{\alpha,C,N-C}\sqrt{\frac{MSE}{2}\left(\frac{1}{n_r}+\frac{1}{n_s}\right)}$$

where

$\quad$ MSE $\quad$ = mean square error
$\quad n_r \quad\quad$ = sample size for rth sample
$\quad n_s \quad\quad$ = sample size for sth sample
$\quad q_{\alpha,C,N-C}$ = critical value of the studentized range distribution from Table A.10

As an example of the application of the Tukey-Kramer procedure, consider the machine operator example in Section 11.2. A one-way ANOVA was used to test for any difference in the mean valve openings produced by four different machine operators. An overall F of 10.18 was computed, which was significant at $\alpha = .05$. Because the ANOVA hypothesis test is significant and the null hypothesis is rejected, this problem is a candidate for multiple comparisons. Because the sample sizes are not equal, Tukey's HSD cannot be used to determine which pairs are significantly different. However, the Tukey-Kramer procedure can be applied. Shown in Table 11.7 are the means and sample sizes for the valve openings for valves produced by the four different operators.

The mean square error for this problem, MSE, is shown in Table 11.3 as .007746. The four operators in the problem represent the four levels of the independent variable, port. Thus, $C = 4$, $N = 24$, and $N - C = 20$. The value of alpha in the problem is .05. With this information, the value of q is obtained from Table A.10 as

$$q_{.05,4,20} = 3.96$$

The distance necessary for the difference in the means of two samples to be statistically significant must be computed by using the Tukey-Kramer procedure for each pair because the sample sizes differ. In this problem with $C = 4$, there are $C(C-1)/2$ or six possible pairwise comparisons. The computations follow.

For operators 1 and 2,

$$3.96\sqrt{\frac{.007746}{2}\left(\frac{1}{5}+\frac{1}{8}\right)} = .1405$$

The difference between the means of Operator 1 and Operator 2 is

$$6.3180 - 6.2775 = .0405.$$

Because this result is less than the critical difference of .1405, there is no significant difference between the average valve openings of valves produced by machine operators 1 and 2.

Table 11.8 reports the critical differences for each of the six pairwise comparisons as computed by using the Tukey-Kramer procedure, along with the absolute value of the actual distances between the means. Any actual distance between means that is greater than the critical distance is significant. As shown in the table, the means of three pairs of samples, operators 1 and 3, operators 2 and 3, and operators 3 and 4 are significantly different.

Table 11.9 shows the MINITAB output for this problem. MINITAB uses the Tukey-Kramer procedure for unequal values of n. As before with the HSD test, MINITAB produces a confidence interval for the differences in means for pairs of treatment levels. If the confidence interval includes zero, there is no significant difference in the pairs of means. If the signs over the interval are the same (zero is not in the interval), there is a significant difference in the means. Note that the signs over the intervals for pairs (1, 3), (2, 3) and (3, 4) are the same, indicating a significant difference in the means of those two pairs. This conclusion agrees with the results determined through the calculations reported in Table 11.8.

TABLE 11.7

Means and Sample Sizes for the Valves Produced by Four Operators

Operator	Sample Size	Mean
1	5	6.3180
2	8	6.2775
3	7	6.4886
4	4	6.2300

TABLE 11.8

Results of Pairwise Comparisions for the Machine Operators Example Using the Tukey-Kramer Procedure

Pair	Critical Difference	Actual Difference
1 and 2	.1405	.0405
1 and 3	.1443	.1706*
1 and 4	.1653	.0880
2 and 3	.1275	.2111*
2 and 4	.1509	.0475
3 and 4	.1545	.2586*

*Significant at $\alpha = .05$.

TABLE 11.9

MINITAB Multiple Comparisons in the Machine Operator Example Using the Tukey-Kramer Procedure

```
Tukey's pairwise comparisons
Family error rate = 0.0500
Individual error rate = 0.0111
Critical value = 3.96
Intervals for (column level mean) - (row level mean)
           1          2          3
2   -0.09999
     0.18099
3   -0.31487   -0.33862
    -0.02627   -0.08353
4   -0.07732   -0.10341    0.10411
     0.25332    0.19841    0.41304
```

11.3 PROBLEMS

11.17 Suppose an ANOVA has been performed on a completely randomized design containing six treatment levels. The mean for group 3 is 15.85, and the sample size for group 3 is eight. The mean for group 6 is 17.21, and the sample size for group 6 is seven. MSE is .3352. The total number of observations is 46. Compute the significant difference for the means of these two groups by using the Tukey-Kramer procedure.

11.18 A completely randomized design has been analyzed by using a one-way ANOVA. There are four treatment groups in the design, and each sample size is six. MSE is equal to 2.389. Using $\alpha = .05$, compute Tukey's HSD for this ANOVA.

11.19 Using the results of Problem 11.5, compute a critical value by using the Tukey-Kramer procedure for groups 1 and 2. Use $\alpha = .05$. Determine whether there is a significant difference between these two groups.

11.20 Use the Tukey-Kramer procedure to determine whether there is a significant difference between the means of groups 2 and 4 in Problem 11.6. Let $\alpha = .01$.

11.21 Using the results from Problem 11.7, compute a Tukey's HSD to determine whether there are any significant differences between group means. Let $\alpha = .01$.

11.22 Using Problem 11.8, compute Tukey's HSD and determine whether there is a significant difference in means by using this methodology. Let $\alpha = .05$.

11.23 Use the Tukey-Kramer procedure to do multiple comparisons for Problem 11.11. Let $\alpha = .01$. State which pairs of machines, if any, produce significantly different mean fills.

11.24 Use Tukey's HSD test to compute multiple comparisons for the data in Problem 11.12. Let $\alpha = .01$. State which regions, if any, are significantly different from other regions in mean starting salary figures.

11.25 Using $\alpha = .05$, compute critical values using the Tukey-Kramer procedure for the pairwise groups in Problem 11.13. Determine which pairs of groups are significantly different, if any.

11.26 Do multiple comparisons on the data in Problem 11.14 using Tukey's HSD test and $\alpha = .05$. State which pairs of cities, if any, have significantly different mean costs.

11.27 Problem 11.16 analyzed the number of weekly hours worked per person at five different plants. An F value of 3.10 was obtained with a probability of .0266. Because the probability is less than .05, the null hypothesis is rejected at $\alpha = .05$. There is an overall difference in the mean weekly hours worked by plant. Which pairs of plants have significant differences in the means, if any? To answer this question, a MINITAB computer analysis was done. The data follow. Study the output in light of Problem 11.16 and discuss the results.

STATISTICS IN BUSINESS TODAY

Does National Ideology Affect a Firm's Definition of Success?

One researcher, G. C. Lodge, proposed that companies pursue different performance goals based on the ideology of their home country. L. Thurow went further by suggesting that such national ideologies drive U.S. firms to be short-term profit maximizers, Japanese firms to be growth maximizers, and European firms to be a mix of the two.

Three other researchers, J. Katz, S. Werner, and L. Brouthers, decided to test these suggestions by studying 114 international banks from the United States, the European Union (EU), and Japan listed in the Global 1000. Specifically, there were 34 banks from the United States, 45 banks from the European Union, and 35 banks from Japan in the study. Financial and market data were gathered and averaged on each bank over a five-year period to limit the effect of single-year variations. All statistics were converted by Morgan Stanley Capital International to U.S. dollar denominations on the same day of each year to ensure consistency of measurement.

The banks were compared on general measures of success such as profitability, capitalization, growth, size, risk, and earnings distribution by specifically examining 11 measures. Eleven one-way analyses of variance designs were computed, one for each dependent variable. These included return on equity, return on assets, yield, capitalization, assets, market value, growth, Tobin's Q, price-to-earnings ratio, payout ratio, and risk. The independent variable in each ANOVA was country, with three levels: U.S., EU, and Japan.

In all 11 ANOVAs, there was a significant difference between banks in the three countries ($\alpha = .01$) supporting the theme of different financial success goals for different national cultures. Because of the overall significant difference attained in the ANOVAs, each analysis of variance was followed by a Duncan's multiple range test (multiple comparison) to determine which, if any, of the pairs were significantly different. These comparisons revealed that U.S. and EU banks maintained significantly higher levels than Japanese banks on return on equity, return on assets, and yield. This result underscores the notion that U.S. and EU banks have more of a short-term profit orientation than do Japanese banks. There was a significant difference in banks from each of the three countries on amount of capitalization. U.S. banks had the highest level of capitalization followed by EU banks and then Japanese banks. This result may reflect the cultural attitude about how much capital is needed to ensure a sound economy, with U.S. banks maintaining higher levels of capital.

The study found that Japanese banks had significantly higher levels on growth, Tobin's Q, and price-to-earnings ratio than did the other two national entities. This result confirms the hypothesis that Japanese firms are more interested in growth. In addition, Japanese banks had a significantly higher asset size and market value of equity than did U.S. banks. The researchers had hypothesized that EU banks would have a greater portfolio risk than that of U.S. or Japanese banks. They found that EU banks did have significantly higher risk and paid out significantly higher dividends than did either Japanese or U.S. banks.

Source: Adapted from Jeffrey P. Katz, Steve Werner, and Lance Brouthers, "Does Winning Mean the Same Thing around the World? National Ideology and the Performance of Global Competitors," *Journal of Business Research*, vol. 44, no. 2 (February 1999), 117–126.

```
Tukey's pairwise comparisons
Family error rate = 0.0500
Individual error rate = 0.00678
Critical value = 4.05
Intervals for (column level mean) - (row level mean)
         1         2         3         4
2    -2.47
     17.91
3   -14.94   -22.46
      7.74    -0.18
4    -4.50   -12.05    -1.65
     21.83    13.94    26.18
5   -10.88   -18.41    -8.11   -22.04
     12.72     4.81    17.15     6.55
```

11.4 THE RANDOMIZED BLOCK DESIGN

A second research design is the **randomized block design.** The randomized block design is similar to the completely randomized design in that it focuses on one independent variable (treatment variable) of interest. However, the randomized block design also includes a second variable, referred to as a blocking variable, that can be used to control for confounding or concomitant variables.

Confounding variables, or **concomitant variables,** are *variables that are not being controlled by the researcher in the experiment but can have an effect on the outcome of the treatment being studied.* For example, Demonstration Problem 11.2 showed how a completely randomized design could be used to analyze the effects of temperature on the tensile strengths of metal. However, other variables not being controlled by the researcher in this experiment may affect the tensile strength of metal, such as humidity, raw materials, machine, and shift. One way to control for these variables is to include them in the experimental design. The randomized block design has the capability of adding one of these variables into the analysis as a blocking variable. A **blocking variable** is *a variable that the researcher wants to control but is not the treatment variable of interest.*

One of the first people to use the randomized block design was Sir Ronald A. Fisher. He applied the design to the field of agriculture, where he was interested in studying the growth patterns of varieties of seeds for a given type of plant. The seed variety was his independent variable. However, he realized that as he experimented on different plots of ground, the "block" of ground might make some difference in the experiment. Fisher designated several different plots of ground as blocks, which he controlled as a second variable. Each of the seed varieties was planted on each of the blocks. The main thrust of his study was to compare the seed varieties (independent variable). He merely wanted to control for the difference in plots of ground (blocking variable).

In Demonstration Problem 11.2, examples of blocking variables might be machine number (if several machines are used to make the metal), worker, shift, or day of the week. The researcher probably already knows that different workers or different machines will produce at least slightly different metal tensile strengths because of individual differences. However, designating the variable (machine or worker) as the blocking variable and computing a randomized block design affords the potential for a more powerful analysis. In other experiments, some other possible variables that might be used as blocking variables include gender of subject, age of subject, intelligence of subject, economic level of subject, brand, supplier, or vehicle.

A special case of the randomized block design is the repeated measures design. The **repeated measures design** is a randomized block design in which each block level is an individual item or person, and that person or item is measured across all treatments. Thus, where a block level in a randomized block design is night shift and items produced under different treatment levels on the night shift are measured, in a repeated measures design, a block level might be an individual machine or person; items produced by that person or machine are then randomly chosen across all treatments. Thus, a repeated measure of the person or machine is made across all treatments. This repeated measures design is an extension of the *t* test for dependent samples presented in Section 10.3.

The sum of squares in a completely randomized design is

$$SST = SSC + SSE$$

In a randomized block design, the sum of squares is

$$SST = SSC + SSR + SSE$$

where

$\quad\quad$ SST $\;=$ sum of squares total
$\quad\quad$ SSC $=$ sum of squares columns (treatment)
$\quad\quad$ SSR $=$ sum of squares rows (blocking)
$\quad\quad$ SSE $\;=$ sum of squares error

SST and SSC are the same for a given analysis whether a completely randomized design or a randomized block design is used. For this reason, the SSR (blocking effects) comes out of the SSE; that is, some of the error variation in the completely randomized design is accounted for in the blocking effects of the randomized block design, as shown in Figure 11.6. By reducing the error term, it is possible that the value of F for treatment will increase (the denominator of the F value is decreased). However, if there is not sufficient difference between levels of the blocking variable, the use of a randomized block design can lead to a less powerful result than would a completely randomized design computed on the same problem. Thus, the researcher should seek out blocking variables that he or she believes are significant contributors to variation among measurements of the dependent variable. Figure 11.7 shows the layout of a randomized block design.

In each of the intersections of independent variable and blocking variable in Figure 11.7, one measurement is taken. In the randomized block design, one measurement is given for each treatment level under each blocking level.

The null and alternate hypotheses for the treatment effects in the randomized block design are

$H_0: \mu_{.1} = \mu_{.2} = \mu_{.3} = \ldots = \mu_{.C}$
H_a: At least one of the treatment means is different from the others.

For the blocking effects, they are

$H_0: \mu_{1.} = \mu_{2.} = \mu_{3.} = \ldots = \mu_{R.}$
H_a: At least one of the blocking means is different from the others.

Essentially, we are testing the null hypothesis that the population means of the treatment groups are equal. If the null hypothesis is rejected, at least one of the population means does not equal the others.

The formulas for computing a randomized block design follow on the next page.

FIGURE 11.6

Partitioning the Total Sum of Squares in a Randomized Block Design

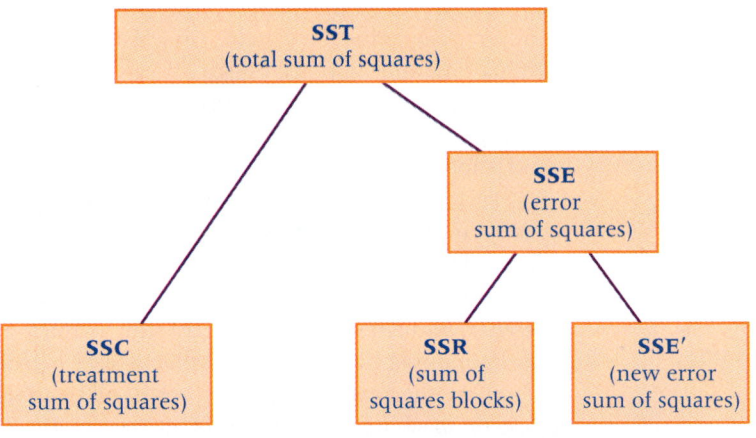

FIGURE 11.7

A Randomized Block Design

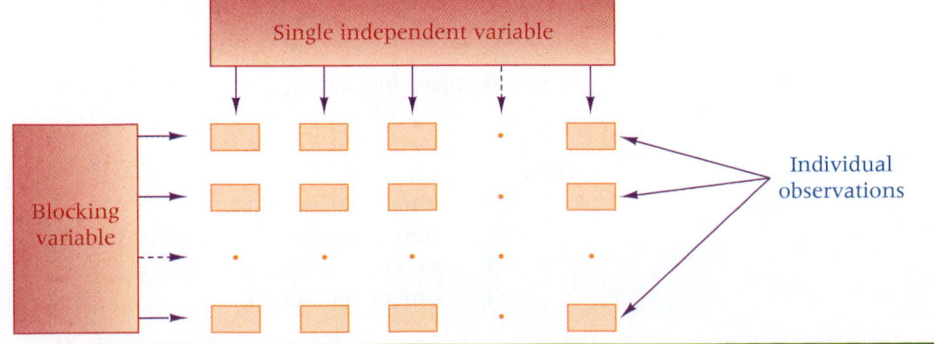

FORMULAS FOR COMPUTING A RANDOMIZED BLOCK DESIGN

$$SSC = n \sum_{j=1}^{C} (\bar{x}_j - \bar{x})^2$$

$$SSR = C \sum_{i=1}^{n} (\bar{x}_i - \bar{x})^2$$

$$SSE = \sum_{i=1}^{n} \sum_{j=1}^{C} (x_{ij} - \bar{x}_j - \bar{x}_i + \bar{x})^2$$

$$SST = \sum_{i=1}^{n} \sum_{j=1}^{C} (x_{ij} - \bar{x})^2$$

where

i = block group (row)
j = treatment level (column)
C = number of treatment levels (columns)
n = number of observations in each treatment level (number of blocks or rows)
x_{ij} = individual observation
$\bar{x}_j$ = treatment (column) mean
$\bar{x}_i$ = block (row) mean
$\bar{x}$ = grand mean
N = total number of observations

$$df_C = C - 1$$
$$df_R = n - 1$$
$$df_E = (C - 1)(n - 1) = N - n - C + 1$$

$$MSC = \frac{SSC}{C - 1}$$

$$MSR = \frac{SSR}{n - 1}$$

$$MSE = \frac{SSE}{N - n - C + 1}$$

$$F_{treatments} = \frac{MSC}{MSE}$$

$$F_{blocks} = \frac{MSR}{MSE}$$

The observed F value for treatments computed using the randomized block design formula is tested by comparing it to a table F value, which is ascertained from Appendix A.7 by using α, df_C (treatment), and df_E (error). If the observed F value is greater than the table value, the null hypothesis is rejected for that alpha value. Such a result would indicate that not all population treatment means are equal. At this point, the business researcher has the option of computing multiple comparisons if the null hypothesis has been rejected.

Some researchers also compute an F value for blocks even though the main emphasis in the experiment is on the treatments. The observed F value for blocks is compared to a critical table F value determined from Appendix A.7 by using α, df_R (blocks), and df_E (error). If the F value for blocks is greater than the critical F value, the null hypothesis that all block population means are equal is rejected. This result tells the business researcher that including the blocking in the design was probably worthwhile and that a significant amount of variance was drawn off from the error term, thus increasing the power of the treatment test. In this text, we have omitted F_{blocks} from the normal presentation and problem solving. We leave the use of this F value to the discretion of the reader.

As an example of the application of the randomized block design, consider a tire company that developed a new tire. The company conducted tread-wear tests on the tire to determine whether there is a significant difference in tread wear if the average speed with which the automobile is driven varies. The company set up an experiment in which the independent variable was speed of automobile. There were three treatment levels: slow speed (car is driven 20 miles per hour), medium speed (car is driven 40 miles per hour), and high speed (car is driven 60 miles per hour). Company researchers realized that several possible variables could confound the study. One of these variables was supplier. The company uses five suppliers to provide a major component of the rubber from which the tires are made. To control for this variable experimentally, the researchers used supplier as a blocking variable. Fifteen tires were randomly selected for the study, three from each supplier. Each of the three was assigned to be tested under a different speed condition. The data are given here, along with treatment and block totals. These figures represent tire wear in units of 10,000 miles.

	Speed			Block Means $\bar{x}_i$
Supplier	**Slow**	**Medium**	**Fast**	
1	3.7	4.5	3.1	3.77
2	3.4	3.9	2.8	3.37
3	3.5	4.1	3.0	3.53
4	3.2	3.5	2.6	3.10
5	3.9	4.8	3.4	4.03
Treatment Means $\bar{x}_j$	3.54	4.16	2.98	$\bar{x} = 3.56$

To analyze this randomized block design using $\alpha = .01$, the computations are as follows.

$$C = 3$$
$$n = 5$$
$$N = 15$$

$$SSC = n\sum_{j=1}^{C}(\bar{x}_j - \bar{x})^2$$

$$= 5[(3.54 - 3.56)^2 + (4.16 - 3.56)^2 + (2.98 - 3.56)^2]$$
$$= 3.484$$

$$SSR = C\sum_{i=1}^{n}(\bar{x}_i - \bar{x})^2$$

$$= 3[(3.77 - 3.56)^2 + (3.37 - 3.56)^2 + (3.53 - 3.56)^2 + (4.03 - 3.56)^2]$$
$$= 1.549$$

$$SSE = \sum_{i=1}^{n}\sum_{j=1}^{C}(x_{ij} - \bar{x}_j - \bar{x}_i + \bar{x})^2$$

$$= (3.7 - 3.54 - 3.77 + 3.56)^2 + (3.4 - 3.54 - 3.37 + 3.56)^2$$
$$+ \ldots + (2.6 - 2.98 - 3.10 + 3.56)^2 + (3.4 - 2.98 - 4.03 + 3.56)^2$$
$$= .143$$

$$SST = \sum_{i=1}^{n}\sum_{j=1}^{C}(x_{ij} - \bar{x})^2$$

$$= (3.7 - 3.56)^2 + (3.4 - 3.56)^2 + \ldots + (2.6 - 3.56)^2 + (3.4 - 3.56)^2$$
$$= 5.176$$

$$MSC = \frac{SSC}{C-1} = \frac{3.484}{2} = 1.742$$

$$MSR = \frac{SSR}{n-1} = \frac{1.549}{4} = .387$$

$$MSE = \frac{SSE}{N-n-C+1} = \frac{.143}{8} = .018$$

$$F = \frac{MSC}{MSE} = \frac{1.742}{0.018} = 96.78$$

Source of Variation	SS	df	MS	F
Treatment	3.484	2	1.742	96.78
Block	1.549	4	.387	
Error	.143	8	.018	
Total	5.176	14		

For alpha of .01, the critical *F* value is

$$F_{.01,2,8} = 8.65$$

Because the observed value of *F* for treatment (96.78) is greater than this critical *F* value, the null hypothesis is rejected. At least one of the population means of the treatment levels is not the same as the others; that is, there is a significant difference in tread wear for cars driven at different speeds. If this problem had been set up as a completely randomized design, the SSR would have been a part of the SSE. The degrees of freedom for the blocking effects would have been combined with degrees of freedom of error. Thus, the value of SSE would have been 1.549 + .143 = 1.692, and df_E would have been 4 + 8 = 12. These would then have been used to recompute MSE = 1.692/12 = .141. The value of *F* for treatments would have been

$$F = \frac{\text{MSC}}{\text{MSE}} = \frac{1.742}{0.141} = 12.35$$

Thus, the *F* value for treatment with the blocking was 96.78 and *without* the blocking was 12.35. By using the random block design, a much larger observed *F* value was obtained.

Using the Computer to Analyze Randomized Block Designs

Both MINITAB and Excel have the capability of analyzing a randomized block design. The computer output from each of these software packages for the tire-tread-wear example is displayed in Table 11.10. The randomized block design analysis is done on MINITAB by using the same process as the two-way ANOVA, which will be discussed in Section 11.5.

The MINITAB output includes *F* values and their associated *p*-values for both the treatment and the blocking effects. As with most standard ANOVA tables, the sum of squares, mean squares, and degrees of freedom for each source of variation are included.

Excel treats a randomized block design like a two-way ANOVA (Section 11.5) that has only one observation per cell. The Excel output includes sums, averages, and variances for each row and column. The Excel ANOVA table displays the observed F values for the treatment (columns) and the blocks (rows). An important inclusion in the Excel output is the *p*-value for each F, along with the critical (table) F values.

DEMONSTRATION PROBLEM 11.3

Suppose a national travel association studied the cost of premium unleaded gasoline in the United States during the summer of 2002. From experience, association directors believed there was a significant difference in the average cost of a gallon of premium gasoline among urban areas in different parts of the country. To test this belief, they placed random calls to gasoline stations in five different cities. In addition, the researchers realized that the brand of gasoline might make a difference. They were mostly interested in the differences between cities, so they made city their treatment variable. To control for the fact that pricing varies with brand, the researchers included brand as a blocking variable and selected six different brands to participate. The researchers randomly telephoned one gasoline station for each brand in each city, resulting in 30 measurements (five cities and six brands). Each station operator was asked to report the current cost of a gallon of premium unleaded gasoline at that station. The data are shown here. Test these data by using a randomized block design analysis to determine whether there is a significant difference in the average cost of premium unleaded gasoline by city. Let α = .01.

TABLE 11.10	MINITAB and Excel Output for the Tread-Wear Example

MINITAB Output

Two-way ANOVA: Tire Wear versus Speed, Supplier

```
Analysis of Variance for Tire Wear
Source     DF     SS       MS      F       P
Speed       2   3.4840   1.7420   97.68   0.000
Supplier    4   1.5493   0.3873   21.72   0.000
Error       8   0.1427   0.0178
Total      14   5.1760
```

Excel Output:

	A	B	C	D	E	F	G
1	Anova: Two-Factor Without Replication						
2							
3	SUMMARY	Count	Sum	Average	Variance		
4	Supplier 1	3	11.3	3.767	0.4933		
5	Supplier 2	3	10.1	3.367	0.3033		
6	Supplier 3	3	10.6	3.533	0.3033		
7	Supplier 4	3	9.3	3.100	0.2100		
8	Supplier 5	3	12.1	4.033	0.5033		
9							
10	Slow	5	17.7	3.54	0.073		
11	Medium	5	20.8	4.16	0.258		
12	Fast	5	14.9	2.98	0.092		
13							
14							
15	ANOVA						
16	Source of Variation	SS	df	MS	F	P-value	F crit
17	Rows	1.549333	4	0.387333	21.72	0.0002357	3.84
18	Columns	3.484000	2	1.742	97.68	0.0000024	4.46
19	Error	0.142667	8	0.017833			
20	Total	5.176000	14				

Geographic Region

Brand	Miami	Philadelphia	Minneapolis	San Antonio	Oakland	$\bar{x}_i$
A	1.47	1.40	1.38	1.32	1.50	1.414
B	1.43	1.41	1.42	1.35	1.44	1.410
C	1.44	1.41	1.43	1.36	1.45	1.418
D	1.46	1.45	1.40	1.30	1.45	1.412
E	1.46	1.40	1.39	1.39	1.48	1.424
F	1.44	1.43	1.42	1.39	1.49	1.434
$\bar{x}_j$	1.450	1.417	1.407	1.352	1.468	$\bar{x}$ = 1.419

Solution

HYPOTHESIZE:

STEP 1. The hypotheses follow.

For treatments,

$H_0: \mu_{.1} = \mu_{.2} = \mu_{.3} = \mu_{.4} = \mu_{.5}$
H_a: At least one of the treatment means is different from the others.

For blocks,

$H_0: \mu_{1.} = \mu_{2.} = \mu_{3.} = \mu_{4.} = \mu_{5.} = \mu_{6.}$
H_a: At least one of the blocking means is different from the others.

TEST:

STEP 2. The appropriate statistical test is the F test in the ANOVA for randomized block designs.

STEP 3. Let $\alpha = .01$.

STEP 4. There are four degrees of freedom for the treatment ($C - 1 = 5 - 1 = 4$), five degrees of freedom for the blocks ($n - 1 = 6 - 1 = 5$), and 20 degrees of freedom for error [$(C - 1)(n - 1) = (4)(5) = 20$]. Using these, $\alpha = .01$, and Table A.7, we find the critical F values.

$$F_{.01,4,20} = 4.43 \text{ for treatments}$$
$$F_{.01,5,20} = 4.10 \text{ for blocks}$$

The decision rule is to reject the null hypothesis for treatments if the observed F value for treatments is greater than 4.43 and to reject the null hypothesis for blocking effects if the observed F value for blocks is greater than 4.10.

STEP 5. The sample data including row and column means and the grand mean are given in the preceding table.

STEP 6.

$$SSC = n \sum_{j=1}^{C} (\bar{x}_j - \bar{x})^2$$

$$= 6[(1.450 - 1.419)^2 + (1.417 - 1.419)^2 + (1.407 - 1.419)^2 + (1.352 - 1.419)^2 + (1.468 - 1.419)^2]$$
$$= .04851$$

$$SSR = C \sum_{i=1}^{n} (\bar{x}_i - \bar{x})^2$$

$$= 5[(1.414 - 1.419)^2 + (1.410 - 1.419)^2 + (1.418 - 1.419)^2 + (1.412 - 1.419)^2 + (1.424 - 1.419)^2 + (1.434 - 1.419)^2]$$
$$= .00203$$

$$SSE = \sum_{i=1}^{n} \sum_{j=1}^{C} (x_{ij} - \bar{x}_j - \bar{x}_i + \bar{x})^2$$

$$= (1.47 - 1.450 - 1.414 + 1.419)^2 + (1.43 - 1.450 - 1.410 + 1.419)^2 + \ldots$$
$$+ (1.48 - 1.468 - 1.424 + 1.419)^2 + (1.49 - 1.468 - 1.434 + 1.419)^2 = .01281$$

$$SST = \sum_{i=1}^{n} \sum_{j=1}^{C} (x_{ij} - \bar{x})^2$$

$$= (1.47 - 1.419)^2 + (1.43 - 1.419)^2 + \ldots + (1.48 - 1.419)^2 + (1.49 - 1.419)^2$$
$$= .06335$$

$$MSC = \frac{SSC}{C - 1} = \frac{.04851}{4} = .01213$$

$$MSR = \frac{SSR}{n - 1} = \frac{.00203}{5} = .00041$$

$$MSE = \frac{SSE}{(C - 1)(n - 1)} = \frac{.01281}{20} = .00064$$

$$F = \frac{MSC}{MSE} = \frac{.01213}{.00064} = 18.95$$

Source of Variance	SS	df	MS	F
Treatment	.04851	4	.01213	18.95
Block	.00203	5	.00041	
Error	.01281	20	.00064	
Total	.06335	29		

ACTION:

STEP 7. Because $F_{treat} = 18.95 > F_{.01,4,20} = 4.43$, the null hypothesis is rejected for the treatment effects. There is a significant difference in the average price of a gallon of premium unleaded gasoline in various cities.

A glance at the MSR reveals that there appears to be relatively little blocking variance. The result of determining an F value for the blocking effects is

$$F = \frac{MSR}{MSE} = \frac{.00041}{.00064} = .64$$

The value of F for blocks is not significant at $\alpha = .01$ ($F_{.01,5,20} = 4.10$). This result indicates that the blocking portion of the experimental design did not contribute significantly to the analysis. If the blocking effects (SSR) are added back into SSE and the df_R are included with df_E, the MSE becomes .00059 instead of .00064. Using the value .00059 in the denominator for the treatment F increases the observed treatment F value to 20.56. Thus, including nonsignificant blocking effects in the original analysis caused a loss of power.

Shown here are the MINITAB and Excel ANOVA table outputs for this problem.

MINITAB Output

```
Two-way ANOVA: Price versus City, Brand

Analysis of Variance for Price

Source  DF      SS          MS          F       P
City    4     0.048513   0.012128   18.94    0.000
Brand   5     0.002027   0.000405    0.63    0.677
Error   20    0.012807   0.000640
Total   29    0.063347
```

Excel Output

Anova: Two-Factor Without Replication

	A	B	C	D	E	F	G
1	ANOVA						
2							
3	Source of Variation	SS	df	MS	F	P-value	F crit
4	Rows	0.002027	5	0.000405	0.63	0.676888	4.10
5	Columns	0.048513	4	0.012128	18.94	0.0000014	4.43
6	Error	0.012807	20	0.000640			
7	Total	0.063347	29				

BUSINESS IMPLICATIONS:

STEP 8. The fact that there is a significant difference in the price of gasoline in different parts of the country can be useful information to decision makers. For example, companies in the ground transportation business are greatly affected by increases in the cost of fuel. Knowledge of price differences in fuel can help these companies plan strategies and routes. Fuel price differences can sometimes be indications of cost-of-living differences or distribution problems, which can affect a company's relocation decision or cost-of-living increases given to employees who transfer to the higher-priced locations. Knowing that the price of gasoline varies around the country can generate interest among market researchers who might want to study why the differences are there and what drives them. This information can sometimes result in a better understanding of the marketplace.

11.4 PROBLEMS

11.28 Use ANOVA to analyze the data from the randomized block design given here. Let $\alpha = .05$. State the null and alternative hypotheses and determine whether the null hypothesis is rejected.

		Treatment Level			
		1	*2*	*3*	*4*
	1	23	26	24	24
	2	31	35	32	33
Block	3	27	29	26	27
	4	21	28	27	22
	5	18	25	27	20

11.29 The following data were gathered from a randomized block design. Use $\alpha = .01$ to test for a significant difference in the treatment levels. Establish the hypotheses and reach a conclusion about the null hypothesis.

		Treatment Level		
		1	*2*	*3*
	1	1.28	1.29	1.29
Block	2	1.40	1.36	1.35
	3	1.15	1.13	1.19
	4	1.22	1.18	1.24

11.30 A randomized block design has a treatment variable with six levels and a blocking variable with 10 blocks. Using this information and $\alpha = .05$, complete the following table and reach a conclusion about the null hypothesis.

Source of Variance	SS	df	MS	F
Treatment	2,477.53			
Blocks	3,180.48			
Error	11,661.38			
Total				

11.31 A randomized block design has a treatment variable with four levels and a blocking variable with seven blocks. Using this information and $\alpha = .01$, complete the following table and reach a conclusion about the null hypothesis.

Source of Variance	SS	df	MS	F
Treatment	199.48			
Blocks	265.24			
Error	306.59			
Total				

11.32 Safety in motels and hotels is a growing concern among travelers. Suppose a survey was conducted by the National Motel and Hotel Association to determine U.S. travelers' perception of safety in various motel chains. The association chose four different national chains from the economy lodging sector and randomly selected 10 people who had stayed overnight in a motel in each of the four chains in the past two years. Each selected traveler was asked to rate each motel chain on a scale from 0 to 100 to indicate how safe he or she felt at that motel. A score of 0 indicates completely unsafe and a score of 100 indicates perfectly safe. The scores follow. Test this randomized block design to determine whether there is a significant difference in the safety ratings of the four motels. Use $\alpha = .05$.

Traveler	Motel 1	Motel 2	Motel 3	Motel 4
1	40	30	55	45
2	65	50	80	70
3	60	55	60	60
4	20	40	55	50
5	50	35	65	60
6	30	30	50	50
7	55	30	60	55
8	70	70	70	70
9	65	60	80	75
10	45	25	45	50

11.33 In recent years, the debate over the U.S. economy has been constant. The electorate seems somewhat divided as to whether the economy is in a recovery or not. Suppose a survey was undertaken to ascertain whether the perception of economic recovery differs according to political affiliation. People were selected for the survey from the Democratic party, the Republican party, and those classifying themselves as independents. A 25-point scale was developed in which respondents gave a score of 25 if they felt the economy was definitely in complete recovery, a 0 if the economy was definitely not in a recovery, and some value in between for more uncertain responses. To control for differences in socioeconomic class, a blocking variable was maintained using five different socioeconomic categories. The data are given here in the form of a randomized block design. Use $\alpha = .01$ to determine whether there is a significant difference in mean responses according to political affiliation.

Socioeconomic Class	Political Affiliation		
	Democrat	Republican	Independent
Upper	11	5	8
Upper middle	15	9	8
Middle	19	14	15
Lower middle	16	12	10
Lower	9	8	7

11.34 As part of a manufacturing process, a plastic container is supposed to be filled with 46 ounces of saltwater solution. The plant has three machines that fill the containers. Managers are concerned that the machines might not be filling the containers with the same amount of saltwater solution, so they set up a randomized block design to test this concern. A pool of five machine operators operates each of the three machines at different times. Company technicians randomly select five containers filled by each machine (one container for each of the five operators). The measurements are gathered and analyzed. The MINITAB output from this analysis follows. What was the structure of the design? How many blocks were there? How many treatment classifications? Is there a statistical difference in the treatment means? Are the blocking effects significant? Discuss the implications of the output.

```
Two-way ANOVA: Measurement versus Machine, Operator
Source    df    SS       MS      F      p
Machine   2     78.30    39.15   6.72   .019
Operator  4      5.09     1.27   0.22   .807
Error     8     46.66     5.83
Total     14   130.06
```

11.35 The comptroller of a company is interested in determining whether the average length of long-distance calls by managers varies according to type of telephone. A randomized block design experiment is set up in which a long-distance call by each of five managers is sampled for four different types of telephones: cellular, computer, regular, and cordless. The treatment is type of telephone and the blocks are the managers. The results of analysis by Excel are shown here. Discuss the results and any implications they might have for the company.

Anova: Two-Factor Without Replication

	A	B	C	D	E	F	G
1	ANOVA						
2							
3	Source of Variation	SS	df	MS	F	P-value	F crit
4	Managers	11.3346	4	2.8336	12.74	0.00028	3.26
5	Phone Type	10.6043	3	3.5348	15.89	0.00018	3.49
6	Error	2.6696	12	0.2225			
7	Total	24.6085	19				

11.5 A FACTORIAL DESIGN (TWO-WAY ANOVA)

Some experiments are designed so that *two or more treatments* (independent variables) *are explored simultaneously.* Such experimental designs are referred to as **factorial designs.** In factorial designs, *every level of each treatment is studied under the conditions of every level of all other treatments.* Factorial designs can be arranged such that three, four, or *n* treatments or independent variables are studied simultaneously in the same experiment. As an example, consider the valve opening data in Table 11.1. The mean valve opening for the 24 measurements is 6.34 centimeters. However, every valve but one in the sample measures something other than the mean. Why? Company management realizes that valves at this firm are made on different machines, by different operators, on different shifts, on different days, with raw materials from different suppliers. Business researchers who are interested in finding the sources of variation might decide to set up a factorial design that incorporates all five of these independent variables in one study. In this text, we explore the factorial designs with two treatments only.

Advantages of the Factorial Design

If two independent variables are analyzed by using a completely randomized design, the effects of each variable are explored separately (one per design). Thus, it takes two completely randomized designs to analyze the effects of the two independent variables. By using a factorial design, the business researcher can analyze both variables at the same time in one design, saving the time and effort of doing two different analyses and minimizing the experiment-wise error rate.

Some business researchers use the factorial design as a way to control confounding or concomitant variables in a study. By building variables into the design, the researcher attempts to control for the effects of multiple variables *in* the experiment. With the completely randomized design, the variables are studied in isolation. With the factorial design, there is potential for increased power over the completely randomized design because the additional effects of the second variable are removed from the error sum of squares.

The researcher can explore the possibility of interaction between the two treatment variables in a two-factor factorial design if multiple measurements are taken under every combination of levels of the two treatments. Interaction will be discussed later.

Factorial designs with two treatments are similar to randomized block designs. However, whereas randomized block designs focus on one treatment variable and *control* for a blocking effect, a two-treatment factorial design focuses on the effects of both variables. Because the randomized block design contains only one measure for each (treatment-block) combination, interaction cannot be analyzed in randomized block designs.

Factorial Designs with Two Treatments

The structure of a two-treatment factorial design is featured in Figure 11.8. Note that there are two independent variables (two treatments) and that there is an intersection of each

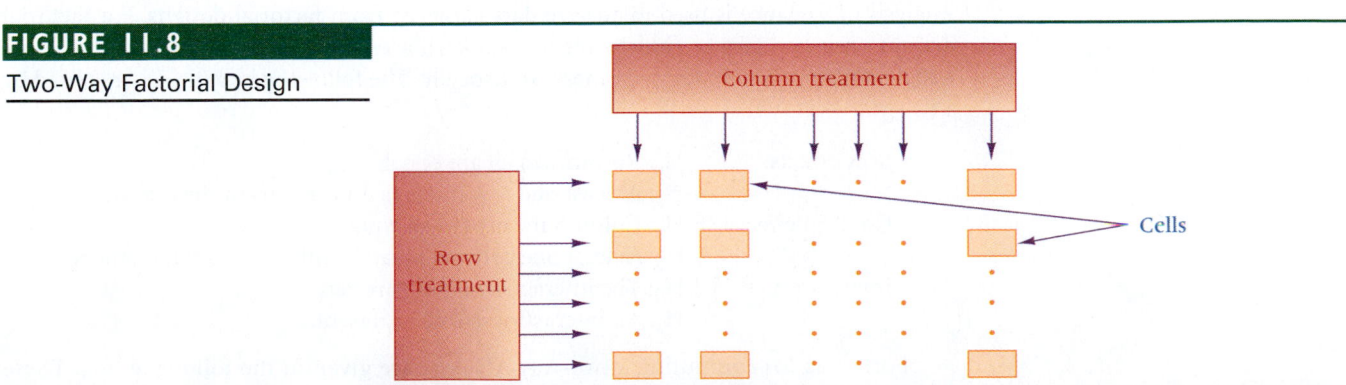

FIGURE 11.8

Two-Way Factorial Design

level of each treatment. These intersections are referred to as *cells*. One treatment is arbitrarily designated as *row* treatment (forming the rows of the design) and the other treatment is designated as *column* treatment (forming the columns of the design). Although it is possible to analyze factorial designs with unequal numbers of items in the cells, the analysis of unequal cell designs is beyond the scope of this text. All factorial designs discussed here have cells of equal size.

Treatments (independent variables) of factorial designs must have at least two levels each. The simplest factorial design is a 2×2 factorial design, where each treatment has two levels. If such a factorial design were diagrammed in the manner of Figure 11.8, it would include two rows and two columns, forming four cells.

In this section, we study only factorial designs with $n > 1$ measurements for each combination of treatment levels (cells). This approach allows us to attempt to measure the interaction of the treatment variables. As with the completely randomized design and the randomized block design, a factorial design contains only *one* dependent variable.

Applications

Many applications of the factorial design are possible in business research. For example, the natural gas industry can design an experiment to study usage rates and how they are affected by temperature and precipitation. Theorizing that the outside temperature and type of precipitation make a difference in natural gas usage, industry researchers can gather usage measurements for a given community over a variety of temperature and precipitation conditions. At the same time, they can make an effort to determine whether certain types of precipitation, combined with certain temperature levels, affect usage rates differently than other combinations of temperature and precipitation (interaction effects).

Stock market analysts can select a company from an industry such as the construction industry and observe the behavior of its stock under different conditions. A factorial design can be set up by using volume of the stock market and prime interest rate as two independent variables. For volume of the market, business researchers can select some days when the volume is up from the day before, some days when the volume is down from the day before, and some other days when the volume is essentially the same as on the preceding day. These groups of days would constitute three levels of the independent variable, market volume. Business researchers can do the same thing with prime rate. Levels can be selected such that the prime rate is (1) up, (2) down, and (3) essentially the same. For the dependent variable, the researchers would measure how much the company's stock rises or falls on those randomly selected days (stock change). Using the factorial design, the business researcher can determine whether stock changes are different under various levels of market volume, whether stock changes are different under various levels of the prime interest rate, and whether stock changes react differently under various combinations of volume and prime rate (interaction effects).

Statistically Testing the Factorial Design

Analysis of variance is used to analyze data gathered from factorial designs. For factorial designs with two factors (independent variables), a **two-way analysis of variance (two-way ANOVA)** is used to test hypotheses statistically. The following hypotheses are tested by a two-way ANOVA.

Row effects:	H_0: Row means all are equal.
	H_a: At least one row mean is different from the others.
Column effects:	H_0: Column means are all equal.
	H_a: At least one column mean is different from the others.
Interaction effects:	H_0: The interaction effects are zero.
	H_a: An interaction effect is present.

Formulas for computing a two-way ANOVA are given in the following box. These formulas are computed in a manner similar to computations for the completely randomized design and the randomized block design. F values are determined for three effects:

1. Row effects
2. Column effects
3. Interaction effects

The row effects and the column effects are sometimes referred to as the main effects. Although F values are determined for these main effects, an F value is also computed for interaction effects. Using these observed F values, the researcher can make a decision about the null hypotheses for each effect.

Each of these observed F values is compared to a table F value. The table F value is determined by α, df_{num}, and df_{denom}. The degrees of freedom for the numerator (df_{num}) are determined by the effect being studied. If the observed F value is for columns, the degrees of freedom for the numerator are $C - 1$. If the observed F value is for rows, the degrees of freedom for the numerator are $R - 1$. If the observed F value is for interaction, the degrees of freedom for the numerator are $(R - 1) \cdot (C - 1)$. The number of degrees of freedom for the denominator of the table value for each of the three effects is the same, the error degrees of freedom, $RC(n - 1)$. The table F values (critical F) for a two-way ANOVA follow.

TABLE F VALUES FOR A TWO-WAY ANOVA		
Row effects:	$F_{\alpha, R-1, RC(n-1)}$	
Column effects:	$F_{\alpha, C-1, RC(n-1)}$	
Interaction effects:	$F_{\alpha, (R-1)(C-1), RC(n-1)}$	

FORMULAS FOR COMPUTING A TWO-WAY ANOVA	
	$$SSR = nC\sum_{i=1}^{R}(\bar{x}_i - \bar{x})^2$$
	$$SSC = nR\sum_{j=1}^{C}(\bar{x}_j - \bar{x})^2$$
	$$SSI = n\sum_{i=1}^{R}\sum_{j=1}^{C}(\bar{x}_{ij} - \bar{x}_i - \bar{x}_j + \bar{x})^2$$
	$$SSE = \sum_{i=1}^{R}\sum_{j=1}^{C}\sum_{k=1}^{n}(x_{ijk} - \bar{x}_{ij})^2$$
	$$SST = \sum_{i=1}^{R}\sum_{j=1}^{C}\sum_{k=1}^{n}(x_{ijk} - \bar{x})^2$$
	$df_R = R - 1$
	$df_C = C - 1$
	$df_I = (R - 1)(C - 1)$
	$df_E = RC(n - 1)$
	$df_T = N - 1$
	$$MSR = \frac{SSR}{R-1}$$
	$$MSC = \frac{SSC}{C-1}$$
	$$MSI = \frac{SSI}{(R-1)(C-1)}$$
	$$MSE = \frac{SSE}{RC(n-1)}$$

continued on the following page

$$F_R = \frac{MSR}{MSE}$$

$$F_C = \frac{MSC}{MSE}$$

$$F_I = \frac{MSI}{MSE}$$

where:

n = number of observations per cell
C = number of column treatments
R = number of row treatments
i = row treatment level
j = column treatment level
k = cell member
x_{ijk} = individual observation

$\bar{x}_{ij}$ = cell mean
$\bar{x}_i$ = row mean

$\bar{x}_j$ = column mean
$\bar{x}$ = grand mean

Interaction

As noted before, along with testing the effects of the two treatments in a factorial design, it is possible to test for the interaction effects of the two treatments whenever multiple measures are taken in each cell of the design. **Interaction** occurs *when the effects of one treatment vary according to the levels of treatment of the other effect.* For example, in a study examining the impact of temperature and humidity on a manufacturing process, it is possible that temperature and humidity will interact in such a way that the effect of temperature on the process varies with the humidity. Low temperatures might not be a significant manufacturing factor when humidity is low but might be a factor when humidity is high. Similarly, high temperatures might be a factor with low humidity but not with high humidity.

As another example, suppose a business researcher is studying the amount of red meat consumed by families per month and is examining economic class and religion as two independent variables. Class and religion might interact in such a way that with certain religions, economic class does not matter in the consumption of red meat, but with other religions, class does make a difference.

In terms of the factorial design, interaction occurs when the pattern of cell means in one row (going across columns) varies from the pattern of cell means in other rows. This variation indicates that the differences in column effects depend on which row is being examined. Hence, an interaction of the rows and columns occurs. The same thing can happen when the pattern of cell means within a column is different from the pattern of cell means in other columns.

Interaction can be depicted graphically by plotting the cell means within each row (and can also be done by plotting the cell means within each column). The means within each row (or column) are then connected by a line. If the broken lines for the rows (or columns) are parallel, no interaction is indicated.

Figure 11.9 is a graph of the means for each cell in each row in a 2 × 3 (2 rows, 3 columns) factorial design with interaction. Note that the lines connecting the means in each row cross each other. In Figure 11.10 the lines converge, indicating the likely presence of some interaction. Figure 11.11 depicts a 2 × 3 factorial design with no interaction.

When the interaction effects are significant, the main effects (row and column) are confounded and should not be analyzed in the usual manner. In this case, it is not possible to state unequivocally that the row effects or the column effects are significantly different because the difference in means of one main effect varies according to the level of the other main effect (interaction is present). Some specific procedures are recommended for examining main effects when significant interaction is present. However, these techniques

FIGURE 11.9

A 2 × 3 Factorial Design with Interaction

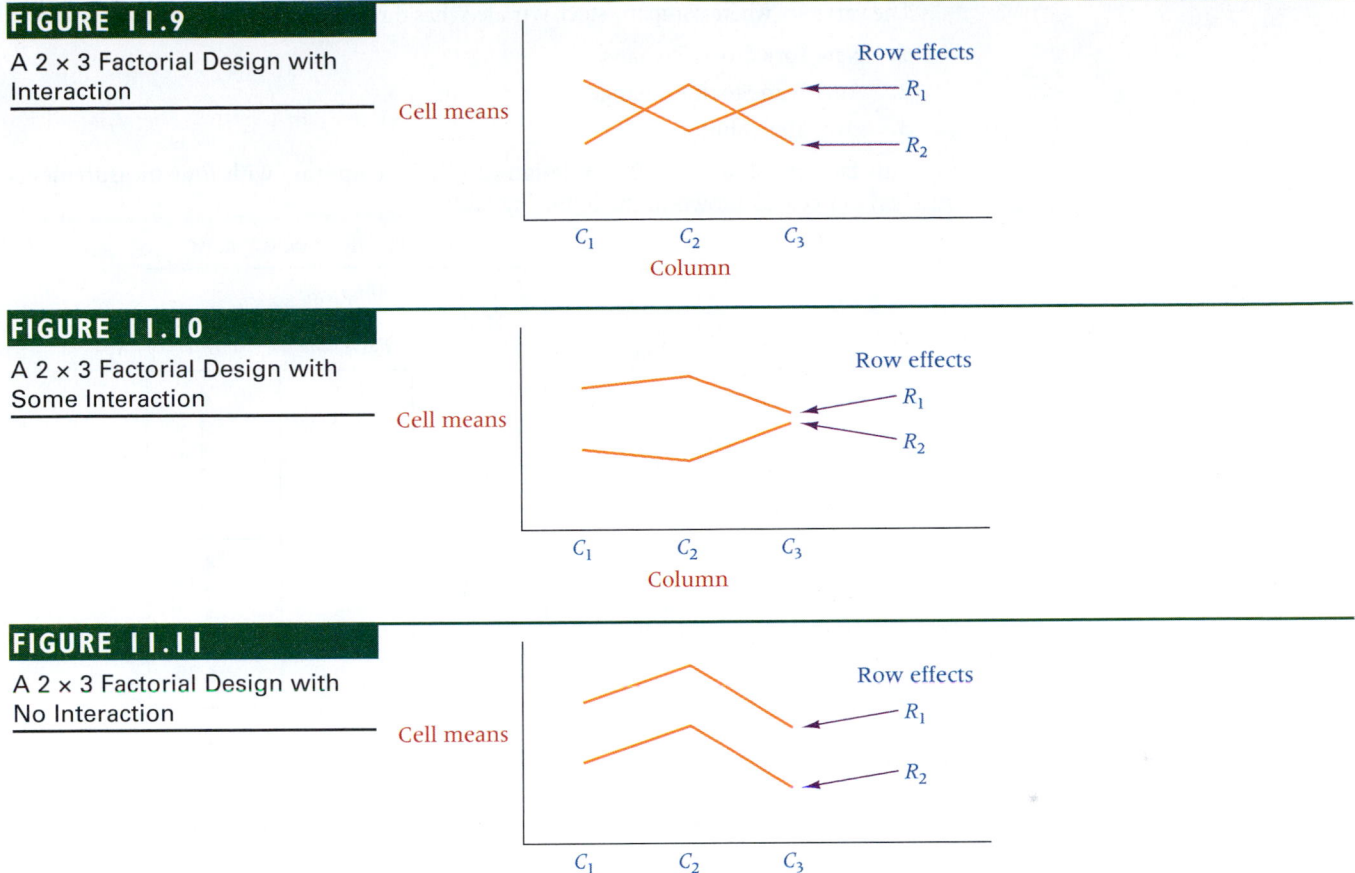

FIGURE 11.10

A 2 × 3 Factorial Design with Some Interaction

FIGURE 11.11

A 2 × 3 Factorial Design with No Interaction

are beyond the scope of material presented here. Hence, in this text, whenever interaction effects are present (F_{inter} is significant), the researcher should *not* attempt to interpret the main effects (F_{row} and F_{col}).

As an example of a factorial design, consider the fact that at the end of a financially successful fiscal year, CEOs often must decide whether to award a dividend to stockholders or to make a company investment. One factor in this decision would seem to be whether attractive investment opportunities are available.* To determine whether this factor is important, business researchers randomly select 24 CEOs and ask them to rate how important "availability of profitable investment opportunities" is in deciding whether to pay dividends or invest. The CEOs are requested to respond to this item on a scale from 0 to 4, where 0 = no importance, 1 = slight importance, 2 = moderate importance, 3 = great importance, and 4 = maximum importance. The 0–4 response is the dependent variable in the experimental design.

The business researchers are concerned that where the company's stock is traded (New York Stock Exchange, American Stock Exchange, and over-the-counter) might make a difference in the CEOs' response to the question. In addition, the business researchers believe that how stockholders are informed of dividends (annual reports versus presentations) might affect the outcome of the experiment. Thus, a two-way ANOVA is set up with "where the company's stock is traded" and "how stockholders are informed of dividends" as the two independent variables. The variable "how stockholders are informed of dividends" has two treatment levels, or classifications.

1. Annual/quarterly reports
2. Presentations to analysts

---

* Adapted from H. Kent Baker, "Why Companies Pay No Dividends," *Akron Business and Economic Review*, vol. 20 (Summer 1989), pp. 48–61.

The variable "where company stock is traded" has three treatment levels, or classifications.

1. New York Stock Exchange
2. American Stock Exchange
3. Over-the-counter

This factorial design is a 2×3 design (2 rows, 3 columns) with four measurements (ratings) per cell, as shown in the following table.

		Where Company Stock is Traded			
		New York Stock Exchange	*American Stock Exchange*	*Over the Counter*	$\overline{X}_i=$
How Stockholders Are Informed of Dividends	*Annual Quarterly Reports*	2 1 2 1 $\overline{X}_{11}=1.5$	2 3 3 2 $\overline{X}_{12}=2.5$	4 3 4 3 $\overline{X}_{13}=3.5$	2.5
	Presentations to Analysts	2 3 1 2 $\overline{X}_{21}=2.0$	3 3 2 4 $\overline{X}_{22}=3.0$	4 4 3 4 $\overline{X}_{23}=3.75$	2.9167
	$\overline{X}_j=$	1.75	2.75	3.625	
			$\overline{X}= 2.7083$		

These data are analyzed by using a two-way analysis of variance and $\alpha = .05$.

$$SSR=nC\sum_{i=1}^{R}(\overline{x}_i - \overline{x})^2$$

$$= 4(3)[(2.5 - 2.7083)^2 + (2.9167 - 2.7083)^2] = 1.0418$$

$$SSC=nR\sum_{j=1}^{C}(\overline{x}_j - \overline{x})^2$$

$$= 4(2)[(1.75 - 2.7083)^2 + (2.75 - 2.7083)^2 + (3.625 - 2.7083)^2] = 14.0833$$

$$SSI=n\sum_{i=1}^{R}\sum_{j=1}^{C}(\overline{x}_{ij} - \overline{x}_i - \overline{x}_j + \overline{x})^2$$

$$= 4[(1.5 - 2.5 - 1.75 + 2.7083)^2 + (2.5 - 2.5 - 2.75 + 2.7083)^2 +$$
$$(3.5 - 2.5 - 3.625 + 2.7083)^2 + (2.0 - 2.9167 - 1.75 + 2.7083)^2 +$$
$$(3.0 - 2.9167 - 2.75 + 2.7083)^2 + (3.75 - 2.9167 - 3.625 + 2.7083)^2] = .0833$$

$$SSE=\sum_{i=1}^{R}\sum_{j=1}^{C}\sum_{k=1}^{n}(x_{ijk} - \overline{x}_{ij})^2$$

$$= (2 - 1.5)^2 + (1 - 1.5)^2 + \ldots +$$
$$(3 - 3.75)^2 + (4 - 3.75)^2 = 7.7500$$

$$SST=\sum_{i=1}^{R}\sum_{j=1}^{C}\sum_{k=1}^{n}(x_{ijk} - \overline{x})^2$$

$$= (2 - 2.7083)^2 + (1 - 2.7083)^2 + \ldots + (3 - 2.7083)^2 + (4 - 2.7083)^2 = 22.9583$$

$$MSR = \frac{SSR}{R-1} = \frac{1.0418}{1} = 1.0418$$

$$MSC = \frac{SSC}{C-1} = \frac{14.0833}{2} = 7.0417$$

$$MSI = \frac{SSI}{(R-1)(C-1)} = \frac{.0833}{2} = .0417$$

$$MSE = \frac{SSE}{RC(n-1)} = \frac{7.7500}{18} = .4306$$

$$F_R = \frac{MSR}{MSE} = \frac{1.0418}{.4306} = 2.42$$

$$F_C = \frac{MSC}{MSE} = \frac{7.0417}{.4306} = 16.35$$

$$F_I = \frac{MSI}{MSE} = \frac{.0417}{.4306} = 0.10$$

Source of Variation	SS	df	MS	F
Row	1.0418	1	1.0418	2.42
Column	14.0833	2	7.0417	16.35*
Interaction	.0833	2	.0417	0.10
Error	7.7500	18	.4306	
Total	22.9583	23		

*Denotes significance at $\alpha = .01$.

The critical F value for the interaction effects at $\alpha = .05$ is

$$F_{.05,2,18} = 3.55.$$

The observed F value for interaction effects is 0.10. Because this value is less than the critical table value (3.55), no significant interaction effects are evident. Because no significant interaction effects are present, it is possible to examine the main effects.

The critical F value of the row effects at $\alpha = .05$ is $F_{.05,1,18} = 4.41$. The observed F value of 2.42 is less than the table value. Hence, no significant row effects are present.

The critical F value of the column effects at $\alpha = .05$ is $F_{.05,2,18} = 3.55$. This value is coincidently the same as the critical table value for interaction because in this problem the degrees of freedom are the same for interaction and column effects. The observed F value for columns (16.35) is greater than this critical value. Hence, a significant difference in row effects is evident at $\alpha = .05$.

A significant difference is noted in the CEOs' mean ratings of the item "availability of profitable investment opportunities" according to where the company's stock is traded. A cursory examination of the means for the three levels of the column effects (where stock is traded) reveals that the lowest mean was from CEOs whose company traded stock on the New York Stock Exchange. The highest mean rating was from CEOs whose company traded stock over-the-counter. Using multiple comparison techniques, the business researchers can statistically test for differences in the means of these three groups.

Because the sample sizes within each column are equal, Tukey's HSD test can be used to compute multiple comparisons. The value of MSE is .431 for this problem. In testing the column means with Tukey's HSD test, the value of n is the number of items in a column, which is eight. The number of treatments is $C = 3$ for columns and $N - C = 24 - 3 = 21$.

With these two values and $\alpha = .05$, a value for q can be determined from Table A.10:

$$q_{.05,3,21} = 3.58$$

From these values, the honestly significant difference can be computed:

$$HSD = q\sqrt{\frac{MSE}{n}} = 3.58\sqrt{\frac{.431}{8}} = .831$$

FIGURE 11.12

MINITAB and Excel Output for the CEO Dividend Problem

MINITAB Output:

```
Two-way ANOVA: Rating versus How Reported, Where Traded

Analysis of Variance for Rating
Source          DF         SS          MS          F         P
How Repo         1      1.042       1.042       2.42     0.137
Where Tr         2     14.083       7.042      16.35     0.000
Interaction      2      0.083       0.042       0.10     0.908
Error           18      7.750       0.431
Total           23     22.958

                        Individual 95% CI
How Repo     Mean     ——— + ——— + ——— + ——— +
1            2.50     (—————————*—————————)
2            2.92                  (—————————*—————————)
                      ——— + ——— + ——— + ——— +
                      2.40    2.70    3.00    3.30

                        Individual 95% CI
Where Tr     Mean     — + ——— + ——— + ——— + ———
1            1.75     (———*———)
2            2.75                (———*———)
3            3.63                            (———*———)
                      — + ——— + ——— + ——— + ———
                      1.40    2.10    2.80    3.50
```

Excel Output:

	A	B	C	D	E	F	G
1	Anova: Two-Factor With Replication						
2							
3	SUMMARY	NYSE	ASE	OTC	Total		
4	A.Q. Reports						
5	Count	4	4	4	12		
6	Sum	6	10	14	30		
7	Average	1.5	2.5	3.5	2.5		
8	Variance	0.3333	0.3333	0.3333	1		
9							
10	Pres. to Analysts						
11	Count	4	4	4	12		
12	Sum	8	12	15	35		
13	Average	2	3	3.75	2.9167		
14	Variance	0.666667	0.666667	0.25	0.9924		
15							
16	Total						
17	Count	8	8	8			
18	Sum	14	22	29			
19	Average	1.75	2.75	3.625			
20	Variance	0.5	0.5	0.2679			
21							
22							
23	ANOVA						
24	Source of Variation	SS	df	MS	F	P-value	F crit
25	Sample	1.04167	1	1.04167	2.42	0.137251	4.41
26	Columns	14.08333	2	7.04167	16.35	0.000089	3.55
27	Interaction	0.08333	2	0.04167	0.10	0.90823	3.55
28	Within	7.75	18	0.43056			
29							
30	Total	22.95833	23				

The mean ratings for the three columns are

$$\bar{x}_1 = 1.75, \bar{x}_2 = 2.75, \bar{x}_3 = 3.625$$

The absolute value of differences between means are as follows:

$$|\bar{x}_1 - \bar{x}_2| = |1.75 - 2.75| = 1.00$$

$$|\bar{x}_1 - \bar{x}_3| = |1.75 - 3.625| = 1.875$$

$$|\bar{x}_2 - \bar{x}_3| = |2.75 - 3.625| = .875$$

FIGURE 11.13

Tukey's Pairwise Comparisons for Column Means

```
Tukey's pairwise comparisons
Family error rate = 0.0500
Individual error rate = 0.0200
Critical value = 3.56
Intervals for (column level mean) - (row level mean)
            1         2
2   -1.8182
    -0.1818
3   -2.6932   -1.6932
    -1.0568   -0.0568
```

All three differences are greater than .831 and are therefore significantly different at $\alpha = .05$ by the HSD test. Where a company's stock is traded makes a difference in the way a CEO responds to the question.

Using a Computer to Do a Two-Way ANOVA

A two-way ANOVA can be computed by using either MINITAB or Excel. Figure 11.12 displays the MINITAB and Excel output for the CEO example. The MINITAB output contains an ANOVA table with each of the three F values and their associated p-values. In addition, there are individual 95% confidence intervals for means of both row and column effects. These intervals give the researcher a visual idea of differences between means. A more formal test of multiple comparisons of the column means is done with MINITAB by using Tukey's HSD test. This output is displayed in Figure 11.13. Observe that in all three comparisons the signs on each end of the particular confidence interval are the same (and thus zero is not included); hence there is a significant difference in the means in each of the three pairs.

The Excel output for two-way ANOVA with replications on the CEO dividend example is included in Figure 11.12. The Excel output contains cell, column, and row means along with observed F values for rows (sample), columns, and interaction. The Excel output also contains p-values and critical F values for each of these Fs. Note that the output here is virtually identical to the findings obtained by the manual calculations.

DEMONSTRATION PROBLEM 11.4	Some theorists believe that training warehouse workers can reduce absenteeism.* Suppose an experimental design is structured to test this belief. Warehouses in which training sessions have been held for workers are selected for the study. The four types of warehouses are (1) general merchandise, (2) commodity, (3) bulk storage, and (4) cold storage. The training sessions are differentiated by length. Researchers identify three levels of training sessions according to the length of sessions: (1) 1–20 days, (2) 21–50 days, and (3) more than 50 days. Three warehouse workers are selected randomly for each particular combination of type of warehouse and session length. The workers are monitored for the next year to determine how many days they are absent. The resulting data are in the following 4 × 3 design (4 rows, 3 columns) structure. Using this information, calculate a two-way ANOVA to determine whether there are any significant differences in effects. Use $\alpha = .05$.

Solution

HYPOTHESIZE:

STEP 1. The following hypotheses are being tested.
For row effects:

$$H_0: \mu_{1.} = \mu_{2.} = \mu_{3.} = \mu_{4.}$$
$$H_a: \text{At least one of the row means is different from the others.}$$

For column effects:

$$H_0: \mu_{.1} = \mu_{.2} = \mu_{.3}$$
$$H_a: \text{At least one of the column means is different from the others.}$$

---

*Adapted from Paul R. Murphy and Richard F. Poist, "Managing the Human Side of Public Warehousing: An Overview of Modern Practices," *Transportation Journal*, vol. 31 (Spring 1992), pp. 54–63.

For interaction effects:

H_0: The interaction effects are zero.

H_a: There is an interaction effect.

TEST:

STEP 2. The two-way ANOVA with the F test is the appropriate statistical test.

STEP 3. $\alpha = .05$

STEP 4.

$$df_{rows} = 4 - 1 = 3$$
$$df_{columns} = 3 - 1 = 2$$
$$df_{interation} = (3)(2) = 6$$
$$df_{error} = (4)(3)(2) = 24$$

For row effects, $F_{.05,3,24} = 3.01$; for column effects, $F_{.05,2,24} = 3.40$; and for interaction effects, $F_{.05,6,24} = 2.51$. For each of these effects, if any observed F value is greater than its associated critical F value, the respective null hypothesis will be rejected.

STEP 5.

		Length of Training Session (Days)			
		1–20	21–50	More than 50	$\overline{X}_r$
	General Merchandise	3 4.5 4	2 2.5 2	2.5 1 1.5	2.5556
Types of Warehouses	Commodity	5 4.5 4	1 3 2.5	0 1.5 2	2.6111
	Bulk Storage	2.5 3 3.5	1 3 1.5	3.5 3.5 4	2.8333
	Cold Storage	2 2 3	5 4.5 2.5	4 4.5 5	3.6111
	$\overline{X}_c$	3.4167	2.5417	2.75	

$$\overline{X} = 2.9028$$

STEP 6. The MINITAB and Excel (ANOVA table only) output for this problem follows.

MINITAB Output

```
Two-way ANOVA: Absences versus Type of Warehouse, Length of Training
   Analysis of Variance for Absences
   Source          DF        SS        MS       F       P
   Type of          3     6.410     2.137    3.46   0.032
   Length           2     5.014     2.507    4.06   0.030
   Interaction      6    33.153     5.525    8.94   0.000
   Error           24    14.833     0.618
   Total           35    59.410

Individual 95% CI
   Type of   Mean    ----+-----+-----+-----+---
      1      2.56    (----*----)
      2      2.61     (----*----)
      3      2.83      (----*----)
      4      3.61                 (----*----)
                      ----+-----+-----+-----+---
                      2.40  3.00  3.60  4.20

Individual 95% CI
   Length    Mean    ----+-----+-----+-----+---
      1      3.42                 (----*----)
      2      2.54    (----*----)
      3      2.75      (----*----)
                      ----+-----+-----+-----+---
                      2.50  3.00  3.50  4.00
```

Excel Output
Anova: Two-Factor With Replication

	A	B	C	D	E	F	G
1	ANOVA						
2	Source of Variation	SS	df	MS	F	P-value	F crit
3	Sample	6.409722	3	2.136574	3.46	0.032205	3.01
4	Columns	5.013889	2	2.506944	4.06	0.030372	3.40
5	Interaction	33.15278	6	5.525463	8.94	0.000035	2.51
6	Within	14.83333	24	0.618056			
7							
8	Total	59.40972	35				

ACTION:

STEP 7. Looking at the source of variation table, we must first examine the inter-action effects. The observed F value for interaction is 8.94 for both Excel and MINITAB. The observed F value for interaction is greater than the critical F value. The interaction effects are statistically significant at $\alpha = .05$. The p-value for interaction shown in Excel is .000035. The interaction effects are significant at $\alpha = .0001$. The business researcher should not bother to examine the main effects because the sig-nificant interaction confounds the main effects.

BUSINESS IMPLICATIONS:

STEP 8. The significant interaction effects indicate that certain warehouse types in combination with certain lengths of training session result in different absenteeism rates than do other combinations of levels for these two variables. Using the cell means shown here, we can depict the interactions graphically.

		Length of Training Session (Days)		
		1–20	**21–50**	**More than 50**
	General Merchandise	3.8	2.2	1.7
	Commodity	4.5	2.2	1.2
Types of Warehouses	Bulk Storage	3.0	1.8	3.7
	Cold Storage	2.3	4.0	4.5

MINITAB produces the following graph of the interaction.

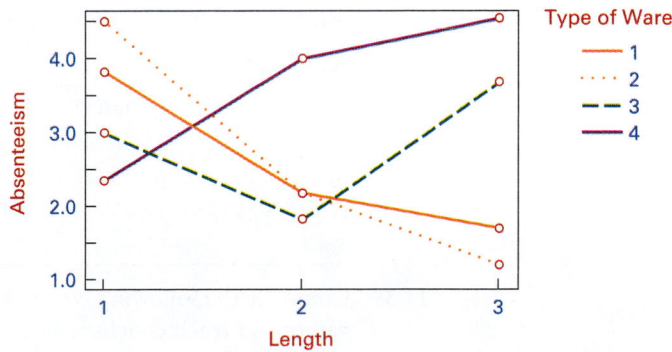

Note the intersecting and crossing lines, which indicate interaction. Under the short-length training sessions, 1, cold-storage workers had the lowest rate of absen-teeism and workers at commodity warehouses had the highest. However, for medium-length sessions, 2, cold-storage workers had the highest rate of absen-teeism and bulk-storage had the lowest. For the longest training sessions, 3, com-modity warehouse workers had the lowest rate of absenteeism, even though these workers had the highest rate of absenteeism for short-length sessions. Thus, the rate of absenteeism for workers at a particular type of warehouse depended on length of session. There was an interaction between type of warehouse and length of session. This graph could be constructed with the row levels along the bottom axis instead of column levels.

11.5 PROBLEMS

11.36 Describe the following factorial design. How many independent and dependent variables are there? How many levels are there for each treatment? If the data were known, could interaction be determined from this design? Compute all degrees of freedom. Each data value is represented by an x.

	Variable 1			
	x_{111}	x_{121}	x_{131}	x_{141}
	x_{112}	x_{122}	x_{132}	x_{142}
	x_{113}	x_{123}	x_{133}	x_{143}
Variable 2				
	x_{211}	x_{221}	x_{231}	x_{241}
	x_{212}	x_{222}	x_{232}	x_{242}
	x_{213}	x_{223}	x_{233}	x_{243}

11.37 Describe the following factorial design. How many independent and dependent variables are there? How many levels are there for each treatment? If the data were known, could interaction be determined from this design? Compute all degrees of freedom. Each data value is represented by an x.

	Variable 1		
	x_{111}	x_{121}	x_{131}
	x_{112}	x_{122}	x_{132}
	x_{211}	x_{221}	x_{231}
	x_{212}	x_{222}	x_{232}
Variable 2	x_{311}	x_{321}	x_{331}
	x_{312}	x_{322}	x_{332}
	x_{411}	x_{421}	x_{431}
	x_{412}	x_{422}	x_{432}

11.38 Complete the following two-way ANOVA table. Determine the critical table F values and reach conclusions about the hypotheses for effects. Let $\alpha = .05$.

Source of Variance	SS	df	MS	F
Row	126.98	3		
Column	37.49	4		
Interaction	380.82			
Error	733.65	60		
Total				

11.39 Complete the following two-way ANOVA table. Determine the critical table F values and reach conclusions about the hypotheses for effects. Let $\alpha = .05$.

Source of Variance	SS	df	MS	F
Row	1.047	1		
Column	3.844	3		
Interaction	0.773			
Error				
Total	12.632	23		

11.40 The data gathered from a two-way factorial design follow. Use the two-way ANOVA to analyze these data. Let $\alpha = .01$.

	Treatment 1		
	A	B	C
A	23	21	20
	25	21	22
Treatment 2			
B	27	24	26
	28	27	27

11.41 Suppose the following data have been gathered from a study with a two-way factorial design. Use $\alpha = .05$ and a two-way ANOVA to analyze the data. State your conclusions.

		Treatment 1	
		A	B
	A	1.2	1.9
		1.3	1.6
		1.3	1.7
		1.5	2.0
	B	2.2	2.7
		2.1	2.5
		2.0	2.8
Treatment 2		2.3	2.8
	C	1.7	1.9
		1.8	2.2
		1.7	1.9
		1.6	2.0
	D	2.4	2.8
		2.3	2.6
		2.5	2.4
		2.4	2.8

11.42 Children are generally believed to have considerable influence over their parents in the purchase of certain items, particularly food and beverage items. To study this notion further, a study is conducted in which parents are asked to report how many food and beverage items purchased by the family per week are purchased mainly because of the influence of their children. Because the age of the child may have an effect on the study, parents are asked to focus on one particular child in the family for the week, and to report the age of the child. Four age categories are selected for the children: 4–5 years, 6–7 years, 8–9 years, and 10–12 years. Also, because the number of children in the family might make a difference, three different sizes of families are chosen for the study: families with one child, families with two children, and families with three or more children. Suppose the following data represent the reported number of child-influenced buying incidents per week. Use the data to compute a two-way ANOVA. Let $\alpha = .05$.

		Number of Children in Family		
		1	2	3 or more
	4–5	2	1	1
		4	2	1
Age of	6–7	5	3	2
Child		4	1	1
(years)	8–9	8	4	2
		6	5	3
	10–12	7	3	4
		8	5	3

11.43 A shoe retailer conducted a study to determine whether there is a difference in the number of pairs of shoes sold per day by stores according to the number of competitors within a 1-mile radius and the location of the store. The company researchers selected three types of stores for consideration in the study: stand-alone suburban stores, mall stores, and downtown stores. These stores vary in the numbers of competing stores within a 1-mile radius, which have been reduced to four categories: 0 competitors, 1 competitor, 2 competitors, and 3 or more competitors. Suppose the following data represent the number of pairs of shoes sold per day for each of these types of stores with the given number of competitors. Use $\alpha = .05$ and a two-way ANOVA to analyze the data.

		Number of Competitors			
		0	**1**	**2**	**3 or more**
	Stand-Alone	41	38	59	47
		30	31	48	40
		45	39	51	39
Store	*Mall*	25	29	44	43
Location		31	35	48	42
		22	30	50	53
	Downtown	18	22	29	24
		29	17	28	27
		33	25	26	32

11.44 Study the following analysis of variance table that was produced by using MINITAB. Describe the design (number of treatments, sample sizes, etc.). Are there any significant effects? Discuss the output. The MINITAB graph that follows the ANOVA table was produced on these same data. Analyze the graph.

```
Two-way Analysis of Variance

Analysis of Variance for Dependent Variable
Source          DF         SS         MS         F          p
RowEffects       2      92.31      46.16      13.23      0.000
ColEffects       4     998.80     249.70      71.57      0.000
Interaction      8     442.13      55.27      15.84      0.000
Error           30     104.67       3.49
Total           44    1637.91
```

Interaction Plot—Data Means for DV

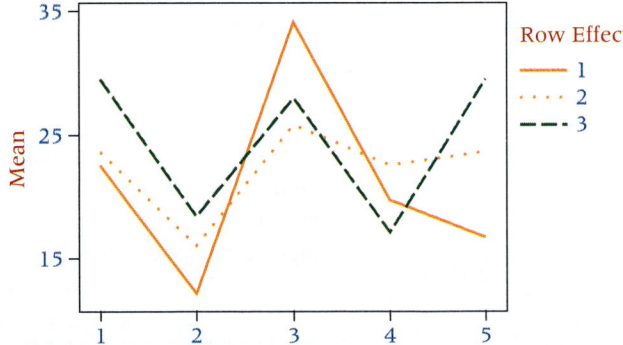

11.45 Consider the valve opening data displayed in Table 11.1. Suppose the data represent valves produced on four different machines on three different shifts and that the quality controllers want to know whether there is any difference in the mean measurements of valve openings by shift or by machine. The data are given here, organized by machine and shift. In addition, Excel has been used to analyze the data with a two-way ANOVA. What are the hypotheses for this problem? Study the output in terms of significant differences. Discuss the results obtained. What conclusions might the quality controllers reach from this analysis?

		Valve Openings (cm)		
		Shift 1	Shift 2	Shift 3
	1	6.56	6.38	6.29
		6.40	6.19	6.23
	2	6.54	6.26	6.19
		6.34	6.23	6.33
Machine	3	6.58	6.22	6.26
		6.44	6.27	6.31
	4	6.36	6.29	6.21
		6.50	6.19	6.58

Anova: Two-Factor With Replication

	A	B	C	D	E	F	G
1	ANOVA						
2							
3	Source of Variation	SS	df	MS	F	P-value	F crit
4	Sample	0.00538	3	0.00179	0.14	0.9368	3.49
5	Columns	0.19731	2	0.09865	7.47	0.0078	3.89
6	Interaction	0.03036	6	0.00506	0.38	0.8760	3.00
7	Within	0.15845	12	0.01320			
8	Total	0.39150	23				

11.46 Finish the computations in the MINITAB ANOVA table shown here and determine the critical table *F* values. Interpret the analysis. Examine the associated MINITAB graph and interpret the results. Discuss this problem, including the structure of the design, the sample sizes, and decisions about the hypotheses.

```
Two-way ANOVA: depvar versus row, column

Analysis of Variance for depvar

Source        DF        SS        MS
Row            2     0.296     0.148
Column         2     1.852     0.926
Interaction    4     4.370     1.093
Error         18    14.000     0.778
Total         26    20.519
```

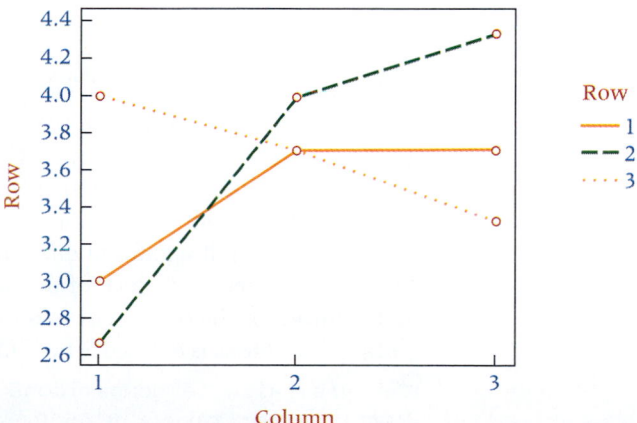

Analyzing the Differences in Profitability of Companies in Three Countries

The Decision Dilemma presents portions of a study to determine differences in the profitability of large companies in three countries. In particular, the question was posed: Is there a difference in the profitability of large companies between Germany, Japan, and the United States? This chapter explained how error rate can build up if a series of *t* tests is used to test the differences by pairs. In comparing the three countries, it would take three t tests to analyze all possibilities: $_3C_2 = 3$. If $\alpha = .05$ for each test, then the probability of at least one of the three t tests being significant by chance when the null hypothesis is true is $1 - (.95)(.95)(.95) = .143$. If seven countries are included in the study and the t test is used to analyze data representing each pair of countries, then $_7C_2 = 21$ different tests will be required. Using $\alpha = .05$ for each test, there is a probability of $1 - (.95)^{21} = .66$ that at least one of the pairwise t tests will be significant by chance even if there are no differences between countries. For this reason, the ANOVA is the preferred methodology for analyzing the data presented in the Decision Dilemma.

The Decision Dilemma presents a completely randomized design if the years are viewed merely as different observations of the dependent variable. The business researcher analyzed the data using three one-way ANOVAs with country being the independent variable and Germany, Japan, and the United States being the three levels of the independent variable. The dependent variable in one analysis is return on assets, in the second analysis is return on equity, and in the third analysis is operating margin. MINITAB and EXCEL output for return on assets follows. You are encouraged to analyze return on equity and operating margin by using a computer package on your own. What did you find?

MINITAB Output

One-way ANOVA: Return on Assets versus Country

```
Analysis of Variance
Source      DF      SS         MS        F         P
Country      2    25.743    12.872    17.37    0.000
Error       15    11.116     0.741
Total       17    36.860
```

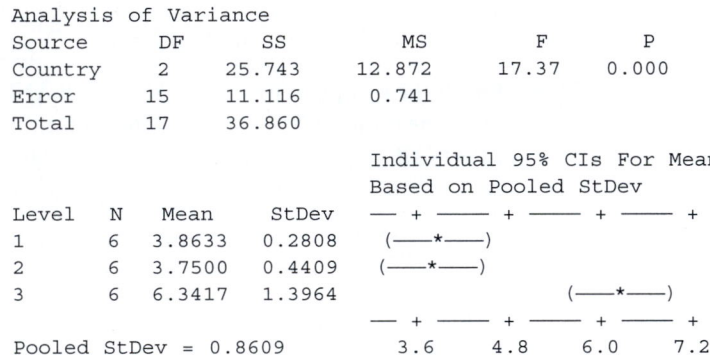

```
                                  Individual 95% CIs For Mean
                                  Based on Pooled StDev
Level   N    Mean     StDev    — + —— + —— + —— +
1       6   3.8633   0.2808   (——*——)
2       6   3.7500   0.4409   (——*——)
3       6   6.3417   1.3964                    (——*——)
                              — + —— + —— + —— +
Pooled StDev = 0.8609          3.6    4.8    6.0    7.2
```

EXCEL Output

	A	B	C	D	E	F	G
1	ANOVA						
2	Source of Variation	SS	df	MS	F	P-value	F crit
3	Between Groups	25.74	2	12.872	17.37	0.0001	3.68
4	Within Groups	11.12	15	0.741			
5	Total	36.86	17				

The results of the one-way ANOVA show that there is a significant difference among the three countries for return on assets. The p-value is .0001, which indicates statistical significance at $\alpha = .001$. Examining the MINITAB confidence intervals shown graphically suggests that there might be a significant difference between some pairs of countries. Because there was an overall significant difference in the countries, it is appropriate to use Tukey's HSD test to determine which of the pairs of countries are significantly different. Tukey's test controls for the overall error so that the problem mentioned previously about computing three t tests is avoided. The MINITAB output for Tukey's test is:

```
Tukey's pairwise comparisons
Family error rate = 0.0500
Individual error rate = 0.0203
Critical value = 3.67
Intervals for (column level mean) - (row level mean)

            1         2
2    -1.1765
      1.4031

3    -3.7681   -3.8815
     -1.1885   -1.3019
```

Note that the confidence intervals for pairs (Germany, United States) and (Japan, United States) contain the same sign throughout the interval indicating that zero is not in the interval and that there is a significant difference between the pair in each case. An examination of the means from previous output indicates that the U.S. large companies are significantly more profitable for return on assets than German or Japanese companies.

Suppose "year" is viewed as a block. The data presented in the Decision Dilemma could be analyzed using the randomized block design. An Excel analysis (ANOVA table only) of the return on assets data with year as a blocking variable follows.

EXCEL Output

Anova: Two-Factor Without Replication

	A	B	C	D	E	F	G
1	ANOVA						
2	Source of Variation	SS	df	MS	F	P-value	F crit
3	Rows	3.99212	5	0.79842	1.12	0.40886	3.33
4	Columns	25.74343	2	12.87172	18.07	0.00048	4.10
5	Error	7.1243	10	0.71243			
6	Total	36.85985	17				

Note that because the p-value for rows (years) is 0.409, there is no significant difference in the blocking effects.

Further studies could be done to examine such additional independent variables as size of company (perhaps a breakdown into small, medium, and large companies). If the study included two independent variables such as country and size of company, then a two-way ANOVA could be used to analyze the data. If more than one observation is taken on each cell (particular combination of country and size of company), then interaction effects could also be analyzed.

What conclusions can be reached from this analysis? On return of assets, there is a significant difference between companies in these three countries. In particular, companies in the United States showed significantly higher profitability than those in Japan or Germany on this measure. Does this result mean that we do not truly have a global economy? The author of the study suggests that differences in governmental regulations and national accounting standards may have affected the dependent variable measurements and that this factor should be taken into consideration in reaching conclusions. In addition, particular countries such as Germany in the late 1980s experienced economic downturns, which can also affect the outcome of such experiments. However, as the global economy grows, there will likely be more studies to determine its affect on the profitability of companies.

ETHICAL CONSIDERATIONS

In theory, any phenomenon that affects the dependent variable in an experiment should be either entered into the experimental design or controlled in the experiment. Researchers will sometimes report statistical findings from an experiment and fail to mention the possible concomitant variables that were neither controlled by the experimental setting nor controlled by the experimental design. The findings from such studies are highly questionable and often lead to spurious conclusions. Scientifically, the researcher needs to conduct the experiment in an environment such that as many concomitant variables are controlled as possible. To the extent that they are not controlled, the researcher has an ethical responsibility to report that fact in the findings.

Other ethical considerations enter into conducting research with experimental designs. Selection of treatment levels should be done with fairness or even randomness in cases where the treatment has several possibilities for levels. A researcher can build in skewed views of the treatment effects by erroneously selecting treatment levels to be studied. Some researchers believe that reporting significant main effects from a factorial design when there are confounding interaction effects is unethical or at least misleading.

Another ethical consideration is the leveling of sample sizes. Some designs, such as the two-way factorial design or completely randomized design with Tukey's HSD, require equal sample sizes. Sometimes unequal sample sizes arise either through the selection process or through attrition. A number of techniques for approaching this problem are not presented in this book. It remains highly unethical to make up data values or to eliminate values arbitrarily to produce equal sample sizes.

SUMMARY

Sound business research requires that the researcher plan and establish a design for the experiment before a study is undertaken. The design of the experiment should encompass the treatment variables to be studied, manipulated, and controlled. These variables are often referred to as the independent variables. It is possible to study several independent variables and several levels, or classifications, of each of those variables in one design. In addition, the researcher selects one measurement to be taken from sample items under the conditions of the experiment. This measurement is referred to as the dependent variable because if the treatment effect is significant, the measurement of the dependent variable will "depend" on the independent variable(s) selected. This chapter explored three types of experimental designs: completely randomized design, randomized block design, and the factorial experimental designs.

The completely randomized design is the simplest of the experimental designs presented in this chapter. It has only one independent, or treatment, variable. With the completely randomized design, subjects are assigned randomly to treatments. If the treatment variable has only two levels, the design becomes identical to the one used to test the difference in means of independent populations presented in Chapter 10. The data from a completely randomized design are analyzed by a one-way analysis of variance (ANOVA). A one-way ANOVA produces an F value that can be compared to table F values in Appendix A.7 to determine whether the ANOVA F value is statistically significant. If it is, the null hypothesis that all population means are equal is rejected and at least one of the means is different from the others. Analysis of variance does not tell the researcher which means, if any, are significantly different from others. Although the researcher can visually examine means to determine which ones are greater and lesser, statistical techniques called multiple comparisons must be used to determine statistically whether pairs of means are significantly different.

Two types of multiple comparison techniques are presented and used in this chapter: Tukey's HSD test and the Tukey-Kramer procedure. Tukey's HSD test requires that equal sample sizes be used. It utilizes the mean square of error from the ANOVA, the sample size, and a q value that is obtained from Table A.10 to solve for the least difference between a pair of means that would be significant (HSD). The absolute value of the difference in sample means is compared to the HSD value to determine statistical significance. The Tukey-Kramer procedure is used in the case of unequal sample sizes.

A second experimental design is the randomized block design. This design contains a treatment variable (independent variable) and a blocking variable. The independent variable is the main variable of interest in this design. The blocking variable is a variable the researcher is interested in controlling rather than studying. A special case of randomized block design is the repeated measures design, in which the blocking variable represents subjects or items for which repeated measures are taken across the full range of treatment levels.

In randomized block designs, the variation of the blocking variable is removed from the error variance. This approach can potentially make the test of treatment effects more powerful. If the blocking variable contains no significant differences, the blocking can make the treatment effects test less powerful. Usually an F is computed only for the treatment effects in a randomized block design. Sometimes an F value is computed for blocking effects to determine whether the blocking was useful in the experiment.

A third experimental design is the factorial design. A factorial design enables the researcher to test the effects of two or more independent variables simultaneously. In complete factorial designs, every treatment level of each independent variable is studied under the conditions of every other treatment level for all independent variables. This chapter focused only on factorial designs with two independent variables. Each independent variable can have two or more treatment levels. These two-way factorial designs are analyzed by two-way analysis of variance (ANOVA). This analysis produces an F value for each of the two treatment effects and for interaction. Interaction is present when the results of one treatment vary significantly according to the levels of the other treatment. At least two measurements per cell must be present in order to compute interaction. If the F value for interaction is statistically significant, the main effects of the experiment are confounded and should not be examined in the usual manner.

KEY TERMS

a posteriori

a priori

analysis of variance
(ANOVA)

blocking variable

classification variable

classifications

completely randomized
design

concomitant variables

confounding variables

dependent variable

experimental design

F distribution

F value

factorial design

factors

independent variable

interaction

levels

multiple comparisons

one-way analysis of variance

post hoc

randomized block design

repeated measures design

treatment variable

Tukey-Kramer procedure

Tukey's HSD test

two-way analysis of variance

FORMULAS

Formulas for computing a one-way ANOVA

$$SSC = \sum_{j=1}^{C} n_j(\bar{x}_j - \bar{x})^2$$

$$SSE = \sum_{i=1}^{n_j}\sum_{j=1}^{C}(x_{ij} - \bar{x}_j)^2$$

$$SST = \sum_{i=1}^{n_j}\sum_{j=1}^{C}(x_{ij} - \bar{x})^2$$

$df_C = C - 1$
$df_E = N - C$
$df_T = N - 1$

$$MSC = \frac{SSC}{df_C}$$

$$MSE = \frac{SSE}{df_E}$$

$$F = \frac{MSC}{MSE}$$

Tukey's HSD test

$$HSD = q_{\alpha,C,N-C}\sqrt{\frac{MSE}{n}}$$

Tukey-Kramer formula

$$q_{\alpha,C,N-C}\sqrt{\frac{MSE}{2}\left(\frac{1}{n_r}+\frac{1}{n_s}\right)}$$

Formulas for computing a randomized block design

$$SSC = n\sum_{j=1}^{C}(\bar{x}_j - \bar{x})^2$$

$$SSR = C\sum_{i=1}^{n}(\bar{x}_i - \bar{x})^2$$

$$SSE = \sum_{i=1}^{n}\sum_{j=1}^{C}(x_{ij} - \bar{x}_j - \bar{x}_i + \bar{x})^2$$

$$SST = \sum_{i=1}^{n}\sum_{j=1}^{C}(x_{ij} - \bar{x})^2$$

$df_C = C - 1$
$df_R = R - 1$
$df_E = (C-1)(n-1) = N - n - C + 1$

$$MSC = \frac{SSC}{C-1}$$

$$MSR = \frac{SSR}{n-1}$$

$$MSE = \frac{SSE}{N-n-C+1}$$

$$F_{treatments} = \frac{MSC}{MSE}$$

$$F_{blocks} = \frac{MSR}{MSE}$$

Formulas for computing a two-way ANOVA

$$SSR = nC\sum_{i=1}^{R}(\bar{x}_i - \bar{x})^2$$

$$SSC = nR\sum_{j=1}^{C}(\bar{x}_j - \bar{x})^2$$

$$SSI = n\sum_{i=1}^{R}\sum_{j=1}^{C}(\bar{x}_{ij} - \bar{x}_i - \bar{x}_j + \bar{x})^2$$

$$SSE = \sum_{i=1}^{R}\sum_{j=1}^{C}\sum_{k=1}^{n}(x_{ijk} - \bar{x}_{ij})^2$$

$$SST = \sum_{i=1}^{R}\sum_{j=1}^{C}\sum_{k=1}^{n}(x_{ijk} - \bar{x})^2$$

$df_R = R - 1$
$df_C = C - 1$
$df_I = (R-1)(C-1)$
$df_E = RC(n-1)$
$df_T = N - 1$

$$MSR = \frac{SSR}{R-1}$$

$$MSC = \frac{SSC}{C-1}$$

$$MSI = \frac{SSI}{(R-1)(C-1)}$$

$$MSE = \frac{SSE}{RC(n-1)}$$

$$F_R = \frac{MSR}{MSE}$$

$$F_C = \frac{MSC}{MSE}$$

$$F_I = \frac{MSI}{MSE}$$

SUPPLEMENTARY PROBLEMS

CALCULATING THE STATISTICS

11.47 Compute a one-way ANOVA on the following data. Use $\alpha = .05$. If there is a significant difference in treatment levels, use Tukey's HSD to compute multiple comparisons. Let $\alpha = .05$ for the multiple comparisons.

Treatment			
1	2	3	4
10	9	12	10
12	7	13	10
15	9	14	13
11	6	14	12

11.48 Complete the following ANOVA table.

Source of Variance	SS	df	MS	F
Treatment				
Error	249.61	19		
Total	317.80	25		

11.49 You are asked to analyze a completely randomized design that has six treatment levels and a total of 42 measurements. Complete the following table, which contains some information from the study.

Source of Variance	SS	df	MS	F
Treatment	210			
Error	655			
Total				

11.50 Compute a one-way ANOVA of the following data. Let $\alpha = .01$. Use the Tukey-Kramer procedure to conduct multiple comparisons for the means.

Treatment		
1	2	3
7	11	8
12	17	6
9	16	10
11	13	9
8	10	11
9	15	7
11	14	10
10	18	
7		
8		

11.51 Examine the structure of the following experimental design. Determine which of the three designs presented in the chapter would be most likely to characterize this structure. Discuss the variables and the levels of variables. Determine the degrees of freedom.

	Methodology		
Person	Method 1	Method 2	Method 3
1	x_{11}	x_{12}	x_{13}
2	x_{21}	x_{22}	x_{23}
3	x_{31}	x_{32}	x_{33}
4	x_{41}	x_{42}	x_{43}
5	x_{51}	x_{52}	x_{53}
6	x_{61}	x_{62}	x_{63}

11.52 Complete the following ANOVA table and determine whether there is any significance in treatment effects. Let $\alpha = .05$.

Source of Variance	SS	df	MS	F
Treatment	20,994	3		
Blocking		9		
Error	33,891			
Total	71,338			

11.53 Analyze the following data, gathered from a randomized block design using $\alpha = .05$. If there is a significant difference in the treatment effects, use Tukey's HSD test to do multiple comparisons.

		Treatment			
		A	B	C	D
	1	17	10	9	21
	2	13	9	8	16
Blocking	3	20	17	18	22
Variable	4	11	6	5	10
	5	16	13	14	22
	6	23	19	20	28

11.54 A two-way ANOVA has been computed on a factorial design. Treatment 1 has five levels and treatment 2 has two levels. Each cell contains four measures. Complete the following ANOVA table. Use $\alpha = .05$ to test to determine significance of the effects. Comment on your findings.

Source of Variance	SS	df	MS	F
Treatment 1	29.13			
Treatment 2	12.67			
Interaction	73.49			
Error	110.38			
Total				

11.55 Compute a two-way ANOVA on the following data ($\alpha = .01$).

		Treatment 1		
		A	B	C
		5	2	2
	A	3	4	3
		6	4	5
		11	9	13
	B	8	10	12
Treatment 2		12	8	10
		6	7	4
	C	4	6	6
		5	7	8
		9	8	8
	D	11	12	9
		9	9	11

TESTING YOUR UNDERSTANDING

11.56 A company conducted a consumer research project to ascertain customer service ratings from its customers. The customers were asked to rate the company on a scale from 1 to 7 on various quality characteristics. One question was the promptness of company response to a repair problem. The following data represent customer responses to this question. The customers were divided by geographic region and by age. Use analysis of variance to analyze the responses. Let $\alpha = .05$. Compute multiple comparisons where they are appropriate. Graph the cell means and observe any interaction.

		Geographic Region			
		Southeast	*West*	*Midwest*	*Northeast*
		3	2	3	2
	21–35	2	4	3	3
		3	3	2	2
		5	4	5	6
Age	36–50	5	4	6	4
		4	6	5	5
		3	2	3	3
	Over 50	1	2	2	2
		2	3	3	1

11.57 A major automobile manufacturer wants to know whether there is any difference in the average mileage of four different brands of tires (A, B, C, and D), because the manufacturer is trying to select the best supplier in terms of tire durability. The manufacturer selects comparable levels of tires from each company and tests some on comparable cars. The mileage results follow.

A	B	C	D
31,000	24,000	30,500	24,500
25,000	25,500	28,000	27,000
28,500	27,000	32,500	26,000
29,000	26,500	28,000	21,000
32,000	25,000	31,000	25,500
27,500	28,000		26,000
	27,500		

Use $\alpha = .05$ to test whether there is a significant difference in the mean mileage of these four brands. Assume tire mileage is normally distributed.

11.58 Agricultural researchers are studying three different ways of planting peanuts to determine whether significantly different levels of production yield will result. The researchers have access to a large peanut farm on which to conduct their tests. They identify six blocks of land. In each block of land, peanuts are planted in each of the three different ways. At the end of the growing season, the peanuts are harvested and the average number of pounds per acre is determined for peanuts planted under each method in each block. Using the following data and $\alpha = .01$, test to determine whether there is a significant difference in yields among the planting methods.

Block	Method 1	Method 2	Method 3
1	1310	1080	850
2	1275	1100	1020
3	1280	1050	780
4	1225	1020	870
5	1190	990	805
6	1300	1030	910

11.59 The Construction Labor Research Council lists a number of construction labor jobs that seem to pay approximately the same wages per hour. Some of these are bricklaying, iron working, and crane operation. Suppose a labor researcher takes a random sample of workers from each of these types of construction jobs and from across the country and asks what their hourly wages are. If this survey yields the following data, is there a significant difference in mean hourly wages for these three jobs? If there is a significant difference, use the Tukey-Kramer procedure to determine which pairs, if any, are also significantly different. Let $\alpha = .05$.

	Job Type	
Bricklaying	*Iron Working*	*Crane Operation*
19.25	26.45	16.20
17.80	21.10	23.30
20.50	16.40	22.90
24.33	22.86	19.50
19.81	25.55	27.00
22.29	18.50	22.95
21.20		25.52
		21.20

11.60 Why are mergers attractive to CEOs? One of the reasons might be a potential increase in market share that can come with the pooling of company markets. Suppose a random survey of CEOs is taken, and they are asked to respond on a scale from 1 to 5 (5 representing strongly agree) whether increase in market share is a good reason for considering a merger of their company with another. Suppose also that the data are as given here and that CEOs have been categorized by size of company and years they have been with their company. Use a two-way ANOVA to determine whether there are any significant differences in the responses to this question. Let $\alpha = .05$.

Company Size ($ million per year in sales)					
		0–5	6–20	21–100	>100
		2	2	3	3
		3	1	4	4
	0–2	2	2	4	4
		2	3	5	3
Years		2	2	3	3
with the		1	3	2	3
Company	3–5	2	2	4	3
		3	3	4	4
		2	2	3	2
		1	3	2	3
	Over 5	1	1	3	2
		2	2	3	3

11.61 Are some unskilled office jobs viewed as having more status than others? Suppose a study is conducted in which eight unskilled, unemployed people are interviewed. The people are asked to rate each of five positions on a scale from 1 to 10 to indicate the status of the position, with 10 denoting most status and 1 denoting least status. The resulting data are given here. Use $\alpha = .05$ to analyze these repeated measures randomized block design data.

		Job				
		Mail Clerk	Typist	Recep-tionist	Secre-tary	Telephone Operator
	1	4	5	3	7	6
	2	2	4	4	5	4
	3	3	3	2	6	7
Respondent	4	4	4	4	5	4
	5	3	5	1	3	5
	6	3	4	2	7	7
	7	2	2	2	4	4
	8	3	4	3	6	6

INTERPRETING THE OUTPUT

11.62 Analyze the following MINITAB output. Describe the design of the experiment. Using $\alpha = .05$, determine whether there are any significant effects; if so, explain why. Discuss any other ramifications of the output.

```
One-way ANOVA: Dependent Variable versus Factor
Analysis of Variance
Source      DF    SS      MS      F     p
Factor       3   876.6   292.2   3.01  0.045
Error       32  3107.5    97.1
Total       35  3984.1
                            Individual 95% CIs for
                            Mean Based on Pooled
                            StDev
Level  N   Mean    StDev  -+----+----+----+--
C1     8  307.73   5.98   (----*----)
C2     7  313.20   9.71        (----*----)
C3    11  308.60   9.78      (----*----)
C4    10  319.74  12.18               (---*---)
                         -+----+----+----+--
Pooled StDev = 9.85      301.0 308.0 315.0 322.0
```

11.63 Following is Excel output for an ANOVA problem. Describe the experimental design. The given value of alpha was .05. Discuss the output in terms of significant findings.

Anova: Two-Factor Without Replication

	A	B	C	D	E	F	G
1	ANOVA						
2	Source of Variation	SS	df	MS	F	P-value	F crit
3	Rows	48.278	5	9.656	3.16	0.057	3.33
4	Columns	10.111	2	5.056	1.65	0.239	4.10
5	Error	30.556	10	3.056			
6	Total	88.944	17				

11.64 Study the following MINITAB output and graph. Discuss the meaning of the output.

```
Two-way ANOVA: Dep. Var. versus Row Effects,
Col. Effects
Analysis of Variance for Dep. Var
Source          DF      SS      MS      F      P
Row Eff          4     4.70    1.17    0.98   0.461
Col. Eff         1     3.20    3.20    2.67   0.134
Interaction      4    22.30    5.57    4.65   0.022
Error           10    12.00    1.20
Total           19    42.20
```

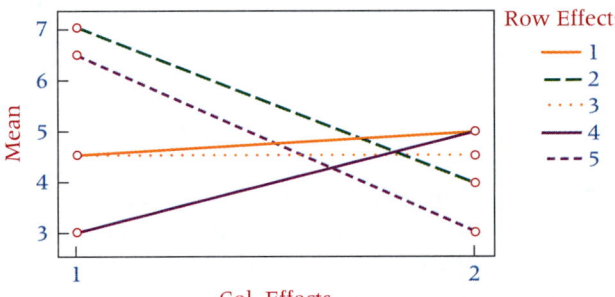

11.65 Interpret the following Excel output. Discuss the structure of the experimental design and any significant effects. Alpha is .01.

Anova: Two-Factor With Replication

	A	B	C	D	E	F	G
1	ANOVA						
2	Source of Variation	SS	df	MS	F	P-value	F crit
3	Sample	2913.889	3	971.296	4.30	0.0146	3.01
4	Columns	240.389	2	120.194	0.53	0.5940	3.40
5	Interaction	1342.944	6	223.824	0.99	0.4533	2.51
6	Within	5419.333	24	225.806			
7	Total	9916.556	35				

11.66 Study the following MINITAB output. Determine whether there are any significant effects and discuss the results. What kind of design was used and what was the size of it?

```
Two-Way Analysis of Variance
Analysis of Variance for Dep. Var.
Source      df     SS       MS
Blocking     4    41.44    10.36
Treatment    4   143.93    35.98
Error       16   117.82     7.36
Total       24   303.19
```

11.67 Discuss the following MINITAB output.

```
One-Way Analysis of Variance          Tukey's pairwise comparisons
Analysis of Variance on depvar        Family error rate = 0.0500
Source      df   SS     MS    F    p   Individual error rate = 0.0111
Treatment   3    138.0  46.0  3.51 0.034  Critical value = 3.96
Error       20   262.2  13.1      Intervals for (column level mean) - (row level
Total       23   400.3           mean)
Individual 95% CIs For Mean Based on Pooled
StDev                                    1          2          3
                                    2   -6.741
Level N  Mean    StDev ----+----+----+----+    4.967
1     6  53.778  5.470  (----*----)
2     6  54.665  1.840  (----*----)       3   -11.987   -11.100
3     6  59.911  3.845          (----*----)    -0.279    0.608
4     6  57.293  2.088     (----*----)
                      ---+----+----+----+    4   -9.369   -8.482   -3.236
                                              2.339    3.225    8.472
Pooled StDev = 3.621    52.5 56.0 59.5 63.0
```

see www.wiley.com/college/black

ANALYZING THE DATABASES

1. Do various financial indicators differ significantly according to type of company? Use a one-way ANOVA and the financial database to answer this question. Let Type of Company be the independent variable with seven levels (Apparel, Chemical, Electric Power, Grocery, Healthcare Products, Insurance, and Petroleum). Compute three one-way ANOVAs, one for each of the following dependent variables: Earnings Per Share, Dividend, and Average P/E Ratio. On each ANOVA, if there is a significant overall difference between Type of Company, compute multiple comparisons to determine which pairs of types of companies, if any, are significantly different.

2. Use the stock market database to determine whether there is any difference in stock market statistics for different parts of the month. Use a one-way ANOVA with Composite Index as the dependent variable and Part of the Month (1 = 10th, 2 = 20th, and 3 = 30th) as the independent variable with three levels. Compute a second ANOVA with Stock Volume as the dependent variable and Part of the Month as the independent variable. Is there a significant difference in Part of the Month on either of these variables? If there is, compute multiple comparisons to determine which parts of the month, if any, are significantly different from the others.

3. In the manufacturing database, the Value of Industrial Shipments has been precoded into four classifications (1–4) according to magnitude of value. Let this value be the independent variable with four levels of classifications. Compute a one-way ANOVA to determine whether there is any significant difference in classification of the Value of Industrial Shipments on the Number of Production Workers (dependent variable). Perform the same analysis using End-of-Year Inventory as the dependent variable. Now change the independent variable to Industry Group, of which there are 20, and perform first a one-way ANOVA using Number of Production Workers as the dependent variable and then a one-way ANOVA using End-of-Year Inventory as the dependent variable.

4. The hospital database contains data on hospitals from seven different geographic regions. Let this variable be the independent variable. Determine whether there is a significant difference in Admissions for these geographic regions using a one-way ANOVA. Perform the same analysis using Births as the dependent variable. Control is a variable with four levels of classification denoting the type of control the hospital is under (such as federal government or for-profit). Use this variable as the independent variable and test to determine whether there is a significant difference in the Admissions of a hospital by Control. Perform the same test using Births as the dependent variable.

CASE: J.R. CLARKSON COMPANY

The J. R. Clarkson Company, founded in 1950 by J. Robert Clarkson, is a family-owned industrial valve design and manufacturing company located in Sparks, Nevada. The Clarkson Company currently employs between 50 and 100 people and specializes in abrasion resistant valves and reagent feeders.

Clarkson has been working to advance metal and mineral processing for more than 65 years. Clarkson, known for its knife-gate and control valves that are able to halt and isolate sections of slurry flow, first introduced such valves in the 1970s. The company is now a key supplier of knife-gate valves helping to control the flow in many of the piping systems around the world. Their knife-gate valves are used in many different industries including mining, energy, wastewater treatment, and other industries that have industrial scrubber systems. Clarkson continually works to improve these valves and has developed several generations of valves. Clarkson has become world renowned for their valves with about half of their products exported.

The knife-gate valve uses a steel gate like a blade that lowers into a slurry flow to create a bubble-tight seal. Conventional metal gates fill with hardened slurry and fail easily thus requiring high maintenance, but Clarkson's design introduced an easily replaceable snap-in elastomer sleeve that is durable, versatile, and handles high pressure and various temperatures. Pipeline operators value Clarkson's elastomer sleeve because traditional seals cost between $75 and $500 to replace. Considerable lost revenue that occurs when the slurry system is stopped for maintenance repairs is avoided, and Clarkson's product lasts longer and is easier to replace.

Clarkson developed a variety of elastomer seals to increase the efficiency and reliability in its various applications. Power companies prefer synthetic types of elastomers that can handle high temperatures; whereas, mining companies prefer natural gum rubber elastomers that can handle abrasive slurries.

Discussion

1. Clarkson's successful knife-gate valve contains a wafer that is thin and light. Yet, the wafer is so strong it can operate with up to 150 pounds-per-square-inch (psi) of pressure on it making it much stronger than those of competing brands. Suppose Clarkson engineers have developed a new wafer that is even stronger. They want to set up an experimental design to test the strength of the wafer but they want to conduct the tests under three different temperature conditions, 70°, 110°, and 150°. In addition, suppose Clarkson uses two different suppliers (company A and company B) of the synthetic materials that are used to manufacturer the wafers. Some wafers are made primarily of raw materials supplied by company A, and some are made primarily of raw materials from Company B. Thus, the engineers have set up a 2 × 3 factorial design with temperature and supplier as the independent variables and pressure (measured in psi) as the dependent variable. Data are gathered and are shown here. Analyze the data and discuss the business implications of the findings. If you were conducting the study, what would you report to the engineers?

	Temperature		
	70°	110°	150°
	163	157	146
Supplier A	159	162	137
	161	155	140
	158	159	150
Supplier B	154	157	142
	164	160	155

2. Pipeline operators estimate that it costs between $75 and $500 in U.S. currency to replace each seal, thus making Clarkson's longer-lasting valves more attractive. Clarkson does business with pipeline companies around the world. Suppose in an attempt to develop marketing materials, Clarkson marketers are interested in determining whether there is a significant difference in the cost of replacing pipeline seals in different countries. Four countries, Canada, Colombia, Taiwan, and the United States are chosen for the study. Pipeline operators from equivalent operations are selected from companies in each country. The operators keep a cost log of seal replacements. A random sample of the data follows. Use these data to help Clarkson determine whether there is a difference in the cost of seal replacements in the various countries. Explain your answer and tell how Clarkson might use the information in their marketing materials.

Canada	Colombia	Taiwan	United States
$215	$355	$170	$230
205	280	190	190
245	300	235	225
270	330	195	220
290	360	205	215
260	340	180	245
225	300	190	230

3. In the late 1980s, Clarkson passed through a difficult time in which virtually no planning was done in the firm. No assessment system was in place to determine demand versus availability. Little communication took place between marketing and manufacturing. The order priority system was first-in, first-out or "whoever yells the loudest." Complaints abounded from customers and sales representatives. In an effort to turn things around, Clarkson installed a manufacturing resource planning system after a project team was formed to study the available computer hardware and software. Using this and other quality improvement approaches, Clarkson was able to reduce lead-time from 6–8 weeks to less than 2 weeks. In a study of lead-times, suppose Clarkson wants to test to determine whether lead-times differ significantly according to the type of valve it is manufacturing. As a control of the experiment, they are including in the study, as a blocking variable, the day of the week the valve was ordered. One lead-time was selected per valve per day of the week. The data are given here in weeks. Analyze the data and discuss your findings.

	Type of Valve					
	Safety	Butterfly	Clack	Slide	Poppet	Needle
Monday	1.6	2.2	1.3	1.8	2.5	0.8
Tuesday	1.8	2.0	1.4	1.5	2.4	1.0
Wednesday	1.0	1.8	1.0	1.6	2.0	0.8
Thursday	1.8	2.2	1.4	1.6	1.8	0.6
Friday	2.0	2.4	1.5	1.8	2.2	1.2

Source: Adapted from "J. R. Clarkson Co., From Afterthought to Forethought," Real-World Lessons for America's Small Businesses: Insights from the Blue Chip Enterprise Initiative. Published by Nation's Business magazine on behalf of Connecticut Mutual Life Insurance Company and the U.S. Chamber of Commerce in association with The Blue Chip Enterprise Initiative, 1992; The Clarkson Co., Company Profile, Thomas Register Industry Answer Results, available at http://www.thomasregister.com; "The Clarkson Company Saves Time and Money Improving Piping Valves," ALGOR, pp. 1–4, available at http://www.algor.com; "Controlling the Flow," Mechanical Engineering, December 1998, pp. 1–5, available at http://www.memagazine.org.

USING THE COMPUTER

EXCEL

Excel has the capability to analyze data from a completely randomized design, a randomized block design, and a two-way factorial design. With each design, the data are loaded into the spreadsheet in the usual way. The one-way ANOVA and the random block design require that treatment observations be loaded into columns. The Excel two-way ANOVA expects the data to be located in rows and columns as with most two-way designs. For each of these analyses, the data should be located in adjacent columns. One-way ANOVAs and block design problems can be loaded into Excel either with or without labels (for appropriate rows or columns). The Excel two-way ANOVA requires labels for both rows and columns.

In each of these cases, after loading the data into the spreadsheet, select **Tools** from the menu bar. A pull-down menu will appear. From this menu, select **Data Analysis.** From the **Data Analysis** dialog box that appears for one-way ANOVA, select **Anova: Single Factor.** For the randomized block design or a two-way ANOVA with only one observation per cell, select **Anova: Two-Factor Without Replication.** For two-way ANOVA with more than one observation per cell, select **Anova: Two-Factor With Replication.**

In computing an **ANOVA: Single Factor,** give the location of the data under **Input Range** in the usual Excel manner. If there are column labels, include the labels in the **Input Range,** and then check the slot **Labels in the First Row** (the labels must be in the first row above the columns). Otherwise, leave **Labels in First Row** blank. Set **Alpha.** Check one of the **Output options.** The output is produced.

In computing an **ANOVA: Two-Factor Without Replication,** give the location of the data under **Input Range** in the usual Excel manner. If there are labels, include the labels in the **Input Range,** and then check the slot **Labels.** Because Excel knows what design you are using, it will expect both row and column labels if you check this box. Set **Alpha.** Check one of the output options. The output is produced.

In computing an **ANOVA: Two-Factor With Replication,** give the location of the data under **Input Range** in the usual Excel manner. There must be both row and column labels. You need not label every row line in the spreadsheet, because there are multiple observations per row treatment. Excel knows you have multiple observations per cell, and it will next ask you to supply the number of **Rows per sample** (number of observations per cell). Set **Alpha.** Check one of the output options. The output is produced.

MINITAB

MINITAB windows has the capability of computing ANOVAs on each of the three experimental designs discussed in the chapter. For any of these designs, select **Stat** from the menu bar. A pull-down menu will appear. From this menu, select **ANOVA.**

There are two ways to compute one-way ANOVA using MINITAB. The first is to select **One-way** from the ANOVA pull-down menu. This selection expects that you have the data "stacked" in one column with group identifiers (numbers representing each group) in another column. In the dialog box that appears, insert the location of the column with the observations (dependent variable) in the box titled **Response.** Place the column location of the group identifiers in the slot titled **Factor.** If you want to do multiple comparisons, click on **Comparisons** and make your selection from the dialog box that will appear. The multiple comparison options are Tukey's, Fisher's, Dunnett's, or Hsu's MCB tests. You can insert the family error rate for which you want to control. Click **OK** on this dialog box to go back to the **One-way** box. Click **OK.** The output includes the standard ANOVA table plus a table containing the group means and standard deviations. The output also contains confidence intervals for the means.

The second way to compute a one-way ANOVA is to select the command **One-way (Unstacked).** The dialog box that appears expects that you have the data (dependent variable) in separate columns. In the slot titled **Responses,** list all the columns containing the data. There is no option of computing multiple comparisons with this dialog box. The output is the same as that obtained using the One-way command.

Both the randomized block design and the two-way ANOVA can be analyzed using MINITAB in at least two ways. One way is to select **Two-way** from the ANOVA pull-down menu. A dialog box will appear. The observations (dependent variable) should be "stacked" in one column. A second column should be created for row (block) identifiers and a third column for column (treatment) identifiers. The output is the standard ANOVA table including the F values and p-values.

A second way to analyze random block designs and two-way ANOVAs is by using the **Balanced ANOVA** command from the ANOVA pull-down menu. The ensuing dialog box contains a slot for the Responses (observations), which are stacked, and a slot to specify the **Model.** In the **Model** box, enter the columns containing group identifiers for any desired effects (e.g., row, column). If you want to analyze the interaction of any two effects, use the * to do so. For example, if the row effects are in C2 and the column effects are in C3, then enter C2*C3 into the **Model** box along with C2 and C3. The output is the standard ANOVA table including the F values and p-values.

CHAPTER 12

Analysis of Categorical Data

LEARNING OBJECTIVES

The overall objective of this chapter is to give you an understanding of two statistical techniques used to analyze categorical data, thereby enabling you to:

1. Understand the chi-square goodness-of-fit test and how to use it.
2. Analyze data by using the chi-square test of independence.

Selecting Suppliers: A Comparison of Small and Large Firms in the Electronics Industry

What criteria are used in the electronics industry to select a supplier? In years past, one dominant criterion of suppliers in many industries was price. The supplier with the low bid often got the job. In more recent years, companies have been forced by global competition and a marked increase in quality to examine other aspects of potential suppliers.

Pearson and Ellram investigated the techniques currently used by firms in the electronics industry in the selection of suppliers. They set out to determine whether there is a difference between small and large firms in supplier selection methodology and criteria. They sent out a survey instrument with questions about criteria used to select and evaluate suppliers, the participation of various functional areas in the selection process, and the formality of methods used in the selection. Of the 210 survey responses received, 87 were from small companies and 123 from large companies. The average sales were $33 million for the small companies and $583 million for the large companies.

Survey questions were stated in such a way as to generate frequencies. The respondents were given a series of supplier selection and evaluation criteria such as quality, cost, current technology, design capabilities, speed to market, manufacturing process, location, and so on. They were asked to check off the criteria used in supplier selection and evaluation and to rank the criteria that they checked. As part of the analysis, the researchers recorded how many of each of the small and large company respondents ranked a criterion first, how many ranked it second, and how many ranked it third. The results are shown in the following table of raw numbers for the criteria of quality, cost, and current technology.

In addition, companies in the study sometimes involved departments such research/development or engineering in the supplier search process. For example, 41.38% of the small companies in the study included research/development in the supplier search process versus 48.78% of the large companies. For engineering, the figures were 81.6% (small) to 91.1% (large).

Quality	Company Size	
	Small	Large
1	48	70
2	17	27
3	7	6

Cost	Company Size	
	Small	Large
1	8	14
2	29	36
3	26	37

Current Technology	Company Size	
	Small	Large
1	5	13
2	8	11
3	5	12

Managerial and Statistical Questions

1. Is there a difference between small and large companies in the ranking of criteria for the evaluation and selection of suppliers in the electronics industry?

2. The authors of the study used frequencies to measure the relative rankings of criteria. What is the appropriate statistical technique to analyze these data?

3. In comparing the participation of company employees in the process of selection and evaluation of suppliers by function and by company size, the researchers reported percentages. Are the differences in percentages merely chance differences from samples or is there a significant difference between small and large companies in the extent to which they involve people from various functional areas in the supplier selection and evaluation process? What statistical technique is appropriate for analyzing these data?

Source: Adapted from John N. Pearson and Lisa M. Ellram. "Supplier Selection and Evaluation in Small Versus Large Electronics Firms," *Journal of Small Business Management*, vol. 33, no. 4 (October 1995), pp. 53–65.

In this chapter, we explore techniques for analyzing categorical data. **Categorical data** are *nonnumerical data that are frequency counts of categories from one or more variables.* For example, it is determined that of the 790 people attending a convention, 240 are engineers, 160 are managers, 310 are sales reps, and 80 are information technologists. The variable is "position in company" with four categories: engineers, managers, sales reps, and information technologists. The data are not ratings or sales figures but rather frequency counts of how many of each position attended. Research questions producing this type of data are often analyzed using chi-square techniques. The chi-square distribution was introduced in Chapters 8 and 9. The techniques presented here for analyzing categorical data, the *chi-square goodness-of-fit test* and *the chi-square test of independence,* are an outgrowth of the binomial distribution and the inferential techniques for analyzing population proportions.

12.1 CHI-SQUARE GOODNESS-OF-FIT TEST

In Chapter 5, we studied the binomial distribution in which only two possible outcomes could occur on a single trial in an experiment. An extension of the binomial distribution is a multinomial distribution in which more than two possible outcomes can occur in a single trial. **The chi-square goodness-of-fit test** is *used to analyze probabilities of multinomial distribution trials along a single dimension.* For example, if the variable being studied is economic class with three possible outcomes of lower income class, middle income class, and upper income class, the single dimension is economic class and the three possible outcomes are the three classes. On each trial, one and only one of the outcomes can occur. In other words, a family unit must be classified either as lower income class, middle income class, or upper income class and cannot be in more than one class.

The chi-square goodness-of-fit test compares the *expected,* or theoretical, *frequencies* of categories from a population distribution to the *observed,* or actual, *frequencies* from a distribution to determine whether there is a difference between what was expected and what was observed. For example, airline industry officials might theorize that the ages of airline ticket purchasers are distributed in a particular way. To validate or reject this expected distribution, an actual sample of ticket purchaser ages can be gathered randomly, and the observed results can be compared to the expected results with the chi-square goodness-of-fit test. This test also can be used to determine whether the observed arrivals at teller windows at a bank are Poisson distributed, as might be expected. In the paper industry, manufacturers can use the chi-square goodness-of-fit test to determine whether the demand for paper follows a uniform distribution throughout the year.

Formula (12.1) is used to compute a chi-square goodness-of-fit test.

CHI-SQUARE GOODNESS-OF-FIT TEST (12.1)	$$\chi^2 = \sum \frac{(f_o - f_e)^2}{f_e}$$ $$df = k - 1 - c$$

where:

f_o = frequency of observed values
f_e = frequency of expected values
k = number of categories
c = number of parameters being estimated from the sample data

This formula compares the frequency of observed values to the frequency of the expected values across the distribution. The test loses one degree of freedom because the total number of expected frequencies must equal the number of observed frequencies; that is, the observed total taken from the sample is used as the total for the expected frequencies. In addition, in some instances a population parameter, such as λ, μ, or σ, is estimated from the sample data to determine the frequency distribution of expected values. Each time this estimation occurs, an additional degree of freedom is lost. As a rule, if a uniform distribution is being used as the expected distribution or if an expected distribution of values is given, $k - 1$ degrees of freedom are used in the test. In testing to determine whether an observed distribution is Poisson, the degrees of freedom are $k - 2$ because an additional degree of freedom is lost in estimating λ. In testing to determine whether an observed distribution is normal, the degrees of freedom are $k - 3$ because two additional degrees of freedom are lost in estimating μ and σ from the observed sample data.

Karl Pearson introduced the chi-square test in 1900. The **chi-square distribution** is *the sum of the squares of k independent random variables* and therefore can never be less than zero; it extends indefinitely in the positive direction. Actually the chi-square distributions constitute a family, with each distribution defined by the degrees of freedom (df) associated with it. For small df values the chi-square distribution is skewed considerably to the right (positive values). As the df increase, the chi-square distribution begins to approach the normal curve. Table values for the chi-square distribution are given in Appendix A. Because of space limitations, chi-square values are listed only for certain probabilities.

How can the chi-square goodness-of-fit test be applied to business situations? One survey of U.S. consumers conducted by *The Wall Street Journal* and NBC News asked the question: "In general, how would you rate the level of service that American businesses provide?" The distribution of responses to this question was as follows:

Excellent	8%
Pretty good	47%
Only fair	34%
Poor	11%

Suppose a store manager wants to find out whether the results of this consumer survey apply to customers of supermarkets in her city. To do so, she interviews 207 randomly selected consumers as they leave supermarkets in various parts of the city. She asks the customers how they would rate the level of service at the supermarket from which they had just exited. The response categories are excellent, pretty good, only fair, and poor. The observed responses from this study are given in Table 12.1. Now the manager can use a chi-square goodness-of-fit test to determine whether the observed frequencies of responses from this survey are the same as the frequencies that would be expected on the basis of the national survey.

HYPOTHESIZE:

STEP 1. The hypotheses for this example follows.

H_0: The observed distribution is the same as the expected distribution.
H_a: The observed distribution is not the same as the expected distribution.

TABLE 12.1

Results of a Local Survey of Consumer Satisfaction

Response	Frequency (f_o)
Excellent	21
Pretty good	109
Only fair	62
Poor	15

TEST:

STEP 2. The statistical test being used is

$$\chi^2 = \sum \frac{(f_o - f_e)^2}{f_e}$$

STEP 3. Let $\alpha = .05$.

STEP 4. Chi-square goodness-of-fit tests are one-tailed because a chi-square of zero indicates perfect agreement between distributions. Any deviation from zero difference occurs in the positive direction only because chi-square is determined by a sum of squared values and can never be negative. With four categories in this example (excellent, pretty good, only fair, and poor), $k = 4$. The degrees of freedom are $k - 1$ because the expected distribution is given: $k - 1 = 4 - 1 = 3$. For $\alpha = .05$ and df = 3, the critical chi-square value is

$$\chi^2_{.05,3} = 7.815$$

After the data are analyzed, an observed chi-square greater than 7.815 must be computed in order to reject the null hypothesis.

STEP 5. The observed values gathered in the sample data from Table 12.1 sum to 207. Thus $n = 207$. The expected proportions are given, but the expected frequencies must be calculated by multiplying the expected proportions by the sample total of the observed frequencies, as shown in Table 12.2.

STEP 6. The chi-square goodness-of-fit can then be calculated, as shown in Table 12.3.

ACTION:

STEP 7. Because the observed value of chi-square of 6.25 is not greater than the critical table value of 7.815, the store manager will not reject the null hypothesis.

TABLE 12.2

Construction of Expected Values for Service Satisfaction Study

Response	Expected Proportion	Expected Frequency (f_e) (proportion × sample total)	
Excellent	.08	(.08)(207) =	16.56
Pretty good	.47	(.47)(207) =	97.29
Only fair	.34	(.34)(207) =	70.38
Poor	.11	(.11)(207) =	22.77
			207.00

TABLE 12.3

Calculation of Chi-Square for Service Satisfaction Example

Response	f_o	f_e	$\frac{(f_o - f_e)^2}{f_e}$
Excellent	21	16.56	1.19
Pretty good	109	97.29	1.41
Only fair	62	70.38	1.00
Poor	15	22.77	2.65
	207	207.00	6.25

FIGURE 12.1

MINITAB Graph of Chi-Square Distribution for Service Satisfaction Example

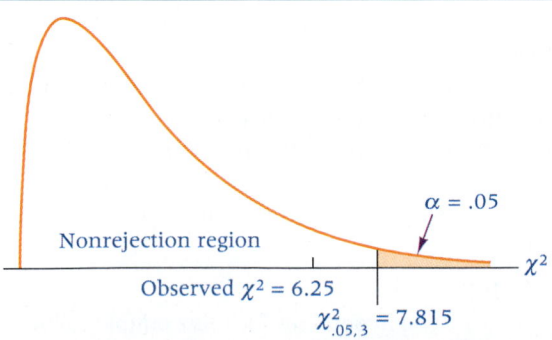

BUSINESS IMPLICATIONS:

STEP 8. Thus the data gathered in the sample of 207 supermarket shoppers indicate that the distribution of responses of supermarket shoppers in the manager's city is not significantly different from the distribution of responses to the national survey.

The store manager may conclude that her customers do not appear to have attitudes different from those people who took the survey. Figure 12.1 depicts the chi-square distribution produced by using MINITAB for this example, along with the observed and critical values.

<table><tr><td>**DEMONSTRATION PROBLEM 12.1**</td><td>Dairies would like to know whether the sales of milk are distributed uniformly over a year so they can plan for milk production and storage. A uniform distribution means that the frequencies are the same in all categories. In this situation, the producers are attempting to determine whether the amounts of milk sold are the same for each month of the year. They ascertain the number of gallons of milk sold by sampling one large supermarket each month during a year, obtaining the following data. Use $\alpha = .01$ to test whether the data fit a uniform distribution.</td></tr></table>

Month	Gallons	Month	Gallons
January	1,610	August	1,350
February	1,585	September	1,495
March	1,649	October	1,564
April	1,590	November	1,602
May	1,540	December	1,655
June	1,397	Total	18,447
July	1,410		

Solution

HYPOTHESIZE:

STEP 1. The hypotheses follow.

H_0: The monthly figures for milk sales are uniformly distributed.
H_a: The monthly figures for milk sales are not uniformly distributed.

TEST:

STEP 2. The statistical test used is

$$\chi^2 = \sum \frac{(f_o - f_e)^2}{f_e}$$

STEP 3. Alpha is .01.

STEP 4. There are 12 categories and a uniform distribution is the expected distribution, so the degrees of freedom are $k - 1 = 12 - 1 = 11$. For $\alpha = .01$, the critical value is $\chi^2_{.01,11} = 24.725$. An observed chi-square value of more than 24.725 must be obtained to reject the null hypothesis.

STEP 5. The data are given in the preceding table.

STEP 6. The first step in calculating the test statistic is to determine the expected frequencies. The total for the expected frequencies must equal the total for the observed frequencies (18,447). If the frequencies are uniformly distributed, the same number of gallons of milk is expected to be sold each month. The expected monthly figure is

$$\frac{18,447}{12} = 1537.25 \text{ gallons}$$

The following table shows the observed frequencies, the expected frequencies, and the chi-square calculations for this problem.

Month	f_o	f_e	$\dfrac{(f_o - f_e)^2}{f_e}$
January	1,610	1,537.25	3.44
February	1,585	1,537.25	1.48
March	1,649	1,537.25	8.12
April	1,590	1,537.25	1.81
May	1,540	1,537.25	0.00
June	1,397	1,537.25	12.80
July	1,410	1,537.25	10.53
August	1,350	1,537.25	22.81
September	1,495	1,537.25	1.16
October	1,564	1,537.25	0.47
November	1,602	1,537.25	2.73
December	1,655	1,537.25	9.02
Total	18,447	18,447.00	$\chi^2 = 74.37$

ACTION:

STEP 7. The observed χ^2 value of 74.37 is greater than the critical table value of $\chi^2_{.01,11} = 24.725$, so the decision is to reject the null hypothesis. This problem provides enough evidence to indicate that the distribution of milk sales is not uniform.

BUSINESS IMPLICATIONS:

STEP 8. Because retail milk demand is not uniformly distributed, sales and production managers need to generate a production plan to cope with uneven demand. In times of heavy demand, more milk will need to be processed or on reserve; in times of less demand, provision for milk storage or for a reduction in the purchase of milk from dairy farmers will be necessary.

The following MINITAB graph depicts the chi-square distribution, critical chi-square value, and observed chi-square value.

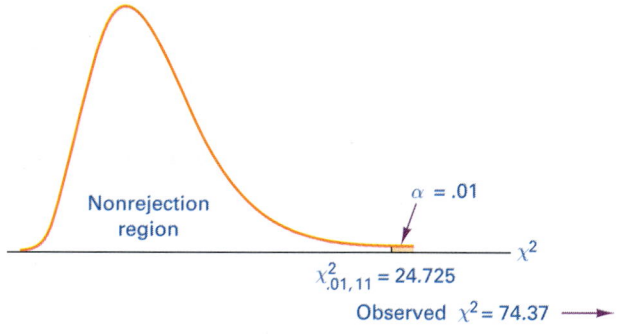

DEMONSTRATION PROBLEM 12.2

Chapter 5 indicated that, quite often in the business world, random arrivals are Poisson distributed. This distribution is characterized by an average arrival rate, λ, per some interval. Suppose a teller supervisor believes the distribution of random arrivals at a local bank is Poisson and sets out to test this hypothesis by gathering information. The following data represent a distribution of frequency of arrivals during one-minute intervals at the bank. Use $\alpha = .05$ to test these data in an effort to determine whether they are Poisson distributed.

Number of Arrivals	Observed Frequencies
0	7
1	18
2	25
3	17
4	12
≥ 5	5

Solution

HYPOTHESIZE:

STEP 1. The hypotheses follow.

H_0: The frequency distribution is Poisson.
H_a: The frequency distribution is not Poisson.

TEST:

STEP 2. The appropriate statistical test for this problem is

$$\chi^2 = \sum \frac{(f_o - f_e)^2}{f_e}$$

STEP 3. Alpha is .05.

STEP 4. The degrees of freedom are $k - 2 = 6 - 1 - 1 = 4$ because the expected distribution is Poisson. An extra degree of freedom is lost, because the value of lambda must be calculated by using the observed sample data. For $\alpha = .05$, the critical table value is $\chi^2_{.05,4} = 9.488$. The decision rule is to reject the null hypothesis if the observed chi-square is greater than $\chi^2_{.05,4} = 9.488$.

STEP 5. To determine the expected frequencies, the supervisor must obtain the probability of each category of arrivals and then multiply each by the total of the observed frequencies. These probabilities are obtained by determining lambda and then using the Poisson table. As it is the mean of a Poisson distribution, lambda can be determined from the observed data by computing the mean of the data. In this case, the supervisor computes a weighted average by summing the product of number of arrivals and frequency of those arrivals and dividing that sum by the total number of observed frequencies.

Number of Arrivals	Observed Frequencies	Arrival · Observed
0	7	0
1	18	18
2	25	50
3	17	51
4	12	48
≥ 5	5	25
	84	192

$$\lambda = \frac{192}{84} = 2.3$$

With this value of lambda and the Poisson distribution table in Appendix A, the supervisor can determine the probabilities of the number of arrivals in each category. The expected probabilities are determined from Table A.3 by looking up the values of $x = 0, 1, 2, 3$, and 4 in the column under $\lambda = 2.3$, shown in the following table as expected probabilities. The probability for $x \geq 5$ is determined by summing the probabilities for the values of $x = 5, 6, 7, 8$, and so on. Using these probabilities and the total of 84 from the observed data, the supervisor computes the expected frequencies by multiplying each expected probability by the total (84).

Arrivals	Expected Probabilities	Expected Frequencies
0	.1003	8.42
1	.2306	19.37
2	.2652	22.28
3	.2033	17.08
4	.1169	9.82
≥ 5	.0837	7.03
		84.00

STEP 6. The supervisor uses these expected frequencies and the observed frequencies to compute the observed value of chi-square.

Arrivals	Observed Frequencies	Expected Frequencies	$\dfrac{(f_o - f_e)^2}{f_e}$
0	7	8.42	.24
1	18	19.37	.10
2	25	22.28	.33
3	17	17.08	.00
4	12	9.82	.48
≥ 5	5	7.03	.59
	84	84.00	$\chi^2 = 1.74$

ACTION:

STEP 7. The observed value is not greater than the critical chi-square value of 9.488, so the supervisor's decision is to not reject the null hypothesis. In other words, he fails to reject the hypothesis that the distribution of bank arrivals is Poisson.

BUSINESS IMPLICATIONS:

STEP 8. The supervisor can use the Poisson distribution as the basis for other types of analysis, such as queuing modeling.

The following MINITAB graph depicts the chi-square distribution, critical value, and computed value.

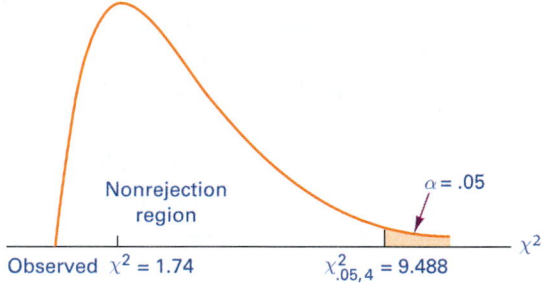

Caution: *When the expected value of a category is small, a large chi-square value can be obtained erroneously, leading to a Type I error. To control for this potential error, the chi-square goodness-of-fit test should not be used when any of the expected frequencies is less than 5. If the observed data produce expected values of less than 5, combining adjacent categories (when meaningful) to create larger frequencies may be possible.*

Testing a Population Proportion by Using the Chi-Square Goodness-of-Fit Test as an Alternative Technique to the *z* Test

In Chapter 9 we discussed a technique for testing the value of a population proportion. When sample size is large enough ($n \cdot p \geq 5$ and $n \cdot q \geq 5$), sample proportions are normally distributed and the following formula can be used to test hypotheses about p.

$$Z = \frac{\hat{p} - p}{\sqrt{\dfrac{p \cdot q}{n}}}$$

The chi-square goodness-of-fit test can also be used to conduct tests about p; this situation can be viewed as a special case of the chi-square goodness-of-fit test where the number of classifications equals two (binomial distribution situation). The observed chi-square is computed in the same way as in any other chi-square goodness-of-fit test, but because the test contains only two classifications (success or failure), $k = 2$ and the degrees of freedom are $k - 1 = 2 - 1 = 1$.

As an example, we will work two problems from Section 9.4 by using chi-square methodology. The first example in Section 9.4 tests the hypothesis that exactly 8% of a manufacturer's products are defective. The following hypotheses are being tested.

$$H_0: p = .08$$
$$H_a: p \neq .08$$

The value of alpha was given to be .10. To test these hypotheses, a business researcher randomly selected a sample of 200 items and determined that 33 of the items had at least one flaw.

Working this problem by the chi-square goodness-of-fit test, we view it as a two-category expected distribution in which we expect .08 defects and .92 nondefects. The observed categories are 33 defects and $200 - 33 = 167$ nondefects. Using the total observed items (200), we can determine an expected distribution as $.08(200) = 16$ and $.92(200) = 184$. Shown here are the observed and expected frequencies.

	f_o	f_e
Defects	33	16
Nondefects	167	184

Alpha is .10 and this test is two-tailed, so $\alpha/2 = .05$. The degrees of freedom are 1. The critical table chi-square value is

$$\chi^2_{.05,1} = 3.841$$

An observed chi-square value greater than this value must be obtained to reject the null hypothesis. The chi-square for this problem is calculated as follows.

$$\chi^2 = \sum \frac{(f_o - f_e)^2}{f_e} = \frac{(33-16)^2}{16} + \frac{(167-184)^2}{184} = 18.06 + 1.57 = 19.63$$

Notice that this observed value of chi-square, 19.63, is greater than the critical table value, 3.841. The decision is to reject the null hypotheses. The manufacturer does not produce 8% defects according to this analysis. Observing the actual sample result, in which .165 of the sample was defective, indicates that the proportion of the population that is defective might be greater than 8%.

The results obtained are approximately the same as those computed in Chapter 9, in which an observed z value of 4.43 was determined and compared to a critical z value of 1.645, causing us to reject the null hypothesis. This result is not surprising to researchers who understand that when the degrees of freedom equal 1, the value of χ^2 equals z^2.

DEMONSTRATION PROBLEM 12.3

Rework Demonstration Problem 9.3 using the chi-square goodness-of-fit technique.

Solution

In this problem, we tested to determine whether the residents of Wisconsin consume a significantly higher proportion of milk as their primary breakfast beverage than the .17 figure for the United States. The hypotheses were

$$H_0: p = .17$$
$$H_a: p > .17$$

The value of alpha was .05, and it is a one-tailed test. The degrees of freedom are $k - 1 = 2 - 1 = 1$, as there are $k = 2$ categories (milk or not milk). The critical table value for chi-square is

$$\chi^2_{.05,1} = 3.841$$

To test these hypotheses, a sample of 550 people were contacted. Of these, 115 declared that milk was their primary breakfast beverage. The observed categories are 115 and $550 - 115 = 435$. The expected categories are determined by multiplying .17

and .83 by the observed total number (550). Thus, the expected categories are .17(550) = 93.5 and .83(550) = 456.5. These frequencies follow.

	f_o	f_e
Milk	115	93.5
Not milk	435	456.5

The observed chi-square is determined by

$$\chi^2 = \sum \frac{(f_o - f_e)^2}{f_e} = \frac{(115 - 93.5)^2}{93.5} + \frac{(435 - 456.5)^2}{456.5} = 4.94 + 1.01 = 5.95$$

This observed chi-square, 5.95, is greater than the critical chi-square value of 3.841. The decision is to reject the null hypothesis. The proportion of residents who drink milk as their primary breakfast beverage is higher in Wisconsin than in the United States as a whole. In Demonstration Problem 9.3, an observed z value of 2.44 was obtained, which was greater than the critical value of 1.645, allowing us to reject the null hypothesis. The results obtained by the two different methods (χ^2 and z) are essentially the same, with the observed value of χ^2 approximately equal to z^2 (z = 2.44, z^2 = 5.95 = χ^2).

12.1 PROBLEMS

12.1 Use a chi-square goodness-of-fit test to determine whether the observed frequencies are distributed the same as the expected frequencies ($\alpha = .05$).

Category	f_o	f_e
1	53	68
2	37	42
3	32	33
4	28	22
5	18	10
6	15	8

12.2 Use the following data and $\alpha = .01$ to determine whether the observed frequencies represent a uniform distribution.

Category	f_o
1	19
2	17
3	14
4	18
5	19
6	21
7	18
8	18

12.3 Are the following data Poisson distributed? Use $\alpha = .05$ and the chi-square goodness-of-fit test to answer this question. What is your estimated lambda?

Number of Arrivals	f_o
0	28
1	17
2	11
3	5

12.4 Use the chi-square goodness-of-fit to test to determine if the following observed data are normally distributed. Let $\alpha = .05$. What are your estimated mean and standard deviation?

Category	Observed
10–under 20	6
20–under 30	14
30–under 40	29
40–under 50	38
50–under 60	25
60–under 70	10
70–under 80	7

12.5 In one survey, successful female entrepreneurs were asked to state their personal definition of success in terms of several categories from which they could select. Thirty-nine percent responded that happiness was their definition of success, 12% said that sales/profit was their definition, 18% responded that helping others was their definition, and 31% responded that achievements/challenge was their definition. Suppose you wanted to determine whether male entrepreneurs felt the same way and took a random sample of men, resulting in the following data. Use the chi-square goodness-of-fit test to determine whether the observed frequency distribution of data for men is the same as the distribution for women. Let $\alpha = .05$.

Definition	f_o
Happiness	42
Sales/profit	95
Helping others	27
Achievements/challenge	63

12.6 The following percentages come from a national survey of the ages of prerecorded-music shoppers. A local survey produced the observed values. Does the evidence in the observed data indicate that we should reject the national survey distribution for local prerecorded-music shoppers? Use $\alpha = .01$.

Age	Percent from Survey	f_o
10–14	9	22
15–19	23	50
20–24	22	43
25–29	14	29
30–34	10	19
≥ 35	22	49

12.7 The general manager of a major league baseball team believes the ages of purchasers of game tickets are normally distributed. The following data represent the distribution of ages for a sample of observed purchasers of major league baseball game tickets. Use the chi-square goodness-of-fit test to determine whether this distribution is significantly different from the normal distribution. Assume that $\alpha = .05$.

Age of Purchaser	Frequency
10–under 20	16
20–under 30	44
30–under 40	61
40–under 50	56
50–under 60	35
60–under 70	19

12.8 The Springfield Emergency Medical Service keeps records of emergency telephone calls. A study of 150 five-minute time intervals resulted in the distribution of number of calls as follows. For example, during 18 of the five-minute intervals, no calls occurred. Use the chi-square goodness-of-fit test and $\alpha = .01$ to determine whether this distribution is Poisson.

Number of Calls (per 5-minute interval)	Frequency
0	18
1	28
2	47
3	21
4	16
5	11
6 or more	9

12.9 According to an extensive survey conducted for *Business Marketing* by Leo J. Shapiro & Associates, 66% of all computer companies are going to spend more on marketing this year than in previous years. Only 33% of other information technology companies and 28% of non–information technology companies are going to spend more. Suppose a researcher wanted to conduct a survey of her own to test the claim that 28% of all non–information technology companies are spending more on marketing next year than this year. She randomly selects 270 companies and determines that 62 of the companies do plan to spend more on marketing next year. Use $\alpha = .05$, the chi-square goodness-of-fit test, and the sample data to test to determine whether the 28% figure holds for all non–information technology companies.

12.10 Cross-cultural training is rapidly becoming a popular way to prepare executives for foreign management positions within their company. This training includes such aspects as foreign language, previsit orientations, meetings with former expatriates, and cultural background information on the country. According to Runzheimer International, 30% of all major companies provide formal cross-cultural programs to their executives being relocated in foreign countries. Suppose a researcher wants to test this figure for companies in the communications industry to determine whether the figure is too high for that industry. In a random sample, 180 communications firms are contacted; 42 provide such a program. Let $\alpha = .05$ and use the chi-square goodness-of-fit test to determine whether the .30 proportion for all major companies is too high for this industry.

12.2 CONTINGENCY ANALYSIS: CHI-SQUARE TEST OF INDEPENDENCE

The chi-square goodness-of-fit test is used to analyze the distribution of frequencies for categories of *one* variable, such as age or number of bank arrivals, to determine whether the distribution of these frequencies is the same as some hypothesized or expected distribution. However, the goodness-of-fit test cannot be used to analyze *two* variables simultaneously. A different chi-square test, the **chi-square test of independence,** can be *used to analyze the frequencies of two variables with multiple categories to determine whether the two variables are independent.* Many times this type of analysis is desirable. For example, a market researcher might want to determine whether the type of soft drink preferred by a consumer is independent of the consumer's age. An organizational behaviorist might want to know whether absenteeism is independent of job classification. Financial investors might want to determine whether type of preferred stock investment is independent of the region where the investor resides.

The chi-square test of independence can be used to analyze any level of data measurement, but it is particularly useful in analyzing nominal data. Suppose a business researcher is interested in determining whether geographic region is independent of type of financial investment. On a questionnaire, the following two questions might be used to measure geographic region and type of financial investment.

In which region of the country do you reside?

      A. Northeast   B. Midwest   C. South   D. West

Which type of financial investment are you most likely to make today?

      E. Stocks   F. Bonds   G. Treasury Bills

The business researcher would *tally the frequencies of responses* to these two questions into a two-way table called a **contingency table.** Because the chi-square test of independence uses a contingency table, this test is sometimes referred to as **contingency analysis.**

Depicted in Table 12.4 is a contingency table for these two variables. Variable 1, geographic region, uses four categories: A, B, C, and D. Variable 2, type of financial investment, uses three categories: E, F, and G. The observed frequency for each cell is denoted as o_{ij}, where i is the row and j is the column. Thus, o_{13} is the observed frequency for the cell in the first row and third column. The expected frequencies are denoted in a similar manner.

If the two variables are independent, they are not related. In a sense, the chi-square test of independence is a test of whether the variables are related. The null hypothesis for a chi-square test of independence is that the two variables are independent (not related). If the null hypothesis is rejected, the conclusion is that the two variables are not independent and are related.

Assume at the beginning that variable 1 and variable 2 are independent. The probability of the intersection of two of their respective categories, A and F, can be found by using the multiplicative law for independent events presented in Chapter 4:

$$P(A \cap F) = P(A) \cdot P(F)$$

if A and F are independent. Then

$$P(A) = \frac{n_A}{N}, \; P(F) = \frac{n_F}{N}, \; \text{and} \; P(A \cap F) = \frac{n_A}{N} \cdot \frac{n_F}{N}$$

If $P(A \cap F)$ is multiplied by the total number of frequencies, N, the expected frequency for the cell of A and F can be determined.

$$e_{AF} = \frac{n_A}{N} \cdot \frac{n_F}{N}(N) = \frac{n_A \cdot n_F}{N}$$

TABLE 12.4

Contingency Table for the Investment Example

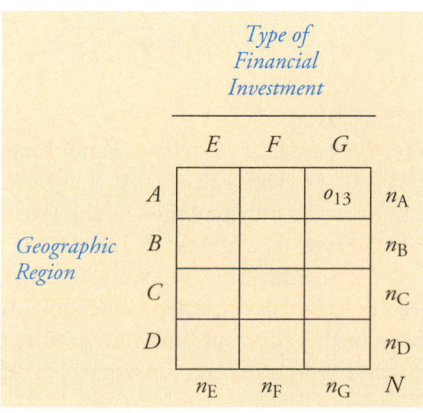

		Type of Financial Investment			
		E	F	G	
	A			o_{13}	n_A
Geographic Region	B				n_B
	C				n_C
	D				n_D
		n_E	n_F	n_G	N

In general, if the two variables are independent, the expected frequency values of each cell can be determined by

$$e_{ij} = \frac{n_i \cdot n_j}{N}$$

where:

i = the row
j = the column
n_i = the total of row i
n_j = the total of column j
N = the total of all frequencies

Using these expected frequency values and the observed frequency values, we can compute a chi-square test of independence to determine whether the variables are independent. Formula (12.2) is the formula for accomplishing this test.

CHI-SQUARE TEST OF INDEPENDENCE (12.2)	$\chi^2 = \sum\sum \dfrac{(f_o - f_e)^2}{f_e}$

where:

df $= (r - 1)(c - 1)$
r = number of rows
c = number of columns

The null hypothesis for a chi-square test of independence is that the two variables are independent. The alternative hypothesis is that the variables are not independent. This test is one-tailed. The degrees of freedom are $(r - 1)(c - 1)$. Note that formula (12.2) is similar to formula (12.1), with the exception that the values are summed across both rows and columns and the degrees of freedom are different.

Suppose a business researcher wants to determine whether type of gasoline preferred is independent of a person's income. She takes a random survey of gasoline purchasers, asking them one question about gasoline preference and a second question about income. The respondent is to check whether he or she prefers (1) regular gasoline, (2) premium gasoline, or (3) extra premium gasoline. The respondent also is to check his or her income brackets as being (1) less than $30,000, (2) $30,000 to $49,999, (3) $50,000 to $99,999, or (4) more than $100,000. The business researcher tallies the responses and obtains the results in Table 12.5. Using $\alpha = .01$, she can use the chi-square test of independence to determine whether type of gasoline preferred is independent of income level.

HYPOTHESIZE:

STEP 1. The hypotheses follow.

H_0: Type of gasoline is independent of income.
H_a: Type of gasoline is not independent of income.

TEST:

STEP 2. The appropriate statistical test is

$$\chi^2 = \sum\sum \frac{(f_o - f_e)^2}{f_e}$$

STEP 3. Alpha is .01.

STEP 4. Here, there are four rows ($r = 4$) and three columns ($c = 3$). The degrees of freedom are $(4 - 1)(3 - 1) = 6$. The critical value of chi-square for $\alpha = .01$ is $\chi^2_{.01,6} = 16.812$. The decision rule is to reject the null hypothesis if the observed chi-square is greater than 16.812.

STEP 5. The observed data appear in Table 12.5.

STEP 6. To determine the observed value of chi-square, the researcher must compute the expected frequencies. The expected values for this example are calculated as follows, with the first term in the subscript (and numerator) representing the row and the second term in the subscript (and numerator) representing the column.

TABLE 12.5

Contingency Table for the
Gasoline Consumer Example

		Type of Gasoline		
		Regular	Premium	Extra Premium	
Less than $30,000		85	16	6	107
$30,000 to $49,999		102	27	13	142
Income $50,000 to $99,999		36	22	15	73
More than $100,000		15	23	25	63
		238	88	59	385

$$e_{11} = \frac{(n_{1.})(n_{.1})}{N} = \frac{(107)(238)}{385} = 66.15$$

$$e_{12} = \frac{(n_{1.})(n_{.2})}{N} = \frac{(107)(88)}{385} = 24.46$$

$$e_{13} = \frac{(n_{1.})(n_{.3})}{N} = \frac{(107)(59)}{385} = 16.40$$

$$e_{21} = \frac{(n_{2.})(n_{.1})}{N} = \frac{(142)(238)}{385} = 87.78$$

$$e_{22} = \frac{(n_{2.})(n_{.2})}{N} = \frac{(142)(88)}{385} = 32.46$$

$$e_{23} = \frac{(n_{2.})(n_{.3})}{N} = \frac{(142)(59)}{385} = 21.76$$

$$e_{31} = \frac{(n_{3.})(n_{.1})}{N} = \frac{(73)(238)}{385} = 45.13$$

$$e_{32} = \frac{(n_{3.})(n_{.2})}{N} = \frac{(73)(88)}{385} = 16.69$$

$$e_{33} = \frac{(n_{3.})(n_{.3})}{N} = \frac{(73)(59)}{385} = 11.19$$

$$e_{41} = \frac{(n_{4.})(n_{.1})}{N} = \frac{(63)(238)}{385} = 38.95$$

$$e_{42} = \frac{(n_{4.})(n_{.2})}{N} = \frac{(63)(88)}{385} = 14.40$$

$$e_{43} = \frac{(n_{4.})(n_{.3})}{N} = \frac{(63)(59)}{385} = 9.65$$

The researcher then lists the expected frequencies in the cells of the contingency tables along with observed frequencies. In this text, expected frequencies are enclosed in parentheses. Table 12.6 provides the contingency table for this example.

Next, the researcher computes the chi-square value by summing $(f_o - f_e)^2/f_e$ for all cells.

$$\chi^2 = \frac{(85-66.15)^2}{66.15} + \frac{(16-24.46)^2}{24.46} + \frac{(6-16.40)^2}{16.40} + \frac{(102-87.78)^2}{87.78} + \frac{(27-32.46)^2}{32.46}$$

$$+ \frac{(13-21.76)^2}{21.76} + \frac{(36-45.13)^2}{45.13} + \frac{(22-16.69)^2}{16.69} + \frac{(15-11.19)^2}{11.19} + \frac{(15-38.95)^2}{38.95}$$

$$+ \frac{(23-14.40)^2}{14.40} + \frac{(25-9.65)^2}{9.65} = 5.37 + 2.93 + 6.60 + 2.30 + 0.92 +$$

$$3.53 + 1.85 + 1.69 + 1.30 + 14.73 + 5.14 + 24.42 = 70.78$$

TABLE 12.6

Contingency Table of Observed and Expected Frequencies for Gasoline Consumer Example

Income		Type of Gasoline			
		Regular	Premium	Extra Premium	
	Less than $30,000	(66.15) 85	(24.46) 16	(16.40) 6	107
	$30,000 to $49,999	(87.78) 102	(32.46) 27	(21.76) 13	142
	$50,000 to $99,999	(45.13) 36	(16.69) 22	(11.19) 15	73
	More than $100,000	(38.95) 15	(14.40) 23	(9.65) 25	63
		238	88	59	385

FIGURE 12.2

MINITAB Output for Gasoline Consumer Example

```
Chi-Square Test: Regular, Premium, Extra Premium

Expected counts are printed below observed counts
        Regular   Premium   Extra Pr   Total
  1        85        16         6        107
          66.15     24.46     16.40

  2       102        27        13        142
          87.78     32.46     21.76

  3        36        22        15         73
          45.13     16.69     11.19

  4        15        23        25         63
          38.95     14.40      9.65

Total     238        88        59        385

Chi-Sq = 5.374 + 2.924 + 6.593 +
         2.303 + 0.918 + 3.527 +
         1.846 + 1.693 + 1.300 +
         14.723 + 5.136 + 24.391 = 70.727

DF = 6, P-Value = 0.000
```

FIGURE 12.3

MINITAB Graph of Chi-Square Distribution for Gasoline Consumer Example

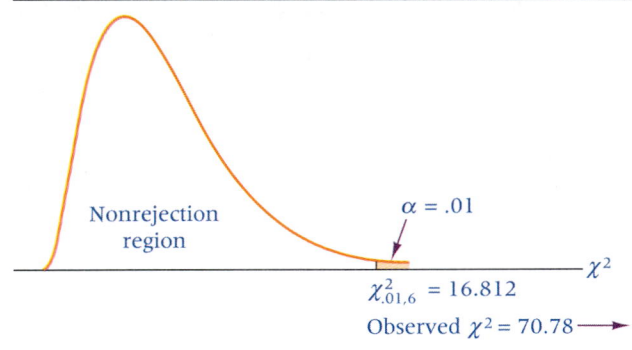

Nonrejection region

$\alpha = .01$

$\chi^2_{.01,6} = 16.812$

Observed $\chi^2 = 70.78 \longrightarrow$

ACTION:

STEP 7. The observed value of chi-square, 70.78, is greater than the critical value of chi-square, 16.812, obtained from Table A.8. The business researcher's decision is to reject the null hypothesis; that is, type of gasoline preferred is not independent of income.

BUSINESS IMPLICATION:

STEP 8. Having established that conclusion, the business researcher can then examine the outcome to determine which people, by income brackets, tend to purchase which type of gasoline and use this information in market decisions.

Figure 12.2 is the MINITAB output for calculating the chi-square value. Figure 12.3 is the MINITAB chi-square graph with the critical value, the rejection region, and the observed χ^2.

DEMONSTRATION PROBLEM 12.4

Is the type of beverage ordered with lunch at a restaurant independent of the age of the consumer? A random poll of 309 lunch customers is taken, resulting in the following contingency table of observed values. Use $\alpha = .01$ to determine whether the two variables are independent.

STATISTICS IN BUSINESS TODAY

Risk-Taking by Ad Agencies

A study was conducted by Douglas C. West to examine under what conditions, if any, advertising agencies take more risk. The primary statistical technique used to analyze the data in the study was the chi-square test of independence. Although several studies previously examined risk on the part of advertisers, little research addresses the willingness of advertising agencies to take risks on behalf of their clients. West theorized that people are more apt to take risks when the outcome affects someone else's livelihood and income rather than their own; consequently, advertising agencies might be more willing to take risks than advertisers. In addition, he theorized that advertising agencies might be more willing to take risks with smaller clients rather than large clients and that newer agencies might tend to be more willing to take risks than older agencies.

The study involved 64 account directors and/or heads of creative departments of advertising agencies selected from a standard directory. Respondents were presented with two advertising options under a plan to launch a new product. Plan A was a standard one with an average rate of return (risk-averse), and Plan B was an uncertain one in which there is a 50 percent chance of getting a lower rate of return than the client's worst forecast and a 50 percent chance of getting a better rate of return than the client's highest forecast (risk-seeking). Using a chi-square test of independence, the percentages of respondents selecting each plan were compared to percentages produced in a similar study with advertisers. The result was that the proportions of agency respondents that were risk-averse/risk-seeking were not significantly different from the proportions of advertisers that

were risk-averse/risk-seeking ($\chi^2 = 3.165$, $p = .076$). Agencies and advertisers were also compared on four degrees of risk in light of the risk taken with their most recent client. The result showed no significant difference between agencies and advertisers on the amount of risk taken with their most recent client ($\chi^2 = 3.165$, $p = .076$, $\alpha = .05$). Thus, on two questions, there was no difference in the risk taking between agencies and advertisers.

Are there circumstances under which an advertising agency might be more willing to take risks? Respondents were asked to what degree they were willing to take risks if the client is their smallest client versus if the client is their largest client. A 4×2 contingency table was constructed with four degrees of risk and the two client sizes. Analysis of these data produced a significant chi-square of 9.819 ($p = .021$) showing that agencies tended to be more risk taking with smaller clients than with large clients.

The effect of agency age on participant selection of Plan A versus Plan B was analyzed using a 2×2 contingency table. Agencies were separated into two age categories (3–19 years versus 20–135 years) with Plan A and Plan B as the risk options. Using a chi-square test of independence, it was determined that a significantly higher proportion of the younger agencies were more risk-seeking than older agencies ($\chi^2 = 6.75$, $p = .01$).

In this study, the chi-square test of independence allowed for categorical comparisons between agencies and advertisers, between small clients and large clients, and between young and old agencies. In many other studies chi-square categorical statistics can be used to study business phenomena.

Source: Adapted from Douglas C. West, "360° of Creative Risk," *Journal of Advertising Research*, vol. 39, no. 1 (January/February 1999), pp. 39–50.

Preferred Beverage

Age		Coffee/Tea	Soft Drink	Other (Milk, etc.)	
	21-34	26	95	18	139
	35-55	41	40	20	101
	>55	24	13	32	69
		91	148	70	309

Solution

HYPOTHESIZE:

STEP 1. The hypotheses follow.

H_0: Type of beverage preferred is independent of age.
H_a: Type of beverage preferred is not independent of age.

TEST:

STEP 2. The appropriate statistical test is

$$\chi^2 = \sum \sum \frac{(f_o - f_e)^2}{f_e}$$

STEP 3. Alpha is .01.

STEP 4. The degrees of freedom are $(3 - 1)(3 - 1) = 4$, and the critical value is $\chi^2_{.01,4} = 13.277$. The decision rule is to reject the null hypothesis if the observed value of chi-square is greater than 13.277.

STEP 5. The sample data were shown previously.

STEP 6. The expected frequencies are the product of the row and column totals divided by the grand total. The contingency table, with expected frequencies, follows.

Preferred Beverage

		Coffee/Tea	Soft Drink	Other (Milk, etc.)	
Age	21-34	(40.94) 26	(66.58) 95	(31.49) 18	139
	35-55	(29.74) 41	(48.38) 40	(22.88) 20	101
	>55	(20.32) 24	(33.05) 13	(15.63) 32	69
		91	148	70	309

For these values, the observed χ^2 is

$$\chi^2 = \frac{(26 - 40.94)^2}{40.94} + \frac{(95 - 66.58)^2}{66.58} + \frac{(18 - 31.49)^2}{31.49} + \frac{(41 - 29.74)^2}{29.74} +$$

$$\frac{(40 - 48.38)^2}{48.38} + \frac{(20 - 22.88)^2}{22.88} + \frac{(24 - 20.32)^2}{20.32} + \frac{(13 - 33.05)^2}{33.05} + \frac{(32 - 15.63)^2}{15.63} =$$

$$5.45 + 12.13 + 5.78 + 4.26 + 1.45 + 0.36 + 0.67 + 12.16 + 17.15 = 59.41$$

ACTION:

STEP 7. The observed value of chi-square, 59.41, is greater than the critical value, 13.277, so the null hypothesis is rejected.

BUSINESS IMPLICATIONS:

STEP 8. The two variables—preferred beverage and age—are not independent. The type of beverage that a customer orders with lunch is related to or dependent on age. Examination of the categories reveals that younger people tend to prefer soft drinks and older people prefer other types of beverages. Managers of eating establishments and marketers of beverage products can utilize such information in targeting their market and in providing appropriate products.

Caution: *As with the chi-square goodness-of-fit test, small expected frequencies can lead to inordinately large chi-square values with the chi-square test of independence. Hence contingency tables should not be used with expected cell values of less than 5. One way to avoid small expected values is to collapse (combine) columns or rows whenever possible and whenever doing so makes sense.*

12.2 PROBLEMS

12.11 Use the following contingency table to test whether variable 1 is independent of variable 2. Let $\alpha = .01$.

Variable 2

Variable 1	203	326
	68	110

12.12 Use the following contingency table to determine whether variable 1 is independent of variable 2. Let $\alpha = .01$.

	Variable 2			
Variable 1	24	13	47	58
	93	59	187	244

12.13 Use the following contingency table and the chi-square test of independence to determine whether social class is independent of number of children in a family. Let $\alpha = .05$.

		Social Class		
		Lower	*Middle*	*Upper*
	0	7	18	6
Number of	*1*	9	38	23
Children	*2 or 3*	34	97	58
	More than 3	47	31	30

12.14 A group of 30-year-olds is interviewed to determine whether the type of music most listened to by people in their age category is independent of the geographic location of their residence. Use the chi-square test of independence, $\alpha = .01$, and the following contingency table to determine whether music preference is independent of geographic location.

		Type of Music Preferred			
		Rock	*R & B*	*Country*	*Classical*
	Northeast	140	32	5	18
Geographic Region	*South*	134	41	52	8
	West	154	27	8	13

12.15 Is the transportation mode used to ship goods independent of type of industry? Suppose the following contingency table represents frequency counts of types of transportation used by the publishing and the computer hardware industries. Analyze the data by using the chi-square test of independence to determine whether type of industry is independent of transportation mode. Let $\alpha = .05$.

		Transportation Mode		
		Air	*Train*	*Truck*
	Publishing	32	12	41
Industry	*Computer Hardware*	5	6	24

12.16 According to data released by the U.S. Department of Housing and Urban Development about new homes built in the United States, there is an almost 50–50 split between one-story and two-story homes. In addition, more than half of all new homes have three bedrooms. Suppose a study is done to determine whether the number of bedrooms in a new home is independent of the number of stories. Use $\alpha = .10$ and the following contingency table to conduct a chi-square test of independence to determine whether, in fact, the number of bedrooms is independent of the number of stories.

		Number of Bedrooms		
		≤2	*3*	*≥4*
Number of Stories	*1*	116	101	57
	2	90	325	160

12.17 A study was conducted to determine the impact of a major Mexican peso devaluation on U.S. border retailers. As a part of the study, data were gathered on the magnitude of business that U.S. border retailers were doing with Mexican citizens. Forty-one shoppers of border city department stores were interviewed; 24 were Mexican citizens, and the rest were U.S. citizens. Thirty-five discount store shoppers were interviewed, as were 30 hardware store and 60 shoe store customers. In these three groups, 20, 11, and 32 were Mexican citizens, and the remaining shoppers were U.S. citizens. Use a chi-square contingency analysis to determine whether the shoppers' citizenship (Mexican versus U.S.) is independent of type of border city retailer (department, discount, hardware, shoe) for these data. Let $\alpha = .05$.

IN RESPONSE

Selecting Suppliers

Pearson and Ellram examined the comparative rankings of selection and evaluation criteria for suppliers of small and large electronics firms. These researchers chose to analyze the relative rankings by using frequency counts for various categories of rankings. The three tables of data displayed in the Decision Dilemma contain frequencies for small and large company respondents on three of these criteria: quality, cost, and current technology. Because each of these tables contains categorical data with two variables, company size and rank category, a contingency analysis (chi-square test of independence) is an appropriate statistical technique for analyzing the data. The null hypothesis is that company size is independent of category of rank for each criterion. The alternative hypothesis is that category of rank for each criterion is not independent of company size (company size makes a difference in how the criterion is ranked). MINITAB chi-square analysis produced the following output. For quality:

$$Chi\text{-}Sq = 0.006 + 0.004 + 0.067 + 0.047 + 0.510 + 0.356 = 0.991$$
$$DF = 2, P\text{-Value} = 0.609$$

The *p*-value of .609 indicates that we fail to reject the null hypothesis. On quality as a criterion, rankings of small company respondents are independent of rankings of large company respondents. There appears to be no difference between small and large company respondents on the importance of quality as a selection and evaluation criterion. Observe in looking at the table that more than half of the respondents for both small and large companies ranked quality as the number 1 criterion.

For cost:

$$Chi\text{-}Sq = 0.166 + 0.121 + 0.106 + 0.077 + 0.008 + 0.006 = 0.483$$
$$DF = 2, P\text{-Value} = 0.785$$

The *p*-value of .785 indicates failure to reject the null hypothesis. Company size is independent of the ranking of this criterion as a supplier selection and evaluation tool. In perusing the raw data, it is evident that about one-third of the respondents in both large and small companies ranked cost either as the second or third most important criterion.

For current technology:

$$Chi\text{-}Sq = 0.167 + 0.083 + 0.439 + 0.219 + 0.078 + 0.039 = 1.026$$
$$DF = 2, P\text{-Value} = 0.599$$

The *p*-value of .599 indicates failure to reject the null hypothesis. Company size is independent of the ranking of this criterion as a supplier selection and evaluation tool.

Pearson and Ellram also found that of small companies' responses to the question of what functional areas are involved in the selection and evaluation of suppliers, 41.38% included research and development. For large companies, 48.6% included research and development. Because sample statistics are used, is enough evidence provided to declare that there is a significant difference in proportions between small and large companies? Techniques presented in Chapter 10 can be used to statistically test this hypothesis. However, the chi-square test of independence can also be used. The two variables are company size (small, large) and whether or not the functional area is included (Yes, No) producing a 2 × 2 table:

	Company Size	
	Small	Large
Yes	36	60
No	51	63

Recall that 87 small companies and 123 large companies took part in the study. The raw numbers are obtained by multiplying the samples sizes by the percentages [e.g., sample size for small companies = 87 and 87(.4138) = 36]. MINITAB gives a chi-square value of 1.125 with a *p*-value of 0.289. Based on this result, there is no significant difference between small and large companies on the inclusion of research and development in the supplier selection and evaluation process.

ETHICAL CONSIDERATIONS

The usage of chi-square goodness-of-fit tests and chi-square tests of independence becomes an issue when the expected frequencies are too small. Considerable debate surrounds the discussion of how small is too small. In this chapter, we used an expected frequency of less than 5 as too small. As an example, suppose an expected frequency is 2. If the observed value is 6, then the calculation of $(f_0 - f_e)^2/f_e$ results in $(6 - 2)^2/2 = 8$ just for this pair of observed and expected frequencies. Such a contribution to the overall computed chi-square can inordinately affect the total chi-square value and skew the analysis. Researchers should exercise caution in using small expected frequencies with chi-square tests lest they arrive at an incorrect statistical outcome.

SUMMARY

The chapter presented two techniques for analyzing categorical data. Categorical data are *nonnumerical data that are frequency counts of categories from one or more variables.* Categorical data producing this type of data are often analyzed using chi-square techniques. The two techniques presented for analyzing categorical data are the chi-square goodness-of-fit test and the chi-square test of independence. These techniques are an outgrowth of the binomial distribution and the inferential techniques for analyzing population proportions.

The chi-square goodness-of-fit test is used to compare a theoretical or expected distribution of measurements for several categories of a variable with the actual or observed distribution of measurements. It can be used to determine whether a distribution of values fits a given distribution, such as the Poisson or normal distribution. If only two categories are used, the test offers the equivalent of a *z* test for a single proportion.

The chi-square test of independence is used to analyze frequencies for categories of two variables to determine whether the two variables are independent. The data used in analysis by a chi-square test of independence are arranged in a two-dimensional table called a contingency table. For this reason, the test is sometimes referred to as contingency analysis. A chi-square test of independence is computed in a manner similar to that used with the chi-square goodness-of-fit test. Expected values are computed for each cell of the contingency table and then compared to observed values with the chi-square statistic. Both the chi-square test of independence and the chi-square goodness-of-fit test require that expected values be greater than or equal to 5.

KEY TERMS

categorical data	chi-square goodness-of-	chi-square test of	contingency analysis
chi-square distribution	fit test	independence	contingency table

FORMULAS

χ^2 goodness-of-fit test

$$\chi^2 = \sum \frac{(f_o - f_e)^2}{f_e}$$

$df = k - 1 - c$

χ^2 test of independence

$$\chi^2 = \sum\sum \frac{(f_o - f_e)^2}{f_e}$$

$df = (r - 1)(c - 1)$

SUPPLEMENTARY PROBLEMS

CALCULATING THE STATISTICS

12.18 Use a chi-square goodness-of-fit test to determine whether the following observed frequencies are distributed the same as the expected frequencies. Let $\alpha = .01$.

Category	f_o	f_e
1	214	206
2	235	232
3	279	268
4	281	284
5	264	268
6	254	232
7	211	206

12.19 Use the chi-square contingency analysis to test to determine whether variable 1 is independent of variable 2. Use a 5% level of significance.

	Variable 2		
	12	23	21
Variable 1	8	17	20
	7	11	18

TESTING YOUR UNDERSTANDING

12.20 Is a manufacturer's geographic location independent of type of customer? Use the following data for companies with primarily industrial customers and companies with primarily retail customers to test this question. Let $\alpha = .10$.

		Geographic Location		
		Northeast	West	South
Customer Type	Industrial Customer	230	115	68
	Retail Customer	185	143	89

12.21 A national youth organization sells six different kinds of cookies during its annual cookie campaign. A local leader is curious about whether national sales of the six kinds of cookies are uniformly distributed. He randomly selects the amounts of each kind of cookies sold from five youths and combines them into the observed data that follow. Use $\alpha = .05$ to determine whether the data indicate that sales for these six kinds of cookies are uniformly distributed.

Kind of Cookie	Observed Frequency
Chocolate chip	189
Peanut butter	168
Cheese cracker	155
Lemon flavored	161
Chocolate mint	216
Vanilla filled	165

12.22 A researcher interviewed 2,067 people and asked whether they were the primary decision makers in the household when buying a new car last year. Two hundred seven were men and had bought a new car last year. Sixty-five were women and had bought a new car last year. Eight hundred eleven of the responses were from men who did not buy a car last year. Nine hundred eighty-four were from women who did not buy a car last year. Use these data to determine whether gender is independent of being a major decision maker in purchasing a car last year. Let $\alpha = .05$.

12.23 Are random arrivals at a shoe store at the local mall Poisson distributed? Suppose a mall employee researches this question by gathering data for arrivals during one-minute intervals on a weekday between 6:30 P.M. and 8:00 P.M. The data obtained follow. Use $\alpha = .05$ to determine whether the observed data seem to be from a Poisson distribution.

Arrivals per Minute	Observed Frequency
0	26
1	40
2	57
3	32
4	17
5	12
6	8

12.24 According to *Beverage Digest/Maxwell Report*, the distribution of market share for the top six soft drinks in the United States was Coca-Cola Classic 20.6%, Pepsi 14.5%, Diet Coke 8.5%, Mountain Dew 6.3%, Sprite 6.2%, Dr. Pepper 5.9%, and others 38%. Suppose a marketing analyst wants to determine whether this distribution fits that of her geographic region. She randomly surveys 1,726 local people and asks them to name their favorite soft drink. The responses are Classic Coke 361, Pepsi 272, Diet Coke 192, Mountain Dew 121, Sprite

102, Dr. Pepper 94, and others 584. She then tests to determine whether the local distribution of soft drink preferences is the same or different from the national figures, using $\alpha = .05$. What does she find?

12.25 Are the types of professional jobs held in the computing industry independent of the number of years a person has worked in the industry? Suppose 246 workers are interviewed. Use the results obtained to determine whether type of professional job held in the computer industry is independent of years worked in the industry. Let $\alpha = .01$.

Professional Position

	Manager	Programmer	Operator	Systems Analyst
0-3	6	37	11	13
4-8	28	16	23	24
More than 8	47	10	12	19

Years

12.26 A study by Market Facts/TeleNation for Personnel Decisions International (PDI) found that the average workweek is getting longer for U.S. full-time workers. Forty-three percent of the responding workers in the survey cited "more work, more business" as the number one reason for this increase in workweek. Suppose you want to test this figure in California to determine whether California workers feel the same way. A random sample of 315 California full-time workers whose workweek has been getting longer is chosen. They are offered a selection of possible reasons for this increase and 120 pick "more work, more business." Use techniques presented in this chapter and an alpha of .05 to test to determine whether the 43% U.S. figure for this reason holds true in California.

12.27 Is the number of children that a college student currently has independent of the type of college or university being attended? Suppose students were randomly selected from three types of colleges and universities and the data shown represent the results of a survey of those students. Use a chi-square test of independence of answer the question. Let $\alpha = .05$.

Type of College or University

	Community College	Large University	Small College
0	25	178	31
1	49	141	12
2	31	54	8
3 or more	22	14	6

Number of Children

INTERPRETING THE OUTPUT

12.28 A survey by Ipsos-Reid reported in *American Demographics* showed that if a person was given a $1,000 windfall, 36% would spend the money on home improvement, 24% on leisure travel/vacation, 15% on clothing, 15% on home entertainment or electronic products, and 10% on local entertainment including restaurants and movies. Suppose a researcher believes that these results would not be the same if posed to adults between 21 and 30 years of age. The researcher conducts a new survey interviewing 200 adults between 21 and 30 years of age asking these same questions. A chi-square goodness-of-fit test is conducted to compare the results of the new survey to the one taken by Ipsos-Reid. The Excel results follow. The observed and expected values are for the categories as already listed and appear in the same order. Discuss the findings. How did the distribution of results from the new survey compare to the old? Discuss the business implications of this outcome.

21-30 years of age	General Population
Observed	Expected
36	72
64	48
42	30
38	30
20	20

The p-value for the chi-square goodness-of-fit test is: **0.0000043**

The observed chi-square for the goodness-of-fit test is: **30.18**

12.29 Do men and women prefer the same colors of cars? That is, is gender independent of color preference for cars? Suppose a study is undertaken to address this question. A random sample of men and women are asked which of five colors (silver, white, black, green, blue) they prefer in a car. The results as analyzed using MINITAB are shown here. Discuss the test used, the hypotheses, the findings, and the business implications.

Chi-Square Test: Men, Women

```
Expected counts are printed below observed
counts
                 Men      Women     Total
Silver           90         52       142
               85.20      56.80
White            75         58       133
               79.80      53.20
Black            63         30        93
               55.80      37.20
Green            39         33        72
               43.20      28.80
Blue             33         27        60
               36.00      24.00
Total           300        200       500
Chi-Sq = 0.270 + 0.406 + 0.289 + 0.433 + 0.929
+ 1.394 + 0.408 + 0.612 + 0.250 + 0.375 = 5.366
DF = 4, P-Value = 0.252
```

ANALYZING THE DATABASES

see www.wiley.com/college/black

1. The financial database contains seven different types of companies. These seven are denoted by the variable, Type. Use a chi-square goodness-of-fit test to determine whether the seven types of companies are uniformly distributed in this database. In the manufacturing database, is the Value of Industrial Shipments (a four-category variable) uniformly distributed across the database?

2. Use a chi-square test of independence to determine whether Control is independent of Service in the hospital database. Comment on the results of this test.

CASE: FOOT LOCKER IN THE SHOE MIX

Foot Locker is the world's number one retailer of athletic shoes and apparel. The company has approximately 3,600 retail stores under various names located in 14 different countries across North America, Europe, and Australia. A majority of its stores are based in malls. In addition, Foot Locker has a large Internet sales operation. Foot Locker estimates that it controls about 18% of the U.S. $15 billion athletic footwear market. The company intends to increase its share of the worldwide market by adding additional stores and by growing its Internet and catalog business.

Recently, Foot Locker officials have been rethinking the company's retail mix. By mid-2002, the company had cut in half its inventory of sneakers priced at $120 or more. Interestingly enough, about 90% of sneakers priced at $100 or more carry the Nike logo; and Foot Locker is Nike's biggest customer. In fact, Nike products generate about $1 of every $2 in sales at Foot Locker. This apparent conflict in pricing may create an opportunity for Nike competitors at Foot Locker in the United States. On the other hand, sales of the more expensive sneakers seem to be holding firm in Europe. Some important decision making appears to be looming on the horizon for both Nike and Foot Locker in determining the shoe mix that will maximize profits.

Discussion

According to Wells Fargo Securities and the NPDFashionworld Consumer Panel, approximately 115 million units of sales of sneakers were made in the under-$30 range in 2000. Sales for this and other price categories are shown here along with the same data for the year 2001. Has the distribution of unit sales changed from 2000 to 2001? Use techniques presented in the chapter to analyze this question. Discuss the business implications for both Foot Locker and Nike. (Units are given in millions.)

Price Category	2000	2001
Less than $30	115	126
$30–less than $40	38	40
$40–less than $50	37	35
$50–less than $60	30	27
$60–less than $70	22	20
$70–less than $85	21	20
$85–less than $100	11	11
$100 or more	17	18

Suppose Foot Locker strongly encourages its employees to make formal suggestions to improve the store, the product, and the working environment. Suppose a quality auditor keeps records of the suggestions, the persons who submitted them, and the geographic region from which they come. A possible breakdown of the number of suggestions over a three-year period by employee gender and geographic location follows. Is there any relationship between the gender of the employee and the geographic location in terms of number of suggestions? If they are related, what does this relationship mean to the company? What business implications might there be for such an analysis?

		Gender	
		Male	Female
	U.S. West	29	43
	U.S. South	48	20
Location	U.S. East	52	61
	U.S. North	28	25
	Europe	78	32
	Australia	47	29

According to Wells Fargo Securities and the NPDFashionworld Consumer Panel, Foot Locker holds 19.4% of the sneaker market. Suppose that due to its relationship with Nike and Nike's presence in the U.S. West region, Foot Locker believes that its share of the market in that region is higher than it is in the rest of the country. Foot Locker hires a market research company to test this notion. The research company randomly samples 1,000 people in the U.S. West who have just purchased a pair of sneakers and 230 of the sampled shoppers purchased their sneakers at Foot Locker. Is this result enough evidence to declare that Foot Locker's share of the market in the U.S. West is significantly higher than it is otherwise? Use techniques from this chapter to test this hypothesis. What business implications might there be for Foot Locker if this market share information is true?

Source: Adapted from Christopher Lawton and Maureen Tkacik. "Foot Locker Changes Mix of Sneakers," *Wall Street Journal*, 22 July 2002, p. B3; Foot Locker, Inc., available at: http://www.footlocker-inc.com; "Venator Group, Inc. Announces Name Change to Foot Locker, Inc.," *PR NEWSWIRE*, 1 November 2001, p. 1.

USING THE COMPUTER

The chi-square goodness-of-fit test can be computed directly using Excel but not by MINITAB. The chi-square test of independence can be computed directly by MINITAB but not by Excel.

EXCEL AND THE CHI-SQUARE GOODNESS-OF-FIT TEST

To compute a chi-square goodness-of-fit test in Excel, begin with the paste function, f_X. From the left side of the dialog box that appears, select **Statistical**. From the right side of the dialog box, select **CHITEST**. In the **CHITEST** dialog box, place the location of the observed values in the first slot, **Actual_range.** Place the location of the expected values in the second slot, **Expected_range.** The output of **CHITEST** is the p-value of the observed chi-square. To determine the observed chi-square from this p-value, go back to the paste function, f_X, select **Statistical** from the left side, and select **CHIINV** from the right side. In the **CHIINV** dialog box that appears, place the p-value in the first slot, **Probability,** and the degrees of freedom in the second slot, **Deg_freedom.** The output from **CHIINV** is the observed chi-square value.

MINITAB AND THE CHI-SQUARE TEST OF INDEPENDENCE

From the **Stat** pull-down menu, select **Tables.** From the pull-down menu that appears, select **Chi-Square Test.** Supply the column locations containing the data in **Columns containing the table.** The output in the session window will include a contingency table with observed values, expected values, row and column totals, calculated chi-square, degrees of freedom, and a p-value.

Simple Regression Analysis

LEARNING OBJECTIVES

The overall objective of this chapter is to give you an understanding of bivariate linear regression analysis, thereby enabling you to:

1. Compute the equation of a simple regression line from a sample of data and interpret the slope and intercept of the equation.
2. Understand the usefulness of residual analysis in testing the assumptions underlying regression analysis and in examining the fit of the regression line to the data.
3. Compute a standard error of the estimate and interpret its meaning.
4. Compute a coefficient of determination and interpret it.
5. Test hypotheses about the slope of the regression model and interpret the results.
6. Estimate values of y by using the regression model.

DECISION DILEMMA

Predicting the Annual Sales Volume of Real Estate Brokerage Firms by the Average Price of the Sale

What are some of the factors that determine the total annual sales volume of a real estate brokerage firm? Certainly, number of units sold would be a factor. Selling more houses/properties would result in higher total sales revenue for a real estate firm. Other factors might also play a role, such as size of houses/properties, location of houses/properties, number of realtors, amount spent on advertising, number of real estate offices, number of cities with real estate offices, and so on. Still another possibility is the average price of a unit sold by a company. It seems feasible that if the average price per sale at a firm is higher, then the total sales volume would be higher.

The following total sales volumes for the top 25 real estate brokerage firms in the United States are given here for a recent year along with the average price of a sale for that same year for each company. Sales volume is given in millions of dollars and the sales prices are given in thousands of dollars.

Company	Sales Volume	Average Price
NRT	50,031	244
Weichert, Realtors	13,000	205
Long & Foster Real Estate	7,791	175
Burnet Financial Group	6,603	176
Prudential Florida Realty	4,927	170
Fred Sands Realtors	4,410	367
Edina Realty	4,055	137
John L. Scott Real Estate	3,721	189
Coldwell Banker Hunneman & Co.	3,700	273
DeWolfe New England	3,593	209
Prudential California Realty	3,439	311
Realty Executives	3,355	138
Fox & Roach Realtors	3,194	179
Realty One	2,712	135
O'Conor, Piper & Flynn	2,711	127
Baird & Warner	2,400	200
Gundaker Realtors/Better Homes and Gardens	2,210	121
Ebby Halliday, Realtors	2,164	166
Prudential Connecticut Realty	2,140	221
Coldwell Banker Premier Van Schaack	2,024	156
Crye-Leike	1,969	126
Henry S. Miller Co., Realtors	1,918	157
Smythe, Cramer	1,912	156
RE/MAX North Atlanta	1,845	174
Pacific Union Residential Brokerage	1,829	439

Managerial and Statistical Questions

1. What variables among the several mentioned are related to the total sales volume for a brokerage firm in any given year? How strongly related to total sales volume are they? What are some other variables besides those mentioned that might be related to total sales volume? How do we determine how strongly one variable is related to another variable?

2. Data are given for the top 25 real estate brokerage firms in the United States for a recent year. In particular, the dollar figures are shown for the two variables, sales volume and average price. Are these two variables related; and if so, how strongly are they related? Just because a firm sells more expensive properties/houses does that mean the firm has higher total revenues? Why or why not?

3. Is there a way to predict a firm's total sales volume for the year by using the average price of a sale? If it were possible to predict a firm's total sales volume by the average price of a sale, how good would the prediction be?

Source: Adapted from data appearing in "REAL Trends, Dallas, Texas," *The Wall Street Journal Almanac 1999.* Ronald J. Alsop, ed. (New York: Ballantine Books), 1999, p. 336.

In many business research situations, the key to decision making lies in understanding the relationships between two or more variables. For example, in an effort to predict the value of airline stock from day to day, an analyst might find it helpful to determine whether the price of an airline stock is related to the price of West Texas intermediate (WTI) crude oil. In studying the behavior of the bond market, a broker might find it useful to know whether the interest rate of bonds is related to the prime interest rate. In studying the effect of advertising on sales, an account executive might find it useful to know how strong the relationship is between advertising dollars and sales dollars for a company. What variables are related to unemployment rates? Are minimum hourly wage rates, the inflation rate, or the wholesale price index usable for predicting an unemployment rate?

This chapter presents regression analysis in which mathematical models are developed to predict one variable from another. Using regression analysis, business researchers attempt to determine the functional relationship between the variables. Also, included in this chapter are statistical tools for testing the strength and predictability of the regression model.

13.1 INTRODUCTION TO SIMPLE REGRESSION ANALYSIS

Regression analysis is the process of constructing a mathematical model or function that can be used to predict or determine one variable by another variable. The most elementary regression model is called **simple regression**, which is *bivariate linear regression,* which means that it involves only two variables. One variable is predicted by another variable. *The variable to be predicted* is called the **dependent variable** and is designated as *y. The predictor* is called the **independent variable,** or *explanatory variable,* and is designated as *x.* In simple regression analysis, only a straight-line relationship between two variables is examined. Nonlinear relationships and regression models with more than one independent variable can be explored by using multiple regression models, which are presented in Chapters 14 and 15.

Can the cost of flying a commercial airliner be predicted using regression analysis? If so, what variables are related to such cost? A few of the many variables that can potentially contribute are type of plane, distance, number of passengers, amount of luggage/freight, weather conditions, direction of destination, and perhaps even pilot skill. Suppose a study is conducted using only Boeing 737s traveling 500 miles on comparable routes during the same season of the year in an effort to reduce the number of possible predictor variables. Can the number of passengers predict the cost of flying such routes? It seems logical that more passengers result in more weight and more baggage, which could, in turn, result in increased fuel consumption and other costs. Suppose the data displayed in Table 13.1 are the costs and associated number of passengers for twelve 500-mile commercial airline flights using Boeing 737s during the same season of the year. We will use these data to develop a regression model to predict cost by number of passengers.

Usually, the first step in simple regression analysis is to construct a **scatter plot** (or scatter diagram), discussed in Chapter 2. Graphing the data in this way yields preliminary information about the shape and spread of the data. Figure 13.1 is an Excel scatter plot of the data in Table 13.1. Figure 13.2 is a close-up view of the scatter plot produced by MINITAB. Try to imagine a line passing through the points. Is a linear fit possible? Would a curve fit the data better? The scatter plot gives some idea of how well a regression line fits the data. Later in the chapter, we present statistical techniques that can be used to determine more precisely how well a regression line fits the data.

13.2 DETERMINING THE EQUATION OF THE REGRESSION LINE

The first step in determining the equation of the regression line that passes through the sample data is to establish the equation's form. Several different types of equations of lines are discussed in algebra, finite math, or analytic geometry courses. Recall that among these equations of a line are the two-point form, the point-slope form, and the slope-intercept form. In regression analysis, researchers use the slope-intercept equation of a line. In math courses, the slope-intercept form of the equation of a line often takes the form

$$y = mx + b$$

where

m = slope of the line
b = y intercept of the line

In statistics, the slope-intercept form of the equation of the regression line through the population points is

$$\hat{y} = \beta_0 + \beta_1 x$$

where

$\hat{y}$ = the predicted value of y
β_0 = the population y intercept
β_1 = the population slope

For any specific dependent variable value, y_i,

$$y_i = \beta_0 + \beta_1 x_i + \in_i$$

where

x_i = the value of the independent variable for the ith value

TABLE 13.1

Airline Cost Data

Number of Passengers	Cost ($1,000)
61	4.280
63	4.080
67	4.420
69	4.170
70	4.480
74	4.300
76	4.820
81	4.700
86	5.110
91	5.130
95	5.640
97	5.560

FIGURE 13.1

Excel Scatter Plot of Airline Cost Data

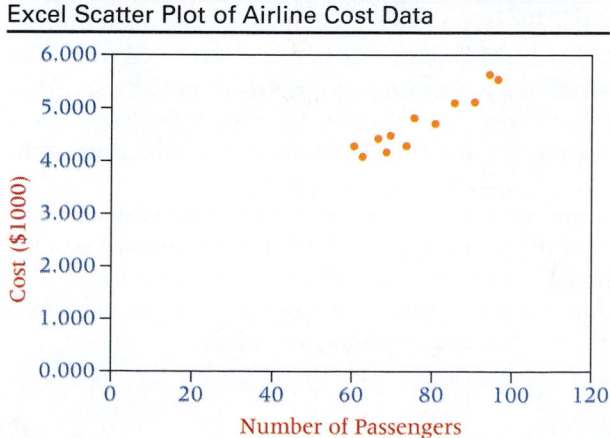

FIGURE 13.2

Close-Up MINITAB Scatter Plot of Airline Cost Data

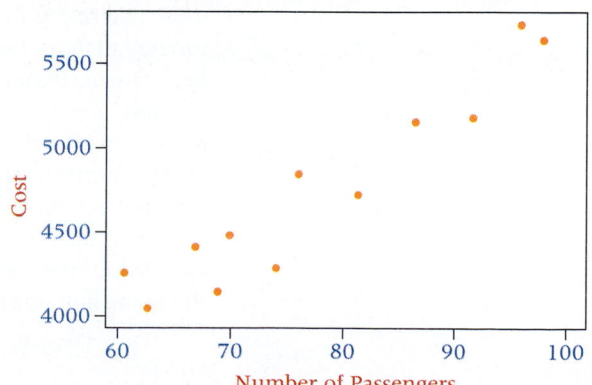

y_i = the value of the dependent variable for the ith value
β_0 = the population y intercept
β_1 = the population slope
ϵ_i = the error of prediction for the ith value

Unless the points being fitted by the regression equation are in perfect alignment, the regression line will miss at least some of the points. In the preceding equation, ϵ_i represents the error of the regression line in fitting these points. If a point is on the regression line, $\epsilon_i = 0$.

These mathematical models can be either deterministic models or probabilistic models. **Deterministic models** are *mathematical models that produce an "exact" output for a given input.* For example, suppose the equation of a regression line is

$$y = 1.68 + 2.40x$$

For a value of $x = 5$, the exact predicted value of y is

$$y = 1.68 + 2.40(5) = 13.68$$

We recognize, however, that most of the time the values of y will not equal exactly the values yielded by the equation. Random error will occur in the prediction of the y values for values of x because it is likely that the variable x does not explain all the variability of the variable y. For example, suppose we are trying to predict the volume of sales (y) for a company through regression analysis by using the annual dollar amount of advertising (x) as the predictor. Although sales are often related to advertising, other factors related to sales are not accounted for by amount of advertising. Hence, a regression model to predict sales volume by amount of advertising probably involves some error. For this reason, in regression, we present the general model as a probabilistic model. A **probabilistic model** is *one that includes an error term that allows for the y values to vary for any given value of x.*

A deterministic regression model is

$$y = \beta_0 + \beta_1 x$$

The probabilistic regression model is

$$y = \beta_0 + \beta_1 x + \epsilon$$

$\beta_0 + \beta_1 x$ is the deterministic portion of the probabilistic model, $\beta_0 + \beta_1 x + \epsilon$. In a deterministic model, all points are assumed to be on the line and in all cases ϵ is zero.

Virtually all regression analyses of business data involve sample data, not population data. As a result, β_0 and β_1 are unattainable and must be estimated by using the sample statistics, b_0 and b_1. Hence the equation of the regression line contains the sample y intercept, b_0, and the sample slope, b_1.

EQUATION OF THE SIMPLE REGRESSION LINE

$$\hat{y} = b_0 + b_1 x$$

where

b_0 = the sample intercept
b_1 = the sample slope

To determine the equation of the regression line for a sample of data, the researcher must determine the values for b_0 and b_1. This process is sometimes referred to as least squares analysis. **Least squares analysis** is *a process whereby a regression model is developed by producing the minimum sum of the squared error values.* On the basis of this premise and calculus, a particular set of equations has been developed to produce components of the regression model.*

Examine the regression line fit through the points in Figure 13.3. Observe that the line does not actually pass through any of the points. The vertical distance from each point to the line is the error of the prediction. In theory, an infinite number of lines could be constructed to pass through these points in some manner. The least squares regression line is the regression line that results in the smallest sum of errors squared.

*Derivation of these formulas is beyond the scope of information being discussed here, but is presented on the CD-ROM.

Formula (13.1) is an equation for computing the value of the sample slope. Several versions of the equation are given to afford latitude in doing the computations.

SLOPE OF THE REGRESSION LINE (13.1)	$$b_1 = \frac{\Sigma(x-\bar{x})(y-\bar{y})}{\Sigma(x-\bar{x})^2} = \frac{\Sigma xy - n\bar{x}\bar{y}}{\Sigma x^2 - n\bar{x}^2} = \frac{\Sigma xy - \dfrac{(\Sigma x)(\Sigma y)}{n}}{\Sigma x^2 - \dfrac{(\Sigma x)^2}{n}}$$

The expression in the numerator of the slope formula (13.1) appears frequently in this chapter and is denoted as SS_{xy}.

$$SS_{xy} = \Sigma(x-\bar{x})(y-\bar{y}) = \Sigma xy - \frac{(\Sigma x)(\Sigma y)}{n}$$

The expression in the denominator of the slope formula (13.1) also appears frequently in this chapter and is denoted as SS_{xx}.

$$SS_{xx} = \Sigma(x-\bar{x})^2 = \Sigma x^2 - \frac{(\Sigma x)^2}{n}$$

With these abbreviations, the equation for the slope can be expressed as in Formula (13.2).

ALTERNATIVE FORMULA FOR SLOPE (13.2)	$$b_1 = \frac{SS_{xy}}{SS_{xx}}$$

Formula (13.3) is used to compute the sample y intercept. The slope must be computed before the y intercept.

y INTERCEPT OF THE REGRESSION LINE (13.3)	$$b_0 = \bar{y} - b_1\bar{x} = \frac{\Sigma y}{n} - b_1\frac{(\Sigma x)}{n}$$

Formulas 13.1, 13.2, and 13.3 show that the following data are needed from sample information to compute the slope and intercept: Σx, Σy, Σx^2, and Σxy, unless sample means are used. Table 13.2 contains the results of solving for the slope and intercept and determining the equation of the regression line for the data in Table 13.1.

The least squares equation of the regression line for this problem is

$$\hat{y} = 1.57 + .0407x$$

The slope of this regression line is .0407. Because the x values were recoded for the ease of computation and are actually in $1,000 denominations, the slope is actually $40.70. One interpretation of the slope in this problem is that for every unit increase in x (every person added to the flight of the airplane), there is a $40.70 increase in the cost of the flight. The y intercept is the point where the line crosses the y axis (where x is zero). Sometimes in regression analysis, the y intercept is meaningless in terms of the variables studied. However, in this problem, one interpretation of the y intercept, which is 1.570 or $1,570, is that even if there were no passengers on the commercial flight, it would still cost $1,570. In other words, costs are associated with a flight that carries no passengers.

FIGURE 13.3

MINITAB Plot of a Regression Line

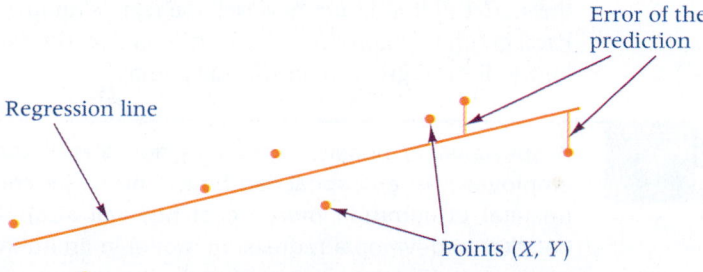

TABLE 13.2

Solving for the Slope and the y Intercept of the Regression Line for the Airline Cost Example

Number of Passengers	Cost ($1,000)		
x	y	x^2	xy
61	4.280	3,721	261.080
63	4.080	3,969	257.040
67	4.420	4,489	296.140
69	4.170	4,761	287.730
70	4.480	4,900	313.600
74	4.300	5,476	318.200
76	4.820	5,776	366.320
81	4.700	6,561	380.700
86	5.110	7,396	439.460
91	5.130	8,281	466.830
95	5.640	9,025	535.800
97	5.560	9,409	539.320
$\Sigma x = 930$	$\Sigma y = 56.690$	$\Sigma x^2 = 73,764$	$\Sigma xy = 4462.220$

$$SS_{xy} = \Sigma xy - \frac{(\Sigma x)(\Sigma y)}{n} = 4462.22 - \frac{(930)(56.69)}{12} = 68.745$$

$$SS_{xx} = \Sigma x^2 - \frac{(\Sigma x)^2}{n} = 73,764 - \frac{(930)^2}{12} = 1689$$

$$b_1 = \frac{SS_{xy}}{SS_{xx}} = \frac{68.745}{1689} = .0407$$

$$b_0 = \frac{\Sigma y}{n} - b_1 \frac{\Sigma x}{n} = \frac{56.69}{12} - (.0407)\frac{930}{12} = 1.57$$

$$\hat{y} = 1.57 + .0407x$$

FIGURE 13.4

Excel Graph of Regression Line for the Airline Cost Example

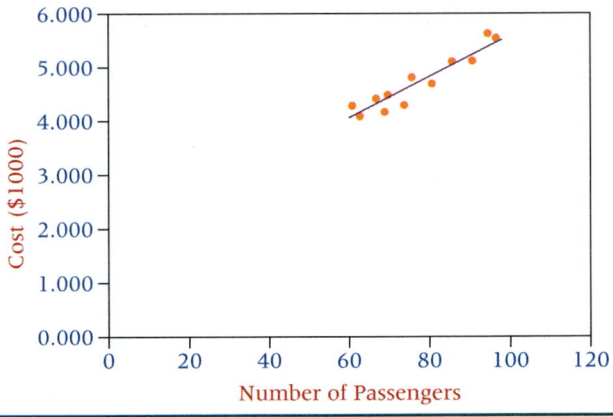

Superimposing the line representing the least squares equation for this problem on the scatter plot indicates how well the regression line fits the data points, as shown in the Excel graph in Figure 13.4. The next several sections explore mathematical ways of testing how well the regression line fits the points.

DEMONSTRATION PROBLEM 13.1

A specialist in hospital administration stated that the number of FTEs (full-time employees) in a hospital can be estimated by counting the number of beds in the hospital (a common measure of hospital size). A healthcare business researcher decided to develop a regression model in an attempt to predict the number of FTEs of a hospital by the number of beds. She surveyed 12 hospitals and obtained the following data. The data are presented in sequence, according to the number of beds.

Number of Beds	FTEs	Number of Beds	FTEs
23	69	50	138
29	95	54	178
29	102	64	156
35	118	66	184
42	126	76	176
46	125	78	225

Solution

The following MINITAB graph is a scatter plot of these data. Note the linear appearance of the data.

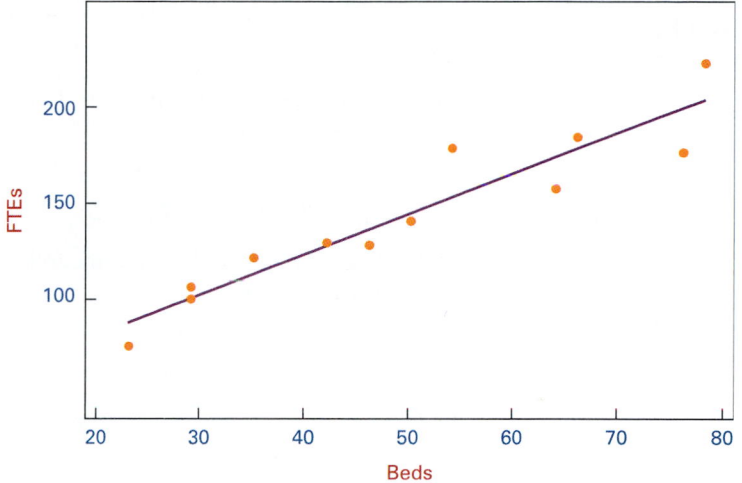

Next, the researcher determined the values of Σx, Σy, Σx^2, and Σxy.

Hospital	Number of Beds x	FTEs y	x^2	xy
1	23	69	529	1,587
2	29	95	841	2,755
3	29	102	841	2,958
4	35	118	1,225	4,130
5	42	126	1,764	5,292
6	46	125	2,116	5,750
7	50	138	2,500	6,900
8	54	178	2,916	9,612
9	64	156	4,096	9,984
10	66	184	4,356	12,144
11	76	176	5,776	13,376
12	78	225	6,084	17,550
	$\Sigma x = 592$	$\Sigma y = 1,692$	$\Sigma x^2 = 33,044$	$\Sigma xy = 92,038$

Using these values, the researcher solved for the sample slope (b_1) and the sample y intercept (b_0).

$$SS_{xy} = \Sigma xy - \frac{(\Sigma x)(\Sigma y)}{n} = 92,038 - \frac{(592)(1692)}{12} = 8566$$

$$SS_{xx} = \Sigma x^2 - \frac{(\Sigma x)^2}{n} = 33,044 - \frac{(592)^2}{12} = 3838.667$$

$$b_1 = \frac{SS_{xy}}{SS_{xx}} = \frac{8566}{3838.667} = 2.232$$

$$b_0 = \frac{\Sigma y}{n} - b_1\frac{\Sigma x}{n} = \frac{1692}{12} - (2.232)\frac{592}{12} = 30.888$$

The least squares equation of the regression line is

$$\hat{y} = 30.888 + 2.232x$$

The slope of the line, $b_1 = 2.232$, means that for every unit increase of x (every bed), y (number of FTEs) is predicted to increase by 2.232. Even though the y intercept helps the researcher sketch the graph of the line by being one of the points on the line (0, 30.888), it has limited usefulness in terms of this solution because $x = 0$ denotes a hospital with no beds. On the other hand, it could be interpreted that a hospital has to have at least 31 FTEs to open its doors even with no patients—a sort of "fixed cost" of personnel.

13.2 PROBLEMS

13.1 Sketch a scatter plot from the following data, and determine the equation of the regression line.

x	12	21	28	8	20
y	17	15	22	19	24

13.2 Sketch a scatter plot from the following data, and determine the equation of the regression line.

x	140	119	103	91	65	29	24
y	25	29	46	70	88	112	128

13.3 A corporation owns several companies. The strategic planner for the corporation believes dollars spent on advertising can to some extent be a predictor of total sales dollars. As an aid in long-term planning, she gathers the following sales and advertising information from several of the companies for 2002 ($ millions).

Advertising	Sales
12.5	148
3.7	55
21.6	338
60.0	994
37.6	541
6.1	89
16.8	126
41.2	379

Develop the equation of the simple regression line to predict sales from advertising expenditures using these data.

13.4 Investment analysts generally believe the interest rate on bonds is inversely related to the prime interest rate for loans; that is, bonds perform well when lending rates are down and perform poorly when interest rates are up. Can the bond rate be predicted by the prime interest rate? Use the following data to construct a least squares regression line to predict bond rates by the prime interest rate.

Bond Rate	Prime Interest Rate
5%	16%
12	6
9	8
15	4
7	7

13.5 Is it possible to predict the annual number of business failures in the United States by the number of business starts the previous year? It might seem that the more business starts there are in a given year, the more potential there is for business failure the next year. The following data from Dun & Bradstreet show the number of business failures from 1989 to 1999 and the number of business starts for each of the previous years. Use these data to develop the equation of a regression line to predict the number of business failures from the number of business starts the previous year. Discuss the slope and y intercept of the model.

Number of Business Starts for the Previous Year	Number of Business Failures
233,710	57,097
199,091	50,361
181,645	60,747
158,930	88,140
155,672	97,069
164,086	86,133
166,154	71,558
188,387	71,128
168,158	71,931
170,475	83,384
166,740	71,857

13.6 It appears that over the past 35 years, the number of farms in the United States declined while the average size of farms increased. The following data provided by the U.S. Department of Agriculture show five-year interval data for U.S. farms. Use these data to develop the equation of a regression line to predict the average size of a farm by the number of farms. Discuss the slope and y intercept of the model.

Year	Number of Farms (millions)	Average Size (acres)
1950	5.65	213
1955	4.65	258
1960	3.96	297
1965	3.36	340
1970	2.95	374
1975	2.52	420
1980	2.44	426
1985	2.29	441
1990	2.15	460
1995	2.07	469
2000	2.17	434

13.7 Can the annual new orders for manufacturing in the United States be predicted by the raw steel production in the United States? Shown here are the annual new orders for 10 years according to the U.S. Census Bureau and the raw steel production for the same 10 years as published by the American Iron & Steel Institute. Use these data to develop a regression model to predict annual new orders by raw steel production. Construct a scatter plot and draw the regression line through the points.

Raw Steel Production (100,000s of net tons)	New Orders ($ trillions)
99.9	2.74
97.9	2.87
98.9	2.93
87.9	2.87
92.9	2.98
97.9	3.09
100.6	3.36
104.9	3.61
105.3	3.75
108.6	3.95

13.3 RESIDUAL ANALYSIS

How does a researcher test a regression line to determine mathematically whether the line is a good fit of the data? One type of information available is the *historical data* used to construct the equation of the line. In other words, actual y values correspond to the x values used in constructing the regression line. Why not insert the historical x values into the equation of the sample regression line and get predicted y values (denoted $\hat{y}$) and then compare these predicted values to the actual y values to determine how much error the equation of the regression line produced? *Each difference between the actual y values and the predicted y values is the error of the regression line at a given point, $y - \hat{y}$,* and is referred to as the **residual.** It is the sum of squares of these residuals that is minimized to find the least squares line.

Table 13.3 shows $\hat{y}$ values and the residuals for each pair of data for the airline cost regression model developed in Section 13.2. The predicted values are calculated by inserting an x value into the equation of the regression line and solving for $\hat{y}$. For example, when $x = 61$, $\hat{y} = 1.57 + .0407(61) = 4.053$, as displayed in column 3 of the table. Each of these predicted y values is subtracted from the actual y value to determine the error, or residual. For example, the first y value listed in the table is 4.280 and the first predicted value is 4.053, resulting in a residual of $4.280 - 4.053 = .227$. The residuals for this problem are given in column 4 of the table.

Note that the sum of the residuals is approximately zero. Except for rounding error, the sum of the residuals is *always zero.* The reason is that a residual is geometrically the vertical distance from the regression line to a data point. The equations used to solve for the slope and intercept place the line geometrically in the middle of all points. Therefore, vertical distances from the line to the points will cancel each other and sum to zero. Figure 13.5 is a MINITAB-produced scatter plot of the data and the residuals for the airline cost example.

An examination of the residuals may give the researcher an idea of how well the regression line fits the historical data points. The largest residual for the airline cost example is –.282, and the smallest is .040. Because the objective of the regression analysis was to predict the cost of flight in $1,000s, the regression line produces an error of $282 when there are 74 passengers and an error of only $40 when there are 86 passengers. This result presents the *best* and *worst* cases for the residuals. The researcher must examine other residuals to determine how well the regression model fits other data points.

Sometimes residuals are used to locate outliers. **Outliers** are *data points that lie apart from the rest of the points.* Outliers can produce residuals with large magnitudes and are usually easy to identify on scatter plots. Outliers can be the result of misrecorded or miscoded data, or they may simply be data points that do not conform to the general trend.

TABLE 13.3			
Predicted Values and Residuals for the Airline Cost Example			
Number of Passengers x	**Cost ($1,000)** y	**Predicted Value** $\hat{y}$	**Residual** $y - \hat{y}$
61	4.280	4.053	.227
63	4.080	4.134	−.054
67	4.420	4.297	.123
69	4.170	4.378	−.208
70	4.480	4.419	.061
74	4.300	4.582	−.282
76	4.820	4.663	.157
81	4.700	4.867	−.167
86	5.110	5.070	.040
91	5.130	5.274	−.144
95	5.640	5.436	.204
97	5.560	5.518	.042

$$\Sigma(y - \hat{y}) = -.001$$

FIGURE 13.5

Close-up MINITAB Scatter Plot with Residuals for the Airline Cost Example

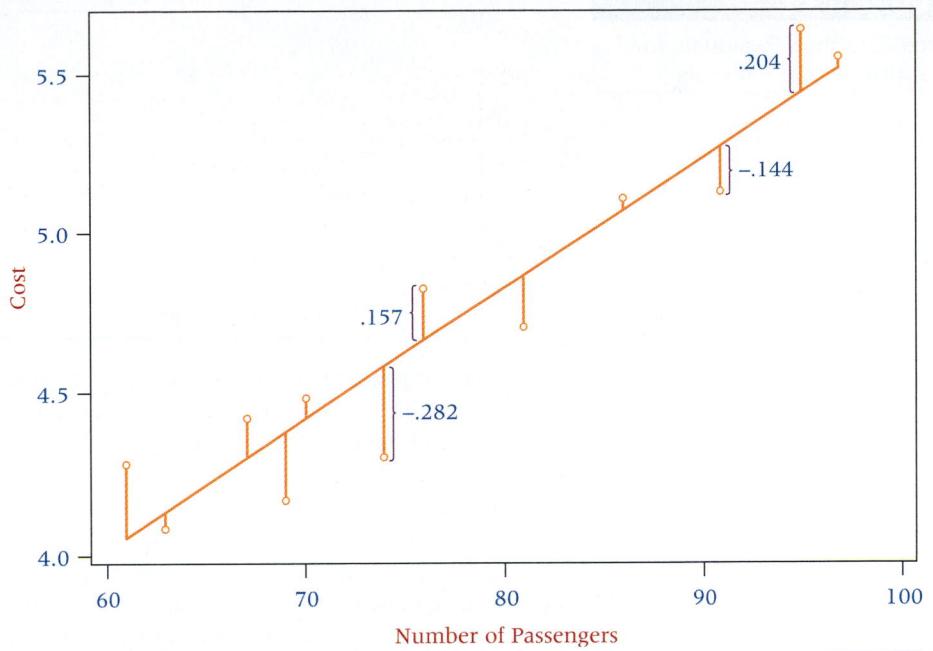

The equation of the regression line is influenced by every data point used in its calculation in a manner similar to the arithmetic mean. Therefore, outliers sometimes can unduly influence the regression line by "pulling" the line toward the outliers. The origin of outliers must be investigated to determine whether they should be retained or whether the regression equation should be recomputed without them.

Residuals are usually plotted against the x axis, which reveals a view of the residuals as x increases. Figure 13.6 shows the residuals plotted by Excel against the x axis for the airline cost example.

Using Residuals to Test the Assumptions of the Regression Model

One of the major uses of residual analysis is to test some of the assumptions underlying regression. The following are the assumptions of simple regression analysis.

1. The model is linear.
2. The error terms have constant variances.
3. The error terms are independent.
4. The error terms are normally distributed.

A particular method for studying the behavior of residuals is the residual plot. The **residual plot** is *a type of graph in which the residuals for a particular regression model are plotted along with their associated value of x as an ordered pair (x, y − ŷ).* Information about how well the regression assumptions are met by the particular regression model can be gleaned by examining the plots. Residual plots are more meaningful with larger sample sizes. For small sample sizes, residual plot analyses can be problematic and subject to over-interpretation. Hence, because the airline cost example is constructed from only 12 pairs of data, one should be cautious in reaching conclusions from Figure 13.6. The residual plots in Figures 13.7, 13.8, and 13.9, however, represent large numbers of data points and therefore are more likely to depict overall trends accurately.

If a residual plot such as the one in Figure 13.7 appears, the assumption that the model is linear does not hold. Note that the residuals are negative for low and high values of x and are positive for middle values of x. The graph of these residuals is parabolic, not linear. The residual plot does not have to be shaped in this manner for a nonlinear relationship to exist. Any significant deviation from an approximately linear residual plot may mean that a nonlinear relationship exists between the two variables.

FIGURE 13.6

Excel Graph of Residuals for
the Airline Cost Example

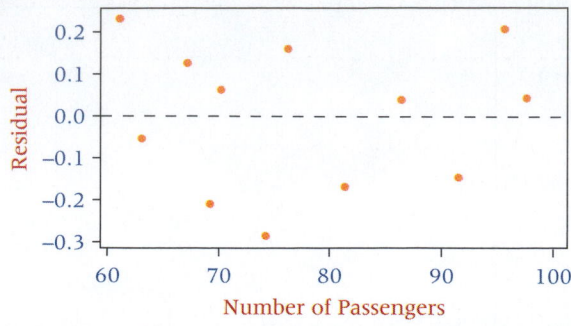

The assumption of *constant error variance* sometimes is called **homoscedasticity.** If *the error variances are not constant* (called **heteroscedasticity**), the residual plots might look like one of the two plots in Figure 13.8. Note in Figure 13.8(a) that the error variance is greater for small values of x and smaller for large values of x. The situation is reversed in Figure 13.8(b).

If the error terms are not independent, the residual plots could look like one of the graphs in Figure 13.9. According to these graphs, instead of each error term being independent of the one next to it, the value of the residual is a function of the residual value next to it. For example, a large positive residual is next to a large positive residual and a small negative residual is next to a small negative residual.

The graph of the residuals from a regression analysis that meets the assumptions—a *healthy residual graph*—might look like the graph in Figure 13.10. The plot is relatively linear; the variances of the errors are about equal for each value of x, and the error terms do not appear to be related to adjacent terms.

Using the Computer for Residual Analysis

Some computer programs contain mechanisms for analyzing residuals for violations of the regression assumptions. MINITAB has the capability of providing graphical analysis of residuals. Figure 13.11 displays MINITAB's residual graphic analyses for a regression model developed to predict the production of carrots in the United States per month by the total production of sweet corn. The data were gathered over a time period of 168 consecutive months (see the CD-ROM for the agricultural database).

These MINITAB residual model diagnostics consist of four different plots. The graph on the lower right is a plot of the residuals versus the fits. Note that this residual plot "flares out" as x gets larger. This pattern is an indication of heteroscedasticity, which is a violation of the assumption of constant variance for error terms. The graph in the upper left is a normal probability plot of the residuals. A straight line indicates that the residuals are normally distributed. Observe that this normal plot is relatively close to being a straight line, indicating that the residuals are nearly normal in shape. This normal distribution is confirmed by the graph on the lower left, which is a histogram of the residuals. The histogram groups residuals in classes so the researcher can observe where groups of the residuals lie without having to rely on the residual plot and to validate the notion that the residuals are approximately normally distributed. In this

FIGURE 13.7

Nonlinear Residual Plot

FIGURE 13.8

Nonconstant Error Variance

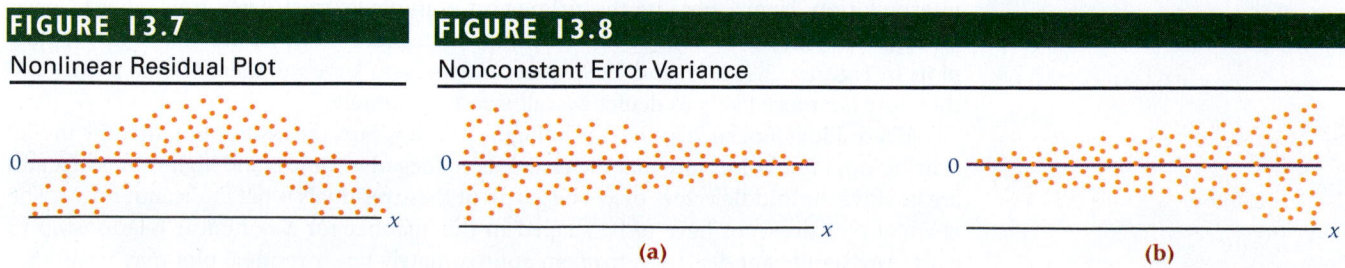

(a) (b)

FIGURE 13.9
Graphs of Nonindependent Error Terms

FIGURE 13.10
Healthy Residual Graph

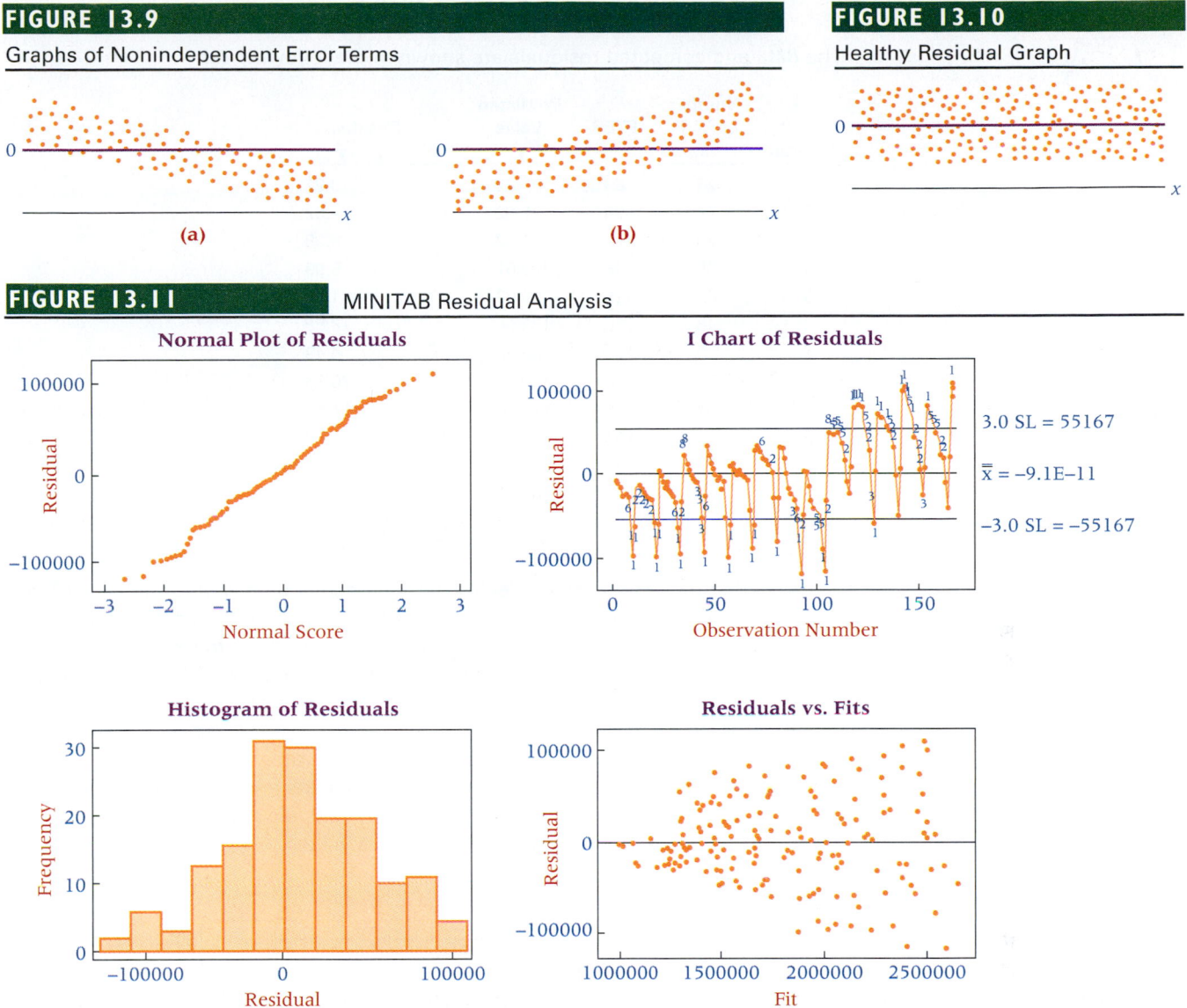

FIGURE 13.11   MINITAB Residual Analysis

problem, the pattern is indicative of at least a mound-shaped distribution of residuals. The I Chart of Residuals on the upper right is a presentation of the residuals in a control chart form (see Chapter 18). UCL is the upper control limit and is generally located three standard deviations above the centerline, which here is 0.000. The LCL is the lower control limit and is generally located three standard deviations below the centerline. In control chart analysis, observations outside UCL or LCL are an indication of an out-of-control system. In addition, a relatively random pattern of residuals should occur above and below the centerline. In this chart, a few residuals fall outside the UCL and LCL. In addition, it appears that the residuals are not independent as evidenced by the apparent patterns in the I Chart. The data used to produce this regression model are time-series data, which are discussed in further detail in Chapter 16. However, the seasonal effect in these agricultural data is likely to account for the lack of independence of error terms.

DEMONSTRATION PROBLEM 13.2

Compute the residuals for Demonstration Problem 13.1 in which a regression model was developed to predict the number of full-time equivalent workers (FTEs) by the number of beds in a hospital. Analyze the residuals by using MINITAB graphic diagnostics.

Solution

The data and computed residuals are shown in the following table.

Hospital	Number of Beds x	FTES y	Predicted Value $\hat{y}$	Residuals $y - \hat{y}$
1	23	69	82.22	−13.22
2	29	95	95.62	−.62
3	29	102	95.62	6.38
4	35	118	109.01	8.99
5	42	126	124.63	1.37
6	46	125	133.56	−8.56
7	50	138	142.49	−4.49
8	54	178	151.42	26.58
9	64	156	173.74	−17.74
10	66	184	178.20	5.80
11	76	176	200.52	−24.52
12	78	225	204.98	20.02

$$\Sigma(y - \hat{y}) = -.01$$

Note that the regression model fits these particular data well for hospitals 2 and 5, as indicated by residuals of −.62 and 1.37 FTEs, respectively. For hospitals 1, 8, 9, 11, and 12, the residuals are relatively large, indicating that the regression model does not fit the data for these hospitals well. The Residuals vs. Fits graph indicates that the residuals seem to increase as x increases, indicating a potential problem with heteroscedasticity. This is confirmed by examining the I Chart, which shows that while the residuals appear to be "under control," the variance of them is increasing. The normal plot of residuals indicates that the residuals are nearly normally distributed. The histogram of residuals shows that the residuals pile up in the middle, but are somewhat skewed toward the larger positive values.

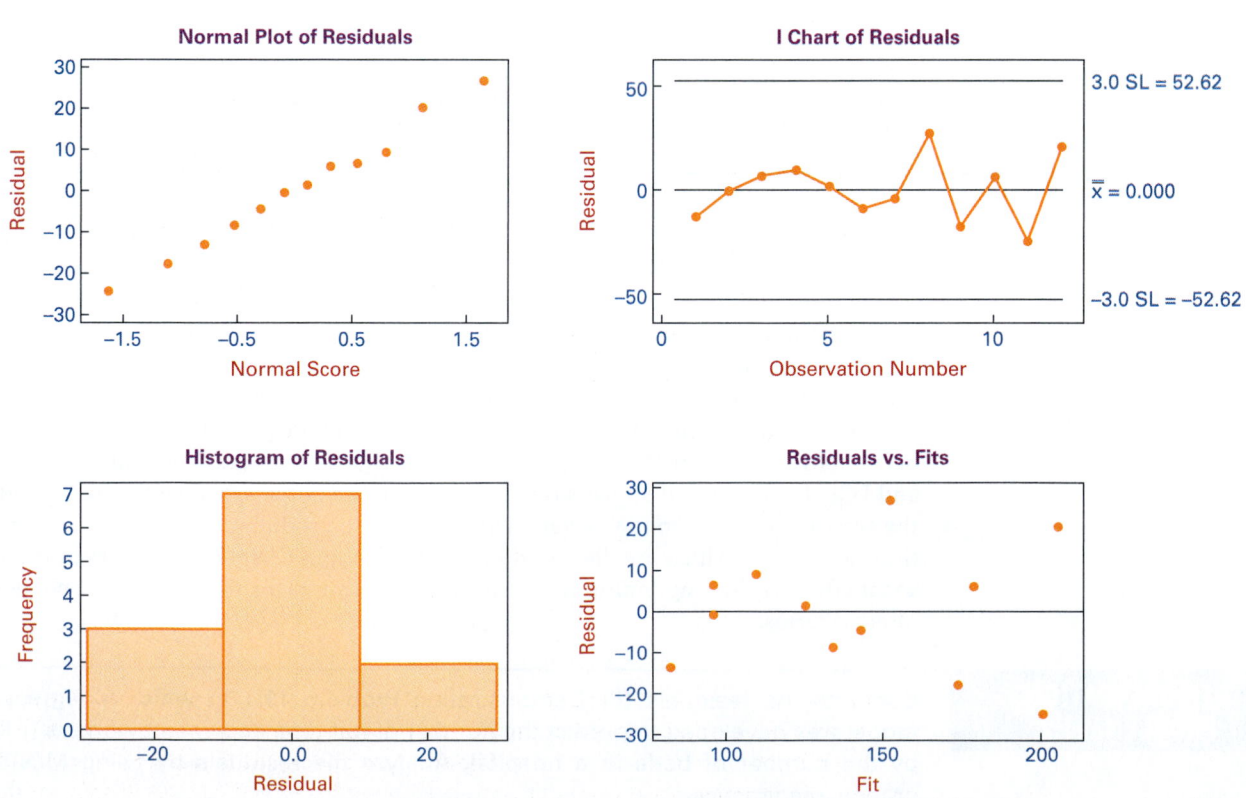

13.3 PROBLEMS

13.8 Determine the equation of the regression line for the following data, and compute the residuals.

x	15	8	19	12	5
y	47	36	56	44	21

13.9 Solve for the predicted values of y and the residuals for the data in Problem 13.1. The data are provided here again:

x	12	21	28	8	20
y	17	15	22	19	24

13.10 Solve for the predicted values of y and the residuals for the data in Problem 13.2. The data are provided here again:

x	140	119	103	91	65	29	24
y	25	29	46	70	88	112	128

13.11 Solve for the predicted values of y and the residuals for the data in Problem 13.3. The data are provided here again:

Advertising	12.5	3.7	21.6	60.0	37.6	6.1	16.8	41.2
Sales		148	55	338	994	541	89	126	379

13.12 Solve for the predicted values of y and the residuals for the data in Problem 13.4. The data are provided here again:

Bond Rate		5%	12%	9%	15%	7%
Prime Interest Rate	16%	6%	8%	4%	7%

13.13 The equation of a regression line is

$$\hat{y} = 50.506 - 1.646x$$

and the data are as follows.

x	5	7	11	12	19	25
y	47	38	32	24	22	10

Solve for the residuals and graph a residual plot. Do these data seem to violate any of the assumptions of regression?

13.14 Wisconsin is an important milk-producing state. Some people might argue that because of transportation costs, the cost of milk increases with the distance of markets from Wisconsin. Suppose the milk prices in eight cities are as follows.

Cost of Milk (per gallon)	Distance from Madison (miles)
$2.64	1,245
2.31	425
2.45	1,346
2.52	973
2.19	255
2.55	865
2.40	1,080
2.37	296

Use the prices along with the distance of each city from Madison, Wisconsin, to develop a regression line to predict the price of a gallon of milk by the number of miles the city is from Madison. Use the data and the regression equation to compute residuals for this model. Sketch a graph of the residuals in the order of the x values. Comment on the shape of the residual graph.

13.15 Graph the following residuals, and indicate which of the assumptions underlying regression appear to be in jeopardy on the basis of the graph.

x	y − ŷ
213	−11
216	−5
227	−2
229	−1
237	+6
247	+10
263	+12

13.16 Graph the following residuals, and indicate which of the assumptions underlying regression appear to be in jeopardy on the basis of the graph.

x	y − ŷ	x	y − ŷ
5	−21	13	−7
6	+16	14	+5
8	+14	17	−2
9	−11	18	+1
12	−8		

13.17 Graph the following residuals, and indicate which of the assumptions underlying regression appear to be in jeopardy on the basis of the graph.

x	y − ŷ	x	y − ŷ
10	+6	14	−3
11	+3	15	+2
12	−1	16	+5
13	−11	17	+8

13.18 Study the following MINITAB Residuals vs. Fits graphic for a simple regression analysis. Comment on the residual evidence of lack of compliance with the regression assumptions.

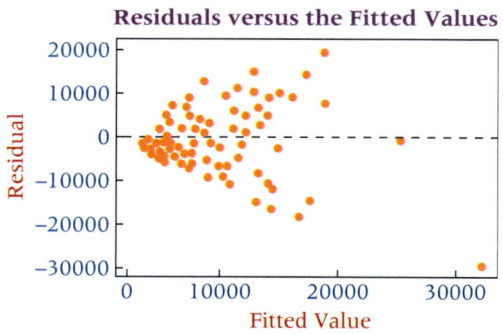

Residuals versus the Fitted Values

13.4 STANDARD ERROR OF THE ESTIMATE

Residuals represent errors of estimation for individual points. With large samples of data, residual computations become laborious. Even with computers, a researcher sometimes has difficulty working through pages of residuals in an effort to understand the error of the regression model. An alternative way of examining the error of the model is the standard error of the estimate, which provides a single measurement of the regression error.

Because the sum of the residuals is zero, attempting to determine the total amount of error by summing the residuals is fruitless. This zero-sum characteristic of residuals can be avoided by squaring the residuals and then summing them.

Table 13.4 contains the airline cost data from Table 13.1, along with the residuals and the residuals squared. The *total of the residuals squared* column is called the **sum of squares of error (SSE)**.

| SUM OF SQUARES OF ERROR | $SSE = \Sigma(y - \hat{y})^2$ |

In theory, infinitely many lines can be fit to a sample of points. However, formulas (13.1) and (13.3) produce a line of best fit for which the SSE is the smallest for any line that can be fit to the sample data. This result is guaranteed, because formulas (13.1) and (13.3) are derived from calculus to minimize SSE. For this reason, the regression process used in this chapter is called *least squares* regression.

A computational version of the equation for computing SSE is less meaningful in terms of interpretation than $\Sigma(y - \hat{y})^2$ but it is usually easier to compute. The computational formula for SSE follows.

| COMPUTATIONAL FORMULA FOR SSE | $SSE = \Sigma y^2 - b_0\Sigma y - b_1\Sigma xy$ |

For the airline cost example,

$$\Sigma y^2 = \Sigma\,[(4.280)^2 + (4.080)^2 + (4.420)^2 + (4.170)^2 + (4.480)^2 + (4.300)^2 + (4.820)^2 + (4.700)^2 + (5.110)^2 + (5.130)^2 + (5.640)^2 + (5.560)^2] = 270.9251$$

$$b_0 = 1.5697928$$
$$b_1 = .0407016^*$$
$$\Sigma y = 56.69$$
$$\Sigma xy = 4462.22$$
$$SSE = \Sigma y^2 - b_0\Sigma y - b_1\Sigma xy$$
$$= 270.9251 - (1.5697928)(56.69) - (.0407016)(4462.22) = .31405$$

The slight discrepancy between this value and the value computed in Table 13.4 is due to rounding error.

The sum of squares error is in part a function of the number of pairs of data being used to compute the sum, which lessens the value of SSE as a measurement of error. A more useful measurement of error is the standard error of the estimate. The **standard error of the estimate,** denoted s_e, is *a standard deviation of the error of the regression model* and has a more practical use than SSE. The standard error of the estimate follows.

*Note: In previous sections, the values of the slope and intercept were rounded off for ease of computation and interpretation. They are shown here with more precision in an effort to reduce rounding error.

TABLE 13.4	Number of Passengers x	Cost ($1,000) y	Residual $y - \hat{y}$	$(y - \hat{y})^2$
Determining SSE for the Airline Cost Example	61	4.280	.227	.05153
	63	4.080	−.054	.00292
	67	4.420	.123	.01513
	69	4.170	−.208	.04326
	70	4.480	.061	.00372
	74	4.300	−.282	.07952
	76	4.820	.157	.02465
	81	4.700	−.167	.02789
	86	5.110	.040	.00160
	91	5.130	−.144	.02074
	95	5.640	.204	.04162
	97	5.560	.042	.00176
			$\Sigma(y-\hat{y})=-.001$	$\Sigma(y-\hat{y})^2=.31434$
		Sum of squares of error = SSE = .31434		

**STANDARD ERROR
OF THE ESTIMATE**

$$s_e = \sqrt{\frac{SSE}{n-2}}$$

The standard error of the estimate for the airline cost example is

$$s_e = \sqrt{\frac{SSE}{n-2}} = \sqrt{\frac{.31434}{10}} = .1773$$

How is the standard error of the estimate used? As previously mentioned, the standard error of the estimate is a standard deviation of error. Recall from Chapter 3 that if data are approximately normally distributed, the empirical rule states that about 68% of all values are within $\mu \pm 1\sigma$ and that about 95% of all values are within $\mu \pm 2\sigma$. One of the assumptions for regression states that for a given x the error terms are normally distributed. Because the error terms are normally distributed, s_e is the standard deviation of error, and the average error is zero, approximately 68% of the error values (residuals) should be within $0 \pm 1s_e$ and 95% of the error values (residuals) should be within $0 \pm 2s_e$. By having knowledge of the variables being studied and by examining the value of s_e, the researcher can often make a judgment about the fit of the regression model to the data by using s_e. How can the s_e value for the airline cost example be interpreted?

The regression model in that example is used to predict airline cost by number of passengers. Note that the range of the airline cost data in Table 13.1 is from 4.08 to 5.64 ($4,080 to $5,640). The regression model for the data yields an s_e of .1773. An interpretation of s_e is that the standard deviation of error for the airline cost example is $177.30. If the error terms were normally distributed about the given values of x, approximately 68% of the error terms would be within $\pm$$177.30 and 95% would be within $\pm 2($177.30) = \pm$$354.60. Examination of the residuals reveals that 100% of the residuals are within $2s_e$. The standard error of the estimate provides a single measure of error, which, if the researcher has enough background in the area being analyzed, can be used to understand the magnitude of errors in the model. In addition, some researchers use the standard error of the estimate to identify outliers. They do so by looking for data that are outside $\pm 2s_e$ or $\pm 3s_e$.

**DEMONSTRATION
PROBLEM 13.3**

Compute the sum of squares of error and the standard error of the estimate for Demonstration Problem 13.1, in which a regression model was developed to predict the number of FTEs at a hospital by the number of beds.

Solution

Hospital	Number of Beds x	FTES y	Residuals $y - \hat{y}$	$(y - \hat{y})^2$
1	23	69	−13.22	174.77
2	29	95	−.62	−0.38
3	29	102	6.38	40.70
4	35	118	8.99	80.82
5	42	126	1.37	1.88
6	46	125	−8.56	73.27
7	50	138	−4.49	20.16
8	54	178	26.58	706.50
9	64	156	−17.74	314.71
10	66	184	5.80	33.64
11	76	176	−24.52	601.23
12	78	225	20.02	400.80
	$\Sigma x = 592$	$\Sigma y = 1692$	$\Sigma(y - \hat{y}) = -.01$	$\Sigma(y - \hat{y})^2 = 2448.86$

SSE = 2448.86

$$s_e = \sqrt{\frac{SSE}{n-2}} = \sqrt{\frac{2448.86}{10}} = 15.65$$

The standard error of the estimate is 15.65 FTEs. An examination of the residuals for this problem reveals that eight of 12 (67%) are within $\pm 1 s_e$ and 100% are within $\pm 2 s_e$. Is this size of error acceptable? Hospital administrators probably can best answer that question.

13.4 PROBLEMS

13.19 Determine the sum of squares of error (SSE) and the standard error of the estimate (s_e) for Problem 13.1. Determine how many of the residuals computed in Problem 13.9 (for Problem 13.1) are within one standard error of the estimate. If the error terms are normally distributed, approximately how many of these residuals should be within $\pm 1 s_e$?

13.20 Determine the SSE and the s_e for Problem 13.2. Use the residuals computed in Problem 13.10 (for Problem 13.2) and determine how many of them are within $\pm 1 s_e$ and $\pm 2 s_e$. How do these numbers compare with what the empirical rule says should occur if the error terms are normally distributed?

13.21 Determine the SSE and the s_e for Problem 13.3. Think about the variables being analyzed by regression in this problem and comment on the value of s_e.

13.22 Determine the SSE and s_e for Problem 13.4. Examine the variables being analyzed by regression in this problem and comment on the value of s_e.

13.23 Use the data from Problem 13.13 and determine the s_e.

13.24 Determine the SSE and the s_e for Problem 13.14. Comment on the size of s_e for this regression model, which is used to predict the cost of milk.

13.25 Determine the equation of the regression line to predict annual sales of a company from the yearly stock market volume of shares sold in a recent year. Compute the standard error of the estimate for this model. Does volume of shares sold appear to be a good predictor of a company's sales? Why or why not?

Company	Annual Sales ($ billions)	Annual Volume (millions of shares)
Merck	10.5	728.6
Philip Morris	48.1	497.9
IBM	64.8	439.1
Eastman Kodak	20.1	377.9
Bristol-Myers Squibb	11.4	375.5
General Motors	123.8	363.8
Ford Motors	89.0	276.3

13.5 COEFFICIENT OF DETERMINATION

A widely used measure of fit for regression models is the **coefficient of determination,** or r^2. The coefficient of determination is *the proportion of variability of the dependent variable (y) accounted for or explained by the independent variable (x).*

The coefficient of determination ranges from 0 to 1. An r^2 of zero means that the predictor accounts for none of the variability of the dependent variable and that there is no regression prediction of y by x. An r^2 of 1 means perfect prediction of y by x and that 100% of the variability of y is accounted for by x. Of course, most r^2 values are between the extremes. The researcher must interpret whether a particular r^2 is high or low, depending on the use of the model and the context within which the model was developed.

In exploratory research where the variables are less understood, low values of r^2 are likely to be more acceptable than they are in areas of research where the parameters are more developed and understood. One NASA researcher who uses vehicular weight to predict mission cost searches for the regression models to have an r^2 of .90 or higher. However, a business researcher who is trying to develop a model to predict the motivation level of employees might be pleased to get an r^2 near .50 in the initial research.

The dependent variable, y, being predicted in a regression model has a variation that is measured by the sum of squares of y (SS_{yy}):

$$SS_{yy} = \Sigma(y - \bar{y})^2 = \Sigma y^2 - \frac{(\Sigma y)^2}{n}$$

and is the sum of the squared deviations of the y values from the mean value of y. This variation can be broken into two additive variations: the *explained variation*, measured by the sum of squares of regression (SSR), and the *unexplained variation*, measured by the sum of squares of error (SSE). This relationship can be expressed in equation form as

$$SS_{yy} = SSR + SSE$$

If each term in the equation is divided by SS_{yy}, the resulting equation is

$$1 = \frac{SSR}{SS_{yy}} + \frac{SSE}{SS_{yy}}$$

The term r^2 is the proportion of the y variability that is explained by the regression model and represented here as

$$r^2 = \frac{SSR}{SS_{yy}}$$

Substituting this equation into the preceding relationship gives

$$1 = r^2 + \frac{SSE}{SS_{yy}}$$

Solving for r^2 yields formula (13.4).

COEFFICIENT OF DETERMINATION (13.4)	$$r^2 = 1 - \frac{SSE}{SS_{yy}} = 1 - \frac{SSE}{\Sigma y^2 - \frac{(\Sigma y)^2}{n}}$$
Note: $0 \le r^2 \le 1$	

The value of r^2 for the airline cost example is solved as follows:

$$SSE = .31434$$

$$SS_{yy} = \Sigma y^2 - \frac{(\Sigma y)^2}{n} = 270.9251 - \frac{(56.69)^2}{12} = 3.11209$$

$$r^2 = 1 - \frac{SSE}{SS_{yy}} = 1 - \frac{.31434}{3.11209} = .899$$

That is, 89.9% of the variability of the cost of flying a Boeing 737 airplane on a commercial flight is explained by variations in the number of passengers. This result also means that 11.1% of the variance in airline flight cost, y, is unaccounted for by x or unexplained by the regression model.

The coefficient of determination can be solved for directly by using

$$r^2 = \frac{SSR}{SS_{yy}}$$

It can be shown through algebra that

$$SSR = b_1^2 SS_{xx}$$

From this equation, a computational formula for r^2 can be developed.

COMPUTATIONAL FORMULA FOR r^2	$$r^2 = \frac{b_1^2 SS_{xx}}{SS_{yy}}$$

For the airline cost example, $b_1 = .0407016$, $SS_{xx} = 1689$, and $SS_{yy} = 3.11209$. Using the computational formula for r^2 yields

$$r^2 = \frac{(.0407016)^2(1689)}{3.11209} = .899$$

DEMONSTRATION PROBLEM 13.4

Compute the coefficient of determination (r^2) for Demonstration Problem 13.1, in which a regression model was developed to predict the number of FTEs of a hospital by the number of beds.

Solution

$$SSE = 2448.6$$

$$SS_{yy} = 260,136 - \frac{(1692)^2}{12} = 21,564$$

$$r^2 = 1 - \frac{SSE}{SS_{yy}} = 1 - \frac{2448.6}{21,564} = .886$$

This regression model accounts for 88.6% of the variance in FTEs, leaving only 11.4% unexplained variance.

Using $SS_{xx} = 3838.667$ and $b_1 = 2.232$ from Demonstration Problem 13.1, we can solve for r^2 with the computational formula:

$$r^2 = \frac{b_1^2 SS_{xx}}{SS_{yy}} = \frac{(2.232)^2(3838.667)}{21,564} = .886$$

Relationship between r and r^2

Is r, the coefficient of correlation (introduced in Chapter 3), related to r^2, the coefficient of determination in linear regression? The answer is yes: r^2 equals $(r)^2$. The coefficient of determination is the square of the coefficient of correlation. In Demonstration Problem 13.1, a regression model was developed to predict FTEs by number of hospital beds. The r^2 value for the model was .886. Taking the square root of this value yields $r = .941$, which is the correlation between the sample number of beds and FTEs. A word of caution here: Because r^2 is always positive, solving for r by taking $\sqrt{r^2}$ gives the correct magnitude of r but may give the wrong sign. The researcher must examine the sign of the slope of the regression line to determine whether a positive or negative relationship exists between the variables and then assign the appropriate sign to the correlation value.

13.5 PROBLEMS

13.26 Compute r^2 for Problem 13.19 (Problem 13.1). Discuss the value of r^2 obtained.

13.27 Compute r^2 for Problem 13.20 (Problem 13.2). Discuss the value of r^2 obtained.

13.28 Compute r^2 for Problem 13.21 (Problem 13.3). Discuss the value of r^2 obtained.

13.29 Compute r^2 for Problem 13.22 (Problem 13.4). Discuss the value of r^2 obtained.

13.30 Compute r^2 for Problem 13.23 (Problem 13.13). Discuss the value of r^2 obtained.

13.31 The Conference Board produces a Consumer Confidence Index (CCI) that reflects people's feelings about general business conditions, employment opportunities, and their own income prospects. Some researchers may feel that consumer confidence is a function of the median household income. Shown here are the CCIs for 9 years and the median household incomes for the same 9 years published by the U.S. Census Bureau. Determine the equation of the regression line to predict the CCI from the median household income. Compute the standard error of the estimate for this model. Compute the value of r^2. Does median household income appear to be a good predictor of the CCI? Why or why not?

CCI	Median Household Income ($1,000)
116.8	37.415
91.5	36.770
68.5	35.501
61.6	35.047
65.9	34.700
90.6	34.942
100.0	35.887
104.6	36.306
125.4	37.005

13.6 HYPOTHESIS TESTS FOR THE SLOPE OF THE REGRESSION MODEL AND TESTING THE OVERALL MODEL

Testing the Slope

A hypothesis test can be conducted on the sample slope of the regression model to determine whether the population slope is significantly different from zero. This test is another way to determine how well a regression model fits the data. Suppose a researcher decides that it is not worth the effort to develop a linear regression model to predict y from x. An alternative approach might be to average the y values and use $\bar{y}$ as the predictor of y for all values of x. For the airline cost example, instead of using number of passengers as the predictor, the researcher would use the average value of airline cost, $\bar{y}$, as the predictor. In this case the average value of y is

$$\bar{y} = \frac{56.69}{12} = 4.7242, \text{ or } \$4,724.20$$

Using this result as a model to predict y, if the number of passengers is 61, 70, or 95—or any other number—the predicted value of y is still 4.7242. Essentially, this approach fits the line of $\bar{y} = 4.7242$ through the data, which is a horizontal line with a slope of zero. Would a regression analysis offer anything more than the $\bar{y}$ model? Using this nonregression model (the $\bar{y}$ model) as a worst case, the researcher can analyze the regression line to determine whether it adds a more significant amount of predictability of y than does the $\bar{y}$ model. Because the slope of the $\bar{y}$ line is zero, one way to determine whether the regression line adds significant predictability is to test the population slope of the regression line to find out whether the slope is different from zero. As the slope of the regression line diverges from zero, the regression model is adding predictability that the $\bar{y}$ line is not generating. For this reason, testing the slope of the regression line to determine whether the slope is different from zero is important. If the slope is not different from zero, the regression line is doing nothing more than the $\bar{y}$ line in predicting y.

How does the researcher go about testing the slope of the regression line? Why not just examine the observed sample slope? For example, the slope of the regression line for the airline cost data is .0407. This value is obviously not zero. The problem is that this slope is obtained from a sample of 12 data points; and if another sample was taken, it is likely that a different slope would be obtained. For this reason, the population slope is statistically tested using the sample slope. The question is: If all the pairs of data points for the population were available, would the slope of that regression line be different from zero? Here the sample slope, b_1, is used as evidence to test whether the population slope is different from zero. The hypotheses for this test follow.

$$H_0: \beta_1 = 0$$

$$H_a: \beta_1 \neq 0$$

Note that this test is two-tailed. The null hypothesis can be rejected if the slope is either negative or positive. A negative slope indicates an inverse relationship between x and y. That is, larger values of x are related to smaller values of y, and vice versa. Both negative and positive slopes can be different from zero. To determine whether there is a significant positive relationship between two variables, the hypotheses would be one-tailed, or

$$H_0: \beta_1 = 0$$
$$H_a: \beta_1 > 0$$

To test for a significant negative relationship between two variables, the hypotheses also would be one-tailed, or

$$H_0: \beta_1 = 0$$
$$H_a: \beta_1 < 0$$

In each case, testing the null hypothesis involves a t test of the slope.

---

t TEST OF SLOPE

$$t = \frac{b_1 - \beta_1}{s_b}$$

where

$$s_b = \frac{s_e}{\sqrt{SS_{xx}}}$$

$$s_e = \sqrt{\frac{SSE}{n-2}}$$

$$SS_{xx} = \Sigma x^2 - \frac{(\Sigma x)^2}{n}$$

β_1 = the hypothesized slope
df $= n - 2$

The test of the slope of the regression line for the airline cost regression model for $\alpha = .05$ follows. The regression line derived for the data is

$$\hat{y} = 1.57 + .0407x$$

The sample slope is $.0407 = b_1$. The value of s_e is .1773, $\Sigma x = 930$, $\Sigma x^2 = 73,764$, and $n = 12$. The hypotheses are

$$H_0: \beta_1 = 0$$
$$H_a: \beta 1 \neq 0$$

The df $= n - 2 = 12 - 2 = 10$. As this test is two-tailed, $\alpha/2 = .025$. The table t value is $t_{.025,10} = \pm 2.228$. The observed t value for this sample slope is

$$t = \frac{.0407 - 0}{.1773 \Big/ \sqrt{73,764 - \frac{(930)^2}{12}}} = 9.43$$

As shown in Figure 13.12, the t value calculated from the sample slope falls in the rejection region. The null hypothesis that the population slope is zero is rejected. This linear regression model is adding significantly more predictive information to the $\bar{y}$ model (no regression).

It is desirable to reject the null hypothesis in testing the slope of the regression model. In rejecting the null hypothesis of a zero population slope, we are stating that the regression model is adding something to the explanation of the variation of the dependent variable that the average value of y model does not. Failure to reject the null hypothesis in this test causes the researcher to conclude that the regression model has no predictability of the dependent variable, and the model, therefore, has little or no use.

FIGURE 13.12

t Test of Slope from
Airline Cost Example

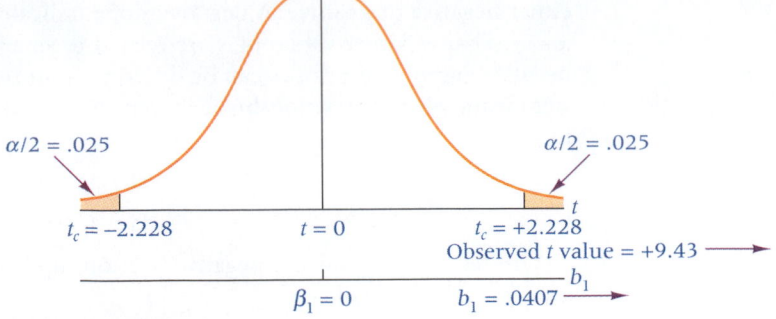

$\alpha/2 = .025$ $\alpha/2 = .025$

$t_c = -2.228$ $t = 0$ $t_c = +2.228$

Observed *t* value = +9.43 ⟶

$\beta_1 = 0$ $b_1 = .0407$ ⟶ b_1

STATISTICS IN BUSINESS TODAY

Predicting the Price of an SUV

What variables are good predictors of the base price of a new car? In a *Wall Street Journal* article on the 2003 Ford Expedition, data are displayed for five variables on five different makes of large SUVs. The variables are base price, engine horsepower, weight (in pounds), towing capacity (in pounds), and city EPA mileage. The SUV makes are Ford Expedition Eddie Bauer 4×4, Toyota Sequoia Limited, Chevrolet Tahoe LT, Acura MDX, and Dodge Durango R/T. The base prices of these five models ranged from $34,700 to $42,725. Suppose a business researcher wanted to develop a regression model to predict the base price of these cars. What variable would be the strongest predictor and how strong would the prediction be?

Using a correlation matrix (coefficient of correlation was discussed in Chapter 3) constructed from the data for the five variables, it was determined that weight was most correlated with base price and had the greatest potential as a predictor. Towing capacity had the second highest correlation with base price, followed by city EPA mileage, and horsepower. City EPA mileage was negatively related to base price indicating that the more expensive SUVs tended to be "gas guzzlers."

A regression model was developed using weight as a predictor of base price. The MINITAB output from the data follows. Excel output contains similar items.

Regression Analysis: Base Price versus Weight

```
The regression equation is
Base Price = 10140 + 5.77 Weight

Predictor  Coef   SE Coef     T      P
Constant   10140     8473   1.20  0.317
Weight     5.769    1.679   3.44  0.041
S = 1699  R-Sq = 79.7%  R-Sq(adj) = 73.0%
```

Note that the r^2 for this model is almost 80% and that the *t* statistic is significant at $\alpha = .05$. In the regression equation, the slope indicates that for every pound of weight increase there is a $5.77 increase in the price. The *y* intercept indicates that if the SUV weighed nothing at all, it would still cost $10,140! The standard error of the estimate is $1,699.

Regression models were developed for each of the other possible predictor variables. Towing capacity was the next best predictor variable producing an r^2 of 31.4%. City EPA mileage produced an r^2 of 20%, and horsepower produced an r^2 of 6.9%.

Source: Adapted from Jonathan Welsh, "The Biggest Station Wagon of Them All," *The Wall Street Journal*, 7 June 2002, p. W15C.

DEMONSTRATION PROBLEM 13.5

Test the slope of the regression model developed in Demonstration Problem 13.1 to predict the number of FTEs in a hospital from the number of beds to determine whether there is a significant positive slope. Use $\alpha = .01$.

Solution

The hypotheses for this problem are

$$H_0: \beta_1 = 0$$
$$H_a: \beta_1 > 0$$

The level of significance is .01. With 12 pairs of data, df = 10. The critical table *t* value is $t_{.01,10} = 2.764$. The regression line equation for this problem is

$$\hat{y} = 30.888 + 2.232x$$

The sample slope, b_1, is 2.232, and $s_e = 15.65$, $\Sigma x = 592$, $\Sigma x^2 = 33{,}044$, and $n = 12$. The observed *t* value for the sample slope is

$$t = \frac{2.232 - 0}{\dfrac{15.65}{\sqrt{33{,}044 - \dfrac{(592)^2}{12}}}} = 8.84$$

The observed t value (8.84) is in the rejection region because it is greater than the critical table t value of 2.764. The null hypothesis is rejected. The population slope for this regression line is significantly different from zero in the positive direction. This regression model is adding significant predictability over the $\bar{y}$ model.

Testing the Overall Model

It is common in regression analysis to compute an F test to determine the overall significance of the model. Most computer software packages include the F test and its associated ANOVA table as standard regression output. In multiple regression (Chapters 14 and 15), this test determines whether at least one of the regression coefficients (from multiple predictors) is different from zero. Simple regression provides only one predictor and only one regression coefficient to test. Because the regression coefficient is the slope of the regression line, the F test for overall significance is testing the same thing as the t test in simple regression. The hypotheses being tested in simple regression by the F test for overall significance are

$$H_0: \beta_1 = 0$$
$$H_a: \beta_1 \neq 0$$

In the case of simple regression analysis, $F = t^2$. Thus, for the airline cost example, the F value is

$$F = t^2 = (9.43)^2 = 88.92$$

The F value is computed directly by

$$F = \frac{SS_{reg}/df_{reg}}{SS_{err}/df_{err}} = \frac{MS_{reg}}{MS_{err}}$$

where

$$df_{reg} = k$$
$$df_{err} = n - k - 1$$
$$k = \text{the number of independent variables}$$

The values of the sum of squares (SS), degrees of freedom (df), and mean squares (MS) are obtained from the analysis of variance table, which is produced with other regression statistics as standard output from statistical software packages. Shown here is the analysis of variance table produced by MINITAB for the airline cost example.

```
Analysis of Variance
Source            DF      SS      MS       F       p
Regression         1   2.7980  2.7980   89.09   0.000
Residual Error    10   0.3141  0.0314
Total             11   3.1121
```

The F value for the airline cost example is calculated from the analysis of variance table information as

$$F = \frac{2.7980/1}{.3141/10} = \frac{2.7980}{.03141} = 89.09$$

The difference between this value (89.09) and the value obtained by squaring the t statistic (88.92) is due to rounding error. The probability of obtaining an F value this large or larger by chance if there is no regression prediction in this model is .000 according to the ANOVA output (the p-value). This output value means it is highly unlikely that the population slope is zero and that there is no prediction due to regression from this model given the sample statistics obtained. Hence, it is highly likely that this regression model adds significant predictability of the dependent variable.

Note from the ANOVA table that the degrees of freedom due to regression are equal to 1. Simple regression models have only one independent variable; therefore, $k = 1$. The degrees of freedom error in simple regression analysis is always $n - k - 1 = n - 1 - 1 = n - 2$. With the degrees of freedom due to regression (1) as the numerator degrees of freedom and the degrees of freedom due to error $(n - 2)$ as the denominator degrees of freedom, Table A.7 can be used to obtain the critical F value $(F_{\alpha,1,n-2})$ to help make the hypothesis-testing decision about the overall regression model if the p-value of F is not given in the computer output. This critical F value is always found in the right tail of the distribution. In simple regression, the relationship between the critical t value to test the slope and the critical F value of overall significance is

$$t^2_{\alpha/2,\, n-2} = F_{\alpha,1,n-2}$$

For the airline cost example with a two-tailed test and $\alpha = .05$, the critical value of $t_{.025,10}$ is ± 2.228 and the critical value of $F_{.05,1,10}$ is 4.96.

$$t^2_{.025,10} = (\pm 2.228)^2 = 4.96 = F_{.05,1,10}$$

13.6 PROBLEMS

13.32 Test the slope of the regression line determined in Problem 13.1. Use $\alpha = .05$.

13.33 Test the slope of the regression line determined in Problem 13.2. Use $\alpha = .01$.

13.34 Test the slope of the regression line determined in Problem 13.3. Use $\alpha = .10$.

13.35 Test the slope of the regression line determined in Problem 13.4. Use a 5% level of significance.

13.36 Shown here is an incomplete analysis of variance table produced by using MINITAB for a simple regression analysis. Compute the value of F and determine whether it is statistically significant by using Table A.7. From this value, compute the value of t. What is the statistical significance of the overall model? Is the slope of the regression line significant? Explain.

```
Analysis of Variance

Source        DF      SS      MS    F
Regression     1    5165
Error          7   18554
Total          8   23718
```

13.37 Study the following analysis of variance table, which was generated from a simple regression analysis. Discuss the F test of the overall model. Determine the value of t and test the slope of the regression line.

```
Analysis of Variance

Source        DF       SS       MS       F       p
Regression     1   116.65   116.65    8.26   0.021
Error          8   112.95    14.12
Total          9   229.60
```

13.7 ESTIMATION

One of the main uses of regression analysis is as a prediction tool. If the regression function is a good model, the researcher can use the regression equation to determine values of the dependent variable from various values of the independent variable. For example, financial brokers would like to have a model with which they could predict the selling price of a particular stock on a certain day by a variable such as unemployment rate or producer price index. Marketing managers would like to have a site location model with which they could predict the sales volume of a new location by variables such as population density or number of competitors. The airline cost example presents a regression model that has the potential to predict the cost of flying an airplane by the number of passengers.

In simple regression analysis, a point estimate prediction of y can be made by substituting the associated value of x into the regression equation and solving for y. From the airline cost example, if the number of passengers is $x = 73$, the predicted cost of the airline flight can be computed by substituting the x value into the regression equation determined in Section 13.2:

$$\hat{y} = 1.57 + .0407x = 1.57 + .0407(73) = 4.5411$$

The point estimate of the predicted cost is 4.5411 or $4,541.10.

Confidence Intervals to Estimate the Conditional Mean of y: $\mu_{y|x}$

Although a point estimate is often of interest to the researcher, the regression line is determined by a sample set of points; and if a different sample is taken, a different line will result, yielding a different point estimate. Hence computing a *confidence interval* for the estimation is often useful. Because for any value of x (independent variable) there can be many values of y (dependent variable), one type of **confidence interval** is *an estimate of the average value of y for a given x.* This average value of y is denoted $E(y_x)$—the expected value of y and can be computed using formula (13.5).

CONFIDENCE INTERVAL TO ESTIMATE $E(y_x)$ FOR A GIVEN VALUE OF x (13.5)	$$\hat{y} \pm t_{\alpha/2, n-2} s_e \sqrt{\frac{1}{n} + \frac{(x_0 - \bar{x})^2}{SS_{xx}}}$$

where

$x_0 = $ a particular value of x

$$SS_{xx} = \Sigma x^2 - \frac{(\Sigma x)^2}{n}$$

The application of this formula can be illustrated with construction of a 95% confidence interval to estimate the average value of y (airline cost) for the airline cost example when x (number of passengers) is 73. For a 95% confidence interval, $\alpha = .05$ and $\alpha/2 = .025$. The df $= n - 2 = 12 - 2 = 10$. The table t value is $t_{.025,10} = 2.228$. Other needed values for this problem, which were solved for previously, are

$$s_e = .1773 \quad \Sigma x = 930 \quad \bar{x} = 77.5 \quad \Sigma x^2 = 73,764$$

For $x_0 = 73$, the value of $\hat{y}$ is 4.5411. The computed confidence interval for the average value of y, $E(y_{73})$, is

$$4.5411 \pm (2.228)(.1773) \sqrt{\frac{1}{12} + \frac{(73 - 77.5)^2}{73,764 - \frac{(930)^2}{12}}} = 4.5411 \pm .1220$$

$$4.4191 \leq E(y_{73}) \leq 4.6631$$

That is, with 95% confidence the average value of y for $x = 73$ is between 4.4191 and 4.6631.

Table 13.5 shows confidence intervals computed for the airline cost example for several values of x to estimate the average value of y. Note that as x values get farther from the mean x value (77.5), the confidence intervals get wider; as the x values get closer to the mean, the confidence intervals narrow. The reason is that the numerator of the second term under the radical sign approaches zero as the value of x nears the mean and increases as x departs from the mean.

Prediction Intervals to Estimate a Single Value of y

A second type of interval in regression estimation is a **prediction interval** to *estimate a single value of y for a given value of x.*

PREDICTION INTERVAL TO ESTIMATE y FOR A GIVEN VALUE OF x (13.6)	$$\hat{y} \pm t_{\alpha/2, n-2} s_e \sqrt{1 + \frac{1}{n} + \frac{(x_0 - \bar{x})^2}{SS_{xx}}}$$

where

$x_0 = $ a particular value of x

$$SS_{xx} = \Sigma x^2 - \frac{(\Sigma x)^2}{n}$$

TABLE 13.5	x	Confidence Interval	
Confidence Intervals to Estimate the Average Value of y for Some x Values in the Airline Cost Example	62	4.0934 ± .1876	3.9058 to 4.2810
	68	4.3376 ± .1461	4.1915 to 4.4837
	73	4.5411 ± .1220	4.4191 to 4.6631
	85	5.0295 ± .1349	4.8946 to 5.1644
	90	5.2230 ± .1656	5.0674 to 5.3986

Formula (13.6) is virtually the same as formula (13.5), except for the additional value of 1 under the radical. This additional value widens the prediction interval to estimate a single value of y from the confidence interval to estimate the average value of y. This result seems logical because the average value of y is toward the middle of a group of y values. Thus the confidence interval to estimate the average need not be as wide as the prediction interval produced by formula (13.6), which takes into account all the y values for a given x.

A 95% prediction interval can be computed to estimate the single value of y for $x = 73$ from the airline cost example by using formula (13.6). The same values used to construct the confidence interval to estimate the average value of y are used here.

$$t_{.025,10} = 2.228, s_e = .1773, \Sigma x = 930, \bar{x} = 77.5, \Sigma x^2 = 73,764$$

For $x_0 = 73$, the value of $\hat{y} = 4.5411$. The computed prediction interval for the single value of y is

$$4.5411 \pm (2.228)(.1773)\sqrt{1 + \frac{1}{12} + \frac{(73-77.5)^2}{73,764 - \frac{(930)^2}{12}}} = 4.5411 \pm .4134$$

$$4.1277 \le y \le 4.9545$$

Prediction intervals can be obtained by using the computer. Shown in Figure 13.13 is the computer output for the airline cost example. The output displays the predicted value for $x = 73$ ($\hat{y} = 4.5411$), a 95% confidence interval for the average value of y for $x = 73$, and a 95% prediction interval for a single value of y for $x = 73$. Note that the resulting values are virtually the same as those calculated in this section.

Figure 13.14 displays MINITAB confidence intervals for various values of x for the average y value and the prediction intervals for a single y value. Note that the intervals flare out toward the ends, as the values of x depart from the average x value. Note also that the intervals for a single y value are always wider than the intervals for the average y value for any given value of x.

An examination of the prediction interval formula to estimate y for a given value of x explains why the intervals flare out.

$$\hat{y} \pm t_{\alpha/2,n-2} s_e \sqrt{1 + \frac{1}{n} + \frac{(x_0 - \bar{x})^2}{SS_{xx}}}$$

As we enter different values of x_0 from the regression analysis into the equation, the only thing that changes in the equation is $(x_0 - \bar{x})^2$. This expression increases as individual values of x_0 get farther from the mean, resulting in an increase in the width of the interval. The interval is narrower for values of x_0 nearer $\bar{x}$ and wider for values of x_0 farther from $\bar{x}$. A comparison of formulas (13.5) and (13.6) reveals them to be identical except that formula (13.6)—to compute a prediction interval to estimate y for a given value of

FIGURE 13.13	Fit	StDev Fit	95.0% CI	95.0% PI
MINITAB Output for Prediction Intervals	4.5410	0.0547	(4.4191, 4.6629)	(4.1278, 4.9543)

FIGURE 13.14

MINITAB Intervals
for Estimation

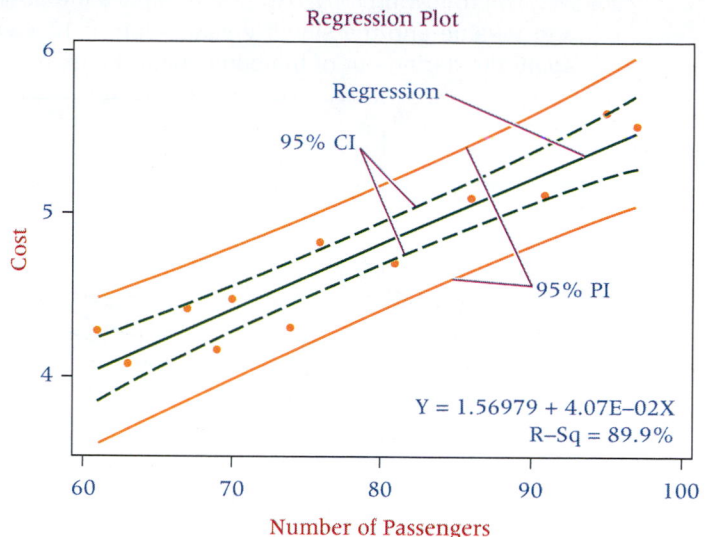

Regression Plot

$Y = 1.56979 + 4.07E{-}02X$
$R{-}Sq = 89.9\%$

x—contains a 1 under the radical sign. This distinction ensures that formula (13.6) will yield wider intervals than (13.5) for otherwise identical data.

Caution: *A regression line is determined from a sample of points. The line, the r^2, the s_e, and the confidence intervals change for different sets of sample points. That is, the linear relationship developed for a set of points does not necessarily hold for values of x outside the domain of those used to establish the model. In the airline cost example, the domain of x values (number of passengers) varied from 61 to 97. The regression model developed from these points may not be valid for flights of say 40, 50, or 100 because the regression model was not constructed with x values of those magnitudes. However, decision makers sometimes extrapolate regression results to values of x beyond the domain of those used to develop the formulas (often in time-series sales forecasting). Understanding the limitations of this type of use of regression analysis is essential.*

DEMONSTRATION PROBLEM 13.6

Construct a 95% confidence interval to estimate the average value of *y* (FTEs) for Demonstration Problem 13.1 when *x* = 40 beds. Then construct a 95% prediction interval to estimate the single value of *y* for *x* = 40 beds.

Solution

For a 95% confidence interval, $\alpha = .05$, $n = 12$, and df = 10. The table *t* value is $t_{.025,10} = 2.228$; $s_e = 15.65$, $\Sigma x = 592$, $\bar{x} = 49.33$, and $\Sigma x^2 = 33{,}044$. For $x_0 = 40$, $\hat{y} = 120.17$. The computed confidence interval for the average value of *y* is

$$120.17 \pm (2.228)(15.65)\sqrt{\frac{1}{12} + \frac{(40 - 49.33)^2}{33{,}044 - \frac{(592)^2}{12}}} = 120.17 \pm 11.35$$

$$108.82 \leq E(y_{40}) \leq 131.52$$

With 95% confidence, the statement can be made that the average number of FTEs for a hospital with 40 beds is between 108.82 and 131.52.

The computed prediction interval for the single value of *y* is

$$120.17 \pm (2.228)(15.65)\sqrt{1 + \frac{1}{12} + \frac{(40 - 49.33)^2}{33{,}044 - \frac{(592)^2}{12}}} = 120.17 \pm 36.67$$

$$83.5 \leq y \leq 156.84$$

With 95% confidence, the statement can be made that a single number of FTEs for a hospital with 40 beds is between 83.5 and 156.84. Obviously this interval is much wider than the 95% confidence interval for the average value of *y* for *x* = 40.

The following MINITAB graph depicts the 95% interval bands for both the average y value and the single y values for all 12 x values in this problem. Note once again the flaring out of the bands near the extreme values of x.

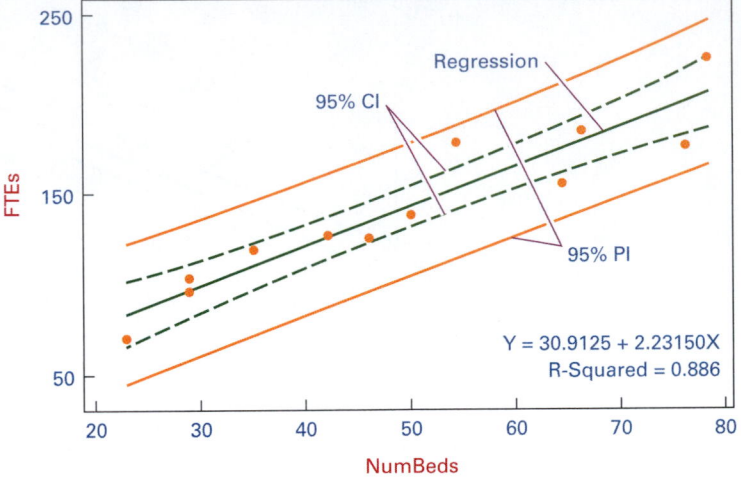

13.7 PROBLEMS

13.38   Construct a 95% confidence interval for the average value of y for Problem 13.1. Use $x = 25$.

13.39   Construct a 90% prediction interval for a single value of y for Problem 13.2; use $x = 100$. Construct a 90% prediction interval for a single value of y for Problem 13.2; use $x = 130$. Compare the results. Which prediction interval is greater? Why?

13.40   Construct a 98% confidence interval for the average value of y for Problem 13.3; use $x = 20$. Construct a 98% prediction interval for a single value of y for Problem 13.3; use $x = 20$. Which is wider? Why?

13.41   Construct a 99% confidence interval for the average bond rate in Problem 13.4 for a prime interest rate of 10%. Discuss the meaning of this confidence interval.

13.8 INTERPRETING THE OUTPUT

Although manual computations can be done, most regression problems are analyzed by using a computer. In this section, computer output from both MINITAB and Excel will be presented and discussed.

At the top of the MINITAB regression output, shown in Figure 13.15, is the regression equation. Next is a table that describes the model in more detail. "Coef" stands for coefficient of the regression terms. The coefficient of "Number of Passengers," the x variable, is 0.040702. This value is equal to the slope of the regression line and is reflected in the regression equation. The coefficient shown next to the constant term (1.5698) is the value of the constant, which is the y intercept and also a part of the regression equation. The "T" values are a t test for the slope and a t test for the intercept or constant. (We generally do not interpret the t test for the constant.) The t value for the slope, $t = 9.44$ with an associated probability of .000, is the same as the value obtained manually in section 13.6. Because the probability of the t value is given, the p-value method can be used to interpret the t value.

The next row of output is the standard error of the estimate s_e, S = 0.1772; the coefficient of determination, r^2, R-Sq = 89.9%; and the adjusted value of r^2, R-Sq(adj) = 88.9%.

FIGURE 13.15

MINITAB Regression Analysis of the Airline Cost Example

Regression Analysis: Cost versus Passengers

```
The regression equation is
Cost = 1.57 + 0.0407 Passengers

Predictor        Coef     SE Coef      T       P
Constant       1.5698      0.3381   4.64   0.001
Passenge     0.040702    0.004312   9.44   0.000
S = 0.1772   R-Sq = 89.9%   R-Sq(adj) = 88.9%

Analysis of Variance

Source            DF        SS       MS       F       P
Regression         1    2.7980   2.7980   89.09   0.000
Residual Error    10    0.3141   0.0314
Total             11    3.1121

Obs    Passenge     Cost      Fit     SE Fit   Residual   St Resid
 1       61.0      4.2800   4.0526   0.0876    0.2274       1.48
 2       63.0      4.0800   4.1340   0.0808   -0.0540      -0.34
 3       67.0      4.4200   4.2968   0.0683    0.1232       0.75
 4       69.0      4.1700   4.3782   0.0629   -0.2082      -1.26
 5       70.0      4.4800   4.4189   0.0605    0.0611       0.37
 6       74.0      4.3000   4.5817   0.0533   -0.2817      -1.67
 7       76.0      4.8200   4.6631   0.0516    0.1569       0.93
 8       81.0      4.7000   4.8666   0.0533   -0.1666      -0.99
 9       86.0      5.1100   5.0701   0.0629    0.0399       0.24
10       91.0      5.1300   5.2736   0.0775   -0.1436      -0.90
11       95.0      5.6400   5.4364   0.0912    0.2036       1.34
12       97.0      5.5600   5.5178   0.0984    0.0422       0.29
```

(Adjusted r^2 will be discussed in Chapter 14.) Following these items is the analysis of variance table. Note that the value of $F = 89.09$ is used to test the overall model of the regression line. The final item of the output is the predicted value and the corresponding residual for each pair of points.

Although the Excel regression output, shown in Figure 13.16 for Demonstration Problem 13.1, is somewhat different from the MINITAB output, the same essential regression features are present. The regression equation is found under Coefficients at the bottom of ANOVA. The slope or coefficient of x is 2.2315 and the y intercept is 30.9125. The standard error of the estimate for the hospital problem is given as the fourth statistic under Regression Statistics at the top of the output, Standard Error = 15.6491. The r^2 value is given as 0.886 on the second line. The t test for the slope is found under t Stat near the bottom of the ANOVA section on the "Number of beds" (x variable) row, $t = 8.83$. Adjacent to the t Stat is the P-value, which is the probability of the t statistic occurring by chance if the null hypothesis is true. For this slope, the probability shown is 0.000005. The ANOVA table is in the middle of the output with the F value having the same probability as the t statistic, 0.000005, and equaling t^2. The predicted values and the residuals are shown in the Residual Output section.

IN RESPONSE

Predicting the Annual Sales Volume

Chapter 13 contains techniques for bivariate regression. Using these techniques along with the coefficient of correlation presented in Chapter 3, it is possible to measure the strength of the relationship between two variables. The Decision Dilemma posed several possible

FIGURE 13.16

Excel Regression Output for Demonstration Problem 13.1

	A	B	C	D	E	F
1	SUMMARY OUTPUT					
2	Regression Statistics					
3	Multiple R	0.942				
4	R Square	0.886				
5	Adjusted R Square	0.875				
6	Standard Error	15.6491				
7	Observations	12				
8						
9	ANOVA					
10		df	SS	MS	F	Significance F
11	Regression	1	19115.0632	19115.0632	78.05	.000005
12	Residual	10	2448.9368	244.8937		
13	Total	11	21564			
14						
15		Coefficients	Standard Error	t Stat	P-value	
16	Intercepts	30.9125	13.2542	2.33	0.041888	
17	Beds	2.2315	0.2526	8.83	0.000005	
18						
19	RESIDUAL OUTPUT					
20	Observation	Predicted FTEs	Residuals			
21	1	82.237	−13.237			
22	2	95.626	−0.626			
23	3	95.626	6.374			
24	4	109.015	8.985			
25	5	124.636	1.364			
26	6	133.562	−8.562			
27	7	142.488	−4.488			
28	8	151.414	26.586			
29	9	173.729	−17.729			
30	10	178.192	5.808			
31	11	200.507	−24.507			
32	12	204.970	20.030			

variables that might be related to the total annual sales volume of a real estate brokerage firm. Some of the more promising variables are number of offices, size of sales force, and number of houses/properties sold. In particular, data were given on total annual sales volume and average price of a sale for the top 25 firms in the United States for a recent year. A regression model can be developed in an attempt to predict sales volume (y) by average price (x). What are the results of such an effort? Both the Excel output and MINITAB output for a regression analysis to predict sales volume by average price follow.

Excel Regression Output

	A	B	C	D	E	F
1	SUMMARY OUTPUT					
2	Regression Statistics					
3	Multiple R	0.129				
4	R Square	0.017				
5	Adjusted R Square	−0.026				
6	Standard Error	9719				
7	Observations	25				
8						
9	ANOVA					
10		df	SS	MS	F	Significance F
11	Regression	1	36477544.53	36477544.53	0.39	0.540
12	Residual	23	2172553428	94458844.7		
13	Total	24	2209030973			
14						
15		Coefficients	Standard Error	t Stat	P-value	
16	Intercept	2357.92	5426.17	0.43	0.668	
17	Average Price	15.90	25.58	0.62	0.540	

MINITAB Regression Output:

Regression Analysis: Sales Volume versus Average Price

```
The regression equation is
Sales Volume = 2358 + 15.9 Average Price

Predictor          Coef         SE Coef      T      P
Constant           2358            5426    0.43  0.668
Average           15.90           25.58    0.62  0.540

S = 9719   R-Sq = 1.7%   R-Sq(adj) = 0.0%

Analysis of Variance
Source           DF         SS          MS      F      P
Regression        1   36477545    36477545   0.39  0.540
Residual Error   23 2172553428    94458845
Total            24 2209030973
```

In studying the regression output, we find several indicators that tell us the model is weak. The r^2 value (.017 = 1.7%) is almost zero showing virtually no predictability in the model. In addition, the value of F yields a p-value of .540, indicating no overall significance in the predictability of this model. The standard error of the estimate is more than \$9.7 billion, which is more than all but two of the companies' annual sales volume.

This example shows how a regression model can be made to fit virtually any two variables of data. It becomes imperative that the researcher is able to study the output and determine the strength of the predictability of the model (if any at all). Presenting this regression model as a way to predict the overall sales volume of a real estate firm would be a misuse of statistics. The student is encouraged to find other data that are more useful in establishing relationships between total sales volume in the real estate industry and other variables.

ETHICAL CONSIDERATIONS

Regression analysis offers several opportunities for unethical behavior. Business researchers who knowingly violate the assumptions underlying statistical techniques are acting unethically. Regression analysis requires equal error variance and independence of error terms. Through the use of residual plots and other statistical techniques, a researcher can search to determine whether such assumptions are being met. To present a regression model as fact when the assumptions underlying regression are being grossly violated is unethical behavior.

Another ethical problem that arises in regression analysis is using the regression model to predict values of the independent variable that are outside the domain of values used to develop the model. The airline cost model used in this chapter was built with between 61 and 97 passengers. A linear relationship appeared to be evident between flight costs and number of passengers over this domain. This model is not guaranteed to fit values outside the domain of 61 to 97 passengers, however. In fact, either a nonlinear relationship or no relationship may be present between flight costs and number of passengers if values from outside this domain are included in the model-building process. It is a mistake and probably unethical behavior to make claims for a regression model outside the perview of the domain of values for which the model was developed.

SUMMARY

Regression is a procedure that produces a mathematical model (function) that can be used to predict one variable by other variables. Simple regression is bivariate (two variables) and linear (only a line fit is attempted). Simple regression analysis produces a model that attempts to predict a y variable, referred to as the dependent variable, by an x variable, referred to as the independent variable. The general form of the equation of the simple regression line is the slope-intercept equation of a line. The equation of the simple regression model consists of a slope of the line as a coefficient of x and a y intercept value as a constant.

After the equation of the line has been developed, several statistics are available that can be used to determine how well the line fits the data. Using the historical data values of x, predicted values of y (denoted as $\hat{y}$) can be calculated by inserting values of x into the regression equation. The predicted values can then be compared to the actual values of y to determine how well the regression equation fits the known data. The difference between a specific y value and its associated predicted y value is called the residual or error of prediction. Examination of the residuals can offer insight into the magnitude of the errors produced by a model. In addition, residual analysis can be used to help determine whether the assumptions underlying the regression analysis have been met. Specifically, graphs of the residuals can reveal (1) lack of linearity, (2) lack of homogeneity of error variance, and (3) independence of error terms. Geometrically, the residuals are the vertical distances from the y values to the regression line. Because the equation that yields the regression line is derived in such a way that the line is in the geometric middle of the points, the sum of the residuals is zero.

A single value of error measurement called the standard error of the estimate, s_e, can be computed. The standard error of the estimate is the standard deviation of error of a model. The value of s_e can be used as a single guide to the magnitude of the error produced by the regression model as opposed to examining all the residuals.

Another widely used statistic for testing the strength of a regression model is r^2, or the coefficient of determination. The coefficient of determination is the proportion of total variance of the y variable accounted for or predicted by x. The coefficient of determination ranges from 0 to 1. The higher the r^2 is, the stronger is the predictability of the model.

Testing to determine whether the slope of the regression line is different from zero is another way to judge the fit of the regression model to the data. If the population slope of the regression line is not different from zero, the regression model is not adding significant predictability to the dependent variable. A t statistic is used to test the significance of the slope. The overall significance of the regression model can be tested using an F statistic. In simple regression, because only one predictor is present, this test accomplishes the same thing as the t test of the slope and $F = t^2$.

One of the most prevalent uses of a regression model is to predict the values of y for given values of x. Recognizing that the predicted value is often not the same as the actual value, a confidence interval has been developed to yield a range within which the mean y value for a given x should fall. A prediction interval for a single y value for a given x value also is specified. This second interval is wider because it allows for the wide diversity of individual values, whereas the confidence interval for the mean y value reflects only the range of average y values for a given x.

KEY TERMS

coefficient of
    determination (r^2)
confidence interval
dependent variable
deterministic model

heteroscedasticity
homoscedasticity
independent variable
least squares analysis
outliers

prediction interval
probabilistic model
regression analysis
residual
residual plot

scatter plot
simple regression
standard error of the
    estimate (s_e)
sum of squares of error (SSE)

FORMULAS

Equation of the simple regression line

$$\hat{y} = \beta_0 + \beta_1 x$$

Sum of squares

$$SS_{xx} = \Sigma x^2 - \frac{(\Sigma x)^2}{n}$$

$$SS_{yy} = \Sigma y^2 - \frac{(\Sigma y)^2}{n}$$

$$SS_{xy} = \Sigma xy - \frac{\Sigma x \Sigma y}{n}$$

Slope of the regression line

$$b_1 = \frac{\Sigma(x-\bar{x})(y-\bar{y})}{\Sigma(x-\bar{x})^2} = \frac{\Sigma xy - n\bar{x}\bar{y}}{\Sigma x^2 - n\bar{x}^2} = \frac{\Sigma xy - \dfrac{(\Sigma x)(\Sigma y)}{n}}{\Sigma x^2 - \dfrac{(\Sigma x)^2}{n}}$$

y intercept of the regression line

$$b_0 = \bar{y} - b_1\bar{x} = \frac{\Sigma y}{n} - b_1\frac{(\Sigma x)}{n}$$

Sum of Squares of Error

$$SSE = \Sigma(y - \hat{y})^2 = \Sigma y^2 - b_0 \Sigma y - b_1 \Sigma xy$$

Standard error of the estimate

$$s_e = \sqrt{\frac{SSE}{n-2}}$$

Coefficient of determination

$$r^2 = 1 - \frac{SSE}{SS_{yy}} = 1 - \frac{SSE}{\Sigma y^2 - \frac{(\Sigma y)^2}{n}}$$

Computational formula for r^2

$$r^2 = \frac{b_1^2 SS_{xx}}{SS_{yy}}$$

t test of slope

$$t = \frac{b_1 - \beta_1}{s_b}$$

$$s_b = \frac{s_e}{\sqrt{SS_{xx}}}$$

Confidence interval to estimate $E(y_x)$ for a given value of x

$$\hat{y} \pm t_{\alpha/2, n-2} s_e \sqrt{\frac{1}{n} + \frac{(x_0 - \bar{x})^2}{SS_{xx}}}$$

Prediction interval to estimate y for a given value of x

$$\hat{y} \pm t_{\alpha/2, n-2} s_e \sqrt{1 + \frac{1}{n} + \frac{(x_0 - \bar{x})^2}{SS_{xx}}}$$

SUPPLEMENTARY PROBLEMS

CALCULATING THE STATISTICS

13.42 Use the following data for parts (a) through (f).

x	5	7	3	16	12	9
y	8	9	11	27	15	13

a. Determine the equation of the least squares regression line to predict y by x.
b. Using the x values, solve for the predicted values of y and the residuals.
c. Solve for s_e.
d. Solve for r^2.
e. Test the slope of the regression line. Use $\alpha = .01$.
f. Comment on the results determined in parts (b) through (e), and make a statement about the fit of the line.

13.43 Use the following data for parts (a) through (g).

x	53	47	41	50	58	62	45	60
y	5	5	7	4	10	12	3	11

a. Determine the equation of the simple regression line to predict y from x.
b. Using the x values, solve for the predicted values of y and the residuals.
c. Solve for SSE.
d. Calculate the standard error of the estimate.
e. Determine the coefficient of determination.
f. Test the slope of the regression line. Assume $\alpha = .05$. What do you conclude about the slope?
g. Comment on parts (d) and (e).

13.44 If you were to develop a regression line to predict y by x, what value would the coefficient of determination have?

x	213	196	184	202	221	247
y	76	65	62	68	71	75

13.45 Determine the equation of the least squares regression line to predict y from the following data.

x	47	94	68	73	80	49	52	61
y	14	40	34	31	36	19	20	21

a. Construct a 95% confidence interval to estimate the mean y value for $x = 60$.
b. Construct a 95% prediction interval to estimate an individual y value for $x = 70$.
c. Interpret the results obtained in parts (a) and (b).

TESTING YOUR UNDERSTANDING

13.46 A manager of a car dealership believes there is a relationship between the number of salespeople on duty and the number of cars sold. Suppose the following sample is used to develop a simple regression model to predict the number of cars sold by the number of salespeople. Solve for r^2 and explain what r^2 means in this problem.

Week	Number of Cars Sold	Number of Salespeople
1	79	6
2	64	6
3	49	4
4	23	2
5	52	3

13.47 Executives of a video rental chain want to predict the success of a potential new store. The company's researcher begins by gathering information on number of rentals and average family income from several of the chain's present outlets.

Rentals	Average Family Income ($1,000)
710	65
529	43
314	29
504	47
619	52
428	50
317	46
205	29
468	31
545	43
607	49
694	64

Develop a regression model to predict the number of rentals per day by the average family income. Comment on the output.

13.48 It seems logical that restaurant chains with more units (restaurants) would have greater sales. This assumption is mitigated, however, by several possibilities: some units may be more profitable than others, some units may be larger, some units may serve more meals, some units may serve more expensive meals, and so on. The data shown here were published by Technomic. Perform a simple regression analysis to predict a restaurant chain's sales by its number of units. How strong is the relationship?

Chain	Sales ($ billions)	Number of Units (1,000)
McDonald's	17.1	12.4
Burger King	7.9	7.5
Taco Bell	4.8	6.8
Pizza Hut	4.7	8.7
Wendy's	4.6	4.6
KFC	4.0	5.1
Subway	2.9	11.2
Dairy Queen	2.7	5.1
Hardee's	2.7	2.9

13.49 According to the National Marine Fisheries Service, the current landings in millions of pounds of fish by U.S. fleets are almost double what they were in the 1970s. In other words, fishing has not faded as an industry. However, the growth of this industry has varied by region as shown in the following data. Some regions have remained relatively constant, the South Atlantic region has dropped in pounds caught, and the Pacific-Alaska region has grown more than threefold.

Fisheries	1977	2000
New England	581	571
Mid-Atlantic	213	220
Chesapeake	668	492
South Atlantic	345	221
Gulf of Mexico	1,476	1,760
Pacific-Alaska	1,776	5,750

Develop a simple regression model to predict the 2000 landings by the 1977 landings. According to the model, if a region had 700 landings in 1977, what would the predicted number be for 2000? Construct a confidence interval for the average y value for the 700 landings. Use the t statistic to test to determine whether the slope is significantly different from zero. Use $\alpha = .05$.

13.50 People in the aerospace industry believe the cost of a space project is a function of the weight of the major object being sent into space. Use the following data to develop a regression model to predict the cost of a space project by the weight of the space object. Determine r^2 and s_e.

Weight (tons)	Cost ($ millions)
1.897	$ 53.6
3.019	184.9
0.453	6.4
0.988	23.5
1.058	33.4
2.100	110.4
2.387	104.6

13.51 The following data represent a breakdown of state banks and all savings organizations in the United States every five years over a 60-year span according to the Federal Reserve System.

Time Period	State Banks	All Savings
1	1,342	2,330
2	1,864	2,667
3	1,912	3,054
4	1,847	3,764
5	1,641	4,423
6	1,405	4,837
7	1,147	4,694
8	1,046	4,407
9	997	4,328
10	1,070	3,626
11	1,009	2,815
12	1,042	2,030
13	992	1,779

Develop a regression model to predict the total number of state banks by the number of all savings organizations. Comment on the strength of the model.

13.52 Is the amount of money spent by companies on advertising a function of the total sales of the company? Shown are sales income and advertising cost data for seven companies, published by *Advertising Age*.

Company	Advertising ($ millions)	Sales ($ billions)
Procter & Gamble	$1,703.1	37.1
Philip Morris	1,319.0	56.1
Ford Motor	973.1	153.6
PepsiCo	797.4	20.9
Time Warner	779.1	13.3
Johnson & Johnson	738.7	22.6
MCI	455.4	19.7

Use the data to develop a regression line to predict the amount of advertising by sales. Compute s_e and r^2. Assuming $\alpha = .05$, test the slope of the regression line. Comment on the strength of the regression model.

13.53 Can the consumption of water in a city be predicted by temperature? The following data represent a sample of a day's water consumption and the high temperature for that day.

Water Use (millions of gallons)	Temperature (degrees Fahrenheit)
219	103°
56	39
107	77
129	78
68	50
184	96
150	90
112	75

Develop a least squares regression line to predict the amount of water used in a day in a city by the high temperature for that day. What would be the predicted water usage for a temperature of 100°? Evaluate the regression model by calculating s_e, by calculating r^2, and by testing the slope. Let $\alpha = .01$.

INTERPRETING THE OUTPUT

13.54 Study the following MINITAB output from a regression analysis to predict y from x.

a. What is the equation of the regression model?
b. What is the meaning of the coefficient of x?
c. What is the result of the test of the slope of the regression model? Let $\alpha = .10$. Why is the t ratio negative?
d. Comment on r^2 and the standard error of the estimate.
e. Comment on the relationship of the F value to the t ratio for x.
f. The correlation coefficient for these two variables is $-.7918$. Is this result surprising to you? Why or why not?

```
Regression Analysis: Y versus X

The regression equation is
Y = 67.2 - 0.0565 X

Predictor    Coef      SE Coef      T        p
Constant     67.231    5.046        13.32    0.000
X            -0.05650  0.01027      -5.50    0.000

S = 10.32    R-Sq = 62.7%    R-Sq(adj) = 60.6%

Analysis of Variance
Source           DF    SS        MS       F       P
Regression       1     3222.9    3222.9   30.25   0.000
Residual Error   18    1918.0    106.6
Total            19    5141.0
```

13.55 Study the following Excel regression output for an analysis attempting to predict the number of union members in the United States by the size of the labor force for selected years over a 30-year period from data published by the U.S. Bureau of Labor Statistics. Analyze the computer output. Discuss the strength of the model in terms of proportion of variation accounted for, slope, and overall predictability. Using the equation of the regression line, attempt to predict the number of union members when the labor force is 100,000. Note that the model was developed with data already recoded in 1,000 units. Use the data in the model as is.

	A	B	C	D	E	F
1	SUMMARY OUTPUT					
2	Regression Statistics					
3	Multiple R	0.610				
4	R Square	0.372				
5	Adjusted R Square	0.320				
6	Standard Error	982.219				
7	Observations	14				
8						
9	ANOVA					
10		df	SS	MS	F	Significance F
11	Regression	1	6868285.79	6868286	7.12	0.0205
12	Residual	12	11577055.64	967455		
13	Total	13	18445341.43			
14						
15		Coefficients	Standard Error	t Stat	P-value	
16	Intercept	22348.97	1846.37	12.10	.000000044	
17	X Variable 1	-0.0524	0.02	-2.67	0.0205	
18						
19	RESIDUAL OUTPUT					
20	Observation	Predicted Y	Residuals			
21	1	19161.39	-1862.39			
22	2	18631.75	749.25			
23	3	18315.95	1295.05			
24	4	17602.12	2240.88			
25	5	17516.68	-176.68			
26	6	17394.71	-398.71			
27	7	17269.86	-294.86			
28	8	17144.07	-231.07			
29	9	17033.79	-31.79			
30	10	16925.13	34.87			
31	11	16902.86	-162.86			
32	12	16961.51	-393.51			
33	13	16914.23	-524.23			
34	14	16841.95	-243.95			

13.56 Study the following MINITAB residual diagnostic graphs. Comment on any possible violations of regression assumptions.

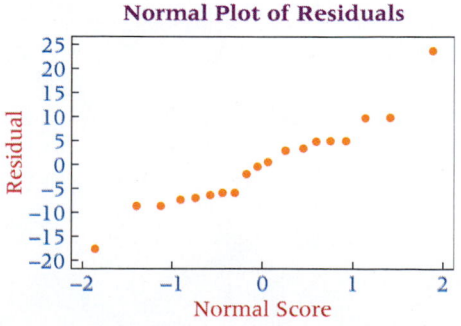

Normal Plot of Residuals

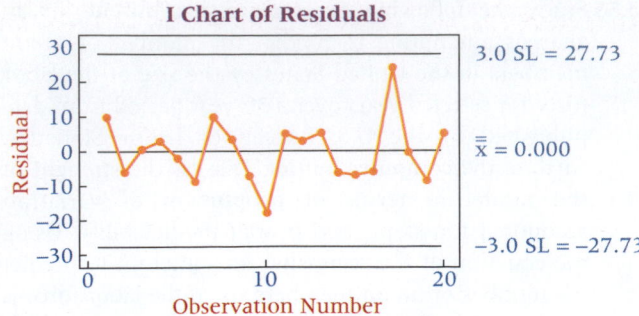

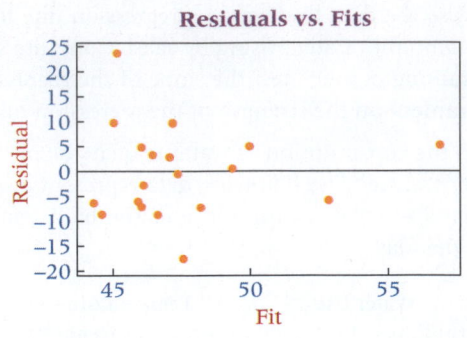

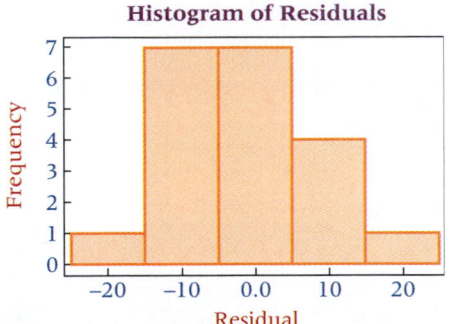

ANALYZING THE DATABASES

see www.wiley.com/college/black

1. Develop a regression model from the manufacturing database to predict New Capital Expenditures from Value Added by Manufacture. Discuss the model and its strength on the basis of indicators presented in this chapter. Does it seem logical that dollars spent on New Capital Expenditure could be predicted by Value Added by Manufacture?

2. Using the hospital database, develop a regression model to predict the number of Personnel by the number of Births. Now develop a regression model to predict number of Personnel by number of Beds. Examine the regression output. Which model is stronger in predicting number of Personnel? Explain why, using techniques presented in this chapter. Use the second regression model to predict the number of Personnel in a hospital that has 110 beds. Construct a 95%

confidence interval around this prediction for the average value of y.

3. Analyze all the variables except Type in the financial database by using a correlation matrix. The seven variables in this database are capable of producing 21 pairs of correlations. Which are most highly correlated? Select the variable that is most highly correlated with P/E ratio and use it as a predictor to develop a regression model to predict P/E ratio. How did the model do?

4. Use the stock market database to develop a regression model to predict the Utility Index by the Stock Volume. How well did the model perform? Did it perform as you expected? Why or why not? Construct a correlation matrix for the variables of this database (excluding Part of Month) so that you can explore the stock market. Did you discover any apparent relationships between variables?

CASE: DELTA WIRE USES TRAINING AS A WEAPON

The Delta Wire Corporation was founded in 1978 in Clarksdale, Mississippi. The company manufactures high-carbon specialty steel wire for global markets and at present employs about 100 people. For the past few years, sales increased each year.

A few years ago, however, things did not look as bright for Delta Wire because it was caught in a potentially disastrous bind. With the dollar declining in value, foreign competition was becoming a growing threat to Delta's market position. In addition to the growing foreign competition, industry quality requirements were becoming tougher each year.

Delta officials realized that some conditions, such as the value of the dollar, were beyond their control. However, one area that they could improve upon was employee education. The company worked with training programs developed by the state of Mississippi and a local community college to set up its own school. Delta employees were introduced to statistical process control and other quality assurance techniques. Delta reassured its customers that the company was working hard on improving quality and staying competitive. Customers were invited to sit in on the educational sessions. Because of this effort, Delta has been able to weather the storm and continues to sustain a leadership position in the highly competitive steel wire industry.

Delta continued its training and education program. In the 1990s, Delta instituted a basic skills training program that eventually led to a decrease in nonconforming material from 6 percent to 2 percent and a productivity increase from 70,000 to 90,000 pounds per week. In addition, this initiative resulted in a "best in class" award from Goodyear, its largest customer.

Discussion

1. Delta Wire prides itself on its efforts in the area of employee education. Employee education can pay off in many ways. Discuss some of them. One payoff can be the renewed interest and excitement generated toward the job and the company. Some people theorize that because of a more positive outlook and interest in implementing things learned, the more education received by a worker, the less likely he or she is to miss work days. Suppose the following data represent the number of days of sick leave taken by 20 workers last year along with the number of contact hours of employee education/training they each received in the past year. Use the techniques learned in this chapter to analyze the data. Include both regression and correlation techniques. Discuss the strength of the relationship and any models that are developed.

Employee	Hours of Education	Sick Days	Employee	Hours of Education	Sick Days
1	24	5	11	8	8
2	16	4	12	60	1
3	48	0	13	0	9
4	120	1	14	28	3
5	36	5	15	15	8
6	10	7	16	88	2
7	65	0	17	120	1
8	36	3	18	15	8
9	0	12	19	48	0
10	12	8	20	5	10

2. Many companies find that the implementation of total quality management eventually results in improved sales. Companies that fail to adopt quality efforts lose market share in many cases or go out of business. One measure of the effect of a company's quality improvement efforts is customer satisfaction. Suppose Delta Wire hired a research firm to measure customer satisfaction each year. The research firm developed a customer satisfaction scale in which totally satisfied customers can award a score as high as 50 and totally unsatisfied customers can award scores as low as 0. The scores are measured across many different industrial customers and averaged for a yearly mean customer score. Do sales increase with increases in customer satisfaction scores? To study this notion, suppose the average customer satisfaction score each year for Delta Wire is paired with the company's total sales of that year for the last 15 years, and a regression analysis is run on the data. Assume the following MINITAB and Excel outputs are the result. Suppose you were asked by Delta Wire to analyze the data and summarize the results. What would you find?

MINITAB OUTPUT

Regression Analysis: Sales versus Satisfaction

```
The regression equation is
Sales = 1.73 + 0.162 CustSat

Predictor     Coef     StDev      T       p
Constant    1.7332    0.4364    3.97    0.002
CustSat     0.16245   0.01490   10.90   0.000

S = 0.4113   R-Sq = 90.1%  R-Sq(adj) = 89.4%

Analysis of Variance

Source          DF   SS      MS      F       p
Regression       1   20.098  20.098  118.80  0.000
Residual Error  13   2.199   0.169
Total           14   22.297
```

EXCEL OUTPUT

	A	B	C	D	E	F
1	SUMMARY OUTPUT					
2	Regression Statistics					
3	Multiple R	0.949				
4	R Square	0.901				
5	Adjusted R Square	0.894				
6	Standard Error	0.411				
7	Observations	15				
8						
9	ANOVA					
10		df	SS	MS	F	Significance F
11	Regression	1	20.098	20.098	118.80	0.000
12	Residual	13	2.199	0.169		
13	Total	14	22.297			
14						
15		Coefficients	Standard Error	t Stat	P-value	
16	Intercept	1.733	0.436	3.97	0.0016	
17	CustSat	0.162	0.015	10.90	0.0000	

3. Delta Wire increased productivity from 70,000 to 90,000 pounds per week during a time when it instituted a basic skills training program. Suppose this program was implemented over an 18-month period and that the following data are the number of total cumulative basic skills hours of training and the per week productivity figures taken once a month over this time. Use techniques from this chapter to analyze the data and make a brief report to Delta about the predictability of productivity from cumulative hours of training.

Cumulative Hours of Training	Productivity (in pounds per week)
0	70,000
100	70,350
250	70,500
375	72,600
525	74,000
750	76,500
875	77,000
1,100	77,400
1,300	77,900
1,450	77,200
1,660	78,900
1,900	81,000
2,300	82,500
2,600	84,000
2,850	86,500
3,150	87,000
3,500	88,600
4,000	90,000

Source: Adapted from "Delta Wire Corporation," *Strengthening America's Competitiveness: Resource Management Insights for Small Business Success.* Published by Warner Books on behalf of Connecticut Mutual Life Insurance Company and the U.S. Chamber of Commerce in association with The Blue Chip Enterprise Initiative, 1991, International Monetary Fund; Terri Bergman, "TRAINING: The Case for Increased Investment," *Employment Relations Today,* Winter 1994–1995, pp. 381–391, available at http://www.ed.psu.edu/nwac/document/train/invest.html.

USING THE COMPUTER

EXCEL

Excel has the capability of doing simple regression analysis. For a more inclusive analysis, use the Data Analysis dialog box. Begin the procedure by selecting **Tools** on the menu bar. From the pull-down menu that appears, choose **Data Analysis.** From the **Data Analysis** dialog box select **Regression.** In the **Regression** dialog box, input the location of the y values in **Input Y Range.** Input the location of the x values in **Input X Range.** If you so desire, input **Labels** and the **Confidence Level.** If you want the line to pass through the origin, check the **Constant is Zero** slot. A variety of output features are available by checking the appropriate slot, including a printout of raw residuals (**Residuals**), residuals converted to z scores (**Standardized Residuals**), a plot of the residuals (**Residual Plots**), and a plot of the line through the points (**Line Fit Plots**). The standard output includes such features as r, r^2, s_e, and an ANOVA table with the F test for overall significance, the slope and intercept, t statistic and associated p-value, and any optional requested output such as graphs or residuals.

By using Excel's Paste function, several of the individual measures presented in this chapter can be produced. Begin the process by clicking on the Paste function key, f_x, on the standard toolbar. The Paste function dialog box will appear. Select **Statistical** from the choices on the left side. Several measures of regression can be obtained by selecting the desired measure from the right side of this dialog box. We present four here. Select the desired measure, either **INTERCEPT** (returns the intercept of the linear regression line), **RSQ** (returns the square of the Pearson product-moment correlation coefficient), **SLOPE** (returns the slope of the linear regression line), or **STEYX** (returns the standard error of the predicted y value for each x in the regression). For each of these measures, a dialog box appears. Input the location of the range of data points for each of x and y. The output is the numerical value of the measure.

MINITAB WINDOWS

MINITAB Windows has a relatively thorough capability to perform regression analysis. Begin by selecting **Stat** on the menu bar and producing the **Stat** pull-down menu.

To perform a regression analysis, select **Regression** from the pull-down menu. A second pull-down menu will appear. Select **Regression** from this menu. A regression dialog box will appear. In the **Response** slot, place the location of the y variable. In the **Predictors** slot, place the location of the x variable.

Four buttons in the dialog box can be used to alter output. The **Graphs** button yields a dialog box with several options for residual plots. The **Options** button allows you to select confidence intervals and prediction intervals for particular values of x. The **Results** button allows you to control the regression display, including such things as unusual observations and residuals along with typical regression output. The **Storage** button allows you to store such things as fits and/or residuals for use in other analyses. The standard output for the **Regression** feature includes the regression equation, the t and F statistics and their associated p-values, an ANOVA table, standard error of the estimate, and the coefficient of determination.

The rather extensive residual diagnosis displayed in this chapter can be obtained through MINITAB. Some preliminary setup is necessary. In performing the initial regression analysis, select the **Storage** button in the **Regression** dialog box. In the **Storage** dialog box, check **Fits** and **Residuals** and click OK. When you run the regression analysis, two columns of additional data will be computed and placed into your worksheet: the regression line fits and the residuals. Now, go back to the menu bar and select **Stat;** from the pull-down menu that appears, select **Regression.** From the **Regression** pull-down menu, select **Residual Plots.** In the Residuals slot, place the column location containing the residuals that were just produced (the column with the residuals may be titled RESI1). In the Fits slot, place the column location containing the regression fits that were just produced (the column with the fits may be titled FITS1). Placing a title on the graph is optional. Click OK to get the residual diagnosis output with the four graphs.

To obtain a fitted line plot for the regression analysis, select **Stat** on the menu bar. From the pull-down menu that appears, select **Regression.** From the next pull-down menu that appears, select **Fitted Line Plot.** A dialog box will appear. Place the column location of the y values in the first slot and the location of the x values in the second slot. Select either the **Linear, Quadratic,** or **Cubic** model. (This chapter examined only linear models.) To display confidence bands and/or prediction bands (as discussed in section 13.7), select **Options.** From the **Options** dialog box, check **Display confidence bands** and/or **Display prediction bands.** MINITAB will default to 95% confidence. For other levels of confidence, place the level desired in the slot labeled **Confidence level.** Placing a title on the graph is optional. The output is a scatter plot of the ordered pairs of points along with a regression line fit through the data. If the confidence bands and/or prediction bands are selected as an option, they will appear in the graph also.

CHAPTER 14

Multiple Regression Analysis

LEARNING OBJECTIVES

This chapter presents the potential of multiple regression analysis as a tool in business decision making and its applications, thereby enabling you to:

1. Develop a multiple regression model.

2. Understand and apply significance tests of the regression model and its coefficients.

3. Compute and interpret residuals, the standard error of the estimate, and the coefficient of multiple determination.

4. Interpret multiple regression computer output.

Are You Going to Hate Your New Job?

Getting a new job can be an exciting and energizing event in your life.

But what if you discover after a short time on the job that you hate your job? Is there any way to determine ahead of time whether you will love or hate your job? Sue Shellenbarger of *The Wall Street Journal* discusses some of the things to look for when interviewing for a position that may provide clues as to whether you will be happy on that job.

Among other things, work cultures vary from hip, freewheeling start-ups to old-school organizational-driven domains. Some organizations place pressure on workers to feel tense and to work long hours while others place more emphasis on creativity and the bottom line. Shellenbarger suggests that job interviewees pay close attention to how they are treated in an interview. Are they just another cog in the wheel or are they valued as an individual? Is a work-life balance apparent within the company? Ask what a typical workday is like at that firm. Inquire about the values that undergird the management by asking questions such as "What is your proudest accomplishment?" Ask about flexible schedules and how job training is managed. For example, does the worker have to go to job training on their own time?

A "Work Trends" survey undertaking by the John J. Heldrich Center for Workforce Development at Rutgers University and the Center for Survey Research and Analysis at the University of Connecticut posed several questions to employees in a survey to ascertain their job satisfaction. Some of the themes included in these questions were relationship with your supervisor, overall quality of the work environment, total hours worked each week, and opportunities for advancement at the job.

Suppose another researcher gathered survey data from 19 employees on these questions and also asked the employees to rate their job satisfaction on a scale from 0 to 100 (with 100 being perfectly satisfied). Suppose the following data represent the results of this survey. Assume that relationship with supervisor is rated on a scale from 1 to 5 (1 represents poor relationship and 5 represents an excellent relationship), overall quality of the work environment is rated on a scale from 0 to 10 (0 represents poor work environment and 10 represents an excellent work environment), and opportunities for advancement is rated on a scale from 1 to 5 (1 represents no opportunities and 5 represents excellent opportunities).

Job Satisfaction	Relationship with Supervisor	Overall Quality of Work Environment	Total Hours Worked per Week	Opportunities for Advancement
55	3	6	55	4
20	1	1	60	3
85	4	8	45	1
65	4	5	65	5
45	3	4	40	3
70	4	6	50	4
35	2	2	75	2
60	4	7	40	3
95	5	8	45	5
65	3	7	60	1
85	3	7	55	3
10	1	1	50	2
75	4	6	45	4
80	4	8	40	5
50	3	5	60	5
90	5	10	55	3
75	3	8	70	4
45	2	4	40	2
65	3	7	55	1

Managerial and Statistical Questions

1. Several variables are presented that may be related to job satisfaction. Which variables are stronger predictors of job satisfaction? Might other variables not mentioned here be related to job satisfaction?

2. Is it possible to develop a mathematical model to predict job satisfaction using the data given? If so, how strong is the model? With four independent variables, will we need to develop four different simple regression models and compare their results?

Source: Adapted from Sue Shellenbarger, "How to Find Out If You're Going to Hate a New Job Before You Agree to Take It," *The Wall Street Journal*, 13 June 2002, p. D1.

Simple regression analysis (discussed in Chapter 13) is bivariate linear regression in which one **dependent variable,** *y,* is predicted by one **independent variable,** *x.* Examples of simple regression applications include models to predict retail sales by population density, Dow Jones averages by prime interest rates, crude oil production by energy consumption, and CEO compensation by quarterly sales. However, in many cases, other independent variables, taken in conjunction with these variables, can make the regression model a better fit in predicting the dependent variable. For example, sales could be predicted by the size of store and number of competitors in addition to population density. A model to predict the Dow Jones average of 30 industrials could include, in addition to the prime interest rate, such predictors as yesterday's volume, the bond interest rate, and the producer price index. A model to predict CEO compensation could be developed by using variables such as company earnings per share, age of CEO, and size of company in addition to quarterly sales. A model could perhaps be developed to predict the cost of outsourcing by such variables as unit price, export taxes, cost of money, damage in transit, and other factors. Each of these examples contains only one dependent variable, *y,* as with simple regression analysis. However, multiple independent variables, *x* (predictors) are involved. *Regression analysis with two or more independent variables or with at least one nonlinear predictor* is called **multiple regression** analysis.

14.1 THE MULTIPLE REGRESSION MODEL

Multiple regression analysis is similar in principle to simple regression analysis. However, it is more complex conceptually and computationally. Recall from Chapter 13 that the equation of the probabilistic simple regression model is

$$y = \beta_0 + \beta_1 x + \epsilon$$

where

y = the value of the dependent variable
β_0 = the population y intercept
β_1 = the population slope
ϵ = the error of prediction

Extending this notion to multiple regression gives the general equation for the probabilistic multiple regression model.

$$y = \beta_0 + \beta_1 x_1 + \beta_2 x_2 + \beta_3 x_3 + \ldots + \beta_k x_k + \epsilon$$

where

y = the value of the dependent variable
β_0 = the regression constant
β_1 = the partial regression coefficient for independent variable 1
β_2 = the partial regression coefficient for independent variable 2
β_3 = the partial regression coefficient for independent variable 3
β_k = the partial regression coefficient for independent variable k
k = the number of independent variables

In multiple regression analysis, the dependent variable, y, is sometimes referred to as the **response variable.** The **partial regression coefficient** of an independent variable, β_i, *represents the increase that will occur in the value of y from a 1-unit increase in that independent variable if all other variables are held constant.* The "full" (versus partial) regression coefficient of an independent variable is a coefficient obtained from the bivariate model (simple regression) in which the independent variable is the sole predictor of y. The partial regression coefficients occur because more than one predictor is included in a model. The partial regression coefficients are analogous to β_1, the slope of the simple regression model in Chapter 13.

In actuality, the partial regression coefficients and the regression constant of a multiple regression model are population values and are unknown. In virtually all research, these values are estimated by using sample information. Shown here is the form of the equation for estimating y with sample information.

$$\hat{y} = b_o + b_1x_1 + b_2x_2 + b_3x_3 + \ldots + b_kx_k$$

where

$\hat{y}$ = the predicted value of y
β_0 = the estimate of the regression constant
β_1 = the estimate of regression coefficient 1
β_2 = the estimate of regression coefficient 2
β_3 = the estimate of regression coefficient 3
β_k = the estimate of regression coefficient k
k = the number of independent variables

Multiple Regression Model with Two Independent Variables (First-Order)

The simplest multiple regression model is one constructed with two independent variables, where the highest power of either variable is 1 (first-order regression model). The regression model is

$$y = \beta_0 + \beta_1x_1 + \beta_2x_2 + \in$$

The constant and coefficients are estimated from sample information, resulting in the following model.

$$\hat{y} = b_o + b_1x_1 + b_2x_2$$

Figure 14.1 is a three-dimensional graph of a series of points (x_1, x_2, y) representing values from three variables used in a multiple regression model to predict the sales price of a house by the number of square feet in the house and the age of the house. Simple regression models yield a line that is fit through data points in the xy plane. In multiple regression analysis, the resulting model produces a **response surface.** In the multiple regression model shown here with two independent first-order variables, the response surface is a **response plane.** The response plane for such a model is fit in a three-dimensional space (x_1, x_2, y).

If such a response plane is fit into the points shown in Figure 14.1, the result is the graph in Figure 14.2. Notice that most of the points are not on the plane. As in simple regression, an error in the fit of the model in multiple regression is usually present. The distances shown in the graph from the points to the response plane are the errors of fit, or residuals $(y - \hat{y})$. Multiple regression models with three or more independent variables involve more than three dimensions and are difficult to depict geometrically.

Observe in Figure 14.2 that the regression model attempts to fit a plane into the three-dimensional plot of points. Notice that the plane intercepts the y axis. Figure 14.2 depicts some values of y for various values of x_1 and x_2. The error of the response plane ($\in$) in predicting or determining the y values is the distance from the points to the plane.

FIGURE 14.1

Points in a Sample Space

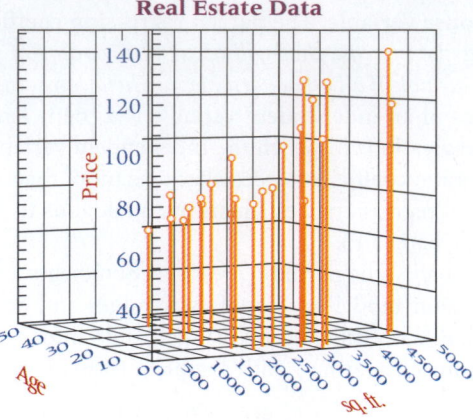

FIGURE 14.2

Response Plane for a First-Order Two-Predictor Multiple Regression Model

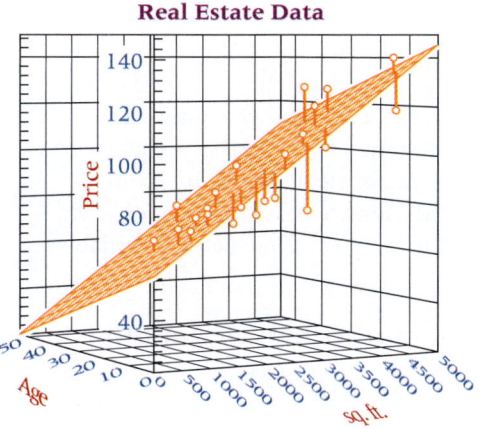

Determining the Multiple Regression Equation

The simple regression equations for determining the sample slope and intercept given in Chapter 13 are the result of using methods of calculus to minimize the sum of squares of error for the regression model. The procedure for developing these equations involves solving two simultaneous equations with two unknowns, b_0 and b_1. Finding the sample slope and intercept from these formulas requires the values of Σx, Σy, Σxy, and Σx^2.

The procedure for determining formulas to solve for multiple regression coefficients is similar. The formulas are established to meet an objective of *minimizing the sum of squares of error for the model.* Hence, the regression analysis shown here is referred to as **least squares analysis.** Methods of calculus are applied, resulting in $k + 1$ equations with $k + 1$ unknowns (b_0 and k values of b_i) for multiple regression analyses with k independent variables. Thus, a regression model with six independent variables will generate seven simultaneous equations with seven unknowns (b_0, b_1, b_2, b_3, b_4, b_5, b_6).

For multiple regression models with two independent variables, the result is three simultaneous equations with three unknowns (b_0, b_1, and b_2).

$$b_0 n + b_1 \Sigma x_1 + b_2 \Sigma x_2 = \Sigma y$$
$$b_0 \Sigma x_1 + b_1 \Sigma x_1^2 + b_2 \Sigma x_1 x_2 = \Sigma x_1 y$$
$$b_0 \Sigma x_2 + b_1 \Sigma x_1 x_2 + b_2 \Sigma x_2^2 = \Sigma x_2 y$$

The process of solving these equations by hand is tedious and time-consuming. Solving for the regression coefficients and regression constant in a multiple regression model with two independent variables requires Σx_1, Σx_2, Σy, Σx_1^2, Σx_2^2, $\Sigma x_1 x_2$, $\Sigma x_1 y$, and $\Sigma x_2 y$. In actuality, virtually all business researchers use computer statistical software packages to solve for the regression coefficients, the regression constant, and other pertinent information. In this chapter, we will discuss computer output and assume little or no hand calculation. The emphasis will be on the interpretation of the computer output.

A Multiple Regression Model

A real estate study was conducted in a small Louisiana city to determine what variables, if any, are related to the market price of a home. Several variables were explored, including the number of bedrooms, the number of bathrooms, the age of the house, the number of square feet of living space, the total number of square feet of space, and the number of garages. Suppose the researcher wants to develop a regression model to predict the market price of a home by two variables, "total number of square feet in the house" and "the age of the house." Listed in Table 14.1 are the data for these three variables.

A number of statistical software packages can perform multiple regression analysis, including Excel and MINITAB. The output for the MINITAB multiple regression analysis on the real estate data is given in Figure 14.3. (Excel output is shown in Demonstration Problem 14.1.)

The MINITAB output for regression analysis begins with "The regression equation is." From Figure 14.3, the regression equation for the real estate data in Table 14.1 is

$$\hat{y} = 57.4 + .0177x_1 - .666x_2$$

The regression constant, 57.4, is the y intercept. The y intercept is the value of $\hat{y}$ if both x_1 (number of square feet) and x_2 (age) are zero. In this example, a practical understanding of the y intercept is meaningless. It makes little sense to say that a house containing no square feet ($x_1 = 0$) and no years of age ($x_2 = 0$) would cost \$57,400. Note in Figure 14.2 that the response plane crosses the y (price) axis at 57.4.

The coefficient of x_1 (total number of square feet in the house) is .0177, which means that a 1-unit increase in square footage would result in a predicted increase of .0177 · (\$1,000) = \$17.70 in the price of the home if age were held constant. All other variables being held constant, the addition of 1 square foot of space in the house results in a predicted increase of \$17.70 in the price of the home.

TABLE 14.1

Real Estate Data

Market Price ($1,000)	Total Number of Square Feet	Age of House (Years)
y	x_1	x_2
63.0	1605	35
65.1	2489	45
69.9	1553	20
76.8	2404	32
73.9	1884	25
77.9	1558	14
74.9	1748	8
78.0	3105	10
79.0	1682	28
83.4	2470	30
79.5	1820	2
83.9	2143	6
79.7	2121	14
84.5	2485	9
96.0	2300	19
109.5	2714	4
102.5	2463	5
121.0	3076	7
104.9	3048	3
128.0	3267	6
129.0	3069	10
117.9	4765	11
140.0	4540	8

FIGURE 14.3

MINITAB Output of Regression for the Real Estate Example

Regression Analysis: Price versus Square Feet, Age

```
The regression equation is
Price = 57.4 + 0.0177 Square Feet - 0.666 Age
Predictor            Coef       SE Coef        T        P
Constant            57.35         10.01     5.73    0.000
Square Feet      0.017718      0.003146     5.63    0.000
Age               -0.6663        0.2280    -2.92    0.008
S = 11.96     R-Sq = 74.1%      R-Sq(adj) = 71.5%

Analysis of Variance

Source          DF        SS        MS        F        P
Regression       2    8189.7    4094.9    28.63    0.000
Error           20    2861.0     143.1
Total           22   11050.7
```

The coefficient of x_2 (age) is $-.666$. The negative sign on the coefficient denotes an inverse relationship between the age of a house and the price of the house: the older the house, the lower the price. In this case, if the total number of square feet in the house is kept constant, a 1-unit increase in the age of the house (1 year) will result in $-.666 \cdot (\$1000) = -\$666$, a predicted \$666 drop in the price.

In examining the regression coefficients, it is important to remember that the independent variables are often measured in different units. It is usually not wise to compare the regression coefficients of predictors in a multiple regression model and decide that the variable with the largest regression coefficient is the best predictor. In this example, the two variables are in different units, square feet and years. Just because x_2 has the larger coefficient (.666) does not necessarily make x_2 the strongest predictor of y.

Some statistical software packages do not specifically print as output "The regression equation is," but rather produce a table, as shown here.

Predictor	Coef
Constant	57.35
Square Feet	0.017718
Age	−0.6663

The table is also part of MINITAB regression output. In this case, Coef means regression coefficient and the value given beside Constant is the regression constant value. Hence, the regression equation given previously for the data from Table 14.1 can also be gleaned from the output shown here. Note that the columns in MINITAB were named for the variables of interest and that MINITAB prints out values with more precision in the table than in the regression equation model shown previously. The remaining portion of this computer output will be discussed in Section 14.2.

This regression model can be used to predict the price of a house in this small Louisiana city. If the house has 2,500 square feet total and is 12 years old, $x_1 = 2,500$ and $x_2 = 12$. Substituting these values into the regression model yields

$$\hat{y} = 57.4 + .0177x_1 - .666x_2$$
$$= 57.4 + .0177(2,500) - .666(12) = 93.658$$

The predicted price of the house is \$93,658. Figure 14.2 is a graph of these data with the response plane and the residual distances.

DEMONSTRATION PROBLEM 14.1*

Much of the freight cargo in the world is transported over roads. The volume of freight cargo shipped over roads varies from country to country depending on the size of the country, the amount of commerce, the wealth of the country, and other

---

* *Source*: World Data; World Road Statistics; George Thomas Kurian, *The Illustrated Book of World Rankings* (Armonk, NY: M.E. Sharpe, Inc., 1997).

factors. Shown here are seven of the top 10 countries in which freight cargo is shipped over roads, along with the number of miles of roads and the number of commercial vehicles (trucks and buses) for each country. Use these data to develop a multiple regression model to predict the volume of freight cargo shipped over roads by the length of roads and the number of commercial vehicles. Determine the predicted volume of freight cargo over roads if the length of roads is 600,000 miles and the number of commercial vehicles is 3 million.

Country	Freight Cargo Shipped by Road (millions of short-ton miles)	Length of Roads (miles)	Number of Commercial Vehicles
China	278,806	673,239	5,010,000
Brazil	178,359	1,031,693	1,371,127
India	144,000	1,342,000	1,980,000
Germany	138,975	395,367	2,923,000
Italy	125,171	188,597	2,745,500
Spain	105,824	206,271	2,859,438
Mexico	96,049	157,036	3,758,034

Solution

The following output shows the results of analyzing the data by using the regression portion of Excel.

	A	B	C	D	E	F
	Summary Output					
	Regression Statistics					
1	Multiple R	0.812				
2	R Square	0.659				
3	Adjusted R Square	0.488				
4	Standard Error	44273.86677				
5	Observations	7				
6						
7	ANOVA					
8		df	SS	MS	F	Significance F
9	Regression	2	15148592381	7574296191	3.86	0.116
10	Residual	4	784070114	1960175278		
11	Total	6	22989293495			
12						
13		Coefficients	Standard Error	t Stat	P-value	
14	Intercept	−26425.45085	67624.938	-0.39	0.716	
15	Length	0.101820862	0.0435	2.34	0.079	
16	Vehicles	0.04094856	0.0171	2.39	0.075	

The regression equation is

$$\hat{y} = -26{,}425.45 + .1018x_1 + .0410x_2$$

where

$\hat{y}$ = volume of freight cargo shipped
x_1 = length of roads
x_2 = number of commercial vehicles

The model indicates that for every 1-unit (1 mile) increase in length of roads, the predicted volume of freight cargo shipped increases by .1018 million short-ton miles, or 101,800 short-ton miles, if the number of commercial vehicles is held constant. If the number of commercial vehicles is increased by 1 unit, the predicted volume of freight cargo shipped increases by .0410 million short-ton miles, or 41,000 short-ton miles, if the length of roads is held constant.

If x_1 (length of roads) is 600,000 and x_2 (number of commercial vehicles) is 3 million, the model predicts that the volume of freight cargo shipped will be 157,655 million short-ton miles:

$$\hat{y} = 26{,}425.45 + .1018(600{,}000) + .0410(3{,}000{,}000) = 157{,}655$$

14.1 PROBLEMS

14.1 Use a computer to develop the equation of the regression model for the following data. Comment on the regression coefficients. Determine the predicted value of y for $x_1 = 200$ and $x_2 = 7$.

y	x_1	x_2
12	174	3
18	281	9
31	189	4
28	202	8
52	149	9
47	188	12
38	215	5
22	150	11
36	167	8
17	135	5

14.2 Use a computer to develop the equation of the regression model for the following data. Comment on the regression coefficients. Determine the predicted value of y for $x_1 = 33$, $x_2 = 29$, and $x_3 = 13$.

y	x_1	x_2	x_3
114	21	6	5
94	43	25	8
87	56	42	25
98	19	27	9
101	29	20	12
85	34	45	21
94	40	33	14
107	32	14	11
119	16	4	7
93	18	31	16
108	27	12	10
117	31	3	8

14.3 Using the following data, determine the equation of the regression model. How many independent variables are there? Comment on the meaning of these regression coefficients.

Predictor	Coefficient
Constant	121.62
x_1	−.174
x_2	6.02
x_3	.00026
x_4	.0041

14.4 Use the following data to determine the equation of the multiple regression model. Comment on the regression coefficients.

Predictor	Coefficient
Constant	31,409.5
x_1	.08425
x_2	289.62
x_3	−.0947

14.5 Is there a particular product that is an indicator of per capita consumption around the world? Shown here are data on per capita consumption, paper consumption, fish consumption, and gasoline consumption for nine countries. Use the data to determine the equation of the multiple regression model to predict per capita consumption by paper consumption, fish consumption, and gasoline consumption. Discuss the impact of increasing paper consumption by 1 unit on the predicted per capita consumption. Discuss the impact of a 1-unit increase in fish consumption on the predicted per capita consumption and the impact of a 1-unit increase in gasoline consumption on the predicted per capita consumption.

Country	Per Capita Consumption	Paper Consumption (kg per 1,000 people)	Fish Consumption (pounds)	Gasoline Consumption (1,000 barrels per day)
Japan	$19,700	76,892	158.7	5,454
Portugal	5,570	24,126	132.7	277
United States	16,500	84,579	47.0	17,033
Venezuela	2,090	6,860	31.1	430
Greece	4,490	15,641	42.1	331
Italy	10,790	43,098	44.3	1,936
Norway	13,400	41,575	90.6	183
United Kingdom	9,040	52,335	43.9	1,803
Philippines	640	940	76.3	235

Sources: World Development Report; Pulp & Paper Industry; *Fishery Statistic Yearbook; Energy Statistics Yearbook;* George Thomas Kurian, *The Illustrated Book of World Rankings* (Armonk, NY: M. E. Sharpe, Inc., 1997).

14.6 Jensen, Solberg, and Zorn investigated the relationship of insider ownership, debt, and dividend policies in companies. One of their findings was that firms with high insider ownership choose lower levels of both debt and dividends. Shown here is a sample of data of these three variables for 11 different industries. Use the data to develop the equation of the regression model to predict insider ownership by debt ratio and dividend payout. Comment on the regression coefficients.

Industry	Insider Ownership	Debt Ratio	Dividend Payout
Mining	8.2	14.2	10.4
Food and beverage	18.4	20.8	14.3
Furniture	11.8	18.6	12.1
Publishing	28.0	18.5	11.8
Petroleum refining	7.4	28.2	10.6
Glass and cement	15.4	24.7	12.6
Motor vehicle	15.7	15.6	12.6
Department store	18.4	21.7	7.2
Restaurant	13.4	23.0	11.3
Amusement	18.1	46.7	4.1
Hospital	10.0	35.8	9.0

Source: R. Gerald Jensen, Donald P. Solberg, and Thomas S. Zorn, "Simultaneous Determination of Insider Ownership, Debt, and Dividend Policies," *Journal of Financial and Quantitative Analysis,* vol. 27, no. 2 (June 1992).

14.2 SIGNIFICANCE TESTS OF THE REGRESSION MODEL AND ITS COEFFICIENTS

Multiple regression models can be developed to fit almost any data set if the level of measurement is adequate and enough data points are available. Once a model has been constructed, it is important to test the model to determine whether it fits the data well and whether the assumptions underlying regression analysis are met. Assessing the adequacy of the regression model can be done in several ways, including testing the overall significance of the model, studying the significance tests of the regression coefficients, computing the residuals, examining the standard error of the estimate, and observing the coefficient of determination. In this section, we examine significance tests of the regression model and of its coefficients.

Testing the Overall Model

With simple regression, a t test of the slope of the regression line is used to determine whether the population slope of the regression line is different from zero—that is, whether the independent variable contributes significantly in linearly predicting the dependent variable. The hypotheses for this test, presented in Chapter 13, are

$$H_0: \beta_1 = 0$$
$$H_a: \beta_1 \neq 0$$

For multiple regression, an analogous test makes use of the F statistic. The overall significance of the multiple regression model is tested with the following hypotheses.

$$H_0: \beta_1 = \beta_2 = \beta_3 = \ldots = \beta_k = 0$$
$$H_a: \text{At least one of the regression coefficients is} \neq 0.$$

If we fail to reject the null hypothesis, we are stating that the regression model has no significant predictability for the dependent variable. A rejection of the null hypothesis indicates that at least one of the independent variables is adding significant predictability for y.

This F test of overall significance is often printed as a part of the standard multiple regression output from statistical software packages. The output appears as an analysis of variance (ANOVA) table. Shown here is the ANOVA table for the real estate example taken from the MINITAB output in Figure 14.3.

Analysis of Variance

Source	DF	SS	MS	F	P
Regression	2	8189.7	4094.9	28.63	0.000
Residual Error	20	2861.0	143.1		
Total	22	11050.7			

The F value is 28.63; because $p = .000$, the F value is significant at $\alpha = .001$. The null hypothesis is rejected, and there is at least one significant predictor of house price in this analysis.

The F value is calculated by the following equation.

$$F = \frac{MS_{reg}}{MS_{err}} = \frac{SS_{reg} / df_{reg}}{SS_{err} / df_{err}} = \frac{SSR / k}{SSE / N - k - 1}$$

where

$$
\begin{aligned}
MS &= \text{mean square} \\
SS &= \text{sum of squares} \\
df &= \text{degrees of freedom} \\
k &= \text{number of independent variables} \\
N &= \text{number of observations}
\end{aligned}
$$

Note that in the ANOVA table for the real estate example, $df_{reg} = 2$. The degrees of freedom formula for regression is the number of regression coefficients plus the regression constant minus 1. The net result is the number of regression coefficients, which equals the number of independent variables, k. The real estate example uses two independent variables, so $k = 2$. Degrees of freedom error in multiple regression equals the total number of observations minus the number of regression coefficients minus the regression constant, or $N - k - 1$. For the real estate example, $N = 23$; thus, $df_{err} = 23 - 2 - 1 = 20$.

As shown in Chapter 11, $MS = SS/df$. The F ratio is formed by dividing MS_{reg} by MS_{err}. In using the F distribution table to determine a critical value against which to test the observed F value, the degrees of freedom numerator is df_{reg} and the degrees of freedom denominator is df_{err}. The table F value is obtained in the usual manner, as presented in Chapter 11. With $\alpha = .01$ for the real estate example, the table value is

$$F_{.01,2,20} = 5.85$$

Comparing the observed F of 28.63 to this table value shows that the decision is to reject the null hypothesis. This same conclusion was reached using the p-value method from the computer output.

If a regression model has only one linear independent variable, it is a simple regression model. In that case, the F test for the overall model is the same as the t test for significance of the population slope. The F value displayed in the regression ANOVA table is related to the t test for the slope in the simple regression case as follows.

$$F = t^2$$

In simple regression, the F value and the t value give redundant information about the overall test of the model.

Most researchers who use multiple regression analysis will observe the value of F and its p-value rather early in the process. If F is not significant, then no population regression coefficient is significantly different from zero, and the regression model has no predictability for the dependent variable.

Significance Tests of the Regression Coefficients

In multiple regression, individual significance tests can be computed for each regression coefficient using a t test. Each of these t tests is analogous to the t test for the slope used in Chapter 13 for simple regression analysis. The hypotheses for testing the regression coefficient of each independent variable take the following form:

$$H_0: \beta_1 = 0$$
$$H_a: \beta_1 \neq 0$$
$$H_0: \beta_2 = 0$$
$$H_a: \beta_2 \neq 0$$
$$\vdots$$
$$H_0: \beta_k = 0$$
$$H_a: \beta_k \neq 0$$

Most multiple regression computer packages yield observed t values to test the individual regression coefficients as standard output. Shown here are the t values and their associated probabilities for the real estate example as displayed with the multiple regression output in Figure 14.3.

Variable	T	p
Square feet	5.63	.000
Age	−2.92	.008

At $\alpha = .05$, the null hypothesis is rejected for both variables because the probabilities (p) associated with their t values are less than .05. If the t ratios for any predictor variables are not significant (fail to reject the null hypothesis), the researcher might decide to drop that variable(s) from the analysis as a nonsignificant predictor(s). Other factors can enter into this decision. In Chapter 15, we will explore techniques for model building in which some variable sorting is required.

The degrees of freedom for each of these individual tests of regression coefficients are $n - k - 1$. In this particular example because there are $k = 2$ predictor variables, the degrees of freedom are $23 - 2 - 1 = 20$. With $\alpha = .05$ and a two-tailed test, the critical table t value is

$$t_{.025,20} = \pm 2.086$$

Notice from the t ratios shown here that if this critical table t value had been used as the hypothesis test criterion instead of the p-value method, the results would have been the same. Testing the regression coefficients not only gives the researcher some insight into the fit of the regression model, but it also helps in the evaluation of how worthwhile individual independent variables are in predicting y.

14.2 PROBLEMS

14.7   Examine the MINITAB output shown here for a multiple regression analysis. How many predictors were there in this model? Comment on the overall significance of the regression model. Discuss the t ratios of the variables and their significance.

```
The regression equation is
```

$$Y = 4.096 - 5.111\ X_1 + 2.662\ X_2 + 1.557\ X_3 + 1.141\ X_4 + 1.650$$
$$X_5 - 1.248\ X_6 + 0.436\ X_7 + 0.962\ X_8 + 1.289\ X_9$$

Predictor	Coef	Stdev	T	p
Constant	4.096	1.2884	3.24	.006
X_1	-5.111	1.8700	2.73	.011
X_2	2.662	2.0796	1.28	.212
X_3	1.557	1.2811	1.22	.235
X_4	1.141	1.4712	0.78	.445
X_5	1.650	1.4994	1.10	.281
X_6	-1.248	1.2735	0.98	.336
X_7	0.436	0.3617	1.21	.239
X_8	0.962	1.1896	0.81	.426
X_9	1.289	1.9182	0.67	.508

```
S = 3.503 R-sq = 40.8%R-sq(adj.) = 20.3%
```

```
Analysis of Variance
```

Source	DF	SS	MS	F	p
Regression	9	219.746	24.416	1.99	.0825
Error	26	319.004	12.269		
Total	35	538.750			

14.8   Displayed here is the MINITAB output for a multiple regression analysis. Study the ANOVA table and the t ratios and use these to discuss the strengths of the regression model and the predictors. Does this model appear to fit the data well? From the information here, what recommendations would you make about the predictor variables in the model?

```
The regression equation is
```

$$Y = 34.7 + 0.0763\ X_1 + 0.00026\ X_2 - 1.12\ X_3$$

Predictor	Coef	Stdev	T	p
Constant	34.672	5.256	6.60	.000
X_1	0.07629	0.02234	3.41	.005
X_2	0.000259	0.001031	0.25	.805
X_3	-1.1212	0.9955	-1.13	.230

```
S = 9.722   R-sq = 51.5%   R-sq(adj) = 40.4%
```

Analysis of Variance

Source	DF	SS	MS	F	p
Regression	3	1306.99	435.66	4.61	.021
Error	13	1228.78	94.52		
Total	16	2535.77			

14.9 Using the data in Problem 14.5, develop a multiple regression model to predict per capita consumption by the consumption of paper, fish, and gasoline. Discuss the output and pay particular attention to the F test and the t tests.

14.10 Using the data from Problem 14.6, develop a multiple regression model to predict insider ownership from debt ratio and dividend payout. Comment on the strength of the model and the predictors by examining the ANOVA table and the t tests.

14.11 Develop a multiple regression model to predict y from x_1, x_2, and x_3 using the following data. Discuss the values of F and t.

y	x_1	x_2	x_3
5.3	44	11	401
3.6	24	40	219
5.1	46	13	394
4.9	38	18	362
7.0	61	3	453
6.4	58	5	468
5.2	47	14	386
4.6	36	24	357
2.9	19	52	206
4.0	31	29	301
3.8	24	37	243
3.8	27	36	228
4.8	36	21	342
5.4	50	11	421
5.8	55	9	445

14.12 Use the following data to develop a regression model to predict y from x_1 and x_2. Comment on the output. Develop a regression model to predict y from x_1 only. Compare the results of this model with those of the model using both predictors. What might you conclude by examining the output from both regression models?

y	x_1	x_2
28	12.6	134
43	11.4	126
45	11.5	143
49	11.1	152
57	10.4	143
68	9.6	147
74	9.8	128
81	8.4	119
82	8.8	130
86	8.9	135
101	8.1	141
112	7.6	123
114	7.8	121
119	7.4	129
124	6.4	135

14.13 Study the following Excel multiple regression output. How many predictors are in this model? How many observations? What is the equation of the regression line? Discuss the strength of the model in terms F. Which predictors, if any, are significant? Why or why not? Comment on the overall effectiveness of the model.

	A	B	C	D	E	F
1	Summary Output					
2	Regression Statistics					
3	Multiple R	0.842				
4	R Square	0.710				
5	Adjusted R Square	0.630				
6	Standard Error	109.430				
7	Observations	15				
8						
9	ANOVA					
10		df	SS	MS	F	Significance F
11	Regression	3	321946.82	107315.6	8.96	0.0027
12	Residual	11	131723.20	11974.8		
13	Total	14	453670			
14						
15		Coefficents	Standard Error	t Stat	P-value	
16	Intercept	657.053	167.460	3.92	.0024	
17	X Variable 1	5.7103	1.792	3.19	.0087	
18	X Variable 2	-0.4169	0.322	-1.29	.2222	
19	X Variable 3	-3.4715	1.443	-2.41	.0349	

14.3 RESIDUALS, STANDARD ERROR OF THE ESTIMATE, AND R^2

Three more statistical tools for examining the strength of a regression model are the residuals, the standard error of the estimate, and the coefficient of multiple determination.

Residuals

The **residual**, or error, of the regression model is *the difference between the y value and the predicted value, $\hat{y}$.*

$$\text{Residual} = y - \hat{y}$$

The residuals for a multiple regression model are solved for in the same manner as they are with simple regression. First, a predicted value, $\hat{y}$, is determined by entering the value for each independent variable for a given set of observations into the multiple regression equation and solving for $\hat{y}$. Next, the value of $y - \hat{y}$ is computed for each set of observations. Shown here are the calculations for the residuals of the first set of observations from Table 14.1. The predicted value of y for $x_1 = 1605$ and $x_2 = 35$ is

$$\hat{y} = 57.4 + .0177(1605) - .666(35) = 62.50$$

Actual value of y = 63.0
Residual = $y - \hat{y}$ = 63.0 − 62.50 = 0.50

All residuals for the real estate data and the regression model displayed in Table 14.1 and Figure 14.3 are displayed in Table 14.2.

An examination of the residuals in Table 14.2 can reveal some information about the fit of the real estate regression model. The business researcher can observe the residuals and decide whether the errors are small enough to support the accuracy of the model. The house price figures are in units of $1,000. Two of the 23 residuals are more than 20.00, or more than $20,000 off in their prediction. On the other hand, two residuals are less than 1, or $1,000 off in their prediction.

Residuals are also helpful in locating outliers. **Outliers** are *data points that are apart, or far, from the mainstream of the other data.* They are sometimes data points that were mistakenly recorded or measured. Because every data point influences the regression model,

TABLE 14.2

Residuals for the Real Estate
Regression Model

y	$\hat{y}$	$y - \hat{y}$
63.0	62.499	.501
65.1	71.485	−6.385
69.9	71.568	−1.668
76.8	78.639	−1.839
73.9	74.097	−.197
77.9	75.653	2.247
74.9	83.012	−8.112
78.0	105.699	−27.699
79.0	68.523	10.477
83.4	81.139	2.261
79.5	88.282	−8.782
83.9	91.335	−7.435
79.7	85.618	−5.918
84.5	95.391	−10.891
96.0	85.456	10.544
109.5	102.774	6.726
102.5	97.665	4.835
121.0	107.183	13.817
104.9	109.352	−4.452
128.0	111.230	16.770
129.0	105.061	23.939
117.9	134.415	−16.515
140.0	132.430	7.570

outliers can exert an overly important influence on the model based on their distance from other points. In examining the residuals in Table 14.2 for outliers, the eighth residual listed is −27.699. This error indicates that the regression model was not nearly as successful in predicting house price on this particular house as it was with others (an error of more than $27,000). For whatever reason, this data point stands somewhat apart from other data points and may be considered an outlier.

Residuals are also useful in testing the assumptions underlying regression analysis. Figure 14.4 displays MINITAB diagnostic techniques for the real estate example. In the bottom right is a graph of the residuals. Notice that residual variance seems to increase in the right half of the plot, indicating potential heteroscedasticity. As discussed in Chapter 13, one of the assumptions underlying regression analysis is that the error terms have homoscedasticity or homogeneous variance. That assumption might be violated in this example. The normal plot of residuals is nearly a straight line, indicating that the assumption of normally distributed error terms probably has not been violated.

SSE and Standard Error of the Estimate

One of the properties of a regression model is that the residuals sum to zero. As pointed out in Chapter 13, this property precludes the possibility of computing an "average" residual as a single measure of error. In an effort to compute a single statistic that can represent the error in a regression analysis, the zero-sum property can be overcome by *squaring the residuals and then summing the squares*. Such an operation produces the sum of squares of error (SSE).

The formula for computing the sum of squares error (SSE) for multiple regression is the same as it is for simple regression.

$$SSE = \Sigma(y - \hat{y})^2$$

For the real estate example, SSE can be computed by squaring and summing the residuals displayed in Table 14.2.

$$
\begin{aligned}
SSE = \ & [(.501)^2 + (-6.385)^2 + (-1.668)^2 + (-1.839)^2 \\
& + (-.197)^2 + (2.247)^2 + (-8.112)^2 + (-27.699)^2 \\
& + (10.477)^2 + (2.261)^2 + (-8.782)^2 + (-7.435)^2 \\
& + (-5.918)^2 + (-10.891)^2 + (10.544)^2 + (6.726)^2 \\
& + (4.835)^2 + (13.817)^2 + (-4.452)^2 + (16.770)^2 \\
& + (23.939)^2 + (-16.515)^2 + (7.570)^2] \\
= \ & 2861.0
\end{aligned}
$$

FIGURE 14.4

MINITAB Residual Diagnosis
for the Real Estate Example

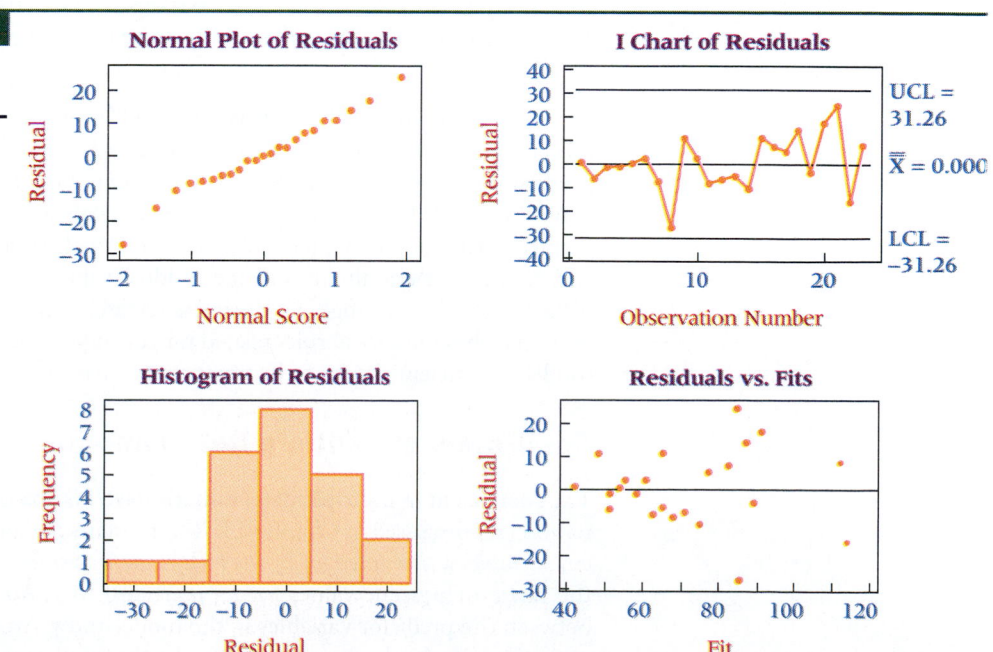

SSE can also be obtained directly from the multiple regression computer output by selecting the value of SS (sum of squares) listed beside error. Shown here is the ANOVA portion of the output displayed in Figure 14.3, which is the result of a multiple regression analysis model developed to predict house prices. Note that the SS for error shown in the ANOVA table equals the value of $\Sigma(y - \hat{y})^2$ just computed (2861.0).

Analysis of Variance

Source	DF	SS	MS	F	p
Regression	2	8189.7	4094.9	28.63	.000
Error	20	2861.0	143.1		
Total	22	11050.7			

SSE has limited usage as a measure of error. However, it is a tool used to solve for other, more useful measures. One of those is the **standard error of the estimate** s_e, which is essentially *the standard deviation of residuals (error) for the regression model*. As explained in Chapter 13, an assumption underlying regression analysis is that the error terms are approximately normally distributed with a mean of zero. With this information and by the empirical rule, approximately 68% of the residuals should be within $\pm 1 s_e$ and 95% should be within $\pm 2 s_e$. This property makes the standard error of the estimate a useful tool in estimating how accurately a regression model is fitting the data.

The standard error of the estimate is computed by dividing SSE by the degrees of freedom of error for the model and taking the square root.

$$s_e = \sqrt{\frac{SSE}{n - k - 1}}$$

where

n = number of observations
k = number of independent variables

The value of s_e can be computed for the real estate example as follows.

$$s_e = \sqrt{\frac{SSE}{n - k - 1}} = \sqrt{\frac{2861}{23 - 2 - 1}} = 11.96$$

The standard error of the estimate, s_e, is usually given as standard output from regression analysis by computer software packages. The MINITAB output displayed in Figure 14.3 contains the standard error of the estimate for the real estate example.

$$S = 11.96$$

By the empirical rule, approximately 68% of the residuals should be within $\pm 1 s_e = \pm 1(11.96) = \pm 11.96$. Because house prices are in units of $1,000, approximately 68% of the predictions are within $\pm 11.96(\$1,000)$, or $\pm\$11,960$. Examining the output displayed in Table 14.2, 18/23, or about 78%, of the residuals are within this span. According to the empirical rule, approximately 95% of the residuals should be within $\pm 2 s_e$, or $\pm 2(11.96) = \pm 23.92$. Further examination of the residual values in Table 14.2 shows that 21 of 23, or 91%, fall within this range. The business researcher can study the standard error of the estimate and these empirical rule–related ranges and decide whether the error of the regression model is sufficiently small to justify further use of the model.

Coefficient of Multiple Determination (R^2)

The **coefficient of multiple determination (R^2)** is analogous to the coefficient of determination (r^2) discussed in Chapter 13. R^2 represents *the proportion of variation of the dependent variable, y, accounted for by the independent variables in the regression model*. As with r^2, the range of possible values for R^2 is from 0 to 1. An R^2 of 0 indicates no relationship between the predictor variables in the model and y. An R^2 of 1 indicates that 100% of the variability of y has been accounted for by the predictors. Of course, it is desirable for R^2 to be high, indicating the strong predictability of a regression model. The coefficient of multiple determination can be calculated by the following formula:

$$R^2 = \frac{\text{SSR}}{\text{SS}_{yy}} = 1 - \frac{\text{SSE}}{\text{SS}_{yy}}$$

R^2 can be calculated in the real estate example by using the sum of squares regression (SSR), the sum of squares error (SSE), and sum of squares total (SS$_{yy}$) from the ANOVA portion of Figure 14.3.

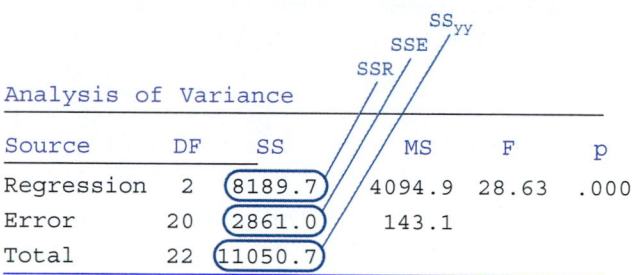

```
                                        SS_yy
                              SSE /
                        SSR /
Analysis of Variance

Source        DF    SS        MS      F       p
Regression     2   8189.7    4094.9  28.63   .000
Error         20   2861.0     143.1
Total         22  11050.7
```

$$R^2 = \frac{\text{SSR}}{\text{SS}_{yy}} = \frac{8189.7}{11050.7} = .741$$

or

$$R^2 = 1 - \frac{\text{SSE}}{\text{SS}_{yy}} = 1 - \frac{2861.0}{11050.7} = .741$$

In addition, virtually all statistical software packages print out R^2 as standard output with multiple regression analysis. A reexamination of Figure 14.3 reveals that R^2 is given as

R-sq = 74.1%

This result indicates that a relatively high proportion of the variation of the dependent variable, house price, is accounted for by the independent variables in this regression model.

Adjusted R^2

As additional independent variables are added to a regression model, the value of R^2 cannot decrease, and in most cases it will increase. In the formulas for determining R^2,

$$R^2 = \frac{\text{SSR}}{\text{SS}_{yy}} = 1 - \frac{\text{SSE}}{\text{SS}_{yy}}$$

The value of SS$_{yy}$ for a given set of observations will remain the same as independent variables are added to the regression analysis because SS$_{yy}$ is the sum of squares for the dependent variable. Because additional independent variables are likely to increase SSR at least by some amount, the value of R^2 will probably increase for any additional independent variables.

However, sometimes additional independent variables add no *significant* information to the regression model, yet R^2 increases. R^2 therefore may yield an inflated figure. Statisticians have developed an **adjusted R^2** *to take into consideration both the additional information each new independent variable brings to the regression model and the changed degrees of freedom of regression.* Many standard statistical computer packages now compute and report adjusted R^2 as part of the output. The formula for computing adjusted R^2 is

$$\text{Adjusted } R^2 = 1 - \frac{\text{SSE}/n-k-1}{\text{SS}_{yy}/n-1}$$

The value of adjusted R^2 for the real estate example can be solved by using information from the ANOVA portion of the computer output in Figure 14.3.

```
                              n - 1              SS_yy
                    n - k - 1               SSE

        Analysis of Variance
        ─────────────────────────────────────────────────────────────
        Source       DF        SS         MS         F        p
        Regression    2       8189.7     4094.9     28.63    .000
        Error        (20)    (2861.0)    143.1
        Total        (22)   (11050.7)
        ─────────────────────────────────────────────────────────────
        SSE = 2861     SS_YY = 11050.7    n - k - 1 = 20    n - 1 = 22
```

$$\text{Adj. } R^2 = 1 - \left[\frac{2861/20}{11050.7/22} \right] = 1 - .285 = .715$$

The standard MINITAB regression output in Figure 14.3 contains the value of the adjusted R^2 already computed. For the real estate example, this value is shown as

R-sq (adj.) = 71.5%

A comparison of R^2 (.741) with the adjusted R^2 (.715) for this example shows that the adjusted R^2 reduces the overall proportion of variation of the dependent variable accounted for by the independent variables by a factor of .026, or 2.6%. The gap between the R^2 and adjusted R^2 tends to increase as nonsignificant independent variables are added to the regression model. As n increases, the difference between R^2 and adjusted R^2 becomes less.

14.3 PROBLEMS

14.14 Study the MINITAB output shown in Problem 14.7. Comment on the overall strength of the regression model in light of S, R^2, and adjusted R^2

STATISTICS IN BUSINESS TODAY

Using Regression Analysis to Help Select a Robot

Several factors contribute to the success of a manufacturing firm in the world markets. Some examples are creating more efficient plants, lowering labor costs, increasing the quality of products, improving the standards of supplier materials, and learning more about international markets. Basically, success boils down to producing a better product for less cost.

One way to achieve that goal is to improve the technology of manufacturing facilities. Many companies are now using robots in plants to increase productivity and reduce labor costs. The use of such technology is relatively new. The science of selecting and purchasing robots is imperfect and often involves considerable subjectivity.

Two researchers, Moutaz Khouja and David Booth, devised a way to use multiple regression to assist decision makers in robot selection. After sorting through 20 of the more promising variables, they found that the most important variables related to robot performance are repeatability, accuracy, load capacity, and velocity. Accuracy is measured by the distance between where the robot goes on a single trial and the center of all points to which it goes on repeated trials. Repeatability is the radius of the circle that just includes all points to which the robot goes on repeated trials. Repeatability is of most concern to decision makers because it is hardest to correct. Accuracy can be viewed as bias and is easier to correct. Load capacity is the maximum weight that the robot can handle, and velocity is the maximum tip velocity of the robot arm.

Khouja and Booth used data gathered from 27 robots and regression analysis to develop a multiple regression model that attempts to predict repeatability of robots (the variable of most concern for decision makers) by the velocity and load capacity of robots. Using the resulting regression model and the residuals of the fit, they developed a ranking system for selecting robots that takes into account repeatability, load capacity, velocity, and cost.

Source: Adapted from Moutaz Khouja and David E. Booth, "A Decision Model for the Robot Selection Problem Using Robust Regression," *Decision Sciences* 22, no. 3 (July/August 1991): 656–62. The *Decision Sciences* journal is published by the Decision Sciences Institute, located at Georgia State University.

14.15 Study the MINITAB output shown in Problem 14.8. Comment on the overall strength of the regression model in light of S, R^2, and adjusted R^2.

14.16 Using the regression output obtained by working Problem 14.5, comment on the overall strength of the regression model using S, R^2, and adjusted R^2.

14.17 Using the regression output obtained by working Problem 14.6, comment on the overall strength of the regression model using S, R^2, and adjusted R^2.

14.18 Using the regression output obtained by working Problem 14.11, comment on the overall strength of the regression model using S, R^2, and adjusted R^2.

14.19 Using the regression output obtained by working Problem 14.12, comment on the overall strength of the regression model using S, R^2, and adjusted R^2.

14.20 Study the Excel output shown in Problem 14.13. Comment on the overall strength of the regression model in light of S, R^2, and adjusted R^2.

14.21 Study the MINITAB residual diagnostic output that follows. Discuss any potential problems with meeting the regression assumptions for this regression analysis based on the residual graphics.

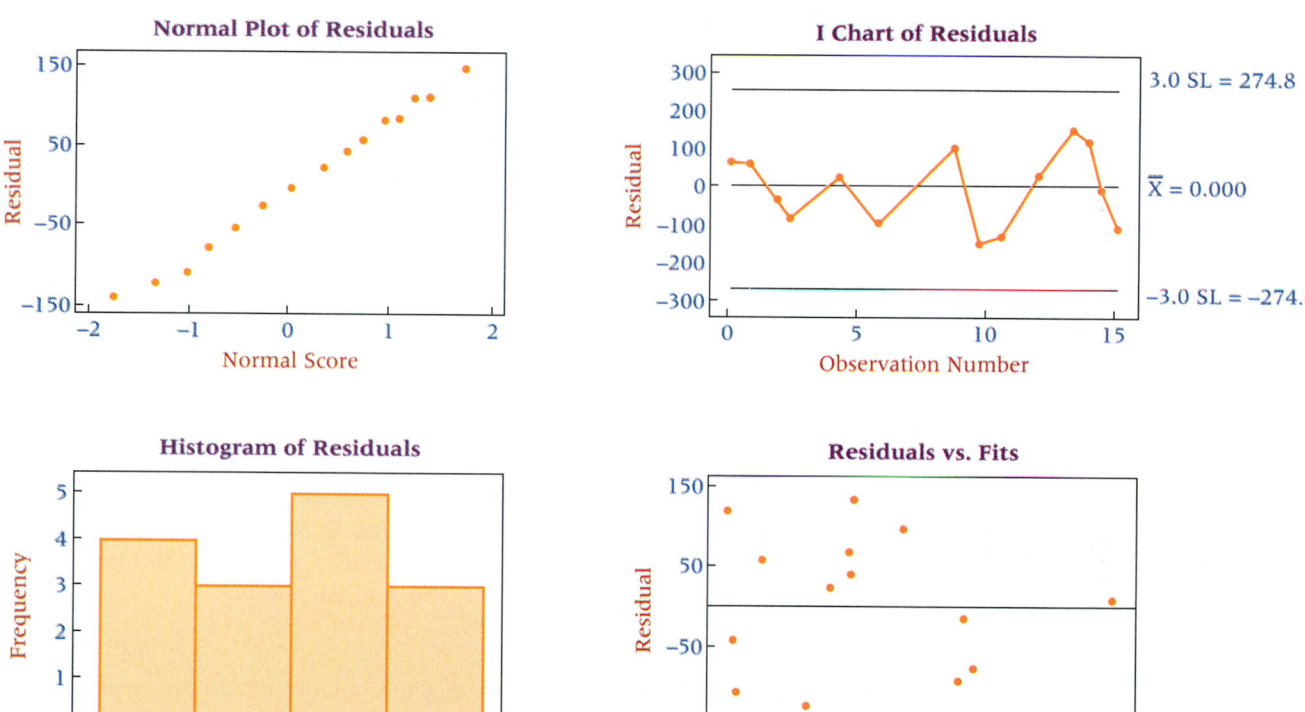

14.4 INTERPRETING MULTIPLE REGRESSION COMPUTER OUTPUT

A Reexamination of the Multiple Regression Output

Figure 14.5 shows again the MINITAB multiple regression output for the real estate example. Many of the concepts discussed thus far in the chapter are highlighted. Note the following items:

1. The equation of the regression model
2. The ANOVA table with the F value for the overall test of the model
3. The t ratios, which test the significance of the regression coefficients
4. The value of SSE
5. The value of s_e
6. The value of R^2
7. The value of adjusted R^2

FIGURE 14.5

Annotated Version of the
MINTAB Output of Regression
for the Real Estate Example

Regression equation

The regression equation is
$\hat{Y} = 57.4 + 0.0177\ X_1 - 0.666\ X_2$

t tests of
regression equation

Predictor	Coef	Stdev	T	p
Constant	57.35	10.01	5.73	.000
X_1	0.017718	0.003146	5.63	.000
X_2	-0.6663	0.2280	-2.92	.008

Standard error of estimate (S_e)

Coefficient of multiple determination (R^2)

Adjusted R^2

S = 11.96   R-sq = 74.1%   R-sq (adj.) = 71.5%

ANOVA table and F test for overall model

Analysis of Variance

Source	DF	SS	MS	F	p
Regression	2	8189.7	4094.9	28.63	.000
Error	20	2861.0	143.1		
Total	22	11050.7			

DEMONSTRATION PROBLEM 14.2

Discuss the Excel multiple regression output for Demonstration Problem 14.1. Comment on the F test for the overall significance of the model, the t tests of the regression coefficients, and the values of s_e, R^2, and adjusted R^2.

Solution

This regression analysis was done to predict the volume of freight cargo shipped annually in a country by road using the predictors "length of roads" and "number of commercial vehicles." The equation of the regression model was presented in the solution of Demonstration Problem 14.1. Shown here is the complete multiple regression output from the Excel analysis of the data.

The value of F for this problem is 3.86, with a p-value of .1163, which is not significant at $\alpha = .05$. On the basis of this information, the null hypothesis would not be rejected for the overall test of significance. None of the regression coefficients are significantly different from zero, and no significant predictability of the volume of freight cargo shipped by road is given from this regression model.

An examination of the t ratios support this conclusion using an $\alpha = .05$. The t ratio for length of roads is 2.34 with an associated p-value of .0793, and the t ratio for number of commercial vehicles is 2.39 with an associated p-value of .0750. Neither p-value is less than .05.

The standard error of the estimate is $s_e = 44,273.87$, indicating that approximately 68% of the residuals are within ±44,273.87. An examination of the Excel-produced residuals shows that actually five out of seven, or 71.4%, of the residuals fall in this interval. Approximately 95% of the residuals should be within ±2(44,273.87) = ±88,547.74, and an examination of the Excel-produced residuals shows that seven out of seven, or 100%, of the residuals are within this interval. Shipping industry researchers could examine the value of the standard error of the estimate to determine whether this model produces results with small enough error to suit their needs.

	A	B	C	D	E	F
1	Summary Output					
2	Regression Statistics					
3	Multiple R	0.812				
4	R Square	0.659				
5	Adjusted R Square	0.488				
6	Standard Error	44273.87				
7	Obervations	7				
8						
9	ANOVA					
10		df	SS	MS	F	Significance F
11	Regression	2	15148592381	7574296191	3.86	0.1163
12	Residual	4	7840701114	1960175278		
13	Total	6	22989293495			
14						
15		Coefficients	Standard Error	t Stat	P-value	
16	Intercept	-26425.45	67624.94	-0.39	0.7159	
17	Length	0.10182	0.04350	2.34	0.0793	
18	Vehicles	0.04095	0.01712	2.39	0.0750	
19						
20	Residual Output					
21	Observation	Predicted Miles	Residuals			
22	1	247276.61	31529.39			
23	2	134768.10	43590.90			
24	3	191296.29	-47296.29			
25	4	133523.80	5451.20			
26	5	105201.93	19969.07			
27	6	111667.11	-5843.11			
	7	143450.17	-47401.17			

R^2 for this regression analysis is .659 or 65.9%; that is, 65.9% of the variation in the volume of freight cargo is accounted for by these two independent variables. Conversely, 34.1% of the variation is unaccounted for by this model. The adjusted R^2 is only .488 or 48.8%, indicating that the value of R^2 is considerably inflated. Thus, it could be that the two predictors of the regression model actually account for less than half of the variation of the dependent variable when R^2 is adjusted.

This problem highlights the notion that a regression model can be developed for data and not really fit the data in a significant way. By examining the values of F, t, s_e, R^2, and adjusted R^2, the business researcher can begin to understand whether the regression model is providing any significant predictability for y.

14.4 PROBLEMS

14.22 Study the MINITAB regression output that follows. How many predictors are there? What is the equation of the regression model? Using the key statistics discussed in this chapter, discuss the strength of the model and the predictors.

Regression Analysis: Y versus X1, X2, X3, X4

```
The regression equation is
Y = - 55.9 + 0.0105 X1 - 0.107 X2 + 0.579 X3 - 0.870 X4
Predictor        Coef   SE Coef        T        P
Constant       -55.93     24.22    -2.31    0.025
      X1       0.01049   0.02100     0.50    0.619
      X2      -0.10720   0.03503    -3.06    0.003
      X3       0.57922   0.07633     7.59    0.000
      X4       -0.8695    0.1498    -5.81    0.000
S = 9.025   R-Sq = 80.2%   R-Sq(adj) = 78.7%
```

Analysis of Variance

Source	DF	SS	MS	F	P
Regression	4	18088.5	4522.1	55.52	0.000
Residual Error	55	4479.7	81.4		
Total	59	22568.2			

14.23 Study the Excel regression output that follows. How many predictors are there? What is the equation of the regression model? Using the key statistics discussed in this chapter, discuss the strength of the model and its predictors.

	A	B	C	D	E	F
1	Summary Output					
2	Regression Statistics					
3	Multiple R	0.814				
4	R Square	0.663				
5	Adjusted R Square	0.636				
6	Standard Error	51.761				
7	Obervations	28				
8						
9	ANOVA					
10		df	SS	MS	F	Significance F
11	Regression	2	131567.0243	65783.5121	24.55	0.0000013
12	Residual	25	66979.6543	2679.1862		
13	Total	27	198546.6786			
14						
15		Coefficients	Standard Error	t Stat	P-value	
16	Intercept	203.3937	67.5177	3.01	0.0059	
17	X1	1.1151	0.5278	2.11	0.0448	
18	X2	-2.2115	0.5667	-3.90	0.0006	

IN RESPONSE

Are You Going to Hate Your New Job?

In the Decision Dilemma, several variables are considered in attempting to determine whether a person will like his or her new job. Four predictor (independent) variables are given with the data set: relationship with supervisor, overall quality of work environment, total hours worked per week, and opportunities for advancement. Other possible variables might include openness of work culture, amount of pressure, how the interviewee is treated during the interview, availability of flexible scheduling, size of office, amount of time allotted for lunch, availability of management, interesting work, and many others.

Using the data that are given, a multiple regression model can be developed to predict job satisfaction from the four independent variables. Such an analysis allows the business researcher to study the entire data set in one model rather than constructing four differ-ent simple regression models, one for each independent variable. In the multiple regres-sion model, job satisfaction is the dependent variable. There are 19 observations. The Excel regression output for this problem follows.

The test for overall significance of the model produced an F of 33.89 with a p-value of .00000046 (significant at $\alpha = .000001$). The R^2 of .906 and adjusted R^2 of .880 indicate strong predictability in the model. The standard error of the estimate, 8.03, can be viewed in light of the job satisfaction values that ranged from 10 to 95 and the residuals, which are not shown here. Sixteen of the 19 residuals (over 84%) are within the standard error of the esti-mate. Examining the t statistics and their associated p-values reveals that only one independ-ent variable, "overall quality of work environment" ($t = 3.92$, p-value = .0015), is significant at $\alpha = .01$. Using a more generous α of .10, one could argue that "relationship with supervisor" is also a significant predictor of job satisfaction. Judging by their large p-values, it appears that "total hours worked per week" and "opportunities for advancement" are not good predictors of job satisfaction.

	A	B	C	D	E	F
1	Summary Output					
2	Regression					
3	Multiple R	0.952				
4	R Square	0.906				
5	Adjusted R Square	0.880				
6	Standard Error	8.03				
7	Observations	19				
8						
9	ANOVA					
10		df	SS	MS	F	Significance F
11	Regression	4	8748.967	2187.242	33.89	0.00000046
12	Residual	14	903.664	64.547		
13	Total	18	9652.632			
14						
15		Coefficients	Standard Error	t Stat	P-value	
16	Intercept	-2.6961	13.0047	-0.21	0.8387	
17	Relationship with Supervisior	6.9211	3.7741	1.83	0.0880	
18	Overall Quality of Work Environment	6.0814	1.5499	3.92	0.0015	
19	Total Hours Worked per Week	0.1063	0.1925	0.55	0.5895	
20	Opportunities for Advancement	0.3881	1.6322	0.24	0.8155	

ETHICAL CONSIDERATIONS

Multiple regression analysis can be used either intentionally or unintentionally in questionable or unethical ways. When degrees of freedom are small, an inflated value of R^2 can be obtained, leading to overenthusiastic expectations about the predictability of a regression model. To prevent this type of reliance, a researcher should take into account the nature of the data, the variables, and the value of the adjusted R^2.

Another misleading aspect of multiple regression can be the tendency of researchers to assume cause-and-effect relationships between the dependent variable and predictors. Just because independent variables produce a significant R^2 does not necessarily mean those variables are causing the deviation of the y values. Indeed, some other force not in the model may be driving both the independent variables and the dependent variable over the range of values being studied.

Some people use the estimates of the regression coefficients to compare the worth of the predictor variables; the larger the coefficient, the greater is its worth. At least two problems can be found in this approach. The first is that most variables are measured in different units. Thus, regression coefficient weights are partly a function of the unit of measurement of the variable. Second, if multicollinearity (discussed in Chapter 15) is present, the interpretation of the regression coefficients is questionable. In addition, the presence of multicollinearity raises several issues about the interpretation of other regression output. Researchers who ignore this problem are at risk of presenting spurious results.

Another danger in using regression analysis is in the extrapolation of the model to values beyond the range of values used to derive the model. A regression model that fits data within a given range does not necessarily fit data outside that range. One of the uses of regression analysis is in the area of forecasting. Users need to be aware that what has occurred in the past is not guaranteed to continue to occur in the future. Unscrupulous and sometimes even well-intentioned business decision makers can use regression models to project conclusions about the future that have little or no basis. The receiver of such messages should be cautioned that regression models may lack validity outside the range of values in which the models were developed.

SUMMARY

Multiple regression analysis is a statistical tool in which a mathematical model is developed in an attempt to predict a dependent variable by two or more independent variables or in which at least one predictor is nonlinear. Because doing multiple regression analysis by hand is extremely tedious and time-consuming, it is almost always done on a computer.

The standard output from a multiple regression analysis is similar to that of simple regression analysis. A regression equation is produced with a constant that is analogous to the y intercept in simple regression and with estimates of the regression coefficients that are analogous to the estimate of the slope in simple regression. An F test for the overall model is computed to determine whether at least one of the regression coefficients is significantly different from zero. This F value is usually displayed in an ANOVA table, which is part of the regression output. The ANOVA table also contains the sum of squares of error and sum of

squares of regression, which are used to compute other statistics in the model.

Most multiple regression computer output contains t values, which are used to determine the significance of the regression coefficients. Using these t values, statisticians can make decisions about including or excluding variables from the model.

Residuals, standard error of the estimate, and R^2 are also standard computer regression output with multiple regression. The coefficient of determination for simple regression models is denoted r^2, whereas for multiple regression it is R^2. The interpretation of residuals, standard error of the estimate, and R^2 in multiple regression is similar to that in simple regression. Because R^2 can be inflated with nonsignificant variables in the mix, an adjusted R^2 is often computed. Unlike R^2, adjusted R^2 takes into account the degrees of freedom and the number of observations.

KEY TERMS

adjusted R^2

coefficient of multiple
    determination (R^2)

dependent variable

independent variable

least squares analysis

multiple regression

outliers

partial regression coefficient

R^2

residual

response plane

response surface

response variable

standard error of the
    estimate (s_e)

sum of squares of error
    (SSE)

FORMULAS

The F value

$$F = \frac{MS_{reg}}{MS_{err}} = \frac{SS_{reg}/df_{reg}}{SS_{err}/df_{err}} = \frac{SSR/k}{SSE/N-k-1}$$

Sum of squares of error

$$SSE = \Sigma(y - \hat{y})^2$$

Standard error of the estimate

$$s_e = \sqrt{\frac{SSE}{n-k-1}}$$

Coefficient of multiple determination

$$R^2 = \frac{SSR}{SS_{yy}} = 1 - \frac{SSE}{SS_{yy}}$$

Adjusted R^2

$$\text{Adjusted } R^2 = 1 - \frac{SSE/n-k-1}{SS_{yy}/n-1}$$

SUPPLEMENTARY PROBLEMS

CALCULATING THE STATISTICS

14.24 Use the following data to develop a multiple regression model to predict y from x_1 and x_2. Discuss the output, including comments about the overall strength of the model, the significance of the regression coefficients, and other indicators of model fit.

y	x_1	x_2
198	29	1.64
214	71	2.81
211	54	2.22
219	73	2.70
184	67	1.57
167	32	1.63
201	47	1.99
204	43	2.14
190	60	2.04
222	32	2.93
197	34	2.15

14.25 Given here are the data for a dependent variable, y, and independent variables. Use these data to develop a regression model to predict y. Discuss the output.

y	x_1	x_2	x_3
14	51	16.4	56
17	48	17.1	64
29	29	18.2	53
32	36	17.9	41
54	40	16.5	60
86	27	17.1	55
117	14	17.8	71
120	17	18.2	48
194	16	16.9	60
203	9	18.0	77
217	14	18.9	90
235	11	18.5	67

TESTING YOUR UNDERSTANDING

14.26 The U.S. Bureau of Mines produces data on the price of minerals. Shown here are the average prices per year for several minerals over a decade. Use these data and multiple regression to produce a model to predict the average price of gold from the other variables. Comment on the results of the process.

Gold ($ per oz.)	Copper (cents per lb.)	Silver ($ per oz.)	Aluminum (cents per lb.)
161.1	64.2	4.4	39.8
308.0	93.3	11.1	61.0
613.0	101.3	20.6	71.6
460.0	84.2	10.5	76.0
376.0	72.8	8.0	76.0
424.0	76.5	11.4	77.8
361.0	66.8	8.1	81.0
318.0	67.0	6.1	81.0
368.0	66.1	5.5	81.0
448.0	82.5	7.0	72.3
438.0	120.5	6.5	110.1
382.6	130.9	5.5	87.8

14.27 The Shipbuilders Council of America in Washington, D.C., publishes data about private shipyards. Among the variables reported by this organization are the employment figures (per 1,000), the number of naval vessels under construction, and the number of repairs or conversions done to commercial ships (in $ millions). Shown here are the data for these three variables over a 7-year period. Use the data to develop a regression model to predict private shipyard employment from number of naval vessels under construction and repairs or conversions of commercial ships. Comment on the regression model and its strengths and its weaknesses.

	Commercial Ship	
Employment	Naval Vessels	Repairs or Conversions
133.4	108	431
177.3	99	1,335
143.0	105	1,419
142.0	111	1,631
130.3	100	852
120.6	85	847
120.4	79	806

14.28 The U.S. Bureau of Labor Statistics produces consumer price indexes for several different categories. Shown here are the percentage changes in consumer price indexes over a period of 20 years for food, shelter, apparel, and fuel oil. Also displayed are the percentage changes in consumer price indexes for all commodities. Use these data and multiple regression to develop a model that attempts to predict all commodities by the other four variables. Comment on the result of this analysis.

All Commodities	Food	Shelter	Apparel	Fuel Oil
.9	1.0	2.0	1.6	3.7
.6	1.3	.8	.9	2.7
.9	.7	1.6	.4	2.6
.9	1.6	1.2	1.3	2.6
1.2	1.3	1.5	.9	2.1
1.1	2.2	1.9	1.1	2.4
2.6	5.0	3.0	2.5	4.4
1.9	.9	3.6	4.1	7.2
3.5	3.5	4.5	5.3	6.0
4.7	5.1	8.3	5.8	6.7
4.5	5.7	8.9	4.2	6.6
3.6	3.1	4.2	3.2	6.2
3.0	4.2	4.6	2.0	3.3
7.4	14.5	4.7	3.7	4.0
11.9	14.3	9.6	7.4	9.3
8.8	8.5	9.9	4.5	12.0
4.3	3.0	5.5	3.7	9.5
5.8	6.3	6.6	4.5	9.6
7.2	9.9	10.2	3.6	8.4
11.3	11.0	13.9	4.3	9.2

14.29 The U.S. Department of Agriculture publishes data annually on various selected farm products. Shown here are the unit production figures (in millions of bushels) for three farm products for 10 years during a 20-year period. Use these data and multiple regression analysis to predict corn production by the production of soybeans and wheat. Comment on the results.

Corn	Soybeans	Wheat
4,152	1,127	1,352
6,639	1,798	2,381
4,175	1,636	2,420
7,672	1,861	2,595
8,876	2,099	2,424
8,226	1,940	2,091
7,131	1,938	2,108
4,929	1,549	1,812
7,525	1,924	2,037
7,933	1,922	2,739

14.30 The American Chamber of Commerce Researchers Association compiles cost-of-living indexes for selected metropolitan areas. Shown here are cost-of-living

indexes for 25 different cities on five different items for a recent year. Use the data to develop a regression model to predict the grocery cost-of-living index by the indexes of housing, utilities, transportation, and healthcare. Discuss the results, highlighting both the significant and nonsignificant predictors.

City	Grocery Items	Housing	Utilities	Transportation	Healthcare
Albany	108.3	106.8	127.4	89.1	107.5
Albuquerque	96.3	105.2	98.8	100.9	102.1
Augusta, GA	96.2	88.8	115.6	102.3	94.0
Austin	98.0	83.9	87.7	97.4	94.9
Baltimore	106.0	114.1	108.1	112.8	111.5
Buffalo	103.1	117.3	127.6	107.8	100.8
Colorado Springs	94.5	88.5	74.6	93.3	102.4
Dallas	105.4	98.9	108.9	110.0	106.8
Denver	91.5	108.3	97.2	105.9	114.3
Des Moines	94.3	95.1	111.4	105.7	96.2
El Paso	102.9	94.6	90.9	104.2	91.4
Indianapolis	96.0	99.7	92.1	102.7	97.4
Jacksonville	96.1	90.4	96.0	106.0	96.1
Kansas City	89.8	92.4	96.3	95.6	93.6
Knoxville	93.2	88.0	91.7	91.6	82.3
Los Angeles	103.3	211.3	75.6	102.1	128.5
Louisville	94.6	91.0	79.4	102.4	88.4
Memphis	99.1	86.2	91.1	101.1	85.5
Miami	100.3	123.0	125.6	104.3	137.8
Minneapolis	92.8	112.3	105.2	106.0	107.5
Mobile	99.9	81.1	104.9	102.8	92.2
Nashville	95.8	107.7	91.6	98.1	90.9
New Orleans	104.0	83.4	122.2	98.2	87.0
Oklahoma City	98.2	79.4	103.4	97.3	97.1
Phoenix	95.7	98.7	96.3	104.6	115.2

INTERPRETING THE OUTPUT

14.31 Shown here are the data for y and three predictors, x_1, x_2, and x_3. A multiple regression analysis has been done on these data; the MINITAB results are given. Comment on the outcome of the analysis in light of the data.

y	x_1	x_2	x_3
94	21	1	204
97	25	0	198
93	22	1	184
95	27	0	200
90	29	1	182
91	20	1	159
91	18	1	147
94	25	0	196
98	26	0	228
99	24	0	242
90	28	1	162
92	23	1	180
96	25	0	219

Regression Analysis: Y versus X1, X2, X3

The regression equation is

Y = 87.9 - 0.256 X1 - 2.71 X2 + 0.0706 X3

Predictor	Coef	SE Coef	T	P
Constant	87.890	3.445	25.51	0.000
X1	-0.25612	0.08317	-3.08	0.013
X2	-2.7137	0.7306	-3.71	0.005
X3	0.07061	0.01353	5.22	0.001

S = 0.8503   R-Sq = 94.1%   R-Sq(adj) = 92.1%

Analysis of Variance

Source	DF	SS	MS	F	P
Regression	3	103.185	34.395	47.57	0.000
Residual Error	9	6.507	0.723		
Total	12	109.692			

14.32 MINITAB residual diagnostic output from the multiple regression analysis for the data given in Problem 14.30 follows. Discuss any potential problems with meeting the regression assumptions for this regression analysis based on the residual graphics.

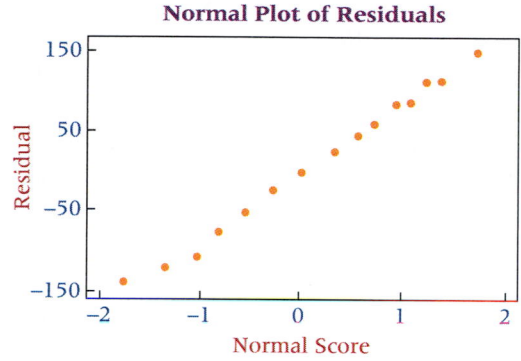

Normal Plot of Residuals

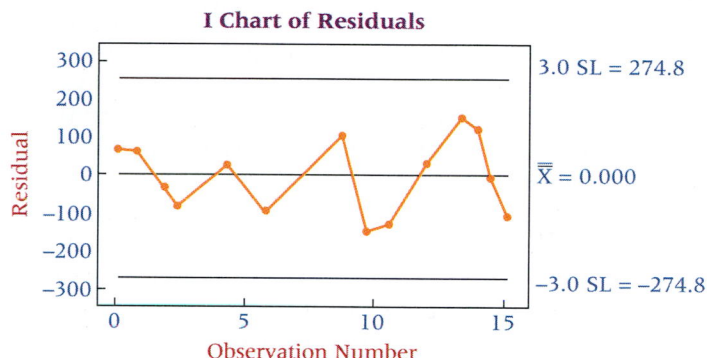

I Chart of Residuals

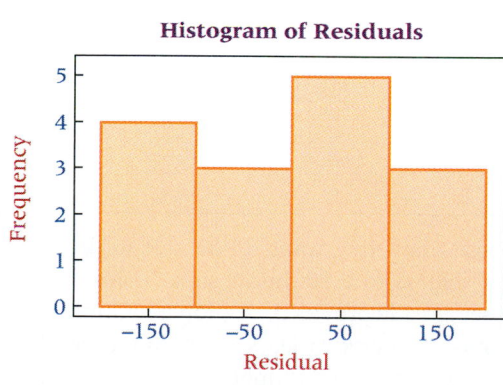

Histogram of Residuals

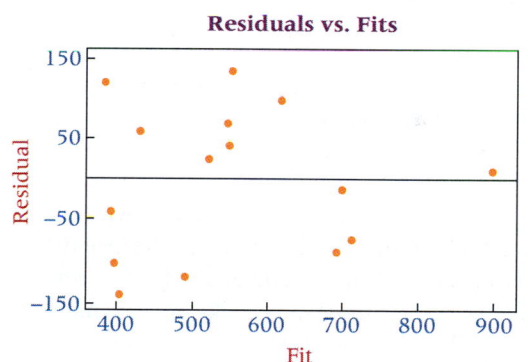

Residuals vs. Fits

ANALYZING THE DATABASES

see www.wiley.com/college/black

1. Use the manufacturing database to develop a multiple regression model to predict Cost of Materials by Number of Employees, New Capital Expenditures, Value Added by Manufacture, and End-of-Year Inventories. Discuss the results of the analysis.

2. Develop a regression model using the financial database. Use Total Revenues, Total Assets, Return on Equity, Earnings Per Share, Average Yield, and Dividends Per Share to predict the average P/E ratio for a company. How strong is the model? Which variables seem to be the best predictors?

3. Use the stock market database to develop a regression model to predict the composite index from Stock Volume, Reported Trades, Dollar Value, and Warrants Volume. Discuss the outcome including the model, the strength of the model, and the strength of the predictors.

CASE: STARBUCKS INTRODUCES DEBIT CARD

Starbucks is a resounding restaurant success story. Beginning with its first coffee house in 1971, Starbucks has grown to more than 5,200 locations with projections of reaching 10,000 by the year 2005. Opening up its first international outlet in the mid 1990s, Starbucks now operates in more than 22 countries (900 coffee houses) outside of North America. Besides selling beverages, pastries, confections, and coffee-related accessories and equipment at its retail outlets, Starbucks also purchases and roasts high-quality coffee beans in several locations. The company's objective is to become the most recognized and respected brand in the world. Starbucks maintains a strong environmental orientation and is committed to taking a leadership position environmentally. In addition, the company has won awards for corporate social responsibility through its community building programs, its strong commitment to its origins (coffee producers, family, community), and the Starbucks Foundation, which is dedicated to creating hope, discovery, and opportunity in the communities where Starbucks resides.

In November 2001, Starbucks launched its prepaid (debit) Starbucks Card. The card, which holds between $5 and $500, can be used at virtually any Starbucks location. The card was so popular when it first was released that many stores ran out. By mid-2002, Starbucks had activated more than 5 million of these cards. It is believed that the card accounted for a large portion of the company's 7% same store increase in sales in early 2002 and that it is responsible for attracting many new patrons to the store. As customers "reload" the cards, it appears they are placing more money on them than the initial value of the card.

Discussion

1. Starbucks enjoyed considerable success with its debit cards, which they sell for $5 to $500. Since the card was introduced in November 2001, sales revenues increased. Suppose Starbucks management wants to study the reasons why some people purchase debit cards with higher prepaid amounts than do other people. Suppose a study of 25 randomly selected prepaid card purchasers is taken. Respondents are asked the amount of the prepaid card, the customer's age, the number of days per month the customer makes a purchase at Starbucks, the number of cups of coffee the customer drinks per day, and the customer's income. The data follow. Using these data, develop a multiple regression model to study how well the amount of the prepaid card can be predicted by the other variables and which variables seem to be more promising in doing

the prediction. What sales implications might be evident from this analysis?

Amount of Prepaid Card ($)	Age	Days per Month at Starbucks	Cups of Coffee per Day	Income ($1,000)
5	25	4	1	20
25	30	12	5	35
10	27	10	4	30
5	42	8	5	30
15	29	11	8	25
50	25	12	5	60
10	50	8	3	30
15	45	6	5	35
5	32	16	7	25
5	23	10	1	20
20	40	18	5	40
35	35	12	3	40
40	28	10	3	50
15	33	12	2	30
200	40	15	5	80
15	37	3	1	30
40	51	10	8	35
5	20	8	4	25
30	26	15	5	35
100	38	19	10	45
30	27	12	3	35
25	29	14	6	35
25	34	10	4	45
50	30	6	3	55
15	22	8	5	30

2. Suppose marketing wants to be able to profile frequent visitors to a Starbucks store. Using the same data set already provided, develop a multiple regression model to predict Days per month at Starbucks by Age, Income, and Number of cups of coffee per day. How strong is the model? Which particular independent variables seem to have more promise in predicting how many days per month a customer visits Starbucks? What marketing implications might be evident from this analysis?

3. Over the past decade or so, Starbucks has grown quite rapidly. As they add stores and increase the number of drinks, their sales revenues increase. In reflecting about this growth, think about some other variables that might be related to the increase in Starbucks sales revenues. Some data for the past

seven years on the number of Starbucks stores (worldwide), approximate sales revenue (in $ millions), number of different drinks sold, and average weekly earnings of U.S. production workers are given here. Most figures are approximate. Develop a multiple regression model to predict sales revenue by number of drinks sold, number of stores, and average weekly earnings. How strong is the model? What are the key predictors, if any? How might this analysis help Starbucks management in attempting to determine what drives sales revenues?

Sales Year	Revenue	Number of Stores	Number of Drinks	Average Weekly Earnings
1	400	676	15	386
2	700	1015	15	394
3	1000	1412	18	407
4	1350	1886	22	425
5	1650	2135	27	442
6	2200	3300	27	457
7	2600	4709	30	474

Source: Adapted from Shirley Leung, "Starbucks May Indeed be a Robust Staple," The Wall Street Journal, 26 July 2002, p. B4; Starbucks, available at http://www.starbucks.com/aboutus; James Peters, "Starbucks' Growth Still Hot; Gift Card Jolts Chain's Sales," Nation's Restaurant News, 11 February, 2002, pp. 1–2.

USING THE COMPUTER

EXCEL

The Using the Computer section at the end of Chapter 13 contains directions for doing simple regression analysis by using Excel. Multiple regression analysis can be performed by using the same commands as those used for simple regression and explained in Chapter 13. Select **Tools** on the menu bar. From the pull-down menu that appears choose **Data Analysis.** This selection will produce the **Data Analysis** dialog box. From this, select **Regression.** In the dialog box shown, input the range of the *y* values in the first slot, **Input Y Range.** In the second slot, **Input X Range,** input the range of the *x* values. The *x* value range may include several columns and Excel will determine the number of predictor variables from the number of columns entered in this box. Other options and the standard output features are presented and explained in Chapter 13.

MINITAB WINDOWS

MINITAB Windows has the capability of generating multiple regression models and other regression techniques (explained and presented in Chapter 15). To analyze data with a multiple regression model, follow the procedures outlined in the Using the Computer section at the end of Chapter 13. Select **Stat** on the menu bar, followed by the selection of **Regression** on the pull-down menu and **Regression** again on the next pull-down menu. In the dialog box that appears, enter the column name of the dependent variable in the slot beside **Response** and the column names of the independent variables in the slot beside **Predictors.** The output described in Chapter 13 will result. The graphical residual analysis and other options are explained in Chapter 13.

Building Multiple Regression Models

Chief executive officers for large companies receive widely varying amounts of compensation for their work. Why is the range so wide? What are some of the variables that seem to contribute to the diversity of CEO compensation packages?

As a starting place, one might examine the role of company size as measured by sales volume, number of employees, number of plants, and so on in driving CEO compensation. It could be argued that CEOs of larger companies carry larger responsibilities and hence should receive higher compensation. Some researchers believe CEO compensation is related to such things as industry performance of the firm, percentage of stock that has outside ownership, and proportion of insiders on the board. At least a significant proportion of CEOs are likely to be compensated according to the performance of their companies during the fiscal period preceding compensation. Company performance can be measured by such variables as earnings per share, percentage change in profit, sales, and profit. In addition, some theorize that companies with outside ownership are more oriented toward declaring dividends to stockholders than toward large CEO compensation packages.

Do CEOs' individual and family characteristics play a role in their compensation? Do such things as CEO age, degrees obtained, marital status, military experience, and number of children matter in compensation? Do type of industry and geographic location of the company matter? What are the significant factors in determining CEO compensation?

What follow are CEO compensation data generated by using management compensation models published by Wyatt Data Services. In the first column on the left are cash compensation figures (in $1,000) for 20 CEOs. Those figures represent salary, bonuses, and any other cash remuneration given to the CEO as part of compensation. The four columns to the right contain data on four variables associated with each CEO's company: sales, number of employees, capital investment, and whether the company is in manufacturing. Sales figures and capital investment figures are given in $ millions.

Cash Compensation	Sales	Number of Employees	Capital Investment	Manufacturing
212	35.0	248.00	10.5	1
226	27.2	156.00	3.8	0
237	49.5	348.00	14.9	1
239	34.0	196.00	5.0	0
242	52.8	371.00	15.9	1
245	37.6	216.00	5.7	0
253	60.7	425.00	18.3	1
262	49.2	285.00	8.0	0
271	75.1	524.00	22.6	1
285	69.0	401.00	12.3	0
329	137.2	947.00	41.4	1
340	140.1	825.00	30.3	0
353	162.9	961.00	36.7	0
384	221.7	1,517.00	67.1	1
405	261.6	1,784.00	79.2	1
411	300.1	1,788.00	79.8	0
456	455.5	2,733.00	135.7	0
478	437.6	2,957.00	132.7	1
525	802.1	4,857.00	278.4	0
564	731.5	4,896.00	222.2	1

Managerial and Statistical Questions

1. Is it possible to sort out variables that appear to be related to CEO compensation and determine which variables are more significant predictors?
2. Can a model be developed to predict CEO compensation?
3. If a model is developed, how can the model be evaluated to determine whether it is valid?
4. Are some of the variables related to CEO compensation but in a nonlinear manner?
5. Are some variables highly interrelated and redundant in their potential for determining CEO compensation?

Sources: Adapted from Jeffrey L. Kerr and Leslie Kren, "Effect of Relative Decision Monitoring on Chief Executive Compensation," *Academy of Management Journal*, vol. 35, no. 2 (June 1992). Used with permission. Robin L. Bartlett, James H. Grant, and Timothy I. Miller, "The Earnings of Top Executives: Compensating Differentials for Risky Business," *Quarterly Reviews of Economics and Finance*, vol. 32, no. 1 (Spring 1992). Used with permission. Database derived using models published in *1993/1994 Top Management Compensation Regression Analysis Report*, 44th ed. (Fort Lee, NJ: Wyatt Data Services/ECS, December 1994).

15.1 NONLINEAR MODELS: MATHEMATICAL TRANSFORMATION

The regression models presented thus far are based on the general linear regression model, which has the form

(15.1)
$$y = \beta_0 + \beta_1 x_1 + \beta_2 x_2 + \ldots + \beta_k x_k + \epsilon,$$

where

β_0 = the regression constant
$\beta_1, \beta_2, \ldots, \beta_k$ are the partial regression coefficients for the k independent variables
$x_1, \ldots, x_k$ are the independent variables
k = the number of independent variables

In this general linear model, the parameters, β_i, are linear. It does not mean, however, that the dependent variable, y, is necessarily linearly related to the predictor variables. Scatter plots sometimes reveal a curvilinear relationship between x and y. Multiple regression response surfaces are not restricted to linear surfaces and may be curvilinear.

To this point, the variables, x_i, have represented different predictors. For example, in the real estate example presented in Chapter 14, the variables, x_1, x_2, represented two predictors: number of square feet in the house and the age of the house, respectively. Certainly, regression models can be developed for more than two predictors. For example, a marketing site location model could be developed in which sales, as the response variable, is predicted by population density, number of competitors, size of the store, and number of salespeople. Such a model could take the form

$$y = \beta_0 + \beta_1 x_1 + \beta_2 x_2 + \beta_3 x_3 + \beta_4 x_4 + \epsilon$$

This regression model has four x_i variables, each of which represents a different predictor.

The general linear model also applies to situations in which some x_i represent recoded data from a predictor variable already represented in the model by another independent variable. In some models, x_i represents variables that have undergone a mathematical transformation to allow the model to follow the form of the general linear model.

In this section of this chapter, we explore some of these other models, including polynomial regression models, regression models with interaction, and models with transformed variables.

Polynomial Regression

Regression models in which the highest power of any predictor variable is 1 and in which there are no interaction terms—cross products $(x_i \cdot x_j)$—are referred to as *first-order models*. Simple regression models like those presented in Chapter 13 are *first-order models with one independent variable*. The general model for simple regression is

$$y = \beta_0 + \beta_1 x_1 + \epsilon$$

If a second independent variable is added, the model is referred to as a first-order model with two independent variables and appears as

$$y = \beta_0 + \beta_1 x_1 + \beta_2 x_2 + \epsilon$$

Polynomial regression models are regression models that are second- or higher-order models. They contain squared, cubed, or higher powers of the predictor variable(s) and contain response surfaces that are curvilinear. Yet, they are still special cases of the general linear model given in formula (15.1).

Consider a regression model with one independent variable where the model includes a second predictor, which is the independent variable squared. Such a model is referred to as a second-order model with one independent variable because the highest power among the predictors is 2, but there is still only one independent variable. This model takes the following form:

$$y = \beta_0 + \beta_1 x_1 + \beta_2 x_1^2 + \epsilon$$

This model can be used to explore the possible fit of a quadratic model in predicting a dependent variable. A **quadratic model** is *a multiple regression model in which the predictors are a variable and the square of the variable.* How can this be a special case of the general linear model? Let x_2 of the general linear model be equal to x_1^2 then $y = \beta_0 + \beta_1 x_1 + \beta_2 x_1^2 + \epsilon$, becomes $y = \beta_0 + \beta_1 x_1 + \beta_2 x_2 + \epsilon$. Through what process does a researcher go to develop the regression constant and coefficients for a curvilinear model such as this one?

Multiple regression analysis assumes a linear fit of the regression coefficients and regression constant, but not necessarily a linear relationship of the independent variable values (x). Hence, a researcher can often accomplish curvilinear regression by recoding the data before the multiple regression analysis is attempted.

As an example, consider the data given in Table 15.1. This table contains sales volumes (in $ millions) for 13 manufacturing companies along with the number of manufacturer's representatives associated with each firm. A simple regression analysis to predict sales by the number of manufacturer's representatives results in the Excel output in Figure 15.1.

TABLE 15.1			
Sales Data for 13 Manufacturing Companies	Manufacturer	Sales ($ millions)	Number of Manufacturing Representatives
	1	2.1	2
	2	3.6	1
	3	6.2	2
	4	10.4	3
	5	22.8	4
	6	35.6	4
	7	57.1	5
	8	83.5	5
	9	109.4	6
	10	128.6	7
	11	196.8	8
	12	280.0	10
	13	462.3	11

FIGURE 15.1

Excel Simple Regression Output for Manufacturing Example

	A	B	C	D	E	F
1	SUMMARY OUTPUT					
2	Regression Statistics					
3	Multiple R	0.933				
4	R Square	0.870				
5	Adjusted R Square	0.858				
6	Standard Error	51.098				
7	Observations	13				
8						
9	ANOVA					
10		df	SS	MS	F	Significant F
11	Regression	1	192395.416	192395.416	73.69	0.0000033
12	Residual	11	28721.452	2611.041		
13	Total	12	221116.868			
14						
15		Coefficients	Standard Error	t Stat	P-value	
16	Intercept	-107.029	28.7373	-3.72	0.0033561	
17	Reps	41.026	4.7794	8.58	0.0000033	

This regression output shows a regression model with an r^2 of 87.0%, a standard error of the estimate equal to 51.10, a significant overall F test for the model, and a significant t ratio for the predictor number of manufacturer's representatives.

Figure 15.2(a) is a scatter plot for the data in Table 15.1. Notice that the plot of number of representatives and sales is not a straight line and is an indication that the relationship between the two variables may be curvilinear. To explore the possibility that a quadratic relationship may exist between sales and number of representatives, the business researcher creates a second predictor variable, (number of manufacturer's representatives)^2, to use in the regression analysis to predict sales along with number of manufacturer's representatives, as shown in Table 15.2. Thus, a variable can be created to explore second-order parabolic relationships by squaring the data from the independent variable of the linear model and entering it into the analysis. Figure 15.2(b) is a scatter plot of sales with (number of manufacturer's reps)^2. Note that this graph, with the squared term, more closely approaches a straight line than does the graph in Figure 15.2(a). By recoding the predictor variable, the researcher creates a potentially better regression fit.

With these data, a multiple regression model can be developed. Figure 15.3 shows the Excel output for the regression analysis to predict sales by number of manufacturer's representatives and (number of manufacturer's representatives)^2.

Examine the output in Figure 15.3 and compare it with the output in Figure 15.1 for the simple regression model. The R^2 for this model is 97.3%, which is an increase from the r^2 of 87.0% for the single linear predictor model. The standard error of the estimate for this model is 24.59, which is considerably lower than the 51.10 value obtained from the

FIGURE 15.2

MINITAB Scatter Plots of Manufacturing Data

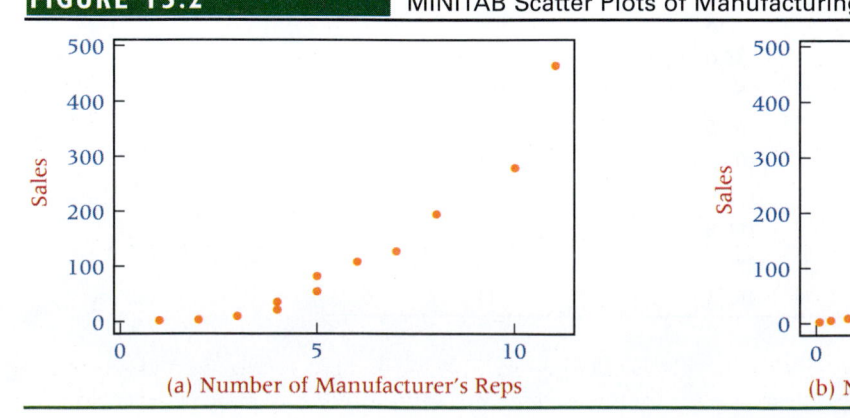

(a) Number of Manufacturer's Reps

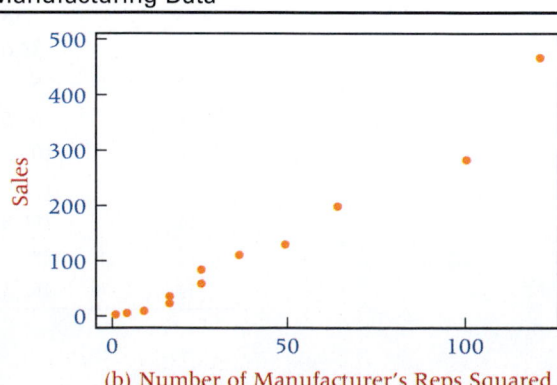

(b) Number of Manufacturer's Reps Squared

TABLE 15.2

Display of Manufacturing Data with Newly Created Variable

Manufacturer	Sales ($ millions) y	Number of Mgfr. Reps x_1	(Mgfr. Reps)^2 $x_2 = (x_1)^2$
1	2.1	2	4
2	3.6	1	1
3	6.2	2	4
4	10.4	3	9
5	22.8	4	16
6	35.6	4	16
7	57.1	5	25
8	83.5	5	25
9	109.4	6	36
10	128.6	7	49
11	196.8	8	64
12	280.0	10	100
13	462.3	11	121

FIGURE 15.3

Excel Output for Quadratic Model of Manufacturing Example

	A	B	C	D	E	F
1	SUMMARY OUTPUT					
2	Regression Statistics					
3	Multiple R	0.986				
4	R Square	0.973				
5	Adjusted R Square	0.967				
6	Standard Error	24.593				
7	Observations	13				
8						
9	ANOVA					
10		df	SS	MS	F	Significant F
11	Regression	2	215068.6001	107534.3	177.79	0.000000015
12	Residual	10	6048.3	604.8		
13	Total	12	221116.8677			
14						
15		Coefficients	Standard Error	t Stat	P-value	
16	Intercept	18.067	24.673	0.73	0.4808	
17	Reps	-15.723	9.550	-1.65	0.1307	
18	RepsSq	4.750	0.776	6.12	0.0001	

simple regression model. Remember, the sales figures were $ millions. The quadratic model reduced the standard error of the estimate by 26.51($1,000,000), or $26,510,000. It appears that the quadratic model is a better model for predicting sales.

An examination of the t statistic for the squared term and its associated probability in Figure 15.3 shows that it is statistically significant at $\alpha = .001$ ($t = 6.12$ with a probability of .0001). If this t statistic were not significant, the researcher would most likely drop the squared term and revert to the first-order model (simple regression model).

In theory, third- and higher-order models can be explored. Generally, business researchers tend to utilize first- and second-order regression models more than higher-order models. Remember that most regression analysis is used in business to aid decision making. Higher-power models (third, fourth, etc.) become difficult to interpret and difficult to explain to decision makers. In addition, the business researcher is usually looking for trends and general directions. The higher the order in regression modeling, the more the model tends to follow irregular fluctuations rather than meaningful directions.

Tukey's Ladder of Transformations

As just shown with the manufacturing example, recoding data can be a useful tool in improving the regression model fit. Many other ways of recoding data can be explored in this process. John W. Tukey* presents a "ladder of expressions" that can be explored to straighten out a plot of x and y, thereby offering potential improvement in the predictability of the regression model. **Tukey's ladder of transformations** gives the following expressions for both x and y.

Ladder for x
$\leftarrow$ Up Ladder $\downarrow$ Neutral Down Ladder $\rightarrow$

$$\ldots, x^4, x^3, x^2, x, \sqrt{x}, x, \log x, -\frac{1}{\sqrt{x}}, -\frac{1}{x}, -\frac{1}{x^2}, -\frac{1}{x^3}, -\frac{1}{x^4}, \ldots$$

Ladder for y
$\leftarrow$ Up Ladder $\downarrow$ Neutral Down Ladder $\rightarrow$

$$\ldots, y^4, y^3, y^2, y, \sqrt{y}, y, \log y, -\frac{1}{\sqrt{y}}, -\frac{1}{y}, -\frac{1}{y^2}, -\frac{1}{y^3}, -\frac{1}{y^4}, \ldots$$

These ladders suggest to the user potential ways to recode the data. Tukey published a **four-quadrant approach** to determining which expressions on the ladder are more appropriate for a given situation. This approach is based on the shape of the scatter plot of x and y. Figure 15.4 shows the four quadrants and the associated recoding expressions. For example, if the scatter plot of x and y indicates a shape like that shown in the upper left quadrant, recoding should move "down the ladder" for the x variable toward

$$\log x, -\frac{1}{\sqrt{x}}, -\frac{1}{x}, -\frac{1}{x^2}, -\frac{1}{x^3}, -\frac{1}{x^4}, \ldots$$

or "up the ladder" for the y variable toward

$$y^2, y^3, y^4, \ldots$$

Or, if the scatter plot of x and y indicates a shape like that of the lower right quadrant, the recoding should move "up the ladder" for the x variable toward

$$x^2, x^3, x^4, \ldots$$

or "down the ladder" for the y variable toward

$$\log y, -\frac{1}{\sqrt{y}}, -\frac{1}{y}, -\frac{1}{y^2}, -\frac{1}{y^3} -\frac{1}{y^4}, \ldots$$

In the manufacturing example, the graph in Figure 15.2(a) is shaped like the curve in the lower right quadrant of Tukey's four-quadrant approach. His approach suggests that

---

FIGURE 15.4

Tukey's Four-Quadrant Approach

Move toward $y^2, y^3, \ldots$ or toward $\log x, -1/\sqrt{x}, \ldots$	Move toward $y^2, y^3, \ldots$ or toward x^2, x^3
Move toward $\log y, -1/\sqrt{y}, \ldots$ or toward $\log x, -1/\sqrt{x}, \ldots$	Move toward $\log y, -1/\sqrt{y}, \ldots$ or toward $x^2, x^3, \ldots$

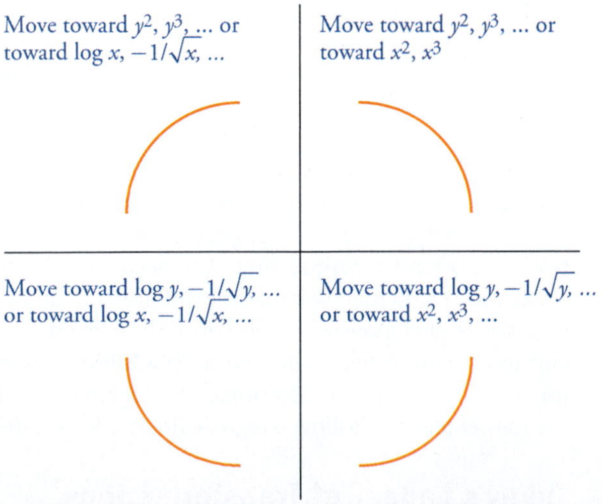

*John W. Tukey, *Exploratory Data Analysis.* Reading, MA, Addison-Wesley, 1977.

the business researcher move "up the ladder" on x as was done by using the squared term. The researcher could have explored other options such as continuing on up the ladder of x or going down the ladder of y. Tukey's ladder is a continuum and leaves open other recoding possibilities between the expressions. For example, between x^2 and x^3 are many possible powers of x that can be explored, such as $x^{2.1}$, $x^{2.5}$, or $x^{2.86}$.

Regression Models with Interaction

Often when two different independent variables are used in a regression analysis, an *interaction* occurs between the two variables. This interaction was discussed in Chapter 11 in two-way analysis of variance, where one variable will act differently over a given range of values for the second variable than it does over another range of values for the second variable. For example, in a manufacturing plant, temperature and humidity might interact in such a way as to have an effect on the hardness of the raw material. The air humidity may affect the raw material differently at different temperatures.

In regression analysis, interaction can be examined as a separate independent variable. An interaction predictor variable can be designed by multiplying the data values of one variable by the values of another variable, thereby creating a new variable. A model that includes an interaction variable is

$$y = \beta_0 + \beta_1 x_1 + \beta_2 x_2 + \beta_3 x_1 x_2 + \in$$

The $x_1 x_2$ term is the interaction term. Even though this model has 1 as the highest power of any one variable, it is considered to be a second-order equation because of the $x_1 x_2$ term.

Suppose the data in Table 15.3 represent the closing stock prices for three corporations over a period of 15 months. An investment firm wants to use the prices for stocks 2 and 3 to develop a regression model to predict the price of stock 1. The form of the general linear regression equation for this model is

$$y = \beta_0 + \beta_1 x_1 + \beta_2 x_2 + \in$$

where

y = price of stock 1
x_1 = price of stock 2
x_2 = price of stock 3

Using MINITAB to develop this regression model, the firm's researcher obtains the first output displayed in Figure 15.5. This regression model is a first-order model with two predictors, x_1 and x_2. This model produced a modest R^2 of .472. Both of the t ratios are small and statistically nonsignificant ($t = -.62$ with a p-value of .549 and $t = -.36$ with a p-value of .728). Although the overall model is statistically significant, $F = 5.37$ with probability of .022, neither predictor is significant.

Sometimes the effects of two variables are not additive because of the interacting effects between the two variables. In such a case, the researcher can use multiple regression analysis to explore the interaction effects by including an interaction term in the equation.

$$y = \beta_0 + \beta_1 x_1 + \beta_2 x_2 + \beta_3 x_1 x_2 + \in$$

The equation fits the form of the general linear model

$$y = \beta_0 + \beta_1 x_1 + \beta_2 x_2 + \beta_3 x_3 + \in$$

where $x_3 = x_1 x_2$. Each individual observation of x_3 is obtained through a recoding process by multiplying the associated observations of x_1 and x_2.

Applying this procedure to the stock example, the researcher uses the interaction term and MINITAB to obtain the second regression output shown in Figure 15.5. This output contains x_1, x_2, and the interaction term, $x_1 x_2$. Observe the R^2, which equals .804 for this model. The introduction of the interaction term caused the R^2 to increase from 47.2% to 80.4%. In addition, the standard error of the estimate decreased from 4.570 in the first model to 2.909 in the second model. The t ratios for both the x_1 term and the interaction term are statistically significant in the second model ($t = 3.36$ with a p-value of .006 for x_1 and $t = -4.31$ with a probability of .001 for $x_1 x_2$). The inclusion of the interaction term

TABLE 15.3

Prices of Three Stocks over a 15 Month Period

Stock 1	Stock 2	Stock 3
41	36	35
39	36	35
38	38	32
45	51	41
41	52	39
43	55	55
47	57	52
49	58	54
41	62	65
35	70	77
36	72	75
39	74	74
33	83	81
28	101	92
31	107	91

FIGURE 15.5

Two MINITAB Regression Outputs—without and with Interaction

Regression Analysis: Stock 1 versus Stock 2, Stock 3

The regression equation is
Stock 1 = 50.9 - 0.119 Stock 2 - 0.071 Stock 3

Predictor	Coef	SE Coef	T	P
Constant	50.855	3.791	13.41	0.000
Stock 2	-0.1190	0.1931	-0.62	0.549
Stock 3	-0.0708	0.1990	-0.36	0.728

S = 4.570   R-Sq = 47.2%   R-Sq(adj) = 38.4%

Analysis of Variance

Source	DF	SS	MS	F	P
Regression	2	224.29	112.15	5.37	0.022
Residual Error	12	250.64	20.89		
Total	14	474.93			

Regression Analysis: Stock 1 versus Stock 2, Stock 3, Interaction

The regression equation is
Stock 1 = 12.0 + 0.879 Stock 2 + 0.220 Stock 3 - 0.00998 Interaction

Predictor	Coef	SE Coef	T	P
Constant	12.046	9.312	1.29	0.222
Stock 2	0.8788	0.2619	3.36	0.006
Stock 3	0.2205	0.1435	1.54	0.153
Interact	-0.009985	0.002314	-4.31	0.001

S = 2.909   R-Sq = 80.4% R-Sq(adj) = 75.1%

Analysis of Variance

Source	DF	SS	MS	F	P
Regression	3	381.85	127.28	15.04	0.000
Residual Error	11	93.09	8.46		
Total	14	474.93			

helped the regression model account for a substantially greater amount of the dependent variable and is a significant contributor to the model.

Figure 15.6(a) is the response surface for the first regression model presented in Figure 15.5 (the model without interaction). As you observe the response plane with stock 3 as the point of reference, you see the plane moving upward with increasing values of stock 1 as the plane moves away from you toward smaller values of stock 2. Now examine Figure 15.6(b), the response surface for the second regression model presented in Figure 15.5 (the model with interaction). Note how the response plane is twisted, with its slope changing as it moves along stock 2. This pattern is caused by the interaction effects of stock 2 prices and

FIGURE 15.6

Response Surfaces for the Stock Example—without and with Interaction

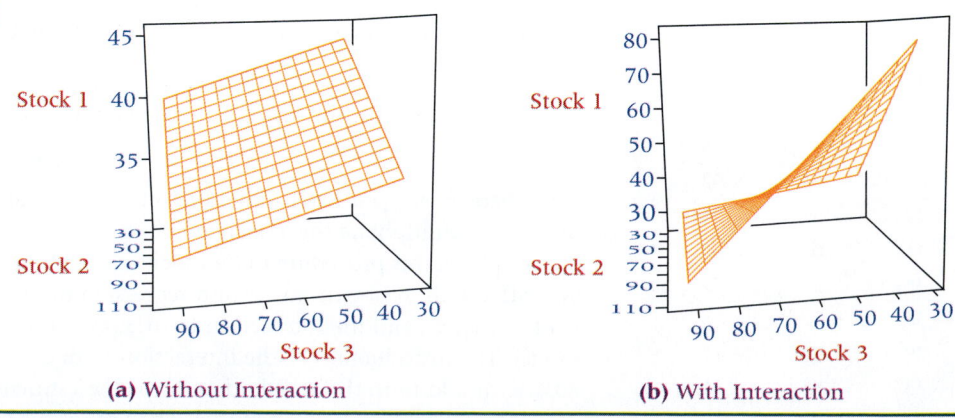

(a) Without Interaction   (b) With Interaction

stock 3 prices. A cross-section of the plane taken from left to right at any given stock 2 price produces a line that attempts to predict the price of stock 3 from the price of stock 1. As you move back through different prices of stock 2, the slope of that line changes, indicating that the relationship between stock 1 and stock 3 varies according to stock 2.

A researcher also could develop a model using two independent variables with their squares and interaction. Such a model would be a second-order model with two independent variables. The model would look like this.

$$y = \beta_0 + \beta_1 x_1 + \beta_2 x_2 + \beta_3 x_1^2 + \beta_4 x_2^2 + \beta_5 x_1 x_2 + \in$$

Model Transformation

To this point in examining polynomial and interaction models, the focus has been on recoding values of x variables. Some multiple regression situations require that the dependent variable, y, be recoded. To examine different relationships between x and y, Tukey's four-quadrant analysis and ladder of transformations can be used to explore ways to recode x or y in attempting to construct regression models with more predictability. Included on the ladder are such y transformations as log y and $1/y$.

Suppose the following data represent the annual sales and annual advertising expenditures for seven companies. Can a regression model be developed from these figures that can be used to predict annual sales by annual advertising expenditures?

Company	Sales ($ million/year)	Advertising ($ million/year)
1	2,580	1.2
2	11,942	2.6
3	9,845	2.2
4	27,800	3.2
5	18,926	2.9
6	4,800	1.5
7	14,550	2.7

One mathematical model that is a good candidate for fitting these data is an exponential model of the form

$$y = \beta_0 \beta_1^x \in$$

This model can be transformed (by taking the log of each side) so that it is in the form of the general linear equation.

$$\log y = \log \beta_0 + x \log \beta_1$$

This transformed model requires a recoding of the y data through the use of logarithms. Notice that x is not recoded but that the regression constant and coefficient are in logarithmic scale. If we let $y' = \log y$, $\beta_0' = \log \beta_0$, and $\beta_1' = \log \beta_1$, the exponential model is in the form of the general linear model.

$$y' = \beta_0' + \beta_1' x$$

The process begins by taking the log of the y values. The data used to build the regression model and the Excel regression output for these data follow.

Log Sales (y)	Advertising (x)
3.4116	1.2
4.0771	2.6
3.9932	2.2
4.4440	3.2
4.2771	2.9
3.6812	1.5
4.1629	2.7

	A	B	C	D	E	F
1	SUMMARY OUTPUT					
2	Regression Statistics					
3	Multiple R	0.990				
4	R Square	0.980				
5	Adjusted R Square	0.977				
6	Standard Error	0.0543				
7	Observations	7				
8						
9	ANOVA					
10		df	SS	MS	F	Significant F
11	Regression	1	0.739215	0.739215	250.36	0.000018
12	Residual	5	0.014763	0.002953		
13	Total	6	0.753979			
14						
15		Coefficients	Standard Error	t Stat	P-value	
16	Intercept	2.9003	0.0729	39.80	0.00000019	
17	Advertising	0.4751	0.0300	15.82	0.00001834	

A simple regression model (without the log recoding of the y variable) yields an R^2 of 87% whereas the exponential model R^2 is 98%. The t statistic for advertising is 15.82 with a p-value of 0.00001834 in the exponential model and 5.77 with a p-value of 0.00219 in the simple regression model. Thus the exponential model gives a better fit than does the simple regression model. An examination of (x^2, y) and (x^3, y) models reveals R^2 of .930 and .969, respectively, which are quite high but still not as good as the R^2 yielded by the exponential model.

The resulting equation of the exponential regression model is

$$y = 2.9003 + .4751x$$

In using this regression equation to determine predicted values of y for x, remember that the resulting predicted y value is in logarithmic form and the antilog of the predicted y must be taken to get the predicted y value in raw units. For example, to get the predicted y value (sales) for an advertising figure of 2.0 ($ million), substitute $x = 2.0$ into the regression equation.

$$y = 2.9003 + .4751x = 2.9003 + .4751(2.0) = 3.8505$$

The log of sales is 3.8505. Taking the antilog of 3.8505 results in the predicted sales in raw units.

$$\text{antilog}(3.8505) = 7087.61 \ (\$ \text{ million})$$

Thus, the exponential regression model predicts that $2.0 million of advertising will result in $7,087.61 million of sales.

Other ways can be used to transform mathematical models so that they can be treated like the general linear model. One example is an inverse model such as

$$y = \frac{1}{\beta_0 + \beta_1 x_1 + \beta_2 x_2 + \in}$$

Such a model can be manipulated algebraically into the form

$$\frac{1}{y} = \beta_0 + \beta_1 x_1 + \beta_2 x_2 + \in$$

Substituting $y' = 1/y$ into this equation results in an equation that is in the form of the general linear model.

$$y' = \beta_0 + \beta_1 x_1 + \beta_2 x_2 + \in$$

To use this "inverse" model, recode the data values for y by using $1/y$. The regression analysis is done on the $1/y$, x_1, and x_2 data. To get predicted values of y from this model, enter the raw values of x_1 and x_2. The resulting predicted value of y from the regression equation will be the inverse of the actual predicted y value.

DEMONSTRATION PROBLEM 15.1

In the aerospace and defense industry, some cost estimators predict the cost of new space projects by using mathematical models that take the form

$$y = \beta_0 x^{\beta_1} \in$$

These cost estimators often use the weight of the object being sent into space as the predictor (x) and the cost of the object as the dependent variable (y). Quite often β_1 turns out to be a value between 0 and 1, resulting in the predicted value of y equaling some root of x.

Use the sample cost data given here to develop a cost regression model in the form just shown to determine the equation for the predicted value of y. Use this regression equation to predict the value of y for $x = 3,000$.

y (cost in billions)	x (weight in tons)
1.2	450
9.0	20,200
4.5	9,060
3.2	3,500
13.0	75,600
0.6	175
1.8	800
2.7	2,100

Solution

The equation

$$y = \beta_0 x^{\beta_1} \in$$

is not in the form of the general linear model, but it can be transformed by using logarithms:

$$\log y = \log \beta_0 + \beta_1 \log x + \in$$

which takes on the general linear form

$$y' = \beta_0' + \beta_1 x'$$

where

$$y' = \log y$$
$$\beta_0' = \log \beta_0$$
$$x' = \log x$$

This equation requires that both x and y be recoded by taking the logarithm of each.

log y	log x
.0792	2.6532
.9542	4.3054
.6532	3.9571
.5051	3.5441
1.1139	4.8785
−.2218	2.2430
.2553	2.9031
.4314	3.3222

Using these data, the computer produces the following regression constant and coefficient:

$$b_0' = -1.25292 \qquad b_1 = .49606$$

From these values, the equation of the predicted y value is determined to be

$$\log \hat{y} = -1.25292 + .49606 \log x$$

If $x = 3{,}000$, log $x = 3.47712$, and

$$\log \hat{y} = -1.25292 + .49606(3.47712) = .47194$$

then

$$\hat{y} = \text{antilog}(\log \hat{y}) = \text{antilog}(.47194) = 2.9644$$

The predicted value of y is \$2.9644 billion for $x = 3{,}000$ tons of weight. Taking the antilog of $b_0' = -1.25292$ yields .055857. From this and $b_1 = .49606$, the model can be written in the original form:

$$y = (.055857)x^{.49606}$$

Substituting $x = 3{,}000$ into this formula also yields \$2.9645 billion for the predicted value of y.

15.1 PROBLEMS

15.1 Use the following data to develop a quadratic model to predict y from x. Develop a simple regression model from the data and compare the results of the two models. Does the quadratic model seem to provide any better predictability? Why or why not?

x	y	x	y
14	200	15	247
9	74	8	82
6	29	5	21
21	456	10	94
17	320		

15.2 Develop a multiple regression model of the form

$$y = b_0 b_1^x \in$$

using the following data to predict y from x. From a scatter plot and Tukey's ladder of transformation, explore ways to recode the data and develop an alternative regression model. Compare the results.

y	x	y	x
2,485	3.87	740	2.83
1,790	3.22	4,010	3.62
874	2.91	3,629	3.52
2,190	3.42	8,010	3.92
3,610	3.55	7,047	3.86
2,847	3.61	5,680	3.75
1,350	3.13	1,740	3.19

15.3 The Publishers Information Bureau in New York City released magazine advertising expenditure data compiled by leading national advertisers. The data were organized by product type over several years. Shown here are data on total magazine advertising expenditures and household equipment and supplies advertising expenditures. Using these data, develop a regression model to predict total magazine advertising expenditures by household equipment and supplies advertising expenditures and by (household equipment and supplies advertising expenditures)^2. Compare this model to a regression model to predict total magazine advertising expenditures by only household equipment and supplies advertising expenditures. Construct a scatter plot of the data. Does the shape of the plot suggest some alternative models in light of Tukey's four-quadrant approach? If so, develop at least one other model and compare the model to the other two previously developed.

Total Magazine Advertising Expenditures ($ millions)	Household Equipment and Supplies Expenditures ($ millions)
1,193	34
2,846	65
4,668	98
5,120	93
5,943	102
6,644	103

15.4 Dun & Bradstreet reports, among other things, information about new business incorporations and number of business failures over the years. Shown here are data on business failures since 1970 and current liabilities of the failing companies. Use these data and the following model to predict current liabilities of the failing companies by the number of business failures. Discuss the strength of the model.

$$y = b_0 b_1^x \in$$

Now develop a different regression model by recoding x. Use Tukey's four-quadrant approach as a resource. Compare your models.

Rate of Business Failures Since 1970 (10,000)	Current Liabilities of Failing Companies ($ millions)
44	1,888
43	4,380
42	4,635
61	6,955
88	15,611
110	16,073
107	29,269
115	36,937
120	44,724
102	34,724
98	39,126
65	44,261

15.5 Use the following data to develop a curvilinear model to predict y. Include both x_1 and x_2 in the model in addition to x_1^2 and x_2^2, and the interaction term $x_1 x_2$. Comment on the overall strength of the model and the significance of each predictor. Develop a regression model with the same independent variables as the first model but without the interaction variable. Compare this model to the model with interaction.

y	x_1	x_2
47.8	6	7.1
29.1	1	4.2
81.8	11	10.0
54.3	5	8.0
29.7	3	5.7
64.0	9	8.8
37.4	3	7.1
44.5	4	5.4
42.1	4	6.5
31.6	2	4.9
78.4	11	9.1
71.9	9	8.5
17.4	2	4.2
28.8	1	5.8
34.7	2	5.9
57.6	6	7.8
84.2	12	10.2
63.2	8	9.4
39.0	3	5.7
47.3	5	7.0

15.6   What follows is Excel output from a regression model to predict y using x_1, x_2, x_1^2, x_2^2, and the interaction term, x_1x_2. Comment on the overall strength of the model and the significance of each predictor. The data follow the Excel output. Develop a regression model with the same independent variables as the first model but without the interaction variable. Compare this model to the model with interaction.

	A	B	C	D	E	F
1	SUMMARY OUTPUT					
2	Regression Statistics					
3	Multiple R	0.954				
4	R Square	0.910				
5	Adjusted R Square	0.878				
6	Standard Error	7.544				
7	Observations	20				
8						
9	ANOVA					
10		df	SS	MS	F	Significant F
11	Regression	5	8089.275	1617.855	28.43	0.00000073
12	Residual	14	796.725	56.909		
13	Total	19	8886			
14						
15		Coefficients	Standard Error	t Stat	P-value	
16	Intercept	464.4433	503.0955	0.92	0.3716	
17	x1	-10.5101	6.0074	-1.75	0.1021	
18	x2	-1.2212	1.9791	-0.62	0.5471	
19	x1Sq	0.0357	0.0195	1.84	0.0876	
20	x2Sq	-0.0002	0.0021	-0.08	0.9394	
21	x1*x2	0.0243	0.0107	2.28	0.0390	

y	x_1	x_2	y	x_1	x_2
34	120	190	45	96	245
56	105	240	34	79	288
78	108	238	23	66	312
90	110	250	89	88	315
23	78	255	76	80	320
34	98	230	56	73	335
45	89	266	43	69	335
67	92	270	23	75	250
78	95	272	45	63	372
65	85	288	56	74	360

15.2 INDICATOR (DUMMY) VARIABLES

Some variables are referred to as **qualitative variables** (as opposed to *quantitative* variables) because qualitative variables do not yield quantifiable outcomes. Instead, *qualitative variables yield nominal- or ordinal-level information,* which is used more to categorize items. These variables have a role in multiple regression and are referred to as **indicator,** or **dummy variables.** In this section, we will examine the role of indicator, or dummy variables as predictors or independent variables in multiple regression analysis.

Indicator variables arise in many ways in business research. Mail questionnaire or personal interview demographic questions are prime candidates because they tend to generate qualitative measures on such items as gender, geographic region, occupation, marital status, level of education, economic class, political affiliation, religion, management/nonmanagement status, buying/leasing a home, method of transportation, or type of broker. In one business study, business researchers were attempting to develop a multiple regression model to predict the distances shoppers drive to malls in the greater Cleveland area. One independent variable was whether the mall was located on the shore of Lake Erie. In a second study, a site location model for pizza restaurants included indicator variables for (1) whether the restaurant served beer and (2) whether the restaurant had a salad bar.

These indicator variables are qualitative in that no interval or ratio level measurement is assigned to a response. For example, if a mall is located on the shore of Lake Erie, awarding it a score of 20 or 30 or 75 because of its location makes no sense. In terms of gender, what value would you assign to a man or a woman in a regression study? Yet these types of indicator, or dummy, variables are often useful in multiple regression studies and can be included if they are coded in the proper format.

Most researchers code indicator variables by using 0 or 1. For example, in the shopping mall study, malls located on the shore of Lake Erie could be assigned a 1, and all other malls would then be assigned a 0. The assignment of 0 or 1 is arbitrary, with the number merely holding a place for the category. For this reason, the coding is referred to as "dummy" coding; the number represents a category by holding a place and is not a measurement.

Many indicator, or dummy, variables are dichotomous, such as male/female, salad bar/no salad bar, employed/not employed, and rent/own. For these variables, a value of 1 is arbitrarily assigned to one category and a value of 0 is assigned to the other category. Some qualitative variables contain several categories, such as the variable "type of job," which might have the categories assembler, painter, and inspector. In this case, using a coding of 1, 2, and 3, respectively, is tempting. However, that type of coding creates problems for multiple regression analysis. For one thing, the category "inspector" would receive a value that is three times that of "painter." In addition, the values of 1, 2, and 3 indicate a hierarchy of job types: assembler < painter < inspector. The proper way to code such indicator variables is with the 0, 1 coding. Two separate independent variables should be used to code the three categories of type of job. The first variable is assembler, where a 1 is recorded if the person's job is assembler and a 0 is recorded if it is not. The second variable is painter, where a 1 is recorded if the person's job is painter and a 0 is recorded if it is not. A variable should not be assigned to inspector, because all workers in the study for whom a 1 was not recorded either for the assembler variable or the painter variable must be inspectors. Thus, coding the inspector variable would result in redundant information and is not necessary. This reasoning holds for all indicator variables with more than two categories. If an indicator variable has c categories, then $c - 1$ dummy variables must be created and inserted into the regression analysis in order to include the indicator variable in the multiple regression.*

An example of an indicator variable with more than two categories is the result of the following question taken from a typical questionnaire.

Your office is located in which region of the country?

_____ Northeast _____ Midwest _____ South _____ West

Suppose a researcher is using a multiple regression analysis to predict the cost of doing business and believes geographic location of the office is a potential predictor. How does the researcher insert this qualitative variable into the analysis? Because $c = 4$ for this question, three dummy variables are inserted into the analysis. Table 15.4 shows one possible way this process works with 13 respondents. Note that rows 2, 7, and 11 contain all zeros, which indicate that those respondents have offices in the West. Thus, a fourth dummy variable for the West region is not necessary and, indeed, should not be included because the information contained in such a fourth variable is contained in the other three variables.

A word of caution is in order. Because of degrees of freedom and interpretation considerations, it is important that a multiple regression analysis have enough observations to handle adequately the number of independent variables entered. Some researchers recommend as a rule of thumb at least three observations per independent variable. If a qualitative variable has multiple categories, resulting in several dummy independent variables, and if several qualitative variables are being included in an analysis, the number of predictors can rather quickly exceed the limit of recommended number of variables per number of observations. Nevertheless, dummy variables can be useful and are a way in which nominal or ordinal information can be recoded and incorporated into a multiple regression model.

As an example, consider the issue of gender discrimination in the salary earnings of workers in some industries. In examining this issue, suppose a random sample of 15 workers is drawn from a pool of employed laborers in a particular industry and the workers' average monthly salaries are determined, along with their age and gender. The data are shown in Table 15.5. As gender can be only male or female, this variable is a dummy variable requiring 0, 1 coding. Suppose we arbitrarily let 1 denote male and 0 denote female. Figure 15.7 is the multiple regression model developed from the data of Table 15.5 by using MINITAB to predict the dependent variable, monthly salary, by two independent variables, age and gender.

The computer output in Figure 15.7 contains the regression equation for this model.

$$\text{Salary} = 0.732 + 0.111 \text{ Age} + 0.459 \text{ Gender}$$

An examination of the t ratios reveals that the dummy variable "gender" has a regression coefficient that is significant at $\alpha = .001$ ($t = 8.58$, $p = .000$). The overall

TABLE 15.4

Coding for the Indicator Variable of Geographic Location for Regression Analysis

Northeast x_1	Midwest x_2	South x_3
1	0	0
0	0	0
1	0	0
0	0	1
0	1	0
0	1	0
0	0	0
0	0	1
1	0	0
1	0	0
0	0	0
0	1	0
0	0	1

---

*If c indicator variables are included in the analysis, no unique estimators of the regression coefficients can be found. [J. Neter, M. H. Kutner, W. Wasserman, and C. Nachtsheim. *Applied Linear Regression Models*, 3rd ed. (Chicago, Richard D. Irwin, 1996).

TABLE 15.5

Data for the Monthly Salary Example

Monthly Salary ($1,000)	Age (10 years)	Gender (1 = male, 0 = female)
1.548	3.2	1
1.629	3.8	1
1.011	2.7	0
1.229	3.4	0
1.746	3.6	1
1.528	4.1	1
1.018	3.8	0
1.190	3.4	0
1.551	3.3	1
0.985	3.2	0
1.610	3.5	1
1.432	2.9	1
1.215	3.3	0
.990	2.8	0
1.585	3.5	1

FIGURE 15.7

MINITAB Regression Output for the Monthly Salary Example

```
Regression Analysis: Salary versus Age, Gender

The regression equation is
Salary = 0.732 + 0.111 Age + 0.459 Gender

Predictor      Coef    SE Coef      T       P
Constant     0.7321    0.2356    3.11    0.009
Age          0.11122   0.07208   1.54    0.149
Gender       0.45868   0.05346   8.58    0.000

S = 0.09679     R-Sq = 89.0%      R-Sq(adj) = 87.2%

Analysis of Variance

Source          DF       SS        MS       F       P
Regression       2    0.90949   0.45474   48.54   0.000
Residual Error  12    0.11242   0.00937
Total           14    1.02191
```

model is significant at $\alpha = .001$ ($F = 48.54$, $p = .000$). The standard error of the estimate, $s_e = .09679$, indicates that approximately 68% of the errors of prediction are within $\pm$ \$96.79 ($.09679 \cdot \$1,000$). The R^2 is relatively high at 89.0%, and the adjusted R^2 is 87.2%.

The t value for gender indicates that it is a significant predictor of monthly salary in this model. This significance is apparent when one looks at the effects of this dummy variable another way. Figure 15.8 shows the graph of the regression equation when gender = 1 (male) and the graph of the regression equation when gender = 0 (female). When gender = 1 (male), the regression equation becomes

$$.732 + .111(\text{Age}) + .459(1) = 1.191 + .111(\text{Age})$$

When gender = 0 (female), the regression equation becomes

$$.732 + .111(\text{Age}) + .459(0) = .732 + .111(\text{Age}).$$

The full regression model (with both predictors) has a response surface that is a plane in a three-dimensional space. However, if a value of 1 is entered for gender into the full regression model, as just shown, the regression model is reduced to a line passing through the plane formed by monthly salary and age. If a value of 0 is entered for gender, as shown, the full regression model also reduces to a line passing through the plane formed by

Predicting Export Intensity of Chinese Manufacturing Firms Using Multiple Regression Analysis

According to business researchers, Hongxin Zhao and Shaoming Zou, little research has been done on the impact of external or uncontrollable variables on the export performance of a company. These two researchers conducted a study of Chinese manufacturing firms and used multiple regression to determine whether both domestic market concentration and firm location are good predictors of a firm's export intensity. The study included 999 Chinese manufacturing firms that exported. The dependent variable was "export intensity," which was defined to be the proportion of production output that is exported and was computed by dividing the firm's export value by its production output value. The higher the proportion was, the higher the export intensity. Zhao and Zou used covariate techniques (beyond the scope of this text) to control for the fact that companies in the study varied by size, capital intensity, innovativeness, and industry. The independent variables were industry concentration and location. Industry concentration was computed as a ratio, with higher values indicating more

concentration in the industry. The location variable was a composite index taking into account total freight volume, available modes of transportation, number of telephones, and size of geographic area.

The multiple regression model produced an R^2 of approximately 52%. Industry concentration was a statistically significant predictor at $\alpha = .01$, and the sign on the regression coefficient indicated that a negative relationship may exist between industry concentration and export intensity. It means export intensity is lower in highly concentrated industries and higher in lower concentrated industries. The researchers believe that in a more highly concentrated industry, the handful of firms dominating the industry will stifle the export competitiveness of firms. In the absence of dominating firms in a more fragmented setting, more competition and an increasing tendency to export are noted. The location variable was also a significant predictor at $\alpha = .01$. Firms located in coastal areas had higher export intensities than did those located in inland areas.

Source: Hongxin Zhao and Shaoming Zou, "The Impact of Industry Concentration and Firm Location on Export Propensity and Intensity: An Empirical Analysis of Chinese Manufacturing Firms," *Journal of International Marketing*, vol. 10, no. 1 (2002), pp. 52–71.

FIGURE 15.8

Regression Model for Male and Female Gender

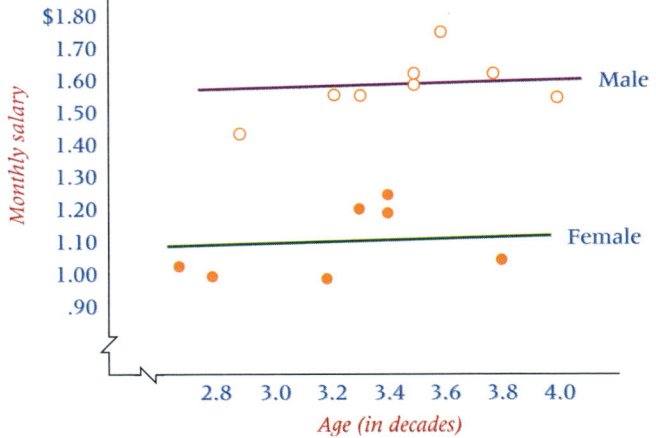

monthly salary and age. Figure 15.8 displays these two lines. Notice that the only difference in the two lines is the y intercept. Observe the monthly salary with male gender, as depicted by ○, versus the monthly salary with female gender, depicted by ●. The difference in the y intercepts of these two lines is .459, which is the value of the regression coefficient for gender. This intercept figure signifies that, on average, men earn $459 per month more than women for this population.

15.2 PROBLEMS

15.7 Analyze the following data by using a multiple regression computer software package to predict y using x_1 and x_2. Notice that x_2 is a dummy variable. Discuss the output from the regression analysis; in particular, comment on the predictability of the dummy variable.

y	x_1	x_2
16.8	27	1
13.2	16	0
14.7	13	0
15.4	11	1
11.1	17	0
16.2	19	1
14.9	24	1
13.3	21	0
17.8	16	1
17.1	23	1
14.3	18	0
13.9	16	0

15.8 Given here are the data from a dependent variable and two independent variables. The second independent variable is an indicator variable with several categories. Hence, this variable is represented by x_2, x_3, and x_4. How many categories are needed in total for this independent variable? Use a computer to perform a multiple regression analysis on this data to predict y from the x values. Discuss the output and pay particular attention to the dummy variables.

y	x_1	x_2	x_3	x_4
11	1.9	1	0	0
3	1.6	0	1	0
2	2.3	0	1	0
5	2.0	0	0	1
9	1.8	0	0	0
14	1.9	1	0	0
10	2.4	1	0	0
8	2.6	0	0	0
4	2.0	0	1	0
9	1.4	0	0	0
11	1.7	1	0	0
4	2.5	0	0	1
6	1.0	1	0	0
10	1.4	0	0	0
3	1.9	0	1	0
4	2.3	0	1	0
9	2.2	0	0	0
6	1.7	0	0	1

15.9   The MINITAB output displayed here is the result of a multiple regression analysis with three independent variables. Variable x_1 is a dummy variable. Discuss the computer output and the role x_1 plays in this regression model.

```
The regression equation is
Y = 121 + 13.4 X₁ -0.632 X₂ + 1.42 X₃

Predictor        Coef     Stdev       T       p
Constant       121.31     11.56   10.50    .000
      X₁        13.355     4.714    2.83    .014
      X₂       -0.6322    0.2270   -2.79    .015
      X₃         1.421     3.342    0.43    .678

S = 7.041      R-sq =79.5%      R-sq(adj) = 74.7%

Analysis of Variance

Source        df        SS       MS       F       p
Regression     3   2491.98   830.66   16.76    .000
Error         13    644.49    49.58
Total         16   3136.47
```

15.10   Given here is Excel output for a multiple regression model that was developed to predict y from two independent variables, x_1 and x_2. Variable x_2 is a dummy variable. Discuss the strength of the multiple regression model on the basis of the output. Focus on the contribution of the dummy variable. Plot x_1 and y with x_2 as 0, and then plot x_1 and y with x_2 as 1. Compare the two lines and discuss the differences.

	A	B	C	D	E	F
1	SUMMARY OUTPUT					
2	Regression Statistics					
3	Multiple R	0.623				
4	R Square	0.388				
5	Adjusted R Square	0.341				
6	Standard Error	11.744				
7	Observations	29				
8						
9	ANOVA					
10		df	SS	MS	F	Significant F
11	Regression	2	2270.11	1135.05	8.23	0.0017
12	Residual	26	3585.75	137.91		
13	Total	28	5855.86			
14						
15		Coefficients	Standard Error	t Stat	P-value	
16	Intercept	41.225	6.380	6.46	.00000076	
17	x1	1.081	1.353	0.80	.4316	
18	x2	-18.404	4.547	-4.05	.0004	

15.11   Falvey, Fried, and Richards[*] developed a multiple regression model to predict the average price of a meal at New Orleans restaurants. The variables explored included such indicator variables as the following: Accepts reservations, Accepts credit cards, Has its own parking lot, Has a separate bar or lounge, Has a maitre d', Has a dress code, Is candlelit, Has live entertainment, Serves alcoholic beverages, Is a steakhouse, Is in the French Quarter. Suppose a relatively simple model is developed to predict the average price of a meal at a restaurant in New Orleans from the number of hours the restaurant is open per week, the probability of being seated upon arrival, and whether the restaurant is located in the French

[*] *Adapted from* Rodney E. Falvey, Harold O. Fried, and Bruce Richards, "An Hedonic Guide to New Orleans Restaurants," *Quarterly Review of Economics and Finance*, vol. 32, no. 1 (Spring 1992).

Quarter. Use the following data and a computer to develop such a model. Comment on the output.

Price	Hours	Probability of Being Seated	French Quarter
$ 8.52	65	.62	0
21.45	45	.43	1
16.18	52	.58	1
6.21	66	.74	0
12.19	53	.19	1
25.62	55	.49	1
13.90	60	.80	0
18.66	72	.75	1
5.25	70	.37	0
7.98	55	.64	0
12.57	48	.51	1
14.85	60	.32	1
8.80	52	.62	0
6.27	64	.83	0

15.12 A researcher gathered 155 observations on four variables: job satisfaction, occupation, industry, and marital status. She wants to develop a multiple regression model to predict job satisfaction by the other three variables. All three predictor variables are qualitative variables with the following categories.

1. Occupation: accounting, management, marketing, finance
2. Industry: manufacturing, healthcare, transportation
3. Marital status: married, single

How many variables will be in the regression model? Delineate the number of predictors needed in each category and discuss the total number of predictors.

15.3 MODEL-BUILDING: SEARCH PROCEDURES

To this point in the chapter, we have explored various types of multiple regression models. We evaluated the strengths of regression models and learned how to understand more about the output from multiple regression computer packages. In this section we examine procedures for developing several multiple regression model options to aid in the decision-making process.

Suppose a researcher wants to develop a multiple regression model to predict the world production of crude oil. The researcher realizes that much of the world crude oil market is driven by variables related to usage and production in the United States. The researcher decides to use as predictors the following five independent variables.

1. U.S. energy consumption
2. Gross U.S. nuclear electricity generation
3. U.S. coal production
4. Total U.S. dry gas (natural gas) production
5. Fuel rate of U.S.-owned automobiles

The researcher measured data for each of these variables for the year preceding each data point of world crude oil production, figuring that the world production is driven by the previous year's activities in the United States. It would seem that as the energy consumption of the United States increases, so would world production of crude oil. In addition, it makes sense that as nuclear electricity generation, coal production, dry gas production, and fuel rates increase, world crude oil production would decrease if energy consumption stays approximately constant.

Table 15.6 shows data for the five independent variables along with the dependent variable, world crude oil production. Using the data presented in Table 15.6, the researcher attempted to develop a multiple regression model using five different independent variables. The result of this process was the MINITAB output in Figure 15.9. Examining the output, the researcher can reach some conclusions about that particular model and its variables.

The output contains an R^2 value of 92.1%, a standard error of the estimate of 1.215, and an overall significant F value of 46.62. Notice from Figure 15.9 that the t ratios indicate that the regression coefficients of four of the predictor variables, nuclear, coal, dry gas, and fuel rate, are not significant at $\alpha = .05$. If the researcher were to drop these four variables out of the regression analysis and rerun the model with the other predictor only, what would happen to the model? What if the researcher ran a regression model with only three predictors? How would these models compare to the full model with all five predictors? Are all the predictors necessary?

Developing regression models for business decision making involves at least two considerations. The first is to develop a regression model that accounts for the most variation of the dependent variable—that is, develop models that maximize the explained proportion of the deviation of the y values. At the same time, the regression model should be as parsimonious (simple and economical) as possible. The more complicated a quantitative

TABLE 15.6 — Data for Multiple Regression Model to Predict Crude Oil Production

World Crude Oil Production (million barrels per day)	U.S. Energy Consumption (quadrillion BTUs generation per year)	U.S. Nuclear Electricity (billion kilowatt-hours)	U.S. Coal Gross Production (million short-tons)	U.S. Total Dry Gas Production (trillion cubic feet)	U.S. Fuel Rate for Automobiles (miles per gallon)
55.7	74.3	83.5	598.6	21.7	13.4
55.7	72.5	114.0	610.0	20.7	13.6
52.8	70.5	172.5	654.6	19.2	14.0
57.3	74.4	191.1	684.9	19.1	13.8
59.7	76.3	250.9	697.2	19.2	14.1
60.2	78.1	276.4	670.2	19.1	14.3
62.7	78.9	255.2	781.1	19.7	14.6
59.6	76.0	251.1	829.7	19.4	16.0
56.1	74.0	272.7	823.8	19.2	16.5
53.5	70.8	282.8	838.1	17.8	16.9
53.3	70.5	293.7	782.1	16.1	17.1
54.5	74.1	327.6	895.9	17.5	17.4
54.0	74.0	383.7	883.6	16.5	17.5
56.2	74.3	414.0	890.3	16.1	17.4
56.7	76.9	455.3	918.8	16.6	18.0
58.7	80.2	527.0	950.3	17.1	18.8
59.9	81.4	529.4	980.7	17.3	19.0
60.6	81.3	576.9	1029.1	17.8	20.3
60.2	81.1	612.6	996.0	17.7	21.2
60.2	82.2	618.8	997.5	17.8	21.0
60.2	83.9	610.3	945.4	18.1	20.6
61.0	85.6	640.4	1033.5	18.8	20.8
62.3	87.2	673.4	1033.0	18.6	21.1
64.1	90.0	674.7	1063.9	18.8	21.2
66.3	90.6	628.6	1089.9	18.9	21.5
67.0	89.7	666.8	1109.8	18.9	21.6

FIGURE 15.9

MINITAB Output of Regression for Crude Oil Production Example

```
Regression Analysis: CrOilPrd versus USEnCons, USNucGen, ...

The regression equation is
CrOilPrd = 2.71 + 0.836 USEnCons - 0.00654 USNucGen + 0.00983
           USCoalPr -0.143 USDryGas - 0.734 FuelRate

Predictor        Coef   SE Coef       T      P
Constant        2.708     8.909    0.30  0.764
USEnCons       0.8357    0.1802    4.64  0.000
USNucGen    -0.006544  0.009854   -0.66  0.514
USCoalPr     0.009825  0.007286    1.35  0.193
USDryGas      -0.1432    0.4484   -0.32  0.753
FuelRate      -0.7341    0.5488   -1.34  0.196

S = 1.215     R-Sq = 92.1% R-Sq(adj) = 90.1%

Analysis of Variance

Source           DF        SS       MS       F      P
Regression        5   343.916   68.783   46.62  0.000
Residual Error   20    29.510    1.476
Total            25   373.427
```

model becomes, the harder it is for managers to understand and implement the model. In addition, as more variables are included in a model, it becomes more expensive to gather historical data or update present data for the model. These two considerations (dependent variable explanation and parsimony of the model) are quite often in opposition to each other. Hence the business researcher, as the model builder, often needs to explore many model options.

In the world crude oil production regression model, if three variables explain the deviation of world crude oil production nearly as well as five variables, the simpler model is more attractive. How might researchers conduct regression analysis so that they can examine several models and then choose the most attractive one? The answer is to use search procedures.

Search Procedures

Search procedures are *processes whereby more than one multiple regression model is developed for a given database, and the models are compared and sorted by different criteria, depending on the given procedure.* Virtually all search procedures are done on a computer. Several search procedures are discussed in this section, including all possible regressions, stepwise regression, forward selection, and backward elimination.

All Possible Regressions

The **all possible regressions** search procedure *computes all possible linear multiple regression models from the data using all variables.* If a data set contains k independent variables, all possible regressions will determine $2^k - 1$ different models.

For the crude oil production example, the procedure of all possible regressions would produce $2^5 - 1 = 31$ different models from the $k = 5$ independent variables. With $k = 5$ predictors, the procedure produces all single-predictor models, all models with two predictors, all models with three predictors, all models with four predictors, and all models with five predictors, as shown in Table 15.7.

The all possible regressions procedure enables the business researcher to examine every model. In theory, this method eliminates the chance that the business researcher will never consider some models, as can be the case with other search procedures. On the other hand, the search through all possible models can be tedious, time-consuming, inefficient, and perhaps overwhelming.

Single Predictor	Two Predictors	Three Predictors	Four Predictors	Five Predictors
x_1	x_1, x_2	x_1, x_2, x_3	x_1, x_2, x_3, x_4	x_1, x_2, x_3, x_4, x_5
x_2	x_1, x_3	x_1, x_2, x_4	x_1, x_2, x_3, x_5	
x_3	x_1, x_4	x_1, x_2, x_5	x_1, x_2, x_4, x_5	
x_4	x_1, x_5	x_1, x_3, x_4	x_1, x_3, x_4, x_5	
x_5	x_2, x_3	x_1, x_3, x_5	x_2, x_3, x_4, x_5	
	x_2, x_4	x_1, x_4, x_5		
	x_2, x_5	x_2, x_3, x_4		
	x_3, x_4	x_2, x_3, x_5		
	x_3, x_5	x_2, x_4, x_5		
	x_4, x_5	x_3, x_4, x_5		

Stepwise Regression

Perhaps the most widely known and used of the search procedures is stepwise regression.
Stepwise regression is *a step-by-step process that begins by developing a regression model with
a single predictor variable and adds and deletes predictors one step at a time,* examining the fit
of the model at each step until no more significant predictors remain outside the model.

STEP 1. In step 1 of a stepwise regression procedure, the k independent variables are
examined one at a time by developing a simple regression model for each independent variable to predict the dependent variable. The model containing the
largest absolute value of t for an independent variable is selected, and the independent variable associated with the model is selected as the "best" single predictor of y at the first step. Some computer software packages use an F value
instead of a t value to make this determination. Most of these computer programs allow the researcher to predetermine critical values for t or F, but most
also contain a default value as an option. If the first independent variable
selected at step 1 is denoted x_1, the model appears in the form

$$\hat{y} = b_o + b_1 x_1$$

If, after examining all possible single-predictor models, it is concluded that
none of the independent variables produces a t value that is significant at α,
then the search procedure stops at step 1 and recommends no model.

STEP 2. In step 2, the stepwise procedure examines all possible two-predictor regression models with x_1 as one of the independent variables in the model and
determines which of the other $k - 1$ independent variables in conjunction with
x_1 produces the highest absolute t value in the model. If this other variable
selected from the remaining independent variables is denoted x_2 and is
included in the model selected at step 2 along with x_1, the model appears in
the form

$$\hat{y} = b_o + b_1 x_1 + b_2 x_2$$

At this point, stepwise regression pauses and examines the t value of the
regression coefficient for x_1. Occasionally, the regression coefficient for x_1 will
become statistically nonsignificant when x_2 is entered into the model. In that
case, stepwise regression will drop x_1 out of the model and go back and examine which of the other $k - 2$ independent variables, if any, will produce the
largest significant absolute t value when that variable is included in the model
along with x_2. If no other variables show significant t values, the procedure
halts. It is worth noting that the regression coefficients are likely to change
from step to step to account for the new predictor being added in the process.
Thus, if x_1 stays in the model at step 2, the value of b_1 at step 1 will probably be
different from the value of b_1 at step 2.

STEP 3. Step 3 begins with independent variables, x_1 and x_2 (the variables that were finally selected at step 2), in the model. At this step, a search is made to determine which of the $k-2$ remaining independent variables in conjunction with x_1 and x_2 produces the largest significant absolute t value in the regression model. Let us denote the one that is selected as x_3. If no significant t values are acknowledged at this step, the process stops here and the model determined in step 2 is the final model. At step 3, the model appears in the form

$$\hat{y} = b_o + b_1 x_1 + b_2 x_2 + b_3 x_3$$

In a manner similar to step 2, stepwise regression now goes back and examines the t values of the regression coefficients of x_1 and x_2 in this step 3 model. If either or both of the t values are now nonsignificant, the variables are dropped out of the model and the process calls for a search through the remaining $k-3$ independent variables to determine which, if any, in conjunction with x_3 produce the largest significant t values in this model. The stepwise regression process continues step by step until no significant independent variables remain that are not in the model.

In the crude oil production example, recall that Table 15.6 contained data that can be used to develop a regression model to predict world crude oil production from as many as five different independent variables. Figure 15.9 displayed the results of a multiple regression analysis to produce a model using all five predictors. Suppose the researcher were to use a stepwise regression search procedure on these data to find a regression model. Recall that the following independent variables were being considered.

1. U.S. energy consumption
2. U.S. nuclear generation
3. U.S. coal production
4. U.S. dry gas production
5. U.S. fuel rate

STEP 1. Each of the independent variables is examined one at a time to determine the strength of each predictor in a simple regression model. The results are reported in Table 15.8.

Note that the independent variable "energy consumption" was selected as the predictor variable, x_1, in step 1. An examination of Table 15.8 reveals that energy consumption produced the largest absolute t value (11.77) of the single predictors. By itself, energy consumption accounted for 85.2% of the variation of the y values (world crude oil production). The regression equation taken from the computer output for this model is

$$y = 13.075 + .580x_1$$

where

y = world crude oil production
x_1 = U.S. energy consumption

STEP 2. In step 2, x_1 was retained initially in the model and a search was conducted among the four remaining independent variables to determine which of those variables in conjunction with x_1 produced the largest significant t value. Table 15.9 reports the results of this search.

The information in Table 15.9 shows that the model selected in step 2 includes the independent variables "energy consumption" and "fuel rate." Fuel rate has the largest absolute t value (−3.75), and it is significant at $\alpha = .05$. Other variables produce varying sizes of t values. The model produced at step 2 has an R^2 of 90.8%. These two variables taken together account for almost 91% of the variation of world crude oil production in this sample.

From other computer information, it is ascertained that the t value for the x_1 variable in this model is 11.91, which is even higher than in step 1.

TABLE 15.8

Step 1: Results of Simple Regression Using Each Independent Variable to Predict Oil Production

Dependent Variable	Independent Variable	t Ratio	R^2
Oil production	Energy consumption	11.77	85.2%
Oil production	Nuclear	4.43	45.0
Oil production	Coal	3.91	38.9
Oil production	Dry gas	1.08	4.6
Oil production	Fuel rate	3.54	34.2

→ Variable selected to serve as x_1

TABLE 15.9

Step 2: Regression Results with Two Predictors

Dependent Variable y	Independent Variable x_1	Independent Variable x_2	t Ratio of x_2	R^2
Oil production	Energy consumption	Nuclear	−3.60	90.6%
Oil production	Energy consumption	Coal	−2.44	88.3
Oil production	Energy consumption	Dry gas	2.23	87.9
Oil production	Energy consumption	Fuel rate	−3.75	90.8

→ Variables selected at step 2

Therefore, x_1 will not be dropped from the model by the stepwise regression procedure. The step 2 regression model from the computer output is

$$y = 7.14 + 0.772x_1 - 0.517x_2$$

where

y = world crude oil production
x_1 = U.S. energy consumption
x_2 = U.S. fuel rate

Note that the regression coefficient for x_1 changed from .580 at step 1 in the model to .772 at step 2.

The R^2 for the model in step 1 was 85.2%. Notice that none of the R^2 values produced from step 2 models is less than 85.2%. The reason is that x_1 is still in the model, so the R^2 at this step must be at least as high as it was in step 1, when only x_1 was in the model. In addition, by examining the R^2 values in Table 15.9, you can get a feel for how much the prospective new predictor adds to the model by seeing how much R^2 increases from 85.2%. For example, with x_2 (fuel rate) added to the model, the R^2 goes up to 90.8%. However, adding the variable "dry gas" to x_1 increases R^2 very little (it goes up 87.9%).

STEP 3.   In step 3, the search procedure continues to look for an additional predictor variable from the three independent variables remaining out of the solution. Variables x_1 and x_2 are retained in the model. Table 15.10 reports the result of this search.

In this step, regression models are explored that contain x_1 (energy consumption) and x_2 (fuel rate) in addition to one of the three remaining variables. None of the three models produce t ratios that are significant at $\alpha = .05$. No new variables are added to the model produced in step 2. The stepwise regression process ends.

Figure 15.10 shows the MINITAB stepwise regression output for the world crude oil production example. The results printed in the table are virtually identical to the step-by-step results discussed in this section, but are in a different format.

Each column in Figure 15.10 contains information about the regression model at each step. Thus, column 1 contains data on the regression model for step 1. In each column at each step you can see the variables in the model. As an example, at step 2, energy consumption and fuel rate are in the model. The numbers above the t ratios are the

TABLE 15.10	Dependent Variable y	Independent Variable x_1	Independent Variable x_2	Independent Variable x_3	t Ratio of x_3	R^2
Step 3: Regression Results with Three Predictors	Oil production	Energy consumption	Fuel rate	Nuclear	−0.43	90.9%
	Oil production	Energy consumption	Fuel rate	Coal	1.71	91.9
	Oil production	Energy consumption	Fuel rate	Dry gas	−0.46	90.9

No t ratio is significant at $\alpha = .05$.
No new variables are added to the model.

FIGURE 15.10

MINITAB Stepwise Regression Output for the Crude Oil Production Example

```
Stepwise Regression: CrOilPrd versus USEnCons, USNucGen, ...
Alpha-to-Enter: 0.1 Alpha-to-Remove: 0.1
Response is CrOilPrd on 5 predictors, with N =   26
Step              1        2
Constant     13.075    7.140

USEnCons      0.580    0.772
T-Value       11.77    11.91
P-Value       0.000    0.000

FuelRate               -0.52
T-Value                -3.75
P-Value                 0.001

S              1.52     1.22
R-Sq          85.24    90.83
R-Sq(adj)     84.62    90.03
C-p            15.4      3.2
```

regression coefficients. The coefficients and the constant in column 2, for example, yield the regression model equation values for step 2.

$$\hat{y} = 7.140 + 0.772x_1 - 0.52x_2$$

The values of R^2 (R-Sq) and the standard error of the estimate (S) are displayed on the bottom row of the output along with the adjusted value of R^2 and the C_p (C-p) statistic, which is a measure of the difference between the estimated model and the true model.

Forward Selection

Another search procedure is forward selection. **Forward selection** is essentially the same as stepwise regression, but once a variable is entered into the process, it is never dropped out. Forward selection begins by finding the independent variable that will produce the largest absolute value of t (and largest R^2) in predicting y. The selected variable is denoted here as x_1 and is part of the model

$$\hat{y} = b_0 + b_1x_1$$

Forward selection proceeds to step 2. While retaining x_1, it examines the other $k-1$ independent variables and determines which variable in the model with x_1 produces the highest absolute value of t that is significant. To this point, forward selection is the same as stepwise regression. If this second variable is designated x_2, the model is

$$\hat{y} = b_0 + b_1x_1 + b_2x_2$$

At this point, forward selection does not reexamine the t value of x_1. Both x_1 and x_2 remain in the model as other variables are examined and included. When independent variables are correlated in forward selection, the overlapping of information can limit the potential predictability of two or more variables in combination. Stepwise regression takes this into account, in part, when it goes back to reexamine the t values of predictors already in the model to determine whether they are still significant predictors of y given the variables that have now entered the process. In other words, stepwise regression acknowledges that the strongest single predictor of y that is selected at step 1 may not be a significant predictor of y when taken in conjunction with other variables.

Using a forward selection procedure to develop multiple regression models for the world crude oil production example would result in the same outcome as that provided by stepwise regression because neither x_1 nor x_2 were removed from the model in that particular stepwise regression. The difference in the two procedures is more apparent in examples where variables selected at earlier steps in the process are removed during later steps in stepwise regression.

Backward Elimination

The **backward elimination** search procedure is *a step-by-step process that begins with the "full" model (all k predictors)*. Using the t values, a search is made to determine whether any nonsignificant independent variables are in the model. If no nonsignificant predictors are found, the backward process ends with the full model. If nonsignificant predictors are found, the predictor with the smallest absolute value of t is eliminated and a new model is developed with $k - 1$ independent variables.

This model is then examined to determine whether it contains any independent variables with nonsignificant t values. If it does, the predictor with the smallest absolute t value is eliminated from the process and a new model is developed for the next step.

This procedure of identifying the smallest nonsignificant t value and eliminating that variable continues until all variables left in the model have significant t values. Sometimes this process yields results similar to those obtained from forward selection and other times it does not. A word of caution is in order. Backward elimination always begins with all possible predictors in the model. Sometimes the sample data do not provide enough observations to justify the use of all possible predictors at the same time in the model. In this case, backward elimination is not a suitable option with which to build regression models.

The following steps show how the backward elimination process can be used to develop multiple regression models to predict world crude oil production using the data and five predictors displayed in Table 15.6.

STEP 1. A full model is developed with all predictors. The results are shown in Table 15.11. The R^2 for this model is 92.1%. A study of Table 15.11 reveals that the predictor "dry gas" has the smallest absolute value of a nonsignificant t ($t = -.32$, $p = .753$). In step 2, this variable will be dropped from the model.

STEP 2. A second regression model is developed with $k - 1 = 4$ predictors. Dry gas has been eliminated from consideration. The results of this multiple regression analysis are presented in Table 15.12. The computer results in Table 15.12 indicate that the variable "nuclear" has the smallest absolute value of a nonsignificant t of the variables remaining in the model ($t = -.64$, $p = .528$). In step 3, this variable will be dropped from the model.

STEP 3. A third regression model is developed with $k - 2 = 3$ predictors. Both nuclear and dry gas variables have been removed from the model. The results of this multiple regression analysis are reported in Table 15.13. The computer results in Table 15.13 indicate that the variable "coal" has the smallest absolute value of a nonsignificant t of the variables remaining in the model ($t = 1.71$, $p = .102$). In step 4, this variable will be dropped from the model.

STEP 4. A fourth regression model is developed with $k - 3 = 2$ predictors. Nuclear, dry gas, and coal variables have been removed from the model. The results of this multiple regression analysis are reported in Table 15.14. Observe that all p-values are less than $\alpha = .05$, indicating that all t values are significant, so no

TABLE 15.11
Step 1: Backward Elimination, Full Model

Predictor	Coefficient	t Ratio	p
Energy consumption	.8357	4.64	.000
Nuclear	−.00654	−0.66	.514
Coal	.00983	1.35	.193
Dry gas	−.1432	−0.32	.753
Fuel rate	−.7341	−1.34	.196

Variable to be dropped from the model

TABLE 15.12
Step 2: Backward Elimination, Four Predictors

Predictor	Coefficient	t Ratio	p
Energy consumption	.7843	9.85	.000
Nuclear	−.004261	−0.64	.528
Coal	.010933	1.74	.096
Fuel rate	−.8253	−1.80	.086

Variable to be dropped from the model

TABLE 15.13
Step 3: Backward Elimination, Three Predictors

Predictor	Coefficient	t Ratio	p
Energy consumption	.75394	11.94	.000
Coal	.010479	1.71	.102
Fuel rate	−1.0283	−3.14	.005

Variable to be dropped from the model

TABLE 15.14
Step 4: Backward Elimination, Two Predictors

Predictor	Coefficient	t Ratio	p
Energy consumption	.77201	11.91	.000
Fuel rate	−.5173	−3.75	.001

All variables are significant at $\alpha = .05$.
No variables will be dropped from this model.
The process stops.

additional independent variables need to be removed. The backward elimination process ends with two predictors in the model. The final model obtained from this backward elimination process is the same model as that obtained by using stepwise regression.

15.3 PROBLEMS

15.13 Use a stepwise regression procedure and the following data to develop a multiple regression model to predict y. Discuss the variables that enter at each step, commenting on their t values and on the value of R^2.

y	x_1	x_2	x_3	y	x_1	x_2	x_3
21	5	108	57	22	13	105	51
17	11	135	34	20	10	111	43
14	14	113	21	16	20	140	20
13	9	160	25	13	19	150	14
19	16	122	43	18	14	126	29
15	18	142	40	12	21	175	22
24	7	93	52	23	6	98	38
17	9	128	38	18	15	129	40

15.14 Given here are data for a dependent variable and four potential predictors. Use these data and a stepwise regression procedure to develop a multiple regression model to predict y. Examine the values of t and R^2 at each step and comment on those values. How many steps did the procedure use? Why do you think the process stopped?

y	x_1	x_2	x_3	x_4
101	2	77	1.2	42
127	4	72	1.7	26
98	9	69	2.4	47
79	5	53	2.6	65
118	3	88	2.9	37
114	1	53	2.7	28
110	3	82	2.8	29
94	2	61	2.6	22
96	8	60	2.4	48
73	6	64	2.1	42
108	2	76	1.8	34
124	5	74	2.2	11
82	6	50	1.5	61
89	9	57	1.6	53
76	1	72	2.0	72
109	3	74	2.8	36
123	2	99	2.6	17
125	6	81	2.5	48

15.15 The computer output given here is the result of a stepwise multiple regression analysis to predict a dependent variable by using six predictor variables. The number of observations was 108. Study the output and discuss the results. How many predictors ended up in the model? Which predictors, if any, did not enter the model?

```
STEPWISE REGRESSION OF Y ON 6  PREDICTORS, WITH N = 108
STEP              1        2        3        4
CONSTANT       8.71     6.82     6.57     5.96

X4            -2.85    -4.92    -4.97    -5.00
T-RATIO        2.11     2.94     3.04     3.07

X2                      4.42     3.72     3.22
T-RATIO                 2.64     2.20     2.05

X3                               1.91     1.78
T-RATIO                          2.07     2.02

X7                                        1.56
T-RATIO                                   1.98

S              3.81     3.51     3.43     3.36
R-SQ          29.20    49.45    54.72    59.29
```

15.16 Study the output given here from a stepwise multiple regression analysis to predict *y* from four variables. Comment on the output at each step.

```
STEPWISE REGRESSION OF Y ON 4  PREDICTORS, WITH N = 63
STEP              1        2
CONSTANT      27.88    22.30

X3             0.89
T-RATIO        2.26

X2                     12.38
T-RATIO                 2.64

X4                     0.0047
T-RATIO                 2.01

S             16.52     9.47
R-SQ          42.39    68.20
```

15.17 The National Underwriter Company in Cincinnati, Ohio, publishes property and casualty insurance data. Given here is a portion of the data published. These data include information from the U.S. insurance industry about (1) net income after taxes, (2) dividends to policyholders, (3) net underwriting gain/loss, and (4) premiums earned. Use the data and stepwise regression to predict premiums earned from the other three variables.

Premiums Earned	Net Income	Dividends	Underwriting Gain/Loss
30.2	1.6	.6	.1
47.2	.6	.7	−3.6
92.8	8.4	1.8	−1.5
95.4	7.6	2.0	−4.9
100.4	6.3	2.2	−8.1
104.9	6.3	2.4	−10.8
113.2	2.2	2.3	−18.2
130.3	3.0	2.4	−21.4
161.9	13.5	2.3	−12.8
182.5	14.9	2.9	−5.9
193.3	11.7	2.9	−7.6

15.18 The U.S. Energy Information Administration releases figures in their publication, *Monthly Energy Review*, about the cost of various fuels and electricity. Shown here are the figures for four different items over a 12-year period. Use the data and stepwise regression to predict the cost of residential electricity from the cost of residential natural gas, residual fuel oil, and leaded regular gasoline. Examine the data and discuss the output.

Residential Electricity (kWh)	Residential Natural Gas (1000 ft³)	Residual Fuel Oil (gal)	Leaded Regular Gasoline (gal)
2.54	1.29	.21	.39
3.51	1.71	.31	.57
4.64	2.98	.44	.86
5.36	3.68	.61	1.19
6.20	4.29	.76	1.31
6.86	5.17	.68	1.22
7.18	6.06	.65	1.16
7.54	6.12	.69	1.13
7.79	6.12	.61	1.12
7.41	5.83	.34	.86
7.41	5.54	.42	.90
7.49	4.49	.33	.90

15.4 MULTICOLLINEARITY

One problem that can arise in multiple regression analysis is multicollinearity. **Multicollinearity** is *when two or more of the independent variables of a multiple regression model are highly correlated.* Technically, if two of the independent variables are correlated, we have collinearity; when three or more independent variables are correlated, we have multicollinearity. However, the two terms are frequently used interchangeably.

The reality of business research is that most of the time some correlation between predictors (independent variables) will be present. The problem of multicollinearity arises when the intercorrelation between predictor variables is high. This relationship causes several other problems, particularly in the interpretation of the analysis.

1. It is difficult, if not impossible, to interpret the estimates of the regression coefficients.
2. Inordinately small t values for the regression coefficients may result.
3. The standard deviations of regression coefficients are overestimated.
4. The algebraic sign of estimated regression coefficients may be the opposite of what would be expected for a particular predictor variable.

The problem of multicollinearity can arise in regression analysis in a variety of business research situations. For example, suppose a model is being developed to predict salaries in a given industry. Independent variables such as years of education, age, years in management, experience on the job, and years of tenure with the firm might be considered as predictors. It is obvious that several of these variables are correlated (virtually all of these variables have something to do with number of years, or time) and yield redundant information. Suppose a financial regression model is being developed to predict bond market rates by such independent variables as Dow Jones average, prime interest rates, GNP, producer price index, and consumer price index. Several of these predictors are likely to be intercorrelated.

In the world crude oil production example used in section 15.3, several of the independent variables are intercorrelated, leading to the potential of multicollinearity problems. Table 15.15 gives the correlations of the predictor variables for this example. Note that r values are quite high ($r > .90$) for fuel rate and nuclear (.972), fuel rate and coal (.968), and coal and nuclear (.952).

Table 15.15 shows that fuel rate and coal production are highly correlated. Using fuel rate as a single predictor of crude oil production produces the following simple regression model.

$$\hat{y} = 44.869 + .7838(\text{fuel rate})$$

Notice that the estimate of the regression coefficient, .7838, is positive, indicating that as fuel rate increases, oil production increases. Using coal as a single predictor of crude oil production yields the following simple regression model.

$$\hat{y} = 45.072 + .0157(\text{coal})$$

The multiple regression model developed using both fuel rate and coal to predict crude oil production is

$$\hat{y} = 45.806 + .0227(\text{coal}) - .3934(\text{fuel rate})$$

Observe that this regression model indicates a *negative* relationship between fuel rate and oil production ($-.3934$), which is in opposition to the *positive* relationship shown in the regression equation for fuel rate as a single predictor. Because of the multicollinearity between coal and fuel rate, these two independent variables interact in the regression analysis in such a way as to produce regression coefficient estimates that are difficult to interpret. Extreme caution should be exercised before interpreting these regression coefficient estimates.

The problem of multicollinearity can also affect the t values that are used to evaluate the regression coefficients. Because the problems of multicollinearity among predictors can result in an overestimation of the standard deviation of the regression coefficients, the t values tend to be underrepresentative when multicollinearity is present. In some regression

TABLE 15.15		Energy Consumption	Nuclear	Dry Coal	Fuel Gas	Rate
Correlations Among Oil Production Predictor Variables	Energy consumption	1	.856	.791	.057	.791
	Nuclear	.856	1	.952	−.404	.972
	Coal	.791	.952	1	−.448	.968
	Dry gas	.057	−.404	−.448	1	−.423
	Fuel rate	.796	.972	.968	−.423	1

models containing multicollinearity in which all t values are nonsignificant, the overall F value for the model is highly significant. In Section 15.1, an example was given of how including interaction when it is significant strengthens a regression model. The computer output for the regression models both with and without the interaction term was shown in Figure 15.5. The model without interaction produced a statistically significant F value but neither predictor variable was significant. Further investigation of this model reveals that the correlation between the two predictors, x_1 and x_2, is .945. This extremely high correlation indicates a strong collinearity between the two predictor variables.

This collinearity may explain the fact that the overall model is significant but neither predictor is significant. It also underscores one of the problems with multicollinearity: underrepresented t values. The t values test the strength of the predictor given the other variables in the model. If a predictor is highly correlated with other independent variables, it will appear not to add much to the explanation of y and produce a low t value. However, had the predictor not been in the presence of these other correlated variables, the predictor might have explained a high proportion of variation of y.

Many of the problems created by multicollinearity are interpretation problems. The business researcher should be alert to and aware of multicollinearity potential with the predictors in the model and view the model outcome in light of such potential.

The problem of multicollinearity is not a simple one to overcome. However, several methods offer an approach to the problem. One way is to examine a correlation matrix like the one in Table 15.15 to search for possible intercorrelations among potential predictor variables. If several variables are highly correlated, the researcher can select the variable that is most correlated to the dependent variable and use that variable to represent the others in the analysis. One problem with this idea is that correlations can be more complex than simple correlation among variables. In other words, simple correlation values do not always reveal multiple correlation between variables. In some instances, variables may not appear to be correlated as pairs, but one variable is a linear combination of several other variables. This situation is also an example of multicollinearity, and a cursory observation of the correlation matrix will probably not reveal the problem.

Stepwise regression is another way to prevent the problem of multicollinearity. The search process enters the variables one at a time and compares the new variable to those in solution. If a new variable is entered and the t values on old variables become nonsignificant, the old variables are dropped out of solution. In this manner, it is more difficult for the problem of multicollinearity to affect the regression analysis. Of course, because of multicollinearity, some important predictors may not enter in to the analysis.

Other techniques are available to attempt to control for the problem of multicollinearity. One is called a **variance inflation factor,** in which a regression analysis is conducted to predict an independent variable by the other independent variables. In this case, the independent variable being predicted becomes the dependent variable. As this process is done for each of the independent variables, it is possible to determine whether any of the independent variables are a function of the other independent variables, yielding evidence of multicollinearity. By using the results from such a model, a variance inflation factor (VIF) can be computed to determine whether the standard errors of the estimates are inflated:

$$\text{VIF} = \frac{1}{1 - R_i^2}$$

where R_i^2 is the coefficient of determination for any of the models, used to predict an independent variable by the other $k - 1$ independent variables. Some researchers follow a guideline that any variance inflation factor greater than 10 or R_i^2 value more than .90 for the largest variance inflation factors indicates a severe multicollinearity problem.*

---

*William Mendenhall and Terry Sincich, *A Second Course in Business Statistics: Regression Analysis* (San Francisco: Dellen Publishing Company, 1989); John Neter, William Wasserman, and Michael H. Kutner, *Applied Linear Regression Models*, 2nd ed. (Homewood, IL: Richard D. Irwin, 1989).

15.4 PROBLEMS

15.19 Develop a correlation matrix for the independent variables in Problem 15.13. Study the matrix and make a judgment as to whether substantial multicollinearity is present among the predictors. Why or why not?

15.20 Construct a correlation matrix for the four independent variables for Problem 15.14 and search for possible multicollinearity. What did you find and why?

15.21 In Problem 15.17, you were asked to use stepwise regression to predict premiums earned by net income, dividends, and underwriting gain or loss. Study the stepwise results, including the regression coefficients, to determine whether there may be a problem with multicollinearity. Construct a correlation matrix of the three variables to aid you in this task.

15.22 Study the three predictor variables in Problem 15.18 and attempt to determine whether substantial multicollinearity is present between the predictor variables. If there is a problem of multicollinearity, how might it affect the outcome of the multiple regression analysis?

Determining Compensation for CEOs

One statistical tool that can be used to study CEO compensation is multiple regression analysis. Regression models can be developed using predictor variables, such as age, years of experience, worth of company, or others, for analyzing CEO compensation. Search procedures such as stepwise regression can be used to sort out the more significant predictors of CEO compensation.

The researcher prepares for the multiple regression analysis by conducting a study of CEOs and gathering data on several variables. The data presented in the Decision Dilemma could be used for such an analysis. It seems reasonable to believe that CEO compensation is related to the size and worth of a company, therefore it makes sense to attempt to develop a regression model or models to predict CEO compensation by the variables company sales, number of employees in the company, and the capital investment of a company. Qualitative or dummy variables can also be used in such an analysis. In the database given in the Decision Dilemma, one variable indicates whether a company is a manufacturing company. One way to recode this variable for regression analysis is to assign a 1 to companies that are manufacturers and a 0 to others.

A stepwise regression procedure can sort out the variables that seem to be more important predictors of CEO compensation. A stepwise regression analysis was conducted on the Decision Dilemma database using sales, number of employees, capital investment, and whether a company is in manufacturing as the four independent variables. The result of this analysis follows.

```
Stepwise Regression: Cash Compen versus Sales, No. of Emp.,  ...
Alpha-to-Enter: 0.15 Alpha-to-Remove: 0.15
Response is Cash Com on 4 predictors, with N =   20
```

Step	1	2	3	4
Constant	243.9	232.2	223.8	223.3
No. of E	0.0696	0.1552	0.0498	
T-Value	13.67	4.97	0.98	
P-Value	0.000	0.000	0.343	
Cap. Inv		−1.66	−2.92	−3.06
T-Value		−2.77	−3.97	−4.27
P-Value		0.013	0.001	0.001
Sales			1.08	1.45
T-Value			2.46	6.10
P-Value			0.026	0.000
S	32.6	27.9	24.5	24.5
R-Sq	91.22	93.95	95.61	95.34
R-Sq(adj)	90.73	93.24	94.78	94.80
C-p	15.9	8.0	4.0	2.9

The stepwise regression analysis produces a single predictor model at step 1 with a high R^2 value of .9122. The number of employees variable used in a simple regression model accounts for over 91.2% of the variation of CEO compensation data. An examination of the regression coefficient of number of employees at the first step (.0696) indicates that a one-employee increase results in a predicted increase of (.0696 · $1,000) about $70 in the CEO's compensation.

At step 2, the company's capital investment enters the model. Notice that the R^2 increases only by .0273 and that the regression coefficient on capital investment is negative. This result seems counterintuitive because we would expect that the more capital investment a company has, the more the CEO should be compensated for the responsibility. A MINITAB simple regression analysis using only capital investment produces the following model:

The regression equation is

CashCompen = 257 + 1.29 CapInv

Notice that the regression coefficient in this model is positive as we would suppose. Multicollinearity is likely. In fact, multicollinearity is evident among sales, number of employees, and capital investment. Each is a function or determiner of company size. Examine the following correlation coefficient:

Correlations

	Sales	No. Employees
No. Employees	0.997	1
Cap. Invest	0.995	.999

Notice that these three predictors are highly interrelated. Therefore, the interpretation of the regression coefficients and the order of entry of these variables in the stepwise regression become more difficult. Nevertheless, number of employees is most highly related to CEO compensation in these data. Observe also in the stepwise regression output that number of employees actually drops out of the model at step 4. The t ratio for number of employees is not significant ($t = 0.98$) at step 3. However, the R^2 actually drops slightly when number of employees are removed. In searching for a model that is both parsimonious and explanatory, the researcher could do worse than to merely select the model at step 1.

Researchers might want to explore more complicated nonlinear models. Some of the independent variables might be related to CEO compensation but in some nonlinear manner.

A brief study of the predictor variables in the Decision Dilemma database reveals that as compensation increases, the values of the data in the independent variables do not increase at a linear rate. Scatter plots of sales, number of employees, and capital investment with CEO compensation confirm this suspicion. Shown here is a scatter plot of sales with cash compensation.

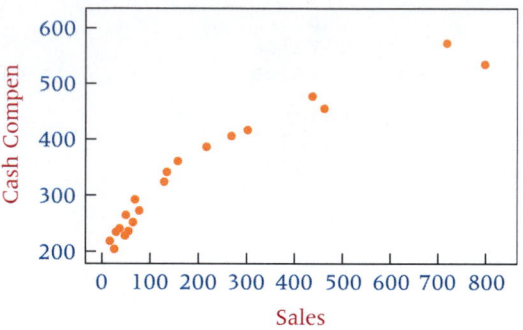

Observe that, the graph suggests more of a logarithmic fit than a linear one. We can use recoding techniques presented in the chapter to conduct a multiple regression analysis to predict compensation using the log of each of these variables. In the analysis, the compensation figures remain the same, but each of the three quantitative independent variables are recoded by taking the log of each value and entering the resultant variable in the model. A second stepwise regression analysis is undertaken with the log variables in the mix along with the original variables. The results follow:

Stepwise Regression: Cash Compen versus Sales, No. of Emp., ...

Alpha-to-Enter: 0.1 Alpha-to-Remove: 0.1

Response is Cash Com on 7 predictors, with N = 20

Step	1	2	3	4	5
Constant	-129.61	-13.23	-122.53	-147.22	-120.74
Log Sale	224.3	152.2	281.4	307.8	280.8
T-Value	22.22	8.75	11.08	32.75	26.81
P-Value	0.000	0.000	0.000	0.000	0.000
No. Emp		0.0251	0.0233	0.0903	0.0828
T-Value		4.53	6.97	13.94	15.52
P-Value		0.000	0.000	0.000	0.000
Log Cap			-106.4	-126.0	-109.8
T-Value			-5.58	-17.87	-15.56
P-Value			0.000	0.000	0.000
Sales				-0.434	-0.250
T-Value				-10.52	-4.11
P-Value				0.000	0.001
Cap. Inv					-0.37
T-Value					-3.51
P-Value					0.003
S	20.7	14.3	8.59	3.07	2.32
R-Sq	96.48	98.41	99.46	99.94	99.97
R-Sq(adj)	96.29	98.22	99.36	99.92	99.95

Note that in this stepwise regression analysis, the variable log sales has the highest single predictability of compensation producing an R^2 of .9648, which is higher than the value at step 1 in the first stepwise regression analysis. Number of employees enters at step 2 and log of capital investment at step 3. However, such a high R^2 at step 1 leaves little room for improved predictability. Our search through the variables may well end with the decision to use the log of sales as the efficient, predictable model of compensation. The final model might be:

$$\text{CEO Compensation} = -129.61 + 224.3 \text{ Log sales}$$

Human resource managers sometimes use compensation tables to assist them in determining ranges and ballparks for salary offers. Company boards of directors can use such models as the one developed here to assist them in negotiations with possible candidates for CEO positions or to aid them in determining whether a presently employed CEO is over- or undercompensated. In addition, candidates who are searching for new CEO opportunities can use models like these to determine the potential compensation for a new position and to help them be more adequately prepared for salary negotiations should they be offered a CEO position.

Some of the variables in this study will undoubtedly produce redundant information. The use of a correlation matrix and a stepwise regression process can protect the analysis from some of the problems of multicollinearity.

The use of multiple regression analysis on a large sample of CEO compensation data with many independent variables could provide some interesting and exciting results. What are the real factors in determining how much compensation a CEO receives? Multiple regression can help answer that question.

ETHICAL CONSIDERATIONS

Some business researchers misuse the results of search procedures by using the order in which variables come into a model (on stepwise and forward selection) to rank the variables in importance. They state that the variable entered at step 1 is the most important predictor of y, the variable entering at step 2 is second most important, and so on. In actuality, variables entering the analysis after step 1 are being analyzed by how much of the unaccounted-for variation (residual variation) they are explaining, not how much they are related to y by themselves. A variable that comes into the model at the fourth step is the variable that most greatly accounts for the variation of the y values leftover after the first three variables have explained the rest. However, the fourth variable taken by itself might explain more variation of y than the second or third variable when seen as single predictors.

Some people use the estimates of the regression coefficients to compare the worth of the predictor variables; the larger the coefficient is, the greater its worth. At least two problems plague this approach. The first is that most variables are measured in different units. Thus, regression coefficient weights are partly a function of the unit of measurement of the variable. Second, if multicollinearity is present, the interpretation of the regression coefficients is questionable. In addition, the presence of multicollinearity raises several issues about the interpretation of other regression output. Researchers who ignore this problem are at risk of presenting spurious results.

SUMMARY

Multiple regression analysis can handle nonlinear independent variables. One way to accommodate this issue is to recode the data and enter the variables into the analysis in the normal way. Other nonlinear regression models, such as exponential models, require that the entire model be transformed. Often the transformation involves the use of logarithms. In some cases, the resulting value of the regression model is in logarithmic form and the antilogarithm of the answer must be taken to determine the predicted value of y.

Indicator, or dummy, variables are qualitative variables used to represent categorical data in the multiple regression model. These variables are coded as 0, 1 and are often used to represent nominal or ordinal classification data that the researcher wants to include in the regression analysis. If a qualitative variable contains more than two categories, it generates multiple dummy variables. In general, if a qualitative variable contains c categories, $c - 1$ dummy variables should be created.

Search procedures are used to help sort through the independent variables as predictors in the examination of various possible models. Several search procedures are available, including all possible regressions, stepwise regression, forward selection, and backward elimination. The all possible regressions procedure computes every possible regression model for a set of data. The drawbacks of this procedure include the time and energy required to compute all possible regressions and the difficulty of deciding which models are most appropriate. The stepwise regression procedure involves selecting and adding one independent variable at a time to the regression process after beginning with a one-predictor model. Variables are added to the model at each step if they contain the most significant t value associated with the remaining variables. If no additional t value is statistically significant at any given step, the procedure stops. With stepwise regression, at each step the process examines the variables already in the model to determine whether their t values are still significant. If not, they are dropped from the model, and the process searches for other independent variables with large, significant t values to replace the variable(s) dropped. The forward selection procedure is the same as stepwise regression but does not drop variables out of the model once they have been included. The backward elimina-

tion procedure begins with a "full" model, a model that contains all the independent variables. The sample size must be large enough to justify a full model, which can be a limiting factor. Backward elimination drops out the least important predictors one at a time until only significant predictors are left in the regression model. The variable with the smallest absolute t value of the statistically nonsignificant t values is the independent variable that is dropped out of the model at each step.

One of the problems in using multiple regression is multicollinearity, or correlations among the predictor variables. This problem can cause overinflated estimates of the standard deviations of regression coefficients, misinterpretation of regression coefficients, undersized t values, and misleading signs on the regression coefficients. It can be lessened by using an intercorrelation matrix of independent variables to help recognize bivariate correlation; by using stepwise regression to sort the variables one at a time; or by using statistics such as a variance inflation factor.

KEY TERMS

all possible regressions	indicator variable	search procedures	Tukey's ladder of
backward elimination	multicollinearity	stepwise regression	transformations
dummy variable	quadratic model	Tukey's four-quadrant	variance inflation factor
forward selection	qualitative variable	approach	

FORMULAS

Variance inflation factor

$$VIF = \frac{1}{1 - R_i^2}$$

SUPPLEMENTARY PROBLEMS

CALCULATING THE STATISTICS

15.23 Given here are the data for a dependent variable, y, and independent variables. Use these data to develop a regression model to predict y. Discuss the output. Which variable is an indicator variable? Was it a significant predictor of y?

x_1	x_2	x_3	y
0	51	16.4	14
0	48	17.1	17
1	29	18.2	29
0	36	17.9	32
0	40	16.5	54
1	27	17.1	86
1	14	17.8	117
0	17	18.2	120
1	16	16.9	194
1	9	18.0	203
1	14	18.9	217
0	11	18.5	235

15.24 Use the following data and a stepwise regression analysis to predict y. In addition to the two independent variables given here, include three other predictors in your analysis: the square of each x as a predictor and an interaction predictor. Discuss the results of the process.

x_1	x_2	y	x_1	x_2	y
10	3	2002	5	12	1750
5	14	1747	6	8	1832
8	4	1980	5	18	1795
7	4	1902	7	4	1917
6	7	1842	8	5	1943
7	6	1883	6	9	1830
4	21	1697	5	12	1786
11	4	2021			

15.25 Use the x_1 values and the log of the x_1 values given here to predict the y values by using a stepwise regression procedure. Discuss the output. Were either or both of the predictors significant?

y	x_1	y	x_1
20.4	850	13.2	204
11.6	146	17.5	487
17.8	521	12.4	192
15.3	304	10.6	98
22.4	1029	19.8	703
21.9	910	17.4	394
16.4	242	19.4	647

Gold ($ per oz.)	Copper (cents per lb.)	Silver ($ per oz.)	Aluminum (cents per lb.)
161.1	64.2	4.4	39.8
308.0	93.3	11.1	61.0
613.0	101.3	20.6	71.6
460.0	84.2	10.5	76.0
376.0	72.8	8.0	76.0
424.0	76.5	11.4	77.8
361.0	66.8	8.1	81.0
318.0	67.0	6.1	81.0
368.0	66.1	5.5	81.0
448.0	82.5	7.0	72.3
438.0	120.5	6.5	110.1
382.6	130.9	5.5	87.8

TESTING YOUR UNDERSTANDING

15.26 The U.S. Commodities Futures Trading Commission reports on the volume of trading in the U.S. commodity futures exchanges. Shown here are the figures for grain, oilseeds, and livestock products over a period of several years. Use these data to develop a multiple regression model to predict grain futures volume of trading from oilseeds volume and livestock products volume. All figures are given in units of millions. Graph each of these predictors separately with the response variable and use Tukey's four-quadrant approach to explore possible recoding schemes for nonlinear relationships. Include any of these in the regression model. Comment on the results.

Grain	Oilseeds	Livestock
2.2	3.7	3.4
18.3	15.7	11.8
19.8	20.3	9.8
14.9	15.8	11.0
17.8	19.8	11.1
15.9	23.5	8.4
10.7	14.9	7.9
10.3	13.8	8.6
10.9	14.2	8.8
15.9	22.5	9.6
15.9	21.1	8.2

15.27 The U.S. Bureau of Mines produces data on the price of minerals. Shown here are the average prices per year for several minerals over a decade. Use these data and a stepwise regression procedure to produce a model to predict the average price of gold from the other variables. Comment on the results of the process.

15.28 The Shipbuilders Council of America in Washington, D.C., publishes data about private shipyards. Among the variables reported by this organization are the employment figures (per 1,000), the number of naval vessels under construction, and the number of repairs or conversions done to commercial ships (in $ millions). Shown here are the data for these three variables over a 7-year period. Use the data to develop a regression model to predict private shipyard employment from number of naval vessels under construction and repairs or conversions of commercial ships. Graph each of these predictors separately with the response variable and use Tukey's four-quadrant approach to explore possible recoding schemes for nonlinear relationships. Include any of these in the regression model. Comment on the regression model and its strengths and its weaknesses.

Employment	Naval Vessels	Commercial Ship Repairs or Conversions
133.4	108	431
177.3	99	1335
143.0	105	1419
142.0	111	1631
130.3	100	852
120.6	85	847
120.4	79	806

15.29 The U.S. Bureau of Labor Statistics produces consumer price indexes for several different categories. Shown here are the percentage changes in consumer price indexes over a period of 20 years for food, shelter, apparel, and fuel oil. Also displayed are the percentage changes in consumer price indexes for all commodities. Use these data and a stepwise regression procedure to develop a model that attempts to predict all commodities by the other four variables. Construct scatter plots of each of these variables with all commodities. Examine the graphs in light of Tukey's four-quadrant approach. Develop any other appropriate predictor variables by recoding data and include them in the analysis. Comment on the result of this analysis.

All Commodities	Food	Shelter	Apparel	Fuel Oil
.9	1.0	2.0	1.6	3.7
.6	1.3	.8	.9	2.7
.9	.7	1.6	.4	2.6
.9	1.6	1.2	1.3	2.6
1.2	1.3	1.5	.9	2.1
1.1	2.2	1.9	1.1	2.4
2.6	5.0	3.0	2.5	4.4
1.9	.9	3.6	4.1	7.2
3.5	3.5	4.5	5.3	6.0
4.7	5.1	8.3	5.8	6.7
4.5	5.7	8.9	4.2	6.6
3.6	3.1	4.2	3.2	6.2
3.0	4.2	4.6	2.0	3.3
7.4	14.5	4.7	3.7	4.0
11.9	14.3	9.6	7.4	9.3
8.8	8.5	9.9	4.5	12.0
4.3	3.0	5.5	3.7	9.5
5.8	6.3	6.6	4.5	9.6
7.2	9.9	10.2	3.6	8.4
11.3	11.0	13.9	4.3	9.2

15.30 The U.S. Department of Agriculture publishes data annually on various selected farm products. Shown here are the unit production figures for three farm products for 10 years during a 20-year period. Use these data and a stepwise regression analysis to predict corn production by the production of soybeans and wheat. Comment on the results.

Corn (million bushels)	Soybeans (million bushels)	Wheat (million bushels)
4152	1127	1352
6639	1798	2381
4175	1636	2420
7672	1861	2595
8876	2099	2424
8226	1940	2091
7131	1938	2108
4929	1549	1812
7525	1924	2037
7933	1922	2739

15.31 The American Chamber of Commerce Researchers Association compiles cost-of-living indexes for selected metropolitan areas. Shown here are cost-of-living indexes for 25 different cities on five different items for a recent year. Use the data to develop a regression model to predict the grocery cost-of-living index by the indexes of housing, utilities, transportation, and healthcare. Discuss the results, highlighting both the significant and nonsignificant predictors.

City	Grocery Items	Housing	Utilities	Transportation	Healthcare
Albany	108.3	106.8	127.4	89.1	107.5
Albuquerque	96.3	105.2	98.8	100.9	102.1
Augusta, GA	96.2	88.8	115.6	102.3	94.0
Austin	98.0	83.9	87.7	97.4	94.9
Baltimore	106.0	114.1	108.1	112.8	111.5
Buffalo	103.1	117.3	127.6	107.8	100.8
Colorado Springs	94.5	88.5	74.6	93.3	102.4
Dallas	105.4	98.9	108.9	110.0	106.8
Denver	91.5	108.3	97.2	105.9	114.3
Des Moines	94.3	95.1	111.4	105.7	96.2
El Paso	102.9	94.6	90.9	104.2	91.4
Indianapolis	96.0	99.7	92.1	102.7	97.4
Jacksonville	96.1	90.4	96.0	106.0	96.1
Kansas City	89.8	92.4	96.3	95.6	93.6
Knoxville	93.2	88.0	91.7	91.6	82.3
Los Angeles	103.3	211.3	75.6	102.1	128.5
Louisville	94.6	91.0	79.4	102.4	88.4
Memphis	99.1	86.2	91.1	101.1	85.5
Miami	100.3	123.0	125.6	104.3	137.8
Minneapolis	92.8	112.3	105.2	106.0	107.5
Mobile	99.9	81.1	104.9	102.8	92.2
Nashville	95.8	107.7	91.6	98.1	90.9
New Orleans	104.0	83.4	122.2	98.2	87.0
Oklahoma City	98.2	79.4	103.4	97.3	97.1
Phoenix	95.7	98.7	96.3	104.6	115.2

INTERPRETING THE OUTPUT

15.32 A stepwise regression procedure was used to analyze a set of 20 observations taken on four predictor variables to predict a dependent variable. The results of this procedure are given next. Discuss the results.

```
STEPWISE REGRESSION OF Y ON 4 PREDICTORS,
WITH N = 20
STEP            1        2
CONSTANT    152.2    124.5

X₁          -50.6    -43.4
T-RATIO      7.42     6.13

X₂                    1.36
T-RATIO              2.13

S            15.2     13.9
R-SQ        75.39    80.59
```

15.33 Shown here are the data for y and three predictors, x_1, x_2, and x_3. A stepwise regression procedure has been done on these data; the results are also given. Comment on the outcome of the stepwise analysis in light of the data.

y	x_1	x_2	x_3
94	21	1	204
97	25	0	198
93	22	1	184
95	27	0	200
90	29	1	182
91	20	1	159
91	18	1	147
94	25	0	196
98	26	0	228
99	24	0	242
90	28	1	162
92	23	1	180
96	25	0	219

```
STEP            1        2        3
CONSTANT    74.81    82.18    87.89

X₃          0.099    0.067    0.071
T-RATIO      6.90     3.65     5.22

X₂                   -2.26    -2.71
T-RATIO             -2.32    -3.71

X₁                           -0.256
T-RATIO                      -3.08

S            1.37     1.16    0.850
R-SQ        81.24    87.82   94.07
```

15.34 Shown below is output from two Excel regression analyses on the same problem. The first output was done on a "full" model. In the second output, the variable with the smallest absolute t value has been removed, and the regression has been rerun like a second step of a backward elimination process. Examine the two outputs. Explain what happened, what the results mean, and what might happen in a third step.

	A	B	C	D	E	F
1	FULL MODEL:					
2	Regression Statistics					
3	Multiple R	0.567				
4	R Square	0.321				
5	Adjusted R Square	0.208				
6	Standard Error	159.681				
7	Observations	29				
8						
9	ANOVA					
10		df	SS	MS	F	Significant F
11	Regression	4	289856.08	72464.02	2.84	0.046
12	Residual	24	611955.23	25498.13		
13	Total	28	901811.31			
14		Coefficients	Standard Error	Stat	P-value	
15	Intercept	336.79	124.08	2.71	0.012	
16	X1	1.65	1.78	0.93	0.363	
17	X2	-5.63	13.47	-0.42	0.680	
18	X3	0.26	1.68	0.16	0.878	
19	X4	185.50	66.22	2.80	0.010	
20						
21	SECOND MODEL:					
22	Regression Statistics					
23	Multiple R	0.566				
24	R Square	0.321				
25	Adjusted R Square	0.239				
26	Standard Error	156.534				
27	Observations	29				
28						
29	ANOVA					
30		df	SS	MS	F	Significant F
31	Regression	3	289238.1	96412.7	3.93	0.020
32	Residual	25	612573.2	24502.9		
33	Total	28	901811.3			
34		Coefficients	Standard Error	Stat	P-value	
35	Intercept	342.919	115.34	2.97	0.006	
36	X1	1.834	1.31	1.40	0.174	
37	X2	-5.749	13.18	-0.44	0.667	
38	X4	181.220	59.05	3.07	0.005	

ANALYZING THE DATABASES

1. Use the manufacturing database to develop a multiple regression model to predict Cost of Materials by Number of Employees, New Capital Expenditures, Value Added by Manufacture, Value of Industry Shipments, and End-of-Year Inventories. Create indicator variables for values of industry shipments that have been coded from 1 to 4. Use a stepwise regression procedure. Does multicollinearity appear to be a problem in this analysis? Discuss the results of the analysis.

2. Construct a correlation matrix for the hospital database variables. Are some of the variables highly correlated? Which ones and why? Perform a stepwise multiple regression analysis to predict Personnel by Control, Service, Beds, Admissions, Census, Outpatients, and Births. The variables Region, Control, and Service will need to be coded as indicator variables. Control has two subcategories, and Service has three.

3. Develop a regression model using the financial database. Use Total Revenues, Total Assets, Return on Equity, Earnings Per Share, Average Yield, and Dividends Per Share to predict the average P/E ratio for a company. How strong is the model? Use stepwise regression to help sort out the variables. Several of these variables may be measuring similar things. Construct a correlation matrix to explore the possibility of multicollinearity among the predictors.

4. Use the stock market database to develop a regression model to predict the composite index from Part of the Month, Stock Volume, Reported Trades, Dollar Value, and Warrants Volume. You will need to treat Part of the Month as a qualitative variable with three subcategories. Drop out the least significant variable if it is not significant at $\alpha = .05$ and rerun the model. How much did R^2 drop? Continue this process until only significant predictors are left. Describe the final model.

CASE: VIRGINIA SEMICONDUCTOR

Virginia Semiconductor is a producer of silicon wafers used in the manufacture of microelectronic products. The company, situated in Fredericksburg, Virginia, was founded in 1978 by two brothers, Thomas and Robert Digges. Virginia Semiconductor was growing and prospering in the early 1980s by selling a high volume of low-profit-margin wafers. However, in 1985, without notice, Virginia Semiconductor lost two major customers that represented 65% of its business. Left with only 35% of its sales base, the company desperately needed customers.

Thomas Digges, Jr., CEO of Virginia Semiconductor, decided to seek markets where his company's market share would be small but profit margin would be high because of the value of its engineering research and its expertise. This decision turned out to be a wise direction for the small, versatile company.

Virginia Semiconductor developed a silicon wafer that was two inches in diameter, 75 microns thick, and polished on both sides. Such wafers were needed by several customers, but had never been produced before. The company produced a number of these wafers and sold them for more than 10 times the price of conventional wafers.

Soon the company was making wafers from two to four microns thick (extremely thin), wafers with textured surfaces for infrared applications, and wafers with micromachined holes or shapes and selling them in specialized markets. It was able to deliver these products faster than competitors were able to deliver standard wafers.

Having made inroads at replacing lost sales, Virginia Semiconductor still had to streamline operations and control inventory and expenses. No layoffs occurred, but the average workweek dropped to 32 hours and the president took an 80% pay reduction for a time. Expenses were cut as far as seemed possible.

The company had virtually no long-term debt and fortunately was able to make it through this period without incurring any additional significant debt. The absence of large monthly debt payments enabled the company to respond quickly to new production needs.

Virginia Semiconductor improved production quality by cross-training employees. In addition, the company participated in the State of Virginia's economic development efforts to find markets in Europe, Japan, Korea, and Israel. Exports, which were 1% of the company's business in 1985, now represent 40%.

The company continues to find new customers because of new products. One new ultramachining wafer has become a key component in auto airbags. Today the company has more than 300 active customers, a significant jump from fewer than 50 in 1985.

Discussion

1. It is often useful to decision makers at a company to determine what factors enter into the size of a customer's purchase. Suppose decision makers at Virginia Semiconductor want to determine from past data what variables might be predictors of size of purchase and are able to gather some data on various customer companies. Assume the following data represent information gathered for 16 companies on five variables: the total amount of purchases

made during a one-year period (size of purchase), the size of the purchasing company (in total sales volume), the percentage of all purchases made by the customer company that were imports, the distance of the customer company from Virginia Semiconductor, and whether the customer company had a single central purchasing agent. Use these data to generate a multiple regression model to predict size of purchase by the other variables. Summarize your findings in terms of the strength of the model, significant predictor variables, and any new variables generated by recoding.

Size of Purchase ($1,000)	Company Size ($ million sales)	Percent of Customer Imports	Distance from Virginia Semiconductor	Central Purchaser?
27.9	25.6	41	18	1
89.6	109.8	16	75	0
12.8	39.4	29	14	0
34.9	16.7	31	117	0
408.6	278.4	14	209	1
173.5	98.4	8	114	1
105.2	101.6	20	75	0
510.6	139.3	17	50	1
382.7	207.4	53	35	1
84.6	26.8	27	15	1
101.4	13.9	31	19	0
27.6	6.8	22	7	0
234.8	84.7	5	89	1
464.3	180.3	27	306	1
309.8	132.6	18	73	1
294.6	118.9	16	11	1

2. Suppose that the next set of data is Virginia Semiconductor's sales figures for the past 11 years, along with the average number of hours worked per week by a full-time employee and the number of different customers the company has for its unique wafers. How do the average workweek length and number of customers relate to total sales figures? Use scatter plots to examine possible relationships between sales and hours per week and sales and number of customers. Use Tukey's four-quadrant approach for possible ways to recode the data. Use stepwise regression analysis to explore the relationships. Let the response variable be "sales" and the predictors be "average number of hours worked per week," "number of customers," and any new variables created by recoding. Explore quadratic relationships, interaction, and other relationships that seem appropriate by using stepwise regression. Summarize your findings in terms of model strength and significant predictors.

Average Sales ($ million)	Hours Worked per Week	Number of Customers
15.6	44	54
15.7	43	52
15.4	41	55
14.3	41	55
11.8	40	39
9.7	40	28
9.6	40	37
10.2	38	58
11.3	38	67
14.3	32	186
14.8	37	226

3. As Virginia Semiconductor continues to grow and prosper, the potential for slipping back into inefficient ways is always present. Suppose that after a few years the company's sales begin to level off, but it continues hiring employees. Such figures over a

10-year period of time may look like the data given here. Graph these data, using sales as the response variable and number of employees as the predictor. Study the graph in light of Tukey's four-quadrant approach. Using the information learned, develop a regression model to predict sales by the number of employees. On the basis of what you find, what would you recommend to management about the trend if it were to continue? What do you see in these data that would concern management?

Sales ($ million)	Number of Employees
20.2	120
24.3	122
28.6	127
33.7	135
35.2	142
35.9	156
36.3	155
36.2	167
36.5	183
36.6	210

Source: Adapted from "Virginia Semiconductor: A New Beginning," *Real-World Lessons for America's Small Businesses: Insights from the Blue Chip Enterprise Initiative 1994.* Published by *Nation's Business* magazine on behalf of Connecticut Mutual Life Insurance Company and the U.S. Chamber of Commerce in association with The Blue Chip Enterprise Initiative, 1994.

USING THE COMPUTER

EXCEL

The Using the Computer section at the end of Chapter 13 contains directions for doing simple regression analysis by using Excel. Multiple regression analysis can be performed by using the same commands as those used for simple regression and explained in Chapter 13. Select **Tools** on the menu bar. From the pull-down menu that appears choose **Data Analysis.** This selection will produce the **Data Analysis** dialog box. Then, select **Regression.** In the dialog box shown, input the range of the *y* values in the first slot, **Input Y Range.** In the second slot, **Input X Range,** input the range of the *x* values. The *x* value range may include several columns and Excel will determine the number of predictor variables from the number of columns entered in this box. Other options and the standard output features are presented and explained in Chapter 13. Nonlinear models can by created in Excel through data recoding using the usual cell and column operations. Excel does not have the capability of directly doing stepwise regression.

MINITAB WINDOWS

MINITAB Windows has the capability of generating multiple regression models, performing various stepwise regression procedures, along with other regression procedures. Chapter 14 contains an explanation for developing multiple regression models. Nonlinear variables can be created by recoding using the MINITAB calculator. First select **Calc** on the Menu bar. From the pull-down menu, select **Calculator.** In the **Calculator** dialog box beside **Store result in variable,** list the name of the column where the new variable is to be located. In the space beside **Expression,** perform the recoding operation on the column where the original linear data are located. After selecting **OK,** the recoded data will appear in the new column.

Stepwise regression procedures can be accessed in MINITAB Windows by selecting **Stat** on the menu bar. From the pull-down menu select **Regression.** From the second pull-down menu that appears, select **Stepwise.** A dialog box will appear. Enter the location of the *y* variable in the **Response** space. Enter all predictor variables that you want to have considered in the procedure in the **Predictors** space. You have the option of selecting which type of regression modeling you want to use by choosing the **Methods** option. In the **Methods** dialog box, you have the option of selecting **Stepwise regression, Forward selection,** or **Backward elimination.**

The output includes the α used to enter variables and the α used to remove variables, the response variable, the number of predictors, the number of observations, and a stepwise output that includes the regression constant, the partial regression weights, the *t* ratio, *s*, R^2 and adjusted R^2.

CHAPTER 16

Time-Series Forecasting and Index Numbers

LEARNING OBJECTIVES

This chapter discusses the general use of forecasting in business, several tools that are available for making business forecasts, the nature of time-series data, and the role of index numbers in business, thereby enabling you to:

1. Gain a general understanding of time-series forecasting techniques.
2. Understand the four possible components of time-series data.
3. Understand stationary forecasting techniques.
4. Understand how to use regression models for trend analysis.
5. Learn how to decompose time-series data into their various elements and to forecast by using decomposition techniques.
6. Understand the nature of autocorrelation and how to test for it.
7. Understand autoregression in forecasting.

Forecasting Air Pollution

The decade of the 1990s brought a heightened awareness of and increased concern over pollution in various forms in the United States. Air pollution is one of the main areas of environmental concern. The U.S. Environmental Protection Agency (EPA) monitors the quality of air around the country. Some of the air pollutants monitored include carbon monoxide emissions, nitrogen oxide emissions, volatile organic compounds, sulfur dioxide emissions, particulate matter, fugitive dust, and lead emissions.

Carbon monoxide is a colorless, odorless, poisonous gas caused mainly by automobile emissions. Nitrogen oxides are produced by motor vehicle exhausts and as by-products of electric utilities and industrial boilers. These oxides can result in respiratory problems. Sulfur dioxide can also cause respiratory problems and is formed when sulfur-containing fuels are burned. Particulate matter is solid or liquid airborne particles that can come from different sources including power plants and diesel trucks. These substances have the potential to cause cancer and respiratory problems. Lead emissions usually come from smelters and battery plants. Lead exposure can result in kidney disease, anemia, and reproductive problems.

Has air quality in the United States been improving or deteriorating over time? The following emission data for two air pollution variables, carbon monoxide and nitrogen oxides, come from a 15-year period and are given in thousands of short-tons.

Year	Carbon Monoxide	Nitrogen Oxides
1985	115,644	23,488
1986	110,437	23,329
1987	108,879	22,806
1988	117,169	24,526
1989	104,447	24,057
1990	96,535	23,792
1991	98,461	23,772
1992	95,123	24,137
1993	95,291	24,482
1994	99,677	24,892
1995	89,721	23,935
1996	90,611	23,391
1997	94,410	24,824
1998	89,454	24,454
1999	97,441	25,393

Managerial and Statistical Questions

1. Is it possible to forecast the emissions of carbon monoxide or nitrogen oxides for the year 2004, 2007, or 2020 using these data?

2. What techniques best forecast the emissions of carbon monoxide or nitrogen oxides in the future from these data?

Sources: Adapted from U.S. Environmental Protection Agency; information published in *The Wall Street Journal Almanac 1999,* Ronald J. Alsop, ed. (New York: Ballantine Books, 1999), p. 628; *The World Almanac 2002* (New York: World Almanac Books, 2002), p. 165; *The New York Times Almanac* 2002. John W. Wright, ed. (New York: Penguin Putnam, 2002) p. 776.

Every day, **forecasting**—*the art or science of predicting the future*—is used in the decision-making process to help businesspeople reach conclusions about buying, selling, producing, hiring, and many other actions. As an example, consider the following items:

- Market watchers predict a resurgence of stock values next year.
- City planners forecast a water crisis in Southern California.
- The price of gasoline will increase sharply in the next several months.
- Increased competition from overseas businesses will result in significant layoffs in the U.S. computer chip industry.

How are these and other conclusions reached? What forecasting techniques are used? Are the forecasts accurate? In this chapter we discuss several forecasting techniques, how to measure the error of a forecast, and some of the problems that can occur in forecasting. In addition, this chapter will focus only on data that occur over time, time-series data.

Time-series data are *data gathered on a given characteristic over a period of time at regular intervals.* Time-series forecasting techniques attempt to account for changes over time by examining patterns, cycles, or trends, or using information about previous time periods to predict the outcome for a future time period. Time-series methods include naive methods, averaging, smoothing, regression trend analysis, and the decomposition of the possible time-series factors, all of which are discussed in subsequent sections.

16.1 INTRODUCTION TO FORECASTING

Virtually all areas of business, including production, sales, employment, transportation, distribution, and inventory, produce and maintain time-series data. Table 16.1 provides an example of time-series data released by the Office of Market Finance, U.S. Department of the Treasury. The table contains the bond yield rates of three-month Treasury Bills for a 17-year period.

Why does the average yield differ from year to year? Is it possible to use these time-series data to predict average yields for year 18 or ensuing years? Figure 16.1 is a graph of these data over time. Often graphical depiction of time-series data can give a clue about any trends, cycles, or relationships that might exist there. Does the graph in Figure 16.1 show that bond yields are decreasing? Will next year's yield rate be lower or is a cycle occurring in these data that will result in an increase? To answer such questions, it is sometimes helpful to determine which of the four components of time-series data exist in the data being studied.

Time-Series Components

It is generally believed that time-series data are composed of four elements: trend, cyclicality, seasonality, and irregularity. Not all time-series data have all these elements. Consider Figure 16.2, which shows the effects of these time-series elements on data over a period of 13 years.

The long-term general direction of data is referred to as **trend.** Notice that even though the data depicted in Figure 16.2 move through upward and downward periods, the general direction or trend is increasing (denoted in Figure 16.2 by the line). **Cycles** are *patterns of highs and lows through which data move over time periods usually of more than a year.* Notice that the data in Figure 16.2 seemingly move through two periods or cycles of highs and lows over a 13-year period. Time-series data that do not extend over a long period of time may not have enough "history" to show **cyclical effects. Seasonal effects,** on the other hand, are *shorter cycles, which usually occur in time periods of less than one year.* Often seasonal effects are measured by the month, but they may occur by quarter, or may be measured in as small a time frame as a week or even a day. Note the seasonal effects shown in Figure 16.2 as up and down cycles, many of which occur during a one-year period. **Irregular fluctuations** are *rapid changes or "bleeps" in the data, which occur in even shorter time frames than seasonal effects.* Irregular fluctuations can happen as often as day to day. They are subject to momentary change and are often unexplained. Note the irregular fluctuations in the data of Figure 16.2.

TABLE 16.1

Bond Yields of Three-Month Treasury Bills

Year	Average Yield
1	14.03%
2	10.69
3	8.63
4	9.58
5	7.48
6	5.98
7	5.82
8	6.69
9	8.12
10	7.51
11	5.42
12	3.45
13	3.02
14	4.29
15	5.51
16	5.02
17	5.07

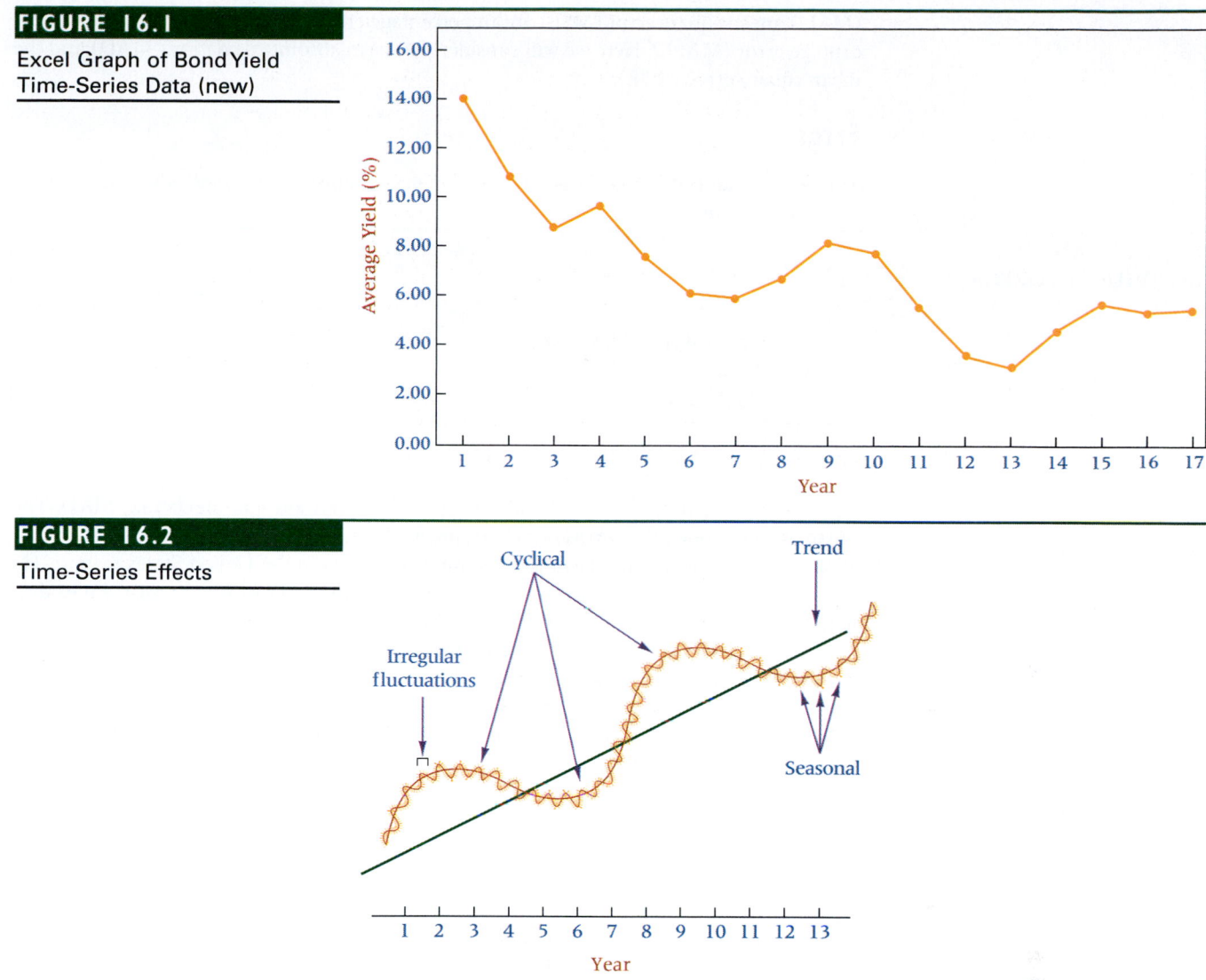

FIGURE 16.1

Excel Graph of Bond Yield
Time-Series Data (new)

FIGURE 16.2

Time-Series Effects

Observe again the bond yield data depicted in Figure 16.1. The general trend seems to move downward and contain two cycles. Each of the cycles traverses approximately five to eight years. It is possible, although not displayed here, that seasonal periods of highs and lows within each year result in seasonal bond yields. In addition, irregular daily fluctuations of bond yield rates may occur but are unexplainable.

Time-series data that contain no trend, cyclical, or seasonal effects are said to be **stationary.** Techniques used to forecast stationary data analyze only the irregular fluctuation effects.

The Measurement of Forecasting Error

In this chapter, several forecasting techniques will be introduced that typically produce different forecasts. How does a decision maker know which forecasting technique is doing the best job in predicting the future? One way is to compare forecast values with actual values and determine the amount of **forecasting error** a technique produces. An examination of individual errors gives some insight into the accuracy of the forecasts. However, this process can be tedious, especially for large data sets, and often a single measurement of overall forecasting error is needed for the entire set of data under consideration. Any of several methods can be used to compute error in forecasting. The choice depends on the forecaster's objective, the forecaster's familiarity with the technique, and the method of error measurement used by the computer forecasting software. Several techniques can be used to measure overall error, including mean error (ME), mean absolute deviation

(MAD), mean square error (MSE), mean percentage error (MPE), and mean absolute percentage error (MAPE). Here we will consider the mean absolute deviation (MAD) and the mean square error (MSE).

Error

The **error of an individual forecast** is *the difference between the actual value and the forecast of that value.*

ERROR OF AN INDIVIDUAL FORECAST	$$e_t = x_t - F_t$$

where

e_t = the error of the forecast
x_t = the actual value
F_t = the forecast value

Mean Absolute Deviation (MAD)

One measure of overall error in forecasting is the mean absolute deviation, MAD. The **mean absolute deviation (MAD)** is *the mean, or average, of the absolute values of the errors.* Table 16.2 presents the nonfarm partnership tax returns in the United States over an 11-year period along with the forecast for each year and the error of the forecast. An examination of these data reveals that some of the forecast errors are positive and some are negative. In summing these errors in an attempt to compute an overall measure of error, the negative and positive values offset each other resulting in an underestimation of the total error. The mean absolute deviation overcomes this problem by taking the absolute value of the error measurement, thereby analyzing the magnitude of the forecast errors without regard to direction.

MEAN ABSOLUTE DEVIATION	$$MAD = \frac{\Sigma |e_i|}{\text{Number of Forecasts}}$$

The mean absolute error can be computed for the forecast errors in Table 16.2 as follows.

$$MAD = \frac{|56.0| + |111.8| + |93.5| + |91.0| + |106.3| + |83.9| + |42.2| + |14.7| + |-41.6| + |-33.5|}{10} = 67.5$$

Mean Square Error (MSE)

The **mean square error (MSE)** is another way to circumvent the problem of the canceling effects of positive and negative forecast errors. The MSE is *computed by squaring each error*

TABLE 16.2	Year	Actual	Forecast	Error
Nonfarm Partnership Tax Returns	1	1,402	—	—
	2	1,458	1,402	56.0
	3	1,553	1,441.2	111.8
	4	1,613	1,519.5	93.5
	5	1,676	1,585.0	91.0
	6	1,755	1,648.7	106.3
	7	1,807	1,723.1	83.9
	8	1,824	1,781.8	42.2
	9	1,826	1,811.3	14.7
	10	1,780	1,821.6	−41.6
	11	1,759	1,792.5	−33.5

(thus creating a positive number) and averaging the squared errors. The following formula states it more formally.

MEAN SQUARE ERROR

$$MSE = \frac{\Sigma e_i^2}{\text{Number of Forecasts}}$$

The mean square error can be computed for the errors shown in Table 16.2 as follows.

$$MSE = \frac{(56.0)^2 + (111.8)^2 + (93.5)^2 + (91.0)^2 + (106.3)^2 + (83.9)^2 + (42.2)^2 + (14.7)^2 + (-41.6)^2 + (-33.5)^2}{10} = 5,584.7$$

Selection of a particular mechanism for computing error is up to the forecaster. It is important to understand that different error techniques will yield different information. The business researcher should be informed enough about the various error measurement techniques to make an educated evaluation of the forecasting results.

16.1 PROBLEMS

16.1 Use the forecast errors given here to compute MAD and MSE. Discuss the information yielded by each type of error measurement.

Period	e
1	2.3
2	1.6
3	−1.4
4	1.1
5	.3
6	−.9
7	−1.9
8	−2.1
9	.7

16.2 Determine the error for each of the following forecasts. Compute MAD and MSE.

Period	Value	Forecast	Error
1	202	—	—
2	191	202	
3	173	192	
4	169	181	
5	171	174	
6	175	172	
7	182	174	
8	196	179	
9	204	189	
10	219	198	
11	227	211	

16.3 Using the following data, determine the values of MAD and MSE. Which of these measurements of error seems to yield the best information about the forecasts? Why?

Period	Value	Forecast
1	19.4	16.6
2	23.6	19.1
3	24.0	22.0
4	26.8	24.8
5	29.2	25.9
6	35.5	28.6

16.4 Figures for acres of tomatoes harvested in the United States from 1988 through 1998 follow. The data are published by the U.S. Department of Agriculture. With these data, forecasts have been made by using techniques presented later in this chapter. Compute MAD and MSE on these forecasts. Comment on the errors.

Year	Number of Acres	Forecast
1988	140,000	—
1989	141,730	140,000
1990	134,590	141,038
1991	131,710	137,169
1992	131,910	133,894
1993	134,250	132,704
1994	135,220	133,632
1995	131,020	134,585
1996	120,640	132,446
1997	115,190	125,362
1998	114,510	119,259

16.2 SMOOTHING TECHNIQUES

Several techniques are available to forecast time-series data that are stationary, or that include no significant trend, cyclical, or seasonal effects. These techniques are often referred to as **smoothing techniques** because they *produce forecasts based on "smoothing out" the irregular fluctuation effects in the time-series data*. Three general categories of smoothing techniques are presented here: (1) naïve forecasting models, (2) averaging models, and (3) exponential smoothing.

Naïve Forecasting Models

Naïve forecasting models are *simple models in which it is assumed that the more recent time periods of data represent the best predictions or forecasts for future outcomes*. Naïve models do not take into account data trend, cyclical effects, or seasonality. For this reason, naïve models seem to work better with data that are reported on a daily or weekly basis or in situations that show no trend or seasonality. The simplest of the naïve forecasting methods is the model in which the forecast for a given time period is the value for the previous time period.

$$F_t = x_{t-1}$$

where

F_t = the forecast value for time period t

x_{t-1} = the value for time period $t - 1$

As an example, if 532 pairs of shoes were sold by a retailer last week, this naïve forecasting model would predict that the retailer will sell 532 pairs of shoes this week. With this naïve model, the actual sales for this week will be the forecast for next week.

Observe the agricultural data in Table 16.3 representing the total reported domestic rail, truck, and air shipments of bell peppers in the United States for a given year. Figure 16.3 presents an Excel graph of these shipments over the 12-month period. From these data, we can make a naïve forecast of the total number of reported shipments of bell peppers for January of the next year by using the figure for December, which is 412.

Another version of the naïve forecast might be to use the number of shipments for January of the previous year as the forecast for January of next year, because the business researcher may believe a relationship exists between bell pepper shipments and the month of the year. In this case, the naïve forecast for next January from Table 16.3 is 336 (January of the previous year). The forecaster is free to be creative with the naïve forecast model method and search for other relationships or rationales within the limits of the time-series data that would seemingly produce a valid forecast.

TABLE 16.3

Total Reported Domestic Shipments of Bell Peppers

Month	Shipments (millions of pounds)
January	336
February	308
March	582
April	771
May	935
June	808
July	663
August	380
September	333
October	412
November	458
December	412

Source: Agricultural Statistics 1999, U.S. Department of Agriculture.

FIGURE 16.3

Excel Graph of Shipments of Bell Peppers over a 12-Month Period

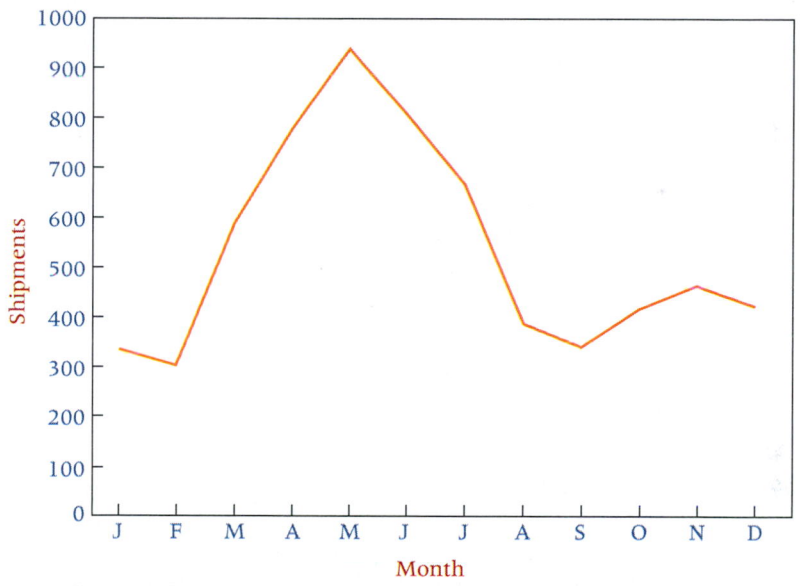

Averaging Models

Many naïve model forecasts are based on the value of one time period. Often such forecasts become a function of irregular fluctuations of the data; as a result, the forecasts are "oversteered." Using averaging models, a forecaster enters information from several time periods into the forecast and "smoothes" the data. **Averaging models** are computed by *averaging data from several time periods and using the average as the forecast for the next time period.*

Simple Averages

The most elementary of the averaging models is the **simple average model.** With this model, *the forecast for time period t is the average of the values for a given number of previous time periods,* as shown in the following equation.

$$F_t = \frac{X_{t-1} + X_{t-2} + X_{t-3} + \cdots + X_{t-n}}{n}$$

The data in Table 16.4 provide the costs of residential heating oil in the United States for three years. Figure 16.4 displays a MINITAB graph of these data.

TABLE 16.4

Cost of Residential Heating Oil
(cents per gallon)

Time Frame	Cost of Heating Oil
January (year 1)	66.1
February	66.1
March	66.4
April	64.3
May	63.2
June	61.6
July	59.3
August	58.1
September	58.9
October	60.9
November	60.7
December	59.4
January (year 2)	61.3
February	63.3
March	62.1
April	59.8
May	58.4
June	57.6
July	55.7
August	55.1
September	55.7
October	56.7
November	57.2
December	58.0
January (year 3)	58.2
February	58.3
March	57.7
April	56.7
May	56.8
June	55.5
July	53.8
August	52.8

FIGURE 16.4

MINITAB Graph of Heating Oil
Cost Data

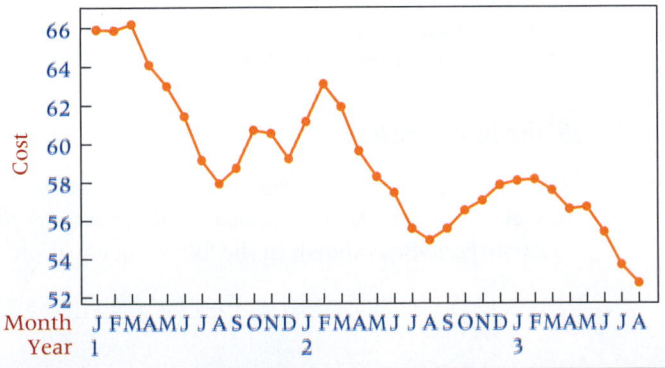

A simple 12-month average could be used to forecast the cost of residential heating oil for September of year 3 from the data in Table 16.4 by averaging the values for September of year 2 through August of year 3 (the preceding 12 months).

$$F_{\text{Sept, year 3}} = \frac{55.7+56.7+57.2+58.0+58.2+58.3+57.7+56.7+56.8+55.5+53.8+52.8}{12} = 56.45$$

With this **simple average,** the forecast for year 3 September heating oil cost is 56.45 cents. Note that none of the previous 12-month figures equal this value and that this average is not necessarily more closely related to values early in the period than to those late in the period. The use of the simple average over 12 months tends to smooth the variations, or fluctuations, that occur during this time.

Moving Averages

Suppose we were to attempt to forecast the heating oil cost for October of year 3 by using averages as the forecasting method. Would we still use the simple average for September of year 2 through August of year 3 as we did to forecast for September of year 3? Instead of using the same 12 months' average used to forecast September of year 3, it would seem to make sense to use the 12 months prior to October of year 3 (October of year 2 through September of year 3) to average for the new forecast. Suppose in September of year 3 the cost of heating oil is 53.3 cents. We could forecast October of year 3 with a new average that includes the same months used to forecast September of year 3, but without the value for September of year 2 and with the value of September of year 3 added.

$$F_{\text{Sept, year 3}} = \frac{56.7+57.2+58.0+58.2+58.3+57.7+56.7+56.8+55.5+53.8+52.8+53.3}{12} = 56.25$$

Computing an average of the values from October of year 2 through September of year 3 produces a moving average, which can be used to forecast the cost of heating oil for October of year 3. In computing this moving average, the earliest of the previous 12 values, September of year 2, is dropped and the most recent value, September of year 3, is included.

A **moving average** is *an average that is updated or recomputed for every new time period being considered.* The most recent information is utilized in each new moving average. This advantage is offset by the disadvantages that (1) it is difficult to choose the optimal length of time for which to compute the moving average, and (2) moving averages do not usually adjust for such time-series effects as trend, cycles, or seasonality. To determine the more optimal lengths for which to compute the moving averages, we would need to forecast with several different average lengths and compare the errors produced by them.

DEMONSTRATION PROBLEM 16.1

Shown here are shipments (in millions of dollars) for electric lighting and wiring equipment over a 12-month period. Use these data to compute a 4-month moving average for all available months.

Month	Shipments
January	1,056
February	1,345
March	1,381
April	1,191
May	1,259
June	1,361
July	1,110
August	1,334
September	1,416
October	1,282
November	1,341
December	1,382

Solution

The first moving average is

$$\text{4-Month Moving Average} = \frac{1{,}056 + 1{,}345 + 1{,}381 + 1{,}191}{4} = 1{,}243.25$$

This first 4-month moving average can be used to forecast the shipments in May. Because 1,259 shipments were actually made in May, the error of the forecast is

$$\text{Error}_{\text{May}} = 1{,}259 - 1{,}243.25 = 15.75$$

Shown next, along with the monthly shipments, are the 4-month moving averages and the errors of forecast when using the 4-month moving averages to predict the next month's shipments. The first moving average is displayed beside the month of May because it is computed by using January, February, March, and April and because it is being used to forecast the shipments for May. The rest of the 4-month moving averages and errors of forecast are as shown.

4-Month Moving Forecast

Month	Shipments	Average	Error
January	1,056	—	—
February	1,345	—	—
March	1,381	—	—
April	1,191	—	—
May	1,259	1,243.25	15.75
June	1,361	1,294.00	67.00
July	1,110	1,298.00	−188.00
August	1,334	1,230.25	103.75
September	1,416	1,266.00	150.00
October	1,282	1,305.25	−23.25
November	1,341	1,285.50	55.50
December	1,382	1,343.25	38.75

The following MINITAB graph shows the actual shipment values and the forecast shipment values based on the 4-month moving averages. Notice that the moving averages are "smoothed" in comparison with the individual data values. They appear to be less volatile and seem to be attempting to follow the general trend of the data.

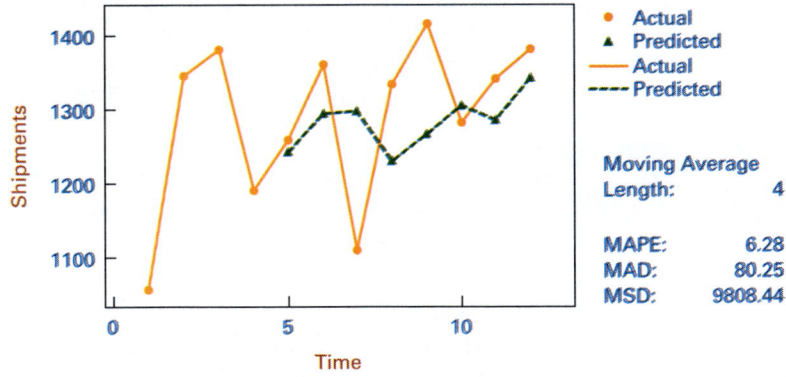

Weighted Moving Averages

A forecaster may want to place more weight on certain periods of time than on others. For example, a forecaster might believe that the previous month's value is three times as important in forecasting as other months. *A moving average in which some time periods are weighted differently than others* is called a **weighted moving average.**

As an example, suppose a 3-month weighted average is computed by weighting last month's value by 3, the value for the previous month by 2, and the value for the month before that by 1. This weighted average is computed as

$$\bar{x}\ _{weighted} = \frac{3(M_{t-1}) + 2(M_{t-2}) + 1(M_{t-3})}{6}$$

where

M_{t-1} = last month's value

M_{t-2} = value for the previous month

M_{t-3} = value for the month before previous month

Notice that the divisor is 6. With a weighted average, the divisor always equals the total number of weights. In this example, the value of M_{t-1} counts three times as much as the value for M_{t-3}.

DEMONSTRATION PROBLEM 16.2	Compute a 4-month weighted moving average for the electric lighting and wiring data from Demonstration Problem 16.1, using weights of 4 for last month's value, 2 for the previous month's value, and 1 for each of the values from the 2 months prior to that.

Solution

The first weighted average is

$$\frac{4(1,191) + 2(1,381) + 1(1,345) + 1(1,056)}{8} = 1,240.875$$

This moving average is recomputed for each ensuing month. Displayed next are the monthly values, the weighted moving averages, and the forecast error for the data.

Month	Shipments	4-Month Weighted Moving Average Forecast	Error
January	1,056	—	—
February	1,345	—	—
March	1,381	—	—
April	1,191	—	—
May	1,259	1,240.9	18.1
June	1,361	1,268.0	93.0
July	1,110	1,316.8	−206.8
August	1,334	1,201.5	132.5
September	1,416	1,272.0	144.0
October	1,282	1,350.4	−68.4
November	1,341	1,300.5	40.5
December	1,382	1,334.8	47.2

Note that in this problem the errors obtained by using the 4-month weighted moving average were greater than most of the errors obtained by using an unweighted 4-month moving average, as shown here.

Forecast Error, Unweighted 4-Month Moving Average	Forecast Error, Weighted 4-Month Moving Average
—	—
—	—
—	—
—	—
15.8	18.1
67.0	93.0
−188.0	−206.8
103.8	132.5
150.0	144.0
−23.3	−68.4
55.5	40.5
38.8	47.2

Smaller errors with weighted averages are not always the case. The forecaster can experiment with different weights in using the weighted moving average as a technique. Many possible weighting schemes can be used.

Exponential Smoothing

Another forecasting technique, **exponential smoothing,** is *used to weight data from previous time periods with exponentially decreasing importance in the forecast.* Exponential smoothing is accomplished by multiplying the actual value for the present time period, X_t, by a value between 0 and 1 (the exponential smoothing constant) referred to as α (not the same α used for a Type I error) and adding that result to the product of the present time period's forecast, F_t, and $(1 - \alpha)$. The following is a more formalized version.

EXPONENTIAL SMOOTHING	$$F_{t+1} = \alpha \cdot X_t + (1 - \alpha) \cdot F_t$$

where

F_{t+1} = the forecast for the next time period $(t + 1)$
F_t = the forecast for the present time period (t)
X_t = the actual value for the present time period
α = a value between 0 and 1 referred to as the exponential smoothing constant.

The value of α is determined by the forecaster. The essence of this procedure is that the new forecast is a combination of the present forecast and the present actual value. If α is chosen to be less than .5, less weight is placed on the actual value than on the forecast of that value. If α is chosen to be greater than .5, more weight is being put on the actual value than on the forecast value.

As an example, suppose the prime interest rate for a time period is 5% and the forecast of the prime interest rate for this time period was 6%. If the forecast of the prime interest rate for the next period is determined by exponential smoothing with $\alpha = .3$, the forecast is

$$F_{t+1} = (.3)(5\%) + (1.0 - .3)(6\%) = 5.7\%$$

Notice that the forecast value of 5.7% for the next period is weighted more toward the previous forecast of 6% than toward the actual value of 5% because α is .3. Suppose we use $\alpha = .7$ as the exponential smoothing constant. Then,

$$F_{t+1} = (.7)(5\%) + (1.0 - .7)(6\%) = 5.3\%$$

This value is closer to the actual value of 5% than the previous forecast of 6% because the exponential smoothing constant, α, is greater than .5.

To see why this procedure is called exponential smoothing, examine the formula for exponential smoothing again.

$$F_{t+1} = \alpha \cdot X_t + (1 - \alpha) \cdot F_t$$

If exponential smoothing has been used over a period of time, the forecast for F_t will have been obtained by

$$F_t = \alpha \cdot X_{t-1} + (1 - \alpha) \cdot F_{t-1}$$

Substituting this forecast value, F_t, into the preceding equation for F_{t+1} produces

$$F_{t+1} = \alpha \cdot X_t + (1 - \alpha)[\alpha \cdot X_{t-1} + (1 - \alpha) \cdot F_{t-1}]$$
$$= \alpha \cdot X_t + \alpha (1 - \alpha) \cdot X_{t-1} + (1 - \alpha)^2 F_{t-1}$$

but

$$F_{t-1} = \alpha \cdot X_{t-2} + (1 - \alpha)F_{t-2}$$

Substituting this value of F_{t-1} into the preceding equation for F_{t+1} produces

$$F_{t+1} = \alpha \cdot X_t + \alpha(1-\alpha) \cdot X_{t-1} + (1-\alpha)^2 F_{t-1}$$
$$= \alpha \cdot X_t + \alpha(1-\alpha) \cdot X_{t-1} + (1-\alpha)^2[\alpha \cdot X_{t-2} + (1-\alpha) F_{t-2}]$$
$$= \alpha \cdot X_t + \alpha(1-\alpha) \cdot X_{t-1} + \alpha(1-\alpha)^2 \cdot X_{t-2} + (1-\alpha)^3 F_{t-2}$$

Continuing this process shows that the weights on previous-period values and forecasts include $(1-\alpha)^n$ (exponential values). The following chart shows the values of α, $(1-\alpha)$, $(1-\alpha)^2$, and $(1-\alpha)^3$ for three different values of α. Included is the value of $\alpha(1-\alpha)^3$, which is the weight of the actual value for three time periods back. Notice the rapidly decreasing emphasis on values for earlier time periods. The impact of exponential smoothing on time-series data is to place much more emphasis on recent time periods. The choice of α determines the amount of emphasis.

α	$1-\alpha$	$(1-\alpha)^2$	$(1-\alpha)^3$	$\alpha(1-\alpha)^3$
.2	.8	.64	.512	.1024
.5	.5	.25	.125	.0625
.8	.2	.04	.008	.0064

Some forecasters use the computer to analyze time-series data for various values of α. By setting up criteria with which to judge the forecasting errors, forecasters can select the value of α that best fits the data.

The exponential smoothing formula

$$F_{t+1} = \alpha \cdot X_t + (1-\alpha) \cdot F_t$$

can be rearranged algebraically as

$$F_{t+1} = F_t + \alpha(X_t - F_t)$$

This form of the equation shows that the new forecast, F_{t+1}, equals the old forecast, F_t, plus an adjustment based on α times the error of the old forecast $(X_t - F_t)$. The smaller α is, the less impact the error has on the new forecast and the more the new forecast is like the old. It demonstrates the dampening effect of α on the forecasts.

DEMONSTRATION PROBLEM 16.3

The U.S. Census Bureau reports housing data in the publication *Current Construction Reports.* The total units of new privately owned housing started between 1984 and 1999 in the United States are given here. Use exponential smoothing to forecast the values for each ensuing time period. Work the problem using α = .2, .5, and .8.

Year	Total Units (1,000)
1984	1,750
1985	1,742
1986	1,805
1987	1,620
1988	1,488
1989	1,376
1990	1,193
1991	1,014
1992	1,200
1993	1,288
1994	1,457
1995	1,354
1996	1,477
1997	1,474
1998	1,617
1999	1,666

Solution

An Excel graph of these data is shown here.

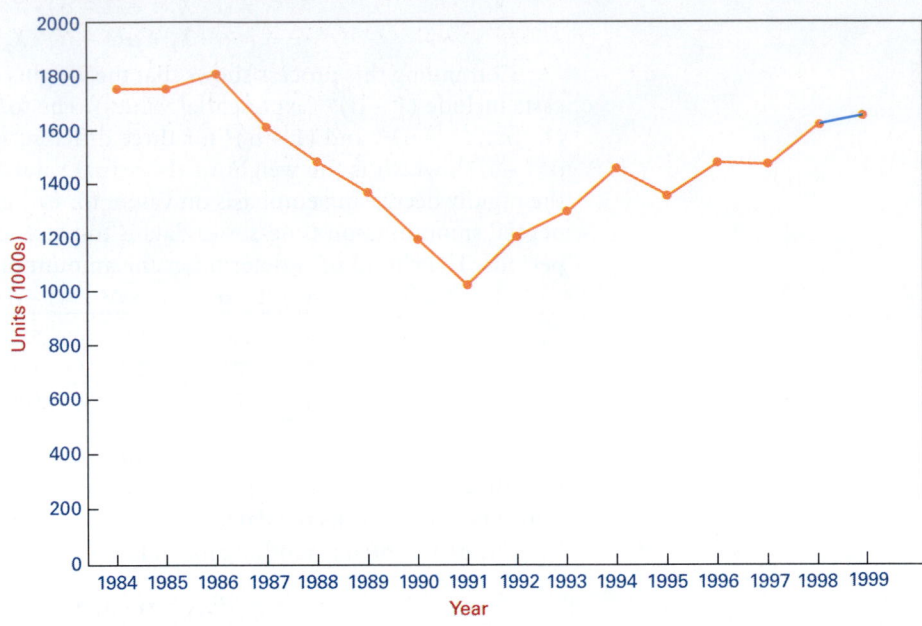

The following table provides the forecasts with each of the three values of alpha. Note that because no forecast is given for the first time period, we cannot compute a forecast based on exponential smoothing for the second period. Instead, we use the actual value for the first period as the forecast for the second period to get started. As examples, the forecasts for the third, fourth, and fifth periods are computed for $\alpha = .2$ as follows.

$$F_3 = .2(1,742) + .8(1,750) = 1,748.4$$
$$F_4 = .2(1,805) + .8(1,748.4) = 1,759.7$$
$$F_5 = .2(1,620) + .8(1,759.7) = 1,731.8$$

Year	Housing Units (1,000)	$\alpha = .2$ F	$\alpha = .2$ e	$\alpha = .5$ F	$\alpha = .5$ e	$\alpha = .8$ F	$\alpha = .8$ e
1984	1,750	—	—	—	—	—	—
1985	1,742	1,750.0	−8.0	1,750.0	−8.0	1,750.0	−8.0
1986	1,805	1,748.4	56.6	1,746.0	59.0	1,743.6	61.4
1987	1,620	1,759.7	−139.7	1,775.5	−155.5	1,792.7	−172.7
1988	1,488	1,731.8	−243.8	1,697.8	−209.8	1,654.5	−166.5
1989	1,376	1,683.0	−307.0	1,592.9	−216.9	1,521.3	−145.3
1990	1,193	1,621.6	−428.6	1,484.5	−291.5	1,405.1	−212.1
1991	1,014	1,535.9	−521.9	1,338.8	−324.8	1,235.4	−221.4
1992	1,200	1,431.5	−231.5	1,176.4	23.6	1,058.3	141.7
1993	1,288	1,385.2	−97.2	1,188.2	99.8	1,171.7	116.3
1994	1,457	1,365.8	91.2	1,238.1	218.9	1,264.7	192.3
1995	1,354	1,384.0	−30.0	1,347.6	6.4	1,418.5	−64.5
1996	1,477	1,378.0	99.0	1,350.8	126.2	1,366.9	110.1
1997	1,474	1,397.8	76.2	1,413.9	60.1	1,455.0	19.0
1998	1,617	1,413.0	204.0	1,444.0	173.0	1,470.2	146.8
1999	1,666	1,453.8	212.2	1,530.5	135.5	1,587.6	78.4

	$\alpha = .2$	$\alpha = .5$	$\alpha = .8$
MAD:	183.1	140.6	123.8
MSE:	53,803.9	29,037.1	19,428.1

Which value of alpha works best on the data? At the bottom of the preceding analysis are the values of two different measurements of error for each of the three different values of alpha. With each measurement of error, $\alpha = .8$ produces the smallest measurement of error. Observe from the Excel graph of the original data that the data vary up and down considerably. In exponential smoothing, the value of alpha is multiplied by the actual value and $1 - \alpha$ is multiplied by the forecast value to get the next forecast. Because the actual values are varying considerably, the exponential smoothing value with the largest alpha seems to be forecasting the best. By placing the greatest weight on the actual values, the new forecast seems to predict the new value better.

The MINITAB graphs shown next depict each of the exponential smoothing analyses used in this problem.

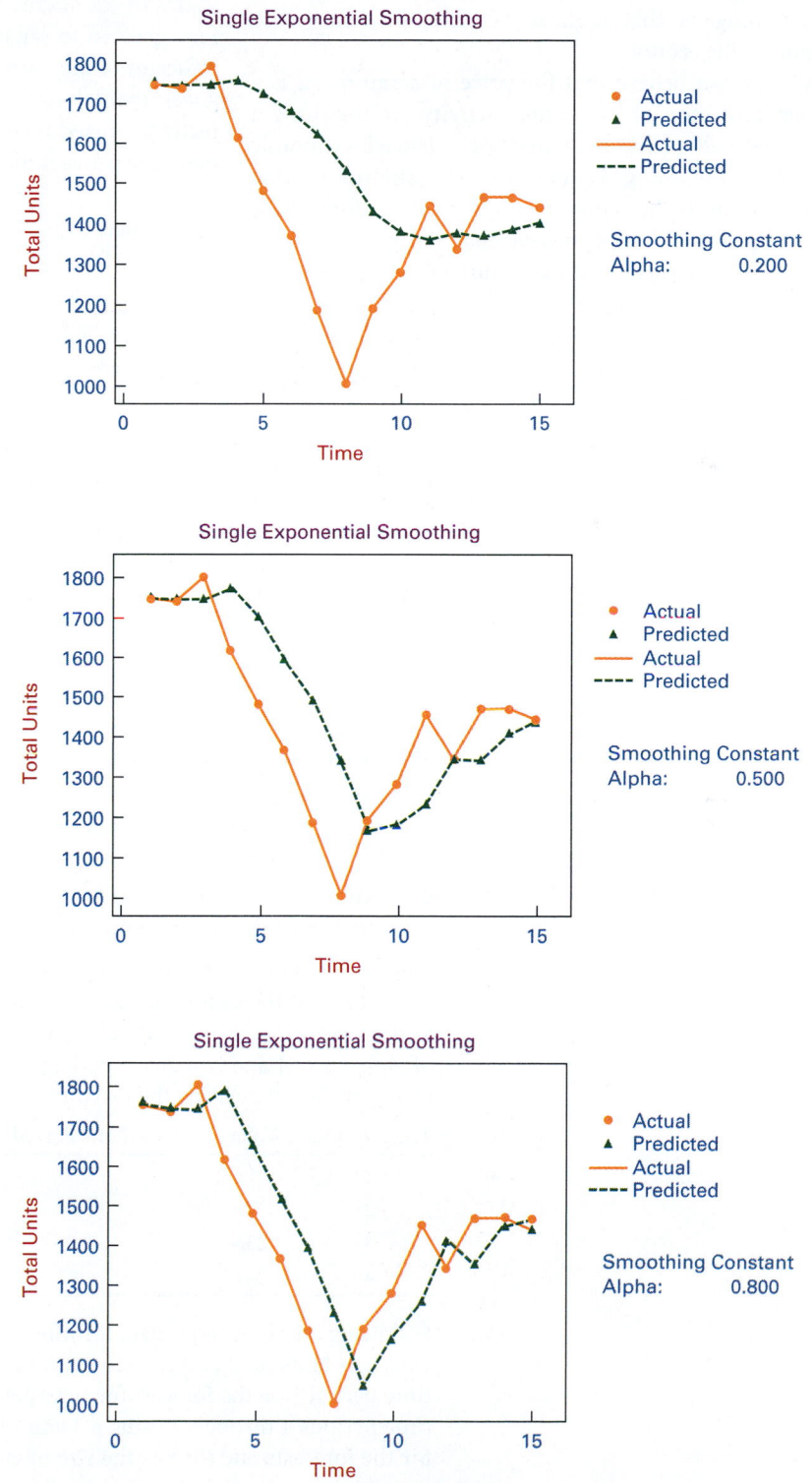

STATISTICS IN BUSINESS TODAY

Forecasting the Economy by Scrap Metal Prices?

Economists are constantly on the lookout for valid indicators of a country's economy. Forecasters have sifted through oil indicators (for example, West Texas intermediate crude), the price of gold on the world markets, the Dow Jones averages, government-published indexes, and practically anything else that might seem related in some way to the state of the economy.

Would you believe that the price of scrap metal is a popular indicator of economic activity in the United States? Several well-known and experienced economic forecasters, including Federal Reserve chairman Alan Greenspan and the chief market analyst for Chase Manhattan, Donald Fine, believe that the price of scrap metal is a good indicator of the industrial economy.

Scrap metal is leftover copper, steel, aluminum, and other metals. Scrap metal is a good indicator of industrial activity because as manufacturing increases, the demand for scrap metals increases, as does the price of scrap metal. Donald Fine says that "scrap metal is the beginning of the production chain"; hence, an increasing demand for it is an indicator of increasing manufacturing production. Mr. Fine goes on to say that scrap metal is sometimes a better indicator of the future direction of the economy than many governmental statistics. In some cases, scrap metal correctly predicted no economic recovery when some government measures indicated that a recovery was underway.

Source: Anita Raghavan and David Wessel, "In Scraping Together Economic Data, Forecasters Turn to Scrap-Metal Prices," *The Wall Street Journal*, April 27, 1992, C1.

16.2 PROBLEMS

16.5 Use the following time-series data to answer the given questions.

Time Period	Value	Time Period	Value
1	27	6	66
2	31	7	71
3	58	8	86
4	63	9	101
5	59	10	97

a. Develop forecasts for periods 5 through 10 using 4-month moving averages.

b. Develop forecasts for periods 5 through 10 using 4-month weighted moving averages. Weight the most recent month by a factor of 4, the previous month by 2, and the other months by 1.

c. Compute the errors of the forecasts in parts (a) and (b) and observe the differences in the errors forecast by the two different techniques.

16.6 Following are time-series data for eight different periods. Use exponential smoothing to forecast the values for periods 3 through 8. Use the value for the first period as the forecast for the second period. Compute forecasts using two different values of alpha, $\alpha = .1$ and $\alpha = .8$. Compute the errors for each forecast and compare the errors produced by using the two different exponential smoothing constants.

Time Period	Value	Time Period	Value
1	211	5	242
2	228	6	227
3	236	7	217
4	241	8	203

16.7 Following are time-series data for nine time periods. Use exponential smoothing with constants of .3 and .7 to forecast time periods 3 through 9. Let the value for time period 1 be the forecast for time period 2. Compute additional forecasts for time periods 4 through 9 using a 3-month moving average. Compute the errors for the forecasts and discuss the size of errors under each method.

Time Period	Value	Time Period	Value
1	9.4	6	11.0
2	8.2	7	10.3
3	7.9	8	9.5
4	9.0	9	9.1
5	9.8		

16.8 The U.S. Census Bureau publishes data on factory orders for all manufacturing, durable goods, and nondurable goods industries. Shown here are factory orders in the United States from 1987 through 1999 ($ billion).

  a. Use these data to develop forecasts for the years 1992 through 1999 using a 5-year moving average.

  b. Use these data to develop forecasts for the years 1992 through 1999 using a 5-year weighted moving average. Weight the most recent year by 6, the previous year by 4, the year before that by 2, and the other years by 1.

  c. Compute the errors of the forecasts in parts (a) and (b) and observe the differences in the errors of the forecasts.

Year	Factory Orders ($ billion)
1987	2,512.7
1988	2,739.2
1989	2,874.9
1990	2,934.1
1991	2,865.7
1992	2,978.5
1993	3,092.4
1994	3,356.8
1995	3,607.6
1996	3,749.3
1997	3,952.0
1998	3,949.0
1999	4,137.0

16.9 The following data show the number of issues from Initial Public Offerings (IPOs) for a 13-year period released by the Securities Data Company. Use these data to develop forecasts for the years 3 through 13 using exponential smoothing techniques with alpha values of .2 and .9. Let the forecast for year 2 be the value for year 1. Compare the results by examining the errors of the forecasts.

Year	Number of Issues
1	332
2	694
3	518
4	222
5	209
6	172
7	366
8	512
9	667
10	571
11	575
12	865
13	609

16.3 TREND ANALYSIS

One of the four elements of time-series data is trend. A trend is the long-run general direction of a business climate over a period of several years. Data trends can be ascertained in several ways. One particular technique is regression analysis. In time-series regression trend analysis, the response variable, Y, is the item being forecast. The independent variable, X, represents the time periods.

Many possible trend fits can be explored with time-series data. In this section we examine only the linear model and the quadratic model because they are the easiest to understand and simplest to compute. Because seasonal effects can confound trend analysis, it is assumed here that no seasonal effects occur in the data or they were removed prior to determining the trend.

Linear Regression Trend Analysis

The data in Table 16.5 represent 35 years of data on the average length of the workweek in Canada for manufacturing workers. A regression line can be fit to these data by using the time periods as the independent variable and length of work week as the dependent variable. Because the time periods are consecutive, they can be renumbered from 1 to 35 and entered along with the time-series data (Y) into a regression analysis. The linear model explored in this example is

$$Y_i = \beta_0 + \beta_1 X_{ti} + \epsilon_i$$

where

Y_i = data value for period i
X_{ti} = ith time period

Figure 16.5 shows the Excel regression output for this example. By using the coefficients of the X variable and intercept, the equation of the trend line can be determined to be

$$\hat{Y} = 37.4161 - .0614 X_t$$

The slope indicates that for every unit increase in time period, X_t, a predicted decrease of .0614 occurs in the length of the average work week in manufacturing. Because the

TABLE 16.5	Time Period	Hours	Time Period	Hours
Average Hours per Week in Manufacturing by Canadian Workers	1	37.2	19	36.0
	2	37.0	20	35.7
	3	37.4	21	35.6
	4	37.5	22	35.2
	5	37.7	23	34.8
	6	37.7	24	35.3
	7	37.4	25	35.6
	8	37.2	26	35.6
	9	37.3	27	35.6
	10	37.2	28	35.9
	11	36.9	29	36.0
	12	36.7	30	35.7
	13	36.7	31	35.7
	14	36.5	32	35.5
	15	36.3	33	35.6
	16	35.9	34	36.3
	17	35.8	35	36.5
	18	35.9		

Source: Data prepared by the U.S. Bureau of Labor Statistics, Office of Productivity and Technology.

FIGURE 16.5

Excel Regression Output for Hours Worked Using Linear Trend

	A	B	C	D	E	F
1	SUMMARY OUTPUT					
2	Regression Statistics					
3	Multiple R	0.782				
4	R Square	0.611				
5	Adjusted R Square	0.600				
6	Standard Error	0.5090				
7	Observations	35				
8						
9	ANOVA					
10		df	SS	MS	F	Significance F
11	Regression	1	13.4467	13.4467	51.91	0.000000029
12	Residual	33	8.5487	0.2591		
13	Total	34	21.9954			
14						
15		Coefficients	Standard Error	t Stat	P-value	
16	Intercept	37.4161	0.1758	212.81	0.00000000	
17	Year	-0.0614	0.0085	-7.20	0.00000003	

workweek is measured in hours, the length of the average workweek decreases by an average of $(.0614)(60 \text{ minutes}) = 3.7$ minutes each year in Canada in manufacturing. The Y intercept, 37.4161, indicates that in the year prior to the first period of these data the average workweek was 37.4161 hours.

The probability of the t ratio (.00000003) indicates that significant linear trend is present in the data. In addition, $R^2 = .611$ indicates considerable predictability in the model. Inserting the various period values (1, 2, 3, ... , 35) into the preceding regression equation produces the predicted values of Y that are the trend. For example, for period 23 the predicted value is

$$\hat{Y} = 37.4161 - .0614(23) = 36.0 \text{ hours}$$

The model was developed with 35 periods (years). From this model, the average workweek in Canada in manufacturing for period 41 (the forty-first year) can be forecast:

$$\hat{Y} = 37.4161 - .0614(41) = 34.9 \text{ hours}$$

Figure 16.6 presents an Excel scatter plot of the average workweek lengths over the 35 periods (years). In this Excel plot, the trend line has been fitted through the points. Observe the general downward trend of the data, but also note the somewhat cyclical nature of the points. Because of this pattern, a forecaster might want to determine whether a quadratic model is a better fit for trend.

FIGURE 16.6

Excel Graph of Canadian Manufacturing Data with Trend Line

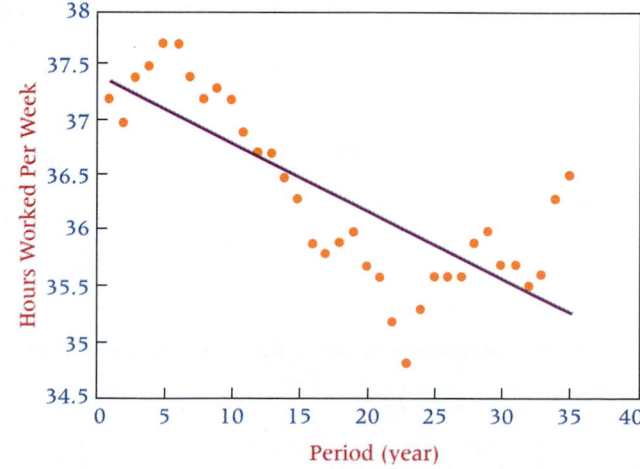

Regression Trend Analysis Using Quadratic Models

In addition to linear regression, forecasters can explore using quadratic regression models to predict data by using the time-series periods. The quadratic regression model is

$$Y_i = \beta_0 + \beta_1 X_{ti} + \beta_2 X_{ti}^2 + \epsilon_i$$

where

Y_i = the time-series data value for period i
X_{ti} = the ith period
X_{ti}^2 = the square of the ith period

This model can be implemented in time-series trend analysis by using the time periods squared as an additional predictor. Thus, in the hours worked example, besides using $X_t = 1, 2, 3, 4, \ldots, 35$ as a predictor, we would also use $X_t^2 = 1, 4, 9, 16, \ldots, 1225$ as a predictor.

Table 16.6 provides the data needed to compute a quadratic regression trend model on the manufacturing workweek data. Note that the table includes the original data, the time periods, and the time periods squared.

The Excel computer output for this quadratic trend regression analysis is shown in Figure 16.7. We see that the quadratic regression model produces an R^2 of .761 with both X_t and X_t^2 in the model. The linear model produced an R^2 of .611 with X_t alone. The quadratic regression seems to add some predictability to the trend model.

Figure 16.8 displays an Excel scatter plot of the week work data with a second-degree polynomial fit through the data.

TABLE 16.6	Time Period	(Time Period)^2	Hours	Time Period	(Time Period)^2	Hours
Data for Quadratic Fit of Manufacturing Workweek Example	1	1	37.2	19	361	36.0
	2	4	37.0	20	400	35.7
	3	9	37.4	21	441	35.6
	4	16	37.5	22	484	35.2
	5	25	37.7	23	529	34.8
	6	36	37.7	24	576	35.3
	7	49	37.4	25	625	35.6
	8	64	37.2	26	676	35.6
	9	81	37.3	27	729	35.6
	10	100	37.2	28	784	35.9
	11	121	36.9	29	841	36.0
	12	144	36.7	30	900	35.7
	13	169	36.7	31	961	35.7
	14	196	36.5	32	1024	35.5
	15	225	36.3	33	1089	35.6
	16	256	35.9	34	1156	36.3
	17	289	35.8	35	1225	36.5
	18	324	35.9			

Source: Data prepared by the U.S. Bureau of Labor Statistics, Office of Productivity and Technology.

FIGURE 16.7

Excel Regression Output for Canadian Manufacturing Example with Quadratic Trend

	A	B	C	D	E	F
1	SUMMARY OUTPUT					
2	Regression Statistics					
3	Multiple R	0.873				
4	R Square	0.761				
5	Adjusted R Square	0.747				
6	Standard Error	0.4049				
7	Observations	35				
8						
9	ANOVA					
10		df	SS	MS	F	Significance F
11	Regression	2	16.7483	8.3741	51.07	0.0000000001
12	Residual	32	5.2472	0.1640		
13	Total	34	21.9954			
14						
15		Coefficients	Standard Error	t Stat	P-value	
16	Intercept	38.1644	0.2177	175.34	0.0000000	
17	Year	-0.1827	0.0279	-6.55	0.0000002	
18	YearSq	0.0034	0.0008	4.49	0.0000876	

FIGURE 16.8

Excel Graph of Canadian Manufacturing Data with a Second-Degree Polynomial Fit

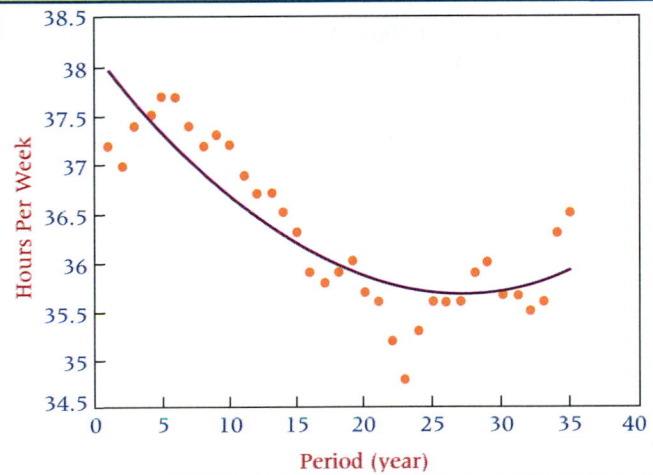

DEMONSTRATION PROBLEM 16.4

Following are data on the U.S. civilian labor force (100,000) for 1988 through 2000, obtained from the U.S. Bureau of Labor Statistics. Use regression analysis to fit a trend line through the data. Explore a quadratic regression trend also. Does either model do well? Compare the two models.

Year	Labor Force (100,000)
1988	114.968
1989	117.342
1990	118.793
1991	117.718
1992	118.492
1993	120.259
1994	123.060
1995	124.900
1996	126.708
1997	129.558
1998	131.463
1999	133.488
2000	134.337

Solution

Recode the time periods as 1 through 13 and let that be X. Run the regression analysis with the labor force members as Y, the dependent variable, and the time period as the independent variable. Now square all the X values, resulting in 1, 4, 9, ... , 121, 144, 169 and let those formulate a second predictor (X^2). Run the regression analysis to predict the number in the labor force with both the time period variable (X) and the (time period)^2 variable. The MINITAB output for each of these regression analyses follows.

LINEAR TREND ANALYSIS

Regression Analysis: Labor Force versus Year

The regression equation is
Labor Force = 112 + 1.67 Year

Predictor	Coef	SE Coef	T	P
Constant	112.229	0.808	138.93	0.000
Year	1.6715	0.1018	16.42	0.000

S = 1.373   R-Sq = 96.1%   R-Sq(adj) = 95.7%

Analysis of Variance

Source	DF	SS	MS	F	P
Regression	1	508.51	508.51	269.75	0.000
Residual Error	11	20.74	1.89		
Total	12	529.24			

QUADRATIC TREND ANALYSIS

Regression Analysis: Labor Force versus Year, YearSq

The regression equation is
Labor Force = 115 + 0.650 Year + 0.0730 YearSq

Predictor	Coef	SE Coef	T	P
Constant	114.783	0.983	116.81	0.000
Year	0.6501	0.3228	2.01	0.072
YearSq	0.07296	0.02244	3.25	0.009

S = 1.004   R-Sq = 98.1%   R-Sq(adj) = 97.7%

Analysis of Variance

Source	DF	SS	MS	F	P
Regression	2	519.16	259.58	257.54	0.000
Residual Error	10	10.08	1.01		
Total	12	529.24			

A comparison of the models shows that the linear model accounts for more than 96% of the variability in the labor force figures, but the quadratic model increases that predictability to greater than 98%. In addition, the standard error of the estimate for the linear model (1.373) is lowered to 1.004 when the quadratic model is used. In the quadratic model, the t test for the squared term is significant at $\alpha = .05$ but is not significant (p-value = .072) for the linear term, indicating that the squared term is the stronger predictor of the labor force figures. Shown next are MINITAB scatter plots of the data. First is the linear model, and then the quadratic model is presented.

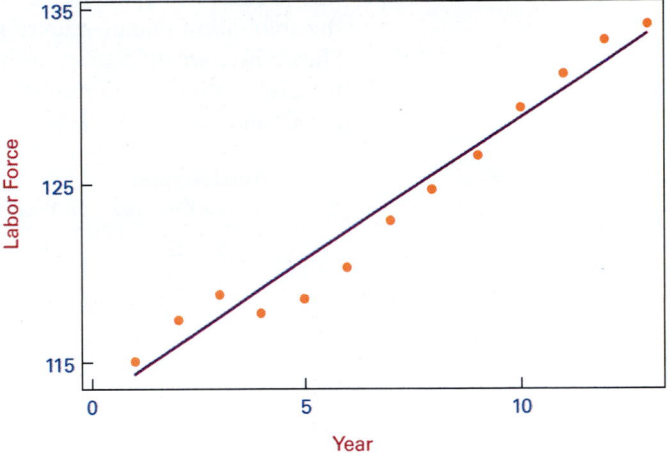

Regression Plot
Labor Force = 112.229 + 1.67152 Year
$S = 1.37299$ $R\text{-}Sq = 96.1\%$ $R\text{-}Sq(adj) = 95.7\%$

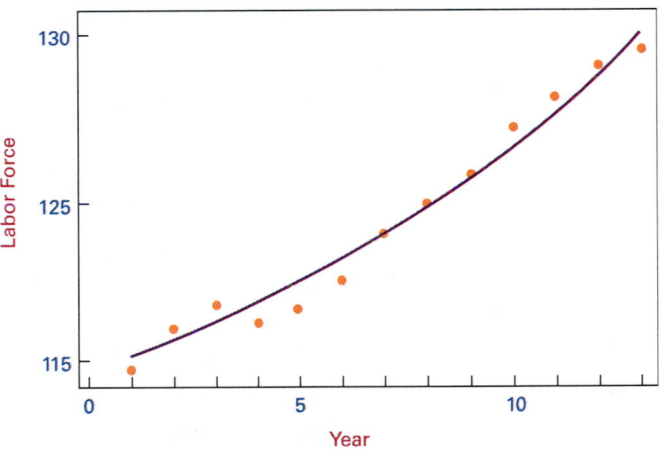

Regression Plot
Labor Force = 114.783 + 0.650088 Year
+ 0.0729595 Year**2
$S = 1.00396$ $R\text{-}Sq = 98.1\%$ $R\text{-}Sq(adj) = 97.7\%$

Holt's Two-Parameter Exponential Smoothing Method

The exponential smoothing technique presented in Section 16.2 (single exponential smoothing) is appropriate to use in forecasting stationary time-series data but is ineffective in forecasting time-series data with a trend because the forecasts will lag behind the trend. However, another exponential smoothing technique, Holt's two-parameter exponential smoothing method, can be used for trend analysis. Holt's technique uses weights (β) to smooth the trend in a manner similar to the smoothing used in single exponential smoothing (α). Using these two weights and several equations, Holt's method is able to develop forecasts that include both a smoothing value and a trend value. A more detailed explanation of Holt's two-parameter exponential smoothing method, along with examples and practice problems, is presented on the CD-ROM that accompanies this text.

16.3 PROBLEMS

16.10 The "Economic Report to the President of the United States" included data on the amounts of manufacturers' new and unfilled orders in millions of dollars. Shown here are the figures for new orders over a 21-year period. Use a computer to develop a regression model to fit the trend effects for these data. Use a linear model and then try a quadratic model. How well does either model fit the data?

Year	Total Number of New Orders	Year	Total Number of New Orders
1	55,022	12	168,025
2	55,921	13	162,140
3	64,182	14	175,451
4	76,003	15	192,879
5	87,327	16	195,706
6	85,139	17	195,204
7	99,513	18	209,389
8	115,109	19	227,025
9	131,629	20	240,758
10	147,604	21	243,643
11	156,359		

16.11 The following data on the number of union members in the United States for the years 1984 through 2000 are provided by the U.S. Bureau of Labor Statistics. Using regression techniques discussed in this section, analyze the data for trend. Develop a scatter plot of the data and fit the trend line through the data. Discuss the strength of the model.

Year	Union Members (1,000s)	Year	Union Members (1,000s)
1984	17,340	1993	16,598
1985	16,996	1994	16,748
1986	16,975	1995	16,360
1987	16,913	1996	16,269
1988	17,002	1997	16,110
1989	16,960	1998	16,211
1990	16,740	1999	16,477
1991	16,568	2000	16,258
1992	16,390		

16.12 The following data list worldwide shipments of personal computers (1,000) according to Dataquest. Plot the data, fit a trend line, and discuss the strength of prediction of the regression model. In addition, explore a quadratic trend. Compare the results of the two models.

Year	Shipments (1,000)
1985	14,705
1986	15,064
1987	16,676
1988	18,061
1989	21,327
1990	23,738
1991	26,966
1992	32,411
1993	38,851
1994	47,894
1995	60,171
1996	71,065
1997	82,400
1998	97,321

16.4 SEASONAL EFFECTS

Earlier in the chapter, we discussed the notion that time-series data consist of four elements: trend, cyclical effects, seasonality, and irregularity. In this section, we examine techniques for identifying seasonal effects. **Seasonal effects** are *patterns of data behavior that occur in periods of time of less than one year.* How can we separate out the seasonal effects?

Decomposition

One of the main techniques for isolating the effects of seasonality is **decomposition.** The decomposition methodology presented here uses the multiplicative model as its basis. The multiplicative model is:

$$T \cdot C \cdot S \cdot I$$

where

T = trend
C = cyclicality
S = seasonality
I = irregularity

To illustrate the decomposition process, we will use the 5-year quarterly time-series data on U.S. shipments of household appliances given in Table 16.7. Figure 16.9 provides a graph of these data.

According to the multiplicative time-series model, $T \cdot C \cdot S \cdot I$, the data can contain the elements of trend, cyclical effects, seasonal effects, and irregular fluctuations. The process of isolating the seasonal effects begins by determining $T \cdot C$ for each value and dividing the time-series data ($T \cdot C \cdot S \cdot I$) by $T \cdot C$. The result is

$$\frac{T \cdot C \cdot S \cdot I}{T \cdot C} = S \cdot I$$

TABLE 16.7

Shipments of Household Appliances

Year	Quarter	Shipments
1	1	4,009
	2	4,321
	3	4,224
	4	3,944
2	1	4,123
	2	4,522
	3	4,657
	4	4,030
3	1	4,493
	2	4,806
	3	4,551
	4	4,485
4	1	4,595
	2	4,799
	3	4,417
	4	4,258
5	1	4,245
	2	4,900
	3	4,585
	4	4,533

FIGURE 16.9

MINITAB Time-Series Graph of Household Appliance Data

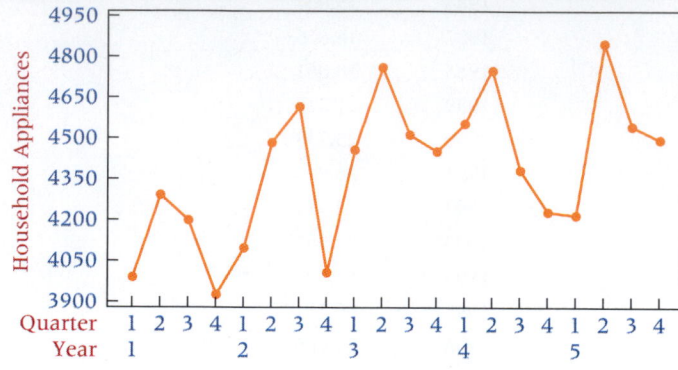

The resulting expression contains seasonal effects along with irregular fluctuations. After reducing the time-series data to the effects of *SI* (seasonality and irregularity), a method for eliminating the irregular fluctuations can be applied, leaving only the seasonal effects.

Suppose we start with time-series data that cover several years and are measured in quarterly increments. If we average the data over four quarters, we will have "dampened" the seasonal effects of the data because the rise and fall of values during the quarterly periods will have been averaged out over the year.

We begin by computing a 4-quarter moving average for quarter 1 through quarter 4 of year 1, using the data from Table 16.7.

$$\text{4-quarter average} = \frac{4,009 + 4,321 + 4,224 + 3,944}{4} = 4,124.5$$

The 4-quarter moving average for quarter 1 through quarter 4 of year 1 is 4,124.5 ($ million) worth of shipments. Because the 4-quarter average is in the middle of the four quarters, it would be placed in the decomposition table between quarter 2 and quarter 3.

Quarter 1
Quarter 2
——— 4,124.5
Quarter 3
Quarter 4

To remove seasonal effects, we need to determine a value that is "centered" with each month. To find this value, instead of using a 4-quarter moving average, we use 4-quarter moving totals and then sum two consecutive moving totals. This 8-quarter total value is divided by 8 to produce a "centered" 4-quarter moving average that lines up across from a quarter. Using this method is analogous to computing two consecutive 4-quarter moving averages and averaging them, thus producing a value that falls on line with a quarter, in between the two averages. The results of using this procedure on the data from Table 16.7 are shown in Table 16.8 in column 5.

A 4-quarter moving total can be computed on these data starting with quarter 1 of year 1 through quarter 4 of year 1 as follows:

First Moving Total = 4,009 + 4,321 + 4,224 + 3,944 = 16,498

In Table 16.8, 16,498 is between quarter 2 and quarter 3 of year 1. The 4-month moving total for quarter 2 of year 1 through quarter 1 of year 2 is

Second Moving Total = 4,321 + 4,224 + 3,944 + 4,123 = 16,612

In Table 16.8, this value is between quarter 3 and quarter 4 of year 1. The 8-quarter (2-year) moving total is computed for quarter 3 of year 1 as

8-Quarter Moving Total = 16,498 + 16,612 = 33,110

| TABLE 16.8 | | | Development of 4-Quarter Moving Averages for the Household Appliance Data | | |

Quarter	Actual Values $(T \cdot C \cdot S \cdot I)$	4-Quarter Moving Total	4-Quarter 2-Year Moving Total	Ratios of Actual Centered Moving Average $(T \cdot C)$	Values to Moving Averages $(S \cdot I) \cdot (100)$
1 (year 1)	4,009				
2	4,321	16,498			
3	4,224		33,110	4,139	102.05
4	3,944	16,612	33,425	4,178	94.40
1 (year 2)	4,123	16,813	34,059	4,257	96.85
2	4,522	17,246	34,578	4,322	104.63
3	4,657	17,332	35,034	4,379	106.35
4	4,030	17,702	35,688	4,461	90.34
1 (year 3)	4,493	17,986	35,866	4,483	100.22
2	4,806	17,880	36,215	4,527	106.16
3	4,551	18,335	36,772	4,597	99.00
4	4,485	18,437	36,867	4,608	97.33
1 (year 4)	4,595	18,430	36,726	4,591	100.09
2	4,799	18,296	36,365	4,546	105.57
3	4,417	18,069	35,788	4,474	98.73
4	4,258	17,719	35,539	4,442	95.86
1 (year 5)	4,245	17,820	35,808	4,476	94.84
2	4,900	17,988	36,251	4,531	108.14
3	4,585	18,263			
4	4,533				

Notice that in Table 16.8 this value is centered with quarter 3 of year 1 because it is between the two adjacent 4-quarter moving totals. Dividing this total by 8 produces the 4-quarter moving average for quarter 3 of year 1 shown in column 5 of Table 16.8:

$$\frac{33,110}{8} = 4,139$$

Column 3 contains the uncentered 4-quarter moving totals, column 4 contains the 2-year centered moving totals, and column 5 contains the 4-quarter centered moving averages.

The 4-quarter centered moving averages shown in column 5 of Table 16.8 represent $T \cdot C$. Seasonal effects have been removed from the original data (actual values) by summing across the 4-quarter periods. Seasonal effects are removed when the data are summed across the time periods that include the seasonal periods and the irregular effects are smoothed, leaving only trend and cycle.

Column 2 of Table 16.8 contains the original data (actual values), which include all effects $(T \cdot C \cdot S \cdot I)$. Column 5 contains only the trend and cyclical effects, $T \cdot C$. If column 2 is divided by column 5, the result is $S \cdot I$, which is displayed in column 6 of Table 16.8.

The values in column 6, sometimes called ratios of actuals to moving average, have been multiplied by 100 to index the values. These values are thus seasonal indexes. An **index number** is *a ratio of a measure taken during one time frame to that same measure taken during another time frame, usually denoted as the time period.* Often the ratio is multiplied by 100 and expressed as a percentage. Index numbers will be discussed more fully in section 16.6. Column 6 contains the effects of seasonality and irregular fluctuations. Now we must remove the irregular effects.

TABLE 16.9

Seasonal Indexes for the
Household Appliance Data

Quarter	Year 1	Year 2	Year 3	Year 4	Year 5
1	—	96.85	100.22	100.09	94.84
2	—	104.63	106.16	105.57	108.14
3	102.05	106.35	99.00	98.73	—
4	94.40	90.34	97.33	95.86	—

TABLE 16.10

Final Seasonal Indexes for the
Household Appliance Data

Quarter	Index
1	98.47
2	105.87
3	100.53
4	95.13

Table 16.9 contains the values from column 6 of Table 16.8 organized by quarter and year. Each quarter in these data has four seasonal indexes. Throwing out the high and low index for each quarter eliminates the extreme values. The remaining two indexes are averaged as follows for quarter 1.

Quarter 1: 96.85   100.22   100.09   94.84
Eliminate: 94.84 and 100.22
Average the Remaining Indexes:

$$\overline{X}_{Q1\,index} = \frac{96.85 + 100.09}{2} = 98.47$$

Table 16.10 gives the final seasonal indexes for all the quarters of these data.

After the final adjusted seasonal indexes are determined, the original data can be **deseasonalized.** The deseasonalization of actual values is relatively common with data published by the government and other agencies. Data can be deseasonalized by dividing the actual values, which consist of $T \cdot C \cdot S \cdot I$, by the final adjusted seasonal effects.

$$\text{Deseasonalized Data} = \frac{T \cdot C \cdot S \cdot I}{S} = T \cdot C \cdot I$$

Because the seasonal effects are in terms of index numbers, the seasonal indexes must be divided by 100 before deseasonalization. Shown here are the computations for deseasonalizing the household appliance data from Table 16.7 for quarter 1 of year 1.

Year 1 Quarter 1 Actual = 4,009
Year 1 Quarter 1 Seasonal Index = 98.47

$$\text{Year 1 Quarter 1 Deseasonalized Value} = \frac{4,009}{.9847} = 4,071.3$$

Table 16.11 gives the deseasonalized data for this example for all years.
Figure 16.10 is a graph of the deseasonalized data.

Finding Seasonal Effects with the Computer

Through MINITAB, decomposition can be performed on the computer with relative ease. The commands for this procedure are given at the end of the chapter in the Using the Computer section. Figure 16.11 displays MINITAB output for seasonal decomposition of the household appliance example. Note that the seasonal indexes are virtually identical to those shown in Table 16.10 computed by hand.

Winters' Three-Parameter Exponential Smoothing Method

Holt's two-parameter exponential smoothing method, can be extended to include seasonal analysis. This technique, referred to as Winters' method, not only smoothes observations and trend but also smoothes the seasonal effects. In addition to the single exponential smoothing weight of α and the trend weight of β, Winters' method introduces γ, a weight for seasonality. Using these three weights and several equations, Winters' method is able to develop forecasts that include a smoothing value for observations, a trend value, and a seasonal value. A more detailed explanation of Winters' three-parameter exponential smoothing method along with examples and practice problems is presented on the CD-Rom that accompanies this text.

TABLE 16.11

Deseasonalized Household
Appliance Data

Year	Quarter	Shipments Actual Values $(T \cdot C \cdot S \cdot I)$	Seasonal Indexes S	Deseasonalized Data $T \cdot C \cdot I$
1	1	4,009	98.47	4,071
	2	4,321	105.87	4,081
	3	4,224	100.53	4,202
	4	3,944	95.13	4,146
2	1	4,123	98.47	4,187
	2	4,522	105.87	4,271
	3	4,657	100.53	4,632
	4	4,030	95.13	4,236
3	1	4,493	98.47	4,563
	2	4,806	105.87	4,540
	3	4,551	100.53	4,527
	4	4,485	95.13	4,715
4	1	4,595	98.47	4,666
	2	4,799	105.87	4,533
	3	4,417	100.53	4,394
	4	4,258	95.13	4,476
5	1	4,245	98.47	4,311
	2	4,900	105.87	4,628
	3	4,585	100.53	4,561
	4	4,533	95.13	4,765

FIGURE 16.10

Graph of the Deseasonalized
Household Appliance Data

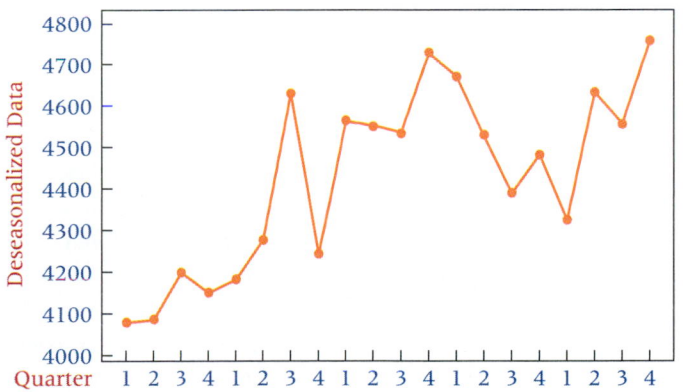

FIGURE 16.11

MINITAB Output for Seasonal
Decomposition of the
Household Appliance Data

```
Time-Series Decomposition
Data: House Appliances
Length: 20.0000
NMissing: 0
Seasonal Indices
Period     Index
    1   0.984691
    2   1.05871
    3   1.00536
    4   0.951239
```

16.4 PROBLEMS

16.13 The U.S. Department of Agriculture publishes statistics on the production of various types of food commodities by month. Shown here are the production figures on broccoli for January of a recent year through December of the next year. Use these data to compute 12-month centered moving averages $(T \cdot C)$. Using these computed values, determine the seasonal effects $(S \cdot I)$.

Month	Broccoli (million pounds)	Month	Broccoli (million pounds)
January (1st year)	132.5	January (2nd year)	104.9
February	164.8	February	99.3
March	141.2	March	102.0
April	133.8	April	122.4
May	138.4	May	112.1
June	150.9	June	108.4
July	146.6	July	119.0
August	146.9	August	119.0
September	138.7	September	114.9
October	128.0	October	106.0
November	112.4	November	111.7
December	121.0	December	112.3

16.14 The U.S. Department of Commerce publishes census information on manufacturing. Included in these figures are monthly shipment data for the paperboard container and box industry shown here for six years. The shipment figures are given in millions of dollars. Use the data to analyze the effects of seasonality, trend, and cycle. Develop the trend model with a linear model only.

Month	Shipments	Month	Shipments
January (year 1)	1,891	January (year 3)	2,183
February	1,986	February	2,230
March	1,987	March	2,222
April	1,987	April	2,319
May	2,000	May	2,369
June	2,082	June	2,529
July	1,878	July	2,267
August	2,074	August	2,457
September	2,086	September	2,524
October	2,045	October	2,502
November	1,945	November	2,314
December	1,861	December	2,277

Month	Shipments	Month	Shipments
January (year 2)	1,936	January (year 4)	2,336
February	2,104	February	2,474
March	2,126	March	2,546
April	2,131	April	2,566
May	2,163	May	2,473
June	2,346	June	2,572
July	2,109	July	2,336
August	2,211	August	2,518
September	2,268	September	2,454
October	2,285	October	2,559
November	2,107	November	2,384
December	2,077	December	2,305

Month	Shipments	Month	Shipments
January (year 5)	2,389	January (year 6)	2,377
February	2,463	February	2,381
March	2,522	March	2,268
April	2,417	April	2,407
May	2,468	May	2,367
June	2,492	June	2,446
July	2,304	July	2,341
August	2,511	August	2,491
September	2,494	September	2,452
October	2,530	October	2,561
November	2,381	November	2,377
December	2,211	December	2,277

16.5 AUTOCORRELATION AND AUTOREGRESSION

Data values gathered over time are often correlated with values from past time periods. This characteristic can cause problems in the use of regression in forecasting and at the same time can open some opportunities. One of the problems that can occur in regressing data over time is autocorrelation.

Autocorrelation

Autocorrelation, or **serial correlation,** occurs in data *when the error terms of a regression forecasting model are correlated.* The likelihood of this occurring with business data increases over time, particularly with economic variables. Autocorrelation can be a problem in using regression analysis as the forecasting method because one of the assumptions underlying regression analysis is that the error terms are independent or random (not correlated). In most business analysis situations, the correlation of error terms is likely to occur as positive autocorrelation (positive errors are associated with positive errors of comparable magnitude and negative errors are associated with negative errors of comparable magnitude).

When autocorrelation occurs in a regression analysis, several possible problems might arise. First, the estimates of the regression coefficients no longer have the minimum variance property and may be inefficient. Second, the variance of the error terms may be greatly underestimated by the mean square error value. Third, the true standard deviation of the estimated regression coefficient may be seriously underestimated. Fourth, the confidence intervals and tests using the t and F distributions are no longer strictly applicable.

First-order autocorrelation results from correlation between the error terms of adjacent time periods (as opposed to two or more previous periods). If first-order autocorrelation is present, the error for one time period, e_t, is a function of the error of the previous time period, e_{t-1}, as follows.

$$e_t = \rho e_{t-1} + v_t$$

The first-order autocorrelation coefficient, ρ, measures the correlation between the error terms. It is a value that lies between −1 and 0 and +1, as does the coefficient of correlation discussed in Chapter 3. v_t is a normally distributed independent error term. If positive autocorrelation is present, the value of ρ is between 0 and +1. If the value of ρ is 0, $e_t = v_t$, which means there is no autocorrelation and e_t is just a random, independent error term.

One way to *test to determine whether autocorrelation is present in a time-series regression analysis* is by using the **Durbin-Watson test** for autocorrelation. Shown next is the formula for computing a Durbin-Watson test for autocorrelation.

DURBIN-WATSON TEST

$$D = \frac{\sum\limits_{t=2}^{n} (e_t - e_{t-1})^2}{\sum\limits_{t=1}^{n} e_t^2}$$

where

n = the number of observations

Note from the formula that the Durbin-Watson test involves finding the difference between successive values of error $(e_t - e_{t-1})$. If errors are positively correlated, this difference will be smaller than with random or independent errors. Squaring this term eliminates the cancellation effects of positive and negative terms.

The null hypothesis for this test is that there is *no* autocorrelation. For a two-tailed test, the alternative hypothesis is that there *is* autocorrelation.

$$H_0: \rho = 0$$
$$H_a: \rho \neq 0$$

As mentioned before, most business forecasting autocorrelation is positive autocorrelation. In most cases, a one-tailed test is used.

$$H_0: \rho = 0$$
$$H_a: \rho > 0$$

In the Durbin-Watson test, D is the observed value of the Durbin-Watson statistic using the residuals from the regression analysis. A critical value for D can be obtained from the values of α, n, and k by using Table A.9 in the appendix, where α is the level of significance, n is the number of data items, and k is the number of predictors. Two Durbin-Watson tables are given in the appendix. One table contains values for $\alpha = .01$ and the other for $\alpha = .05$. The Durbin-Watson tables in Appendix A include values for d_U and d_L. These values range from 0 to 4. If the observed value of D is above d_U, we fail to reject the null hypothesis and there is no significant autocorrelation. If the observed value of D is below d_L, the null hypothesis is rejected and there is autocorrelation. Sometimes the observed statistic, D, is between the values of d_U and d_L. In this case, the Durbin-Watson test is inconclusive.

As an example, consider Table 16.12, which lists drilling data for oil wells and gas wells from 1973 through 1998 (in thousands). A regression line can be fit through these data to determine whether the number of oil wells drilled in a given year can be predicted by the number of gas wells drilled in a year. The resulting errors of prediction can be tested by the Durbin-Watson statistic for the presence of significant positive autocorrelation by using $\alpha = .05$. The hypotheses are

$$H_0: \rho = 0$$
$$H_a: \rho > 0$$

The following regression equation was obtained by means of a MINITAB computer analysis.

Oil Wells = −11.337 + 2.6106 (Gas Wells)

With the values for the number of gas wells being drilled (X) from Table 16.12 and the regression model equation shown here, predicted values of Y (number of oil wells being drilled) can be computed. From the predicted values and the actual values, the errors of prediction for each time interval, e_t, can be calculated. Table 16.13 shows the values of $\hat{Y}$, e_t, e_t^2, $(e_t - e_{t-1})$, and $(e_t - e_{t-1})^2$ for this example. Note that the first predicted value of Y is

$$\hat{Y}_{1973} = -11.337 + 2.6106(6.933) = 6.7623$$

The error for 1973 is

$$\text{Actual}_{1973} - \text{Predicted}_{1973} = 10.167 - 6.7623 = 3.4047$$

The value of $e_t - e_{t-1}$ for 1973 and 1974 is computed by subtracting the error for 1973 from the error of 1974.

$$e_{1974} - e_{1973} = 6.3495 - 3.4047 = 2.9448$$

TABLE 16.12
U.S. Oil and Gas Well Drilling, 1973–1998

Year	Oil Wells (1,000)	Gas Wells (1,000)
1973	10.167	6.933
1974	13.647	7.138
1975	16.948	8.127
1976	17.688	9.409
1977	18.745	12.122
1978	19.181	14.413
1979	20.851	15.254
1980	32.639	17.333
1981	43.598	20.166
1982	39.199	18.979
1983	37.120	14.564
1984	42.605	17.127
1985	35.118	14.168
1986	19.097	8.516
1987	16.164	8.055
1988	13.636	8.555
1989	10.204	9.539
1990	12.198	11.044
1991	11.770	9.526
1992	8.757	8.209
1993	8.407	10.017
1994	6.721	9.538
1995	7.627	8.354
1996	8.314	9.302
1997	10.436	11.327
1998	7.118	12.106

Source: Monthly Energy Review, June 1998.

TABLE 16.13
Predicted Values and Error Terms for the Oil and Gas Well Data

Year	$\hat{Y}$	e_t	e_t^2	$e_t - e_{t-1}$	$(e_t - e_{t-1})^2$
1973	6.7623	3.4047	11.592	—	—
1974	7.2975	6.3495	40.317	2.9448	8.6718
1975	9.8793	7.0687	49.966	0.7191	0.5171
1976	13.2261	4.4619	19.908	−2.6068	6.7954
1977	20.3087	−1.5637	2.445	−6.0256	36.3078
1978	26.2896	−7.1086	50.532	−5.5449	30.7459
1979	28.4851	−7.6341	58.279	−0.5255	0.2762
1980	33.9125	−1.2735	1.622	6.3606	40.4572
1981	41.3084	2.2896	5.242	3.5632	12.6964
1982	38.2096	0.9894	0.979	−1.3002	1.6905
1983	26.6838	10.4362	108.915	9.4468	89.2420
1984	33.3747	9.2303	85.198	−1.2060	1.4544
1985	25.6500	9.4680	89.643	0.2378	0.0565
1986	10.8949	8.2021	67.275	−1.2659	1.6025
1987	9.6914	6.4726	41.895	−1.7295	2.9912
1988	10.9967	2.6393	6.966	−3.8333	14.6942
1989	13.5655	−3.3615	11.300	−6.0008	36.0100
1990	17.4945	−5.2965	28.053	−1.9350	3.7442
1991	13.5316	−1.7616	3.103	3.5349	12.4955
1992	10.0934	−1.3364	1.786	0.4252	0.1808
1993	14.8134	−6.4064	41.042	−5.0700	25.7049
1994	13.5629	−6.8419	46.812	−0.4355	0.1897
1995	10.4720	−2.8450	8.094	3.9970	15.9760
1996	12.9468	−4.6328	21.463	−1.7879	3.1966
1997	18.2333	−7.7973	60.797	−3.1645	10.0141
1998	20.2669	−13.1489	172.894	−5.3517	28.6407

$\sum e_t = 0.0043 \qquad \sum e_t^2 = 1036.118 \qquad \sum (e_t - e_{t-1})^2 = 384.3516$

The Durbin-Watson statistic can now be computed:

$$D = \frac{\sum_{t=2}^{n}(e_t - e_{t-1})^2}{\sum_{t=1}^{n} e_t^2} = \frac{384.3516}{1,036.118} = .371$$

Because we used a simple linear regression, the value of k is 1. The sample size, n, is 26, and $\alpha = .05$. The critical values in Table A.9 are

$$d_U = 1.46 \text{ and } d_L = 1.30$$

Because the computed D statistic, .371, is less than the value of $d_L = 1.30$, the null hypothesis is rejected. A positive autocorrelation is present in this example.

Figure 16.12 provides the graph of the residuals given in Table 16.13. Note that several "runs" of positive and negative error terms are evident instead of a random distribution of error terms, which indicates the presence of autocorrelation.

FIGURE 16.12

Excel Graph of the Residuals of the Oil and Gas Well Example

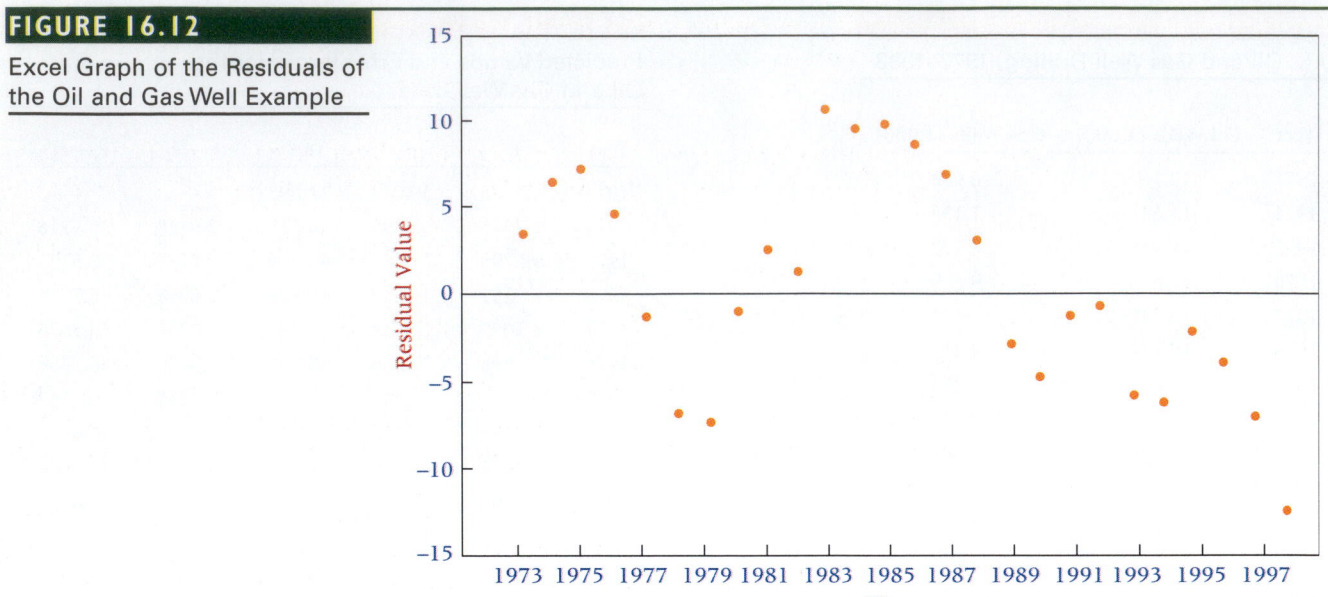

Ways to Overcome the Autocorrelation Problem

Several approaches to data analysis can be used when autocorrelation is present. One uses additional independent variables and another transforms the independent variable.

Addition of Independent Variables

Often the reason autocorrelation occurs in regression analyses is that one or more important predictor variables have been left out of the analysis. For example, suppose a researcher develops a regression forecasting model that attempts to predict sales of new homes by sales of used homes over some period of time. Such a model might contain significant autocorrelation. The exclusion of the variable "prime mortgage interest rate" might be a factor driving the autocorrelation between the other two variables. Adding this variable to the regression model might significantly reduce the autocorrelation.

Transforming Variables

When the inclusion of additional variables is not helpful in reducing autocorrelation to an acceptable level, transforming the data in the variables may help to solve the problem. One such method is the **first-differences approach.** With the first-differences approach, *each value of X is subtracted from each succeeding time period value of X;* these "differences" become the new and transformed X variable. The same process is used to transform the Y variable. The regression analysis is then computed on the transformed X and transformed Y variables to compute a new model that is hopefully free of significant autocorrelation effects.

Another way is to generate new variables by using the percentage changes from period to period and regressing these new variables. A third way is to use autoregression models.

Autoregression

A forecasting technique that takes advantage of the relationship of values (Y_t) to previous-period values ($Y_{t-1}, Y_{t-2}, Y_{t-3}, \ldots$) is called autoregression. **Autoregression** is *a multiple regression technique in which the independent variables are time-lagged versions of the dependent variable,* which means we try to predict a value of Y from values of Y from previous time periods. The independent variable can be lagged for one, two, three, or more time periods. An autoregressive model containing independent variables for three time periods looks like this:

$$\hat{Y} = b_o + b_1 Y_{t-1} + b_2 Y_{t-2} + b_3 Y_{t-3}$$

As an example, suppose we take the oil well data from Table 16.12 and attempt to predict the number of oil wells drilled by using data lagged for two time periods. The data for this analysis are displayed in Table 16.14.

Using Excel, a multiple regression model is developed to predict the values of Y_t by the values of Y_{t-1} and Y_{t-2}. The results appear in Figure 16.13.

The autoregression model is

$$Y_t = 2.3304 + 1.2822 Y_{t-1} - 0.4151 Y_{t-2}$$

The relatively high value of R^2 (83.5%) and relatively small value of S (5.1583) indicate that this regression model provides fairly strong predictability. In addition, both predictors have statistically significant t ratios ($t = 6.40$ with $p = .0000024$, and $t = -2.08$ with $p = .0504475$).

Autoregression can be a useful tool in locating seasonal or cyclical effects in time-series data. For example, if the data are given in monthly increments, autoregression using variables lagged by as much as 12 months can search for the predictability of previous monthly time periods. If data are given in quarterly time periods, autoregression of up to four periods removed can be a useful tool in locating the predictability of data from previous quarters. When the time periods are in years, lagging the data by yearly periods and using autoregression can help in locating cyclical predictability.

TABLE 16.14

Time-Lagged Oil Well Data

Year	Oil Wells Y_t	One Period Lagged Y_{t-1} (X_1)	Two Periods Lagged Y_{t-2} (X_2)
1973	10.167		
1974	13.647	10.167	
1975	16.948	13.647	10.167
1976	17.688	16.948	13.647
1977	18.745	17.688	16.948
1978	19.181	18.745	17.688
1979	20.851	19.181	18.745
1980	32.639	20.851	19.181
1981	43.598	32.639	20.851
1982	39.199	43.598	32.639
1983	37.120	39.199	43.598
1984	42.605	37.120	39.199
1985	35.118	42.605	37.120
1986	19.097	35.118	42.605
1987	16.164	19.097	35.118
1988	13.636	16.164	19.097
1989	10.204	13.636	16.164
1990	12.198	10.204	13.636
1991	11.770	12.198	10.204
1992	8.757	11.770	12.198
1993	8.407	8.757	11.770
1994	6.721	8.407	8.757
1995	7.627	6.721	8.407
1996	8.314	7.627	6.721
1997	10.436	8.314	7.627
1998	7.118	10.436	8.314

Adapted from: Data in *Monthly Energy Review,* June 1998.

FIGURE 16.13

Excel Autoregression Results for Oil Well Data

	A	B	C	D	E	F
1	SUMMARY OUTPUT					
2	Regression Statistics					
3	Multiple R	0.914				
4	R Square	0.835				
5	Adjusted R Square	0.819				
6	Standard Error	5.1583				
7	Observations	24				
8						
9	ANOVA					
10		df	SS	MS	F	Significant F
11	Regression	2	2831.0351	1415.5176	53.20	0.000000006
12	Residual	21	558.7621	26.6077		
13	Total	23	3389.7972			
14						
15		Coefficients	Standard Error	t Stat	P-value	
16	Intercept	2.3304	2.1000	1.11	0.2796706	
17	1-lag	1.2822	0.2002	6.40	0.0000024	
18	2-lags	−0.4151	0.2001	−2.08	0.0504475	

16.5 PROBLEMS

16.15 The U.S. Bureau of Labor Statistics publishes consumer price indexes (CPIs) on many commodities. Following are the percentage changes in the CPIs for food and for shelter for 1974 through 1999. Use these data to develop a linear regression model to forecast the percentage change in food CPIs by the percentage change in shelter CPIs. Compute a Durbin-Watson statistic to determine whether significant autocorrelation is present in the model. Let $\alpha = .05$.

Year	Food	Shelter	Year	Food	Shelter
1974	14.3	9.6	1986	3.2	5.5
1975	8.5	9.9	1987	4.1	4.7
1976	3.0	5.5	1988	4.1	4.8
1977	6.3	6.6	1989	5.8	4.5
1978	9.9	10.2	1990	5.8	5.4
1979	11.0	13.9	1991	2.9	4.5
1980	8.6	17.6	1992	1.2	3.3
1981	7.8	11.7	1993	2.2	3.0
1982	4.1	7.1	1994	2.4	3.1
1983	2.1	2.3	1995	2.8	3.2
1984	3.8	4.9	1996	3.3	3.2
1985	2.3	5.6	1997	2.6	3.1
			1998	2.2	3.3
			1999	2.1	2.9

16.16 Use the data from Problem 16.15 to create a regression forecasting model using the first-differences data transformation. How do the results from this model differ from those obtained in Problem 16.15?

16.17 The Federal Deposit Insurance Corporation (FDIC) releases data on bank failures. Following are data on the number of U.S. bank failures in a given year and the total amount of bank deposits (in $ millions) involved in such failures for a given year. Use these data to develop a simple regression forecasting model that attempts to predict the failed bank assets involved in bank closings by the number of bank failures. Compute a Durbin-Watson statistic for this regression model and determine whether significant autocorrelation is present. Let $\alpha = .05$.

Year	Failures	Failed Bank Assets
1	11	8,189
2	7	104
3	34	1,862
4	45	4,137
5	79	36,394
6	118	3,034
7	144	7,609
8	201	7,538
9	221	56,620
10	206	28,507
11	159	10,739
12	108	43,552
13	100	16,915
14	42	2,588
15	11	825
16	6	753
17	5	186
18	1	27

16.18 Use the data in Problem 16.17 to compute a regression model after recoding the data by the first-differences approach. Compute a Durbin-Watson statistic to determine whether significant autocorrelation is present in this first-differences model. Compare this model with the model determined in Problem 16.17, and compare the significance of the Durbin-Watson statistics for the two problems. Let $\alpha = .05$.

16.19 *Current Construction Reports* from the U.S. Census Bureau contain data on new privately owned housing units. Data on new privately owned housing units (1,000s) built in the West between 1970 and 1997 follow. Use these time-series data to develop an autoregression model with a one-period lag. Now try an autoregression model with a two-period lag. Discuss the results and compare the two models.

Year	Housing Starts (1,000)	Year	Housing Starts (1,000)
1970	311	1984	436
1971	486	1985	468
1972	527	1986	483
1973	429	1987	420
1974	285	1988	404
1975	275	1989	396
1976	400	1990	329
1977	538	1991	254
1978	545	1992	288
1979	470	1993	302
1980	306	1994	351
1981	240	1995	331
1982	205	1996	361
1983	382	1997	364

16.20 The U.S. Department of Agriculture publishes data on the production, utilization, and value of fruits in the United States. Shown here are the amounts of noncitrus fruit processed into juice (in kilotons) for a 25-year period. Use these data to develop an autoregression forecasting model with a two-period lag. Discuss the results of this analysis.

Year	Processed Juice	Year	Processed Juice
1	598	14	1,135
2	768	15	1,893
3	863	16	1,372
4	818	17	1,547
5	841	18	1,450
6	1,140	19	1,557
7	1,285	20	1,742
8	1,418	21	1,736
9	1,235	22	1,886
10	1,255	23	1,857
11	1,445	24	1,582
12	1,336	25	1,675
13	1,226		

16.6 INDEX NUMBERS

One particular type of descriptive measure that is useful in allowing comparisons of data over time is the index number. An index number is, in part, a ratio of a measure taken during one time frame to that same measure taken during another time frame, usually denoted as the base period. Often the ratio is multiplied by 100 and is expressed as a percentage. When expressed as a percentage, index numbers serve as an alternative to comparing raw numbers. Index number users become accustomed to interpreting measures for a given time period in light of a base period on a scale in which the base period has an index of 100(%). Index numbers are used to compare phenomena from one time period to another and are especially helpful in highlighting interperiod differences.

Index numbers are widely used around the world to relate information about stock markets, inflation, sales, exports and imports, agriculture, and many other things. Some examples of specific indexes are the employment cost index, price index for construction, index of manufacturing capacity, producer price index, consumer price index, Dow Jones industrial average, index of output, and Nikkei 225 average. This section, although recognizing the importance of stock indexes and others, will focus on price indexes.

The motivation for using an index number is to reduce data to an easier-to-use, more convenient form. As an example, examine the raw data on number of business starts in the United States from 1985 through 1999 shown in Table 16.15. An analyst can describe these data by observing that, in general, the number of business starts has been decreasing since 1986. How do the number of business starts in 1995 compare to 1985? How do the number of business starts in 1997 compare to 1990 or 1991? To answer these questions without index numbers, a researcher would probably resort to subtracting the number of business starts for the years of interest and comparing the corresponding increases or decreases. This process can be tedious and frustrating for decision makers who must maximize their effort in minimal time. Using simple index numbers, the researcher can transform these data into values that are more usable. In addition, it is sometimes easier to compare other years to one particular key year.

Simple Index Numbers and Unweighted Aggregate Price Indexes

How are index numbers computed? The equation for computing a **simple index number** follows.

TABLE 16.15

Business Starts in the United States

Year	Starts
1985	249,770
1986	253,092
1987	233,710
1988	199,091
1989	181,645
1990	158,930
1991	155,672
1992	164,086
1993	166,154
1994	188,387
1995	168,158
1996	170,475
1997	166,740
1998	155,141
1999	151,016

SIMPLE INDEX NUMBER	$$I_i = \frac{X_i}{X_0}(100)$$

where

X_0 = the quantity, price, or cost in the base year
X_i = the quantity, price, or cost in the year of interest
I_i = the index number for the year of interest

Suppose cost-of-living researchers examining the data from Table 16.15 decide to compute index numbers using 1985 as the base year. The index number for the year 1997 is

$$I_{1997} = \frac{X_{1997}}{X_{1985}}(100) = \frac{166,740}{249,770}(100) = 66.8$$

Table 16.16 displays all the index numbers for the data in Table 16.15, with 1985 as the base year, along with the raw data. A cursory glance at these index numbers reveals a decrease in the number of business starts for most of the years since 1985 (because the index has been going down). In particular, the greatest drop in number seems to have occurred between 1987 and 1988—a drop of nearly 14 in the index. Because most people are easily able to understand the concept of 100%, it is likely that decision makers can make quick judgments on the number of business starts in the United States from one year relative to another by examining the index numbers over this period.

Unweighted Aggregate Price Index Numbers

The use of simple index numbers makes possible the conversion of prices, costs, quantities, and so on for different time periods into a number scale with the base year equaling 100%. One of the drawbacks of simple index numbers, however, is that each time period is represented by only one item or commodity. When multiple items are involved, multiple sets of index numbers are possible. Suppose a decision maker is interested in combining or pooling the prices of several items, creating a "market basket" in order to compare the prices for several years. Fortunately, a technique does exist for combining several items and determining index numbers for the total (aggregate). Because this technique is used mostly in determining price indexes, the focus in this section is on developing aggregate price indexes. The formula for constructing the **unweighted aggregate price index number** follows.

UNWEIGHTED AGGREGATE PRICE INDEX NUMBER	$$I_i = \frac{\Sigma P_i}{\Sigma P_0}(100)$$

where

P_i = the price of an item in the year of interest (i)
P_0 = the price of an item in the base year (0)
I_i = the index number for the year of interest (i)

Suppose a state's department of labor wants to compare the cost of family food buying over the years. Department officials decide that instead of using a single food item to do this comparison, they will use a food basket that consists of five items: eggs, milk, bananas, potatoes, and sugar. They gathered price information on these five items for the years 1990, 1995, and 2000. The items and the prices are listed in Table 16.17.

From the data in Table 16.17 and the formula, the unweighted aggregate price indexes for the years 1990, 1995, and 2000 can be computed by using 1990 as the base year. The first step is to add together, or aggregate, the prices for all the food basket items in a given year. These totals are shown in the last row of Table 16.17. The index numbers are constructed by using these totals (not individual item prices): $\Sigma P_{1990} = 2.91$, $\Sigma P_{1995} = 3.44$, and $\Sigma P_{2000} = 3.93$. From these figures, the unweighted aggregate price index for 1995 is computed as follows.

For 1995: $I_{1995} = \dfrac{\Sigma P_{1995}}{\Sigma P_{1990}}(100) = \dfrac{3.44}{2.91}(100) = 118.2$

TABLE 16.16

Index Numbers for Business Starts in the United States

Year	Starts	Index Number
1985	249,770	100.0
1986	253,092	101.3
1987	233,710	93.6
1988	199,091	79.7
1989	181,645	72.7
1990	158,930	63.6
1991	155,672	62.3
1992	164,086	65.7
1993	166,154	66.5
1994	188,387	75.4
1995	168,158	67.3
1996	170,475	68.3
1997	166,740	66.8
1998	155,141	62.1
1999	151,016	60.5

TABLE 16.17

Prices for a Basket of Food Items

Item	Year 1990	1995	2000
Eggs (dozen)	.78	.86	1.06
Milk (1/2 gallon)	1.14	1.39	1.59
Bananas (per lb.)	.36	.46	.49
Potatoes (per lb.)	.28	.31	.36
Sugar (per lb.)	.35	.42	.43
Total of Items	2.91	3.44	3.93

Weighted Aggregate Price Index Numbers

A major drawback to unweighted aggregate price indexes is that they are *unweighted*—that is, equal weight is put on each item by assuming the market basket contains only one of each item. This assumption may or may not be true. For example, a household may consume 5 pounds of bananas per year but drink 50 gallons of milk. In addition, unweighted aggregate index numbers are dependent on the units selected for various items. For example, if milk is measured in quarts instead of gallons, the price of milk used in determining the index numbers is considerably lower. A class of index numbers that can be used to avoid these problems is weighted aggregate price index numbers.

Weighted aggregate price index numbers are *computed by multiplying quantity weights and item prices in determining the market basket worth for a given year.* Sometimes when price and quantity are multiplied to construct index numbers, the index numbers are referred to as *value indexes.* Thus, weighted aggregate price index numbers are also value indexes.

Including quantities eliminates the problems caused by how many of each item are consumed per time period and the units of items. If 50 gallons of milk but only 5 pounds of bananas are consumed, weighted aggregate price index numbers will reflect those weights. If the business researcher switches from gallons of milk to quarts, the prices will change downward but the quantity will increase fourfold (4 quarts in a gallon).

In general, weighted aggregate price indexes are constructed by multiplying the price of each item by its quantity and then summing these products for the market basket over a given time period (often a year). The ratio of this sum for one time period of interest (year) to a base time period of interest (base year) is multiplied by 100. The following formula reflects a weighted aggregate price index computed by using quantity weights from each time period (year).

$$I_i = \frac{\sum P_i Q_i}{\sum P_0 Q_0}(100)$$

One of the problems with this formula is the implication that new and possibly different quantities apply for each time period. However, business researchers expend much time and money ascertaining the quantities used in a market basket. Redetermining quantity weights for each year is therefore often prohibitive for most organizations (even the government). Two particular types of weighted aggregate price indexes offer a solution to the problem of which quantity weights to use. The first and most widely used is the Laspeyres price index. The second and less widely used is the Paasche price index.

Laspeyres Price Index

The **Laspeyres price index** is *a weighted aggregate price index computed by using the quantities of the base period (year) for all other years.* The advantages of this technique are that the price indexes for all years can be compared, and new quantities do not have to be determined for each year. The formula for constructing the Laspeyres price index follows.

LASPEYRES PRICE INDEX	$I_L = \dfrac{\Sigma P_i Q_0}{\Sigma P_0 Q_0}(100)$

Notice that the formula requires the base period quantities (Q_0) in both the numerator and the denominator.

In Table 16.17, a food basket is presented in which aggregate price indexes are computed. This food basket consisted of eggs, milk, bananas, potatoes, and sugar. The prices of these items were combined (aggregated) for a given year and the price indexes were computed from these aggregate figures. The unweighted aggregate price indexes computed on these data gave all items equal importance. Suppose that the business researchers realize that applying equal weight to these five items is probably not a representative way to construct this food basket and consequently ascertain quantity weights on each food item for one year's consumption. Table 16.18 lists these five items, their prices, and their quantity usage weights for the base year (1990). From these data, the business researchers can compute Laspeyres price indexes.

The Laspeyres price index for 1995 with 1990 as the base year is:

$$\Sigma P_i Q_0 = \Sigma P_{1995} Q_{1990}$$
$$= \Sigma\,[(.86)(45) + (1.39)(60) + (.46)(12) + (.31)(55) + (.42)(36)]$$
$$= 38.70 + 83.40 + 5.52 + 17.05 + 15.12 = 159.79$$

$$\Sigma P_0 Q_0 = \Sigma P_{1990} Q_{1990}$$
$$= \Sigma\,[(.78)(45) + (1.14)(60) + (.36)(12) + (.28)(55) + (.35)(36)]$$
$$= 35.10 + 68.40 + 4.32 + 15.40 + 12.60 = 135.82$$

$$I_{1995} = \frac{\Sigma P_{1995} Q_{1990}}{\Sigma P_{1990} Q_{1990}}(100) = \frac{159.79}{135.82}(100) = 117.6$$

Paasche Price Index

The **Paasche price index** is *a weighted aggregate price index computed by using the quantities for the year of interest in computations for a given year.* The advantage of this technique is that it incorporates current quantity figures in the calculations. One disadvantage is that ascertaining quantity figures for each time period is expensive. The formula for computing Paasche price indexes follows.

PAASCHE PRICE INDEX	$I_P = \dfrac{\Sigma P_i Q_i}{\Sigma P_0 Q_i}(100)$

Suppose the yearly quantities for the basket of food items listed in Table 16.18 are determined. The result is the quantities and prices shown in Table 16.19 for the years 1990 and 1995 that can be used to compute Paasche price index numbers.

TABLE 16.18

Food Basket Items with Quantity Weights

Item	Quantity 1990	Price 1990	1995	2000
Eggs (dozen)	45	.78	.86	1.06
Milk (1/2 gal.)	60	1.14	1.39	1.59
Bananas (per lb.)	12	.36	.46	.49
Potatoes (per lb.)	55	.28	.31	.36
Sugar (per lb.)	36	.35	.42	.43

TABLE 16.19

Food Basket Items with Yearly Quantity Weights for 1990 and 1995

Item	P_{1990}	Q_{1990}	P_{1995}	Q_{1995}
Eggs (dozen)	.78	45	.86	42
Milk (1/2 gal.)	1.14	60	1.39	57
Bananas (per lb.)	.36	12	.46	13
Potatoes (per lb.)	.28	55	.31	52
Sugar (per lb.)	.35	36	.42	36

The Paasche price index numbers can be determined for 1995 by using a base year of 1990 as follows.

For 1995:

$$\Sigma P_{1995}Q_{1995} = [(.86)(42) + (1.39)(57) + (.46)(13) + (.31)(52) + .42)(36)]$$
$$= 36.12 + 79.23 + 5.98 + 16.12 + 15.12$$
$$= 152.57$$

$$\Sigma P_{1990}Q_{1995} = [(.78)(42) + (1.14)(57) + (.36)(13) + (.28)(52) + (.35)(36)]$$
$$= 32.76 + 64.98 + 4.68 + 14.56 + 12.60$$
$$= 129.58$$

$$I_{1995} = \frac{\Sigma P_{1995}Q_{1995}}{\Sigma P_{1990}Q_{1995}}(100) = \frac{152.57}{129.58}(100) = 117.7$$

DEMONSTRATION PROBLEM 16.5

The Arapaho Valley Pediatrics Clinic has been in business for 18 years. The office manager noticed that prices of clinic materials and office supplies fluctuate over time. To get a handle on the price trends for running the clinic, the office manager examined prices of six items the clinic uses as part of its operation. Shown here are the items, their prices, and the quantities for the years 1999 and 2000. Use these data to develop unweighted aggregate price indexes for 2000 with a base year of 1999. Compute the Laspeyres price index for the year 2000 using 1999 as the base year. Compute the Paasche index number for 2000 using 1999 as the base year.

Item	1999		2000	
	Price	**Quantity**	**Price**	**Quantity**
Syringes (dozen)	6.70	150	6.95	135
Cotton swabs (box)	1.35	60	1.45	65
Patient record forms (pad)	5.10	8	6.25	12
Children's Tylenol (bottle)	4.50	25	4.95	30
Computer paper (box)	11.95	6	13.20	8
Thermometers	7.90	4	9.00	2
Totals	37.50		41.80	

Solution

Unweighted Aggregate Index for 2000:

$$I_{2000} = \frac{\Sigma P_{2000}}{\Sigma P_{1999}}(100) = \frac{41.80}{37.50}(100) = 111.5$$

Laspeyres Index for 2000:

$$\Sigma P_{2000}Q_{1999} = [(6.95)(150) + (1.45)(60) + (6.25)(8) + (4.95)(25) + (13.20)(6)$$
$$+ (9.00)(4)]$$
$$= 1{,}042.50 + 87.00 + 50.00 + 123.75 + 79.20 + 36.00$$
$$= 1{,}418.45$$

$$\Sigma P_{1999}Q_{1999} = [(6.70)(150) + (1.35)(60) + (5.10)(8) + (4.50)(25) + (11.95)(6)$$
$$+ (7.90)(4)]$$
$$= 1{,}005.00 + 81.00 + 40.80 + 112.50 + 71.70 + 31.60$$
$$= 1{,}342.6$$

$$I_{2000} = \frac{\Sigma P_{2000}Q_{1999}}{\Sigma P_{1999}Q_{1999}}(100) = \frac{1418.45}{1342.6}(100) = 105.6$$

Paasche Index for 2000:

$$\Sigma P_{2000}Q_{2000} = [(6.95)(135) + (1.45)(65) + (6.25)(12) + (4.95)(30) + (13.20)(8)$$
$$+ (9.00)(2)]$$
$$= 938.25 + 94.25 + 75.00 + 148.50 + 105.60 + 18.00$$
$$= 1,379.60$$

$$\Sigma P_{1999}Q_{2000} = [(6.70)(135) + (1.35)(65) + (5.10)(12) + (4.50)(30) + (11.95)(8)$$
$$+ (7.90)(2)]$$
$$= 904.50 + 87.75 + 61.20 + 135.00 + 95.60 + 15.80$$
$$= 1,299.85$$

$$I_{2000} = \frac{\Sigma P_{2000}Q_{2000}}{\Sigma P_{1999}Q_{2000}}(100) = \frac{1,379.60}{1,299.85}(100) = 106.1$$

16.6 PROBLEMS

16.21 Suppose the following data represent the price of 20 reams of office paper over a 50-year time frame. Find the simple index numbers for the data.

a. Let 1950 be the base year.

b. Let 1980 be the base year.

Year	Price	Year	Price
1950	$22.45	1980	$69.75
1955	31.40	1985	73.44
1960	32.33	1990	80.05
1965	36.50	1995	84.61
1970	44.90	2000	87.28
1975	61.24		

16.22 The U.S. Patent and Trademark Office reports fiscal year figures for patents issued in the United States. Following are the numbers of patents issued for the years 1980 through 1997. Using these data and a base year of 1990, determine the simple index numbers for each year.

Year	Number of Patents (1,000s)
1980	66.0
1981	70.8
1982	63.1
1983	61.7
1984	72.5
1985	77.1
1986	76.7
1987	89.3
1988	84.2
1989	102.4
1990	98.9
1991	106.8
1992	107.7
1993	110.1
1994	124.1
1995	114.4
1996	122.6
1997	125.5
1998	163.1

16.23 Using the U.S. Bureau of Labor Statistics data that follow, compute the aggregate index numbers for the four types of meat. Let 1987 be the base year for this market basket of goods.

	Year		
Items	1987	1992	1997
Ground beef (per lb.)	1.31	1.53	1.40
Sausage (per lb.)	1.99	2.21	2.15
Bacon (per lb.)	2.14	1.92	2.68
Round steak (per lb.)	2.89	3.38	3.10

16.24 Suppose the following data are prices of market goods involved in household transportation for the years 1994 through 2002. Using 1998 as a base year, compute aggregate transportation price indexes for this data.

	Year								
Items	1994	1995	1996	1997	1998	1999	2000	2001	2002
Gasoline (per gal.)	1.06	1.21	1.09	1.13	1.10	1.16	1.23	1.23	1.08
Oil (per qt.)	1.47	1.65	1.60	1.62	1.58	1.61	1.78	1.77	1.61
Transmission fluid (per qt.)	1.70	1.70	1.80	1.85	1.80	1.82	1.98	1.96	1.94
Radiator coolant (per gal.)	6.65	6.90	7.50	8.10	7.95	7.96	8.24	8.21	8.19

16.25 Calculate Laspeyres price indexes for 2000–2002 from the following data. Use 1995 as the base year.

	Quantity	Price			
Item	1995	1995	2000	2001	2002
1	21	$0.50	$0.67	$0.68	$0.71
2	6	1.23	1.85	1.90	1.91
3	17	0.84	.75	.75	.80
4	43	0.15	.21	.25	.25

16.26 Calculate Paasche price indexes for 2001 and 2002 using the following data and 1997 as the base year.

		2001		2002	
Item	1997 Price	Price	Quantity	Price	Quantity
1	$22.50	$27.80	13	$28.11	12
2	10.90	13.10	5	13.25	8
3	1.85	2.25	41	2.35	44

Forecasting Air Pollution

In searching for the most effective forecasting technique to use to forecast either the carbon monoxide emission or the nitrogen oxide, it is useful to determine whether a trend is evident in either set of time-series data. MINITAB's trend analysis output is presented on the next page for each of the variables.

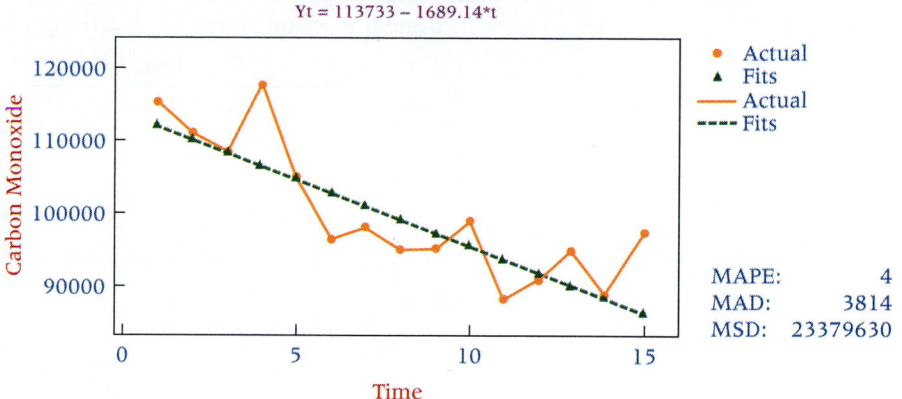

Trend Analysis for Carbon Monoxide
Linear Trend Model
$Yt = 113733 - 1689.14*t$

MAPE: 4
MAD: 3814
MSD: 23379630

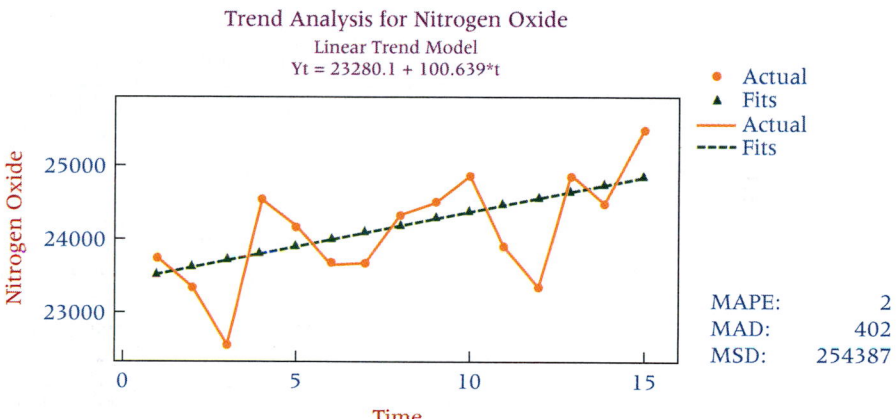

Trend Analysis for Nitrogen Oxide
Linear Trend Model
$Yt = 23280.1 + 100.639*t$

MAPE: 2
MAD: 402
MSD: 254387

Regression trend analysis produces an R^2 of 69.5% for carbon monoxide and 41.8% for nitrogen oxide. It appears, based on the trend analysis graphs, and the R^2 values that more trend is evident in the carbon monoxide data than in the nitrogen oxide data. Is a quadratic trend present in either of these variables? The output for a MINITAB quadratic trend analysis for carbon monoxide is shown next. Notice the error, MAD, has been reduced from 3814 with a linear trend to 2961 with a quadratic trend. Using multiple regression to determine trend with a quadratic model (results not shown here) for carbon monoxide produces an R^2 of 79.8%, an increase of 10.3% over the linear regression trend model. This same analysis on the nitrogen oxide data produces no improvement in the trend fit using a quadratic model.

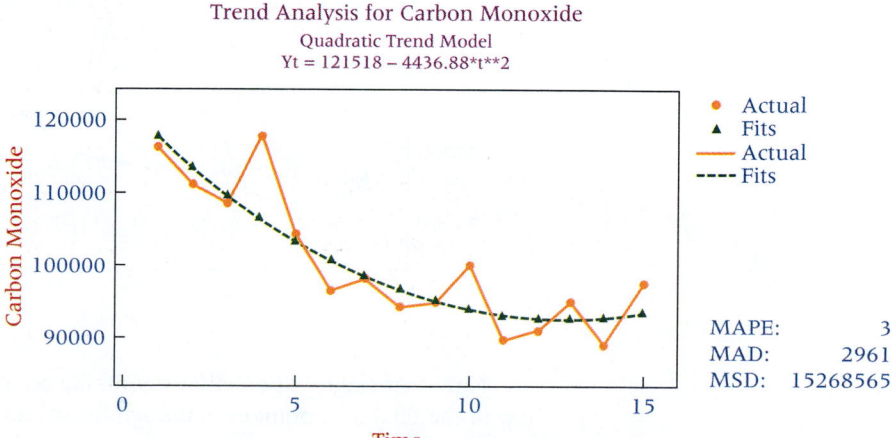

Trend Analysis for Carbon Monoxide
Quadratic Trend Model
$Yt = 121518 - 4436.88*t**2$

MAPE: 3
MAD: 2961
MSD: 15268565

Smoothing techniques can be used to forecast time-series data when no significant trend characterizes the data. A MINITAB moving average graphical analysis of the nitrogen oxide data and the carbon monoxide data using a 5-year moving average are provided here.

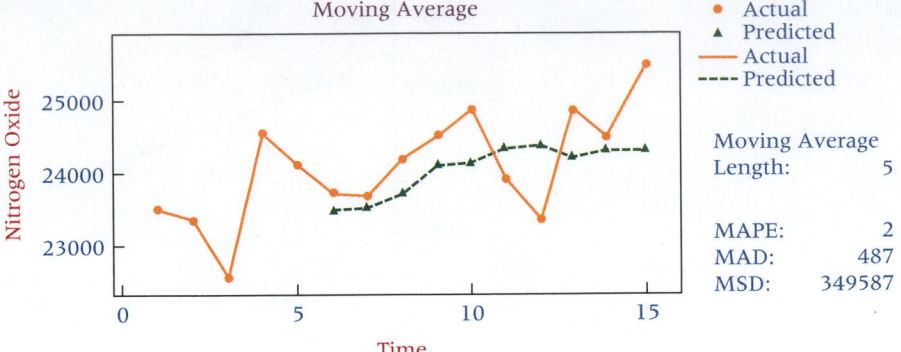

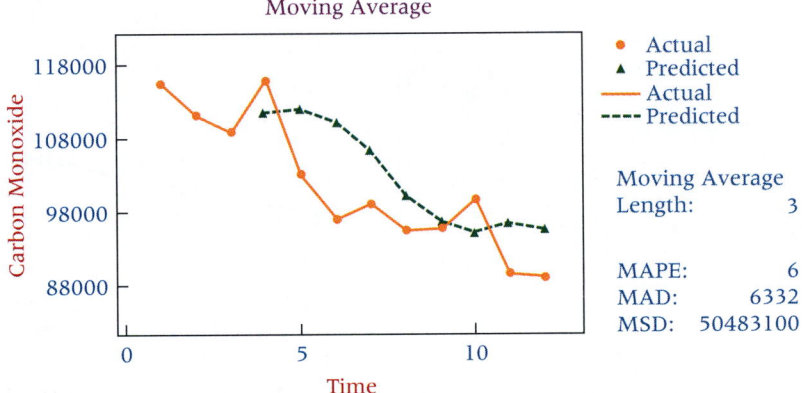

Observe the fit of the moving averages to the data. The moving average forecasts seem to be somewhat linear while the actual data are moving up and down. Also of concern might be that the moving average forecast is in a slightly downward trend on the last data point whereas the data are rapidly increasing.

MINITAB has the capability of administering exponential smoothing to time-series data in such a way as to determine the optimum value of alpha by comparing error values. Shown here is MINITAB output from exponential smoothing analysis on the nitrogen oxide data. The optimum value of alpha for this analysis is .322.

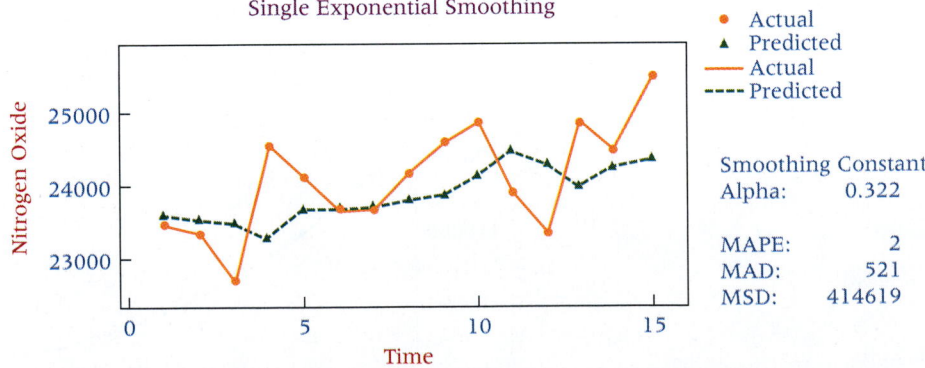

Note that single exponential smoothing seems to be responding better to the rapid rise in the final data point even though the overall MAD is greater than that of the moving average model. It does not make sense to explore seasonal effects with these data since the time period is years.

ETHICAL CONSIDERATIONS

The true test of a forecast is the accuracy of the prediction. Until the actual value is obtained for a given time period, the accuracy of the forecast is unknown. Many forecasters make predictions in society, including card readers, religious leaders, and self-proclaimed prophets. The proof of the forecast is in the outcome. The same holds true in the business world. Forecasts are made about everything from market share to interest rates to number of international air travelers. Many businesses fail because of faulty forecasts.

Forecasting is perhaps as much an art as a science. To keep forecasting ethical, the consumer of the forecast should be given the caveats and limitations of the forecast. The forecaster should be honestly cautious in selling the predictions to a client. In addition, the forecaster should be constantly on the lookout for changes in the business setting being modeled and quickly translate and incorporate those changes into the forecasting model.

Unethical behavior can occur in forecasting when particular data are selected to develop a model that has been predetermined to produce certain results. As mentioned previously, statistics can be used to "prove" almost anything. The ethical forecaster lets the data drive the model and is constantly seeking honest input from new variables to revise the forecast. He or she strives to communicate the limitations of both the forecasts and the models to clients.

SUMMARY

Time-series data are data that have been gathered at regular intervals over a period of time. It is generally believed that time-series data are composed of four elements—trend, cyclical effects, seasonality, and irregularity. Trend is the long-term general direction of the time-series data. Cyclical effects are the business and economic cycles that occur over periods of more than one year. Seasonal effects are patterns or cycles of data behavior that occur over time periods of less than one year. Irregular fluctuations are unaccounted-for "bleeps" or variations that occur over short periods of time.

One way to establish the validity of a forecast is to examine the forecasting error. The error of a forecast is the difference between the actual value and the forecast value. Computing a value to measure forecasting error can be done in several different ways. This chapter presents mean absolute deviation and mean square error for this task.

Regression analysis with either linear or quadratic models can be used to explore trend. Regression trend analysis is a special case of regression analysis in which the dependent variable is the data to be forecast and the independent variable is the time periods numbered consecutively from 1 to k, where k is the number of time periods. For the quadratic model, a second independent variable is constructed by squaring the values in the first independent variable, and both independent variables are included in the analysis.

One group of time-series forecasting methods contains smoothing techniques. Among these techniques are naïve models, averaging techniques, and simple exponential smoothing. These techniques do much better if the time-series data are stationary or show no significant trend or seasonal effects. Naïve forecasting models are models in which it is assumed that the more recent time periods of data represent the best predictions or forecasts for future outcomes.

Simple averages use the average value for some given length of previous time periods to forecast the value for the next period. Moving averages are time period averages that are revised for each time period by including the most recent value(s) in the computation of the average and deleting the value or values that are farthest away from the present time period. A special case of the moving average is the weighted moving average, in which different weights are placed on the values from different time periods.

Simple (single) exponential smoothing is a technique in which data from previous time periods are weighted exponentially to forecast the value for the present time period. The forecaster has the option of selecting how much to weight more recent values versus those of previous time periods.

Decomposition is a method for isolating the four possible effects in time-series data, trend, cyclical effects, seasonality, and irregular fluctuations.

Autocorrelation or serial correlation occurs when the error terms from forecasts are correlated over time. In regression analysis, this effect is particularly disturbing because one of the assumptions is that the error terms are independent. One way to test for autocorrelation is to use the Durbin-Watson test.

A number of methods attempt to overcome the effects of autocorrelation on the data. One way is to determine whether at least one independent variable is missing and, if so, include it or them in the model. Another way is to transform the variables. One transformation technique is the first-differences approach, in which each value of X is subtracted from the succeeding time period value of X and the differences are used as the values of the X variable. The same approach is used to transform the Y variable. The forecasting model is then developed from the transformed variables.

Autoregression is a forecasting technique in which time-series data are predicted by independent variables that are lagged versions of the original dependent variable data. A variable that is lagged one period is derived from values of the previous time period. Other variables can be lagged two or more periods.

Index numbers can be used to translate raw data into numbers that are more readily comparable. Simple index numbers are constructed by creating the ratio of the raw data value for a given time period to the raw data value for the base period and multiplying the ratio by 100. The index number for the base time period is designated to be 100.

Unweighted aggregate price index numbers are constructed by summing the prices of several items for a time period and comparing that sum to the sum of the prices of the same items during a base time period and multiplying the ratio by 100. Weighted aggregate price indexes are index numbers utilizing the prices of several items, and the items are weighted by their quantity usage.

The Laspeyres price index uses the quantity weights from the base year in all calculations. The Paasche price index uses the quantity weights for the current time period for both the current time period and the base time period in calculations.

KEY TERMS

autocorrelation	exponential smoothing	mean square error (MSE)	smoothing techniques
autoregression	first-differences approach	moving average	stationary
averaging models	forecasting	naïve forecasting models	time-series data
cycles	forecasting error	Paasche price index	trend
cyclical effects	index number	seasonal effects	unweighted aggregate price index number
decomposition	irregular fluctuations	serial correlation	weighted aggregate price index numbers
deseasonalized data	Laspeyres price index	simple average	
Durbin-Watson test	mean absolute deviation (MAD)	simple average model	
error of an individual forecast		simple index number	weighted moving average

FORMULAS

Individual forecast error

$$e_t = X_t - F_t$$

Mean absolute deviation

$$\text{MAD} = \frac{\Sigma|e_i|}{\text{Number of Forecasts}}$$

Mean square error

$$\text{MSE} = \frac{\Sigma e_i^2}{\text{Number of Forecasts}}$$

Exponential smoothing

$$F_{t+1} = \alpha \cdot X_t + (1 - \alpha) \cdot F_t$$

Durbin-Watson test

$$D = \frac{\sum_{t=2}^{n}(e_t - e_{t-1})^2}{\sum_{t=1}^{n}e_t^2}$$

SUPPLEMENTARY PROBLEMS

CALCULATING THE STATISTICS

16.27 Following are the average yields of long-term new corporate bonds over a several-month period published by the Office of Market Finance of the U.S. Department of the Treasury.

Month	Yield	Month	Yield
1	10.08	13	7.91
2	10.05	14	7.73
3	9.24	15	7.39
4	9.23	16	7.48
5	9.69	17	7.52
6	9.55	18	7.48
7	9.37	19	7.35
8	8.55	20	7.04
9	8.36	21	6.88
10	8.59	22	6.88
11	7.99	23	7.17
12	8.12	24	7.22

a. Explore trends in these data by using regression trend analysis. How strong are the models? Is the quadratic model significantly stronger than the linear trend model?

b. Use a 4-month moving average to forecast values for each of the ensuing months.

c. Use simple exponential smoothing to forecast values for each of the ensuing months. Let $\alpha = .3$ and then let $\alpha = .7$. Which weight produces better forecasts?

d. Compute MAD for the forecasts obtained in parts (b) and (c) and compare the results.

e. Determine seasonal effects using decomposition on these data. Let the seasonal effects have four periods. After determining the seasonal indexes, deseasonalize the data.

16.28 Compute index numbers for the following data using 1988 as the base year.

Year	Quantity	Year	Quantity
1988	2,073	1996	2,520
1989	2,290	1997	2,529
1990	2,349	1998	2,483
1991	2,313	1999	2,467
1992	2,456	2000	2,397
1993	2,508	2001	2,351
1994	2,463	2002	2,308
1995	2,499		

16.29 Compute unweighted aggregate price index numbers for each of the given years using 1998 as the base year.

Item	1998	1999	2000	2001	2002
1	3.21	3.37	3.80	3.73	3.65
2	.51	.55	.68	.62	.59
3	.83	.90	.91	1.02	1.06
4	1.30	1.32	1.33	1.32	1.30
5	1.67	1.72	1.90	1.99	1.98
6	.62	.67	.70	.72	.71

16.30 Using the following data and 1999 as the base year, compute the Laspeyres price index for 2002 and the Paasche price index for 2001.

Item	1999 Price	1999 Quantity	2000 Price	2000 Quantity
1	$2.75	12	$2.98	9
2	0.85	47	0.89	52
3	1.33	20	1.32	28

Item	2001 Price	2001 Quantity	2002 Price	2002 Quantity
1	$3.10	9	$3.21	11
2	0.95	61	0.98	66
3	1.36	25	1.40	32

TESTING YOUR UNDERSTANDING

16.31 Following are data on the quantity (million pounds) of the U.S. domestic fishing catch for human food from 1980 through 2000. The data are published by the U.S. National Oceanic and Atmospheric Administration.

a. Use a 3-year moving average to forecast the quantity of fish for the years 1983 through 2000 for these data. Compute the error of each forecast and then determine the mean absolute deviation of error for the forecast.

b. Use exponential smoothing and $\alpha = .2$ to forecast the data from 1983 through 2000. Let the forecast for 1981 equal the actual value for 1980. Compute the error of each forecast and then determine the mean absolute deviation of error for the forecast.

c. Compare the results obtained in parts (a) and (b) using MAD. Which technique seems to perform better? Why?

Year	Quantity	Year	Quantity
1980	3,654	1989	6,204
1981	3,547	1990	7,041
1982	3,285	1991	7,031
1983	3,238	1992	7,618
1984	3,320	1993	8,214
1985	3,294	1994	7,936
1986	3,393	1995	7,667
1987	3,946	1996	7,474
1988	4,588	1997	7,244
		1998	7,173
		1999	6,832
		2000	6,912

16.32 The U.S. Department of Commerce publishes a series of census documents referred to as *Current Industrial Reports*. Included in these documents are the Manufacturers' Shipments, Inventories, and Orders over a five-year period. Displayed here is a portion of these data representing the shipments of chemicals and allied products from January of year 1 through December of year 5. Use time-series decomposition methods to develop the seasonal indexes for these data.

Time Period	Chemicals and Allied Products ($ billion)	Time Period	Chemicals and Allied Products ($ billion)
January (year1)	23.701	January (year 2)	23.347
February	24.189	February	24.122
March	24.200	March	25.282
April	24.971	April	25.426
May	24.560	May	25.185
June	24.992	June	26.486
July	22.566	July	24.088
August	24.037	August	24.672
September	25.047	September	26.072
October	24.115	October	24.328
November	23.034	November	23.826
December	22.590	December	24.373
January (year 3)	24.207	January (year 4)	25.316
February	25.772	February	26.435
March	27.591	March	29.346
April	26.958	April	28.983
May	25.920	May	28.424
June	28.460	June	30.149
July	24.821	July	26.746
August	25.560	August	28.966
September	27.218	September	30.783
October	25.650	October	28.594
November	25.589	November	28.762
December	25.370	December	29.018

Time Period	Chemicals and Allied Products ($ billion)
January (year 5)	28.931
February	30.456
March	32.372
April	30.905
May	30.743
June	32.794
July	29.342
August	30.765
September	31.637
October	30.206
November	30.842
December	31.090

16.33 Use the seasonal indexes computed to deseasonalize the data in Problem 16.32.

16.34 Determine the trend for the data in Problem 16.32 using the deseasonalized data from Problem 16.33. Explore both a linear and a quadratic model in an attempt to develop the better trend model.

16.35 The U.S. Department of Labor reports the prices of some food commodities. Shown here are the average retail price figures for five different food commodities over three years. In addition, quantity estimates are included. Use these data and a base year of 1999 to compute unweighted aggregate price indexes for this market basket of food. Using a base year of 1999, calculate Laspeyres price indexes and Paasche price indexes for 2000 and 2001.

Item	1999 Price	1999 Quantity	2000 Price	2000 Quantity
Margarine (lb.)	.83	21	.81	23
Shortening (lb.)	.89	5	.87	3
Milk (1/2 gal.)	1.43	70	1.56	68
Cola (2 l)	1.05	12	1.02	13
Potato chips (16 oz.)	3.01	27	3.06	29

Item	2001 Price	2001 Quantity
Margarine (lb.)	.83	22
Shortening (lb.)	.87	4
Milk (1/2 gal.)	1.59	65
Cola (2 l)	1.01	11
Potato chips (16 oz.)	3.13	28

16.36 The National Cable Television Association publishes data on the cable television market. Shown here are "the number of basic cable subscribers" and "as percentage of household with TVs" for the years 1976 to 2001. Develop a regression model to predict the number of basic cable subscribers from the variable "as percentage of households with TVs" using these data. Use this model to predict the number of basic cable subscribers if the value of the variable "as percentage of households with TVs" is 55%. Discuss the strength of the regression model. Use the data and the regression model to compute a Durbin-Watson test to determine whether significant autocorrelation is present. Let $\alpha = .05$.

Year	Basic Cable Subscribers	As Percentage of Households with TVS
1976	10,787,970	15.1
1977	12,168,450	16.6
1978	13,391,910	17.9
1979	14,814,380	19.4
1980	17,671,490	22.6
1981	23,219,200	28.3
1982	29,340,570	35.0
1983	34,113,790	40.5
1984	37,290,870	43.7
1985	39,872,520	46.2
1986	42,237,140	48.1
1987	44,970,880	50.5
1988	48,636,520	53.8
1989	52,564,470	57.1
1990	54,871,330	59.0
1991	55,786,390	60.6
1992	57,211,600	61.5
1993	58,834,440	62.5
1994	60,483,600	63.4
1995	62,956,470	65.7
1996	64,654,180	66.7
1997	65,929,420	67.3
1998	67,011,180	67.4
1999	68,537,980	68.0
2000	69,368,920	67.9
2001	69,501,440	68.0

16.37 The U.S. Bureau of Labor Statistics releases consumer price indexes (CPIs) for selected items in the publication *Monthly Labor Review*. Shown here are the CPIs for apparel and upkeep for the years 1983 through 2000. Use the data to answer the following questions.

a. Compute a 4-year moving average to forecast the CPIs from 1987 through 2000.

b. Compute a 4-year weighted moving average to forecast the CPIs from 1987 through 2000. Weight the most recent year by 4, the next most recent year by 3, and the next year by 2, and the last year of the four by 1.

c. Determine the errors for parts (a) and (b). Compute MSE for parts (a) and (b). Compare the MSE values

and comment on the effectiveness of the moving average versus the weighted moving average for these data.

Year	Apparel and Upkeep
1983	100.2
1984	102.1
1985	105.0
1986	105.9
1987	110.6
1988	115.4
1989	118.6
1990	124.1
1991	128.7
1992	131.9
1993	133.7
1994	133.4
1995	132.0
1996	131.7
1997	132.9
1998	133.0
1999	131.3
2000	129.6

16.38 In the *Survey of Current Business*, the U.S. Department of Commerce publishes data on farm commodity prices. Given are the cotton prices from November of year 1 through February of year 4. The prices are indexes with a base of 100 from the period of 1910 through 1914. Use these data to develop autoregression models for a 1-month lag and a 4-month lag. Compare the results of these two models. Which model seems to yield better predictions? Why?

Time Period	Cotton Prices	Time Period	Cotton Prices
November (year 1)	552	January (year 3)	571
December	519	February	573
		March	582
January (year 2)	505	April	587
February	512	May	592
March	541	June	570
April	549	July	560
May	552	August	565
June	526	September	547
July	531	October	529
August	545	November	514
September	549	December	469
October	570		
November	576	January (year 4)	436
December	568	February	419

16.39 The U.S. Department of Commerce publishes data on industrial machinery and equipment. Shown here are the shipments (in $ billions) of industrial machinery and equipment from the first quarter of year 1 through the fourth quarter of year 6. Use these data to determine the seasonal indexes for the data through time-series decomposition methods. Use the four-quarter centered moving average in the computations.

Time Period	Industrial Machinery and Equipment Shipments
1st quarter (year 1)	54.019
2nd quarter	56.495
3rd quarter	50.169
4th quarter	52.891
1st quarter (year 2)	51.915
2nd quarter	55.101
3rd quarter	53.419
4th quarter	57.236
1st quarter (year 3)	57.063
2nd quarter	62.488
3rd quarter	60.373
4th quarter	63.334
1st quarter (year 4)	62.723
2nd quarter	68.380
3rd quarter	63.256
4th quarter	66.446
1st quarter (year 5)	65.445
2nd quarter	68.011
3rd quarter	63.245
4th quarter	66.872
1st quarter (year 6)	59.714
2nd quarter	63.590
3rd quarter	58.088
4th quarter	61.443

16.40 Use the seasonal indexes computed to deseasonalize the data in Problem 16.39.

16.41 Use both a linear and quadratic model to explore trends in the deseasonalized data from Problem 16.40. Which model seems to produce a better fit of the data?

16.42 The Board of Governors of the Federal Reserve System publishes data on mortgage debt outstanding by type of property and holder. The following data give the amounts of residential nonfarm debt (in $ billions) held by savings institutions in the United States over a 10-year period. Use these data to develop an autoregression model with a 1-period lag. Discuss the strength of the model.

Year	Debt
1	529
2	554
3	559
4	602
5	672
6	669
7	600
8	538
9	490
10	470

16.43 The data shown here, from the Investment Company Institute, show that the equity fund assets of mutual funds have been growing since 1981. At the same time, the assets of mutual funds in taxable money markets have been increasing since 1980. Use these data to develop a regression model to forecast the equity fund assets by the taxable money market assets. All figures are given in billion-dollar units. Conduct a Durbin-Watson test on the data and the regression model to determine whether significant autocorrelation is present. Let $\alpha = .01$.

Year	Equity Funds	Taxable Money Markets
1980	44.4	74.5
1981	41.2	181.9
1982	53.7	206.6
1983	77.0	162.5
1984	83.1	209.7
1985	116.9	207.5
1986	161.5	228.3
1987	180.7	254.7
1988	194.8	272.3
1989	249.0	358.7
1990	245.8	414.7
1991	411.6	452.6
1992	522.8	451.4
1993	749.0	461.9
1994	866.4	500.4
1995	1,269.0	629.7
1996	1,750.9	761.8
1997	2,399.3	898.1
1998	2,978.2	1,163.2
1999	4,041.9	1,408.7
2000	3,962.3	1,607.2

16.44 The purchasing-power value figures for the minimum wage in 1997 dollars for the years 1980 through 1997 are shown here. Use these data and exponential smoothing to develop forecasts for the years 1981 through 1997. Try $\alpha = .1, .5,$ and $.8,$ and compare the results using MAD. Discuss your findings. Select the value of alpha that worked best and use your exponential smoothing results to predict the figure for 1998.

Year	Purchasing Power	Year	Purchasing Power
1980	$6.04	1989	$4.34
1981	5.92	1990	4.67
1982	5.57	1991	5.01
1983	5.40	1992	4.86
1984	5.17	1993	4.72
1985	5.00	1994	4.60
1986	4.91	1995	4.48
1987	4.73	1996	4.86
1988	4.55	1997	5.15

INTERPRETING THE OUTPUT

16.45 Shown below is the Excel output for a regression analysis to predict the number of business bankruptcy filings over a 16-year period by the number of consumer bankruptcy filings. How strong is the model? Note the residuals. Compute a Durbin-Watson statistic from the data and discuss the presence of autocorrelation in this model.

	A	B	C	D	E	F
1	SUMMARY OUTPUT					
2	Regression Statistics					
3	Multiple R	0.529				
4	R Square	0.280				
5	Adjusted R Square	0.228				
6	Standard Error	8179.84				
7	Observations	16				
8						
9	ANOVA					
10		df	SS	MS	F	Significant F
11	Regression	1	364069877.4	364069877.4	5.44	0.0351
12	Residual	14	936737379.6	66909812.8		
13	Total	15	1300807257			
14						
15		Coefficients	Standard Error	t Stat	P-value	
16	Intercept	75532.43621	4980.08791	15.17	0.0000	
17	Consumer Bankrupcies	–0.01574	0.00675	–2.33	0.0351	
18						
19	RESIDUAL OUTPUT					
20	Observation	Predicted Bus. Bankruptcies	Residuals			
21	1	70638.58	–1338.6			
22	2	71024.28	–8588.3			
23	3	71054.61	–7050.6			
24	4	70161.99	1115.0			
25	5	68462.72	12772.3			
26	6	67733.25	14712.8			
27	7	66882.45	–3029.4			
28	8	65834.05	–2599.1			
29	9	64230.61	622.4			
30	10	61801.70	9747.3			
31	11	61354.16	9288.8			
32	12	62738.76	–434.8			
33	13	63249.36	–10875.4			
34	14	61767.01	–9808.0			
35	15	57826.69	–4277.7			
36	16	54283.80	–256.8			

1. Use the agricultural time-series database and the variable Green Beans to forecast the number of green beans for period 169 by using the following techniques.

   a. Five-period moving average
   b. Simple exponential smoothing with $\alpha = .6$
   c. Time-series linear trend model
   d. Decomposition

2. Use decomposition on Carrots in the agricultural database to determine the seasonal indexes? These data actually represent 14 years of 12-month data. Do the seasonal indexes indicate the presence of some seasonal effects? Run an autoregression model to predict Carrots by a 1-month lag and another by a 12-month lag. Compare the two models. Because vegetables are somewhat seasonal, is the 12-month lag model significant?

3. Use the energy database to forecast 1999 U.S. Coal Production by using simple exponential smoothing of previous U.S. Coal Production data. Let $\alpha = .2$ and $\alpha = .8$. Compare the forecast with the actual figure. Which of the two models produces the forecast with the least error?

4. Use the international labor database to develop a regression model to predict the Unemployment Rate for Germany by the Unemployment Rate of Italy. Test for autocorrelation and discuss its presence or absence in this regression analysis.

CASE: DEBOURGH MANUFACTURING COMPANY

The DeBourgh Manufacturing Company was founded in 1909 as a metal-fabricating company in Minnesota by the four Berg brothers. In the 1980s, the company ran into hard times, as did the rest of the metal-fabricating industry. Among the problems that DeBourgh faced were declining sales, deteriorating labor relations, and increasing costs. Labor unions had resisted cost-cutting measures. Losses were piling up in the heavy job-shop fabrication division, which was the largest of the company's three divisions. A division that made pedestrian steel bridges closed in 1990. The remaining company division, producer of All-American lockers, had to move to a lower-cost environment.

In 1990, with the company's survival at stake, the firm made a risky decision and moved everything from its high-cost location in Minnesota to a lower-cost area in La Junta, Colorado. Eighty semitrailer trucks were used to move equipment and inventory 1,000 miles at a cost of $1.2 million. The company was relocated to a building in La Junta that had stood vacant for three years. Only 10 of the Minnesota workers transferred with the company, which quickly hired and trained 80 more workers in La Junta. By moving to La Junta, the company was able to go nonunion.

DeBourgh also faced a financial crisis. A bank that had been loaning the company money for 35 years would no longer do so. In addition, a costly severance package was worked out with Minnesota workers to keep production going during the move. An internal stock-purchase "earnout" was arranged between company president Steven C. Berg and his three aunts, who were the other principal owners.

The roof of the building that was to be the new home of DeBourgh Manufacturing in La Junta was badly in need of repair. During the first few weeks of production, heavy rains fell on the area and production was all but halted. However, DeBourgh was able to overcome these obstacles. One year later, locker sales achieved record-high sales levels each month. The company is now more profitable than ever with sales topping $6 million. Much credit has been given to the positive spirit of teamwork fostered among its approximately 80 employees. Emphasis shifted to employee involvement in decision making, quality, teamwork, employee participation in compensation action, and shared profits. In addition, DeBourgh became a more socially responsible company by doing more for the town in which it is located and by using paints that are more environmentally friendly.

Discussion

1. After its move in 1990 to La Junta, Colorado, and its new initiatives, the DeBourgh Manufacturing Company began an upward climb of record sales. Suppose the figures shown here are the DeBourgh monthly sales figures from January 1993 through December 2001 (in $1,000s). Are any trends evident in the data? Does DeBourgh have a seasonal component to its sales? Shown after the sales figures is MINITAB output from a decomposition analysis of the sales figures using 12-month seasonality. Next an Excel graph displays the data with a trend line. Examine the data, the output, and any additional analysis you feel is helpful, and write a short report on DeBourgh sales. Include a discussion of the general direction of sales and any seasonal tendencies that might be occurring.

Month	1993	1994	1995	1996	1997	1998	1999	2000	2001
January	139.7	165.1	177.8	228.6	266.7	431.8	381.0	431.8	495.3
February	114.3	177.8	203.2	254.0	317.5	457.2	406.4	444.5	533.4
March	101.6	177.8	228.6	266.7	368.3	457.2	431.8	495.3	635.0
April	152.4	203.2	279.4	342.9	431.8	482.6	457.2	533.4	673.1
May	215.9	241.3	317.5	355.6	457.2	533.4	495.3	558.8	749.3
June	228.6	279.4	330.2	406.4	571.5	622.3	584.2	647.7	812.8
July	215.9	292.1	368.3	444.5	546.1	660.4	609.6	673.1	800.1
August	190.5	317.5	355.6	431.8	482.6	520.7	558.8	660.4	736.6
September	177.8	203.2	241.3	330.2	431.8	508.0	508.0	609.6	685.8
October	139.7	177.8	215.9	330.2	406.4	482.6	495.3	584.2	635.0
November	139.7	165.1	215.9	304.8	393.7	457.2	444.5	520.7	622.3
December	152.4	177.8	203.2	292.1	406.4	431.8	419.1	482.6	622.3

```
Time-series Decomposition
Data: DeBourgh
Length: 108.000
NMissing: 0
Seasonal Indices
Period      Index
   1      0.794869
   2      0.851250
   3      0.926003
   4      1.02227
   5      1.11591
   6      1.24281
   7      1.31791
   8      1.16422
   9      0.992014
  10      0.915239
  11      0.850714
  12      0.806788
Accuracy of Model
MAPE:   48.1
MAD:   141.1
MSD: 26153.6
```

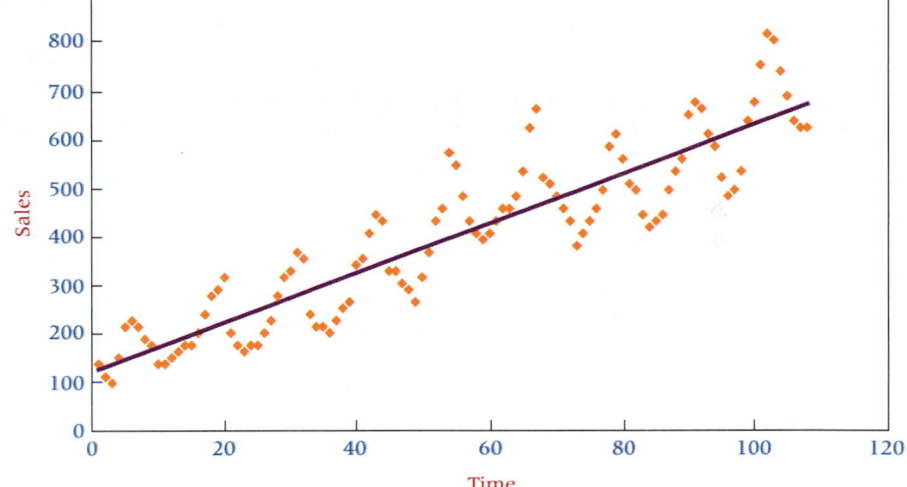

2. Suppose DeBourgh accountants computed a per-unit cost of lockers for each year since 1988, as reported here. Use techniques in this chapter to analyze the data. Forecast the per-unit labor costs through the year 2002. Use smoothing techniques, moving averages, trend analysis, and any others that seem appropriate. Calculate the error of the forecasts and determine which forecasting method seems to do the best job of minimizing error. Study the data and explain the behavior of the per-unit labor cost since 1988. Think about the company history and objectives since 1988.

Year	Per-Unit Labor Cost
1988	$80.15
1989	85.29
1990	85.75
1991	64.23
1992	63.70
1993	62.54
1994	60.19
1995	59.84
1996	57.29
1997	58.74
1998	55.01
1999	56.20
2000	55.93
2001	55.60

Source: Adapted from "DeBourgh Manufacturing Company: A Move That Saved a Company," Real-World Lessons for America's Small Businesses: Insights from the Blue Chip Enterprise Initiative. Published by *Nation's Business* magazine on behalf of Connecticut Mutual Life Insurance Company and the U.S. Chamber of Commerce in association with the Blue Chip Enterprise Initiative, 1992. See also DeBourgh, available at http://www.debourgh.com: and the Web site containing Colorado Springs top business stories, available at http://www.csbj.com/1998/981113/top_stor.htm.

USING THE COMPUTER

EXCEL

Excel has the capability of doing several of the forecasting techniques presented in this chapter. Two of the techniques, exponential smoothing and moving averages, are accessed by using the **Data Analysis** selection. Begin the process by selecting **Tools** on the menu bar. A pull-down menu will appear. Select **Data Analysis** from this menu to produce the **Data Analysis** dialog box.

Exponential Smoothing

From the **Data Analysis** dialog box, select **Exponential Smoothing**. A dialog box will appear. Input the location of the data to be smoothed in the **Input Range** space. Place the value of the dampening factor in the **Damping Factor** space. The default value is .3. In the **Output Range** space, place the location of the upper left cell of the output table. The output consists of forecast values of the data using the smoothing constant. If the **Standard Errors** slot is checked, a second column of output will be given with the standard errors.

Moving Average

From the **Data Analysis** dialog box, select **Moving Average.** A dialog box will appear. Place the location of the data in the **Input Range** space. In the **Interval** space, record how many data values you want to include in the moving average. The default is three values. In the **Output Range** space, place the location of the upper left cell for the moving averages. The output consists of the moving averages. If the **Standard Errors** slot is checked, a second column of output will be given with the standard errors.

Two other forecasting techniques can be accessed in Excel by using the Paste Function. Begin the process by clicking on the Paste Function key, f_x, on the standard tool bar. The Paste Function dialog box will appear. From the left side menu, select **Statistical.** From the choices on the right side, select **FORECAST** to compute forecasts and **TREND** to fit trend to the data.

Forecast

From the Paste Function box, select **FORECAST.** This feature enables you to forecast a value by using linear regression. A dialog box will appear. Place in the space on the first line the value of X for which you want a predicted value. You must place an entry here. Place in the space on the second line the location of X values to be used in development of the regression model; and in the space on the third line, place the location of the Y values. The output consists of the predicted value.

Trend

This Paste Function selection fits a straight line (by using least squares analysis) to the arrays of X and Y. It returns the Y values along the line for the array of new Xs that you specify.

From the Paste Function box, select **TREND.** A dialog box will appear. In the space on the first line, place the location of the known Y values; in the space on the second line, place the location of the known X values. The X values can consist of more than one column if you want to fit a polynomial curve. Merely place squared values of X, cubed values of X, and so on as desired in other columns and include those columns in the **known X** space. In the **new X's** box, place the values for which you want to return corresponding Y values. If you want to compute linear trend based on Y values for consecutive periods, you can choose to omit the known X values and Excel will default to $(1, 2, 3, 4, \ldots)$. Then under **new X's** place the period (e.g., 15) or periods for which you want to forecast using trend. The space on the fourth line in the dialog box is **Const,** which is a logical value specifying whether to force the regression constant to be zero. If you place **TRUE** in the box, you will get a value for the constant as usual (default option). If you place **FALSE** in the box, b_0 will be set to zero.

MINITAB

MINITAB Windows offers much in the way of forecasting analysis. Begin by selecting **Stat** on the menu bar. A pull-down menu will appear. Select **Time-Series** from the menu. Another pull-down menu will appear. From this pull-down menu, you can make your forecasting analysis selections. The appropriate dialog box will appear.

Time-Series Plot

A time-series plot can be obtained by using the command, **Time-Series Plot.** Enter the column containing the Y values under **Graph variables.** Under **Time Scale,** you can define what scale you want to use for X. You have the option of checking whether you want to use an **Index** (scale of 1 to n consecutive numbers), a **Calender** (with various options and combinations of days, weeks, months, quarters, years, etc.), or some **Clock** scales such as day, hour, or minute. The output is a time-series plot with time on the X axis.

Trend Analysis

The **Trend Analysis** option on the pull-down menu enables you to fit a trend through the data. Place the location of the time-series data in the **Variable** slot. Under **Model Type,** you have four options: linear, quadratic, exponential growth, or S-curve. Select the model desired. You have the option of generating forecasts.

Decomposition

Select the **Decomposition** option to perform classical decomposition on time-series data. Under **Variable,** place the location of the time-series data. Under **Seasonal Length,** enter a positive integer greater than or equal to 2. Under **Model Type,** select either the multiplicative model (the one presented in the chapter) or the additive model. Under **Model**

Components, select either seasonal only or trend plus seasonal. Select an initial seasonal period (the default is 1). The output is a summary table and a set of plots. The summary table includes the trend equation, the seasonal indexes, and three measures of error. The plots include a time-series plot, a component analysis, and a seasonal analysis.

Moving Average

The **Moving Average** choice produces moving averages. Enter the location of the data under **Variable.** Under **M**A Length, enter the number of values to be averaged. Check whether you want to center the moving averages. If you check this, MINITAB will compute the moving average values at the period that is at the center of the range rather than at the end of it. The default output consists of a time-series plot displaying the data and one-period-ahead forecasts along with three measures of forecast error.

Single Exponential Smoothing

The selection of **Single Exp Smoothing** allows you to smooth time-series data with a single exponential smoothing weight. Enter the location of the data under **Variable.** You can attempt to optimize the smoothing process by checking Optimize. This option allows MINITAB to attempt to minimize the sum of squares errors. If you choose to enter your own weight, select **Use** and enter the value. You have the option of generating forecasts, selecting the number of forecasts, and/or selecting the starting point (**Starting from origin**). The output is a time-series plot displaying the data and one-period-ahead forecasts. Also displayed are the smoothing weight used and three measures of error.

Double Exponential Smoothing

The **Double Exp Smoothing** option enables you to smooth the data and smooth for trend. Enter the location of the data under **Variable.** Check whether you want MINITAB to optimize the model or whether you want to enter your own weights. If you choose **Use,** you will enter a smoothing constant (weight) for both leveling and trend. The output is similar to that obtained under Single Exponential Smoothing, but includes the trend component.

Winters' Method

The selection of **Winters' Method** produces an exponential smoothing using both seasonality and trend. Enter the location of the data in **Variable;** the seasonal length (greater than or equal to 2) under **Seasonal length;** and the smoothing weights (constants between 0 and 1) for leveling, trend, and seasonality. By default, all three smoothing weights will be set at .2. The output is a time-series plot similar to that of Single Exponential Smoothing but includes the smoothing weights used.

Differences

The **Differences** command enables you to compute the differences between the data elements in a column. Under **Series,** select the column containing the data for which you want to compute the differences. Under **Store differences in,** enter the location of a storage column for the differences. Using the **Lag** slot, specify the value for the lag. MINITAB subtracts from each value the element k rows above, where k is the lag specified, and stores the resulting values in a new column.

Lag

The **Lag** command moves data values in a column down a specified number of rows. MINITAB stores the results in a new column of the same length. Enter the column containing the data in **Series.** Enter the column location for the results under **Store lags in.** Specify the value for the lag under **Lag.**

Autocorrelation Function

The **Autocorrelation** command computes and plots the autocorrelation of a set of time-series data. In the **Series** slot, enter the column location of the data. If you check **Default number of lags,** MINITAB will default to $n/4$ if there are less than 240 observations and to $\sqrt{n} + 45$ for more than 240 observations. If you check **Number of lags,** you can specify the number of lags. Check either **Graphical ACF** or **Nongraphical ACF,** depending on the output you desire.

CHAPTER 17

Nonparametric Statistics

LEARNING OBJECTIVES

This chapter presents several nonparametric statistics that can be used to analyze data specifically, thereby enabling you to:

1. Recognize the advantages and disadvantages of nonparametric statistics.
2. Understand how to use the runs test to test for randomness.
3. Know when and how to use the Mann-Whitney U test, the Wilcoxon matched-pairs signed rank test, the Kruskal-Wallis test, and the Friedman test.
4. Learn when and how to measure correlation by using Spearman's rank correlation measurement.

How Is the Doughnut Business?

Krispy Kreme is a rapidly growing international company specializing in doughnuts. The company, established in 1937 by Vernon Rudolph, began as a small manufacturer and supplier of doughnuts to local grocery stores in Winston-Salem, North Carolina. Because customers made their way to the plant in search of hot versions of Krispy Kreme doughnuts, Rudolph cut a hole in a wall and began selling doughnuts directly to customers. In the 1940s and 1950s, the company grew to become a small chain of mostly family-owned stores. For quality reasons, Krispy Kreme built its own mix plant and developed a distribution system to each store. In addition, they designed and built their own doughnut-making equipment. The 1960s and 1970s showed steady growth in the number of Krispy Kreme outlets. Vernon Rudolph died in 1973, and the company was sold to Beatrice Foods in 1976. However, in 1982 a small group of early franchisees bought Krispy Kreme back from Beatrice and made a renewed focus on hot doughnuts a priority. In the 1990s, the company began its rapid expansion out of the Southeast. The first New York City store was opened in 1996; and in 1999, Krispy Kreme began its first California operation. The initial public common stock offering of Krispy Kreme occurred in April 2000. In December 2001 the company opened its first international store near Toronto. Currently, the company is working on an improved coffee program. The twenty-first century will bring expansion of Krispy Kreme to other countries around the world.

Suppose researchers at Krispy Kreme are studying several manufacturing and marketing questions in an effort to improve the consistency of their products and understand their market. Manufacturing engineers are concerned that the various machines produce a consistent doughnut size. In an effort to test this issue, four machines are selected for a study. Each machine is set to produce a doughnut that is supposed to be about 7.62 cm (3 inches) in diameter. A random sample of doughnuts is taken from each machine and the diameters of the doughnuts are measured. The result is the data shown as follows:

Machine 1	Machine 2	Machine 3	Machine 4
7.58	7.41	7.56	7.72
7.52	7.44	7.55	7.65
7.50	7.42	7.50	7.67
7.52	7.38	7.58	7.70
	7.45	7.53	7.69
	7.40		7.71
			7.73

Suppose Krispy Kreme implements a national advertising campaign in the United States. Marketing researchers want to determine whether the campaign has increased the number of doughnuts sold at various outlets around the country. Ten stores are randomly selected and the number of doughnuts sold between 8 and 9 A.M. on a Tuesday is measured both before and after the campaign is implemented. The data follow:

Outlet	Before	After
1	301	374
2	198	187
3	278	332
4	205	212
5	249	243
6	410	478
7	360	386
8	124	141
9	253	251
10	190	264

Do bigger stores have greater sales? To test this question, suppose sales data were gathered from seven Krispy Kreme stores along with store size. These figures are used to rank the seven stores on each variable. The ranked data follow.

Store	Sales Rank	Size Rank
1	6	7
2	2	2
3	3	6
4	7	5
5	5	4
6	1	1
7	4	3

Managerial and Statistical Questions:

1. The manufacturing researchers who are testing to determine whether there is a difference in the size of doughnuts by machine want to run a one-way ANOVA, but they have serious doubts that the ANOVA assumptions can be met by these data. Is it still possible to analyze the data using statistics?

2. The market researchers are uncertain that normal distribution assumptions underlying the matched-pairs t test can be met with the number of doughnuts data. How can the before-and-after data still be used to test the effectiveness of the advertisements?

3. If the sales and store size data are given as ranks, how do we compute a correlation to answer the research question about the relationship of sales and store size? The Pearson product-moment correlation coefficient requires at least interval-level data, and these data are given as ordinal level.

Source: Adapted from the Krispy Kreme website at: http://www.krispykreme.com/history.html. Please note that the data set forth in the above problem is fictional, was not supplied by Krispy Kreme, and does not necessarily represent Krispy Kreme's experience.

Except for the chi-square analyses presented in Chapter 12, all statistical techniques presented in the text thus far are parametric techniques. **Parametric statistics** are *statistical techniques based on assumptions about the population from which the sample data are selected.* For example, if a t statistic is being used to conduct a hypothesis test about a population mean, the assumption is that the data being analyzed are randomly selected from a *normally* distributed population. The name *parametric statistics* refers to the fact that an assumption (here, normally distributed data) is being made about the data used to test or estimate the parameter (in this case, the population mean). In addition, the use of parametric statistics requires quantitative measurements that yield interval- or ratio-level data.

For data that do not meet the assumptions made about the population, or when the level of data being measured is qualitative, statistical techniques called nonparametric, or distribution-free, techniques are used. **Nonparametric statistics** *are based on fewer assumptions about the population and the parameters than are parametric statistics.* Sometimes they are referred to as *distribution-free* statistics because many of them can be used regardless of the shape of the population distribution. A variety of nonparametric statistics are available for use with nominal or ordinal data. Some require at least ordinal-level data, but others can be specifically targeted for use with nominal-level data.

Nonparametric techniques have the following advantages.

1. Sometimes there is no parametric alternative to the use of nonparametric statistics.
2. Certain nonparametric tests can be used to analyze nominal data.

3. Certain nonparametric tests can be used to analyze ordinal data.

4. The computations on nonparametric statistics are usually less complicated than those for parametric statistics, particularly for small samples.

5. Probability statements obtained from most nonparametric tests are exact probabilities.

Using nonparametric statistics also has some disadvantages.

1. Nonparametric tests can be wasteful of data if parametric tests are available for use with the data.

2. Nonparametric tests are usually not as widely available and well known as parametric tests.

3. For large samples, the calculations for many nonparametric statistics can be tedious.

Entire courses and texts are dedicated to the study of nonparametric statistics. This text presents only some of the more important techniques: runs test, Mann-Whitney U test, Wilcoxon matched-pairs signed ranks test, Kruskal-Wallis test, Friedman test, Spearman's rank correlation coefficient, chi-square test of goodness-of-fit, and chi-square test of independence. The chi-square goodness-of-fit test and the chi-square test of independence were presented in Chapter 12. The others are presented in this chapter.

17.1 RUNS TEST

The one-sample **runs test** is *a nonparametric test of randomness.* The runs test is *used to determine whether the order or sequence of observations in a sample is random.* The runs test examines the number of "runs" of each of two possible characteristics that sample items may have. A *run* is a succession of observations that have a particular one of the characteristics. For example, if a sample of people contains both men and women, one run could be a continuous succession of women. In tossing coins, the outcome of three heads in a row would constitute a run, as would a succession of seven tails.

Suppose a researcher takes a random sample of 15 people who arrive at a Wal-Mart to shop. Eight of the people are women and seven are men. If these people arrive randomly at the store, it makes sense that the sequence of arrivals would have some mix of men and women, but not probably a perfect mix. That is, it seems unlikely (although possible) that the sequence of a random sample of such shoppers would be first eight women and then seven men. In such a case, there are two runs. Suppose, however, the sequence of shoppers is woman, man, woman, man, woman, and so on all the way through the sample. This would result in 15 "runs." Each of these cases is possible, but neither is highly likely in a random scenario. In fact, if there are just two runs, it seems possible that a group of women came shopping together followed by a group of men who did likewise. In that case, the observations would not be random. Similarly, a pattern of woman-man all the way through may make the business researcher suspicious that what has been observed is not really individual random arrivals, but actually random arrivals of couples.

In a random sample, the number of runs is likely to be somewhere between these extremes. What number of runs is reasonable? The one-sample runs test takes into consideration the size of the sample, n, the number observations in the sample having each characteristic, n_1, n_2 (man, woman, etc.), and the number of runs in the sample, R, to reach conclusions about hypotheses of randomness. The following hypotheses are tested by the one-sample runs test.

H_0: The observations in the sample are randomly generated.

H_a: The observations in the sample are not randomly generated.

The one-sample runs test is conducted differently for small samples than it is for large samples. Each test is presented here. First, we consider the small-sample case.

Small-Sample Runs Test

If both n_1 and n_2 are less than or equal to 20, the small-sample runs test is appropriate. In the example of shoppers with $n_1 = 7$ men and $n_2 = 8$ women, the small-sample runs test could be used to test for randomness. The test is carried out by comparing the observed number of runs, R, to critical values of runs for the given values of n_1 and n_2. The critical values of R are given in Tables A.11 and A.12 in the appendix for $\alpha = .05$. Table A.11 contains critical values of R for the lower tail of the distribution in which so few runs occur that the probability of that many runs or fewer runs occurring is less than .025 ($\alpha/2$). Table A.12 contains critical values of R for the upper tail of the distribution in which so many runs occur that the probability of that many runs or more occurring is less than .025 ($\alpha/2$). Any observed value of R that is less than or equal to the critical value of the lower tail (Table A.11) results in the rejection of the null hypothesis and the conclusion that the sample data are not random. Any observed value of R that is equal to or greater than the critical value in the upper tail (Table A.12) also results in the rejection of the null hypothesis and the conclusion that the sample data are not random.

As an example, suppose 26 cola drinkers are sampled randomly to determine whether they prefer regular cola or diet cola. The random sample contains 18 regular cola drinkers and eight diet cola drinkers. Let C denote regular cola drinkers and D denote diet cola drinkers. Suppose the sequence of sampled cola drinkers is DCCCCCDCCDCCCCDCD-CCCDDDCCC. Is this sequence of cola drinkers evidence that the sample is not random? Applying the HTAB system of hypothesis testing to this problem results in:

HYPOTHESIZE:

STEP 1. The hypotheses tested follow.

H_0: The observations in the sample were generated randomly.
H_a: The observations in the sample were not generated randomly.

TEST:

STEP 2. Let n_1 denote the number of regular cola drinkers and n_2 denote the number of diet cola drinkers. Because $n_1 = 18$ and $n_2 = 8$, the small-sample runs test is the appropriate test.

STEP 3. Alpha is .05.

STEP 4. With $n_1 = 18$ and $n_2 = 8$, Table A.11 yields a critical value of 7 and Table A.12 yields a critical value of 17. If there are seven or fewer runs or 17 or more runs, the decision rule is to reject the null hypothesis.

STEP 5. The sample data are given as
DCCCCCDCCDCCCCDCDCCCDDDCCC

STEP 6. Tally the number of runs in this sample.

1	2	3	4	5	6	7	8	9	10	11	12
D	CCCCC	D	CC	D	CCCC	D	C	D	CCC	DDD	CCC

The number of runs, R, is 12.

ACTION:

STEP 7. Because the value of R falls between the critical values of 7 and 17, the decision is to not reject the null hypothesis. Not enough evidence is provided to declare that the data are not random.

BUSINESS IMPLICATION:

STEP 8. The cola researcher can proceed with the study under the assumption that the sample represents randomly selected cola drinkers.

MINITAB has the capability of analyzing data by using the runs test. Figure 17.1 is the MINITAB output for the cola example runs test. Notice that the output includes the number of runs, 12, and the significance level of the test. For this analysis, diet cola was coded as a 1 and regular cola coded as a 2. The MINITAB runs test is a two-tailed test and the reported significance of the test is equivalent to a p-value. Because the significance is .9710, the decision is to not reject the null hypothesis.

FIGURE 17.1

MINITAB Output for the Cola
Example

```
Runs Test: Cola

Cola

K = 1.6923

The observed number of runs = 12
The expected number of runs = 12.0769
18 Observations above K      8 below
 * N Small — The following approximation may be invalid
The test is significant at 0.9710
Cannot reject at alpha = 0.05
```

Large-Sample Runs Test

Tables A.11 and A.12 do not contain critical values for n_1 and n_2 greater than 20. Fortunately, the sampling distribution of R is approximately normal with a mean and standard deviation of

$$\mu_R = \frac{2n_1 n_2}{n_1 + n_2} + 1 \quad \text{and} \quad \sigma_R = \sqrt{\frac{2n_1 n_2 (2n_1 n_2 - n_1 - n_2)}{(n_1 + n_2)^2 (n_1 + n_2 - 1)}}$$

The test statistic is a z statistic computed as

$$z = \frac{R - \mu_R}{\sigma_R} = \frac{R - \left(\dfrac{2n_1 n_2}{n_1 + n_2} + 1\right)}{\sqrt{\dfrac{2n_1 n_2 (2n_1 n_2 - n_1 - n_2)}{(n_1 + n_2)^2 (n_1 + n_2 - 1)}}}$$

The following hypotheses are being tested.

H_0: The observations in the sample were generated randomly.
H_a: The observations in the sample were not generated randomly.

The critical z values are obtained in the usual way by using alpha and Table A.5.

Consider the following manufacturing example. A machine produces parts that are occasionally flawed. When the machine is working in adjustment, flaws still occur but seem to happen randomly. A quality control person randomly selects 50 of the parts produced by the machine today and examines them one at a time in the order that they were made. The result is 40 parts with no flaws and 10 parts with flaws. The sequence of no flaws (denoted by N) and flaws (denoted by F) is shown here. Using an alpha of .05, the quality controller tests to determine whether the machine is producing randomly (the flaws are occurring randomly).

NNN F NNNNNNN F NN FF NNNNNN F NNNN F NNNNNN
FFFF NNNNNNNNNNNN

HYPOTHESIZE:

STEP 1. The hypotheses follow.
H_0: The observations in the sample were generated randomly.
H_a: The observations in the sample were not generated randomly.

TEST:

STEP 2. The appropriate statistical test is the large-sample runs test. The test statistic is

$$z = \frac{R - \mu_R}{\sigma_R} = \frac{R - \left(\dfrac{2n_1 n_2}{n_1 + n_2} + 1\right)}{\sqrt{\dfrac{2n_1 n_2 (2n_1 n_2 - n_1 - n_2)}{(n_1 + n_2)^2 (n_1 + n_2 - 1)}}}$$

STEP 3. The value of alpha is .05.

STEP 4. This test is two-tailed. Too few or too many runs could indicate that the machine is not producing flaws randomly. With $\alpha = .05$ and $\alpha/2 = .025$, the critical values are $z_{.025} = \pm 1.96$. The decision rule is to reject the null hypothesis if the observed value of the test statistic is greater than 1.96 or less than -1.96.

STEP 5. The preceding sequence provides the sample data. The value of n_1 is 40 and the value of n_2 is 10. The number of runs (R) is 13.

$$\mu_R = \frac{2(40)(10)}{40+10} + 1 = 17$$

$$\sigma_R = \sqrt{\frac{2(40)(10)[2(40)(10)-40-10]}{(40+10)^2(40+10-1)}} = 2.213$$

$$z = \frac{13-17}{2.213} = -1.81$$

STEP 6.

ACTION:

STEP 7. Because the observed value of the test statistic, $z = -1.81$, is greater than the lower-tail critical value, $z = -1.96$, the decision is to not reject the null hypothesis.

BUSINESS IMPLICATION:

STEP 8. There is no evidence that the machine is not producing flaws randomly. If the null hypothesis had been rejected, there might be concern that the machine is producing flaws systematically and thereby is in need of inspection or repair.

Figure 17.2 is the MINITAB output for this example. The value of K is the average of the observations. The data were entered into MINITAB with a nonflaw coded as a 0 and a flaw as a 1. The value $K = .20$ is merely the average of these coded values. In MINITAB, a run is a sequence of observations above or below this mean, which effectively yields the same thing as the number of 0s in a row (nonflaws) or number of 1s in a row (flaws). The nonflaws and flaws could have been coded as any two different numbers and the same results would have been achieved. The output shows the number of runs as 13 (the same number obtained manually) and a test significance (p-value) equal to .0710. The test statistic is not significant at $\alpha = .05$ because the p-value is greater than .05.

17.1 PROBLEMS

17.1 Test the following sequence of observations by using the runs test and $\alpha = .05$ to determine whether the process produced random results.

X X X Y X X X Y Y Y X Y X Y X X X Y Y Y Y X

17.2 Test the following sequence of observations by using the runs test and $\alpha = .05$ to determine whether the process produced random results.

M M N N N N N M M M M M M N N M M M M M N M M

N N N N N N N N N N N N N M M M M M M M M M M M

FIGURE 17.2	
| MINITAB Output for the Flawed Parts Example | ```
Runs Test: Flaws

Flaws

K = 0.2000


The observed number of runs = 13
The expected number of runs = 17.0000
10 Observations above K    40 below
* N Small — The following approximation may be invalid
The test is significant at 0.0707
Cannot reject at alpha = 0.05
``` |
```

17.3   A process produced good parts and defective parts. A sample of 60 parts was taken and inspected. Eight defective parts were found. The sequence of good and defective parts was analyzed by using MINITAB. The output is given here. With a two-tailed test and $\alpha = .05$, what conclusions can be reached about the randomness of the sample?

```
Runs Test: Defects
      Defects
      K = 0.1333

      The observed number of runs = 11
      The expected number of runs = 14.8667
      8 Observations above K  52 below
             The test is significant at 0.0264
```

17.4   A Watson Wyatt Worldwide survey showed that 58% of all Hispanic Americans are satisfied with their salary. Suppose a researcher randomly samples 27 Hispanic American workers and asks whether they are satisfied with their salary with the result that 15 say yes. The sequence of Yes and No responses is recorded and tested for randomness by means of MINITAB. The output follows. Using an alpha of .05 and a two-tailed test, what could you conclude about the randomness of the sample?

```
Runs Test: Yes/No
      Yes/No
      K = 0.5556

      The observed number of runs = 18
      The expected number of runs = 14.3333
      15 Observations above K  12 below
      The test is significant at 0.1452
             Cannot reject at alpha = 0.05
```

17.5   A Virginia Slims Opinion Poll by Roper Starch found that more than 70% of the women interviewed believe they have had more opportunity to succeed than their parents. Suppose a researcher in your state conducts a similar poll and asks the same question with the result that of 64 women interviewed, 40 believe they have had more opportunity to succeed than their parents. The sequence of responses to this question is given below with Y denoting yes and N denoting no. Use the runs test and $\alpha = .05$ to test this sequence and determine whether the responses are random.

Y Y N Y Y N N Y Y Y N N Y N N Y Y Y Y Y N Y Y Y Y N N Y Y N N N Y Y Y N
N Y Y Y Y N Y N Y Y Y Y N N N Y N N Y Y Y Y Y N N Y Y Y Y

17.6   A survey conducted by the Ethics Resource Center discovered that 35% of all workers say that coworkers have committed some kind of office theft. Suppose a survey is conducted in your large company to ask the same question of 13 randomly selected employees. The results are that five of the sample say coworkers have committed some kind of office theft and eight say they are not aware of such infractions. The sequence of responses follows. (Y denotes a Yes answer and N denotes a No answer.) Use $\alpha = .05$ to test to determine whether this sequence represents a random sample.

N N N N Y Y Y N N N N Y Y

17.2 MANN-WHITNEY *U* TEST

The **Mann-Whitney *U* test** is a *nonparametric counterpart of the t test used to compare the means of two independent populations.* This test was developed by Henry B. Mann and D. R. Whitney in 1947. Recall that the *t* test for independent samples presented in Chapter 10 can be used when data are at least interval in measurement and the populations are normally distributed. However, if the assumption of a normally distributed population is invalid or if the data are only ordinal in measurement, the *t* test should not be used. In such cases, the Mann-Whitney *U* test is an acceptable option for analyzing the data. The following assumptions underlie the use of the Mann-Whitney *U* test.

1. The samples are independent.
2. The level of data is at least ordinal.

The two-tailed hypotheses being tested with the Mann-Whitney *U* test are as follows.

H_0: The two populations are identical.
H_a: The two populations are not identical.

Computation of the *U* test begins by arbitrarily designating two samples as group 1 and group 2. The data from the two groups are combined into one group, with each data value retaining a group identifier of its original group. The pooled values are then ranked from 1 to *n*, with the smallest value being assigned a rank of 1. The sum of the ranks of values from group 1 is computed and designated as W_1 and the sum of the ranks of values from group 2 is designated as W_2.

The Mann-Whitney *U* test is implemented differently for small samples than for large samples. If both $n_1, n_2 \le 10$, the samples are considered small. If either n_1 or n_2 is greater than 10, the samples are considered large.

Small-Sample Case

With small samples, the next step is to calculate a *U* statistic for W_1 and for W_2 as

$$U_1 = n_1 n_2 + \frac{n_1(n_1+1)}{2} - W_1 \text{ and } U_2 = n_1 n_2 + \frac{n_2(n_2+1)}{2} - W_1$$

The test statistic is the smallest of these two *U* values. Both values do not need to be calculated; instead, one value of *U* can be calculated and the other can be found by using the transformation

$$U' = n_1 \cdot n_2 - U$$

Table A.13 contains *p*-values for *U*. To determine the *p*-value for a *U* from the table, let n_1 denote the size of the smaller sample and n_2 the size of the larger sample. Using the particular table in Table A.13 for n_1, n_2, locate the value of *U* in the left column. At the intersection of the *U* and n_1 is the *p*-value for a one-tailed test. For a two-tailed test, double the *p*-value shown in the table.

DEMONSTRATION PROBLEM 17.1	

Is there a difference between health service workers and educational service workers in the amount of compensation employers pay them per hour? Suppose a random sample of seven health service workers is taken along with a random sample of eight educational service workers from different parts of the country. Each of their employers is interviewed and figures are obtained on the amount paid per hour for employee compensation for these workers. The following data indicate total compensation per hour. Use a Mann-Whitney *U* test to determine whether these two populations are different in employee compensation.

Health Service Worker	Educational Service Worker
$20.10	$26.19
19.80	23.88
22.36	25.50
18.75	21.64
21.90	24.85
22.96	25.30
20.75	24.12
	23.45

Solution

HYPOTHESIZE:

STEP 1. The hypotheses are as follows.

H_0: The health service population is identical to the educational service population on employee compensation.

H_a: The health service population is not identical to the educational service population on employee compensation.

TEST:

STEP 2. Because we cannot be certain the populations are normally distributed, we chose a nonparametric alternative to the *t* test for independent populations: the small-sample Mann-Whitney *U* test.

STEP 3. Let alpha be .05.

STEP 4. If the final *p*-value from Table A.13 (after doubling for a two-tailed test here) is less than .05, the decision is to reject the null hypothesis.

STEP 5. The sample data were already provided.

STEP 6. We combine scores from the two groups and rank them from smallest to largest while retaining group identifier information.

Total Employee Compensation	Rank	Group
$18.75	1	H
19.80	2	H
20.10	3	H
20.75	4	H
21.64	5	E
21.90	6	H
22.36	7	H
22.96	8	H
23.45	9	E
23.88	10	E
24.12	11	E
24.85	12	E
25.30	13	E
25.50	14	E
26.19	15	E

$W_1 = 1 + 2 + 3 + 4 + 6 + 7 + 8 = 31$

$W_2 = 5 + 9 + 10 + 11 + 12 + 13 + 14 + 15 = 89$

$$U_1 = (7)(8) + \frac{(7)(8)}{2} - 31 = 53$$

$$U_2 = (7)(8) + \frac{(8)(9)}{2} - 89 = 3$$

Because U_2 is the smaller value of U, we use $U = 3$ as the test statistic for Table A.13. Because it is the smallest size, let $n_1 = 7$; $n_2 = 8$.

ACTION:

STEP 7. Table A.13 yields a *p*-value of .0011. Because this test is two-tailed, we double the table *p*-value, producing a final *p*-value of .0022. Because the *p*-value is less than $\alpha = .05$, the null hypothesis is rejected. The statistical conclusion is that the populations are not identical.

BUSINESS IMPLICATIONS:

STEP 8. An examination of the total compensation figures from the samples indicates that employers pay educational service workers more per hour than they pay health service workers.

As shown in Figure 17.3, MINITAB has the capability of computing a Mann-Whitney *U* test. The output includes a *p*-value of .0046 for the two-tailed test for Demonstration

FIGURE 17.3

MINITAB Output for
Demonstration Problem 17.1

```
Mann-Whitney Test and CI: Health, Education

Health    N = 7   Median =  20.750
Educatio  N = 8   Median =  24.485
Point estimate for ETA1-ETA2 is  -3.385
95.7 Percent CI for ETA1-ETA2 is (-5.370, -1.551)
W = 31.0
Test of ETA1 = ETA2  vs  ETA1 not = ETA2 is significant at 0.0046
```

Problem 17.1. The decision based on the computer output is to reject the null hypothesis, which is consistent with what we computed. The difference in p-values is due to rounding error in the table.

Large-Sample Case

For large sample sizes, the value of U is approximately normally distributed. Using an average expected U value for groups of this size and a standard deviation of Us allows computation of a z score for the U value. The probability of yielding a z score of this magnitude, given no difference between the groups, is computed. A decision is then made whether to reject the null hypothesis. A z score can be calculated from U by the following formulas.

LARGE-SAMPLE FORMULAS
MANN-WHITNEY U TEST (17.1)

$$\mu_U = \frac{n_1 \cdot n_2}{2}, \quad \sigma_U = \sqrt{\frac{n_1 \cdot n_2 (n_1 + n_2 + 1)}{12}}, \quad z = \frac{U - \mu_U}{\sigma_U}$$

For example, the Mann-Whitney U test can be used to determine whether there is a difference in the average income of families who view PBS television and families who do not view PBS television. Suppose a sample of 14 families that have identified themselves as PBS television viewers and a sample of 13 families that have identified themselves as non–PBS television viewers are selected randomly.

HYPOTHESIZE:

STEP 1. The hypotheses for this example are as follows.

H_0: The incomes of PBS and non-PBS viewers are identical.
H_a: The incomes of PBS and non-PBS viewers are not identical.

TEST:

STEP 2. Use the Mann-Whitney U test for large samples.

STEP 3. Let $\alpha = .05$.

STEP 4. Because this test is two-tailed with $\alpha = .05$, the critical values are $z_{.025} = \pm 1.96$. If the test statistic is greater than 1.96 or less than -1.96, the decision is to reject the null hypothesis.

STEP 5. The average annual reported income for each family in the two samples is given in Table 17.1.

STEP 6. The first step toward computing a Mann-Whitney U test is to combine these two columns of data into one group and rank the data from lowest to highest, while maintaining the identification of each original group. Table 17.2 shows the results of this step.

Note that in the case of a tie, the ranks associated with the tie are averaged across the values that tie. For example, two incomes of \$43,500 appear in the sample. These incomes represent ranks 19 and 20. Each value therefore is awarded a ranking of 19.5, or the average of 19 and 20.

If PBS viewers are designated as group 1, W_1 can be computed by summing the ranks of all the incomes of PBS viewers in the sample.

$$W_1 = 4 + 7 + 11 + 12 + 13 + 14 + 18 + 19.5 + 22 + 23 + 24 + 25 + 26 + 27 = 245.5$$

Then W_1 is used to compute the U value. Because $n_1 = 14$ and $n_2 = 13$, then

$$U = n_1 n_2 + \frac{n_1(n_1 + 1)}{2} - W_1$$

$$= (14)(13) + \frac{(14)(15)}{2} - 245.5 = 41.5$$

TABLE 17.1

Incomes of PBS and
Non-PBS Viewers

PBS	Non–PBS
\$24,500	\$41,000
39,400	32,500
36,800	33,000
43,000	21,000
57,960	40,500
32,000	32,400
61,000	16,000
34,000	21,500
43,500	39,500
55,000	27,600
39,000	43,500
62,500	51,900
61,400	27,800
53,000	
$n_1 = 14$	$n_2 = 13$

TABLE 17.2

Ranks of Incomes from Combined Groups of PBS and Non-PBS Viewers

Income	Rank	Group	Income	Rank	Group
$16,000	1	Non–PBS	39,500	15	Non–PBS
21,000	2	Non–PBS	40,500	16	Non–PBS
21,500	3	Non–PBS	41,000	17	Non–PBS
24,500	4	PBS	43,000	18	PBS
27,600	5	Non–PBS	43,500	19.5	PBS
27,800	6	Non–PBS	43,500	19.5	Non–PBS
32,000	7	PBS	51,900	21	Non–PBS
32,400	8	Non–PBS	53,000	22	PBS
32,500	9	Non–PBS	55,000	23	PBS
33,000	10	Non–PBS	57,960	24	PBS
34,000	11	PBS	61,000	25	PBS
36,800	12	PBS	61,400	26	PBS
39,000	13	PBS	62,500	27	PBS
39,400	14	PBS			

Because $n_1, n_2 > 10$, U is approximately normally distributed, with a mean of

$$\mu_U = \frac{n_1 \cdot n_2}{2} = \frac{(14)(13)}{2} = 91$$

and a standard deviation of

$$\sigma_U = \sqrt{\frac{n_1 \cdot n_2 (n_1 + n_2 + 1)}{12}} = \sqrt{\frac{(14)(13)(28)}{12}} = 20.6$$

A z value now can be computed to determine the probability of the sample U value coming from the distribution with $\mu_U = 91$ and $\sigma_U = 20.6$ if there is no difference in the populations.

$$z = \frac{U - \mu_U}{\sigma_U} = \frac{41.5 - 91}{20.6} = \frac{-49.5}{20.6} = -2.40$$

ACTION:

STEP 7. The observed value of z is –2.40, so the results are in the rejection region. That is, there is a difference between the income of a PBS viewer and that of a non–PBS viewer. Examination of the sample data confirms that in general, the income of a PBS viewer is higher than that of a non–PBS viewer.

BUSINESS IMPLICATIONS:

STEP 8. The fact that PBS viewers have higher average income can affect the type of programming on PBS in terms of both trying to please present viewers and offering programs that might attract viewers of other income levels. In addition, fund-raising drives can be made to appeal to the viewers with higher incomes.

Assignment of PBS viewers to group 1 was arbitrary. If non–PBS viewers had been designated as group 1, the results would have been the same but the observed z value would have been positive.

Figure 17.4 is the MINITAB output for this example. Note that MINITAB does not produce a z value but rather yields the value of W and the probability of the test results

FIGURE 17.4

MINITAB Output for the PBS Viewer Example

```
Mann-Whitney Test and CI: PBS, NON-PBS

PBS       N =   14   Median =   43250
NON-PBS   N =   13   Median =   32500
Point estimate for ETA1-ETA2 is   12500
95.1 Percent CI for ETA1-ETA2 is (3000,22000)
W = 245.5
Test of ETA1 = ETA2   vs   ETA1 not = ETA2 is significant at 0.0174
The test is significant at 0.0174 (adjusted for ties)
```

occurring by chance (.0174). Because the *p*-value (.0174) is less than $\alpha = .05$, the decision based on the computer output is to reject the null hypothesis. The *p*-value of the observed test statistic ($z = 2.40$) is .0164. The difference is likely to be due to rounding error.

<table>
<tr><td>**DEMONSTRATION PROBLEM 17.2**</td><td>Do construction workers who purchase lunch from street vendors spend less per meal than construction workers who go to restaurants for lunch? To test this question, a researcher selects two random samples of construction workers, one group that purchases lunch from street vendors and one group that purchases lunch from restaurants. Workers are asked to record how much they spend on lunch that day. The data follow. Use the data and a Mann-Whitney *U* test to analyze the data to determine whether street-vendor lunches are significantly cheaper than restaurant lunches. Let $\alpha = .01$.</td></tr>
</table>

Vendor	Restaurant
$2.75	$4.10
3.29	4.75
4.53	3.95
3.61	3.50
3.10	4.25
4.29	4.98
2.25	5.75
2.97	4.10
4.01	2.70
3.68	3.65
3.15	5.11
2.97	4.80
4.05	6.25
3.60	3.89
	4.80
	5.50
$n_1 = 14$	$n_2 = 16$

Solution

HYPOTHESIZE:

STEP 1. The hypotheses follow.

> H_0: The populations of construction-worker spending for lunch at vendors and restaurants are the same.
>
> H_a: The population of construction-worker spending at vendors is shifted to the left of the population of construction-worker spending at restaurants.

TEST:

STEP 2. The large-sample Mann-Whitney *U* test is appropriate. The test statistic is the *z*.

STEP 3. Alpha is .01.

STEP 4. If the *p*-value of the sample statistic is less than .01, the decision is to reject the null hypothesis.

STEP 5. The sample data are given.

STEP 6. Determine the value of W_1 by combining the groups, while retaining group identification, and ranking all the values from 1 to 30 (14 + 16), with 1 representing the smallest value.

Value	Rank	Group	Value	Rank	Group
$2.25	1	V	$4.01	16	V
2.70	2	R	4.05	17	V
2.75	3	V	4.10	18.5	R
2.97	4.5	V	4.10	18.5	R
2.97	4.5	V	4.25	20	R
3.10	6	V	4.29	21	V
3.15	7	V	4.53	22	V
3.29	8	V	4.75	23	R
3.50	9	R	4.80	24.5	R
3.60	10	V	4.80	24.5	R
3.61	11	V	4.98	26	R
3.65	12	R	5.11	27	R
3.68	13	V	5.50	28	R
3.89	14	R	5.75	29	R
3.95	15	R	6.25	30	R

Summing the ranks for the vendor sample gives

$$W_1 = 1 + 3 + 4.5 + 4.5 + 6 + 7 + 8 + 10 + 11 + 13 + 16 + 17 + 21 + 22 = 144$$

Solving for U, μ_U, and α_U yields

$$U = (14)(16) + \frac{(14)(15)}{2} - 144 = 185$$

$$\mu_U = \frac{(14)(16)}{2} = 112$$

$$\sigma_U = \sqrt{\frac{(14)(16)(31)}{12}} = 24.1$$

Solving for the observed z value gives

$$z = \frac{185 - 112}{24.1} = 3.03$$

ACTION:

STEP 7. The p-value associated with $z = 3.03$ is .0012. The null hypothesis is rejected.

BUSINESS IMPLICATIONS:

STEP 8. The business researcher concludes that construction-worker spending at vendors is less than the spending at restaurants for lunches.

17.2 PROBLEMS

17.7 Use the Mann-Whitney U test and the following data to determine whether there is a significant difference between the values of group 1 and group 2. Let $\alpha = .05$.

Group 1	Group 2
15	23
17	14
26	24
11	13
18	22
21	23
13	18
29	21

17.8 The data shown represent two random samples gathered from two populations. Is there sufficient evidence in the data to determine whether the values of population 1 are significantly larger than the values of population 2? Use the Mann-Whitney U test and $\alpha = .01$.

Sample 1	Sample 2
224	203
256	218
231	229
222	230
248	211
283	230
241	209
217	223
240	219
255	236
216	227
	208
	214

17.9 Results of a survey by the National Center for Health Statistics indicated that people between 65 and 74 years of age contact a physician an average of 9.8 times per year. People 75 and older contact doctors an average of 12.9 times per year. Suppose you want to validate these results by taking your own samples. The following data represent the number of annual contacts people make with a physician. The samples are independent. Use a Mann-Whitney U test to determine whether the number of contacts with physicians by people 75 and older is greater than the number by people 65 to 74 years old. Let $\alpha = .01$.

65 to 74	75 and Older
12	16
13	15
8	10
11	17
9	13
6	12
11	14
	9
	13

17.10 Suppose 12 urban households and 12 rural households are selected randomly and each family is asked to report the amount spent on food at home annually. The results follow. Use a Mann-Whitney U test to determine whether there is a significant difference between urban and rural households in the amounts spent for food at home. Use $\alpha = .05$.

Urban	Rural	Urban	Rural
$2,110	$2,050	$1,950	$2,770
2,655	2,800	2,480	3,100
2,710	2,975	2,630	2,685
2,540	2,075	2,750	2,790
2,200	2,490	2,850	2,995
2,175	2,585	2,850	2,995

17.11 Does the male stock market investor earn significantly more than the female stock market investor? One study by the New York Stock Exchange showed that the male investor has an income of $46,400 and that the female investor has an income of $39,400. Suppose an analyst wanted to "prove" that the male investor earns more than the female investor. The following data represent random samples of male and female investors from across the United States. The analyst uses the Mann-Whitney U test to determine whether the male investor earns significantly more than the female investor for $\alpha = .01$. What does the analyst find?

Male	Female
$50,100	$41,200
47,800	36,600
45,000	44,500
51,500	47,800
55,000	42,500
53,850	47,500
51,500	40,500
63,900	28,900
57,800	48,000
61,100	42,300
51,000	40,000
	31,400

17.12 The National Association of Realtors reports that the median price of an existing single-family home in Denver, Colorado, is $140,600 and the median price of an existing single-family home in Hartford, Connecticut, is $138,000. Suppose a survey of 13 randomly selected single-family homes is taken in Denver and a survey of 15 randomly selected single-family homes is taken in Hartford with the resulting prices shown here. Use a Mann-Whitney U test to determine whether there is a significant difference in the price of a single-family home in these two cities. Let $\alpha = .05$.

Denver	Hartford
$134,157	$143,947
138,057	134,127
135,062	135,238
137,016	137,359
135,940	140,031
136,981	139,114
140,479	142,012
140,102	144,500
139,638	136,419
141,861	137,867
141,408	137,741
132,405	134,514
141,730	142,136
	136,333
	143,968

17.3 WILCOXON MATCHED-PAIRS SIGNED RANK TEST

The Mann-Whitney U test presented in Section 17.2 is a nonparametric alternative to the t test for two *independent* samples. If the two samples are *related*, the U test is not applicable. A test that does handle related data is the **Wilcoxon matched-pairs signed rank test,** which serves as *a nonparametric alternative to the t test for two related samples*. Developed by Frank Wilcoxon in 1945, the Wilcoxon test, like the t test for two related samples, is used to analyze several different types of studies when the data of one group are related to the data in the other group, including before-and-after studies, studies in which measures are taken on the same person or object under two different conditions, and studies of twins or other relatives.

The Wilcoxon test utilizes the differences of the scores of the two matched groups in a manner similar to that of the t test for two related samples. After the difference scores have been computed, the Wilcoxon test ranks all differences regardless of whether the difference is positive or negative. The values are ranked from smallest to largest, with a rank of 1 assigned to the smallest difference. If a difference is negative, the rank is given a negative sign. The sum of the positive ranks is tallied along with the sum of the negative ranks. Zero differences representing ties between scores from the two groups are ignored, and the value of n is reduced accordingly. When ties occur between ranks, the ranks are averaged over the values. The smallest sum of ranks (either + or −) is used in the analysis and is represented by T. The Wilcoxon matched-pairs signed rank test procedure for determining statistical significance differs with sample size. When the number of matched pairs, n, is greater than 15, the value of T is approximately normally distributed and a z score is computed to test the null hypothesis. When sample size is small, $n \leq 15$, a different procedure is followed.

Two assumptions underlie the use of this technique.

1. The paired data are selected randomly.
2. The underlying distributions are symmetrical.

The following hypotheses are being tested.

For two-tailed tests:

$$H_0: M_d = 0 \qquad H_a: M_d \neq 0$$

For one-tailed tests:

$$H_0: M_d = 0 \qquad H_a: M_d > 0$$

or

$$H_0: M_d = 0 \qquad H_a: M_d < 0$$

where M_d is the median.

Small-Sample Case ($n \leq 15$)

When sample size is small, a critical value against which to compare T can be found in Table A.14 to determine whether the null hypothesis should be rejected. The critical value is located by using n and α. Critical values are given in the table for $\alpha = .05, .025, .01,$ and $.005$ for two-tailed tests and $\alpha = .10, .05, .02,$ and $.01$ for one-tailed tests. If the observed value of T is less than or equal to the critical value of T, the decision is to reject the null hypothesis.

As an example, consider the survey by American Demographics that estimated the average annual household spending on healthcare. The U.S. metropolitan average was $1,800. Suppose six families in Pittsburgh, Pennsylvania, are matched demographically with six families in Oakland, California, and their amounts of household spending on healthcare for last year are obtained. The data follow.

Family Pair	Pittsburgh	Oakland
1	$1,950	$1,760
2	1,840	1,870
3	2,015	1,810
4	1,580	1,660
5	1,790	1,340
6	1,925	1,765

A healthcare analyst uses $\alpha = .05$ to test to determine whether there is a significant difference in annual household healthcare spending between these two cities.

HYPOTHESIZE:

STEP 1. The following hypotheses are being tested.
$$H_0: M_d = 0$$
$$H_a: M_d \neq 0$$

TEST:

STEP 2. Because the sample size of pairs is six, the small-sample Wilcoxon matched-pairs signed ranks test is appropriate if the underlying distributions are assumed to be symmetrical.

STEP 3. Alpha is .05.

STEP 4. From Table A.14, if the observed value of T is less than or equal to 1, the decision is to reject the null hypothesis.

STEP 5. The sample data were listed earlier.

STEP 6.

Family Pair	Pittsburgh	Oakland	d	Rank
1	$1950	$1760	+190	+4
2	1840	1870	−30	−1
3	2015	1810	+205	+5
4	1580	1660	−80	−2
5	1790	1340	+450	+6
6	1925	1765	+160	+3

$$T = \text{minimum of } (T_+, T_-)$$
$$T_+ = 4 + 5 + 6 + 3 = 18$$
$$T_- = 1 + 2 = 3$$
$$T = \text{minimum of } (18, 3) = 3$$

ACTION:

STEP 7. Because $T = 3$ is greater than critical $T = 1$, the decision is not to reject the null hypothesis.

BUSINESS IMPLICATIONS:

STEP 8. Not enough evidence is provided to declare that Pittsburgh and Oakland differ in annual household spending on healthcare. This information may be useful to healthcare providers and employers in the two cities and particularly to businesses that either operate in both cities or are planning to move from one to the other. Rates can be established on the notion that healthcare costs are about the same in both cities. In addition, employees considering transfers from one city to the other can expect their annual healthcare costs to remain about the same.

Large-Sample Case ($n > 15$)

For large samples, the T statistic is approximately normally distributed and a z score can be used as the test statistic. Formula (17.2) contains the necessary formulas to complete this procedure.

WILCOXON MATCHED-PAIRS SIGNED RANK TEST (17.2)	$$\mu_T = \frac{(n)(n+1)}{4}$$ $$\sigma_T = \sqrt{\frac{(n)(n+1)(2n+1)}{24}}$$ $$z = \frac{T - \mu_T}{\sigma_T}$$

where

n = number of pairs

T = total ranks for either + or − differences, whichever is less in magnitude

This technique can be applied to the airline industry, where an analyst might want to determine whether there is a difference in the cost per mile of airfares in the United States between 1979 and 2002 for various cities. The data in Table 17.3 represent the costs per mile of airline tickets for a sample of 17 cities for both 1979 and 2002.

HYPOTHESIZE:

STEP 1. The analyst states the hypotheses as follows.

$$H_0: M_d = 0$$
$$H_a: M_d \neq 0$$

TEST:

STEP 2. The analyst applies a Wilcoxon matched-pairs signed rank test to the data to test the difference in cents per mile for the two periods of time. She assumes the underlying distributions are symmetrical.

City	1979	2002	d	Rank
1	20.3	22.8	−2.5	−8
2	19.5	12.7	+6.8	+17
3	18.6	14.1	+4.5	+13
4	20.9	16.1	+4.8	+15
5	19.9	25.2	−5.3	−16
6	18.6	20.2	−1.6	−4
7	19.6	14.9	+4.7	+14
8	23.2	21.3	+1.9	+6.5
9	21.8	18.7	+3.1	+10
10	20.3	20.9	−0.6	−1
11	19.2	22.6	−3.4	−11.5
12	19.5	16.9	+2.6	+9
13	18.7	20.6	−1.9	−6.5
14	17.7	18.5	−0.8	−2
15	21.6	23.4	−1.8	−5
16	22.4	21.3	+1.1	+3
17	20.8	17.4	+3.4	+11.5

STEP 3. Use $\alpha = .05$.

STEP 4. Because this test is two-tailed, $\alpha/2 = .025$ and the critical values are $z = \pm 1.96$. If the observed value of the test statistic is greater than 1.96 or less than −1.96, the null hypothesis is rejected.

STEP 5. The sample data are given in Table 17.3.

STEP 6. The analyst begins the process by computing a difference score, d. Which year's data are subtracted from the other does not matter as long as consistency in direction is maintained. For the data in Table 17.3, the analyst subtracted the 2002 figures from the 1979 figures. The sign of the difference is left on the difference score. Next, she ranks the differences without regard to sign, but the sign is left on the rank as an identifier. Note the tie for ranks 6 and 7; each is given a rank of 6.5, the average of the two ranks. The same applies to ranks 11 and 12.

After the analyst ranks all difference values regardless of sign, she sums the positive ranks (T_1) and the negative ranks (T_2). She then determines the T value from these two sums as the smallest T_1 or T_2.

$$T = \text{minimum of } (T_+, T_-)$$
$$T_+ = 17 + 13 + 15 + 14 + 6.5 + 10 + 9 + 3 + 11.5 = 99$$
$$T_- = 8 + 16 + 4 + 1 + 11.5 + 6.5 + 2 + 5 = 54$$
$$T = \text{minimum of } (99, 54) = 54$$

The T value is normally distributed for large sample sizes, with a mean and standard deviation of

$$\mu_T = \frac{(n)(n+1)}{4} = \frac{(17)(18)}{4} = 76.5$$

$$\sigma_T = \sqrt{\frac{(n)(n+1)(2n+1)}{24}} = \sqrt{\frac{(17)(18)(35)}{24}} = 21.1$$

The observed z value is

$$z = \frac{T - \mu_T}{\sigma_T} = \frac{54 - 76.5}{21.1} = -1.07$$

ACTION:

STEP 7. The critical z value for this two-tailed test is $z_{.025} = \pm 1.96$. The observed $z = -1.07$, so the analyst fails to reject the null hypothesis. There is no significant difference in the cost of airline tickets between 1979 and 2002.

BUSINESS IMPLICATIONS:

STEP 8. Promoters in the airline industry can use this type of information (the fact that ticket prices have not increased significantly in 23 years) to sell their product as a good buy. In addition, industry managers could use it as an argument for raising prices.

DEMONSTRATION PROBLEM 17.3

During the 1980s and 1990s, U.S. businesses increasingly emphasized quality control. One of the arguments in favor of quality control programs is that quality control can increase productivity. Suppose a company implemented a quality control program and has been operating under it for two years. The company's president wants to determine whether worker productivity significantly increased since installation of the program. Company records contain the figures for items produced per worker during a sample of production runs two years ago. Productivity figures on the same workers are gathered now and compared to the previous figures. The following data represent items produced per hour. The company's statistical analyst uses the Wilcoxon matched-pairs signed rank test to determine whether there is a significant increase in per worker production for $\alpha = .01$.

Worker	Before	After	Worker	Before	After
1	5	11	11	2	6
2	4	9	12	5	10
3	9	9	13	4	9
4	6	8	14	5	7
5	3	5	15	8	9
6	8	7	16	7	6
7	7	9	17	9	10
8	10	9	18	5	8
9	3	7	19	4	5
10	7	9	20	3	6

Solution

HYPOTHESIZE:

STEP 1. The hypotheses are as follows.

$$H_0: M_d = 0$$
$$H_a: M_d < 0$$

TEST:

STEP 2. The analyst applies a Wilcoxon matched-pairs signed rank test to the data to test the difference in productivity from before to after. He assumes the underlying distributions are symmetrical.

STEP 3. Use $\alpha = .01$.

STEP 4. This test is one-tailed. The critical value is $z = -2.33$. If the observed value of the test statistic is less than -2.33, the null hypothesis is rejected.

STEP 5. The sample data are as already given.

STEP 6. The analyst computes the difference values, and, because zero differences are to be eliminated, deletes worker 3 from the study. This reduces n from 20 to 19. He then ranks the differences regardless of sign. The differences that are the same (ties) receive the average rank for those values. For example, the differences for workers 4, 5, 7, 10, and 14 are the same. The ranks for these five are 7, 8, 9, 10, and 11, so each worker receives the rank of 9, the average of these five ranks.

Worker	Before	After	d	Rank
1	5	11	−6	−19
2	4	9	−5	−17
3	9	9	0	delete
4	6	8	−2	−9
5	3	5	−2	−9
6	8	7	+1	+3.5
7	7	9	−2	−9
8	10	9	+1	+3.5
9	3	7	−4	−14.5
10	7	9	−2	−9
11	2	6	−4	−14.5
12	5	10	−5	−17
13	4	9	−5	−17
14	5	7	−2	−9
15	8	9	−1	−3.5
16	7	6	+1	+3.5
17	9	10	−1	−3.5
18	5	8	−3	−12.5
19	4	5	−1	−3.5
20	3	6	−3	−12.5

The analyst determines the values of T_+, T_-, and T to be

$$T_+ = 3.5 + 3.5 + 3.5 = 10.5$$
$$T_- = 19 + 17 + 9 + 9 + 9 + 14.5 + 9 + 14.5 + 17 + 17$$
$$+ 9 + 3.5 + 3.5 + 12.5 + 3.5 + 12.5 = 179.5$$
$$T = \text{minimum of } (10.5, 179.5) = 10.5$$

The mean and standard deviation of T are

$$\mu_T = \frac{(n)(n+1)}{4} = \frac{(19)(20)}{4} = 95$$

$$\sigma_T = \sqrt{\frac{(n)(n+1)(2n+1)}{24}} = \sqrt{\frac{(19)(20)(39)}{24}} = 24.8$$

The observed z value is

$$z = \frac{T - \mu_T}{\sigma_T} = \frac{10.5 - 95}{24.8} = -3.41$$

ACTION:

STEP 7. The observed z value (−3.41) is in the rejection region, so the analyst rejects the null hypothesis. The productivity is significantly greater after the implementation of quality control at this company.

BUSINESS IMPLICATIONS:

STEP 8. Managers, the quality team, and any consultants can point to the figures as validation of the efficacy of the quality program. Such results could be used to justify further activity in the area of quality.

Figure 17.5 is MINITAB output for Demonstration Problem 17.3. MINITAB does not produce a z test statistic for the Wilcoxon matched-pairs signed rank test. Instead, it calculates a Wilcoxon statistic that is equivalent to T. A p-value of .001 is produced for this T value. The p-value of the observed $z = -3.41$ determined in Demonstration Problem 17.3 is .0003. The difference in the two p-values is due to rounding error.

FIGURE 17.5

MINITAB Output for
Demonstration Problem 17.3

```
Wilcoxon Signed Rank Test: difference
Test of median = 0.000000 versus median not = 0.000000
                    N for    Wilcoxon   Estimated
               N    Test    Statistic           P   Median
differen      20     19        10.5       0.001   -2.000
```

17.3 PROBLEMS

17.13 Use the Wilcoxon matched-pairs signed rank test to determine whether there is a significant difference between the two groups of related data given. Use $\alpha = .10$. Assume the underlying distributions are symmetrical.

1	2	1	2
212	179	220	223
234	184	218	217
219	213	234	208
199	167	212	215
194	189	219	187
206	200	196	198
234	212	178	189
225	221	213	201

17.14 Use the Wilcoxon matched-pairs signed rank test and $\alpha = .05$ to analyze the before-and-after measurements given. Assume the underlying distributions are symmetrical.

Before	After
49	43
41	29
47	30
39	38
53	40
51	43
51	46
49	40
38	42
54	50
46	47
50	47
44	39
49	49
45	47

17.15 A corporation owns a chain of several hundred gasoline stations on the eastern seaboard. The marketing director wants to test a proposed marketing campaign by running ads on some local television stations and determining whether gasoline sales at a sample of the company's stations increase after the advertising. The following data represent gasoline sales for a day before and a day after the advertising campaign. Use the Wilcoxon matched-pairs signed rank test to determine whether sales increased significantly after the advertising campaign. Let $\alpha = .05$. Assume the underlying distributions are symmetrical.

Station	Before	After
1	$10,500	$12,600
2	8,870	10,660
3	12,300	11,890
4	10,510	14,630
5	5,570	8,580
6	9,150	10,115
7	11,980	14,350
8	6,740	6,900
9	7,340	8,890
10	13,400	16,540
11	12,200	11,300
12	10,570	13,330
13	9,880	9,990
14	12,100	14,050
15	9,000	9,500
16	11,800	12,450
17	10,500	13,450

17.16 Many supermarkets across the United States invest heavily in optical scanner systems to expedite customer checkout, increase checkout productivity, and improve product accountability. These systems are not 100% effective, and items often have to be scanned several times. Sometimes items are manually entered into the cash register because the scanner cannot read the item number. In general, do optical scanners register significantly more items than manual entry systems do? The following data are from an experiment in which a supermarket selected 14 of its best checkers and measured their productivity both when using a scanner and when working manually. The data show the number of items checked per hour by each method. Use a Wilcoxon matched-pairs signed rank test and $\alpha = .05$ to test the difference. Assume the underlying distributions are symmetrical.

Checker	Manual	Scanner
1	426	473
2	387	446
3	410	421
4	506	510
5	411	465
6	398	409
7	427	414
8	449	459
9	407	502
10	438	439
11	418	456
12	482	499
13	512	517
14	402	437

17.17 American attitudes toward big business change over time and probably are cyclical. Suppose the following data represent a survey of 20 American adults taken in 1990 and again in 2002 in which each adult was asked to rate American big business overall on a scale from 1 to 100 in terms of positive opinion. A response of 1 indicates a low opinion and a response of 100 indicates a high opinion. Use a Wilcoxon matched-pairs signed rank test to determine whether the scores from 2002 are significantly higher than the scores from 1990. Use $\alpha = .10$. Assume the underlying distributions are symmetrical.

Person	1990	2002
1	49	54
2	27	38
3	39	38
4	75	80
5	59	53
6	67	68
7	22	43
8	61	67
9	58	73
10	60	55
11	72	58
12	62	57
13	49	63
14	48	49
15	19	39
16	32	34
17	60	66
18	80	90
19	55	57
20	68	58

17.18 Suppose 16 people in various industries are contacted in 2001 and asked to rate business conditions on several factors. The ratings of each person are tallied into a "business optimism" score. The same people are contacted in 2002 and asked to do the same thing. The higher the score, the more optimistic the person is. Shown here are the 2001 and 2002 scores for the 16 people. Use a Wilcoxon matched-pairs signed rank test to determine whether people were less optimistic in 2002 than in 2001. Assume the underlying distributions are symmetrical and that alpha is .05.

Industry	April 2001	April 2002
1	63.1	57.4
2	67.1	66.4
3	65.5	61.8
4	68.0	65.3
5	66.6	63.5
6	65.7	66.4
7	69.2	64.9
8	67.0	65.2
9	65.2	65.1
10	60.7	62.2
11	63.4	60.3
12	59.2	57.4
13	62.9	58.2
14	69.4	65.3
15	67.3	67.2
16	66.8	64.1

17.4 KRUSKAL-WALLIS TEST

The *nonparametric alternative to the one-way analysis of variance* is the **Kruskal-Wallis test,** developed in 1952 by William H. Kruskal and W. Allen Wallis. Like the one-way analysis of variance, the Kruskal-Wallis test is used to determine whether $c \geq 3$ samples come from the same or different populations. Whereas the one-way ANOVA is based on the assumptions of normally distributed populations, independent groups, at least interval level data, and equal population variances, the Kruskal-Wallis test can be used to analyze ordinal data and is not based on any assumption about population shape. The Kruskal-Wallis test is based on the assumption that the c groups are independent and that individual items are selected randomly.

The hypotheses tested by the Kruskal-Wallis test follow.

H_0: The c populations are identical.
H_a: At least one of the c populations is different.

This test determines whether all of the groups come from the same or equal populations or whether at least one group comes from a different population.

The process of computing a Kruskal-Wallis K statistic begins with ranking the data in all the groups together, as though they were from one group. The smallest value is awarded a 1. As usual, for ties, each value is given the average rank for those tied values. Unlike one-way ANOVA, in which the raw data are analyzed, the Kruskal-Wallis test analyzes the ranks of the data.

Formula (17.3) is used to compute a Kruskal-Wallis K statistic.

KRUSKAL-WALLIS TEST (17.3)

$$K = \frac{12}{n(n+1)} \left(\sum_{j=1}^{c} \frac{T_j^2}{n_j} \right) - 3(n+1)$$

where

c = number of groups
n = total number of items
T_j = total of ranks in a group
n_j = number of items in a group
$K \approx \chi^2$, with df = $c - 1$

The K value is approximately chi-square distributed, with $c - 1$ degrees of freedom as long as n_j is not less than 5 for any group.

Suppose a researcher wants to determine whether the number of physicians in an office produces significant differences in the number of office patients seen by each physician per day. She takes a random sample of physicians from practices in which (1) there are only two partners, (2) there are three or more partners, or (3) the office is a health maintenance organization (HMO). Table 17.4 shows the data she obtained.

Three groups are targeted in this study, so $c = 3$, and $n = 18$ physicians, with the numbers of patients ranked for these physicians. The researcher sums the ranks within each column to obtain T_j, as shown in Table 17.5.

TABLE 17.4

Number of Office Patients per Doctor

Two Partners	Three or More Partners	HMO
13	24	26
15	16	22
20	19	31
18	22	27
23	25	28
	14	33
	17	

TABLE 17.5

Kruskal-Wallis Analysis of Physicians' Patients

Two Partners	Three or More Partners	HMO
1	12	14
3	4	9.5
8	7	17
6	9.5	15
11	13	16
	2	18
	5	
$T_1 = 29$	$T_2 = 52.5$	$T_3 = 89.5$
$n_1 = 5$	$n_2 = 7$	$n_3 = 6 \qquad n = 18$

$$\sum_{j=1}^{3} \frac{T_j^2}{n_j} = \frac{(29)^2}{5} + \frac{(52.5)^2}{7} + \frac{(89.5)^2}{6} = 1897$$

FIGURE 17.6	Kruskal-Wallis Test: No. Patients versus Type Office

MINITAB Output for the Physicians' Patients Example

```
Kruskal-Wallis Test: No. Patients versus Type Office
Kruskal-Wallis Test on No. Patients
C39         N   Median   Ave Rank      Z
HMO         6    27.50      14.9     3.04
Three or    7    19.00       7.5    -1.27
Two         5    18.00       5.8    -1.82
Overall    18                9.5

H = 9.56  DF = 2   P = 0.008
H = 9.57  DF = 2   P = 0.008  (adjusted for ties)
```

The Kruskal-Wallis K is

$$K = \frac{12}{18(18+1)}(1897) - 3(18+1) = 9.56$$

The critical chi-square value is $\chi^2_{\alpha,df}$. If $\alpha = .05$ and df for $c - 1 = 3 - 1 = 2$, $\chi^2_{.05,2} = 5.991$. This test is always one-tailed, and the rejection region is always in the right tail of the distribution. Because $K = 9.56$ is larger than the critical χ^2 value, the researcher rejects the null hypothesis. The number of patients seen in the office by a physician is not the same in these three sizes of offices. Examination of the values in each group reveals that physicians in two-partner offices see fewer patients per physician in the office, and HMO physicians see more patients per physician in the office.

Figure 17.6 is the MINITAB computer output for this example. The statistic H printed in the output is equivalent to the K statistic calculated here (both K and H are 9.56).

DEMONSTRATION PROBLEM 17.4

Agribusiness researchers are interested in determining the conditions under which Christmas trees grow fastest. A random sample of equivalent-size seedlings is divided into four groups. The trees are all grown in the same field. One group is left to grow naturally, one group is given extra water, one group is given fertilizer spikes, and one group is given fertilizer spikes and extra water. At the end of one year, the seedlings are measured for growth (in height). These measurements are shown for each group. Use the Kruskal-Wallis test to determine whether there is a significant difference in the growth of trees in these groups. Use $\alpha = .05$.

Group 1 (native)	Group 2 (+ water)	Group 3 (+ fertilizer)	Group 4 (+ water and fertilizer)
8 in.	10 in.	11 in.	18 in.
5	12	14	20
7	11	10	16
11	9	16	15
9	13	17	14
6	12	12	22

Solution

Here, $n = 24$, and $n_j = 6$ in each group.

HYPOTHESIZE:

STEP 1. The hypotheses follow.

H_0: group 1 = group 2 = group 3 = group 4
H_a: At least one group is different.

TEST:

STEP 2. The Kruskal-Wallis K is the appropriate test statistic.

STEP 3. Alpha is .01.

STEP 4. The degrees of freedom are $c - 1 = 4 - 1 = 3$. The critical value of chi-square is $\chi^2_{.01,3} = 11.345$. If the observed value of K is greater than 11.345, the decision is to reject the null hypothesis.

STEP 5. The data are as shown previously.

STEP 6. Ranking all group values yields the following.

1	2	3	4
4	7.5	10	22
1	13	16.5	23
3	10	7.5	19.5
10	5.5	19.5	18
5.5	15	21	16.5
2	13	13	24
$T_1 = 25.5$	$T_2 = 64.0$	$T_3 = 87.5$	$T_4 = 123.0$
$n_1 = 6$	$n_2 = 6$	$n_3 = 6$	$n_4 = 6$ $\quad n = 24$

$$\sum_{j=1}^{c} \frac{T_j^2}{n_j} = \frac{(25.5)^2}{6} + \frac{(64)^2}{6} + \frac{(87.5)^2}{6} + \frac{(123)^2}{6} = 4{,}588.6$$

$$K = \frac{12}{24(24+1)}(4588.6) - 3(24+1) = 16.77$$

ACTION:

STEP 7. The observed K value is 16.77 and the critical $\chi^2_{.01,3} = 11.345$. Because the observed value is greater than the table value, the null hypothesis is rejected. There is a significant difference in the way the trees grow.

BUSINESS IMPLICATIONS:

STEP 8. From the increased heights in the original data, the trees with both water and fertilizer seem to be doing the best. However, these are sample data; without analyzing the pairs of samples with nonparametric multiple comparisons (not included in this text), it is difficult to conclude whether the water/fertilizer group is actually growing faster than the others. It appears that the trees under natural conditions are growing more slowly than the others. The following diagram shows the relationship of the observed K value and the critical chi-square value.

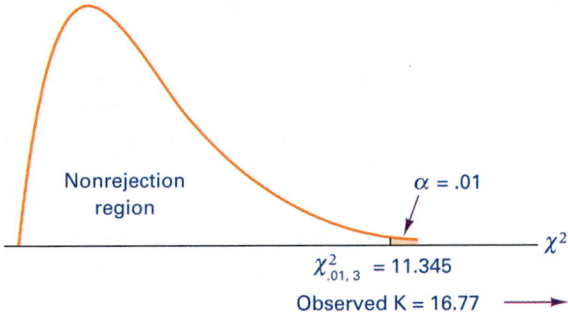

Nonrejection region

$\alpha = .01$

χ^2

$\chi^2_{.01,3} = 11.345$

Observed K = 16.77

17.4 PROBLEMS

17.19 Use the Kruskal-Wallis test to determine whether groups 1 through 5 come from different populations. Let $\alpha = .01$.

1	2	3	4	5
157	165	219	286	197
188	197	257	243	215
175	204	243	259	235
174	214	231	250	217
201	183	217	279	240
203		203		233
				213

Profiling Online Users

According to Jupiter Media Metrix, nearly 30% of all online users are in the 35- to 49-year-old age bracket. This age group is the most prevalent online age group followed by 25- to 34-year-olds and 2- to 17-year-olds each of whom represent 19.2% of the users. Of the nine U.S. geographic regions represented in the analysis, the Pacific region has the largest percentage of online users with 18.5%. This region is followed closely by East North Central with 18.2%. By gender, online users are split 50-50, with females holding a slight edge. Income-wise, the largest online user group is the $60K–$100K group, which represents 28.4% of online users. The second highest income group of online users is the Under $40K group, which represents 27.8% of the users.

Jupiter Media Metrix also presents the average minutes spent per month online for various variables. Nonparametric statistics can be applied to test various hypotheses about online usage. For example, according to Jupiter Media Metrix, males average 1,320.8 minutes per month online compared to 1,184.4 for females. Does this result mean a significant difference between males and females in online usage? To test this issue, a study can be designed, controlling for region, age, and income, where male and female online users are independently randomly selected and the number of minutes of online usage recorded for each person. If distribution characteristics are unknown, the Mann-Whitney U test can be used to test to determine whether there is a significant difference between men and women for online usage.

Online usage is also given by age, region, and income. Each of these three demographic variables contains classification levels. For example, income usage levels are given for Under $40K, $40K–$60K, $60K–$100K, and $100K+. If random samples of online users are taken from each of these four levels of income, online usage minutes per month can be compared using the Kruskal-Wallis test to determine whether there is a significant difference by income level. This test is particularly useful if the business researcher is uncertain about whether normal distribution assumptions underlying the one-way ANOVA are being met.

Online usage seems to grow every year. Suppose a business researcher wants to conduct a statistical test to determine whether online usage is significantly greater this year than last year. A representative cross-section of online users representing various demographic groups can be randomly selected. The minutes of online usage for one month are recorded. One year later, the same measurement is recorded for these same users. A Wilcoxon matched-pairs signed rank test can be used to determine whether there was a significant difference between last year's usage and this year's usage.

Source: Adapted from "Who Goes There?" *The Wall Street Journal*, 29 October 2001, p. R4.

17.20 Use the Kruskal-Wallis test to determine whether there is a significant difference in the following groups. Use $\alpha = .05$.

Group 1	19	21	29	22	37	42	
Group 2	30	38	35	24	29		
Group 3	39	32	41	44	30	27	33

17.21 Is there a difference in the amount of customers' initial deposits when they open savings accounts according to geographic region of the United States? To test this question, an analyst selects savings and loan offices of equal size from four regions of the United States. The offices selected are located in areas having similar economic and population characteristics. The analyst randomly selects adult customers who are opening their first savings account and obtains the following dollar amounts. Use the Kruskal-Wallis test to determine whether there is a significant difference between geographic regions. Use $\alpha = .05$.

Region 1	Region 2	Region 3	Region 4
$1,200	$225	$675	$1,075
450	950	500	1,050
110	100	1,100	750
800	350	310	180
375	275	660	330
200			680
			425

17.22 Does the asking price of a new car vary according to whether the dealership is in a small town, a city, or a suburban area? To test this question, a researcher randomly selects dealerships selling Pontiacs in the state of Illinois. The researcher goes to these dealerships posing as a prospective buyer and makes a serious inquiry as to the asking price of a new Pontiac Grand Am (each having the same equipment). The following data represent the results of this sample. Is there a significant difference between prices according to the area in which the dealership is located? Use the Kruskal-Wallis test and $\alpha = .05$.

Small Town	City	Suburb
$15,800	$16,300	$16,000
16,500	15,900	16,600
15,750	15,900	16,800
16,200	16,650	16,050
15,600	15,800	15,250
		16,550

17.23 A survey by the U.S. Travel Data Center showed that a higher percentage of Americans travel to the ocean/beach for vacation than to any other destination. Much further behind in the survey, and virtually tied for second place, were the mountains and small/rural towns. How long do people stay at vacation destinations? Does the length of stay differ according to location? Suppose the following data were taken from a survey of vacationers who were asked how many nights they stay at a destination when on vacation. Use a Kruskal-Wallis test to determine whether there is a significant difference in the duration of stay by type of vacation destination. Let $\alpha = .05$.

Amusement Park	Lake Area	City	National Park
0	3	2	2
1	2	2	4
1	3	3	3
0	5	2	4
2	4	3	3
1	4	2	5
0	3	3	4
	5	3	4
	2	1	
		3	

17.24 Do workers on different shifts get different amounts of sleep per week? Some people believe that shift workers who regularly work the graveyard shift (12:00 A.M. to 8:00 A.M.) or swing shift (4:00 P.M. to 12:00 A.M.) are unable to get the same amount of sleep as day workers because of family schedules, noise, amount of daylight, and other factors. To test this theory, a researcher samples workers from day, swing, and graveyard shifts and asks each worker to keep a sleep journal for one week. The following data represent the number of hours of sleep per week per worker for the different shifts. Use the Kruskal-Wallis test to determine whether there is a significant difference in the number of hours of sleep per week for workers on these shifts. Use $\alpha = .05$.

Day Shift	Swing Shift	Graveyard Shift
52	45	41
57	48	46
53	44	39
56	51	49
55	48	42
50	54	35
51	49	52
	43	

17.5 FRIEDMAN TEST

The **Friedman test,** developed by M. Friedman in 1937, is *a nonparametric alternative to the randomized block design* discussed in Chapter 11. The randomized block design has the same assumptions as other ANOVA procedures: observations are drawn from normally distributed populations. When this assumption cannot be met or when the researcher has ranked data, the Friedman test provides a nonparametric alternative.

Three assumptions underlie the Friedman test.

1. The blocks are independent.
2. No interaction is present between blocks and treatments.
3. Observations within each block can be ranked.

The hypotheses being tested are as follows.

H_0: The treatment populations are equal.
H_a: At least one treatment population yields larger values than at least one other treatment population.

The first step in computing a Friedman test is to convert all raw data to ranks (unless the data are already ranked). However, unlike the Kruskal-Wallis test where all data are ranked together, the data in a Friedman test are ranked *within* each block from smallest (1) to largest (c). Each block contains c ranks, where c is the number of treatment levels. Using these ranks, the Friedman test will test to determine whether it is likely that the different treatment levels (columns) came from the same population. Formula (17.4) is used to calculate the test statistic, which is approximately chi-square distributed with df $= c - 1$ if $c > 4$ or when $c = 3$ and $b > 9$, or when $c = 4$ and $b > 4$.

FRIEDMAN TEST (17.4)

$$\chi_r^2 = \frac{12}{bc(c+1)} \sum_{j=1}^{c} R_j^2 - 3b(c+1)$$

where

c = number of treatment levels (columns)
b = number of blocks (rows)
R_j = total of ranks for a particular treatment level (column)
j = particular treatment level (column)
$\chi_r^2 \approx \chi^2$, with df $= c - 1$

As an example, suppose a manufacturing company assembles microcircuits that contain a plastic housing. Managers are concerned about an unacceptably high number of the products that sustained housing damage during shipment. The housing component is made by four different suppliers. Managers have decided to conduct a study of the plastic housing by randomly selecting five housings made by each of the four suppliers. To determine whether a supplier is consistent during the production week, one housing is selected for each day of the week. That is, for each supplier, a housing made on Monday is selected, one made on Tuesday is selected, and so on.

In analyzing the data, the treatment variable is supplier and the treatment levels are the four suppliers. The blocking effect is day of the week with each day representing a block level. The quality control team wants to determine whether there is any significant difference in the tensile strength of the plastic housing by supplier. The data are given here (in pounds per inch).

Day	Supplier 1	Supplier 2	Supplier 3	Supplier 4
Monday	62	63	57	61
Tuesday	63	61	59	65
Wednesday	61	62	56	63
Thursday	62	60	57	64
Friday	64	63	58	66

HYPOTHESIZE:

STEP 1. The hypotheses follow.

H_0: The supplier populations are equal.
H_a: At least one supplier population yields larger values than at least one other supplier population.

TEST:

STEP 2. The quality researchers do not feel they have enough evidence to conclude that the observations come from normally distributed populations. Because they are analyzing a randomized block design, the Friedman test is appropriate.

STEP 3. Let $\alpha = .05$.

STEP 4. For four treatment levels (suppliers), $c = 4$ and df $= 4 - 1 = 3$. The critical value is $\chi^2_{.05,3} = 7.81473$. If the observed chi-square is greater than 7.81473, the decision is to reject the null hypothesis.

STEP 5. The sample data are as given.

STEP 6. The calculations begin by ranking the observations in each row with 1 designating the rank of the smallest observation. The ranks are then summed for each column, producing R_j. The values of R_j are squared and then summed. Because the study is concerned with five days of the week, five blocking levels are used and $b = 5$. The value of R_j is computed as shown in the following table.

Day	Supplier 1	Supplier 2	Supplier 3	Supplier 4
Monday	3	4	1	2
Tuesday	3	2	1	4
Wednesday	2	3	1	4
Thursday	3	2	1	4
Friday	3	2	1	4
R_j	14	13	5	18
R^2_j	196	169	25	324

$$\sum_{j=1}^{4} R_j^2 = (196 + 169 + 25 + 324) = 714$$

$$\chi_r^2 = \frac{12}{bc(c+1)} \sum_{j=1}^{c} R_j^2 - 3b(c+1) = \frac{12}{5(4)(4+1)}(714) - 3(5)(4+1) = 10.68$$

ACTION:

STEP 7. Because the observed value of $\chi^2_r = 10.68$ is greater than the critical value, $\chi^2_{.05,3} = 7.81473$, the decision is to reject the null hypothesis.

BUSINESS IMPLICATIONS:

STEP 8. Statistically, there is a significant difference in the tensile strength of housings made by different suppliers. The sample data indicate that supplier 3 is producing housings with a lower tensile strength than those made by other suppliers and that supplier 4 is producing housings with higher tensile strength. Further study by managers and a quality team may result in attempts to bring supplier 3 up to standard on tensile strength or perhaps cancellation of the contract.

Figure 17.7 displays the chi-square distribution for df $= 3$ along with the critical value, the observed value of the test statistic, and the rejection region. Figure 17.8 is the MINITAB output for the Friedman test. The computer output contains the value of χ^2_r referred to as S along with the p-value of .014, which informs the researcher that the null

FIGURE 17.7

Distribution for Tensile
Strength Example

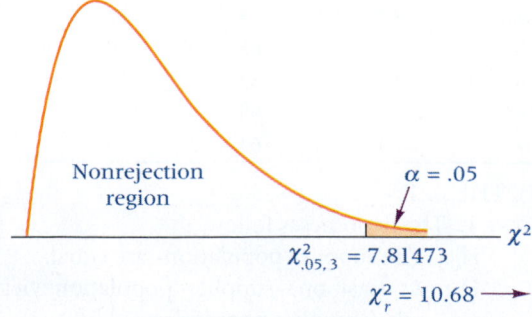

FIGURE 17.8

MINITAB Output for the Tensile Strength Example

```
Friedman Test: Strength versus Supplier, Day
Friedman test for Strength by Supplier blocked by Day
S = 10.68   DF = 3   P = 0.014
                      Est    Sum of
Supplier   N   Median    Ranks
1          5   62.125    14.0
2          5   61.375    13.0
3          5   56.875     5.0
4          5   64.125    18.0
Grand median = 61.125
```

hypothesis is rejected at an alpha of .05. Additional information is given about the medians and the column sum totals of ranks.

DEMONSTRATION PROBLEM 17.5

A market research company wants to determine brand preference for refrigerators. Five companies contracted with the research company to have their products be included in the study. As part of the study, the research company randomly selects 10 potential refrigerator buyers and shows them one of each of the five brands. Each survey participant is then asked to rank the refrigerator brands from 1 to 5. The results of these rankings are given in the table. Use the Friedman test and $\alpha = .01$ to determine whether there are any significant differences between the rankings of these brands.

Solution

HYPOTHESIZE:

STEP 1. The hypotheses are as follows.

H_0: The brand populations are equal.

H_a: At least one brand population yields larger values than at least one other brand population.

TEST:

STEP 2. The market researchers collected ranked data that are ordinal in level. The Friedman test is the appropriate test.

STEP 3. Let $\alpha = .01$.

STEP 4. Because the study uses five treatment levels (brands), $c = 5$ and df = 5 − 1 = 4. The critical value is $\chi^2_{.01,4} = 13.2767$. If the observed chi-square is greater than 13.2767, the decision is to reject the null hypothesis.

STEP 5. The sample data follow.

STEP 6. The ranks are totaled for each column, squared, and then summed across the column totals. The results are shown in the table.

Individual	Brand A	Brand B	Brand C	Brand D	Brand E
1	3	5	2	4	1
2	1	3	2	4	5
3	3	4	5	2	1
4	2	3	1	4	5
5	5	4	2	1	3
6	1	5	3	4	2
7	4	1	3	2	5
8	2	3	4	5	1
9	2	4	5	3	1
10	3	5	4	2	1
R_j	26	37	31	31	25
R_j^2	676	1,369	961	961	625

$\Sigma R_j^2 = 4{,}592$

The value of χ_r^2 is

$$\chi_r^2 = \frac{12}{bc(c+1)}\sum_{j=1}^{c} R_j^2 - 3b(c+1) = \frac{12}{10(5)(5+1)}(4{,}592) - 3(10)(5+1) = 3.68$$

ACTION:

STEP 7. Because the observed value of $\chi_r^2 = 3.68$ is not greater than the critical value, $\chi^2_{.01,4} = 13.2767$, the researchers fail to reject the null hypothesis.

BUSINESS IMPLICATIONS:

STEP 8. Potential refrigerator purchasers appear to have no significant brand preference. Marketing managers for the various companies might want to develop strategies for positively distinguishing their product from the others.

The chi-square distribution for four degrees of freedom, produced by MINITAB, is shown with the observed test statistic and the critical value. In addition, MINITAB output for the Friedman test is shown. Note that the p-value is .451, which underscores the decision not to reject the null hypothesis at $\alpha = .01$.

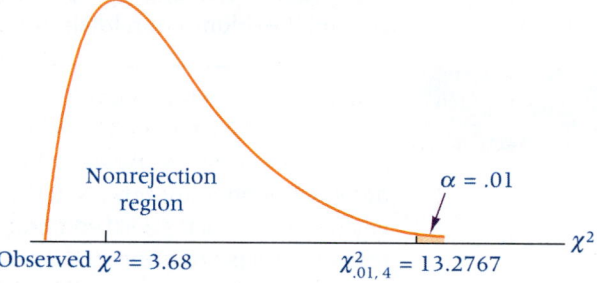

MINITAB Friedman Output:

```
Friedman Test: Rating versus Brand, Indiv.
Friedman test for Rating by Brand blocked by Indiv.
S = 3.68   DF = 4   P = 0.451

            Est      Sum of
Brand   N   Median   Ranks
1       10  2.300    26.0
2       10  4.000    37.0
3       10  3.000    31.0
4       10  3.000    31.0
5       10  1.700    25.0
Grand median = 2.800
```

17.5 PROBLEMS

17.25 Use the following data to test to determine whether there are any differences between treatment levels. Let $\alpha = .05$.

		Treatment				
		1	2	3	4	5
	1	200	214	212	215	208
	2	198	211	214	217	206
Block	3	207	206	213	216	207
	4	213	210	215	219	204
	5	211	209	210	221	205

17.26 Use the Friedman test and $\alpha = .05$ to test the following data to determine whether there is a significant difference between treatment levels.

		Treatment					
		1	**2**	**3**	**4**	**5**	**6**
	1	29	32	31	38	35	33
	2	33	35	30	42	34	31
	3	26	34	32	39	36	35
	4	30	33	35	41	37	32
Block	5	33	31	32	35	37	36
	6	31	34	33	37	36	35
	7	26	32	35	43	36	34
	8	32	29	31	38	37	35
	9	30	31	34	41	39	35

17.27 An experiment is undertaken to study the effects of four different medical treatments on the recovery time for a medical disorder. Six physicians are involved in the study. One patient with the disorder is sampled for each physician under each treatment, resulting in 24 patients in the study. Recovery time in days is the observed measurement. The data are given here. Use the Friedman test and $\alpha = .01$ to determine whether there is a significant difference in recovery times for the four different medical treatments.

		Treatment			
		1	**2**	**3**	**4**
	1	3	7	5	4
	2	4	5	6	3
Physician	3	3	6	5	4
	4	3	6	7	4
	5	2	6	7	3
	6	4	5	7	3

17.28 Does the configuration of the workweek have any impact on productivity? This question is raised by a researcher who wants to compare the traditional five-day workweek with a four-day workweek and a workweek with three 12-hour days and one 4-hour day. The researcher conducts the experiment in a factory making small electronic parts. He selects seven workers who spend a month working under each type of workweek configuration. The researcher randomly selects one day from each of the three months (three workweek configurations) for each of the seven workers. The observed measurement is the number of parts produced per day by each worker. Use the Friedman test to determine whether there is a difference in productivity by workweek configuration.

		Workweek Configuration		
		Five Days	**Four Days**	**Three-and-a-Half Days**
	1	37	33	28
	2	44	38	36
	3	35	29	31
	4	41	40	36
Worker	5	38	39	35
	6	34	27	23
	7	43	38	39
	8	39	35	32
	9	41	38	37
	10	36	30	31

17.29 Shown here is MINITAB output from a Friedman test. What is the size of the experimental design in terms of treatment levels and blocks? Discuss the outcome of the experiment in terms of any statistical conclusions.

```
FRIEDMAN TEST
Friedman test of Observations by Treatment blocked by Block
S = 2.04   DF = 3   P = 0.564

                      Est.     Sum of
Treatment    N     Median     Ranks
    1        5     3.250      15.0
    2        5     2.000      10.0
    3        5     2.750      11.0
    4        5     4.000      14.0
Grand median = 3.000
```

17.30 Shown here is MINITAB output for a Friedman test. Discuss the experimental design and the outcome of the experiment.

```
FRIEDMAN TEST
Friedman test of Observations by Treatment blocked by Block
S = 13.71   DF = 4   P = 0.009

                      Est.     Sum of
Treatment    N     Median     Ranks
    1        7     21.000     12.0
    2        7     24.000     14.0
    3        7     29.800     30.0
    4        7     27.600     26.0
    5        7     27.600     23.0
Grand median = 26.000
```

17.6 SPEARMAN'S RANK CORRELATION

In Chapter 3, the Pearson product-moment correlation coefficient, r, was presented and discussed as a technique to measure the amount or degree of association between two variables. The Pearson r requires at least interval level of measurement for the data. When only ordinal-level data or ranked data are available, **Spearman's rank correlation,** r_s, can be used to analyze the degree of association of two variables. Charles E. Spearman (1863–1945) developed this correlation coefficient.

The formula for calculating a Spearman's rank correlation is as follows:

SPEARMAN'S RANK CORRELATION (16.7)	$$r_s = 1 - \frac{6\sum d^2}{n(n^2 - 1)}$$

where

n = number of pairs being correlated
d = the difference in the ranks of each pair

The Spearman's rank correlation formula is derived from the Pearson product-moment formula and utilizes the ranks of the n pairs instead of the raw data. The value of d is the difference in the ranks of each pair.

The process begins by the assignment of ranks within each group. The difference in ranks between each group (d) is calculated by subtracting the rank of a member of one group from the rank of its associated member of the other group. The differences (d) are then squared and summed. The number of pairs in the groups is represented by n.

The interpretation of r_s values is similar to the interpretation of r values. Positive correlations indicate that high values of one variable tend to be associated with high values of the other variable, and low values of one variable tend to be associated with low values of the other variable. Correlations near +1 indicate high positive correlations, and correlations near −1 indicate high negative correlations. Negative correlations indicate that high values of one variable tend to be associated with low values of the other variable, and vice versa. Correlations near zero indicate little or no association between variables.

TABLE 17.6
Cattle and Lamb Prices from 1988 through 2000

Year	Cattle Prices ($/100 lbs.)	Lamb Prices ($/100 lbs.)
1988	66.60	69.10
1989	69.50	66.10
1990	74.60	55.50
1991	72.70	52.20
1992	71.30	59.50
1993	72.60	64.40
1994	66.70	65.60
1995	61.80	78.20
1996	58.70	82.20
1997	63.10	90.30
1998	59.60	72.30
1999	63.40	74.50
2000	68.60	79.40

TABLE 17.7
Calculations of Spearman's Rank Correlation for Cattle and Lamb Prices

Year	Rank: Cattle	Rank: Lambs	d	d^2
1988	6	7	−1	1
1989	9	6	3	9
1990	13	2	11	121
1991	12	1	11	121
1992	10	3	7	49
1993	11	4	7	49
1994	7	5	2	4
1995	3	10	−7	49
1996	1	12	−11	121
1997	4	13	−9	81
1998	2	8	−6	36
1999	5	9	−4	16
2000	8	11	−3	9
				$\Sigma d^2 = 666$

$$r_S = 1 - \frac{6\sum d^2}{n(n^2 - 1)} = 1 - \frac{6(666)}{13(13^2 - 1)} = -.830$$

Listed in Table 17.6 are the average prices in dollars per 100 pounds for cattle and lambs from 1988 through 2000. The data were published by the National Agricultural Statistics Service of the U.S. Department of Agriculture. Suppose we want to determine the strength of association of the prices between these two commodities over this 13-year period by using Spearman's rank correlation.

The cattle prices are ranked and the lamb prices are ranked. The difference in ranks is computed for each year. The differences are squared and summed, producing $\Sigma d^2 = 666$. The number of pairs, n, is 13. The value of $r_s = -.830$ indicates a strong inverse correlation between cattle and lamb prices. There appears to be a tendency toward lower lamb prices when cattle prices are higher, and vice versa. The calculations of this Spearman's rank correlation are enumerated in Table 17.7.

DEMONSTRATION PROBLEM 17.6

How strong is the correlation between crude oil prices and prices of gasoline at the pump? In an effort to estimate this association, an oil company analyst gathered the data shown over a period of several months. She lets crude oil prices be represented by the market value of a barrel of West Texas intermediate crude and gasoline prices be the estimated average price of regular unleaded gasoline in a certain city. She computes a Spearman's rank correlation for these data.

Crude Oil	Gasoline
$14.60	$1.05
10.50	1.06
12.30	1.08
15.10	1.06
18.35	1.12
22.60	1.24
28.90	1.36
31.40	1.40
26.75	1.34

Solution

Here, $n = 9$. When the analyst ranks the values within each group and computes the values of d and d^2, she obtains the following.

Crude Oil	Gasoline	d	d²
3	1	+2	4
1	2.5	−1.5	2.25
2	4	−2	4
4	2.5	+1.5	2.25
5	5	0	0
6	6	0	0
8	8	0	0
9	9	0	0
7	7	0	0
			$\Sigma d^2 = 12.5$

$$r_S = 1 - \frac{6\sum d^2}{n(n^2 - 1)} = 1 - \frac{6(12.5)}{9(9^2 - 1)} = +.90$$

A high positive correlation is computed between the price of a barrel of West Texas intermediate crude and a gallon of regular unleaded gasoline.

17.6 PROBLEMS

17.31 Compute a Spearman's rank correlation for the following variables to determine the degree of association between the two variables.

x	y
23	201
41	259
37	234
29	240
25	231
17	209
33	229
41	246
40	248
28	227
19	200

17.32 The following data are the ranks for values of the two variables, x and y. Compute a Spearman's rank correlation to determine the degree of relation between the two variables.

x	y	x	y
4	6	3	2
5	8	1	3
8	7	2	1
11	10	9	11
10	9	6	4
7	5		

17.33 Compute a Spearman's rank correlation for the following data.

x	y	x	y
99	108	80	124
67	139	57	162
82	117	49	145
46	168	91	102

17.34 Over a period of a few months, is there a strong correlation between the value of the U.S. dollar and the prime interest rate? The following data represent a sample of these quantities over a period of time. Compute a Spearman's rank correlation to determine the strength of the relationship between prime interest rates and the value of the dollar.

Dollar Value	Prime Rate	Dollar Value	Prime Rate
92	9.3	88	8.4
96	9.0	84	8.1
91	8.5	81	7.9
89	8.0	83	7.2
91	8.3		

17.35 Shown here are the percentages of consumer loans with payments that are 30 days or more overdue for both bank credit cards and home equity loans over a 14-year period according to the American Bankers Association. Compute a Spearman's rank correlation to determine the degree of association between these two variables.

Year	Bank Credit Card	Home Equity Loan
1	2.51%	2.07%
2	2.86	1.95
3	2.33	1.66
4	2.54	1.77
5	2.54	1.51
6	2.18	1.47
7	3.34	1.75
8	2.86	1.73
9	2.74	1.48
10	2.54	1.51
11	3.18	1.25
12	3.53	1.44
13	3.51	1.38
14	3.11	1.30

17.36 Shown here are the net tonnage figures for total pig iron and raw steel output in the United States as reported by the American Iron and Steel Institute over a 12-year period. Use these data to calculate a Spearman's rank correlation to determine the degree of association between production of pig iron and raw steel over this period. Was the association strong? Comment.

Year	Total Pig Iron (net tons)	Raw Steel (net tons)
1	43,952,000	81,606,000
2	48,410,000	89,151,000
3	55,745,000	99,924,000
4	55,873,000	97,943,000
5	54,750,000	98,906,000
6	48,637,000	87,896,000
7	52,224,000	92,949,000
8	53,082,000	97,877,000
9	54,426,000	100,579,000
10	56,097,000	104,930,000
11	54,485,000	105,309,478
12	54,679,000	108,561,182

17.37 Is there a correlation between the number of companies listed on the New York Stock Exchange in a given year and the number of equity issues on the American Stock Exchange? Shown here are the values for these two variables over an 8-year period. Compute a Spearman's rank correlation to determine the degree of association between these two variables.

Year	Number of Companies on NYSE	Number of Equity Issues on AMEX
1990	1,774	1,063
1991	1,885	1,055
1992	2,088	943
1993	2,361	1,005
1994	2,570	981
1995	2,675	936
1996	2,907	896
1997	3,047	893
1998	3,114	862
1999	3,025	769
2000	2,862	765

IN RESPONSE

How Is the Doughnut Business?

The Krispy Kreme researchers' dilemma is that in each of the three studies presented, the assumptions underlying the use of parametric statistics are in question or have not been met. The distribution of the data is unknown bringing into question the normal distribution assumption or the level of data is only ordinal. For each study, a nonparametric technique presented in this chapter could be appropriately used to analyze the data.

The differences in doughnut sizes according to machine can be analyzed using the Kruskal-Wallis test. The independent variable is machine with four levels of classification. The dependent variable is size of doughnut in centimeters. The Kruskal-Wallis test is not based on any assumption about population shape. The following MINITAB output is from a Kruskal-Wallis test on the machine data presented in the Decision Dilemma.

```
Kruskal-Wallis Test: Size versus Machine
Kruskal-Wallis Test on Size
 Machine   N    Median   Ave Rank     Z
    1      4    7.520     10.3      -0.43
    2      6    7.415      3.5      -3.54
    3      5    7.550     11.6       0.04
    4      7    7.700     19.0       3.70
Overall   22              11.5
H = 18.59  DF = 3   P = 0.000
H = 18.63  DF = 3   P = 0.000 (adjusted for ties)
```

Because the H statistic (MINITAB's equivalent to the K statistic) has a p-value of .000, there is a significant difference in the diameter of the doughnut according to machine at $\alpha = .001$. An examination of median values reveals that machine 4 is producing the largest doughnuts and machine 2 the smallest.

How well did the advertising work? One way to address this question is to perform a before-and-after test of the number of doughnuts sold. The nonparametric alternative to the matched-pairs t test is the Wilcoxon matched-pairs signed rank test. The analysis for these data is:

Before	After	d	Rank
301	374	−73	−9
198	187	11	4
278	332	−54	−7
205	212	−7	−3
249	243	6	2
410	478	−68	-8
360	386	−26	−6
124	141	−17	−5
253	251	2	1
190	264	−74	−10

$T_+ = 4 + 2 + 1 = 7$ $T_- = 9 + 7 + 3 + 8 + 6 + 5 + 10 = 48$

observed $T = \min(T_+, T_-) = 7$ critical T for .025 and $n = 10$ is 8

Using a two-sided test and $\alpha = .05$, the critical T value is 8. Because the observed T is 7, the decision is to reject the null hypothesis. There is a significant difference between the before and after number of donuts sold. An observation of the ranks and raw data reveals that a majority of the stores experienced an increase in sales after the advertising campaign.

Do bigger stores have greater sales? Because the data are given as ranks, it is appropriate to use Spearman's Rank Correlation to determine the extent of the correlation between these two variables. Shown here are the calculations of a Spearman's Rank correlation for this problem.

Sales	Size	d	d²
6	7	−1	1
2	2	0	0
3	6	−3	9
7	5	2	4
5	4	1	1
1	1	0	0
4	3	1	1
			$\sum d^2 = 16$

$$r_s = 1 - \frac{6\sum d^2}{n(n^2-1)} = 1 - \frac{6(16)}{7(49-1)} = .714$$

There is a relatively strong correlation (.714) between sales and size of store. It is not, however, a perfect correlation, which leaves room for other factors that may determine a store's sales such as location, attractiveness of store, population density, number of employees, management style, and others.

ETHICAL CONSIDERATIONS

The researcher should be aware of all assumptions underlying the usage of statistical techniques. Many parametric techniques have level-of-data requirements and assumptions about the distribution of the population or assumptions about the parameters. Inasmuch as these assumptions and requirements are not met, the researcher sets herself or himself up for misuse of statistical analysis. Spurious results can follow, and misguided conclusions can be reached. Nonparametric statistics can be used in many cases to avoid such pitfalls. In addition, some nonparametric statistics require at least ordinal-level data.

SUMMARY

Nonparametric statistics are a group of techniques that can be used for statistical analysis when the data are less than interval in measurement or when assumptions about population parameters, such as shape of the distribution, cannot be met. Nonparametric tests offer several advantages. Sometimes the nonparametric test is the only technique available, with no parametric alternative. Nonparametric tests can be used to analyze nominal- or ordinal-level data. Computations from nonparametric tests are usually simpler than those used with parametric tests. Probability statements obtained from most nonparametric tests are exact probabilities. Nonparametric techniques also have some disadvantages. They are wasteful of data whenever a parametric technique can be used. Nonparametric tests are not as widely available as parametric tests. For large sample sizes, the calculations of nonparametric statistics can be tedious.

Many of the parametric techniques presented in this text have corresponding nonparametric techniques. The six nonparametric statistical techniques presented here are the runs test, the Mann-Whitney U test, the Wilcoxon matched-pairs signed rank test, the Kruskal-Wallis test, the Friedman test, and Spearman's rank correlation.

The runs test is a nonparametric test of randomness. It is used to determine whether the order of sequence of observations in a sample is random. A run is a succession of observations that have a particular characteristic. If data are truly random, neither a very high number of runs nor a very small number of runs is likely to be present.

The Mann-Whitney U test is a nonparametric version of the t test of the means from two independent samples. When the assumption of normally distributed data cannot be met or if the data are only ordinal in level of measurement, the Mann-Whitney U test can be used in place of the t test. The Mann-Whitney U test—like many nonparametric tests—works with the ranks of data rather than the raw data.

The Wilcoxon matched-pairs signed rank test is used as an alternative to the t test for related measures when assumptions cannot be met or if the data are ordinal in measurement. In contrast to the Mann-Whitney U test, the Wilcoxon test is used when the data are related in some way. The Wilcoxon test is used to analyze the data by ranks of the differences of the raw data.

The Kruskal-Wallis test is a nonparametric one-way analysis of variance technique. It is particularly useful when the assumptions underlying the F test of the parametric one-way ANOVA cannot be met. The Kruskal-Wallis test is usually used when the researcher wants to determine whether three or more groups or samples are from the same or equivalent populations. This test is based on the assumption that the sample items are selected randomly and that the groups are independent. The raw data are converted to ranks and the Kruskal-Wallis test is used to analyze the ranks with the equivalent of a chi-square statistic.

The Friedman test is a nonparametric alternative to the randomized block design. Friedman's test is computed by ranking the observations within each block and then summing the ranks for each treatment level. The resulting test statistic χ^2 is approximately chi-square distributed.

If two variables contain data that are ordinal in level of measurement, a Spearman's rank correlation can be used to determine the amount of relationship or association between the variables. Spearman's rank correlation coefficient is a nonparametric alternative to Pearson's product-moment correlation coefficient. Spearman's rank correlation coefficient is interpreted in a manner similar to the Pearson r.

KEY TERMS

Friedman test

Kruskal-Wallis test

Mann-Whitney U test

nonparametric statistics

parametric statistics

runs test

Spearman's rank correlation

Wilcoxon matched-pairs
  signed rank test

FORMULAS

Large-sample runs test

$$\mu_R = \frac{2n_1 n_2}{n_1 + n_2} + 1$$

$$\sigma_R = \sqrt{\frac{2n_1 n_2 (2n_1 n_2 - n_1 - n_2)}{(n_1 + n_2)^2 (n_1 + n_2 - 1)}}$$

$$z = \frac{R - \mu_R}{\sigma_R} = \frac{R - \left(\frac{2n_1 n_2}{n_1 + n_2} + 1\right)}{\sqrt{\frac{2n_1 n_2 (2n_1 n_2 - n_1 - n_2)}{(n_1 + n_2)^2 (n_1 + n_2 - 1)}}}$$

Mann-Whitney U test

Small sample:

$$U_1 = n_1 n_2 + \frac{n_1 (n_1 + 1)}{2} - W_1$$

$$U_2 = n_1 n_2 + \frac{n_2 (n_2 + 1)}{2} - W_2$$

$$U' = n_1 \cdot n_2 - U$$

Large sample:

$$\mu_U = \frac{n_1 \cdot n_2}{2}$$

$$\sigma_U = \sqrt{\frac{n_1 \cdot n_2 (n_1 + n_2 + 1)}{12}}$$

$$z = \frac{U - \mu_U}{\sigma_U}$$

Wilcoxon matched-pair signed rank test

$$\mu_T = \frac{(n)(n+1)}{4}$$

$$\sigma_T = \sqrt{\frac{(n)(n+1)(2n+1)}{24}}$$

$$z = \frac{T - \mu_T}{\sigma_T}$$

Kruskal-Wallis test

$$K = \frac{12}{n(n+1)} \left(\sum_{j=1}^{c} \frac{T_j^2}{n_j} \right) - 3(n+1)$$

Friedman test

$$\chi_r^2 = \frac{12}{bc(c+1)} \sum_{j=1}^{c} R_j^2 - 3b(c+1)$$

Spearman's rank correlation

$$r_s = 1 - \frac{6 \sum d^2}{n(n^2 - 1)}$$

SUPPLEMENTARY PROBLEMS

CALCULATING THE STATISTICS

17.38 Use the runs test to determine whether the sample is random. Let alpha be .05.

1 1 1 1 1 2 2 2 2 2 2 2 2 1 1 1 2 2 2
2 2 2 2 2 1 2 1 2 2 1 1 1 1 2 2 2

17.39 Use the Mann-Whitney U test and $\alpha = .01$ to determine whether there is a significant difference between the populations represented by the two samples given here.

Sample 1	Sample 2
573	547
532	566
544	551
565	538
540	557
548	560
536	557
523	547

17.40 Use the Wilcoxon matched-pairs signed rank test to determine whether there is a significant difference between the related populations represented by the matched pairs given here. Assume $\alpha = .05$.

Group 1	Group 2
5.6	6.4
1.3	1.5
4.7	4.6
3.8	4.3
2.4	2.1
5.5	6.0
5.1	5.2
4.6	4.5
3.7	4.5

17.41 Use the Kruskal-Wallis test and $\alpha = .01$ to determine whether the four groups come from different populations.

Group 1	Group 2	Group 3	Group 4
6	4	3	1
11	13	7	4
8	6	7	5
10	8	5	6
13	12	10	9
7	9	8	6
10	8	5	7

17.42 Use the Friedman test to determine whether the treatment groups come from different populations. Let alpha be .05.

Block	Group 1	Group 2	Group 3	Group 4
1	16	14	15	17
2	8	6	5	9
3	19	17	13	18
4	24	26	25	21
5	13	10	9	11
6	19	11	18	13
7	21	16	14	15

17.43 Compute a Spearman's rank correlation to determine the degree of association between the two variables.

Variable 1	Variable 2
101	87
129	89
133	84
147	79
156	70
179	64
183	67
190	71

TESTING YOUR UNDERSTANDING

17.44 Commercial fish raising is a growing industry in the United States. What makes fish raised commercially grow faster and larger? Suppose that a fish industry study is conducted over the three summer months in an effort to determine whether the amount of water allotted per fish makes any difference in the speed with which the fish grow. The following data represent the inches of growth of marked catfish in fish farms for different volumes of water per fish. Use $\alpha = .01$ to test whether there is a significant difference in fish growth by volume of allotted water.

1 Gallon per Fish	5 Gallons per Fish	10 Gallons per Fish
1.1 inches	2.9 inches	3.1 inches
1.4	2.5	2.4
1.7	2.6	3.0
1.3	2.2	2.3
1.9	2.1	2.9
1.4	2.0	1.9
2.1	2.7	

17.45 Manchester Partners International claims that 60% of the banking executives who lose their job stay in banking whereas 40% leave banking. Suppose 40 people who have lost their job as a banking executive are contacted and are asked whether they are still in banking. The results follow. Test to determine whether this sample appears to be random on the basis of the sequence of those who have left banking and those who have not. Let L denote left banking and S denote stayed in banking. Let $\alpha = .05$.

S S L S L L S S S S S L S S L L L S S L
L L L S S L S S S S S S L L S L S S L S

17.46 Three machines produce the same part. Ten different machine operators work these machines. A quality team wants to determine whether the machines are producing parts that are significantly different from each other in weight. The team devises an experimental design in which a random part is selected from each of the 10 machine operators on each machine. The results follow.

Using alpha of .05, test to determine whether there is a difference in machines.

Operator	Machine 1	Machine 2	Machine 3
1	231	229	234
2	233	232	231
3	229	233	230
4	232	235	231
5	235	228	232
6	234	237	231
7	236	233	230
8	230	229	227
9	228	230	229
10	237	238	234

17.47 In some fire-fighting organizations, you must serve as a fire fighter for some period of time before you can become part of the emergency medical service arm of the organization. Does that mean EMS workers are older, on average, than traditional fire fighters? Use the data shown and $\alpha = .05$ to test whether EMS workers are significantly older than fire fighters. Assume the two groups are independent and you do no want to use a t test to analyze the data.

Fire Fighters	EMS Workers	Fire Fighters	EMS Workers
23	27	32	39
37	29	24	33
28	30	21	30
25	33	27	28
41	28		27
36	36		30

17.48 Automobile dealers usually advertise in the yellow pages of the telephone book. Sometimes they have to pay to be listed in the white pages, and some dealerships opt to save money by omitting that listing, assuming most people will use the yellow pages to find the telephone number. A two-year study is conducted with 20 car dealerships where in one year the dealer is listed in the white pages and the other year it is not. Ten of the dealerships are listed in the white pages the first year and the other 10 are listed there in the second year in an attempt to control for economic cycles. The following data represent the numbers of units sold per year. Is there a significant difference between the number of units sold when the dealership is listed in the white pages and the number sold when it is not listed? Assume all companies are continuously listed in the yellow pages, that the t test is not appropriate, and that $\alpha = .01$.

Dealer	With Listing	Without Listing
1	1,180	1,209
2	874	902
3	1,071	862
4	668	503
5	889	974
6	724	675
7	880	821
8	482	567
9	796	602
10	1,207	1,097
11	968	962
12	1,027	1,045
13	1,158	896
14	670	708
15	849	642
16	559	327
17	449	483
18	992	978
19	1,046	973
20	852	841

17.49 Suppose you want to take a random sample of GMAT test scores to determine whether there is any significant difference between the GMAT scores for the test given in March and the scores for the test given in June. You gather the following data from a sample of persons who took each test. Use the Mann-Whitney U test to determine whether there is a significant difference in the two test results. Let $\alpha = .10$.

March	June
490	300
520	420
550	580
380	540
450	560
460	470
480	410
510	500
500	480
440	520

17.50 Does impulse buying really increase sales? A market researcher is curious to find out whether the location of packages of chewing gum in a grocery store really has anything to do with volume of gum sales. As a test, gum is moved to a different location in the store every Monday for four weeks (four locations). To control the experiment for type of gum, six different brands are moved around. Sales representatives keep track of how many packs of each type of gum are sold every Monday for the four weeks. The results follow. Test to determine whether there are any differences in the volume of gum sold at the various locations. Let $\alpha = .05$.

		Location			
		1	**2**	**3**	**4**
	A	176	58	111	120
	B	156	62	98	117
Brand	C	203	89	117	105
	D	183	73	118	113
	E	147	46	101	114
	F	190	83	113	115

17.51 Does deodorant sell better in a box or without additional packaging? An experiment in a large store is designed in which, for one month, all deodorants are sold packaged in a box and, during a second month, all deodorants are removed from the box and sold without packaging. Is there a significant difference in the number of units of deodorant sold with and without the additional packaging? Let $\alpha = .05$.

Deodorant	Box	No Box
1	185	170
2	109	112
3	92	90
4	105	87
5	60	51
6	45	49
7	25	11
8	58	40
9	161	165
10	108	82
11	89	94
12	123	139
13	34	21
14	68	55
15	59	60
16	78	52

17.52 Some people drink coffee to relieve stress on the job. Is there a correlation between the number of cups of coffee consumed on the job and perceived job stress? Suppose the data shown represent the number of cups of coffee consumed per week and a stress rating for the job on a scale of 0 to 100 for nine managers in the same industry. Determine the correlation between these two variables, assuming you do not want to use the Pearson product-moment correlation coefficient.

Cups of Coffee per Week	Job Stress
25	80
41	85
16	35
0	45
11	30
28	50
34	65
18	40
5	20

17.53 A Gallup/Air Transport Association survey showed that in a recent year, 52% of all air trips were for pleasure/personal and 48% were for business. Suppose the organization randomly samples 30 air travelers and asks them to state the purpose of their trip. The results are shown here with B denoting business and P denoting personal. Test the sequence of these data to determine whether the data are random. Let $\alpha = .05$.

B P B P B B P B P P B P B P P
P B P B B P B P P B B P P B B

17.54 Does a statistics course improve a student's mathematics skills, as measured by a national test? Suppose a random sample of 13 students takes the same national mathematics examination just prior to enrolling in a statistics course and just after completing the course. Listed are the students' quantitative scores from both examinations. Use $\alpha = .01$ to determine whether the scores after the statistics course are significantly higher than the scores before.

Student	Before	After
1	430	465
2	485	475
3	520	535
4	360	410
5	440	425
6	500	505
7	425	450
8	470	480
9	515	520
10	430	430
11	450	460
12	495	500
13	540	530

17.55 Should male managers wear a tie during the workday to command respect and demonstrate professionalism? Suppose a measurement scale has been developed that generates a management professionalism score. A random sample of managers in a high-tech industry is selected for the study, some of whom wear ties at work and others of whom do not. One subordinate is selected randomly from each manager's department and asked to complete the scale on their boss's professionalism. Analyze the data taken from these independent groups to determine whether the managers with the ties received significantly higher professionalism scores. Let $\alpha = .05$.

With Tie	Without Tie
27	22
23	16
25	25
22	19
25	21
26	24
21	20
25	19
26	23
28	26
22	17

17.56 Many fast-food restaurants have soft drink dispensers with present amounts, so that when the operator merely pushes a button for the desired drink the cup is automatically filled. This method apparently saves time and seems to increase worker productivity. To test this conclusion, a researcher randomly selects 18 workers from the fast-food industry, nine from a restaurant with automatic soft drink dispensers and nine from a comparable restaurant with manual soft drink dispensers. The samples are independent. During a comparable hour, the amount of sales rung up by the worker is recorded. Assume that $\alpha = .01$ and that a t test is not appropriate. Test whether workers with automatic dispensers are significantly more productive (higher sales per hour).

Automatic Dispenser	Manual Dispenser
$153	$105
128	118
143	129
110	114
152	125
168	117
144	106
137	92
118	126

17.57 A particular metal part can be produced at different temperatures. All other variables being equal, a company would like to determine whether the strength of the metal part is significantly different for different temperatures. Given are the strengths of random samples of parts produced under different temperatures. Use $\alpha = .01$ and determine whether there is a significant difference in the strength of the part for different temperatures.

45°	55°	70°	85°
216	228	219	218
215	224	220	216
218	225	221	217
216	222	223	221
219	226	224	218
214	225		217

17.58 Is there a strong correlation between the number of miles driven by a salesperson and sales volume achieved? Data were gathered from nine salespeople who worked territories of similar size and potential. Determine the correlation coefficient for these data. Assume the data are ordinal in level of measurement.

Sales	Miles per Month
$150,000	1,500
210,000	2,100
285,000	3,200
301,000	2,400
335,000	2,200
390,000	2,500
400,000	3,300
425,000	3,100
440,000	3,600

17.59 Workers in three different but comparable companies were asked to rate the use of quality control techniques in their firms on a 50-point scale. A score of 50 represents nearly perfect implementation of quality control techniques and 0 represents no implementation. Workers are divided into three independent groups. One group worked in a company that had required all its workers to attend a 3-day seminar on quality control one year ago. A second group worked in a company in which each worker was part of a quality circle group that had been meeting at least once a month for a year. The third group of workers was employed by a company in which management had been actively involved in the quality control process for more than a year. Use $\alpha = .10$ to determine whether there is a significant difference between the three groups, as measured by the ratings.

Attended 3-Day Seminar	Quality Circles	Management Involved
9	27	16
11	38	21
17	25	18
10	40	28
22	31	29
15	19	20
6	35	31

17.60 The scores given are husband-wife scores on a marketing measure. Use the Wilcoxon matched-pairs signed rank test to determine whether the wives' scores are significantly higher on the marketing measure than the husbands'. Assume that $\alpha = .01$.

Husbands	Wives
27	35
22	29
28	30
19	20
28	27
29	31
18	22
21	19
25	29
18	28
20	21
24	22
23	33
25	38
22	34
16	31
23	36
30	31

INTERPRETING THE OUTPUT

17.61 Study the following MINITAB output. What statistical test was run? What type of design was it? What was the result of the test?

```
Friedman test of Observations by
Treatment blocked by Block

S = 11.31   DF = 3   P = 0.010
S = 12.16   DF = 3   P = 0.007 (adjusted
for ties)
                   Est.    Sum of
Treatment   N    Median   Ranks
    1       10   20.125   17.0
    2       10   25.875   33.0
    3       10   24.500   30.5
    4       10   22.500   19.5
        Grand median = 23.250
```

17.62 Examine the following MINITAB output. Discuss the statistical test, its intent, and its outcome.

```
Runs Test

K = 1.4200

The observed number of runs = 28
The expected number of runs = 25.3600
21 Observations above K 29 below
    The test is significant at 0.4387
    Cannot reject an alpha = 0.05
```

17.63 Study the following MINITAB output. What statistical test was being computed by MINITAB? What are the results of this analysis?

```
Mann-Whitney Confidence Interval and
Test

C1   N = 16   Median = 37.000
C2   N = 16   Median = 46.500
Point estimate for ETA1-ETA2 is -8.000
95.2 Percent C.I. For ETA1-ETA2 is
(-13.999, -2.997)
W = 191.5
Test of ETA1 = ETA2 vs. ETA1~=ETA2 is
significant at 0.0067
The test is significant at 0.0066
(adjusted for ties)
```

17.64 Study the following MINITAB output. What type of statistical test was done? What were the hypotheses and what was the outcome? Discuss.

```
Kruskal-Wallis test on Observations

Group    N   Median   Ave Rank    Z
  1      5   35.00     14.8      0.82
  2      6   25.50      4.2     -3.33
  3      7   35.00     15.0      1.11
  4      6   35.00     16.0      1.40
Overall 24            12.5

H = 11.21   DF = 3   P5 0.011
H = 11.28   DF = 3   P5 0.010 (adjusted
for ties)
```

ANALYZING THE DATABASES

see www.wiley.com/college/black

1. Compute a Spearman's rank correlation between New Capital Expenditures and End-of-Year Inventories in the manufacturing database. Is the amount spent annually on New Capital Expenditures related to the End-of-Year Inventories? Are these two variables highly correlated? Explain.

2. Use a Kruskal-Wallis test to determine whether there is a significant difference between the four levels of Value of Industry Shipments on Number of Employees for the manufacturing database. Discuss the results.

3. Use a Mann-Whitney U test to determine whether there is a significant difference between hospitals that are general hospitals and those that are Psychiatric (Service variable) on Personnel for the hospital database. Discuss the results.

4. Use the stock market database and the Kruskal-Wallis test to determine whether there is a significant difference in Stock Volume by Time of the Month.

CASE: SCHWINN

In 1895, Ignaz Schwinn and his partner, Adolph Arnold, incorporated the Arnold, Schwinn & Company in Chicago to produce bicycles. In the early years with bicycle products such as the "Roadster," a single speed bike that weighed 19 pounds, Schwinn products appealed to people of all ages as a means of transportation. By 1900, bicycles could go as fast as 60 miles per hour. Because of the advent of the auto in 1909, the use of bicycles as a means of transportation in the United States waned. In that same year, Schwinn developed manufacturing advances that allowed bicycles to be made more cheaply and sturdily. These advances opened a new market to the company as they manufactured and sold bicycles for children for the first time. Meanwhile, Ignaz Schwinn bought out Arnold to become the sole owner of the company. Over the next 20 years, Schwinn bought out two motorcycle companies and developed mudguards as its major technological achievement. In the 1930s, Schwinn developed a series of quality, appearance, and technological breakthroughs including the balloon tire, which some say was the biggest innovation in mountain bike technology; the forewheel brake; the cantilever frame; and the spring fork. In 1946, built-in kickstands were added to their bikes. In the 1950s, Schwinn began an authorized dealer network and expanded its parts and accessory programs.

In the 1960s, Schwinn expanded into the fitness arena with in-home workout machines. In 1967, the company became the Schwinn Bicycle Company. The company introduced the airdyne stationary bike in the late 1970s. In 1993, the company filed for bankruptcy; and in 1994, it was moved from Chicago to Boulder, Colorado, to be nearer the mountain bike scene. In the next several years, Schwinn's mountain bike products won accolades and awards. In 2001, Pacific Cycle purchased Schwinn; but Schwinn products continue to enjoy a lofty place in bicycle manufacturing circles as a premier producer of bicycles.

Discussion

1. What is the age of the target market for Schwinn bikes? One theory is that in locales where mountain bikes are more popular, the mean age of their customers is older than in locales where relatively little mountain biking is done. In an attempt to test this theory, a random sample of Colorado Springs customers is taken along with a random sample of customers in St. Louis. The ages for these customers are given here. The customer is defined as "the person for whom the bike is primarily purchased." The shape of the population distribution of bicycle customer ages is unknown. Analyze the data and discuss the implications for Schwinn manufacturing and sales.

Colorado Springs	St. Louis
29	11
38	14
31	15
17	12
36	14
28	25
44	14
9	11
32	8
23	
35	

2. Suppose for a particular model of bike, the specified weight of a handle bar is 200 grams and Schwinn uses three different suppliers of handle bars. Suppose Schwinn conducts a quality control study in which handle bars are randomly selected from each supplier and weighed. The results (in grams) are shown next. It is uncertain whether handle bar weight is normally distributed in the population. Analyze the data and discuss what the business implications are to Schwinn.

Supplier 1	Supplier 2	Supplier 3
200.76	197.38	192.63
202.63	207.24	199.68
198.03	201.56	203.07
201.24	194.53	195.18
202.88	197.21	189.11
194.62	198.94	
203.58		
205.41		

3. Quality technicians at Schwinn's manufacturing plant examine their finished products for paint flaws. Paint inspections are done on a production run of 75 bicycles. The inspection data are coded and the data analyzed using MINITAB. If a bicycle's paint job contained no flaws, a 0 is recorded; and if it contained at least one flaw, the code used is a 1. Inspectors want to determine whether the flawed bikes occur in a random fashion or in a nonrandom pattern. Study the MINITAB output. Determine whether the flaws occur randomly. Report on the proportion of flawed bikes and discuss the implications of these results to Schwinn's production management.

```
Runs Test: Paint Flaw
Paint Flaw
K = 0.2533
The observed number of runs = 29
The expected number of runs = 29.3733
19 Observations above K    56 below
The test is significant at 0.9083
Cannot reject at alpha = 0.05
```

Source: Adapted from Schwinn, available at http://www.schwinnbike.com/heritage.

USING THE COMPUTER

MINITAB

Five of the nonparametric statistics presented in this chapter can be accessed on MINITAB Windows by selecting **Stat** on the menu bar.

For the runs test, the Mann-Whitney U test, the Wilcoxon matched-pairs signed rank test, Kruskal-Wallis test, and Friedman test, select **Nonparametrics** from the **Stat** pull-down menu.

Runs Test

From the **Nonparametrics** menu, select **Runs Test.** Supply the column(s) that contain the data in **Variables.** The test defaults to "above and below the mean"; that is, it will use the mean of the numbers to determine when the runs stop. If you want to supply your own value, click the other circle and supply the value. The output in the sessions window will include K, which is the average of the values (usually used as the divider of runs), the observed number of runs, the expected number of runs, the p-value, and decision information about rejecting the null hypothesis.

Mann-Whitney U Test

From the **Nonparametrics** menu, select **Mann-Whitney.** You will be asked for the column location of the first sample, the column location of the second sample, the confidence level, and the form of the alternative hypothesis (choose from: not equal, less than, greater than). The output will include sample sizes, medians, a confidence interval, W, a p-value, and decision information about rejecting the null hypothesis.

Wilcoxin Matched-Pairs Signed Rank Test

There is no Wilcoxon matched-pairs signed rank test as such in MINITAB. Instead, to manipulate MINITAB's one-sample Wilcoxon to perform the test, you must either enter the two related samples in columns and use the calculator under **Calc** on the main menu bar to subtract the two columns, thereby creating a third column, or enter the differences in a column at the start. From the **Nonparametrics** menu, select **1-sample Wilcoxon.** Under variables, list the column where the differences are located. If you are testing a 0.0 median, the **1-Sample Wilcoxon** will default to the zero value. To test any other value of the median, list the value under Test Median. The three options for hypothesis testing under Alternative are not equal, less than, or greater than. The output includes a statement of the hypotheses, the number of differences, the Wilcoxon statistic, and the p-value.

Kruskal-Wallis Test

The Kruskal-Wallis test is set up so that all observations from all treatment levels should be located in one column. In a second column, stack the treatment levels to match the observations. From the **Nonparametrics** menu, select **Kruskal-Wallis.** You will be asked for the location of the **Response** variable. Give the column location of the observations. Next you will be asked for the **Factor** location. Give the column location with the treatment levels in it. The output includes treatment ns, treatment means, the average rank for a treatment, an H value, degrees of freedom, and a p-value.

Friedman Test

As in the Kruskal-Wallis test, for the Friedman test MINITAB expects the observations to be one column, the treatment levels to be in a second column, and the blocks to be in a third column. From the **Nonparametrics** menu, select **Friedman.** You will be asked the location of the observations as **Response,** the location of the treatment levels as **Treatment,** and the location of the blocks as **Blocks.** You also have the option of storing the residuals and storing the fits by clicking on those boxes. The output includes an S value, the degrees of freedom, and the p-value. It provides information about the treatment levels including the value of n, estimated median, and the sum of ranks. The grand median is also part of the output.

Statistical Quality Control

LEARNING OBJECTIVES

This chapter presents basic concepts in quality control, with a particular emphasis on statistical quality control techniques, thereby enabling you to:

1. Understand the concepts of quality, quality control, and total quality management.

2. Understand the importance of statistical quality control in total quality management.

3. Learn about process analysis and some process analysis tools, including Pareto charts, fishbone diagrams, and control charts.

4. Learn how to construct $\bar{x}$ charts, R charts, p charts, and c charts.

5. Understand the theory and application of acceptance sampling.

Quality Control at Xerox

Xerox was the pioneer company in photocopying. In fact, the first photocopy ever made was from a Xerox machine, and over the years Xerox has been a successful American company. In particular, the decade of the 1960s has been referred to as the "golden years" for Xerox. During that time, the company introduced the 9-14 copier, which has been called the most successful product introduction in U.S. history, and Xerox was one of America's most highly regarded companies.

The years between the 1960s and the 1990s were not all easy years. Beginning in 1976, the company was, as one executive said, "attacked by the Japanese." Japanese companies began introducing lines of low-priced copiers. Included in this cadre were name brands such as Canon, Mita, Toshiba, Sanyo, and Sharp. Gradually, these Japanese companies took market share away from Xerox. By 1982, Xerox had lost close to 40 points of market share. Profits fell from $1.149 billion in 1981 to $0.6 billion in 1982. This situation caused great concern within the corporation.

What happened? After self-examination, Xerox managers found that the company was a victim of its own success. Employees felt good about themselves, and they were proud of their product and company name. They were also proud of their reputation. However, in this self-focus, they had lost sight of their customers' needs. In addition, by the late 1970s, it became clear that Japanese companies could sell a copier for what it cost Xerox to build one.

In response to this dilemma, Xerox launched its Leadership Through Quality campaign in 1983. Leadership Through Quality is credited for turning Xerox around and possibly for saving it from disaster. Using this strategy, Xerox changed its company culture by educating and empowering its employees and by giving them the tools and techniques to produce quality products. The strategy worked. In the decade from 1983 to 1993, Xerox regained the market share it had lost to the Japanese and received more than 20 awards worldwide for quality achievements. The price of Xerox shares rose from a low of $29 in 1990 to a high of $145 in 1995.

Xerox has chosen to not rest on its laurels. One of the things that got Xerox into trouble in the late 1970s and early 1980s was being complacent about the company's achievements. Company managers want to make certain that it will not happen again. Late in 1994, then Xerox chairman and CEO, Paul Allaire, outlined a strategy for Xerox 2000, a quality initiative to update and improve Leadership Through Quality and position the company for continuous business success as a world leader in its field through the year 2000.

In 1975, the return on assets for Xerox was at 25%. By 1984, the company hit what officials called a "crisis of survival" when the return on assets dropped to about 7%. The Leadership Through Quality effort paid off as return on assets climbed back to about 14% in 1990. However, return on assets did not change for the next three years. Some company officials referred to this time as a "crisis of opportunity." What would it take to grow and expand its opportunities? A company self-analysis revealed that several areas still needed improvement. For example, greater speed was needed not only in producing products, but also in making decisions, implementing them, and evaluating them. Further, the company needed to make more efficient and effective use of its available quality tools.

The Xerox 2000 concept addressed these and other quality issues. A plan was implemented for linking quality to productivity improvement. An effort was made to broaden the Leadership Through Quality program from a strategic approach to a method by which total quality management could be integrated into business planning and daily operations. A Xerox Management Model was developed and more than 35 nonfinancial measurements for continuous improvement were identified as useful tools to measure and track quality with seven different business results. Some of the measurements included customer satisfaction and loyalty, process measures, employee involvement, people development, and vision and strategic direction. Some of the business results were market share, return on assets, productivity, and employee motivation and satisfaction. Today, Xerox employs 79,000 worldwide, earns $16 billion in revenue per year, and commits $1 billion per year to research and development. As Xerox enters the twenty-first century, the company follows a course of continuous improvement of their total quality management effort.

Managerial and Statistical Questions:

1. Xerox uses tens of thousands of processes: manufacturing processes, order processing, hiring and firing processes, marketing processes, distribution processes, quality evaluation processes, and many more. How can Xerox begin to study these processes in order to improve them?

2. Whenever problems arise, Xerox has quality teams and participating employees involved in trying to solve them. How do these problem solvers go about sorting through the myriad of possible causes for problems? How could problem causes be displayed to aid in decision making?

3. Xerox's massive quality undertaking in the 1980s resulted in the implementation of statistical process control. As samples of products are tested at various stages in the production process, what mechanism is available for monitoring the measurements and depicting them in such a way as to alert management to possible situations in which the process is out of control?

4. Xerox has hundreds of suppliers. Mass inspection of all raw materials is not feasible. How does Xerox go about deciding whether to accept a batch of supplies?

Source: Adapted from Richard J. Leo, "Xerox 2000: From Survival to Opportunity," *Quality Progress*, March 1996, vol. 29, no. 3, pp. 65–71. Also, Xerox Fact Sheet, available at http://www.xerox.com/go/xrx/template /009.jsp?view=About%20Xerox&Xcntry=USA&Xlang=en_US.

What is *quality?* Quality means different things to different people. If you asked commuters whether their automobiles have quality, the response would vary according to each individual's perspective. One person's view of a quality automobile is one that goes 75,000 miles without needing any major repair work. Other people perceive automobile quality as comfortable seats and extra electronic gadgetry. These people look for "bells and whistles" along with form-fitting, cushy seats in a quality car. Still other automobile consumers define automobile quality as the presence of numerous safety features.

In this chapter, we examine various definitions of quality and discuss some of the main concepts of quality and quality control. We explore some techniques for analyzing processes. In addition, we learn how to construct and interpret control charts. Finally, we examine the concept of acceptance sampling.

18.1 INTRODUCTION TO QUALITY CONTROL

There are almost as many definitions of quality as there are people and products. Assume, however, that in the marketplace buyer and seller agree on the specifications of a product. One definition of **quality,** then, is *when a product delivers what is stipulated for it in its specifications.*

From this point of view, quality is present when the producer delivers what has been specified in the product description, as agreed upon by both buyer and seller.

Most automobile purchasers agree that a Lexus or a Cadillac has quality. If a buyer agrees to purchase a Saturn with few extra accessories and if the Saturn is delivered to the buyer in the condition specified, the Saturn is a quality car even if it is not a Lexus or a Cadillac.

Other definitions of quality are also used. Philip B. Crosby, author of *Quality Is Free* and *Quality Without Tears* and a well-known expert on quality, has said that "quality is conformance to requirements."[*] The product requirements must be met by the producer to assure quality. This notion of quality is similar to the one based on specifications. Armand V. Feigenbaum, a well-known quality authority, says in his book *Total Quality Control* that "quality is a customer determination" as opposed to management's determination or a designer's determination.[†] He states that this determination is based on the customer's experience with the product or service and that it is always a moving target.

Another authority on quality control is David A. Garvin, author of *Managing Quality*. Garvin advocates defining quality along at least five dimensions: transcendent, product, user, manufacturing, and value.[‡] **Transcendent quality** *implies that a product has an "innate excellence."* It has *"uncompromising standards and high achievement."* Garvin says that this definition offers little practical guidance to business people. **Product quality** *is measurable in the product.* Consumers perceive differences in products, *and quality products have more attributes.* For example, a baseball glove with more stitching has more quality. A personal computer with more memory has more quality. Tires with more tread have more quality.

User quality means that the *quality of a product is determined by the consumer.* This dimension of quality is based on customer requirements and product specifications. **Manufacturing quality** derives mainly from engineering and manufacturing practices. Once the specifications are determined, *quality is measured by the manufacturer's ability to target the requirements consistently with little variability.* The fifth dimension of quality according to Garvin is **value quality,** which *has to do with price and costs*—that is, did the customer get his or her money's worth?

What Is Quality Control?

How does a company know whether it is producing a quality product? One way is to practice quality control. **Quality control** (sometimes referred to as quality assurance) is *the collection of strategies, techniques, and actions taken by an organization to assure itself that it is producing a quality product.*

The process begins at the product planning and design phase, where attributes of the product are determined and specified. Each attribute of the product is a potential contributor to overall product quality. For quality control to be possible, measurable attributes and specifications must be established against which the actual attributes of the product can be compared.

Quality control can be undertaken in two distinct ways: after-process control and in-process control. **After-process quality control** involves *inspecting the attributes of a finished product to determine whether the product is acceptable, is in need of rework, or is to be rejected and scrapped.* The after-process quality control method was the leading quality control technique for U.S. manufacturers for several decades until the 1980s. The after-process method emphasizes weeding out defective products before they reach the consumer. The problem with this method is that it does not generate information that can correct in-process problems or raw materials problems nor does it generate much information about how to improve quality. Two main outcomes of the after-process methodology are (1) reporting the number of defects produced during a specific period of time and (2) screening defective products from consumers. Because U.S. companies dominated world markets in many areas for several decades during and after World War II, their managers had little interest in changing from the after-process method.

---

[*]Philip B. Crosby, *Quality Without Tears* (New York: McGraw-Hill, 1984).
[†]Armand V. Feigenbaum, *Total Quality Control*, 3rd ed. (New York: McGraw-Hill, 1991).
[‡]David A. Garvin, *Managing Quality* (New York: The Free Press, 1988).

However, as Japan, other Asian nations, and Western European countries began to compete strongly with the United States in the world market in the late 1970s and 1980s, U.S. companies began to reexamine quality control methods. As a result, many U.S. companies, following the example of Japanese and European manufacturers, developed quality control programs based on in-process control. **In-process quality control** *techniques measure product attributes at various intervals throughout the manufacturing process in an effort to pinpoint problem areas.* This information enables quality control personnel in conjunction with production personnel to make corrections in operations as products are being made. This intervention in turn opens the door to opportunities for improving the process and the product.

Total Quality Management

W. Edwards Deming, who has been referred to as the "father of the quality movement," advocated that the achievement of quality is an organic phenomenon that begins with top managers' commitment and extends all the way to suppliers on one side and consumers on the other. Deming believed that quality control is a long-term total company effort. The effort called for by Deming is **total quality management (TQM).** Total quality management involves all members of the organization—from the CEO to the line worker—in improving quality. In addition, the goals and objectives of the organization come under the purview of quality control and can be measured in quality terms. Suppliers, raw materials, worker training, and opportunity for workers to make improvements all are part of total quality management. The antithesis of total quality management is when a company gives a quality control department total responsibility for improving product quality.

Deming presented a cause-and-effect explanation of the impact of total quality management on a company. This idea has become known as the Deming chain reaction.* The chain reaction begins with improving quality. Improving quality will decrease costs because of less reworking, fewer mistakes, fewer delays and snags, and better use of machine time and materials. From the reduced costs comes an improvement in productivity because

$$\text{Productivity} = \frac{\text{Output}}{\text{Input}}$$

A reduction of costs generates more output for less input and, hence, increases productivity. As productivity improves, a company is more able to capture the market with better quality and lower prices. This capability enables a company to stay in business and provide more jobs.

Deming listed 14 points which, if followed, can lead to improved total quality management.†

1. Create constancy of purpose for improvement of product and service.
2. Adopt the new philosophy.
3. Cease dependence on mass inspection.
4. End the practice of awarding business on price tag alone.
5. Improve constantly and forever the system of production and service.
6. Institute training.
7. Institute leadership.
8. Drive out fear.
9. Break down barriers between staff areas.
10. Eliminate slogans.
11. Eliminate numerical quotas.
12. Remove barriers to pride of workmanship.
13. Institute a vigorous program of education and retraining.
14. Take action to accomplish the transformation.

---

*W. Edwards Deming, *Out of the Crisis* (Cambridge, MA: Massachusetts Institute of Technology Center for Advanced Engineering Study, 1986).
†Mary Walton, *The Deming Management Method* (New York: Perigee Books, 1986).

The first point indicates the need to seek constant improvement in process, innovation, design, and technique. The second point suggests that to truly make changes, a new, positive point of view must be taken; in other words, the viewpoint that poor quality is acceptable must be changed. The third point is a call for change from after-process inspection to in-process inspection. Deming pointed out that after-process inspection has nothing to do with improving the product or the service. The fourth point indicates that a company should be careful in awarding contracts to suppliers and vendors. Purchasers should look more for quality and reliability in a supplier than for just low price. Deming called for long-term supplier relationships in which the company and supplier agree on quality standards.

Point 5 conveys the message that quality is not a one-time activity. Management and labor should be constantly on the lookout for ways to improve the product. Institute training, the sixth point, implies that training is an essential element in total quality management. Workers need to learn how to do their jobs correctly and learn techniques that will result in higher quality. Point 7, institute leadership, is a call for a new management based on showing, doing, and supporting rather than ordering and punishing. The eighth point results in establishing a "safe" work environment, where workers feel free to share ideas and make suggestions without the threat of punitive measures. Point 9, breaking down barriers, emphasizes reducing competition and conflicts between departments and groups. It is a call for more of a team approach—the notion that "we're all in this together."

Deming did not believe that slogans help affect quality products, as stated in point 10. Quality control is not a movement of slogans. Point 11 indicates that quotas do not help companies make quality products. In fact, pressure to make quotas can result in inefficiencies, errors, and lack of quality. Point 12 says that managers must find ways to make it easier for workers to produce quality products; faulty equipment and poor-quality supplies do not allow workers to take pride in what is produced. Point 13 calls for total reeducation and training within a company about new methods and how to more effectively do one's job. Point 14 implies that rhetoric is not the answer; a call for action is necessary in order to institute change and promote higher quality.

Some Important Quality Concepts

Of the several widely used techniques in quality control, five in particular warrant discussion: benchmarking, just-in-time inventory systems, reengineering, Six Sigma, and team building.

Benchmarking

One practice used by U.S. companies to improve quality is benchmarking. **Benchmarking** is *a method in which a company attempts to develop and establish total quality management from product to process by examining and emulating the "best practices" and techniques used in its industry.* The ultimate objective of benchmarking is to use a positive, proactive process to make changes that will affect superior performance. The process of benchmarking involves studying competitors and learning from the best in the industry.

One of the American pioneers in what is called "competitive benchmarking" was Xerox. Xerox was struggling to hold on to its market share against foreign competition. At one point, other companies could sell a machine for what it cost Xerox to make a machine. Xerox set out to find out why. The company instituted a benchmarking process in which the internal workings and features of competing machines were studied in depth. Xerox attempted to emulate and learn from the best of these features in developing its own products. In time, benchmarking was so successful within the company that top managers included benchmarking as a major corporate effort.*

Just-in-Time Inventory Systems

Another technique used to improve quality control is the just-in-time system for inventory, which focuses on raw materials, subparts, and suppliers. Ideally, a **just-in-time inventory system** means that *no extra raw materials or inventory of parts for production are stored.*

---

*Robert C. Camp, *Benchmarking* (Milwaukee, WI: Quality Press, ASQC, 1989).

Necessary supplies and parts needed for production arrive "just in time." The advantage of this system is that holding costs, personnel, and space needed to manage inventory are reduced. Even within the production process, as subparts are assembled and merged, the just-in-time philosophy can be applied to smooth the process and eliminate bottlenecks.

A production facility is unlikely to become 100% just-in-time. One of the residual effects of installing a just-in-time system throughout the production process is that, as the inventory "fat" is trimmed from the production process, the pressure on the system to produce often discloses problems previously undetected. For example, one subpart being made on two machines may not be produced in enough quantity to supply the next step. Installation of the just-in-time system shows that this station is a bottleneck. The company might choose to add another machine to produce more subparts, change the production schedule, or develop another strategy. As the bottleneck is loosened and the problem is corrected, other areas of weakness may emerge. Thus, the residual effect of a just-in-time inventory system can be the opportunity for production managers to work their way methodically through a maze of previously unidentified problems that would not normally be recognized.

A just-in-time inventory system typically changes the relationship between supplier and producer. Most companies using this system have fewer suppliers than they did before installing the system. The tendency is for manufacturers to give suppliers longer contracts under the just-in-time system. However, the suppliers are expected to produce raw materials and subparts to a specified quality and to deliver the goods as near to just in time as possible. Just-in-time suppliers may even build production or warehouse facilities next to the producer's. In the just-in-time system, the suppliers become part of total quality management.

Reengineering

A more radical approach to improving quality is reengineering. Whereas total quality approaches like Deming's 14 points call for continuous improvement, **reengineering** is *the complete redesigning of the core business process in a company.* It involves innovation and is often a complete departure from the company's usual way of doing business.

Reengineering is not a fine-tuning of the present process nor is it mere downsizing of a company. Reengineering starts with a blank sheet of paper and an idea about where the company would like to be in the future. Without considering the present limitations or constraints of the company, the reengineering process works backward from where the company wants to be in the future and then attempts to determine what it would take to get there. From this information, the company cuts or adds, reshapes, or redesigns itself to achieve the new goal. In other words, the reengineering approach involves determining what the company would be like if it could start from scratch and then redesigning the process to make it work that way.

Reengineering affects almost every functional area of the company, including information systems, financial reporting systems, the manufacturing environment, suppliers, shipping, and maintenance. Reengineering is usually painful and difficult for a company. Companies that have been most successful in implementing reengineering are those that faced big shifts in the nature of competition and that required major changes to stay in business.

Some recommendations to consider in implementing reengineering in a company are to (1) get the strategy straight first, (2) lead from the top, (3) create a sense of urgency, (4) design from the outside in, (5) manage the firm's consultant, and (6) combine top-down and bottom-up initiatives. Getting the strategy straight is crucial because the strategy drives the changes. The company must determine what business it wants to be in and how to make money in it. The company's strategy determines its operations.

Reengineering involves cross-functional operation. It must be led by top managers who have the authority and the leadership capacity to oversee, direct, and facilitate the implementation of tough decisions. Because internal political pressure or the satisfaction of making small gains can bog down the process, a sense of urgency must be created for reengineering to be successful and to sustain the energy needed to complete the changes.

The focus of reengineering is outside the company; the process begins with the customer. Current operations may have some merit, but time is spent determining the need of the marketplace and how to meet that need.

Although the leadership for reengineering must come from the top, employees must buy into the changes through participation. Often, line workers have useful ideas and suggestions that can make the company more profitable and productive. Hence, both top-down and bottom-up participation in the process is required.*

Six Sigma

Currently, a popular approach to total quality management is Six Sigma. **Six Sigma** is both a methodology and a measurement. Originally developed in the electronics industry, Six Sigma measures the capability of a process to perform defect-free work, where a defect is defined as anything that results in customer dissatisfaction. Six Sigma is derived from a previous quality scheme in which a process was considered to be producing quality results if $\pm 3\sigma$ or 99.74% of the products or attributes were within specification. (Note: The standard normal distribution table, Table A.5, produces an area of .4987 for a z score of 3. Doubling that and converting to a percentage yields 99.74%, which is the portion of a normal distribution that falls within $\mu \pm 3\sigma$.) Six Sigma methodology requires that $\pm 6\sigma$ of the product be within specification. The goal of Six Sigma methodology is to have 99.99966% of the product or attributes be within specification, or no more than .00034% = .0000034 out of specification. This means that no more than 3.4 of the product or attributes per million can be defective. Essentially, it calls for the process to approach a defect-free status.

Why Six Sigma? Several reasons highlight the importance of adoption of a Six Sigma philosophy. First, in some industries the three sigma philosophy is simply unacceptable. For example, the three sigma goal of having 99.74% of the product or attribute be in specification in the prescription drug industry implies that it is acceptable to have .26% incorrectly filled prescriptions, or 2,600 out of every million prescriptions filled. In the airline industry, the three sigma goal implies that it is acceptable to have 2,600 unsatisfactory landings by commercial aircraft out of every million landings. In contrast, a Six Sigma approach would require that there be no more than 3.4 incorrectly filled prescriptions or 3.4 unsatisfactory landings per million, with a goal of approaching zero.

A second reason for adopting a Six Sigma approach is that it forces companies that adopt it to work much harder and more quickly to discover and reduce sources of variation in processes. It "raises the bar" of the quality goals of a firm, causing the company to place even more emphasis on continuous quality improvement. A third reason is that Six Sigma dedication to quality may be required to attain world-class status and be a top competitor in the international market.

The first step in implementing Six Sigma is to determine the number of opportunities or chances to perform an operation successfully for each component. More complex parts or products contain larger opportunity counts. The occurrence of defects is characterized by the defects per unit (dpu). The dpu is then normalized by the total number of opportunities yielding defects per million opportunities, which is then related to the level of sigma using the normal distribution.†

Implementing a Six Sigma approach to quality requires a company to commit additional resources to quality improvement. Six Sigma is based on measurement and is data driven. Time and money must be allocated to data gathering, storage, and analysis. Another Six Sigma resource commitment is an in-house person who receives special training in Six Sigma and is referred to as a "black belt." Six Sigma black belts are in-company

---

*This section adapted from Thomas A. Stewart, "Reengineering: The Hot New Managing Tool," *Fortune*, 23 August 1993, pp. 40–48. Copyright © 1993 Time Inc. All rights reserved.

†This section adapted from "Six-Sigma Analysis: A Route to Quality and Affordability," University of Delaware Center for Composite Materials, available at http://www.ccm.udel.edu/reports-pubs/tech-briefs/110.html "Program Background," American Society of Quality (ASQ), available at http://www.asq.org ; Peter Pande, Robert P. Neuman and Roland R. Cavanaugh, *The Six Sigma Way* (New York: McGraw-Hill, 2000).

experts who teach and implement Six Sigma ideas and tools within the company. Originating from various areas within the firm, black belts serve as change agents who lead improvement projects and interact with management on improvement plans.

Team Building

In years past, the traditional business approach to decision making in the United States allowed managers to decide what was best for the company and act upon that decision. In the past decade or so, the U.S. business culture underwent major changes as total quality management was adopted. One aspect of total quality management is team building. **Team building** occurs *when a group of employees are organized as an entity to undertake management tasks and perform other functions such as organizing, developing, and overseeing projects.*

The result of team building is that more workers take over managerial responsibilities. Fewer lines of demarcation separate workers from managers and union from nonunion. Workers are invited to work on a par with managers to remove obstacles that prevent a company from delivering a quality product. The old "us and them" point of view is being replaced by a cooperative relationship between managers and workers in reaching common goals under team building.

People on teams often represent different business functions such as design, production, marketing, and finance. Working together, team members are able to incorporate input from a variety of viewpoints; their decisions result in more comprehensive thinking, more effective time utilization, and fewer instances of mistaken direction due to failure to consider all factors. For example, teams are organized to design, develop, and produce new products; to oversee the building of new plants; and to reorganize and restructure office layouts for more efficient operation, among other things.

One particular type of team that was introduced to U.S. companies by the Japanese is the quality circle. A **quality circle** is *a small group of workers,* usually from the same department or work area, and their supervisor, *who meet regularly to consider quality issues.* The size of the group ranges from 4 to 15 members, and they meet as often as once a week.* The meetings are usually on company time and members of the circle are compensated. The supervisor may be the leader of the circle, but the members of the group determine the agenda and reach their own conclusions.

Because a great amount of brainstorming occurs in quality circles, employees need to feel that they will not be penalized for ideas shared. Each person is to be respected as an integral, important part of the team. Because employees may hold negative attitudes toward such groups—remembering similar meetings in the past—a few meetings may be necessary before a quality circle becomes effective. Eventually, if the participants realize that the quality circle is a serious, useful endeavor, they may begin to offer information about specific items in the production process that need attention. It is essential, however, that top managers support such efforts and provide the impetus for these groups. The quality circle movement has failed more often than not because of lack of support from top managers.

Quality circles and other teams tend to elevate workers from a level of "just installing their part" to a level of "analyst." The team concept has potential for generating communication and cooperation in a company. The concepts of team building and quality circles have been introduced in various types of businesses, ranging from hospitals to chemical production facilities.

18.2 PROCESS ANALYSIS

Much of what transpires in the business world involves processes. A **process** is *"a series of actions, changes, or functions that bring about a result."* Processes usually involve the manufacturing, production, assembling, or development of some output from a given input. Generally, in a meaningful system, value is added to the input as part of the process. In the area of production, processes are often the main focus of decision makers. Production

---

*The American Heritage Dictionary of the English Language, 3d ed. (Boston: Houghton Mifflin, 1992).

Six Sigma Focus at GE

GE's focus on quality began late in the 1980s with a movement called Work-Out® which reduced company bureaucracy, opened their culture to new ideas, and helped create a learning environment that eventually led to Six Sigma. In the mid-1990s, General Electric established a goal of attaining Six Sigma quality by the year 2000. By 1999, GE had already invested more than $1 billion in their quality effort. Today at General Electric, Six Sigma defines the way they do business. They continue to strive for greater quality by following a Six Sigma philosophy. In their push for Six Sigma status, they engaged more than 5,000 employees in Six Sigma methodology in more than 25,000 completed projects.

GE's Six Sigma approach is data-driven and customer-focused. All of their employees are trained in the techniques, strategy, and statistical tools of Six Sigma. The focus of Six Sigma at GE is on reducing process variation and process capability. The benefits delivered by this process include reduced cycle times, accelerated product designs, consistent efforts to eliminate variation, and increased probabilities of meeting customer requirements. The adoption of Six Sigma resulted in a culture in which quality thinking is embedded at every level in every operation throughout the company.

Why has GE pursued a Six Sigma philosophy? GE discovered that their customers were demanding better quality, and their employees thought they could be doing a better job. Their peer competitors such as Motorola, Texas Instruments, and Allied Signal had proven that following a disciplined, rigorous approach to quality significantly improved customer service and resulted in greater productivity. Internal process defects had been limiting GE's ability to achieve growth objectives. With increased globalization and information access, GE believes that products and services continually change the way their customers do business, and the highly competitive worldwide marketplace leaves no room for error in designing, producing, and delivering products. Six Sigma provides the philosophy and approach needed to meet these goals.

The GE people point out the difference between three sigma and Six Sigma: With three sigma, 1.5 misspelled words per page in book in a small library; with Six Sigma there is 1 misspelled word in all the books in a small library. In a post office with three sigma, there are 20,000 lost articles of mail per hour; with Six Sigma, there are only 7 per hour. They also claim that Six Sigma can improve your golf score. If you played 100 rounds of golf per year, under a two sigma philosophy you would miss six putts per round. Under three sigma, you would miss one putt per round. Under Six Sigma, you would miss only one putt every 163 years!

Source: Adapted from General Electric, "Quality: GE's Evolution Towards Quality, What Is Six Sigma?" and "Achieving Quality for the Customer," available at http:///www.ge.com/commitment/quality.htm; "Tip 'Six Sigma' Quality," accessed (formerly available) at http://trailers.ge.com/getip/news/june.html, and "What We Do," accessed (formerly available) at http://www.crd.ge.com/whatwedo/sixsigma.html.

processes abound in the chemical, steel, automotive, appliance, computer, furniture, and clothing manufacture industries, as well as many others. Production layouts vary, but it is not difficult to picture an assembly line with its raw materials, parts, and supplies being processed into a finished product that becomes worth more than the sum of the parts and materials that went into it. However, processes are not limited to the area of production. Virtually all other areas of business involve processes. The processing of a check from the moment it is used for a purchase, through the financial institution, and back to the user is one example. The hiring of new employees by a human resources department involves a process that might begin with a job description and end with the training of a new employee. Many different processes occur within healthcare facilities. One process involves the flow of a patient from check-in at a hospital through an operation to recovery and release. Meanwhile, the dietary and foods department prepares food and delivers it to various points in the hospital as part of another process. The patient's paperwork follows still another process, and central supply processes medical supplies from the vendor to the floor supervisor.

Identifying and understanding the role of bottlenecks in a process are key to quality improvement. Finding ways to smooth the flow and shorten the cycle can result in greater productivity and higher quality. For these and other reasons, process analysis is an important component of total quality management. Several diagnostic techniques are available as process analysis tools. Among the more prominent ones are flowcharts, Pareto analysis, cause-and-effect (fishbone) diagrams, and control charts.

Flowcharts

Commonly, particularly in nonmanufacturing settings, no one maps out the complete flow of sequential stages of various processes in a business. For example, one NASA subcontractor was responsible for processing the paperwork for change items on space projects.

Change requests would begin at NASA and be sent to the subcontractor's building. The requests would be processed there and returned to NASA in about 14 days. Exactly what happened to the paperwork during the two-week period? As part of a quality effort, NASA asked the contractor to study the process. No one had taken a hard look at where the paperwork went, how long it sat on various people's desks, and how many different people handled it. The contractor soon became involved in process analysis.

One of the first activities that should take place in process analysis is the flowcharting of the process from beginning to end. A **flowchart** is *a schematic representation of all the activities and interactions that occur in a process.* It includes decision points, activities, input/output, start/stop, and a flowline. Figure 18.1 displays some of the symbols used in flowcharting.

The parallelogram represents input into the process or output from the process. In the case of the dietary/foods department at the hospital, the input includes uncooked food, utensils, plates, containers, and liquids. The output is the prepared meal delivered to the patient's room. The processing symbol is a rectangle that represents an activity. For the dietary/foods department, that activity could include cooking carrots or loading food carts. The decision symbol, a diamond, is used at points in the process where decisions are made that can result in different pathways. In some hospitals, the dietary/foods department supports a hospital cafeteria as well as patient meals. At some point in the process, the decision must be made as to whether the food is destined for a patient room or the cafeteria. The cafeteria food may follow a general menu whereas patient food may have to be individualized for particular health conditions. The arrow is the flowline symbol designating to the flowchart user the sequence of activities of the process. The flowline in the hospital food example would follow the pathway of the food from raw ingredients (vegetables, meat, flour, etc.) to the delivered product in patient rooms or in the cafeteria. The elongated oval represents the starting and stopping points in the process.

As an example, suppose we want to flowchart the process of obtaining a home improvement loan of $10,000 from a bank. The process begins with the customer entering the bank. The flow takes the customer to a receptionist, who poses a decision dilemma. For what purpose has the customer come to the bank? Is it to get information, to cash a check, to deposit money, to buy a money order, to get a loan, or to invest money? Because we are charting the loan process, we follow the flowline to the loan department. The customer arrives in the loan department and is met by another receptionist who asks what type and size of loan the person needs. For small personal loans, the customer is given a form to submit for loan consideration with no need to see a loan officer. For larger loans, such as the home improvement loan, the customer is given a form to fill out and is assigned to see a loan officer. The small personal loans are evaluated and the customer is given a response immediately. If the answer is yes, word of the decision is conveyed to a teller who cuts a check for the customer. For larger loans, the customer is interviewed by a loan officer, who then makes a decision. If the answer is yes, a contract is drawn up and signed. The customer is then sent to a teller who has the check for the loan. Figure 18.2 provides a possible flowchart for this scenario.

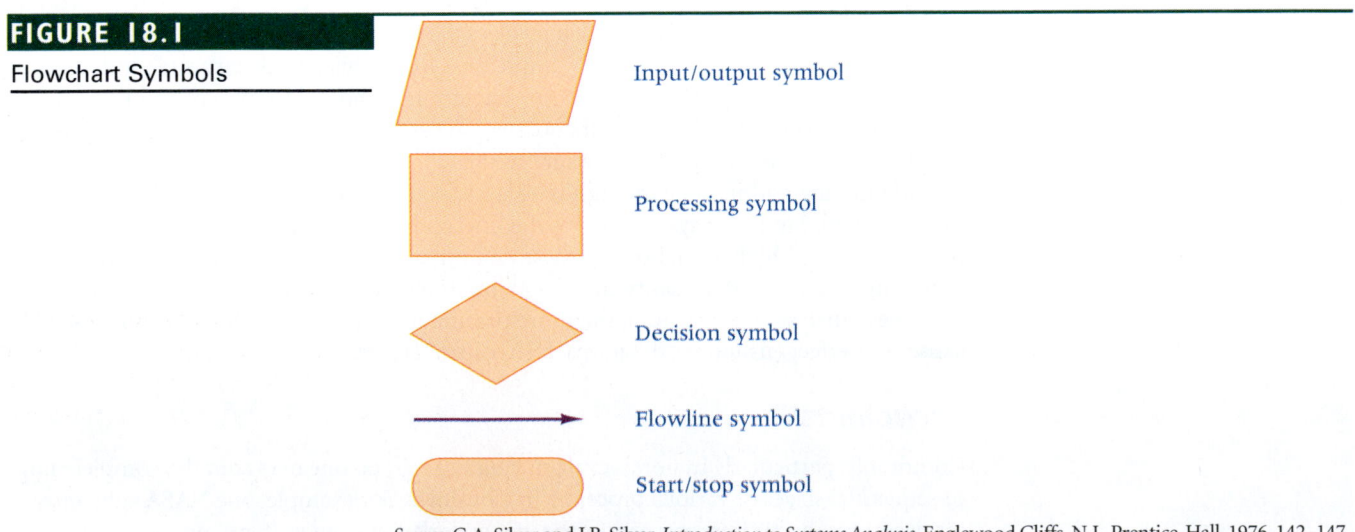

FIGURE 18.1

Flowchart Symbols

Input/output symbol

Processing symbol

Decision symbol

Flowline symbol

Start/stop symbol

Source: G.A. Silver and J.B. Silver. *Introduction to Systems Analysis*. Englewood Cliffs, N.J., Prentice-Hall, 1976, 142–147..

FIGURE 18.2   Flowchart of Loan Process

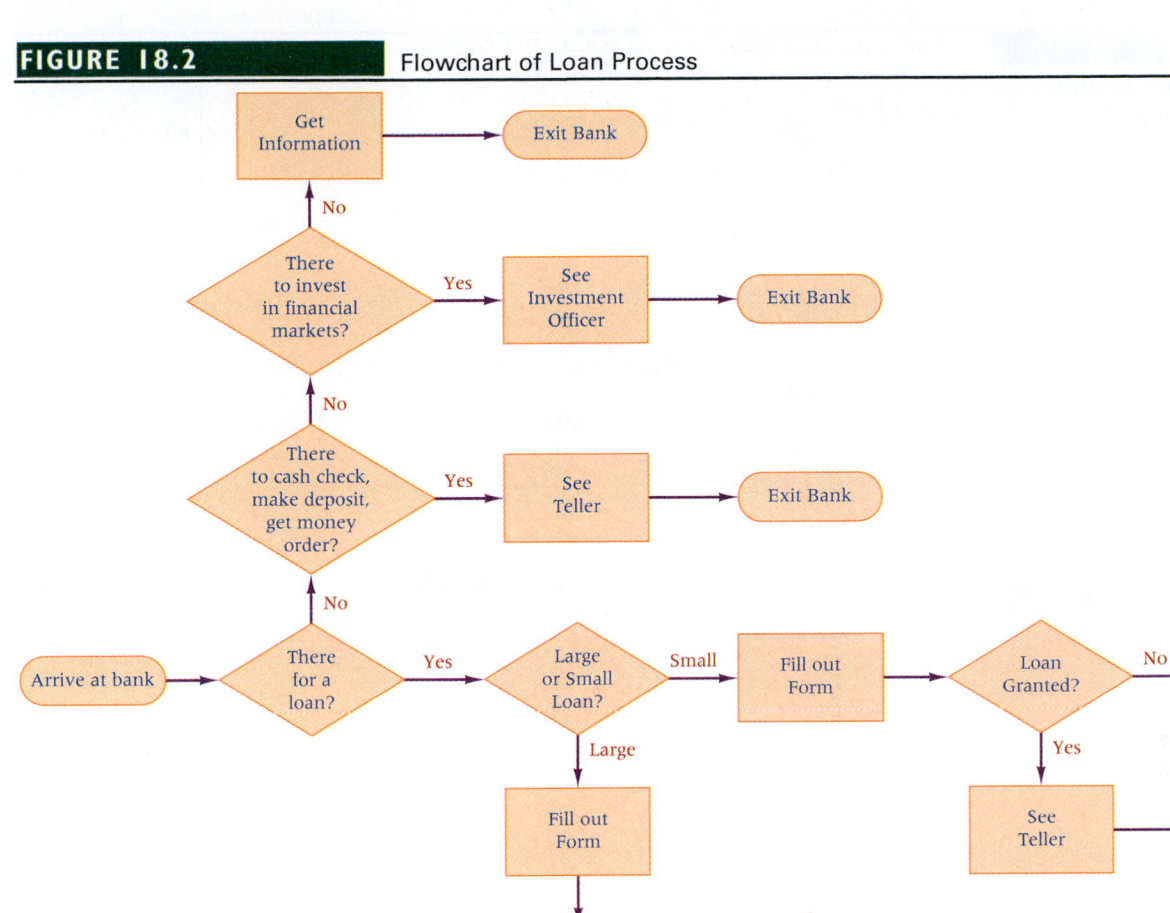

Pareto Analysis

Once the process has been mapped by such techniques as the flowchart, procedures for identifying bottlenecks and problem causes can begin. One technique for displaying problem causes is Pareto analysis. **Pareto analysis** is *a quantitative tallying of the number and types of defects that occur with a product or service.* Analysts use this tally to produce *a vertical bar chart that displays the most common types of defects, ranked in order of occurrence from left to right.* The bar chart is called a **Pareto chart.** Pareto charts are presented and explained in greater detail in Section 2.2 of Chapter 2. Figure 18.3 contains a MINITAB Pareto chart depicting various potential sources of medication error in a hospital. Figure 18.4 redisplays Figure 2.8, which depicts the possible causes of motor problems.

Cause-and-Effect (Fishbone) Diagrams

Another tool for identifying problem causes is the **cause-and-effect diagram,** sometimes referred to as **fishbone, or Ishikawa, diagram.** This diagram was developed by Kaoru Ishikawa in the 1940s as a way to *display possible causes of a problem and the interrelationships among the causes.* The causes can be uncovered through brainstorming, investigating, surveying, observing, and other information-gathering techniques.

The name *fishbone diagram* comes from the shape of the diagram, which looks like a fish skeleton with the problem at the head of the fish and possible causes flaring out on both sides of the main "bone." Subcauses can be included along each "fishbone."

FIGURE 18.3

Pareto Chart of Medication Errors in a Hospital

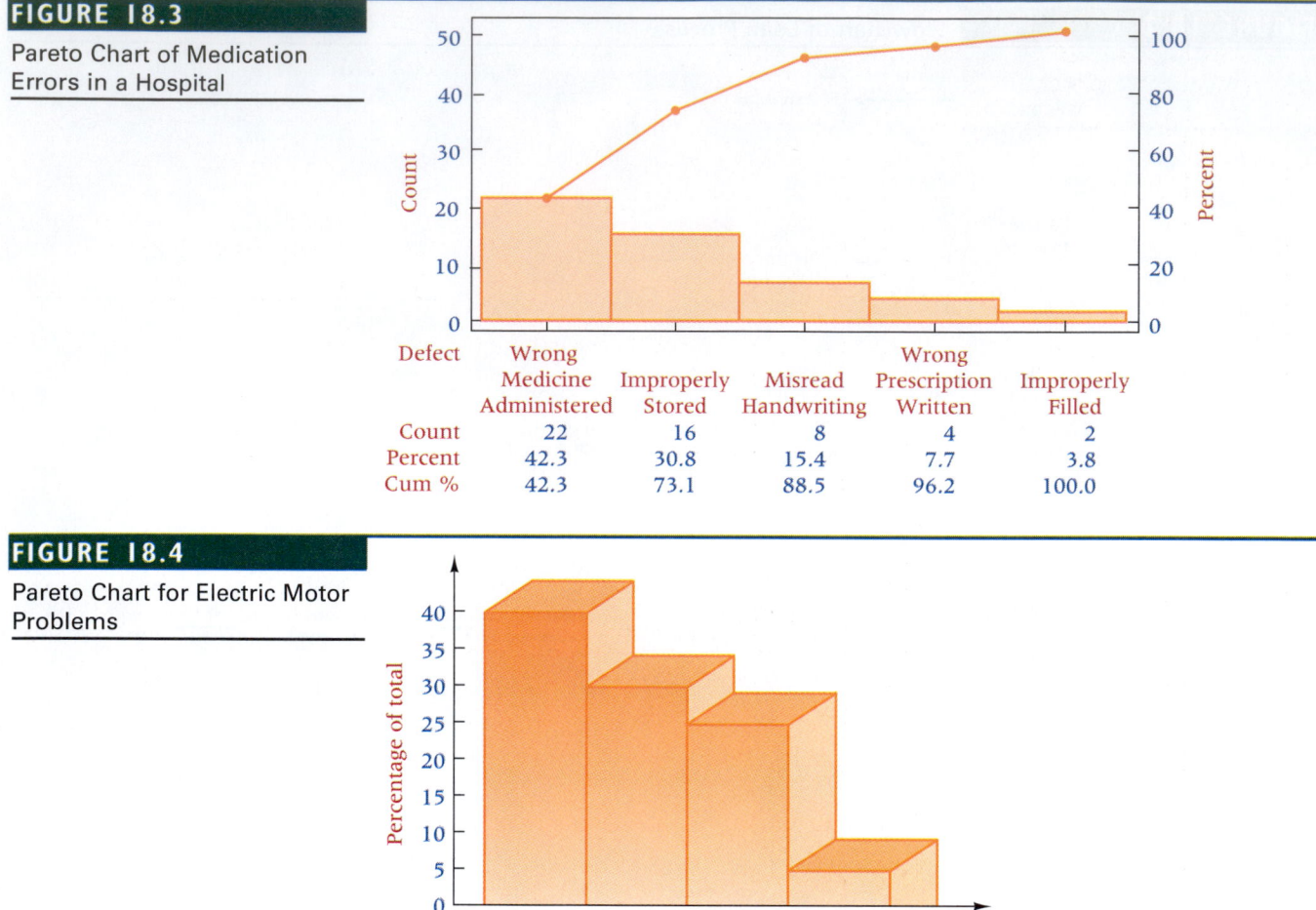

Defect	Wrong Medicine Administered	Improperly Stored	Misread Handwriting	Wrong Prescription Written	Improperly Filled
Count	22	16	8	4	2
Percent	42.3	30.8	15.4	7.7	3.8
Cum %	42.3	73.1	88.5	96.2	100.0

FIGURE 18.4

Pareto Chart for Electric Motor Problems

Suppose officials at the company producing the electric motor want to construct a fishbone diagram for the poor wiring problem shown as the major problem in Figure 18.4. Some of the possible causes of poor wiring might be raw materials, equipment, workers, or methods. Some possible raw material causes might be vendor problems (and their source of materials), transportation damage, or damage during storage (inventory). Possible causes of equipment failure might be out-of-date equipment, equipment that is out of adjustment, poor maintenance of equipment, or lack of effective tools. Poor wiring might also be the result of worker error, which can include lack of training or improper training, poor attitude, or excessive absenteeism that results in lack of consistency. Methods causes can include poor wiring schemes and inefficient plant layouts. Figure 18.5 presents a MINITAB fishbone diagram of this problem and its possible causes.

Control Charts

A fourth diagnostic technique that has worldwide acceptance is the control chart. According to Armand V. Feigenbaum, a renowned expert on control charts, a **control chart** is *a graphical method for evaluating whether a process is or is not in a "state of statistical control."*[*] Several kinds of control charts are used. Figure 18.6 is an $\bar{x}$ control chart. In the next section, we will explore control charts in more detail.

---

*Armand V. Feigenbaum, *Total Quality Control* (New York, McGraw-Hill, 1991).

FIGURE 18.5

MINITAB Cause-and-Effect
Diagram for Electric Motor
Problems

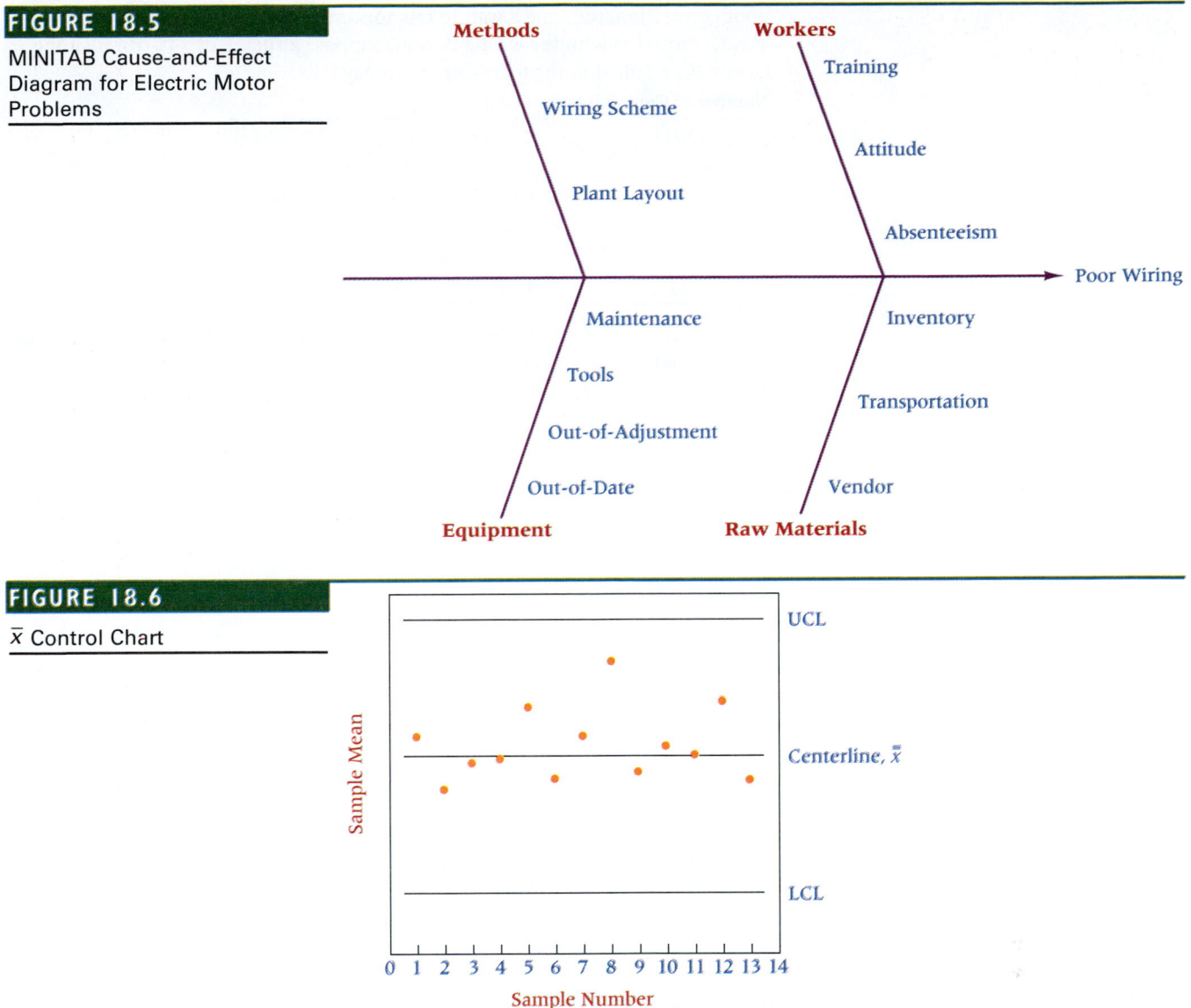

FIGURE 18.6

$\bar{x}$ Control Chart

18.2 PROBLEMS

18.1 For each of the following scenarios, sketch the process with activities and decision points. Construct a flowchart by using the symbols depicted in Figure 18.1.

    a. A customer enters the office of an insurance agent wanting to purchase auto
insurance and leaves the office with a paid policy in hand.

    b. A truckload of men's shirts enters a warehouse at the main distribution cen-
ter for a men's retail clothing company that has four stores in that area. The
shirts are on the racks inside the stores ready for sale.

    c. A couple enters a restaurant to enjoy dinner out. An hour and a half later,
they leave, satisfied, having paid their bill. Construct the flowchart from the
restaurant's point of view.

18.2 An airline company uses a central telephone bank and a semiautomated telephone process to take reservations. It has been receiving an unusually high number of customer complaints about its reservation system. The company
conducted a survey of customers, asking them whether they had encountered any
of the following problems in making reservations: busy signal, disconnection,

poor connection, too long a wait to talk to someone, could not get through to an agent, connected with the wrong person. Suppose a survey of 744 complaining customers resulted in the following frequency tally.

Number of Complaints	Complaints
184	Too long a wait
10	Transferred to the wrong person
85	Could not get through to an agent
37	Got disconnected
420	Busy signal
8	Poor connection

Construct a Pareto chart from this information to display the various problems encountered in making reservations.

18.3   A bank has just sent out a monthly reconciliation statement to a customer with an error in the person's monthly income. Brainstorm to determine some possible causes of this error. Try to think of some possible reasons for the causes. Construct a fishbone diagram to display your results.

18.3 CONTROL CHARTS

Control charts have been in existence for nearly 70 years. Walter A. Shewhart is credited with developing control charts at Bell Laboratories in the 1920s. Shewhart and others, including one of his understudies at Bell Laboratories, W. Edwards Deming, were able to apply control charts to industrial processes as a tool to assist in controlling variation. The use of control charts in the United States failed to gain momentum after World War II because the success of U.S. manufacturers in the world market reduced the apparent need for such a tool. As the Japanese and other international manufacturers became more competitive by using such tools, the control chart increased in popularity in the United States.

Control charts are easy to use and understand. Often it is the line workers who record and plot product measurements on the charts. In more automated settings, sensors record chart values and send them into an information system, which compiles the charts. Control charts are used mainly to monitor product variation. The charts enable operators, technicians, and managers to see when a process gets out of control, which in turn improves quality and increases productivity.

Variation

If no variations occurred between manufactured items, control charts would be pointless. However, variation occurs for virtually any product or service. Variation can occur among units within a lot and can occur between lots. Among the reasons for product variation are differences in raw materials, differences in workers, differences in machines, changes in the environment, and wear and tear of machinery. Small variations can be caused by unnoticeable events, such as a passing truck that creates vibrations or dust that affects machine operation. Variations need to be measured, recorded, and studied so that out-of-control conditions can be identified and corrections can be made in the process.

Types of Control Charts

The two general types of control charts are (1) control charts for measurements and (2) control charts for compliance items. In this section, we discuss two types of control charts for measurements, $\bar{x}$ charts and R charts. We also discuss two types of control charts for attribute compliance, p charts and c charts.

Each control chart has a **centerline,** an **upper control limit (UCL),** and a **lower control limit (LCL).** Data are recorded on the control chart, and the chart is examined for disturbing patterns or for data points that indicate a process is out of control. Once a process is determined to be out of control, measures can be taken to correct the problem causing the deviation.

$\bar{x}$ Chart

An $\bar{x}$ **chart** is *a graph of sample means computed for a series of small random samples over a period of time.* The means are average measurements of some product characteristic. For example, the measurement could be the volume of fluid in a liter of rubbing alcohol, the thickness of a piece of sheet metal, or the size of a hole in a plastic part. These sample means are plotted on a graph that contains a centerline and upper and lower control limits (UCL and LCL).

$\bar{x}$ charts can be made from standards or without standards.[*] Companies sometimes have smoothed their process to the point where they have standard centerlines and control limits for a product. These standards are usually used when a company is producing products that have been made for some time and in situations where managers have little interest in monitoring the overall measure of location for the product. In this text, we will study only situations in which no standard is given. It is fairly common to compute $\bar{x}$ charts without existing standards—especially if a company is producing a new product, is closely monitoring proposed standards, or expects a change in the process. Many firms want to monitor the standards, so they recompute the standards for each chart. In the no-standards situation, the standards (such as mean and standard deviation) are estimated by using the sample data.

The centerline for an $\bar{x}$ chart is the average of the sample means, $\bar{\bar{x}}$. The $\bar{x}$ chart has an upper control limit (UCL) that is three standard deviations of means above the centerline $(+3\sigma_{\bar{x}})$ The lower boundary of the $\bar{x}$ chart, called the lower control limit (LCL), is three standard deviations of means below the centerline $(-3\sigma_{\bar{x}})$. Recall the empirical rule presented in Chapter 3 stating that if data are normally distributed, approximately 99.7% of all values will be within three standard deviations of the mean. Because the shape of the sampling distribution of $\bar{x}$ is normal for large sample sizes regardless of the population shape, the empirical rule applies. However, because small samples are often used, an approximation of the three standard deviations of means is used to determine UCL and LCL. This approximation can be made using either sample ranges or sample standard deviations. For small sample sizes ($n \leq 15$ is acceptable, but $n \leq 10$ is preferred), a weighted value of the average range is a good approximation of the three-standard-deviation distance to UCL and LCL. The range is easy to compute (difference of extreme values), which is particularly useful when a wide array of nontechnical workers are involved in control chart computations. When sample sizes are larger, a weighted average of the sample standard deviations ($\bar{s}$) is a good estimate of the three standard deviations of means. The drawback of using the sample standard deviation is that it must always be computed, whereas the sample range can often be determined at a glance. Most control charts are constructed with small sample sizes; therefore, the range is more widely used in constructing control charts.

Table A.15 contains the weights applied to the average sample range or the average sample standard deviation to compute upper and lower control limits. The value of A_2 is used for ranges and the value of A_3 is used for standard deviations. The following steps are used to produce an $\bar{x}$ chart.

1. Decide on the quality to be measured.
2. Determine a sample size.
3. Gather 20 to 30 samples.
4. Compute the sample average, $\bar{x}$, for each sample.
5. Compute the sample range, R, for each sample.

---

[*]Armand V. Feigenbaum, *Total Quality Control* (New York, McGraw-Hill, 1991).

6. Determine the average sample mean for all samples, $\bar{\bar{x}}$, as

$$\bar{\bar{x}} = \frac{\sum \bar{x}}{k}$$

where k is the number of samples.

7. Determine the average sample range for all samples, $\bar{R}$, as

$$\bar{R} = \frac{\sum R}{k}$$

or determine the average sample standard deviation for all samples, $\bar{s}$, as

$$\bar{s} = \frac{\sum s}{k}$$

8. Using the size of the samples, n_i, determine the value of A_2 if using the range and A_3 if using standard deviations.

9. Construct the centerline, the upper control limit, and the lower control limit. For ranges:

$$\bar{\bar{x}} \text{ is the centerline}$$

$$\bar{\bar{x}} + A_2 \bar{R} \text{ is the UCL}$$

$$\bar{\bar{x}} - A_2 \bar{R} \text{ is the LCL}$$

For standard deviations:

$$\bar{\bar{x}} \text{ is the centerline}$$

$$\bar{\bar{x}} + A_3 \bar{s} \text{ is the UCL}$$

$$\bar{\bar{x}} - A_3 \bar{s} \text{ is the LCL}$$

DEMONSTRATION PROBLEM 18.1

A manufacturing facility produces bearings. The diameter specified for the bearings is 5 millimeters. Every 10 minutes, six bearings are sampled and their diameters are measured and recorded. Twenty of these samples of six bearings are gathered. Use the resulting data and construct an $\bar{x}$ chart.

Sample 1	Sample 2	Sample 3	Sample 4	Sample 5
5.13	4.96	5.21	5.02	5.12
4.92	4.98	4.87	5.09	5.08
5.01	4.95	5.02	4.99	5.09
4.88	4.96	5.08	5.02	5.13
5.05	5.01	5.12	5.03	5.06
4.97	4.89	5.04	5.01	5.13

Sample 6	Sample 7	Sample 8	Sample 9	Sample 10
4.98	4.99	4.96	4.96	5.03
5.02	5.00	5.01	5.00	4.99
4.97	5.00	5.02	4.91	4.96
4.99	5.02	5.05	4.87	5.14
4.98	5.01	5.04	4.96	5.11
4.99	5.01	5.02	5.01	5.04

Sample 11	Sample 12	Sample 13	Sample 14	Sample 15
4.91	4.97	5.09	4.96	4.99
4.93	4.91	4.96	4.99	4.97
5.04	5.02	5.05	4.82	5.01
5.00	4.93	5.12	5.03	4.98
4.90	4.95	5.06	5.00	4.96
4.82	4.96	5.01	4.96	5.02

Sample 16	Sample 17	Sample 18	Sample 19	Sample 20
5.01	5.05	4.96	4.90	5.04
5.04	4.97	4.93	4.85	5.03
5.09	5.04	4.97	5.02	4.97
5.07	5.03	5.01	5.01	4.99
5.12	5.09	4.98	4.88	5.05
5.13	5.01	4.92	4.86	5.06

Solution

Compute the value of $\bar{x}$ for each sample and average these values, obtaining $\bar{\bar{x}}$

$$\bar{\bar{x}} = \frac{\bar{x}_1 + \bar{x}_2 + \bar{x}_3 + \cdots + \bar{x}_{20}}{20}$$

$$= \frac{4.9933 + 4.9583 + 5.0566 + \cdots + 5.0233}{20}$$

$$= \frac{100.043}{20} = 5.00215 \text{ (the centerline)}$$

Compute the values of R and average them, obtaining $\bar{R}$.

$$\bar{R} = \frac{R_1 + R_2 + R_3 + \cdots + R_{20}}{20}$$

$$= \frac{.25 + .12 + .34 + \cdots + .09}{20}$$

$$= \frac{2.72}{20} = .136$$

Determine the value of A_2 by using $n_i = 6$ (size of the sample) from Table A.15: $A_2 = .483$.

The UCL is

$$\bar{\bar{x}} + A_2\bar{R} = 5.00215 + (.483)(.136) = 5.00215 + .06569 = 5.06784$$

The LCL is

$$\bar{\bar{x}} - A_2\bar{R} = 5.00215 - (.483)(.136) = 5.00215 - .06569 = 4.93646$$

Using the standard deviation instead of the range,

$$\bar{s} = \frac{s_1 + s_2 + s_3 + \cdots + s_{20}}{20}$$

$$= \frac{.0905 + .0397 + .1136 + \cdots + .0356}{20}$$

$$= .0494$$

Determine the value of A_3 by using $n_i = 6$ (sample size) from Table A.15:

$$A_3 = 1.287$$

The UCL is

$$\bar{\bar{x}} + A_3\bar{s} = 5.00215 + (1.287)(.0494) = 5.00215 + .06385 = 5.06573$$

The LCL is

$$\bar{\bar{x}} - A_3\bar{s} = 5.00215 - (1.287)(.0494) = 5.00215 - .06385 = 4.93857$$

The following graph depicts the $\bar{x}$ control chart using the range (rather than the standard deviation) as the measure of dispersion to compute LCL and UCL. Observe that if the standard deviation is used instead of the range to compute LCL and UCL, because of the precision (or lack thereof) of this chart, there is little, if any, perceptible difference in LCL and UCL by the two methods.

Note that the sample means for samples 5 and 16 are above the UCL and the sample means for samples 11 and 19 are below the LCL. This result indicates that these four samples are out of control and alerts the production supervisor or worker to initiate further investigation of bearings produced during these periods. All other samples are within the control limits.

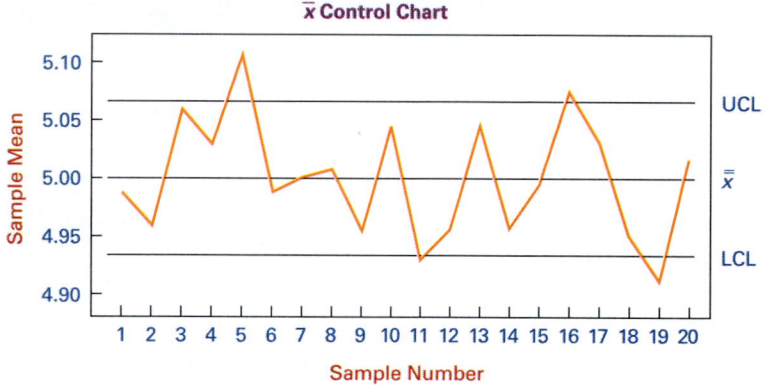

Shown next is the MINITAB output for this problem. Note that the MINITAB output is nearly identical to the control chart just shown.

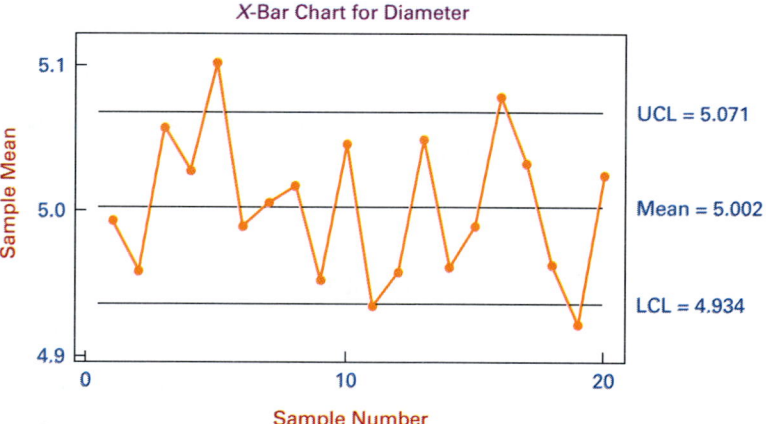

R Charts

An **R chart** is a plot of the sample ranges and often is used in conjunction with an $\bar{x}$ chart. Whereas $\bar{x}$ charts are used to plot the location values, $\bar{x}$, for each sample, R charts are used to plot the variation of each sample as measured by the sample range. The centerline of an R chart is the average range, $\bar{R}$. Lower control limits (LCLs) are determined by $D_3\bar{R}$ where D_3 is a weight applied to $\bar{R}$ reflecting sample size. The value of D_3 can be obtained from Table A.15. Upper control limits (UCLs) are determined by $D_4\bar{R}$ where D_4 is a value obtained from Table A.15, which also reflects sample size. The following steps lead to an R chart.

1. Decide on the quality to be measured.
2. Determine a sample size.

3. Gather 20 to 30 samples.
4. Compute the sample range, R, for each sample.
5. Determine the average sample range for all samples, $\bar{R}$, as

$$\bar{R} = \frac{\sum R}{k}$$

where k = the number of samples.

6. Using the size of the samples, n_i, find the values of D_3 and D_4 in Table A.15.
7. Construct the centerline and control limits.

$$\text{Centerline} = \bar{R}$$
$$\text{UCL} = D_4\,\bar{R}$$
$$\text{LCL} = D_3\,\bar{R}$$

DEMONSTRATION PROBLEM 18.2	Construct an R chart for the 20 samples of data in Demonstration Problem 18.1 on bearings.

Solution

Compute the sample ranges shown.

Sample	Range
1	.25
2	.12
3	.34
4	.10
5	.07
6	.05
7	.03
8	.09
9	.14
10	.18
11	.22
12	.11
13	.16
14	.21
15	.06
16	.12
17	.12
18	.09
19	.17
20	.09

Compute $\bar{R}$

$$\bar{R} = \frac{.25 + .12 + .34 + \cdots + .09}{20} = \frac{2.72}{20} = .136$$

For $n_i = 6$, $D_3 = 0$, and $D_4 = 2.004$ (from Table A.15):

$$\text{Centerline } \bar{R} = .136$$
$$\text{LCL} = D_3\bar{R} = (0)(.136) = 0$$
$$\text{UCL} = D_4\bar{R} = (2.004)(.136) = .2725$$

The resulting R chart for these data is shown next, followed by the MINITAB output. Note that the range for sample 3 is out of control (beyond the UCL). The range of values in sample 3 appears to be unacceptable. Further investigation of the population from which this sample was drawn is warranted.

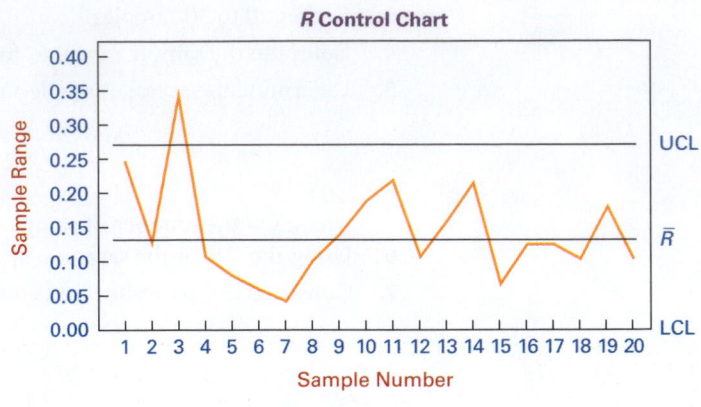

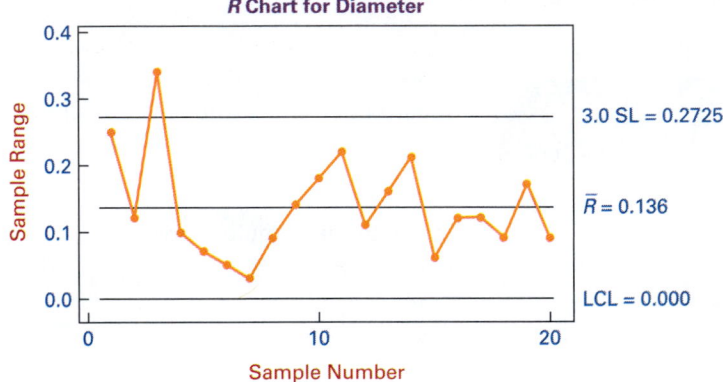

p Charts

When product attributes are measurable, $\bar{x}$ charts and R charts can be formulated from the data. Sometimes, however, product inspection yields no measurement—only a yes-or-no type of conclusion based on whether the item complies with the specifications. For this type of data, no measure is available from which to average or determine the range. However, attribute compliance can be depicted graphically by a *p* chart. A **p chart** *graphs the proportion of sample items in noncompliance for multiple samples.*

For example, suppose a company producing electric motors samples 40 motors three times a week for a month. For each group of 40 motors, it determines the proportion of the sample group that does not comply with the specifications. It then plots these sample proportions, $\hat{p}$, on a *p* chart to identify trends or samples with unacceptably high proportions of nonconformance. Other *p* chart applications include determining whether a gallon of paint has been manufactured with acceptable texture, a pane of glass contains cracks, or a tire has a defective tread.

Like the $\bar{x}$ chart and the R chart, a *p* chart contains a centerline. The centerline is the average of the sample proportions. Upper and lower control limits are computed from the average of the sample proportions plus or minus three standard deviations of proportions. The following are the steps for constructing a *p* chart.

1. Decide on the quality to be measured.
2. Determine a sample size.
3. Gather 20 to 30 samples.
4. Compute the sample proportion:

$$\hat{p} = \frac{n_{\text{non}}}{n}$$

where

n_{non} = the number of items in the sample in noncompliance
n = the number of items in the sample

5. Compute the average proportion:

$$p = \frac{\sum \hat{p}}{k}$$

where:

$$\hat{p} = \frac{n_{non}}{n} = \text{the sample proportion}$$

k = the number of samples

6. Determine the centerline, UCL, and LCL, when $q = 1 - p$.

$$\text{Centerline} = p$$

$$\text{UCL} = p + 3\sqrt{\frac{p \cdot q}{n}}$$

$$\text{LCL} = p - 3\sqrt{\frac{p \cdot q}{n}}$$

DEMONSTRATION PROBLEM 18.3

A company produces bond paper and, at regular intervals, samples of 50 sheets of paper are inspected. Suppose 20 random samples of 50 sheets of paper each are taken during a certain period of time, with the following numbers of sheets in non-compliance per sample. Construct a p chart from these data.

Sample	n	Out of Compliance
1	50	4
2	50	3
3	50	1
4	50	0
5	50	5
6	50	2
7	50	3
8	50	1
9	50	4
10	50	2
11	50	2
12	50	6
13	50	0
14	50	2
15	50	1
16	50	6
17	50	2
18	50	3
19	50	1
20	50	5

Solution

From the data, $n = 50$. The values of $\hat{p}$ follow.

Sample	$\hat{p}$ (out of compliance)
1	4/50 = .08
2	3/50 = .06
3	1/50 = .02
4	0/50 = .00
5	5/50 = .10
6	2/50 = .04
7	3/50 = .06
8	1/50 = .02
9	4/50 = .08
10	2/50 = .04
11	2/50 = .04
12	6/50 = .12
13	0/50 = .00
14	2/50 = .04
15	1/50 = .02
16	6/50 = .12
17	2/50 = .04
18	3/50 = .06
19	1/50 = .02
20	5/50 = .10

The value of p is obtained by averaging these $\hat{p}$ values.

$$p = \frac{\hat{p}_1 + \hat{p}_2 + \hat{p}_3 + \cdots \hat{p}_{20}}{20}$$

$$= \frac{.08 + .06 + .02 + \cdots + .10}{20} = \frac{1.06}{20} = .053$$

The centerline is $p = .053$.
The UCL is

$$p + 3\sqrt{\frac{p \cdot q}{n}} = .053 + 3\sqrt{\frac{(.053)(.947)}{50}} = .053 + .095 = .148$$

The LCL is

$$p - 3\sqrt{\frac{p \cdot q}{n}} = .053 - 3\sqrt{\frac{(.053)(.947)}{50}} = .053 - .095 = -.042$$

To have $-.042$ item in noncompliance is impossible, so the lower control limit is 0. Following is the p chart for this problem. Note that all 20 proportions are within the quality control limits.

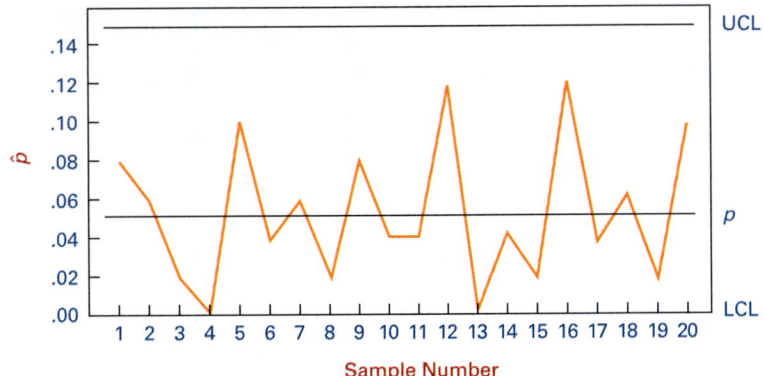

Shown next is the MINITAB output for this p chart. Note that the computer output is essentially the same as the graph just shown.

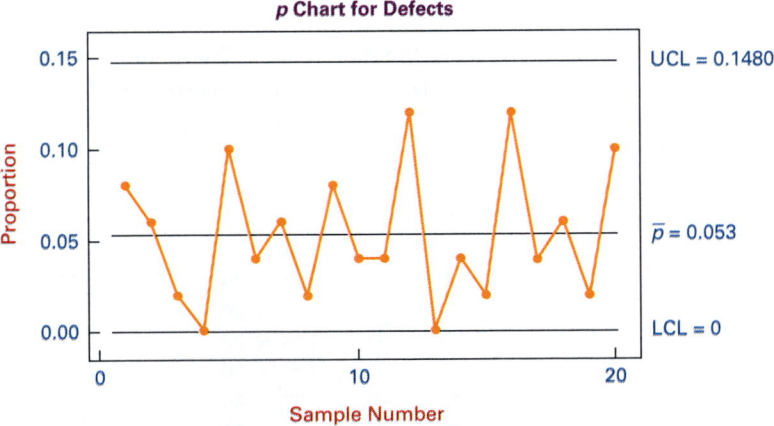

p Chart for Defects

c Charts

The c chart is less widely used than the $\bar{x}$, the R, or the p chart. Like the p chart, the c chart attempts to formulate information about defective items. However, whereas the p chart is a control chart that displays the proportion of items in a sample that are out of compliance with specifications, a *c chart* displays *the number of nonconformances per item or unit*. Examples of nonconformances could be paint flaws, scratches, openings drilled too large or too small, or shorts in electric wires. The c chart allows for multiple nonconforming features per item or unit. For example, if an item is a radio, there can be scratches (multiple) in the paint, poor soldering, bad wiring, broken dials, burned-out light bulbs, and broken antennae. A unit need not be an item such as a computer chip. It can be a bolt of cloth, 4 feet of wire, or a 2×4 board. The requirement is that the unit remain consistent throughout the test or experiment.

In computing a c chart, a c value is determined for each item or unit by tallying the total nonconformances for the item or unit. The centerline is computed by averaging the c values for all items or units. Because in theory nonconformances per item or unit are rare, the Poisson distribution is used as the basis for the c chart. The long-run average for the Poisson distribution is λ, and the analogous long-run average for a c chart is $\bar{c}$ (the average of the c values for the items or units studied), which is used as the centerline value. Upper control limits (UCL) and lower control limits (LCL) are computed by adding or subtracting three standard deviations of the mean, $\bar{c}$ from the centerline value, $\bar{c}$. The standard deviation of a Poisson distribution is the square root of λ; likewise, the standard deviation of $\bar{c}$ is the square root of $\bar{c}$. The UCL is thus determined by $\bar{c} + 3\sqrt{\bar{c}}$ and the LCL is given by $\bar{c} - 3\sqrt{\bar{c}}$. The following steps are used for constructing a c chart.

1. Decide on nonconformances to be evaluated.

2. Determine the number of items of units to be studied. (This number should be at least 25.)

3. Gather items or units.

4. Determine the value of c for each item or unit by summing the number of nonconformances in the item or unit.

5. Calculate the value of $\bar{c}$.

$$\bar{c} = \frac{c_1 + c_2 + c_3 + \cdots + c_i}{i}$$

where

i = number of items

c_i = number of nonconformances per item

6. Determine the centerline, UCL, and LCL.

$$\text{Centerline} = \bar{c}$$

$$\text{UCL} = \bar{c} + 3\sqrt{\bar{c}}$$

$$\text{LCL} = \bar{c} - 3\sqrt{\bar{c}}$$

DEMONSTRATION PROBLEM 18.4

A manufacturer produces gauges to measure oil pressure. As part of the company's statistical process control, 25 gauges are randomly selected and tested for nonconformances. The results are shown here. Use these data to construct a c chart that displays the nonconformances per item.

Item Number	Number of Nonconformances	Item Number	Number of Nonconformances
1	2	14	2
2	0	15	1
3	3	16	4
4	1	17	0
5	2	18	2
6	5	19	3
7	3	20	2
8	2	21	1
9	0	22	3
10	0	23	2
11	4	24	0
12	3	25	3
13	2		

Solution

Determine the centerline, UCL, and LCL.

$$\text{Centerline} = \bar{c} = \frac{2 + 0 + 3 + \cdots + 3}{25} = \frac{50}{25} = 2.0$$

$$\text{UCL} = \bar{c} + 3\sqrt{\bar{c}} = 2.0 + 3\sqrt{2.0} = 2.0 + 4.2 = 6.2$$

$$\text{LCL} = \bar{c} - 3\sqrt{\bar{c}} = 2.0 - 3\sqrt{2.0} = 2.0 - 4.2 = -2.2$$

The lower control limit cannot be less than zero; thus, the LCL is 0. The graph of the control chart, followed by the MINITAB c chart, is shown next. Note that none of the points are beyond the control limits and there is a healthy deviation of points both above and below the centerline. This chart indicates a process that is relatively in control, with an average of two nonconformances per item.

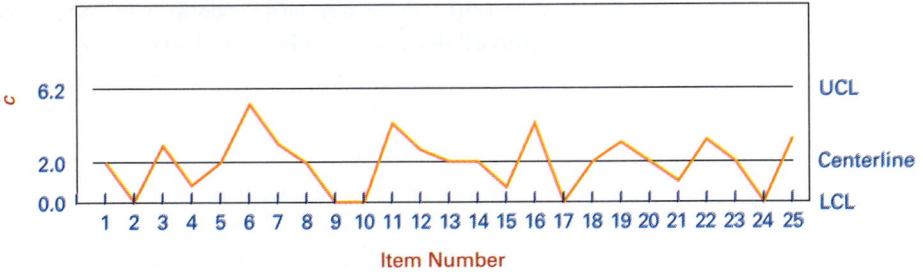

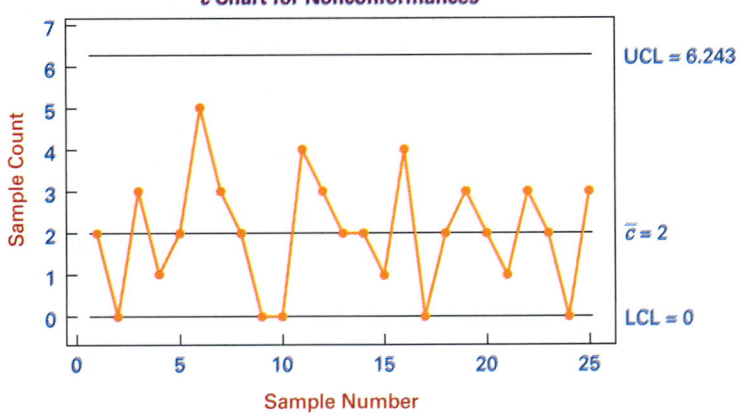

Interpreting Control Charts

How can control charts be used to monitor processes? When is a process out of control? An evaluation of the points plotted on a control chart examines several things. Obviously, one concern is points that are outside the control limits. Control chart outer limits (UCL and LCL) are established at three standard deviations above and below the centerline. The empirical rule discussed in Chapter 3 and the z table value for $z = 3$ indicate that approximately 99.7% of all values should be within three standard deviations of the mean of the statistic. Applying this rule to control charts suggests that fewer than .3% of all points should be beyond the upper and lower control limits by chance. Thus, one of the more elementary items a control chart observer looks for is points outside LCL and UCL. If the system is "in control," virtually no data points should be outside these limits. Workers responsible for process control should investigate samples in which sample members are outside the LCL and UCL. In the case of the c chart, items that are above the UCL line contain an inordinate number of nonconformances in relation to the average. The occurrence of points beyond the control limits call for further investigation.

Several other criteria can be used to determine whether a control chart is plotting a process that is out of control. In general, there *should* be random fluctuation above and below the centerline within the UCL and LCL. However, a process can be out of control if too many consecutive points are above or below the centerline. Eight or more consecutive points on one side of the centerline are considered too many. In addition, if 10 of 11 or 12 of 14 points are on the same side of the center, the process may be out of control.[*]

Another criterion for process control operators to look for is trends in the control charts. At any point in the process, is a trend emerging in the data? As a rule of thumb, if six or more points are increasing or are decreasing, the process may be out of control.[†] Such a trend can indicate that points will eventually deviate increasingly from the centerline (the gap between the centerline and the points will increase).

Another concern with control charts is an overabundance of points in the outer one-third of the region between the centerline and the outer limits (LCL and UCL). By a rationalization similar to that imposed on LCL and UCL, the empirical rule and the table of z values show that approximately 95% of all points should be within two standard deviations of the centerline. With this in mind, fewer than 5% of the points should be in the outer one-third of the region between the centerline and the outer control limits (because 95% should be within two-thirds of the region). A rule to follow is that if two out of three consecutive points are in the outer one-third of the chart, a control problem may be present. Likewise, because approximately 68% of all values should be within one standard deviation of the mean (empirical rule, z table for $z = 1$), only 32% should be in the outer two-thirds of the control chart above and below the centerline. As a rule, if four out of five successive points are in the outer two-thirds of the control chart, the process should be investigated.[‡]

Another consideration in evaluating control charts is the location of the centerline. With each successive batch of samples, it is important to observe whether the centerline is shifting away from specifications.

The following list provides a summary of the control chart abnormalities for which a statistical process controller should be determined.

1. Points are above UCL and/or below LCL.
2. Eight or more consecutive points are above or below the centerline. Ten out of 11 points are above or below the centerline. Twelve out of 14 points are above or below the centerline.
3. A trend of six or more consecutive points (increasing or decreasing) is present.
4. Two out of three consecutive values are in the outer one-third.
5. Four out of five consecutive values are in the outer two-thirds.
6. The centerline shifts from chart to chart.

Figure 18.7 contains several control charts, each of which has one of these types of problems. The chart in (a) contains points above and below the outer control limits. The one in (b) has eight consecutive points on one side of the centerline. The chart in (c) has seven consecutive increasing points. In (d), at least two out of three consecutive points are in the outer one-third of the control chart. In (e), at least four out of five consecutive points are in the outer two-thirds of the chart.

In investigating control chart abnormalities, several possible causes may be found. Some of them are listed here.[**]

1. Changes in the physical environment
2. Worker fatigue
3. Worn tools
4. Changes in operators or machines
5. Maintenance
6. Changes in worker skills
7. Changes in materials
8. Process modification

[*]James R. Evans and William M. Lindsay, *The Management and Control of Quality*. 4th ed. (Cincinnati: South-Western College Publishing, 1999).

[†]Richard E. DeVor, Tsong-how Chang, and John W. Sutherland, *Statistical Quality Design and Control* (New York, Macmillan, 1992).

[‡]DeVor, Chang, and Sutherland; Evans and Lindsay.

[**]Eugene L. Grant and Richard S. Leavenworth, *Statistical Quality Control*, 5th ed. (New York, McGraw-Hill, 1980).

FIGURE 18.7

Control Charts with Problems

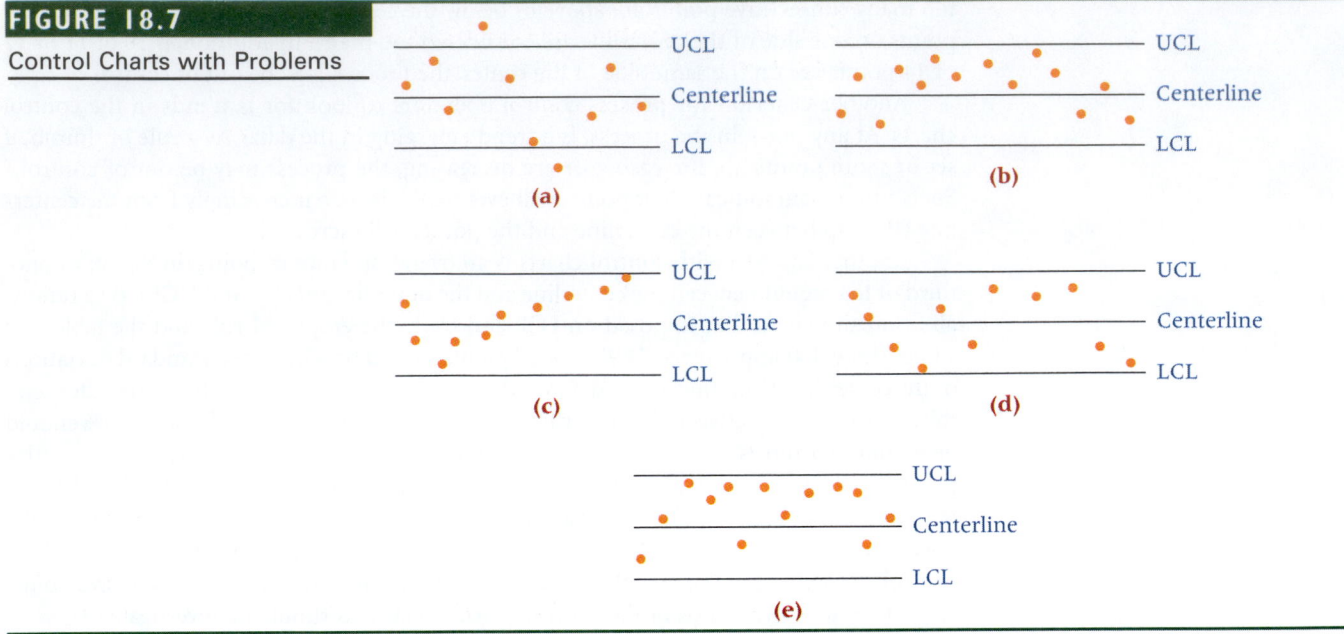

The statistical process control person should beware that control chart abnormalities can arise because of measurement errors or incorrect calculation of control limits. Judgment should be exercised so as not to overcontrol the process by readjusting to every oddity that appears to be out of the ordinary on a control chart.

18.3 PROBLEMS

18.4 A food-processing company makes potato chips, pretzels, and cheese chips. Although its products are packaged and sold by weight, the company has been taking sample bags of cheese chips and counting the number of chips in each bag. Shown here is the number of chips per bag for five samples of seven bags of chips. Use these data to construct an $\bar{x}$ chart and an R chart. Discuss the results.

Sample 1	Sample 2	Sample 3	Sample 4	Sample 5
25	22	30	32	25
23	21	23	26	23
29	24	22	27	29
31	25	26	28	27
26	23	28	25	27
28	26	27	25	26
27	29	21	31	24

18.5 A toy-manufacturing company has been given a large order for small plastic whistles that will be given away by a large fast-food hamburger chain with its kid's meal. Seven random samples of four whistles have been taken. The weight of each whistle has been ascertained in grams. The data are shown here. Use these data to construct an $\bar{x}$ chart and an R chart. What managerial decisions should be made on the basis of these findings?

Sample 1	Sample 2	Sample 3	Sample 4	Sample 5	Sample 6	Sample 7
4.1	3.6	4.0	4.6	3.9	5.1	4.6
5.2	4.3	4.8	4.8	3.8	4.7	4.4
3.9	3.9	5.1	4.7	4.6	4.8	4.0
5.0	4.6	5.3	4.7	4.9	4.3	4.5

18.6 A machine operator at a pencil-manufacturing facility gathered 10 different random samples of 100 pencils. The operator's inspection was to determine whether the pencils were in compliance or out of compliance with specifications. The results of this inspection are shown here. Use these data to construct a *p* chart. Comment on the results of this chart.

Sample	Size	Number out of Compliance
1	100	2
2	100	7
3	100	4
4	100	3
5	100	3
6	100	5
7	100	2
8	100	0
9	100	1
10	100	6

18.7 A large manufacturer makes valves. Currently it is producing a particular valve for use in industrial engines. As a part of a quality control effort, the company engineers randomly sample seven groups of 40 valves and inspect them to determine whether they are in or out of compliance. Results are shown here. Use the information to construct a *p* chart. Comment on the chart.

Sample	Size	Number out of Compliance
1	40	1
2	40	0
3	40	1
4	40	3
5	40	2
6	40	5
7	40	2

18.8 A firm in the upper Midwest manufactures light bulbs. Before the bulbs are released for shipment, a sample of bulbs is selected for inspection. Inspectors look for nonconformances such as scratches, weak or broken filaments, incorrectly bored turns, insufficient outside contacts, and others. A sample of 35 60-watt bulbs has just been inspected, and the results are shown here. Use these data to construct a *c* chart. Discuss the findings.

Bulb Number	Number of Nonconformances	Bulb Number	Number of Nonconformances
1	0	19	2
2	1	20	0
3	0	21	0
4	0	22	1
5	3	23	0
6	0	24	0
7	1	25	0
8	0	26	2
9	0	27	0
10	0	28	0
11	2	29	1
12	0	30	0
13	0	31	0
14	2	32	0
15	0	33	0
16	1	34	3
17	3	35	0
18	0		

18.9 A soft drink bottling company just ran a long line of 12-ounce soft drink cans filled with cola. A sample of 32 cans is selected by inspectors looking for nonconforming items. Among the things the inspectors look for are paint defects on the can, improper seal, incorrect volume, leaking contents, incorrect mixture of carbonation and syrup in the soft drink, and out-of-spec syrup mixture. The results of this inspection are given here. Construct a *c* chart from the data and comment on the results.

Can Number	Number of Nonconformances	Can Number	Number of Nonconformances
1	2	17	3
2	1	18	1
3	1	19	2
4	0	20	0
5	2	21	0
6	1	22	1
7	2	23	4
8	0	24	0
9	1	25	2
10	3	26	1
11	1	27	1
12	4	28	3
13	2	29	0
14	1	30	1
15	0	31	2
16	1	32	0

18.10 Examine the three control charts shown. Discuss any and all control problems that may be apparent from these control charts.

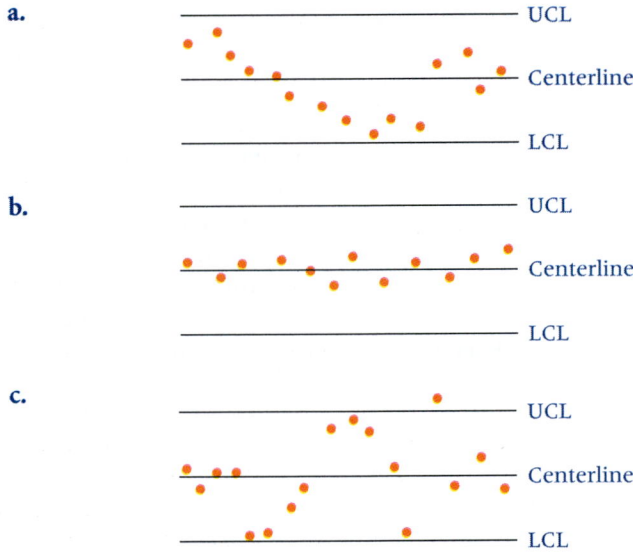

18.11 Study each of the following MINITAB control charts and determine whether any of them indicate problems in the processes. Comment on each chart.

a.

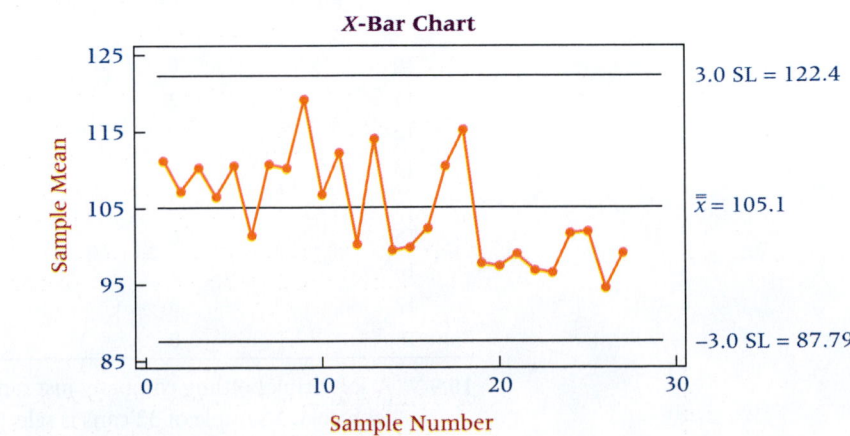

X-Bar Chart

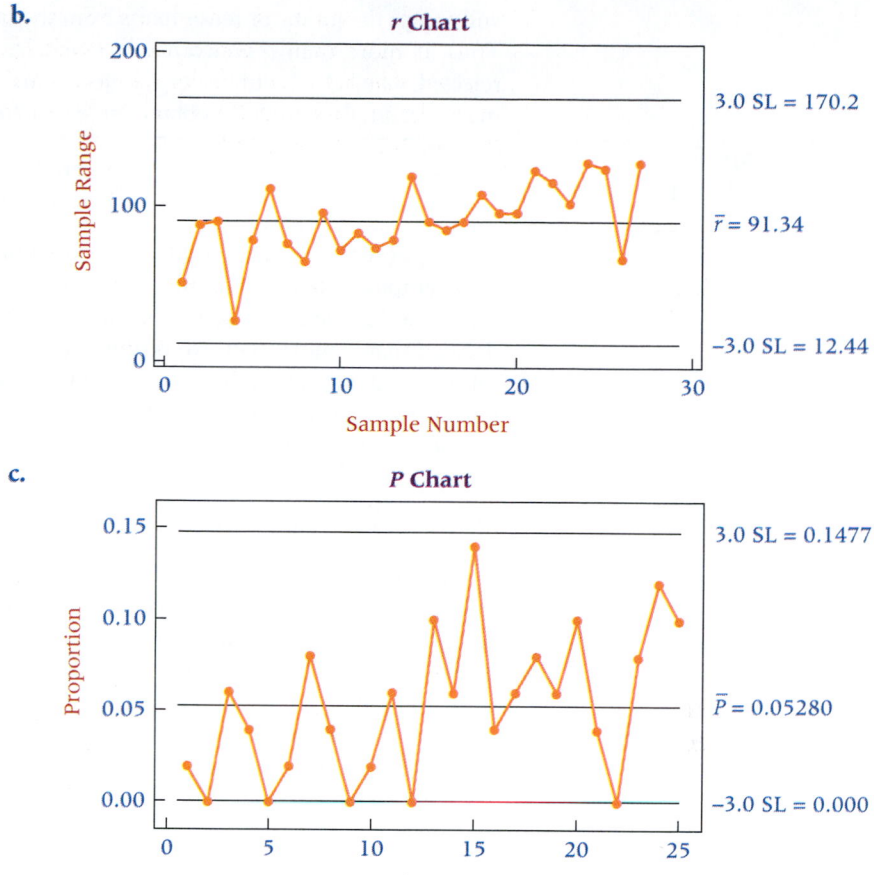

b.

r Chart

3.0 SL = 170.2

$\bar{r}$ = 91.34

−3.0 SL = 12.44

c.

P Chart

3.0 SL = 0.1477

$\bar{P}$ = 0.05280

−3.0 SL = 0.000

18.4 ACCEPTANCE SAMPLING

Another type of quality control is acceptance sampling, which involves after-process inspection. **Acceptance sampling** is *the inspection of a sample from a batch or lot of goods to determine whether the batch or lot will be accepted or rejected.* Suppose, for example, a large bicycle manufacturer has a contract with a supplier for braces that support the bicycle headlight. The braces are shipped to the bicycle manufacturer in lots of 3,000. How does the bicycle manufacturer determine whether a lot is acceptable? One way is to do 100% inspection.

In acceptance sampling, the lot is the population; hence, with 100% inspection every item of the lot is examined and the process becomes a census. This technique is costly and can bring diminishing returns due to inspector fatigue. However, in cases where safety is important, 100% inspection might be the only alternative. For example, 100% of all airplane hydraulic systems should be inspected. In some manufacturing plants where assembly is highly automated, it may be possible to do 100% inspection on incoming supplies and unfinished products online in a relatively inexpensive way. However, most businesses opt for acceptance sampling instead of 100% inspection.

Acceptance sampling is a method in which a random sample of size *n* items is selected from a population of size *N* (lot size). Each of the *n* items in the sample is inspected and labeled as acceptable or unacceptable. On the basis of the number of unacceptable items in the sample, the entire lot is accepted or rejected. If the lot is rejected, the receiver of the lot (who has just done the acceptance sampling) has such options as returning the lot to the supplier or negotiating for a reduced price on the lot. The different types of acceptance sampling plans include the single-sample plan, double-sample plan, and multiple-sample plan.

Single-Sample Plan

In a **single-sample plan,** *one sample of size n is sampled from a lot that contains N items.* The inspector determines from previous studies and from company specifications that it will accept the lot if c or fewer items from the sample of size n are rejected (unacceptable). Thus, if more than c unacceptable items are identified in the sample, the lot will be rejected. The actual number of rejected items in a sample is often denoted by x. In summary, the single-sample acceptance rule is as follows.

SINGLE-SAMPLE ACCEPTANCE RULE	Accept lot if $x \leq c$ Reject lot if $x > c$

Suppose the bicycle manufacturer mentioned previously uses a single-sample acceptance sampling plan to determine whether to accept or reject a lot of braces from the supplier. The bicycle manufacturer decides to sample $n = 20$ braces for inspection and has decided that if more than two of the sampled braces are defective, it will reject the entire lot of $N = 3,000$. Thus, for this problem, the value of c is two. If a sample produces zero, one, or two defective braces, the lot is accepted. If a sample produces three or more defective braces, the lot is rejected.

Double-Sample Plan

Sometimes an inspection team will determine that if the number of rejected items in a sample is marginal, they will take a second sample and see whether the results from the second sample in conjunction with the results from the first sample produce conclusive evidence to reject or accept the lot. This procedure is called the **double-sample plan.** In this case, a first sample is taken. The decision rule is to accept the lot if the number of rejects in the first sample, x_1, is less than or equal to a prespecified number, c_1. The lot is rejected if the number of rejects, x_1, is greater than or equal to a prespecified number of rejects, r_1, where $r_1 > c_1$. If the number of rejects from the first sample is between c_1 and r_1, a second sample is taken.

The number of rejects, x_2, in the second sample is determined. This number is combined with the number of rejects in the first sample to give $x_1 + x_2$. If this total is less than or equal to some prespecified value, c_2, the lot is accepted. If the total of x_1 and x_2 is greater than c_2, the lot is rejected. Shown here is a summary of the decision rules for the double-sample acceptance sampling plan.

DOUBLE-SAMPLE PLAN ACCEPTANCE RULE		
First Sample:	Accept if	$x_1 \leq c_1$
	Reject if	$x_1 \geq r_1$
Take second sample if		$c_1 < x_1 < r_1$
Second sample:	Accept if	$x_1 + x_2 \leq c_2$
	Reject if	$x_1 + x_2 > c_2$

Suppose the bicycle manufacturer decides to use a double-sample plan. The manufacturer decides to take a first sample of size 20 and use $c_1 = 2$ and $r_1 = 5$. If the number of rejects in the first sample is less than or equal to two (0, 1, or 2 defects), the lot of 3,000 braces is accepted. If the number of rejects in the first sample is five or more, the lot is rejected. However, if the number of rejects is between two and five—that is, the number of rejects is three or four—a second sample of size 20 will be taken. The number of items in a second sample does not necessarily have to be the same as the number in the first sample. Suppose the company officials have determined that c_2 is four. If the sum of the number of rejects from the first and second samples is less than or equal to four, the lot is accepted. If the sum is more than four, the lot is rejected.

Multiple-Sample Plan

An extension of the single- and double-sample plans is the **multiple-sample plan.** In this plan, three or more samples are taken in sequence in an effort to determine whether a lot is to be accepted or rejected. In a manner analogous to the double-sample plan, a cumulative sum of the number of rejects is compared to a value of c_i after each sample. If the sum is less than or equal to that value of c_i, the lot is accepted and the sampling process is stopped for that lot. If the sum of rejects is greater than or equal to the value of r_i, the lot is rejected and the sampling process ceases for that lot. If the sum of rejects is between the values of c_i and r_i after a sample is inspected, an additional sample is taken and inspected. The values of r_i and c_i change every time a new sample is taken. The process continues until the lot is accepted or rejected or the inspection team determines enough samples have been taken.

Determining Error and OC Curves

In acceptance sampling, as in hypothesis testing, once a researcher makes a decision about a lot from the sample information, he or she either made a correct decision or an error. As described in Chapter 9, if a researcher rejects a true null hypothesis, the researcher commits a Type I error. A researcher who fails to reject (accepts) a false null hypothesis commits a Type II error. These principles can be applied to acceptance sampling. When the decision maker rejects a lot on the basis of sample information, he or she either makes a correct decision about the lot or commits a Type I error. If the lot is acceptable and the sample data indicate rejection, a Type I error occurs. If the lot should be rejected and the sample information indicates a rejection of the lot, a correct decision is made.

When a decision maker accepts (fails to reject) a lot on the basis of sample information, he or she either makes a correct decision about the lot or commits a Type II error. If the lot is acceptable and the sample information leads to acceptance, a correct decision is made. If the lot should be rejected but the sample information leads to acceptance of (failure to reject) the lot, a Type II error occurs.

In acceptance sampling, the *consumer* (customer, buyer) is usually doing the testing and decision making about the lot. The *producer* ships the lot to the consumer and waits for a decision while the consumer tests the lot. For this reason, Type I error is sometimes referred to as the **producer's risk.** The probability of committing a Type I error, or the producer's risk, is α. A Type I error can be committed only when the lot made by the producer is rejected by the consumer. The producer is particularly concerned about instances in which the lot follows specifications and should be acceptable, but the sample information leads the consumer to reject it.

The Type II error in acceptance sampling is sometimes referred to as the **consumer's risk.** The probability of committing a Type II error, or the consumer's risk, is β. A Type II error occurs when an unacceptable lot is accepted by the consumer. By accepting the lot, the consumer takes on the risk. Table 18.1 combines the concepts of Type I and Type II errors as outlined in Chapter 9 with the notion of consumer's and producer's risk discussed here.

The values of α and β can be computed in acceptance sampling by using specific percentage of nonconforming items for a given sample size and value of c. In the example of the bicycle manufacturer, suppose the brace supplier sends a lot of 3,000 braces. The bicycle manufacturer decides to sample 15 braces randomly selected from the lot and accept the lot if the number of nonconformances does not exceed one ($c = 1$). Suppose also that in the lot shipped by the brace supplier, 2% of the items actually are in nonconformance. What is the probability that the bicycle manufacturer will accept the lot?

This problem can be solved using the binomial distribution, provided the population is large in relation to the sample size. Recall from Chapter 5 that when sampling is done

TABLE 18.1		State of Nature	
Producer and Consumer Errors		*Null True*	*Null False*
Action — *Fail to Reject Null*		Correct decision	Type II error – consumer's risk
Reject Null		Type I error – producer's risk	Correct decision

without replacement, the binomial distribution is a close enough approximation to use if the sample size is less than 5% of the population size. If the sample size is greater than or equal to 5% of the population size, the hypergeometric distribution should be used. The value of p for the binomial distribution is denoted p_0 in acceptance sampling if the lot contains an acceptable proportion of nonconforming items. If the proportion of nonconforming items in the lot would be unacceptable to the receiver (customer), it is denoted p_1. For the bicycle problem, p_0 is .02, n is 15, and $c = 1$. Because $c = 1$, the lot will be accepted if the number of nonconformances in the sample is $x = 0$ or $x = 1$. Shown next are the binomial probability computations to determine what the chances are of the bicycle manufacturing company accepting the lot with the $c = 1$ decision rule if the supplier has shipped a lot of braces with 2% defects.

Probability of accepting the lot:

$$P(x = 0) + P(x = 1) = {}_{15}C_0(.02)^0(.98)^{15} + {}_{15}C_1(.02)^1(.98)^{14}$$
$$= .7386 + .2261 = .9647$$

Probability of rejecting the lot:

$$1 - [P(x = 0) + P(x = 1)] = 1 - [.9647] = .0353$$

If 2% is an acceptable level to the bicycle manufacturer and the lot of braces contains 2% nonconformances, there is a .9647 probability of correctly accepting the lot of braces. However, there is a .0353 probability of committing a Type I error and rejecting the lot even though its population proportion of nonconformances is acceptable. This .0353 is the producer's risk because the producer is shipping according to specifications but the lot is being rejected.

Now suppose the producer's lot contains 12% braces in nonconformance and that this proportion is unacceptable to the consumer (the bicycle manufacturer). What is the probability that the bicycle manufacturer will incorrectly accept the lot on the basis of the sample results even though the lot proportion would be unacceptable? The unacceptable population proportion is denoted p_1, and $p_1 = .12$. With $n = 15$ and $c = 1$, the probability of acceptance is

$$P(x = 0) + P(x = 1) = {}_{15}C_0(.12)^0(.88)^{15} + {}_{15}C_1(.12)^1(.88)^{14}$$
$$= .1470 + .3006 = .4476$$

This probability, .4476, is the probability of committing a Type II error. It is the consumer's risk because there is a 44.76% chance that, with the $c = 1$ criterion, the bicycle manufacturer will accept this lot even though the lot contains an unacceptable 12% of braces in nonconformance. Similarly, there is a $1 - .4476 = .5524$ probability of correctly rejecting the lot.

Suppose the bicycle manufacturer changes the value of c from 1 to 0. How do the risks change? For $n = 15$, $c = 0$, $p_0 = .02$, and $p_1 = .12$, we compute the producer's risk (α) as follows.

Determine the probability of accepting an acceptable lot.

$$P(x = 0) = {}_{15}C_0(.02)^0(.98)^{15} = .7386$$

Find the probability of rejecting an acceptable lot.

$$1 - P(x = 0) = 1 - .7386 = .2614 \text{ (producer's risk and } \alpha)$$

There is a .7386 probability that the lot will be accepted. Accepting the lot represents a correct decision if the $p_0 = .02$ for the entire lot is acceptable. There is also a $1 - .7386$, or .2614, probability of incorrectly rejecting the lot—that is, a .2614 probability of committing a Type I error, the producer's risk. To compute the consumer's risk (β), use the unacceptable (alternative) proportion of nonconformances, p_1, along with c to determine the probability of incorrectly accepting the lot.

$$P(x = 0) = {}_{15}C_0(.12)^0(.88)^{15} = .1470$$

There is a .1470 probability that the lot will be accepted because the sample contains no items in nonconformance, even though the lot contains 12% items in nonconformance, which is unacceptable to the bicycle manufacturer (the consumer). This .1470 is the value of β and is the consumer's risk.

In any given acceptance sampling plan, there are myriad possible values for n, c, p_0, and p_1. To enable decision makers to take a closer look at the possible risks involved, graphs called OC curves can be constructed. An **operating characteristic (OC) curve** *depicts the probabilities of accepting a lot based on the proportion of nonconformances in the lot, the sample size, and the value of c.* These curves are constructed by using the proportion of nonconformances as the *x* axis and the probability of acceptance as the *y* axis. Each curve is constructed for a given value of n and a given value of c.

As an example, suppose the bicycle manufacturer decides to inspect a sample of size $n = 15$, using $c = 0$ as the acceptance measure. The probability of acceptance can be computed for various possible proportions of nonconformance in a lot.

$$
\begin{aligned}
p = .00 \qquad & {}_{15}C_0(.00)^0(1.00)^{15} = 1.00 \\
p = .01 \qquad & {}_{15}C_0(.01)^0(.99)^{15} = .86 \\
p = .02 \qquad & {}_{15}C_0(.02)^0(.98)^{15} = .74 \\
p = .03 \qquad & {}_{15}C_0(.03)^0(.97)^{15} = .63 \\
p = .04 \qquad & {}_{15}C_0(.04)^0(.96)^{15} = .54 \\
p = .05 \qquad & {}_{15}C_0(.05)^0(.95)^{15} = .46 \\
p = .06 \qquad & {}_{15}C_0(.06)^0(.94)^{15} = .40 \\
p = .07 \qquad & {}_{15}C_0(.07)^0(.93)^{15} = .34 \\
p = .08 \qquad & {}_{15}C_0(.08)^0(.92)^{15} = .29 \\
p = .09 \qquad & {}_{15}C_0(.09)^0(.91)^{15} = .24 \\
p = .10 \qquad & {}_{15}C_0(.10)^0(.90)^{15} = .21 \\
p = .15 \qquad & {}_{15}C_0(.15)^0(.85)^{15} = .09
\end{aligned}
$$

From these and other values, an OC curve can be constructed for $n = 15$ and $c = 0$. This curve is displayed in Figure 18.8. Notice that as the actual percentage of nonconforming items increases toward 15%, the probability of accepting the lot based on a sample of size 15 and a c value of 0 decreases to less than .10. It becomes more and more difficult to get zero nonconforming items in a sample of 15 as the percentage of nonconformity in the population increases.

Suppose the brace producer shipped a lot with .02 nonconforming braces and that the .02 is acceptable to the bicycle manufacturer. There is a .26 chance that the lot will be rejected by the bicycle manufacturer. This probability is determined by computing the complement of accepting the lot.

$$
1 - {}_{15}C_0(.02)^0(.98)^{15} = 1 - .74 = .26
$$

This probability is the producer's risk. In Figure 18.9 it is superimposed on the OC curve from Figure 18.8.

Now suppose the lot contains 10% nonconforming braces and would be unacceptable to the bicycle manufacturer (the consumer). From the OC curve and the previous figures,

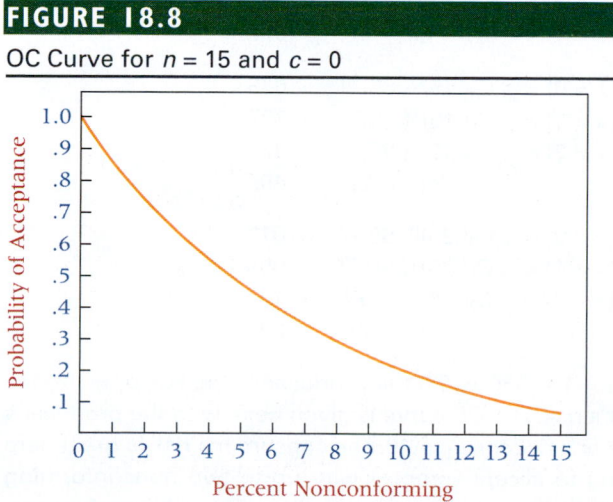

FIGURE 18.8

OC Curve for $n = 15$ and $c = 0$

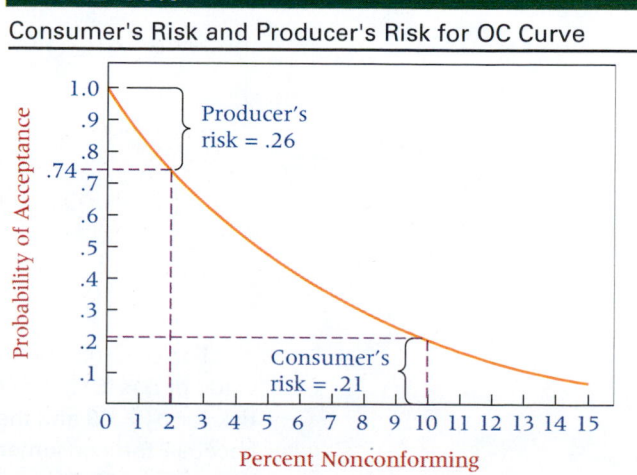

FIGURE 18.9

Consumer's Risk and Producer's Risk for OC Curve

the probability of the consumer accepting a lot with $n = 15$, $c = 0$, and $p_1 = .10$ is .21. This consumer's risk is also displayed in Figure 18.9.

Decision makers can balance the values of α and β for acceptance sampling schemes by examining various OC curves. From these results, they can select a plan that will help them control risk in the manner they desire. Organizations such as the U.S. military establishment have constructed tables and charts to meet this need.

DEMONSTRATION PROBLEM 18.5

A computer manufacturer purchases circuit boards from a supplier in lots of 5,000. The computer manufacturer (consumer) decided to use single-sample acceptance sampling to decide whether to accept or reject the lot. The sample size is 20 and $C = 2$. Construct an OC chart for this acceptance plan. Suppose $p_0 = .03$ is acceptable to the computer manufacturer but $p_1 = .10$ is not. Determine the producer's and consumer's risks for these values.

Solution

$n = 20$, $c = 2$

The lot will be accepted if $x \leq 2$. The probability computations for various selected values of p follow.

$$p = .01: \quad P(x = 0) = {}_{20}C_0(.01)^0(.99)^{20} = .818$$
$$P(x = 1) = {}_{20}C_1(.01)^1(.99)^{19} = .165$$
$$P(x = 2) = {}_{20}C_2(.01)^2(.99)^{18} = .016$$
$$P(x \leq 2) = .999$$

$$p = .02: \quad P(x = 0) = {}_{20}C_0(.02)^0(.98)^{20} = .668$$
$$P(x = 1) = {}_{20}C_1(.02)^1(.98)^{19} = .272$$
$$P(x = 2) = {}_{20}C_2(.02)^2(.98)^{18} = .053$$
$$\text{Prob}(x \leq 2) = .993$$

$$p = .03: \quad P(x = 0) = {}_{20}C_0(.03)^0(.97)^{20} = .544$$
$$P(x = 1) = {}_{20}C_1(.03)^1(.97)^{19} = .336$$
$$P(x = 2) = {}_{20}C_2(.03)^2(.97)^{18} = .100$$
$$P(x \leq 2) = .980$$

$$p = .05: \quad P(x = 0) = {}_{20}C_0(.05)^0(.95)^{20} = .358$$
$$P(x = 1) = {}_{20}C_1(.05)^1(.95)^{19} = .377$$
$$P(x = 2) = {}_{20}C_2(.05)^2(.95)^{18} = .189$$
$$P(x \leq 2) = .924$$

$$p = .10: \quad P(x = 0) = {}_{20}C_0(.10)^0(.90)^{20} = .122$$
$$P(x = 1) = {}_{20}C_1(.10)^1(.90)^{19} = .270$$
$$P(x = 2) = {}_{20}C_2(.10)^2(.90)^{18} = .285$$
$$P(x \leq 2) = .677$$

$$p = .15: \quad P(x = 0) = {}_{20}C_0(.15)^0(.85)^{20} = .039$$
$$P(x = 1) = {}_{20}C_1(.15)^1(.85)^{19} = .137$$
$$P(x = 2) = {}_{20}C_2(.15)^2(.85)^{18} = .229$$
$$P(x \leq 2) = .405$$

$$p = .20: \quad P(x = 0) = {}_{20}C_0(.20)^0(.80)^{20} = .012$$
$$P(x = 1) = {}_{20}C_1(.20)^1(.80)^{19} = .058$$
$$P(x = 2) = {}_{20}C_2(.20)^2(.80)^{18} = .137$$
$$P(x \leq 2) = .207$$

For $p_0 = .03$, the value of $\alpha = 1 - .980 = .02$, the producer's risk. For $p_1 = .10$, the value of β is .677, the consumer's risk. The OC curve is given next, with the producer's risk for $p_0 = .03$ and the consumer's risk for $p_1 = .10$. The consumer's risk is great here because the consumer is willing to accept samples with up to two nonconforming items out of 20. This sample acceptance value, $c = 2$, represents a possibility of accepting $2/20 = .10 = 10\%$ defective items in the sample. If the computer manufacturer is unwilling to accept $p_1 = .10$ in the population, it will have trouble rejecting such a population when accepting up to 10% defective items in the sample.

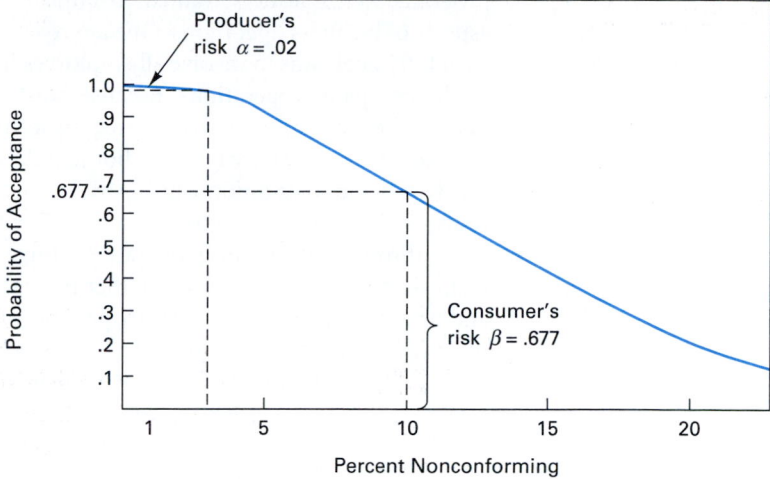

18.4 PROBLEMS

18.12 An office supply company ordered a lot of 4,000 pens. When the lot arrives, the company inspector will randomly inspect 15 pens. If more than four pens in the sample are nonconforming, the lot will be rejected. If fewer than two pens are nonconforming, the lot will be accepted. If two, three, or four pens are nonconforming, a second sample of size 10 will be taken. The value of c_2 is 3. Suppose the inspector finds two nonconforming items in the first sample and two in the second sample. What is the inspector's decision? Why? What type of acceptance plan is used here?

18.13 A manufacturer purchased a lot of 1,700 ring seals from a producer. The manufacturer's inspectors are using a single-sample acceptance sampling plan to decide whether to accept the lot. The sample size is 10, and if the inspectors find any seals out of conformance in the sample, the lot will be rejected. Suppose the lot has 5% nonconforming seals, which is acceptable to the manufacturer (consumer). What is the producer's risk? Suppose the lot contains 14% nonconforming seals, which is unacceptable to the manufacturer. What is the consumer's risk?

18.14 A book wholesaler received a lot of 2,000 books from a printer. The wholesaler plans to sample 12 books and use single-sample acceptance sampling to reach a decision about the lot. If more than one book is defective, the wholesaler will reject the lot. Suppose the printer is fairly certain that only 4% of the books are defective. What is the producer's risk? Suppose 15% of the lot of books is defective and that this rate would be too high for the wholesaler to accept. What is the wholesaler's risk in using this acceptance sampling?

18.15 Construct an OC curve for $n = 8$ and $c = 0$. Determine the producer's risk for $p_0 = .03$ and consumer's risk for $p_1 = .10$. Display these values on the curve.

18.16 Construct an OC curve for $n = 11$ and $c = 1$. Show the producer's risk for $p_0 = .08$ and the consumer's risk for $p_1 = .20$ on the curve.

Quality Control at Xerox

Xerox uses thousands of processes. In investigating each process, Xerox could likely discover barriers to productivity and quality. Under the Leadership Through Quality thrust of the 1980s, Xerox spent four years training more than 100,000 employees in the principles of quality. In an effort to take the quality effort to another level through its Xerox 2000 program, Xerox leaders wanted to improve productivity and integrate quality into all aspects of business operations. One approach Xerox may have taken in an attempt to meet such lofty goals was to involve all employees in a drive to flowchart processes in all aspects of the company's operations. Because most employees received TQM training, they are likely to be familiar with process analysis techniques and flowcharting.

As the processes are laid out, bottlenecks and problems begin to manifest themselves. Workers begin to question why a particular sequence of activities is followed in a process. Brainstorming may begin to occur as quality teams study the process flowcharts. Such an effort throughout the company can pay huge dividends through waste reduction and the identification of problem areas. Other process diagnostic techniques such as Pareto charts and fishbone diagrams can identify possible problem causes and determine which ones are most common.

Xerox stands as a world leader in the area of benchmarking. The company developed a competitive products laboratory where products from competing companies were disassembled and analyzed. From this work, the company learned how other firms could produce quality products at low prices. Xerox was able to improve its designs and its processes.

Once standards are set either on the assembly line or in such areas as customer service, how can these standards be monitored? One useful tool for constant monitoring is the control chart. By use of statistical process control techniques, product samples can be tested and statistically measured. Control charts can be drawn to display product attributes on a regular basis from samples. This tool enables workers to determine when processes are getting out of control and to take action to prevent further deterioration of the process. Using control charts can result in less scrap and waste because the system responds much faster to off-specifications product.

Customer satisfaction, employee attitude, and many other quality issues can be monitored using control charts. For example, if a sudden persistent downturn in average customer satisfaction scores is noted, then the company would want to investigate so that they can reverse the trend.

Xerox adopted just-in-time inventory practices as part of their Leadership Through Quality effort. During this period, they reduced the number of suppliers from 5,000 to about 300. Dealing with fewer suppliers afforded Xerox an opportunity to greatly improve relations and communications with its suppliers. The suppliers began working hand-in-hand with Xerox in planning, designing, and producing. Xerox was able to realize many just-in-time advantages in its system. In addition, Xerox offered its suppliers access to much of the training that Xerox employees were receiving. Xerox does not mass inspect supplies and materials coming from its suppliers, and it is likely that Xerox's suppliers themselves test the batches of goods and materials. Whether Xerox or the suppliers test batches to determine whether they will be acceptable, acceptance sampling can be a part of the procedure. With acceptance sampling, only a portion of the lot needs to be tested. Probabilities can be used to determine whether the evidence of the sample indicates the lot or batch is acceptable.

Xerox continues to be a world leader in copiers and other related products. Through Xerox 2000 and other new initiatives, company leaders hope not only to continue the total quality management that shaped their culture for the past 20 years, but also to propel Xerox to ever-high levels of quality.

SUMMARY

Quality means many different things to different people. According to one definition, a quality product delivers to the customer those attributes that have been agreed upon by both buyer and seller. Leading quality experts such as Philip B. Crosby, Armand V. Feigenbaum, and David A. Garvin suggest various divergent views on the notion of quality.

Quality control is the collection of strategies, techniques, and actions an organization can use to ensure the production of a quality product. For decades, U.S. companies used after-process quality control, which essentially consisted of inspectors determining whether a product complied with its specifications. During the 1980s, U.S. companies joined Western European and Asian businesses in instituting in-process quality control, which enables the producer to determine weaknesses and flaws during the production process.

Total quality management occurs when all members of an organization—from the CEO to the line worker—are involved in improving quality. One of the main proponents of total quality management was W. Edwards Deming. Deming was known for his cause-and-effect explanation of total quality management in a company, which is sometimes referred to as the Deming chain reaction. In addition, Deming presented 14 points that can lead to improved total quality management.

Five important quality concepts are benchmarking, just-in-time inventory systems, reengineering, Six Sigma, and team building. Benchmarking is a technique through which a company attempts to develop product and process excellence by examining and emulating the best practices and techniques used in the industry. Just-in-time inventory systems are inventory systems that focus on raw materials, subparts, and suppliers. Just-in-time is a philosophy of coordination and cooperation between supplier and manufacturer such that a part or raw material arrives just as it is needed. This approach saves on inventory and also serves as a catalyst for discovering bottlenecks and inefficiencies. It changes the manufacturer-supplier relationship. Reengineering is a radical approach to total quality management in which the core business process is redesigned. Six Sigma is a methodology and a measurement. A goal of Six Sigma is that no more than 3.4 attributes or products per million be defective. It is essentially a philosophy of zero defects. Team building is the creation of organized groups of employees that undertake management tasks and perform other functions, such as overseeing projects.

Four diagnostic techniques used in analyzing processes are flowcharts, Pareto analysis, fishbone (cause-and-effect) diagrams, and control charts. Flowcharts are schematic representations of all activities that occur in a process. Pareto analysis is a method of examining types of defects that occur with a product. The result is usually a vertical bar chart that depicts the most common types of defects ranked in order of occurrence. The fishbone diagram displays potential causes of quality problems. The diagram is shaped like a fish skeleton,

with the head being the problem and the skeletal bones being the potential causes. A control chart is a graphic method of evaluating whether a process is or is not in a state of statistical control.

Control charts are used to monitor product variation, thus enabling operators, technicians, and managers to see when a process gets out of control. The $\bar{x}$ chart and the R chart are two types of control charts for measurements. The $\bar{x}$ chart is a graph of sample means computed on a series of small random samples over time. The R chart is a plot of sample ranges. The $\bar{x}$ chart plots the measure of location, whereas the R chart plots a measure of variability. The p chart and the c chart are two types of control charts for nonconformance. The p chart graphs the proportions of sample items that are in noncompliance. The c chart displays the number of nonconformances per item for a series of sampled items. All four types of control chart are plotted around a centerline and upper and lower control limits. The control limits are located three standard deviations from the centerline.

Acceptance sampling is another type of statistical quality control technique. It involves inspecting a random sample of items taken from a lot and determining whether to accept the lot on the basis of the sample results. Single-sample acceptance sampling plans allow for taking only one sample per lot and reaching a conclusion based on the inspection of that sample. Double-sample acceptance sampling plans allow for taking a second sample and considering the results of tests on that sample along with those from the first sample if the results obtained from the first sample are not conclusive. Researchers can examine the potential error risks in acceptance sampling by constructing operating characteristic (OC) curves. The producer's risk is the probability of committing a Type I error. The consumer's risk is the probability of committing a Type II error.

KEY TERMS

acceptance sampling	in-process quality control	process	total quality management
after-process quality control	Ishikawa diagram	producer's risk	(TQM)
benchmarking	just-in-time inventory system	product quality	transcendent quality
c chart	lower control limit (LCL)	quality	upper control limit (UCL)
cause-and-effect diagram	manufacturing quality	quality circle	user quality
centerline	multiple-sample plan	quality control	value quality
consumer's risk	operating characteristic	R chart	$\bar{x}$ chart
control chart	(OC) curve	reengineering	
double-sample plan	p chart	single-sample plan	
fishbone diagram	Pareto analysis	Six Sigma	
flowchart	Pareto chart	team building	

FORMULAS

$\bar{x}$ Charts

Centerline: $\bar{\bar{x}} = \dfrac{\sum \bar{x}}{k}$

UCL: $\bar{\bar{x}} + A_2 \bar{R}$

LCL: $\bar{\bar{x}} - A_2 \bar{R}$

or

UCL: $\bar{\bar{x}} + A_3 s$

LCL: $\bar{\bar{x}} - A_3 \bar{s}$

R Charts

Centerline: $\bar{R} = \dfrac{\sum R}{k}$

UCL: $D_4 \bar{R}$

LCL: $D_3 \bar{R}$

p Charts

Centerline: $p = \dfrac{\sum \hat{p}}{k}$

UCL: $p + 3\sqrt{\dfrac{p \cdot q}{n}}$

LCL: $p - 3\sqrt{\dfrac{p \cdot q}{n}}$

c Charts

Centerline: $\bar{c} = \dfrac{c_1 + c_2 + c_3 + \cdots + c_i}{i}$

UCL: $\bar{c} + 3\sqrt{\bar{c}}$

LCL: $\bar{c} - 3\sqrt{\bar{c}}$

ETHICAL CONSIDERATIONS

Unethical or borderline ethical behavior can occur in many areas of total quality management. At the top, CEOs and other high-level managers can profess to the world that the company is committed to quality and not truly promote quality in the organization. Managers who use the quality movement only as a tool for attention and leverage and do not actually intend to implement the process may be acting unethically.

Some of the specifics of quality control and statistical process control lend themselves to unethical behavior. Just-in-time systems can be used as an excuse to implement favoritism among suppliers. With the move to reduce the number of suppliers, contracting managers can be more selective in choosing suppliers. This practice can give contracting agents or purchasing agents more leverage in securing deals through unethical means.

Just-in-time systems often encourage the supplier to do the testing rather than the manufacturer. This self-evaluation opens opportunity for the falsification of records and tests. It is hoped that such behavior is uncovered by just-in-time systems that place pressure on suppliers to ship on-specification parts and materials. The customer or user of the supplies in a just-in-time system is more likely to discover off-specification material than users in traditional systems.

Benchmarking could easily lend itself to violation of patent laws if a company is not careful. It could also encourage business espionage and unfair competitive practices. Benchmarking could create an atmosphere of continually seeking ways to "steal" competitive ideas and innovations.

Control charts and acceptance sampling present the same potential for unethical behavior as any sampling process. Those workers constructing the charts have opportunity to falsify data, selectively choose favorable items, or graphically misrepresent data to make a system look in control or a lot seem acceptable when in fact it is not.

The implementation of a sound quality program in a company must be based on teamwork, mutual support, trust, and honesty. Unethical behavior in quality control can set the process back for years, if not permanently. The intent in the quality movement is to bring out the best in people so as to optimize the quality of the product.

SUPPLEMENTARY PROBLEMS

CALCULATING THE STATISTICS

18.17 Create a flowchart from the following sequence of activities: Begin. Flow to activity A. Flow to decision B. If Yes, flow to activity C. If No, flow to activity D. From C flow to activity E and to activity F. From F, flow to decision G. If Yes, flow to decision H. If No at G, stop. At H, if Yes, flow to activity I and on to activity J and then stop. If No at H, flow to activity J and stop. At D, flow to activity K, flow to L, and flow to decision M. If Yes at M, stop. If No at M, flow to activity N, then stop.

18.18 An examination of rejects shows at least 10 problems. A frequency tally of the problems follows. Construct a Pareto chart for these data.

Problem	Frequency
1	673
2	29
3	108
4	379
5	73
6	564
7	12
8	402
9	54
10	202

18.19 A brainstorm session on possible causes of a problem resulted in five possible causes: A, B, C, D, and E. Cause A has three possible subcauses, cause B has four, cause C has two, cause D has five, and cause E has three. Construct a fishbone diagram for this problem and its possible causes.

18.20 Solve the following.

a. A random sample of 13 items is taken from a lot. If fewer than two items are defective, the lot will be accepted. If two or more are defective, the lot will be rejected. Suppose the lot contains 5% defective items, and that proportion is acceptable to the customer. What is the probability the lot will be rejected? What is the probability it will be accepted? Suppose the lot contains 12% defective items, which is unacceptable to the customer. What is the probability that the customer will incorrectly accept the lot?

b. A lot has 8,575 items. The customer plans to sample 20 of these items randomly to determine whether to accept the lot. If no more than two of the sample are defective, the customer will accept the lot. Suppose the lot contains only 3% defective items, which is quite acceptable to the customer. What is the producer's risk?

TESTING YOUR UNDERSTANDING

18.21 A bottled-water company has been randomly inspecting bottles of water to determine whether they are acceptable for delivery and sale. The inspectors are looking at water quality, bottle condition, and seal tightness. A series of 10 random samples of 50 bottles each is taken. Some bottles are rejected. Use the following information on the number of bottles from each batch that were rejected as being out of compliance to construct a p chart.

Sample	N	Number out of Compliance
1	50	3
2	50	11
3	50	7
4	50	2
5	50	5
6	50	8
7	50	0
8	50	9
9	50	1
10	50	6

18.22 A fruit juice company sells a glass container filled with 24 ounces of cranapple juice. Inspectors are concerned about the consistency of volume of fill in these containers. Every 2 hours for 3 days of production, a sample of five containers is randomly selected and the volume of fill is measured. The results follow.

Sample 1	Sample 2	Sample 3	Sample 4
24.05	24.01	24.03	23.98
24.01	24.02	23.95	24.00
24.02	24.10	24.00	24.01
23.99	24.03	24.01	24.01
24.04	24.08	23.99	24.00

Sample 5	Sample 6	Sample 7	Sample 8
23.97	24.02	24.01	24.08
23.99	24.05	24.00	24.03
24.02	24.01	24.00	24.00
24.01	24.00	23.97	24.05
24.00	24.01	24.02	24.01

Sample 9	Sample 10	Sample 11	Sample 12
24.00	24.00	24.01	24.00
24.02	24.01	23.99	24.05
24.03	24.00	24.02	24.04
24.01	24:00	24.03	24.02
24.01	24.00	24.01	24.00

Use this information to construct $\bar{x}$ and R charts and comment on any samples that are out of compliance.

18.23 A motor company purchases industrial hoses in lots of 500. The company uses acceptance sampling to determine whether it will accept or reject the hoses. It uses a single-sample plan with $n = 15$. The company will not accept a lot unless the lot contains no nonconforming hoses. Construct an OC curve for this situation. Suppose 2% of the hoses in a lot are nonconforming, which is acceptable to the motor company. What is the producer's risk? Suppose the lot contains .10 that are in nonconformance, which is unacceptable. What is the consumer's risk?

18.24 A metal-manufacturing company produces sheet metal. Statistical quality control technicians randomly select sheets to be inspected for blemishes and size problems. The number of nonconformances per sheet is tallied. Shown here are the results of testing 36 sheets of metal. Use the data to construct a c chart. What is the centerline? What is the meaning of the centerline value?

Sheet Number	Number of Nonconformances	Sheet Number	Number of Nonconformances
1	4	19	1
2	2	20	3
3	1	21	4
4	1	22	0
5	3	23	2
6	0	24	3
7	4	25	0
8	5	26	0
9	2	27	4
10	1	28	2
11	2	29	5
12	0	30	3
13	5	31	1
14	4	32	2
15	1	33	0
16	2	34	4
17	1	35	2
18	0	36	3

18.25 A manufacturing company produces cylindrical tubes for engines that are specified to be 1.20 centimeters thick. As part of the company's statistical quality control effort, random samples of four tubes are taken each hour. The tubes are measured to determine whether they are within thickness tolerances. Shown here are the thickness data in centimeters for nine samples of tubes. Use these data to develop an $\bar{x}$ chart and an R chart. Comment on whether or not the process appears to be in control at this point.

Sample 1	Sample 2	Sample 3	Sample 4	Sample 5
1.22	1.20	1.21	1.16	1.24
1.19	1.20	1.18	1.17	1.20
1.20	1.22	1.17	1.20	1.21
1.23	1.20	1.20	1.16	1.18

Sample 6	Sample 7	Sample 8	Sample 9
1.19	1.24	1.17	1.22
1.21	1.17	1.23	1.17
1.21	1.18	1.22	1.16
1.20	1.19	1.16	1.19

18.26 A manufacturer produces digital watches. Every 2 hours a sample of six watches is selected randomly to be tested. Each watch is run for exactly 15 minutes and is timed by an accurate, precise timing device. Because of the variation among watches, they do not all run the same. Shown here are the data from eight different samples given in minutes. Use these data to construct $\bar{x}$ and R charts. Observe the results and comment on whether the process is in control.

Sample 1	Sample 2	Sample 3	Sample 4
15.01	15.03	14.96	15.00
14.99	14.96	14.97	15.01
14.99	15.01	14.96	14.97
15.00	15.02	14.99	15.01
14.98	14.97	15.01	14.99
14.99	15.01	14.98	14.96

Sample 5	Sample 6	Sample 7	Sample 8
15.02	15.02	15.03	14.96
15.03	15.01	15.04	14.99
14.99	14.97	15.03	15.02
15.01	15.00	15.00	15.01
15.02	15.01	15.01	14.98
15.01	14.99	14.99	15.02

18.27 A company produces outdoor home thermometers. For a variety of reasons, a thermometer can be tested and found to be out of compliance with company specification. The company takes samples of thermometers on a regular basis and tests each one to determine whether it meets company standards. Shown here are data from 12 different random samples of 75 thermometers. Use these data to construct a p chart. Comment on the pattern of points in the chart.

Sample	n	Number out of Compliance
1	75	9
2	75	3
3	75	0
4	75	2
5	75	7
6	75	14
7	75	11
8	75	8
9	75	5
10	75	4
11	75	0
12	75	7

18.28 A plastics company makes thousands of plastic bottles for another company that manufactures saline solution for users of soft contact lenses. The plastics company randomly inspects a sample of its bottles as part of its quality control program. Inspectors look for blemishes on the bottle, size and thickness, ability to close, leaks, labeling problems, and so on. Shown here are the results of tests completed on 25 bottles. Use these data to construct a c chart. Observe the results and comment on the chart.

Bottle Number	Number of Nonconformances	Bottle Number	Number of Nonconformances
1	1	14	0
2	0	15	0
3	1	16	0
4	0	17	1
5	0	18	0
6	2	19	0
7	1	20	1
8	1	21	0
9	0	22	1
10	1	23	2
11	0	24	0
12	2	25	1
13	1		

18.29 A manufacturer of men's jeans purchases zippers in lots of 800. The jeans manufacturer uses single-sample acceptance sampling with a sample size of 10 to determine whether to accept the lot. The manufacturer uses $c = 2$ as the acceptance number. Construct an OC curve for this problem. Suppose the lot actually contains 10% nonconforming zippers, which is acceptable to the manufacturer. What is the producer's risk? Suppose the lot contains 30% unacceptable zippers, which is not acceptable. What is the consumer's risk? (*Hint:* Use Table A.2 to work this problem.)

18.30 A bathtub manufacturer closely inspects several tubs on every shift for nonconformances such as leaks, lack of symmetry, unstable base, drain malfunctions, and so on. The following list gives the number of nonconformances per tub for 40 tubs. Use these data to construct a c chart of nonconformances for bathtubs. Comment on the results of this chart.

Tub	Number of Nonconformances	Tub	Number of Nonconformances
1	3	21	2
2	2	22	5
3	3	23	1
4	1	24	3
5	4	25	4
6	2	26	3
7	2	27	2
8	1	28	0
9	4	29	1
10	2	30	0
11	3	31	2
12	0	32	1
13	3	33	2
14	2	34	1
15	2	35	1
16	1	36	1
17	0	37	3
18	4	38	0
19	3	39	1
20	2	40	4

18.31 A glass manufacturer produces hand mirrors. Each mirror is supposed to meet company standards for such things as glass thickness, ability to reflect, size of handle, quality of glass, color of handle, and so on. To control for these features, the company quality people randomly sample 40 mirrors every shift and determine how many of the mirrors are out of compliance on at least one feature. Shown here are the data for 15 such samples. Use the data to construct a p chart. Observe the results and comment on the control of the process as indicated by the chart.

Sample	n	Number out of Compliance
1	40	2
2	40	0
3	40	6
4	40	3
5	40	1
6	40	1
7	40	5
8	40	0
9	40	4
10	40	3
11	40	2
12	40	2
13	40	6
14	40	1
15	40	0

INTERPRETING THE OUTPUT

18.32 Study the MINITAB chart on the fill of a product that is supposed to contain 12 ounces. Does the process appear to be out of control? Why or why not?

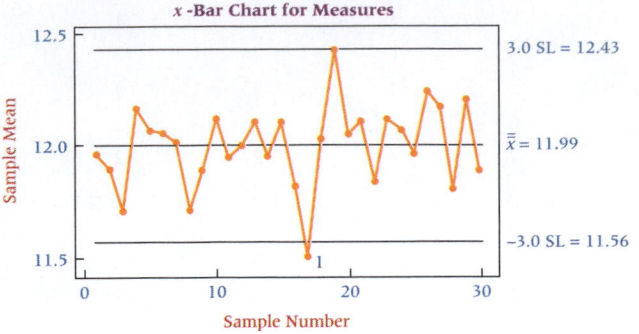

x-Bar Chart for Measures

18.33 Study the MINITAB R chart for the product and data used in Problem 18.32. Comment on the state of the production process for this item.

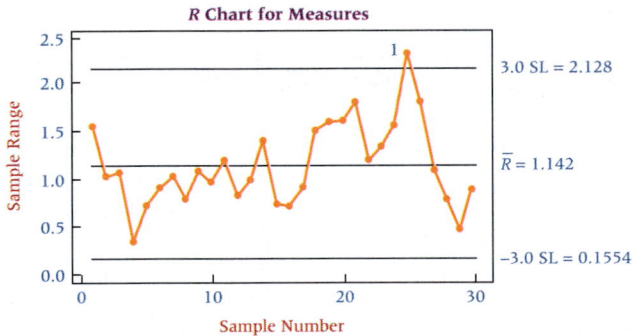

R Chart for Measures

18.34 Study the MINITAB p chart for a manufactured item. The chart represents the results of testing 30 items at a

time for compliance. Sixty different samples were taken for this chart. Discuss the results and the implications for the production process.

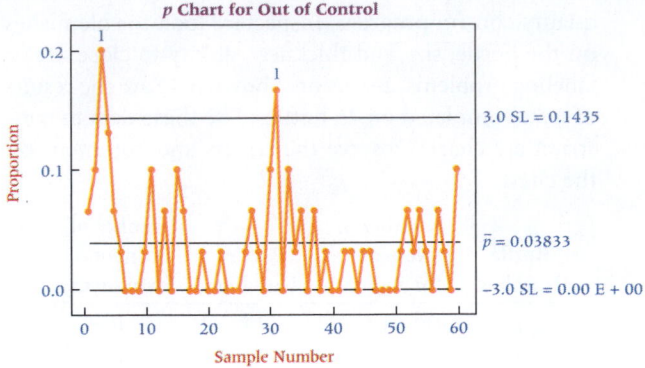

p Chart for Out of Control

18.35 Study the MINITAB c chart for nonconformances for a part produced in a manufacturing process. Comment on the results.

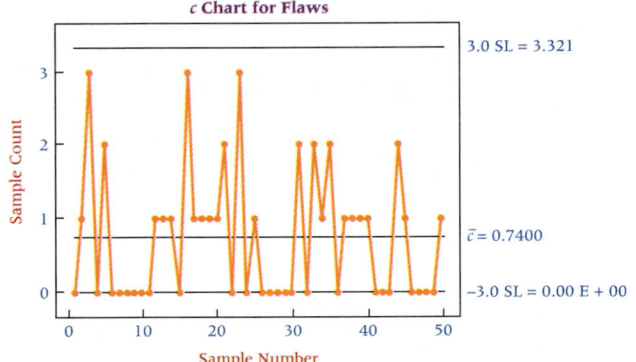

c Chart for Flaws

ANALYZING THE DATABASES

see **www.wiley.com/college/black**

1. A dairy company in the manufacturing database tests its quart milk container fills for volume in four-container samples. Shown here are the results of 10 such samples and the volume measurements in quarts. Use the information to construct both an $\bar{x}$ and an R chart for the data. Discuss the results. What are the centerline, LCL, and UCL for each of these charts?

Sample Number	Measurements			
1	.98	1.01	1.05	1.03
2	1.02	.94	.97	1.02
3	1.11	1.02	.93	1.01
4	.95	.98	1.02	.96
5	1.03	1.01	1.01	.95
6	1.04	.93	.91	.96
7	.94	1.12	1.10	1.03
8	1.03	.92	.98	1.03
9	1.01	1.01	.99	1.00
10	1.05	.96	1.00	1.04

2. A hospital in the hospital database takes weekly samples of patient account statements for 12 weeks with each sample containing 40 accounts. Auditors analyze the account statements, looking for nonconforming statements. Shown here are the results of the 12 samples. Use these data to construct a p chart

for proportion of nonconforming statements. What is the centerline? What are UCL and LCL? Comment on the control chart.

Sample	Number of Nonconforming Statements
1	1
2	0
3	6
4	3
5	0
6	2
7	8
8	3
9	5
10	2
11	2
12	1

3. A company in the financial database manufactures laptop computers. A supplier is shipping the company a particular part in lots of 5,000. The computer manufacturing company (consumer) is doing acceptance sampling with samples of size 25. If the supplier is actually producing lots with only 3% defective parts and if this proportion is acceptable to the consumer, what is the producer's risk if $c = 1$? Suppose the supplier is actually producing the part in lots with 12% defective parts, which is unacceptable to the consumer. If c is still 1, what is the consumer's risk? Construct an OC curve for $n = 25$ and $c = 1$. Comment on the curve.

CASE: ROBOTRON

Robotron Corporation manufactured bonding products for the automobile industry for more than two decades. For several years, Robotron felt it produced and delivered a high-quality product because it rarely received complaints from customers. However, early in the 1980s General Motors gave Robotron an order for induction bonding machines to cure adhesive in auto door joints. Actually, the machines were shipped to a Michigan plant of Sanyo Manufacturing that GM was using as a door builder.

The Japanese firm was unhappy with the quality of the machines. Robotron president Leonard Brzozowski went to the Sanyo plant to investigate the situation in person and learned that the Japanese had a much higher quality standard than the usual American customers. Tolerances were much smaller and inspection was more demanding. Brzozowski said that he realized for the first time that the philosophy, engineering, management, and shop practices of Robotron did not qualify the company for world competition. Brzozowski said that this was the most embarrassing time of his professional career. What should Robotron do about this situation?

Brzozowski began by sending a group of hourly employees to the Sanyo plant. There they met the customer and heard firsthand the many complaints about their product. The workers could see the difference in quality between their machines and those of Sanyo. The plant visit was extremely effective. On the way home, the Robotron workers started discussing what they could do to improve quality.

The company took several steps to begin the process of quality improvement. It established new inspection procedures, bought more accurate inspection tools, changed internal control procedures, and developed baselines against which to measure progress. Teams were organized and sent out to customers six months after a purchase to determine customer satisfaction. A hotline was established for customers to call to report product dissatisfaction.

For one month, engineers assembled machinery in the shop under the direction of hourly employees. This exercise gave the engineers a new awareness of the importance of accurate, clear drawings; designing smaller, lighter weight details; and minimizing the number of machined surfaces.

Robotron's effort paid off handsomely. Claims under warranty dropped 40% in three years, during which time orders rose at a compound annual rate of 13.5%. The company cut costs and streamlined procedures and processes. Sales increased and new markets opened.

In 1997, Robotron received ISO-9001 certification. Early in 1998, Robotron merged with ELOTHERM, a European company, so that Robotron could more easily enjoy a presence in the European market and at the same time provide ELOTHERM opportunities in North America. Robotron's bonding business expanded into induction heating systems, heat treating, tube welding, and electrical discharge machines. The company maintains a quality system that takes corrective action in response to customer complaints, employee suggestions, or supplier defects. Robotron-Elotherm's U.S. headquarters are located in Southfield, Michigan, and its European headquarters in Remscheid, Germany.

Discussion

1. As a part of quality improvement, it is highly likely that Robotron analyzed its manufacturing processes. Suppose that as Robotron improved quality, the company wanted to examine other processes including the flow of work orders from the time they are received until they are filled. Use the following verbal sketch of some of the activities that might take place in such a flow as a start, and add some of your own ideas as you draw a flowchart for the process of work orders.

Work order flow: Received at mailroom. Sent to order processing office. Examined by order processing clerk who decides whether the item is a standard item or a custom item. If it is a standard item, the order is sent to the warehouse. If the item is available, the item is shipped and the order is sent to the billing department. If the item is not available, the order is sent to the plant where it is received by a manufacturing clerk. The clerk checks to determine whether such an item is being manufactured. If so, the order is sent to the end of the assembly line where it will be tagged with one such item. If not, the order is sent to the beginning of the assembly line and flows along the assembly line with the item as it is being made. In either case, when the part comes off the assembly line, the order is attached to the item and sent to shipping. The shipping clerk then ships the item and sends the order to billing. If the ordered item is a customized part, the order is sent straight from the order processing clerk to manufacturing where it follows the same procedures as already described for standard items that have not been manufactured yet.

2. Virtually all quality manufacturers use some type of control chart to monitor performance. Suppose the MINITAB control charts shown here are for two different parts produced by Robotron during a particular period. Part 173 is specified to weigh 183 grams. Part 248 contains an opening that is specified to be 35 millimeters in diameter. Study these charts and report to Robotron what you found. Is there any reason for concern? Is everything in control?

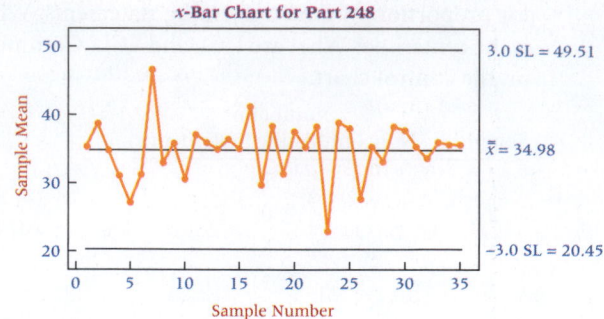

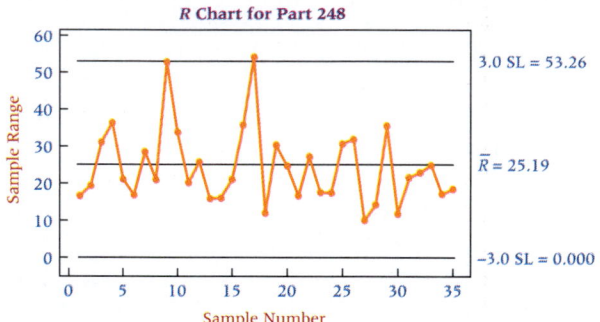

3. Suppose Robotron also keeps p charts on nonconformance. The MINITAB chart shown here represents the proportion of nonconforming items for a given part over 100 samples. Study the chart and write a brief report to Robotron about what you learned from the chart. Think about overall performance, out-of-control samples, samples that have outstanding performance, and any general trends that you see.

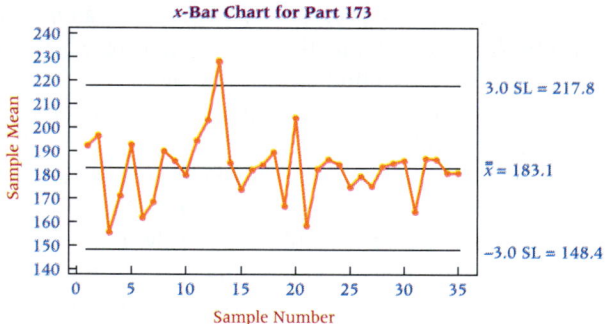

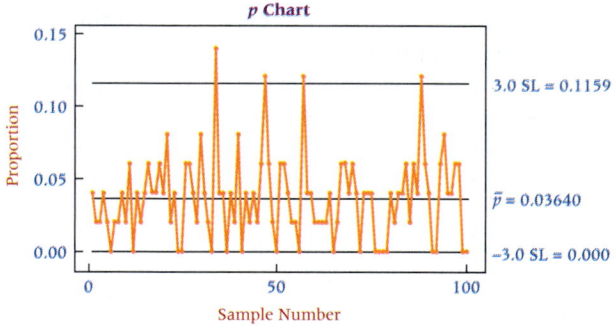

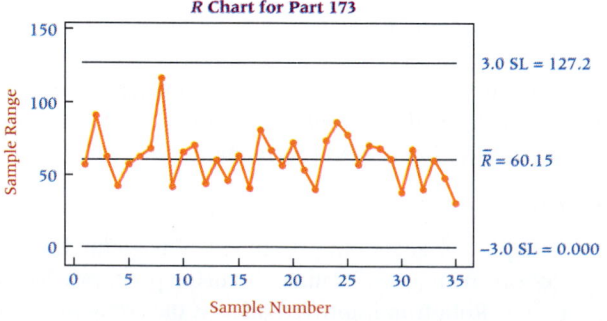

Source: Adapted from "ROBOTRON: Qualifying For Global Competition," *Real-World Lessons for America's Small Businesses: Insights from the Blue Chip Enterprise Initiative.* Published by *Nation's Business* magazine on behalf of Connecticut Mutual Life Insurance Company and the U.S. Chamber of Commerce in association with The Blue Chip Enterprise Initiative 1994. See also Robotron, available at http://www.robotron.com/ aboutus/iso9001.html; http://www.robotron.com/products; http://www.robotron.com/aboutus /merger.html; http://www.robotron.com/aboutus/jobs.html.

USING THE COMPUTER

MINITAB Windows has the capability of producing several different types of quality charts and graphs. All of the quality analyses begin with the selection of **Stat** from the menu bar. From the pull-down menu that appears, two options can be used to generate quality analyses. The first option is **Control Charts,** which can be used to produce control charts. The **Control Charts** pull-down menu offers many options. We will focus on the four types of control charts presented in the chapter. To construct an $\bar{x}$ chart, select **Xbar** from the pull-down menu. To construct an R chart, select **R** from the pull-down menu. To construct a p chart, select **P** from the pull-down menu. To construct a c chart, select **C** from the pull-down menu. The specific dialog box will appear.

In using the **Xbar** option, you can choose the data stacked in one column or in multiple columns. If the data are all in a single column, select **Single column.** After entering the location containing the data in this box, insert the size of the samples in the second box, **Subgroup size.** If your samples are arranged in rows across several columns, choose **Subgroups across rows of** and place the columns that contain these data. You can place a historical mean or standard deviation in the dialog box or allow MINITAB to compute estimates for you using the sample data. Several options are available, including one called **Tests** that allows you to select which of several types of problems in the data you would like the control chart to display (e.g., nine points in a row on the same side of the centerline). The **R** chart dialog box looks similar to the $\bar{x}$ chart dialog box and has basically the same options except that fewer tests are offered and you are not given the option of inputting a historical mean.

With **P** charts, the defects per sample are entered into one column. In the dialog box, enter the location of the column containing these data in the **Variable** space. In the line, **Subgroup size,** enter the number in each sample size if all sample sizes are the same. If the sample sizes are different, enter these in a separate column from the original data and enter the column location of these sample sizes under **Subgroups in.** You are offered the option of entering a historical value of p, otherwise MINITAB will estimate it from the data. Several options are offered in the dialog box. One of these is **Tests,** which allows you to select several tests to be displayed on the chart. The **C** chart dialog box assumes that all the data (defects per unit) are in one column. Enter the location of the data under **Variable.** You may enter a historical value of the mean. If you do not enter anything, MINITAB will compute an estimate based on the sample data. As with the p chart, several options are available. The **Tests** option works the same as it does for the p chart.

The second option from the pull-down menu under **Stat** is **Quality Tools.** Pareto charts and fishbone (cause-and-effect) diagrams can be constructed. To construct a Pareto chart, select **Pareto Chart.** If you recorded the frequencies in one column and the labels in another, check **Chart defects table** and enter the column locations of the frequencies and the labels. If the chart defects are individually entered rather than tallied, check the **Chart defects data in** selection. To construct a fishbone diagram, select **Cause-and-Effect** under **Quality Tools.** In the dialog box that appears, list the columns containing the causes in the spaces provided under the **Causes** label. To change the default branch labels, fill in the spaces under **Label** with the labels that you want to use. You may forgo labeling the branches and delete any missing or empty branches (if you have fewer than six branches) by checking the appropriate box.

APPENDIX A: TABLES

TABLE A.1 — Random Numbers

12651	61646	11769	75109	86996	97669	25757	32535	07122	76763
81769	74436	02630	72310	45049	18029	07469	42341	98173	79260
36737	98863	77240	76251	00654	64688	09343	70278	67331	98729
82861	54371	76610	94934	72748	44124	05610	53750	95938	01485
21325	15732	24127	37431	09723	63529	73977	95218	96074	42138
74146	47887	62463	23045	41490	07954	22597	60012	98866	90959
90759	64410	54179	66075	61051	75385	51378	08360	95946	95547
55683	98078	02238	91540	21219	17720	87817	41705	95785	12563
79686	17969	76061	83748	55920	83612	41540	86492	06447	60568
70333	00201	86201	69716	78185	62154	77930	67663	29529	75116
14042	53536	07779	04157	41172	36473	42123	43929	50533	33437
59911	08256	06596	48416	69770	68797	56080	14223	59199	30162
62368	62623	62742	14891	39247	52242	98832	69533	91174	57979
57529	97751	54976	48957	74599	08759	78494	52785	68526	64618
15469	90574	78033	66885	13936	42117	71831	22961	94225	31816
18625	23674	53850	32827	81647	80820	00420	63555	74489	80141
74626	68394	88562	70745	23701	45630	65891	58220	35442	60414
11119	16519	27384	90199	79210	76965	99546	30323	31664	22845
41101	17336	48951	53674	17880	45260	08575	49321	36191	17095
32123	91576	84221	78902	82010	30847	62329	63898	23268	74283
26091	68409	69704	82267	14751	13151	93115	01437	56945	89661
67680	79790	48462	59278	44185	29616	76531	19589	83139	28454
15184	19260	14073	07026	25264	08388	27182	22557	61501	67481
58010	45039	57181	10238	36874	28546	37444	80824	63981	39942
56425	53996	86245	32623	78858	08143	60377	42925	42815	11159
82630	84066	13592	60642	17904	99718	63432	88642	37858	25431
14927	40909	23900	48761	44860	92467	31742	87142	03607	32059
23740	22505	07489	85986	74420	21744	97711	36648	35620	97949
32990	97446	03711	63824	07953	85965	87089	11687	92414	67257
05310	24058	91946	78437	34365	82469	12430	84754	19354	72745
21839	39937	27534	88913	49055	19218	47712	67677	51889	70926
08833	42549	93981	94051	28382	83725	72643	64233	97252	17133
58336	11139	47479	00931	91560	95372	97642	33856	54825	55680
62032	91144	75478	47431	52726	30289	42411	91886	51818	78292
45171	30557	53116	04118	58301	24375	65609	85810	18620	49198
91611	62656	60128	35609	63698	78356	50682	22505	01692	36291
55472	63819	86314	49174	93582	73604	78614	78849	23096	72825
18573	09729	74091	53994	10970	86557	65661	41854	26037	53296
60866	02955	90288	82136	83644	94455	06560	78029	98768	71296
45043	55608	82767	60890	74646	79485	13619	98868	40857	19415
17831	09737	79473	75945	28394	79334	70577	38048	03607	06932
40137	03981	07585	18128	11178	32601	27994	05641	22600	86064
77776	31343	14576	97706	16039	47517	43300	59080	80392	63189
69605	44104	40103	95635	05635	81673	68657	09559	23510	95875
19916	52934	26499	09821	97331	80993	61299	36979	73599	35055
02606	58552	07678	56619	65325	30705	99582	53390	46357	13244
65183	73160	87131	35530	47946	09854	18080	02321	05809	04893
10740	98914	44916	11322	89717	88189	30143	52687	19420	60061
98642	89822	71691	51573	83666	61642	46683	33761	47542	23551
60139	25601	93663	25547	02654	94829	48672	28736	84994	13071

TABLE A.2
Binomial Probability Distribution

n = 1

x	Probability .1	.2	.3	.4	.5	.6	.7	.8	.9
0	.900	.800	.700	.600	.500	.400	.300	.200	.100
1	.100	.200	.300	.400	.500	.600	.700	.800	.900

n = 2

x	Probability .1	.2	.3	.4	.5	.6	.7	.8	.9
0	..810	.640	.490	.360	.250	.160	.090	.040	.010
1	.180	.320	.420	.480	.500	.480	.420	.320	.180
2	.010	.040	.090	.160	.250	.360	.490	.640	.810

n = 3

x	Probability .1	.2	.3	.4	.5	.6	.7	.8	.9
0	.729	.512	.343	.216	.125	.064	.027	.008	.001
1	.243	.384	.441	.432	.375	.288	.189	.096	.027
2	.027	.096	.189	.288	.375	.432	.441	.384	.243
3	.001	.008	.027	.064	.125	.216	.343	.512	.729

n = 4

x	Probability .1	.2	.3	.4	.5	.6	.7	.8	.9
0	.656	.410	.240	.130	.063	.026	.008	.002	.000
1	.292	.410	.412	.346	.250	.154	.076	.026	.004
2	.049	.154	.265	.346	.375	.346	.265	.154	.049
3	.004	.026	.076	.154	.250	.346	.412	.410	.292
4	.000	.002	.008	.026	.063	.130	.240	.410	.656

n = 5

x	Probability .1	.2	.3	.4	.5	.6	.7	.8	.9
0	.590	.328	.168	.078	.031	.010	.002	.000	.000
1	.328	.410	.360	.259	.156	.077	.028	.006	.000
2	.073	.205	.309	.346	.313	.230	.132	.051	.008
3	.008	.051	.132	.230	.313	.346	.309	.205	.073
4	.000	.006	.028	.077	.156	.259	.360	.410	.328
5	.000	.000	.002	.010	.031	.078	.168	.328	.590

n = 6

x	Probability .1	.2	.3	.4	.5	.6	.7	.8	.9
0	.531	.262	.118	.047	.016	.004	.001	.000	.000
1	.354	.393	.303	.187	.094	.037	.010	.002	.000
2	.098	.246	.324	.311	.234	.138	.060	.015	.001
3	.015	.082	.185	.276	.313	.276	.185	.082	.015
4	.001	.015	.060	.138	.234	.311	.324	.246	.098
5	.000	.002	.010	.037	.094	.187	.303	.393	.354
6	.000	.000	.001	.004	.016	.047	.118	.262	.531

Continued

n = 7

					Probability				
x	.1	.2	.3	.4	.5	.6	.7	.8	.9
0	.478	.210	.082	.028	.008	.002	.000	.000	.000
1	.372	.367	.247	.131	.055	.017	.004	.000	.000
2	.124	.275	.318	.261	.164	.077	.025	.004	.000
3	.023	.115	.227	.290	.273	.194	.097	.029	.003
4	.003	.029	.097	.194	.273	.290	.227	.115	.023
5	.000	.004	.025	.077	.164	.261	.318	.275	.124
6	.000	.000	.004	.017	.055	.131	.247	.367	.372
7	.000	.000	.000	.002	.008	.028	.082	.210	.478

n = 8

					Probability				
x	.1	.2	.3	.4	.5	.6	.7	.8	.9
0	.430	.168	.058	.017	.004	.001	.000	.000	.000
1	.383	.336	.198	.090	.031	.008	.001	.000	.000
2	.149	.294	.296	.209	.109	.041	.010	.001	.000
3	.033	.147	.254	.279	.219	.124	.047	.009	.000
4	.005	.046	.136	.232	.273	.232	.136	.046	.005
5	.000	.009	.047	.124	.219	.279	.254	.147	.033
6	.000	.001	.010	.041	.109	.209	.296	.294	.149
7	.000	.000	.001	.008	.031	.090	.198	.336	.383
8	.000	.000	.000	.001	.004	.017	.058	.168	.430

n = 9

					Probability				
x	.1	.2	.3	.4	.5	.6	.7	.8	.9
0	.387	.134	.040	.010	.002	.000	.000	.000	.000
1	.387	.302	.156	.060	.018	.004	.000	.000	.000
2	.172	.302	.267	.161	.070	.021	.004	.000	.000
3	.045	.176	.267	.251	.164	.074	.021	.003	.000
4	.007	.066	.172	.251	.246	.167	.074	.017	.001
5	.001	.017	.074	.167	.246	.251	.172	.066	.007
6	.000	.003	.021	.074	.164	.251	.267	.176	.045
7	.000	.000	.004	.021	.070	.161	.267	.302	.172
8	.000	.000	.000	.004	.018	.060	.156	.302	.387
9	.000	.000	.000	.000	.002	.010	.040	.134	.387

					n = 10				
					Probability				
x	**.1**	**.2**	**.3**	**.4**	**.5**	**.6**	**.7**	**.8**	**.9**
0	.349	.107	.028	.006	.001	.000	.000	.000	.000
1	.387	.268	.121	.040	.010	.002	.000	.000	.000
2	.194	.302	.233	.121	.044	.011	.001	.000	.000
3	.057	.201	.267	.215	.117	.042	.009	.001	.000
4	.011	.088	.200	.251	.205	.111	.037	.006	.000
5	.001	.026	.103	.201	.246	.201	.103	.026	.001
6	.000	.006	.037	.111	.205	.251	.200	.088	.011
7	.000	.001	.009	.042	.117	.215	.267	.201	.057
8	.000	.000	.001	.011	.044	.121	.233	.302	.194
9	.000	.000	.000	.002	.010	.040	.121	.268	.387
10	.000	.000	.000	.000	.001	.006	.028	.107	.349

					n = 11				
					Probability				
x	**.1**	**.2**	**.3**	**.4**	**.5**	**.6**	**.7**	**.8**	**.9**
0	.314	.086	.020	.004	.000	.000	.000	.000	.000
1	.384	.236	.093	.027	.005	.001	.000	.000	.000
2	.213	.295	.200	.089	.027	.005	.001	.000	.000
3	.071	.221	.257	.177	.081	.023	.004	.000	.000
4	.016	.111	.220	.236	.161	.070	.017	.002	.000
5	.002	.039	.132	.221	.226	.147	.057	.010	.000
6	.000	.010	.057	.147	.226	.221	.132	.039	.002
7	.000	.002	.017	.070	.161	.236	.220	.111	.016
8	.000	.000	.004	.023	.081	.177	.257	.221	.071
9	.000	.000	.001	.005	.027	.089	.200	.295	.213
10	.000	.000	.000	.001	.005	.027	.093	.236	.384
11	.000	.000	.000	.000	.000	.004	.020	.086	.314

					n = 12				
					Probability				
x	**.1**	**.2**	**.3**	**.4**	**.5**	**.6**	**.7**	**.8**	**.9**
0	.282	.069	.014	.002	.000	.000	.000	.000	.0001
1	.377	.206	.071	.017	.003	.000	.000	.000	.000
2	.230	.283	.168	.064	.016	.002	.000	.000	.000
3	.085	.236	.240	.142	.054	.012	.001	.000	.000
4	.021	.133	.231	.213	.121	.042	.008	.001	.000
5	.004	.053	.158	.227	.193	.101	.029	.003	.000
6	.000	.016	.079	.177	.226	.177	.079	.016	.000
7	.000	.003	.029	.101	.193	.227	.158	.053	.004
8	.000	.001	.008	.042	.121	.213	.231	.133	.021
9	.000	.000	.001	.012	.054	.142	.240	.236	.085
10	.000	.000	.000	.002	.016	.064	.168	.283	.230
11	.000	.000	.000	.000	.003	.017	.071	.206	.377
12	.000	.000	.000	.000	.000	.002	.014	.069	.282

Continued

				$n = 13$					
				Probability					
x	.1	.2	.3	.4	.5	.6	.7	.8	.9
0	.254	.055	.010	.001	.000	.000	.000	.000	.000
1	.367	.179	.054	.011	.002	.000	.000	.000	.000
2	.245	.268	.139	.045	.010	.001	.000	.000	.000
3	.100	.246	.218	.111	.035	.006	.001	.000	.000
4	.028	.154	.234	.184	.087	.024	.003	.000	.000
5	.006	.069	.180	.221	.157	.066	.014	.001	.000
6	.001	.023	.103	.197	.209	.131	.044	.006	.000
7	.000	.006	.044	.131	.209	.197	.103	.023	.001
8	.000	.001	.014	.066	.157	.221	.180	.069	.006
9	.000	.000	.003	.024	.087	.184	.234	.154	.028
10	.000	.000	.001	.006	.035	.111	.218	.246	.100
11	.000	.000	.000	.001	.010	.045	.139	.268	.245
12	.000	.000	.000	.000	.002	.011	.054	.179	.367
13	.000	.000	.000	.000	.000	.001	.010	.055	.254

				$n = 14$					
				Probability					
x	.1	.2	.3	.4	.5	.6	.7	.8	.9
0	.229	.044	.007	.001	.000	.000	.000	.000	.000
1	.356	.154	.041	.007	.001	.000	.000	.000	.000
2	.257	.250	.113	.032	.006	.001	.000	.000	.000
3	.114	.250	.194	.085	.022	.003	.000	.000	.000
4	.035	.172	.229	.155	.061	.014	.001	.000	.000
5	.008	.086	.196	.207	.122	.041	.007	.000	.000
6	.001	.032	.126	.207	.183	.092	.023	.002	.000
7	.000	.009	.062	.157	.209	.157	.062	.009	.000
8	.000	.002	.023	.092	.183	.207	.126	.032	.001
9	.000	.000	.007	.041	.122	.207	.196	.086	.008
10	.000	.000	.001	.014	.061	.155	.229	.172	.035
11	.000	.000	.000	.003	.022	.085	.194	.250	.114
12	.000	.000	.000	.001	.006	.032	.113	.250	.257
13	.000	.000	.000	.000	.001	.007	.041	.154	.356
14	.000	.000	.000	.000	.000	.001	.007	.044	.229

					n = 15				
					Probability				
x	.1	.2	.3	.4	.5	.6	.7	.8	.9
0	.206	.035	.005	.000	.000	.000	.000	.000	.000
1	.343	.132	.031	.005	.000	.000	.000	.000	.000
2	.267	.231	.092	.022	.003	.000	.000	.000	.000
3	.129	.250	.170	.063	.014	.002	.000	.000	.000
4	.043	.188	.219	.127	.042	.007	.001	.000	.000
5	.010	.103	.206	.186	.092	.024	.003	.000	.000
6	.002	.043	.147	.207	.153	.061	.012	.001	.000
7	.000	.014	.081	.177	.196	.118	.035	.003	.000
8	.000	.003	.035	.118	.196	.177	.081	.014	.000
9	.000	.001	.012	.061	.153	.207	.147	.043	.002
10	.000	.000	.003	.024	.092	.186	.206	.103	.010
11	.000	.000	.001	.007	.042	.127	.219	.188	.043
12	.000	.000	.000	.002	.014	.063	.170	.250	.129
13	.000	.000	.000	.000	.003	.022	.092	.231	.267
14	.000	.000	.000	.000	.000	.005	.031	.132	.343
15	.000	.000	.000	.000	.000	.000	.005	.035	.206

					n = 16				
					Probability				
x	.1	.2	.3	.4	.5	.6	.7	.8	.9
0	.185	.028	.003	.000	.000	.000	.000	.000	.000
1	.329	.113	.023	.003	.000	.000	.000	.000	.000
2	.275	.211	.073	.015	.002	.000	.000	.000	.000
3	.142	.246	.146	.047	.009	.001	.000	.000	.000
4	.051	.200	.204	.101	.028	.004	.000	.000	.000
5	.014	.120	.210	.162	.067	.014	.001	.000	.000
6	.003	.055	.165	.198	.122	.039	.006	.000	.000
7	.000	.020	.101	.189	.175	.084	.019	.001	.000
8	.000	.006	.049	.142	.196	.142	.049	.006	.000
9	.000	.001	.019	.084	.175	.189	.101	.020	.000
10	.000	.000	.006	.039	.122	.198	.165	.055	.003
11	.000	.000	.001	.014	.067	.162	.210	.120	.014
12	.000	.000	.000	.004	.028	.101	.204	.200	.051
13	.000	.000	.000	.001	.009	.047	.146	.246	.142
14	.000	.000	.000	.000	.002	.015	.073	.211	.275
15	.000	.000	.000	.000	.000	.003	.023	.113	.329
16	.000	.000	.000	.000	.000	.000	.003	.028	.185

Continued

					n = 17				
					Probability				
x	**.1**	**.2**	**.3**	**.4**	**.5**	**.6**	**.7**	**.8**	**.9**
0	.167	.023	.002	.000	.000	.000	.000	.000	.000
1	.315	.096	.017	.002	.000	.000	.000	.000	.000
2	.280	.191	.058	.010	.001	.000	.000	.000	.000
3	.156	.239	.125	.034	.005	.000	.000	.000	.000
4	.060	.209	.187	.080	.018	.002	.000	.000	.000
5	.017	.136	.208	.138	.047	.008	.001	.000	.000
6	.004	.068	.178	.184	.094	.024	.003	.000	.000
7	.001	.027	.120	.193	.148	.057	.009	.000	.000
8	.000	.008	.064	.161	.185	.107	.028	.002	.000
9	.000	.002	.028	.107	.185	.161	.064	.008	.000
10	.000	.000	.009	.057	.148	.193	.120	.027	.001
11	.000	.000	.003	.024	.094	.184	.178	.068	.004
12	.000	.000	.001	.008	.047	.138	.208	.136	.017
13	.000	.000	.000	.002	.018	.080	.187	.209	.060
14	.000	.000	.000	.000	.005	.034	.125	.239	.156
15	.000	.000	.000	.000	.001	.010	.058	.191	.280
16	.000	.000	.000	.000	.000	.002	.017	.096	.315
17	.000	.000	.000	.000	.000	.000	.002	.023	.167

					n = 18				
					Probability				
x	**.1**	**.2**	**.3**	**.4**	**.5**	**.6**	**.7**	**.8**	**.9**
0	.150	.018	.002	.000	.000	.000	.000	.000	.000
1	.300	.081	.013	.001	.000	.000	.000	.000	.000
2	.284	.172	.046	.007	.001	.000	.000	.000	.000
3	.168	.230	.105	.025	.003	.000	.000	.000	.000
4	.070	.215	.168	.061	.012	.001	.000	.000	.000
5	.022	.151	.202	.115	.033	.004	.000	.000	.000
6	.005	.082	.187	.166	.071	.015	.001	.000	.000
7	.001	.035	.138	.189	.121	.037	.005	.000	.000
8	.000	.012	.081	.173	.167	.077	.015	.001	.000
9	.000	.003	.039	.128	.185	.128	.039	.003	.000
10	.000	.001	.015	.077	.167	.173	.081	.012	.000
11	.000	.000	.005	.037	.121	.189	.138	.035	.001
12	.000	.000	.001	.015	.071	.166	.187	.082	.005
13	.000	.000	.000	.004	.033	.115	.202	.151	.022
14	.000	.000	.000	.001	.012	.061	.168	.215	.070
15	.000	.000	.000	.000	.003	.025	.105	.230	.168
16	.000	.000	.000	.000	.001	.007	.046	.172	.284
17	.000	.000	.000	.000	.000	.001	.013	.081	.300
18	.000	.000	.000	.000	.000	.000	.002	.018	.150

					$n = 19$				
					Probability				
x	.1	.2	.3	.4	.5	.6	.7	.8	.9
0	.135	.014	.001	.000	.000	.000	.000	.000	.000
1	.285	.068	.009	.001	.000	.000	.000	.000	.000
2	.285	.154	.036	.005	.000	.000	.000	.000	.000
3	.180	.218	.087	.017	.002	.000	.000	.000	.000
4	.080	.218	.149	.047	.007	.001	.000	.000	.000
5	.027	.164	.192	.093	.022	.002	.000	.000	.000
6	.007	.095	.192	.145	.052	.008	.001	.000	.000
7	.001	.044	.153	.180	.096	.024	.002	.000	.000
8	.000	.017	.098	.180	.144	.053	.008	.000	.000
9	.000	.005	.051	.146	.176	.098	.022	.001	.000
10	.000	.001	.022	.098	.176	.146	.051	.005	.000
11	.000	.000	.008	.053	.144	.180	.098	.017	.000
12	.000	.000	.002	.024	.096	.180	.153	.044	.001
13	.000	.000	.001	.008	.052	.145	.192	.095	.007
14	.000	.000	.000	.002	.022	.093	.192	.164	.027
15	.000	.000	.000	.001	.007	.047	.149	.218	.080
16	.000	.000	.000	.000	.002	.017	.087	.218	.180
17	.000	.000	.000	.000	.000	.005	.036	.154	.285
18	.000	.000	.000	.000	.000	.001	.009	.068	.285
19	.000	.000	.000	.000	.000	.000	.001	.014	.135

					$n = 20$				
					Probability				
x	.1	.2	.3	.4	.5	.6	.7	.8	.9
0	.122	.012	.001	.000	.000	.000	.000	.000	.000
1	.270	.058	.007	.000	.000	.000	.000	.000	.000
2	.285	.137	.028	.003	.000	.000	.000	.000	.000
3	.190	.205	.072	.012	.001	.000	.000	.000	.000
4	.090	.218	.130	.035	.005	.000	.000	.000	.000
5	.032	.175	.179	.075	.015	.001	.000	.000	.000
6	.009	.109	.192	.124	.037	.005	.000	.000	.000
7	.002	.055	.164	.166	.074	.015	.001	.000	.000
8	.000	.022	.114	.180	.120	.035	.004	.000	.000
9	.000	.007	.065	.160	.160	.071	.012	.000	.000
10	.000	.002	.031	.117	.176	.117	.031	.002	.000
11	.000	.000	.012	.071	.160	.160	.065	.007	.000
12	.000	.000	.004	.035	.120	.180	.114	.022	.000
13	.000	.000	.001	.015	.074	.166	.164	.055	.002
14	.000	.000	.000	.005	.037	.124	.192	.109	.009
15	.000	.000	.000	.001	.015	.075	.179	.175	.032
16	.000	.000	.000	.000	.005	.035	.130	.218	.090
17	.000	.000	.000	.000	.001	.012	.072	.205	.190
18	.000	.000	.000	.000	.000	.003	.028	.137	.285
19	.000	.000	.000	.000	.000	.000	.007	.058	.270
20	.000	.000	.000	.000	.000	.000	.001	.012	.122

Continued

					n = 25				
					Probability				
x	.1	.2	.3	.4	.5	.6	.7	.8	.9
0	.072	.004	.000	.000	.000	.000	.000	.000	.000
1	.199	.024	.001	.000	.000	.000	.000	.000	.000
2	.266	.071	.007	.000	.000	.000	.000	.000	.000
3	.226	.136	.024	.002	.000	.000	.000	.000	.000
4	.138	.187	.057	.007	.000	.000	.000	.000	.000
5	.065	.196	.103	.020	.002	.000	.000	.000	.000
6	.024	.163	.147	.044	.005	.000	.000	.000	.000
7	.007	.111	.171	.080	.014	.001	.000	.000	.000
8	.002	.062	.165	.120	.032	.003	.000	.000	.000
9	.000	.029	.134	.151	.061	.009	.000	.000	.000
10	.000	.012	.092	.161	.097	.021	.001	.000	.000
11	.000	.004	.054	.147	.133	.043	.004	.000	.000
12	.000	.001	.027	.114	.155	.076	.011	.000	.000
13	.000	.000	.011	.076	.155	.114	.027	.001	.000
14	.000	.000	.004	.043	.133	.147	.054	.004	.000
15	.000	.000	.001	.021	.097	.161	.092	.012	.000
16	.000	.000	.000	.009	.061	.151	.134	.029	.000
17	.000	.000	.000	.003	.032	.120	.165	.062	.002
18	.000	.000	.000	.001	.014	.080	.171	.111	.007
19	.000	.000	.000	.000	.005	.044	.147	.163	.024
20	.000	.000	.000	.000	.002	.020	.103	.196	.065
21	.000	.000	.000	.000	.000	.007	.057	.187	.138
22	.000	.000	.000	.000	.000	.002	.024	.136	.226
23	.000	.000	.000	.000	.000	.000	.007	.071	.266
24	.000	.000	.000	.000	.000	.000	.001	.024	.199
25	.000	.000	.000	.000	.000	.000	.000	.004	.072

TABLE A.3   Poisson Probabilities

x	.005	.01	.02	.03	.04	.05	.06	.07	.08	.09
0	.9950	.9900	.9802	.9704	.9608	.9512	.9418	.9324	.9231	.9139
1	.0050	.0099	.0196	.0291	.0384	.0476	.0565	.0653	.0738	.0823
2	.0000	.0000	.0002	.0004	.0008	.0012	.0017	.0023	.0030	.0037
3	.0000	.0000	.0000	.0000	.0000	.0000	.0000	.0001	.0001	.0001

x	.1	.2	.3	.4	.5	.6	.7	.8	.9	1.0
0	.9048	.8187	.7408	.6703	.6065	.5488	.4966	.4493	.4066	.3679
1	.0905	.1637	.2222	.2681	.3033	.3293	.3476	.3595	.3659	.3679
2	.0045	.0164	.0333	.0536	.0758	.0988	.1217	.1438	.1647	.1839
3	.0002	.0011	.0033	.0072	.0126	.0198	.0284	.0383	.0494	.0613
4	.0000	.0001	.0003	.0007	.0016	.0030	.0050	.0077	.0111	.0153
5	.0000	.0000	.0000	.0001	.0002	.0004	.0007	.0012	.0020	.0031
6	.0000	.0000	.0000	.0000	.0000	.0000	.0001	.0002	.0003	.0005
7	.0000	.0000	.0000	.0000	.0000	.0000	.0000	.0000	.0000	.0001

x	1.1	1.2	1.3	1.4	1.5	1.6	1.7	1.8	1.9	2.0
0	.3329	.3012	.2725	.2466	.2231	.2019	.1827	.1653	.1496	.1353
1	.3662	.3614	.3543	.3452	.3347	.3230	.3106	.2975	.2842	.2707
2	.2014	.2169	.2303	.2417	.2510	.2584	.2640	.2678	.2700	.2707
3	.0738	.0867	.0998	.1128	.1255	.1378	.1496	.1607	.1710	.1804
4	.0203	.0260	.0324	.0395	.0471	.0551	.0636	.0723	.0812	.0902
5	.0045	.0062	.0084	.0111	.0141	.0176	.0216	.0260	.0309	.0361
6	.0008	.0012	.0018	.0026	.0035	.0047	.0061	.0078	.0098	.0120
7	.0001	.0002	.0003	.0005	.0008	.0011	.0015	.0020	.0027	.0034
8	.0000	.0000	.0001	.0001	.0001	.0002	.0003	.0005	.0006.	.0009
9	.0000	.0000	.0000	.0000	.0000	.0000	.0001	.0001	.0001	.0002

x	2.1	2.2	2.3	2.4	2.5	2.6	2.7	2.8	2.9	3.0
0	.1225	.1108	.1003	.0907	.0821	.0743	.0672	.0608	.0550	.0498
1	.2572	.2438	.2306	.2177	.2052	.1931	.1815	.1703	.1596	.1494
2	.2700	.2681	.2652	.2613	.2565	.2510	.2450	.2384	.2314	.2240
3	.1890	.1966	.2033	.2090	.2138	.2176	.2205	.2225	.2237	.2240
4	.0992	.1082	.1169	.1254	.1336	.1414	.1488	.1557	.1622	.1680
5	.0417	.0476	.0538	.0602	.0668	.0735	.0804	.0872	.0940	.1008
6	.0146	.0174	.0206	.0241	.0278	.0319	.0362	.0407	.0455	.0504
7	.0044	.0055	.0068	.0083	.0099	.0118	.0139	.0163	.0188	.0216
8	.0011	.0015	.0019	.0025	.0031	.0038	.0047	.0057	.0068	.0081
9	.0003	.0004	.0005	.0007	.0009	.0011	.0014	.0018	.0022	.0027
10	.0001	.0001	.0001	.0002	.0002	.0003	.0004	.0005	.0006	.0008
11	.0000	.0000	.0000	.0000	.0000	.0001	.0001	.0001	.0002	.0002
12	.0000	.0000	.0000	.0000	.0000	.0000	.0000	.0000	.0000	.0001

Continued

					λ					
x	3.1	3.2	3.3	3.4	3.5	3.6	3.7	3.8	3.9	4.0
0	.0450	.0408	.0369	.0334	.0302	.0273	.0247	.0224	.0202	.0183
1	.1397	.1304	.1217	.1135	.1057	.0984	.0915	.0850	.0789	.0733
2	.2165	.2087	.2008	.1929	.1850	.1771	.1692	.1615	.1539	.1465
3	.2237	.2226	.2209	.2186	.2158	.2125	.2087	.2046	.2001	.1954
4	.1733	.1781	.1823	.1858	.1888	.1912	.1931	.1944	.1951	.1954
5	.1075	.1140	.1203	.1264	.1322	.1377	.1429	.1477	.1522	.1563
6	.0555	.0608	.0662	.0716	.0771	.0826	.0881	.0936	.0989	.1042
7	.0246	.0278	.0312	.0348	.0385	.0425	.0466	.0508	.0551	.0595
8	.0095	.0111	.0129	.0148	.0169	.0191	.0215	.0241	.0269	.0298
9	.0033	.0040	.0047	.0056	.0066	.0076	.0089	.0102	.0116	.0132
10	.0010	.0013	.0016	.0019	.0023	.0028	.0033	.0039	.0045	.0053
11	.0003	.0004	.0005	.0006	.0007	.0009	.0011	.0013	.0016	.0019
12	.0001	.0001	.0001	.0002	.0002	.0003	.0003	.0004	.0005	.0006
13	.0000	.0000	.0000	.0000	.0001	.0001	.0001	.0001	.0002	.0002
14	.0000	.0000	.0000	.0000	.0000	.0000	.0000	.0000	.0000	.0001

x	4.1	4.2	4.3	4.4	4.5	4.6	4.7	4.8	4.9	5.0
0	.0166	.0150	.0136	.0123	.0111	.0101	.0091	.0082	.0074	.0067
1	.0679	.0630	.0583	.0540	.0500	.0462	.0427	.0395	.0365	.0337
2	.1393	.1323	.1254	.1188	.1125	.1063	.1005	.0948	.0894	.0842
3	.1904	.1852	.1798	.1743	.1687	.1631	.1574	.1517	.1460	.1404
4	.1951	.1944	.1933	.1917	.1898	.1875	.1849	.1820	.1789	.1755
5	.1600	.1633	.1662	.1687	.1708	.1725	.1738	.1747	.1753	.1755
6	.1093	.1143	.1191	.1237	.1281	.1323	.1362	.1398	.1432	.1462
7	.0640	.0686	.0732	.0778	.0824	.0869	.0914	.0959	.1002	.1044
8	.0328	.0360	.0393	.0428	.0463	.0500	.0537	.0575	.0614	.0653
9	.0150	.0168	.0188	.0209	.0232	.0255	.0281	.0307	.0334	.0363
10	.0061	.0071	.0081	.0092	.0104	.0118	.0132	.0147	.0164	.0181
11	.0023	.0027	.0032	.0037	.0043	.0049	.0056	.0064	.0073	.0082
12	.0008	.0009	.0011	.0013	.0016	.0019	.0022	.0026	.0030	.0034
13	.0002	.0003	.0004	.0005	.0006	.0007	.0008	.0009	.0011	.0013
14	.0001	.0001	.0001	.0001	.0002	.0002	.0003	.0003	.0004	.0005
15	.0000	.0000	.0000	.0000	.0001	.0001	.0001	.0001	.0001	.0002

					λ					
x	5.1	5.2	5.3	5.4	5.5	5.6	5.7	5.8	5.9	6.0
0	.0061	.0055	.0050	.0045	.0041	.0037	.0033	.0030	.0027	.0025
1	.0311	.0287	.0265	.0244	.0225	.0207	.0191	.0176	.0162	.0149
2	.0793	.0746	.0701	.0659	.0618	.0580	.0544	.0509	.0477	.0446
3	.1348	.1293	.1239	.1185	.1133	.1082	.1033	.0985	.0938	.0892
4	.1719	.1681	.1641	.1600	.1558	.1515	.1472	.1428	.1383	.1339
5	.1753	.1748	.1740	.1728	.1714	.1697	.1678	.1656	.1632	.1606
6	.1490	.1515	.1537	.1555	.1571	.1584	.1594	.1601	.1605	.1606
7	.1086	.1125	.1163	.1200	.1234	.1267	.1298	.1326	.1353	.1377
8	.0692	.0731	.0771	.0810	.0849	.0887	.0925	.0962	.0998	.1033
9	.0392	.0423	.0454	.0486	.0519	.0552	.0586	.0620	.0654	.0688
10	.0200	.0220	.0241	.0262	.0285	.0309	.0334	.0359	.0386	.0413
11	.0093	.0104	.0116	.0129	.0143	.0157	.0173	.0190	.0207	.0225
12	.0039	.0045	.0051	.0058	.0065	.0073	.0082	.0092	.0102	.0113
13	.0015	.0018	.0021	.0024	.0028	.0032	.0036	.0041	.0046	.0052
14	.0006	.0007	.0008	.0009	.0011	.0013	.0015	.0017	.0019	.0022
15	.0002	.0002	.0003	.0003	.0004	.0005	.0006	.0007	.0008	.0009
16	.0001	.0001	.0001	.0001	.0001	.0002	.0002	.0002	.0003	.0003
17	.0000	.0000	.0000	.0000	.0000	.0001	.0001	.0001	.0001	.0001

x	6.1	6.2	6.3	6.4	6.5	6.6	6.7	6.8	6.9	7.0
0	.0022	.0020	.0018	.0017	.0015	.0014	.0012	.0011	.0010	.0009
1	.0137	.0126	.0116	.0106	.0098	.0090	.0082	.0076	.0070	.0064
2	.0417	.0390	.0364	.0340	.0318	.0296	.0276	.0258	.0240	.0223
3	.0848	.0806	.0765	.0726	.0688	.0652	.0617	.0584	.0552	.0521
4	.1294	.1249	.1205	.1162	.1118	.1076	.1034	.0992	.0952	.0912
5	.1579	.1549	.1519	.1487	.1454	.1420	.1385	.1349	.1314	.1277
6	.1605	.1601	.1595	.1586	.1575	.1562	.1546	.1529	.1511	.1490
7	.1399	.1418	.1435	.1450	.1462	.1472	.1480	.1486	.1489	.1490
8	.1066	.1099	.1130	.1160	.1188	.1215	.1240	.1263	.1284	.1304
9	.0723	.0757	.0791	.0825	.0858	.0891	.0923	.0954	.0985	.1014
10	.0441	.0469	.0498	.0528	.0558	.0588	.0618	.0649	.0679	.0710
11	.0244	.0265	.0285	.0307	.0330	.0353	.0377	.0401	.0426	.0452
12	.0124	.0137	.0150	.0164	.0179	.0194	.0210	.0227	.0245	.0263
13	.0058	.0065	.0073	.0081	.0089	.0099	.0108	.0119	.0130	.0142
14	.0025	.0029	.0033	.0037	.0041	.0046	.0052	.0058	.0064	.0071
15	.0010	.0012	.0014	.0016	.0018	.0020	.0023	.0026	.0029	.0033
16	.0004	.0005	.0005	.0006	.0007	.0008	.0010	.0011	.0013	.0014
17	.0001	.0002	.0002	.0002	.0003	.0003	.0004	.0004	.0005	.0006
18	.0000	.0001	.0001	.0001	.0001	.0001	.0001	.0002	.0002	.0002
19	.0000	.0000	.0000	.0000	.0000	.0000	.0001	.0001	.0001	.0001

Continued

					λ					
x	7.1	7.2	7.3	7.4	7.5	7.6	7.7	7.8	7.9	8.0
0	.0008	.0007	.0007	.0006	.0006	.0005	.0005	.0004	.0004	.0003
1	.0059	.0054	.0049	.0045	.0041	.0038	.0035	.0032	.0029	.0027
2	.0208	.0194	.0180	.0167	.0156	.0145	.0134	.0125	.0116	.0107
3	.0492	.0464	.0438	.0413	.0389	.0366	.0345	.0324	.0305	.0286
4	.0874	.0836	.0799	.0764	.0729	.0696	.0663	.0632	.0602	.0573
5	.1241	.1204	.1167	.1130	.1094	.1057	.1021	.0986	.0951	.0916
6	.1468	.1445	.1420	.1394	.1367	.1339	.1311	.1282	.1252	.1221
7	.1489	.1486	.1481	.1474	.1465	.1454	.1442	.1428	.1413	.1396
8	.1321	.1337	.1351	.1363	.1373	.1381	.1388	.1392	.1395	.1396
9	.1042	.1070	.1096	.1121	.1144	.1167	.1187	.1207	.1224	.1241
10	.0740	.0770	.0800	.0829	.0858	.0887	.0914	.0941	.0967	.0993
11	.0478	.0504	.0531	.0558	.0585	.0613	.0640	.0667	.0695	.0722
12	.0283	.0303	.0323	.0344	.0366	.0388	.0411	.0434	.0457	.0481
13	.0154	.0168	.0181	.0196	.0211	.0227	.0243	.0260	.0278	.0296
14	.0078	.0086	.0095	.0104	.0113	.0123	.0134	.0145	.0157	.0169
15	.0037	.0041	.0046	.0051	.0057	.0062	.0069	.0075	.0083	.0090
16	.0016	.0019	.0021	.0024	.0026	.0030	.0033	.0037	.0041	.0045
17	.0007	.0008	.0009	.0010	.0012	.0013	.0015	.0017	.0019	.0021
18	.0003	.0003	.0004	.0004	.0005	.0006	.0006	.0007	.0008	.0009
19	.0001	.0001	.0001	.0002	.0002	.0002	.0003	.0003	.0003	.0004
20	.0000	.0000	.0001	.0001	.0001	.0001	.0001	.0001	.0001	.0002
21	.0000	.0000	.0000	.0000	.0000	.0000	.0000	.0000	.0001	.0001

x	8.1	8.2	8.3	8.4	8.5	8.6	8.7	8.8	8.9	9.0
0	.0003	.0003	.0002	.0002	.0002	.0002	.0002	.0002	.0001	.0001
1	.0025	.0023	.0021	.0019	.0017	.0016	.0014	.0013	.0012	.0011
2	.0100	.0092	.0086	.0079	.0074	.0068	.0063	.0058	.0054	.0050
3	.0269	.0252	.0237	.0222	.0208	.0195	.0183	.0171	.0160	.0150
4	.0544	.0517	.0491	.0466	.0443	.0420	.0398	.0377	.0357	.0337
5	.0882	.0849	.0816	.0784	.0752	.0722	.0692	.0663	.0635	.0607
6	.1191	.1160	.1128	.1097	.1066	.1034	.1003	.0972	.0941	.0911
7	.1378	.1358	.1338	.1317	.1294	.1271	.1247	.1222	.1197	.1171
8	.1395	.1392	.1388	.1382	.1375	.1366	.1356	.1344	.1332	.1318
9	.1256	.1269	.1280	.1290	.1299	.1306	.1311	.1315	.1317	.1318
10	.1017	.1040	.1063	.1084	.1104	.1123	.1140	.1157	.1172	.1186
11	.0749	.0776	.0802	.0828	.0853	.0878	.0902	.0925	.0948	.0970
12	.0505	.0530	.0555	.0579	.0604	.0629	.0654	.0679	.0703	.0728
13	.0315	.0334	.0354	.0374	.0395	.0416	.0438	.0459	.0481	.0504
14	.0182	.0196	.0210	.0225	.0240	.0256	.0272	.0289	.0306	.0324
15	.0098	.0107	.0116	.0126	.0136	.0147	.0158	.0169	.0182	.0194
16	.0050	.0055	.0060	.0066	.0072	.0079	.0086	.0093	.0101	.0109
17	.0024	.0026	.0029	.0033	.0036	.0040	.0044	.0048	.0053	.0058
18	.0011	.0012	.0014	.0015	.0017	.0019	.0021	.0024	.0026	.0029
19	.0005	.0005	.0006	.0007	.0008	.0009	.0010	.0011	.0012	.0014
20	.0002	.0002	.0002	.0003	.0003	.0004	.0004	.0005	.0005	.0006
21	.0001	.0001	.0001	.0001	.0001	.0002	.0002	.0002	.0002	.0003
22	.0000	.0000	.0000	.0000	.0001	.0001	.0001	.0001	.0001	.0001

x	9.1	9.2	9.3	9.4	9.5	9.6	9.7	9.8	9.9	10.0
0	.0001	.0001	.0001	.0001	.0001	.0001	.0001	.0001	.0001	.0000
1	.0010	.0009	.0009	.0008	.0007	.0007	.0006	.0005	.0005	.0005
2	.0046	.0043	.0040	.0037	.0034	.0031	.0029	.0027	.0025	.0023
3	.0140	.0131	.0123	.0115	.0107	.0100	.0093	.0087	.0081	.0076
4	.0319	.0302	.0285	.0269	.0254	.0240	.0226	.0213	.0201	.0189
5	.0581	.0555	.0530	.0506	.0483	.0460	.0439	.0418	.0398	.0378
6	.0881	.0851	.0822	.0793	.0764	.0736	.0709	.0682	.0656	.0631
7	.1145	.1118	.1091	.1064	.1037	.1010	.0982	.0955	.0928	.0901
8	.1302	.1286	.1269	.1251	.1232	.1212	.1191	.1170	.1148	.1126
9	.1317	.1315	.1311	.1306	.1300	.1293	.1284	.1274	.1263	.1251
10	.1198	.1210	.1219	.1228	.1235	.1241	.1245	.1249	.1250	.1251
11	.0991	.1012	.1031	.1049	.1067	.1083	.1098	.1112	.1125	.1137
12	.0752	.0776	.0799	.0822	.0844	.0866	.0888	.0908	.0928	.0948
13	.0526	.0549	.0572	.0594	.0617	.0640	.0662	.0685	.0707	.0729
14	.0342	.0361	.0380	.0399	.0419	.0439	.0459	.0479	.0500	.0521
15	.0208	.0221	.0235	.0250	.0265	.0281	.0297	.0313	.0330	.0347
16	.0118	.0127	.0137	.0147	.0157	.0168	.0180	.0192	.0204	.0217
17	.0063	.0069	.0075	.0081	.0088	.0095	.0103	.0111	.0119	.0128
18	.0032	.0035	.0039	.0042	.0046	.0051	.0055	.0060	.0065	.0071
19	.0015	.0017	.0019	.0021	.0023	.0026	.0028	.0031	.0034	.0037
20	.0007	.0008	.0009	.0010	.0011	.0012	.0014	.0015	.0017	.0019
21	.0003	.0003	.0004	.0004	.0005	.0006	.0006	.0007	.0008	.0009
22	.0001	.0001	.0002	.0002	.0002	.0002	.0003	.0003	.0004	.0004
23	.0000	.0001	.0001	.0001	.0001	.0001	.0001	.0001	.0002	.0002
24	.0000	.0000	.0000	.0000	.0000	.0000	.0000	.0001	.0001	.0001

TABLE A.4　　　　The e^{-x} Table

x	e^{-x}	x	e^{-x}	x	e^{-x}	x	e^{-x}
0.0	1.0000	3.0	0.0498	6.0	0.00248	9.0	0.00012
0.1	0.9048	3.1	0.0450	6.1	0.00224	9.1	0.00011
0.2	0.8187	3.2	0.0408	6.2	0.00203	9.2	0.00010
0.3	0.7408	3.3	0.0369	6.3	0.00184	9.3	0.00009
0.4	0.6703	3.4	0.0334	6.4	0.00166	9.4	0.00008
0.5	0.6065	3.5	0.0302	6.5	0.00150	9.5	0.00007
0.6	0.5488	3.6	0.0273	6.6	0.00136	9.6	0.00007
0.7	0.4966	3.7	0.0247	6.7	0.00123	9.7	0.00006
0.8	0.4493	3.8	0.0224	6.8	0.00111	9.8	0.00006
0.9	0.4066	3.9	0.0202	6.9	0.00101	9.9	0.00005
1.0	0.3679	4.0	0.0183	7.0	0.00091	10.0	0.00005
1.1	0.3329	4.1	0.0166	7.1	0.00083		
1.2	0.3012	4.2	0.0150	7.2	0.00075		
1.3	0.2725	4.3	0.0136	7.3	0.00068		
1.4	0.2466	4.4	0.0123	7.4	0.00061		
1.5	0.2231	4.5	0.0111	7.5	0.00055		
1.6	0.2019	4.6	0.0101	7.6	0.00050		
1.7	0.1827	4.7	0.0091	7.7	0.00045		
1.8	0.1653	4.8	0.0082	7.8	0.00041		
1.9	0.1496	4.9	0.0074	7.9	0.00037		
2.0	0.1353	5.0	0.0067	8.0	0.00034		
2.1	0.1225	5.1	0.0061	8.1	0.00030		
2.2	0.1108	5.2	0.0055	8.2	0.00027		
2.3	0.1003	5.3	0.0050	8.3	0.00025		
2.4	0.0907	5.4	0.0045	8.4	0.00022		
2.5	0.0821	5.5	0.0041	8.5	0.00020		
2.6	0.0743	5.6	0.0037	8.6	0.00018		
2.7	0.0672	5.7	0.0033	8.7	0.00017		
2.8	0.0608	5.8	0.0030	8.8	0.00015		
2.9	0.0550	5.9	0.0027	8.9	0.00014		

TABLE A.5 Areas of the Standard Normal Distribution

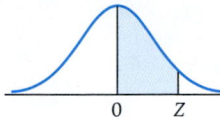

The entries in this table are the probabilities that a standard normal random variable is between 0 and Z (the shaded area).

Z	0.00	0.01	0.02	0.03	0.04	0.05	0.06	0.07	0.08	0.09
0.0	.0000	.0040	.0080	.0120	.0160	.0199	.0239	.0279	.0319	.0359
0.1	.0398	.0438	.0478	.0517	.0557	.0596	.0636	.0675	.0714	.0753
0.2	.0793	.0832	.0871	.0910	.0948	.0987	.1026	.1064	.1103	.1141
0.3	.1179	.1217	.1255	.1293	.1331	.1368	.1406	.1443	.1480	.1517
0.4	.1554	.1591	.1628	.1664	.1700	.1736	.1772	.1808	.1844	.1879
0.5	.1915	.1950	.1985	.2019	.2054	.2088	.2123	.2157	.2190	.2224
0.6	.2257	.2291	.2324	.2357	.2389	.2422	.2454	.2486	.2517	.2549
0.7	.2580	.2611	.2642	.2673	.2704	.2734	.2764	.2794	.2823	.2852
0.8	.2881	.2910	.2939	.2967	.2995	.3023	.3051	.3078	.3106	.3133
0.9	.3159	.3186	.3212	.3238	.3264	.3289	.3315	.3340	.3365	.3389
1.0	.3413	.3438	.3461	.3485	.3508	.3531	.3554	.3577	.3599	.3621
1.1	.3643	.3665	.3686	.3708	.3729	.3749	.3770	.3790	.3810	.3830
1.2	.3849	.3869	.3888	.3907	.3925	.3944	.3962	.3980	.3997	.4015
1.3	.4032	.4049	.4066	.4082	.4099	.4115	.4131	.4147	.4162	.4177
1.4	.4192	.4207	.4222	.4236	.4251	.4265	.4279	.4292	.4306	.4319
1.5	.4332	.4345	.4357	.4370	.4382	.4394	.4406	.4418	.4429	.4441
1.6	.4452	.4463	.4474	.4484	.4495	.4505	.4515	.4525	.4535	.4545
1.7	.4554	.4564	.4573	.4582	.4591	.4599	.4608	.4616	.4625	.4633
1.8	.4641	.4649	.4656	.4664	.4671	.4678	.4686	.4693	.4699	.4706
1.9	.4713	.4719	.4726	.4732	.4738	.4744	.4750	.4756	.4761	.4767
2.0	.4772	.4778	.4783	.4788	.4793	.4798	.4803	.4808	.4812	.4817
2.1	.4821	.4826	.4830	.4834	.4838	.4842	.4846	.4850	.4854	.4857
2.2	.4861	.4864	.4868	.4871	.4875	.4878	.4881	.4884	.4887	.4890
2.3	.4893	.4896	.4898	.4901	.4904	.4906	.4909	.4911	.4913	.4916
2.4	.4918	.4920	.4922	.4925	.4927	.4929	.4931	.4932	.4934	.4936
2.5	.4938	.4940	.4941	.4943	.4945	.4946	.4948	.4949	.4951	.4952
2.6	.4953	.4955	.4956	.4957	.4959	.4960	.4961	.4962	.4963	.4964
2.7	.4965	.4966	.4967	.4968	.4969	.4970	.4971	.4972	.4973	.4974
2.8	.4974	.4975	.4976	.4977	.4977	.4978	.4979	.4979	.4980	.4981
2.9	.4981	.4982	.4982	.4983	.4984	.4984	.4985	.4985	.4986	.4986
3.0	.4987	.4987	.4987	.4988	.4988	.4989	.4989	.4989	.4990	.4990
3.1	.4990	.4991	.4991	.4991	.4992	.4992	.4992	.4992	.4993	.4993
3.2	.4993	.4993	.4994	.4994	.4994	.4994	.4994	.4995	.4995	.4995
3.3	.4995	.4995	.4995	.4996	.4996	.4996	.4996	.4996	.4996	.4997
3.4	.4997	.4997	.4997	.4997	.4997	.4997	.4997	.4997	.4997	.4998
3.5	.4998									
4.0	.49997									
4.5	.499997									
5.0	.4999997									
6.0	.499999999									

TABLE A.6 — Critical Values from the *t* Distribution

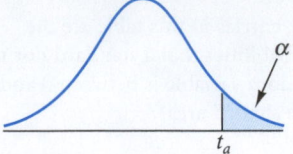

df	$t_{.100}$	$t_{.050}$	$t_{.025}$	$t_{.010}$	$t_{.005}$	$t_{.001}$
1	3.078	6.314	12.706	31.821	63.656	318.289
2	1.886	2.920	4.303	6.965	9.925	22.328
3	1.638	2.353	3.182	4.541	5.841	10.214
4	1.533	2.132	2.776	3.747	4.604	7.173
5	1.476	2.015	2.571	3.365	4.032	5.894
6	1.440	1.943	2.447	3.143	3.707	5.208
7	1.415	1.895	2.365	2.998	3.499	4.785
8	1.397	1.860	2.306	2.896	3.355	4.501
9	1.383	1.833	2.262	2.821	3.250	4.297
10	1.372	1.812	2.228	2.764	3.169	4.144
11	1.363	1.796	2.201	2.718	3.106	4.025
12	1.356	1.782	2.179	2.681	3.055	3.930
13	1.350	1.771	2.160	2.650	3.012	3.852
14	1.345	1.761	2.145	2.624	2.977	3.787
15	1.341	1.753	2.131	2.602	2.947	3.733
16	1.337	1.746	2.120	2.583	2.921	3.686
17	1.333	1.740	2.110	2.567	2.898	3.646
18	1.330	1.734	2.101	2.552	2.878	3.610
19	1.328	1.729	2.093	2.539	2.861	3.579
20	1.325	1.725	2.086	2.528	2.845	3.552
21	1.323	1.721	2.080	2.518	2.831	3.527
22	1.321	1.717	2.074	2.508	2.819	3.505
23	1.319	1.714	2.069	2.500	2.807	3.485
24	1.318	1.711	2.064	2.492	2.797	3.467
25	1.316	1.708	2.060	2.485	2.787	3.450
26	1.315	1.706	2.056	2.479	2.779	3.435
27	1.314	1.703	2.052	2.473	2.771	3.421
28	1.313	1.701	2.048	2.467	2.763	3.408
29	1.311	1.699	2.045	2.462	2.756	3.396
30	1.310	1.697	2.042	2.457	2.750	3.385
40	1.303	1.684	2.021	2.423	2.704	3.307
50	1.299	1.676	2.009	2.403	2.678	3.261
60	1.296	1.671	2.000	2.390	2.660	3.232
70	1.294	1.667	1.994	2.381	2.648	3.211
80	1.292	1.664	1.990	2.374	2.639	3.195
90	1.291	1.662	1.987	2.368	2.632	3.183
100	1.290	1.660	1.984	2.364	2.626	3.174
150	1.287	1.655	1.976	2.351	2.609	3.145
200	1.286	1.653	1.972	2.345	2.601	3.131
∞	1.282	1.645	1.960	2.326	2.576	3.090

Values of α for one-tailed test and $\alpha/2$ for two-tailed test

TABLE A.7

Percentage Points of the *F* Distribution

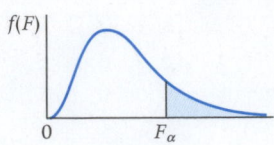

v_2	\multicolumn{9}{c}{$\alpha = .10$ — Numerator Degrees of Freedom}								
	1	2	3	4	5	6	7	8	9
1	39.86	49.50	53.59	55.83	57.24	58.20	58.91	59.44	59.86
2	8.53	9.00	9.16	9.24	9.29	9.33	9.35	9.37	9.38
3	5.54	5.46	5.39	5.34	5.31	5.28	5.27	5.25	5.24
4	4.54	4.32	4.19	4.11	4.05	4.01	3.98	3.95	3.94
5	4.06	3.78	3.62	3.52	3.45	3.40	3.37	3.34	3.32
6	3.78	3.46	3.29	3.18	3.11	3.05	3.01	2.98	2.96
7	3.59	3.26	3.07	2.96	2.88	2.83	2.78	2.75	2.72
8	3.46	3.11	2.92	2.81	2.73	2.67	2.62	2.59	2.56
9	3.36	3.01	2.81	2.69	2.61	2.55	2.51	2.47	2.44
10	3.29	2.92	2.73	2.61	2.52	2.46	2.41	2.38	2.35
11	3.23	2.86	2.66	2.54	2.45	2.39	2.34	2.30	2.27
12	3.18	2.81	2.61	2.48	2.39	2.33	2.28	2.24	2.21
13	3.14	2.76	2.56	2.43	2.35	2.28	2.23	2.20	2.16
14	3.10	2.73	2.52	2.39	2.31	2.24	2.19	2.15	2.12
15	3.07	2.70	2.49	2.36	2.27	2.21	2.16	2.12	2.09
16	3.05	2.67	2.46	2.33	2.24	2.18	2.13	2.09	2.06
17	3.03	2.64	2.44	2.31	2.22	2.15	2.10	2.06	2.03
18	3.01	2.62	2.42	2.29	2.20	2.13	2.08	2.04	2.00
19	2.99	2.61	2.40	2.27	2.18	2.11	2.06	2.02	1.98
20	2.97	2.59	2.38	2.25	2.16	2.09	2.04	2.00	1.96
21	2.96	2.57	2.36	2.23	2.14	2.08	2.02	1.98	1.95
22	2.95	2.56	2.35	2.22	2.13	2.06	2.01	1.97	1.93
23	2.94	2.55	2.34	2.21	2.11	2.05	1.99	1.95	1.92
24	2.93	2.54	2.33	2.19	2.10	2.04	1.98	1.94	1.91
25	2.92	2.53	2.32	2.18	2.09	2.02	1.97	1.93	1.89
26	2.91	2.52	2.31	2.17	2.08	2.01	1.96	1.92	1.88
27	2.90	2.51	2.30	2.17	2.07	2.00	1.95	1.91	1.87
28	2.89	2.50	2.29	2.16	2.06	2.00	1.94	1.90	1.87
29	2.89	2.50	2.28	2.15	2.06	1.99	1.93	1.89	1.86
30	2.88	2.49	2.28	2.14	2.05	1.98	1.93	1.88	1.85
40	2.84	2.44	2.23	2.09	2.00	1.93	1.87	1.83	1.79
60	2.79	2.39	2.18	2.04	1.95	1.87	1.82	1.77	1.74
120	2.75	2.35	2.13	1.99	1.90	1.82	1.77	1.72	1.68
∞	2.71	2.30	2.08	1.94	1.85	1.77	1.72	1.67	1.63

Denominator Degrees of Freedom (left axis label for v_2)

				$\alpha = .10$							v_1	
			Numerator Degrees of Freedom									
10	**12**	**15**	**20**	**24**	**30**	**40**	**60**	**120**	**∞**		v_2
60.19	60.71	61.22	61.74	62.00	62.26	62.53	62.79	63.06	63.33	1
9.39	9.41	9.42	9.44	9.45	9.46	9.47	9.47	9.48	9.49	2
5.23	5.22	5.20	5.18	5.18	5.17	5.16	5.15	5.14	5.13	3
3.92	3.90	3.87	3.84	3.83	3.82	3.80	3.79	3.78	3.76	4
3.30	3.27	3.24	3.21	3.19	3.17	3.16	3.14	3.12	3.10	5
2.94	2.90	2.87	2.84	2.82	2.80	2.78	2.76	2.74	2.72	6
2.70	2.67	2.63	2.59	2.58	2.56	2.54	2.51	2.49	2.47	7
2.54	2.50	2.46	2.42	2.40	2.38	2.36	2.34	2.32	2.29	8
2.42	2.38	2.34	2.30	2.28	2.25	2.23	2.21	2.18	2.16	9
2.32	2.28	2.24	2.20	2.18	2.16	2.13	2.11	2.08	2.06	10
2.25	2.21	2.17	2.12	2.10	2.08	2.05	2.03	2.00	1.97	11
2.19	2.15	2.10	2.06	2.04	2.01	1.99	1.96	1.93	1.90	12
2.14	2.10	2.05	2.01	1.98	1.96	1.93	1.90	1.88	1.85	13
2.10	2.05	2.01	1.96	1.94	1.91	1.89	1.86	1.83	1.80	14
2.06	2.02	1.97	1.92	1.90	1.87	1.85	1.82	1.79	1.76	15
2.03	1.99	1.94	1.89	1.87	1.84	1.81	1.78	1.75	1.72	16
2.00	1.96	1.91	1.86	1.84	1.81	1.78	1.75	1.72	1.69	17
1.98	1.93	1.89	1.84	1.81	1.78	1.75	1.72	1.69	1.66	18
1.96	1.91	1.86	1.81	1.79	1.76	1.73	1.70	1.67	1.63	19
1.94	1.89	1.84	1.79	1.77	1.74	1.71	1.68	1.64	1.61	20
1.92	1.87	1.83	1.78	1.75	1.72	1.69	1.66	1.62	1.59	21
1.90	1.86	1.81	1.76	1.73	1.70	1.67	1.64	1.60	1.57	22
1.89	1.84	1.80	1.74	1.72	1.69	1.66	1.62	1.59	1.55	23
1.88	1.83	1.78	1.73	1.70	1.67	1.64	1.61	1.57	1.53	24
1.87	1.82	1.77	1.72	1.69	1.66	1.63	1.59	1.56	1.52	25
1.86	1.81	1.76	1.71	1.68	1.65	1.61	1.58	1.54	1.50	26
1.85	1.80	1.75	1.70	1.67	1.64	1.60	1.57	1.53	1.49	27
1.84	1.79	1.74	1.69	1.66	1.63	1.59	1.56	1.52	1.48	28
1.83	1.78	1.73	1.68	1.65	1.62	1.58	1.55	1.51	1.47	29
1.82	1.77	1.72	1.67	1.64	1.61	1.57	1.54	1.50	1.46	30
1.76	1.71	1.66	1.61	1.57	1.54	1.51	1.47	1.42	1.38	40
1.71	1.66	1.60	1.54	1.51	1.48	1.44	1.40	1.35	1.29	60
1.65	1.60	1.55	1.48	1.45	1.41	1.37	1.32	1.26	1.19	120
1.60	1.55	1.49	1.42	1.38	1.34	1.30	1.24	1.17	1.00	∞

Denominator Degrees of Freedom

Continued

v_2 \ v_1	$\alpha = .05$ Numerator Degrees of Freedom								
	1	2	3	4	5	6	7	8	9
1	161.45	199.50	215.71	224.58	230.16	233.99	236.77	238.88	240.54
2	18.51	19.00	19.16	19.25	19.30	19.33	19.35	19.37	19.38
3	10.13	9.55	9.28	9.12	9.01	8.94	8.89	8.85	8.81
4	7.71	6.94	6.59	6.39	6.26	6.16	6.09	6.04	6.00
5	6.61	5.79	5.41	5.19	5.05	4.95	4.88	4.82	4.77
6	5.99	5.14	4.76	4.53	4.39	4.28	4.21	4.15	4.10
7	5.59	4.74	4.35	4.12	3.97	3.87	3.79	3.73	3.68
8	5.32	4.46	4.07	3.84	3.69	3.58	3.50	3.44	3.39
9	5.12	4.26	3.86	3.63	3.48	3.37	3.29	3.23	3.18
10	4.96	4.10	3.71	3.48	3.33	3.22	3.14	3.07	3.02
11	4.84	3.98	3.59	3.36	3.20	3.09	3.01	2.95	2.90
12	4.75	3.89	3.49	3.26	3.11	3.00	2.91	2.85	2.80
13	4.67	3.81	3.41	3.18	3.03	2.92	2.83	2.77	2.71
14	4.60	3.74	3.34	3.11	2.96	2.85	2.76	2.70	2.65
15	4.54	3.68	3.29	3.06	2.90	2.79	2.71	2.64	2.59
16	4.49	3.63	3.24	3.01	2.85	2.74	2.66	2.59	2.54
17	4.45	3.59	3.20	2.96	2.81	2.70	2.61	2.55	2.49
18	4.41	3.55	3.16	2.93	2.77	2.66	2.58	2.51	2.46
19	4.38	3.52	3.13	2.90	2.74	2.63	2.54	2.48	2.42
20	4.35	3.49	3.10	2.87	2.71	2.60	2.51	2.45	2.39
21	4.32	3.47	3.07	2.84	2.68	2.57	2.49	2.42	2.37
22	4.30	3.44	3.05	2.82	2.66	2.55	2.46	2.40	2.34
23	4.28	3.42	3.03	2.80	2.64	2.53	2.44	2.37	2.32
24	4.26	3.40	3.01	2.78	2.62	2.51	2.42	2.36	2.30
25	4.24	3.39	2.99	2.76	2.60	2.49	2.40	2.34	2.28
26	4.23	3.37	2.98	2.74	2.59	2.47	2.39	2.32	2.27
27	4.21	3.35	2.96	2.73	2.57	2.46	2.37	2.31	2.25
28	4.20	3.34	2.95	2.71	2.56	2.45	2.36	2.29	2.24
29	4.18	3.33	2.93	2.70	2.55	2.43	2.35	2.28	2.22
30	4.17	3.32	2.92	2.69	2.53	2.42	2.33	2.27	2.21
40	4.08	3.23	2.84	2.61	2.45	2.34	2.25	2.18	2.12
60	4.00	3.15	2.76	2.53	2.37	2.25	2.17	2.10	2.04
120	3.92	3.07	2.68	2.45	2.29	2.18	2.09	2.02	1.96
∞	3.84	3.00	2.60	2.37	2.21	2.10	2.01	1.94	1.88

Denominator Degrees of Freedom

$\alpha = .05$										ν_1	
Numerator Degrees of Freedom											
10	**12**	**15**	**20**	**24**	**30**	**40**	**60**	**120**	**∞**		ν_2
241.88	243.90	245.90	248.00	249.10	250.10	251.10	252.20	253.30	254.30	1	
19.40	19.41	19.43	19.45	19.45	19.46	19.47	19.48	19.49	19.50	2	
8.79	8.74	8.70	8.66	8.64	8.62	8.59	8.57	8.55	8.53	3	
5.96	5.91	5.86	5.80	5.77	5.75	5.72	5.69	5.66	5.63	4	
4.74	4.68	4.62	4.56	4.53	4.50	4.46	4.43	4.40	4.36	5	
4.06	4.00	3.94	3.87	3.84	3.81	3.77	3.74	3.70	3.67	6	
3.64	3.57	3.51	3.44	3.41	3.38	3.34	3.30	3.27	3.23	7	
3.35	3.28	3.22	3.15	3.12	3.08	3.04	3.01	2.97	2.93	8	
3.14	3.07	3.01	2.94	2.90	2.86	2.83	2.79	2.75	2.71	9	
2.98	2.91	2.85	2.77	2.74	2.70	2.66	2.62	2.58	2.54	10	
2.85	2.79	2.72	2.65	2.61	2.57	2.53	2.49	2.45	2.40	11	
2.75	2.69	2.62	2.54	2.51	2.47	2.43	2.38	2.34	2.30	12	
2.67	2.60	2.53	2.46	2.42	2.38	2.34	2.30	2.25	2.21	13	
2.60	2.53	2.46	2.39	2.35	2.31	2.27	2.22	2.18	2.13	14	
2.54	2.48	2.40	2.33	2.29	2.25	2.20	2.16	2.11	2.07	15	
2.49	2.42	2.35	2.28	2.24	2.19	2.15	2.11	2.06	2.01	16	
2.45	2.38	2.31	2.23	2.19	2.15	2.10	2.06	2.01	1.96	17	
2.41	2.34	2.27	2.19	2.15	2.11	2.06	2.02	1.97	1.92	18	
2.38	2.31	2.23	2.16	2.11	2.07	2.03	1.98	1.93	1.88	19	
2.35	2.28	2.20	2.12	2.08	2.04	1.99	1.95	1.90	1.84	20	
2.32	2.25	2.18	2.10	2.05	2.01	1.96	1.92	1.87	1.81	21	
2.30	2.23	2.15	2.07	2.03	1.98	1.94	1.89	1.84	1.78	22	
2.27	2.20	2.13	2.05	2.01	1.96	1.91	1.86	1.81	1.76	23	
2.25	2.18	2.11	2.03	1.98	1.94	1.89	1.84	1.79	1.73	24	
2.24	2.16	2.09	2.01	1.96	1.92	1.87	1.82	1.77	1.71	25	
2.22	2.15	2.07	1.99	1.95	1.90	1.85	1.80	1.75	1.69	26	
2.20	2.13	2.06	1.97	1.93	1.88	1.84	1.79	1.73	1.67	27	
2.19	2.12	2.04	1.96	1.91	1.87	1.82	1.77	1.71	1.65	28	
2.18	2.10	2.03	1.94	1.90	1.85	1.81	1.75	1.70	1.64	29	
2.16	2.09	2.01	1.93	1.89	1.84	1.79	1.74	1.68	1.62	30	
2.08	2.00	1.92	1.84	1.79	1.74	1.69	1.64	1.58	1.51	40	
1.99	1.92	1.84	1.75	1.70	1.65	1.59	1.53	1.47	1.39	60	
1.91	1.83	1.75	1.66	1.61	1.55	1.50	1.43	1.35	1.25	120	
1.83	1.75	1.67	1.57	1.52	1.46	1.39	1.32	1.22	1.00	∞	

Denominator Degrees of Freedom

Continued

v_2	$\alpha = .025$ Numerator Degrees of Freedom								
	1	2	3	4	5	6	7	8	9
1	647.79	799.48	864.15	899.60	921.83	937.11	948.20	956.64	963.28
2	38.51	39.00	39.17	39.25	39.30	39.33	39.36	39.37	39.39
3	17.44	16.04	15.44	15.10	14.88	14.73	14.62	14.54	14.47
4	12.22	10.65	9.98	9.60	9.36	9.20	9.07	8.98	8.90
5	10.01	8.43	7.76	7.39	7.15	6.98	6.85	6.76	6.68
6	8.81	7.26	6.60	6.23	5.99	5.82	5.70	5.60	5.52
7	8.07	6.54	5.89	5.52	5.29	5.12	4.99	4.90	4.82
8	7.57	6.06	5.42	5.05	4.82	4.65	4.53	4.43	4.36
9	7.21	5.71	5.08	4.72	4.48	4.32	4.20	4.10	4.03
10	6.94	5.46	4.83	4.47	4.24	4.07	3.95	3.85	3.78
11	6.72	5.26	4.63	4.28	4.04	3.88	3.76	3.66	3.59
12	6.55	5.10	4.47	4.12	3.89	3.73	3.61	3.51	3.44
13	6.41	4.97	4.35	4.00	3.77	3.60	3.48	3.39	3.31
14	6.30	4.86	4.24	3.89	3.66	3.50	3.38	3.29	3.21
15	6.20	4.77	4.15	3.80	3.58	3.41	3.29	3.20	3.12
16	6.12	4.69	4.08	3.73	3.50	3.34	3.22	3.12	3.05
17	6.04	4.62	4.01	3.66	3.44	3.28	3.16	3.06	2.98
18	5.98	4.56	3.95	3.61	3.38	3.22	3.10	3.01	2.93
19	5.92	4.51	3.90	3.56	3.33	3.17	3.05	2.96	2.88
20	5.87	4.46	3.86	3.51	3.29	3.13	3.01	2.91	2.84
21	5.83	4.42	3.82	3.48	3.25	3.09	2.97	2.87	2.80
22	5.79	4.38	3.78	3.44	3.22	3.05	2.93	2.84	2.76
23	5.75	4.35	3.75	3.41	3.18	3.02	2.90	2.81	2.73
24	5.72	4.32	3.72	3.38	3.15	2.99	2.87	2.78	2.70
25	5.69	4.29	3.69	3.35	3.13	2.97	2.85	2.75	2.68
26	5.66	4.27	3.67	3.33	3.10	2.94	2.82	2.73	2.65
27	5.63	4.24	3.65	3.31	3.08	2.92	2.80	2.71	2.63
28	5.61	4.22	3.63	3.29	3.06	2.90	2.78	2.69	2.61
29	5.59	4.20	3.61	3.27	3.04	2.88	2.76	2.67	2.59
30	5.57	4.18	3.59	3.25	3.03	2.87	2.75	2.65	2.57
40	5.42	4.05	3.46	3.13	2.90	2.74	2.62	2.53	2.45
60	5.29	3.93	3.34	3.01	2.79	2.63	2.51	2.41	2.33
120	5.15	3.80	3.23	2.89	2.67	2.52	2.39	2.30	2.22
∞	5.02	3.69	3.12	2.79	2.57	2.41	2.29	2.19	2.11

v_1

Denominator Degrees of Freedom

10	12	15	20	24	30	40	60	120	∞	v_1	v_2
					$\alpha = .025$						
			Numerator Degrees of Freedom								
968.63	976.72	984.87	993.08	997.27	1001.40	1005.60	1009.79	1014.04	1018.00	1	
9.40	39.41	39.43	39.45	39.46	39.46	39.47	39.48	39.49	39.50	2	
14.42	14.34	14.25	14.17	14.12	14.08	14.04	13.99	13.95	13.90	3	
8.84	8.75	8.66	8.56	8.51	8.46	8.41	8.36	8.31	8.26	4	
6.62	6.52	6.43	6.33	6.28	6.23	6.18	6.12	6.07	6.02	5	
5.46	5.37	5.27	5.17	5.12	5.07	5.01	4.96	4.90	4.85	6	
4.76	4.67	4.57	4.47	4.41	4.36	4.31	4.25	4.20	4.14	7	
4.30	4.20	4.10	4.00	3.95	3.89	3.84	3.78	3.73	3.67	8	
3.96	3.87	3.77	3.67	3.61	3.56	3.51	3.45	3.39	3.33	9	
3.72	3.62	3.52	3.42	3.37	3.31	3.26	3.20	3.14	3.08	10	
3.53	3.43	3.33	3.23	3.17	3.12	3.06	3.00	2.94	2.88	11	
3.37	3.28	3.18	3.07	3.02	2.96	2.91	2.85	2.79	2.72	12	
3.25	3.15	3.05	2.95	2.89	2.84	2.78	2.72	2.66	2.60	13	
3.15	3.05	2.95	2.84	2.79	2.73	2.67	2.61	2.55	2.49	14	
3.06	2.96	2.86	2.76	2.70	2.64	2.59	2.52	2.46	2.40	15	
2.99	2.89	2.79	2.68	2.63	2.57	2.51	2.45	2.38	2.32	16	
2.92	2.82	2.72	2.62	2.56	2.50	2.44	2.38	2.32	2.25	17	
2.87	2.77	2.67	2.56	2.50	2.44	2.38	2.32	2.26	2.19	18	
2.82	2.72	2.62	2.51	2.45	2.39	2.33	2.27	2.20	2.13	19	
2.77	2.68	2.57	2.46	2.41	2.35	2.29	2.22	2.16	2.09	20	
2.73	2.64	2.53	2.42	2.37	2.31	2.25	2.18	2.11	2.04	21	
2.70	2.60	2.50	2.39	2.33	2.27	2.21	2.14	2.08	2.00	22	
2.67	2.57	2.47	2.36	2.30	2.24	2.18	2.11	2.04	1.97	23	
2.64	2.54	2.44	2.33	2.27	2.21	2.15	2.08	2.01	1.94	24	
2.61	2.51	2.41	2.30	2.24	2.18	2.12	2.05	1.98	1.91	25	
2.59	2.49	2.39	2.28	2.22	2.16	2.09	2.03	1.95	1.88	26	
2.57	2.47	2.36	2.25	2.19	2.13	2.07	2.00	1.93	1.85	27	
2.55	2.45	2.34	2.23	2.17	2.11	2.05	1.98	1.91	1.83	28	
2.53	2.43	2.32	2.21	2.15	2.09	2.03	1.96	1.89	1.81	29	
2.51	2.41	2.31	2.20	2.14	2.07	2.01	1.94	1.87	1.79	30	
2.39	2.29	2.18	2.07	2.01	1.94	1.88	1.80	1.72	1.64	40	
2.27	2.17	2.06	1.94	1.88	1.82	1.74	1.67	1.58	1.48	60	
2.16	2.05	1.94	1.82	1.76	1.69	1.61	1.53	1.43	1.31	120	
2.05	1.94	1.83	1.71	1.64	1.57	1.48	1.39	1.27	1.00	∞	

Denominator Degrees of Freedom

Continued

v_1				$\alpha = .01$					
	\multicolumn{9}{c}{**Numerator Degrees of Freedom**}								
v_2	**1**	**2**	**3**	**4**	**5**	**6**	**7**	**8**	**9**
1	4052.18	4999.34	5403.53	5624.26	5763.96	5858.95	5928.33	5980.95	6022.40
2	98.50	99.00	99.16	99.25	99.30	99.33	99.36	99.38	99.39
3	34.12	30.82	29.46	28.71	28.24	27.91	27.67	27.49	27.34
4	21.20	18.00	16.69	15.98	15.52	15.21	14.98	14.80	14.66
5	16.26	13.27	12.06	11.39	10.97	10.67	10.46	10.29	10.16
6	13.75	10.92	9.78	9.15	8.75	8.47	8.26	8.10	7.98
7	12.25	9.55	8.45	7.85	7.46	7.19	6.99	6.84	6.72
8	11.26	8.65	7.59	7.01	6.63	6.37	6.18	6.03	5.91
9	10.56	8.02	6.99	6.42	6.06	5.80	5.61	5.47	5.35
10	10.04	7.56	6.55	5.99	5.64	5.39	5.20	5.06	4.94
11	9.65	7.21	6.22	5.67	5.32	5.07	4.89	4.74	4.63
12	9.33	6.93	5.95	5.41	5.06	4.82	4.64	4.50	4.39
13	9.07	6.70	5.74	5.21	4.86	4.62	4.44	4.30	4.19
14	8.86	6.51	5.56	5.04	4.69	4.46	4.28	4.14	4.03
15	8.68	6.36	5.42	4.89	4.56	4.32	4.14	4.00	3.89
16	8.53	6.23	5.29	4.77	4.44	4.20	4.03	3.89	3.78
17	8.40	6.11	5.19	4.67	4.34	4.10	3.93	3.79	3.68
18	8.29	6.01	5.09	4.58	4.25	4.01	3.84	3.71	3.60
19	8.18	5.93	5.01	4.50	4.17	3.94	3.77	3.63	3.52
20	8.10	5.85	4.94	4.43	4.10	3.87	3.70	3.56	3.46
21	8.02	5.78	4.87	4.37	4.04	3.81	3.64	3.51	3.40
22	7.95	5.72	4.82	4.31	3.99	3.76	3.59	3.45	3.35
23	7.88	5.66	4.76	4.26	3.94	3.71	3.54	3.41	3.30
24	7.82	5.61	4.72	4.22	3.90	3.67	3.50	3.36	3.26
25	7.77	5.57	4.68	4.18	3.85	3.63	3.46	3.32	3.22
26	7.72	5.53	4.64	4.14	3.82	3.59	3.42	3.29	3.18
27	7.68	5.49	4.60	4.11	3.78	3.56	3.39	3.26	3.15
28	7.64	5.45	4.57	4.07	3.75	3.53	3.36	3.23	3.12
29	7.60	5.42	4.54	4.04	3.73	3.50	3.33	3.20	3.09
30	7.56	5.39	4.51	4.02	3.70	3.47	3.30	3.17	3.07
40	7.31	5.18	4.31	3.83	3.51	3.29	3.12	2.99	2.89
60	7.08	4.98	4.13	3.65	3.34	3.12	2.95	2.82	2.72
120	6.85	4.79	3.95	3.48	3.17	2.96	2.79	2.66	2.56
∞	6.63	4.61	3.78	3.32	3.02	2.80	2.64	2.51	2.41

Denominator Degrees of Freedom

$\alpha = .01$											v_1
Numerator Degrees of Freedom											
10	**12**	**15**	**20**	**24**	**30**	**40**	**60**	**120**	**∞**		v_2
6055.93	6106.68	6156.97	6208.66	6234.27	6260.35	6286.43	6312.97	6339.51	6366.00	1	
99.40	99.42	99.43	99.45	99.46	99.47	99.48	99.48	99.49	99.50	2	
27.23	27.05	26.87	26.69	26.60	26.50	26.41	26.32	26.22	26.13	3	
14.55	14.37	14.20	14.02	13.93	13.84	13.75	13.65	13.56	13.46	4	
10.05	9.89	9.72	9.55	9.47	9.38	9.29	9.20	9.11	9.02	5	
7.87	7.72	7.56	7.40	7.31	7.23	7.14	7.06	6.97	6.88	6	
6.62	6.47	6.31	6.16	6.07	5.99	5.91	5.82	5.74	5.65	7	
5.81	5.67	5.52	5.36	5.28	5.20	5.12	5.03	4.95	4.86	8	
5.26	5.11	4.96	4.81	4.73	4.65	4.57	4.48	4.40	4.31	9	
4.85	4.71	4.56	4.41	4.33	4.25	4.17	4.08	4.00	3.91	10	
4.54	4.40	4.25	4.10	4.02	3.94	3.86	3.78	3.69	3.60	11	
4.30	4.16	4.01	3.86	3.78	3.70	3.62	3.54	3.45	3.36	12	
4.10	3.96	3.82	3.66	3.59	3.51	3.43	3.34	3.25	3.17	13	
3.94	3.80	3.66	3.51	3.43	3.35	3.27	3.18	3.09	3.00	14	
3.80	3.67	3.52	3.37	3.29	3.21	3.13	3.05	2.96	2.87	15	
3.69	3.55	3.41	3.26	3.18	3.10	3.02	2.93	2.84	2.75	16	
3.59	3.46	3.31	3.16	3.08	3.00	2.92	2.83	2.75	2.65	17	
3.51	3.37	3.23	3.08	3.00	2.92	2.84	2.75	2.66	2.57	18	
3.43	3.30	3.15	3.00	2.92	2.84	2.76	2.67	2.58	2.49	19	
3.37	3.23	3.09	2.94	2.86	2.78	2.69	2.61	2.52	2.42	20	
3.31	3.17	3.03	2.88	2.80	2.72	2.64	2.55	2.46	2.36	21	
3.26	3.12	2.98	2.83	2.75	2.67	2.58	2.50	2.40	2.31	22	
3.21	3.07	2.93	2.78	2.70	2.62	2.54	2.45	2.35	2.26	23	
3.17	3.03	2.89	2.74	2.66	2.58	2.49	2.40	2.31	2.21	24	
3.13	2.99	2.85	2.70	2.62	2.54	2.45	2.36	2.27	2.17	25	
3.09	2.96	2.81	2.66	2.58	2.50	2.42	2.33	2.23	2.13	26	
3.06	2.93	2.78	2.63	2.55	2.47	2.38	2.29	2.20	2.10	27	
3.03	2.90	2.75	2.60	2.52	2.44	2.35	2.26	2.17	2.06	28	
3.00	2.87	2.73	2.57	2.49	2.41	2.33	2.23	2.14	2.03	29	
2.98	2.84	2.70	2.55	2.47	2.39	2.30	2.21	2.11	2.01	30	
2.80	2.66	2.52	2.37	2.29	2.20	2.11	2.02	1.92	1.80	40	
2.63	2.50	2.35	2.20	2.12	2.03	1.94	1.84	1.73	1.60	60	
2.47	2.34	2.19	2.03	1.95	1.86	1.76	1.66	1.53	1.38	120	
2.32	2.18	2.04	1.88	1.79	1.70	1.59	1.47	1.32	1.00	∞	

Denominator Degrees of Freedom

Continued

ν_1	$\alpha = .005$								
	Numerator Degrees of Freedom								
ν_2	**1**	**2**	**3**	**4**	**5**	**6**	**7**	**8**	**9**
1	16212.46	19997.36	21614.13	22500.75	23055.82	23439.53	23715.20	23923.81	24091.45
2	198.50	199.01	199.16	199.24	199.30	199.33	199.36	199.38	199.39
3	55.55	49.80	47.47	46.20	45.39	44.84	44.43	44.13	43.88
4	31.33	26.28	24.26	23.15	22.46	21.98	21.62	21.35	21.14
5	22.78	18.31	16.53	15.56	14.94	14.51	14.20	13.96	13.77
6	18.63	14.54	12.92	12.03	11.46	11.07	10.79	10.57	10.39
7	16.24	12.40	10.88	10.05	9.52	9.16	8.89	8.68	8.51
8	14.69	11.04	9.60	8.81	8.30	7.95	7.69	7.50	7.34
9	13.61	10.11	8.72	7.96	7.47	7.13	6.88	6.69	6.54
10	12.83	9.43	8.08	7.34	6.87	6.54	6.30	6.12	5.97
11	12.23	8.91	7.60	6.88	6.42	6.10	5.86	5.68	5.54
12	11.75	8.51	7.23	6.52	6.07	5.76	5.52	5.35	5.20
13	11.37	8.19	6.93	6.23	5.79	5.48	5.25	5.08	4.94
14	11.06	7.92	6.68	6.00	5.56	5.26	5.03	4.86	4.72
15	10.80	7.70	6.48	5.80	5.37	5.07	4.85	4.67	4.54
16	10.58	7.51	6.30	5.64	5.21	4.91	4.69	4.52	4.38
17	10.38	7.35	6.16	5.50	5.07	4.78	4.56	4.39	4.25
18	10.22	7.21	6.03	5.37	4.96	4.66	4.44	4.28	4.14
19	10.07	7.09	5.92	5.27	4.85	4.56	4.34	4.18	4.04
20	9.94	6.99	5.82	5.17	4.76	4.47	4.26	4.09	3.96
21	9.83	6.89	5.73	5.09	4.68	4.39	4.18	4.01	3.88
22	9.73	6.81	5.65	5.02	4.61	4.32	4.11	3.94	3.81
23	9.63	6.73	5.58	4.95	4.54	4.26	4.05	3.88	3.75
24	9.55	6.66	5.52	4.89	4.49	4.20	3.99	3.83	3.69
25	9.48	6.60	5.46	4.84	4.43	4.15	3.94	3.78	3.64
26	9.41	6.54	5.41	4.79	4.38	4.10	3.89	3.73	3.60
27	9.34	6.49	5.36	4.74	4.34	4.06	3.85	3.69	3.56
28	9.28	6.44	5.32	4.70	4.30	4.02	3.81	3.65	3.52
29	9.23	6.40	5.28	4.66	4.26	3.98	3.77	3.61	3.48
30	9.18	6.35	5.24	4.62	4.23	3.95	3.74	3.58	3.45
40	8.83	6.07	4.98	4.37	3.99	3.71	3.51	3.35	3.22
60	8.49	5.79	4.73	4.14	3.76	3.49	3.29	3.13	3.01
120	8.18	5.54	4.50	3.92	3.55	3.28	3.09	2.93	2.81
∞	7.88	5.30	4.28	3.72	3.35	3.09	2.90	2.74	2.62

Denominator Degrees of Freedom

$\alpha = .005$											v_1
Numerator Degrees of Freedom											
10	**12**	**15**	**20**	**24**	**30**	**40**	**60**	**120**	**∞**		v_2
24221.84	24426.73	24631.62	24836.51	24937.09	25041.40	25145.71	25253.74	25358.05	25465.00	1	
199.39	199.42	199.43	199.45	199.45	199.48	199.48	199.48	199.49	199.50	2	
43.68	43.39	43.08	42.78	42.62	42.47	42.31	42.15	41.99	41.83	3	
20.97	20.70	20.44	20.17	20.03	19.89	19.75	19.61	19.47	19.32	4	
13.62	13.38	13.15	12.90	12.78	12.66	12.53	12.40	12.27	12.14	5	
10.25	10.03	9.81	9.59	9.47	9.36	9.24	9.12	9.00	8.88	6	
8.38	8.18	7.97	7.75	7.64	7.53	7.42	7.31	7.19	7.08	7	
7.21	7.01	6.81	6.61	6.50	6.40	6.29	6.18	6.06	5.95	8	
6.42	6.23	6.03	5.83	5.73	5.62	5.52	5.41	5.30	5.19	9	
5.85	5.66	5.47	5.27	5.17	5.07	4.97	4.86	4.75	4.64	10	
5.42	5.24	5.05	4.86	4.76	4.65	4.55	4.45	4.34	4.23	11	
5.09	4.91	4.72	4.53	4.43	4.33	4.23	4.12	4.01	3.90	12	
4.82	4.64	4.46	4.27	4.17	4.07	3.97	3.87	3.76	3.65	13	
4.60	4.43	4.25	4.06	3.96	3.86	3.76	3.66	3.55	3.44	14	
4.42	4.25	4.07	3.88	3.79	3.69	3.59	3.48	3.37	3.26	15	
4.27	4.10	3.92	3.73	3.64	3.54	3.44	3.33	3.22	3.11	16	
4.14	3.97	3.79	3.61	3.51	3.41	3.31	3.21	3.10	2.98	17	
4.03	3.86	3.68	3.50	3.40	3.30	3.20	3.10	2.99	2.87	18	
3.93	3.76	3.59	3.40	3.31	3.21	3.11	3.00	2.89	2.78	19	
3.85	3.68	3.50	3.32	3.22	3.12	3.02	2.92	2.81	2.69	20	
3.77	3.60	3.43	3.24	3.15	3.05	2.95	2.84	2.73	2.61	21	
3.70	3.54	3.36	3.18	3.08	2.98	2.88	2.77	2.66	2.55	22	
3.64	3.47	3.30	3.12	3.02	2.92	2.82	2.71	2.60	2.48	23	
3.59	3.42	3.25	3.06	2.97	2.87	2.77	2.66	2.55	2.43	24	
3.54	3.37	3.20	3.01	2.92	2.82	2.72	2.61	2.50	2.38	25	
3.49	3.33	3.15	2.97	2.87	2.77	2.67	2.56	2.45	2.33	26	
3.45	3.28	3.11	2.93	2.83	2.73	2.63	2.52	2.41	2.29	27	
3.41	3.25	3.07	2.89	2.79	2.69	2.59	2.48	2.37	2.25	28	
3.38	3.21	3.04	2.86	2.76	2.66	2.56	2.45	2.33	2.21	29	
3.34	3.18	3.01	2.82	2.73	2.63	2.52	2.42	2.30	2.18	30	
3.12	2.95	2.78	2.60	2.50	2.40	2.30	2.18	2.06	1.93	40	
2.90	2.74	2.57	2.39	2.29	2.19	2.08	1.96	1.83	1.69	60	
2.71	2.54	2.37	2.19	2.09	1.98	1.87	1.75	1.61	1.43	120	
2.52	2.36	2.19	2.00	1.90	1.79	1.67	1.53	1.36	1.00	∞	

TABLE A.8 The Chi-Square Table

Values of χ^2 for Selected Probabilities

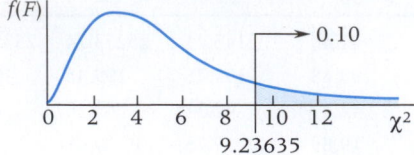

Example: df (Number of degrees of freedom) = 5, the tail above χ^2 = 9.23635 represents 0.10 or 10% of the area under the curve.

Degrees of Freedom	Area in Upper Tail									
	.995	.99	.975	.95	.9	.1	.05	.025	.01	.005
1	0.0000393	0.0001571	0.0009821	0.0039322	0.0157907	2.7055	3.8415	5.0239	6.6349	7.8794
2	0.010025	0.020100	0.050636	0.102586	0.210721	4.6052	5.9915	7.3778	9.2104	10.5965
3	0.07172	0.11483	0.21579	0.35185	0.58438	6.2514	7.8147	9.3484	11.3449	12.8381
4	0.20698	0.29711	0.48442	0.71072	1.06362	7.7794	9.4877	11.1433	13.2767	14.8602
5	0.41175	0.55430	0.83121	1.14548	1.61031	9.2363	11.0705	12.8325	15.0863	16.7496
6	0.67573	0.87208	1.23734	1.63538	2.20413	10.6446	12.5916	14.4494	16.8119	18.5475
7	0.98925	1.23903	1.68986	2.16735	2.83311	12.0170	14.0671	16.0128	18.4753	20.2777
8	1.34440	1.64651	2.17972	2.73263	3.48954	13.3616	15.5073	17.5345	20.0902	21.9549
9	1.73491	2.08789	2.70039	3.32512	4.16816	14.6837	16.9190	19.0228	21.6660	23.5893
10	2.15585	2.55820	3.24696	3.94030	4.86518	15.9872	18.3070	20.4832	23.2093	25.1881
11	2.60320	3.05350	3.81574	4.57481	5.57779	17.2750	19.6752	21.9200	24.7250	26.7569
12	3.07379	3.57055	4.40378	5.22603	6.30380	18.5493	21.0261	23.3367	26.2170	28.2997
13	3.56504	4.10690	5.00874	5.89186	7.04150	19.8119	22.3620	24.7356	27.6882	29.8193
14	4.07466	4.66042	5.62872	6.57063	7.78954	21.0641	23.6848	26.1189	29.1412	31.3194
15	4.60087	5.22936	6.26212	7.26093	8.54675	22.3071	24.9958	27.4884	30.5780	32.8015
16	5.14216	5.81220	6.90766	7.96164	9.31224	23.5418	26.2962	28.8453	31.9999	34.2671
17	5.69727	6.40774	7.56418	8.67175	10.08518	24.7690	27.5871	30.1910	33.4087	35.7184
18	6.26477	7.01490	8.23074	9.39045	10.86494	25.9894	28.8693	31.5264	34.8052	37.1564
19	6.84392	7.63270	8.90651	10.11701	11.65091	27.2036	30.1435	32.8523	36.1908	38.5821
20	7.43381	8.26037	9.59077	10.85080	12.44260	28.4120	31.4104	34.1696	37.5663	39.9969
21	8.03360	8.89717	10.28291	11.59132	13.23960	29.6151	32.6706	35.4789	38.9322	41.4009
22	8.64268	9.54249	10.98233	12.33801	14.04149	30.8133	33.9245	36.7807	40.2894	42.7957
23	9.26038	10.19569	11.68853	13.09051	14.84795	32.0069	35.1725	38.0756	41.6383	44.1814
24	9.88620	10.85635	12.40115	13.84842	15.65868	33.1962	36.4150	39.3641	42.9798	45.5584
25	10.51965	11.52395	13.11971	14.61140	16.47341	34.3816	37.6525	40.6465	44.3140	46.9280
26	11.16022	12.19818	13.84388	15.37916	17.29188	35.5632	38.8851	41.9231	45.6416	48.2898
27	11.80765	12.87847	14.57337	16.15139	18.11389	36.7412	40.1133	43.1945	46.9628	49.6450
28	12.46128	13.56467	15.30785	16.92788	18.93924	37.9159	41.3372	44.4608	48.2782	50.9936
29	13.12107	14.25641	16.04705	17.70838	19.76774	39.0875	42.5569	45.7223	49.5878	52.3355
30	13.78668	14.95346	16.79076	18.49267	20.59924	40.2560	43.7730	46.9792	50.8922	53.6719
40	20.70658	22.16420	24.43306	26.50930	29.05052	51.8050	55.7585	59.3417	63.6908	66.7660
50	27.99082	29.70673	32.35738	34.76424	37.68864	63.1671	67.5048	71.4202	76.1538	79.4898
60	35.53440	37.48480	40.48171	43.18797	46.45888	74.3970	79.0820	83.2977	88.3794	91.9518
70	43.27531	45.44170	48.75754	51.73926	55.32894	85.5270	90.5313	95.0231	100.4251	104.2148
80	51.17193	53.53998	57.15315	60.39146	64.27784	96.5782	101.8795	106.6285	112.3288	116.3209
90	59.19633	61.75402	65.64659	69.12602	73.29108	107.5650	113.1452	118.1359	124.1162	128.2987
100	67.32753	70.06500	74.22188	77.92944	82.35813	118.4980	124.3421	129.5613	135.8069	140.1697

TABLE A.9 — Critical Values for the Durbin-Watson Test

Entries in the table give the critical values for a one-tailed Durbin-Watson test for autocorrelation. For a two-tailed test, the level of significance is doubled.

Significant Points of d_L and d_U: $\alpha = .05$
Number of Independent Variables

	k	1		2		3		4		5	
n	d_L	d_U	d_L	d_U	d_L	d_U	d_L	d_U	d_L	d_U
15	1.08	1.36	0.95	1.54	0.82	1.75	0.69	1.97	0.56	2.21
16	1.10	1.37	0.98	1.54	0.86	1.73	0.74	1.93	0.62	2.15
17	1.13	1.38	1.02	1.54	0.90	1071	0.78	1.90	0.67	2.10
18	1.16	1.39	1.05	1.53	0.93	1.69	0.82	1.87	0.71	2.06
19	1.18	1.40	1.08	1.53	0.97	1.68	0.86	1.85	0.75	2.02
20	1.20	1.41	1.10	1.54	1.00	1.68	0.90	1.83	0.79	1.99
21	1.22	1.42	1.13	1.54	1.03	1.67	0.93	1.81	0.83	1.96
22	1.24	1.43	1.15	1.54	1.05	1.66	0.96	1.80	0.86	1.94
23	1.26	1.44	1.17	1.54	1.08	1.66	0.99	1.79	0.90	1.92
24	1.27	1.45	1.19	1.55	1.10	1.66	1.01	1.78	0.93	1.90
25	1.29	1.45	1.21	1.55	1.12	1.66	1.04	1.77	0.95	1.89
26	1.30	1.46	1.22	1.55	1.14	1.65	1.06	1.76	0.98	1.88
27	1.32	1.47	1.24	1.56	1.16	1.65	1.08	1.76	1.01	1.86
28	1.33	1.48	1.26	1.56	1.18	1.65	1.10	1.75	1.03	1085
29	1.34	1.48	1.27	1.56	1.20	1.65	1.12	1.74	1.05	1.84
30	1.35	1.49	1.28	1.57	1.21	1.65	1.14	1.74	1.07	1.83
31	1.36	1.50	1.30	1.57	1.23	1.65	1.16	1.74	1.09	1.83
32	1.37	1.50	1.31	1.57	1.24	1.65	1.18	1.73	1.11	1.82
33	1.38	1.51	1.32	1.58	1.26	1.65	1.19	1.73	1.13	1.81
34	1.39	1.51	1.33	1.58	1.27	1.65	1.21	1.73	1.15	1.81
35	1.40	1.52	1.34	1.58	1.28	1.65	1.22	1.73	1.16	1.80
36	1.41	1.52	1.35	1.59	1.29	1.65	1.24	1.73	1.18	1.80
37	1.42	1.53	1.36	1.59	1.31	1.66	1.25	1.72	1.19	1.80
38	1.43	1.54	1.37	1.59	1.32	1.66	1.26	1.72	1.21	1.79
39	1.43	1.54	1.38	1.60	1.33	1.66	1.27	1.72	1.22	1.79
40	1.44	1.54	1.39	1.60	1.34	1.66	1.29	1.72	1.23	1.79
45	1.48	1.57	1.43	1.62	1.38	1.67	1.34	1.72	1.29	1.78
50	1.50	1.59	1.46	1.63	1.421	1.67	1.38	1.72	1.34	1.77
55	1.53	1.60	1.49	1.64	1.45	1.68	1.41	1.72	1.38	1.77
60	1.55	1.62	1.51	1.65	1.48	1.69	1.44	1.73	1.41	1.77
65	1.57	1.63	1.54	1.66	1.50	1.70	1.47	1.73	1.44	1.77
70	1.58	1.64	1.55	1.67	1.52	1.70	1.49	1.74	1.46	1.77
75	1.60	1.65	1.57	1.68	1.54	1.71	1.51	1.74	1.49	1.77
80	1.61	1.66	1.59	1.69	1.56	1.72	1.53	1.74	1.51	1.77
85	1.62	1.67	1.60	1.70	1.57	1.72	1.55	1.75	1.52	1.77
90	1.63	1.68	1.61	1.70	1.59	1.73	1.57	1.75	1.54	1.78
95	1.64	1.69	1.62	1.71	1.60	1.73	1.58	1.75	1.56	1.78
100	1.65	1.69	1.63	1.72	1.61	1.74	1.59	1.76	1.57	1.78

Continued

Significant Points of d_L and d_U: $\alpha = .01$
Number of Independent Variables

k	1		2		3		4		5	
n	d_L	d_U	d_L	d_U	d_L	d_U	d_L	d_U	d_L	d_U
15	0.81	1.07	0.70	1.25	0.59	1.46	0.49	1.70	0.39	1.96
16	0.84	1.09	0.74	1.25	0.63	1044	0.53	1.66	0.44	1.90
17	0.87	1.10	0.77	1.25	0.67	1.43	0.57	1.63	0.48	1.85
18	0.90	1.12	0.80	1.26	0.71	1.42	0.61	1.60	0.52	1.80
19	0.93	1.13	0.83	1.26	0.74	1.41	0.65	1.58	0.56	1.77
20	0.95	1.15	0.86	1.27	0.77	1.41	0.68	1.57	0.60	1.74
21	0.97	1.16	0.89	1.27	0.80	1.41	0.72	1.55	0.63	1.71
22	1.00	1.17	0.91	1.28	0.83	1.40	0.75	1.54	0.66	1.69
23	1.02	1.19	0.94	1.29	0.86	1.40	0.77	1.53	0.70	1.67
24	1.04	1.20	0.96	1.30	0.88	1.41	0.80	1.53	0.72	1.66
25	1.05	1.21	0.98	1.30	0.90	1.41	0.83	1.52	0.75	1.65
26	1.07	1.22	1.00	1.31	0.93	1.41	0.85	1.52	0.78	1.64
27	1.09	1.23	1.02	1.32	0.95	1.41	0.88	1.51	0.81	1.63
28	1.10	1.24	1.04	1.32	0.97	1.41	0.90	1.51	0.83	1.62
29	1.12	1.25	1.05	1.33	0.99	1.42	0.92	1.51	0.85	1.61
30	1.13	1.26	1.07	1.34	1.01	1.42	0.94	1.51	0.88	1.61
31	1.15	1.27	1.08	1.34	1.02	1.42	0.96	1.51	0.90	1.60
32	1.16	1.28	1.10	1.35	1.04	1.43	0.98	1.51	0.92	1.60
33	1.17	1.29	1.11	1.36	1.05	1.43	1.00	1.51	0.94	1.59
34	1.18	1.30	1.13	1.36	1.07	1.43	1.01	1.51	0.95	1.59
35	1.19	1.31	1.14	1.37	1.08	1.44	1.03	1.51	0.97	1.59
36	1.21	1.32	1.15	1.38	1.10	1.44	1.04	1.51	0.99	1.59
37	1.22	1.32	1.16	1.38	1.11	1.45	1.06	1.51	1.00	1.59
38	1.23	1.33	1.18	1.39	1.12	1.45	1.07	1.52	1.02	1.58
39	1.24	1.34	1.19	1.39	1.14	1.45	1.09	1.52	1.03	1.58
40	1.25	1.34	1.20	1.40	1.15	1.46	1.10	1.52	1.05	1.58
45	1.29	1.38	1.24	1.42	1.20	1.48	1.16	1.53	1.11	1.58
50	1.32	1.40	1.28	1.45	1.24	1.49	1.20	1.54	1.16	1.59
55	1.36	1.43	1.32	1.47	1.28	1.51	1.25	1.55	1.21	1.59
60	1.38	1.45	1.35	1.48	1.32	1.52	1.28	1.56	1.25	1.60
65	1.41	1.47	1.38	1.50	1.35	1.53	1.31	1.57	1.28	1.61
70	1.43	1.49	1.40	1.52	1.37	1.55	1.34	1.58	1.31	1.61
75	1.45	1.50	1.42	1.53	1.39	1.56	1.37	1.59	1.34	1.62
80	1.47	1.52	1.44	1.54	1.42	1.57	1.39	1.60	1.36	1.62
85	1.48	1.53	1.46	1.55	1.43	1.58	1.41	1.60	1.39	1.63
90	1.50	1.54	1.47	1.56	1.45	1.59	1.43	1.61	1.41	1.64
95	1.51	1.55	1.49	1.57	1.47	1.60	1.45	1.62	1.42	1.64
100	1.52	1.56	1.50	1.58	1.48	1.60	1.46	1.63	1.44	1.65

TABLE A.10	Critical Values of the Studentized Range (*q*) Distribution

$\alpha = .05$

Degrees of Freedom	2	3	4	5	6	7	8	9	10	11	12	13	14	15	16	17	18	19	20
1	18.0	27.0	32.8	37.1	40.4	43.1	45.4	47.4	49.1	50.6	52.0	53.2	54.3	55.4	56.3	57.2	58.0	58.8	59.6
2	6.08	8.33	9.80	10.9	11.7	12.4	13.0	13.5	14.0	14.4	14.7	15.1	15.4	15.7	15.9	16.1	16.4	16.6	16.8
3	4.50	5.91	6.82	7.50	8.04	8.48	8.85	9.18	9.46	9.72	9.95	10.2	10.3	10.5	10.7	10.8	11.0	11.1	11.2
4	3.93	5.04	5.76	6.29	6.71	7.05	7.35	7.60	7.83	8.03	8.21	8.37	8.52	8.66	8.79	8.91	9.03	9.13	9.23
5	3.64	4.60	5.22	5.67	6.03	6.33	6.58	6.80	6.99	7.17	7.32	7.47	7.60	7.72	7.83	7.93	8.03	8.12	8.21
6	3.46	4.34	4.90	5.30	5.63	5.90	6.12	6.32	6.49	6.65	6.79	6.92	7.03	7.14	7.24	7.34	7.43	7.51	7.59
7	3.34	4.16	4.68	5.06	5.36	5.61	5.82	6.00	6.16	6.30	6.43	6.55	6.66	6.76	6.85	6.94	7.02	7.10	7.17
8	3.26	4.04	4.53	4.89	5.17	5.40	5.60	5.77	5.92	6.05	6.18	6.29	6.39	6.48	6.57	6.65	6.73	6.80	6.87
9	3.20	3.95	4.41	4.76	5.02	5.24	5.43	5.59	5.74	5.87	5.98	6.09	6.19	6.28	6.36	6.44	6.51	6.58	6.64
10	3.15	3.88	4.33	4.65	4.91	5.12	5.30	5.46	5.60	5.72	5.83	5.93	6.03	6.11	6.19	6.27	6.34	6.40	6.47
11	3.11	3.82	4.26	4.57	4.82	5.03	5.20	5.35	5.49	5.61	5.71	5.81	5.90	5.98	6.06	6.13	6.20	6.27	6.33
12	3.08	3.77	4.20	4.51	4.75	4.95	5.12	5.27	5.39	5.51	5.61	5.71	5.80	5.88	5.95	6.02	6.09	6.15	6.21
13	3.06	3.73	4.15	4.45	4.69	4.88	5.05	5.19	5.32	5.43	5.53	5.63	5.71	5.79	5.86	5.93	5.99	6.05	6.11
14	3.03	3.70	4.11	4.41	4.64	4.83	4.99	5.13	5.25	5.36	5.46	5.55	5.64	5.71	5.79	5.85	5.91	5.97	6.03
15	3.01	3.67	4.08	4.37	4.59	4.78	4.94	5.08	5.20	5.31	5.40	5.49	5.57	5.65	5.72	5.78	5.85	5.90	5.96
16	3.00	3.65	4.05	4.33	4.56	4.74	4.90	5.03	5.15	5.26	5.35	5.44	5.52	5.59	5.66	5.73	5.79	5.84	5.90
17	2.98	3.63	4.02	4.30	4.52	4.70	4.86	4.99	5.11	5.21	5.31	5.39	5.47	5.54	5.61	5.67	5.73	5.79	5.84
18	2.97	3.61	4.00	4.28	4.49	4.67	4.82	4.96	5.07	5.17	5.27	5.35	5.43	5.50	5.57	5.63	5.69	5.74	5.79
19	2.96	3.59	3.98	4.25	4.47	4.65	4.79	4.92	5.04	5.14	5.23	5.31	5.39	5.46	5.53	5.59	5.65	5.70	5.75
20	2.95	3.58	3.96	4.23	4.45	4.62	4.77	4.90	5.01	5.11	5.20	5.28	5.36	5.43	5.49	5.55	5.61	5.66	5.71
24	2.92	3.53	3.90	4.17	4.37	4.54	4.68	4.81	4.92	5.01	5.10	5.18	5.25	5.32	5.38	5.44	5.49	5.55	5.59
30	2.89	3.49	3.85	4.10	4.30	4.46	4.60	4.72	4.82	4.92	5.00	5.08	5.15	5.21	5.27	5.33	5.38	5.43	5.47
40	2.86	3.44	3.79	4.04	4.23	4.39	4.52	4.63	4.73	4.82	4.90	4.98	5.04	5.11	5.16	5.22	5.27	5.31	5.36
60	2.83	3.40	3.74	3.98	4.16	4.31	4.44	4.55	4.65	4.73	4.81	4.88	4.94	5.00	5.06	5.11	5.15	5.20	5.24
120	2.80	3.36	3.68	3.92	4.10	4.24	4.36	4.47	4.56	4.64	4.71	4.78	4.84	4.90	4.95	5.00	5.04	5.09	5.13
∞	2.77	3.31	3.63	3.86	4.03	4.17	4.29	4.39	4.47	4.55	4.62	4.68	4.74	4.80	4.85	4.89	4.93	4.97	5.01

	$\alpha = .01$																		
Degrees of Freedom	**Number of Populations**																		
	2	**3**	**4**	**5**	**6**	**7**	**8**	**9**	**10**	**11**	**12**	**13**	**14**	**15**	**16**	**17**	**18**	**19**	**20**
1	90.0	135.	164.	186.	202.	216.	227.	237.	246.	253.	260.	266.	272.	277.	282.	286.	290.	294.	298.
2	14.0	19.0	22.3	24.7	26.6	28.2	29.5	30.7	31.7	32.6	33.4	34.1	34.8	35.4	36.0	36.5	37.0	37.5	37.9
3	8.26	10.6	12.2	13.3	14.2	15.0	15.6	16.2	16.7	17.1	17.5	17.9	18.2	18.5	18.8	19.1	19.3	19.5	19.8
4	6.51	8.12	9.17	9.96	10.6	11.1	11.5	11.9	12.3	12.6	12.8	13.1	13.3	13.5	13.7	13.9	14.1	14.2	14.4
5	5.70	6.97	7.80	8.42	8.91	9.32	9.67	9.97	10.2	10.5	10.7	10.9	11.1	11.2	11.4	11.6	11.7	11.8	11.9
6	5.24	6.33	7.03	7.56	7.97	8.32	8.61	8.87	9.10	9.30	9.49	9.65	9.81	9.95	10.1	10.2	10.3	10.4	10.5
7	4.95	5.92	6.54	7.01	7.37	7.68	7.94	8.17	8.37	8.55	8.71	8.86	9.00	9.12	9.24	9.35	9.46	9.55	9.65
8	4.74	5.63	6.20	6.63	6.96	7.24	7.47	7.68	7.87	8.03	8.18	8.31	8.44	8.55	8.66	8.76	8.85	8.94	9.03
9	4.60	5.43	5.96	6.35	6.66	6.91	7.13	7.32	7.49	7.65	7.78	7.91	8.03	8.13	8.23	8.32	8.41	8.49	8.57
10	4.48	5.27	5.77	6.14	6.43	6.67	6.87	7.05	7.21	7.36	7.48	7.60	7.71	7.81	7.91	7.99	8.07	8.15	8.22
11	4.39	5.14	5.62	5.97	6.25	6.48	6.67	6.84	6.99	7.13	7.25	7.36	7.46	7.56	7.65	7.73	7.81	7.88	7.95
12	4.32	5.04	5.50	5.84	6.10	6.32	6.51	6.67	6.81	6.94	7.06	7.17	7.26	7.36	7.44	7.52	7.59	7.66	7.73
13	4.26	4.96	5.40	5.73	5.98	6.19	6.37	6.53	6.67	6.79	6.90	7.01	7.10	7.19	7.27	7.34	7.42	7.48	7.55
14	4.21	4.89	5.32	5.63	5.88	6.08	6.26	6.41	6.54	6.66	6.77	6.87	6.96	7.05	7.12	7.20	7.27	7.33	7.39
15	4.17	4.83	5.25	5.56	5.80	5.99	6.16	6.31	6.44	6.55	6.66	6.76	6.84	6.93	7.00	7.07	7.14	7.20	7.26
16	4.13	4.78	5.19	5.49	5.72	5.92	6.08	6.22	6.35	6.46	6.56	6.66	6.74	6.82	6.90	6.97	7.03	7.09	7.15
17	4.10	4.74	5.14	5.43	5.66	5.85	6.01	6.15	6.27	6.38	6.48	6.57	6.66	6.73	6.80	6.87	6.94	7.00	7.05
18	4.07	4.70	5.09	5.38	5.60	5.79	5.94	6.08	6.20	6.31	6.41	6.50	6.58	6.65	6.72	6.79	6.85	6.91	6.96
19	4.05	4.67	5.05	5.33	5.55	5.73	5.89	6.02	6.14	6.25	6.34	6.43	6.51	6.58	6.65	6.72	6.78	6.84	6.89
20	4.02	4.64	5.02	5.29	5.51	5.69	5.84	5.97	6.09	6.19	6.29	6.37	6.45	6.52	6.59	6.65	6.71	6.76	6.82
24	3.96	4.54	4.91	5.17	5.37	5.54	5.69	5.81	5.92	6.02	6.11	6.19	6.26	6.33	6.39	6.45	6.51	6.56	6.61
30	3.89	4.45	4.80	5.05	5.24	5.40	5.54	5.65	5.76	5.85	5.93	6.01	6.08	6.14	6.20	6.26	6.31	6.36	6.41
40	3.82	4.37	4.70	4.93	5.11	5.27	5.39	5.50	5.60	5.69	5.77	5.84	5.90	5.96	6.02	6.07	6.12	6.17	6.21
60	3.76	4.28	4.60	4.82	4.99	5.13	5.25	5.36	5.45	5.53	5.60	5.67	5.73	5.79	5.84	5.89	5.93	5.98	6.02
120	3.70	4.20	4.50	4.71	4.87	5.01	5.12	5.21	5.30	5.38	5.44	5.51	5.56	5.61	5.66	5.71	5.75	5.79	5.83
∞	3.64	4.12	4.40	4.60	4.76	4.88	4.99	5.08	5.16	5.23	5.29	5.35	5.40	5.45	5.49	5.54	5.57	5.61	5.65

TABLE A.11 — Critical Values of R for the Runs Test: Lower Tail

n_1 \ n_2	2	3	4	5	6	7	8	9	10	11	12	13	14	15	16	17	18	19	20
2											2	2	2	2	2	2	2	2	2
3					2	2	2	2	2	2	2	2	2	3	3	3	3	3	3
4				2	2	2	3	3	3	3	3	3	3	3	4	4	4	4	4
5			2	2	3	3	3	3	3	4	4	4	4	4	4	4	5	5	5
6		2	2	3	3	3	3	4	4	4	4	5	5	5	5	5	5	6	6
7		2	2	3	3	3	4	4	5	5	5	5	5	6	6	6	6	6	6
8		2	3	3	3	4	4	5	5	5	6	6	6	6	6	7	7	7	7
9		2	3	3	4	4	5	5	5	6	6	6	7	7	7	7	8	8	8
10		2	3	3	4	5	5	5	6	6	7	7	7	7	8	8	8	8	9
11		2	3	4	4	5	5	6	6	7	7	7	8	8	8	9	9	9	9
12	2	2	3	4	4	5	6	6	7	7	7	8	8	8	9	9	9	10	10
13	2	2	3	4	5	5	6	6	7	7	8	8	9	9	9	10	10	10	10
14	2	2	3	4	5	5	6	7	7	8	8	9	9	9	10	10	10	11	11
15	2	3	3	4	5	6	6	7	7	8	8	9	9	10	10	11	11	11	12
16	2	3	4	4	5	6	6	7	8	8	9	9	10	10	11	11	11	12	12
17	2	3	4	4	5	6	7	7	8	9	9	10	10	11	11	11	12	12	13
18	2	3	4	5	5	6	7	8	8	9	9	10	10	11	11	12	12	13	13
19	2	3	4	5	6	6	7	8	8	9	10	10	11	11	12	12	13	13	13
20	2	3	4	5	6	6	7	8	9	9	10	10	11	12	12	13	13	13	14

$\alpha = .025$

Source: Adapted from F.S. Swed and C. Eisenhart, *Ann. Math. Statist.*, vol. 14, 1943, pp. 83-86.

TABLE A.12 — Critical Values of R for the Runs Test: Upper Tail

n_1 \ n_2	2	3	4	5	6	7	8	9	10	11	12	13	14	15	16	17	18	19	20
2																			
3																			
4				9	9														
5			9	10	10	11	11												
6			9	10	11	12	12	13	13	13	13								
7				11	12	13	13	14	14	14	14	15	15	15					
8				11	12	13	14	14	15	15	16	16	16	16	17	17	17	17	17
9					13	14	14	15	16	16	16	17	17	18	18	18	18	18	18
10					13	14	15	16	16	17	17	18	18	18	19	19	19	20	20
11					13	14	15	16	17	17	18	19	19	19	20	20	20	21	21
12					13	14	16	16	17	18	19	19	20	20	21	21	21	22	22
13						15	16	17	18	19	19	20	20	21	21	22	22	23	23
14						15	16	17	18	19	20	20	21	22	22	23	23	23	24
15						15	16	18	18	19	20	21	22	22	23	23	24	24	25
16							17	18	19	20	21	21	22	23	23	24	25	25	25
17							17	18	19	20	21	22	23	23	24	25	25	26	26
18							17	18	19	20	21	22	23	24	25	25	26	26	27
19							17	18	20	21	22	23	23	24	25	26	26	27	27
20							17	18	20	21	22	23	24	25	25	26	27	27	28

$\alpha = .025$

TABLE A.13

p-Values for Mann-Whitney *U* Statistic Small Samples ($n_1 \leq n_2$)

$n_2 = 3$	U_0	n_1 1	2	3		
	0	.25	.10	.05		
	1	.50	.20	.10		
	2		.40	.20		
	3		.60	.35		
	4			.50		

$n_2 = 4$	U_0	n_1 1	2	3	4	
	0	.2000	.0667	.0286	.0143	
	1	.4000	.1333	.0571	.0286	
	2	.6000	.2667	.1143	.0571	
	3		.4000	.2000	.1000	
	4		.6000	.3143	.1714	
	5			.4286	.2429	
	6			.5714	.3429	
	7				.4429	
	8				.5571	

$n_2 = 5$	U_0	n_1 1	2	3	4	5
	0	.1667	.0476	.0179	.0079	.0040
	1	.3333	.0952	.0357	.0159	.0079
	2	.5000	.1905	.0714	.0317	.0159
	3		.2857	.1250	.0556	.0278
	4		.4286	.1964	.0952	.0476
	5		.5714	.2857	.1429	.0754
	6			.3929	.2063	.1111
	7			.5000	.2778	.1548
	8				.3651	.2103
	9				.4524	.2738
	10				.5476	.3452
	11					.4206
	12					.5000

Computed by M. Pagano, Dept. of Statistics, University of Florida. Reprinted by permission from *Statistics for Management and Economics,* 5th ed., by William Mendenhall and James E. Reinmuth. Copyright © 1986 by PWS-KENT Publishers, Boston.

$n_2 = 6$	U_0	n_1 1	2	3	4	5	6
	0	.1429	.0357	.0119	.0048	.0022	.0011
	1	.2857	.0714	.0238	.0095	.0043	.0022
	2	.4286	.1429	.0476	.0190	.0087	.0043
	3	.5714	.2143	.0833	.0333	.0152	.0076
	4		.3214	.1310	.0571	.0260	.0130
	5		.4286	.1905	.0857	.0411	.0206
	6		.5714	.2738	.1286	.0628	.0325
	7			.3571	.1762	.0887	.0465
	8			.4524	.2381	.1234	.0660
	9			.5476	.3048	.1645	.0898
	10				.3810	.2143	.1201
	11				.4571	.2684	.1548
	12				.5429	.3312	.1970
	13					.3961	.2424
	14					.4654	.2944
	15					.5346	.3496
	16						.4091
	17						.4686
	18						.5314

$n_2 = 7$	U_0	n_1 1	2	3	4	5	6	7
	0	.1250	.0278	.0083	.0030	.0013	.0006	.0003
	1	.2500	.0556	.0167	.0061	.0025	.0012	.0006
	2	.3750	.1111	.0333	.0121	.0051	.0023	.0012
	3	.5000	.1667	.0583	.0212	.0088	.0041	.0020
	4		.2500	.0917	.0364	.0152	.0070	.0035
	5		.3333	.1333	.0545	.0240	.0111	.0055
	6		.4444	.1917	.0818	.0366	.0175	.0087
	7		.5556	.2583	.1152	.0530	.0256	.0131
	8			.3333	.1576	.0745	.0367	.0189
	9			.4167	.2061	.1010	.0507	.0265
	10			.5000	.2636	.1338	.0688	.0364
	11				.3242	.1717	.0903	.0487
	12				.3939	.2159	.1171	.0641
	13				.4636	.2652	.1474	.0825
	14				.5364	.3194	.1830	.1043
	15					.3775	.2226	.1297
	16					.4381	.2669	.1588
	17					.5000	.3141	.1914
	18						.3654	.2279
	19						.4178	.2675
	20						.4726	.3100
	21						.5274	.3552
	22							.4024
	23							.4508
	24							.5000

Continued

$n_2 = 8$	U_0	n_1							
		1	2	3	4	5	6	7	8
	0	.1111	.0222	.0061	.0020	.0008	.0003	.0002	.0001
	1	.2222	.0444	.0121	.0040	.0016	.0007	.0003	.0002
	2	.3333	.0889	.0242	.0081	.0031	.0013	.0006	.0003
	3	.4444	.1333	.0424	.0141	.0054	.0023	.0011	.0005
	4	.5556	.2000	.0667	.0242	.0093	.0040	.0019	.0009
	5		.2667	.0970	.0364	.0148	.0063	.0030	.0015
	6		.3556	.1394	.0545	.0225	.0100	.0047	.0023
	7		.4444	.1879	.0768	.0326	.0147	.0070	.0035
	8		.5556	.2485	.1071	.0466	.0213	.0103	.0052
	9			.3152	.1414	.0637	.0296	.0145	.0074
	10			.3879	.1838	.0855	.0406	.0200	.0103
	11			.4606	.2303	.1111	.0539	.0270	.0141
	12			.5394	.2848	.1422	.0709	.0361	.0190
	13				.3414	.1772	.0906	.0469	.0249
	14				.4040	.2176	.1142	.0603	.0325
	15				.4667	.2618	.1412	.0760	.0415
	16				.5333	.3108	.1725	.0946	.0524
	17					.3621	.2068	.1159	.0652
	18					.4165	.2454	.1405	.0803
	19					.4716	.2864	.1678	.0974
	20					.5284	.3310	.1984	.1172
	21						.3773	.2317	.1393
	22						.4259	.2679	.1641
	23						.4749	.3063	.1911
	24						.5251	.3472	.2209
	25							.3894	.2527
	26							.4333	.2869
	27							.4775	.3227
	28							.5225	.3605
	29								.3992
	30								.4392
	31								.4796
	32								.5204

$n_2 = 9$	U_0	1	2	3	4	5	6	7	8	9
						n_1				
	0	.1000	.0182	.0045	.0014	.0005	.0002	.0001	.0000	.0000
	1	.2000	.0364	.0091	.0028	.0010	.0004	.0002	.0001	.0000
	2	.3000	.0727	.0182	.0056	.0020	.0008	.0003	.0002	.0001
	3	.4000	.1091	.0318	.0098	.0035	.0014	.0006	.0003	.0001
	4	.5000	.1636	.0500	.0168	.0060	.0024	.0010	.0005	.0002
	5		.2182	.0727	.0252	.0095	.0038	.0017	.0008	.0004
	6		.2909	.1045	.0378	.0145	.0060	.0026	.0012	.0006
	7		.3636	.1409	.0531	.0210	.0088	.0039	.0019	.0009
	8		.4545	.1864	.0741	.0300	.0128	.0058	.0028	.0014
	9		.5455	.2409	.0993	.0415	.0180	.0082	.0039	.0020
	10			.3000	.1301	.0559	.0248	.0115	.0056	.0028
	11			.3636	.1650	.0734	.0332	.0156	.0076	.0039
	12			.4318	.2070	.0949	.0440	.0209	.0103	.0053
	13			.5000	.2517	.1199	.0567	.0274	.0137	.0071
	14				.3021	.1489	.0723	.0356	.0180	.0094
	15				.3552	.1818	.0905	.0454	.0232	.0122
	16				.4126	.2188	.1119	.0571	.0296	.0157
	17				.4699	.2592	.1361	.0708	.0372	.0200
	18				.5301	.3032	.1638	.0869	.0464	.0252
	19					.3497	.1942	.1052	.0570	.0313
	20					.3986	.2280	.1261	.0694	.0385
	21					.4491	.2643	.1496	.0836	.0470
	22					.5000	.3035	.1755	.0998	.0567
	23						.3445	.2039	.1179	.0680
	24						.3878	.2349	.1383	.0807
	25						.4320	.2680	.1606	.0951
	26						.4773	.3032	.1852	.1112
	27						.5227	.3403	.2117	.1290
	28							.3788	.2404	.1487
	29							.4185	.2707	.1701
	30							.4591	.3029	.1933
	31							.5000	.3365	.2181
	32								.3715	.2447
	33								.4074	.2729
	34								.4442	.3024
	35								.4813	.3332
	36								.5187	.3652
	37									.3981
	38									.4317
	39									.4657
	40									.5000

Continued

		n_1									
$n_2 = 10$	U_0	1	2	3	4	5	6	7	8	9	10
	0	.0909	.0152	.0035	.0010	.0003	.0001	.0001	.0000	.0000	.0000
	1	.1818	.0303	.0070	.0020	.0007	.0002	.0001	.0000	.0000	.0000
	2	.2727	.0606	.0140	.0040	.0013	.0005	.0002	.0001	.0000	.0000
	3	.3636	.0909	.0245	.0070	.0023	.0009	.0004	.0002	.0001	.0000
	4	.4545	.1364	.0385	.0120	.0040	.0015	.0006	.0003	.0001	.0001
	5	.5455	.1818	.0559	.0180	.0063	.0024	.0010	.0004	.0002	.0001
	6		.2424	.0804	.0270	.0097	.0037	.0015	.0007	.0003	.0002
	7		.3030	.1084	.0380	.0140	.0055	.0023	.0010	.0005	.0002
	8		.3788	.1434	.0529	.0200	.0080	.0034	.0015	.0007	.0004
	9		.4545	.1853	.0709	.0276	.0112	.0048	.0022	.0011	.0005
	10		.5455	.2343	.0939	.0376	.0156	.0068	.0031	.0015	.0008
	11			.2867	.1199	.0496	.0210	.0093	.0043	.0021	.0010
	12			.3462	.1518	.0646	.0280	.0125	.0058	.0028	.0014
	13			.4056	.1868	.0823	.0363	.0165	.0078	.0038	.0019
	14			.4685	.2268	.1032	.0467	.0215	.0103	.0051	.0026
	15			.5315	.2697	.1272	.0589	.0277	.0133	.0066	.0034
	16				.3177	.1548	.0736	.0351	.0171	.0086	.0045
	17				.3666	.1855	.0903	.0439	.0217	.0110	.0057
	18				.4196	.2198	.1099	.0544	.0273	.0140	.0073
	19				.4725	.2567	.1317	.0665	.0338	.0175	.0093
	20				.5275	.2970	.1566	.0806	.0416	.0217	.0116
	21					.3393	.1838	.0966	.0506	.0267	.0144
	22					.3839	.2139	.1148	.0610	.0326	.0177
	23					.4296	.2461	.1349	.0729	.0394	.0216
	24					.4765	.2811	.1574	.0864	.0474	.0262
	25					.5235	.3177	.1819	.1015	.0564	.0315
	26						.3564	.2087	.1185	.0667	.0376
	27						.3962	.2374	.1371	.0782	.0446
	28						.4374	.2681	.1577	.0912	.0526
	29						.4789	.3004	.1800	.1055	.0615
	30						.5211	.3345	.2041	.1214	.0716
	31							.3698	.2299	.1388	.0827
	32							.4063	.2574	.1577	.0952
	33							.4434	.2863	.1781	.1088
	34							.4811	.3167	.2001	.1237
	35							.5189	.3482	.2235	.1399
	36								.3809	.2483	.1575
	37								.4143	.2745	.1763
	38								.4484	.3019	.1965
	39								.4827	.3304	.2179
	40								.5173	.3598	.2406
	41									.3901	.2644
	42									.4211	.2894
	43									.4524	.3153
	44									.4841	.3421
	45									.5159	.3697
	46										.3980
	47										.4267
	48										.4559
	49										.4853
	50										.5147

TABLE A.14 — Critical Values of *T* for the Wilcoxon Matched-Pairs Signed Rank Test (Small Samples)

1-SIDED	2-SIDED	n = 5	n = 6	n = 7	n = 8	n = 9	n = 10
α=.05	α=.10	1	2	4	6	8	11
α=.025	α=.05		1	2	4	6	8
α=.01	α=.02			0	2	3	5
α=.005	α=.01				0	2	3

1-SIDED	2-SIDED	n = 11	n = 12	n = 13	n = 14	n = 15	n = 16
α=.05	α=.10	14	17	21	26	30	36
α=.025	α=.05	11	14	17	21	25	30
α=.01	α=.02	7	10	13	16	20	24
α=.005	α=.01	5	7	10	13	16	19

1-SIDED	2-SIDED	n = 17	n = 18	n = 19	n = 20	n = 21	n = 22
α=.05	α=.10	41	47	54	60	68	75
α=.025	α=.05	35	40	46	52	59	66
α=.01	α=.02	28	33	38	43	49	56
α=.005	α=.01	23	28	32	37	43	49

1-SIDED	2-SIDED	n = 23	n = 24	n = 25	n = 26	n = 27	n = 28
α=.05	α=.10	83	92	101	110	120	130
α=.025	α=.05	73	81	90	98	107	117
α=.01	α=.02	62	69	77	85	93	102
α=.005	α=.01	55	61	68	76	84	92

1-SIDED	2-SIDED	n = 29	n = 30	n = 31	n = 32	n = 33	n = 34
α=.05	α=.10	141	152	163	175	188	201
α=.025	α=.05	127	137	148	159	171	183
α=.01	α=.02	111	120	130	141	151	162
α=.005	α=.01	100	109	118	128	138	149

1-SIDED	2-SIDED	n = 35	n = 36	n = 37	n = 38	n = 39	
α=.05	α=.10	214	228	242	256	271	
α=.025	α=.05	195	208	222	235	250	
α=.01	α=.02	174	186	198	211	224	
α=.005	α=.01	160	171	183	195	208	

1-SIDED	2-SIDED	n = 40	n = 41	n = 42	n = 43	n = 44	n = 45
α=.05	α=.10	287	303	319	336	353	371
α=.025	α=.05	264	279	295	311	327	344
α=.01	α=.02	238	252	267	281	297	313
α=.005	α=.01	221	234	248	262	277	292

1-SIDED	2-SIDED	n = 46	n = 47	n = 48	n = 49	n = 50	
α=.05	α=.10	389	408	427	446	466	
α=.025	α=.05	361	379	397	415	434	
α=.01	α=.02	329	345	362	380	398	
α=.005	α=.01	307	323	339	356	373	

From E. Wilcoxon and R.A. Wilcox, "Some Rapid Approximate Statistical Procedures," 1964. Reprinted by permission of Lederle Labs, a division of The American Cyanamid Co.

TABLE A.15

Factors for Control Charts

Number of Items In Sample	AVERAGES			RANGES	
	Factors for Control Limits		Factors for Central Line	Factors for Control Limits	
n	A_2	A_3	d_2	D_3	D_4
2	1.880	2.659	1.128	0	3.267
3	1.023	1.954	1.693	0	2.575
4	0.729	1.628	2.059	0	2.282
5	0.577	1.427	2.326	0	2.115
6	0.483	1.287	2.534	0	2.004
7	0.419	1.182	2.704	0.076	1.924
8	0.373	1.099	2.847	0.136	1.864
9	0.337	1.032	2.970	0.184	1.816
10	0.308	0.975	3.078	0.223	1.777
11	0.285	0.927	3.173	0.256	1.744
12	0.266	0.886	3.258	0.284	1.716
13	0.249	0.850	3.336	0.308	1.692
14	0.235	0.817	3.407	0.329	1.671
15	0.223	0.789	3.472	0.348	1.652

Adapted from American Society for Testing and Materials, *Manual on Quality Control of Materials,* 1951, Table B2, p. 115. For a more detailed table and explanation, see Acheson J. Duncan, *Quality Control and Industrial Statistics,* 3d ed. (Homewood, Ill.: Richard D. Irwin, 1974), Table M, p. 927.

APPENDIX B: ANSWERS TO SELECTED ODD-NUMBERED QUANTITATIVE PROBLEMS

CHAPTER 1

1.5
  a. ratio
  b. ratio
  c. ordinal
  d. nominal
  e. ratio
  f. ratio
  g. nominal
  h. ratio

1.7
  a. 900 electric contractors
  b. 35 electric contractors
  c. average score for 35 participants
  d. average score for all 900 electric contractors

CHAPTER 2

No answers given

CHAPTER 3

3.1 4
3.3 294
3.5 −1
3.7 107, 127, 145, 114, 127.5, 143.5
3.9 624, 751, 486, 677, 775.5, 1096
3.11
  a. 8
  b. 2.041
  c. 6.204

  d. 2.491
  e. 4
  f. 0.69, −0.92, −0.11, 1.89, −1.32, −0.52, 0.29

3.13
  a. 4.598
  b. 4.598

3.15 58,631.359; 242.139

3.17
  a. .75
  b. .84
  c. .609
  d. .902

3.19
  a. 2.667
  b. 11.060
  c. 3.326
  d. 2.5
  e. −0.85
  f. 37.65%

3.21 Between 113 and 137
     Between 101 and 149
     Between 89 and 161

3.23 2.236

3.25 95%, 2.5%, .15%, 16%

3.27 4.64, 1

3.29 185.694, 13.627

3.31
  a. 44.9
  b. 39
  c. 187.2
  d. 13.7

3.33
  a. 38
  b. 25

c.   251

d.   15.843

3.35   skewed right

3.37   0.726

3.39   no outliers. negatively skewed

3.41   −0.927

3.43   0.645

3.45   0.975, 0.985, 0.957

3.47   23, 49.5, 27.5, 47.5, 20, 62

3.49   933, 290.8, 438, 789.2

3.51   a.   2031, 1795, no mode

b.   2030, 980, 525.2, 441387.78, 664.37

c.   1.066

d.   no outliers

3.53   a.   42.89, 10

b.   31.346

3.55   10.78%, 6.43%

3.57   a.   392 to 446, 365 to 473, 338 to 500

b.   79.7%

c.   −0.704

3.59   skewed right

3.61 $Q_1 = 43.85$, $Q_2 = 53.15$, $Q_3 = 73.7$, no outliers

CHAPTER 4

4.1   15, .60

4.3   {4, 8, 10, 14, 16, 18, 20, 22, 26, 28, 30}

4.5   20, combinations, .60

4.7   38,760

4.9   a.   .7167

b.   .5000

c.   .65

d.   .5167

4.11   not solvable

4.13   a.   .86

b.   .31

c.   .14

4.15   a.   .2807

b.   .0526

c.   .0000

d.   .0000

4.17   a.   .0122

b.   .0144

4.19   a.   .57

b.   .3225

c.   .4775

d.   .5225

e.   .6775

f.   .0475

4.21   a.   .039

b.   .571

c.   .129

4.23   a.   .2286

b.   .2297

c.   .3231

d.   .0000

4.25   not independent

4.27   a.   .4054

b.   .3261

c.   .4074

d.   .32

4.29   a.   .03

b.   .2875

c.   .3354

d.   .9759

4.31   a.   .45

b.   .95

c.   .4743, .4269, .0988

d.   .2748, .4533, .2719

4.33   .65, .859, .6205

4.35   a.   .0897

b.   .0000

c.   .2821

d.   .0000

e.   .3636

f.   .3810

g.   .4615

h.   .2051

4.37   a.   .91

b.   .09

c.   .3462

d.   .13

4.39   a.   .042

b.   .034

c.   .2625

d.   .1976

e.   .525

4.41   a.   .43

b.   .189

c.   .6143

d. .699

4.43 **a.** .312

b. .572

c. .9176

d. .22

e. .9533

4.45 **a.** .20

b. .6429

c. .40

d. .60

e. .40

f. .33

4.47 .329, .0623

4.49 .8456, .1149, .0396

CHAPTER 5

5.1 2.666, 1.8364, 1.3552

5.3 0.956, 1.1305

5.5 **a.** .0036

b. .1147

c. .3822

d. .5838

5.7 **a.** 14, 2.05

b. 24.5, 3.99

c. 50, 5

5.9 **a.** .1356

b. .0032

c. .113

5.11 **a.** .585

b. .009

c. .013

5.13 **a.** .1032

b. .0000

c. .0352

d. .3480

5.15 **a.** .0538

b. .1539

c. .4142

d. .0672

e. .0244

f. .3702

5.17 **a.** 6.3, 2.51

b. 1.3, 1.14

c. 8.9, 2.98

d. 0.6, .775

5.19 3.5

a. .0302

b. .1424

c. .0817

d. .42

e. .1009

5.21 **a.** .5488

b. .3293

c. .1220

d. .8913

e. .1912

5.23 **a.** .3012

b. .0000

c. .0336

5.25 .0104, .0000, .1653, .9636

5.27 **a.** .5091

b. .2937

c. .4167

d. .0014

5.29 .0529, .0294, .4235

5.31 **a.** .30

b. .0238

c. .2381

5.33 .0474

5.35 **a.** .124

b. .849

c. .090

d. .000

5.37 **a.** .1607

b. .7626

c. .3504

d. .5429

5.39 .111, .017, 5, .180, .125, .000, .056, 8, 8

5.41 .2644, .0694, .0029, .7521

5.43 **a.** 5

b. .0244

5.45 .0687, .020, .1032, 2.28

5.47 .174

5.49 .5488, .0232, .3012

5.51 .0002, .0595, .2330

5.53 **a.** .0907

b. .0358

c. .1517

d. .8781

5.55   **a.**   .265

   b.   .0136

   c.   .0067

5.57   **a.**   .1377

   b.   .5790

   c.   .0922

5.59   **a.**   .0215

   b.   .1317

   c.   .7907

CHAPTER 6

6.1   **a.**   1/40

   b.   220, 11.547

   c.   .25

   d.   .3750

   e.   .6250

6.3   2.94, 0.10, .2941

6.5   981.5, .000294, .2353, .0000, .2353

6.7   **a.**   .7088

   b.   .0099

   c.   .5042

   d.   .1030

   e.   .6772

   f.   .1093

6.9   **a.**   .0139

   b.   .6097

   c.   .0582

   d.   .2806

6.11   **a.**   .9050

   b.   .0132

   c.   .1308

   d.   17293.23

   e.   25440

6.13   **a.**   63.285

   b.   46.85

6.15   22.2

6.17   **a.** $P(x \leq 16.5 \mid \mu = 21 \text{ and } \sigma = 2.51)$

   b. $P(10.5 \leq x \leq 20.5 \mid \mu = 12.5 \text{ and } \sigma = 2.5)$

   c. $P(21.5 \leq x \leq 22.5 \mid \mu = 24 \text{ and } \sigma = 3.10)$

   d. $P(x > 14.5 \mid \mu = 7.2 \text{ and } \sigma = 1.99)$

6.19   **a.**   .1170, .120

   b.   .4090, .415

   c.   .1985, .196

   d.   fails test

6.21   .0495

6.23   **a.**   .1314

   b.   .6767

   c.   .0132

   d.   .0916

6.27   **a.**   .0012

   b.   .8700

   c.   .0011

   d.   .9918

6.29   **a.**   .0000

   b.   .0000

   c.   .0872

   d.   .41 minutes

6.31   295, .1836, .4924

6.33   15, 15, .1254

6.35   **a.**   .1587

   b.   .0013

   c.   .6915

   d.   .9270

   e.   .0000

6.37   **a.**   .0202

   b.   .9817

   c.   .1849

   d.   .4449

6.39   .0000

6.41   .1131, .2912, .1543

6.43   .5319, 41.5, .0213

6.45   **a.**   .3050

   b.   .6413

   c.   .2985

   d.   .0045

6.47   **a.**   .1251

   b.   .1131

   c.   .9913

   d.   .5951

6.49   **a.**   .0025

   b.   .8944

   c.   .3482

6.51   .0655, .6502, .9993

6.53 $11428.57

6.55   .5488, .2592, 1.67 months

6.57   1940, 2018.75, 2267.25

6.59   .0436, .0026

CHAPTER 7

7.7	825
7.13	**a.** .0548
	b. .7881
	c. .0082
	d. .8575
	e. .1664
7.15	11.11
7.17	**a.** .9772
	b. .2385
	c. .1469
	d. .1230
7.19	.0000
7.21	**a.** .1894
	b. .0559
	c. .0000
	d. 16.4964
7.23	**a.** .1492
	b. .9404
	c. .1985
	d. .1445
	e. .0000
7.25	.26
7.27	**a.** .1977
	b. .2843
	c. .9881
7.29	**a.** .1020
	b. .7568
	c. .2981
7.31	55, 45, 90, 25, 35
7.37	**a.** .3156
	b. .00003
	c. .1736
7.41	.0021, .9265, .0281
7.43	**a.** .0314
	b. .2420
	c. .2250
	d. .1469
	e. .0000
7.45	**a.** .8534
	b. .0256
	c. .0007
7.49	.6402, .0174, .0217

7.51 .9147

CHAPTER 8

8.1	**a.** $24.11 \leq \mu \leq 25.89$
	b. $113.17 \leq \mu \leq 126.03$
	c. $3.136 \leq \mu \leq 3.702$
	d. $54.55 \leq \mu \leq 58.85$
8.3	$45.92 \leq \mu \leq 48.08$
8.5	$66, 62.75 \leq \mu \leq 69.25$
8.7	$5.3, 5.13 \leq \mu \leq 5.47$
8.9	$2.853 \leq \mu \leq 3.759$
8.11	$23.036 \leq \mu \leq 26.030$
8.13	$42.18 \leq \mu \leq 49.06$
8.15	$118.57 \leq \mu \leq 138.23, 128.4$
8.17	$15.631 \leq \mu \leq 16.545, 16.088$
8.19	$2.26886 \leq \mu \leq 2.45346, 2.36116, .0923$
8.21	$36.77 \leq \mu \leq 62.83$
8.23	**a.** $.316 \leq p \leq .704$
	b. $.777 \leq p \leq .863$
	c. $.456 \leq p \leq .504$
	d. $.246 \leq p \leq .394$
8.25	$.38 \leq p \leq .56$
	$.364 \leq p \leq .576$
	$.33 \leq p \leq .61$
8.27	$.4287 \leq p \leq .5113$
	$.2488 \leq p \leq .3112$
8.29	**a.** .266
	b. $.246 \leq p \leq .286$
8.31	$.5935 \leq p \leq .6665$
8.33	$18.24 \leq \sigma^2 \leq 106.66$
8.35	$1.37 \leq \sigma^2 \leq 10.54$
8.37	**a.** 200
	b. 114
	c. 299
	d. 57
8.39	166
8.41	62
8.43	385
8.45	$43.924 \leq \mu \leq 47.276, 43.138 \leq \mu \leq 48.062,$ $42.549 \leq \mu \leq 48.651$
8.47	**a.** $.4235 \leq p \leq .4965$
	b. $.6657 \leq p \leq .7543$
	c. $.4523 \leq p \leq .5077$

    d. $.5374 \leq p \leq .6446$

8.49 **a.** 827

    b. 196

    c. 849

    d. 897

8.51 722

8.53 $196.33 \leq \mu \leq 229.67$

8.55 196

8.57 $117.534 \leq \mu \leq 138.466, 20.932$

8.59 196

8.61 $.233 \leq p \leq .427$

8.63 $4.6736 \leq \mu \leq 4.9664$

8.65 $.28 \leq p \leq .38$

8.67 $1.69 \leq \mu \leq 2.51$

8.69 $1.209 \leq \mu \leq 1.379$

CHAPTER 9

9.1 **a.** $z = 2.77$, reject

    b. .0028

    c. 22.115, 27.885

9.3 **a.** $z = 1.59$, reject

    b. .0559

    c. 1212.04

9.5 $z = 1.84$, fail to reject

9.7 $z = 1.41$, fail to reject

9.9 $z = -5.46$, reject

9.11 $t = 0.56$, fail to reject

9.13 $t = 2.44$, reject

9.15 $t = 1.59$, fail to reject

9.17 $t = -2.06$, fail to reject

9.19 $z = 0.53$, fail to reject

9.21 $z = -0.60$, fail to reject

    .2743, .257 and .323

9.23 $z = -3.00$, reject

9.25 $z = 2.02$, fail to reject

9.27 $z = 2.08$, reject

9.29 $\chi^2 = 23.64$, reject

9.31 $\chi^2 = 49.93$, reject

9.33 **a.** .7852

    b. .8749

    c. .9671

9.35 .5160

9.37 $z = 0.96$, fail to reject, .8599, .5832, .2514, .0618

9.39 $z = 3.21$, reject

9.41 **a.** $z = 0.85$, fail to reject

    b. $z = -2.05$, reject

9.43 **a.** $\beta = .1003$

    b. $\beta = .6255$

9.45 $z = 1.05$, fail to reject

9.47 $\chi^2 = 24.63$, reject

9.49 **a.** $z = 1.38$, fail to reject

    b. $z = -2.52, \beta = .0059$

9.51 $z = 1.53$, fail to reject, .7704

9.53 $z = 2.05$, fail to reject, .01, .3300

9.55 $\chi^2 = 47.25$, reject

9.57 **a.** $z = -1.43$, fail to reject

    b. .3156

CHAPTER 10

10.1 **a.** $z = -1.02$, fail to reject

    b. ± 3.08

    c. .1539

10.3 **a.** $z = 5.48$, reject

    b. $4.04 \leq \mu_1 - \mu_2 \leq 10.02$

10.5 $-1.86 \leq \mu_1 - \mu_2 \leq -0.54$

10.7 $z = -2.32$, fail to reject

10.9 $z = 2.27$, reject

10.11 $t = -1.05$, fail to reject

10.13 $t = 4.64$, reject

10.15 $1905.38 \leq \mu_1 - \mu_2 \leq 3894.62$

10.17 $t = 2.06$, fail to reject

10.19 $t = 4.95$, reject

10.21 $t = 3.31$, reject

10.23 $26.29 \leq D \leq 54.83$

10.25 $-3415.6 \leq D \leq 6021.2$

10.27 $6.58 \leq D \leq 49.60$

10.29 $63.71 \leq D \leq 86.29$

10.31 **a.** $z = 0.75$, fail to reject

    b. $z = 4.83$, reject

10.33 $z = -3.35$, reject

10.35 $z = -0.94$, fail to reject

10.37 $z = 2.35$, reject

10.39 $F = 1.80$, fail to reject

10.41 $F = 0.81$, fail to reject

10.43 $F = 1.53$, fail to reject

10.45 $z = -2.38$, reject

10.47 $t = 0.85$, fail to reject

10.49 $t = -5.26$, reject

10.51 $z = -1.20$, fail to reject

10.53 $F = 1.24$, fail to reject

10.55 $-3.201 \leq D \leq 2.313$

10.57 $F = 1.31$, fail to reject

10.59 $-256.7 \leq \mu_1 - \mu_2 \leq -177.3$

10.61 $z = 7.37$, reject

10.63 $F = 2.01$, reject

10.65 $t = -2.44$, reject

10.67 $z = 2.64$, reject

10.69 $6.28 \leq \mu_1 - \mu_2 \leq 9.32$

10.71 $t = 4.78$, reject

CHAPTER 11

11.5 $F = 11.07$, reject

11.7 $F = 13.00$, reject

11.9 4, 50, 54, 145.8975, 19.4436, $F = 7.501$, reject

11.11 $F = 10.10$, reject

11.13 $F = 11.76$ reject

11.15 4 levels; sizes 18, 15, 21, and 11; $F = 2.95$, $p = .04$; means = 226.73, 238.79, 232.58, and 239.82.

11.17 HSD = 0.896

11.19 HSD = 1.584, groups 1&2 significantly different

11.21 HSD = 10.29, groups 1&3 significantly different

11.23 $HSD_{1,3} = .0381$, groups 1&3 significantly different

11.25 $HSD_{1,3} = 1.764$, HSD2,3 = 1.621, groups 1&3 and 2&3 significantly different

11.29 $F = 1.48$, fail to reject

11.31 $F = 3.90$, fail to reject

11.33 $F = 15.37$, reject

11.37 2, 1, 4 row levels, 3 column levels, yes

$df_{row} = 3$, $df_{col.} = 2$, $df_{int.} = 6$, $df_{error} = 12$, $df_{total} = 23$

11.39 $MS_{row} = 1.047$, $MS_{col.} = 1.281$, $MS_{int.} = 0.258$, $MS_{error} = 0.436$,

$F_{row} = 2.40$, $F_{col.} = 2.94$, $F_{int.} = 0.59$, fail to reject any hypothesis

11.41 $F_{row} = 87.25$, reject; $F_{col.} = 63.67$, reject; $F_{int.} = 2.07$, fail to reject

11.43 $F_{row} = 34.31$, reject; $F_{col.} = 14.20$, reject; $F_{int.} = 3.32$, reject

11.45 no significant interaction or row effects; significant column effects.

11.47 $F = 8.82$, reject; HSD = 3.33 groups 1&2, 2&3, and 2&4 significantly different.

11.49 $df_{treat.} = 5$, $MS_{treat.} = 42.0$, $df_{error} = 36$, $MS_{error} = 18.194$, $F = 2.31$

11.51 1 treatment variable, 3 levels; 1 blocking variable, 6 levels; $df_{treat.} = 2$, $df_{block} = 5$, $df_{error} = 10$

11.53 $F_{treat.} = 31.51$, reject; $F_{blocks} = 43.20$, reject; HSD = 8.757, no pairs significant

11.55 $F_{rows} = 38.21$, reject; $F_{col.} = 0.23$, fail to reject; $F_{inter.} = 1.30$, fail to reject

11.57 $F = 7.38$, reject

11.59 $F = 0.46$, fail to reject

11.61 $F_{treat.} = 13.64$, reject

CHAPTER 12

12.1 $\chi^2 = 18.095$, reject.

12.3 $\chi^2 = 2.001$, fail to reject, $l = 0.9$.

12.5 $\chi^2 = 198.48$, reject.

12.7 $\chi^2 = 2.45$, fail to reject

12.9 $\chi^2 = 3.398$, fail to reject

12.11 $\chi^2 = 0.00$, fail to reject

12.13 $\chi^2 = 34.97$, reject

12.15 $\chi^2 = 6.43$, reject

12.17 $\chi^2 = 3.93$, fail to reject

12.19 $\chi^2 = 1.652$, fail to reject

12.21 $\chi^2 = 14.91$, reject

12.23 $\chi^2 = 8.44$, fail to reject

12.25 $\chi^2 = 59.63$, reject

12.27 $\chi^2 = 54.63$, reject

CHAPTER 13

13.1 $\hat{y} = 16.5 + 0.162x$

13.3 $\hat{y} = -46.29 + 15.24x$

13.5 $\hat{y} = 158881.1 - 0.48042x$

13.7 $\hat{y} = -2.31307 + 0.05557x$

13.9 18.4582, 19.9196, 21.0563, 17.8087, 19.7572, −1.4582, −4.9196, 0.9437, 1.1913, 4.2428

13.11 144.2053, 10.0953, 282.8873, 868.0945, 526.7236, 46.6708, 209.7364, 581.5868, 3.7947, 44.9047, 55.1127, 125.9055, 14.2764, 42.3292, −83.7364, −202.5868

13.13 4.7244, −0.9836, −0.3996, −6.7537, 2.7683, 0.6442

13.15 Error terms nonindependent.

13.17 Nonlinear regression.

13.19 SSE = 46.5692, $s_e = 3.94$, 3 out of 5

13.21 SSE = 70940, $s_e = 108.7$, 6 out of 8

13.23 $s_e = 4.391$

13.25 $\hat{y} = 118.257 - 0.1504x$, $s_e = 40.5256$

13.27 $r^2 = .972$

13.29 $r^2 = .685$

13.31 $\hat{y} = -599.3674 + 19.2204x$; $s_e = 13.539$; $r^2 = .688$

13.33 $t = -13.18$, reject

13.35 $t = -2.56$, fail to reject

13.37 $F = 8.26$, p-value $= .021$, not significant at $\alpha = .01$, $t = 2.874$, not significant at $\alpha = .01$.

13.39 $38.523 \le y \le 70.705$, $10.447 \le y \le 44.901$

13.41 $0.97 \le E(y_{10}) \le 15.65$

13.43 a. $\hat{y} = -11.335 + 0.355x$

   b. 7.48, 5.35, 3.22, 6.415, 9.255, 10.675, 4.64, 9.965; -2.48, -0.35, 3.78, -2.415, 0.745, 1.325, -1.64, 1.035

   c. SSE $= 32.4649$

   d. $s_e = 2.3261$

   e. $r^2 = .608$

   f. $t = 3.05$, reject

13.45 a. $20.92 < E(y_{60}) < 26.8$

   b. $20.994 < y < 37.688$

13.47 $\hat{y} = 9.728511 + 10.626383x$, $s_e = 97.1277$, $r^2 = .652$, $t = 4.33$, reject

13.49 $\hat{y} = -1004.9575 + 2.97366x$; $\hat{y}(700) = 1076.6044$; -287.5588 to 2440.7676; $t = 3.6124$, reject

13.51 $\hat{y} = 1268.685 + 0.01835x$

13.53 $\hat{y} = -54.35604 + 2.40107x$; $s_e = 17.886$; $r^2 = .91$; $t = 7.80$, reject; $\hat{y}(100) = 185.75$

CHAPTER 14

14.1 $\hat{y} = 25.03 - 0.0497x_1 + 1.928x_2$, 28.586

14.3 $\hat{y} = 121.62 - 0.174x_1 + 6.02x2 + 0.00026x_3 + 0.0041x_4$, 4

14.5 Per capita consumption $= -538 + 0.23368$ paper consumption $+ 18.09$ fish consumption $- 0.2116$ gasoline consumption

14.7 9, fail to reject null overall at $\alpha = .05$, only $t = 2.73$ for x_1, significant at $\alpha = .05$, $s_e = 3.503$, $R^2 = .408$, adj. $R^2 = .203$

14.9 Per capita consumption $= -538 + 0.23368$ paper consumption $+ 18.09$ fish consumption $- 0.2116$ gasoline consumption; $F = 24.63$, $p = .002$; $t_1 = 5.31$, $p = .003$; $t_2 = 0.98$, $p = .373$; $t_3 = -0.93$, $p = .397$; $s_e = 2085$; $R^2 = .937$; adj. $R^2 = .899$

14.11 $\hat{y} = 3.981 + 0.07322x_1 - 0.03232x_2 - 0.003886x_3$, $F = 100.47$ significant at $\alpha = .01$, $t = 3.50$ for x_1 significant at $\alpha = .01$, $s_e = 0.2331$, $R^2 = .965$, adj. $R^2 = .955$

14.13 3 predictors, 15 observations, $\hat{y} = 657.053 + 5.710$ $x_1 - 0.417\,x_2 - 3.471\,x_3$, $R^2 = .842$, adjusted $R^2 = .630$, $s_e = 109.43$, $F = 8.96$ with $p = .0027$, x_1 significant at $\alpha = .01$, x_3 significant at $\alpha = .05$

14.15 $s_e = 9.722$, $R^2 = .515$, adjusted $R^2 = .404$

14.17 $s_e = 6.544$, $R^2 = .005$, adjusted $R^2 = .000$

14.19 model with x_1, x_2: $s_e = 6.333$, $R^2 = .963$, adjusted $R^2 = .957$

   model with x_1: $s_e = 6.124$, $R^2 = .963$, adjusted $R^2 = .960$

14.21 heterogeneity of variance

14.23 2, $\hat{y} = 203.3937 + 1.1151x_1 - 2.2115x_2$, $F = 24.55$, reject, $R^2 = .663$, adjusted $R^2 = .636$

14.25 $\hat{y} = 362 - 4.75x_1 - 13.9x_2 + 1.87x_3$; $F = 16.05$, reject; $s_e = 37.07$; $R^2 = .858$; adjusted $R^2 = .804$; x_1 only significant predictor

14.27 Employment $= 71.03 + 0.4620$ Naval Vessels $+ 0.02082$ Commercial

   $F = 1.22$, fail to reject; $R^2 = .379$; adjusted $R^2 = .068$; no significant predictors

14.29 Corn $= -2718 + 6.26$ Soybeans $- 0.77$ Wheat; $F = 14.25$, reject; $s_e = 862.4$; $R^2 = .803$; adjusted $R^2 = .746$; Soybeans was a significant predictor

CHAPTER 15

15.1 Simple Model: $\hat{y} = -147.27 + 27.128\,x$, $F = 229$ with $p = .000$, $s_e = 27.27$, $R^2 = .97$, adjusted $R^2 = .966$

   Quadratic Model: $\hat{y} = -22.01 + 3.385x_1 + 0.9373x_2$, $F = 578.76$ with $p = .000$, $s_e = 12.3$, $R^2 = .995$, adjusted $R^2 = .993$, for x_1: $t = 0.75$, for x_2: $t = 5.33$

15.3 $\hat{y} = 1012 - 14.1x + 0.611x^2$; $R^2 = .947$; S $= 605.7$; adjusted $R^2 = .911$; $t(x) = -0.17$, fail to reject; $t(x^2) = 1.03$, fail to reject

15.5 $\hat{y} = -28.61 - 2.68x_1 + 18.25x_2 - 0.2135x_1^2 - 1.533x_2^2 + 1.226x_1x_2$; $F = 63.43$, reject; $s_e = 4.669$, $R^2 = .958$; adjusted $R^2 = .943$; no significant t ratios. Model with no interaction term: $R^2 = .957$

15.7 $\hat{y} = 13.619 - 0.01201x_1 + 2.988x_2$, $F = 8.43$ significant at $\alpha = .01$, $t = 3.88$ for x_2, (dummy variable) significant at $\alpha = .01$, $s_e = 1.245$, $R^2 = .652$, adj. $R^2 = .575$

15.9 x_1 is a significant predictor at $\alpha = .05$

15.11 Price $= 7.066 - 0.0855$ Hours $+ 9.614$ Probability $+ 10.507$ French Quarter, $F = 6.80$ significant at $\alpha = .01$, $t = 3.97$ for French Quarter (dummy variable) significant at $\alpha = .01$, $s_e = 4.02$, $R^2 = .671$, adj. $R^2 = .573$

15.13 Step 1: x_2 entered, $t = -7.53$, $r^2 = .794$
   Step 2: x_3 entered, $t_2 = -4.60$, $t_3 = 2.93$, $R^2 = .876$

15.15 4 predictors, x_2 (c3) and x_5(c6) not in model.

15.17 Step 1: Dividends in the model, $t = 6.69$, $r^2 = .833$

Step 2: Net income and dividends in model, $t = 2.24$ and $t = 4.36$, $R^2 = .897$

15.19

	y	x_1	x_2
x_1	−.653		
x_2	−.891	.650	
x_3	.821	−.615	−.688

15.21

	Net Income	Dividends
Dividends	.682	
Underwriting	.092	−.522

15.23 $\hat{y} = 564 − 27.99\, x_1 − 6.155\, x_2 − 15.90\, x_3$, $R^2 = .809$, adjusted $R^2 = .738$, $s_e = 42.88$, $F = 11.32$ with $p = .003$, x_2 only significant predictor x_1 is a non significant indicator variable

15.25 The procedure stopped at step 1 with only log x in the model, $= −13.20 + 11.64 \log x_1$, $R^2 = .9617$

15.27 The procedure went 2 steps, step 1: silver entered, $R^2 = .5244$, step 2: aluminum entered, $R^2 = .8204$, final model: gold $= −50.19 + 18.9$ silver $+ 3.59$ aluminum

15.29 The procedure went 3 steps, step 1: food entered, $R^2 = .84$, step 2: fuel oil entered, $R^2 = .95$, step 3: shelter entered, $R^2 = .96$, final model: All $= −1.0615 + 0.474$ food $+ 0.269$ fuel oil $+ 0.249$ shelter

15.31 Grocery $= 76.23 + 0.08592$ Housing $+ 0.16767$ Utility $+ 0.0284$ Transportation $− 0.0659$ Healthcare, $F = 2.29$ not significant; $s_e = 4.416$; $R^2 = .315$; Adjusted $R^2 = .177$; Utility only significant predictor.

CHAPTER 16

16.1 MAD $= 1.367$, MSE $= 2.27$

16.3 MAD $= 5.375$, MSE $= 23.65$

16.5 a. 44.75, 52.75, 61.50, 64.75, 70.50, 81

b. 53.25, 56.375, 62.875, 67.25, 76.375, 89.125

16.7 $\alpha = .3$: 9.4, 9, 8.7, 8.8, 9.1, 9.7, 9.9, 9.8

$\alpha = .7$: 9.4, 8.6, 8.1, 8.7, 9.5, 10.6, 10.4, 9.8

16.9 $\alpha = .2$: 332, 404.4, 427.1, 386.1, 350.7, 315, 325.2, 362.6, 423.5, 453, 477.4, 554.9

$\alpha = .9$: 332, 657.8, 532, 253, 213.4, 176.1, 347, 495.5, 649.9, 578.9, 575.4, 836; MAD$_{\alpha=.2} = 190.8$; MAD$_{\alpha=.9} = 168.6$

16.11 Members $= 17206 − 62.7$ Year; $R^2 = .809$; $s_e = 158.8$; $F = 63.54$, reject

16.13 TC: 136.78, 132.90, 128.54, 126.43, 124.86, 122, 119.08, 116.76, 114.61, 112.70, 111.75, 111.36

SI: 93.30, 90.47, 92.67, 98.77, 111.09, 100.83, 113.52, 117.58, 112.36, 92.08, 99.69, 102.73

16.15 $D = 1.12$, reject

16.17 Assets $= 1379 + 136.68$ failures, $R^2 = .379$, $D = 2.49$, fail to reject

16.19 1 lag model: $= 158 + 0.589\, x$, $R^2 = .353$

2 lag model: $= 401 − 0.065\, x$, $R^2 = .05$

16.21 a. 100, 139.9, 144.0, 162.6, 200, 272.8, 310.7, 327.1, 356.6, 376.9, 388.8

b. 32.2, 45.0, 46.4, 52.3, 64.4, 87.8, 100, 105.3, 114.8, 121.3, 125.1

16.23 100, 108.5, 112.0

16.25 121.6, 127.4, 131.4

16.27 a. Linear: $= 9.96 − 0.14\, x$, $R^2 = 90.9\%$,

Quadratic: $= 10.4 − 0.252\, x + .00445\, x_2$, $R^2 = 94.4\%$

b. MAD $= .3585$

c. MAD ($\alpha = .3$) $= .4374$, MAD ($\alpha = .7$) $= .2596$

d. $\alpha = .7$ did best

16.29 100, 104.8, 114.5, 115.5, 114.1

16.31 MAD$_{mov.avg.} = 653.63$, MAD$_{\alpha=.2} = 1054.11$

16.33 Jan. 95.35, Feb. 99.69, March 106.75, April 103.99, May 100.99, June 106.96, July 94.53, Aug. 99.60, Sept. 104.16, Oct. 97.04, Nov. 95.75, Dec. 95.19

16.35 unweighted: 100, 101.5, 103.05; Laspeyres: 104.4, 106.4; Paasche: 104.3, 106.3

16.37 MSE$_{ma} = 49.06$; MSE$_{wma} = 32.07$

16.39 98.07, 103.84, 97.04, 101.05

16.43 $D = 0.99$, inconclusive

16.45 $D = 0.98$, reject

CHAPTER 17

17.1 $R = 11$, fail to reject

17.3 $\alpha/2 = .025$, p-value $= .0264$, fail to reject

17.5 $R = 27$, $z = −1.08$, fail to reject

17.7 $U = 26.5$, p-value $= .6454$, fail to reject

17.9 $U = 11$, p-value $= .0156$, fail to reject

17.11 $z = −3.78$, reject

17.13 $z = −2.59$, reject

17.15 $z = −3.20$, reject

17.17 $z = −1.75$, reject

17.19 $K = 21.21$, reject

17.21 $K = 2.75$, fail to reject

17.23 $K = 18.99$, reject

17.25 $\chi^2 = 13.8$, reject

17.27 $\chi^2 = 14.8$, reject

17.29 4, 5, $S = 2.04$, fail to reject

17.31 $r_s = .893$

17.33 $r_s = -.952$

17.35 $r_s = -.398$

17.37 $r_s = -.855$

17.39 $U = 20$, p-value $= .2344$, fail to reject

17.41 $K = 7.75$, fail to reject

17.43 $r_s = -.81$

17.45 $z = -0.40$, fail to reject

17.47 $z = 0.96$, fail to reject

17.49 $U = 45.5$, p-value $= .739$, fail to reject

17.51 $z = -1.91$, fail to reject

17.53 $R = 21$, fail to reject

17.55 $z = -2.43$, reject

17.57 $K = 17.21$, reject

17.59 $K = 11.96$, reject

CHAPTER 18

18.5 $\bar{\bar{x}} = 4.51$, UCL $= 5.17$, LCL $= 3.85$

$\bar{R} = 0.90$, UCL $= 2.05$, LCL $= 0$

18.7 $p = .05$, UCL $= .1534$, LCL $= .000$

18.9 $\bar{c} = 1.34375$, UCL $= 4.82136$, LCL $= .000$

18.11 Chart 1: nine consecutive points below centerline, four out of five points in the outer 2/3 of the lower region

Chart 2: eight consecutive points above the centerline

Chart 3: in control

18.13 .4013, .2213

18.15 .2163, .4305

18.21 $p = .104$, LCL $= 0.000$, UCL $= .234$

18.23 .2614, .2059

18.25 $\bar{\bar{x}} = 1.196$, LCL $= 1.161$, UCL $= 1.231$, $\bar{R} = 0.0477$, LCL $= 0.000$, UCL $= 0.1089$

18.27 $p = .07778$, LCL $= .000$, UCL $= .1706$

18.29 .0702, .3828

18.31 $p = 0.06$, LCL $= 0.000$, UCL $= .1726$

CHAPTER 19 (ON ACCOMPANYING CD)

19.1 **a.** 390

b. 70

c. 82, 296

d. 140

19.3 60, 10

19.7 31.75, 6.50

19.9 Lock in $= 85$, 182.5, 97.5

19.11 **a.** 75,000

b. Avoider

c. >75,000

19.13 244.275, 194.275

19.15 21012.32, 12.32

19.17 **b.** 267.5, 235

c. 352.5, 85

19.19 **a.** 2000, 200

b. 500

19.21 875,650

19.23 Reduction: .60, .2333, .1667

Constant: .10, .6222, .2778

Increase: .0375, .0875, .8750, 21425.55, 2675.55

GLOSSARY

A

a posteriori   After the experiment; pairwise comparisons made by the researcher *after* determining that there is a significant overall F value from ANOVA; also called *post hoc*.

a priori   Determined before, or prior to, an experiment.

acceptance sampling   A type of quality control that involves after-process inspection; the inspection of a sample from a batch or lot of goods to determine whether the batch or lot will be accepted or rejected.

adjusted R^2   A modified value of R^2 in which the degrees of freedom are taken into account, thereby allowing the researcher to determine whether the value of R^2 is inflated for a particular multiple regression model.

after-process quality control   A type of quality control in which product attributes are measured by inspection after the manufacturing process is completed to determine whether the product is acceptable.

all possible regressions   A multiple regression search procedure in which all possible multiple linear regression models are determined from the data using all variables.

alpha (α)   The probability of committing a Type I error; also called the level of significance.

alternative hypothesis   The hypothesis that complements the null hypothesis; usually it is the hypothesis that the researcher is interested in proving.

analysis of variance (ANOVA)   A technique for statistically analyzing the data from a completely randomized design; uses the F test to determine whether there is a significant difference in two or more independent groups.

arithmetic mean   The average of a group of numbers.

autocorrelation   A problem that arises in regression analysis when the data occur over time and the error terms are correlated; also called serial correlation.

autoregression   A multiple regression forecasting technique in which the independent variables are time-lagged versions of the dependent variable.

averaging models   Forecasting models in which the forecast is the average of several preceding time periods.

B

backward elimination   A step-by-step multiple regression search procedure that begins with a full model containing all predictors. A search is made to determine if there are any nonsignificant independent variables in the model. If there are no nonsignificant predictors, then the backward process ends with the full model. If there are nonsignificant predictors, then the predictor with the smallest absolute value of t is eliminated and a new model is developed with the remaining variables. This procedure continues until only variables with significant t values remain in the model.

Bayes' rule   An extension of the conditional law of probabilities discovered by Thomas Bayes that can be used to revise probabilities.

benchmarking   A quality control method in which a company attempts to develop and establish total quality management from product to process by examining and emulating the best practices and techniques used in their industry.

beta (β)   The probability of committing a Type II error.

bimodal   Data sets that have two modes.

binomial distribution   Widely known discrete distribution in which there are only two possibilities on any one trial.

blocking variable   A variable that the researcher wants to control but is not the treatment variable of interest.

bounds   The error portion of the confidence interval that is added and/or subtracted from the point estimate to form the confidence interval.

box and whisker plot   A diagram that utilizes the upper and lower quartiles along with the median and the two most extreme values to depict a distribution graphically; sometimes called a box plot.

C

c chart   A quality control chart for attribute compliance that displays the number of nonconformances per item or unit.

cause-and-effect diagram   A tool for displaying possible causes for a quality problem and the interrelationships among the causes; also called a fishbone diagram or an Ishikawa diagram.

census   A process of gathering data from the whole population for a given measurement of interest.

centerline   The middle horizontal line of a control chart, often determined either by a product or service specification or by computing an expected value from sample information.

central limit theorem   A theorem that states that regardless of the shape of a population, the distributions of sample means and proportions are normal if sample sizes are large.

Chebyshev's theorem   A theorem stating that at least $1 - 1/k^2$ values will fall within $\pm k$ standard deviations of the mean regardless of the shape of the distribution.

chi-square distribution   A continuous distribution determined by the sum of the squares of k independent random variables.

chi-square goodness-of-fit test   A statistical test used to analyze probabilities of multinomial distribution trials along a single dimension; compares expected, or theoretical, frequencies of categories from a population distribution to the observed, or actual, frequencies from a distribution.

chi-square test of independence   A statistical test used to analyze the frequencies of two variables with multiple categories to determine whether the two variables are independent.

class midpoint   For any given class interval of a frequency distribution, the value halfway across the class interval; the average of the two class endpoints.

classical method of assigning probabilities   Probabilities assigned based on rules and laws.

classification variable   The independent variable of an experimental design that was present prior to the experiment and is not the result of the researcher's manipulations or control.

classifications   The subcategories of the independent variable used by the researcher in the experimental design; also called levels.

class mark   Another name for class midpoint; the midpoint of each class interval in grouped data.

cluster (or area) sampling   A type of random sampling in which the population is divided into nonoverlapping areas or clusters and elements are randomly sampled from the areas or clusters.

coefficient of determination (r^2)   The proportion of variability of the dependent variable accounted for or explained by the independent variable in a regression model.

coefficient of multiple determination (R^2)   The proportion of variation of the dependent variable accounted for by the independent variables in the regression model.

coefficient of skewness   A measure of the degree of skewness that exists in a distribution of numbers; compares the mean and the median in light of the magnitude of the standard deviation.

coefficient of variation (CV)   The ratio of the standard deviation to the mean, expressed as a percentage.

collectively exhaustive events   A list containing all possible elementary events for an experiment.

combinations   Used to determine the number of possible ways n things can happen from N total possibilities when sampling without replacement.

complement of a union   The only possible case other than the union of sets X and Y; the probability that neither X nor Y is in the outcome.

complementary events   Two events, one of which comprises all the elementary events of an experiment that are not in the other event.

completely randomized design   An experimental design wherein there is one treatment or independent variable with two or more treatment levels and one dependent variable. This design is analyzed by analysis of variance.

concomitant variables   Variables that are not being controlled by the researcher in the experiment but can have an effect on the outcome of the treatment being studied; also called confounding variables.

conditional probability   The probability of the occurrence of one event given that another event has occurred.

confounding variables   Variables that are not being controlled by the researcher in the experiment but can have an effect on the outcome of the treatment being studied; also called concomitant variables.

consumer price index (CPI)   A popular measure of consumer purchasing power published by the U.S. government as a relative measure of the cost of a market basket of goods and services purchased by either urban wage earners or by all urban consumers.

consumer's risk   The probability of a Type II error occurring in acceptance sampling; the probability that the producer will ship an unacceptable lot to a consumer but the consumer will accept the lot based on sample evidence.

contingency analysis   Another name for the chi-square test of independence.

contingency table   A two-way table that contains the frequencies of responses to two questions; also called a raw values matrix.

continuous distributions   Distributions constructed from continuous random variables.

continuous random variables   Variables that take on values at every point over a given interval.

control chart   A quality control graph that contains an upper control limit, a lower control limit, and a centerline; used to evaluate whether a process is or is not in a state of statistical control.

convenience sampling   A nonrandom sampling technique in which items for the sample are selected for the convenience of the researcher.

correction for continuity   A correction made when a binomial distribution problem is approximated by the normal distribution because a discrete distribution problem is being approximated by a continuous distribution.

correlation   A measure of the degree of relatedness of two or more variables.

covariance   The variance of x and y together.

critical value   The value that divides the nonrejection region from the rejection region.

critical value method   A method of testing hypotheses in which the sample statistic is compared to a critical value in order to reach a conclusion about rejecting or failing to reject the null hypothesis.

cumulative frequency   A running total of frequencies through the classes of a frequency distribution.

cyclical effects   The rise and fall of time-series data over periods longer than 1 year.

D

decision alternatives   The various choices or options available to the decision maker in any given problem situation.

decision analysis   A category of quantitative business techniques particularly targeted at clarifying and enhancing the decision-making process.

decision making under certainty   A decision-making situation in which the states of nature are known.

decision making under risk   A decision-making situation in which it is uncertain which states of nature will occur but the probability of each state of nature occurring has been determined.

decision making under uncertainty   A decision-making situation in which the states of nature that may occur are unknown and the probability of a state of nature occurring is also unknown.

decision table   A matrix that displays the decision alternatives, the states of nature, and the payoffs for a particular decision-making problem; also called a payoff table.

decision trees   A flowchart-like depiction of the decision process that includes the various decision alternatives, the various states of nature, and the payoffs.

decomposition   Breaking down the effects of time-series data into the four component parts of trend, cyclical, seasonal, and irregular.

degrees of freedom   A mathematical adjustment made to the size of the sample; used along with α to locate values in statistical tables.

dependent samples   Two or more samples selected in such a way as to be dependent or related; each item or person in one sample has a corresponding matched or related item in the other samples. Also called related samples.

dependent variable   In regression analysis, the variable that is being predicted.

descriptive statistics   Statistics that have been gathered on a group to describe or reach conclusions about that same group.

deseasonalized data   Time-series data in which the effects of seasonality have been removed.

deterministic model   Mathematical models that produce an "exact" output for a given input.

deviation from the mean   The difference between a number and the average of the set of numbers of which the number is a part.

discrete distributions   Distributions constructed from discrete random variables.

discrete random variables   Random variables in which the set of all possible values is at most a finite or a countably infinite number of possible values.

disproportionate stratified random sampling   A type of stratified random sampling in which the proportions of items selected from the strata for the final sample do not reflect the proportions of the strata in the population.

double-sample plan   An acceptance sampling plan in which an inspector is allowed to take a second sample from a lot to determine whether the lot is to be rejected or accepted if the first sample is inconclusive.

Dow Jones indexes   Four indexes published by Dow Jones & Company that are used to track the performance of stocks on the New York Stock Exchange. Included in these are the Dow Jones industrial average of 30 industrial stocks, the Dow Jones average of 20 transportation stocks, the Dow Jones average of 15 utility stocks, and a composite index of these 65 stocks.

dummy variable   Another name for a qualitative or indicator variable; usually coded as 0 or 1 and represents whether or not a given item or person possesses a certain characteristic.

Durbin-Watson test   A statistical test for determining whether significant autocorrelation is present in a time-series regression model.

E

elementary events   Events that cannot be decomposed or broken down into other events.

empirical rule   A guideline that states the approximate percentage of values that fall within a given number of standard deviations of a mean of a set of data that are normally distributed.

EMV'er   A decision maker who bases his or her decision on the expected monetary value of the decision alternative.

error of an individual forecast   The difference between the actual value and the forecast of that value.

error of estimation   The difference between the statistic computed to estimate a parameter and the parameter.

event   An outcome of an experiment.

expected monetary value (EMV)   A value of a decision alternative computed by multiplying the probability of each state of nature by the state's associated payoff and summing these products across the states of nature.

expected value   The long-run average of occurrences; sometimes referred to as the mean value.

expected value of perfect information   The difference between the payoff that would occur if the decision maker knew which states of nature would occur and the expected monetary payoff from the best decision alternative when there is no information about the occurrence of the states of nature.

expected value of sample information   The difference between the expected monetary value with information and the expected monetary value without information.

experiment   A process that produces outcomes.

experimental design   A plan and a structure to test hypotheses in which the researcher either controls or manipulates one or more variables.

exponential distribution   A continuous distribution closely related to the Poisson distribution that describes the times between random occurrences.

exponential smoothing   A forecasting technique in which a weighting system is used to determine the importance of previous time periods in the forecast.

F

F distribution   A distribution based on the ratio of two random variances; used in testing two variances and in analysis of variance.

F value   The ratio of two sample variances, used to reach statistical conclusions regarding the null hypothesis; in ANOVA, the ratio of the treatment variance to the error variance.

factorial design   An experimental design in which two or more independent variables are studied simultaneously and every level of each treatment is studied under the conditions of every level of all other treatments. Also called a factorial experiment.

factors   Another name for the independent variables of an experimental design.

finite correction factor   A statistical adjustment made to the Z formula for sample means; adjusts for the fact that a population is finite and the size is known.

first-differences approach   A method of transforming data in an attempt to reduce or remove autocorrelation from a time-series regression model; results in each data

value being subtracted from each succeeding time period data value, producing a new, transformed value.

fishbone diagram   A display of possible causes of a quality problem and the interrelationships among the causes. The problem is diagrammed along the main line of the "fish" and possible causes are diagrammed as line segments angled off in such a way as to give the appearance of a fish skeleton. Also called an Ishikawa diagram or a cause-and-effect diagram.

Fisher's ideal price index   A type of weighted aggregate price index computed by taking the square root of the product of the Laspeyres index and the Paasche index.

flowchart   A schematic representation of all the activities and interactions that occur in a process.

forecasting   The art or science of predicting the future.

forecasting error   A single measure of the overall error of a forecast for an entire set of data.

forward selection   A multiple regression search procedure that is essentially the same as stepwise regression analysis except that once a variable is entered into the process, it is never deleted.

frame   A list, map, directory, or some other source that is being used to represent the population in the process of sampling.

frequency distribution   A summary of data presented in the form of class intervals and frequencies.

frequency polygon   A graph constructed by plotting a dot for the frequencies at the class midpoints and connecting the dots.

Friedman test   A nonparametric alternative to the randomized block design.

G

general linear regression model   Regression models that take the form of $y = \beta_0 + \beta_1 x_1 + \beta_2 x_2 + \ldots + \beta_k x_k + \varepsilon$, where the parameters, β_i, are linear.

grouped data   Data that have been organized into a frequency distribution.

H

heteroscedasticity   The condition that occurs when the error variances produced by a regression model are not constant.

histogram   A type of vertical bar chart constructed by graphing line segments for the frequencies of classes across the class intervals and connecting each to the x axis to form a series of rectangles.

homoscedasticity   The condition that occurs when the error variances produced by a regression model are constant.

Hurwicz criterion   An approach to decision making in which the maximum and minimum payoffs selected from each decision alternative are used with a weight, α, between 0 and 1 to determine the alternative with the maximum weighted average. The higher the value of α, the more optimistic is the decision maker.

hypergeometric distribution   A distribution of probabilities of the occurrence of x items in a sample of n when there are A of that same item in a population of N.

hypothesis testing   A process of testing hypotheses about parameters by setting up null and alternative hypotheses, gathering sample data, computing statistics from the samples, and using statistical techniques to reach conclusions about the hypotheses.

I

independent events   Events such that the occurrence or nonoccurrence of one has no effect on the occurrence of the others.

independent samples   Two or more samples in which the selected items are related only by chance.

independent variable   In regression analysis, the predictor variable.

index number   A ratio, often expressed as a percentage, of a measure taken during one time frame to that same measure taken during another time frame, usually denoted as the base period.

indicator variable   Another name for a dummy or qualitative variable; usually coded as 0 or 1 and represents whether or not a given item or person possesses a certain characteristic.

inferential statistics   Statistics that have been gathered from a sample and used to reach conclusions about the population from which the sample was taken.

in-process quality control   A quality control method in which product attributes are measured at various intervals throughout the manufacturing process.

interaction   When the effects of one treatment in an experimental design vary according to the levels of treatment of the other effect(s).

interquartile range   The range of values between the first and the third quartile.

intersection   The portion of the population that contains elements that lie in both or all groups of interest.

interval estimate   A range of values within which it is estimated with some confidence the population parameter lies.

interval level data   Next to highest level of data. These data have all the properties of ordinal level data, but in addition, intervals between consecutive numbers have meaning.

irregular fluctuations   Unexplained or error variation within time-series data.

Ishikawa diagram   A tool developed by Kaoru Ishikawa as a way to display possible causes of a quality problem and the interrelationships of the causes; also called a fishbone diagram or a cause-and-effect diagram.

J

joint probability   The probability of the intersection occurring, or the probability of two or more events happening at once.

judgment sampling   A nonrandom sampling technique in which items selected for the sample are chosen by the judgment of the researcher.

just-in-time inventory system   An inventory system in which little or no extra raw materials or parts for production are stored.

K

Kruskal-Wallis test   The nonparametric alternative to one-way analysis of variance; used to test whether three or more samples come from the same or different populations.

kurtosis   The amount of peakedness of a distribution.

L

lambda (λ)   Denotes the long-run average of a Poisson distribution.

Laspeyres price index   A type of weighted aggregate price index in which the quantity values used in the calculations are from the base year.

least squares analysis   The process by which a regression model is developed based on calculus techniques that attempt to produce a minimum sum of the squared error values.

leptokurtic   Distributions that are high and thin.

level of significance   The probability of committing a Type I error; also known as alpha.

levels   The subcategories of the independent variable used by the researcher in the experimental design; also called classifications.

lower control limit (LCL)   The bottom-end line of a control chart, usually situated approximately three standard deviations of the statistic below the centerline; data points below this line indicate quality control problems.

M

Mann-Whitney U test   A nonparametric counterpart of the t test used to compare the means of two independent populations.

manufacturing quality   A view of quality in which the emphasis is on the manufacturer's ability to target consistently the requirements for the product with little variability.

marginal probability   A probability computed by dividing a subtotal of the population by the total of the population.

matched pairs data   Data or measurements gathered from pairs of items or persons that are matched on some characteristic or from a before-and-after design and then separated into different samples; also called paired data or related measures.

matched-pairs test   A *t* test to test the differences in two related or matched samples; sometimes called the *t* test for related measures or the correlated *t* test.

maximax criterion   An optimistic approach to decision making under uncertainty in which the decision alternative is chosen according to which alternative produces the maximum overall payoff of the maximum payoffs from each alternative.

maximin criterion   A pessimistic approach to decision making under uncertainty in which the decision alternative is chosen according to which alternative produces the maximum overall payoff of the minimum payoffs from each alternative.

mean absolute deviation (MAD)   The average of the absolute values of the deviations around the mean for a set of numbers.

mean absolute percentage error (MAPE)   The average of the absolute values of the percentage errors of a forecast.

mean error (ME)   The average of all the errors of forecast for a group of data.

mean percentage error   The average of the percentage errors of a forecast.

mean square error (MSE)   The average of all errors squared of a forecast for a group of data.

mean value   The long-run average of occurrences; also called the expected value.

measures of central tendency   One type of measure that is used to yield information about the center of a group of numbers.

measures of shape   Tools that can be used to describe the shape of a distribution of data.

measures of variability   Statistics that describe the spread or dispersion of a set of data.

median   The middle value in an ordered array of numbers.

mesokurtic   Distributions that are normal in shape—that is, not too high or too flat.

metric data   Interval and ratio level data; also called quantitative data.

minimax regret   A decision-making strategy in which the decision maker determines the lost opportunity for each decision alternative and selects the decision alternative with the minimum of lost opportunity or regret.

***mn* counting rule**   A rule used in probability to count the number of ways two operations can occur if the first operation has *m* possibilities and the second operation has *n* possibilities.

mode   The most frequently occurring value in a set of data.

moving average   When an average of data from previous time periods is used to forecast the value for ensuing time periods and this average is modified at each new time period by including more recent values not in the previous average and dropping out values from the more distant time periods that were in the average. It is continually updated at each new time period.

multicollinearity   A problematic condition that occurs when two or more of the independent variables of a multiple regression model are highly correlated.

multimodal   Data sets that contain more than two modes.

multiple comparisons   Statistical techniques used to compare pairs of treatment means when the analysis of variance yields an overall significant difference in the treatment means.

multiple regression   Regression analysis with one dependent variable and two or more independent variables or at least one nonlinear independent variable.

multiple-sample plan   An acceptance sampling plan in which the inspector is allowed to take three or more samples in sequence to determine whether a lot is to be accepted or rejected when the previous samples are inconclusive.

mutually exclusive events   Events such that the occurrence of one precludes the occurrence of the other.

N

naïve forecasting models   Simple models in which it is assumed that the more recent time periods of data represent the best predictions or forecasts for future outcomes.

nominal level data   The lowest level of data measurement; used only to classify or categorize.

nonlinear regression model   Multiple regression models in which the models are nonlinear, such as polynomial models, logarithmic models, and exponential models.

nonmetric data   Nominal and ordinal level data; also called qualitative data.

nonparametric statistics   A class of statistical techniques that make few assumptions about the population and are particularly applicable to nominal and ordinal level data.

nonrandom sampling   Sampling in which not every unit of the population has the same probability of being selected into the sample.

nonrandom sampling techniques   Sampling techniques used to select elements from the population by any mechanism that does not involve a random selection process.

nonrejection region   Any portion of a distribution that is not in the rejection region. If the observed statistic falls in this region, the decision is to fail to reject the null hypothesis.

nonsampling errors   All errors other than sampling errors.

normal distribution   A widely known and much-used continuous distribution that fits the measurements of many human characteristics and many machine-produced items.

null hypothesis   The hypothesis that assumes the status quo—that the old theory, method, or standard is still true; the complement of the alternative hypothesis.

O

observed significance level   Another name for the *p*-value method of testing hypotheses.

ogive   A cumulative frequency polygon; plotted by graphing a dot at each class endpoint for the cumulative or decumulative frequency value and connecting the dots.

one-tailed test   A statistical test wherein the researcher is interested only in testing one side of the distribution.

one-way analysis of variance   The process used to analyze a completely randomized experimental design. This process involves computing a ratio of the variance between treatment levels of the independent variable to the error variance. This ratio is an *F* value, which is then used to determine whether there are any significant differences between the means of the treatment levels.

operating-characteristic (OC) curve   In hypothesis testing, a graph of Type II error probabilities for various possible values of an alternative hypotheses. In quality control, a graph of consumer's risk for various values of nonconforming percent.

opportunity loss table   A decision table constructed by subtracting all payoffs for a given state of nature from the maximum payoff for that state of nature and doing this for all states of nature; displays the lost opportunities or regret that would occur for a given decision alternative if that particular state of nature occurred.

ordinal level data   Next-higher level of data from nominal level data; can be used to order or rank items, objects, or people.

outliers   Data points that lie apart from the rest of the points.

P

P chart   A quality control chart for attribute compliance that graphs the proportion of sample items in noncompliance with specifications for multiple samples.

p-value method   A method of testing hypotheses in which there is no preset level of α. The probability of getting a test statistic at least as extreme as the observed test statistic is computed under the assumption that the null hypothesis is true. This probability is called the *p* value, and it is the smallest value of α for which the null hypothesis can be rejected.

Paasche price index   A type of weighted aggregate price index in which the quantity values used in the calculations are from the year of interest.

paired data   Data gathered from pairs of items or persons that are matched on some characteristic or from a before-and-after design and then separated into different samples; also called matched pairs data or related measures.

parameter   A descriptive measure of the population.

parametric statistics   A class of statistical techniques that contain assumptions about the population and that are used only with interval and ratio level data.

Pareto analysis   A quantitative tallying of the number and types of defects that occur with a product or service, often recorded in a Pareto chart.

Pareto chart   A vertical bar chart in which the number and types of defects for a product or service are graphed in order of magnitude from greatest to least.

partial regression coefficient   The coefficient of an independent variable in a multiple regression model that represents the increase that will occur in the value of the dependent variable from a 1-unit increase in the independent variable if all other variables are held constant.

payoff table   A matrix that displays the decision alternatives, the states of nature, and the payoffs for a particular decision-making problem; also called a decision table.

payoffs   The benefits or rewards that result from selecting a particular decision alternative.

Pearson product–moment correlation coefficient (r)   A correlation measure used to determine the degree of relatedness of two variables that are at least of interval level.

percentage error   The ratio of the error of a forecast to the actual value being forecast, multiplied by 100.

percentiles   Measures of central tendency that divide a group of data into 100 parts.

pie chart   A circular depiction of data where the area of the whole pie represents 100% of the data being studied and slices represent a percentage breakdown of the sublevels.

platykurtic   Distributions that are flat and spread out.

point estimate   An estimate of a population parameter constructed from a statistic taken from a sample.

Poisson distribution   A discrete distribution that is constructed from the probability of occurrence of rare events over an interval; focuses only on the number of discrete occurrences over some interval or continuum.

population   A collection of persons, objects, or items of interest.

post hoc   After the experiment; pairwise comparisons made by the researcher *after* determining that there is a significant overall *F* value from ANOVA; also called a *posteriori*.

power   The probability of rejecting a false null hypothesis.

power curve   A graph that plots the power values against various values of the alternative hypothesis.

probabilistic model   A model that includes an error term that allows for various values of output to occur for a given value of input.

probability matrix A two-dimensional table that displays the marginal and intersection probabilities of a given problem.

process A series of actions, changes, or functions that bring about a result.

producer price index (PPI) An index of prices received by producers of all commodities at all stages of processing in the United States, published by the U.S. Bureau of Labor Statistics; formerly called the wholesale price index.

producer's risk The probability of committing a Type I error in acceptance sampling; the probability that the producer will ship an acceptable lot to a consumer but the consumer will reject the lot based on sample evidence.

product quality A view of quality in which quality is measurable in the product based on the fact that there are perceived differences in products and quality products possess more attributes.

proportionate stratified random sampling A type of stratified random sampling in which the proportions of the items selected for the sample from the strata reflect the proportions of the strata in the population.

Q

quadratic regression model A multiple regression model in which the predictors are a variable and the square of the variable.

qualitative variable Another name for a dummy or indicator variable; represents whether or not a given item or person possesses a certain characteristic and is usually coded as 0 or 1.

quality When a product delivers what is stipulated in its specifications.

quality circle A small group of workers consisting of supervisors and six to 10 employees who meet frequently and regularly to consider quality issues in their department or area of the business.

quality control The collection of strategies, techniques, and actions taken by an organization to ensure the production of quality products.

quartiles Measures of central tendency that divide a group of data into four subgroups or parts.

quota sampling A nonrandom sampling technique in which the population is stratified on some characteristic and then elements selected for the sample are chosen by nonrandom processes.

R

R chart A plot of sample ranges used in quality control.

R^2 The coefficient of multiple determination; a value that ranges from 0 to 1 and represents the proportion of the dependent variable in a multiple regression model that is accounted for by the independent variables.

random sampling Sampling in which every unit of the population has the same probability of being selected for the sample.

random variable A variable that contains the outcomes of a chance experiment.

randomized block design An experimental design in which there is one independent variable of interest and a second variable, known as a blocking variable, that is used to control for confounding or concomitant variables.

range The difference between the largest and the smallest values in a set of numbers.

ratio level data Highest level of data measurement; contains the same properties as interval level data, with the additional property that zero has meaning and represents the absence of the phenomenon being measured.

rectangular distribution A relatively simple continuous distribution in which the same height is obtained over a range of values; also referred to as the uniform distribution.

reengineering A radical approach to total quality management in which the core business processes of a company is redesigned.

regression The process of constructing a mathematical model or function that can be used to predict or determine one variable by any other variable.

regression-based forecasting techniques Forecasting techniques using regression analysis that are based on the knowledge or supposition that a variable can be predicted or forecast by at least one variable.

rejection region If a computed statistic lies in this portion of a distribution, the null hypothesis will be rejected.

related measures Another name for matched pairs or paired data in which measurements are taken from pairs of items or persons matched on some characteristic or from a before-and-after design and then separated into different samples.

related samples Another name for dependent samples, where each item in one sample has a corresponding matched or related item in the other sample.

relative frequency The proportion of the total frequencies that fall into any given class interval in a frequency distribution.

relative frequency of occurrence Assigning probability based on cumulated historical data.

repeated measures design A randomized block design in which each block level is an individual item or person, and that person or item is measured across all treatments.

residual The difference between the actual Y value and the Y value predicted by the regression model; the error of the regression model in predicting each value of the dependent variable.

residual plot   A type of graph in which the residuals for a particular regression model are plotted along with their associated values of X.

response plane   A plane fit in a three-dimensional space and that represents the response surface defined by a multiple regression model with two independent first-order variables.

response surface   The surface defined by a multiple regression model.

response variable   The dependent variable in a multiple regression model; the variable that the researcher is trying to predict.

risk avoider   A decision maker who avoids risk whenever possible and is willing to drop out of a game when given the chance even when the payoff is less than the expected monetary value.

risk taker   A decision maker who enjoys taking risk and will not drop out of a game unless the payoff is more than the expected monetary value.

robust   Describes a statistical technique that is relatively insensitive to minor violations in one or more of its underlying assumptions.

run   A succession of observations that have a particular characteristic.

runs test   A nonparametric test of randomness used to determine whether the order or sequence of observations in a sample is random.

S

sample   A portion of the whole.

sample proportion   The quotient of the frequency at which a given characteristic occurs in a sample and the number of items in the sample.

sample-size estimation   An estimate of the size of sample necessary to fulfill the requirements of a particular level of confidence and to be within a specified amount of error.

sample space   A complete roster or listing of all elementary events for an experiment.

sampling error   Error that occurs when the sample is not representative of the population.

scatter plot   A plot or graph of the pairs of data from a simple regression analysis.

search procedures   Processes whereby more than one multiple regression model is developed for a given database, and the models are compared and sorted by different criteria, depending on the given procedure.

seasonal effects   Patterns of data behavior that occur in periods of time of less than 1 year, often measured by the month.

serial correlation   A problem that arises in regression analysis when the error terms of a regression model are correlated due to time-series data; also called autocorrelation.

set notation   The use of braces to group numbers that have some specified characteristic.

simple average   The arithmetic mean or average for the values of a given number of time periods of data.

simple average model   A forecasting averaging model in which the forecast for the next time period is the average of values for a given number of previous time periods.

simple index number   A number determined by computing the ratio of a quantity, price, or cost for a particular year of interest to the quantity price or cost of a base year, expressed as a percentage.

simple random sampling   The most elementary of the random sampling techniques; involves numbering each item in the population and using a list or roster of random numbers to select items for the sample.

simple regression   Bivariate, linear regression.

single-sample plan   An acceptance sampling plan in which only one sample of size n is sampled from a lot of N items in an attempt to determine whether the lot will be accepted.

Six Sigma   A total quality management approach that measures the capability of a process to perform defect-free work, where a defect is defined as anything that results in customer dissatisfaction.

skewness   The lack of symmetry of a distribution of values.

snowball sampling   A nonrandom sampling technique in which survey subjects who fit a desired profile are selected based on referral from other survey respondents who also fit the desired profile.

Spearman's rank correlation   A measure of the correlation of two variables; used when only ordinal level or ranked data are available.

standard deviation   The square root of the variance.

standard error of the estimate (s_e)   A standard deviation of the error of a regression model.

standard error of the mean   The standard deviation of the distribution of sample means.

standard error of the proportion   The standard deviation of the distribution of sample proportions.

standardized normal distribution z distribution; a distribution of z scores produced for values from a normal distribution with a mean of 0 and a standard deviation of 1.

states of nature   The occurrences of nature that can happen after a decision has been made that can affect the outcome of the decision and over which the decision maker has little or no control.

statistic   A descriptive measure of a sample.

statistics   A science dealing with the collection, analysis, interpretation, and presentation of numerical data.

stem and leaf plot   A plot of numbers constructed by separating each number into two groups, a stem and a leaf. The leftmost digits are the stems and the rightmost digits are the leaves.

stepwise regression   A step-by-step multiple regression search procedure that begins by developing a regression model with a single predictor variable and adds and deletes predictors one step at a time, examining the fit of the model at each step until there are no more significant predictors remaining outside the model.

stratified random sampling   A type of random sampling in which the population is divided into various nonoverlapping strata and then items are randomly selected into the sample from each stratum.

subjective probability   A probability assigned based on the intuition or reasoning of the person determining the probability.

sum of squares of error (SSE)   The sum of the residuals squared for a regression model.

sum of squares of x   The sum of the squared deviations about the mean of a set of values.

systematic sampling   A random sampling technique in which every kth item or person is selected from the population.

T

t distribution   A distribution that describes the sample data in small samples when the standard deviation is unknown and the population is normally distributed.

t value   The computed value of t used to reach statistical conclusions regarding the null hypothesis in small-sample analysis.

team building   When a group of employees are organized as an entity to undertake management tasks and perform other functions such as organizing, developing, and overseeing projects.

time-series data   Data gathered on a given characteristic over a period of time at regular intervals.

total quality management (TQM)   A program that occurs when all members of an organization are involved in improving quality; all goals and objectives of the organization come under the purview of quality control and are measured in quality terms.

transcendent quality   A view of quality that implies that a product has an innate excellence, uncompromising standards, and high achievement.

treatment variable   The independent variable of an experimental design that the researcher either controls or modifies.

trend   Long-run general direction of a business climate over a period of several years.

Tukey-Kramer procedure   A modification of the Tukey HSD multiple comparison procedure; used when there are unequal sample sizes.

Tukey's four-quadrant approach   A graphical method using the four quadrants for determining which expressions of Tukey's ladder of transformations to use.

Tukey's honestly significant difference (HSD) test   In analysis of variance, a technique used for pairwise *a posteriori* multiple comparisons to determine if there are significant differences between the means of any pair of treatment levels in an experimental design. This test requires equal sample sizes and uses a q value along with the mean square error in its computation.

Tukey's ladder of transformations   A process used for determining ways to recode data in multiple regression analysis to achieve potential improvement in the predictability of the model.

two-stage sampling   Cluster sampling done in two stages: A first round of samples is taken and then a second round is taken from within the first samples.

two-tailed test   A statistical test wherein the researcher is interested in testing both sides of the distribution.

two-way analysis of variance (two-way ANOVA)   The process used to statistically test the effects of variables in factorial designs with two independent variables.

Type I error   An error committed by rejecting a true null hypothesis.

Type II error   An error committed by failing to reject a false null hypothesis.

U

ungrouped data   Raw data, or data that have not been summarized in any way.

uniform distribution   A relatively simple continuous distribution in which the same height is obtained over a range of values; also called the rectangular distribution.

union   A new set of elements formed by combining the elements of two or more other sets.

union probability   The probability of one event occurring or the other event occurring or both occurring.

unweighted aggregate price index number   The ratio of the sum of the prices of a market basket of items for a particular year to the sum of the prices of those same items in a base year, expressed as a percentage.

upper control limit (UCL)   The top-end line of a control chart, usually situated approximately three standard deviations of the statistic above the centerline; data points above this line indicate quality control problems.

user quality   A view of quality in which the quality of the product is determined by the user.

utility   The degree of pleasure or displeasure a decision maker has in being involved in the outcome selection process given the risks and opportunities available.

V

value quality   A view of quality having to do with price and costs and whether the consumer got his or her money's worth.

variance   The average of the squared deviations about the arithmetic mean for a set of numbers.

variance inflation factor   A statistic computed using the R^2 value of a regression model developed by predicting one independent variable of a regression analysis by other independent variables; used to determine whether there is multicollinearity among the variables.

W

weighted aggregate price index number   A price index computed by multiplying quantity weights and item prices and summing the products to determine a market basket's worth in a given year and then determining the ratio of the market basket's worth in the year of interest to the same value computed for a base year, expressed as a percentage.

weighted moving average   A moving average in which different weights are applied to the data values from different time periods.

Wilcoxon matched-pairs signed rank test   A nonparametric alternative to the t test for two related or dependent samples.

X

$\bar{x}$ chart   A quality control chart for measurements that graphs the sample means computed for a series of small random samples over a period of time.

Z

z distribution   A distribution of z scores; a normal distribution with a mean of 0 and a standard deviation of 1.

z score   The number of standard deviations a value (x) is above or below the mean of a set of numbers when the data are normally distributed.

INDEX

PHOTO CREDITS

CHAPTER 1:

Dinodia/ Omni – Photo Communications

CHAPTER 2:

Digital Vision

CHAPTER 3:

© Frederick Astier/ Corbis Sygma

CHAPTER 4:

PhotoDisc, Inc.

CHAPTER 5:

Chuck Savage/ The Stock Market

CHAPTER 6:

PhotoDisc, Inc.

CHAPTER 7:

Flat Earth

CHAPTER 8:

PhotoDisc Inc

CHAPTER 9:

Corbis Digital Stock

CHAPTER 10:

Corbis Digital Stock

CHAPTER 11:

Charles Hamilton

CHAPTER 12:

PhotoDisc, Inc.

CHAPTER 13:

Michael Coqliantry, The Image Bank

CHAPTER 14:

Keith Brofsky, PhotoDisc, Inc

CHAPTER 15:

PhotoDisc, Inc

CHAPTER 16:

PhotoDisc, Inc

CHAPTER 17:

Krispy Kreme Doughnut Corporation

CHAPTER 18:

David W. Hamilton, The Image Bank